Java™:
The Complete Reference,
Seventh Edition

About the Author

Herbert Schildt is a leading authority on the Java, C, C++, and C# languages, and is a master Windows programmer. His programming books have sold more than 3.5 million copies worldwide and have been translated into all major foreign languages. He is the author of the best-selling *The Art of Java, Java: A Beginner's Guide,* and *Swing: A Beginner's Guide.* Among his other bestsellers are *C++: The Complete Reference, C++: A Beginner's Guide, C#: The Complete Reference,* and *C#: A Beginner's Guide.* Schildt holds both graduate and undergraduate degrees from the University of Illinois. He can be reached at his consulting office at (217) 586-4683. His Web site is **www.HerbSchildt.com**.

Java™:
The Complete Reference, Seventh Edition

Herbert Schildt

New York   Chicago   San Francisco
Lisbon   London   Madrid   Mexico City
Milan   New Delhi   San Juan
Seoul   Singapore   Sydney   Toronto

The **McGraw·Hill** Companies

McGraw-Hill books are available at special quantity discounts to use as premiums and sales promotions, or for use in corporate training programs. For more information, please write to the Director of Special Sales, Professional Publishing, McGraw-Hill, Two Penn Plaza, New York, NY 10121-2298. Or contact your local bookstore.

Java™: The Complete Reference, Seventh Edition

1234567890 DOC DOC 019876

ISBN-13: 978-0-07-226385-5
ISBN-10:   0-07-226385-7

Sponsoring Editor
Wendy Rinaldi

Editorial Supervisor
Janet Walden

Project Editor
LeeAnn Pickrell

Acquisitions Coordinator
Mandy Canales

Technical Editor
Hale Pringle

Copy Editor
LeeAnn Pickrell

Proofreaders
Susie Elkind, LeeAnn Pickrell

Indexer
Sherry Schildt

Production Supervisor
Jean Bodeaux

Composition
Apollo Publishing Service

Illustration
Apollo Publishing Service

Series Design
Peter F. Hancik, Lyssa Wald

Art Director, Cover
Jeff Weeks

Contents at a Glance

Contents

Part III   Software Development Using Java

Preface

As I write this, Java is just beginning its second decade. Unlike many other computer languages whose influence begins to wane over the years, Java's has grown stronger with the passage of time. Java leapt to the forefront of Internet programming with its first release. Each subsequent version has solidified that position. Today, Java is still the first and best choice for developing web-based applications.

One reason for Java's success is its agility. Java has rapidly adapted to changes in the programming environment and to changes in the way that programmers program. Most importantly, it has not just followed the trends, *it has helped create them*. Unlike some other languages that have a revision cycle of approximately 10 years, Java's release cycle averages about 1.5 years! Java's ability to accommodate the fast rate of change in the computing world is a crucial part of why it has stayed at the forefront of computer language design. With the release of Java SE 6, Java's leadership remains unchallenged. If you are programming for the Internet, you have chosen the right language. Java has been and continues to be the preeminent language of the Internet.

As many readers will know, this is the seventh edition of the book, which was first published in 1996. This edition has been updated for Java SE 6. It has also been expanded in several key areas. Here are two examples: it now includes twice as much coverage of Swing and a more detailed discussion of resource bundles. Throughout are many other additions and improvements. In all, dozens of pages of new material have been incorporated.

A Book for All Programmers

This book is for all programmers, whether you are a novice or an experienced pro. The beginner will find its carefully paced discussions and many examples especially helpful. Its in-depth coverage of Java's more advanced features and libraries will appeal to the pro. For both, it offers a lasting resource and handy reference.

What's Inside

This book is a comprehensive guide to the Java language, describing its syntax, keywords, and fundamental programming principles. Significant portions of the Java API library are also examined. The book is divided into four parts, each focusing on a different aspect of the Java programming environment.

Part I presents an in-depth tutorial of the Java language. It begins with the basics, including such things as data types, control statements, and classes. Part I also discusses Java's exception-handling mechanism, multithreading subsystem, packages, and interfaces. Of course, Java's newer features, such as generics, annotations, enumerations, and autoboxing are covered in detail.

Part II examines key aspects of Java's standard API library. Topics include strings, I/O, networking, the standard utilities, the Collections Framework, applets, GUI-based controls, imaging, and concurrency.

Part III looks at three important Java technologies: Java Beans, Swing, and servlets.

Part IV contains two chapters that show examples of Java in action. The first chapter develops several applets that perform various popular financial calculations, such as computing the regular payment on a loan or the minimum investment needed to withdraw a desired monthly annuity. This chapter also shows how to convert those applets into servlets. The second chapter develops a download manager that oversees the downloading of files. It includes the ability to start, stop, and resume a transfer. Both chapters are adapted from my book *The Art of Java*, which I co-authored with James Holmes.

Don't Forget: Code on the Web

Remember, the source code for all of the examples in this book is available free-of-charge on the Web at **www.osborne.com**.

Special Thanks

Special thanks to Patrick Naughton. Patrick was one of the creators of the Java language. He also helped write the first edition of this book. For example, much of the material in Chapters 19, 20, and 25 was initially provided by Patrick. His insights, expertise, and energy contributed greatly to the success of this book.

Thanks also go to Joe O'Neil for providing the initial drafts for Chapters 27, 28, 30, and 31. Joe has helped on several of my books and, as always, his efforts are appreciated.

Finally, many thanks to James Holmes for providing Chapter 32. James is an extraordinary programmer and author. He was my co-author on *The Art of Java* and is the author of *Struts: The Complete Reference* and a co-author of *JSF: The Complete Reference*.

HERBERT SCHILDT
November 8, 2006

For Further Study

Java: The Complete Reference is your gateway to the Herb Schildt series of programming books. Here are some others that you will find of interest.

To learn more about Java programming, we recommend the following:

Java: A Beginner's Guide

Swing: A Beginner's Guide

The Art Of Java

To learn about C++, you will find these books especially helpful:

C++: The Complete Reference

C++: A Beginner's Guide

The Art of C++

C++ From the Ground Up

STL Programming From the Ground Up

To learn about C#, we suggest the following Schildt books:

C#: The Complete Reference

C#: A Beginner's Guide

To learn about the C language, the following titles will be of interest:

C: The Complete Reference

Teach Yourself C

When you need solid answers, fast, turn to Herbert Schildt, the recognized authority on programming.

PART

The Java Language

The History and Evolution of Java

To fully understand Java, one must understand the reasons behind its creation, the forces that shaped it, and the legacy that it inherits. Like the successful computer languages that came before, Java is a blend of the best elements of its rich heritage combined with the innovative concepts required by its unique mission. While the remaining chapters of this book describe the practical aspects of Java—including its syntax, key libraries, and applications—this chapter explains how and why Java came about, what makes it so important, and how it has evolved over the years.

Although Java has become inseparably linked with the online environment of the Internet, it is important to remember that Java is first and foremost a programming language. Computer language innovation and development occurs for two fundamental reasons:

- To adapt to changing environments and uses
- To implement refinements and improvements in the art of programming

As you will see, the development of Java was driven by both elements in nearly equal measure.

Java's Lineage

Java is related to C++, which is a direct descendant of C. Much of the character of Java is inherited from these two languages. From C, Java derives its syntax. Many of Java's object-oriented features were influenced by C++. In fact, several of Java's defining characteristics come from—or are responses to—its predecessors. Moreover, the creation of Java was deeply rooted in the process of refinement and adaptation that has been occurring in computer programming languages for the past several decades. For these reasons, this section reviews the sequence of events and forces that led to Java. As you will see, each innovation in language design was driven by the need to solve a fundamental problem that the preceding languages could not solve. Java is no exception.

The Birth of Modern Programming: C

The C language shook the computer world. Its impact should not be underestimated, because it fundamentally changed the way programming was approached and thought about. The creation of C was a direct result of the need for a structured, efficient, high-level language that could replace assembly code when creating systems programs. As you probably know, when a computer language is designed, trade-offs are often made, such as the following:

- Ease-of-use versus power
- Safety versus efficiency
- Rigidity versus extensibility

Prior to C, programmers usually had to choose between languages that optimized one set of traits or the other. For example, although FORTRAN could be used to write fairly efficient programs for scientific applications, it was not very good for system code. And while BASIC was easy to learn, it wasn't very powerful, and its lack of structure made its usefulness questionable for large programs. Assembly language can be used to produce highly efficient programs, but it is not easy to learn or use effectively. Further, debugging assembly code can be quite difficult.

Another compounding problem was that early computer languages such as BASIC, COBOL, and FORTRAN were not designed around structured principles. Instead, they relied upon the GOTO as a primary means of program control. As a result, programs written using these languages tended to produce "spaghetti code"—a mass of tangled jumps and conditional branches that make a program virtually impossible to understand. While languages like Pascal are structured, they were not designed for efficiency, and failed to include certain features necessary to make them applicable to a wide range of programs. (Specifically, given the standard dialects of Pascal available at the time, it was not practical to consider using Pascal for systems-level code.)

So, just prior to the invention of C, no one language had reconciled the conflicting attributes that had dogged earlier efforts. Yet the need for such a language was pressing. By the early 1970s, the computer revolution was beginning to take hold, and the demand for software was rapidly outpacing programmers' ability to produce it. A great deal of effort was being expended in academic circles in an attempt to create a better computer language. But, and perhaps most importantly, a secondary force was beginning to be felt. Computer hardware was finally becoming common enough that a critical mass was being reached. No longer were computers kept behind locked doors. For the first time, programmers were gaining virtually unlimited access to their machines. This allowed the freedom to experiment. It also allowed programmers to begin to create their own tools. On the eve of C's creation, the stage was set for a quantum leap forward in computer languages.

Invented and first implemented by Dennis Ritchie on a DEC PDP-11 running the UNIX operating system, C was the result of a development process that started with an older language called BCPL, developed by Martin Richards. BCPL influenced a language called B, invented by Ken Thompson, which led to the development of C in the 1970s. For many years, the de facto standard for C was the one supplied with the UNIX operating system and described in *The C Programming Language* by Brian Kernighan and Dennis Ritchie (Prentice-Hall, 1978). C was formally standardized in December 1989, when the American National Standards Institute (ANSI) standard for C was adopted.

The creation of C is considered by many to have marked the beginning of the modern age of computer languages. It successfully synthesized the conflicting attributes that had so troubled earlier languages. The result was a powerful, efficient, structured language that was relatively easy to learn. It also included one other, nearly intangible aspect: it was a *programmer's* language. Prior to the invention of C, computer languages were generally designed either as academic exercises or by bureaucratic committees. C is different. It was designed, implemented, and developed by real, working programmers, reflecting the way that they approached the job of programming. Its features were honed, tested, thought about, and rethought by the people who actually used the language. The result was a language that programmers liked to use. Indeed, C quickly attracted many followers who had a near-religious zeal for it. As such, it found wide and rapid acceptance in the programmer community. In short, C is a language designed by and for programmers. As you will see, Java inherited this legacy.

C++: The Next Step

During the late 1970s and early 1980s, C became the dominant computer programming language, and it is still widely used today. Since C is a successful and useful language, you might ask why a need for something else existed. The answer is *complexity*. Throughout the history of programming, the increasing complexity of programs has driven the need for better ways to manage that complexity. C++ is a response to that need. To better understand why managing program complexity is fundamental to the creation of C++, consider the following.

Approaches to programming have changed dramatically since the invention of the computer. For example, when computers were first invented, programming was done by manually toggling in the binary machine instructions by use of the front panel. As long as programs were just a few hundred instructions long, this approach worked. As programs grew, assembly language was invented so that a programmer could deal with larger, increasingly complex programs by using symbolic representations of the machine instructions. As programs continued to grow, high-level languages were introduced that gave the programmer more tools with which to handle complexity.

The first widespread language was, of course, FORTRAN. While FORTRAN was an impressive first step, it is hardly a language that encourages clear and easy-to-understand programs. The 1960s gave birth to *structured programming*. This is the method of programming championed by languages such as C. The use of structured languages enabled programmers to write, for the first time, moderately complex programs fairly easily. However, even with structured programming methods, once a project reaches a certain size, its complexity exceeds what a programmer can manage. By the early 1980s, many projects were pushing the structured approach past its limits. To solve this problem, a new way to program was invented, called *object-oriented programming (OOP)*. Object-oriented programming is discussed in detail later in this book, but here is a brief definition: OOP is a programming methodology that helps organize complex programs through the use of inheritance, encapsulation, and polymorphism.

In the final analysis, although C is one of the world's great programming languages, there is a limit to its ability to handle complexity. Once the size of a program exceeds a certain point, it becomes so complex that it is difficult to grasp as a totality. While the precise size at which this occurs differs, depending upon both the nature of the program and the programmer, there is always a threshold at which a program becomes unmanageable. C++ added features that enabled this threshold to be broken, allowing programmers to comprehend and manage larger programs.

C++ was invented by Bjarne Stroustrup in 1979, while he was working at Bell Laboratories in Murray Hill, New Jersey. Stroustrup initially called the new language "C with Classes." However, in 1983, the name was changed to C++. C++ extends C by adding object-oriented features. Because C++ is built on the foundation of C, it includes all of C's features, attributes, and benefits. This is a crucial reason for the success of C++ as a language. The invention of C++ was not an attempt to create a completely new programming language. Instead, it was an enhancement to an already highly successful one.

The Stage Is Set for Java

By the end of the 1980s and the early 1990s, object-oriented programming using C++ took hold. Indeed, for a brief moment it seemed as if programmers had finally found the perfect language. Because C++ blended the high efficiency and stylistic elements of C with the object-oriented paradigm, it was a language that could be used to create a wide range of programs. However, just as in the past, forces were brewing that would, once again, drive computer language evolution forward. Within a few years, the World Wide Web and the Internet would reach critical mass. This event would precipitate another revolution in programming.

The Creation of Java

Java was conceived by James Gosling, Patrick Naughton, Chris Warth, Ed Frank, and Mike Sheridan at Sun Microsystems, Inc. in 1991. It took 18 months to develop the first working version. This language was initially called "Oak," but was renamed "Java" in 1995. Between the initial implementation of Oak in the fall of 1992 and the public announcement of Java in the spring of 1995, many more people contributed to the design and evolution of the language. Bill Joy, Arthur van Hoff, Jonathan Payne, Frank Yellin, and Tim Lindholm were key contributors to the maturing of the original prototype.

Somewhat surprisingly, the original impetus for Java was not the Internet! Instead, the primary motivation was the need for a platform-independent (that is, architecture-neutral) language that could be used to create software to be embedded in various consumer electronic devices, such as microwave ovens and remote controls. As you can probably guess, many different types of CPUs are used as controllers. The trouble with C and C++ (and most other languages) is that they are designed to be compiled for a specific target. Although it is possible to compile a C++ program for just about any type of CPU, to do so requires a full C++ compiler targeted for that CPU. The problem is that compilers are expensive and time-consuming to create. An easier—and more cost-efficient—solution was needed. In an attempt to find such a solution, Gosling and others began work on a portable, platform-independent language that could be used to produce code that would run on a variety of CPUs under differing environments. This effort ultimately led to the creation of Java.

About the time that the details of Java were being worked out, a second, and ultimately more important, factor was emerging that would play a crucial role in the future of Java. This second force was, of course, the World Wide Web. Had the Web not taken shape at about the same time that Java was being implemented, Java might have remained a useful but obscure language for programming consumer electronics. However, with the emergence of the World Wide Web, Java was propelled to the forefront of computer language design, because the Web, too, demanded portable programs.

Most programmers learn early in their careers that portable programs are as elusive as they are desirable. While the quest for a way to create efficient, portable (platform-independent) programs is nearly as old as the discipline of programming itself, it had taken a back seat to other, more pressing problems. Further, because (at that time) much of the computer world had divided itself into the three competing camps of Intel, Macintosh, and UNIX, most programmers stayed within their fortified boundaries, and the urgent need for portable code was reduced. However, with the advent of the Internet and the Web, the old problem of portability returned with a vengeance. After all, the Internet consists of a diverse, distributed universe populated with various types of computers, operating systems, and CPUs. Even though many kinds of platforms are attached to the Internet, users would like them all to be able to run the same program. What was once an irritating but low-priority problem had become a high-profile necessity.

By 1993, it became obvious to members of the Java design team that the problems of portability frequently encountered when creating code for embedded controllers are also found when attempting to create code for the Internet. In fact, the same problem that Java was initially designed to solve on a small scale could also be applied to the Internet on a large scale. This realization caused the focus of Java to switch from consumer electronics to Internet programming. So, while the desire for an architecture-neutral programming language provided the initial spark, the Internet ultimately led to Java's large-scale success.

As mentioned earlier, Java derives much of its character from C and C++. This is by intent. The Java designers knew that using the familiar syntax of C and echoing the object-oriented features of C++ would make their language appealing to the legions of experienced C/C++ programmers. In addition to the surface similarities, Java shares some of the other attributes that helped make C and C++ successful. First, Java was designed, tested, and refined by real, working programmers. It is a language grounded in the needs and experiences of the people who devised it. Thus, Java is a programmer's language. Second, Java is cohesive and logically consistent. Third, except for those constraints imposed by the Internet environment, Java gives you, the programmer, full control. If you program well, your programs reflect it. If you program poorly, your programs reflect that, too. Put differently, Java is not a language with training wheels. It is a language for professional programmers.

Because of the similarities between Java and C++, it is tempting to think of Java as simply the "Internet version of C++." However, to do so would be a large mistake. Java has significant practical and philosophical differences. While it is true that Java was influenced by C++, it is not an enhanced version of C++. For example, Java is neither upwardly nor downwardly compatible with C++. Of course, the similarities with C++ are significant, and if you are a C++ programmer, then you will feel right at home with Java. One other point: Java was not designed to replace C++. Java was designed to solve a certain set of problems. C++ was designed to solve a different set of problems. Both will coexist for many years to come.

As mentioned at the start of this chapter, computer languages evolve for two reasons: to adapt to changes in environment and to implement advances in the art of programming. The environmental change that prompted Java was the need for platform-independent programs destined for distribution on the Internet. However, Java also embodies changes in the way that people approach the writing of programs. For example, Java enhanced and refined the object-oriented paradigm used by C++, added integrated support for multithreading, and provided a library that simplified Internet access. In the final analysis, though, it was not the individual features of Java that made it so remarkable. Rather, it was the language as a whole. Java was the perfect response to the demands of the then newly emerging, highly distributed computing universe. Java was to Internet programming what C was to system programming: a revolutionary force that changed the world.

The C# Connection

The reach and power of Java continues to be felt in the world of computer language development. Many of its innovative features, constructs, and concepts have become part of the baseline for any new language. The success of Java is simply too important to ignore.

Perhaps the most important example of Java's influence is C#. Created by Microsoft to support the .NET Framework, C# is closely related to Java. For example, both share the same general syntax, support distributed programming, and utilize the same object model. There are, of course, differences between Java and C#, but the overall "look and feel" of these languages is very similar. This "cross-pollination" from Java to C# is the strongest testimonial to date that Java redefined the way we think about and use a computer language.

How Java Changed the Internet

The Internet helped catapult Java to the forefront of programming, and Java, in turn, had a profound effect on the Internet. In addition to simplifying web programming in general, Java innovated a new type of networked program called the applet that changed the way the online world thought about content. Java also addressed some of the thorniest issues associated with the Internet: portability and security. Let's look more closely at each of these.

Java Applets

An *applet* is a special kind of Java program that is designed to be transmitted over the Internet and automatically executed by a Java-compatible web browser. Furthermore, an applet is downloaded on demand, without further interaction with the user. If the user clicks a link that contains an applet, the applet will be automatically downloaded and run in the browser. Applets are intended to be small programs. They are typically used to display data provided by the server, handle user input, or provide simple functions, such as a loan calculator, that execute locally, rather than on the server. In essence, the applet allows some functionality to be moved from the server to the client.

The creation of the applet changed Internet programming because it expanded the universe of objects that can move about freely in cyberspace. In general, there are two very broad categories of objects that are transmitted between the server and the client: passive information and dynamic, active programs. For example, when you read your e-mail, you are viewing passive data. Even when you download a program, the program's code is still only passive data until you execute it. By contrast, the applet is a dynamic, self-executing program. Such a program is an active agent on the client computer, yet it is initiated by the server.

As desirable as dynamic, networked programs are, they also present serious problems in the areas of security and portability. Obviously, a program that downloads and executes automatically on the client computer must be prevented from doing harm. It must also be able to run in a variety of different environments and under different operating systems. As you will see, Java solved these problems in an effective and elegant way. Let's look a bit more closely at each.

Security

As you are likely aware, every time you download a "normal" program, you are taking a risk, because the code you are downloading might contain a virus, Trojan horse, or other harmful code. At the core of the problem is the fact that malicious code can cause its damage because it has gained unauthorized access to system resources. For example, a virus program might gather private information, such as credit card numbers, bank account balances, and passwords, by searching the contents of your computer's local file system. In order for Java to enable applets to be downloaded and executed on the client computer safely, it was necessary to prevent an applet from launching such an attack.

Java achieved this protection by confining an applet to the Java execution environment and not allowing it access to other parts of the computer. (You will see how this is accomplished shortly.) The ability to download applets with confidence that no harm will be done and that no security will be breached is considered by many to be the single most innovative aspect of Java.

Portability

Portability is a major aspect of the Internet because there are many different types of computers and operating systems connected to it. If a Java program were to be run on virtually any computer connected to the Internet, there needed to be some way to enable that program to execute on different systems. For example, in the case of an applet, the same applet must be able to be downloaded and executed by the wide variety of CPUs, operating systems, and browsers connected to the Internet. It is not practical to have different versions of the applet for different computers. The *same* code must work on *all* computers. Therefore, some means of generating portable executable code was needed. As you will soon see, the same mechanism that helps ensure security also helps create portability.

Java's Magic: The Bytecode

The key that allows Java to solve both the security and the portability problems just described is that the output of a Java compiler is not executable code. Rather, it is bytecode. *Bytecode* is a highly optimized set of instructions designed to be executed by the Java run-time system, which is called the *Java Virtual Machine (JVM)*. In essence, the original JVM was designed as an *interpreter for bytecode*. This may come as a bit of a surprise since many modern languages are designed to be compiled into executable code because of performance concerns. However, the fact that a Java program is executed by the JVM helps solve the major problems associated with web-based programs. Here is why.

Translating a Java program into bytecode makes it much easier to run a program in a wide variety of environments because only the JVM needs to be implemented for each platform. Once the run-time package exists for a given system, any Java program can run on it. Remember, although the details of the JVM will differ from platform to platform, all understand the same Java bytecode. If a Java program were compiled to native code, then different versions of the same program would have to exist for each type of CPU connected to the Internet. This is, of course, not a feasible solution. Thus, the execution of bytecode by the JVM is the easiest way to create truly portable programs.

The fact that a Java program is executed by the JVM also helps to make it secure. Because the JVM is in control, it can contain the program and prevent it from generating side effects outside of the system. As you will see, safety is also enhanced by certain restrictions that exist in the Java language.

In general, when a program is compiled to an intermediate form and then interpreted by a virtual machine, it runs slower than it would run if compiled to executable code. However, with Java, the differential between the two is not so great. Because bytecode has been highly optimized, the use of bytecode enables the JVM to execute programs much faster than you might expect.

Although Java was designed as an interpreted language, there is nothing about Java that prevents on-the-fly compilation of bytecode into native code in order to boost performance. For this reason, Sun began supplying its HotSpot technology not long after Java's initial release. HotSpot provides a Just-In-Time (JIT) compiler for bytecode. When a JIT compiler is part of the JVM, selected portions of bytecode are compiled into executable code in real time, on a piece-by-piece, demand basis. It is important to understand that it is not practical to compile an entire Java program into executable code all at once, because Java performs various run-time checks that can be done only at run time. Instead, a JIT compiler compiles code as it is needed, during execution. Furthermore, not all sequences of bytecode are compiled—only those that will benefit from compilation. The remaining code is simply interpreted. However, the just-in-time approach still yields a significant performance boost. Even when dynamic compilation is applied to bytecode, the portability and safety features still apply, because the JVM is still in charge of the execution environment.

Servlets: Java on the Server Side

As useful as applets can be, they are just one half of the client/server equation. Not long after the initial release of Java, it became obvious that Java would also be useful on the server side. The result was the *servlet*. A servlet is a small program that executes on the server. Just as applets dynamically extend the functionality of a web browser, servlets dynamically extend the functionality of a web server. Thus, with the advent of the servlet, Java spanned both sides of the client/server connection.

Servlets are used to create dynamically generated content that is then served to the client. For example, an online store might use a servlet to look up the price for an item in a database. The price information is then used to dynamically generate a web page that is sent to the browser. Although dynamically generated content is available through mechanisms such as CGI (Common Gateway Interface), the servlet offers several advantages, including increased performance.

Because servlets (like all Java programs) are compiled into bytecode and executed by the JVM, they are highly portable. Thus, the same servlet can be used in a variety of different server environments. The only requirements are that the server support the JVM and a servlet container.

The Java Buzzwords

No discussion of Java's history is complete without a look at the Java buzzwords. Although the fundamental forces that necessitated the invention of Java are portability and security, other factors also played an important role in molding the final form of the language. The key considerations were summed up by the Java team in the following list of buzzwords:

- Simple
- Secure
- Portable
- Object-oriented
- Robust
- Multithreaded
- Architecture-neutral
- Interpreted
- High performance
- Distributed
- Dynamic

Two of these buzzwords have already been discussed: secure and portable. Let's examine what each of the others implies.

Simple

Java was designed to be easy for the professional programmer to learn and use effectively. Assuming that you have some programming experience, you will not find Java hard to master. If you already understand the basic concepts of object-oriented programming, learning Java will be even easier. Best of all, if you are an experienced C++ programmer, moving to Java will require very little effort. Because Java inherits the C/C++ syntax and many of the object-oriented features of C++, most programmers have little trouble learning Java.

Object-Oriented

Although influenced by its predecessors, Java was not designed to be source-code compatible with any other language. This allowed the Java team the freedom to design with a blank slate. One outcome of this was a clean, usable, pragmatic approach to objects. Borrowing liberally from many seminal object-software environments of the last few decades, Java manages to strike a balance between the purist's "everything is an object" paradigm and the pragmatist's "stay out of my way" model. The object model in Java is simple and easy to extend, while primitive types, such as integers, are kept as high-performance nonobjects.

Robust

The multiplatformed environment of the Web places extraordinary demands on a program, because the program must execute reliably in a variety of systems. Thus, the ability to create robust programs was given a high priority in the design of Java. To gain reliability, Java restricts you in a few key areas to force you to find your mistakes early in program development. At the same time, Java frees you from having to worry about many of the most common causes of programming errors. Because Java is a strictly typed language, it checks your code at compile time. However, it also checks your code at run time. Many hard-to-track-down bugs that often turn up in hard-to-reproduce run-time situations are simply impossible to create in Java. Knowing that what you have written will behave in a predictable way under diverse conditions is a key feature of Java.

To better understand how Java is robust, consider two of the main reasons for program failure: memory management mistakes and mishandled exceptional conditions (that is, run-time errors). Memory management can be a difficult, tedious task in traditional programming environments. For example, in C/C++, the programmer must manually allocate and free all dynamic memory. This sometimes leads to problems, because programmers will either forget to free memory that has been previously allocated or, worse, try to free some memory that another part of their code is still using. Java virtually eliminates these problems by managing memory allocation and deallocation for you. (In fact, deallocation is completely automatic, because Java provides garbage collection for unused objects.) Exceptional conditions in traditional environments often arise in situations such as division by zero or "file not found," and they must be managed with clumsy and hard-to-read constructs. Java helps in this area by providing object-oriented exception handling. In a well-written Java program, all run-time errors can—and should—be managed by your program.

Multithreaded

Java was designed to meet the real-world requirement of creating interactive, networked programs. To accomplish this, Java supports multithreaded programming, which allows you to write programs that do many things simultaneously. The Java run-time system comes with an elegant yet sophisticated solution for multiprocess synchronization that enables you to construct smoothly running interactive systems. Java's easy-to-use approach to multithreading allows you to think about the specific behavior of your program, not the multitasking subsystem.

Architecture-Neutral

A central issue for the Java designers was that of code longevity and portability. One of the main problems facing programmers is that no guarantee exists that if you write a program today, it will run tomorrow—even on the same machine. Operating system upgrades, processor upgrades, and changes in core system resources can all combine to make a program malfunction. The Java designers made several hard decisions in the Java language and the Java Virtual Machine in an attempt to alter this situation. Their goal was "write once; run anywhere, any time, forever." To a great extent, this goal was accomplished.

Interpreted and High Performance

As described earlier, Java enables the creation of cross-platform programs by compiling into an intermediate representation called Java bytecode. This code can be executed on any system that implements the Java Virtual Machine. Most previous attempts at cross-platform solutions have done so at the expense of performance. As explained earlier, the Java bytecode was carefully designed so that it would be easy to translate directly into native machine code for very high performance by using a just-in-time compiler. Java run-time systems that provide this feature lose none of the benefits of the platform-independent code.

Distributed

Java is designed for the distributed environment of the Internet because it handles TCP/IP protocols. In fact, accessing a resource using a URL is not much different from accessing a file. Java also supports *Remote Method Invocation (RMI).* This feature enables a program to invoke methods across a network.

Dynamic

Java programs carry with them substantial amounts of run-time type information that is used to verify and resolve accesses to objects at run time. This makes it possible to dynamically link code in a safe and expedient manner. This is crucial to the robustness of the Java environment, in which small fragments of bytecode may be dynamically updated on a running system.

The Evolution of Java

The initial release of Java was nothing short of revolutionary, but it did not mark the end of Java's era of rapid innovation. Unlike most other software systems that usually settle into a pattern of small, incremental improvements, Java continued to evolve at an explosive pace. Soon after the release of Java 1.0, the designers of Java had already created Java 1.1. The features added by Java 1.1 were more significant and substantial than the increase in the minor revision number would have you think. Java 1.1 added many new library elements, redefined the way events are handled, and reconfigured many features of the 1.0 library. It also deprecated (rendered obsolete) several features originally defined by Java 1.0. Thus, Java 1.1 both added to and subtracted from attributes of its original specification.

The next major release of Java was Java 2, where the "2" indicates "second generation." The creation of Java 2 was a watershed event, marking the beginning of Java's "modern age." The first release of Java 2 carried the version number 1.2. It may seem odd that the first release of Java 2 used the 1.2 version number. The reason is that it originally referred to the internal version number of the Java libraries, but then was generalized to refer to the entire release. With Java 2, Sun repackaged the Java product as J2SE (Java 2 Platform Standard Edition), and the version numbers began to be applied to that product.

Java 2 added support for a number of new features, such as Swing and the Collections Framework, and it enhanced the Java Virtual Machine and various programming tools. Java 2 also contained a few deprecations. The most important affected the **Thread** class in which the methods **suspend( )**, **resume( )**, and **stop( )** were deprecated.

J2SE 1.3 was the first major upgrade to the original Java 2 release. For the most part, it added to existing functionality and "tightened up" the development environment. In general, programs written for version 1.2 and those written for version 1.3 are source-code compatible. Although version 1.3 contained a smaller set of changes than the preceding three major releases, it was nevertheless important.

The release of J2SE 1.4 further enhanced Java. This release contained several important upgrades, enhancements, and additions. For example, it added the new keyword **assert**, chained exceptions, and a channel-based I/O subsystem. It also made changes to the Collections Framework and the networking classes. In addition, numerous small changes were made throughout. Despite the significant number of new features, version 1.4 maintained nearly 100 percent source-code compatibility with prior versions.

The next release of Java was J2SE 5, and it was revolutionary. Unlike most of the previous Java upgrades, which offered important, but measured improvements, J2SE 5 fundamentally expanded the scope, power, and range of the language. To grasp the magnitude of the changes that J2SE 5 made to Java, consider the following list of its major new features:

- Generics
- Annotations
- Autoboxing and auto-unboxing

- Enumerations
- Enhanced, for-each style **for** loop
- Variable-length arguments (varargs)
- Static import
- Formatted I/O
- Concurrency utilities

This is not a list of minor tweaks or incremental upgrades. Each item in the list represents a significant addition to the Java language. Some, such as generics, the enhanced **for**, and varargs, introduce new syntax elements. Others, such as autoboxing and auto-unboxing, alter the semantics of the language. Annotations add an entirely new dimension to programming. In all cases, the impact of these additions went beyond their direct effects. They changed the very character of Java itself.

The importance of these new features is reflected in the use of the version number "5." The next version number for Java would normally have been 1.5. However, the new features were so significant that a shift from 1.4 to 1.5 just didn't seem to express the magnitude of the change. Instead, Sun elected to increase the version number to 5 as a way of emphasizing that a major event was taking place. Thus, it was named J2SE 5, and the developer's kit was called JDK 5. However, in order to maintain consistency, Sun decided to use 1.5 as its *internal version* number, which is also referred to as the *developer version* number. The "5" in J2SE 5 is called the *product version* number.

Java SE 6

The newest release of Java is called Java SE 6, and the material in this book has been updated to reflect this latest version of Java. With the release of Java SE 6, Sun once again decided to change the name of the Java platform. First, notice that the "2" has been dropped. Thus, the platform now has the name *Java SE*, and the official product name is *Java Platform, Standard Edition 6*. As with J2SE 5, the 6 in Java SE 6 is the product version number. The internal, developer version number is 1.6.

Java SE 6 builds on the base of J2SE 5, adding incremental improvements. Java SE 6 adds no major features to the Java language proper, but it does enhance the API libraries, add several new packages, and offer improvements to the run time. As it relates to this book, it is the changes to the core API that are the most notable. Many of the packages have new classes, and many of the classes have new methods. These changes are indicated throughout the book. In general, the release of Java SE 6 serves to further solidify the advances made by J2SE 5.

A Culture of Innovation

Since the beginning, Java has been at the center of a culture of innovation. Its original release redefined programming for the Internet. The Java Virtual Machine (JVM) and bytecode changed the way we think about security and portability. The applet (and then the servlet) made the Web come alive. The Java Community Process (JCP) redefined the way that new ideas are assimilated into the language. The world of Java has never stood still for very long. Java SE 6 is the latest release in Java's ongoing, dynamic history.

An Overview of Java

A s in all other computer languages, the elements of Java do not exist in isolation. Rather, they work together to form the language as a whole. However, this interrelatedness can make it difficult to describe one aspect of Java without involving several others. Often a discussion of one feature implies prior knowledge of another. For this reason, this chapter presents a quick overview of several key features of Java. The material described here will give you a foothold that will allow you to write and understand simple programs. Most of the topics discussed will be examined in greater detail in the remaining chapters of Part I.

Object-Oriented Programming

Object-oriented programming (OOP) is at the core of Java. In fact, all Java programs are to at least some extent object-oriented. OOP is so integral to Java that it is best to understand its basic principles before you begin writing even simple Java programs. Therefore, this chapter begins with a discussion of the theoretical aspects of OOP.

Two Paradigms

All computer programs consist of two elements: code and data. Furthermore, a program can be conceptually organized around its code or around its data. That is, some programs are written around "what is happening" and others are written around "who is being affected." These are the two paradigms that govern how a program is constructed. The first way is called the *process-oriented model.* This approach characterizes a program as a series of linear steps (that is, code). The process-oriented model can be thought of as *code acting on data.* Procedural languages such as C employ this model to considerable success. However, as mentioned in Chapter 1, problems with this approach appear as programs grow larger and more complex.

To manage increasing complexity, the second approach, called *object-oriented programming,* was conceived. Object-oriented programming organizes a program around its data (that is, objects) and a set of well-defined interfaces to that data. An object-oriented program can be characterized as *data controlling access to code.* As you will see, by switching the controlling entity to data, you can achieve several organizational benefits.

Abstraction

An essential element of object-oriented programming is *abstraction*. Humans manage complexity through abstraction. For example, people do not think of a car as a set of tens of thousands of individual parts. They think of it as a well-defined object with its own unique behavior. This abstraction allows people to use a car to drive to the grocery store without being overwhelmed by the complexity of the parts that form the car. They can ignore the details of how the engine, transmission, and braking systems work. Instead, they are free to utilize the object as a whole.

A powerful way to manage abstraction is through the use of hierarchical classifications. This allows you to layer the semantics of complex systems, breaking them into more manageable pieces. From the outside, the car is a single object. Once inside, you see that the car consists of several subsystems: steering, brakes, sound system, seat belts, heating, cellular phone, and so on. In turn, each of these subsystems is made up of more specialized units. For instance, the sound system consists of a radio, a CD player, and/or a tape player. The point is that you manage the complexity of the car (or any other complex system) through the use of hierarchical abstractions.

Hierarchical abstractions of complex systems can also be applied to computer programs. The data from a traditional process-oriented program can be transformed by abstraction into its component objects. A sequence of process steps can become a collection of messages between these objects. Thus, each of these objects describes its own unique behavior. You can treat these objects as concrete entities that respond to messages telling them to *do something*. This is the essence of object-oriented programming.

Object-oriented concepts form the heart of Java just as they form the basis for human understanding. It is important that you understand how these concepts translate into programs. As you will see, object-oriented programming is a powerful and natural paradigm for creating programs that survive the inevitable changes accompanying the life cycle of any major software project, including conception, growth, and aging. For example, once you have well-defined objects and clean, reliable interfaces to those objects, you can gracefully decommission or replace parts of an older system without fear.

The Three OOP Principles

All object-oriented programming languages provide mechanisms that help you implement the object-oriented model. They are encapsulation, inheritance, and polymorphism. Let's take a look at these concepts now.

Encapsulation

Encapsulation is the mechanism that binds together code and the data it manipulates, and keeps both safe from outside interference and misuse. One way to think about encapsulation is as a protective wrapper that prevents the code and data from being arbitrarily accessed by other code defined outside the wrapper. Access to the code and data inside the wrapper is tightly controlled through a well-defined interface. To relate this to the real world, consider the automatic transmission on an automobile. It encapsulates hundreds of bits of information about your engine, such as how much you are accelerating, the pitch of the surface you are on, and the position of the shift lever. You, as the user, have only one method of affecting this complex encapsulation: by moving the gear-shift lever. You can't affect the transmission by using the turn signal or windshield wipers, for example. Thus, the gear-shift lever is a well-defined (indeed, unique) interface to the transmission. Further, what occurs inside the transmission does not affect objects outside the transmission. For example, shifting gears does not turn on the headlights! Because an automatic transmission is encapsulated, dozens of car manufacturers can implement one in any way they please. However, from the driver's point of view, they all work the same. This same idea can be applied to programming. The power of encapsulated code is that everyone knows how to access it and thus can use it regardless of the implementation details—and without fear of unexpected side effects.

In Java, the basis of encapsulation is the class. Although the class will be examined in great detail later in this book, the following brief discussion will be helpful now. A *class* defines the structure and behavior (data and code) that will be shared by a set of objects. Each object of a given class contains the structure and behavior defined by the class, as if it were stamped out by a mold in the shape of the class. For this reason, objects are sometimes referred to as *instances of a class.* Thus, a class is a logical construct; an object has physical reality.

When you create a class, you will specify the code and data that constitute that class. Collectively, these elements are called *members* of the class. Specifically, the data defined by the class are referred to as *member variables* or *instance variables.* The code that operates on that data is referred to as *member methods* or just *methods.* (If you are familiar with C/C++, it may help to know that what a Java programmer calls a *method,* a C/C++ programmer calls a *function.*) In properly written Java programs, the methods define how the member variables can be used. This means that the behavior and interface of a class are defined by the methods that operate on its instance data.

Since the purpose of a class is to encapsulate complexity, there are mechanisms for hiding the complexity of the implementation inside the class. Each method or variable in a class may be marked private or public. The *public* interface of a class represents everything that external users of the class need to know, or may know. The *private* methods and data can only be accessed by code that is a member of the class. Therefore, any other code that is not a member of the class cannot access a private method or variable. Since the private members of a class may only be accessed by other parts of your program through the class' public methods, you can ensure that no improper actions take place. Of course, this means that the public interface should be carefully designed not to expose too much of the inner workings of a class (see Figure 2-1).

Inheritance

Inheritance is the process by which one object acquires the properties of another object. This is important because it supports the concept of hierarchical classification. As mentioned earlier, most knowledge is made manageable by hierarchical (that is, top-down) classifications. For example, a Golden Retriever is part of the classification *dog,* which in turn is part of the *mammal* class, which is under the larger class *animal.* Without the use of hierarchies, each object would need to define all of its characteristics explicitly. However, by use of inheritance, an object need only define those qualities that make it unique within its class. It can inherit its general attributes from its parent. Thus, it is the inheritance mechanism that makes it possible for one object to be a specific instance of a more general case. Let's take a closer look at this process.

FIGURE 2-1
Encapsulation:
public methods
can be used to
protect private
data

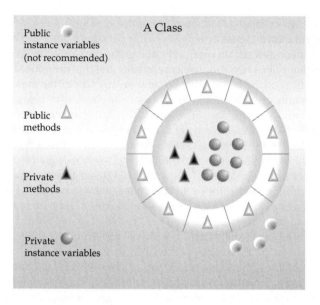

Most people naturally view the world as made up of objects that are related to each other in a hierarchical way, such as animals, mammals, and dogs. If you wanted to describe animals in an abstract way, you would say they have some attributes, such as size, intelligence, and type of skeletal system. Animals also have certain behavioral aspects; they eat, breathe, and sleep. This description of attributes and behavior is the *class* definition for animals.

If you wanted to describe a more specific class of animals, such as mammals, they would have more specific attributes, such as type of teeth, and mammary glands. This is known as a *subclass* of animals, where animals are referred to as mammals' *superclass*.

Since mammals are simply more precisely specified animals, they *inherit* all of the attributes from animals. A deeply inherited subclass inherits all of the attributes from each of its ancestors in the *class hierarchy*.

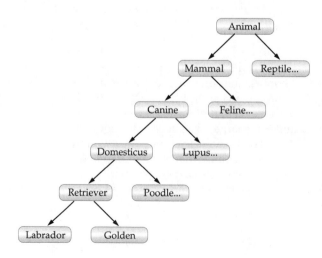

Inheritance interacts with encapsulation as well. If a given class encapsulates some attributes, then any subclass will have the same attributes *plus* any that it adds as part of its specialization (see Figure 2-2). This is a key concept that lets object-oriented programs grow in complexity linearly rather than geometrically. A new subclass inherits all of the attributes of all of its ancestors. It does not have unpredictable interactions with the majority of the rest of the code in the system.

Polymorphism

Polymorphism (from Greek, meaning "many forms") is a feature that allows one interface to be used for a general class of actions. The specific action is determined by the exact nature

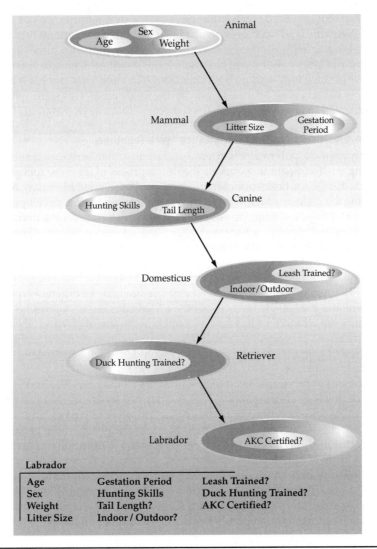

FIGURE 2-2 Labrador inherits the encapsulation of all its superclasses

of the situation. Consider a stack (which is a last-in, first-out list). You might have a program that requires three types of stacks. One stack is used for integer values, one for floating-point values, and one for characters. The algorithm that implements each stack is the same, even though the data being stored differs. In a non–object-oriented language, you would be required to create three different sets of stack routines, with each set using different names. However, because of polymorphism, in Java you can specify a general set of stack routines that all share the same names.

More generally, the concept of polymorphism is often expressed by the phrase "one interface, multiple methods." This means that it is possible to design a generic interface to a group of related activities. This helps reduce complexity by allowing the same interface to be used to specify a *general class of action*. It is the compiler's job to select the *specific action* (that is, method) as it applies to each situation. You, the programmer, do not need to make this selection manually. You need only remember and utilize the general interface.

Extending the dog analogy, a dog's sense of smell is polymorphic. If the dog smells a cat, it will bark and run after it. If the dog smells its food, it will salivate and run to its bowl. The same sense of smell is at work in both situations. The difference is what is being smelled, that is, the type of data being operated upon by the dog's nose! This same general concept can be implemented in Java as it applies to methods within a Java program.

Polymorphism, Encapsulation, and Inheritance Work Together

When properly applied, polymorphism, encapsulation, and inheritance combine to produce a programming environment that supports the development of far more robust and scalable programs than does the process-oriented model. A well-designed hierarchy of classes is the basis for reusing the code in which you have invested time and effort developing and testing. Encapsulation allows you to migrate your implementations over time without breaking the code that depends on the public interface of your classes. Polymorphism allows you to create clean, sensible, readable, and resilient code.

Of the two real-world examples, the automobile more completely illustrates the power of object-oriented design. Dogs are fun to think about from an inheritance standpoint, but cars are more like programs. All drivers rely on inheritance to drive different types (subclasses) of vehicles. Whether the vehicle is a school bus, a Mercedes sedan, a Porsche, or the family minivan, drivers can all more or less find and operate the steering wheel, the brakes, and the accelerator. After a bit of gear grinding, most people can even manage the difference between a stick shift and an automatic, because they fundamentally understand their common superclass, the transmission.

People interface with encapsulated features on cars all the time. The brake and gas pedals hide an incredible array of complexity with an interface so simple you can operate them with your feet! The implementation of the engine, the style of brakes, and the size of the tires have no effect on how you interface with the class definition of the pedals.

The final attribute, polymorphism, is clearly reflected in the ability of car manufacturers to offer a wide array of options on basically the same vehicle. For example, you can get an antilock braking system or traditional brakes, power or rack-and-pinion steering, and 4-, 6-, or 8-cylinder engines. Either way, you will still press the brake pedal to stop, turn the steering wheel to change direction, and press the accelerator when you want to move. The same interface can be used to control a number of different implementations.

As you can see, it is through the application of encapsulation, inheritance, and polymorphism that the individual parts are transformed into the object known as a car. The same is also true of computer programs. By the application of object-oriented principles, the various parts of a complex program can be brought together to form a cohesive, robust, maintainable whole.

As mentioned at the start of this section, every Java program is object-oriented. Or, put more precisely, every Java program involves encapsulation, inheritance, and polymorphism. Although the short example programs shown in the rest of this chapter and in the next few chapters may not seem to exhibit all of these features, they are nevertheless present. As you will see, many of the features supplied by Java are part of its built-in class libraries, which do make extensive use of encapsulation, inheritance, and polymorphism.

A First Simple Program

Now that the basic object-oriented underpinning of Java has been discussed, let's look at some actual Java programs. Let's start by compiling and running the short sample program shown here. As you will see, this involves a little more work than you might imagine.

```
/*
   This is a simple Java program.
   Call this file "Example.java".
*/
class Example {
  // Your program begins with a call to main().
  public static void main(String args[]) {
    System.out.println("This is a simple Java program.");
  }
}
```

NOTE   *The descriptions that follow use the standard Java SE 6 Development Kit (JDK 6), which is available from Sun Microsystems. If you are using a different Java development environment, then you may need to follow a different procedure for compiling and executing Java programs. In this case, consult your compiler's documentation for details.*

Entering the Program

For most computer languages, the name of the file that holds the source code to a program is immaterial. However, this is not the case with Java. The first thing that you must learn about Java is that the name you give to a source file is very important. For this example, the name of the source file should be **Example.java**. Let's see why.

In Java, a source file is officially called a *compilation unit*. It is a text file that contains one or more class definitions. The Java compiler requires that a source file use the **.java** filename extension.

As you can see by looking at the program, the name of the class defined by the program is also **Example**. This is not a coincidence. In Java, all code must reside inside a class. By convention, the name of that class should match the name of the file that holds the program. You should also make sure that the capitalization of the filename matches the class name.

The reason for this is that Java is case-sensitive. At this point, the convention that filenames correspond to class names may seem arbitrary. However, this convention makes it easier to maintain and organize your programs.

Compiling the Program

To compile the **Example** program, execute the compiler, **javac**, specifying the name of the source file on the command line, as shown here:

```
C:\>javac Example.java
```

The **javac** compiler creates a file called **Example.class** that contains the bytecode version of the program. As discussed earlier, the Java bytecode is the intermediate representation of your program that contains instructions the Java Virtual Machine will execute. Thus, the output of **javac** is not code that can be directly executed.

To actually run the program, you must use the Java application launcher, called **java**. To do so, pass the class name **Example** as a command-line argument, as shown here:

```
C:\>java Example
```

When the program is run, the following output is displayed:

```
This is a simple Java program.
```

When Java source code is compiled, each individual class is put into its own output file named after the class and using the **.class** extension. This is why it is a good idea to give your Java source files the same name as the class they contain—the name of the source file will match the name of the **.class** file. When you execute **java** as just shown, you are actually specifying the name of the class that you want to execute. It will automatically search for a file by that name that has the **.class** extension. If it finds the file, it will execute the code contained in the specified class.

A Closer Look at the First Sample Program

Although **Example.java** is quite short, it includes several key features that are common to all Java programs. Let's closely examine each part of the program.

The program begins with the following lines:

```
/*
   This is a simple Java program.
   Call this file "Example.java".
*/
```

This is a *comment*. Like most other programming languages, Java lets you enter a remark into a program's source file. The contents of a comment are ignored by the compiler. Instead, a comment describes or explains the operation of the program to anyone who is reading its source code. In this case, the comment describes the program and reminds you that the source file should be called **Example.java**. Of course, in real applications, comments generally explain how some part of the program works or what a specific feature does.

Java supports three styles of comments. The one shown at the top of the program is called a *multiline comment.* This type of comment must begin with /* and end with */. Anything between these two comment symbols is ignored by the compiler. As the name suggests, a multiline comment may be several lines long.

The next line of code in the program is shown here:

```
class Example {
```

This line uses the keyword **class** to declare that a new class is being defined. **Example** is an *identifier* that is the name of the class. The entire class definition, including all of its members, will be between the opening curly brace ({) and the closing curly brace (}). For the moment, don't worry too much about the details of a class except to note that in Java, all program activity occurs within one. This is one reason why all Java programs are (at least a little bit) object-oriented.

The next line in the program is the *single-line comment,* shown here:

```
// Your program begins with a call to main().
```

This is the second type of comment supported by Java. A *single-line comment* begins with a // and ends at the end of the line. As a general rule, programmers use multiline comments for longer remarks and single-line comments for brief, line-by-line descriptions. The third type of comment, a *documentation comment,* will be discussed in the "Comments" section later in this chapter.

The next line of code is shown here:

```
public static void main(String args[]) {
```

This line begins the **main( )** method. As the comment preceding it suggests, this is the line at which the program will begin executing. All Java applications begin execution by calling **main( )**. The full meaning of each part of this line cannot be given now, since it involves a detailed understanding of Java's approach to encapsulation. However, since most of the examples in the first part of this book will use this line of code, let's take a brief look at each part now.

The **public** keyword is an *access specifier,* which allows the programmer to control the visibility of class members. When a class member is preceded by **public**, then that member may be accessed by code outside the class in which it is declared. (The opposite of **public** is **private**, which prevents a member from being used by code defined outside of its class.) In this case, **main( )** must be declared as **public**, since it must be called by code outside of its class when the program is started. The keyword **static** allows **main( )** to be called without having to instantiate a particular instance of the class. This is necessary since **main( )** is called by the Java Virtual Machine before any objects are made. The keyword **void** simply tells the compiler that **main( )** does not return a value. As you will see, methods may also return values. If all this seems a bit confusing, don't worry. All of these concepts will be discussed in detail in subsequent chapters.

As stated, **main( )** is the method called when a Java application begins. Keep in mind that Java is case-sensitive. Thus, **Main** is different from **main**. It is important to understand that the Java compiler will compile classes that do not contain a **main( )** method. But **java** has no way to run these classes. So, if you had typed **Main** instead of **main**, the compiler would still compile your program. However, **java** would report an error because it would be unable to find the **main( )** method.

Any information that you need to pass to a method is received by variables specified within the set of parentheses that follow the name of the method. These variables are called *parameters*. If there are no parameters required for a given method, you still need to include the empty parentheses. In **main( )**, there is only one parameter, albeit a complicated one. **String args[ ]** declares a parameter named **args**, which is an array of instances of the class **String**. (*Arrays* are collections of similar objects.) Objects of type **String** store character strings. In this case, **args** receives any command-line arguments present when the program is executed. This program does not make use of this information, but other programs shown later in this book will.

The last character on the line is the {. This signals the start of **main( )**'s body. All of the code that comprises a method will occur between the method's opening curly brace and its closing curly brace.

One other point: **main( )** is simply a starting place for your program. A complex program will have dozens of classes, only one of which will need to have a **main( )** method to get things started. When you begin creating applets—Java programs that are embedded in web browsers—you won't use **main( )** at all, since the web browser uses a different means of starting the execution of applets.

The next line of code is shown here. Notice that it occurs inside **main( )**.

```
System.out.println("This is a simple Java program.");
```

This line outputs the string "This is a simple Java program." followed by a new line on the screen. Output is actually accomplished by the built-in **println( )** method. In this case, **println( )** displays the string which is passed to it. As you will see, **println( )** can be used to display other types of information, too. The line begins with **System.out**. While too complicated to explain in detail at this time, briefly, **System** is a predefined class that provides access to the system, and **out** is the output stream that is connected to the console.

As you have probably guessed, console output (and input) is not used frequently in most real-world Java programs and applets. Since most modern computing environments are windowed and graphical in nature, console I/O is used mostly for simple utility programs and for demonstration programs. Later in this book, you will learn other ways to generate output using Java. But for now, we will continue to use the console I/O methods.

Notice that the **println( )** statement ends with a semicolon. All statements in Java end with a semicolon. The reason that the other lines in the program do not end in a semicolon is that they are not, technically, statements.

The first } in the program ends **main( )**, and the last } ends the **Example** class definition.

A Second Short Program

Perhaps no other concept is more fundamental to a programming language than that of a variable. As you probably know, a *variable* is a named memory location that may be assigned a value by your program. The value of a variable may be changed during the execution of the program. The next program shows how a variable is declared and how it is assigned a value. The program also illustrates some new aspects of console output. As the comments at the top of the program state, you should call this file **Example2.java**.

```
/*
   Here is another short example.
   Call this file "Example2.java".
*/

class Example2 {
  public static void main(String args[]) {
    int num; // this declares a variable called num

    num = 100; // this assigns num the value 100

    System.out.println("This is num: " + num);

    num = num * 2;

    System.out.print("The value of num * 2 is ");
    System.out.println(num);
  }
}
```

When you run this program, you will see the following output:

```
This is num: 100
The value of num * 2 is 200
```

Let's take a close look at why this output is generated. The first new line in the program is shown here:

```
int num; // this declares a variable called num
```

This line declares an integer variable called **num**. Java (like most other languages) requires that variables be declared before they are used.

Following is the general form of a variable declaration:

type var-name;

Here, *type* specifies the type of variable being declared, and *var-name* is the name of the variable. If you want to declare more than one variable of the specified type, you may use a comma-separated list of variable names. Java defines several data types, including integer, character, and floating-point. The keyword **int** specifies an integer type.

In the program, the line

```
num = 100; // this assigns num the value 100
```

assigns to **num** the value 100. In Java, the assignment operator is a single equal sign.

The next line of code outputs the value of **num** preceded by the string "This is num:".

```
System.out.println("This is num: " + num);
```

In this statement, the plus sign causes the value of **num** to be appended to the string that precedes it, and then the resulting string is output. (Actually, **num** is first converted from an integer into its string equivalent and then concatenated with the string that precedes it. This process is described in detail later in this book.) This approach can be generalized. Using the + operator, you can join together as many items as you want within a single **println( )** statement.

The next line of code assigns **num** the value of **num** times 2. Like most other languages, Java uses the * operator to indicate multiplication. After this line executes, **num** will contain the value 200.

Here are the next two lines in the program:

```
System.out.print("The value of num * 2 is ");
System.out.println(num);
```

Several new things are occurring here. First, the built-in method **print( )** is used to display the string "The value of num * 2 is ". This string is *not* followed by a newline. This means that when the next output is generated, it will start on the same line. The **print( )** method is just like **println( )**, except that it does not output a newline character after each call. Now look at the call to **println( )**. Notice that **num** is used by itself. Both **print( )** and **println( )** can be used to output values of any of Java's built-in types.

Two Control Statements

Although Chapter 5 will look closely at control statements, two are briefly introduced here so that they can be used in example programs in Chapters 3 and 4. They will also help illustrate an important aspect of Java: blocks of code.

The if Statement

The Java **if** statement works much like the IF statement in any other language. Further, it is syntactically identical to the **if** statements in C, C++, and C#. Its simplest form is shown here:

if(*condition*) *statement*;

Here, *condition* is a Boolean expression. If *condition* is true, then the statement is executed. If *condition* is false, then the statement is bypassed. Here is an example:

```
if(num < 100) System.out.println("num is less than 100");
```

In this case, if **num** contains a value that is less than 100, the conditional expression is true, and **println( )** will execute. If **num** contains a value greater than or equal to 100, then the **println( )** method is bypassed.

As you will see in Chapter 4, Java defines a full complement of relational operators which may be used in a conditional expression. Here are a few:

Operator	Meaning
<	Less than
>	Greater than
==	Equal to

Notice that the test for equality is the double equal sign.

Here is a program that illustrates the **if** statement:

```
/*
  Demonstrate the if.

  Call this file "IfSample.java".
*/
class IfSample {
  public static void main(String args[]) {
    int x, y;

    x = 10;
    y = 20;

    if(x < y) System.out.println("x is less than y");

    x = x * 2;
    if(x == y) System.out.println("x now equal to y");

    x = x * 2;
    if(x > y) System.out.println("x now greater than y");

    // this won't display anything
    if(x == y) System.out.println("you won't see this");
  }
}
```

The output generated by this program is shown here:

```
x is less than y
x now equal to y
x now greater than y
```

Notice one other thing in this program. The line

```
int x, y;
```

declares two variables, **x** and **y**, by use of a comma-separated list.

The for Loop

As you may know from your previous programming experience, loop statements are an important part of nearly any programming language. Java is no exception. In fact, as you will see in Chapter 5, Java supplies a powerful assortment of loop constructs. Perhaps the most versatile is the **for** loop. The simplest form of the **for** loop is shown here:

for(*initialization; condition; iteration*) *statement;*

In its most common form, the *initialization* portion of the loop sets a loop control variable to an initial value. The *condition* is a Boolean expression that tests the loop control variable. If the outcome of that test is true, the **for** loop continues to iterate. If it is false, the loop terminates. The *iteration* expression determines how the loop control variable is changed each time the loop iterates. Here is a short program that illustrates the **for** loop:

```
/*
   Demonstrate the for loop.

   Call this file "ForTest.java".
*/
class ForTest {
  public static void main(String args[]) {
    int x;

    for(x = 0; x<10; x = x+1)
      System.out.println("This is x: " + x);
  }
}
```

This program generates the following output:

```
This is x: 0
This is x: 1
This is x: 2
This is x: 3
This is x: 4
This is x: 5
This is x: 6
This is x: 7
This is x: 8
This is x: 9
```

In this example, **x** is the loop control variable. It is initialized to zero in the initialization portion of the **for**. At the start of each iteration (including the first one), the conditional test **x < 10** is performed. If the outcome of this test is true, the **println( )** statement is executed, and then the iteration portion of the loop is executed. This process continues until the conditional test is false.

As a point of interest, in professionally written Java programs you will almost never see the iteration portion of the loop written as shown in the preceding program. That is, you will seldom see statements like this:

```
x = x + 1;
```

The reason is that Java includes a special increment operator which performs this operation more efficiently. The increment operator is **++**. (That is, two plus signs back to back.) The increment operator increases its operand by one. By use of the increment operator, the preceding statement can be written like this:

```
x++;
```

Thus, the **for** in the preceding program will usually be written like this:

```
for(x = 0; x<10; x++)
```

You might want to try this. As you will see, the loop still runs exactly the same as it did before.

Java also provides a decrement operator, which is specified as − −. This operator decreases its operand by one.

Using Blocks of Code

Java allows two or more statements to be grouped into *blocks of code*, also called *code blocks.* This is done by enclosing the statements between opening and closing curly braces. Once a block of code has been created, it becomes a logical unit that can be used any place that a single statement can. For example, a block can be a target for Java's **if** and **for** statements. Consider this **if** statement:

```
if(x < y) { // begin a block
  x = y;
  y = 0;
} // end of block
```

Here, if **x** is less than **y**, then both statements inside the block will be executed. Thus, the two statements inside the block form a logical unit, and one statement cannot execute without the other also executing. The key point here is that whenever you need to logically link two or more statements, you do so by creating a block.

Let's look at another example. The following program uses a block of code as the target of a **for** loop.

```
/*
  Demonstrate a block of code.

  Call this file "BlockTest.java"
*/
class BlockTest {
  public static void main(String args[]) {
    int x, y;

    y = 20;

    // the target of this loop is a block
    for(x = 0; x<10; x++) {
      System.out.println("This is x: " + x);
      System.out.println("This is y: " + y);
      y = y - 2;
    }
  }
}
```

The output generated by this program is shown here:

```
This is x: 0
This is y: 20
```

```
This is x: 1
This is y: 18
This is x: 2
This is y: 16
This is x: 3
This is y: 14
This is x: 4
This is y: 12
This is x: 5
This is y: 10
This is x: 6
This is y: 8
This is x: 7
This is y: 6
This is x: 8
This is y: 4
This is x: 9
This is y: 2
```

In this case, the target of the **for** loop is a block of code and not just a single statement. Thus, each time the loop iterates, the three statements inside the block will be executed. This fact is, of course, evidenced by the output generated by the program.

As you will see later in this book, blocks of code have additional properties and uses. However, the main reason for their existence is to create logically inseparable units of code.

Lexical Issues

Now that you have seen several short Java programs, it is time to more formally describe the atomic elements of Java. Java programs are a collection of whitespace, identifiers, literals, comments, operators, separators, and keywords. The operators are described in the next chapter. The others are described next.

Whitespace

Java is a free-form language. This means that you do not need to follow any special indentation rules. For instance, the **Example** program could have been written all on one line or in any other strange way you felt like typing it, as long as there was at least one whitespace character between each token that was not already delineated by an operator or separator. In Java, whitespace is a space, tab, or newline.

Identifiers

Identifiers are used for class names, method names, and variable names. An identifier may be any descriptive sequence of uppercase and lowercase letters, numbers, or the underscore and dollar-sign characters. They must not begin with a number, lest they be confused with a numeric literal. Again, Java is case-sensitive, so **VALUE** is a different identifier than **Value**. Some examples of valid identifiers are

AvgTemp	count	a4	$test	this_is_ok

Invalid identifier names include these:

2count	high-temp	Not/ok

Literals

A constant value in Java is created by using a *literal* representation of it. For example, here are some literals:

100	98.6	'X'	"This is a test"

Left to right, the first literal specifies an integer, the next is a floating-point value, the third is a character constant, and the last is a string. A literal can be used anywhere a value of its type is allowed.

Comments

As mentioned, there are three types of comments defined by Java. You have already seen two: single-line and multiline. The third type is called a *documentation comment.* This type of comment is used to produce an HTML file that documents your program. The documentation comment begins with a /** and ends with a */. Documentation comments are explained in Appendix A.

Separators

In Java, there are a few characters that are used as separators. The most commonly used separator in Java is the semicolon. As you have seen, it is used to terminate statements. The separators are shown in the following table:

Symbol	Name	Purpose
( )	Parentheses	Used to contain lists of parameters in method definition and invocation. Also used for defining precedence in expressions, containing expressions in control statements, and surrounding cast types.
{ }	Braces	Used to contain the values of automatically initialized arrays. Also used to define a block of code, for classes, methods, and local scopes.
[ ]	Brackets	Used to declare array types. Also used when dereferencing array values.
;	Semicolon	Terminates statements.
,	Comma	Separates consecutive identifiers in a variable declaration. Also used to chain statements together inside a **for** statement.
.	Period	Used to separate package names from subpackages and classes. Also used to separate a variable or method from a reference variable.

The Java Keywords

There are 50 keywords currently defined in the Java language (see Table 2-1). These keywords, combined with the syntax of the operators and separators, form the foundation of the Java language. These keywords cannot be used as names for a variable, class, or method.

abstract	continue	for	new	switch
assert	default	goto	package	synchronized
boolean	do	if	private	this
break	double	implements	protected	throw
byte	else	import	public	throws
case	enum	instanceof	return	transient
catch	extends	int	short	try
char	final	interface	static	void
class	finally	long	strictfp	volatile
const	float	native	super	while

TABLE 2-1 Java Keywords

The keywords **const** and **goto** are reserved but not used. In the early days of Java, several other keywords were reserved for possible future use. However, the current specification for Java only defines the keywords shown in Table 2-1.

In addition to the keywords, Java reserves the following: **true**, **false**, and **null**. These are values defined by Java. You may not use these words for the names of variables, classes, and so on.

The Java Class Libraries

The sample programs shown in this chapter make use of two of Java's built-in methods: **println( )** and **print( )**. As mentioned, these methods are members of the **System** class, which is a class predefined by Java that is automatically included in your programs. In the larger view, the Java environment relies on several built-in class libraries that contain many built-in methods that provide support for such things as I/O, string handling, networking, and graphics. The standard classes also provide support for windowed output. Thus, Java as a totality is a combination of the Java language itself, plus its standard classes. As you will see, the class libraries provide much of the functionality that comes with Java. Indeed, part of becoming a Java programmer is learning to use the standard Java classes. Throughout Part I of this book, various elements of the standard library classes and methods are described as needed. In Part II, the class libraries are described in detail.

Data Types, Variables, and Arrays

This chapter examines three of Java's most fundamental elements: data types, variables, and arrays. As with all modern programming languages, Java supports several types of data. You may use these types to declare variables and to create arrays. As you will see, Java's approach to these items is clean, efficient, and cohesive.

Java Is a Strongly Typed Language

It is important to state at the outset that Java is a strongly typed language. Indeed, part of Java's safety and robustness comes from this fact. Let's see what this means. First, every variable has a type, every expression has a type, and every type is strictly defined. Second, all assignments, whether explicit or via parameter passing in method calls, are checked for type compatibility. There are no automatic coercions or conversions of conflicting types as in some languages. The Java compiler checks all expressions and parameters to ensure that the types are compatible. Any type mismatches are errors that must be corrected before the compiler will finish compiling the class.

The Primitive Types

Java defines eight *primitive* types of data: **byte**, **short**, **int**, **long**, **char**, **float**, **double**, and **boolean**. The primitive types are also commonly referred to as *simple* types, and both terms will be used in this book. These can be put in four groups:

- Integers   This group includes **byte**, **short**, **int**, and **long**, which are for whole-valued signed numbers.

- Floating-point numbers   This group includes **float** and **double**, which represent numbers with fractional precision.

- Characters   This group includes **char**, which represents symbols in a character set, like letters and numbers.

- Boolean   This group includes **boolean**, which is a special type for representing true/false values.

You can use these types as-is, or to construct arrays or your own class types. Thus, they form the basis for all other types of data that you can create.

The primitive types represent single values—not complex objects. Although Java is otherwise completely object-oriented, the primitive types are not. They are analogous to the simple types found in most other non–object-oriented languages. The reason for this is efficiency. Making the primitive types into objects would have degraded performance too much.

The primitive types are defined to have an explicit range and mathematical behavior. Languages such as C and C++ allow the size of an integer to vary based upon the dictates of the execution environment. However, Java is different. Because of Java's portability requirement, all data types have a strictly defined range. For example, an **int** is always 32 bits, regardless of the particular platform. This allows programs to be written that are guaranteed to run *without porting* on any machine architecture. While strictly specifying the size of an integer may cause a small loss of performance in some environments, it is necessary in order to achieve portability.

Let's look at each type of data in turn.

Integers

Java defines four integer types: **byte**, **short**, **int**, and **long**. All of these are signed, positive and negative values. Java does not support unsigned, positive-only integers. Many other computer languages support both signed and unsigned integers. However, Java's designers felt that unsigned integers were unnecessary. Specifically, they felt that the concept of *unsigned* was used mostly to specify the behavior of the *high-order bit,* which defines the *sign* of an integer value. As you will see in Chapter 4, Java manages the meaning of the high-order bit differently, by adding a special "unsigned right shift" operator. Thus, the need for an unsigned integer type was eliminated.

The *width* of an integer type should not be thought of as the amount of storage it consumes, but rather as the *behavior* it defines for variables and expressions of that type. The Java run-time environment is free to use whatever size it wants, as long as the types behave as you declared them. The width and ranges of these integer types vary widely, as shown in this table:

Name	Width	Range
long	64	−9,223,372,036,854,775,808 to 9,223,372,036,854,775,807
int	32	−2,147,483,648 to 2,147,483,647
short	16	−32,768 to 32,767
byte	8	−128 to 127

Let's look at each type of integer.

byte

The smallest integer type is **byte**. This is a signed 8-bit type that has a range from –128 to 127. Variables of type **byte** are especially useful when you're working with a stream of data from a network or file. They are also useful when you're working with raw binary data that may not be directly compatible with Java's other built-in types.

Byte variables are declared by use of the **byte** keyword. For example, the following declares two **byte** variables called **b** and **c**:

```
byte b, c;
```

short

short is a signed 16-bit type. It has a range from –32,768 to 32,767. It is probably the least-used Java type. Here are some examples of **short** variable declarations:

```
short s;
short t;
```

int

The most commonly used integer type is **int**. It is a signed 32-bit type that has a range from –2,147,483,648 to 2,147,483,647. In addition to other uses, variables of type **int** are commonly employed to control loops and to index arrays. Although you might think that using a **byte** or **short** would be more efficient than using an **int** in situations in which the larger range of an **int** is not needed, this may not be the case. The reason is that when **byte** and **short** values are used in an expression they are *promoted* to **int** when the expression is evaluated. (Type promotion is described later in this chapter.) Therefore, **int** is often the best choice when an integer is needed.

long

long is a signed 64-bit type and is useful for those occasions where an **int** type is not large enough to hold the desired value. The range of a **long** is quite large. This makes it useful when big, whole numbers are needed. For example, here is a program that computes the number of miles that light will travel in a specified number of days.

```
// Compute distance light travels using long variables.
class Light {
  public static void main(String args[]) {
    int lightspeed;
    long days;
    long seconds;
    long distance;

    // approximate speed of light in miles per second
    lightspeed = 186000;

    days = 1000; // specify number of days here
```

```
    seconds = days * 24 * 60 * 60; // convert to seconds

    distance = lightspeed * seconds; // compute distance

    System.out.print("In " + days);
    System.out.print(" days light will travel about ");
    System.out.println(distance + " miles.");
  }
}
```

This program generates the following output:

```
In 1000 days light will travel about 16070400000000 miles.
```

Clearly, the result could not have been held in an **int** variable.

Floating-Point Types

Floating-point numbers, also known as *real* numbers, are used when evaluating expressions that require fractional precision. For example, calculations such as square root, or transcendentals such as sine and cosine, result in a value whose precision requires a floating-point type. Java implements the standard (IEEE–754) set of floating-point types and operators. There are two kinds of floating-point types, **float** and **double**, which represent single- and double-precision numbers, respectively. Their width and ranges are shown here:

Name	Width in Bits	Approximate Range
double	64	4.9e–324 to 1.8e+308
float	32	1.4e–045 to 3.4e+038

Each of these floating-point types is examined next.

float

The type **float** specifies a *single-precision* value that uses 32 bits of storage. Single precision is faster on some processors and takes half as much space as double precision, but will become imprecise when the values are either very large or very small. Variables of type **float** are useful when you need a fractional component, but don't require a large degree of precision. For example, **float** can be useful when representing dollars and cents.

Here are some example **float** variable declarations:

```
float hightemp, lowtemp;
```

double

Double precision, as denoted by the **double** keyword, uses 64 bits to store a value. Double precision is actually faster than single precision on some modern processors that have been optimized for high-speed mathematical calculations. All transcendental math functions, such as **sin( )**, **cos( )**, and **sqrt( )**, return **double** values. When you need to maintain accuracy over many iterative calculations, or are manipulating large-valued numbers, **double** is the best choice.

Here is a short program that uses **double** variables to compute the area of a circle:

```
// Compute the area of a circle.
class Area {
  public static void main(String args[]) {
    double pi, r, a;

    r = 10.8; // radius of circle
    pi = 3.1416; // pi, approximately
    a = pi * r * r; // compute area

    System.out.println("Area of circle is " + a);
  }
}
```

Characters

In Java, the data type used to store characters is **char**. However, C/C++ programmers beware: **char** in Java is not the same as **char** in C or C++. In C/C++, **char** is 8 bits wide. This is *not* the case in Java. Instead, Java uses Unicode to represent characters. *Unicode* defines a fully international character set that can represent all of the characters found in all human languages. It is a unification of dozens of character sets, such as Latin, Greek, Arabic, Cyrillic, Hebrew, Katakana, Hangul, and many more. For this purpose, it requires 16 bits. Thus, in Java **char** is a 16-bit type. The range of a **char** is 0 to 65,536. There are no negative **char**s. The standard set of characters known as ASCII still ranges from 0 to 127 as always, and the extended 8-bit character set, ISO-Latin-1, ranges from 0 to 255. Since Java is designed to allow programs to be written for worldwide use, it makes sense that it would use Unicode to represent characters. Of course, the use of Unicode is somewhat inefficient for languages such as English, German, Spanish, or French, whose characters can easily be contained within 8 bits. But such is the price that must be paid for global portability.

NOTE *More information about Unicode can be found at http://www.unicode.org.*

Here is a program that demonstrates **char** variables:

```
// Demonstrate char data type.
class CharDemo {
  public static void main(String args[]) {
    char ch1, ch2;

    ch1 = 88;  // code for X
    ch2 = 'Y';

    System.out.print("ch1 and ch2: ");
    System.out.println(ch1 + " " + ch2);
  }
}
```

This program displays the following output:

```
ch1 and ch2: X Y
```

Notice that **ch1** is assigned the value 88, which is the ASCII (and Unicode) value that corresponds to the letter X. As mentioned, the ASCII character set occupies the first 127 values in the Unicode character set. For this reason, all the "old tricks" that you may have used with characters in other languages will work in Java, too.

Although **char** is designed to hold Unicode characters, it can also be thought of as an integer type on which you can perform arithmetic operations. For example, you can add two characters together, or increment the value of a character variable. Consider the following program:

```
// char variables behave like integers.
class CharDemo2 {
  public static void main(String args[]) {
    char ch1;

    ch1 = 'X';
    System.out.println("ch1 contains " + ch1);

    ch1++; // increment ch1
    System.out.println("ch1 is now " + ch1);
  }
}
```

The output generated by this program is shown here:

```
ch1 contains X
ch1 is now Y
```

In the program, **ch1** is first given the value X. Next, **ch1** is incremented. This results in **ch1** containing Y, the next character in the ASCII (and Unicode) sequence.

Booleans

Java has a primitive type, called **boolean**, for logical values. It can have only one of two possible values, **true** or **false**. This is the type returned by all relational operators, as in the case of **a < b**. **boolean** is also the type *required* by the conditional expressions that govern the control statements such as **if** and **for**.

Here is a program that demonstrates the **boolean** type:

```
// Demonstrate boolean values.
class BoolTest {
  public static void main(String args[]) {
    boolean b;

    b = false;
    System.out.println("b is " + b);
    b = true;
    System.out.println("b is " + b);

    // a boolean value can control the if statement
```

```
    if(b) System.out.println("This is executed.");

    b = false;
    if(b) System.out.println("This is not executed.");

    // outcome of a relational operator is a boolean value
    System.out.println("10 > 9 is " + (10 > 9));
  }
}
```

The output generated by this program is shown here:

```
b is false
b is true
This is executed.
10 > 9 is true
```

There are three interesting things to notice about this program. First, as you can see, when a **boolean** value is output by **println( )**, "true" or "false" is displayed. Second, the value of a **boolean** variable is sufficient, by itself, to control the **if** statement. There is no need to write an **if** statement like this:

```
if(b == true) ...
```

Third, the outcome of a relational operator, such as **<**, is a **boolean** value. This is why the expression **10 > 9** displays the value "true." Further, the extra set of parentheses around **10 > 9** is necessary because the **+** operator has a higher precedence than the **>**.

A Closer Look at Literals

Literals were mentioned briefly in Chapter 2. Now that the built-in types have been formally described, let's take a closer look at them.

Integer Literals

Integers are probably the most commonly used type in the typical program. Any whole number value is an integer literal. Examples are 1, 2, 3, and 42. These are all decimal values, meaning they are describing a base 10 number. There are two other bases which can be used in integer literals, *octal* (base eight) and *hexadecimal* (base 16). Octal values are denoted in Java by a leading zero. Normal decimal numbers cannot have a leading zero. Thus, the seemingly valid value 09 will produce an error from the compiler, since 9 is outside of octal's 0 to 7 range. A more common base for numbers used by programmers is hexadecimal, which matches cleanly with modulo 8 word sizes, such as 8, 16, 32, and 64 bits. You signify a hexadecimal constant with a leading zero-x, (**0x** or **0X**). The range of a hexadecimal digit is 0 to 15, so *A* through *F* (or *a* through *f*) are substituted for 10 through 15.

Integer literals create an **int** value, which in Java is a 32-bit integer value. Since Java is strongly typed, you might be wondering how it is possible to assign an integer literal to one of Java's other integer types, such as **byte** or **long**, without causing a type mismatch error. Fortunately, such situations are easily handled. When a literal value is assigned to a **byte** or **short** variable, no error is generated if the literal value is within the range of the target type.

An integer literal can always be assigned to a **long** variable. However, to specify a **long** literal, you will need to explicitly tell the compiler that the literal value is of type **long**. You do this by appending an upper- or lowercase L to the literal. For example, 0x7fffffffffffffffL or 9223372036854775807L is the largest **long**. An integer can also be assigned to a **char** as long as it is within range.

Floating-Point Literals

Floating-point numbers represent decimal values with a fractional component. They can be expressed in either standard or scientific notation. *Standard notation* consists of a whole number component followed by a decimal point followed by a fractional component. For example, 2.0, 3.14159, and 0.6667 represent valid standard-notation floating-point numbers. *Scientific notation* uses a standard-notation, floating-point number plus a suffix that specifies a power of 10 by which the number is to be multiplied. The exponent is indicated by an *E* or *e* followed by a decimal number, which can be positive or negative. Examples include 6.022E23, 314159E–05, and 2e+100.

Floating-point literals in Java default to **double** precision. To specify a **float** literal, you must append an *F* or *f* to the constant. You can also explicitly specify a **double** literal by appending a *D* or *d*. Doing so is, of course, redundant. The default **double** type consumes 64 bits of storage, while the less-accurate **float** type requires only 32 bits.

Boolean Literals

Boolean literals are simple. There are only two logical values that a **boolean** value can have, **true** and **false**. The values of **true** and **false** do not convert into any numerical representation. The **true** literal in Java does not equal 1, nor does the **false** literal equal 0. In Java, they can only be assigned to variables declared as **boolean**, or used in expressions with Boolean operators.

Character Literals

Characters in Java are indices into the Unicode character set. They are 16-bit values that can be converted into integers and manipulated with the integer operators, such as the addition and subtraction operators. A literal character is represented inside a pair of single quotes. All of the visible ASCII characters can be directly entered inside the quotes, such as 'a', 'z', and '@'. For characters that are impossible to enter directly, there are several escape sequences that allow you to enter the character you need, such as '\'' for the single-quote character itself and '**\n**' for the newline character. There is also a mechanism for directly entering the value of a character in octal or hexadecimal. For octal notation, use the backslash followed by the three-digit number. For example, '\141' is the letter 'a'. For hexadecimal, you enter a backslash-u (**\u**), then exactly four hexadecimal digits. For example, '\u0061' is the ISO-Latin-1 'a' because the top byte is zero. '\ua432' is a Japanese Katakana character. Table 3-1 shows the character escape sequences.

String Literals

String literals in Java are specified like they are in most other languages—by enclosing a sequence of characters between a pair of double quotes. Examples of string literals are

    "Hello World"
    "two\nlines"
    "\"This is in quotes\""

	Escape Sequence	Description
TABLE 3-1 Character Escape Sequences	\ddd	Octal character (ddd)
	\uxxxx	Hexadecimal Unicode character (xxxx)
	\'	Single quote
	\"	Double quote
	\\	Backslash
	\r	Carriage return
	\n	New line (also known as line feed)
	\f	Form feed
	\t	Tab
	\b	Backspace

The escape sequences and octal/hexadecimal notations that were defined for character literals work the same way inside of string literals. One important thing to note about Java strings is that they must begin and end on the same line. There is no line-continuation escape sequence as there is in some other languages.

NOTE *As you may know, in some other languages, including C/C++, strings are implemented as arrays of characters. However, this is not the case in Java. Strings are actually object types. As you will see later in this book, because Java implements strings as objects, Java includes extensive string-handling capabilities that are both powerful and easy to use.*

Variables

The variable is the basic unit of storage in a Java program. A variable is defined by the combination of an identifier, a type, and an optional initializer. In addition, all variables have a scope, which defines their visibility, and a lifetime. These elements are examined next.

Declaring a Variable

In Java, all variables must be declared before they can be used. The basic form of a variable declaration is shown here:

type identifier [= *value*][, *identifier* [= *value*] ...] ;

The *type* is one of Java's atomic types, or the name of a class or interface. (Class and interface types are discussed later in Part I of this book.) The *identifier* is the name of the variable. You can initialize the variable by specifying an equal sign and a value. Keep in mind that the initialization expression must result in a value of the same (or compatible) type as that specified for the variable. To declare more than one variable of the specified type, use a comma-separated list.

Here are several examples of variable declarations of various types. Note that some include an initialization.

```
int a, b, c;          // declares three ints, a, b, and c.
int d = 3, e, f = 5;  // declares three more ints, initializing
                      // d and f.
byte z = 22;          // initializes z.
double pi = 3.14159;  // declares an approximation of pi.
char x = 'x';         // the variable x has the value 'x'.
```

The identifiers that you choose have nothing intrinsic in their names that indicates their type. Java allows any properly formed identifier to have any declared type.

Dynamic Initialization

Although the preceding examples have used only constants as initializers, Java allows variables to be initialized dynamically, using any expression valid at the time the variable is declared.

For example, here is a short program that computes the length of the hypotenuse of a right triangle given the lengths of its two opposing sides:

```
// Demonstrate dynamic initialization.
class DynInit {
    public static void main(String args[]) {
        double a = 3.0, b = 4.0;

        // c is dynamically initialized
        double c = Math.sqrt(a * a + b * b);

        System.out.println("Hypotenuse is " + c);
    }
}
```

Here, three local variables—**a**, **b**, and **c**—are declared. The first two, **a** and **b**, are initialized by constants. However, **c** is initialized dynamically to the length of the hypotenuse (using the Pythagorean theorem). The program uses another of Java's built-in methods, **sqrt( )**, which is a member of the **Math** class, to compute the square root of its argument. The key point here is that the initialization expression may use any element valid at the time of the initialization, including calls to methods, other variables, or literals.

The Scope and Lifetime of Variables

So far, all of the variables used have been declared at the start of the **main( )** method. However, Java allows variables to be declared within any block. As explained in Chapter 2, a block is begun with an opening curly brace and ended by a closing curly brace. A block defines a *scope*. Thus, each time you start a new block, you are creating a new scope. A scope determines what objects are visible to other parts of your program. It also determines the lifetime of those objects.

Many other computer languages define two general categories of scopes: global and local. However, these traditional scopes do not fit well with Java's strict, object-oriented model. While it is possible to create what amounts to being a global scope, it is by far the exception, not the rule. In Java, the two major scopes are those defined by a class and those defined by a method. Even this distinction is somewhat artificial. However, since the class scope has several unique properties and attributes that do not apply to the scope defined by a method, this distinction makes some sense. Because of the differences, a discussion of class scope (and variables declared within it) is deferred until Chapter 6, when classes are described. For now, we will only examine the scopes defined by or within a method.

The scope defined by a method begins with its opening curly brace. However, if that method has parameters, they too are included within the method's scope. Although this book will look more closely at parameters in Chapter 6, for the sake of this discussion, they work the same as any other method variable.

As a general rule, variables declared inside a scope are not visible (that is, accessible) to code that is defined outside that scope. Thus, when you declare a variable within a scope, you are localizing that variable and protecting it from unauthorized access and/or modification. Indeed, the scope rules provide the foundation for encapsulation.

Scopes can be nested. For example, each time you create a block of code, you are creating a new, nested scope. When this occurs, the outer scope encloses the inner scope. This means that objects declared in the outer scope will be visible to code within the inner scope. However, the reverse is not true. Objects declared within the inner scope will not be visible outside it.

To understand the effect of nested scopes, consider the following program:

```
// Demonstrate block scope.
class Scope {
  public static void main(String args[]) {
    int x; // known to all code within main

    x = 10;
    if(x == 10) { // start new scope
     int y = 20; // known only to this block

      // x and y both known here.
      System.out.println("x and y: " + x + " " + y);
      x = y * 2;
    }
    // y = 100; // Error! y not known here

    // x is still known here.
    System.out.println("x is " + x);
  }
}
```

As the comments indicate, the variable **x** is declared at the start of **main( )**'s scope and is accessible to all subsequent code within **main( )**. Within the **if** block, **y** is declared. Since a block defines a scope, **y** is only visible to other code within its block. This is why outside of its block, the line **y = 100;** is commented out. If you remove the leading comment symbol, a compile-time error will occur, because **y** is not visible outside of its block. Within the **if** block, **x** can be used because code within a block (that is, a nested scope) has access to variables declared by an enclosing scope.

Within a block, variables can be declared at any point, but are valid only after they are declared. Thus, if you define a variable at the start of a method, it is available to all of the code within that method. Conversely, if you declare a variable at the end of a block, it is effectively useless, because no code will have access to it. For example, this fragment is invalid because **count** cannot be used prior to its declaration:

```
// This fragment is wrong!
count = 100; // oops!  cannot use count before it is declared!
int count;
```

Here is another important point to remember: variables are created when their scope is entered, and destroyed when their scope is left. This means that a variable will not hold its value once it has gone out of scope. Therefore, variables declared within a method will not hold their values between calls to that method. Also, a variable declared within a block will lose its value when the block is left. Thus, the lifetime of a variable is confined to its scope.

If a variable declaration includes an initializer, then that variable will be reinitialized each time the block in which it is declared is entered. For example, consider the next program.

```
// Demonstrate lifetime of a variable.
class LifeTime {
  public static void main(String args[]) {
    int x;

    for(x = 0; x < 3; x++) {
      int y = -1; // y is initialized each time block is entered
      System.out.println("y is: " + y); // this always prints -1
      y = 100;
      System.out.println("y is now: " + y);
    }
  }
}
```

The output generated by this program is shown here:

```
y is: -1
y is now: 100
y is: -1
y is now: 100
y is: -1
y is now: 100
```

As you can see, **y** is reinitialized to –1 each time the inner **for** loop is entered. Even though it is subsequently assigned the value 100, this value is lost.

One last point: Although blocks can be nested, you cannot declare a variable to have the same name as one in an outer scope. For example, the following program is illegal:

```
// This program will not compile
class ScopeErr {
  public static void main(String args[]) {
```

```
    int bar = 1;
    {                // creates a new scope
      int bar = 2;  // Compile-time error - bar already defined!
    }
  }
}
```

Type Conversion and Casting

If you have previous programming experience, then you already know that it is fairly common to assign a value of one type to a variable of another type. If the two types are compatible, then Java will perform the conversion automatically. For example, it is always possible to assign an **int** value to a **long** variable. However, not all types are compatible, and thus, not all type conversions are implicitly allowed. For instance, there is no automatic conversion defined from **double** to **byte**. Fortunately, it is still possible to obtain a conversion between incompatible types. To do so, you must use a *cast*, which performs an explicit conversion between incompatible types. Let's look at both automatic type conversions and casting.

Java's Automatic Conversions

When one type of data is assigned to another type of variable, an *automatic type conversion* will take place if the following two conditions are met:

- The two types are compatible.
- The destination type is larger than the source type.

When these two conditions are met, a *widening conversion* takes place. For example, the **int** type is always large enough to hold all valid **byte** values, so no explicit cast statement is required.

For widening conversions, the numeric types, including integer and floating-point types, are compatible with each other. However, there are no automatic conversions from the numeric types to **char** or **boolean**. Also, **char** and **boolean** are not compatible with each other.

As mentioned earlier, Java also performs an automatic type conversion when storing a literal integer constant into variables of type **byte**, **short**, **long**, or **char**.

Casting Incompatible Types

Although the automatic type conversions are helpful, they will not fulfill all needs. For example, what if you want to assign an **int** value to a **byte** variable? This conversion will not be performed automatically, because a **byte** is smaller than an **int**. This kind of conversion is sometimes called a *narrowing conversion*, since you are explicitly making the value narrower so that it will fit into the target type.

To create a conversion between two incompatible types, you must use a cast. A *cast* is simply an explicit type conversion. It has this general form:

(target-type) value

Here, *target-type* specifies the desired type to convert the specified value to. For example, the following fragment casts an **int** to a **byte**. If the integer's value is larger than the range of a **byte**, it will be reduced modulo (the remainder of an integer division by the) **byte**'s range.

```
int a;
byte b;
// ...
b = (byte) a;
```

A different type of conversion will occur when a floating-point value is assigned to an integer type: *truncation*. As you know, integers do not have fractional components. Thus, when a floating-point value is assigned to an integer type, the fractional component is lost. For example, if the value 1.23 is assigned to an integer, the resulting value will simply be 1. The 0.23 will have been truncated. Of course, if the size of the whole number component is too large to fit into the target integer type, then that value will be reduced modulo the target type's range.

The following program demonstrates some type conversions that require casts:

```
// Demonstrate casts.
class Conversion {
  public static void main(String args[]) {
    byte b;
    int i = 257;
    double d = 323.142;

    System.out.println("\nConversion of int to byte.");
    b = (byte) i;
    System.out.println("i and b " + i + " " + b);

    System.out.println("\nConversion of double to int.");
    i = (int) d;
    System.out.println("d and i " + d + " " + i);

    System.out.println("\nConversion of double to byte.");
    b = (byte) d;
    System.out.println("d and b " + d + " " + b);
  }
}
```

This program generates the following output:

```
Conversion of int to byte.
i and b 257 1

Conversion of double to int.
d and i 323.142 323

Conversion of double to byte.
d and b 323.142 67
```

Let's look at each conversion. When the value 257 is cast into a **byte** variable, the result is the remainder of the division of 257 by 256 (the range of a **byte**), which is 1 in this case. When the **d** is converted to an **int**, its fractional component is lost. When **d** is converted to a **byte**, its fractional component is lost, *and* the value is reduced modulo 256, which in this case is 67.

Automatic Type Promotion in Expressions

In addition to assignments, there is another place where certain type conversions may occur: in expressions. To see why, consider the following. In an expression, the precision required of an intermediate value will sometimes exceed the range of either operand. For example, examine the following expression:

```
byte a = 40;
byte b = 50;
byte c = 100;
int d = a * b / c;
```

The result of the intermediate term **a * b** easily exceeds the range of either of its **byte** operands. To handle this kind of problem, Java automatically promotes each **byte**, **short**, or **char** operand to **int** when evaluating an expression. This means that the subexpression **a * b** is performed using integers—not bytes. Thus, 2,000, the result of the intermediate expression, **50 * 40**, is legal even though **a** and **b** are both specified as type **byte**.

As useful as the automatic promotions are, they can cause confusing compile-time errors. For example, this seemingly correct code causes a problem:

```
byte b = 50;
b = b * 2; // Error! Cannot assign an int to a byte!
```

The code is attempting to store 50 * 2, a perfectly valid **byte** value, back into a **byte** variable. However, because the operands were automatically promoted to **int** when the expression was evaluated, the result has also been promoted to **int**. Thus, the result of the expression is now of type **int**, which cannot be assigned to a **byte** without the use of a cast. This is true even if, as in this particular case, the value being assigned would still fit in the target type.

In cases where you understand the consequences of overflow, you should use an explicit cast, such as

```
byte b = 50;
b = (byte) (b * 2);
```

which yields the correct value of 100.

The Type Promotion Rules

Java defines several *type promotion* rules that apply to expressions. They are as follows: First, all **byte**, **short**, and **char** values are promoted to **int**, as just described. Then, if one operand is a **long**, the whole expression is promoted to **long**. If one operand is a **float**, the entire expression is promoted to **float**. If any of the operands is **double**, the result is **double**.

The following program demonstrates how each value in the expression gets promoted to match the second argument to each binary operator:

```
class Promote {
  public static void main(String args[]) {
    byte b = 42;
    char c = 'a';
    short s = 1024;
    int i = 50000;
    float f = 5.67f;
    double d = .1234;
    double result = (f * b) + (i / c) - (d * s);
    System.out.println((f * b) + " + " + (i / c) + " - " + (d * s));
    System.out.println("result = " + result);
  }
}
```

Let's look closely at the type promotions that occur in this line from the program:

```
double result = (f * b) + (i / c) - (d * s);
```

In the first subexpression, **f** * **b**, **b** is promoted to a **float** and the result of the subexpression is **float**. Next, in the subexpression **i** / **c**, **c** is promoted to **int**, and the result is of type **int**. Then, in **d** * **s**, the value of **s** is promoted to **double**, and the type of the subexpression is **double**. Finally, these three intermediate values, **float**, **int**, and **double**, are considered. The outcome of **float** plus an **int** is a **float**. Then the resultant **float** minus the last **double** is promoted to **double**, which is the type for the final result of the expression.

Arrays

An *array* is a group of like-typed variables that are referred to by a common name. Arrays of any type can be created and may have one or more dimensions. A specific element in an array is accessed by its index. Arrays offer a convenient means of grouping related information.

NOTE   *If you are familiar with C/C++, be careful. Arrays in Java work differently than they do in those languages.*

One-Dimensional Arrays

A *one-dimensional array* is, essentially, a list of like-typed variables. To create an array, you first must create an array variable of the desired type. The general form of a one-dimensional array declaration is

   type var-name[ ];

Here, *type* declares the base type of the array. The base type determines the data type of each element that comprises the array. Thus, the base type for the array determines what type of data the array will hold. For example, the following declares an array named **month_days** with the type "array of int":

```
int month_days[];
```

Although this declaration establishes the fact that **month_days** is an array variable, no array actually exists. In fact, the value of **month_days** is set to **null**, which represents an array with no value. To link **month_days** with an actual, physical array of integers, you must allocate one using **new** and assign it to **month_days**. **new** is a special operator that allocates memory.

You will look more closely at **new** in a later chapter, but you need to use it now to allocate memory for arrays. The general form of **new** as it applies to one-dimensional arrays appears as follows:

> *array-var* = new *type*[*size*];

Here, *type* specifies the type of data being allocated, *size* specifies the number of elements in the array, and *array-var* is the array variable that is linked to the array. That is, to use **new** to allocate an array, you must specify the type and number of elements to allocate. The elements in the array allocated by **new** will automatically be initialized to zero. This example allocates a 12-element array of integers and links them to **month_days**.

```
month_days = new int[12];
```

After this statement executes, **month_days** will refer to an array of 12 integers. Further, all elements in the array will be initialized to zero.

Let's review: Obtaining an array is a two-step process. First, you must declare a variable of the desired array type. Second, you must allocate the memory that will hold the array, using **new**, and assign it to the array variable. Thus, in Java all arrays are dynamically allocated. If the concept of dynamic allocation is unfamiliar to you, don't worry. It will be described at length later in this book.

Once you have allocated an array, you can access a specific element in the array by specifying its index within square brackets. All array indexes start at zero. For example, this statement assigns the value 28 to the second element of **month_days**.

```
month_days[1] = 28;
```

The next line displays the value stored at index 3.

```
System.out.println(month_days[3]);
```

Putting together all the pieces, here is a program that creates an array of the number of days in each month.

```java
// Demonstrate a one-dimensional array.
class Array {
  public static void main(String args[]) {
    int month_days[];
    month_days = new int[12];
    month_days[0] = 31;
    month_days[1] = 28;
    month_days[2] = 31;
    month_days[3] = 30;
    month_days[4] = 31;
    month_days[5] = 30;
    month_days[6] = 31;
```

```
    month_days[7] = 31;
    month_days[8] = 30;
    month_days[9] = 31;
    month_days[10] = 30;
    month_days[11] = 31;
    System.out.println("April has " + month_days[3] + " days.");
  }
}
```

When you run this program, it prints the number of days in April. As mentioned, Java array indexes start with zero, so the number of days in April is **month_days[3]** or 30.

It is possible to combine the declaration of the array variable with the allocation of the array itself, as shown here:

```
int month_days[] = new int[12];
```

This is the way that you will normally see it done in professionally written Java programs. Arrays can be initialized when they are declared. The process is much the same as that used to initialize the simple types. An *array initializer* is a list of comma-separated expressions surrounded by curly braces. The commas separate the values of the array elements. The array will automatically be created large enough to hold the number of elements you specify in the array initializer. There is no need to use **new**. For example, to store the number of days in each month, the following code creates an initialized array of integers:

```
// An improved version of the previous program.
class AutoArray {
  public static void main(String args[]) {

    int month_days[] = { 31, 28, 31, 30, 31, 30, 31, 31, 30, 31,
                         30, 31 };
    System.out.println("April has " + month_days[3] + " days.");
  }
}
```

When you run this program, you see the same output as that generated by the previous version.

Java strictly checks to make sure you do not accidentally try to store or reference values outside of the range of the array. The Java run-time system will check to be sure that all array indexes are in the correct range. For example, the run-time system will check the value of each index into **month_days** to make sure that it is between 0 and 11 inclusive. If you try to access elements outside the range of the array (negative numbers or numbers greater than the length of the array), you will cause a run-time error.

Here is one more example that uses a one-dimensional array. It finds the average of a set of numbers.

```
// Average an array of values.
class Average {
  public static void main(String args[]) {
    double nums[] = {10.1, 11.2, 12.3, 13.4, 14.5};
    double result = 0;
    int i;
```

```
   for(i=0; i<5; i++)
     result = result + nums[i];

   System.out.println("Average is " + result / 5);
  }
}
```

Multidimensional Arrays

In Java, *multidimensional arrays* are actually arrays of arrays. These, as you might expect, look and act like regular multidimensional arrays. However, as you will see, there are a couple of subtle differences. To declare a multidimensional array variable, specify each additional index using another set of square brackets. For example, the following declares a two-dimensional array variable called **twoD**.

```
int twoD[][] = new int[4][5];
```

This allocates a 4 by 5 array and assigns it to **twoD**. Internally this matrix is implemented as an *array* of *arrays* of **int**. Conceptually, this array will look like the one shown in Figure 3-1.

The following program numbers each element in the array from left to right, top to bottom, and then displays these values:

```
// Demonstrate a two-dimensional array.
class TwoDArray {
  public static void main(String args[]) {
    int twoD[][]= new int[4][5];
    int i, j, k = 0;

    for(i=0; i<4; i++)
      for(j=0; j<5; j++) {
        twoD[i][j] = k;
        k++;

      }

    for(i=0; i<4; i++) {
      for(j=0; j<5; j++)
        System.out.print(twoD[i][j] + " ");
      System.out.println();
    }
  }
}
```

This program generates the following output:

```
0  1  2  3  4
5  6  7  8  9
10 11 12 13 14
15 16 17 18 19
```

When you allocate memory for a multidimensional array, you need only specify the memory for the first (leftmost) dimension. You can allocate the remaining dimensions

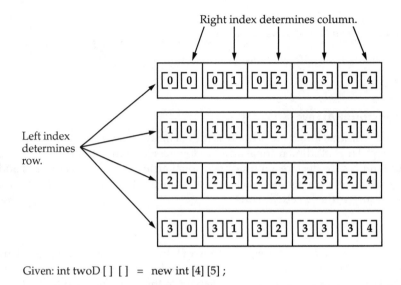

Right index determines column.

Left index determines row.

Given: int twoD [ ] [ ] = new int [4] [5] ;

FIGURE 3-1   A conceptual view of a 4 by 5, two-dimensional array

separately. For example, this following code allocates memory for the first dimension of **twoD** when it is declared. It allocates the second dimension manually.

```
int twoD[] [] = new int[4] [];
twoD[0] = new int[5];
twoD[1] = new int[5];
twoD[2] = new int[5];
twoD[3] = new int[5];
```

While there is no advantage to individually allocating the second dimension arrays in this situation, there may be in others. For example, when you allocate dimensions manually, you do not need to allocate the same number of elements for each dimension. As stated earlier, since multidimensional arrays are actually arrays of arrays, the length of each array is under your control. For example, the following program creates a two-dimensional array in which the sizes of the second dimension are unequal.

```
// Manually allocate differing size second dimensions.
class TwoDAgain {
  public static void main(String args[]) {
    int twoD[][] = new int[4] [];
    twoD[0] = new int[1];
    twoD[1] = new int[2];
    twoD[2] = new int[3];
    twoD[3] = new int[4];

    int i, j, k = 0;

    for(i=0; i<4; i++)
      for(j=0; j<i+1; j++) {
```

```
        twoD[i][j] = k;
        k++;
      }

    for(i=0; i<4; i++) {
      for(j=0; j<i+1; j++)
        System.out.print(twoD[i][j] + " ");
      System.out.println();
    }
  }
}
```

This program generates the following output:

```
0
1 2
3 4 5
6 7 8 9
```

The array created by this program looks like this:

The use of uneven (or, irregular) multidimensional arrays may not be appropriate for many applications, because it runs contrary to what people expect to find when a multidimensional array is encountered. However, irregular arrays can be used effectively in some situations. For example, if you need a very large two-dimensional array that is sparsely populated (that is, one in which not all of the elements will be used), then an irregular array might be a perfect solution.

It is possible to initialize multidimensional arrays. To do so, simply enclose each dimension's initializer within its own set of curly braces. The following program creates a matrix where each element contains the product of the row and column indexes. Also notice that you can use expressions as well as literal values inside of array initializers.

```
// Initialize a two-dimensional array.
class Matrix {
  public static void main(String args[]) {
    double m[][] = {
      { 0*0, 1*0, 2*0, 3*0 },
      { 0*1, 1*1, 2*1, 3*1 },
      { 0*2, 1*2, 2*2, 3*2 },
```

```
      { 0*3, 1*3, 2*3, 3*3 }
    };
    int i, j;

    for(i=0; i<4; i++) {
      for(j=0; j<4; j++)
        System.out.print(m[i][j] + " ");
      System.out.println();
    }
  }
}
```

When you run this program, you will get the following output:

```
0.0   0.0   0.0   0.0
0.0   1.0   2.0   3.0
0.0   2.0   4.0   6.0
0.0   3.0   6.0   9.0
```

As you can see, each row in the array is initialized as specified in the initialization lists.

Let's look at one more example that uses a multidimensional array. The following program creates a 3 by 4 by 5, three-dimensional array. It then loads each element with the product of its indexes. Finally, it displays these products.

```
// Demonstrate a three-dimensional array.
class ThreeDMatrix {
  public static void main(String args[]) {
    int threeD[][][] = new int[3][4][5];
    int i, j, k;

    for(i=0; i<3; i++)
      for(j=0; j<4; j++)
        for(k=0; k<5; k++)
          threeD[i][j][k] = i * j * k;

    for(i=0; i<3; i++) {
      for(j=0; j<4; j++) {
        for(k=0; k<5; k++)
          System.out.print(threeD[i][j][k] + " ");
        System.out.println();
      }
      System.out.println();
    }
  }
}
```

This program generates the following output:

```
0 0 0 0 0
0 0 0 0 0
0 0 0 0 0
0 0 0 0 0
```

```
0  0  0  0  0
0  1  2  3  4
0  2  4  6  8
0  3  6  9  12

0  0  0  0  0
0  2  4  6  8
0  4  8  12  16
0  6  12  18  24
```

Alternative Array Declaration Syntax

There is a second form that may be used to declare an array:

type[ ] *var-name;*

Here, the square brackets follow the type specifier, and not the name of the array variable. For example, the following two declarations are equivalent:

```
int a1[] = new int[3];
int[] a2 = new int[3];
```

The following declarations are also equivalent:

```
char twod1[][] = new char[3][4];
char[][] twod2 = new char[3][4];
```

This alternative declaration form offers convenience when declaring several arrays at the same time. For example,

```
int[] nums, nums2, nums3; // create three arrays
```

creates three array variables of type **int**. It is the same as writing

```
int nums[], nums2[], nums3[]; // create three arrays
```

The alternative declaration form is also useful when specifying an array as a return type for a method. Both forms are used in this book.

A Few Words About Strings

As you may have noticed, in the preceding discussion of data types and arrays there has been no mention of strings or a string data type. This is not because Java does not support such a type—it does. It is just that Java's string type, called **String**, is not a simple type. Nor is it simply an array of characters. Rather, **String** defines an object, and a full description of it requires an understanding of several object-related features. As such, it will be covered later in this book, after objects are described. However, so that you can use simple strings in example programs, the following brief introduction is in order.

The **String** type is used to declare string variables. You can also declare arrays of strings. A quoted string constant can be assigned to a **String** variable. A variable of type **String** can be assigned to another variable of type **String**. You can use an object of type **String** as an argument to **println( )**. For example, consider the following fragment:

```
String str = "this is a test";
System.out.println(str);
```

Here, **str** is an object of type **String**. It is assigned the string "this is a test". This string is displayed by the **println( )** statement.

As you will see later, **String** objects have many special features and attributes that make them quite powerful and easy to use. However, for the next few chapters, you will be using them only in their simplest form.

A Note to C/C++ Programmers About Pointers

If you are an experienced C/C++ programmer, then you know that these languages provide support for pointers. However, no mention of pointers has been made in this chapter. The reason for this is simple: Java does not support or allow pointers. (Or more properly, Java does not support pointers that can be accessed and/or modified by the programmer.) Java cannot allow pointers, because doing so would allow Java programs to breach the firewall between the Java execution environment and the host computer. (Remember, a pointer can be given any address in memory—even addresses that might be outside the Java run-time system.) Since C/C++ make extensive use of pointers, you might be thinking that their loss is a significant disadvantage to Java. However, this is not true. Java is designed in such a way that as long as you stay within the confines of the execution environment, you will never need to use a pointer, nor would there be any benefit in using one.

Operators

Java provides a rich operator environment. Most of its operators can be divided into the following four groups: arithmetic, bitwise, relational, and logical. Java also defines some additional operators that handle certain special situations. This chapter describes all of Java's operators except for the type comparison operator **instanceof**, which is examined in Chapter 13.

Arithmetic Operators

Arithmetic operators are used in mathematical expressions in the same way that they are used in algebra. The following table lists the arithmetic operators:

Operator	Result
+	Addition
−	Subtraction (also unary minus)
*	Multiplication
/	Division
%	Modulus
++	Increment
+=	Addition assignment
−=	Subtraction assignment
*=	Multiplication assignment
/=	Division assignment
%=	Modulus assignment
− −	Decrement

The operands of the arithmetic operators must be of a numeric type. You cannot use them on **boolean** types, but you can use them on **char** types, since the **char** type in Java is, essentially, a subset of **int**.

The Basic Arithmetic Operators

The basic arithmetic operations—addition, subtraction, multiplication, and division— all behave as you would expect for all numeric types. The minus operator also has a unary form that negates its single operand. Remember that when the division operator is applied to an integer type, there will be no fractional component attached to the result.

The following simple example program demonstrates the arithmetic operators. It also illustrates the difference between floating-point division and integer division.

```java
// Demonstrate the basic arithmetic operators.
class BasicMath {
  public static void main(String args[]) {
    // arithmetic using integers
    System.out.println("Integer Arithmetic");
    int a = 1 + 1;
    int b = a * 3;
    int c = b / 4;
    int d = c - a;
    int e = -d;
    System.out.println("a = " + a);
    System.out.println("b = " + b);
    System.out.println("c = " + c);
    System.out.println("d = " + d);
    System.out.println("e = " + e);

    // arithmetic using doubles
    System.out.println("\nFloating Point Arithmetic");
    double da = 1 + 1;
    double db = da * 3;
    double dc = db / 4;
    double dd = dc - a;
    double de = -dd;
    System.out.println("da = " + da);
    System.out.println("db = " + db);
    System.out.println("dc = " + dc);
    System.out.println("dd = " + dd);
    System.out.println("de = " + de);
  }
}
```

When you run this program, you will see the following output:

```
Integer Arithmetic
a = 2
b = 6
c = 1
d = -1
e = 1

Floating Point Arithmetic
da = 2.0
db = 6.0
```

```
dc = 1.5
dd = -0.5
de = 0.5
```

The Modulus Operator

The modulus operator, %, returns the remainder of a division operation. It can be applied to floating-point types as well as integer types. The following example program demonstrates the %:

```
// Demonstrate the % operator.
class Modulus {
  public static void main(String args[]) {
    int x = 42;
    double y = 42.25;

    System.out.println("x mod 10 = " + x % 10);
    System.out.println("y mod 10 = " + y % 10);
  }
}
```

When you run this program, you will get the following output:

```
x mod 10 = 2
y mod 10 = 2.25
```

Arithmetic Compound Assignment Operators

Java provides special operators that can be used to combine an arithmetic operation with an assignment. As you probably know, statements like the following are quite common in programming:

```
a = a + 4;
```

In Java, you can rewrite this statement as shown here:

```
a += 4;
```

This version uses the **+=** *compound assignment operator*. Both statements perform the same action: they increase the value of **a** by 4.

Here is another example,

```
a = a % 2;
```

which can be expressed as

```
a %= 2;
```

In this case, the **%=** obtains the remainder of **a**/2 and puts that result back into **a**.

There are compound assignment operators for all of the arithmetic, binary operators. Thus, any statement of the form

var = var op expression;

can be rewritten as

var op= expression;

The compound assignment operators provide two benefits. First, they save you a bit of typing, because they are "shorthand" for their equivalent long forms. Second, they are implemented more efficiently by the Java run-time system than are their equivalent long forms. For these reasons, you will often see the compound assignment operators used in professionally written Java programs.

Here is a sample program that shows several *op=* assignments in action:

```java
// Demonstrate several assignment operators.
class OpEquals {
  public static void main(String args[]) {
    int a = 1;
    int b = 2;
    int c = 3;

    a += 5;
    b *= 4;
    c += a * b;
    c %= 6;
    System.out.println("a = " + a);
    System.out.println("b = " + b);
    System.out.println("c = " + c);
  }
}
```

The output of this program is shown here:

```
a = 6
b = 8
c = 3
```

Increment and Decrement

The ++ and the – – are Java's increment and decrement operators. They were introduced in Chapter 2. Here they will be discussed in detail. As you will see, they have some special properties that make them quite interesting. Let's begin by reviewing precisely what the increment and decrement operators do.

The increment operator increases its operand by one. The decrement operator decreases its operand by one. For example, this statement:

```java
x = x + 1;
```

can be rewritten like this by use of the increment operator:

```java
x++;
```

Similarly, this statement:

```java
x = x - 1;
```

is equivalent to

```
x--;
```

These operators are unique in that they can appear both in *postfix* form, where they follow the operand as just shown, and *prefix* form, where they precede the operand. In the foregoing examples, there is no difference between the prefix and postfix forms. However, when the increment and/or decrement operators are part of a larger expression, then a subtle, yet powerful, difference between these two forms appears. In the prefix form, the operand is incremented or decremented before the value is obtained for use in the expression. In postfix form, the previous value is obtained for use in the expression, and then the operand is modified. For example:

```
x = 42;
y = ++x;
```

In this case, **y** is set to 43 as you would expect, because the increment occurs *before* **x** is assigned to **y**. Thus, the line **y = ++x;** is the equivalent of these two statements:

```
x = x + 1;
y = x;
```

However, when written like this,

```
x = 42;
y = x++;
```

the value of **x** is obtained before the increment operator is executed, so the value of **y** is 42. Of course, in both cases **x** is set to 43. Here, the line **y = x++;** is the equivalent of these two statements:

```
y = x;
x = x + 1;
```

The following program demonstrates the increment operator.

```java
// Demonstrate ++.
class IncDec {
  public static void main(String args[]) {
    int a = 1;
    int b = 2;
    int c;
    int d;
    c = ++b;
    d = a++;
    c++;
    System.out.println("a = " + a);
    System.out.println("b = " + b);
    System.out.println("c = " + c);
    System.out.println("d = " + d);
  }
}
```

The output of this program follows:

```
a = 2
b = 3
c = 4
d = 1
```

The Bitwise Operators

Java defines several *bitwise operators* that can be applied to the integer types, **long**, **int**, **short**, **char**, and **byte**. These operators act upon the individual bits of their operands. They are summarized in the following table:

Operator	Result
~	Bitwise unary NOT
&	Bitwise AND
|	Bitwise OR
^	Bitwise exclusive OR
>>	Shift right
>>>	Shift right zero fill
<<	Shift left
&=	Bitwise AND assignment
|=	Bitwise OR assignment
^=	Bitwise exclusive OR assignment
>>=	Shift right assignment
>>>=	Shift right zero fill assignment
<<=	Shift left assignment

Since the bitwise operators manipulate the bits within an integer, it is important to understand what effects such manipulations may have on a value. Specifically, it is useful to know how Java stores integer values and how it represents negative numbers. So, before continuing, let's briefly review these two topics.

All of the integer types are represented by binary numbers of varying bit widths. For example, the **byte** value for 42 in binary is 00101010, where each position represents a power of two, starting with 2^0 at the rightmost bit. The next bit position to the left would be 2^1, or 2, continuing toward the left with 2^2, or 4, then 8, 16, 32, and so on. So 42 has 1 bits set at positions 1, 3, and 5 (counting from 0 at the right); thus, 42 is the sum of $2^1 + 2^3 + 2^5$, which is 2 + 8 + 32.

All of the integer types (except **char**) are signed integers. This means that they can represent negative values as well as positive ones. Java uses an encoding known as *two's complement*, which means that negative numbers are represented by inverting (changing 1's to 0's and vice versa) all of the bits in a value, then adding 1 to the result. For example, –42 is represented by inverting all of the bits in 42, or 00101010, which yields 11010101, then adding 1, which results in 11010110, or –42. To decode a negative number, first invert all of the bits, then add 1. For example, –42, or 11010110 inverted, yields 00101001, or 41, so when you add 1 you get 42.

The reason Java (and most other computer languages) uses two's complement is easy to see when you consider the issue of *zero crossing*. Assuming a **byte** value, zero is represented by 00000000. In one's complement, simply inverting all of the bits creates 11111111, which creates negative zero. The trouble is that negative zero is invalid in integer math. This problem is solved by using two's complement to represent negative values. When using two's complement, 1 is added to the complement, producing 100000000. This produces a 1 bit too far to the left to fit back into the **byte** value, resulting in the desired behavior, where –0 is the same as 0, and 11111111 is the encoding for –1. Although we used a **byte** value in the preceding example, the same basic principle applies to all of Java's integer types.

Because Java uses two's complement to store negative numbers—and because all integers are signed values in Java—applying the bitwise operators can easily produce unexpected results. For example, turning on the high-order bit will cause the resulting value to be interpreted as a negative number, whether this is what you intended or not. To avoid unpleasant surprises, just remember that the high-order bit determines the sign of an integer no matter how that high-order bit gets set.

The Bitwise Logical Operators

The bitwise logical operators are &, |, ^, and ~. The following table shows the outcome of each operation. In the discussion that follows, keep in mind that the bitwise operators are applied to each individual bit within each operand.

A	B	A	B	A & B	A ^ B	~A
0	0	0	0	0	1
1	0	1	0	1	0
0	1	1	0	1	1
1	1	1	1	0	0

The Bitwise NOT

Also called the *bitwise complement,* the unary NOT operator, ~, inverts all of the bits of its operand. For example, the number 42, which has the following bit pattern:

    00101010

becomes

    11010101

after the NOT operator is applied.

The Bitwise AND

The AND operator, &, produces a 1 bit if both operands are also 1. A zero is produced in all other cases. Here is an example:

```
  00101010    42
& 00001111    15
----------
  00001010    10
```

The Bitwise OR

The OR operator, |, combines bits such that if either of the bits in the operands is a 1, then the resultant bit is a 1, as shown here:

```
   00101010    42
|  00001111    15

   00101111    47
```

The Bitwise XOR

The XOR operator, ^, combines bits such that if exactly one operand is 1, then the result is 1. Otherwise, the result is zero. The following example shows the effect of the ^. This example also demonstrates a useful attribute of the XOR operation. Notice how the bit pattern of 42 is inverted wherever the second operand has a 1 bit. Wherever the second operand has a 0 bit, the first operand is unchanged. You will find this property useful when performing some types of bit manipulations.

```
   00101010    42
^  00001111    15

   00100101    37
```

Using the Bitwise Logical Operators

The following program demonstrates the bitwise logical operators:

```java
// Demonstrate the bitwise logical operators.
class BitLogic {
  public static void main(String args[]) {
    String binary[] = {
      "0000", "0001", "0010", "0011", "0100", "0101", "0110", "0111",
      "1000", "1001", "1010", "1011", "1100", "1101", "1110", "1111"
    };
    int a = 3; // 0 + 2 + 1 or 0011 in binary
    int b = 6; // 4 + 2 + 0 or 0110 in binary
    int c = a | b;
    int d = a & b;
    int e = a ^ b;
    int f = (~a & b) | (a & ~b);
    int g = ~a & 0x0f;

    System.out.println("        a = " + binary[a]);
    System.out.println("        b = " + binary[b]);
    System.out.println("      a|b = " + binary[c]);
    System.out.println("      a&b = " + binary[d]);
    System.out.println("      a^b = " + binary[e]);
    System.out.println("~a&b|a&~b = " + binary[f]);
    System.out.println("       ~a = " + binary[g]);
  }
}
```

In this example, **a** and **b** have bit patterns that present all four possibilities for two binary digits: 0-0, 0-1, 1-0, and 1-1. You can see how the | and **&** operate on each bit by the results in **c** and **d**. The values assigned to **e** and **f** are the same and illustrate how the ^ works. The string array named **binary** holds the human-readable, binary representation of the numbers 0 through 15. In this example, the array is indexed to show the binary representation of each result. The array is constructed such that the correct string representation of a binary value **n** is stored in **binary[n]**. The value of ~**a** is ANDed with **0x0f** (0000 1111 in binary) in order to reduce its value to less than 16, so it can be printed by use of the **binary** array. Here is the output from this program:

```
          a = 0011
          b = 0110
        a|b = 0111
        a&b = 0010
        a^b = 0101
~a&b|a&~b = 0101
         ~a = 1100
```

The Left Shift

The left shift operator, <<, shifts all of the bits in a value to the left a specified number of times. It has this general form:

value << num

Here, *num* specifies the number of positions to left-shift the value in *value*. That is, the << moves all of the bits in the specified value to the left by the number of bit positions specified by *num*. For each shift left, the high-order bit is shifted out (and lost), and a zero is brought in on the right. This means that when a left shift is applied to an **int** operand, bits are lost once they are shifted past bit position 31. If the operand is a **long**, then bits are lost after bit position 63.

Java's automatic type promotions produce unexpected results when you are shifting **byte** and **short** values. As you know, **byte** and **short** values are promoted to **int** when an expression is evaluated. Furthermore, the result of such an expression is also an **int**. This means that the outcome of a left shift on a **byte** or **short** value will be an **int**, and the bits shifted left will not be lost until they shift past bit position 31. Furthermore, a negative **byte** or **short** value will be sign-extended when it is promoted to **int**. Thus, the high-order bits will be filled with 1's. For these reasons, to perform a left shift on a **byte** or **short** implies that you must discard the high-order bytes of the **int** result. For example, if you left-shift a **byte** value, that value will first be promoted to **int** and then shifted. This means that you must discard the top three bytes of the result if what you want is the result of a shifted **byte** value. The easiest way to do this is to simply cast the result back into a **byte**. The following program demonstrates this concept:

```
// Left shifting a byte value.
class ByteShift {
  public static void main(String args[]) {
    byte a = 64, b;
    int i;
```

```
    i = a << 2;
    b = (byte) (a << 2);

    System.out.println("Original value of a: " + a);
    System.out.println("i and b: " + i + " " + b);
  }
}
```

The output generated by this program is shown here:

```
Original value of a: 64
i and b: 256 0
```

Since **a** is promoted to **int** for the purposes of evaluation, left-shifting the value 64 (0100 0000) twice results in **i** containing the value 256 (1 0000 0000). However, the value in **b** contains 0 because after the shift, the low-order byte is now zero. Its only 1 bit has been shifted out.

Since each left shift has the effect of doubling the original value, programmers frequently use this fact as an efficient alternative to multiplying by 2. But you need to watch out. If you shift a 1 bit into the high-order position (bit 31 or 63), the value will become negative. The following program illustrates this point:

```
// Left shifting as a quick way to multiply by 2.
class MultByTwo {
  public static void main(String args[]) {
    int i;
    int num = 0xFFFFFFE;

    for(i=0; i<4; i++) {
      num = num << 1;
      System.out.println(num);
    }
  }
}
```

The program generates the following output:

```
536870908
1073741816
2147483632
-32
```

The starting value was carefully chosen so that after being shifted left 4 bit positions, it would produce –32. As you can see, when a 1 bit is shifted into bit 31, the number is interpreted as negative.

The Right Shift

The right shift operator, **>>**, shifts all of the bits in a value to the right a specified number of times. Its general form is shown here:

value >> num

Here, *num* specifies the number of positions to right-shift the value in *value*. That is, the **>>** moves all of the bits in the specified value to the right the number of bit positions specified by *num*.

The following code fragment shifts the value 32 to the right by two positions, resulting in **a** being set to 8:

```
int a = 32;
a = a >> 2; // a now contains 8
```

When a value has bits that are "shifted off," those bits are lost. For example, the next code fragment shifts the value 35 to the right two positions, which causes the two low-order bits to be lost, resulting again in **a** being set to 8.

```
int a = 35;
a = a >> 2; // a still contains 8
```

Looking at the same operation in binary shows more clearly how this happens:

```
00100011    35
>> 2
00001000     8
```

Each time you shift a value to the right, it divides that value by two—and discards any remainder. You can take advantage of this for high-performance integer division by 2. Of course, you must be sure that you are not shifting any bits off the right end.

When you are shifting right, the top (leftmost) bits exposed by the right shift are filled in with the previous contents of the top bit. This is called *sign extension* and serves to preserve the sign of negative numbers when you shift them right. For example, –8 >> 1 is –4, which, in binary, is

```
11111000    -8
>>1
11111100    -4
```

It is interesting to note that if you shift –1 right, the result always remains –1, since sign extension keeps bringing in more ones in the high-order bits.

Sometimes it is not desirable to sign-extend values when you are shifting them to the right. For example, the following program converts a **byte** value to its hexadecimal string representation. Notice that the shifted value is masked by ANDing it with **0x0f** to discard any sign-extended bits so that the value can be used as an index into the array of hexadecimal characters.

```
// Masking sign extension.
class HexByte {
  static public void main(String args[]) {
    char hex[] = {
      '0', '1', '2', '3', '4', '5', '6', '7',
      '8', '9', 'a', 'b', 'c', 'd', 'e', 'f'
    };
```

```
    byte b = (byte) 0xf1;

    System.out.println("b = 0x" + hex[(b >> 4) & 0x0f] + hex[b & 0x0f]);
  }
}
```

Here is the output of this program:

```
  b = 0xf1
```

The Unsigned Right Shift

As you have just seen, the **>>** operator automatically fills the high-order bit with its previous contents each time a shift occurs. This preserves the sign of the value. However, sometimes this is undesirable. For example, if you are shifting something that does not represent a numeric value, you may not want sign extension to take place. This situation is common when you are working with pixel-based values and graphics. In these cases, you will generally want to shift a zero into the high-order bit no matter what its initial value was. This is known as an *unsigned shift*. To accomplish this, you will use Java's unsigned, shift-right operator, **>>>**, which always shifts zeros into the high-order bit.

The following code fragment demonstrates the **>>>**. Here, **a** is set to –1, which sets all 32 bits to 1 in binary. This value is then shifted right 24 bits, filling the top 24 bits with zeros, ignoring normal sign extension. This sets **a** to 255.

```
int a = -1;
a = a >>> 24;
```

Here is the same operation in binary form to further illustrate what is happening:

```
11111111 11111111 11111111 11111111    -1  in binary as an int
>>>24
00000000 00000000 00000000 11111111   255  in binary as an int
```

The **>>>** operator is often not as useful as you might like, since it is only meaningful for 32- and 64-bit values. Remember, smaller values are automatically promoted to **int** in expressions. This means that sign-extension occurs and that the shift will take place on a 32-bit rather than on an 8- or 16-bit value. That is, one might expect an unsigned right shift on a **byte** value to zero-fill beginning at bit 7. But this is not the case, since it is a 32-bit value that is actually being shifted. The following program demonstrates this effect:

```
// Unsigned shifting a byte value.
class ByteUShift {
  static public void main(String args[]) {
    char hex[] = {
      '0', '1', '2', '3', '4', '5', '6', '7',
      '8', '9', 'a', 'b', 'c', 'd', 'e', 'f'
    };
    byte b = (byte) 0xf1;
    byte c = (byte) (b >> 4);
    byte d = (byte) (b >>> 4);
    byte e = (byte) ((b & 0xff) >> 4);
```

```
        System.out.println("                        b = 0x"
          + hex[(b >> 4) & 0x0f] + hex[b & 0x0f]);
        System.out.println("                    b >> 4 = 0x"
          + hex[(c >> 4) & 0x0f] + hex[c & 0x0f]);
        System.out.println("                   b >>> 4 = 0x"
          + hex[(d >> 4) & 0x0f] + hex[d & 0x0f]);
        System.out.println("(b & 0xff) >> 4 = 0x"
          + hex[(e >> 4) & 0x0f] + hex[e & 0x0f]);
    }
}
```

The following output of this program shows how the **>>>** operator appears to do nothing when dealing with bytes. The variable **b** is set to an arbitrary negative **byte** value for this demonstration. Then **c** is assigned the **byte** value of **b** shifted right by four, which is 0xff because of the expected sign extension. Then **d** is assigned the **byte** value of **b** unsigned shifted right by four, which you might have expected to be 0x0f, but is actually 0xff because of the sign extension that happened when **b** was promoted to **int** before the shift. The last expression sets **e** to the **byte** value of **b** masked to 8 bits using the AND operator, then shifted right by four, which produces the expected value of 0x0f. Notice that the unsigned shift right operator was not used for **d**, since the state of the sign bit after the AND was known.

```
                b = 0xf1
           b >> 4 = 0xff
          b >>> 4 = 0xff
  (b & 0xff) >> 4 = 0x0f
```

Bitwise Operator Compound Assignments

All of the binary bitwise operators have a compound form similar to that of the algebraic operators, which combines the assignment with the bitwise operation. For example, the following two statements, which shift the value in **a** right by four bits, are equivalent:

```
a = a >> 4;
a >>= 4;
```

Likewise, the following two statements, which result in **a** being assigned the bitwise expression **a** OR **b**, are equivalent:

```
a = a | b;
a |= b;
```

The following program creates a few integer variables and then uses compound bitwise operator assignments to manipulate the variables:

```
class OpBitEquals {
  public static void main(String args[]) {
    int a = 1;
    int b = 2;
    int c = 3;

    a |= 4;
    b >>= 1;
```

```
   c <<= 1;
   a ^= c;
   System.out.println("a = " + a);
   System.out.println("b = " + b);
   System.out.println("c = " + c);
  }
}
```

The output of this program is shown here:

```
  a = 3
  b = 1
  c = 6
```

Relational Operators

The *relational operators* determine the relationship that one operand has to the other. Specifically, they determine equality and ordering. The relational operators are shown here:

Operator	Result
==	Equal to
!=	Not equal to
>	Greater than
<	Less than
>=	Greater than or equal to
<=	Less than or equal to

The outcome of these operations is a **boolean** value. The relational operators are most frequently used in the expressions that control the **if** statement and the various loop statements.

Any type in Java, including integers, floating-point numbers, characters, and Booleans can be compared using the equality test, ==, and the inequality test, !=. Notice that in Java equality is denoted with two equal signs, not one. (Remember: a single equal sign is the assignment operator.) Only numeric types can be compared using the ordering operators. That is, only integer, floating-point, and character operands may be compared to see which is greater or less than the other.

As stated, the result produced by a relational operator is a **boolean** value. For example, the following code fragment is perfectly valid:

```
int a = 4;
int b = 1;
boolean c = a < b;
```

In this case, the result of **a<b** (which is **false**) is stored in **c**.

If you are coming from a C/C++ background, please note the following. In C/C++, these types of statements are very common:

```
int done;
// ...
if(!done) ... // Valid in C/C++
if(done) ...   // but not in Java.
```

In Java, these statements must be written like this:

```
if(done == 0) ... // This is Java-style.
if(done != 0) ...
```

The reason is that Java does not define true and false in the same way as C/C++. In C/C++, true is any nonzero value and false is zero. In Java, **true** and **false** are nonnumeric values that do not relate to zero or nonzero. Therefore, to test for zero or nonzero, you must explicitly employ one or more of the relational operators.

Boolean Logical Operators

The Boolean logical operators shown here operate only on **boolean** operands. All of the binary logical operators combine two **boolean** values to form a resultant **boolean** value.

Operator	Result
&	Logical AND
		Logical OR
^	Logical XOR (exclusive OR)
||	Short-circuit OR
&&	Short-circuit AND
!	Logical unary NOT
&=	AND assignment
|=	OR assignment
^=	XOR assignment
==	Equal to
!=	Not equal to
?:	Ternary if-then-else

The logical Boolean operators, **&**, **|**, and **^**, operate on **boolean** values in the same way that they operate on the bits of an integer. The logical **!** operator inverts the Boolean state: **!true == false** and **!false == true**. The following table shows the effect of each logical operation:

A	B	A	B	A & B	A ^ B	!A
False	False	False	False	False	True
True	False	True	False	True	False
False	True	True	False	True	True
True	True	True	True	False	False

Here is a program that is almost the same as the **BitLogic** example shown earlier, but it operates on **boolean** logical values instead of binary bits:

```
// Demonstrate the boolean logical operators.
class BoolLogic {
  public static void main(String args[]) {
    boolean a = true;
    boolean b = false;
    boolean c = a | b;
    boolean d = a & b;
    boolean e = a ^ b;
    boolean f = (!a & b) | (a & !b);
    boolean g = !a;
    System.out.println("        a = " + a);
    System.out.println("        b = " + b);
    System.out.println("      a|b = " + c);
    System.out.println("      a&b = " + d);
    System.out.println("      a^b = " + e);
    System.out.println("!a&b|a&!b = " + f);
    System.out.println("       !a = " + g);
  }
}
```

After running this program, you will see that the same logical rules apply to **boolean** values as they did to bits. As you can see from the following output, the string representation of a Java **boolean** value is one of the literal values **true** or **false**:

```
        a = true
        b = false
      a|b = true
      a&b = false
      a^b = true
a&b|a&!b = true
       !a = false
```

Short-Circuit Logical Operators

Java provides two interesting Boolean operators not found in many other computer languages. These are secondary versions of the Boolean AND and OR operators, and are known as *short-circuit* logical operators. As you can see from the preceding table, the OR operator results in **true** when **A** is **true**, no matter what **B** is. Similarly, the AND operator results in **false** when **A** is **false**, no matter what **B** is. If you use the | | and **&&** forms, rather than the | and **&** forms of these operators, Java will not bother to evaluate the right-hand operand when the outcome of the expression can be determined by the left operand alone. This is very useful when the right-hand operand depends on the value of the left one in order to function properly. For example, the following code fragment shows how you can take advantage of short-circuit logical evaluation to be sure that a division operation will be valid before evaluating it:

```
if (denom != 0 && num / denom > 10)
```

Since the short-circuit form of AND (**&&**) is used, there is no risk of causing a run-time exception when **denom** is zero. If this line of code were written using the single **&** version of AND, both sides would be evaluated, causing a run-time exception when **denom** is zero.

It is standard practice to use the short-circuit forms of AND and OR in cases involving Boolean logic, leaving the single-character versions exclusively for bitwise operations. However, there are exceptions to this rule. For example, consider the following statement:

```
if(c==1 & e++ < 100) d = 100;
```

Here, using a single **&** ensures that the increment operation will be applied to **e** whether **c** is equal to 1 or not.

The Assignment Operator

You have been using the assignment operator since Chapter 2. Now it is time to take a formal look at it. The *assignment operator* is the single equal sign, **=**. The assignment operator works in Java much as it does in any other computer language. It has this general form:

var = expression;

Here, the type of *var* must be compatible with the type of *expression.*

The assignment operator does have one interesting attribute that you may not be familiar with: it allows you to create a chain of assignments. For example, consider this fragment:

```
int x, y, z;

x = y = z = 100; // set x, y, and z to 100
```

This fragment sets the variables **x**, **y**, and **z** to 100 using a single statement. This works because the **=** is an operator that yields the value of the right-hand expression. Thus, the value of **z = 100** is 100, which is then assigned to **y**, which in turn is assigned to **x**. Using a "chain of assignment" is an easy way to set a group of variables to a common value.

The ? Operator

Java includes a special *ternary* (three-way) *operator* that can replace certain types of if-then-else statements. This operator is the **?**. It can seem somewhat confusing at first, but the **?** can be used very effectively once mastered. The **?** has this general form:

expression1 **?** *expression2* **:** *expression3*

Here, *expression1* can be any expression that evaluates to a **boolean** value. If *expression1* is **true**, then *expression2* is evaluated; otherwise, *expression3* is evaluated. The result of the **?** operation is that of the expression evaluated. Both *expression2* and *expression3* are required to return the same type, which can't be **void**.

Here is an example of the way that the **?** is employed:

```
ratio = denom == 0 ? 0 : num / denom;
```

When Java evaluates this assignment expression, it first looks at the expression to the *left* of the question mark. If **denom** equals zero, then the expression *between* the question mark and the colon is evaluated and used as the value of the entire **?** expression. If **denom** does not equal zero, then the expression *after* the colon is evaluated and used for the value of the entire **?** expression. The result produced by the **?** operator is then assigned to **ratio**.

Here is a program that demonstrates the **?** operator. It uses it to obtain the absolute value of a variable.

```
// Demonstrate ?.
class Ternary {
  public static void main(String args[]) {
    int i, k;

    i = 10;
    k = i < 0 ? -i : i; // get absolute value of i
    System.out.print("Absolute value of ");
    System.out.println(i + " is " + k);

    i = -10;
    k = i < 0 ? -i : i; // get absolute value of i
    System.out.print("Absolute value of ");
    System.out.println(i + " is " + k);
  }
}
```

The output generated by the program is shown here:

```
Absolute value of 10 is 10
Absolute value of -10 is 10
```

Operator Precedence

Table 4-1 shows the order of precedence for Java operators, from highest to lowest. Notice that the first row shows items that you may not normally think of as operators: parentheses, square brackets, and the dot operator. Technically, these are called *separators*, but they act like operators in an expression. Parentheses are used to alter the precedence of an operation. As you know from the previous chapter, the square brackets provide array indexing. The dot operator is used to dereference objects and will be discussed later in this book.

Using Parentheses

Parentheses raise the precedence of the operations that are inside them. This is often necessary to obtain the result you desire. For example, consider the following expression:

```
a >> b + 3
```

This expression first adds 3 to **b** and then shifts **a** right by that result. That is, this expression can be rewritten using redundant parentheses like this:

```
a >> (b + 3)
```

TABLE 4-1

The Precedence of the Java Operators

Highest			
( )	[ ]	.	
++	– –	~	!
*	/	%	
+	–		
>>	>>>	<<	
>	>=	<	<=
==	!=		
&			
^			
|			
&&			
||			
?:			
=	op=		
Lowest			

However, if you want to first shift **a** right by **b** positions and then add 3 to that result, you will need to parenthesize the expression like this:

```
(a >> b) + 3
```

In addition to altering the normal precedence of an operator, parentheses can sometimes be used to help clarify the meaning of an expression. For anyone reading your code, a complicated expression can be difficult to understand. Adding redundant but clarifying parentheses to complex expressions can help prevent confusion later. For example, which of the following expressions is easier to read?

```
a | 4 + c >> b & 7
(a | (((4 + c) >> b) & 7))
```

One other point: parentheses (redundant or not) do not degrade the performance of your program. Therefore, adding parentheses to reduce ambiguity does not negatively affect your program.

Control Statements

A programming language uses *control* statements to cause the flow of execution to advance and branch based on changes to the state of a program. Java's program control statements can be put into the following categories: selection, iteration, and jump. *Selection* statements allow your program to choose different paths of execution based upon the outcome of an expression or the state of a variable. *Iteration* statements enable program execution to repeat one or more statements (that is, iteration statements form loops). *Jump* statements allow your program to execute in a nonlinear fashion. All of Java's control statements are examined here.

Java's Selection Statements

Java supports two selection statements: **if** and **switch**. These statements allow you to control the flow of your program's execution based upon conditions known only during run time. You will be pleasantly surprised by the power and flexibility contained in these two statements.

if

The **if** statement was introduced in Chapter 2. It is examined in detail here. The **if** statement is Java's conditional branch statement. It can be used to route program execution through two different paths. Here is the general form of the **if** statement:

> if (*condition*) *statement1*;
> else *statement2*;

Here, each *statement* may be a single statement or a compound statement enclosed in curly braces (that is, a *block*). The *condition* is any expression that returns a **boolean** value. The **else** clause is optional.

The **if** works like this: If the *condition* is true, then *statement1* is executed. Otherwise, *statement2* (if it exists) is executed. In no case will both statements be executed. For example, consider the following:

```
int a, b;
// ...
if(a < b) a = 0;
else b = 0;
```

Here, if **a** is less than **b**, then **a** is set to zero. Otherwise, **b** is set to zero. In no case are they both set to zero.

Most often, the expression used to control the **if** will involve the relational operators. However, this is not technically necessary. It is possible to control the **if** using a single **boolean** variable, as shown in this code fragment:

```
boolean dataAvailable;
// ...
if (dataAvailable)
  ProcessData();
else
  waitForMoreData();
```

Remember, only one statement can appear directly after the **if** or the **else**. If you want to include more statements, you'll need to create a block, as in this fragment:

```
int bytesAvailable;
// ...
if (bytesAvailable > 0) {
  ProcessData();
  bytesAvailable -= n;
} else
  waitForMoreData();
```

Here, both statements within the **if** block will execute if **bytesAvailable** is greater than zero.

Some programmers find it convenient to include the curly braces when using the **if**, even when there is only one statement in each clause. This makes it easy to add another statement at a later date, and you don't have to worry about forgetting the braces. In fact, forgetting to define a block when one is needed is a common cause of errors. For example, consider the following code fragment:

```
int bytesAvailable;
// ...
if (bytesAvailable > 0) {
  ProcessData();
  bytesAvailable -= n;
} else
  waitForMoreData();
  bytesAvailable = n;
```

It seems clear that the statement **bytesAvailable = n;** was intended to be executed inside the **else** clause, because of the indentation level. However, as you recall, whitespace is insignificant to Java, and there is no way for the compiler to know what was intended. This code will compile without complaint, but it will behave incorrectly when run. The preceding example is fixed in the code that follows:

```
int bytesAvailable;
// ...
```

```
if (bytesAvailable > 0) {
  ProcessData();
  bytesAvailable -= n;
} else {
  waitForMoreData();
  bytesAvailable = n;
}
```

Nested ifs

A *nested* **if** is an **if** statement that is the target of another **if** or **else**. Nested **if**s are very common in programming. When you nest **if**s, the main thing to remember is that an **else** statement always refers to the nearest **if** statement that is within the same block as the **else** and that is not already associated with an **else**. Here is an example:

```
if(i == 10) {
  if(j < 20) a = b;
  if(k > 100) c = d; // this if is
  else a = c;        // associated with this else
}
else a = d;          // this else refers to if(i == 10)
```

As the comments indicate, the final **else** is not associated with **if(j<20)** because it is not in the same block (even though it is the nearest **if** without an **else**). Rather, the final **else** is associated with **if(i==10)**. The inner **else** refers to **if(k>100)** because it is the closest **if** within the same block.

The if-else-if Ladder

A common programming construct that is based upon a sequence of nested **if**s is the *if-else-if ladder*. It looks like this:

> if(*condition*)
> *statement*;
> else if(*condition*)
> *statement*;
> else if(*condition*)
> *statement*;
> .
> .
> .
> else
> *statement*;

The **if** statements are executed from the top down. As soon as one of the conditions controlling the **if** is **true**, the statement associated with that **if** is executed, and the rest of the ladder is bypassed. If none of the conditions is true, then the final **else** statement will be executed. The final **else** acts as a default condition; that is, if all other conditional tests fail, then the last **else** statement is performed. If there is no final **else** and all other conditions are **false**, then no action will take place.

Here is a program that uses an **if-else-if** ladder to determine which season a particular month is in.

```
// Demonstrate if-else-if statements.
class IfElse {
  public static void main(String args[]) {
    int month = 4; // April
    String season;

    if(month == 12 || month == 1 || month == 2)
      season = "Winter";
    else if(month == 3 || month == 4 || month == 5)
      season = "Spring";
    else if(month == 6 || month == 7 || month == 8)
      season = "Summer";
    else if(month == 9 || month == 10 || month == 11)
      season = "Autumn";
    else
      season = "Bogus Month";

    System.out.println("April is in the " + season + ".");
  }
}
```

Here is the output produced by the program:

```
April is in the Spring.
```

You might want to experiment with this program before moving on. As you will find, no matter what value you give **month**, one and only one assignment statement within the ladder will be executed.

switch

The **switch** statement is Java's multiway branch statement. It provides an easy way to dispatch execution to different parts of your code based on the value of an expression. As such, it often provides a better alternative than a large series of **if-else-if** statements. Here is the general form of a **switch** statement:

```
switch (expression) {
  case value1:
    // statement sequence
    break;
  case value2:
    // statement sequence
    break;
  .
  .
  .
  case valueN:
```

```
        // statement sequence
        break;
    default:
        // default statement sequence
}
```

The *expression* must be of type **byte**, **short**, **int**, or **char**; each of the *values* specified in the **case** statements must be of a type compatible with the expression. (An enumeration value can also be used to control a **switch** statement. Enumerations are described in Chapter 12.) Each **case** value must be a unique literal (that is, it must be a constant, not a variable). Duplicate **case** values are not allowed.

The **switch** statement works like this: The value of the expression is compared with each of the literal values in the **case** statements. If a match is found, the code sequence following that **case** statement is executed. If none of the constants matches the value of the expression, then the **default** statement is executed. However, the **default** statement is optional. If no **case** matches and no **default** is present, then no further action is taken.

The **break** statement is used inside the **switch** to terminate a statement sequence. When a **break** statement is encountered, execution branches to the first line of code that follows the entire **switch** statement. This has the effect of "jumping out" of the **switch**.

Here is a simple example that uses a **switch** statement:

```
// A simple example of the switch.
class SampleSwitch {
  public static void main(String args[]) {
    for(int i=0; i<6; i++)
      switch(i) {
        case 0:
          System.out.println("i is zero.");
          break;
        case 1:
          System.out.println("i is one.");
          break;
        case 2:
          System.out.println("i is two.");
          break;
        case 3:
          System.out.println("i is three.");
          break;
        default:
          System.out.println("i is greater than 3.");
      }
  }
}
```

The output produced by this program is shown here:

```
i is zero.
i is one.
i is two.
i is three.
i is greater than 3.
i is greater than 3.
```

As you can see, each time through the loop, the statements associated with the **case** constant that matches **i** are executed. All others are bypassed. After **i** is greater than 3, no **case** statements match, so the **default** statement is executed.

The **break** statement is optional. If you omit the **break**, execution will continue on into the next **case**. It is sometimes desirable to have multiple **cases** without **break** statements between them. For example, consider the following program:

```
// In a switch, break statements are optional.
class MissingBreak {
  public static void main(String args[]) {
    for(int i=0; i<12; i++)
      switch(i) {
        case 0:
        case 1:
        case 2:
        case 3:
        case 4:
          System.out.println("i is less than 5");
          break;
        case 5:
        case 6:
        case 7:
        case 8:
        case 9:
          System.out.println("i is less than 10");
          break;
        default:
          System.out.println("i is 10 or more");
      }
  }
}
```

This program generates the following output:

```
i is less than 5
i is less than 5
i is less than 5
i is less than 5
i is less than 5
i is less than 10
i is less than 10
i is less than 10
i is less than 10
i is less than 10
i is 10 or more
i is 10 or more
```

As you can see, execution falls through each **case** until a **break** statement (or the end of the **switch**) is reached.

While the preceding example is, of course, contrived for the sake of illustration, omitting the **break** statement has many practical applications in real programs. To sample its more realistic usage, consider the following rewrite of the season example shown earlier. This version uses a **switch** to provide a more efficient implementation.

```
// An improved version of the season program.
class Switch {
    public static void main(String args[]) {
        int month = 4;
        String season;
        switch (month) {
          case 12:
          case 1:
          case 2:
            season = "Winter";
            break;
          case 3:
          case 4:
          case 5:
            season = "Spring";
            break;
          case 6:
          case 7:
          case 8:
            season = "Summer";
            break;
          case 9:
          case 10:
          case 11:
            season = "Autumn";
            break;
          default:
            season = "Bogus Month";
        }
        System.out.println("April is in the " + season + ".");
    }
}
```

Nested switch Statements

You can use a **switch** as part of the statement sequence of an outer **switch**. This is called a *nested* **switch**. Since a **switch** statement defines its own block, no conflicts arise between the **case** constants in the inner **switch** and those in the outer **switch**. For example, the following fragment is perfectly valid:

```
switch(count) {
  case 1:
    switch(target) { // nested switch
      case 0:
        System.out.println("target is zero");
        break;
```

```
      case 1: // no conflicts with outer switch
        System.out.println("target is one");
        break;
    }
    break;
  case 2: // ...
```

Here, the **case 1:** statement in the inner switch does not conflict with the **case 1:** statement in the outer switch. The **count** variable is only compared with the list of cases at the outer level. If **count** is 1, then **target** is compared with the inner list cases.

In summary, there are three important features of the **switch** statement to note:

- The **switch** differs from the **if** in that **switch** can only test for equality, whereas **if** can evaluate any type of Boolean expression. That is, the **switch** looks only for a match between the value of the expression and one of its **case** constants.

- No two **case** constants in the same **switch** can have identical values. Of course, a **switch** statement and an enclosing outer **switch** can have **case** constants in common.

- A **switch** statement is usually more efficient than a set of nested **if**s.

The last point is particularly interesting because it gives insight into how the Java compiler works. When it compiles a **switch** statement, the Java compiler will inspect each of the **case** constants and create a "jump table" that it will use for selecting the path of execution depending on the value of the expression. Therefore, if you need to select among a large group of values, a **switch** statement will run much faster than the equivalent logic coded using a sequence of **if-else**s. The compiler can do this because it knows that the **case** constants are all the same type and simply must be compared for equality with the **switch** expression. The compiler has no such knowledge of a long list of **if** expressions.

Iteration Statements

Java's iteration statements are **for**, **while**, and **do-while**. These statements create what we commonly call *loops*. As you probably know, a loop repeatedly executes the same set of instructions until a termination condition is met. As you will see, Java has a loop to fit any programming need.

while

The **while** loop is Java's most fundamental loop statement. It repeats a statement or block while its controlling expression is true. Here is its general form:

```
while(condition) {
    // body of loop
}
```

The *condition* can be any Boolean expression. The body of the loop will be executed as long as the conditional expression is true. When *condition* becomes false, control passes to the next line of code immediately following the loop. The curly braces are unnecessary if only a single statement is being repeated.

Here is a **while** loop that counts down from 10, printing exactly ten lines of "tick":

```
// Demonstrate the while loop.
class While {
  public static void main(String args[]) {
    int n = 10;

    while(n > 0) {
      System.out.println("tick " + n);
      n--;
    }
  }
}
```

When you run this program, it will "tick" ten times:

```
tick 10
tick 9
tick 8
tick 7
tick 6
tick 5
tick 4
tick 3
tick 2
tick 1
```

Since the **while** loop evaluates its conditional expression at the top of the loop, the body of the loop will not execute even once if the condition is false to begin with. For example, in the following fragment, the call to **println( )** is never executed:

```
int a = 10, b = 20;

while(a > b)
  System.out.println("This will not be displayed");
```

The body of the **while** (or any other of Java's loops) can be empty. This is because a *null statement* (one that consists only of a semicolon) is syntactically valid in Java. For example, consider the following program:

```
// The target of a loop can be empty.
class NoBody {
  public static void main(String args[]) {
    int i, j;

    i = 100;
    j = 200;

    // find midpoint between i and j
    while(++i < --j) ; // no body in this loop
```

```
    System.out.println("Midpoint is " + i);
  }
}
```

This program finds the midpoint between **i** and **j**. It generates the following output:

```
Midpoint is 150
```

Here is how this **while** loop works. The value of **i** is incremented, and the value of **j** is decremented. These values are then compared with one another. If the new value of **i** is still less than the new value of **j**, then the loop repeats. If **i** is equal to or greater than **j**, the loop stops. Upon exit from the loop, **i** will hold a value that is midway between the original values of **i** and **j**. (Of course, this procedure only works when **i** is less than **j** to begin with.) As you can see, there is no need for a loop body; all of the action occurs within the conditional expression, itself. In professionally written Java code, short loops are frequently coded without bodies when the controlling expression can handle all of the details itself.

do-while

As you just saw, if the conditional expression controlling a **while** loop is initially false, then the body of the loop will not be executed at all. However, sometimes it is desirable to execute the body of a loop at least once, even if the conditional expression is false to begin with. In other words, there are times when you would like to test the termination expression at the end of the loop rather than at the beginning. Fortunately, Java supplies a loop that does just that: the **do-while**. The **do-while** loop always executes its body at least once, because its conditional expression is at the bottom of the loop. Its general form is

```
do {
  // body of loop
} while (condition);
```

Each iteration of the **do-while** loop first executes the body of the loop and then evaluates the conditional expression. If this expression is true, the loop will repeat. Otherwise, the loop terminates. As with all of Java's loops, *condition* must be a Boolean expression.

Here is a reworked version of the "tick" program that demonstrates the **do-while** loop. It generates the same output as before.

```
// Demonstrate the do-while loop.
class DoWhile {
  public static void main(String args[]) {
    int n = 10;

    do {
      System.out.println("tick " + n);
      n--;
    } while(n > 0);
  }
}
```

The loop in the preceding program, while technically correct, can be written more efficiently as follows:

```
do {
  System.out.println("tick " + n);
} while(--n > 0);
```

In this example, the expression **(– –n > 0)** combines the decrement of **n** and the test for zero into one expression. Here is how it works. First, the – –n statement executes, decrementing **n** and returning the new value of **n**. This value is then compared with zero. If it is greater than zero, the loop continues; otherwise it terminates.

The **do-while** loop is especially useful when you process a menu selection, because you will usually want the body of a menu loop to execute at least once. Consider the following program, which implements a very simple help system for Java's selection and iteration statements:

```
// Using a do-while to process a menu selection
class Menu {
  public static void main(String args[])
    throws java.io.IOException {
    char choice;

    do {
      System.out.println("Help on:");
      System.out.println("  1. if");
      System.out.println("  2. switch");
      System.out.println("  3. while");
      System.out.println("  4. do-while");
      System.out.println("  5. for\n");
      System.out.println("Choose one:");
      choice = (char) System.in.read();
    } while( choice < '1' || choice > '5');

    System.out.println("\n");

    switch(choice) {
      case '1':
        System.out.println("The if:\n");
        System.out.println("if(condition) statement;");
        System.out.println("else statement;");
        break;
      case '2':
        System.out.println("The switch:\n");
        System.out.println("switch(expression) {");
        System.out.println("  case constant:");
        System.out.println("    statement sequence");
        System.out.println("  break;");
        System.out.println("  // ...");
        System.out.println("}");
        break;
      case '3':
        System.out.println("The while:\n");
        System.out.println("while(condition) statement;");
        break;
      case '4':
```

```
      System.out.println("The do-while:\n");
      System.out.println("do {");
      System.out.println("  statement;");
      System.out.println("} while (condition);");
      break;
    case '5':
      System.out.println("The for:\n");
      System.out.print("for(init; condition; iteration)");
      System.out.println("  statement;");
      break;
  }
 }
}
```

Here is a sample run produced by this program:

```
Help on:
  1. if
  2. switch
  3. while
  4. do-while
  5. for
Choose one:
4
The do-while:
do {
  statement;
} while (condition);
```

In the program, the **do-while** loop is used to verify that the user has entered a valid choice. If not, then the user is reprompted. Since the menu must be displayed at least once, the **do-while** is the perfect loop to accomplish this.

A few other points about this example: Notice that characters are read from the keyboard by calling **System.in.read( )**. This is one of Java's console input functions. Although Java's console I/O methods won't be discussed in detail until Chapter 13, **System.in.read( )** is used here to obtain the user's choice. It reads characters from standard input (returned as integers, which is why the return value was cast to **char**). By default, standard input is line buffered, so you must press ENTER before any characters that you type will be sent to your program.

Java's console input can be a bit awkward to work with. Further, most real-world Java programs will be graphical and window-based. For these reasons, not much use of console input has been made in this book. However, it is useful in this context. One other point to consider: Because **System.in.read( )** is being used, the program must specify the **throws java.io.IOException** clause. This line is necessary to handle input errors. It is part of Java's exception handling features, which are discussed in Chapter 10.

for

You were introduced to a simple form of the **for** loop in Chapter 2. As you will see, it is a powerful and versatile construct.

Beginning with JDK 5, there are two forms of the **for** loop. The first is the traditional form that has been in use since the original version of Java. The second is the new "for-each" form. Both types of **for** loops are discussed here, beginning with the traditional form.

Here is the general form of the traditional **for** statement:

```
for(initialization; condition; iteration) {
  // body
}
```

If only one statement is being repeated, there is no need for the curly braces.

The **for** loop operates as follows. When the loop first starts, the *initialization* portion of the loop is executed. Generally, this is an expression that sets the value of the *loop control variable*, which acts as a counter that controls the loop. It is important to understand that the initialization expression is only executed once. Next, *condition* is evaluated. This must be a Boolean expression. It usually tests the loop control variable against a target value. If this expression is true, then the body of the loop is executed. If it is false, the loop terminates. Next, the *iteration* portion of the loop is executed. This is usually an expression that increments or decrements the loop control variable. The loop then iterates, first evaluating the conditional expression, then executing the body of the loop, and then executing the iteration expression with each pass. This process repeats until the controlling expression is false.

Here is a version of the "tick" program that uses a **for** loop:

```
// Demonstrate the for loop.
class ForTick {
  public static void main(String args[]) {
    int n;

    for(n=10; n>0; n--)
      System.out.println("tick " + n);
  }
}
```

Declaring Loop Control Variables Inside the for Loop

Often the variable that controls a **for** loop is only needed for the purposes of the loop and is not used elsewhere. When this is the case, it is possible to declare the variable inside the initialization portion of the **for**. For example, here is the preceding program recoded so that the loop control variable **n** is declared as an **int** inside the **for**:

```
// Declare a loop control variable inside the for.
class ForTick {
  public static void main(String args[]) {

    // here, n is declared inside of the for loop
    for(int n=10; n>0; n--)
      System.out.println("tick " + n);
  }
}
```

When you declare a variable inside a **for** loop, there is one important point to remember: the scope of that variable ends when the **for** statement does. (That is, the scope of the variable is limited to the **for** loop.) Outside the **for** loop, the variable will cease to exist. If you need to use the loop control variable elsewhere in your program, you will not be able to declare it inside the **for** loop.

When the loop control variable will not be needed elsewhere, most Java programmers declare it inside the **for**. For example, here is a simple program that tests for prime numbers. Notice that the loop control variable, **i**, is declared inside the **for** since it is not needed elsewhere.

```
// Test for primes.
class FindPrime {
  public static void main(String args[]) {
    int num;
    boolean isPrime = true;

    num = 14;
    for(int i=2; i <= num/i; i++) {
      if((num % i) == 0) {
        isPrime = false;
        break;
      }
    }
    if(isPrime) System.out.println("Prime");
    else System.out.println("Not Prime");
  }
}
```

Using the Comma

There will be times when you will want to include more than one statement in the initialization and iteration portions of the **for** loop. For example, consider the loop in the following program:

```
class Sample {
  public static void main(String args[]) {
    int a, b;

    b = 4;
    for(a=1; a<b; a++) {
      System.out.println("a = " + a);
      System.out.println("b = " + b);
      b--;
    }
  }
}
```

As you can see, the loop is controlled by the interaction of two variables. Since the loop is governed by two variables, it would be useful if both could be included in the **for** statement, itself, instead of **b** being handled manually. Fortunately, Java provides a way to accomplish this. To allow two or more variables to control a **for** loop, Java permits you to include multiple statements in both the initialization and iteration portions of the **for**. Each statement is separated from the next by a comma.

Using the comma, the preceding **for** loop can be more efficiently coded as shown here:

```
// Using the comma.
class Comma {
```

```
public static void main(String args[]) {
  int a, b;

  for(a=1, b=4; a<b; a++, b--) {
    System.out.println("a = " + a);
    System.out.println("b = " + b);
  }
}
}
```

In this example, the initialization portion sets the values of both **a** and **b**. The two comma-separated statements in the iteration portion are executed each time the loop repeats. The program generates the following output:

```
a = 1
b = 4
a = 2
b = 3
```

NOTE *If you are familiar with C/C++, then you know that in those languages the comma is an operator that can be used in any valid expression. However, this is not the case with Java. In Java, the comma is a separator.*

Some for Loop Variations

The **for** loop supports a number of variations that increase its power and applicability. The reason it is so flexible is that its three parts—the initialization, the conditional test, and the iteration—do not need to be used for only those purposes. In fact, the three sections of the **for** can be used for any purpose you desire. Let's look at some examples.

One of the most common variations involves the conditional expression. Specifically, this expression does not need to test the loop control variable against some target value. In fact, the condition controlling the **for** can be any Boolean expression. For example, consider the following fragment:

```
boolean done = false;

for(int i=1; !done; i++) {
  // ...
  if(interrupted()) done = true;
}
```

In this example, the **for** loop continues to run until the **boolean** variable **done** is set to **true**. It does not test the value of **i**.

Here is another interesting **for** loop variation. Either the initialization or the iteration expression or both may be absent, as in this next program:

```
// Parts of the for loop can be empty.
class ForVar {
  public static void main(String args[]) {
    int i;
```

```
  boolean done = false;

  i = 0;
  for( ; !done; ) {
    System.out.println("i is " + i);
    if(i == 10) done = true;
    i++;
  }
 }
}
```

Here, the initialization and iteration expressions have been moved out of the **for**. Thus, parts of the **for** are empty. While this is of no value in this simple example—indeed, it would be considered quite poor style—there can be times when this type of approach makes sense. For example, if the initial condition is set through a complex expression elsewhere in the program or if the loop control variable changes in a nonsequential manner determined by actions that occur within the body of the loop, it may be appropriate to leave these parts of the **for** empty.

Here is one more **for** loop variation. You can intentionally create an infinite loop (a loop that never terminates) if you leave all three parts of the **for** empty. For example:

```
for( ; ; ) {
  // ...
}
```

This loop will run forever because there is no condition under which it will terminate. Although there are some programs, such as operating system command processors, that require an infinite loop, most "infinite loops" are really just loops with special termination requirements. As you will soon see, there is a way to terminate a loop— even an infinite loop like the one shown—that does not make use of the normal loop conditional expression.

The For-Each Version of the for Loop

Beginning with JDK 5, a second form of **for** was defined that implements a "for-each" style loop. As you may know, contemporary language theory has embraced the for-each concept, and it is quickly becoming a standard feature that programmers have come to expect. A for-each style loop is designed to cycle through a collection of objects, such as an array, in strictly sequential fashion, from start to finish. Unlike some languages, such as C#, that implement a for-each loop by using the keyword **foreach**, Java adds the for-each capability by enhancing the **for** statement. The advantage of this approach is that no new keyword is required, and no preexisting code is broken. The for-each style of **for** is also referred to as the *enhanced* **for** loop.

The general form of the for-each version of the **for** is shown here:

for(*type itr-var : collection*) *statement-block*

Here, *type* specifies the type and *itr-var* specifies the name of an *iteration variable* that will receive the elements from a collection, one at a time, from beginning to end. The collection being cycled through is specified by *collection*. There are various types of collections that can be used with the **for**, but the only type used in this chapter is the array. (Other types of collections that can be used with the **for**, such as those defined by the Collections Framework, are discussed later in this book.) With each iteration of the loop, the next element in the collection is retrieved and stored in *itr-var*. The loop repeats until all elements in the collection have been obtained.

Because the iteration variable receives values from the collection, *type* must be the same as (or compatible with) the elements stored in the collection. Thus, when iterating over arrays, *type* must be compatible with the base type of the array.

To understand the motivation behind a for-each style loop, consider the type of **for** loop that it is designed to replace. The following fragment uses a traditional **for** loop to compute the sum of the values in an array:

```
int nums[] = { 1, 2, 3, 4, 5, 6, 7, 8, 9, 10 };
int sum = 0;

for(int i=0; i < 10; i++) sum += nums[i];
```

To compute the sum, each element in **nums** is read, in order, from start to finish. Thus, the entire array is read in strictly sequential order. This is accomplished by manually indexing the **nums** array by **i**, the loop control variable.

The for-each style **for** automates the preceding loop. Specifically, it eliminates the need to establish a loop counter, specify a starting and ending value, and manually index the array. Instead, it automatically cycles through the entire array, obtaining one element at a time, in sequence, from beginning to end. For example, here is the preceding fragment rewritten using a for-each version of the **for**:

```
int nums[] = { 1, 2, 3, 4, 5, 6, 7, 8, 9, 10 };
int sum = 0;

for(int x: nums) sum += x;
```

With each pass through the loop, **x** is automatically given a value equal to the next element in **nums**. Thus, on the first iteration, **x** contains 1; on the second iteration, **x** contains 2; and so on. Not only is the syntax streamlined, but it also prevents boundary errors.

Here is an entire program that demonstrates the for-each version of the **for** just described:

```
// Use a for-each style for loop.
class ForEach {
  public static void main(String args[]) {
    int nums[] = { 1, 2, 3, 4, 5, 6, 7, 8, 9, 10 };
    int sum = 0;

    // use for-each style for to display and sum the values
    for(int x : nums) {
      System.out.println("Value is: " + x);
      sum += x;
    }

    System.out.println("Summation: " + sum);
  }
}
```

The output from the program is shown here.

```
Value is: 1
Value is: 2
Value is: 3
Value is: 4
Value is: 5
Value is: 6
Value is: 7
Value is: 8
Value is: 9
Value is: 10
Summation: 55
```

As this output shows, the for-each style **for** automatically cycles through an array in sequence from the lowest index to the highest.

Although the for-each **for** loop iterates until all elements in an array have been examined, it is possible to terminate the loop early by using a **break** statement. For example, this program sums only the first five elements of **nums**:

```
// Use break with a for-each style for.
class ForEach2 {
  public static void main(String args[]) {
    int sum = 0;
    int nums[] = { 1, 2, 3, 4, 5, 6, 7, 8, 9, 10 };

    // use for to display and sum the values
    for(int x : nums) {
      System.out.println("Value is: " + x);
      sum += x;
      if(x == 5) break; // stop the loop when 5 is obtained
    }
    System.out.println("Summation of first 5 elements: " + sum);
  }
}
```

This is the output produced:

```
Value is: 1
Value is: 2
Value is: 3
Value is: 4
Value is: 5
Summation of first 5 elements: 15
```

As is evident, the **for** loop stops after the fifth element has been obtained. The **break** statement can also be used with Java's other loops, and it is discussed in detail later in this chapter.

There is one important point to understand about the for-each style loop. Its iteration variable is "read-only" as it relates to the underlying array. An assignment to the iteration variable has no effect on the underlying array. In other words, you can't change the contents of the array by assigning the iteration variable a new value. For example, consider this program:

```
// The for-each loop is essentially read-only.
class NoChange {
  public static void main(String args[]) {
    int nums[] = { 1, 2, 3, 4, 5, 6, 7, 8, 9, 10 };

    for(int x : nums) {
      System.out.print(x + " ");
      x = x * 10; // no effect on nums
    }

    System.out.println();

    for(int x : nums)
      System.out.print(x + " ");

    System.out.println();
  }
}
```

The first **for** loop increases the value of the iteration variable by a factor of 10. However, this assignment has no effect on the underlying array **nums**, as the second **for** loop illustrates. The output, shown here, proves this point:

```
1 2 3 4 5 6 7 8 9 10
1 2 3 4 5 6 7 8 9 10
```

Iterating Over Multidimensional Arrays

The enhanced version of the **for** also works on multidimensional arrays. Remember, however, that in Java, multidimensional arrays consist of *arrays of arrays*. (For example, a two-dimensional array is an array of one-dimensional arrays.) This is important when iterating over a multidimensional array, because each iteration obtains the *next array*, not an individual element. Furthermore, the iteration variable in the **for** loop must be compatible with the type of array being obtained. For example, in the case of a two-dimensional array, the iteration variable must be a reference to a one-dimensional array. In general, when using the for-each **for** to iterate over an array of N dimensions, the objects obtained will be arrays of $N-1$ dimensions. To understand the implications of this, consider the following program. It uses nested **for** loops to obtain the elements of a two-dimensional array in row-order, from first to last.

```
// Use for-each style for on a two-dimensional array.
class ForEach3 {
  public static void main(String args[]) {
    int sum = 0;
    int nums[][] = new int[3][5];

    // give nums some values
    for(int i = 0; i < 3; i++)
```

```
        for(int j=0; j < 5; j++)
          nums[i][j] = (i+1)*(j+1);

    // use for-each for to display and sum the values
    for(int x[] : nums) {
      for(int y : x) {
        System.out.println("Value is: " + y);
        sum += y;
      }
    }
    System.out.println("Summation: " + sum);
  }
}
```

The output from this program is shown here:

```
Value is: 1
Value is: 2
Value is: 3
Value is: 4
Value is: 5
Value is: 2
Value is: 4
Value is: 6
Value is: 8
Value is: 10
Value is: 3
Value is: 6
Value is: 9
Value is: 12
Value is: 15
Summation: 90
```

In the program, pay special attention to this line:

```
for(int x[] : nums) {
```

Notice how **x** is declared. It is a reference to a one-dimensional array of integers. This is necessary because each iteration of the **for** obtains the next *array* in **nums**, beginning with the array specified by **nums[0]**. The inner **for** loop then cycles through each of these arrays, displaying the values of each element.

Applying the Enhanced for

Since the for-each style **for** can only cycle through an array sequentially, from start to finish, you might think that its use is limited, but this is not true. A large number of algorithms require exactly this mechanism. One of the most common is searching. For example, the following program uses a **for** loop to search an unsorted array for a value. It stops if the value is found.

```
// Search an array using for-each style for.
class Search {
  public static void main(String args[]) {
    int nums[] = { 6, 8, 3, 7, 5, 6, 1, 4 };
    int val = 5;
    boolean found = false;

    // use for-each style for to search nums for val
    for(int x : nums) {
      if(x == val) {
        found = true;
        break;
      }
    }

    if(found)
      System.out.println("Value found!");
  }
}
```

The for-each style **for** is an excellent choice in this application because searching an unsorted array involves examining each element in sequence. (Of course, if the array were sorted, a binary search could be used, which would require a different style loop.) Other types of applications that benefit from for-each style loops include computing an average, finding the minimum or maximum of a set, looking for duplicates, and so on.

Although we have been using arrays in the examples in this chapter, the for-each style **for** is especially useful when operating on collections defined by the Collections Framework, which is described in Part II. More generally, the **for** can cycle through the elements of any collection of objects, as long as that collection satisfies a certain set of constraints, which are described in Chapter 17.

Nested Loops

Like all other programming languages, Java allows loops to be nested. That is, one loop may be inside another. For example, here is a program that nests **for** loops:

```
// Loops may be nested.
class Nested {
  public static void main(String args[]) {
    int i, j;

    for(i=0; i<10; i++) {
      for(j=i; j<10; j++)
        System.out.print(".");
      System.out.println();
    }
  }
}
```

The output produced by this program is shown here:

```
. . . . . . . . . .
 . . . . . . . . .
  . . . . . . . .
   . . . . . . .
    . . . . . .
     . . . . .
      . . . .
       . . .
        . .
         .
```

Jump Statements

Java supports three jump statements: **break**, **continue**, and **return**. These statements transfer control to another part of your program. Each is examined here.

NOTE *In addition to the jump statements discussed here, Java supports one other way that you can change your program's flow of execution: through exception handling. Exception handling provides a structured method by which run-time errors can be trapped and handled by your program. It is supported by the keywords **try**, **catch**, **throw**, **throws**, and **finally**. In essence, the exception handling mechanism allows your program to perform a nonlocal branch. Since exception handling is a large topic, it is discussed in its own chapter, Chapter 10.*

Using break

In Java, the **break** statement has three uses. First, as you have seen, it terminates a statement sequence in a **switch** statement. Second, it can be used to exit a loop. Third, it can be used as a "civilized" form of goto. The last two uses are explained here.

Using break to Exit a Loop

By using **break**, you can force immediate termination of a loop, bypassing the conditional expression and any remaining code in the body of the loop. When a **break** statement is encountered inside a loop, the loop is terminated and program control resumes at the next statement following the loop. Here is a simple example:

```java
// Using break to exit a loop.
class BreakLoop {
  public static void main(String args[]) {
    for(int i=0; i<100; i++) {
      if(i == 10) break; // terminate loop if i is 10
      System.out.println("i: " + i);
    }
    System.out.println("Loop complete.");
  }
}
```

This program generates the following output:

```
i: 0
i: 1
i: 2
i: 3
i: 4
i: 5
i: 6
i: 7
i: 8
i: 9
Loop complete.
```

As you can see, although the **for** loop is designed to run from 0 to 99, the **break** statement causes it to terminate early, when **i** equals 10.

The **break** statement can be used with any of Java's loops, including intentionally infinite loops. For example, here is the preceding program coded by use of a **while** loop. The output from this program is the same as just shown.

```
// Using break to exit a while loop.
class BreakLoop2 {
  public static void main(String args[]) {
    int i = 0;

    while(i < 100) {
      if(i == 10) break; // terminate loop if i is 10
      System.out.println("i: " + i);
      i++;
    }
    System.out.println("Loop complete.");
  }
}
```

When used inside a set of nested loops, the **break** statement will only break out of the innermost loop. For example:

```
// Using break with nested loops.
class BreakLoop3 {
  public static void main(String args[]) {
    for(int i=0; i<3; i++) {
      System.out.print("Pass " + i + ": ");
      for(int j=0; j<100; j++) {
        if(j == 10) break; // terminate loop if j is 10
        System.out.print(j + " ");
      }
      System.out.println();
    }
    System.out.println("Loops complete.");
  }
}
```

This program generates the following output:

```
Pass 0:  0 1 2 3 4 5 6 7 8 9
Pass 1:  0 1 2 3 4 5 6 7 8 9
Pass 2:  0 1 2 3 4 5 6 7 8 9
Loops complete.
```

As you can see, the **break** statement in the inner loop only causes termination of that loop. The outer loop is unaffected.

Here are two other points to remember about **break**. First, more than one **break** statement may appear in a loop. However, be careful. Too many **break** statements have the tendency to destructure your code. Second, the **break** that terminates a **switch** statement affects only that **switch** statement and not any enclosing loops.

REMEMBER   *break was not designed to provide the normal means by which a loop is terminated. The loop's conditional expression serves this purpose. The* **break** *statement should be used to cancel a loop only when some sort of special situation occurs.*

Using break as a Form of Goto

In addition to its uses with the **switch** statement and loops, the **break** statement can also be employed by itself to provide a "civilized" form of the goto statement. Java does not have a goto statement because it provides a way to branch in an arbitrary and unstructured manner. This usually makes goto-ridden code hard to understand and hard to maintain. It also prohibits certain compiler optimizations. There are, however, a few places where the goto is a valuable and legitimate construct for flow control. For example, the goto can be useful when you are exiting from a deeply nested set of loops. To handle such situations, Java defines an expanded form of the **break** statement. By using this form of **break**, you can, for example, break out of one or more blocks of code. These blocks need not be part of a loop or a **switch**. They can be any block. Further, you can specify precisely where execution will resume, because this form of **break** works with a label. As you will see, **break** gives you the benefits of a goto without its problems.

The general form of the labeled **break** statement is shown here:

break *label*;

Most often, *label* is the name of a label that identifies a block of code. This can be a stand-alone block of code but it can also be a block that is the target of another statement. When this form of **break** executes, control is transferred out of the named block. The labeled block must enclose the **break** statement, but it does not need to be the immediately enclosing block. This means, for example, that you can use a labeled **break** statement to exit from a set of nested blocks. But you cannot use **break** to transfer control out of a block that does not enclose the **break** statement.

To name a block, put a label at the start of it. A *label* is any valid Java identifier followed by a colon. Once you have labeled a block, you can then use this label as the target of a **break** statement. Doing so causes execution to resume at the *end* of the labeled block. For example, the following program shows three nested blocks, each with its own label. The **break** statement causes execution to jump forward, past the end of the block labeled **second**, skipping the two **println( )** statements.

```
// Using break as a civilized form of goto.
class Break {
  public static void main(String args[]) {
    boolean t = true;

    first: {
      second: {
        third: {
          System.out.println("Before the break.");
          if(t) break second; // break out of second block
          System.out.println("This won't execute");
        }
        System.out.println("This won't execute");
      }
      System.out.println("This is after second block.");
    }
  }
}
```

Running this program generates the following output:

```
Before the break.
This is after second block.
```

One of the most common uses for a labeled **break** statement is to exit from nested loops. For example, in the following program, the outer loop executes only once:

```
// Using break to exit from nested loops
class BreakLoop4 {
  public static void main(String args[]) {
    outer: for(int i=0; i<3; i++) {
      System.out.print("Pass " + i + ": ");
      for(int j=0; j<100; j++) {
        if(j == 10) break outer; // exit both loops
        System.out.print(j + " ");
      }
      System.out.println("This will not print");
    }
    System.out.println("Loops complete.");
  }
}
```

This program generates the following output:

```
Pass 0:  0 1 2 3 4 5 6 7 8 9 Loops complete.
```

As you can see, when the inner loop breaks to the outer loop, both loops have been terminated. Notice that this example labels the **for** statement, which has a block of code as its target.

Keep in mind that you cannot break to any label which is not defined for an enclosing block. For example, the following program is invalid and will not compile:

```
// This program contains an error.
class BreakErr {
```

```
public static void main(String args[]) {

   one: for(int i=0; i<3; i++) {
     System.out.print("Pass " + i + ": ");
   }

   for(int j=0; j<100; j++) {
     if(j == 10) break one; // WRONG
     System.out.print(j + " ");
   }
 }
}
```

Since the loop labeled **one** does not enclose the **break** statement, it is not possible to transfer control out of that block.

Using continue

Sometimes it is useful to force an early iteration of a loop. That is, you might want to continue running the loop but stop processing the remainder of the code in its body for this particular iteration. This is, in effect, a goto just past the body of the loop, to the loop's end. The **continue** statement performs such an action. In **while** and **do-while** loops, a **continue** statement causes control to be transferred directly to the conditional expression that controls the loop. In a **for** loop, control goes first to the iteration portion of the **for** statement and then to the conditional expression. For all three loops, any intermediate code is bypassed.

Here is an example program that uses **continue** to cause two numbers to be printed on each line:

```
// Demonstrate continue.
class Continue {
  public static void main(String args[]) {
    for(int i=0; i<10; i++) {
      System.out.print(i + " ");
      if (i%2 == 0) continue;
      System.out.println("");
    }
  }
}
```

This code uses the % operator to check if **i** is even. If it is, the loop continues without printing a newline. Here is the output from this program:

```
0 1
2 3
4 5
6 7
8 9
```

As with the **break** statement, **continue** may specify a label to describe which enclosing loop to continue. Here is an example program that uses **continue** to print a triangular multiplication table for 0 through 9.

```
// Using continue with a label.
class ContinueLabel {
  public static void main(String args[]) {
outer: for (int i=0; i<10; i++) {
        for(int j=0; j<10; j++) {
          if(j > i) {
            System.out.println();
            continue outer;
          }
          System.out.print(" " + (i * j));
        }
      }
      System.out.println();
  }
}
```

The **continue** statement in this example terminates the loop counting **j** and continues with the next iteration of the loop counting **i**. Here is the output of this program:

```
0
0 1
0 2 4
0 3 6 9
0 4 8 12 16
0 5 10 15 20 25
0 6 12 18 24 30 36
0 7 14 21 28 35 42 49
0 8 16 24 32 40 48 56 64
0 9 18 27 36 45 54 63 72 81
```

Good uses of **continue** are rare. One reason is that Java provides a rich set of loop statements which fit most applications. However, for those special circumstances in which early iteration is needed, the **continue** statement provides a structured way to accomplish it.

return

The last control statement is **return**. The **return** statement is used to explicitly return from a method. That is, it causes program control to transfer back to the caller of the method. As such, it is categorized as a jump statement. Although a full discussion of **return** must wait until methods are discussed in Chapter 6, a brief look at **return** is presented here.

At any time in a method the **return** statement can be used to cause execution to branch back to the caller of the method. Thus, the **return** statement immediately terminates the method in which it is executed. The following example illustrates this point. Here, **return** causes execution to return to the Java run-time system, since it is the run-time system that calls **main( )**.

```
// Demonstrate return.
class Return {
  public static void main(String args[]) {
    boolean t = true;
```

```
    System.out.println("Before the return.");

    if(t) return; // return to caller

    System.out.println("This won't execute.");
  }
}
```

The output from this program is shown here:

```
Before the return.
```

As you can see, the final **println( )** statement is not executed. As soon as **return** is executed, control passes back to the caller.

One last point: In the preceding program, the **if(t)** statement is necessary. Without it, the Java compiler would flag an "unreachable code" error because the compiler would know that the last **println( )** statement would never be executed. To prevent this error, the **if** statement is used here to trick the compiler for the sake of this demonstration.

Introducing Classes

The class is at the core of Java. It is the logical construct upon which the entire Java language is built because it defines the shape and nature of an object. As such, the class forms the basis for object-oriented programming in Java. Any concept you wish to implement in a Java program must be encapsulated within a class.

Because the class is so fundamental to Java, this and the next few chapters will be devoted to it. Here, you will be introduced to the basic elements of a class and learn how a class can be used to create objects. You will also learn about methods, constructors, and the **this** keyword.

Class Fundamentals

Classes have been used since the beginning of this book. However, until now, only the most rudimentary form of a class has been used. The classes created in the preceding chapters primarily exist simply to encapsulate the **main( )** method, which has been used to demonstrate the basics of the Java syntax. As you will see, classes are substantially more powerful than the limited ones presented so far.

Perhaps the most important thing to understand about a class is that it defines a new data type. Once defined, this new type can be used to create objects of that type. Thus, a class is a *template* for an object, and an object is an *instance* of a class. Because an object is an instance of a class, you will often see the two words *object* and *instance* used interchangeably.

The General Form of a Class

When you define a class, you declare its exact form and nature. You do this by specifying the data that it contains and the code that operates on that data. While very simple classes may contain only code or only data, most real-world classes contain both. As you will see, a class' code defines the interface to its data.

A class is declared by use of the **class** keyword. The classes that have been used up to this point are actually very limited examples of its complete form. Classes can (and usually do) get much more complex. A simplified general form of a **class** definition is shown here:

```
class classname {
    type instance-variable1;
    type instance-variable2;
```

```
// ...
type instance-variableN;

type methodname1(parameter-list) {
  // body of method
}
type methodname2(parameter-list) {
  // body of method
}
// ...
type methodnameN(parameter-list) {
  // body of method
}
}
```

The data, or variables, defined within a **class** are called *instance variables*. The code is contained within *methods*. Collectively, the methods and variables defined within a class are called *members* of the class. In most classes, the instance variables are acted upon and accessed by the methods defined for that class. Thus, as a general rule, it is the methods that determine how a class' data can be used.

Variables defined within a class are called instance variables because each instance of the class (that is, each object of the class) contains its own copy of these variables. Thus, the data for one object is separate and unique from the data for another. We will come back to this point shortly, but it is an important concept to learn early.

All methods have the same general form as **main( )**, which we have been using thus far. However, most methods will not be specified as **static** or **public**. Notice that the general form of a class does not specify a **main( )** method. Java classes do not need to have a **main( )** method. You only specify one if that class is the starting point for your program. Further, applets don't require a **main( )** method at all.

NOTE   *C++ programmers will notice that the class declaration and the implementation of the methods are stored in the same place and not defined separately. This sometimes makes for very large .java files, since any class must be entirely defined in a single source file. This design feature was built into Java because it was felt that in the long run, having specification, declaration, and implementation all in one place makes for code that is easier to maintain.*

A Simple Class

Let's begin our study of the class with a simple example. Here is a class called **Box** that defines three instance variables: **width**, **height**, and **depth**. Currently, **Box** does not contain any methods (but some will be added soon).

```
class Box {
  double width;
  double height;
  double depth;
}
```

As stated, a class defines a new type of data. In this case, the new data type is called **Box**. You will use this name to declare objects of type **Box**. It is important to remember that a **class** declaration only creates a template; it does not create an actual object. Thus, the preceding code does not cause any objects of type **Box** to come into existence.

To actually create a **Box** object, you will use a statement like the following:

```
Box mybox = new Box(); // create a Box object called mybox
```

After this statement executes, **mybox** will be an instance of **Box**. Thus, it will have "physical" reality. For the moment, don't worry about the details of this statement.

As mentioned earlier, each time you create an instance of a class, you are creating an object that contains its own copy of each instance variable defined by the class. Thus, every **Box** object will contain its own copies of the instance variables **width**, **height**, and **depth**. To access these variables, you will use the *dot* (.) operator. The dot operator links the name of the object with the name of an instance variable. For example, to assign the **width** variable of **mybox** the value 100, you would use the following statement:

```
mybox.width = 100;
```

This statement tells the compiler to assign the copy of **width** that is contained within the **mybox** object the value of 100. In general, you use the dot operator to access both the instance variables and the methods within an object.

Here is a complete program that uses the **Box** class:

```
/* A program that uses the Box class.

   Call this file BoxDemo.java
*/
class Box {
  double width;
  double height;
  double depth;
}

// This class declares an object of type Box.
class BoxDemo {
  public static void main(String args[]) {
    Box mybox = new Box();
    double vol;

    // assign values to mybox's instance variables
    mybox.width = 10;
    mybox.height = 20;
    mybox.depth = 15;

    // compute volume of box
    vol = mybox.width * mybox.height * mybox.depth;

    System.out.println("Volume is " + vol);
  }
}
```

You should call the file that contains this program **BoxDemo.java**, because the **main( )** method is in the class called **BoxDemo**, not the class called **Box**. When you compile this program, you will find that two **.class** files have been created, one for **Box** and one for **BoxDemo**. The Java compiler automatically puts each class into its own **.class** file. It is not necessary for both the **Box** and the **BoxDemo** class to actually be in the same source file. You could put each class in its own file, called **Box.java** and **BoxDemo.java**, respectively.

To run this program, you must execute **BoxDemo.class**. When you do, you will see the following output:

```
Volume is 3000.0
```

As stated earlier, each object has its own copies of the instance variables. This means that if you have two **Box** objects, each has its own copy of **depth**, **width**, and **height**. It is important to understand that changes to the instance variables of one object have no effect on the instance variables of another. For example, the following program declares two **Box** objects:

```
// This program declares two Box objects.

class Box {
  double width;
  double height;
  double depth;
}

class BoxDemo2 {
  public static void main(String args[]) {
    Box mybox1 = new Box();
    Box mybox2 = new Box();
    double vol;

    // assign values to mybox1's instance variables
    mybox1.width = 10;
    mybox1.height = 20;
    mybox1.depth = 15;

    /* assign different values to mybox2's
       instance variables */
    mybox2.width = 3;
    mybox2.height = 6;
    mybox2.depth = 9;

    // compute volume of first box
    vol = mybox1.width * mybox1.height * mybox1.depth;
    System.out.println("Volume is " + vol);

    // compute volume of second box
    vol = mybox2.width * mybox2.height * mybox2.depth;
    System.out.println("Volume is " + vol);
  }
}
```

The output produced by this program is shown here:

```
Volume is 3000.0
Volume is 162.0
```

As you can see, **mybox1**'s data is completely separate from the data contained in **mybox2**.

Declaring Objects

As just explained, when you create a class, you are creating a new data type. You can use this type to declare objects of that type. However, obtaining objects of a class is a two-step process. First, you must declare a variable of the class type. This variable does not define an object. Instead, it is simply a variable that can *refer* to an object. Second, you must acquire an actual, physical copy of the object and assign it to that variable. You can do this using the **new** operator. The **new** operator dynamically allocates (that is, allocates at run time) memory for an object and returns a reference to it. This reference is, more or less, the address in memory of the object allocated by **new**. This reference is then stored in the variable. Thus, in Java, all class objects must be dynamically allocated. Let's look at the details of this procedure.

In the preceding sample programs, a line similar to the following is used to declare an object of type **Box**:

```
Box mybox = new Box();
```

This statement combines the two steps just described. It can be rewritten like this to show each step more clearly:

```
Box mybox; // declare reference to object
mybox = new Box(); // allocate a Box object
```

The first line declares **mybox** as a reference to an object of type **Box**. After this line executes, **mybox** contains the value **null**, which indicates that it does not yet point to an actual object. Any attempt to use **mybox** at this point will result in a compile-time error. The next line allocates an actual object and assigns a reference to it to **mybox**. After the second line executes, you can use **mybox** as if it were a **Box** object. But in reality, **mybox** simply holds the memory address of the actual **Box** object. The effect of these two lines of code is depicted in Figure 6-1.

NOTE *Those readers familiar with C/C++ have probably noticed that object references appear to be similar to pointers. This suspicion is, essentially, correct. An object reference is similar to a memory pointer. The main difference—and the key to Java's safety—is that you cannot manipulate references as you can actual pointers. Thus, you cannot cause an object reference to point to an arbitrary memory location or manipulate it like an integer.*

A Closer Look at new

As just explained, the **new** operator dynamically allocates memory for an object. It has this general form:

class-var = new *classname*( );

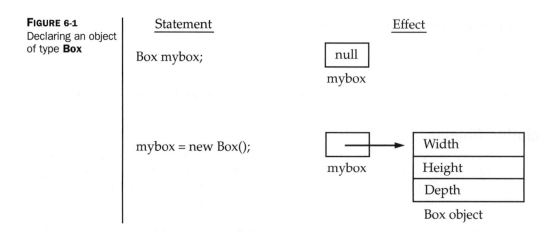

FIGURE 6-1
Declaring an object
of type **Box**

Here, *class-var* is a variable of the class type being created. The *classname* is the name of the class that is being instantiated. The class name followed by parentheses specifies the *constructor* for the class. A constructor defines what occurs when an object of a class is created. Constructors are an important part of all classes and have many significant attributes. Most real-world classes explicitly define their own constructors within their class definition. However, if no explicit constructor is specified, then Java will automatically supply a default constructor. This is the case with **Box**. For now, we will use the default constructor. Soon, you will see how to define your own constructors.

At this point, you might be wondering why you do not need to use **new** for such things as integers or characters. The answer is that Java's primitive types are not implemented as objects. Rather, they are implemented as "normal" variables. This is done in the interest of efficiency. As you will see, objects have many features and attributes that require Java to treat them differently than it treats the primitive types. By not applying the same overhead to the primitive types that applies to objects, Java can implement the primitive types more efficiently. Later, you will see object versions of the primitive types that are available for your use in those situations in which complete objects of these types are needed.

It is important to understand that **new** allocates memory for an object during run time. The advantage of this approach is that your program can create as many or as few objects as it needs during the execution of your program. However, since memory is finite, it is possible that **new** will not be able to allocate memory for an object because insufficient memory exists. If this happens, a run-time exception will occur. (You will learn how to handle this and other exceptions in Chapter 10.) For the sample programs in this book, you won't need to worry about running out of memory, but you will need to consider this possibility in real-world programs that you write.

Let's once again review the distinction between a class and an object. A class creates a new data type that can be used to create objects. That is, a class creates a logical framework that defines the relationship between its members. When you declare an object of a class, you are creating an instance of that class. Thus, a class is a logical construct. An object has physical reality. (That is, an object occupies space in memory.) It is important to keep this distinction clearly in mind.

Assigning Object Reference Variables

Object reference variables act differently than you might expect when an assignment takes place. For example, what do you think the following fragment does?

```
Box b1 = new Box();
Box b2 = b1;
```

You might think that **b2** is being assigned a reference to a copy of the object referred to by **b1**. That is, you might think that **b1** and **b2** refer to separate and distinct objects. However, this would be wrong. Instead, after this fragment executes, **b1** and **b2** will both refer to the *same* object. The assignment of **b1** to **b2** did not allocate any memory or copy any part of the original object. It simply makes **b2** refer to the same object as does **b1**. Thus, any changes made to the object through **b2** will affect the object to which **b1** is referring, since they are the same object.

This situation is depicted here:

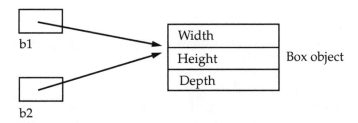

Although **b1** and **b2** both refer to the same object, they are not linked in any other way. For example, a subsequent assignment to **b1** will simply *unhook* **b1** from the original object without affecting the object or affecting **b2**. For example:

```
Box b1 = new Box();
Box b2 = b1;
// ...
b1 = null;
```

Here, **b1** has been set to **null**, but **b2** still points to the original object.

REMEMBER   *When you assign one object reference variable to another object reference variable, you are not creating a copy of the object, you are only making a copy of the reference.*

Introducing Methods

As mentioned at the beginning of this chapter, classes usually consist of two things: instance variables and methods. The topic of methods is a large one because Java gives them so much power and flexibility. In fact, much of the next chapter is devoted to methods. However, there are some fundamentals that you need to learn now so that you can begin to add methods to your classes.

This is the general form of a method:

type name(*parameter-list*) {
    // body of method
}

Here, *type* specifies the type of data returned by the method. This can be any valid type, including class types that you create. If the method does not return a value, its return type must be **void**. The name of the method is specified by *name*. This can be any legal identifier other than those already used by other items within the current scope. The *parameter-list* is a sequence of type and identifier pairs separated by commas. Parameters are essentially variables that receive the value of the *arguments* passed to the method when it is called. If the method has no parameters, then the parameter list will be empty.

Methods that have a return type other than **void** return a value to the calling routine using the following form of the **return** statement:

return *value*;

Here, *value* is the value returned.

In the next few sections, you will see how to create various types of methods, including those that take parameters and those that return values.

Adding a Method to the Box Class

Although it is perfectly fine to create a class that contains only data, it rarely happens. Most of the time, you will use methods to access the instance variables defined by the class. In fact, methods define the interface to most classes. This allows the class implementor to hide the specific layout of internal data structures behind cleaner method abstractions. In addition to defining methods that provide access to data, you can also define methods that are used internally by the class itself.

Let's begin by adding a method to the **Box** class. It may have occurred to you while looking at the preceding programs that the computation of a box's volume was something that was best handled by the **Box** class rather than the **BoxDemo** class. After all, since the volume of a box is dependent upon the size of the box, it makes sense to have the **Box** class compute it. To do this, you must add a method to **Box**, as shown here:

```
// This program includes a method inside the box class.

class Box {
  double width;
  double height;
  double depth;

  // display volume of a box
  void volume() {
    System.out.print("Volume is ");
    System.out.println(width * height * depth);
  }
}
```

```
class BoxDemo3 {
  public static void main(String args[]) {
    Box mybox1 = new Box();
    Box mybox2 = new Box();

    // assign values to mybox1's instance variables
    mybox1.width = 10;
    mybox1.height = 20;
    mybox1.depth = 15;

    /* assign different values to mybox2's
       instance variables */
    mybox2.width = 3;
    mybox2.height = 6;
    mybox2.depth = 9;

    // display volume of first box
    mybox1.volume();

    // display volume of second box
    mybox2.volume();
  }
}
```

This program generates the following output, which is the same as the previous version.

```
Volume is 3000.0
Volume is 162.0
```

Look closely at the following two lines of code:

```
mybox1.volume();
mybox2.volume();
```

The first line here invokes the **volume( )** method on **mybox1**. That is, it calls **volume( )** relative to the **mybox1** object, using the object's name followed by the dot operator. Thus, the call to **mybox1.volume( )** displays the volume of the box defined by **mybox1**, and the call to **mybox2.volume( )** displays the volume of the box defined by **mybox2**. Each time **volume( )** is invoked, it displays the volume for the specified box.

If you are unfamiliar with the concept of calling a method, the following discussion will help clear things up. When **mybox1.volume( )** is executed, the Java run-time system transfers control to the code defined inside **volume( )**. After the statements inside **volume( )** have executed, control is returned to the calling routine, and execution resumes with the line of code following the call. In the most general sense, a method is Java's way of implementing subroutines.

There is something very important to notice inside the **volume( )** method: the instance variables **width**, **height**, and **depth** are referred to directly, without preceding them with an object name or the dot operator. When a method uses an instance variable that is defined by its class, it does so directly, without explicit reference to an object and without use of the dot operator. This is easy to understand if you think about it. A method is always invoked relative to some object of its class. Once this invocation has occurred, the object is known. Thus, within a method, there is no need to specify the object a second time. This means that **width, height,** and **depth** inside **volume( )** implicitly refer to the copies of those variables found in the object that invokes **volume( ).**

Let's review: When an instance variable is accessed by code that is not part of the class in which that instance variable is defined, it must be done through an object, by use of the dot operator. However, when an instance variable is accessed by code that is part of the same class as the instance variable, that variable can be referred to directly. The same thing applies to methods.

Returning a Value

While the implementation of **volume( )** does move the computation of a box's volume inside the **Box** class where it belongs, it is not the best way to do it. For example, what if another part of your program wanted to know the volume of a box, but not display its value? A better way to implement **volume( )** is to have it compute the volume of the box and return the result to the caller. The following example, an improved version of the preceding program, does just that:

```
// Now, volume() returns the volume of a box.

class Box {
  double width;
  double height;
  double depth;

  // compute and return volume
  double volume() {
    return width * height * depth;
  }
}

class BoxDemo4 {
  public static void main(String args[]) {
    Box mybox1 = new Box();
    Box mybox2 = new Box();
    double vol;

    // assign values to mybox1's instance variables
    mybox1.width = 10;
    mybox1.height = 20;
    mybox1.depth = 15;

    /* assign different values to mybox2's
       instance variables */
    mybox2.width = 3;
    mybox2.height = 6;
    mybox2.depth = 9;

    // get volume of first box
    vol = mybox1.volume();
    System.out.println("Volume is " + vol);
```

```
    // get volume of second box
    vol = mybox2.volume();
    System.out.println("Volume is " + vol);
  }
}
```

As you can see, when **volume( )** is called, it is put on the right side of an assignment statement. On the left is a variable, in this case **vol**, that will receive the value returned by **volume( )**. Thus, after

```
vol = mybox1.volume();
```

executes, the value of **mybox1.volume( )** is 3,000 and this value then is stored in **vol**.

There are two important things to understand about returning values:

- The type of data returned by a method must be compatible with the return type specified by the method. For example, if the return type of some method is **boolean**, you could not return an integer.

- The variable receiving the value returned by a method (such as **vol**, in this case) must also be compatible with the return type specified for the method.

One more point: The preceding program can be written a bit more efficiently because there is actually no need for the **vol** variable. The call to **volume( )** could have been used in the **println( )** statement directly, as shown here:

```
System.out.println("Volume is " + mybox1.volume());
```

In this case, when **println( )** is executed, **mybox1.volume( )** will be called automatically and its value will be passed to **println( )**.

Adding a Method That Takes Parameters

While some methods don't need parameters, most do. Parameters allow a method to be generalized. That is, a parameterized method can operate on a variety of data and/or be used in a number of slightly different situations. To illustrate this point, let's use a very simple example. Here is a method that returns the square of the number 10:

```
int square()
{
  return 10 * 10;
}
```

While this method does, indeed, return the value of 10 squared, its use is very limited. However, if you modify the method so that it takes a parameter, as shown next, then you can make **square( )** much more useful.

```
int square(int i)
{
  return i * i;
}
```

Now, **square( )** will return the square of whatever value it is called with. That is, **square( )** is now a general-purpose method that can compute the square of any integer value, rather than just 10.

Here is an example:

```
int x, y;
x = square(5); // x equals 25
x = square(9); // x equals 81
y = 2;
x = square(y); // x equals 4
```

In the first call to **square( )**, the value 5 will be passed into parameter **i**. In the second call, **i** will receive the value 9. The third invocation passes the value of **y**, which is 2 in this example. As these examples show, **square( )** is able to return the square of whatever data it is passed.

It is important to keep the two terms *parameter* and *argument* straight. A *parameter* is a variable defined by a method that receives a value when the method is called. For example, in **square( )**, **i** is a parameter. An *argument* is a value that is passed to a method when it is invoked. For example, **square(100)** passes 100 as an argument. Inside **square( )**, the parameter **i** receives that value.

You can use a parameterized method to improve the **Box** class. In the preceding examples, the dimensions of each box had to be set separately by use of a sequence of statements, such as:

```
mybox1.width = 10;
mybox1.height = 20;
mybox1.depth = 15;
```

While this code works, it is troubling for two reasons. First, it is clumsy and error prone. For example, it would be easy to forget to set a dimension. Second, in well-designed Java programs, instance variables should be accessed only through methods defined by their class. In the future, you can change the behavior of a method, but you can't change the behavior of an exposed instance variable.

Thus, a better approach to setting the dimensions of a box is to create a method that takes the dimensions of a box in its parameters and sets each instance variable appropriately. This concept is implemented by the following program:

```
// This program uses a parameterized method.

class Box {
  double width;
  double height;
  double depth;

  // compute and return volume
  double volume() {
    return width * height * depth;
  }

  // sets dimensions of box
  void setDim(double w, double h, double d) {
    width = w;
```

```
    height = h;
    depth = d;
  }
}

class BoxDemo5 {
  public static void main(String args[]) {
    Box mybox1 = new Box();
    Box mybox2 = new Box();
    double vol;

    // initialize each box
    mybox1.setDim(10, 20, 15);
    mybox2.setDim(3, 6, 9);

    // get volume of first box
    vol = mybox1.volume();
    System.out.println("Volume is " + vol);

    // get volume of second box
    vol = mybox2.volume();
    System.out.println("Volume is " + vol);
  }
}
```

As you can see, the **setDim( )** method is used to set the dimensions of each box. For example, when

```
mybox1.setDim(10, 20, 15);
```

is executed, 10 is copied into parameter **w**, 20 is copied into **h**, and 15 is copied into **d**. Inside **setDim( )** the values of **w**, **h**, and **d** are then assigned to **width**, **height**, and **depth**, respectively.

For many readers, the concepts presented in the preceding sections will be familiar. However, if such things as method calls, arguments, and parameters are new to you, then you might want to take some time to experiment before moving on. The concepts of the method invocation, parameters, and return values are fundamental to Java programming.

Constructors

It can be tedious to initialize all of the variables in a class each time an instance is created. Even when you add convenience functions like **setDim( )**, it would be simpler and more concise to have all of the setup done at the time the object is first created. Because the requirement for initialization is so common, Java allows objects to initialize themselves when they are created. This automatic initialization is performed through the use of a constructor.

A *constructor* initializes an object immediately upon creation. It has the same name as the class in which it resides and is syntactically similar to a method. Once defined, the constructor is automatically called immediately after the object is created, before the **new** operator completes. Constructors look a little strange because they have no return type, not even **void**. This is because the implicit return type of a class' constructor is the class type itself. It is the constructor's job to initialize the internal state of an object so that the code creating an instance will have a fully initialized, usable object immediately.

You can rework the **Box** example so that the dimensions of a box are automatically initialized when an object is constructed. To do so, replace **setDim( )** with a constructor. Let's begin by defining a simple constructor that simply sets the dimensions of each box to the same values. This version is shown here:

```
/* Here, Box uses a constructor to initialize the
   dimensions of a box.
*/
class Box {
  double width;
  double height;
  double depth;

  // This is the constructor for Box.
  Box() {
    System.out.println("Constructing Box");
    width = 10;
    height = 10;
    depth = 10;
  }

  // compute and return volume
  double volume() {
    return width * height * depth;
  }
}

class BoxDemo6 {
  public static void main(String args[]) {
    // declare, allocate, and initialize Box objects
    Box mybox1 = new Box();
    Box mybox2 = new Box();

    double vol;

    // get volume of first box
    vol = mybox1.volume();
    System.out.println("Volume is " + vol);

    // get volume of second box
    vol = mybox2.volume();
    System.out.println("Volume is " + vol);
  }
}
```

When this program is run, it generates the following results:

```
Constructing Box
Constructing Box
Volume is 1000.0
Volume is 1000.0
```

As you can see, both **mybox1** and **mybox2** were initialized by the **Box( )** constructor when they were created. Since the constructor gives all boxes the same dimensions, 10 by 10 by 10, both **mybox1** and **mybox2** will have the same volume. The **println( )** statement inside **Box( )** is for the sake of illustration only. Most constructors will not display anything. They will simply initialize an object.

Before moving on, let's reexamine the **new** operator. As you know, when you allocate an object, you use the following general form:

class-var = new *classname*( );

Now you can understand why the parentheses are needed after the class name. What is actually happening is that the constructor for the class is being called. Thus, in the line

```
Box mybox1 = new Box();
```

new Box( ) is calling the **Box( )** constructor. When you do not explicitly define a constructor for a class, then Java creates a default constructor for the class. This is why the preceding line of code worked in earlier versions of **Box** that did not define a constructor. The default constructor automatically initializes all instance variables to zero. The default constructor is often sufficient for simple classes, but it usually won't do for more sophisticated ones. Once you define your own constructor, the default constructor is no longer used.

Parameterized Constructors

While the **Box( )** constructor in the preceding example does initialize a **Box** object, it is not very useful—all boxes have the same dimensions. What is needed is a way to construct **Box** objects of various dimensions. The easy solution is to add parameters to the constructor. As you can probably guess, this makes them much more useful. For example, the following version of **Box** defines a parameterized constructor that sets the dimensions of a box as specified by those parameters. Pay special attention to how **Box** objects are created.

```
/* Here, Box uses a parameterized constructor to
   initialize the dimensions of a box.
*/
class Box {
  double width;
  double height;
  double depth;

  // This is the constructor for Box.
  Box(double w, double h, double d) {
    width = w;
    height = h;
    depth = d;
  }

  // compute and return volume
  double volume() {
    return width * height * depth;
  }
}
```

```
class BoxDemo7 {
  public static void main(String args[]) {
    // declare, allocate, and initialize Box objects
    Box mybox1 = new Box(10, 20, 15);
    Box mybox2 = new Box(3, 6, 9);

    double vol;

    // get volume of first box
    vol = mybox1.volume();
    System.out.println("Volume is " + vol);

    // get volume of second box
    vol = mybox2.volume();
    System.out.println("Volume is " + vol);
  }
}
```

The output from this program is shown here:

```
Volume is 3000.0
Volume is 162.0
```

As you can see, each object is initialized as specified in the parameters to its constructor. For example, in the following line,

```
Box mybox1 = new Box(10, 20, 15);
```

the values 10, 20, and 15 are passed to the **Box( )** constructor when **new** creates the object. Thus, **mybox1**'s copy of **width**, **height**, and **depth** will contain the values 10, 20, and 15, respectively.

The this Keyword

Sometimes a method will need to refer to the object that invoked it. To allow this, Java defines the **this** keyword. **this** can be used inside any method to refer to the *current* object. That is, **this** is always a reference to the object on which the method was invoked. You can use **this** anywhere a reference to an object of the current class' type is permitted.

To better understand what **this** refers to, consider the following version of **Box( )**:

```
// A redundant use of this.
Box(double w, double h, double d) {
  this.width = w;
  this.height = h;
  this.depth = d;
}
```

This version of **Box( )** operates exactly like the earlier version. The use of **this** is redundant, but perfectly correct. Inside **Box( )**, **this** will always refer to the invoking object. While it is redundant in this case, **this** is useful in other contexts, one of which is explained in the next section.

Instance Variable Hiding

As you know, it is illegal in Java to declare two local variables with the same name inside the same or enclosing scopes. Interestingly, you can have local variables, including formal parameters to methods, which overlap with the names of the class' instance variables. However, when a local variable has the same name as an instance variable, the local variable *hides* the instance variable. This is why **width**, **height**, and **depth** were not used as the names of the parameters to the **Box( )** constructor inside the **Box** class. If they had been, then **width** would have referred to the formal parameter, hiding the instance variable **width**. While it is usually easier to simply use different names, there is another way around this situation. Because **this** lets you refer directly to the object, you can use it to resolve any name space collisions that might occur between instance variables and local variables. For example, here is another version of **Box( )**, which uses **width**, **height**, and **depth** for parameter names and then uses **this** to access the instance variables by the same name:

```
// Use this to resolve name-space collisions.
Box(double width, double height, double depth) {
  this.width = width;
  this.height = height;
  this.depth = depth;
}
```

A word of caution: The use of **this** in such a context can sometimes be confusing, and some programmers are careful not to use local variables and formal parameter names that hide instance variables. Of course, other programmers believe the contrary—that it is a good convention to use the same names for clarity, and use **this** to overcome the instance variable hiding. It is a matter of taste which approach you adopt.

Garbage Collection

Since objects are dynamically allocated by using the **new** operator, you might be wondering how such objects are destroyed and their memory released for later reallocation. In some languages, such as C++, dynamically allocated objects must be manually released by use of a **delete** operator. Java takes a different approach; it handles deallocation for you automatically. The technique that accomplishes this is called *garbage collection*. It works like this: when no references to an object exist, that object is assumed to be no longer needed, and the memory occupied by the object can be reclaimed. There is no explicit need to destroy objects as in C++. Garbage collection only occurs sporadically (if at all) during the execution of your program. It will not occur simply because one or more objects exist that are no longer used. Furthermore, different Java run-time implementations will take varying approaches to garbage collection, but for the most part, you should not have to think about it while writing your programs.

The finalize( ) Method

Sometimes an object will need to perform some action when it is destroyed. For example, if an object is holding some non-Java resource such as a file handle or character font, then you might want to make sure these resources are freed before an object is destroyed. To handle such situations, Java provides a mechanism called *finalization*. By using finalization, you can define specific actions that will occur when an object is just about to be reclaimed by the garbage collector.

To add a finalizer to a class, you simply define the **finalize( )** method. The Java run time calls that method whenever it is about to recycle an object of that class. Inside the **finalize( )** method, you will specify those actions that must be performed before an object is destroyed. The garbage collector runs periodically, checking for objects that are no longer referenced by any running state or indirectly through other referenced objects. Right before an asset is freed, the Java run time calls the **finalize( )** method on the object.

The **finalize( )** method has this general form:

```
protected void finalize( )
{
// finalization code here
}
```

Here, the keyword **protected** is a specifier that prevents access to **finalize( )** by code defined outside its class. This and the other access specifiers are explained in Chapter 7.

It is important to understand that **finalize( )** is only called just prior to garbage collection. It is not called when an object goes out-of-scope, for example. This means that you cannot know when—or even if—**finalize( )** will be executed. Therefore, your program should provide other means of releasing system resources, etc., used by the object. It must not rely on **finalize( )** for normal program operation.

NOTE *If you are familiar with C++, then you know that C++ allows you to define a destructor for a class, which is called when an object goes out-of-scope. Java does not support this idea or provide for destructors. The **finalize( )** method only approximates the function of a destructor. As you get more experienced with Java, you will see that the need for destructor functions is minimal because of Java's garbage collection subsystem.*

A Stack Class

While the **Box** class is useful to illustrate the essential elements of a class, it is of little practical value. To show the real power of classes, this chapter will conclude with a more sophisticated example. As you recall from the discussion of object-oriented programming (OOP) presented in Chapter 2, one of OOP's most important benefits is the encapsulation of data and the code that manipulates that data. As you have seen, the class is the mechanism by which encapsulation is achieved in Java. By creating a class, you are creating a new data type that defines both the nature of the data being manipulated and the routines used to manipulate it. Further, the methods define a consistent and controlled interface to the class' data. Thus, you can use the class through its methods without having to worry about the details of its implementation or how the data is actually managed within the class. In a sense, a class is like a "data engine." No knowledge of what goes on inside the engine is required to use the engine through its controls. In fact, since the details are hidden, its inner workings can be changed as needed. As long as your code uses the class through its methods, internal details can change without causing side effects outside the class.

To see a practical application of the preceding discussion, let's develop one of the archetypal examples of encapsulation: the stack. A *stack* stores data using first-in, last-out ordering. That is, a stack is like a stack of plates on a table—the first plate put down on the table is the last plate to be used. Stacks are controlled through two operations traditionally called *push* and *pop*. To put an item on top of the stack, you will use push. To take an item off the stack, you will use pop. As you will see, it is easy to encapsulate the entire stack mechanism.

Here is a class called **Stack** that implements a stack for integers:

```
// This class defines an integer stack that can hold 10 values.
class Stack {
  int stck[] = new int[10];
  int tos;

  // Initialize top-of-stack
  Stack() {
    tos = -1;
  }

  // Push an item onto the stack
  void push(int item) {
    if(tos==9)
      System.out.println("Stack is full.");
    else
      stck[++tos] = item;
  }

  // Pop an item from the stack
  int pop() {
    if(tos < 0) {
      System.out.println("Stack underflow.");
      return 0;
    }
    else
      return stck[tos--];
  }
}
```

As you can see, the **Stack** class defines two data items and three methods. The stack of integers is held by the array **stck**. This array is indexed by the variable **tos**, which always contains the index of the top of the stack. The **Stack( )** constructor initializes **tos** to –1, which indicates an empty stack. The method **push( )** puts an item on the stack. To retrieve an item, call **pop( )**. Since access to the stack is through **push( )** and **pop( )**, the fact that the stack is held in an array is actually not relevant to using the stack. For example, the stack could be held in a more complicated data structure, such as a linked list, yet the interface defined by **push( )** and **pop( )** would remain the same.

The class **TestStack**, shown here, demonstrates the **Stack** class. It creates two integer stacks, pushes some values onto each, and then pops them off.

```
class TestStack {
  public static void main(String args[]) {
    Stack mystack1 = new Stack();
    Stack mystack2 = new Stack();
```

```
    // push some numbers onto the stack
    for(int i=0; i<10; i++) mystack1.push(i);
    for(int i=10; i<20; i++) mystack2.push(i);

    // pop those numbers off the stack
    System.out.println("Stack in mystack1:");
    for(int i=0; i<10; i++)
       System.out.println(mystack1.pop());

    System.out.println("Stack in mystack2:");
    for(int i=0; i<10; i++)
       System.out.println(mystack2.pop());
  }
}
```

This program generates the following output:

```
Stack in mystack1:
9
8
7
6
5
4
3
2
1
0
Stack in mystack2:
19
18
17
16
15
14
13
12
11
10
```

As you can see, the contents of each stack are separate.

One last point about the **Stack** class. As it is currently implemented, it is possible for the array that holds the stack, **stck**, to be altered by code outside of the **Stack** class. This leaves **Stack** open to misuse or mischief. In the next chapter, you will see how to remedy this situation.

CHAPTER

A Closer Look at Methods and Classes

This chapter continues the discussion of methods and classes begun in the preceding chapter. It examines several topics relating to methods, including overloading, parameter passing, and recursion. The chapter then returns to the class, discussing access control, the use of the keyword **static**, and one of Java's most important built-in classes: **String**.

Overloading Methods

In Java it is possible to define two or more methods within the same class that share the same name, as long as their parameter declarations are different. When this is the case, the methods are said to be *overloaded*, and the process is referred to as *method overloading*. Method overloading is one of the ways that Java supports polymorphism. If you have never used a language that allows the overloading of methods, then the concept may seem strange at first. But as you will see, method overloading is one of Java's most exciting and useful features.

When an overloaded method is invoked, Java uses the type and/or number of arguments as its guide to determine which version of the overloaded method to actually call. Thus, overloaded methods must differ in the type and/or number of their parameters. While overloaded methods may have different return types, the return type alone is insufficient to distinguish two versions of a method. When Java encounters a call to an overloaded method, it simply executes the version of the method whose parameters match the arguments used in the call.

Here is a simple example that illustrates method overloading:

```java
// Demonstrate method overloading.
class OverloadDemo {
  void test() {
    System.out.println("No parameters");
  }

  // Overload test for one integer parameter.
  void test(int a) {
    System.out.println("a: " + a);
  }
```

```
  // Overload test for two integer parameters.
  void test(int a, int b) {
    System.out.println("a and b: " + a + " " + b);
  }

  // overload test for a double parameter
  double test(double a) {
    System.out.println("double a: " + a);
    return a*a;
  }
}

class Overload {
  public static void main(String args[]) {
    OverloadDemo ob = new OverloadDemo();
    double result;

    // call all versions of test()
    ob.test();
    ob.test(10);
    ob.test(10, 20);
    result = ob.test(123.25);
    System.out.println("Result of ob.test(123.25): " + result);
  }
}
```

This program generates the following output:

```
No parameters
a: 10
a and b: 10 20
double a: 123.25
Result of ob.test(123.25): 15190.5625
```

As you can see, **test( )** is overloaded four times. The first version takes no parameters, the second takes one integer parameter, the third takes two integer parameters, and the fourth takes one **double** parameter. The fact that the fourth version of **test( )** also returns a value is of no consequence relative to overloading, since return types do not play a role in overload resolution.

When an overloaded method is called, Java looks for a match between the arguments used to call the method and the method's parameters. However, this match need not always be exact. In some cases, Java's automatic type conversions can play a role in overload resolution. For example, consider the following program:

```
// Automatic type conversions apply to overloading.
class OverloadDemo {
  void test() {
    System.out.println("No parameters");
  }
```

```
  // Overload test for two integer parameters.
  void test(int a, int b) {
    System.out.println("a and b: " + a + " " + b);
  }

  // overload test for a double parameter
  void test(double a) {
    System.out.println("Inside test(double) a: " + a);
  }
}

class Overload {
  public static void main(String args[]) {
    OverloadDemo ob = new OverloadDemo();
    int i = 88;

    ob.test();
    ob.test(10, 20);

    ob.test(i); // this will invoke test(double)
    ob.test(123.2); // this will invoke test(double)
  }
}
```

This program generates the following output:

```
No parameters
a and b: 10 20
Inside test(double) a: 88
Inside test(double) a: 123.2
```

As you can see, this version of **OverloadDemo** does not define **test(int)**. Therefore, when **test( )** is called with an integer argument inside **Overload**, no matching method is found. However, Java can automatically convert an integer into a **double**, and this conversion can be used to resolve the call. Therefore, after **test(int)** is not found, Java elevates **i** to **double** and then calls **test(double)**. Of course, if **test(int)** had been defined, it would have been called instead. Java will employ its automatic type conversions only if no exact match is found.

Method overloading supports polymorphism because it is one way that Java implements the "one interface, multiple methods" paradigm. To understand how, consider the following. In languages that do not support method overloading, each method must be given a unique name. However, frequently you will want to implement essentially the same method for different types of data. Consider the absolute value function. In languages that do not support overloading, there are usually three or more versions of this function, each with a slightly different name. For instance, in C, the function **abs( )** returns the absolute value of an integer, **labs( )** returns the absolute value of a long integer, and **fabs( )** returns the absolute value of a floating-point value. Since C does not support overloading, each function has to have its own name, even though all three functions do essentially the same thing. This makes the situation more complex, conceptually, than it actually is. Although the underlying concept of each function is the same, you still have three names to remember. This situation does not occur in Java, because each absolute value method can use the same name. Indeed, Java's standard class library includes an absolute value method, called **abs( )**. This method is overloaded by Java's **Math** class to handle all numeric types. Java determines which version of **abs( )** to call based upon the type of argument.

The value of overloading is that it allows related methods to be accessed by use of a common name. Thus, the name **abs** represents the *general action* that is being performed. It is left to the compiler to choose the right *specific* version for a particular circumstance. You, the programmer, need only remember the general operation being performed. Through the application of polymorphism, several names have been reduced to one. Although this example is fairly simple, if you expand the concept, you can see how overloading can help you manage greater complexity.

When you overload a method, each version of that method can perform any activity you desire. There is no rule stating that overloaded methods must relate to one another. However, from a stylistic point of view, method overloading implies a relationship. Thus, while you can use the same name to overload unrelated methods, you should not. For example, you could use the name **sqr** to create methods that return the *square* of an integer and the *square root* of a floating-point value. But these two operations are fundamentally different. Applying method overloading in this manner defeats its original purpose. In practice, you should only overload closely related operations.

Overloading Constructors

In addition to overloading normal methods, you can also overload constructor methods. In fact, for most real-world classes that you create, overloaded constructors will be the norm, not the exception. To understand why, let's return to the **Box** class developed in the preceding chapter. Following is the latest version of **Box**:

```
class Box {
  double width;
  double height;
  double depth;

  // This is the constructor for Box.
  Box(double w, double h, double d) {
    width = w;
    height = h;
    depth = d;
  }

  // compute and return volume
  double volume() {
    return width * height * depth;
  }
}
```

As you can see, the **Box( )** constructor requires three parameters. This means that all declarations of **Box** objects must pass three arguments to the **Box( )** constructor. For example, the following statement is currently invalid:

```
Box ob = new Box();
```

Since **Box( )** requires three arguments, it's an error to call it without them. This raises some important questions. What if you simply wanted a box and did not care (or know) what its initial dimensions were? Or, what if you want to be able to initialize a cube by specifying only one value that would be used for all three dimensions? As the **Box** class is currently written, these other options are not available to you.

Fortunately, the solution to these problems is quite easy: simply overload the **Box** constructor so that it handles the situations just described. Here is a program that contains an improved version of **Box** that does just that:

```
/* Here, Box defines three constructors to initialize
   the dimensions of a box various ways.
*/
class Box {
  double width;
  double height;
  double depth;

  // constructor used when all dimensions specified
  Box(double w, double h, double d) {
    width = w;
    height = h;
    depth = d;
  }

  // constructor used when no dimensions specified
  Box() {
    width = -1;   // use -1 to indicate
    height = -1; // an uninitialized
    depth = -1;   // box
  }

  // constructor used when cube is created
  Box(double len) {
    width = height = depth = len;
  }

  // compute and return volume
  double volume() {
    return width * height * depth;
  }
}

class OverloadCons {
  public static void main(String args[]) {
    // create boxes using the various constructors
    Box mybox1 = new Box(10, 20, 15);
    Box mybox2 = new Box();
    Box mycube = new Box(7);

    double vol;
```

```
// get volume of first box
vol = mybox1.volume();
System.out.println("Volume of mybox1 is " + vol);

// get volume of second box
vol = mybox2.volume();
System.out.println("Volume of mybox2 is " + vol);
// get volume of cube
vol = mycube.volume();
System.out.println("Volume of mycube is " + vol);
  }
}
```

The output produced by this program is shown here:

```
Volume of mybox1 is 3000.0
Volume of mybox2 is -1.0
Volume of mycube is 343.0
```

As you can see, the proper overloaded constructor is called based upon the parameters specified when **new** is executed.

Using Objects as Parameters

So far, we have only been using simple types as parameters to methods. However, it is both correct and common to pass objects to methods. For example, consider the following short program:

```
// Objects may be passed to methods.
class Test {
  int a, b;

  Test(int i, int j) {
    a = i;
    b = j;
  }

  // return true if o is equal to the invoking object
  boolean equals(Test o) {
    if(o.a == a && o.b == b) return true;
    else return false;
  }
}

class PassOb {
  public static void main(String args[]) {
    Test ob1 = new Test(100, 22);
    Test ob2 = new Test(100, 22);
    Test ob3 = new Test(-1, -1);

    System.out.println("ob1 == ob2: " + ob1.equals(ob2));
```

```
    System.out.println("ob1 == ob3: " + ob1.equals(ob3));
  }
}
```

This program generates the following output:

```
ob1 == ob2: true
ob1 == ob3: false
```

As you can see, the **equals( )** method inside **Test** compares two objects for equality and returns the result. That is, it compares the invoking object with the one that it is passed. If they contain the same values, then the method returns **true**. Otherwise, it returns **false**. Notice that the parameter **o** in **equals( )** specifies **Test** as its type. Although **Test** is a class type created by the program, it is used in just the same way as Java's built-in types.

One of the most common uses of object parameters involves constructors. Frequently, you will want to construct a new object so that it is initially the same as some existing object. To do this, you must define a constructor that takes an object of its class as a parameter. For example, the following version of **Box** allows one object to initialize another:

```
// Here, Box allows one object to initialize another.

class Box {
  double width;
  double height;
  double depth;

  // Notice this constructor. It takes an object of type Box.
  Box(Box ob) { // pass object to constructor
    width = ob.width;
    height = ob.height;
    depth = ob.depth;
  }

  // constructor used when all dimensions specified
  Box(double w, double h, double d) {
    width = w;
    height = h;
    depth = d;
  }

  // constructor used when no dimensions specified
  Box() {
    width = -1;  // use -1 to indicate
    height = -1; // an uninitialized
    depth = -1;  // box
  }

  // constructor used when cube is created
  Box(double len) {
    width = height = depth = len;
  }
```

```
    // compute and return volume
    double volume() {
      return width * height * depth;
    }
}

class OverloadCons2 {
  public static void main(String args[]) {
    // create boxes using the various constructors
    Box mybox1 = new Box(10, 20, 15);
    Box mybox2 = new Box();
    Box mycube = new Box(7);

    Box myclone = new Box(mybox1); // create copy of mybox1

    double vol;

    // get volume of first box
    vol = mybox1.volume();
    System.out.println("Volume of mybox1 is " + vol);
    // get volume of second box
    vol = mybox2.volume();
    System.out.println("Volume of mybox2 is " + vol);

    // get volume of cube
    vol = mycube.volume();
    System.out.println("Volume of cube is " + vol);

    // get volume of clone
    vol = myclone.volume();
    System.out.println("Volume of clone is " + vol);
  }
}
```

As you will see when you begin to create your own classes, providing many forms of constructors is usually required to allow objects to be constructed in a convenient and efficient manner.

A Closer Look at Argument Passing

In general, there are two ways that a computer language can pass an argument to a subroutine. The first way is *call-by-value*. This approach copies the *value* of an argument into the formal parameter of the subroutine. Therefore, changes made to the parameter of the subroutine have no effect on the argument. The second way an argument can be passed is *call-by-reference*. In this approach, a reference to an argument (not the value of the argument) is passed to the parameter. Inside the subroutine, this reference is used to access the actual argument specified in the call. This means that changes made to the parameter will affect the argument used to call the subroutine. As you will see, Java uses both approaches, depending upon what is passed.

In Java, when you pass a primitive type to a method, it is passed by value. Thus, what occurs to the parameter that receives the argument has no effect outside the method. For example, consider the following program:

```
// Primitive types are passed by value.
class Test {
  void meth(int i, int j) {
    i *= 2;
    j /= 2;
  }
}
class CallByValue {
  public static void main(String args[]) {
    Test ob = new Test();

    int a = 15, b = 20;

    System.out.println("a and b before call: " +
                       a + " " + b);

    ob.meth(a, b);

    System.out.println("a and b after call: " +
                       a + " " + b);
  }
}
```

The output from this program is shown here:

```
a and b before call: 15 20
a and b after call: 15 20
```

As you can see, the operations that occur inside **meth( )** have no effect on the values of **a** and **b** used in the call; their values here did not change to 30 and 10.

When you pass an object to a method, the situation changes dramatically, because objects are passed by what is effectively call-by-reference. Keep in mind that when you create a variable of a class type, you are only creating a reference to an object. Thus, when you pass this reference to a method, the parameter that receives it will refer to the same object as that referred to by the argument. This effectively means that objects are passed to methods by use of call-by-reference. Changes to the object inside the method *do* affect the object used as an argument. For example, consider the following program:

```
// Objects are passed by reference.

class Test {
  int a, b;

  Test(int i, int j) {
    a = i;
    b = j;
  }
  // pass an object
  void meth(Test o) {
    o.a *=  2;
```

```
      o.b /= 2;
  }
}

class CallByRef {
  public static void main(String args[]) {
    Test ob = new Test(15, 20);

    System.out.println("ob.a and ob.b before call: " +
                       ob.a + " " + ob.b);

    ob.meth(ob);

    System.out.println("ob.a and ob.b after call: " +
                       ob.a + " " + ob.b);
  }
}
```

This program generates the following output:

```
ob.a and ob.b before call: 15 20
ob.a and ob.b after call: 30 10
```

As you can see, in this case, the actions inside **meth( )** have affected the object used as an argument.

As a point of interest, when an object reference is passed to a method, the reference itself is passed by use of call-by-value. However, since the value being passed refers to an object, the copy of that value will still refer to the same object that its corresponding argument does.

REMEMBER   *When a primitive type is passed to a method, it is done by use of call-by-value. Objects are implicitly passed by use of call-by-reference.*

Returning Objects

A method can return any type of data, including class types that you create. For example, in the following program, the **incrByTen( )** method returns an object in which the value of **a** is ten greater than it is in the invoking object.

```
// Returning an object.
class Test {
  int a;

  Test(int i) {
    a = i;
  }

  Test incrByTen() {
    Test temp = new Test(a+10);
    return temp;
  }
```

```
}

class RetOb {
  public static void main(String args[]) {
    Test ob1 = new Test(2);
    Test ob2;

    ob2 = ob1.incrByTen();
    System.out.println("ob1.a: " + ob1.a);
    System.out.println("ob2.a: " + ob2.a);

    ob2 = ob2.incrByTen();
    System.out.println("ob2.a after second increase: "
                         + ob2.a);
  }
}
```

The output generated by this program is shown here:

```
ob1.a: 2
ob2.a: 12
ob2.a after second increase: 22
```

As you can see, each time **incrByTen( )** is invoked, a new object is created, and a reference to it is returned to the calling routine.

The preceding program makes another important point: Since all objects are dynamically allocated using **new**, you don't need to worry about an object going out-of-scope because the method in which it was created terminates. The object will continue to exist as long as there is a reference to it somewhere in your program. When there are no references to it, the object will be reclaimed the next time garbage collection takes place.

Recursion

Java supports *recursion*. Recursion is the process of defining something in terms of itself. As it relates to Java programming, recursion is the attribute that allows a method to call itself. A method that calls itself is said to be *recursive*.

The classic example of recursion is the computation of the factorial of a number. The factorial of a number N is the product of all the whole numbers between 1 and N. For example, 3 factorial is $1 \times 2 \times 3$, or 6. Here is how a factorial can be computed by use of a recursive method:

```
// A simple example of recursion.
class Factorial {
  // this is a recursive method
  int fact(int n) {
    int result;

    if(n==1) return 1;
    result = fact(n-1) * n;
    return result;
```

```
    }
}

class Recursion {
  public static void main(String args[]) {
    Factorial f = new Factorial();

    System.out.println("Factorial of 3 is " + f.fact(3));
    System.out.println("Factorial of 4 is " + f.fact(4));
    System.out.println("Factorial of 5 is " + f.fact(5));
  }
}
```

The output from this program is shown here:

```
Factorial of 3 is 6
Factorial of 4 is 24
Factorial of 5 is 120
```

If you are unfamiliar with recursive methods, then the operation of **fact( )** may seem a bit confusing. Here is how it works. When **fact( )** is called with an argument of 1, the function returns 1; otherwise, it returns the product of **fact(n–1)*n**. To evaluate this expression, **fact( )** is called with **n–1**. This process repeats until **n** equals 1 and the calls to the method begin returning.

To better understand how the **fact( )** method works, let's go through a short example. When you compute the factorial of 3, the first call to **fact( )** will cause a second call to be made with an argument of 2. This invocation will cause **fact( )** to be called a third time with an argument of 1. This call will return 1, which is then multiplied by 2 (the value of **n** in the second invocation). This result (which is 2) is then returned to the original invocation of **fact( )** and multiplied by 3 (the original value of **n**). This yields the answer, 6. You might find it interesting to insert **println( )** statements into **fact( )**, which will show at what level each call is and what the intermediate answers are.

When a method calls itself, new local variables and parameters are allocated storage on the stack, and the method code is executed with these new variables from the start. As each recursive call returns, the old local variables and parameters are removed from the stack, and execution resumes at the point of the call inside the method. Recursive methods could be said to "telescope" out and back.

Recursive versions of many routines may execute a bit more slowly than the iterative equivalent because of the added overhead of the additional function calls. Many recursive calls to a method could cause a stack overrun. Because storage for parameters and local variables is on the stack and each new call creates a new copy of these variables, it is possible that the stack could be exhausted. If this occurs, the Java run-time system will cause an exception. However, you probably will not have to worry about this unless a recursive routine runs wild.

The main advantage to recursive methods is that they can be used to create clearer and simpler versions of several algorithms than can their iterative relatives. For example, the QuickSort sorting algorithm is quite difficult to implement in an iterative way. Also, some types of AI-related algorithms are most easily implemented using recursive solutions.

When writing recursive methods, you must have an **if** statement somewhere to force the method to return without the recursive call being executed. If you don't do this, once you call the method, it will never return. This is a very common error in working with recursion. Use **println( )** statements liberally during development so that you can watch what is going on and abort execution if you see that you have made a mistake.

Here is one more example of recursion. The recursive method **printArray( )** prints the first **i** elements in the array **values**.

```
// Another example that uses recursion.

class RecTest {
  int values[];

  RecTest(int i) {
    values = new int[i];
  }

  // display array -- recursively
  void printArray(int i) {
    if(i==0) return;
    else printArray(i-1);
    System.out.println("[" + (i-1) + "] " + values[i-1]);
  }
}

class Recursion2 {
  public static void main(String args[]) {
    RecTest ob = new RecTest(10);
    int i;

    for(i=0; i<10; i++) ob.values[i] = i;

    ob.printArray(10);
  }
}
```

This program generates the following output:

```
[0] 0
[1] 1
[2] 2
[3] 3
[4] 4
[5] 5
[6] 6
[7] 7
[8] 8
[9] 9
```

Introducing Access Control

As you know, encapsulation links data with the code that manipulates it. However, encapsulation provides another important attribute: *access control.* Through encapsulation, you can control what parts of a program can access the members of a class. By controlling access, you can prevent misuse. For example, allowing access to data only through a well-defined set of methods, you can prevent the misuse of that data. Thus, when correctly implemented, a class creates a "black box" which may be used, but the inner workings of which are not open to tampering. However, the classes that were presented earlier do not completely meet this goal. For example, consider the **Stack** class shown at the end of Chapter 6. While it is true that the methods **push( )** and **pop( )** do provide a controlled interface to the stack, this interface is not enforced. That is, it is possible for another part of the program to bypass these methods and access the stack directly. Of course, in the wrong hands, this could lead to trouble. In this section, you will be introduced to the mechanism by which you can precisely control access to the various members of a class.

How a member can be accessed is determined by the *access specifier* that modifies its declaration. Java supplies a rich set of access specifiers. Some aspects of access control are related mostly to inheritance or packages. (A *package* is, essentially, a grouping of classes.) These parts of Java's access control mechanism will be discussed later. Here, let's begin by examining access control as it applies to a single class. Once you understand the fundamentals of access control, the rest will be easy.

Java's access specifiers are **public**, **private**, and **protected**. Java also defines a default access level. **protected** applies only when inheritance is involved. The other access specifiers are described next.

Let's begin by defining **public** and **private**. When a member of a class is modified by the **public** specifier, then that member can be accessed by any other code. When a member of a class is specified as **private**, then that member can only be accessed by other members of its class. Now you can understand why **main( )** has always been preceded by the **public** specifier. It is called by code that is outside the program—that is, by the Java run-time system. When no access specifier is used, then by default the member of a class is public within its own package, but cannot be accessed outside of its package. (Packages are discussed in the following chapter.)

In the classes developed so far, all members of a class have used the default access mode, which is essentially public. However, this is not what you will typically want to be the case. Usually, you will want to restrict access to the data members of a class—allowing access only through methods. Also, there will be times when you will want to define methods that are private to a class.

An access specifier precedes the rest of a member's type specification. That is, it must begin a member's declaration statement. Here is an example:

```
public int i;
private double j;

private int myMethod(int a, char b) { // ...
```

To understand the effects of public and private access, consider the following program:

```
/* This program demonstrates the difference between
   public and private.
*/
class Test {
  int a; // default access
  public int b; // public access
  private int c; // private access

  // methods to access c
  void setc(int i) { // set c's value
    c = i;
  }
  int getc() { // get c's value
    return c;
  }
}

class AccessTest {
  public static void main(String args[]) {
    Test ob = new Test();

    // These are OK, a and b may be accessed directly
    ob.a = 10;
    ob.b = 20;

    // This is not OK and will cause an error
//  ob.c = 100; // Error!

    // You must access c through its methods
    ob.setc(100); // OK
    System.out.println("a, b, and c: " + ob.a + " " +
                        ob.b + " " + ob.getc());
  }
}
```

As you can see, inside the **Test** class, **a** uses default access, which for this example is the same as specifying **public**. **b** is explicitly specified as **public**. Member **c** is given private access. This means that it cannot be accessed by code outside of its class. So, inside the **AccessTest** class, **c** cannot be used directly. It must be accessed through its public methods: **setc( )** and **getc( )**. If you were to remove the comment symbol from the beginning of the following line,

```
//  ob.c = 100; // Error!
```

then you would not be able to compile this program because of the access violation.

To see how access control can be applied to a more practical example, consider the following improved version of the **Stack** class shown at the end of Chapter 6.

```
// This class defines an integer stack that can hold 10 values.
class Stack {
  /* Now, both stck and tos are private.  This means
```

```
    that they cannot be accidentally or maliciously
    altered in a way that would be harmful to the stack.
  */
  private int stck[] = new int[10];
  private int tos;

  // Initialize top-of-stack
  Stack() {
    tos = -1;
  }

  // Push an item onto the stack
  void push(int item) {
    if(tos==9)
      System.out.println("Stack is full.");
    else
      stck[++tos] = item;
  }
  // Pop an item from the stack
  int pop() {
    if(tos < 0) {
      System.out.println("Stack underflow.");
      return 0;
    }
    else
      return stck[tos--];
  }
}
```

As you can see, now both **stck**, which holds the stack, and **tos**, which is the index of the top of the stack, are specified as **private**. This means that they cannot be accessed or altered except through **push( )** and **pop( )**. Making **tos** private, for example, prevents other parts of your program from inadvertently setting it to a value that is beyond the end of the **stck** array.

The following program demonstrates the improved **Stack** class. Try removing the commented-out lines to prove to yourself that the **stck** and **tos** members are, indeed, inaccessible.

```
class TestStack {
  public static void main(String args[]) {
    Stack mystack1 = new Stack();
    Stack mystack2 = new Stack();

    // push some numbers onto the stack
    for(int i=0; i<10; i++) mystack1.push(i);
    for(int i=10; i<20; i++) mystack2.push(i);

    // pop those numbers off the stack
    System.out.println("Stack in mystack1:");
    for(int i=0; i<10; i++)
      System.out.println(mystack1.pop());

    System.out.println("Stack in mystack2:");
```

```
    for(int i=0; i<10; i++)
       System.out.println(mystack2.pop());

    // these statements are not legal
    // mystack1.tos = -2;
    // mystack2.stck[3] = 100;
  }
}
```

Although methods will usually provide access to the data defined by a class, this does not always have to be the case. It is perfectly proper to allow an instance variable to be public when there is good reason to do so. For example, most of the simple classes in this book were created with little concern about controlling access to instance variables for the sake of simplicity. However, in most real-world classes, you will need to allow operations on data only through methods. The next chapter will return to the topic of access control. As you will see, it is particularly important when inheritance is involved.

Understanding static

There will be times when you will want to define a class member that will be used independently of any object of that class. Normally, a class member must be accessed only in conjunction with an object of its class. However, it is possible to create a member that can be used by itself, without reference to a specific instance. To create such a member, precede its declaration with the keyword **static**. When a member is declared **static**, it can be accessed before any objects of its class are created, and without reference to any object. You can declare both methods and variables to be **static**. The most common example of a **static** member is **main( )**. **main( )** is declared as **static** because it must be called before any objects exist.

Instance variables declared as **static** are, essentially, global variables. When objects of its class are declared, no copy of a **static** variable is made. Instead, all instances of the class share the same **static** variable.

Methods declared as **static** have several restrictions:

- They can only call other **static** methods.
- They must only access **static** data.
- They cannot refer to **this** or **super** in any way. (The keyword **super** relates to inheritance and is described in the next chapter.)

If you need to do computation in order to initialize your **static** variables, you can declare a **static** block that gets executed exactly once, when the class is first loaded. The following example shows a class that has a **static** method, some **static** variables, and a **static** initialization block:

```
// Demonstrate static variables, methods, and blocks.
class UseStatic {
  static int a = 3;
  static int b;

  static void meth(int x) {
```

```
    System.out.println("x = " + x);
    System.out.println("a = " + a);
    System.out.println("b = " + b);
  }

  static {
    System.out.println("Static block initialized.");
    b = a * 4;
  }

  public static void main(String args[]) {
    meth(42);
  }
}
```

As soon as the **UseStatic** class is loaded, all of the **static** statements are run. First, **a** is set to **3**, then the **static** block executes, which prints a message and then initializes **b** to **a * 4** or **12**. Then **main( )** is called, which calls **meth( )**, passing **42** to **x**. The three **println( )** statements refer to the two **static** variables **a** and **b**, as well as to the local variable **x**.

Here is the output of the program:

```
Static block initialized.
x = 42
a = 3
b = 12
```

Outside of the class in which they are defined, **static** methods and variables can be used independently of any object. To do so, you need only specify the name of their class followed by the dot operator. For example, if you wish to call a **static** method from outside its class, you can do so using the following general form:

classname.method( )

Here, *classname* is the name of the class in which the **static** method is declared. As you can see, this format is similar to that used to call non-**static** methods through object-reference variables. A **static** variable can be accessed in the same way—by use of the dot operator on the name of the class. This is how Java implements a controlled version of global methods and global variables.

Here is an example. Inside **main( )**, the **static** method **callme( )** and the **static** variable **b** are accessed through their class name **StaticDemo**.

```
class StaticDemo {
  static int a = 42;
  static int b = 99;
  static void callme() {
    System.out.println("a = " + a);
  }
```

```
  }

class StaticByName {
  public static void main(String args[]) {
    StaticDemo.callme();
    System.out.println("b = " + StaticDemo.b);
  }
}
```

Here is the output of this program:

```
a = 42
b = 99
```

Introducing final

A variable can be declared as **final**. Doing so prevents its contents from being modified. This means that you must initialize a **final** variable when it is declared. For example:

```
final int FILE_NEW = 1;
final int FILE_OPEN = 2;
final int FILE_SAVE = 3;
final int FILE_SAVEAS = 4;
final int FILE_QUIT = 5;
```

Subsequent parts of your program can now use **FILE_OPEN**, etc., as if they were constants, without fear that a value has been changed.

It is a common coding convention to choose all uppercase identifiers for **final** variables. Variables declared as **final** do not occupy memory on a per-instance basis. Thus, a **final** variable is essentially a constant.

The keyword **final** can also be applied to methods, but its meaning is substantially different than when it is applied to variables. This second usage of **final** is described in the next chapter, when inheritance is described.

Arrays Revisited

Arrays were introduced earlier in this book, before classes had been discussed. Now that you know about classes, an important point can be made about arrays: they are implemented as objects. Because of this, there is a special array attribute that you will want to take advantage of. Specifically, the size of an array—that is, the number of elements that an array can hold—is found in its **length** instance variable. All arrays have this variable, and it will always hold the size of the array. Here is a program that demonstrates this property:

```
// This program demonstrates the length array member.
class Length {
  public static void main(String args[]) {
    int a1[] = new int[10];
    int a2[] = {3, 5, 7, 1, 8, 99, 44, -10};
    int a3[] = {4, 3, 2, 1};
```

```
    System.out.println("length of a1 is " + a1.length);
    System.out.println("length of a2 is " + a2.length);
    System.out.println("length of a3 is " + a3.length);
  }
}
```

This program displays the following output:

```
length of a1 is 10
length of a2 is 8
length of a3 is 4
```

As you can see, the size of each array is displayed. Keep in mind that the value of **length** has nothing to do with the number of elements that are actually in use. It only reflects the number of elements that the array is designed to hold.

You can put the **length** member to good use in many situations. For example, here is an improved version of the **Stack** class. As you might recall, the earlier versions of this class always created a ten-element stack. The following version lets you create stacks of any size. The value of **stck.length** is used to prevent the stack from overflowing.

```
// Improved Stack class that uses the length array member.
class Stack {
  private int stck[];
  private int tos;

  // allocate and initialize stack
  Stack(int size) {
    stck = new int[size];
    tos = -1;
  }

  // Push an item onto the stack
  void push(int item) {
    if(tos==stck.length-1) // use length member
      System.out.println("Stack is full.");
    else
      stck[++tos] = item;
  }

  // Pop an item from the stack
  int pop() {
    if(tos < 0) {
      System.out.println("Stack underflow.");
      return 0;
    }
    else
      return stck[tos--];
  }
}

class TestStack2 {
  public static void main(String args[]) {
```

```
      Stack mystack1 = new Stack(5);
      Stack mystack2 = new Stack(8);
      // push some numbers onto the stack
      for(int i=0; i<5; i++) mystack1.push(i);
      for(int i=0; i<8; i++) mystack2.push(i);

      // pop those numbers off the stack
      System.out.println("Stack in mystack1:");
      for(int i=0; i<5; i++)
         System.out.println(mystack1.pop());

      System.out.println("Stack in mystack2:");
      for(int i=0; i<8; i++)
         System.out.println(mystack2.pop());
   }
}
```

Notice that the program creates two stacks: one five elements deep and the other eight elements deep. As you can see, the fact that arrays maintain their own length information makes it easy to create stacks of any size.

Introducing Nested and Inner Classes

It is possible to define a class within another class; such classes are known as *nested classes*. The scope of a nested class is bounded by the scope of its enclosing class. Thus, if class B is defined within class A, then B does not exist independently of A. A nested class has access to the members, including private members, of the class in which it is nested. However, the enclosing class does not have access to the members of the nested class. A nested class that is declared directly within its enclosing class scope is a member of its enclosing class. It is also possible to declare a nested class that is local to a block.

There are two types of nested classes: *static* and *non-static*. A static nested class is one that has the **static** modifier applied. Because it is static, it must access the members of its enclosing class through an object. That is, it cannot refer to members of its enclosing class directly. Because of this restriction, static nested classes are seldom used.

The most important type of nested class is the *inner* class. An inner class is a non-static nested class. It has access to all of the variables and methods of its outer class and may refer to them directly in the same way that other non-static members of the outer class do.

The following program illustrates how to define and use an inner class. The class named **Outer** has one instance variable named **outer_x**, one instance method named **test( )**, and defines one inner class called **Inner**.

```
// Demonstrate an inner class.
class Outer {
  int outer_x = 100;

  void test() {
    Inner inner = new Inner();
    inner.display();
  }

  // this is an inner class
```

```
  class Inner {
    void display() {
      System.out.println("display: outer_x = " + outer_x);
    }
  }
}

class InnerClassDemo {
  public static void main(String args[]) {
    Outer outer = new Outer();
    outer.test();
  }
}
```

Output from this application is shown here:

```
display: outer_x = 100
```

In the program, an inner class named **Inner** is defined within the scope of class **Outer**. Therefore, any code in class **Inner** can directly access the variable **outer_x**. An instance method named **display( )** is defined inside **Inner**. This method displays **outer_x** on the standard output stream. The **main( )** method of **InnerClassDemo** creates an instance of class **Outer** and invokes its **test( )** method. That method creates an instance of class **Inner** and the **display( )** method is called.

It is important to realize that an instance of **Inner** can be created only within the scope of class **Outer**. The Java compiler generates an error message if any code outside of class **Outer** attempts to instantiate class **Inner**. (In general, an inner class instance must be created by an enclosing scope.) You can, however, create an instance of **Inner** outside of **Outer** by qualifying its name with **Outer**, as in **Outer.Inner**.

As explained, an inner class has access to all of the members of its enclosing class, but the reverse is not true. Members of the inner class are known only within the scope of the inner class and may not be used by the outer class. For example,

```
// This program will not compile.
class Outer {
  int outer_x = 100;

  void test() {
    Inner inner = new Inner();
    inner.display();
  }

  // this is an inner class
  class Inner {
    int y = 10; // y is local to Inner
    void display() {
      System.out.println("display: outer_x = " + outer_x);
    }
  }

  void showy() {
    System.out.println(y); // error, y not known here!
```

```
    }
}

class InnerClassDemo {
  public static void main(String args[]) {
    Outer outer = new Outer();
    outer.test();
  }
}
```

Here, **y** is declared as an instance variable of **Inner**. Thus, it is not known outside of that class and it cannot be used by **showy( )**.

Although we have been focusing on inner classes declared as members within an outer class scope, it is possible to define inner classes within any block scope. For example, you can define a nested class within the block defined by a method or even within the body of a **for** loop, as this next program shows.

```
// Define an inner class within a for loop.
class Outer {
  int outer_x = 100;

  void test() {
    for(int i=0; i<10; i++) {
      class Inner {
        void display() {
          System.out.println("display: outer_x = " + outer_x);
        }
      }
      Inner inner = new Inner();
      inner.display();
    }
  }
}

class InnerClassDemo {
  public static void main(String args[]) {
    Outer outer = new Outer();
    outer.test();
  }
}
```

The output from this version of the program is shown here.

```
display: outer_x = 100
display: outer_x = 100
display: outer_x = 100
display: outer_x = 100
display: outer_x = 100
display: outer_x = 100
display: outer_x = 100
display: outer_x = 100
```

```
display: outer_x = 100
display: outer_x = 100
```

While nested classes are not applicable to all stiuations, they are particularly helpful when handling events. We will return to the topic of nested classes in Chapter 22. There you will see how inner classes can be used to simplify the code needed to handle certain types of events. You will also learn about *anonymous inner classes*, which are inner classes that don't have a name.

One final point: Nested classes were not allowed by the original 1.0 specification for Java. They were added by Java 1.1.

Exploring the String Class

Although the **String** class will be examined in depth in Part II of this book, a short exploration of it is warranted now, because we will be using strings in some of the example programs shown toward the end of Part I. **String** is probably the most commonly used class in Java's class library. The obvious reason for this is that strings are a very important part of programming.

The first thing to understand about strings is that every string you create is actually an object of type **String**. Even string constants are actually **String** objects. For example, in the statement

```
System.out.println("This is a String, too");
```

the string "This is a String, too" is a **String** constant.

The second thing to understand about strings is that objects of type **String** are immutable; once a **String** object is created, its contents cannot be altered. While this may seem like a serious restriction, it is not, for two reasons:

- If you need to change a string, you can always create a new one that contains the modifications.

- Java defines a peer class of **String**, called **StringBuffer**, which allows strings to be altered, so all of the normal string manipulations are still available in Java. (**StringBuffer** is described in Part II of this book.)

Strings can be constructed in a variety of ways. The easiest is to use a statement like this:

```
String myString = "this is a test";
```

Once you have created a **String** object, you can use it anywhere that a string is allowed. For example, this statement displays **myString**:

```
System.out.println(myString);
```

Java defines one operator for **String** objects: **+**. It is used to concatenate two strings. For example, this statement

```
String myString = "I" + " like " + "Java.";
```

results in **myString** containing "I like Java."

The following program demonstrates the preceding concepts:

```
// Demonstrating Strings.
class StringDemo {
  public static void main(String args[]) {
    String strOb1 = "First String";
    String strOb2 = "Second String";
    String strOb3 = strOb1 + " and " + strOb2;

    System.out.println(strOb1);
    System.out.println(strOb2);
    System.out.println(strOb3);
  }
}
```

The output produced by this program is shown here:

```
First String
Second String
First String and Second String
```

The **String** class contains several methods that you can use. Here are a few. You can test two strings for equality by using **equals( )**. You can obtain the length of a string by calling the **length( )** method. You can obtain the character at a specified index within a string by calling **charAt( )**. The general forms of these three methods are shown here:

boolean equals(String *object*)
int length( )
char charAt(int *index*)

Here is a program that demonstrates these methods:

```
// Demonstrating some String methods.
class StringDemo2 {
  public static void main(String args[]) {
    String strOb1 = "First String";
    String strOb2 = "Second String";
    String strOb3 = strOb1;

    System.out.println("Length of strOb1: " +
                       strOb1.length());

    System.out.println("Char at index 3 in strOb1: " +
                       strOb1.charAt(3));

    if(strOb1.equals(strOb2))
      System.out.println("strOb1 == strOb2");
    else
      System.out.println("strOb1 != strOb2");

    if(strOb1.equals(strOb3))
      System.out.println("strOb1 == strOb3");
    else
```

```
       System.out.println("strOb1 != strOb3");
    }
}
```

This program generates the following output:

```
Length of strOb1: 12
Char at index 3 in strOb1: s
strOb1 != strOb2
strOb1 == strOb3
```

Of course, you can have arrays of strings, just like you can have arrays of any other type of object. For example:

```
// Demonstrate String arrays.
class StringDemo3 {
  public static void main(String args[]) {
    String str[] = { "one", "two", "three" };

    for(int i=0; i<str.length; i++)
      System.out.println("str[" + i + "]: " +
                          str[i]);
  }
}
```

Here is the output from this program:

```
str[0]: one
str[1]: two
str[2]: three
```

As you will see in the following section, string arrays play an important part in many Java programs.

Using Command-Line Arguments

Sometimes you will want to pass information into a program when you run it. This is accomplished by passing *command-line arguments* to **main( )**. A command-line argument is the information that directly follows the program's name on the command line when it is executed. To access the command-line arguments inside a Java program is quite easy—they are stored as strings in a **String** array passed to the **args** parameter of **main( )**. The first command-line argument is stored at **args[0]**, the second at **args[1]**, and so on. For example, the following program displays all of the command-line arguments that it is called with:

```
// Display all command-line arguments.
class CommandLine {
  public static void main(String args[]) {
    for(int i=0; i<args.length; i++)
      System.out.println("args[" + i + "]: " +
                          args[i]);
  }
}
```

Try executing this program, as shown here:

```
java CommandLine this is a test 100 -1
```

When you do, you will see the following output:

```
args[0]: this
args[1]: is
args[2]: a
args[3]: test
args[4]: 100
args[5]: -1
```

REMEMBER   *All command-line arguments are passed as strings. You must convert numeric values to their internal forms manually, as explained in Chapter 16.*

Varargs: Variable-Length Arguments

Beginning with JDK 5, Java has included a feature that simplifies the creation of methods that need to take a variable number of arguments. This feature is called *varargs* and it is short for *variable-length arguments*. A method that takes a variable number of arguments is called a *variable-arity method*, or simply a *varargs method*.

Situations that require that a variable number of arguments be passed to a method are not unusual. For example, a method that opens an Internet connection might take a user name, password, filename, protocol, and so on, but supply defaults if some of this information is not provided. In this situation, it would be convenient to pass only the arguments to which the defaults did not apply. Another example is the **printf( )** method that is part of Java's I/O library. As you will see in Chapter 19, it takes a variable number of arguments, which it formats and then outputs.

Prior to JDK 5, variable-length arguments could be handled two ways, neither of which was particularly pleasing. First, if the maximum number of arguments was small and known, then you could create overloaded versions of the method, one for each way the method could be called. Although this works and is suitable for some cases, it applies to only a narrow class of situations.

In cases where the maximum number of potential arguments was larger, or unknowable, a second approach was used in which the arguments were put into an array, and then the array was passed to the method. This approach is illustrated by the following program:

```
// Use an array to pass a variable number of
// arguments to a method. This is the old-style
// approach to variable-length arguments.
class PassArray {
  static void vaTest(int v[]) {
    System.out.print("Number of args: " + v.length +
                        " Contents: ");

    for(int x : v)
      System.out.print(x + " ");
```

```
      System.out.println();
    }

    public static void main(String args[])
    {
      // Notice how an array must be created to
      // hold the arguments.
      int n1[] = { 10 };
      int n2[] = { 1, 2, 3 };
      int n3[] = { };

      vaTest(n1); // 1 arg
      vaTest(n2); // 3 args
      vaTest(n3); // no args
    }
}
```

The output from the program is shown here:

```
    Number of args: 1 Contents: 10
    Number of args: 3 Contents: 1 2 3
    Number of args: 0 Contents:
```

In the program, the method **vaTest( )** is passed its arguments through the array **v**. This old-style approach to variable-length arguments does enable **vaTest( )** to take an arbitrary number of arguments. However, it requires that these arguments be manually packaged into an array prior to calling **vaTest( )**. Not only is it tedious to construct an array each time **vaTest( )** is called, it is potentially error-prone. The varargs feature offers a simpler, better option.

A variable-length argument is specified by three periods (...). For example, here is how **vaTest( )** is written using a vararg:

```
static void vaTest(int ... v) {
```

This syntax tells the compiler that **vaTest( )** can be called with zero or more arguments. As a result, **v** is implicitly declared as an array of type **int[ ]**. Thus, inside **vaTest( )**, **v** is accessed using the normal array syntax. Here is the preceding program rewritten using a vararg:

```
// Demonstrate variable-length arguments.
class VarArgs {

  // vaTest() now uses a vararg.
  static void vaTest(int ... v) {
    System.out.print("Number of args: " + v.length +
                       " Contents: ");

    for(int x : v)
      System.out.print(x + " ");

    System.out.println();
  }

  public static void main(String args[])
  {
```

```
    // Notice how vaTest() can be called with a
    // variable number of arguments.
    vaTest(10);      // 1 arg
    vaTest(1, 2, 3); // 3 args
    vaTest();        // no args
  }
}
```

The output from the program is the same as the original version.

There are two important things to notice about this program. First, as explained, inside **vaTest( )**, **v** is operated on as an array. This is because **v** *is* an array. The **...** syntax simply tells the compiler that a variable number of arguments will be used, and that these arguments will be stored in the array referred to by **v**. Second, in **main( )**, **vaTest( )** is called with different numbers of arguments, including no arguments at all. The arguments are automatically put in an array and passed to **v**. In the case of no arguments, the length of the array is zero.

A method can have "normal" parameters along with a variable-length parameter. However, the variable-length parameter must be the last parameter declared by the method. For example, this method declaration is perfectly acceptable:

```
int doIt(int a, int b, double c, int ... vals) {
```

In this case, the first three arguments used in a call to **doIt( )** are matched to the first three parameters. Then, any remaining arguments are assumed to belong to **vals**.

Remember, the varargs parameter must be last. For example, the following declaration is incorrect:

```
int doIt(int a, int b, double c, int ... vals, boolean stopFlag) { // Error!
```

Here, there is an attempt to declare a regular parameter after the varargs parameter, which is illegal.

There is one more restriction to be aware of: there must be only one varargs parameter. For example, this declaration is also invalid:

```
int doIt(int a, int b, double c, int ... vals, double ... morevals) { // Error!
```

The attempt to declare the second varargs parameter is illegal.

Here is a reworked version of the **vaTest( )** method that takes a regular argument and a variable-length argument:

```
// Use varargs with standard arguments.
class VarArgs2 {

  // Here, msg is a normal parameter and v is a
  // varargs parameter.
  static void vaTest(String msg, int ... v) {
    System.out.print(msg + v.length +
                        " Contents: ");

    for(int x : v)
      System.out.print(x + " ");

    System.out.println();
  }
```

```
public static void main(String args[])
{
  vaTest("One vararg: ", 10);
  vaTest("Three varargs: ", 1, 2, 3);
  vaTest("No varargs: ");
}
}
```

The output from this program is shown here:

```
One vararg: 1 Contents: 10
Three varargs: 3 Contents: 1 2 3
No varargs: 0 Contents:
```

Overloading Vararg Methods

You can overload a method that takes a variable-length argument. For example, the following program overloads **vaTest( )** three times:

```
// Varargs and overloading.
class VarArgs3 {

  static void vaTest(int ... v) {
    System.out.print("vaTest(int ...): " +
                     "Number of args: " + v.length +
                     " Contents: ");

    for(int x : v)
      System.out.print(x + " ");

    System.out.println();
  }

  static void vaTest(boolean ... v) {
    System.out.print("vaTest(boolean ...) " +
                     "Number of args: " + v.length +
                     " Contents: ");

    for(boolean x : v)
      System.out.print(x + " ");

    System.out.println();
  }

  static void vaTest(String msg, int ... v) {
    System.out.print("vaTest(String, int ...): " +
                     msg + v.length +
                     " Contents: ");

    for(int x : v)
      System.out.print(x + " ");

    System.out.println();
  }
```

```
  public static void main(String args[])
  {
    vaTest(1, 2, 3);
    vaTest("Testing: ", 10, 20);
    vaTest(true, false, false);
  }
}
```

The output produced by this program is shown here:

```
vaTest(int ...): Number of args: 3 Contents: 1 2 3
vaTest(String, int ...): Testing: 2 Contents: 10 20
vaTest(boolean ...) Number of args: 3 Contents: true false false
```

This program illustrates both ways that a vararg method can be overloaded. First, the types of its vararg parameter can differ. This is the case for **vaTest(int ...)** and **vaTest(boolean ...)**. Remember, the ... causes the parameter to be treated as an array of the specified type. Therefore, just as you can overload methods by using different types of array parameters, you can overload vararg methods by using different types of varargs. In this case, Java uses the type difference to determine which overloaded method to call.

The second way to overload a varargs method is to add a normal parameter. This is what was done with **vaTest(String, int ...)**. In this case, Java uses both the number of arguments and the type of the arguments to determine which method to call.

NOTE *A varargs method can also be overloaded by a non-varargs method. For example, **vaTest(int x)** is a valid overload of **vaTest( )** in the foregoing program. This version is invoked only when one **int** argument is present. When two or more **int** arguments are passed, the varargs version **vaTest(int...v)** is used.*

Varargs and Ambiguity

Somewhat unexpected errors can result when overloading a method that takes a variable-length argument. These errors involve ambiguity because it is possible to create an ambiguous call to an overloaded varargs method. For example, consider the following program:

```
// Varargs, overloading, and ambiguity.
//
// This program contains an error and will
// not compile!
class VarArgs4 {

  static void vaTest(int ... v) {
    System.out.print("vaTest(int ...): " +
                     "Number of args: " + v.length +
                     " Contents: ");

    for(int x : v)
      System.out.print(x + " ");

    System.out.println();
  }
```

```
static void vaTest(boolean ... v) {
  System.out.print("vaTest(boolean ...) " +
                   "Number of args: " + v.length +
                   " Contents: ");

  for(boolean x : v)
    System.out.print(x + " ");

  System.out.println();
}


public static void main(String args[])
{
  vaTest(1, 2, 3);  // OK
  vaTest(true, false, false); // OK

  vaTest(); // Error: Ambiguous!
}
}
```

In this program, the overloading of **vaTest( )** is perfectly correct. However, this program will not compile because of the following call:

```
vaTest(); // Error: Ambiguous!
```

Because the vararg parameter can be empty, this call could be translated into a call to **vaTest(int ...)** or **vaTest(boolean ...)**. Both are equally valid. Thus, the call is inherently ambiguous.

Here is another example of ambiguity. The following overloaded versions of **vaTest( )** are inherently ambiguous even though one takes a normal parameter:

```
static void vaTest(int ... v) { // ...

static void vaTest(int n, int ... v) { // ...
```

Although the parameter lists of **vaTest( )** differ, there is no way for the compiler to resolve the following call:

```
    vaTest(1)
```

Does this translate into a call to **vaTest(int ...)**, with one varargs argument, or into a call to **vaTest(int, int ...)** with no varargs arguments? There is no way for the compiler to answer this question. Thus, the situation is ambiguous.

Because of ambiguity errors like those just shown, sometimes you will need to forego overloading and simply use two different method names. Also, in some cases, ambiguity errors expose a conceptual flaw in your code, which you can remedy by more carefully crafting a solution.

Inheritance

Inheritance is one of the cornerstones of object-oriented programming because it allows the creation of hierarchical classifications. Using inheritance, you can create a general class that defines traits common to a set of related items. This class can then be inherited by other, more specific classes, each adding those things that are unique to it. In the terminology of Java, a class that is inherited is called a *superclass*. The class that does the inheriting is called a *subclass*. Therefore, a subclass is a specialized version of a superclass. It inherits all of the instance variables and methods defined by the superclass and adds its own, unique elements.

Inheritance Basics

To inherit a class, you simply incorporate the definition of one class into another by using the **extends** keyword. To see how, let's begin with a short example. The following program creates a superclass called **A** and a subclass called **B**. Notice how the keyword **extends** is used to create a subclass of **A**.

```
// A simple example of inheritance.

// Create a superclass.
class A {
  int i, j;

  void showij() {
    System.out.println("i and j: " + i + " " + j);
  }
}

// Create a subclass by extending class A.
class B extends A {
  int k;

  void showk() {
    System.out.println("k: " + k);
  }
  void sum() {
    System.out.println("i+j+k: " + (i+j+k));
  }
}
```

```
class SimpleInheritance {
  public static void main(String args[]) {
    A superOb = new A();
    B subOb = new B();

    // The superclass may be used by itself.
    superOb.i = 10;
    superOb.j = 20;
    System.out.println("Contents of superOb: ");
    superOb.showij();
    System.out.println();

    /* The subclass has access to all public members of
       its superclass. */
    subOb.i = 7;
    subOb.j = 8;
    subOb.k = 9;
    System.out.println("Contents of subOb: ");
    subOb.showij();
    subOb.showk();
    System.out.println();

    System.out.println("Sum of i, j and k in subOb:");
    subOb.sum();
  }
}
```

The output from this program is shown here:

```
Contents of superOb:
i and j: 10 20

Contents of subOb:
i and j: 7 8
k: 9

Sum of i, j and k in subOb:
i+j+k: 24
```

As you can see, the subclass **B** includes all of the members of its superclass, **A**. This is why **subOb** can access **i** and **j** and call **showij( )**. Also, inside **sum( )**, **i** and **j** can be referred to directly, as if they were part of **B**.

Even though **A** is a superclass for **B**, it is also a completely independent, stand-alone class. Being a superclass for a subclass does not mean that the superclass cannot be used by itself. Further, a subclass can be a superclass for another subclass.

The general form of a **class** declaration that inherits a superclass is shown here:

class *subclass-name* extends *superclass-name* {
    // body of class
}

You can only specify one superclass for any subclass that you create. Java does not support the inheritance of multiple superclasses into a single subclass. You can, as stated, create a hierarchy of inheritance in which a subclass becomes a superclass of another subclass. However, no class can be a superclass of itself.

Member Access and Inheritance

Although a subclass includes all of the members of its superclass, it cannot access those members of the superclass that have been declared as **private**. For example, consider the following simple class hierarchy:

```
/* In a class hierarchy, private members remain
   private to their class.

   This program contains an error and will not
   compile.
*/

// Create a superclass.
class A {
  int i; // public by default
  private int j; // private to A

  void setij(int x, int y) {
    i = x;
    j = y;
  }
}

// A's j is not accessible here.
class B extends A {
  int total;
  void sum() {
    total = i + j; // ERROR, j is not accessible here
  }
}

class Access {
  public static void main(String args[]) {
    B subOb = new B();

    subOb.setij(10, 12);

    subOb.sum();
    System.out.println("Total is " + subOb.total);
  }
}
```

This program will not compile because the reference to **j** inside the **sum( )** method of **B** causes an access violation. Since **j** is declared as **private**, it is only accessible by other members of its own class. Subclasses have no access to it.

***

REMEMBER *A class member that has been declared as private will remain private to its class. It is not accessible by any code outside its class, including subclasses.*

A More Practical Example

Let's look at a more practical example that will help illustrate the power of inheritance. Here, the final version of the **Box** class developed in the preceding chapter will be extended to include a fourth component called **weight**. Thus, the new class will contain a box's width, height, depth, and weight.

```java
// This program uses inheritance to extend Box.
class Box {
  double width;
  double height;
  double depth;

  // construct clone of an object
  Box(Box ob) { // pass object to constructor
    width = ob.width;
    height = ob.height;
    depth = ob.depth;
  }

  // constructor used when all dimensions specified
  Box(double w, double h, double d) {
    width = w;
    height = h;
    depth = d;
  }

  // constructor used when no dimensions specified
  Box() {
    width = -1;  // use -1 to indicate
    height = -1; // an uninitialized
    depth = -1;  // box
  }

  // constructor used when cube is created
  Box(double len) {
    width = height = depth = len;
  }

  // compute and return volume
  double volume() {
    return width * height * depth;
  }
}

// Here, Box is extended to include weight.
class BoxWeight extends Box {
  double weight; // weight of box
```

```
  // constructor for BoxWeight
  BoxWeight(double w, double h, double d, double m) {
    width = w;
    height = h;
    depth = d;
    weight = m;
  }
}

class DemoBoxWeight {
  public static void main(String args[]) {
    BoxWeight mybox1 = new BoxWeight(10, 20, 15, 34.3);
    BoxWeight mybox2 = new BoxWeight(2, 3, 4, 0.076);
    double vol;

    vol = mybox1.volume();
    System.out.println("Volume of mybox1 is " + vol);
    System.out.println("Weight of mybox1 is " + mybox1.weight);
    System.out.println();

    vol = mybox2.volume();
    System.out.println("Volume of mybox2 is " + vol);
    System.out.println("Weight of mybox2 is " + mybox2.weight);
  }
}
```

The output from this program is shown here:

```
Volume of mybox1 is 3000.0
Weight of mybox1 is 34.3

Volume of mybox2 is 24.0
Weight of mybox2 is 0.076
```

BoxWeight inherits all of the characteristics of **Box** and adds to them the **weight** component. It is not necessary for **BoxWeight** to re-create all of the features found in **Box**. It can simply extend **Box** to meet its own purposes.

A major advantage of inheritance is that once you have created a superclass that defines the attributes common to a set of objects, it can be used to create any number of more specific subclasses. Each subclass can precisely tailor its own classification. For example, the following class inherits **Box** and adds a color attribute:

```
// Here, Box is extended to include color.
class ColorBox extends Box {
  int color; // color of box

  ColorBox(double w, double h, double d, int c) {
    width = w;
    height = h;
    depth = d;
    color = c;
  }
}
```

Remember, once you have created a superclass that defines the general aspects of an object, that superclass can be inherited to form specialized classes. Each subclass simply adds its own unique attributes. This is the essence of inheritance.

A Superclass Variable Can Reference a Subclass Object

A reference variable of a superclass can be assigned a reference to any subclass derived from that superclass. You will find this aspect of inheritance quite useful in a variety of situations. For example, consider the following:

```
class RefDemo {
  public static void main(String args[]) {
    BoxWeight weightbox = new BoxWeight(3, 5, 7, 8.37);
    Box plainbox = new Box();
    double vol;

    vol = weightbox.volume();
    System.out.println("Volume of weightbox is " + vol);
    System.out.println("Weight of weightbox is " +
                        weightbox.weight);
    System.out.println();

    // assign BoxWeight reference to Box reference
    plainbox = weightbox;

    vol = plainbox.volume(); // OK, volume() defined in Box
    System.out.println("Volume of plainbox is " + vol);

    /* The following statement is invalid because plainbox
       does not define a weight member. */
//  System.out.println("Weight of plainbox is " + plainbox.weight);
  }
}
```

Here, **weightbox** is a reference to **BoxWeight** objects, and **plainbox** is a reference to **Box** objects. Since **BoxWeight** is a subclass of **Box**, it is permissible to assign **plainbox** a reference to the **weightbox** object.

It is important to understand that it is the type of the reference variable—not the type of the object that it refers to—that determines what members can be accessed. That is, when a reference to a subclass object is assigned to a superclass reference variable, you will have access only to those parts of the object defined by the superclass. This is why **plainbox** can't access **weight** even when it refers to a **BoxWeight** object. If you think about it, this makes sense, because the superclass has no knowledge of what a subclass adds to it. This is why the last line of code in the preceding fragment is commented out. It is not possible for a **Box** reference to access the **weight** field, because **Box** does not define one.

Although the preceding may seem a bit esoteric, it has some important practical applications—two of which are discussed later in this chapter.

Using super

In the preceding examples, classes derived from **Box** were not implemented as efficiently or as robustly as they could have been. For example, the constructor for **BoxWeight** explicitly initializes the **width**, **height**, and **depth** fields of **Box( )**. Not only does this duplicate code found in its superclass, which is inefficient, but it implies that a subclass must be granted access to these members. However, there will be times when you will want to create a superclass that keeps the details of its implementation to itself (that is, that keeps its data members private). In this case, there would be no way for a subclass to directly access or initialize these variables on its own. Since encapsulation is a primary attribute of OOP, it is not surprising that Java provides a solution to this problem. Whenever a subclass needs to refer to its immediate superclass, it can do so by use of the keyword **super**.

super has two general forms. The first calls the superclass' constructor. The second is used to access a member of the superclass that has been hidden by a member of a subclass. Each use is examined here.

Using super to Call Superclass Constructors

A subclass can call a constructor defined by its superclass by use of the following form of **super**:

super(*arg-list*);

Here, *arg-list* specifies any arguments needed by the constructor in the superclass. **super( )** must always be the first statement executed inside a subclass' constructor.

To see how **super( )** is used, consider this improved version of the **BoxWeight( )** class:

```
// BoxWeight now uses super to initialize its Box attributes.
class BoxWeight extends Box {
  double weight; // weight of box

  // initialize width, height, and depth using super()
  BoxWeight(double w, double h, double d, double m) {
    super(w, h, d); // call superclass constructor
    weight = m;
  }
}
```

Here, **BoxWeight( )** calls **super( )** with the arguments **w**, **h**, and **d**. This causes the **Box( )** constructor to be called, which initializes **width**, **height**, and **depth** using these values. **BoxWeight** no longer initializes these values itself. It only needs to initialize the value unique to it: **weight**. This leaves **Box** free to make these values **private** if desired.

In the preceding example, **super( )** was called with three arguments. Since constructors can be overloaded, **super( )** can be called using any form defined by the superclass. The constructor executed will be the one that matches the arguments. For example, here is a complete implementation of **BoxWeight** that provides constructors for the various ways that a box can be constructed. In each case, **super( )** is called using the appropriate arguments. Notice that **width, height,** and **depth** have been made private within **Box**.

```java
// A complete implementation of BoxWeight.
class Box {
  private double width;
  private double height;
  private double depth;

  // construct clone of an object
  Box(Box ob) { // pass object to constructor
    width = ob.width;
    height = ob.height;
    depth = ob.depth;
  }

  // constructor used when all dimensions specified
  Box(double w, double h, double d) {
    width = w;
    height = h;
    depth = d;
  }

  // constructor used when no dimensions specified
  Box() {
    width = -1;  // use -1 to indicate
    height = -1; // an uninitialized
    depth = -1;  // box
  }

  // constructor used when cube is created
  Box(double len) {
    width = height = depth = len;
  }

  // compute and return volume
  double volume() {
    return width * height * depth;
  }
}

// BoxWeight now fully implements all constructors.
class BoxWeight extends Box {
  double weight; // weight of box

  // construct clone of an object
  BoxWeight(BoxWeight ob) { // pass object to constructor
    super(ob);
    weight = ob.weight;
  }

  // constructor when all parameters are specified
  BoxWeight(double w, double h, double d, double m) {
```

```
    super(w, h, d); // call superclass constructor
    weight = m;
  }

  // default constructor
  BoxWeight() {
    super();
    weight = -1;
  }

  // constructor used when cube is created
  BoxWeight(double len, double m) {
    super(len);
    weight = m;
  }
}

class DemoSuper {
  public static void main(String args[]) {
    BoxWeight mybox1 = new BoxWeight(10, 20, 15, 34.3);
    BoxWeight mybox2 = new BoxWeight(2, 3, 4, 0.076);
    BoxWeight mybox3 = new BoxWeight(); // default
    BoxWeight mycube = new BoxWeight(3, 2);
    BoxWeight myclone = new BoxWeight(mybox1);
    double vol;

    vol = mybox1.volume();
    System.out.println("Volume of mybox1 is " + vol);
    System.out.println("Weight of mybox1 is " + mybox1.weight);
    System.out.println();

    vol = mybox2.volume();
    System.out.println("Volume of mybox2 is " + vol);
    System.out.println("Weight of mybox2 is " + mybox2.weight);
    System.out.println();

    vol = mybox3.volume();
    System.out.println("Volume of mybox3 is " + vol);
    System.out.println("Weight of mybox3 is " + mybox3.weight);
    System.out.println();

    vol = myclone.volume();
    System.out.println("Volume of myclone is " + vol);
    System.out.println("Weight of myclone is " + myclone.weight);
    System.out.println();

    vol = mycube.volume();
    System.out.println("Volume of mycube is " + vol);
    System.out.println("Weight of mycube is " + mycube.weight);
    System.out.println();
  }
}
```

This program generates the following output:

```
Volume of mybox1 is 3000.0
Weight of mybox1 is 34.3

Volume of mybox2 is 24.0
Weight of mybox2 is 0.076

Volume of mybox3 is -1.0
Weight of mybox3 is -1.0

Volume of myclone is 3000.0
Weight of myclone is 34.3

Volume of mycube is 27.0
Weight of mycube is 2.0
```

Pay special attention to this constructor in **BoxWeight( )**:

```
// construct clone of an object
BoxWeight(BoxWeight ob) { // pass object to constructor
  super(ob);
  weight = ob.weight;
}
```

Notice that **super( )** is passed an object of type **BoxWeight**—not of type **Box**. This still invokes the constructor **Box(Box ob)**. As mentioned earlier, a superclass variable can be used to reference any object derived from that class. Thus, we are able to pass a **BoxWeight** object to the **Box** constructor. Of course, **Box** only has knowledge of its own members.

Let's review the key concepts behind **super( )**. When a subclass calls **super( )**, it is calling the constructor of its immediate superclass. Thus, **super( )** always refers to the superclass immediately above the calling class. This is true even in a multileveled hierarchy. Also, **super( )** must always be the first statement executed inside a subclass constructor.

A Second Use for super

The second form of **super** acts somewhat like **this**, except that it always refers to the superclass of the subclass in which it is used. This usage has the following general form:

super.*member*

Here, *member* can be either a method or an instance variable.

This second form of **super** is most applicable to situations in which member names of a subclass hide members by the same name in the superclass. Consider this simple class hierarchy:

```
// Using super to overcome name hiding.
class A {
  int i;
}
```

```
// Create a subclass by extending class A.
class B extends A {
  int i; // this i hides the i in A

  B(int a, int b) {
    super.i = a; // i in A
    i = b; // i in B
  }

  void show() {
    System.out.println("i in superclass: " + super.i);
    System.out.println("i in subclass: " + i);
  }
}

class UseSuper {
  public static void main(String args[]) {
    B subOb = new B(1, 2);

    subOb.show();
  }
}
```

This program displays the following:

```
i in superclass: 1
i in subclass: 2
```

Although the instance variable **i** in **B** hides the **i** in **A**, **super** allows access to the **i** defined in the superclass. As you will see, **super** can also be used to call methods that are hidden by a subclass.

Creating a Multilevel Hierarchy

Up to this point, we have been using simple class hierarchies that consist of only a superclass and a subclass. However, you can build hierarchies that contain as many layers of inheritance as you like. As mentioned, it is perfectly acceptable to use a subclass as a superclass of another. For example, given three classes called **A**, **B**, and **C**, **C** can be a subclass of **B**, which is a subclass of **A**. When this type of situation occurs, each subclass inherits all of the traits found in all of its superclasses. In this case, **C** inherits all aspects of **B** and **A**. To see how a multilevel hierarchy can be useful, consider the following program. In it, the subclass **BoxWeight** is used as a superclass to create the subclass called **Shipment**. **Shipment** inherits all of the traits of **BoxWeight** and **Box**, and adds a field called **cost**, which holds the cost of shipping such a parcel.

```
// Extend BoxWeight to include shipping costs.

// Start with Box.
class Box {
  private double width;
  private double height;
  private double depth;
```

```java
  // construct clone of an object
  Box(Box ob) { // pass object to constructor
    width = ob.width;
    height = ob.height;
    depth = ob.depth;
  }

  // constructor used when all dimensions specified
  Box(double w, double h, double d) {
    width = w;
    height = h;
    depth = d;
  }

  // constructor used when no dimensions specified
  Box() {
    width = -1;  // use -1 to indicate
    height = -1; // an uninitialized
    depth = -1;  // box
  }

  // constructor used when cube is created
  Box(double len) {
    width = height = depth = len;
  }

  // compute and return volume
  double volume() {
    return width * height * depth;
  }
}

// Add weight.
class BoxWeight extends Box {
  double weight; // weight of box

  // construct clone of an object
  BoxWeight(BoxWeight ob) { // pass object to constructor
    super(ob);
    weight = ob.weight;
  }
  // constructor when all parameters are specified
  BoxWeight(double w, double h, double d, double m) {
    super(w, h, d); // call superclass constructor
    weight = m;
  }

  // default constructor
  BoxWeight() {
    super();
    weight = -1;
  }
```

```java
    // constructor used when cube is created
    BoxWeight(double len, double m) {
      super(len);
      weight = m;
    }
}

// Add shipping costs.
class Shipment extends BoxWeight {
  double cost;

  // construct clone of an object
  Shipment(Shipment ob) { // pass object to constructor
    super(ob);
    cost = ob.cost;
  }

  // constructor when all parameters are specified
  Shipment(double w, double h, double d,
           double m, double c) {
    super(w, h, d, m); // call superclass constructor
    cost = c;
  }

  // default constructor
  Shipment() {
    super();
    cost = -1;
  }

  // constructor used when cube is created
  Shipment(double len, double m, double c) {
    super(len, m);
    cost = c;
  }
}

class DemoShipment {
  public static void main(String args[]) {
    Shipment shipment1 =
              new Shipment(10, 20, 15, 10, 3.41);
    Shipment shipment2 =
              new Shipment(2, 3, 4, 0.76, 1.28);

    double vol;

    vol = shipment1.volume();
    System.out.println("Volume of shipment1 is " + vol);
    System.out.println("Weight of shipment1 is "
                        + shipment1.weight);
    System.out.println("Shipping cost: $" + shipment1.cost);
    System.out.println();
```

```
    vol = shipment2.volume();
    System.out.println("Volume of shipment2 is " + vol);
    System.out.println("Weight of shipment2 is "
                          + shipment2.weight);
    System.out.println("Shipping cost: $" + shipment2.cost);
  }
}
```

The output of this program is shown here:

```
Volume of shipment1 is 3000.0
Weight of shipment1 is 10.0
Shipping cost: $3.41

Volume of shipment2 is 24.0
Weight of shipment2 is 0.76
Shipping cost: $1.28
```

Because of inheritance, **Shipment** can make use of the previously defined classes of **Box** and **BoxWeight**, adding only the extra information it needs for its own, specific application. This is part of the value of inheritance; it allows the reuse of code.

This example illustrates one other important point: **super( )** always refers to the constructor in the closest superclass. The **super( )** in **Shipment** calls the constructor in **BoxWeight**. The **super( )** in **BoxWeight** calls the constructor in **Box**. In a class hierarchy, if a superclass constructor requires parameters, then all subclasses must pass those parameters "up the line." This is true whether or not a subclass needs parameters of its own.

NOTE *In the preceding program, the entire class hierarchy, including* **Box**, **BoxWeight***, and* **Shipment***, is shown all in one file. This is for your convenience only. In Java, all three classes could have been placed into their own files and compiled separately. In fact, using separate files is the norm, not the exception, in creating class hierarchies.*

When Constructors Are Called

When a class hierarchy is created, in what order are the constructors for the classes that make up the hierarchy called? For example, given a subclass called **B** and a superclass called **A**, is **A**'s constructor called before **B**'s, or vice versa? The answer is that in a class hierarchy, constructors are called in order of derivation, from superclass to subclass. Further, since **super( )** must be the first statement executed in a subclass' constructor, this order is the same whether or not **super( )** is used. If **super( )** is not used, then the default or parameterless constructor of each superclass will be executed. The following program illustrates when constructors are executed:

```
// Demonstrate when constructors are called.

// Create a super class.
class A {
  A() {
    System.out.println("Inside A's constructor.");
  }
}
```

```
// Create a subclass by extending class A.
class B extends A {
  B() {
    System.out.println("Inside B's constructor.");
  }
}

// Create another subclass by extending B.
class C extends B {
  C() {
    System.out.println("Inside C's constructor.");
  }
}

class CallingCons {
  public static void main(String args[]) {
    C c = new C();
  }
}
```

The output from this program is shown here:

```
Inside A's constructor
Inside B's constructor
Inside C's constructor
```

As you can see, the constructors are called in order of derivation.

If you think about it, it makes sense that constructors are executed in order of derivation. Because a superclass has no knowledge of any subclass, any initialization it needs to perform is separate from and possibly prerequisite to any initialization performed by the subclass. Therefore, it must be executed first.

Method Overriding

In a class hierarchy, when a method in a subclass has the same name and type signature as a method in its superclass, then the method in the subclass is said to *override* the method in the superclass. When an overridden method is called from within a subclass, it will always refer to the version of that method defined by the subclass. The version of the method defined by the superclass will be hidden. Consider the following:

```
// Method overriding.
class A {
  int i, j;
  A(int a, int b) {
    i = a;
    j = b;
  }

  // display i and j
  void show() {
    System.out.println("i and j: " + i + " " + j);
  }
}
```

```
class B extends A {
  int k;

  B(int a, int b, int c) {
    super(a, b);
    k = c;
  }

  // display k - this overrides show() in A
  void show() {
    System.out.println("k: " + k);
  }
}

class Override {
  public static void main(String args[]) {
    B subOb = new B(1, 2, 3);

    subOb.show(); // this calls show() in B
  }
}
```

The output produced by this program is shown here:

```
k: 3
```

When **show( )** is invoked on an object of type **B**, the version of **show( )** defined within **B** is used. That is, the version of **show( )** inside **B** overrides the version declared in **A**.

If you wish to access the superclass version of an overridden method, you can do so by using **super**. For example, in this version of **B**, the superclass version of **show( )** is invoked within the subclass' version. This allows all instance variables to be displayed.

```
class B extends A {
  int k;

  B(int a, int b, int c) {
    super(a, b);
    k = c;
  }
  void show() {
    super.show(); // this calls A's show()
    System.out.println("k: " + k);
  }
}
```

If you substitute this version of **A** into the previous program, you will see the following output:

```
i and j: 1 2
k: 3
```

Here, **super.show( )** calls the superclass version of **show( )**.

Method overriding occurs *only* when the names and the type signatures of the two methods are identical. If they are not, then the two methods are simply overloaded. For example, consider this modified version of the preceding example:

```
// Methods with differing type signatures are overloaded - not
// overridden.
class A {
  int i, j;

  A(int a, int b) {
    i = a;
    j = b;
  }

  // display i and j
  void show() {
    System.out.println("i and j: " + i + " " + j);
  }
}

// Create a subclass by extending class A.
class B extends A {
  int k;

  B(int a, int b, int c) {
    super(a, b);
    k = c;
  }

  // overload show()
  void show(String msg) {
    System.out.println(msg + k);
  }
}

class Override {
  public static void main(String args[]) {
    B subOb = new B(1, 2, 3);

    subOb.show("This is k: "); // this calls show() in B
    subOb.show(); // this calls show() in A
  }
}
```

The output produced by this program is shown here:

```
This is k: 3
i and j: 1 2
```

The version of **show( )** in **B** takes a string parameter. This makes its type signature different from the one in **A**, which takes no parameters. Therefore, no overriding (or name hiding) takes place. Instead, the version of **show( )** in **B** simply overloads the version of **show( )** in **A**.

Dynamic Method Dispatch

While the examples in the preceding section demonstrate the mechanics of method overriding, they do not show its power. Indeed, if there were nothing more to method overriding than a name space convention, then it would be, at best, an interesting curiosity, but of little real value. However, this is not the case. Method overriding forms the basis for one of Java's most powerful concepts: *dynamic method dispatch.* Dynamic method dispatch is the mechanism by which a call to an overridden method is resolved at run time, rather than compile time. Dynamic method dispatch is important because this is how Java implements run-time polymorphism.

Let's begin by restating an important principle: a superclass reference variable can refer to a subclass object. Java uses this fact to resolve calls to overridden methods at run time. Here is how. When an overridden method is called through a superclass reference, Java determines which version of that method to execute based upon the type of the object being referred to at the time the call occurs. Thus, this determination is made at run time. When different types of objects are referred to, different versions of an overridden method will be called. In other words, *it is the type of the object being referred to* (not the type of the reference variable) that determines which version of an overridden method will be executed. Therefore, if a superclass contains a method that is overridden by a subclass, then when different types of objects are referred to through a superclass reference variable, different versions of the method are executed.

Here is an example that illustrates dynamic method dispatch:

```
// Dynamic Method Dispatch
class A {
  void callme() {
    System.out.println("Inside A's callme method");
  }
}

class B extends A {
  // override callme()
  void callme() {
    System.out.println("Inside B's callme method");
  }
}

class C extends A {
  // override callme()
  void callme() {
    System.out.println("Inside C's callme method");
  }
}

class Dispatch {
  public static void main(String args[]) {
    A a = new A(); // object of type A
    B b = new B(); // object of type B
    C c = new C(); // object of type C
    A r; // obtain a reference of type A
```

```
    r = a; // r refers to an A object
    r.callme(); // calls A's version of callme

    r = b; // r refers to a B object
    r.callme(); // calls B's version of callme

    r = c; // r refers to a C object
    r.callme(); // calls C's version of callme
  }
}
```

The output from the program is shown here:

```
Inside A's callme method
Inside B's callme method
Inside C's callme method
```

This program creates one superclass called **A** and two subclasses of it, called **B** and **C**. Subclasses **B** and **C** override **callme( )** declared in **A**. Inside the **main( )** method, objects of type **A**, **B**, and **C** are declared. Also, a reference of type **A**, called **r**, is declared. The program then in turn assigns a reference to each type of object to **r** and uses that reference to invoke **callme( )**. As the output shows, the version of **callme( )** executed is determined by the type of object being referred to at the time of the call. Had it been determined by the type of the reference variable, **r**, you would see three calls to **A**'s **callme( )** method.

NOTE   *Readers familiar with C++ or C# will recognize that overridden methods in Java are similar to virtual functions in those languages.*

Why Overridden Methods?

As stated earlier, overridden methods allow Java to support run-time polymorphism. Polymorphism is essential to object-oriented programming for one reason: it allows a general class to specify methods that will be common to all of its derivatives, while allowing subclasses to define the specific implementation of some or all of those methods. Overridden methods are another way that Java implements the "one interface, multiple methods" aspect of polymorphism.

Part of the key to successfully applying polymorphism is understanding that the superclasses and subclasses form a hierarchy which moves from lesser to greater specialization. Used correctly, the superclass provides all elements that a subclass can use directly. It also defines those methods that the derived class must implement on its own. This allows the subclass the flexibility to define its own methods, yet still enforces a consistent interface. Thus, by combining inheritance with overridden methods, a superclass can define the general form of the methods that will be used by all of its subclasses.

Dynamic, run-time polymorphism is one of the most powerful mechanisms that object-oriented design brings to bear on code reuse and robustness. The ability of existing code libraries to call methods on instances of new classes without recompiling while maintaining a clean abstract interface is a profoundly powerful tool.

Applying Method Overriding

Let's look at a more practical example that uses method overriding. The following program creates a superclass called **Figure** that stores the dimensions of a two-dimensional object. It also defines a method called **area( )** that computes the area of an object. The program derives two subclasses from **Figure**. The first is **Rectangle** and the second is **Triangle**. Each of these subclasses overrides **area( )** so that it returns the area of a rectangle and a triangle, respectively.

```java
// Using run-time polymorphism.
class Figure {
  double dim1;
  double dim2;

  Figure(double a, double b) {
    dim1 = a;
    dim2 = b;
  }

  double area() {
    System.out.println("Area for Figure is undefined.");
    return 0;
  }
}

class Rectangle extends Figure {
  Rectangle(double a, double b) {
    super(a, b);
  }

  // override area for rectangle
  double area() {
    System.out.println("Inside Area for Rectangle.");
    return dim1 * dim2;
  }
}

class Triangle extends Figure {
  Triangle(double a, double b) {
    super(a, b);
  }

  // override area for right triangle
  double area() {
    System.out.println("Inside Area for Triangle.");
    return dim1 * dim2 / 2;
  }
}

class FindAreas {
  public static void main(String args[]) {
    Figure f = new Figure(10, 10);
    Rectangle r = new Rectangle(9, 5);
    Triangle t = new Triangle(10, 8);
```

```
        Figure figref;

        figref = r;
        System.out.println("Area is " + figref.area());

        figref = t;
        System.out.println("Area is " + figref.area());

        figref = f;
        System.out.println("Area is " + figref.area());
    }
}
```

The output from the program is shown here:

```
Inside Area for Rectangle.
Area is 45
Inside Area for Triangle.
Area is 40
Area for Figure is undefined.
Area is 0
```

Through the dual mechanisms of inheritance and run-time polymorphism, it is possible to define one consistent interface that is used by several different, yet related, types of objects. In this case, if an object is derived from **Figure**, then its area can be obtained by calling **area( )**. The interface to this operation is the same no matter what type of figure is being used.

Using Abstract Classes

There are situations in which you will want to define a superclass that declares the structure of a given abstraction without providing a complete implementation of every method. That is, sometimes you will want to create a superclass that only defines a generalized form that will be shared by all of its subclasses, leaving it to each subclass to fill in the details. Such a class determines the nature of the methods that the subclasses must implement. One way this situation can occur is when a superclass is unable to create a meaningful implementation for a method. This is the case with the class **Figure** used in the preceding example. The definition of **area( )** is simply a placeholder. It will not compute and display the area of any type of object.

As you will see as you create your own class libraries, it is not uncommon for a method to have no meaningful definition in the context of its superclass. You can handle this situation two ways. One way, as shown in the previous example, is to simply have it report a warning message. While this approach can be useful in certain situations—such as debugging—it is not usually appropriate. You may have methods that must be overridden by the subclass in order for the subclass to have any meaning. Consider the class **Triangle**. It has no meaning if **area( )** is not defined. In this case, you want some way to ensure that a subclass does, indeed, override all necessary methods. Java's solution to this problem is the *abstract method*.

You can require that certain methods be overridden by subclasses by specifying the **abstract** type modifier. These methods are sometimes referred to as *subclasser responsibility* because they have no implementation specified in the superclass. Thus, a subclass must override them—it cannot simply use the version defined in the superclass. To declare an abstract method, use this general form:

abstract *type name(parameter-list);*

As you can see, no method body is present.

Any class that contains one or more abstract methods must also be declared abstract. To declare a class abstract, you simply use the **abstract** keyword in front of the **class** keyword at the beginning of the class declaration. There can be no objects of an abstract class. That is, an abstract class cannot be directly instantiated with the **new** operator. Such objects would be useless, because an abstract class is not fully defined. Also, you cannot declare abstract constructors, or abstract static methods. Any subclass of an abstract class must either implement all of the abstract methods in the superclass, or be itself declared **abstract**.

Here is a simple example of a class with an abstract method, followed by a class which implements that method:

```
// A Simple demonstration of abstract.
abstract class A {
  abstract void callme();

  // concrete methods are still allowed in abstract classes
  void callmetoo() {
    System.out.println("This is a concrete method.");
  }
}

class B extends A {
  void callme() {
    System.out.println("B's implementation of callme.");
  }
}

class AbstractDemo {
  public static void main(String args[]) {
    B b = new B();

    b.callme();
    b.callmetoo();
  }
}
```

Notice that no objects of class **A** are declared in the program. As mentioned, it is not possible to instantiate an abstract class. One other point: class **A** implements a concrete method called **callmetoo( )**. This is perfectly acceptable. Abstract classes can include as much implementation as they see fit.

Although abstract classes cannot be used to instantiate objects, they can be used to create object references, because Java's approach to run-time polymorphism is implemented through the use of superclass references. Thus, it must be possible to create a reference to an abstract class so that it can be used to point to a subclass object. You will see this feature put to use in the next example.

Using an abstract class, you can improve the **Figure** class shown earlier. Since there is no meaningful concept of area for an undefined two-dimensional figure, the following version of the program declares **area( )** as abstract inside **Figure**. This, of course, means that all classes derived from **Figure** must override **area( )**.

```
// Using abstract methods and classes.
abstract class Figure {
  double dim1;
  double dim2;

  Figure(double a, double b) {
    dim1 = a;
    dim2 = b;
  }

  // area is now an abstract method
  abstract double area();
}

class Rectangle extends Figure {
  Rectangle(double a, double b) {
    super(a, b);
  }

  // override area for rectangle
  double area() {
    System.out.println("Inside Area for Rectangle.");
    return dim1 * dim2;
  }
}

class Triangle extends Figure {
  Triangle(double a, double b) {
    super(a, b);
  }

  // override area for right triangle
  double area() {
    System.out.println("Inside Area for Triangle.");
    return dim1 * dim2 / 2;
  }
}

class AbstractAreas {
  public static void main(String args[]) {
// Figure f = new Figure(10, 10); // illegal now
    Rectangle r = new Rectangle(9, 5);
    Triangle t = new Triangle(10, 8);
    Figure figref; // this is OK, no object is created

    figref = r;
    System.out.println("Area is " + figref.area());
```

```
    figref = t;
    System.out.println("Area is " + figref.area());
  }
}
```

As the comment inside **main( )** indicates, it is no longer possible to declare objects of type **Figure**, since it is now abstract. And, all subclasses of **Figure** must override **area( )**. To prove this to yourself, try creating a subclass that does not override **area( )**. You will receive a compile-time error.

Although it is not possible to create an object of type **Figure**, you can create a reference variable of type **Figure**. The variable **figref** is declared as a reference to **Figure**, which means that it can be used to refer to an object of any class derived from **Figure**. As explained, it is through superclass reference variables that overridden methods are resolved at run time.

Using final with Inheritance

The keyword **final** has three uses. First, it can be used to create the equivalent of a named constant. This use was described in the preceding chapter. The other two uses of **final** apply to inheritance. Both are examined here.

Using final to Prevent Overriding

While method overriding is one of Java's most powerful features, there will be times when you will want to prevent it from occurring. To disallow a method from being overridden, specify **final** as a modifier at the start of its declaration. Methods declared as **final** cannot be overridden. The following fragment illustrates **final**:

```
class A {
  final void meth() {
    System.out.println("This is a final method.");
  }
}

class B extends A {
  void meth() { // ERROR! Can't override.
    System.out.println("Illegal!");
  }
}
```

Because **meth( )** is declared as **final**, it cannot be overridden in **B**. If you attempt to do so, a compile-time error will result.

Methods declared as **final** can sometimes provide a performance enhancement: The compiler is free to *inline* calls to them because it "knows" they will not be overridden by a subclass. When a small **final** method is called, often the Java compiler can copy the bytecode for the subroutine directly inline with the compiled code of the calling method, thus eliminating the costly overhead associated with a method call. Inlining is only an option with **final** methods. Normally, Java resolves calls to methods dynamically, at run time. This is called *late binding*. However, since **final** methods cannot be overridden, a call to one can be resolved at compile time. This is called *early binding*.

Using final to Prevent Inheritance

Sometimes you will want to prevent a class from being inherited. To do this, precede the class declaration with **final**. Declaring a class as **final** implicitly declares all of its methods as **final**, too. As you might expect, it is illegal to declare a class as both **abstract** and **final** since an abstract class is incomplete by itself and relies upon its subclasses to provide complete implementations.

Here is an example of a **final** class:

```
final class A {
  // ...
}

// The following class is illegal.
class B extends A { // ERROR! Can't subclass A
  // ...
}
```

As the comments imply, it is illegal for **B** to inherit **A** since **A** is declared as **final**.

The Object Class

There is one special class, **Object**, defined by Java. All other classes are subclasses of **Object**. That is, **Object** is a superclass of all other classes. This means that a reference variable of type **Object** can refer to an object of any other class. Also, since arrays are implemented as classes, a variable of type **Object** can also refer to any array.

Object defines the following methods, which means that they are available in every object.

Method	Purpose
Object clone( )	Creates a new object that is the same as the object being cloned.
boolean equals(Object *object*)	Determines whether one object is equal to another.
void finalize( )	Called before an unused object is recycled.
Class getClass( )	Obtains the class of an object at run time.
int hashCode( )	Returns the hash code associated with the invoking object.
void notify( )	Resumes execution of a thread waiting on the invoking object.
void notifyAll( )	Resumes execution of all threads waiting on the invoking object.
String toString( )	Returns a string that describes the object.
void wait( ) void wait(long *milliseconds*) void wait(long *milliseconds*, int *nanoseconds*)	Waits on another thread of execution.

The methods **getClass( )**, **notify( )**, **notifyAll( )**, and **wait( )** are declared as **final**. You may override the others. These methods are described elsewhere in this book. However, notice two methods now: **equals( )** and **toString( )**. The **equals( )** method compares the contents of two objects. It returns **true** if the objects are equivalent, and **false** otherwise.

The precise definition of equality can vary, depending on the type of objects being compared. The **toString( )** method returns a string that contains a description of the object on which it is called. Also, this method is automatically called when an object is output using **println( )**. Many classes override this method. Doing so allows them to tailor a description specifically for the types of objects that they create.

CHAPTER

Packages and Interfaces

This chapter examines two of Java's most innovative features: packages and interfaces. *Packages* are containers for classes that are used to keep the class name space compartmentalized. For example, a package allows you to create a class named **List**, which you can store in your own package without concern that it will collide with some other class named **List** stored elsewhere. Packages are stored in a hierarchical manner and are explicitly imported into new class definitions.

In previous chapters, you have seen how methods define the interface to the data in a class. Through the use of the **interface** keyword, Java allows you to fully abstract the interface from its implementation. Using **interface**, you can specify a set of methods that can be implemented by one or more classes. The **interface**, itself, does not actually define any implementation. Although they are similar to abstract classes, **interface**s have an additional capability: A class can implement more than one interface. By contrast, a class can only inherit a single superclass (abstract or otherwise).

Packages

In the preceding chapters, the name of each example class was taken from the same name space. This means that a unique name had to be used for each class to avoid name collisions. After a while, without some way to manage the name space, you could run out of convenient, descriptive names for individual classes. You also need some way to be assured that the name you choose for a class will be reasonably unique and not collide with class names chosen by other programmers. (Imagine a small group of programmers fighting over who gets to use the name "Foobar" as a class name. Or, imagine the entire Internet community arguing over who first named a class "Espresso.") Thankfully, Java provides a mechanism for partitioning the class name space into more manageable chunks. This mechanism is the package. The package is both a naming and a visibility control mechanism. You can define classes inside a package that are not accessible by code outside that package. You can also define class members that are only exposed to other members of the same package. This allows your classes to have intimate knowledge of each other, but not expose that knowledge to the rest of the world.

Defining a Package

To create a package is quite easy: simply include a **package** command as the first statement in a Java source file. Any classes declared within that file will belong to the specified package. The **package** statement defines a name space in which classes are stored. If you omit the **package** statement, the class names are put into the default package, which has no name. (This is why you haven't had to worry about packages before now.) While the default package is fine for short, sample programs, it is inadequate for real applications. Most of the time, you will define a package for your code.

This is the general form of the **package** statement:

package *pkg*;

Here, *pkg* is the name of the package. For example, the following statement creates a package called **MyPackage**.

```
package MyPackage;
```

Java uses file system directories to store packages. For example, the **.class** files for any classes you declare to be part of **MyPackage** must be stored in a directory called **MyPackage**. Remember that case is significant, and the directory name must match the package name exactly.

More than one file can include the same **package** statement. The **package** statement simply specifies to which package the classes defined in a file belong. It does not exclude other classes in other files from being part of that same package. Most real-world packages are spread across many files.

You can create a hierarchy of packages. To do so, simply separate each package name from the one above it by use of a period. The general form of a multileveled package statement is shown here:

package *pkg1*[.*pkg2*[.*pkg3*]];

A package hierarchy must be reflected in the file system of your Java development system. For example, a package declared as

```
package java.awt.image;
```

needs to be stored in **java\awt\image** in a Windows environment. Be sure to choose your package names carefully. You cannot rename a package without renaming the directory in which the classes are stored.

Finding Packages and CLASSPATH

As just explained, packages are mirrored by directories. This raises an important question: How does the Java run-time system know where to look for packages that you create? The answer has three parts. First, by default, the Java run-time system uses the current working directory as its starting point. Thus, if your package is in a subdirectory of the current directory, it will be found. Second, you can specify a directory path or paths by setting the

CLASSPATH environmental variable. Third, you can use the **-classpath** option with **java** and **javac** to specify the path to your classes.

For example, consider the following package specification:

```
package MyPack
```

In order for a program to find **MyPack,** one of three things must be true. Either the program can be executed from a directory immediately above **MyPack,** or the **CLASSPATH** must be set to include the path to **MyPack,** or the **-classpath** option must specify the path to **MyPack** when the program is run via **java.**

When the second two options are used, the class path *must not* include **MyPack,** itself. It must simply specify the *path to* **MyPack.** For example, in a Windows environment, if the path to **MyPack** is

```
C:\MyPrograms\Java\MyPack
```

Then the class path to **MyPack** is

```
C:\MyPrograms\Java
```

The easiest way to try the examples shown in this book is to simply create the package directories below your current development directory, put the **.class** files into the appropriate directories, and then execute the programs from the development directory. This is the approach used in the following example.

A Short Package Example

Keeping the preceding discussion in mind, you can try this simple package:

```java
// A simple package
package MyPack;

class Balance {
  String name;
  double bal;

  Balance(String n, double b) {
    name = n;
    bal = b;
  }

  void show() {
    if(bal<0)
      System.out.print("--> ");
    System.out.println(name + ": $" + bal);
  }
}

class AccountBalance {
  public static void main(String args[]) {
    Balance current[] = new Balance[3];
```

```
     current[0] = new Balance("K. J. Fielding", 123.23);
     current[1] = new Balance("Will Tell", 157.02);
     current[2] = new Balance("Tom Jackson", -12.33);

     for(int i=0; i<3; i++) current[i].show();
   }
}
```

Call this file **AccountBalance.java** and put it in a directory called **MyPack**.

Next, compile the file. Make sure that the resulting **.class** file is also in the **MyPack** directory. Then, try executing the **AccountBalance** class, using the following command line:

```
java MyPack.AccountBalance
```

Remember, you will need to be in the directory above **MyPack** when you execute this command. (Alternatively, you can use one of the other two options described in the preceding section to specify the path **MyPack**.)

As explained, **AccountBalance** is now part of the package **MyPack**. This means that it cannot be executed by itself. That is, you cannot use this command line:

```
java AccountBalance
```

AccountBalance must be qualified with its package name.

Access Protection

In the preceding chapters, you learned about various aspects of Java's access control mechanism and its access specifiers. For example, you already know that access to a **private** member of a class is granted only to other members of that class. Packages add another dimension to access control. As you will see, Java provides many levels of protection to allow fine-grained control over the visibility of variables and methods within classes, subclasses, and packages.

Classes and packages are both means of encapsulating and containing the name space and scope of variables and methods. Packages act as containers for classes and other subordinate packages. Classes act as containers for data and code. The class is Java's smallest unit of abstraction. Because of the interplay between classes and packages, Java addresses four categories of visibility for class members:

- Subclasses in the same package
- Non-subclasses in the same package
- Subclasses in different packages
- Classes that are neither in the same package nor subclasses

The three access specifiers, **private**, **public**, and **protected**, provide a variety of ways to produce the many levels of access required by these categories. Table 9-1 sums up the interactions.

While Java's access control mechanism may seem complicated, we can simplify it as follows. Anything declared **public** can be accessed from anywhere. Anything declared **private** cannot be seen outside of its class. When a member does not have an explicit access

TABLE 9-1
Class Member
Access

	Private	No Modifier	Protected	Public
Same class	Yes	Yes	Yes	Yes
Same package subclass	No	Yes	Yes	Yes
Same package non-subclass	No	Yes	Yes	Yes
Different package subclass	No	No	Yes	Yes
Different package non-subclass	No	No	No	Yes

specification, it is visible to subclasses as well as to other classes in the same package. This is the default access. If you want to allow an element to be seen outside your current package, but only to classes that subclass your class directly, then declare that element **protected**.

Table 9-1 applies only to members of classes. A non-nested class has only two possible access levels: default and public. When a class is declared as **public**, it is accessible by any other code. If a class has default access, then it can only be accessed by other code within its same package. When a class is public, it must be the only public class declared in the file, and the file must have the same name as the class.

An Access Example

The following example shows all combinations of the access control modifiers. This example has two packages and five classes. Remember that the classes for the two different packages need to be stored in directories named after their respective packages—in this case, **p1** and **p2**.

The source for the first package defines three classes: **Protection**, **Derived**, and **SamePackage**. The first class defines four **int** variables in each of the legal protection modes. The variable **n** is declared with the default protection, **n_pri** is **private**, **n_pro** is **protected**, and **n_pub** is **public**.

Each subsequent class in this example will try to access the variables in an instance of this class. The lines that will not compile due to access restrictions are commented out. Before each of these lines is a comment listing the places from which this level of protection would allow access.

The second class, **Derived**, is a subclass of **Protection** in the same package, **p1**. This grants **Derived** access to every variable in **Protection** except for **n_pri**, the **private** one. The third class, **SamePackage**, is not a subclass of **Protection**, but is in the same package and also has access to all but **n_pri**.

This is file **Protection.java**:

```
package p1;

public class Protection {
  int n = 1;
  private int n_pri = 2;
  protected int n_pro = 3;
  public int n_pub = 4;

  public Protection() {
    System.out.println("base constructor");
    System.out.println("n = " + n);
    System.out.println("n_pri = " + n_pri);
    System.out.println("n_pro = " + n_pro);
    System.out.println("n_pub = " + n_pub);
  }
}
```

This is file **Derived.java**:

```
package p1;

class Derived extends Protection {
  Derived() {
    System.out.println("derived constructor");
    System.out.println("n = " + n);

// class only
//  System.out.println("n_pri = "4 + n_pri);

    System.out.println("n_pro = " + n_pro);
    System.out.println("n_pub = " + n_pub);
  }
}
```

This is file **SamePackage.java**:

```
package p1;

class SamePackage {
  SamePackage() {

    Protection p = new Protection();
    System.out.println("same package constructor");
    System.out.println("n = " + p.n);

// class only
//  System.out.println("n_pri = " + p.n_pri);
    System.out.println("n_pro = " + p.n_pro);
    System.out.println("n_pub = " + p.n_pub);
  }
}
```

Following is the source code for the other package, **p2**. The two classes defined in **p2** cover the other two conditions that are affected by access control. The first class, **Protection2**, is a subclass of **p1.Protection**. This grants access to all of **p1.Protection**'s variables except for **n_pri** (because it is **private**) and **n**, the variable declared with the default protection. Remember, the default only allows access from within the class or the package, not extra-package subclasses. Finally, the class **OtherPackage** has access to only one variable, **n_pub**, which was declared **public**.

This is file **Protection2.java**:

```java
package p2;

class Protection2 extends p1.Protection {
  Protection2() {
    System.out.println("derived other package constructor");

//  class or package only
//  System.out.println("n = " + n);

//  class only
//  System.out.println("n_pri = " + n_pri);

    System.out.println("n_pro = " + n_pro);
    System.out.println("n_pub = " + n_pub);
  }
}
```

This is file **OtherPackage.java**:

```java
package p2;

class OtherPackage {
  OtherPackage() {
    p1.Protection p = new p1.Protection();
    System.out.println("other package constructor");

//  class or package only
//  System.out.println("n = " + p.n);

//  class only
//  System.out.println("n_pri = " + p.n_pri);

//  class, subclass or package only
//  System.out.println("n_pro = " + p.n_pro);

    System.out.println("n_pub = " + p.n_pub);
  }
}
```

If you wish to try these two packages, here are two test files you can use. The one for package **p1** is shown here:

```
// Demo package p1.
package p1;

// Instantiate the various classes in p1.
public class Demo {
  public static void main(String args[]) {
    Protection ob1 = new Protection();
    Derived ob2 = new Derived();
    SamePackage ob3 = new SamePackage();
  }
}
```

The test file for **p2** is shown next:

```
// Demo package p2.
package p2;

// Instantiate the various classes in p2.
public class Demo {
  public static void main(String args[]) {
    Protection2 ob1 = new Protection2();
    OtherPackage ob2 = new OtherPackage();
  }
}
```

Importing Packages

Given that packages exist and are a good mechanism for compartmentalizing diverse classes from each other, it is easy to see why all of the built-in Java classes are stored in packages. There are no core Java classes in the unnamed default package; all of the standard classes are stored in some named package. Since classes within packages must be fully qualified with their package name or names, it could become tedious to type in the long dot-separated package path name for every class you want to use. For this reason, Java includes the **import** statement to bring certain classes, or entire packages, into visibility. Once imported, a class can be referred to directly, using only its name. The **import** statement is a convenience to the programmer and is not technically needed to write a complete Java program. If you are going to refer to a few dozen classes in your application, however, the **import** statement will save a lot of typing.

In a Java source file, **import** statements occur immediately following the **package** statement (if it exists) and before any class definitions. This is the general form of the **import** statement:

import *pkg1*[.*pkg2*].(*classname* | *);

Here, *pkg1* is the name of a top-level package, and *pkg2* is the name of a subordinate package inside the outer package separated by a dot (.). There is no practical limit on the depth of a package hierarchy, except that imposed by the file system. Finally, you specify either an explicit *classname* or a star (*), which indicates that the Java compiler should import the entire package. This code fragment shows both forms in use:

```
import java.util.Date;
import java.io.*;
```

CAUTION *The star form may increase compilation time—especially if you import several large packages. For this reason it is a good idea to explicitly name the classes that you want to use rather than importing whole packages. However, the star form has absolutely no effect on the run-time performance or size of your classes.*

All of the standard Java classes included with Java are stored in a package called **java**. The basic language functions are stored in a package inside of the **java** package called **java.lang**. Normally, you have to import every package or class that you want to use, but since Java is useless without much of the functionality in **java.lang**, it is implicitly imported by the compiler for all programs. This is equivalent to the following line being at the top of all of your programs:

```
import java.lang.*;
```

If a class with the same name exists in two different packages that you import using the star form, the compiler will remain silent, unless you try to use one of the classes. In that case, you will get a compile-time error and have to explicitly name the class specifying its package.

It must be emphasized that the **import** statement is optional. Any place you use a class name, you can use its *fully qualified name*, which includes its full package hierarchy. For example, this fragment uses an import statement:

```
import java.util.*;
class MyDate extends Date {
}
```

The same example without the **import** statement looks like this:

```
class MyDate extends java.util.Date {
}
```

In this version, **Date** is fully-qualified.

As shown in Table 9-1, when a package is imported, only those items within the package declared as **public** will be available to non-subclasses in the importing code. For example, if you want the **Balance** class of the package **MyPack** shown earlier to be available as a stand-alone class for general use outside of **MyPack**, then you will need to declare it as **public** and put it into its own file, as shown here:

```
package MyPack;

/* Now, the Balance class, its constructor, and its
   show() method are public.  This means that they can
   be used by non-subclass code outside their package.
*/
public class Balance {
```

```
    String name;
    double bal;

    public Balance(String n, double b) {
      name = n;
      bal = b;
    }

    public void show() {
      if(bal<0)
        System.out.print("--> ");
      System.out.println(name + ": $" + bal);
    }
}
```

As you can see, the **Balance** class is now **public**. Also, its constructor and its **show( )** method are **public**, too. This means that they can be accessed by any type of code outside the **MyPack** package. For example, here **TestBalance** imports **MyPack** and is then able to make use of the **Balance** class:

```
import MyPack.*;

class TestBalance {
  public static void main(String args[]) {

    /* Because Balance is public, you may use Balance
       class and call its constructor. */
    Balance test = new Balance("J. J. Jaspers", 99.88);

    test.show(); // you may also call show()
  }
}
```

As an experiment, remove the **public** specifier from the **Balance** class and then try compiling **TestBalance**. As explained, errors will result.

Interfaces

Using the keyword **interface**, you can fully abstract a class' interface from its implementation. That is, using **interface**, you can specify what a class must do, but not how it does it. Interfaces are syntactically similar to classes, but they lack instance variables, and their methods are declared without any body. In practice, this means that you can define interfaces that don't make assumptions about how they are implemented. Once it is defined, any number of classes can implement an **interface**. Also, one class can implement any number of interfaces.

To implement an interface, a class must create the complete set of methods defined by the interface. However, each class is free to determine the details of its own implementation. By providing the **interface** keyword, Java allows you to fully utilize the "one interface, multiple methods" aspect of polymorphism.

Interfaces are designed to support dynamic method resolution at run time. Normally, in order for a method to be called from one class to another, both classes need to be present at compile time so the Java compiler can check to ensure that the method signatures are compatible. This requirement by itself makes for a static and nonextensible classing environment. Inevitably in a system like this, functionality gets pushed up higher and higher in the class hierarchy so that the mechanisms will be available to more and more subclasses. Interfaces are designed to avoid this problem. They disconnect the definition of a method or set of methods from the inheritance hierarchy. Since interfaces are in a different hierarchy from classes, it is possible for classes that are unrelated in terms of the class hierarchy to implement the same interface. This is where the real power of interfaces is realized.

NOTE   *Interfaces add most of the functionality that is required for many applications that would normally resort to using multiple inheritance in a language such as C++.*

Defining an Interface

An interface is defined much like a class. This is the general form of an interface:

```
access interface name {
    return-type method-name1(parameter-list);
    return-type method-name2(parameter-list);
    type final-varname1 = value;
    type final-varname2 = value;
    // ...
    return-type method-nameN(parameter-list);
    type final-varnameN = value;
}
```

When no access specifier is included, then default access results, and the interface is only available to other members of the package in which it is declared. When it is declared as **public**, the interface can be used by any other code. In this case, the interface must be the only public interface declared in the file, and the file must have the same name as the interface. *name* is the name of the interface, and can be any valid identifier. Notice that the methods that are declared have no bodies. They end with a semicolon after the parameter list. They are, essentially, abstract methods; there can be no default implementation of any method specified within an interface. Each class that includes an interface must implement all of the methods.

Variables can be declared inside of interface declarations. They are implicitly **final** and **static**, meaning they cannot be changed by the implementing class. They must also be initialized. All methods and variables are implicitly **public**.

Here is an example of an interface definition. It declares a simple interface that contains one method called **callback( )** that takes a single integer parameter.

```
interface Callback {
  void callback(int param);
}
```

Implementing Interfaces

Once an **interface** has been defined, one or more classes can implement that interface. To implement an interface, include the **implements** clause in a class definition, and then create the methods defined by the interface. The general form of a class that includes the **implements** clause looks like this:

class *classname* [extends *superclass*] [implements *interface* [,*interface*...]] {
    // class-body
}

If a class implements more than one interface, the interfaces are separated with a comma. If a class implements two interfaces that declare the same method, then the same method will be used by clients of either interface. The methods that implement an interface must be declared **public**. Also, the type signature of the implementing method must match exactly the type signature specified in the **interface** definition.

Here is a small example class that implements the **Callback** interface shown earlier.

```
class Client implements Callback {
  // Implement Callback's interface
  public void callback(int p) {

    System.out.println("callback called with " + p);
  }
}
```

Notice that **callback( )** is declared using the **public** access specifier.

REMEMBER *When you implement an interface method, it must be declared as* ***public***.

It is both permissible and common for classes that implement interfaces to define additional members of their own. For example, the following version of **Client** implements **callback( )** and adds the method **nonIfaceMeth( )**:

```
class Client implements Callback {
  // Implement Callback's interface
  public void callback(int p) {
    System.out.println("callback called with " + p);
  }

  void nonIfaceMeth() {
    System.out.println("Classes that implement interfaces " +
                       "may also define other members, too.");
  }
}
```

Accessing Implementations Through Interface References

You can declare variables as object references that use an interface rather than a class type. Any instance of any class that implements the declared interface can be referred to by such a variable. When you call a method through one of these references, the correct version will be called based on the actual instance of the interface being referred to. This is one of the key features of interfaces. The method to be executed is looked up dynamically at run time, allowing classes to be created later than the code which calls methods on them. The calling code can dispatch through an interface without having to know anything about the "callee." This process is similar to using a superclass reference to access a subclass object, as described in Chapter 8.

CAUTION Because dynamic lookup of a method at run time incurs a significant overhead when compared with the normal method invocation in Java, you should be careful not to use interfaces casually in performance-critical code.

The following example calls the **callback( )** method via an interface reference variable:

```
class TestIface {
  public static void main(String args[]) {
    Callback c = new Client();
    c.callback(42);
  }
}
```

The output of this program is shown here:

```
callback called with 42
```

Notice that variable **c** is declared to be of the interface type **Callback**, yet it was assigned an instance of **Client**. Although **c** can be used to access the **callback( )** method, it cannot access any other members of the **Client** class. An interface reference variable only has knowledge of the methods declared by its **interface** declaration. Thus, **c** could not be used to access **nonIfaceMeth( )** since it is defined by **Client** but not **Callback**.

While the preceding example shows, mechanically, how an interface reference variable can access an implementation object, it does not demonstrate the polymorphic power of such a reference. To sample this usage, first create the second implementation of **Callback**, shown here:

```
// Another implementation of Callback.
class AnotherClient implements Callback {
  // Implement Callback's interface
  public void callback(int p) {
    System.out.println("Another version of callback");
    System.out.println("p squared is " + (p*p));
  }
}
```

Now, try the following class:

```
class TestIface2 {
  public static void main(String args[]) {
    Callback c = new Client();
    AnotherClient ob = new AnotherClient();

    c.callback(42);

    c = ob; // c now refers to AnotherClient object
    c.callback(42);
  }
}
```

The output from this program is shown here:

```
callback called with 42
Another version of callback
p squared is 1764
```

As you can see, the version of **callback( )** that is called is determined by the type of object that **c** refers to at run time. While this is a very simple example, you will see another, more practical one shortly.

Partial Implementations

If a class includes an interface but does not fully implement the methods defined by that interface, then that class must be declared as **abstract**. For example:

```
abstract class Incomplete implements Callback {
  int a, b;
  void show() {
    System.out.println(a + " " + b);
  }
  // ...
}
```

Here, the class **Incomplete** does not implement **callback( )** and must be declared as abstract. Any class that inherits **Incomplete** must implement **callback( )** or be declared **abstract** itself.

Nested Interfaces

An interface can be declared a member of a class or another interface. Such an interface is called a *member interface* or a *nested interface*. A nested interface can be declared as **public**, **private**, or **protected**. This differs from a top-level interface, which must either be declared as **public** or use the default access level, as previously described. When a nested interface is used outside of its enclosing scope, it must be qualified by the name of the class or interface of which it is a member. Thus, outside of the class or interface in which a nested interface is declared, its name must be fully qualified.

Here is an example that demonstrates a nested interface:

```
// A nested interface example.

// This class contains a member interface.
class A {
```

```
  // this is a nested interface
  public interface NestedIF {
    boolean isNotNegative(int x);
  }
}

// B implements the nested interface.
class B implements A.NestedIF {
  public boolean isNotNegative(int x) {
    return x < 0 ? false : true;
  }
}

class NestedIFDemo {
  public static void main(String args[]) {

    // use a nested interface reference
    A.NestedIF nif = new B();

    if(nif.isNotNegative(10))
      System.out.println("10 is not negative");
    if(nif.isNotNegative(-12))
      System.out.println("this won't be displayed");
  }
}
```

Notice that **A** defines a member interface called **NestedIF** and that it is declared **public**. Next, **B** implements the nested interface by specifying

```
implements A.NestedIF
```

Notice that the name is fully qualified by the enclosing class' name. Inside the **main( )** method, an **A.NestedIF** reference called **nif** is created, and it is assigned a reference to a **B** object. Because **B** implements **A.NestedIF**, this is legal.

Applying Interfaces

To understand the power of interfaces, let's look at a more practical example. In earlier chapters, you developed a class called **Stack** that implemented a simple fixed-size stack. However, there are many ways to implement a stack. For example, the stack can be of a fixed size or it can be "growable." The stack can also be held in an array, a linked list, a binary tree, and so on. No matter how the stack is implemented, the interface to the stack remains the same. That is, the methods **push( )** and **pop( )** define the interface to the stack independently of the details of the implementation. Because the interface to a stack is separate from its implementation, it is easy to define a stack interface, leaving it to each implementation to define the specifics. Let's look at two examples.

First, here is the interface that defines an integer stack. Put this in a file called **IntStack.java**. This interface will be used by both stack implementations.

```
// Define an integer stack interface.
interface IntStack {
  void push(int item); // store an item
  int pop(); // retrieve an item
}
```

The following program creates a class called **FixedStack** that implements a fixed-length version of an integer stack:

```java
// An implementation of IntStack that uses fixed storage.
class FixedStack implements IntStack {
  private int stck[];
  private int tos;

  // allocate and initialize stack
  FixedStack(int size) {
    stck = new int[size];
    tos = -1;
  }

  // Push an item onto the stack
  public void push(int item) {
    if(tos==stck.length-1) // use length member
      System.out.println("Stack is full.");
    else
      stck[++tos] = item;
  }

  // Pop an item from the stack
  public int pop() {
    if(tos < 0) {
      System.out.println("Stack underflow.");
      return 0;
    }
    else
      return stck[tos--];
  }
}

class IFTest {
  public static void main(String args[]) {
    FixedStack mystack1 = new FixedStack(5);
    FixedStack mystack2 = new FixedStack(8);

    // push some numbers onto the stack
    for(int i=0; i<5; i++) mystack1.push(i);
    for(int i=0; i<8; i++) mystack2.push(i);

    // pop those numbers off the stack
    System.out.println("Stack in mystack1:");
    for(int i=0; i<5; i++)
      System.out.println(mystack1.pop());

    System.out.println("Stack in mystack2:");
    for(int i=0; i<8; i++)
      System.out.println(mystack2.pop());
  }
}
```

Following is another implementation of **IntStack** that creates a dynamic stack by use of the same **interface** definition. In this implementation, each stack is constructed with an initial length. If this initial length is exceeded, then the stack is increased in size. Each time more room is needed, the size of the stack is doubled.

```java
// Implement a "growable" stack.
class DynStack implements IntStack {
  private int stck[];
  private int tos;

  // allocate and initialize stack
  DynStack(int size) {
    stck = new int[size];
    tos = -1;
  }

  // Push an item onto the stack
  public void push(int item) {
    // if stack is full, allocate a larger stack
    if(tos==stck.length-1) {
      int temp[] = new int[stck.length * 2]; // double size
      for(int i=0; i<stck.length; i++) temp[i] = stck[i];
      stck = temp;
      stck[++tos] = item;
    }
    else
      stck[++tos] = item;
  }

  // Pop an item from the stack
  public int pop() {
    if(tos < 0) {
      System.out.println("Stack underflow.");
      return 0;
    }
    else
      return stck[tos--];
  }
}

class IFTest2 {
  public static void main(String args[]) {
    DynStack mystack1 = new DynStack(5);
    DynStack mystack2 = new DynStack(8);

    // these loops cause each stack to grow
    for(int i=0; i<12; i++) mystack1.push(i);
    for(int i=0; i<20; i++) mystack2.push(i);

    System.out.println("Stack in mystack1:");
    for(int i=0; i<12; i++)
      System.out.println(mystack1.pop());

    System.out.println("Stack in mystack2:");
```

```
    for(int i=0; i<20; i++)
       System.out.println(mystack2.pop());
  }
}
```

The following class uses both the **FixedStack** and **DynStack** implementations. It does so through an interface reference. This means that calls to **push( )** and **pop( )** are resolved at run time rather than at compile time.

```
/* Create an interface variable and
   access stacks through it.
*/
class IFTest3 {
  public static void main(String args[]) {
    IntStack mystack; // create an interface reference variable
    DynStack ds = new DynStack(5);
    FixedStack fs = new FixedStack(8);

    mystack = ds; // load dynamic stack
    // push some numbers onto the stack
    for(int i=0; i<12; i++) mystack.push(i);

    mystack = fs; // load fixed stack
    for(int i=0; i<8; i++) mystack.push(i);


    mystack = ds;
    System.out.println("Values in dynamic stack:");
    for(int i=0; i<12; i++)
       System.out.println(mystack.pop());

    mystack = fs;
    System.out.println("Values in fixed stack:");
    for(int i=0; i<8; i++)
       System.out.println(mystack.pop());
  }
}
```

In this program, **mystack** is a reference to the **IntStack** interface. Thus, when it refers to **ds**, it uses the versions of **push( )** and **pop( )** defined by the **DynStack** implementation. When it refers to **fs**, it uses the versions of **push( )** and **pop( )** defined by **FixedStack**. As explained, these determinations are made at run time. Accessing multiple implementations of an interface through an interface reference variable is the most powerful way that Java achieves run-time polymorphism.

Variables in Interfaces

You can use interfaces to import shared constants into multiple classes by simply declaring an interface that contains variables that are initialized to the desired values. When you include that interface in a class (that is, when you "implement" the interface), all of those variable names will be in scope as constants. (This is similar to using a header file in C/C++ to create a large number of **#defined** constants or **const** declarations.) If an interface contains no methods, then any class that includes such an interface doesn't actually implement anything.

It is as if that class were importing the constant fields into the class name space as **final** variables. The next example uses this technique to implement an automated "decision maker":

```
import java.util.Random;

interface SharedConstants {
  int NO = 0;
  int YES = 1;
  int MAYBE = 2;
  int LATER = 3;
  int SOON = 4;
  int NEVER = 5;
}

class Question implements SharedConstants {
  Random rand = new Random();
  int ask() {
    int prob = (int) (100 * rand.nextDouble());
    if (prob < 30)
      return NO;            // 30%
    else if (prob < 60)
      return YES;           // 30%
    else if (prob < 75)
      return LATER;         // 15%
    else if (prob < 98)
      return SOON;          // 13%

    else
      return NEVER;         // 2%
  }
}

class AskMe implements SharedConstants {
  static void answer(int result) {
    switch(result) {
      case NO:
        System.out.println("No");
        break;
      case YES:
        System.out.println("Yes");
        break;
      case MAYBE:
        System.out.println("Maybe");
        break;
      case LATER:
        System.out.println("Later");
        break;
      case SOON:
        System.out.println("Soon");
        break;
      case NEVER:
        System.out.println("Never");
        break;
    }
  }
```

```
  public static void main(String args[]) {
    Question q = new Question();
    answer(q.ask());
    answer(q.ask());
    answer(q.ask());
    answer(q.ask());
  }
}
```

Notice that this program makes use of one of Java's standard classes: **Random**. This class provides pseudorandom numbers. It contains several methods that allow you to obtain random numbers in the form required by your program. In this example, the method **nextDouble( )** is used. It returns random numbers in the range 0.0 to 1.0.

In this sample program, the two classes, **Question** and **AskMe**, both implement the **SharedConstants** interface where **NO, YES, MAYBE, SOON, LATER,** and **NEVER** are defined. Inside each class, the code refers to these constants as if each class had defined or inherited them directly. Here is the output of a sample run of this program. Note that the results are different each time it is run.

```
Later
Soon
No
Yes
```

Interfaces Can Be Extended

One interface can inherit another by use of the keyword **extends**. The syntax is the same as for inheriting classes. When a class implements an interface that inherits another interface, it must provide implementations for all methods defined within the interface inheritance chain. Following is an example:

```
// One interface can extend another.
interface A {
  void meth1();
  void meth2();
}

// B now includes meth1() and meth2() -- it adds meth3().
interface B extends A {
  void meth3();
}

// This class must implement all of A and B
class MyClass implements B {
  public void meth1() {
    System.out.println("Implement meth1().");
  }

  public void meth2() {
    System.out.println("Implement meth2().");
  }

  public void meth3() {
```

```
      System.out.println("Implement meth3().");
   }


}

class IFExtend {
  public static void main(String arg[]) {
    MyClass ob = new MyClass();

    ob.meth1();
    ob.meth2();
    ob.meth3();
  }
}
```

As an experiment, you might want to try removing the implementation for **meth1( )** in **MyClass**. This will cause a compile-time error. As stated earlier, any class that implements an interface must implement all methods defined by that interface, including any that are inherited from other interfaces.

Although the examples we've included in this book do not make frequent use of packages or interfaces, both of these tools are an important part of the Java programming environment. Virtually all real programs that you write in Java will be contained within packages. A number will probably implement interfaces as well. It is important, therefore, that you be comfortable with their usage.

Exception Handling

This chapter examines Java's exception-handling mechanism. An *exception* is an abnormal condition that arises in a code sequence at run time. In other words, an exception is a run-time error. In computer languages that do not support exception handling, errors must be checked and handled manually—typically through the use of error codes, and so on. This approach is as cumbersome as it is troublesome. Java's exception handling avoids these problems and, in the process, brings run-time error management into the object-oriented world.

Exception-Handling Fundamentals

A Java exception is an object that describes an exceptional (that is, error) condition that has occurred in a piece of code. When an exceptional condition arises, an object representing that exception is created and *thrown* in the method that caused the error. That method may choose to handle the exception itself, or pass it on. Either way, at some point, the exception is *caught* and processed. Exceptions can be generated by the Java run-time system, or they can be manually generated by your code. Exceptions thrown by Java relate to fundamental errors that violate the rules of the Java language or the constraints of the Java execution environment. Manually generated exceptions are typically used to report some error condition to the caller of a method.

Java exception handling is managed via five keywords: **try**, **catch**, **throw**, **throws**, and **finally**. Briefly, here is how they work. Program statements that you want to monitor for exceptions are contained within a **try** block. If an exception occurs within the **try** block, it is thrown. Your code can catch this exception (using **catch**) and handle it in some rational manner. System-generated exceptions are automatically thrown by the Java run-time system. To manually throw an exception, use the keyword **throw**. Any exception that is thrown out of a method must be specified as such by a **throws** clause. Any code that absolutely must be executed after a **try** block completes is put in a **finally** block.

This is the general form of an exception-handling block:

```
try {
    // block of code to monitor for errors
}
```

```
catch (ExceptionType1 exOb) {
    // exception handler for ExceptionType1
}

catch (ExceptionType2 exOb) {
    // exception handler for ExceptionType2
}
// ...
finally {
    // block of code to be executed after try block ends
}
```

Here, *ExceptionType* is the type of exception that has occurred. The remainder of this chapter describes how to apply this framework.

Exception Types

All exception types are subclasses of the built-in class **Throwable**. Thus, **Throwable** is at the top of the exception class hierarchy. Immediately below **Throwable** are two subclasses that partition exceptions into two distinct branches. One branch is headed by **Exception**. This class is used for exceptional conditions that user programs should catch. This is also the class that you will subclass to create your own custom exception types. There is an important subclass of **Exception**, called **RuntimeException**. Exceptions of this type are automatically defined for the programs that you write and include things such as division by zero and invalid array indexing.

The other branch is topped by **Error**, which defines exceptions that are not expected to be caught under normal circumstances by your program. Exceptions of type **Error** are used by the Java run-time system to indicate errors having to do with the run-time environment, itself. Stack overflow is an example of such an error. This chapter will not be dealing with exceptions of type **Error**, because these are typically created in response to catastrophic failures that cannot usually be handled by your program.

Uncaught Exceptions

Before you learn how to handle exceptions in your program, it is useful to see what happens when you don't handle them. This small program includes an expression that intentionally causes a divide-by-zero error:

```java
class Exc0 {
  public static void main(String args[]) {
    int d = 0;
    int a = 42 / d;
  }
}
```

When the Java run-time system detects the attempt to divide by zero, it constructs a new exception object and then *throws* this exception. This causes the execution of **Exc0** to stop, because once an exception has been thrown, it must be *caught* by an exception handler and dealt with immediately. In this example, we haven't supplied any exception handlers of our own, so the exception is caught by the default handler provided by the Java run-time system. Any exception that is not caught by your program will ultimately be processed by the default handler. The default handler displays a string describing the exception, prints a stack trace from the point at which the exception occurred, and terminates the program.

Here is the exception generated when this example is executed:

```
java.lang.ArithmeticException: / by zero
        at Exc0.main(Exc0.java:4)
```

Notice how the class name, **Exc0**; the method name, **main**; the filename, **Exc0.java**; and the line number, **4**, are all included in the simple stack trace. Also, notice that the type of exception thrown is a subclass of **Exception** called **ArithmeticException**, which more specifically describes what type of error happened. As discussed later in this chapter, Java supplies several built-in exception types that match the various sorts of run-time errors that can be generated.

The stack trace will always show the sequence of method invocations that led up to the error. For example, here is another version of the preceding program that introduces the same error but in a method separate from **main( )**:

```
class Exc1 {
  static void subroutine() {
    int d = 0;
    int a = 10 / d;
  }
  public static void main(String args[]) {
    Exc1.subroutine();
  }
}
```

The resulting stack trace from the default exception handler shows how the entire call stack is displayed:

```
java.lang.ArithmeticException: / by zero
        at Exc1.subroutine(Exc1.java:4)
        at Exc1.main(Exc1.java:7)
```

As you can see, the bottom of the stack is **main**'s line 7, which is the call to **subroutine( )**, which caused the exception at line 4. The call stack is quite useful for debugging, because it pinpoints the precise sequence of steps that led to the error.

Using try and catch

Although the default exception handler provided by the Java run-time system is useful for debugging, you will usually want to handle an exception yourself. Doing so provides two benefits. First, it allows you to fix the error. Second, it prevents the program from automatically terminating. Most users would be confused (to say the least) if your program stopped running and printed a stack trace whenever an error occurred! Fortunately, it is quite easy to prevent this.

To guard against and handle a run-time error, simply enclose the code that you want to monitor inside a **try** block. Immediately following the **try** block, include a **catch** clause that specifies the exception type that you wish to catch. To illustrate how easily this can be done, the following program includes a **try** block and a **catch** clause that processes the **ArithmeticException** generated by the division-by-zero error:

```
class Exc2 {
  public static void main(String args[]) {
    int d, a;

    try { // monitor a block of code.
      d = 0;
      a = 42 / d;
      System.out.println("This will not be printed.");
    } catch (ArithmeticException e) { // catch divide-by-zero error
      System.out.println("Division by zero.");
    }
    System.out.println("After catch statement.");
  }
}
```

This program generates the following output:

```
Division by zero.
After catch statement.
```

Notice that the call to **println( )** inside the **try** block is never executed. Once an exception is thrown, program control transfers out of the **try** block into the **catch** block. Put differently, **catch** is not "called," so execution never "returns" to the **try** block from a **catch**. Thus, the line "This will not be printed." is not displayed. Once the **catch** statement has executed, program control continues with the next line in the program following the entire **try/catch** mechanism.

A **try** and its **catch** statement form a unit. The scope of the **catch** clause is restricted to those statements specified by the immediately preceding **try** statement. A **catch** statement cannot catch an exception thrown by another **try** statement (except in the case of nested **try** statements, described shortly). The statements that are protected by **try** must be surrounded by curly braces. (That is, they must be within a block.) You cannot use **try** on a single statement.

The goal of most well-constructed **catch** clauses should be to resolve the exceptional condition and then continue on as if the error had never happened. For example, in the next program each iteration of the **for** loop obtains two random integers. Those two integers are divided by each other, and the result is used to divide the value 12345. The final result is put into **a**. If either division operation causes a divide-by-zero error, it is caught, the value of **a** is set to zero, and the program continues.

```
// Handle an exception and move on.
import java.util.Random;

class HandleError {
  public static void main(String args[]) {
```

```
    int a=0, b=0, c=0;
    Random r = new Random();

    for(int i=0; i<32000; i++) {
      try {
        b = r.nextInt();
        c = r.nextInt();
        a = 12345 / (b/c);
      } catch (ArithmeticException e) {
        System.out.println("Division by zero.");
        a = 0; // set a to zero and continue
      }
      System.out.println("a: " + a);
    }
  }
}
```

Displaying a Description of an Exception

Throwable overrides the **toString( )** method (defined by **Object**) so that it returns a string containing a description of the exception. You can display this description in a **println( )** statement by simply passing the exception as an argument. For example, the **catch** block in the preceding program can be rewritten like this:

```
catch (ArithmeticException e) {
  System.out.println("Exception: " + e);
  a = 0; // set a to zero and continue
}
```

When this version is substituted in the program, and the program is run, each divide-by-zero error displays the following message:

```
Exception: java.lang.ArithmeticException: / by zero
```

While it is of no particular value in this context, the ability to display a description of an exception is valuable in other circumstances—particularly when you are experimenting with exceptions or when you are debugging.

Multiple catch Clauses

In some cases, more than one exception could be raised by a single piece of code. To handle this type of situation, you can specify two or more **catch** clauses, each catching a different type of exception. When an exception is thrown, each **catch** statement is inspected in order, and the first one whose type matches that of the exception is executed. After one **catch** statement executes, the others are bypassed, and execution continues after the **try/catch** block. The following example traps two different exception types:

```
// Demonstrate multiple catch statements.
class MultiCatch {
  public static void main(String args[]) {
    try {
```

```
      int a = args.length;
      System.out.println("a = " + a);
      int b = 42 / a;
      int c[] = { 1 };
      c[42] = 99;
    } catch(ArithmeticException e) {
      System.out.println("Divide by 0: " + e);
    } catch(ArrayIndexOutOfBoundsException e) {
      System.out.println("Array index oob: " + e);
    }
    System.out.println("After try/catch blocks.");
  }
}
```

This program will cause a division-by-zero exception if it is started with no command-line arguments, since **a** will equal zero. It will survive the division if you provide a command-line argument, setting **a** to something larger than zero. But it will cause an **ArrayIndexOutOfBoundsException**, since the **int** array **c** has a length of 1, yet the program attempts to assign a value to **c[42]**.

Here is the output generated by running it both ways:

```
C:\>java MultiCatch
a = 0
Divide by 0: java.lang.ArithmeticException: / by zero
After try/catch blocks.

C:\>java MultiCatch TestArg
a = 1
Array index oob: java.lang.ArrayIndexOutOfBoundsException:42
After try/catch blocks.
```

When you use multiple **catch** statements, it is important to remember that exception subclasses must come before any of their superclasses. This is because a **catch** statement that uses a superclass will catch exceptions of that type plus any of its subclasses. Thus, a subclass would never be reached if it came after its superclass. Further, in Java, unreachable code is an error. For example, consider the following program:

```
/* This program contains an error.

   A subclass must come before its superclass in
   a series of catch statements. If not,
   unreachable code will be created and a
   compile-time error will result.
*/
class SuperSubCatch {
  public static void main(String args[]) {
    try {
      int a = 0;
      int b = 42 / a;
    } catch(Exception e) {
```

```
      System.out.println("Generic Exception catch.");
    }
    /* This catch is never reached because
       ArithmeticException is a subclass of Exception. */
    catch(ArithmeticException e) { // ERROR - unreachable
      System.out.println("This is never reached.");
    }
  }
}
```

If you try to compile this program, you will receive an error message stating that the second **catch** statement is unreachable because the exception has already been caught. Since **ArithmeticException** is a subclass of **Exception**, the first **catch** statement will handle all **Exception**-based errors, including **ArithmeticException**. This means that the second **catch** statement will never execute. To fix the problem, reverse the order of the **catch** statements.

Nested try Statements

The **try** statement can be nested. That is, a **try** statement can be inside the block of another **try**. Each time a **try** statement is entered, the context of that exception is pushed on the stack. If an inner **try** statement does not have a **catch** handler for a particular exception, the stack is unwound and the next **try** statement's **catch** handlers are inspected for a match. This continues until one of the **catch** statements succeeds, or until all of the nested **try** statements are exhausted. If no **catch** statement matches, then the Java run-time system will handle the exception. Here is an example that uses nested **try** statements:

```
// An example of nested try statements.
class NestTry {
  public static void main(String args[]) {
    try {
      int a = args.length;

      /* If no command-line args are present,
         the following statement will generate
         a divide-by-zero exception. */
      int b = 42 / a;

      System.out.println("a = " + a);

      try { // nested try block
        /* If one command-line arg is used,
           then a divide-by-zero exception
           will be generated by the following code. */
        if(a==1) a = a/(a-a); // division by zero

        /* If two command-line args are used,
           then generate an out-of-bounds exception. */
        if(a==2) {
          int c[] = { 1 };
```

```
        c[42] = 99; // generate an out-of-bounds exception
      }
    } catch(ArrayIndexOutOfBoundsException e) {
      System.out.println("Array index out-of-bounds: " + e);
    }

  } catch(ArithmeticException e) {
    System.out.println("Divide by 0: " + e);
  }
 }
}
```

As you can see, this program nests one **try** block within another. The program works as follows. When you execute the program with no command-line arguments, a divide-by-zero exception is generated by the outer **try** block. Execution of the program with one command-line argument generates a divide-by-zero exception from within the nested **try** block. Since the inner block does not catch this exception, it is passed on to the outer **try** block, where it is handled. If you execute the program with two command-line arguments, an array boundary exception is generated from within the inner **try** block. Here are sample runs that illustrate each case:

```
C:\>java NestTry
Divide by 0: java.lang.ArithmeticException: / by zero

C:\>java NestTry One
a = 1
Divide by 0: java.lang.ArithmeticException: / by zero

C:\>java NestTry One Two
a = 2
Array index out-of-bounds:
  java.lang.ArrayIndexOutOfBoundsException:42
```

Nesting of **try** statements can occur in less obvious ways when method calls are involved. For example, you can enclose a call to a method within a **try** block. Inside that method is another **try** statement. In this case, the **try** within the method is still nested inside the outer **try** block, which calls the method. Here is the previous program recoded so that the nested **try** block is moved inside the method **nesttry( )**:

```
/* Try statements can be implicitly nested via
   calls to methods. */
class MethNestTry {
  static void nesttry(int a) {
    try { // nested try block
      /* If one command-line arg is used,
         then a divide-by-zero exception
         will be generated by the following code. */
      if(a==1) a = a/(a-a); // division by zero
```

```
      /* If two command-line args are used,
         then generate an out-of-bounds exception. */
      if(a==2) {
        int c[] = { 1 };
        c[42] = 99; // generate an out-of-bounds exception
      }
    } catch(ArrayIndexOutOfBoundsException e) {
      System.out.println("Array index out-of-bounds: " + e);
    }
  }

  public static void main(String args[]) {
    try {
      int a = args.length;

      /* If no command-line args are present,
         the following statement will generate
         a divide-by-zero exception. */
      int b = 42 / a;
      System.out.println("a = " + a);

      nesttry(a);
    } catch(ArithmeticException e) {
      System.out.println("Divide by 0: " + e);
    }
  }
}
```

The output of this program is identical to that of the preceding example.

throw

So far, you have only been catching exceptions that are thrown by the Java run-time system.
However, it is possible for your program to throw an exception explicitly, using the **throw**
statement. The general form of **throw** is shown here:

throw *ThrowableInstance*;

Here, *ThrowableInstance* must be an object of type **Throwable** or a subclass of **Throwable**.
Primitive types, such as **int** or **char**, as well as non-**Throwable** classes, such as **String** and
Object, cannot be used as exceptions. There are two ways you can obtain a **Throwable** object:
using a parameter in a **catch** clause, or creating one with the **new** operator.

The flow of execution stops immediately after the **throw** statement; any subsequent
statements are not executed. The nearest enclosing **try** block is inspected to see if it has a
catch statement that matches the type of exception. If it does find a match, control is
transferred to that statement. If not, then the next enclosing **try** statement is inspected, and
so on. If no matching **catch** is found, then the default exception handler halts the program
and prints the stack trace.

Here is a sample program that creates and throws an exception. The handler that catches the exception rethrows it to the outer handler.

```
// Demonstrate throw.
class ThrowDemo {
  static void demoproc() {
    try {
      throw new NullPointerException("demo");
    } catch(NullPointerException e) {
      System.out.println("Caught inside demoproc.");
      throw e; // rethrow the exception
    }
  }

  public static void main(String args[]) {
    try {
      demoproc();
    } catch(NullPointerException e) {
      System.out.println("Recaught: " + e);
    }
  }
}
```

This program gets two chances to deal with the same error. First, **main( )** sets up an exception context and then calls **demoproc( )**. The **demoproc( )** method then sets up another exception-handling context and immediately throws a new instance of **NullPointerException**, which is caught on the next line. The exception is then rethrown. Here is the resulting output:

```
Caught inside demoproc.
Recaught: java.lang.NullPointerException: demo
```

The program also illustrates how to create one of Java's standard exception objects. Pay close attention to this line:

```
throw new NullPointerException("demo");
```

Here, **new** is used to construct an instance of **NullPointerException**. Many of Java's built-in run-time exceptions have at least two constructors: one with no parameter and one that takes a string parameter. When the second form is used, the argument specifies a string that describes the exception. This string is displayed when the object is used as an argument to **print( )** or **println( )**. It can also be obtained by a call to **getMessage( )**, which is defined by **Throwable**.

throws

If a method is capable of causing an exception that it does not handle, it must specify this behavior so that callers of the method can guard themselves against that exception. You do this by including a **throws** clause in the method's declaration. A **throws** clause lists the types of exceptions that a method might throw. This is necessary for all exceptions, except those of type **Error** or **RuntimeException,** or any of their subclasses. All other exceptions that a method can throw must be declared in the **throws** clause. If they are not, a compile-time error will result.

This is the general form of a method declaration that includes a **throws** clause:

type method-name(parameter-list) throws *exception-list*
{
  // body of method
}

Here, *exception-list* is a comma-separated list of the exceptions that a method can throw.

Following is an example of an incorrect program that tries to throw an exception that it does not catch. Because the program does not specify a **throws** clause to declare this fact, the program will not compile.

```
// This program contains an error and will not compile.
class ThrowsDemo {
  static void throwOne() {
    System.out.println("Inside throwOne.");
    throw new IllegalAccessException("demo");
  }
  public static void main(String args[]) {
    throwOne();
  }
}
```

To make this example compile, you need to make two changes. First, you need to declare that **throwOne( )** throws **IllegalAccessException**. Second, **main( )** must define a **try/catch** statement that catches this exception.

The corrected example is shown here:

```
// This is now correct.
class ThrowsDemo {
  static void throwOne() throws IllegalAccessException {
    System.out.println("Inside throwOne.");
    throw new IllegalAccessException("demo");
  }
  public static void main(String args[]) {
    try {
      throwOne();
    } catch (IllegalAccessException e) {
      System.out.println("Caught " + e);
    }
  }
}
```

Here is the output generated by running this example program:

```
inside throwOne
caught java.lang.IllegalAccessException: demo
```

finally

When exceptions are thrown, execution in a method takes a rather abrupt, nonlinear path that alters the normal flow through the method. Depending upon how the method is coded, it is even possible for an exception to cause the method to return prematurely. This could be a problem in some methods. For example, if a method opens a file upon entry and closes it upon exit, then you will not want the code that closes the file to be bypassed by the exception-handling mechanism. The **finally** keyword is designed to address this contingency.

finally creates a block of code that will be executed after a **try/catch** block has completed and before the code following the **try/catch** block. The **finally** block will execute whether or not an exception is thrown. If an exception is thrown, the **finally** block will execute even if no **catch** statement matches the exception. Any time a method is about to return to the caller from inside a **try/catch** block, via an uncaught exception or an explicit return statement, the **finally** clause is also executed just before the method returns. This can be useful for closing file handles and freeing up any other resources that might have been allocated at the beginning of a method with the intent of disposing of them before returning. The **finally** clause is optional. However, each **try** statement requires at least one **catch** or a **finally** clause.

Here is an example program that shows three methods that exit in various ways, none without executing their **finally** clauses:

```
// Demonstrate finally.
class FinallyDemo {
  // Through an exception out of the method.
  static void procA() {
    try {
      System.out.println("inside procA");
      throw new RuntimeException("demo");
    } finally {
      System.out.println("procA's finally");
    }
  }

  // Return from within a try block.
  static void procB() {
    try {
      System.out.println("inside procB");
      return;
    } finally {
      System.out.println("procB's finally");
    }
  }
  // Execute a try block normally.
  static void procC() {
    try {
      System.out.println("inside procC");
    } finally {
```

```
      System.out.println("procC's finally");
    }
  }

  public static void main(String args[]) {
    try {
      procA();
    } catch (Exception e) {
      System.out.println("Exception caught");
    }
    procB();
    procC();
  }
}
```

In this example, **procA( )** prematurely breaks out of the **try** by throwing an exception. The **finally** clause is executed on the way out. **procB( )**'s **try** statement is exited via a **return** statement. The **finally** clause is executed before **procB( )** returns. In **procC( )**, the **try** statement executes normally, without error. However, the **finally** block is still executed.

REMEMBER   *If a finally block is associated with a **try**, the **finally** block will be executed upon conclusion of the **try**.*

Here is the output generated by the preceding program:

```
inside procA
procA's finally
Exception caught
inside procB
procB's finally
inside procC
procC's finally
```

Java's Built-in Exceptions

Inside the standard package **java.lang**, Java defines several exception classes. A few have been used by the preceding examples. The most general of these exceptions are subclasses of the standard type **RuntimeException**. As previously explained, these exceptions need not be included in any method's **throws** list. In the language of Java, these are called *unchecked exceptions* because the compiler does not check to see if a method handles or throws these exceptions. The unchecked exceptions defined in **java.lang** are listed in Table 10-1. Table 10-2 lists those exceptions defined by **java.lang** that must be included in a method's **throws** list if that method can generate one of these exceptions and does not handle it itself. These are called *checked exceptions*. Java defines several other types of exceptions that relate to its various class libraries.

Exception	Meaning
ArithmeticException	Arithmetic error, such as divide-by-zero.
ArrayIndexOutOfBoundsException	Array index is out-of-bounds.
ArrayStoreException	Assignment to an array element of an incompatible type.
ClassCastException	Invalid cast.
EnumConstantNotPresentException	An attempt is made to use an undefined enumeration value.
IllegalArgumentException	Illegal argument used to invoke a method.
IllegalMonitorStateException	Illegal monitor operation, such as waiting on an unlocked thread.
IllegalStateException	Environment or application is in incorrect state.
IllegalThreadStateException	Requested operation not compatible with current thread state.
IndexOutOfBoundsException	Some type of index is out-of-bounds.
NegativeArraySizeException	Array created with a negative size.
NullPointerException	Invalid use of a null reference.
NumberFormatException	Invalid conversion of a string to a numeric format.
SecurityException	Attempt to violate security.
StringIndexOutOfBounds	Attempt to index outside the bounds of a string.
TypeNotPresentException	Type not found.
UnsupportedOperationException	An unsupported operation was encountered.

TABLE 10-1   Java's Unchecked **RuntimeException** Subclasses Defined in **java.lang**

Exception	Meaning
ClassNotFoundException	Class not found.
CloneNotSupportedException	Attempt to clone an object that does not implement the **Cloneable** interface.
IllegalAccessException	Access to a class is denied.
InstantiationException	Attempt to create an object of an abstract class or interface.
InterruptedException	One thread has been interrupted by another thread.
NoSuchFieldException	A requested field does not exist.
NoSuchMethodException	A requested method does not exist.

TABLE 10-2   Java's Checked Exceptions Defined in **java.lang**

Creating Your Own Exception Subclasses

Although Java's built-in exceptions handle most common errors, you will probably want to create your own exception types to handle situations specific to your applications. This is quite easy to do: just define a subclass of **Exception** (which is, of course, a subclass of **Throwable**). Your subclasses don't need to actually implement anything—it is their existence in the type system that allows you to use them as exceptions.

The **Exception** class does not define any methods of its own. It does, of course, inherit those methods provided by **Throwable**. Thus, all exceptions, including those that you create, have the methods defined by **Throwable** available to them. They are shown in Table 10-3.

Method	Description
Throwable fillInStackTrace( )	Returns a **Throwable** object that contains a completed stack trace. This object can be rethrown.
Throwable getCause( )	Returns the exception that underlies the current exception. If there is no underlying exception, **null** is returned.
String getLocalizedMessage( )	Returns a localized description of the exception.
String getMessage( )	Returns a description of the exception.
StackTraceElement[ ] getStackTrace( )	Returns an array that contains the stack trace, one element at a time, as an array of **StackTraceElement**. The method at the top of the stack is the last method called before the exception was thrown. This method is found in the first element of the array. The **StackTraceElement** class gives your program access to information about each element in the trace, such as its method name.
Throwable initCause(Throwable _causeExc_)	Associates _causeExc_ with the invoking exception as a cause of the invoking exception. Returns a reference to the exception.
void printStackTrace( )	Displays the stack trace.
void printStackTrace(PrintStream _stream_)	Sends the stack trace to the specified stream.
void printStackTrace(PrintWriter _stream_)	Sends the stack trace to the specified stream.
void setStackTrace(StackTraceElement _elements_[ ])	Sets the stack trace to the elements passed in _elements_. This method is for specialized applications, not normal use.
String toString( )	Returns a **String** object containing a description of the exception. This method is called by **println( )** when outputting a **Throwable** object.

TABLE 10-3   The Methods Defined by **Throwable**

You may also wish to override one or more of these methods in exception classes that you create.

Exception defines four constructors. Two were added by JDK 1.4 to support chained exceptions, described in the next section. The other two are shown here:

Exception( )

Exception(String *msg*)

The first form creates an exception that has no description. The second form lets you specify a description of the exception.

Although specifying a description when an exception is created is often useful, sometimes it is better to override **toString( )**. Here's why: The version of **toString( )** defined by **Throwable** (and inherited by **Exception**) first displays the name of the exception followed by a colon, which is then followed by your description. By overriding **toString( )**, you can prevent the exception name and colon from being displayed. This makes for a cleaner output, which is desirable in some cases.

The following example declares a new subclass of **Exception** and then uses that subclass to signal an error condition in a method. It overrides the **toString( )** method, allowing a carefully tailored description of the exception to be displayed.

```
// This program creates a custom exception type.
class MyException extends Exception {
  private int detail;

  MyException(int a) {
    detail = a;
  }

  public String toString() {
    return "MyException[" + detail + "]";
  }
}

class ExceptionDemo {
  static void compute(int a) throws MyException {
    System.out.println("Called compute(" + a + ")");
    if(a > 10)
      throw new MyException(a);
    System.out.println("Normal exit");
  }

  public static void main(String args[]) {
    try {
      compute(1);
      compute(20);
    } catch (MyException e) {
      System.out.println("Caught " + e);
    }
  }
}
```

This example defines a subclass of **Exception** called **MyException**. This subclass is quite simple: it has only a constructor plus an overloaded **toString( )** method that displays the value of the exception. The **ExceptionDemo** class defines a method named **compute( )** that throws a **MyException** object. The exception is thrown when **compute( )**'s integer parameter is greater than 10. The **main( )** method sets up an exception handler for **MyException**, then calls **compute( )** with a legal value (less than 10) and an illegal one to show both paths through the code. Here is the result:

```
Called compute(1)
Normal exit
Called compute(20)
Caught MyException[20]
```

Chained Exceptions

Beginning with JDK 1.4, a new feature has been incorporated into the exception subsystem: *chained exceptions.* The chained exception feature allows you to associate another exception with an exception. This second exception describes the cause of the first exception. For example, imagine a situation in which a method throws an **ArithmeticException** because of an attempt to divide by zero. However, the actual cause of the problem was that an I/O error occurred, which caused the divisor to be set improperly. Although the method must certainly throw an **ArithmeticException**, since that is the error that occurred, you might also want to let the calling code know that the underlying cause was an I/O error. Chained exceptions let you handle this, and any other situation in which layers of exceptions exist.

To allow chained exceptions, two constructors and two methods were added to **Throwable**. The constructors are shown here:

Throwable(Throwable *causeExc*)
Throwable(String *msg*, Throwable *causeExc*)

In the first form, *causeExc* is the exception that causes the current exception. That is, *causeExc* is the underlying reason that an exception occurred. The second form allows you to specify a description at the same time that you specify a cause exception. These two constructors have also been added to the **Error**, **Exception**, and **RuntimeException** classes.

The chained exception methods added to **Throwable** are **getCause( )** and **initCause( )**. These methods are shown in Table 10-3 and are repeated here for the sake of discussion.

Throwable getCause( )
Throwable initCause(Throwable *causeExc*)

The **getCause( )** method returns the exception that underlies the current exception. If there is no underlying exception, **null** is returned. The **initCause( )** method associates *causeExc* with the invoking exception and returns a reference to the exception. Thus, you can associate a cause with an exception after the exception has been created. However, the cause exception can be set only once. Thus, you can call **initCause( )** only once for each exception object. Furthermore, if the cause exception was set by a constructor, then you can't set it again using **initCause( )**. In general, **initCause( )** is used to set a cause for legacy exception classes that don't support the two additional constructors described earlier.

Here is an example that illustrates the mechanics of handling chained exceptions:

```
// Demonstrate exception chaining.
class ChainExcDemo {
  static void demoproc() {
```

```
    // create an exception
    NullPointerException e =
      new NullPointerException("top layer");

    // add a cause
    e.initCause(new ArithmeticException("cause"));

    throw e;
  }

  public static void main(String args[]) {
    try {
      demoproc();
    } catch(NullPointerException e) {
      // display top level exception
      System.out.println("Caught: " + e);

      // display cause exception
      System.out.println("Original cause: " +
                           e.getCause());
    }
  }
}
```

The output from the program is shown here:

```
Caught: java.lang.NullPointerException: top layer
Original cause: java.lang.ArithmeticException: cause
```

In this example, the top-level exception is **NullPointerException**. To it is added a cause exception, **ArithmeticException**. When the exception is thrown out of **demoproc( )**, it is caught by **main( )**. There, the top-level exception is displayed, followed by the underlying exception, which is obtained by calling **getCause( )**.

Chained exceptions can be carried on to whatever depth is necessary. Thus, the cause exception can, itself, have a cause. Be aware that overly long chains of exceptions may indicate poor design.

Chained exceptions are not something that every program will need. However, in cases in which knowledge of an underlying cause is useful, they offer an elegant solution.

Using Exceptions

Exception handling provides a powerful mechanism for controlling complex programs that have many dynamic run-time characteristics. It is important to think of **try**, **throw**, and **catch** as clean ways to handle errors and unusual boundary conditions in your program's logic. Unlike some other languages in which error return codes are used to indicate failure, Java uses exceptions. Thus, when a method can fail, have it throw an exception. This is a cleaner way to handle failure modes.

One last point: Java's exception-handling statements should not be considered a general mechanism for nonlocal branching. If you do so, it will only confuse your code and make it hard to maintain.

Multithreaded Programming

U nlike many other computer languages, Java provides built-in support for *multithreaded programming*. A multithreaded program contains two or more parts that can run concurrently. Each part of such a program is called a *thread*, and each thread defines a separate path of execution. Thus, multithreading is a specialized form of multitasking.

You are almost certainly acquainted with multitasking, because it is supported by virtually all modern operating systems. However, there are two distinct types of multitasking: process-based and thread-based. It is important to understand the difference between the two. For most readers, process-based multitasking is the more familiar form. A *process* is, in essence, a program that is executing. Thus, *process-based* multitasking is the feature that allows your computer to run two or more programs concurrently. For example, process-based multitasking enables you to run the Java compiler at the same time that you are using a text editor. In process-based multitasking, a program is the smallest unit of code that can be dispatched by the scheduler.

In a *thread-based* multitasking environment, the thread is the smallest unit of dispatchable code. This means that a single program can perform two or more tasks simultaneously. For instance, a text editor can format text at the same time that it is printing, as long as these two actions are being performed by two separate threads. Thus, process-based multitasking deals with the "big picture," and thread-based multitasking handles the details.

Multitasking threads require less overhead than multitasking processes. Processes are heavyweight tasks that require their own separate address spaces. Interprocess communication is expensive and limited. Context switching from one process to another is also costly. Threads, on the other hand, are lightweight. They share the same address space and cooperatively share the same heavyweight process. Interthread communication is inexpensive, and context switching from one thread to the next is low cost. While Java programs make use of process-based multitasking environments, process-based multitasking is not under the control of Java. However, multithreaded multitasking is.

Multithreading enables you to write very efficient programs that make maximum use of the CPU, because idle time can be kept to a minimum. This is especially important for the interactive, networked environment in which Java operates, because idle time is common. For example, the transmission rate of data over a network is much slower than the rate at which the computer can process it. Even local file system resources are read and written at a much slower pace than they can be processed by the CPU. And, of course, user input is much slower than the computer. In a single-threaded environment, your program has to wait for each of these tasks to finish before it can proceed to the next one—even though the CPU is sitting idle most of the time. Multithreading lets you gain access to this idle time and put it to good use.

If you have programmed for operating systems such as Windows, then you are already familiar with multithreaded programming. However, the fact that Java manages threads makes multithreading especially convenient, because many of the details are handled for you.

The Java Thread Model

The Java run-time system depends on threads for many things, and all the class libraries are designed with multithreading in mind. In fact, Java uses threads to enable the entire environment to be asynchronous. This helps reduce inefficiency by preventing the waste of CPU cycles.

The value of a multithreaded environment is best understood in contrast to its counterpart. Single-threaded systems use an approach called an *event loop* with *polling*. In this model, a single thread of control runs in an infinite loop, polling a single event queue to decide what to do next. Once this polling mechanism returns with, say, a signal that a network file is ready to be read, then the event loop dispatches control to the appropriate event handler. Until this event handler returns, nothing else can happen in the system. This wastes CPU time. It can also result in one part of a program dominating the system and preventing any other events from being processed. In general, in a singled-threaded environment, when a thread *blocks* (that is, suspends execution) because it is waiting for some resource, the entire program stops running.

The benefit of Java's multithreading is that the main loop/polling mechanism is eliminated. One thread can pause without stopping other parts of your program. For example, the idle time created when a thread reads data from a network or waits for user input can be utilized elsewhere. Multithreading allows animation loops to sleep for a second between each frame without causing the whole system to pause. When a thread blocks in a Java program, only the single thread that is blocked pauses. All other threads continue to run.

Threads exist in several states. A thread can be *running*. It can be *ready to run* as soon as it gets CPU time. A running thread can be *suspended*, which temporarily suspends its activity. A suspended thread can then be *resumed*, allowing it to pick up where it left off. A thread can be *blocked* when waiting for a resource. At any time, a thread can be terminated, which halts its execution immediately. Once terminated, a thread cannot be resumed.

Thread Priorities

Java assigns to each thread a priority that determines how that thread should be treated with respect to the others. Thread priorities are integers that specify the relative priority of one thread to another. As an absolute value, a priority is meaningless; a higher-priority thread doesn't run any faster than a lower-priority thread if it is the only thread running. Instead, a thread's priority is used to decide when to switch from one running thread to the next. This is called a *context switch*. The rules that determine when a context switch takes place are simple:

- *A thread can voluntarily relinquish control.* This is done by explicitly yielding, sleeping, or blocking on pending I/O. In this scenario, all other threads are examined, and the highest-priority thread that is ready to run is given the CPU.

- *A thread can be preempted by a higher-priority thread.* In this case, a lower-priority thread that does not yield the processor is simply preempted—no matter what it is doing— by a higher-priority thread. Basically, as soon as a higher-priority thread wants to run, it does. This is called *preemptive multitasking.*

In cases where two threads with the same priority are competing for CPU cycles, the situation is a bit complicated. For operating systems such as Windows, threads of equal priority are time-sliced automatically in round-robin fashion. For other types of operating systems, threads of equal priority must voluntarily yield control to their peers. If they don't, the other threads will not run.

CAUTION *Portability problems can arise from the differences in the way that operating systems context-switch threads of equal priority.*

Synchronization

Because multithreading introduces an asynchronous behavior to your programs, there must be a way for you to enforce synchronicity when you need it. For example, if you want two threads to communicate and share a complicated data structure, such as a linked list, you need some way to ensure that they don't conflict with each other. That is, you must prevent one thread from writing data while another thread is in the middle of reading it. For this purpose, Java implements an elegant twist on an age-old model of interprocess synchronization: the *monitor.* The monitor is a control mechanism first defined by C.A.R. Hoare. You can think of a monitor as a very small box that can hold only one thread. Once a thread enters a monitor, all other threads must wait until that thread exits the monitor. In this way, a monitor can be used to protect a shared asset from being manipulated by more than one thread at a time.

Most multithreaded systems expose monitors as objects that your program must explicitly acquire and manipulate. Java provides a cleaner solution. There is no class "Monitor"; instead, each object has its own implicit monitor that is automatically entered when one of the object's synchronized methods is called. Once a thread is inside a synchronized method, no other thread can call any other synchronized method on the same object. This enables you to write very clear and concise multithreaded code, because synchronization support is built into the language.

Messaging

After you divide your program into separate threads, you need to define how they will communicate with each other. When programming with most other languages, you must depend on the operating system to establish communication between threads. This, of course, adds overhead. By contrast, Java provides a clean, low-cost way for two or more threads to talk to each other, via calls to predefined methods that all objects have. Java's messaging system allows a thread to enter a synchronized method on an object, and then wait there until some other thread explicitly notifies it to come out.

The Thread Class and the Runnable Interface

Java's multithreading system is built upon the **Thread** class, its methods, and its companion interface, **Runnable**. **Thread** encapsulates a thread of execution. Since you can't directly refer to the ethereal state of a running thread, you will deal with it through its proxy, the **Thread** instance that spawned it. To create a new thread, your program will either extend **Thread** or implement the **Runnable** interface.

The **Thread** class defines several methods that help manage threads. The ones that will be used in this chapter are shown here:

Method	Meaning
getName	Obtain a thread's name.
getPriority	Obtain a thread's priority.
isAlive	Determine if a thread is still running.
join	Wait for a thread to terminate.
run	Entry point for the thread.
sleep	Suspend a thread for a period of time.
start	Start a thread by calling its run method.

Thus far, all the examples in this book have used a single thread of execution. The remainder of this chapter explains how to use **Thread** and **Runnable** to create and manage threads, beginning with the one thread that all Java programs have: the main thread.

The Main Thread

When a Java program starts up, one thread begins running immediately. This is usually called the *main thread* of your program, because it is the one that is executed when your program begins. The main thread is important for two reasons:

- It is the thread from which other "child" threads will be spawned.
- Often, it must be the last thread to finish execution because it performs various shutdown actions.

Although the main thread is created automatically when your program is started, it can be controlled through a **Thread** object. To do so, you must obtain a reference to it by calling the method **currentThread( )**, which is a **public static** member of **Thread**. Its general form is shown here:

static Thread currentThread( )

This method returns a reference to the thread in which it is called. Once you have a reference to the main thread, you can control it just like any other thread.

Let's begin by reviewing the following example:

```
// Controlling the main Thread.
class CurrentThreadDemo {
  public static void main(String args[]) {
    Thread t = Thread.currentThread();

    System.out.println("Current thread: " + t);

    // change the name of the thread
    t.setName("My Thread");
    System.out.println("After name change: " + t);

    try {
      for(int n = 5; n > 0; n--) {
        System.out.println(n);
        Thread.sleep(1000);
      }
    } catch (InterruptedException e) {
      System.out.println("Main thread interrupted");
    }
  }
}
```

In this program, a reference to the current thread (the main thread, in this case) is obtained by calling **currentThread( )**, and this reference is stored in the local variable **t**. Next, the program displays information about the thread. The program then calls **setName( )** to change the internal name of the thread. Information about the thread is then redisplayed. Next, a loop counts down from five, pausing one second between each line. The pause is accomplished by the **sleep( )** method. The argument to **sleep( )** specifies the delay period in milliseconds. Notice the **try/catch** block around this loop. The **sleep( )** method in **Thread** might throw an **InterruptedException**. This would happen if some other thread wanted to interrupt this sleeping one. This example just prints a message if it gets interrupted. In a real program, you would need to handle this differently. Here is the output generated by this program:

```
Current thread: Thread[main,5,main]
After name change: Thread[My Thread,5,main]
5
4
3
2
1
```

Notice the output produced when **t** is used as an argument to **println( )**. This displays, in order: the name of the thread, its priority, and the name of its group. By default, the name of the main thread is **main**. Its priority is 5, which is the default value, and **main** is also the name of the group of threads to which this thread belongs. A *thread group* is a data structure that controls the state of a collection of threads as a whole. After the name of the thread is changed, **t** is again output. This time, the new name of the thread is displayed.

Let's look more closely at the methods defined by **Thread** that are used in the program. The **sleep( )** method causes the thread from which it is called to suspend execution for the specified period of milliseconds. Its general form is shown here:

static void sleep(long *milliseconds*) throws InterruptedException

The number of milliseconds to suspend is specified in *milliseconds*. This method may throw an **InterruptedException**.

The **sleep( )** method has a second form, shown next, which allows you to specify the period in terms of milliseconds and nanoseconds:

static void sleep(long *milliseconds,* int *nanoseconds*) throws InterruptedException

This second form is useful only in environments that allow timing periods as short as nanoseconds.

As the preceding program shows, you can set the name of a thread by using **setName( )**. You can obtain the name of a thread by calling **getName( )** (but note that this is not shown in the program). These methods are members of the **Thread** class and are declared like this:

final void setName(String *threadName*)

final String getName( )

Here, *threadName* specifies the name of the thread.

Creating a Thread

In the most general sense, you create a thread by instantiating an object of type **Thread**. Java defines two ways in which this can be accomplished:

- You can implement the **Runnable** interface.
- You can extend the **Thread** class, itself.

The following two sections look at each method, in turn.

Implementing Runnable

The easiest way to create a thread is to create a class that implements the **Runnable** interface. **Runnable** abstracts a unit of executable code. You can construct a thread on any object that implements **Runnable**. To implement **Runnable**, a class need only implement a single method called **run( )**, which is declared like this:

public void run( )

Inside **run( )**, you will define the code that constitutes the new thread. It is important to understand that **run( )** can call other methods, use other classes, and declare variables, just like the main thread can. The only difference is that **run( )** establishes the entry point for another, concurrent thread of execution within your program. This thread will end when **run( )** returns.

After you create a class that implements **Runnable**, you will instantiate an object of type **Thread** from within that class. **Thread** defines several constructors. The one that we will use is shown here:

Thread(Runnable *threadOb*, String *threadName*)

In this constructor, *threadOb* is an instance of a class that implements the **Runnable** interface. This defines where execution of the thread will begin. The name of the new thread is specified by *threadName*.

After the new thread is created, it will not start running until you call its **start( )** method, which is declared within **Thread**. In essence, **start( )** executes a call to **run( )**. The **start( )** method is shown here:

void start( )

Here is an example that creates a new thread and starts it running:

```
// Create a second thread.
class NewThread implements Runnable {
  Thread t;

  NewThread() {
    // Create a new, second thread
    t = new Thread(this, "Demo Thread");
    System.out.println("Child thread: " + t);
    t.start(); // Start the thread
  }

  // This is the entry point for the second thread.
  public void run() {
    try {
      for(int i = 5; i > 0; i--) {
        System.out.println("Child Thread: " + i);
        Thread.sleep(500);
      }
    } catch (InterruptedException e) {
      System.out.println("Child interrupted.");
    }
    System.out.println("Exiting child thread.");
  }
}

class ThreadDemo {
  public static void main(String args[]) {
    new NewThread(); // create a new thread

    try {
      for(int i = 5; i > 0; i--) {
        System.out.println("Main Thread: " + i);
        Thread.sleep(1000);
      }
    } catch (InterruptedException e) {
```

```
    System.out.println("Main thread interrupted.");
  }
  System.out.println("Main thread exiting.");
 }
}
```

Inside **NewThread**'s constructor, a new **Thread** object is created by the following statement:

```
t = new Thread(this, "Demo Thread");
```

Passing **this** as the first argument indicates that you want the new thread to call the **run( )** method on **this** object. Next, **start( )** is called, which starts the thread of execution beginning at the **run( )** method. This causes the child thread's **for** loop to begin. After calling **start( )**, **NewThread**'s constructor returns to **main( )**. When the main thread resumes, it enters its **for** loop. Both threads continue running, sharing the CPU, until their loops finish. The output produced by this program is as follows. (Your output may vary based on processor speed and task load.)

```
Child thread: Thread[Demo Thread,5,main]
Main Thread: 5
Child Thread: 5
Child Thread: 4
Main Thread: 4
Child Thread: 3
Child Thread: 2
Main Thread: 3
Child Thread: 1
Exiting child thread.
Main Thread: 2
Main Thread: 1
Main thread exiting.
```

As mentioned earlier, in a multithreaded program, often the main thread must be the last thread to finish running. In fact, for some older JVMs, if the main thread finishes before a child thread has completed, then the Java run-time system may "hang." The preceding program ensures that the main thread finishes last, because the main thread sleeps for 1,000 milliseconds between iterations, but the child thread sleeps for only 500 milliseconds. This causes the child thread to terminate earlier than the main thread. Shortly, you will see a better way to wait for a thread to finish.

Extending Thread

The second way to create a thread is to create a new class that extends **Thread**, and then to create an instance of that class. The extending class must override the **run( )** method, which is the entry point for the new thread. It must also call **start( )** to begin execution of the new thread. Here is the preceding program rewritten to extend **Thread**:

```
// Create a second thread by extending Thread
class NewThread extends Thread {

  NewThread() {
    // Create a new, second thread
    super("Demo Thread");
    System.out.println("Child thread: " + this);
    start(); // Start the thread
  }

  // This is the entry point for the second thread.
  public void run() {
    try {
      for(int i = 5; i > 0; i--) {
        System.out.println("Child Thread: " + i);
        Thread.sleep(500);
      }
    } catch (InterruptedException e) {
      System.out.println("Child interrupted.");
    }
    System.out.println("Exiting child thread.");
  }
}

class ExtendThread {
  public static void main(String args[]) {
    new NewThread(); // create a new thread

    try {
      for(int i = 5; i > 0; i--) {
        System.out.println("Main Thread: " + i);
        Thread.sleep(1000);
      }
    } catch (InterruptedException e) {
      System.out.println("Main thread interrupted.");
    }
    System.out.println("Main thread exiting.");
  }
}
```

This program generates the same output as the preceding version. As you can see, the child thread is created by instantiating an object of **NewThread**, which is derived from **Thread**.

Notice the call to **super( )** inside **NewThread**. This invokes the following form of the **Thread** constructor:

public Thread(String *threadName*)

Here, *threadName* specifies the name of the thread.

Choosing an Approach

At this point, you might be wondering why Java has two ways to create child threads, and which approach is better. The answers to these questions turn on the same point. The **Thread** class defines several methods that can be overridden by a derived class. Of these methods, the only one that *must* be overridden is **run( )**. This is, of course, the same method required when you implement **Runnable**. Many Java programmers feel that classes should be extended only when they are being enhanced or modified in some way. So, if you will not be overriding any of **Thread**'s other methods, it is probably best simply to implement **Runnable**. This is up to you, of course. However, throughout the rest of this chapter, we will create threads by using classes that implement **Runnable**.

Creating Multiple Threads

So far, you have been using only two threads: the main thread and one child thread. However, your program can spawn as many threads as it needs. For example, the following program creates three child threads:

```
// Create multiple threads.
class NewThread implements Runnable {
  String name; // name of thread
  Thread t;

  NewThread(String threadname) {
    name = threadname;
    t = new Thread(this, name);
    System.out.println("New thread: " + t);
    t.start(); // Start the thread
  }

  // This is the entry point for thread.
  public void run() {
    try {
      for(int i = 5; i > 0; i--) {
        System.out.println(name + ": " + i);
        Thread.sleep(1000);
      }
    } catch (InterruptedException e) {
      System.out.println(name + "Interrupted");
    }
    System.out.println(name + " exiting.");
  }
}

class MultiThreadDemo {
  public static void main(String args[]) {
    new NewThread("One"); // start threads
    new NewThread("Two");
    new NewThread("Three");
```

```
    try {
      // wait for other threads to end
      Thread.sleep(10000);
    } catch (InterruptedException e) {
      System.out.println("Main thread Interrupted");
    }

    System.out.println("Main thread exiting.");
  }
}
```

The output from this program is shown here:

```
New thread: Thread[One,5,main]
New thread: Thread[Two,5,main]
New thread: Thread[Three,5,main]
One: 5
Two: 5
Three: 5
One: 4
Two: 4
Three: 4
One: 3
Three: 3
Two: 3
One: 2
Three: 2
Two: 2
One: 1
Three: 1
Two: 1
One exiting.
Two exiting.
Three exiting.
Main thread exiting.
```

As you can see, once started, all three child threads share the CPU. Notice the call to
sleep(10000) in **main( )**. This causes the main thread to sleep for ten seconds and ensures
that it will finish last.

Using isAlive( ) and join( )

As mentioned, often you will want the main thread to finish last. In the preceding examples,
this is accomplished by calling **sleep( )** within **main( )**, with a long enough delay to ensure
that all child threads terminate prior to the main thread. However, this is hardly a satisfactory
solution, and it also raises a larger question: How can one thread know when another thread
has ended? Fortunately, **Thread** provides a means by which you can answer this question.

Two ways exist to determine whether a thread has finished. First, you can call **isAlive( )** on the thread. This method is defined by **Thread**, and its general form is shown here:

final boolean isAlive( )

The **isAlive( )** method returns **true** if the thread upon which it is called is still running. It returns **false** otherwise.

While **isAlive( )** is occasionally useful, the method that you will more commonly use to wait for a thread to finish is called **join( )**, shown here:

final void join( ) throws InterruptedException

This method waits until the thread on which it is called terminates. Its name comes from the concept of the calling thread waiting until the specified thread *joins* it. Additional forms of **join( )** allow you to specify a maximum amount of time that you want to wait for the specified thread to terminate.

Here is an improved version of the preceding example that uses **join( )** to ensure that the main thread is the last to stop. It also demonstrates the **isAlive( )** method.

```
// Using join() to wait for threads to finish.
class NewThread implements Runnable {
  String name; // name of thread
  Thread t;

  NewThread(String threadname) {
    name = threadname;
    t = new Thread(this, name);
    System.out.println("New thread: " + t);
    t.start(); // Start the thread
  }

  // This is the entry point for thread.
  public void run() {
    try {
      for(int i = 5; i > 0; i--) {
        System.out.println(name + ": " + i);
        Thread.sleep(1000);
      }
    } catch (InterruptedException e) {
      System.out.println(name + " interrupted.");
    }
    System.out.println(name + " exiting.");
  }
}

class DemoJoin {
  public static void main(String args[]) {
    NewThread ob1 = new NewThread("One");
    NewThread ob2 = new NewThread("Two");
    NewThread ob3 = new NewThread("Three");
```

```
      System.out.println("Thread One is alive: "
                          + ob1.t.isAlive());
      System.out.println("Thread Two is alive: "
                          + ob2.t.isAlive());
      System.out.println("Thread Three is alive: "
                          + ob3.t.isAlive());
    // wait for threads to finish
    try {
      System.out.println("Waiting for threads to finish.");
      ob1.t.join();
      ob2.t.join();
      ob3.t.join();
    } catch (InterruptedException e) {
      System.out.println("Main thread Interrupted");
    }

      System.out.println("Thread One is alive: "
                          + ob1.t.isAlive());
      System.out.println("Thread Two is alive: "
                          + ob2.t.isAlive());
      System.out.println("Thread Three is alive: "
                          + ob3.t.isAlive());

      System.out.println("Main thread exiting.");
  }
}
```

Sample output from this program is shown here. (Your output may vary based on processor speed and task load.)

```
New thread: Thread[One,5,main]
New thread: Thread[Two,5,main]
New thread: Thread[Three,5,main]
Thread One is alive: true
Thread Two is alive: true
Thread Three is alive: true
Waiting for threads to finish.
One: 5
Two: 5
Three: 5
One: 4
Two: 4
Three: 4
One: 3
Two: 3
Three: 3
One: 2
Two: 2
Three: 2
```

```
One: 1
Two: 1
Three: 1
Two exiting.
Three exiting.
One exiting.
Thread One is alive: false
Thread Two is alive: false
Thread Three is alive: false
Main thread exiting.
```

As you can see, after the calls to **join( )** return, the threads have stopped executing.

Thread Priorities

Thread priorities are used by the thread scheduler to decide when each thread should be allowed to run. In theory, higher-priority threads get more CPU time than lower-priority threads. In practice, the amount of CPU time that a thread gets often depends on several factors besides its priority. (For example, how an operating system implements multitasking can affect the relative availability of CPU time.) A higher-priority thread can also preempt a lower-priority one. For instance, when a lower-priority thread is running and a higher-priority thread resumes (from sleeping or waiting on I/O, for example), it will preempt the lower-priority thread.

In theory, threads of equal priority should get equal access to the CPU. But you need to be careful. Remember, Java is designed to work in a wide range of environments. Some of those environments implement multitasking fundamentally differently than others. For safety, threads that share the same priority should yield control once in a while. This ensures that all threads have a chance to run under a nonpreemptive operating system. In practice, even in nonpreemptive environments, most threads still get a chance to run, because most threads inevitably encounter some blocking situation, such as waiting for I/O. When this happens, the blocked thread is suspended and other threads can run. But, if you want smooth multithreaded execution, you are better off not relying on this. Also, some types of tasks are CPU-intensive. Such threads dominate the CPU. For these types of threads, you want to yield control occasionally so that other threads can run.

To set a thread's priority, use the **setPriority( )** method, which is a member of **Thread**. This is its general form:

final void setPriority(int *level*)

Here, *level* specifies the new priority setting for the calling thread. The value of *level* must be within the range **MIN_PRIORITY** and **MAX_PRIORITY**. Currently, these values are 1 and 10, respectively. To return a thread to default priority, specify **NORM_PRIORITY**, which is currently 5. These priorities are defined as **static final** variables within **Thread**.

You can obtain the current priority setting by calling the **getPriority( )** method of **Thread**, shown here:

final int getPriority( )

Implementations of Java may have radically different behavior when it comes to scheduling. The Windows XP/98/NT/2000 versions work, more or less, as you would expect. However, other versions may work quite differently. Most of the inconsistencies arise when you have threads that are relying on preemptive behavior, instead of cooperatively giving up CPU time. The safest way to obtain predictable, cross-platform behavior with Java is to use threads that voluntarily give up control of the CPU.

The following example demonstrates two threads at different priorities, which do not run on a preemptive platform in the same way as they run on a nonpreemptive platform. One thread is set two levels above the normal priority, as defined by **Thread.NORM_ PRIORITY**, and the other is set to two levels below it. The threads are started and allowed to run for ten seconds. Each thread executes a loop, counting the number of iterations. After ten seconds, the main thread stops both threads. The number of times that each thread made it through the loop is then displayed.

```
// Demonstrate thread priorities.
class clicker implements Runnable {
  long click = 0;
  Thread t;
  private volatile boolean running = true;

  public clicker(int p) {
    t = new Thread(this);
    t.setPriority(p);
  }

  public void run() {
    while (running) {
      click++;
    }
  }

  public void stop() {
    running = false;
  }

  public void start() {
    t.start();
  }
}

class HiLoPri {
  public static void main(String args[]) {
    Thread.currentThread().setPriority(Thread.MAX_PRIORITY);
    clicker hi = new clicker(Thread.NORM_PRIORITY + 2);
    clicker lo = new clicker(Thread.NORM_PRIORITY - 2);

    lo.start();
    hi.start();
    try {
      Thread.sleep(10000);
    } catch (InterruptedException e) {
      System.out.println("Main thread interrupted.");
    }
```

```
      lo.stop();
      hi.stop();

      // Wait for child threads to terminate.
      try {
        hi.t.join();
        lo.t.join();
      } catch (InterruptedException e) {
        System.out.println("InterruptedException caught");
      }

      System.out.println("Low-priority thread: " + lo.click);
      System.out.println("High-priority thread: " + hi.click);
    }
}
```

The output of this program, shown as follows when run under Windows, indicates that the threads did context switch, even though neither voluntarily yielded the CPU nor blocked for I/O. The higher-priority thread got the majority of the CPU time.

```
Low-priority thread: 4408112
High-priority thread: 589626904
```

Of course, the exact output produced by this program depends on the speed of your CPU and the number of other tasks running in the system. When this same program is run under a nonpreemptive system, different results will be obtained.

One other note about the preceding program. Notice that **running** is preceded by the keyword **volatile**. Although **volatile** is examined more carefully in Chapter 13, it is used here to ensure that the value of **running** is examined each time the following loop iterates:

```
while (running) {
  click++;
}
```

Without the use of **volatile**, Java is free to optimize the loop in such a way that a local copy of **running** is created. The use of **volatile** prevents this optimization, telling Java that **running** may change in ways not directly apparent in the immediate code.

Synchronization

When two or more threads need access to a shared resource, they need some way to ensure that the resource will be used by only one thread at a time. The process by which this is achieved is called *synchronization*. As you will see, Java provides unique, language-level support for it.

Key to synchronization is the concept of the monitor (also called a *semaphore*). A *monitor* is an object that is used as a mutually exclusive lock, or *mutex*. Only one thread can *own* a monitor at a given time. When a thread acquires a lock, it is said to have *entered* the monitor. All other threads attempting to enter the locked monitor will be suspended until the first thread *exits* the monitor. These other threads are said to be *waiting* for the monitor. A thread that owns a monitor can reenter the same monitor if it so desires.

If you have worked with synchronization when using other languages, such as C or C++, you know that it can be a bit tricky to use. This is because these languages do not, themselves, support synchronization. Instead, to synchronize threads, your programs need to utilize operating system primitives. Fortunately, because Java implements synchronization through language elements, most of the complexity associated with synchronization has been eliminated.

You can synchronize your code in either of two ways. Both involve the use of the **synchronized** keyword, and both are examined here.

Using Synchronized Methods

Synchronization is easy in Java, because all objects have their own implicit monitor associated with them. To enter an object's monitor, just call a method that has been modified with the **synchronized** keyword. While a thread is inside a synchronized method, all other threads that try to call it (or any other synchronized method) on the same instance have to wait. To exit the monitor and relinquish control of the object to the next waiting thread, the owner of the monitor simply returns from the synchronized method.

To understand the need for synchronization, let's begin with a simple example that does not use it—but should. The following program has three simple classes. The first one, **Callme**, has a single method named **call( )**. The **call( )** method takes a **String** parameter called **msg**. This method tries to print the **msg** string inside of square brackets. The interesting thing to notice is that after **call( )** prints the opening bracket and the **msg** string, it calls **Thread .sleep(1000)**, which pauses the current thread for one second.

The constructor of the next class, **Caller**, takes a reference to an instance of the **Callme** class and a **String**, which are stored in **target** and **msg**, respectively. The constructor also creates a new thread that will call this object's **run( )** method. The thread is started immediately. The **run( )** method of **Caller** calls the **call( )** method on the **target** instance of **Callme**, passing in the **msg** string. Finally, the **Synch** class starts by creating a single instance of **Callme**, and three instances of **Caller**, each with a unique message string. The same instance of **Callme** is passed to each **Caller**.

```
// This program is not synchronized.
class Callme {
  void call(String msg) {
    System.out.print("[" + msg);
    try {
      Thread.sleep(1000);
    } catch(InterruptedException e) {
      System.out.println("Interrupted");
    }
    System.out.println("]");
  }
}

class Caller implements Runnable {
  String msg;
  Callme target;
  Thread t;
```

```
  public Caller(Callme targ, String s) {
    target = targ;
    msg = s;
    t = new Thread(this);
    t.start();
  }

  public void run() {
    target.call(msg);
  }
}

class Synch {
  public static void main(String args[]) {
    Callme target = new Callme();
    Caller ob1 = new Caller(target, "Hello");
    Caller ob2 = new Caller(target, "Synchronized");
    Caller ob3 = new Caller(target, "World");

    // wait for threads to end
    try {
      ob1.t.join();
      ob2.t.join();
      ob3.t.join();
    } catch(InterruptedException e) {
      System.out.println("Interrupted");
    }
  }
}
```

Here is the output produced by this program:

```
Hello[Synchronized[World]
]
]
```

As you can see, by calling **sleep( )**, the **call( )** method allows execution to switch to another thread. This results in the mixed-up output of the three message strings. In this program, nothing exists to stop all three threads from calling the same method, on the same object, at the same time. This is known as a *race condition*, because the three threads are racing each other to complete the method. This example used **sleep( )** to make the effects repeatable and obvious. In most situations, a race condition is more subtle and less predictable, because you can't be sure when the context switch will occur. This can cause a program to run right one time and wrong the next.

To fix the preceding program, you must *serialize* access to **call( )**. That is, you must restrict its access to only one thread at a time. To do this, you simply need to precede **call( )**'s definition with the keyword **synchronized**, as shown here:

```
class Callme {
    synchronized void call(String msg) {
      ...
```

This prevents other threads from entering **call( )** while another thread is using it. After **synchronized** has been added to **call( )**, the output of the program is as follows:

```
[Hello]
[Synchronized]
[World]
```

Any time that you have a method, or group of methods, that manipulates the internal state of an object in a multithreaded situation, you should use the **synchronized** keyword to guard the state from race conditions. Remember, once a thread enters any synchronized method on an instance, no other thread can enter any other synchronized method on the same instance. However, nonsynchronized methods on that instance will continue to be callable.

The synchronized Statement

While creating **synchronized** methods within classes that you create is an easy and effective means of achieving synchronization, it will not work in all cases. To understand why, consider the following. Imagine that you want to synchronize access to objects of a class that was not designed for multithreaded access. That is, the class does not use **synchronized** methods. Further, this class was not created by you, but by a third party, and you do not have access to the source code. Thus, you can't add **synchronized** to the appropriate methods within the class. How can access to an object of this class be synchronized? Fortunately, the solution to this problem is quite easy: You simply put calls to the methods defined by this class inside a **synchronized** block.

This is the general form of the **synchronized** statement:

```
synchronized(object) {
   // statements to be synchronized
   }
```

Here, *object* is a reference to the object being synchronized. A synchronized block ensures that a call to a method that is a member of *object* occurs only after the current thread has successfully entered *object*'s monitor.

Here is an alternative version of the preceding example, using a synchronized block within the **run( )** method:

```
// This program uses a synchronized block.
class Callme {
  void call(String msg) {
    System.out.print("[" + msg);
    try {
      Thread.sleep(1000);
    } catch (InterruptedException e) {
      System.out.println("Interrupted");
    }
    System.out.println("]");
  }
}

class Caller implements Runnable {
  String msg;
```

```
  Callme target;
  Thread t;

  public Caller(Callme targ, String s) {
    target = targ;
    msg = s;
    t = new Thread(this);
    t.start();
  }

  // synchronize calls to call()
  public void run() {
    synchronized(target) { // synchronized block
      target.call(msg);
    }
  }
}

class Synch1 {
  public static void main(String args[]) {
    Callme target = new Callme();
    Caller ob1 = new Caller(target, "Hello");
    Caller ob2 = new Caller(target, "Synchronized");
    Caller ob3 = new Caller(target, "World");

    // wait for threads to end
    try {
      ob1.t.join();
      ob2.t.join();
      ob3.t.join();
    } catch(InterruptedException e) {
      System.out.println("Interrupted");
    }
  }
}
```

Here, the **call( )** method is not modified by **synchronized**. Instead, the **synchronized** statement is used inside **Caller**'s **run( )** method. This causes the same correct output as the preceding example, because each thread waits for the prior one to finish before proceeding.

Interthread Communication

The preceding examples unconditionally blocked other threads from asynchronous access to certain methods. This use of the implicit monitors in Java objects is powerful, but you can achieve a more subtle level of control through interprocess communication. As you will see, this is especially easy in Java.

As discussed earlier, multithreading replaces event loop programming by dividing your tasks into discrete, logical units. Threads also provide a secondary benefit: they do away with polling. Polling is usually implemented by a loop that is used to check some condition repeatedly. Once the condition is true, appropriate action is taken. This wastes CPU time. For example, consider the classic queuing problem, where one thread is producing some data and another is consuming it. To make the problem more interesting, suppose that the producer has to wait until the consumer is finished before it generates more data. In a polling system, the consumer would waste many CPU cycles while it waited for the producer to produce. Once the producer was finished, it would start polling, wasting more CPU cycles waiting for the consumer to finish, and so on. Clearly, this situation is undesirable.

To avoid polling, Java includes an elegant interprocess communication mechanism via the **wait( )**, **notify( )**, and **notifyAll( )** methods. These methods are implemented as **final** methods in **Object**, so all classes have them. All three methods can be called only from within a **synchronized** context. Although conceptually advanced from a computer science perspective, the rules for using these methods are actually quite simple:

- **wait( )** tells the calling thread to give up the monitor and go to sleep until some other thread enters the same monitor and calls **notify( )**.

- **notify( )** wakes up a thread that called **wait( )** on the same object.

- **notifyAll( )** wakes up all the threads that called **wait( )** on the same object. One of the threads will be granted access.

These methods are declared within **Object**, as shown here:

```
final void wait( ) throws InterruptedException
final void notify( )
final void notifyAll( )
```

Additional forms of **wait( )** exist that allow you to specify a period of time to wait.

Before working through an example that illustrates interthread communication, an important point needs to be made. Although **wait( )** normally waits until **notify( )** or **notifyAll( )** is called, there is a possibility that in very rare cases the waiting thread could be awakened due to a *spurious wakeup*. In this case, a waiting thread resumes without **notify( )** or **notifyAll( )** having been called. (In essence, the thread resumes for no apparent reason.) Because of this remote possibility, Sun recommends that calls to **wait( )** should take place within a loop that checks the condition on which the thread is waiting. The following example shows this technique.

Let's now work through an example that uses **wait( )** and **notify( )**. To begin, consider the following sample program that incorrectly implements a simple form of the producer/consumer problem. It consists of four classes: **Q**, the queue that you're trying to synchronize; **Producer**, the threaded object that is producing queue entries; **Consumer**, the threaded object that is consuming queue entries; and **PC**, the tiny class that creates the single **Q**, **Producer**, and **Consumer**.

```java
// An incorrect implementation of a producer and consumer.
class Q {
  int n;

  synchronized int get() {
    System.out.println("Got: " + n);
    return n;
  }

  synchronized void put(int n) {
    this.n = n;
    System.out.println("Put: " + n);
  }
}
```

```
class Producer implements Runnable {
  Q q;

  Producer(Q q) {
    this.q = q;
    new Thread(this, "Producer").start();
  }

  public void run() {
    int i = 0;

    while(true) {
      q.put(i++);
    }
  }
}

class Consumer implements Runnable {
  Q q;

  Consumer(Q q) {
    this.q = q;
    new Thread(this, "Consumer").start();
  }

  public void run() {
    while(true) {
      q.get();
    }
  }
}

class PC {
  public static void main(String args[]) {
    Q q = new Q();
    new Producer(q);
    new Consumer(q);

    System.out.println("Press Control-C to stop.");
  }
}
```

Although the **put( )** and **get( )** methods on **Q** are synchronized, nothing stops the producer from overrunning the consumer, nor will anything stop the consumer from consuming the same queue value twice. Thus, you get the erroneous output shown here (the exact output will vary with processor speed and task load):

```
Put: 1
Got: 1
Got: 1
Got: 1
Got: 1
```

```
Got: 1
Put: 2
Put: 3
Put: 4
Put: 5
Put: 6
Put: 7
Got: 7
```

As you can see, after the producer put 1, the consumer started and got the same 1 five times in a row. Then, the producer resumed and produced 2 through 7 without letting the consumer have a chance to consume them.

The proper way to write this program in Java is to use **wait( )** and **notify( )** to signal in both directions, as shown here:

```
// A correct implementation of a producer and consumer.
class Q {
  int n;
  boolean valueSet = false;

  synchronized int get() {
    while(!valueSet)
      try {
        wait();

      } catch(InterruptedException e) {
        System.out.println("InterruptedException caught");
      }

      System.out.println("Got: " + n);
      valueSet = false;
      notify();
      return n;
  }

  synchronized void put(int n) {
    while(valueSet)
      try {
        wait();
      } catch(InterruptedException e) {
        System.out.println("InterruptedException caught");
      }

      this.n = n;
      valueSet = true;
      System.out.println("Put: " + n);
      notify();
  }
}

class Producer implements Runnable {
  Q q;
```

```
    Producer(Q q) {
      this.q = q;
      new Thread(this, "Producer").start();
    }

    public void run() {
      int i = 0;

      while(true) {
        q.put(i++);
      }
    }
}

class Consumer implements Runnable {
  Q q;

  Consumer(Q q) {
    this.q = q;
    new Thread(this, "Consumer").start();
  }

  public void run() {
    while(true) {
      q.get();
    }
  }
}

class PCFixed {
  public static void main(String args[]) {
    Q q = new Q();
    new Producer(q);
    new Consumer(q);

    System.out.println("Press Control-C to stop.");
  }
}
```

Inside **get( )**, **wait( )** is called. This causes its execution to suspend until the **Producer** notifies you that some data is ready. When this happens, execution inside **get( )** resumes. After the data has been obtained, **get( )** calls **notify( )**. This tells **Producer** that it is okay to put more data in the queue. Inside **put( )**, **wait( )** suspends execution until the **Consumer** has removed the item from the queue. When execution resumes, the next item of data is put in the queue, and **notify( )** is called. This tells the **Consumer** that it should now remove it.

Here is some output from this program, which shows the clean synchronous behavior:

```
    Put: 1
    Got: 1
    Put: 2
    Got: 2
    Put: 3
```

```
Got:  3
Put:  4
Got:  4
Put:  5
Got:  5
```

Deadlock

A special type of error that you need to avoid that relates specifically to multitasking is *deadlock*, which occurs when two threads have a circular dependency on a pair of synchronized objects. For example, suppose one thread enters the monitor on object X and another thread enters the monitor on object Y. If the thread in X tries to call any synchronized method on Y, it will block as expected. However, if the thread in Y, in turn, tries to call any synchronized method on X, the thread waits forever, because to access X, it would have to release its own lock on Y so that the first thread could complete. Deadlock is a difficult error to debug for two reasons:

- In general, it occurs only rarely, when the two threads time-slice in just the right way.
- It may involve more than two threads and two synchronized objects. (That is, deadlock can occur through a more convoluted sequence of events than just described.)

To understand deadlock fully, it is useful to see it in action. The next example creates two classes, **A** and **B**, with methods **foo( )** and **bar( )**, respectively, which pause briefly before trying to call a method in the other class. The main class, named **Deadlock**, creates an **A** and a **B** instance, and then starts a second thread to set up the deadlock condition. The **foo( )** and **bar( )** methods use **sleep( )** as a way to force the deadlock condition to occur.

```java
// An example of deadlock.
class A {
  synchronized void foo(B b) {
    String name = Thread.currentThread().getName();

    System.out.println(name + " entered A.foo");

    try {
      Thread.sleep(1000);
    } catch(Exception e) {
      System.out.println("A Interrupted");
    }

    System.out.println(name + " trying to call B.last()");
    b.last();
  }

  synchronized void last() {
    System.out.println("Inside A.last");
  }
}

class B {
```

```
  synchronized void bar(A a) {
    String name = Thread.currentThread().getName();
    System.out.println(name + " entered B.bar");

    try {
      Thread.sleep(1000);
    } catch(Exception e) {
      System.out.println("B Interrupted");
    }

    System.out.println(name + " trying to call A.last()");
    a.last();
  }

  synchronized void last() {
    System.out.println("Inside A.last");
  }
}

class Deadlock implements Runnable {
  A a = new A();
  B b = new B();

  Deadlock() {
    Thread.currentThread().setName("MainThread");
    Thread t = new Thread(this, "RacingThread");
    t.start();

    a.foo(b); // get lock on a in this thread.
    System.out.println("Back in main thread");
  }

  public void run() {
    b.bar(a); // get lock on b in other thread.
    System.out.println("Back in other thread");
  }

  public static void main(String args[]) {
    new Deadlock();
  }
}
```

When you run this program, you will see the output shown here:

```
MainThread entered A.foo
RacingThread entered B.bar
MainThread trying to call B.last()
RacingThread trying to call A.last()
```

Because the program has deadlocked, you need to press CTRL-C to end the program. You can see a full thread and monitor cache dump by pressing CTRL-BREAK on a PC . You will see that **RacingThread** owns the monitor on **b**, while it is waiting for the monitor on **a**. At the same time, **MainThread** owns **a** and is waiting to get **b**. This program will never complete. As this example illustrates, if your multithreaded program locks up occasionally, deadlock is one of the first conditions that you should check for.

Suspending, Resuming, and Stopping Threads

Sometimes, suspending execution of a thread is useful. For example, a separate thread can be used to display the time of day. If the user doesn't want a clock, then its thread can be suspended. Whatever the case, suspending a thread is a simple matter. Once suspended, restarting the thread is also a simple matter.

The mechanisms to suspend, stop, and resume threads differ between early versions of Java, such as Java 1.0, and modern versions, beginning with Java 2. Although you should use the modern approach for all new code, you still need to understand how these operations were accomplished for earlier Java environments. For example, you may need to update or maintain older, legacy code. You also need to understand why a change was made. For these reasons, the next section describes the original way that the execution of a thread was controlled, followed by a section that describes the modern approach.

Suspending, Resuming, and Stopping Threads Using Java 1.1 and Earlier

Prior to Java 2, a program used **suspend( )** and **resume( )**, which are methods defined by **Thread**, to pause and restart the execution of a thread. They have the form shown below:

```
final void suspend( )
final void resume( )
```

The following program demonstrates these methods:

```
// Using suspend() and resume().
class NewThread implements Runnable {
  String name; // name of thread
  Thread t;

  NewThread(String threadname) {
    name = threadname;
    t = new Thread(this, name);
    System.out.println("New thread: " + t);
    t.start(); // Start the thread
  }

  // This is the entry point for thread.
  public void run() {
    try {
      for(int i = 15; i > 0; i--) {
        System.out.println(name + ": " + i);
        Thread.sleep(200);
      }
    } catch (InterruptedException e) {
      System.out.println(name + " interrupted.");
    }
    System.out.println(name + " exiting.");
  }
}
```

```
class SuspendResume {
  public static void main(String args[]) {
    NewThread ob1 = new NewThread("One");
    NewThread ob2 = new NewThread("Two");

    try {
      Thread.sleep(1000);
      ob1.t.suspend();
      System.out.println("Suspending thread One");
      Thread.sleep(1000);
      ob1.t.resume();
      System.out.println("Resuming thread One");
      ob2.t.suspend();
      System.out.println("Suspending thread Two");
      Thread.sleep(1000);
      ob2.t.resume();
      System.out.println("Resuming thread Two");
    } catch (InterruptedException e) {
      System.out.println("Main thread Interrupted");
    }

    // wait for threads to finish
    try {
      System.out.println("Waiting for threads to finish.");
      ob1.t.join();
      ob2.t.join();
    } catch (InterruptedException e) {
      System.out.println("Main thread Interrupted");
    }
    System.out.println("Main thread exiting.");
  }
}
```

Sample output from this program is shown here. (Your output may differ based on processor speed and task load.)

```
New thread: Thread[One,5,main]
One: 15
New thread: Thread[Two,5,main]
Two: 15
One: 14
Two: 14
One: 13
Two: 13
One: 12
Two: 12
One: 11
Two: 11
Suspending thread One
Two: 10
Two: 9
Two: 8
```

```
Two: 7
Two: 6
Resuming thread One
Suspending thread Two
One: 10
One: 9
One: 8
One: 7
One: 6
Resuming thread Two
Waiting for threads to finish.
Two: 5
One: 5
Two: 4
One: 4
Two: 3
One: 3
Two: 2
One: 2
Two: 1
One: 1
Two exiting.
One exiting.
Main thread exiting.
```

The **Thread** class also defines a method called **stop( )** that stops a thread. Its signature is shown here:

final void stop( )

Once a thread has been stopped, it cannot be restarted using **resume( )**.

The Modern Way of Suspending, Resuming, and Stopping Threads

While the **suspend( )**, **resume( )**, and **stop( )** methods defined by **Thread** seem to be a perfectly reasonable and convenient approach to managing the execution of threads, they must not be used for new Java programs. Here's why. The **suspend( )** method of the **Thread** class was deprecated by Java 2 several years ago. This was done because **suspend( )** can sometimes cause serious system failures. Assume that a thread has obtained locks on critical data structures. If that thread is suspended at that point, those locks are not relinquished. Other threads that may be waiting for those resources can be deadlocked.

The **resume( )** method is also deprecated. It does not cause problems, but cannot be used without the **suspend( )** method as its counterpart.

The **stop( )** method of the **Thread** class, too, was deprecated by Java 2. This was done because this method can sometimes cause serious system failures. Assume that a thread is writing to a critically important data structure and has completed only part of its changes. If that thread is stopped at that point, that data structure might be left in a corrupted state.

Because you can't now use the **suspend( )**, **resume( )**, or **stop( )** methods to control a thread, you might be thinking that no way exists to pause, restart, or terminate a thread. But, fortunately, this is not true. Instead, a thread must be designed so that the **run( )** method periodically checks to determine whether that thread should suspend, resume, or stop its own execution. Typically, this is accomplished by establishing a flag variable that indicates the execution state of the thread. As long as this flag is set to "running," the **run( )** method must continue to let the thread execute. If this variable is set to "suspend," the thread must pause. If it is set to "stop," the thread must terminate. Of course, a variety of ways exist in which to write such code, but the central theme will be the same for all programs.

The following example illustrates how the **wait( )** and **notify( )** methods that are inherited from **Object** can be used to control the execution of a thread. This example is similar to the program in the previous section. However, the deprecated method calls have been removed. Let us consider the operation of this program.

The **NewThread** class contains a **boolean** instance variable named **suspendFlag**, which is used to control the execution of the thread. It is initialized to **false** by the constructor. The **run( )** method contains a **synchronized** statement block that checks **suspendFlag**. If that variable is **true**, the **wait( )** method is invoked to suspend the execution of the thread. The **mysuspend( )** method sets **suspendFlag** to **true**. The **myresume( )** method sets **suspendFlag** to **false** and invokes **notify( )** to wake up the thread. Finally, the **main( )** method has been modified to invoke the **mysuspend( )** and **myresume( )** methods.

```
// Suspending and resuming a thread the modern way.
class NewThread implements Runnable {
  String name; // name of thread
  Thread t;
  boolean suspendFlag;

  NewThread(String threadname) {
    name = threadname;
    t = new Thread(this, name);
    System.out.println("New thread: " + t);
    suspendFlag = false;
    t.start(); // Start the thread
  }

  // This is the entry point for thread.
  public void run() {
    try {
      for(int i = 15; i > 0; i--) {
        System.out.println(name + ": " + i);
        Thread.sleep(200);
        synchronized(this) {
          while(suspendFlag) {
            wait();
          }
        }
      }
    } catch (InterruptedException e) {
      System.out.println(name + " interrupted.");
    }
```

```
      System.out.println(name + " exiting.");
    }

  void mysuspend() {
    suspendFlag = true;
  }

  synchronized void myresume() {
    suspendFlag = false;
    notify();
  }
}

class SuspendResume {
  public static void main(String args[]) {
    NewThread ob1 = new NewThread("One");
    NewThread ob2 = new NewThread("Two");

    try {
      Thread.sleep(1000);
      ob1.mysuspend();
      System.out.println("Suspending thread One");
      Thread.sleep(1000);
      ob1.myresume();
      System.out.println("Resuming thread One");
      ob2.mysuspend();
      System.out.println("Suspending thread Two");
      Thread.sleep(1000);
      ob2.myresume();
      System.out.println("Resuming thread Two");
    } catch (InterruptedException e) {
      System.out.println("Main thread Interrupted");
    }

    // wait for threads to finish
    try {
      System.out.println("Waiting for threads to finish.");
      ob1.t.join();
      ob2.t.join();
    } catch (InterruptedException e) {
      System.out.println("Main thread Interrupted");
    }

    System.out.println("Main thread exiting.");
  }
}
```

The output from this program is identical to that shown in the previous section. Later in this book, you will see more examples that use the modern mechanism of thread control. Although this mechanism isn't as "clean" as the old way, nevertheless, it is the way required to ensure that run-time errors don't occur. It is the approach that *must* be used for all new code.

Using Multithreading

The key to utilizing Java's multithreading features effectively is to think concurrently rather than serially. For example, when you have two subsystems within a program that can execute concurrently, make them individual threads. With the careful use of multithreading, you can create very efficient programs. A word of caution is in order, however: If you create too many threads, you can actually degrade the performance of your program rather than enhance it. Remember, some overhead is associated with context switching. If you create too many threads, more CPU time will be spent changing contexts than executing your program!

Enumerations, Autoboxing, and Annotations (Metadata)

This chapter examines three recent additions to the Java language: enumerations, autoboxing, and annotations (also referred to as metadata). Each expands the power of the language by offering a streamlined approach to handling common programming tasks. This chapter also discusses Java's type wrappers and introduces reflection.

Enumerations

Versions prior to JDK 5 lacked one feature that many programmers felt was needed: enumerations. In its simplest form, an *enumeration* is a list of named constants. Although Java offered other features that provide somewhat similar functionality, such as **final** variables, many programmers still missed the conceptual purity of enumerations—especially because enumerations are supported by most other commonly used languages. Beginning with JDK 5, enumerations were added to the Java language, and they are now available to the Java programmer.

In their simplest form, Java enumerations appear similar to enumerations in other languages. However, this similarity is only skin deep. In languages such as C++, enumerations are simply lists of named integer constants. In Java, an enumeration defines a class type. By making enumerations into classes, the concept of the enumeration is greatly expanded. For example, in Java, an enumeration can have constructors, methods, and instance variables. Therefore, although enumerations were several years in the making, Java's rich implementation made them well worth the wait.

Enumeration Fundamentals

An enumeration is created using the **enum** keyword. For example, here is a simple enumeration that lists various apple varieties:

```
// An enumeration of apple varieties.
enum Apple {
  Jonathan, GoldenDel, RedDel, Winesap, Cortland
}
```

The identifiers **Jonathan**, **GoldenDel**, and so on, are called *enumeration constants*. Each is implicitly declared as a public, static final member of **Apple**. Furthermore, their type is the type of the enumeration in which they are declared, which is **Apple** in this case. Thus, in the language of Java, these constants are called *self-typed*, in which "self" refers to the enclosing enumeration.

Once you have defined an enumeration, you can create a variable of that type. However, even though enumerations define a class type, you do not instantiate an **enum** using **new**. Instead, you declare and use an enumeration variable in much the same way as you do one of the primitive types. For example, this declares **ap** as a variable of enumeration type **Apple**:

```
Apple ap;
```

Because **ap** is of type **Apple**, the only values that it can be assigned (or can contain) are those defined by the enumeration. For example, this assigns **ap** the value **RedDel**:

```
ap = Apple.RedDel;
```

Notice that the symbol **RedDel** is preceded by **Apple**.

Two enumeration constants can be compared for equality by using the = = relational operator. For example, this statement compares the value in **ap** with the **GoldenDel** constant:

```
if(ap == Apple.GoldenDel) // ...
```

An enumeration value can also be used to control a **switch** statement. Of course, all of the **case** statements must use constants from the same **enum** as that used by the **switch** expression. For example, this **switch** is perfectly valid:

```
// Use an enum to control a switch statement.
switch(ap) {
  case Jonathan:
    // ...
  case Winesap:
    // ...
```

Notice that in the **case** statements, the names of the enumeration constants are used without being qualified by their enumeration type name. That is, **Winesap**, not **Apple.Winesap**, is used. This is because the type of the enumeration in the **switch** expression has already implicitly specified the **enum** type of the **case** constants. There is no need to qualify the constants in the **case** statements with their **enum** type name. In fact, attempting to do so will cause a compilation error.

When an enumeration constant is displayed, such as in a **println( )** statement, its name is output. For example, given this statement:

```
System.out.println(Apple.Winesap);
```

the name **Winesap** is displayed.

The following program puts together all of the pieces and demonstrates the **Apple** enumeration:

```
// An enumeration of apple varieties.
enum Apple {
  Jonathan, GoldenDel, RedDel, Winesap, Cortland
}

class EnumDemo {
  public static void main(String args[])
  {
    Apple ap;

    ap = Apple.RedDel;

    // Output an enum value.
    System.out.println("Value of ap: " + ap);
    System.out.println();

    ap = Apple.GoldenDel;

    // Compare two enum values.
    if(ap == Apple.GoldenDel)
      System.out.println("ap contains GoldenDel.\n");

    // Use an enum to control a switch statement.
    switch(ap) {
      case Jonathan:
        System.out.println("Jonathan is red.");
        break;
      case GoldenDel:
        System.out.println("Golden Delicious is yellow.");
        break;
      case RedDel:
        System.out.println("Red Delicious is red.");
        break;
      case Winesap:
        System.out.println("Winesap is red.");
        break;
      case Cortland:
        System.out.println("Cortland is red.");
        break;
    }
  }
}
```

The output from the program is shown here:

```
Value of ap: RedDel

ap contains GoldenDel.

Golden Delicious is yellow.
```

The values( ) and valueOf( ) Methods

All enumerations automatically contain two predefined methods: **values( )** and **valueOf( )**.
Their general forms are shown here:

public static *enum-type*[ ] values( )
public static *enum-type* valueOf(String *str*)

The **values( )** method returns an array that contains a list of the enumeration constants. The
valueOf( ) method returns the enumeration constant whose value corresponds to the string
passed in *str*. In both cases, *enum-type* is the type of the enumeration. For example, in the case
of the **Apple** enumeration shown earlier, the return type of **Apple.valueOf("Winesap")** is
Winesap.

The following program demonstrates the **values( )** and **valueOf( )** methods:

```
// Use the built-in enumeration methods.

// An enumeration of apple varieties.
enum Apple {
  Jonathan, GoldenDel, RedDel, Winesap, Cortland
}

class EnumDemo2 {
  public static void main(String args[])
  {
    Apple ap;

    System.out.println("Here are all Apple constants:");

    // use values()
    Apple allapples[] = Apple.values();
    for(Apple a : allapples)
      System.out.println(a);

    System.out.println();

    // use valueOf()
    ap = Apple.valueOf("Winesap");
    System.out.println("ap contains " + ap);

  }
}
```

The output from the program is shown here:

```
Here are all Apple constants:
Jonathan
GoldenDel
RedDel
Winesap
Cortland

ap contains Winesap
```

Notice that this program uses a for-each style **for** loop to cycle through the array of constants obtained by calling **values( )**. For the sake of illustration, the variable **allapples** was created and assigned a reference to the enumeration array. However, this step is not necessary because the **for** could have been written as shown here, eliminating the need for the **allapples** variable:

```
for(Apple a : Apple.values())
  System.out.println(a);
```

Now, notice how the value corresponding to the name **Winesap** was obtained by calling **valueOf( )**.

```
ap = Apple.valueOf("Winesap");
```

As explained, **valueOf( )** returns the enumeration value associated with the name of the constant represented as a string.

NOTE   *C/C++ programmers will notice that Java makes it much easier to translate between the human-readable form of an enumeration constant and its binary value than do these other languages. This is a significant advantage to Java's approach to enumerations.*

Java Enumerations Are Class Types

As explained, a Java enumeration is a class type. Although you don't instantiate an **enum** using **new**, it otherwise has much the same capabilities as other classes. The fact that **enum** defines a class gives powers to the Java enumeration that enumerations in other languages simply do not have. For example, you can give them constructors, add instance variables and methods, and even implement interfaces.

It is important to understand that each enumeration constant is an object of its enumeration type. Thus, when you define a constructor for an **enum**, the constructor is called when each enumeration constant is created. Also, each enumeration constant has its own copy of any instance variables defined by the enumeration. For example, consider the following version of **Apple**:

```
// Use an enum constructor, instance variable, and method.
enum Apple {
  Jonathan(10), GoldenDel(9), RedDel(12), Winesap(15), Cortland(8);

  private int price; // price of each apple

  // Constructor
  Apple(int p) { price = p; }

  int getPrice() { return price; }
}

class EnumDemo3 {
  public static void main(String args[])
  {
    Apple ap;
```

```
    // Display price of Winesap.
    System.out.println("Winesap costs " +
                        Apple.Winesap.getPrice() +
                        " cents.\n");

    // Display all apples and prices.
    System.out.println("All apple prices:");
    for(Apple a : Apple.values())
      System.out.println(a + " costs " + a.getPrice() +
                          " cents.");
  }
}
```

The output is shown here:

```
Winesap costs 15 cents.

All apple prices:
Jonathan costs 10 cents.
GoldenDel costs 9 cents.
RedDel costs 12 cents.
Winesap costs 15 cents.
Cortland costs 8 cents.
```

This version of **Apple** adds three things. The first is the instance variable **price**, which is used to hold the price of each variety of apple. The second is the **Apple** constructor, which is passed the price of an apple. The third is the method **getPrice( )**, which returns the value of **price**.

When the variable **ap** is declared in **main( )**, the constructor for **Apple** is called once for each constant that is specified. Notice how the arguments to the constructor are specified, by putting them inside parentheses after each constant, as shown here:

```
Jonathan(10), GoldenDel(9), RedDel(12), Winesap(15), Cortland(8);
```

These values are passed to the **p** parameter of **Apple( )**, which then assigns this value to **price**. Again, the constructor is called once for each constant.

Because each enumeration constant has its own copy of **price**, you can obtain the price of a specified type of apple by calling **getPrice( )**. For example, in **main( )** the price of a Winesap is obtained by the following call:

```
Apple.Winesap.getPrice()
```

The prices of all varieties are obtained by cycling through the enumeration using a **for** loop. Because there is a copy of **price** for each enumeration constant, the value associated with one constant is separate and distinct from the value associated with another constant. This is a powerful concept, which is only available when enumerations are implemented as classes, as Java does.

Although the preceding example contains only one constructor, an **enum** can offer two or more overloaded forms, just as can any other class. For example, this version of **Apple** provides a default constructor that initializes the price to –1, to indicate that no price data is available:

```
// Use an enum constructor.
enum Apple {
  Jonathan(10), GoldenDel(9), RedDel, Winesap(15), Cortland(8);

  private int price; // price of each apple

  // Constructor
  Apple(int p) { price = p; }

  // Overloaded constructor
  Apple() { price = -1; }

  int getPrice() { return price; }
}
```

Notice that in this version, **RedDel** is not given an argument. This means that the default constructor is called, and **RedDel**'s price variable is given the value –1.

Here are two restrictions that apply to enumerations. First, an enumeration can't inherit another class. Second, an **enum** cannot be a superclass. This means that an **enum** can't be extended. Otherwise, **enum** acts much like any other class type. The key is to remember that each of the enumeration constants is an object of the class in which it is defined.

Enumerations Inherit Enum

Although you can't inherit a superclass when declaring an **enum**, all enumerations automatically inherit one: **java.lang.Enum**. This class defines several methods that are available for use by all enumerations. The **Enum** class is described in detail in Part II, but three of its methods warrant a discussion at this time.

You can obtain a value that indicates an enumeration constant's position in the list of constants. This is called its *ordinal value,* and it is retrieved by calling the **ordinal( )** method, shown here:

final int ordinal( )

It returns the ordinal value of the invoking constant. Ordinal values begin at zero. Thus, in the **Apple** enumeration, **Jonathan** has an ordinal value of zero, **GoldenDel** has an ordinal value of 1, **RedDel** has an ordinal value of 2, and so on.

You can compare the ordinal value of two constants of the same enumeration by using the **compareTo( )** method. It has this general form:

final int compareTo(*enum-type e*)

Here, *enum-type* is the type of the enumeration, and *e* is the constant being compared to the invoking constant. Remember, both the invoking constant and *e* must be of the same enumeration. If the invoking constant has an ordinal value less than *e*'s, then **compareTo( )** returns a negative value. If the two ordinal values are the same, then zero is returned. If the invoking constant has an ordinal value greater than *e*'s, then a positive value is returned.

You can compare for equality an enumeration constant with any other object by using **equals( )**, which overrides the **equals( )** method defined by **Object**. Although **equals( )** can compare an enumeration constant to any other object, those two objects will only be equal if they both refer to the same constant, within the same enumeration. Simply having ordinal values in common will not cause **equals( )** to return true if the two constants are from different enumerations.

Remember, you can compare two enumeration references for equality by using = =.

The following program demonstrates the **ordinal( )**, **compareTo( )**, and **equals( )** methods:

```
// Demonstrate ordinal(), compareTo(), and equals().

// An enumeration of apple varieties.
enum Apple {
  Jonathan, GoldenDel, RedDel, Winesap, Cortland
}

class EnumDemo4 {
  public static void main(String args[])
  {
    Apple ap, ap2, ap3;

    // Obtain all ordinal values using ordinal().
    System.out.println("Here are all apple constants" +
                       " and their ordinal values: ");
    for(Apple a : Apple.values())
      System.out.println(a + " " + a.ordinal());

    ap =  Apple.RedDel;
    ap2 = Apple.GoldenDel;
    ap3 = Apple.RedDel;

    System.out.println();

    // Demonstrate compareTo() and equals()
    if(ap.compareTo(ap2) < 0)
      System.out.println(ap + " comes before " + ap2);

    if(ap.compareTo(ap2) > 0)
      System.out.println(ap2 + " comes before " + ap);

    if(ap.compareTo(ap3) == 0)
      System.out.println(ap + " equals " + ap3);

    System.out.println();

    if(ap.equals(ap2))
      System.out.println("Error!");

    if(ap.equals(ap3))
      System.out.println(ap + " equals " + ap3);

    if(ap == ap3)
      System.out.println(ap + " == " + ap3);

  }
}
```

The output from the program is shown here:

```
Here are all apple constants and their ordinal values:
Jonathan 0
GoldenDel 1
RedDel 2
Winesap 3
Cortland 4

GoldenDel comes before RedDel
RedDel equals RedDel

RedDel equals RedDel
RedDel == RedDel
```

Another Enumeration Example

Before moving on, we will look at a different example that uses an **enum**. In Chapter 9, an automated "decision maker" program was created. In that version, variables called **NO**, **YES**, **MAYBE**, **LATER**, **SOON**, and **NEVER** were declared within an interface and used to represent the possible answers. While there is nothing technically wrong with that approach, the enumeration is a better choice. Here is an improved version of that program that uses an **enum** called **Answers** to define the answers. You should compare this version to the original in Chapter 9.

```
// An improved version of the "Decision Maker"
// program from Chapter 9. This version uses an
// enum, rather than interface variables, to
// represent the answers.

import java.util.Random;

// An enumeration of the possible answers.
enum Answers {
  NO, YES, MAYBE, LATER, SOON, NEVER
}

class Question {
  Random rand = new Random();
  Answers ask() {
    int prob = (int) (100 * rand.nextDouble());

    if (prob < 15)
      return Answers.MAYBE; // 15%
    else if (prob < 30)
      return Answers.NO;    // 15%
    else if (prob < 60)
      return Answers.YES;   // 30%
    else if (prob < 75)
      return Answers.LATER; // 15%
    else if (prob < 98)
      return Answers.SOON;  // 13%
```

```
      else
        return Answers.NEVER; // 2%
  }
}

class AskMe {
  static void answer(Answers result) {
    switch(result) {
      case NO:
        System.out.println("No");
        break;
      case YES:
        System.out.println("Yes");
        break;
      case MAYBE:
        System.out.println("Maybe");
        break;
      case LATER:
        System.out.println("Later");
        break;
      case SOON:
        System.out.println("Soon");
        break;
      case NEVER:
        System.out.println("Never");
        break;
    }
  }

  public static void main(String args[]) {
    Question q = new Question();
    answer(q.ask());
    answer(q.ask());
    answer(q.ask());
    answer(q.ask());
  }
}
```

Type Wrappers

As you know, Java uses primitive types (also called simple types), such as **int** or **double**, to hold the basic data types supported by the language. Primitive types, rather than objects, are used for these quantities for the sake of performance. Using objects for these values would add an unacceptable overhead to even the simplest of calculations. Thus, the primitive types are not part of the object hierarchy, and they do not inherit **Object**.

Despite the performance benefit offered by the primitive types, there are times when you will need an object representation. For example, you can't pass a primitive type by reference to a method. Also, many of the standard data structures implemented by Java operate on objects, which means that you can't use these data structures to store primitive types. To handle these (and other) situations, Java provides *type wrappers*, which are classes that encapsulate a primitive type within an object. The type wrapper classes are described in detail in Part II, but they are introduced here because they relate directly to Java's autoboxing feature.

The type wrappers are **Double, Float, Long, Integer, Short, Byte, Character,** and **Boolean.** These classes offer a wide array of methods that allow you to fully integrate the primitive types into Java's object hierarchy. Each is briefly examined next.

Character

Character is a wrapper around a **char.** The constructor for **Character** is

    Character(char *ch*)

Here, *ch* specifies the character that will be wrapped by the **Character** object being created. To obtain the **char** value contained in a **Character** object, call **charValue( )**, shown here:

    char charValue( )

It returns the encapsulated character.

Boolean

Boolean is a wrapper around **boolean** values. It defines these constructors:

    Boolean(boolean *boolValue*)
    Boolean(String *boolString*)

In the first version, *boolValue* must be either **true** or **false.** In the second version, if *boolString* contains the string "true" (in uppercase or lowercase), then the new **Boolean** object will be true. Otherwise, it will be false.

To obtain a **boolean** value from a **Boolean** object, use **booleanValue( )**, shown here:

    boolean booleanValue( )

It returns the **boolean** equivalent of the invoking object.

The Numeric Type Wrappers

By far, the most commonly used type wrappers are those that represent numeric values. These are **Byte, Short, Integer, Long, Float,** and **Double.** All of the numeric type wrappers inherit the abstract class **Number. Number** declares methods that return the value of an object in each of the different number formats. These methods are shown here:

    byte byteValue( )
    double doubleValue( )
    float floatValue( )
    int intValue( )
    long longValue( )
    short shortValue( )

For example, **doubleValue( )** returns the value of an object as a **double, floatValue( )** returns the value as a **float,** and so on. These methods are implemented by each of the numeric type wrappers.

All of the numeric type wrappers define constructors that allow an object to be constructed from a given value, or a string representation of that value. For example, here are the constructors defined for **Integer**:

Integer(int *num*)
Integer(String *str*)

If *str* does not contain a valid numeric value, then a **NumberFormatException** is thrown.

All of the type wrappers override **toString( )**. It returns the human-readable form of the value contained within the wrapper. This allows you to output the value by passing a type wrapper object to **println( )**, for example, without having to convert it into its primitive type.

The following program demonstrates how to use a numeric type wrapper to encapsulate a value and then extract that value.

```
// Demonstrate a type wrapper.
class Wrap {
  public static void main(String args[]) {

    Integer iOb = new Integer(100);

    int i = iOb.intValue();

    System.out.println(i + " " + iOb); // displays 100 100
  }
}
```

This program wraps the integer value 100 inside an **Integer** object called **iOb**. The program then obtains this value by calling **intValue( )** and stores the result in **i**.

The process of encapsulating a value within an object is called *boxing*. Thus, in the program, this line boxes the value 100 into an **Integer**:

```
Integer iOb = new Integer(100);
```

The process of extracting a value from a type wrapper is called *unboxing*. For example, the program unboxes the value in **iOb** with this statement:

```
int i = iOb.intValue();
```

The same general procedure used by the preceding program to box and unbox values has been employed since the original version of Java. However, with the release of JDK 5, Java fundamentally improved on this through the addition of autoboxing, described next.

Autoboxing

Beginning with JDK 5, Java added two important features: *autoboxing* and *auto-unboxing*. Autoboxing is the process by which a primitive type is automatically encapsulated (boxed) into its equivalent type wrapper whenever an object of that type is needed. There is no need to explicitly construct an object. Auto-unboxing is the process by which the value of a boxed object is automatically extracted (unboxed) from a type wrapper when its value is needed. There is no need to call a method such as **intValue( )** or **doubleValue( )**.

The addition of autoboxing and auto-unboxing greatly streamlines the coding of several algorithms, removing the tedium of manually boxing and unboxing values. It also helps prevent errors. Moreover, it is very important to generics, which operates only on objects. Finally, autoboxing makes working with the Collections Framework (described in Part II) much easier.

With autoboxing it is no longer necessary to manually construct an object in order to wrap a primitive type. You need only assign that value to a type-wrapper reference. Java automatically constructs the object for you. For example, here is the modern way to construct an **Integer** object that has the value 100:

```
Integer iOb = 100; // autobox an int
```

Notice that no object is explicitly created through the use of **new**. Java handles this for you, automatically.

To unbox an object, simply assign that object reference to a primitive-type variable. For example, to unbox **iOb**, you can use this line:

```
int i = iOb; // auto-unbox
```

Java handles the details for you.

Here is the preceding program rewritten to use autoboxing/unboxing:

```
// Demonstrate autoboxing/unboxing.
class AutoBox {
  public static void main(String args[]) {

    Integer iOb = 100; // autobox an int

    int i = iOb; // auto-unbox

    System.out.println(i + " " + iOb);  // displays 100 100
  }
}
```

Autoboxing and Methods

In addition to the simple case of assignments, autoboxing automatically occurs whenever a primitive type must be converted into an object; auto-unboxing takes place whenever an object must be converted into a primitive type. Thus, autoboxing/unboxing might occur when an argument is passed to a method, or when a value is returned by a method. For example, consider this example:

```
// Autoboxing/unboxing takes place with
// method parameters and return values.

class AutoBox2 {
  // Take an Integer parameter and return
  // an int value;
  static int m(Integer v) {
    return v ; // auto-unbox to int
  }
```

```
  public static void main(String args[]) {
    // Pass an int to m() and assign the return value
    // to an Integer.  Here, the argument 100 is autoboxed
    // into an Integer.  The return value is also autoboxed
    // into an Integer.
    Integer iOb = m(100);

    System.out.println(iOb);
  }
}
```

This program displays the following result:

```
100
```

In the program, notice that **m( )** specifies an **Integer** parameter and returns an **int** result. Inside **main( )**, **m( )** is passed the value 100. Because **m( )** is expecting an **Integer**, this value is automatically boxed. Then, **m( )** returns the **int** equivalent of its argument. This causes **v** to be auto-unboxed. Next, this **int** value is assigned to **iOb** in **main( )**, which causes the **int** return value to be autoboxed.

Autoboxing/Unboxing Occurs in Expressions

In general, autoboxing and unboxing take place whenever a conversion into an object or from an object is required. This applies to expressions. Within an expression, a numeric object is automatically unboxed. The outcome of the expression is reboxed, if necessary. For example, consider the following program:

```
// Autoboxing/unboxing occurs inside expressions.

class AutoBox3 {
  public static void main(String args[]) {

    Integer iOb, iOb2;
    int i;

    iOb = 100;
    System.out.println("Original value of iOb: " + iOb);

    // The following automatically unboxes iOb,
    // performs the increment, and then reboxes
    // the result back into iOb.
    ++iOb;
    System.out.println("After ++iOb: " + iOb);

    // Here, iOb is unboxed, the expression is
    // evaluated, and the result is reboxed and
    // assigned to iOb2.
    iOb2 = iOb + (iOb / 3);
    System.out.println("iOb2 after expression: " + iOb2);

    // The same expression is evaluated, but the
```

```
    // result is not reboxed.
    i = iOb + (iOb / 3);
    System.out.println("i after expression: " + i);

  }
}
```

The output is shown here:

```
Original value of iOb: 100
After ++iOb: 101
iOb2 after expression: 134
i after expression: 134
```

In the program, pay special attention to this line:

```
++iOb;
```

This causes the value in **iOb** to be incremented. It works like this: **iOb** is unboxed, the value is incremented, and the result is reboxed.

Auto-unboxing also allows you to mix different types of numeric objects in an expression. Once the values are unboxed, the standard type promotions and conversions are applied. For example, the following program is perfectly valid:

```
class AutoBox4 {
  public static void main(String args[]) {

    Integer iOb = 100;
    Double dOb = 98.6;


    dOb = dOb + iOb;
    System.out.println("dOb after expression: " + dOb);
  }
}
```

The output is shown here:

```
dOb after expression: 198.6
```

As you can see, both the **Double** object **dOb** and the **Integer** object **iOb** participated in the addition, and the result was reboxed and stored in **dOb**.

Because of auto-unboxing, you can use integer numeric objects to control a **switch** statement. For example, consider this fragment:

```
Integer iOb = 2;

switch(iOb) {
  case 1: System.out.println("one");
    break;
  case 2: System.out.println("two");
    break;
```

```
    default: System.out.println("error");
}
```

When the **switch** expression is evaluated, **iOb** is unboxed and its **int** value is obtained.

As the examples in the program show, because of autoboxing/unboxing, using numeric objects in an expression is both intuitive and easy. In the past, such code would have involved casts and calls to methods such as **intValue( )**.

Autoboxing/Unboxing Boolean and Character Values

As described earlier, Java also supplies wrappers for **boolean** and **char**. These are **Boolean** and **Character**. Autoboxing/unboxing applies to these wrappers, too. For example, consider the following program:

```
// Autoboxing/unboxing a Boolean and Character.

class AutoBox5 {
  public static void main(String args[]) {

    // Autobox/unbox a boolean.
    Boolean b = true;

    // Below, b is auto-unboxed when used in
    // a conditional expression, such as an if.
    if(b) System.out.println("b is true");

    // Autobox/unbox a char.
    Character ch = 'x'; // box a char
    char ch2 = ch; // unbox a char

    System.out.println("ch2 is " + ch2);
  }
}
```

The output is shown here:

```
b is true
ch2 is x
```

The most important thing to notice about this program is the auto-unboxing of **b** inside the **if** conditional expression. As you should recall, the conditional expression that controls an **if** must evaluate to type **boolean**. Because of auto-unboxing, the **boolean** value contained within **b** is automatically unboxed when the conditional expression is evaluated. Thus, with the advent of autoboxing/unboxing, a **Boolean** object can be used to control an **if** statement.

Because of auto-unboxing, a **Boolean** object can now also be used to control any of Java's loop statements. When a **Boolean** is used as the conditional expression of a **while**, **for**, or **do/while**, it is automatically unboxed into its **boolean** equivalent. For example, this is now perfectly valid code:

```
Boolean b;
// ...
while(b) { // ...
```

Autoboxing/Unboxing Helps Prevent Errors

In addition to the convenience that it offers, autoboxing/unboxing can also help prevent errors. For example, consider the following program:

```
// An error produced by manual unboxing.
class UnboxingError {
  public static void main(String args[]) {

    Integer iOb = 1000; // autobox the value 1000

    int i = iOb.byteValue(); // manually unbox as byte !!!

    System.out.println(i);  // does not display 1000 !
  }
}
```

This program displays not the expected value of 1000, but –24! The reason is that the value inside **iOb** is manually unboxed by calling **byteValue( )**, which causes the truncation of the value stored in **iOb**, which is 1,000. This results in the garbage value of –24 being assigned to **i**. Auto-unboxing prevents this type of error because the value in **iOb** will always auto-unbox into a value compatible with **int**.

In general, because autoboxing always creates the proper object, and auto-unboxing always produces the proper value, there is no way for the process to produce the wrong type of object or value. In the rare instances where you want a type different than that produced by the automated process, you can still manually box and unbox values. Of course, the benefits of autoboxing/unboxing are lost. In general, new code should employ autoboxing/unboxing. It is the way that modern Java code will be written.

A Word of Warning

Now that Java includes autoboxing and auto-unboxing, some might be tempted to use objects such as **Integer** or **Double** exclusively, abandoning primitives altogether. For example, with autoboxing/unboxing it is possible to write code like this:

```
// A bad use of autoboxing/unboxing!
Double a, b, c;

a = 10.0;
b = 4.0;

c = Math.sqrt(a*a + b*b);

System.out.println("Hypotenuse is " + c);
```

In this example, objects of type **Double** hold values that are used to calculate the hypotenuse of a right triangle. Although this code is technically correct and does, in fact, work properly, it is a very bad use of autoboxing/unboxing. It is far less efficient than the equivalent code written using the primitive type **double**. The reason is that each autobox and auto-unbox adds overhead that is not present if the primitive type is used.

In general, you should restrict your use of the type wrappers to only those cases in which an object representation of a primitive type is required. Autoboxing/unboxing was not added to Java as a "back door" way of eliminating the primitive types.

Annotations (Metadata)

Beginning with JDK 5, a new facility was added to Java that enables you to embed supplemental information into a source file. This information, called an *annotation*, does not change the actions of a program. Thus, an annotation leaves the semantics of a program unchanged. However, this information can be used by various tools during both development and deployment. For example, an annotation might be processed by a source-code generator. The term *metadata* is also used to refer to this feature, but the term *annotation* is the most descriptive and more commonly used.

Annotation Basics

An annotation is created through a mechanism based on the **interface**. Let's begin with an example. Here is the declaration for an annotation called **MyAnno**:

```
// A simple annotation type.
@interface MyAnno {
  String str();
  int val();
}
```

First, notice the @ that precedes the keyword **interface**. This tells the compiler that an annotation type is being declared. Next, notice the two members **str( )** and **val( )**. All annotations consist solely of method declarations. However, you don't provide bodies for these methods. Instead, Java implements these methods. Moreover, the methods act much like fields, as you will see.

An annotation cannot include an **extends** clause. However, all annotation types automatically extend the **Annotation** interface. Thus, **Annotation** is a super-interface of all annotations. It is declared within the **java.lang.annotation** package. It overrides **hashCode( )**, **equals( )**, and **toString( )**, which are defined by **Object**. It also specifies **annotationType( )**, which returns a **Class** object that represents the invoking annotation.

Once you have declared an annotation, you can use it to annotate a declaration. Any type of declaration can have an annotation associated with it. For example, classes, methods, fields, parameters, and **enum** constants can be annotated. Even an annotation can be annotated. In all cases, the annotation precedes the rest of the declaration.

When you apply an annotation, you give values to its members. For example, here is an example of **MyAnno** being applied to a method:

```
// Annotate a method.
@MyAnno(str = "Annotation Example", val = 100)
public static void myMeth() { // ...
```

This annotation is linked with the method **myMeth( )**. Look closely at the annotation syntax. The name of the annotation, preceded by an @, is followed by a parenthesized list of member initializations. To give a member a value, that member's name is assigned a value. Therefore, in the example, the string "Annotation Example" is assigned to the **str** member of **MyAnno**.

Notice that no parentheses follow **str** in this assignment. When an annotation member is given a value, only its name is used. Thus, annotation members look like fields in this context.

Specifying a Retention Policy

Before exploring annotations further, it is necessary to discuss *annotation retention policies*. A retention policy determines at what point an annotation is discarded. Java defines three such policies, which are encapsulated within the **java.lang.annotation.RetentionPolicy** enumeration. They are **SOURCE**, **CLASS**, and **RUNTIME**.

An annotation with a retention policy of **SOURCE** is retained only in the source file and is discarded during compilation.

An annotation with a retention policy of **CLASS** is stored in the **.class** file during compilation. However, it is not available through the JVM during run time.

An annotation with a retention policy of **RUNTIME** is stored in the **.class** file during compilation and is available through the JVM during run time. Thus, **RUNTIME** retention offers the greatest annotation persistence.

A retention policy is specified for an annotation by using one of Java's built-in annotations: **@Retention**. Its general form is shown here:

@Retention(*retention-policy*)

Here, *retention-policy* must be one of the previously discussed enumeration constants. If no retention policy is specified for an annotation, then the default policy of **CLASS** is used.

The following version of **MyAnno** uses **@Retention** to specify the **RUNTIME** retention policy. Thus, **MyAnno** will be available to the JVM during program execution.

```
@Retention(RetentionPolicy.RUNTIME)
@interface MyAnno {
  String str();
  int val();
}
```

Obtaining Annotations at Run Time by Use of Reflection

Although annotations are designed mostly for use by other development or deployment tools, if they specify a retention policy of **RUNTIME**, then they can be queried at run time by any Java program through the use of *reflection*. Reflection is the feature that enables information about a class to be obtained at run time. The reflection API is contained in the **java.lang.reflect** package. There are a number of ways to use reflection, and we won't examine them all here. We will, however, walk through a few examples that apply to annotations.

The first step to using reflection is to obtain a **Class** object that represents the class whose annotations you want to obtain. **Class** is one of Java's built-in classes and is defined in **java.lang**. It is described in detail in Part II. There are various ways to obtain a **Class** object. One of the easiest is to call **getClass( )**, which is a method defined by **Object**. Its general form is shown here:

final Class getClass( )

It returns the **Class** object that represents the invoking object. (**getClass( )** and several other reflection-related methods make use of the generics feature. However, because generics are not discussed until Chapter 14, these methods are shown and used here in their raw form. As a result, you will see a warning message when you compile the following programs. In Chapter 14, you will learn about generics in detail.)

After you have obtained a **Class** object, you can use its methods to obtain information about the various items declared by the class, including its annotations. If you want to obtain the annotations associated with a specific item declared within a class, you must first obtain an object that represents that item. For example, **Class** supplies (among others) the **getMethod( )**, **getField( )**, and **getConstructor( )** methods, which obtain information about a method, field, and constructor, respectively. These methods return objects of type **Method**, **Field**, and **Constructor**.

To understand the process, let's work through an example that obtains the annotations associated with a method. To do this, you first obtain a **Class** object that represents the class, and then call **getMethod( )** on that **Class** object, specifying the name of the method. **getMethod( )** has this general form:

Method getMethod(String *methName*, Class ... *paramTypes*)

The name of the method is passed in *methName*. If the method has arguments, then **Class** objects representing those types must also be specified by *paramTypes*. Notice that *paramTypes* is a varargs parameter. This means that you can specify as many parameter types as needed, including zero. **getMethod( )** returns a **Method** object that represents the method. If the method can't be found, **NoSuchMethodException** is thrown.

From a **Class**, **Method**, **Field**, or **Constructor** object, you can obtain a specific annotation associated with that object by calling **getAnnotation( )**. Its general form is shown here:

Annotation getAnnotation(Class *annoType*)

Here, *annoType* is a **Class** object that represents the annotation in which you are interested. The method returns a reference to the annotation. Using this reference, you can obtain the values associated with the annotation's members. The method returns **null** if the annotation is not found, which will be the case if the annotation does not have **RUNTIME** retention.

Here is a program that assembles all of the pieces shown earlier and uses reflection to display the annotation associated with a method.

```
import java.lang.annotation.*;
import java.lang.reflect.*;

// An annotation type declaration.
@Retention(RetentionPolicy.RUNTIME)
@interface MyAnno {
  String str();
  int val();
}

class Meta {

  // Annotate a method.
  @MyAnno(str = "Annotation Example", val = 100)
  public static void myMeth() {
    Meta ob = new Meta();

    // Obtain the annotation for this method
    // and display the values of the members.
    try {
```

```
      // First, get a Class object that represents
      // this class.
      Class c = ob.getClass();

      // Now, get a Method object that represents
      // this method.
      Method m = c.getMethod("myMeth");

      // Next, get the annotation for this class.
      MyAnno anno = m.getAnnotation(MyAnno.class);

      // Finally, display the values.
      System.out.println(anno.str() + " " + anno.val());
    } catch (NoSuchMethodException exc) {
      System.out.println("Method Not Found.");
    }
  }

  public static void main(String args[]) {
    myMeth();
  }
}
```

The output from the program is shown here:

```
Annotation Example 100
```

This program uses reflection as described to obtain and display the values of **str** and **val** in the **MyAnno** annotation associated with **myMeth( )** in the **Meta** class. There are two things to pay special attention to. First, in this line

```
MyAnno anno = m.getAnnotation(MyAnno.class);
```

notice the expression **MyAnno.class**. This expression evaluates to a **Class** object of type **MyAnno**, the annotation. This construct is called a *class literal*. You can use this type of expression whenever a **Class** object of a known class is needed. For example, this statement could have been used to obtain the **Class** object for **Meta**:

```
Class c = Meta.class;
```

Of course, this approach only works when you know the class name of an object in advance, which might not always be the case. In general, you can obtain a class literal for classes, interfaces, primitive types, and arrays.

The second point of interest is the way the values associated with **str** and **val** are obtained when they are output by the following line:

```
System.out.println(anno.str() + " " + anno.val());
```

Notice that they are invoked using the method-call syntax. This same approach is used whenever the value of an annotation member is required.

A Second Reflection Example

In the preceding example, **myMeth( )** has no parameters. Thus, when **getMethod( )** was called, only the name **myMeth** was passed. However, to obtain a method that has parameters, you must specify class objects representing the types of those parameters as arguments to **getMethod( )**. For example, here is a slightly different version of the preceding program:

```
import java.lang.annotation.*;
import java.lang.reflect.*;

@Retention(RetentionPolicy.RUNTIME)
@interface MyAnno {
  String str();
  int val();
}

class Meta {

  // myMeth now has two arguments.
  @MyAnno(str = "Two Parameters", val = 19)
  public static void myMeth(String str, int i)
  {
    Meta ob = new Meta();

    try {
      Class c = ob.getClass();

      // Here, the parameter types are specified.
      Method m = c.getMethod("myMeth", String.class, int.class);

      MyAnno anno = m.getAnnotation(MyAnno.class);

      System.out.println(anno.str() + " " + anno.val());
    } catch (NoSuchMethodException exc) {
      System.out.println("Method Not Found.");
    }
  }

  public static void main(String args[]) {
    myMeth("test", 10);
  }
}
```

The output from this version is shown here:

```
Two Parameters 19
```

In this version, **myMeth( )** takes a **String** and an **int** parameter. To obtain information about this method, **getMethod( )** must be called as shown here:

```
Method m = c.getMethod("myMeth", String.class, int.class);
```

Here, the **Class** objects representing **String** and **int** are passed as additional arguments.

Obtaining All Annotations

You can obtain all annotations that have **RUNTIME** retention that are associated with an item by calling **getAnnotations( )** on that item. It has this general form:

Annotation[ ] getAnnotations( )

It returns an array of the annotations. **getAnnotations( )** can be called on objects of type **Class**, **Method**, **Constructor**, and **Field**.

Here is another reflection example that shows how to obtain all annotations associated with a class and with a method. It declares two annotations. It then uses those annotations to annotate a class and a method.

```
// Show all annotations for a class and a method.
import java.lang.annotation.*;
import java.lang.reflect.*;

@Retention(RetentionPolicy.RUNTIME)
@interface MyAnno {
  String str();
  int val();
}

@Retention(RetentionPolicy.RUNTIME)
@interface What {
  String description();
}

@What(description = "An annotation test class")
@MyAnno(str = "Meta2", val = 99)
class Meta2 {

  @What(description = "An annotation test method")
  @MyAnno(str = "Testing", val = 100)
  public static void myMeth() {
    Meta2 ob = new Meta2();

    try {
      Annotation annos[] = ob.getClass().getAnnotations();

      // Display all annotations for Meta2.
      System.out.println("All annotations for Meta2:");
      for(Annotation a : annos)
        System.out.println(a);

      System.out.println();

      // Display all annotations for myMeth.
      Method m = ob.getClass( ).getMethod("myMeth");
      annos = m.getAnnotations();

      System.out.println("All annotations for myMeth:");
      for(Annotation a : annos)
```

```
      System.out.println(a);

    } catch (NoSuchMethodException exc) {
      System.out.println("Method Not Found.");
    }
  }

  public static void main(String args[]) {
    myMeth();
  }
}
```

The output is shown here:

```
All annotations for Meta2:
@What(description=An annotation test class)
@MyAnno(str=Meta2, val=99)

All annotations for myMeth:
@What(description=An annotation test method)
@MyAnno(str=Testing, val=100)
```

The program uses **getAnnotations( )** to obtain an array of all annotations associated with the **Meta2** class and with the **myMeth( )** method. As explained, **getAnnotations( )** returns an array of **Annotation** objects. Recall that **Annotation** is a super-interface of all annotation interfaces and that it overrides **toString( )** in **Object**. Thus, when a reference to an **Annotation** is output, its **toString( )** method is called to generate a string that describes the annotation, as the preceding output shows.

The AnnotatedElement Interface

The methods **getAnnotation( )** and **getAnnotations( )** used by the preceding examples are defined by the **AnnotatedElement** interface, which is defined in **java.lang.reflect**. This interface supports reflection for annotations and is implemented by the classes **Method**, **Field**, **Constructor**, **Class**, and **Package**.

In addition to **getAnnotation( )** and **getAnnotations( )**, **AnnotatedElement** defines two other methods. The first is **getDeclaredAnnotations( )**, which has this general form:

Annotation[ ] getDeclaredAnnotations( )

It returns all non-inherited annotations present in the invoking object. The second is **isAnnotationPresent( )**, which has this general form:

boolean isAnnotationPresent(Class *annoType*)

It returns true if the annotation specified by *annoType* is associated with the invoking object. It returns false otherwise.

NOTE *The methods **getAnnotation( )** and **isAnnotationPresent( )** make use of the generics feature to ensure type safety. Because generics are not discussed until Chapter 14, their signatures are shown in this chapter in their raw forms.*

Using Default Values

You can give annotation members default values that will be used if no value is specified when the annotation is applied. A default value is specified by adding a **default** clause to a member's declaration. It has this general form:

type member( ) default *value;*

Here, *value* must be of a type compatible with *type*.

Here is **@MyAnno** rewritten to include default values:

```
// An annotation type declaration that includes defaults.
@Retention(RetentionPolicy.RUNTIME)
@interface MyAnno {
  String str() default "Testing";
  int val() default 9000;
}
```

This declaration gives a default value of "Testing" to **str** and 9000 to **val**. This means that neither value needs to be specified when **@MyAnno** is used. However, either or both can be given values if desired. Therefore, following are the four ways that **@MyAnno** can be used:

```
@MyAnno() // both str and val default
@MyAnno(str = "some string") // val defaults
@MyAnno(val = 100) // str defaults
@MyAnno(str = "Testing", val = 100) // no defaults
```

The following program demonstrates the use of default values in an annotation.

```
import java.lang.annotation.*;
import java.lang.reflect.*;

// An annotation type declaration that includes defaults.
@Retention(RetentionPolicy.RUNTIME)
@interface MyAnno {
  String str() default "Testing";
  int val() default 9000;
}

class Meta3 {

  // Annotate a method using the default values.
  @MyAnno()
  public static void myMeth() {
    Meta3 ob = new Meta3();

    // Obtain the annotation for this method
    // and display the values of the members.
    try {
      Class c = ob.getClass();

      Method m = c.getMethod("myMeth");
```

```
      MyAnno anno = m.getAnnotation(MyAnno.class);

      System.out.println(anno.str() + " " + anno.val());
    } catch (NoSuchMethodException exc) {
      System.out.println("Method Not Found.");
    }
  }

  public static void main(String args[]) {
    myMeth();
  }
}
```

The output is shown here:

```
    Testing 9000
```

Marker Annotations

A *marker* annotation is a special kind of annotation that contains no members. Its sole purpose is to mark a declaration. Thus, its presence as an annotation is sufficient. The best way to determine if a marker annotation is present is to use the method **isAnnotationPresent( )**, which is a defined by the **AnnotatedElement** interface.

Here is an example that uses a marker annotation. Because a marker interface contains no members, simply determining whether it is present or absent is sufficient.

```
import java.lang.annotation.*;
import java.lang.reflect.*;

// A marker annotation.
@Retention(RetentionPolicy.RUNTIME)
@interface MyMarker { }

class Marker {

  // Annotate a method using a marker.
  // Notice that no ( ) is needed.
  @MyMarker
  public static void myMeth() {
    Marker ob = new Marker();

    try {
      Method m = ob.getClass().getMethod("myMeth");

      // Determine if the annotation is present.
      if(m.isAnnotationPresent(MyMarker.class))
        System.out.println("MyMarker is present.");

    } catch (NoSuchMethodException exc) {
      System.out.println("Method Not Found.");
    }
  }
```

```
public static void main(String args[]) {
    myMeth();
  }
}
```

The output, shown here, confirms that **@MyMarker** is present:

```
MyMarker is present.
```

In the program, notice that you do not need to follow **@MyMarker** with parentheses when it is applied. Thus, **@MyMarker** is applied simply by using its name, like this:

```
@MyMarker
```

It is not wrong to supply an empty set of parentheses, but they are not needed.

Single-Member Annotations

A *single-member* annotation contains only one member. It works like a normal annotation except that it allows a shorthand form of specifying the value of the member. When only one member is present, you can simply specify the value for that member when the annotation is applied—you don't need to specify the name of the member. However, in order to use this shorthand, the name of the member must be **value**.

Here is an example that creates and uses a single-member annotation:

```
import java.lang.annotation.*;
import java.lang.reflect.*;

// A single-member annotation.
@Retention(RetentionPolicy.RUNTIME)
@interface MySingle {
  int value(); // this variable name must be value
}

class Single {

  // Annotate a method using a single-member annotation.
  @MySingle(100)
  public static void myMeth() {
    Single ob = new Single();

    try {
      Method m = ob.getClass().getMethod("myMeth");

      MySingle anno = m.getAnnotation(MySingle.class);

      System.out.println(anno.value()); // displays 100

    } catch (NoSuchMethodException exc) {
      System.out.println("Method Not Found.");
    }
  }
}
```

```
public static void main(String args[]) {
    myMeth();
  }
}
```

As expected, this program displays the value 100. In the program, **@MySingle** is used to annotate **myMeth( )**, as shown here:

```
@MySingle(100)
```

Notice that **value =** need not be specified.

You can use the single-value syntax when applying an annotation that has other members, but those other members must all have default values. For example, here the value **xyz** is added, with a default value of zero:

```
@interface SomeAnno {
  int value();
  int xyz() default 0;
}
```

In cases in which you want to use the default for **xyz**, you can apply **@SomeAnno**, as shown next, by simply specifying the value of **value** by using the single-member syntax.

```
@SomeAnno(88)
```

In this case, **xyz** defaults to zero, and **value** gets the value 88. Of course, to specify a different value for **xyz** requires that both members be explicitly named, as shown here:

```
@SomeAnno(value = 88, xyz = 99)
```

Remember, whenever you are using a single-member annotation, the name of that member must be **value**.

The Built-In Annotations

Java defines many built-in annotations. Most are specialized, but seven are general purpose. Of these, four are imported from **java.lang.annotation**: **@Retention**, **@Documented**, **@Target**, and **@Inherited**. Three—**@Override**, **@Deprecated**, and **@SuppressWarnings**—are included in **java.lang**. Each is described here.

@Retention

@Retention is designed to be used only as an annotation to another annotation. It specifies the retention policy as described earlier in this chapter.

@Documented

The **@Documented** annotation is a marker interface that tells a tool that an annotation is to be documented. It is designed to be used only as an annotation to an annotation declaration.

@Target

The **@Target** annotation specifies the types of declarations to which an annotation can be applied. It is designed to be used only as an annotation to another annotation. **@Target** takes one argument, which must be a constant from the **ElementType** enumeration. This argument specifies the types of declarations to which the annotation can be applied. The constants are shown here along with the type of declaration to which they correspond.

Target Constant	Annotation Can Be Applied To
ANNOTATION_TYPE	Another annotation
CONSTRUCTOR	Constructor
FIELD	Field
LOCAL_VARIABLE	Local variable
METHOD	Method
PACKAGE	Package
PARAMETER	Parameter
TYPE	Class, interface, or enumeration

You can specify one or more of these values in a **@Target** annotation. To specify multiple values, you must specify them within a braces-delimited list. For example, to specify that an annotation applies only to fields and local variables, you can use this **@Target** annotation:

```
@Target( { ElementType.FIELD, ElementType.LOCAL_VARIABLE } )
```

@Inherited

@Inherited is a marker annotation that can be used only on another annotation declaration. Furthermore, it affects only annotations that will be used on class declarations. **@Inherited** causes the annotation for a superclass to be inherited by a subclass. Therefore, when a request for a specific annotation is made to the subclass, if that annotation is not present in the subclass, then its superclass is checked. If that annotation is present in the superclass, and if it is annotated with **@Inherited**, then that annotation will be returned.

@Override

@Override is a marker annotation that can be used only on methods. A method annotated with **@Override** must override a method from a superclass. If it doesn't, a compile-time error will result. It is used to ensure that a superclass method is actually overridden, and not simply overloaded.

@Deprecated

@Deprecated is a marker annotation. It indicates that a declaration is obsolete and has been replaced by a newer form.

@SuppressWarnings

@SuppressWarnings specifies that one or more warnings that might be issued by the compiler are to be suppressed. The warnings to suppress are specified by name, in string form. This annotation can be applied to any type of declaration.

Some Restrictions

There are a number of restrictions that apply to annotation declarations. First, no annotation can inherit another. Second, all methods declared by an annotation must be without parameters. Furthermore, they must return one of the following:

- A primitive type, such as **int** or **double**
- An object of type **String** or **Class**
- An **enum** type
- Another annotation type
- An array of one of the preceding types

Annotations cannot be generic. In other words, they cannot take type parameters. (Generics are described in Chapter 14.) Finally, annotation methods cannot specify a **throws** clause.

I/O, Applets, and Other Topics

This chapter introduces two of Java's most important packages: **io** and **applet**. The **io** package supports Java's basic I/O (input/output) system, including file I/O. The **applet** package supports applets. Support for both I/O and applets comes from Java's core API libraries, not from language keywords. For this reason, an in-depth discussion of these topics is found in Part II of this book, which examines Java's API classes. This chapter discusses the foundation of these two subsystems so that you can see how they are integrated into the Java language and how they fit into the larger context of the Java programming and execution environment. This chapter also examines the last of Java's keywords: **transient**, **volatile**, **instanceof**, **native**, **strictfp**, and **assert**. It concludes by examining static import and by describing another use for the **this** keyword.

I/O Basics

As you may have noticed while reading the preceding 12 chapters, not much use has been made of I/O in the example programs. In fact, aside from **print( )** and **println( )**, none of the I/O methods have been used significantly. The reason is simple: most real applications of Java are not text-based, console programs. Rather, they are graphically oriented programs that rely upon Java's Abstract Window Toolkit (AWT) or Swing for interaction with the user. Although text-based programs are excellent as teaching examples, they do not constitute an important use for Java in the real world. Also, Java's support for console I/O is limited and somewhat awkward to use—even in simple example programs. Text-based console I/O is just not very important to Java programming.

The preceding paragraph notwithstanding, Java does provide strong, flexible support for I/O as it relates to files and networks. Java's I/O system is cohesive and consistent. In fact, once you understand its fundamentals, the rest of the I/O system is easy to master.

Streams

Java programs perform I/O through streams. A *stream* is an abstraction that either produces or consumes information. A stream is linked to a physical device by the Java I/O system. All streams behave in the same manner, even if the actual physical devices to which they are linked differ. Thus, the same I/O classes and methods can be applied to any type of device. This means that an input stream can abstract many different kinds of input: from a disk file, a keyboard, or a network socket. Likewise, an output stream may refer to the console, a disk file, or a network connection. Streams are a clean way to deal with input/output without having every part of your code understand the difference between a keyboard and a network, for example. Java implements streams within class hierarchies defined in the **java.io** package.

Byte Streams and Character Streams

Java defines two types of streams: byte and character. *Byte streams* provide a convenient means for handling input and output of bytes. Byte streams are used, for example, when reading or writing binary data. *Character streams* provide a convenient means for handling input and output of characters. They use Unicode and, therefore, can be internationalized. Also, in some cases, character streams are more efficient than byte streams.

The original version of Java (Java 1.0) did not include character streams and, thus, all I/O was byte-oriented. Character streams were added by Java 1.1, and certain byte-oriented classes and methods were deprecated. This is why older code that doesn't use character streams should be updated to take advantage of them, where appropriate.

One other point: at the lowest level, all I/O is still byte-oriented. The character-based streams simply provide a convenient and efficient means for handling characters.

An overview of both byte-oriented streams and character-oriented streams is presented in the following sections.

The Byte Stream Classes

Byte streams are defined by using two class hierarchies. At the top are two abstract classes: **InputStream** and **OutputStream**. Each of these abstract classes has several concrete subclasses that handle the differences between various devices, such as disk files, network connections, and even memory buffers. The byte stream classes are shown in Table 13-1. A few of these classes are discussed later in this section. Others are described in Part II. Remember, to use the stream classes, you must import **java.io**.

The abstract classes **InputStream** and **OutputStream** define several key methods that the other stream classes implement. Two of the most important are **read( )** and **write( )**, which, respectively, read and write bytes of data. Both methods are declared as abstract inside **InputStream** and **OutputStream**. They are overridden by derived stream classes.

The Character Stream Classes

Character streams are defined by using two class hierarchies. At the top are two abstract classes, **Reader** and **Writer**. These abstract classes handle Unicode character streams. Java has several concrete subclasses of each of these. The character stream classes are shown in Table 13-2.

The abstract classes **Reader** and **Writer** define several key methods that the other stream classes implement. Two of the most important methods are **read( )** and **write( )**, which read and write characters of data, respectively. These methods are overridden by derived stream classes.

Stream Class	Meaning
BufferedInputStream	Buffered input stream
BufferedOutputStream	Buffered output stream
ByteArrayInputStream	Input stream that reads from a byte array
ByteArrayOutputStream	Output stream that writes to a byte array
DataInputStream	An input stream that contains methods for reading the Java standard data types
DataOutputStream	An output stream that contains methods for writing the Java standard data types
FileInputStream	Input stream that reads from a file
FileOutputStream	Output stream that writes to a file
FilterInputStream	Implements **InputStream**
FilterOutputStream	Implements **OutputStream**
InputStream	Abstract class that describes stream input
ObjectInputStream	Input stream for objects
ObjectOutputStream	Output stream for objects
OutputStream	Abstract class that describes stream output
PipedInputStream	Input pipe
PipedOutputStream	Output pipe
PrintStream	Output stream that contains **print( )** and **println( )**
PushbackInputStream	Input stream that supports one-byte "unget," which returns a byte to the input stream
RandomAccessFile	Supports random access file I/O
SequenceInputStream	Input stream that is a combination of two or more input streams that will be read sequentially, one after the other

TABLE 13-1   The Byte Stream Classes

Stream Class	Meaning
BufferedReader	Buffered input character stream
BufferedWriter	Buffered output character stream
CharArrayReader	Input stream that reads from a character array
CharArrayWriter	Output stream that writes to a character array
FileReader	Input stream that reads from a file
FileWriter	Output stream that writes to a file
FilterReader	Filtered reader
FilterWriter	Filtered writer

TABLE 13-2   The Character Stream I/O Classes

Stream Class	Meaning
InputStreamReader	Input stream that translates bytes to characters
LineNumberReader	Input stream that counts lines
OutputStreamWriter	Output stream that translates characters to bytes
PipedReader	Input pipe
PipedWriter	Output pipe
PrintWriter	Output stream that contains **print( )** and **println( )**
PushbackReader	Input stream that allows characters to be returned to the input stream
Reader	Abstract class that describes character stream input
StringReader	Input stream that reads from a string
StringWriter	Output stream that writes to a string
Writer	Abstract class that describes character stream output

TABLE 13-2　　The Character Stream I/O Classes *(continued)*

The Predefined Streams

As you know, all Java programs automatically import the **java.lang** package. This package defines a class called **System**, which encapsulates several aspects of the run-time environment. For example, using some of its methods, you can obtain the current time and the settings of various properties associated with the system. **System** also contains three predefined stream variables: **in**, **out**, and **err**. These fields are declared as **public**, **static**, and **final** within **System**. This means that they can be used by any other part of your program and without reference to a specific **System** object.

System.out refers to the standard output stream. By default, this is the console. **System.in** refers to standard input, which is the keyboard by default. **System.err** refers to the standard error stream, which also is the console by default. However, these streams may be redirected to any compatible I/O device.

System.in is an object of type **InputStream**; **System.out** and **System.err** are objects of type **PrintStream**. These are byte streams, even though they typically are used to read and write characters from and to the console. As you will see, you can wrap these within character-based streams, if desired.

The preceding chapters have been using **System.out** in their examples. You can use **System.err** in much the same way. As explained in the next section, use of **System.in** is a little more complicated.

Reading Console Input

In Java 1.0, the only way to perform console input was to use a byte stream, and older code that uses this approach persists. Today, using a byte stream to read console input is still technically possible, but doing so is not recommended. The preferred method of reading console input is to use a character-oriented stream, which makes your program easier to internationalize and maintain.

In Java, console input is accomplished by reading from **System.in**. To obtain a character-based stream that is attached to the console, wrap **System.in** in a **BufferedReader** object. **BufferedReader** supports a buffered input stream. Its most commonly used constructor is shown here:

> BufferedReader(Reader *inputReader*)

Here, *inputReader* is the stream that is linked to the instance of **BufferedReader** that is being created. **Reader** is an abstract class. One of its concrete subclasses is **InputStreamReader**, which converts bytes to characters. To obtain an **InputStreamReader** object that is linked to **System.in**, use the following constructor:

> InputStreamReader(InputStream *inputStream*)

Because **System.in** refers to an object of type **InputStream**, it can be used for *inputStream*. Putting it all together, the following line of code creates a **BufferedReader** that is connected to the keyboard:

```
BufferedReader br = new
                 InputStreamReader(System.in));
```

After this statement executes, **br** is a character-based stream that is linked to the console through **System.in**.

Reading Characters

To read a character from a **BufferedReader**, use **read( )**. The version of **read( )** that we will be using is

> int read( ) throws IOException

Each time that **read( )** is called, it reads a character from the input stream and returns it as an integer value. It returns –1 when the end of the stream is encountered. As you can see, it can throw an **IOException**.

The following program demonstrates **read( )** by reading characters from the console until the user types a "q." Notice that any I/O exceptions that might be generated are simply thrown out of **main( )**. Such an approach is common when reading from the console, but you can handle these types of errors yourself, if you chose.

```
// Use a BufferedReader to read characters from the console.
import java.io.*;

class BRRead {
  public static void main(String args[])
    throws IOException
  {
    char c;
    BufferedReader br = new
            BufferedReader(new InputStreamReader(System.in));
    System.out.println("Enter characters, 'q' to quit.");
```

```
    // read characters
    do {
      c = (char) br.read();
      System.out.println(c);
    } while(c != 'q');
  }
}
```

Here is a sample run:

```
Enter characters, 'q' to quit.
123abcq
1
2
3
a
b
c
q
```

This output may look a little different from what you expected, because **System.in** is line buffered, by default. This means that no input is actually passed to the program until you press ENTER. As you can guess, this does not make **read( )** particularly valuable for interactive console input.

Reading Strings

To read a string from the keyboard, use the version of **readLine( )** that is a member of the **BufferedReader** class. Its general form is shown here:

String readLine( ) throws IOException

As you can see, it returns a **String** object.

The following program demonstrates **BufferedReader** and the **readLine( )** method; the program reads and displays lines of text until you enter the word "stop":

```
// Read a string from console using a BufferedReader.
import java.io.*;

class BRReadLines {
  public static void main(String args[])
    throws IOException
  {
    // create a BufferedReader using System.in
    BufferedReader br = new BufferedReader(new
                          InputStreamReader(System.in));
    String str;

    System.out.println("Enter lines of text.");
    System.out.println("Enter 'stop' to quit.");
    do {
      str = br.readLine();
```

```
      System.out.println(str);
    } while(!str.equals("stop"));
  }
}
```

The next example creates a tiny text editor. It creates an array of **String** objects and then reads in lines of text, storing each line in the array. It will read up to 100 lines or until you enter "stop." It uses a **BufferedReader** to read from the console.

```
// A tiny editor.
import java.io.*;

class TinyEdit {
  public static void main(String args[])
    throws IOException
  {
    // create a BufferedReader using System.in
    BufferedReader br = new BufferedReader(new
                           InputStreamReader(System.in));
    String str[] = new String[100];

    System.out.println("Enter lines of text.");
    System.out.println("Enter 'stop' to quit.");
    for(int i=0; i<100; i++) {
      str[i] = br.readLine();
      if(str[i].equals("stop")) break;
    }

    System.out.println("\nHere is your file:");

    // display the lines
    for(int i=0; i<100; i++) {
      if(str[i].equals("stop")) break;
      System.out.println(str[i]);
    }
  }
}
```

Here is a sample run:

```
Enter lines of text.
Enter 'stop' to quit.
This is line one.
This is line two.
Java makes working with strings easy.
Just create String objects.
stop
Here is your file:
This is line one.
This is line two.
Java makes working with strings easy.
Just create String objects.
```

Writing Console Output

Console output is most easily accomplished with **print( )** and **println( )**, described earlier, which are used in most of the examples in this book. These methods are defined by the class **PrintStream** (which is the type of object referenced by **System.out**). Even though **System.out** is a byte stream, using it for simple program output is still acceptable. However, a character-based alternative is described in the next section.

Because **PrintStream** is an output stream derived from **OutputStream**, it also implements the low-level method **write( )**. Thus, **write( )** can be used to write to the console. The simplest form of **write( )** defined by **PrintStream** is shown here:

    void write(int *byteval*)

This method writes to the stream the byte specified by *byteval*. Although *byteval* is declared as an integer, only the low-order eight bits are written. Here is a short example that uses **write( )** to output the character "A" followed by a newline to the screen:

```
// Demonstrate System.out.write().
class WriteDemo {
  public static void main(String args[]) {
    int b;

    b = 'A';
    System.out.write(b);
    System.out.write('\n');
  }
}
```

You will not often use **write( )** to perform console output (although doing so might be useful in some situations), because **print( )** and **println( )** are substantially easier to use.

The PrintWriter Class

Although using **System.out** to write to the console is acceptable, its use is recommended mostly for debugging purposes or for sample programs, such as those found in this book. For real-world programs, the recommended method of writing to the console when using Java is through a **PrintWriter** stream. **PrintWriter** is one of the character-based classes. Using a character-based class for console output makes it easier to internationalize your program.

PrintWriter defines several constructors. The one we will use is shown here:

    PrintWriter(OutputStream *outputStream*, boolean *flushOnNewline*)

Here, *outputStream* is an object of type **OutputStream**, and *flushOnNewline* controls whether Java flushes the output stream every time a **println( )** method is called. If *flushOnNewline* is **true**, flushing automatically takes place. If **false**, flushing is not automatic.

PrintWriter supports the **print( )** and **println( )** methods for all types including **Object**. Thus, you can use these methods in the same way as they have been used with **System.out**. If an argument is not a simple type, the **PrintWriter** methods call the object's **toString( )** method and then print the result.

To write to the console by using a **PrintWriter**, specify **System.out** for the output stream and flush the stream after each newline. For example, this line of code creates a **PrintWriter** that is connected to console output:

```
PrintWriter pw = new PrintWriter(System.out, true);
```

The following application illustrates using a **PrintWriter** to handle console output:

```
// Demonstrate PrintWriter
import java.io.*;

public class PrintWriterDemo {
  public static void main(String args[]) {
    PrintWriter pw = new PrintWriter(System.out, true);
    pw.println("This is a string");
    int i = -7;
    pw.println(i);
    double d = 4.5e-7;
    pw.println(d);
  }
}
```

The output from this program is shown here:

```
This is a string
-7
4.5E-7
```

Remember, there is nothing wrong with using **System.out** to write simple text output to the console when you are learning Java or debugging your programs. However, using a **PrintWriter** will make your real-world applications easier to internationalize. Because no advantage is gained by using a **PrintWriter** in the sample programs shown in this book, we will continue to use **System.out** to write to the console.

Reading and Writing Files

Java provides a number of classes and methods that allow you to read and write files. In Java, all files are byte-oriented, and Java provides methods to read and write bytes from and to a file. However, Java allows you to wrap a byte-oriented file stream within a character-based object. This technique is described in Part II. This chapter examines the basics of file I/O.

Two of the most often-used stream classes are **FileInputStream** and **FileOutputStream**, which create byte streams linked to files. To open a file, you simply create an object of one of these classes, specifying the name of the file as an argument to the constructor. While both classes support additional, overridden constructors, the following are the forms that we will be using:

FileInputStream(String *fileName*) throws FileNotFoundException
FileOutputStream(String *fileName*) throws FileNotFoundException

Here, *fileName* specifies the name of the file that you want to open. When you create an input stream, if the file does not exist, then **FileNotFoundException** is thrown. For output streams, if the file cannot be created, then **FileNotFoundException** is thrown. When an output file is opened, any preexisting file by the same name is destroyed.

When you are done with a file, you should close it by calling **close( )**. It is defined by both **FileInputStream** and **FileOutputStream**, as shown here:

void close( ) throws IOException

To read from a file, you can use a version of **read( )** that is defined within **FileInputStream**. The one that we will use is shown here:

int read( ) throws IOException

Each time that it is called, it reads a single byte from the file and returns the byte as an integer value. **read( )** returns –1 when the end of the file is encountered. It can throw an **IOException**.

The following program uses **read( )** to input and display the contents of a text file, the name of which is specified as a command-line argument. Note the **try/catch** blocks that handle two errors that might occur when this program is used—the specified file not being found or the user forgetting to include the name of the file. You can use this same approach whenever you use command-line arguments. Other I/O exceptions that might occur are simply thrown out of **main( )**, which is acceptable for this simple example. However, often you will want to handle all I/O exceptions yourself when working with files.

```
/* Display a text file.

   To use this program, specify the name
   of the file that you want to see.
   For example, to see a file called TEST.TXT,
   use the following command line.

   java ShowFile TEST.TXT

*/

import java.io.*;

class ShowFile {
  public static void main(String args[])
    throws IOException
  {
    int i;
    FileInputStream fin;

    try {
      fin = new FileInputStream(args[0]);
    } catch(FileNotFoundException e) {
      System.out.println("File Not Found");
      return;
    } catch(ArrayIndexOutOfBoundsException e) {
      System.out.println("Usage: ShowFile File");
      return;
    }
```

```
  // read characters until EOF is encountered
  do {
    i = fin.read();
    if(i != -1) System.out.print((char) i);
  } while(i != -1);

  fin.close();
  }
}
```

To write to a file, you can use the **write( )** method defined by **FileOutputStream**. Its simplest form is shown here:

void write(int *byteval*) throws IOException

This method writes the byte specified by *byteval* to the file. Although *byteval* is declared as an integer, only the low-order eight bits are written to the file. If an error occurs during writing, an **IOException** is thrown. The next example uses **write( )** to copy a text file:

```
/* Copy a text file.

   To use this program, specify the name
   of the source file and the destination file.
   For example, to copy a file called FIRST.TXT
   to a file called SECOND.TXT, use the following
   command line.

   java CopyFile FIRST.TXT SECOND.TXT
*/

import java.io.*;

class CopyFile {
  public static void main(String args[])
    throws IOException
  {
    int i;
    FileInputStream fin;
    FileOutputStream fout;

    try {
      // open input file
      try {
        fin = new FileInputStream(args[0]);
      } catch(FileNotFoundException e) {
        System.out.println("Input File Not Found");
        return;
      }
```

```
    // open output file
    try {
      fout = new FileOutputStream(args[1]);
    } catch(FileNotFoundException e) {
      System.out.println("Error Opening Output File");
      return;
    }
  } catch(ArrayIndexOutOfBoundsException e) {
    System.out.println("Usage: CopyFile From To");
    return;
  }

  // Copy File
  try {
    do {
      i = fin.read();
      if(i != -1) fout.write(i);
    } while(i != -1);
  } catch(IOException e) {
    System.out.println("File Error");
  }

  fin.close();
  fout.close();
  }
}
```

Notice the way that potential I/O errors are handled in this program. Unlike some other computer languages, including C and C++, which use error codes to report file errors, Java uses its exception handling mechanism. Not only does this make file handling cleaner, but it also enables Java to easily differentiate the end-of-file condition from file errors when input is being performed. In C/C++, many input functions return the same value when an error occurs and when the end of the file is reached. (That is, in C/C++, an EOF condition often is mapped to the same value as an input error.) This usually means that the programmer must include extra program statements to determine which event actually occurred. In Java, errors are passed to your program via exceptions, not by values returned by **read( )**. Thus, when **read( )** returns –1, it means only one thing: the end of the file has been encountered.

Applet Fundamentals

All of the preceding examples in this book have been Java console-based applications. However, these types of applications constitute only one class of Java programs. Another type of program is the applet. As mentioned in Chapter 1, *applets* are small applications that are accessed on an Internet server, transported over the Internet, automatically installed, and run as part of a web document. After an applet arrives on the client, it has limited access to resources so that it can produce a graphical user interface and run complex computations without introducing the risk of viruses or breaching data integrity.

Many of the issues connected with the creation and use of applets are found in Part II, when the **applet** package is examined and also when Swing is described in Part III. However, the fundamentals connected to the creation of an applet are presented here, because applets are not structured in the same way as the programs that have been used thus far. As you will see, applets differ from console-based applications in several key areas.

Let's begin with the simple applet shown here:

```
import java.awt.*;
import java.applet.*;

public class SimpleApplet extends Applet {
  public void paint(Graphics g) {
    g.drawString("A Simple Applet", 20, 20);
  }
}
```

This applet begins with two **import** statements. The first imports the Abstract Window Toolkit (AWT) classes. Applets interact with the user (either directly or indirectly) through the AWT, not through the console-based I/O classes. The AWT contains support for a window-based, graphical user interface. As you might expect, the AWT is quite large and sophisticated, and a complete discussion of it consumes several chapters in Part II of this book. Fortunately, this simple applet makes very limited use of the AWT. (Applets can also use Swing to provide the graphical user interface, but this approach is described later in this book.) The second **import** statement imports the **applet** package, which contains the class **Applet**. Every applet that you create must be a subclass of **Applet**.

The next line in the program declares the class **SimpleApplet**. This class must be declared as **public**, because it will be accessed by code that is outside the program.

Inside **SimpleApplet**, **paint( )** is declared. This method is defined by the AWT and must be overridden by the applet. **paint( )** is called each time that the applet must redisplay its output. This situation can occur for several reasons. For example, the window in which the applet is running can be overwritten by another window and then uncovered. Or, the applet window can be minimized and then restored. **paint( )** is also called when the applet begins execution. Whatever the cause, whenever the applet must redraw its output, **paint( )** is called. The **paint( )** method has one parameter of type **Graphics**. This parameter contains the graphics context, which describes the graphics environment in which the applet is running. This context is used whenever output to the applet is required.

Inside **paint( )** is a call to **drawString( )**, which is a member of the **Graphics** class. This method outputs a string beginning at the specified X,Y location. It has the following general form:

void drawString(String *message*, int *x*, int *y*)

Here, *message* is the string to be output beginning at *x,y*. In a Java window, the upper-left corner is location 0,0. The call to **drawString( )** in the applet causes the message "A Simple Applet" to be displayed beginning at location 20,20.

Notice that the applet does not have a **main( )** method. Unlike Java programs, applets do not begin execution at **main( )**. In fact, most applets don't even have a **main( )** method. Instead, an applet begins execution when the name of its class is passed to an applet viewer or to a network browser.

After you enter the source code for **SimpleApplet**, compile in the same way that you have been compiling programs. However, running **SimpleApplet** involves a different process. In fact, there are two ways in which you can run an applet:

- Executing the applet within a Java-compatible web browser.
- Using an applet viewer, such as the standard tool, **appletviewer**. An applet viewer executes your applet in a window. This is generally the fastest and easiest way to test your applet.

Each of these methods is described next.

To execute an applet in a web browser, you need to write a short HTML text file that contains a tag that loads the applet. Currently, Sun recommends using the APPLET tag for this purpose. Here is the HTML file that executes **SimpleApplet**:

```
<applet code="SimpleApplet" width=200 height=60>
</applet>
```

The **width** and **height** statements specify the dimensions of the display area used by the applet. (The APPLET tag contains several other options that are examined more closely in Part II.) After you create this file, you can execute your browser and then load this file, which causes **SimpleApplet** to be executed.

To execute **SimpleApplet** with an applet viewer, you may also execute the HTML file shown earlier. For example, if the preceding HTML file is called **RunApp.html**, then the following command line will run **SimpleApplet**:

C:\>appletviewer RunApp.html

However, a more convenient method exists that you can use to speed up testing. Simply include a comment at the head of your Java source code file that contains the APPLET tag. By doing so, your code is documented with a prototype of the necessary HTML statements, and you can test your compiled applet merely by starting the applet viewer with your Java source code file. If you use this method, the **SimpleApplet** source file looks like this:

```
import java.awt.*;
import java.applet.*;
/*
<applet code="SimpleApplet" width=200 height=60>
</applet>
*/

public class SimpleApplet extends Applet {
  public void paint(Graphics g) {
    g.drawString("A Simple Applet", 20, 20);
  }
}
```

With this approach, you can quickly iterate through applet development by using these three steps:

1. Edit a Java source file.

2. Compile your program.

3. Execute the applet viewer, specifying the name of your applet's source file. The applet viewer will encounter the APPLET tag within the comment and execute your applet.

The window produced by **SimpleApplet**, as displayed by the applet viewer, is shown in the following illustration:

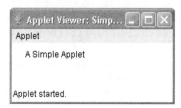

While the subject of applets is more fully discussed later in this book, here are the key points that you should remember now:

- Applets do not need a **main( )** method.
- Applets must be run under an applet viewer or a Java-compatible browser.
- User I/O is not accomplished with Java's stream I/O classes. Instead, applets use the interface provided by the AWT or Swing.

The transient and volatile Modifiers

Java defines two interesting type modifiers: **transient** and **volatile**. These modifiers are used to handle somewhat specialized situations.

When an instance variable is declared as **transient**, then its value need not persist when an object is stored. For example:

```
class T {
  transient int a; // will not persist
  int b; // will persist
}
```

Here, if an object of type **T** is written to a persistent storage area, the contents of **a** would not be saved, but the contents of **b** would.

The **volatile** modifier tells the compiler that the variable modified by **volatile** can be changed unexpectedly by other parts of your program. One of these situations involves multithreaded programs. (You saw an example of this in Chapter 11.) In a multithreaded program, sometimes two or more threads share the same variable. For efficiency considerations, each thread can keep its own, private copy of such a shared variable. The real (or *master*) copy of the variable is updated at various times, such as when a **synchronized** method is entered. While this approach works fine, it may be inefficient at times. In some cases, all that really matters is that the master copy of a variable always reflects its current state. To ensure this, simply specify the variable as **volatile**, which tells the compiler that it must always use the master copy of a **volatile** variable (or, at least, always keep any private copies up-to-date with the master copy, and vice versa). Also, accesses to the master variable must be executed in the precise order in which they are executed on any private copy.

Using instanceof

Sometimes, knowing the type of an object during run time is useful. For example, you might have one thread of execution that generates various types of objects, and another thread that processes these objects. In this situation, it might be useful for the processing thread to know the type of each object when it receives it. Another situation in which knowledge of an object's type at run time is important involves casting. In Java, an invalid cast causes a run-time error. Many invalid casts can be caught at compile time. However, casts involving class hierarchies can produce invalid casts that can be detected only at run time. For example, a superclass called A can produce two subclasses, called B and C. Thus, casting a B object into type A or casting a C object into type A is legal, but casting a B object into type C (or vice versa) isn't legal. Because an object of type A can refer to objects of either B or C, how can you know, at run time, what type of object is actually being referred to before attempting the cast to type C? It could be an object of type A, B, or C. If it is an object of type B, a run-time exception will be thrown. Java provides the run-time operator **instanceof** to answer this question.

The **instanceof** operator has this general form:

objref instanceof *type*

Here, *objref* is a reference to an instance of a class, and *type* is a class type. If *objref* is of the specified type or can be cast into the specified type, then the **instanceof** operator evaluates to **true**. Otherwise, its result is **false**. Thus, **instanceof** is the means by which your program can obtain run-time type information about an object.

The following program demonstrates **instanceof**:

```
// Demonstrate instanceof operator.
class A {
  int i, j;
}

class B {
  int i, j;
}

class C extends A {
  int k;
}

class D extends A {
  int k;
}

class InstanceOf {
  public static void main(String args[]) {
    A a = new A();
    B b = new B();
    C c = new C();
    D d = new D();
```

```
   if(a instanceof A)
     System.out.println("a is instance of A");
   if(b instanceof B)
     System.out.println("b is instance of B");
   if(c instanceof C)
     System.out.println("c is instance of C");
   if(c instanceof A)
     System.out.println("c can be cast to A");

   if(a instanceof C)
     System.out.println("a can be cast to C");

   System.out.println();

   // compare types of derived types
   A ob;

   ob = d; // A reference to d
   System.out.println("ob now refers to d");
   if(ob instanceof D)
     System.out.println("ob is instance of D");

   System.out.println();

   ob = c; // A reference to c
   System.out.println("ob now refers to c");

   if(ob instanceof D)
     System.out.println("ob can be cast to D");
   else
     System.out.println("ob cannot be cast to D");

   if(ob instanceof A)
     System.out.println("ob can be cast to A");

   System.out.println();

   // all objects can be cast to Object
   if(a instanceof Object)
     System.out.println("a may be cast to Object");
   if(b instanceof Object)
     System.out.println("b may be cast to Object");
   if(c instanceof Object)
     System.out.println("c may be cast to Object");
   if(d instanceof Object)
     System.out.println("d may be cast to Object");
  }
}
```

The output from this program is shown here:

```
a is instance of A
b is instance of B
```

```
c is instance of C
c can be cast to A

ob now refers to d
ob is instance of D

ob now refers to c
ob cannot be cast to D
ob can be cast to A

a may be cast to Object
b may be cast to Object
c may be cast to Object
d may be cast to Object
```

The **instanceof** operator isn't needed by most programs, because, generally, you know the type of object with which you are working. However, it can be very useful when you're writing generalized routines that operate on objects of a complex class hierarchy.

strictfp

A relatively new keyword is **strictfp**. With the creation of Java 2, the floating-point computation model was relaxed slightly. Specifically, the new model does not require the truncation of certain intermediate values that occur during a computation. This prevents overflow or underflow in some cases. By modifying a class or a method with **strictfp**, you ensure that floating-point calculations (and thus all truncations) take place precisely as they did in earlier versions of Java. When a class is modified by **strictfp**, all the methods in the class are also modified by **strictfp** automatically.

For example, the following fragment tells Java to use the original floating-point model for calculations in all methods defined within **MyClass**:

```
strictfp class MyClass { //...
```

Frankly, most programmers never need to use **strictfp**, because it affects only a very small class of problems.

Native Methods

Although it is rare, occasionally you may want to call a subroutine that is written in a language other than Java. Typically, such a subroutine exists as executable code for the CPU and environment in which you are working—that is, native code. For example, you may want to call a native code subroutine to achieve faster execution time. Or, you may want to use a specialized, third-party library, such as a statistical package. However, because Java programs are compiled to bytecode, which is then interpreted (or compiled on-the-fly) by the Java run-time system, it would seem impossible to call a native code subroutine from within your Java program. Fortunately, this conclusion is false. Java provides the **native** keyword, which is used to declare native code methods. Once declared, these methods can be called from inside your Java program just as you call any other Java method.

To declare a native method, precede the method with the **native** modifier, but do not define any body for the method. For example:

```
public native int meth() ;
```

After you declare a native method, you must write the native method and follow a rather complex series of steps to link it with your Java code.

Most native methods are written in C. The mechanism used to integrate C code with a Java program is called the *Java Native Interface (JNI)*. A detailed description of the JNI is beyond the scope of this book, but the following description provides sufficient information for most applications.

NOTE *The precise steps that you need to follow will vary between different Java environments. They also depend on the language that you are using to implement the native method. The following discussion assumes a Windows environment. The language used to implement the native method is C.*

The easiest way to understand the process is to work through an example. To begin, enter the following short program, which uses a **native** method called **test( )**:

```
// A simple example that uses a native method.
public class NativeDemo {
  int i;
  public static void main(String args[]) {
    NativeDemo ob = new NativeDemo();

    ob.i = 10;
    System.out.println("This is ob.i before the native method:" +
                       ob.i);
    ob.test(); // call a native method
    System.out.println("This is ob.i after the native method:" +
                       ob.i);
  }
  // declare native method
  public native void test() ;

  // load DLL that contains static method
  static {
    System.loadLibrary("NativeDemo");
  }
}
```

Notice that the **test( )** method is declared as **native** and has no body. This is the method that we will implement in C shortly. Also notice the **static** block. As explained earlier in this book, a **static** block is executed only once, when your program begins execution (or, more precisely, when its class is first loaded). In this case, it is used to load the dynamic link library that contains the native implementation of **test( )**. (You will see how to create this library soon.)

The library is loaded by the **loadLibrary( )** method, which is part of the **System** class. This is its general form:

static void loadLibrary(String *filename*)

Here, *filename* is a string that specifies the name of the file that holds the library. For the Windows environment, this file is assumed to have the .DLL extension.

After you enter the program, compile it to produce **NativeDemo.class**. Next, you must use **javah.exe** to produce one file: **NativeDemo.h**. (**javah.exe** is included in the JDK.) You will include **NativeDemo.h** in your implementation of **test( )**. To produce **NativeDemo.h**, use the following command:

javah -jni NativeDemo

This command produces a header file called **NativeDemo.h**. This file must be included in the C file that implements **test( )**. The output produced by this command is shown here:

```
/* DO NOT EDIT THIS FILE - it is machine generated */
#include <jni.h>
/* Header for class NativeDemo */

#ifndef _Included_NativeDemo
#define _Included_NativeDemo
#ifdef _ _cplusplus
extern "C" {
#endif
/*
 * Class:     NativeDemo
 * Method:    test
 * Signature: ()V
 */
JNIEXPORT void JNICALL Java_NativeDemo_test
  (JNIEnv *, jobject);

#ifdef _ _cplusplus
}
#endif
#endif
```

Pay special attention to the following line, which defines the prototype for the **test( )** function that you will create:

```
JNIEXPORT void JNICALL Java_NativeDemo_test(JNIEnv *, jobject);
```

Notice that the name of the function is **Java_NativeDemo_test( )**. You must use this as the name of the native function that you implement. That is, instead of creating a C function called **test( )**, you will create one called **Java_NativeDemo_test( )**. The **NativeDemo** component of the prefix is added because it identifies the **test( )** method as being part of the **NativeDemo** class. Remember, another class may define its own native **test( )** method that is completely different from the one declared by **NativeDemo**. Including the class name in the prefix provides a way to differentiate between differing versions. As a general rule, native functions will be given a name whose prefix includes the name of the class in which they are declared.

After producing the necessary header file, you can write your implementation of **test( )**
and store it in a file named **NativeDemo.c**:

```
/* This file contains the C version of the
   test() method.
*/

#include <jni.h>
#include "NativeDemo.h"
#include <stdio.h>

JNIEXPORT void JNICALL Java_NativeDemo_test(JNIEnv *env, jobject obj)
{
  jclass cls;
  jfieldID fid;
  jint i;

  printf("Starting the native method.\n");
  cls = (*env)->GetObjectClass(env, obj);
  fid = (*env)->GetFieldID(env, cls, "i", "I");

  if(fid == 0) {
    printf("Could not get field id.\n");
    return;
  }
  i = (*env)->GetIntField(env, obj, fid);
  printf("i = %d\n", i);
  (*env)->SetIntField(env, obj, fid, 2*i);
  printf("Ending the native method.\n");
}
```

Notice that this file includes **jni.h**, which contains interfacing information. This file is provided
by your Java compiler. The header file **NativeDemo.h** was created by **javah** earlier.

In this function, the **GetObjectClass( )** method is used to obtain a C structure that has
information about the class **NativeDemo**. The **GetFieldID( )** method returns a C structure
with information about the field named "i" for the class. **GetIntField( )** retrieves the original
value of that field. **SetIntField( )** stores an updated value in that field. (See the file **jni.h** for
additional methods that handle other types of data.)

After creating **NativeDemo.c**, you must compile it and create a DLL. To do this by using the
Microsoft C/C++ compiler, use the following command line. (You might need to specify the
path to **jni.h** and its subordinate file **jni_md.h**.)

Cl /LD NativeDemo.c

This produces a file called **NativeDemo.dll**. Once this is done, you can execute the Java
program, which will produce the following output:

```
This is ob.i before the native method: 10
Starting the native method.
i = 10
Ending the native method.
This is ob.i after the native method: 20
```

Problems with Native Methods

Native methods seem to offer great promise, because they enable you to gain access to an existing base of library routines, and they offer the possibility of faster run-time execution. But native methods also introduce two significant problems:

- **Potential security risk** Because a native method executes actual machine code, it can gain access to any part of the host system. That is, native code is not confined to the Java execution environment. This could allow a virus infection, for example. For this reason, applets cannot use native methods. Also, the loading of DLLs can be restricted, and their loading is subject to the approval of the security manager.

- **Loss of portability** Because the native code is contained in a DLL, it must be present on the machine that is executing the Java program. Further, because each native method is CPU- and operating system–dependent, each DLL is inherently nonportable. Thus, a Java application that uses native methods will be able to run only on a machine for which a compatible DLL has been installed.

The use of native methods should be restricted, because they render your Java programs nonportable and pose significant security risks.

Using assert

Another relatively new addition to Java is the keyword **assert**. It is used during program development to create an *assertion,* which is a condition that should be true during the execution of the program. For example, you might have a method that should always return a positive integer value. You might test this by asserting that the return value is greater than zero using an **assert** statement. At run time, if the condition actually is true, no other action takes place. However, if the condition is false, then an **AssertionError** is thrown. Assertions are often used during testing to verify that some expected condition is actually met. They are not usually used for released code.

The **assert** keyword has two forms. The first is shown here:

assert *condition*;

Here, *condition* is an expression that must evaluate to a Boolean result. If the result is true, then the assertion is true and no other action takes place. If the condition is false, then the assertion fails and a default **AssertionError** object is thrown.

The second form of **assert** is shown here:

assert *condition* : *expr*;

In this version, *expr* is a value that is passed to the **AssertionError** constructor. This value is converted to its string format and displayed if an assertion fails. Typically, you will specify a string for *expr,* but any non-**void** expression is allowed as long as it defines a reasonable string conversion.

Here is an example that uses **assert**. It verifies that the return value of **getnum( )** is positive.

```
// Demonstrate assert.
class AssertDemo {
  static int val = 3;

  // Return an integer.
  static int getnum() {
    return val--;
  }

  public static void main(String args[])
  {
    int n;

    for(int i=0; i < 10; i++) {
      n = getnum();

      assert n > 0; // will fail when n is 0

      System.out.println("n is " + n);
    }
  }
}
```

To enable assertion checking at run time, you must specify the **-ea** option. For example, to enable assertions for **AssertDemo**, execute it using this line:

```
java -ea AssertDemo
```

After compiling and running as just described, the program creates the following output:

```
n is 3
n is 2
n is 1
Exception in thread "main" java.lang.AssertionError
        at AssertDemo.main(AssertDemo.java:17)
```

In **main( )**, repeated calls are made to the method **getnum( )**, which returns an integer value. The return value of **getnum( )** is assigned to **n** and then tested using this **assert** statement:

```
assert n > 0; // will fail when n is 0
```

This statement will fail when **n** equals 0, which it will after the fourth call. When this happens, an exception is thrown.

As explained, you can specify the message displayed when an assertion fails. For example, if you substitute

```
assert n > 0 : "n is negative!";
```

for the assertion in the preceding program, then the following output will be generated:

```
n is 3
n is 2
n is 1
Exception in thread "main" java.lang.AssertionError: n is
negative!
        at AssertDemo.main(AssertDemo.java:17)
```

One important point to understand about assertions is that you must not rely on them to perform any action actually required by the program. The reason is that normally, released code will be run with assertions disabled. For example, consider this variation of the preceding program:

```
// A poor way to use assert!!!
class AssertDemo {
  // get a random number generator
  static int val = 3;

  // Return an integer.
  static int getnum() {
    return val--;
  }

  public static void main(String args[])
  {
    int n = 0;

    for(int i=0; i < 10; i++) {

      assert (n = getnum()) > 0; // This is not a good idea!

      System.out.println("n is " + n);
    }
  }
}
```

In this version of the program, the call to **getnum( )** is moved inside the **assert** statement. Although this works fine if assertions are enabled, it will cause a malfunction when assertions are disabled, because the call to **getnum( )** will never be executed! In fact, **n** must now be initialized, because the compiler will recognize that it might not be assigned a value by the **assert** statement.

Assertions are a good addition to Java because they streamline the type of error checking that is common during development. For example, prior to **assert**, if you wanted to verify that **n** was positive in the preceding program, you had to use a sequence of code similar to this:

```
if(n < 0) {
   System.out.println("n is negative!");
   return; // or throw an exception
}
```

With **assert**, you need only one line of code. Furthermore, you don't have to remove the **assert** statements from your released code.

Assertion Enabling and Disabling Options

When executing code, you can disable assertions by using the **-da** option. You can enable or disable a specific package by specifying its name after the **-ea** or **-da** option. For example, to enable assertions in a package called **MyPack**, use

```
-ea:MyPack
```

To disable assertions in **MyPack**, use

```
-da:MyPack
```

To enable or disable all subpackages of a package, follow the package name with three dots. For example,

```
-ea:MyPack...
```

You can also specify a class with the **-ea** or **-da** option. For example, this enables **AssertDemo** individually:

```
-ea:AssertDemo
```

Static Import

JDK 5 added a new feature to Java called *static import* that expands the capabilities of the **import** keyword. By following **import** with the keyword **static**, an **import** statement can be used to import the static members of a class or interface. When using static import, it is possible to refer to static members directly by their names, without having to qualify them with the name of their class. This simplifies and shortens the syntax required to use a static member.

To understand the usefulness of static import, let's begin with an example that does *not* use it. The following program computes the hypotenuse of a right triangle. It uses two static methods from Java's built-in math class **Math**, which is part of **java.lang**. The first is **Math.pow( )**, which returns a value raised to a specified power. The second is **Math.sqrt( )**, which returns the square root of its argument.

```
// Compute the hypotenuse of a right triangle.
class Hypot {
  public static void main(String args[]) {
    double side1, side2;
    double hypot;
```

```
    side1 = 3.0;
    side2 = 4.0;

    // Notice how sqrt() and pow() must be qualified by
    // their class name, which is Math.
    hypot = Math.sqrt(Math.pow(side1, 2) +
                      Math.pow(side2, 2));

    System.out.println("Given sides of lengths " +
                       side1 + " and " + side2 +
                       " the hypotenuse is " +
                       hypot);
  }
}
```

Because **pow( )** and **sqrt( )** are static methods, they must be called through the use of their class' name, **Math**. This results in a somewhat unwieldy hypotenuse calculation:

```
hypot = Math.sqrt(Math.pow(side1, 2) +
                  Math.pow(side2, 2));
```

As this simple example illustrates, having to specify the class name each time **pow( )** or **sqrt( )** (or any of Java's other math methods, such as **sin( )**, **cos( )**, and **tan( )**) is used can grow tedious.

You can eliminate the tedium of specifying the class name through the use of static import, as shown in the following version of the preceding program:

```
// Use static import to bring sqrt() and pow() into view.
import static java.lang.Math.sqrt;
import static java.lang.Math.pow;

// Compute the hypotenuse of a right triangle.
class Hypot {
  public static void main(String args[]) {
    double side1, side2;
    double hypot;

    side1 = 3.0;
    side2 = 4.0;

    // Here, sqrt() and pow() can be called by themselves,
    // without their class name.
    hypot = sqrt(pow(side1, 2) + pow(side2, 2));

    System.out.println("Given sides of lengths " +
                       side1 + " and " + side2 +
                       " the hypotenuse is " +
                       hypot);
  }
}
```

In this version, the names **sqrt** and **pow** are brought into view by these static import statements:

```
import static java.lang.Math.sqrt;
import static java.lang.Math.pow;
```

After these statements, it is no longer necessary to qualify **sqrt( )** or **pow( )** with their class name. Therefore, the hypotenuse calculation can more conveniently be specified, as shown here:

```
hypot = sqrt(pow(side1, 2) + pow(side2, 2));
```

As you can see, this form is considerably more readable.

There are two general forms of the **import static** statement. The first, which is used by the preceding example, brings into view a single name. Its general form is shown here:

import static *pkg.type-name.static-member-name*;

Here, *type-name* is the name of a class or interface that contains the desired static member. Its full package name is specified by *pkg*. The name of the member is specified by *static-member-name*.

The second form of static import imports all static members of a given class or interface. Its general form is shown here:

import static *pkg.type-name.**;

If you will be using many static methods or fields defined by a class, then this form lets you bring them into view without having to specify each individually. Therefore, the preceding program could have used this single **import** statement to bring both **pow( )** and **sqrt( )** (and *all other* static members of **Math**) into view:

```
import static java.lang.Math.*;
```

Of course, static import is not limited just to the **Math** class or just to methods. For example, this brings the static field **System.out** into view:

```
import static java.lang.System.out;
```

After this statement, you can output to the console without having to qualify **out** with **System**, as shown here:

```
out.println("After importing System.out, you can use out directly.");
```

Whether importing **System.out** as just shown is a good idea is subject to debate. Although it does shorten the statement, it is no longer instantly clear to anyone reading the program that the **out** being referred to is **System.out**.

One other point: in addition to importing the static members of classes and interfaces defined by the Java API, you can also use static import to import the static members of classes and interfaces that you create.

As convenient as static import can be, it is important not to abuse it. Remember, the reason that Java organizes its libraries into packages is to avoid namespace collisions. When you import static members, you are bringing those members into the global namespace. Thus, you are increasing the potential for namespace conflicts and for the inadvertent hiding of other names. If you are using a static member once or twice in the program, it's best not to import it. Also, some static names, such as **System.out**, are so recognizable that you might not want to import them. Static import is designed for those situations in which you are using a static member repeatedly, such as when performing a series of mathematical computations. In essence, you should use, but not abuse, this feature.

Invoking Overloaded Constructors Through this( )

When working with overloaded constructors, it is sometimes useful for one constructor to invoke another. In Java, this is accomplished by using another form of the **this** keyword. The general form is shown here:

this(*arg-list*)

When **this( )** is executed, the overloaded constructor that matches the parameter list specified by *arg-list* is executed first. Then, if there are any statements inside the original constructor, they are executed. The call to **this( )** must be the first statement within the constructor.

To understand how **this( )** can be used, let's work through a short example. First, consider the following class that *does not* use **this( )**:

```
class MyClass {
  int a;
  int b;

  // initialize a and b individually
  MyClass(int i, int j) {
    a = i;
    b = j;
  }

  // initialize a and b to the same value
  MyClass(int i) {
    a = i;
    b = i;
  }

  // give a and b default values of 0
  MyClass( ) {
    a = 0;
    b = 0;
  }
}
```

This class contains three constructors, each of which initializes the values of **a** and **b**. The first is passed individual values for **a** and **b**. The second is passed just one value, which is assigned to both **a** and **b**. The third gives **a** and **b** default values of zero.

By using **this( )**, it is possible to rewrite **MyClass** as shown here:

```
class MyClass {
  int a;
  int b;

  // initialize a and b individually
  MyClass(int i, int j) {
    a = i;
    b = j;
  }

  // initialize a and b to the same value
  MyClass(int i) {
    this(i, i); // invokes MyClass(i, i)
  }

  // give a and b default values of 0
  MyClass( ) {
    this(0); // invokes MyClass(0)
  }
}
```

In this version of **MyClass**, the only constructor that actually assigns values to the **a** and **b** fields is **MyClass(int, int)**. The other two constructors simply invoke that constructor (either directly or indirectly) through **this( )**. For example, consider what happens when this statement executes:

```
MyClass mc = new MyClass(8);
```

The call to **MyClass(8)** causes **this(8, 8)** to be executed, which translates into a call to **MyClass(8, 8)**, because this is the version of the **MyClass** constructor whose parameter list matches the arguments passed via **this( )**. Now, consider the following statement, which uses the default constructor:

```
MyClass mc2 = new MyClass();
```

In this case, **this(0)** is called. This causes **MyClass(0)** to be invoked because it is the constructor with the matching parameter list. Of course, **MyClass(0)** then calls **MyClass(0, 0)** as just described.

One reason why invoking overloaded constructors through **this( )** can be useful is that it can prevent the unnecessary duplication of code. In many cases, reducing duplicate code decreases the time it takes to load your class because often the object code is smaller. This is especially important for programs delivered via the Internet in which load times are an issue. Using **this( )** can also help structure your code when constructors contain a large amount of duplicate code.

However, you need to be careful. Constructors that call **this( )** will execute a bit slower than those that contain all of their initialization code inline. This is because the call and return mechanism used when the second constructor is invoked adds overhead. If your class will be used to create only a handful of objects, or if the constructors in the class that call **this( )** will be seldom used, then this decrease in run-time performance is probably insignificant. However, if your class will be used to create a large number of objects (on the order of thousands) during program execution, then the negative impact of the increased overhead could be meaningful. Because object creation affects all users of your class, there will be cases in which you must carefully weigh the benefits of faster load time against the increased time it takes to create an object.

Here is another consideration: for very short constructors, such as those used by **MyClass**, there is often little difference in the size of the object code whether **this( )** is used or not. (Actually, there are cases in which no reduction in the size of the object code is achieved.) This is because the bytecode that sets up and returns from the call to **this( )** adds instructions to the object file. Therefore, in these types of situations, even though duplicate code is eliminated, using **this( )** will not obtain significant savings in terms of load time. However, the added cost in terms of overhead to each object's construction will still be incurred. Therefore, **this( )** is most applicable to constructors that contain large amounts of initialization code, not for those that simply set the value of a handful of fields.

There are two restrictions you need to keep in mind when using **this( )**. First, you cannot use any instance variable of the constructor's class in a call to **this( )**. Second, you cannot use **super( )** and **this( )** in the same constructor because each must be the first statement in the constructor.

Generics

Since the original 1.0 release in 1995, many new features have been added to Java. The one that has had the most profound impact is *generics*. Introduced by JDK 5, generics changed Java in two important ways. First, it added a new syntactical element to the language. Second, it caused changes to many of the classes and methods in the core API. Because generics represented such a large change to the language, some programmers were reluctant to adopt its use. However, with the release of JDK 6, generics can no longer be ignored. Simply put, if you will be programming in Java SE 6, you will be using generics. Fortunately, generics are not difficult to use, and they provide significant benefits for the Java programmer.

Through the use of generics, it is possible to create classes, interfaces, and methods that will work in a type-safe manner with various kinds of data. Many algorithms are logically the same no matter what type of data they are being applied to. For example, the mechanism that supports a stack is the same whether that stack is storing items of type **Integer**, **String**, **Object**, or **Thread**. With generics, you can define an algorithm once, independently of any specific type of data, and then apply that algorithm to a wide variety of data types without any additional effort. The expressive power generics add to the language fundamentally changes the way that Java code is written.

Perhaps the one feature of Java that has been most significantly affected by generics is the *Collections Framework*. The Collections Framework is part of the Java API and is described in detail in Chapter 17, but a brief mention is useful now. A *collection* is a group of objects. The Collections Framework defines several classes, such as lists and maps, that manage collections. The collection classes have always been able to work with any type of object. The benefit that generics add is that the collection classes can now be used with complete type safety. Thus, in addition to providing a powerful, new language element, generics also enabled an existing feature to be substantially improved. This is why generics represent such an important addition to Java.

This chapter describes the syntax, theory, and use of generics. It also shows how generics provide type safety for some previously difficult cases. Once you have completed this chapter, you will want to examine Chapter 17, which covers the Collections Framework. There you will find many examples of generics at work.

REMEMBER   *Generics were added by JDK 5. Source code using generics cannot be compiled by earlier versions of* **javac***.*

What Are Generics?

At its core, the term *generics* means *parameterized types.* Parameterized types are important because they enable you to create classes, interfaces, and methods in which the type of data upon which they operate is specified as a parameter. Using generics, it is possible to create a single class, for example, that automatically works with different types of data. A class, interface, or method that operates on a parameterized type is called *generic,* as in *generic class* or *generic method.*

It is important to understand that Java has always given you the ability to create generalized classes, interfaces, and methods by operating through references of type **Object**. Because **Object** is the superclass of all other classes, an **Object** reference can refer to any type object. Thus, in pre-generics code, generalized classes, interfaces, and methods used **Object** references to operate on various types of objects. The problem was that they could not do so with type safety.

Generics add the type safety that was lacking. They also streamline the process, because it is no longer necessary to explicitly employ casts to translate between **Object** and the type of data that is actually being operated upon. With generics, all casts are automatic and implicit. Thus, generics expand your ability to reuse code and let you do so safely and easily.

NOTE *A Warning to C++ Programmers: Although generics are similar to templates in C++, they are not the same. There are some fundamental differences between the two approaches to generic types. If you have a background in C++, it is important not to jump to conclusions about how generics work in Java.*

A Simple Generics Example

Let's begin with a simple example of a generic class. The following program defines two classes. The first is the generic class **Gen**, and the second is **GenDemo**, which uses **Gen**.

```
// A simple generic class.
// Here, T is a type parameter that
// will be replaced by a real type
// when an object of type Gen is created.
class Gen<T> {
  T ob; // declare an object of type T

  // Pass the constructor a reference to
  // an object of type T.
  Gen(T o) {
    ob = o;
  }

  // Return ob.
  T getob() {
    return ob;
  }

  // Show type of T.
  void showType() {
    System.out.println("Type of T is " +
                    ob.getClass().getName());
  }
}
```

```
// Demonstrate the generic class.
class GenDemo {
  public static void main(String args[]) {
    // Create a Gen reference for Integers.
    Gen<Integer> iOb;

    // Create a Gen<Integer> object and assign its
    // reference to iOb.  Notice the use of autoboxing
    // to encapsulate the value 88 within an Integer object.
    iOb = new Gen<Integer>(88);

    // Show the type of data used by iOb.
    iOb.showType();

    // Get the value in iOb. Notice that
    // no cast is needed.
    int v = iOb.getob();
    System.out.println("value: " + v);

    System.out.println();

    // Create a Gen object for Strings.
    Gen<String> strOb = new Gen<String>("Generics Test");

    // Show the type of data used by strOb.
    strOb.showType();

    // Get the value of strOb. Again, notice
    // that no cast is needed.
    String str = strOb.getob();
    System.out.println("value: " + str);
  }
}
```

The output produced by the program is shown here:

```
Type of T is java.lang.Integer
value: 88

Type of T is java.lang.String
value: Generics Test
```

Let's examine this program carefully.

First, notice how **Gen** is declared by the following line:

```
class Gen<T> {
```

Here, **T** is the name of a *type parameter.* This name is used as a placeholder for the actual type that will be passed to **Gen** when an object is created. Thus, **T** is used within **Gen** whenever the type parameter is needed. Notice that **T** is contained within < >. This syntax can be generalized. Whenever a type parameter is being declared, it is specified within angle brackets. Because **Gen** uses a type parameter, **Gen** is a generic class, which is also called a *parameterized type.*

Next, **T** is used to declare an object called **ob**, as shown here:

```
T ob; // declare an object of type T
```

As explained, **T** is a placeholder for the actual type that will be specified when a **Gen** object is created. Thus, **ob** will be an object of the type passed to **T**. For example, if type **String** is passed to **T**, then in that instance, **ob** will be of type **String**.

Now consider **Gen**'s constructor:

```
Gen(T o) {
  ob = o;
}
```

Notice that its parameter, **o**, is of type **T**. This means that the actual type of **o** is determined by the type passed to **T** when a **Gen** object is created. Also, because both the parameter **o** and the member variable **ob** are of type **T**, they will both be of the same actual type when a **Gen** object is created.

The type parameter **T** can also be used to specify the return type of a method, as is the case with the **getob( )** method, shown here:

```
T getob() {
  return ob;
}
```

Because **ob** is also of type **T**, its type is compatible with the return type specified by **getob( )**.

The **showType( )** method displays the type of **T** by calling **getName( )** on the **Class** object returned by the call to **getClass( )** on **ob**. The **getClass( )** method is defined by **Object** and is thus a member of all class types. It returns a **Class** object that corresponds to the type of the class of the object on which it is called. **Class** defines the **getName( )** method, which returns a string representation of the class name.

The **GenDemo** class demonstrates the generic **Gen** class. It first creates a version of **Gen** for integers, as shown here:

```
Gen<Integer> iOb;
```

Look closely at this declaration. First, notice that the type **Integer** is specified within the angle brackets after **Gen**. In this case, **Integer** is a *type argument* that is passed to **Gen**'s type parameter, **T**. This effectively creates a version of **Gen** in which all references to **T** are translated into references to **Integer**. Thus, for this declaration, **ob** is of type **Integer**, and the return type of **getob( )** is of type **Integer**.

Before moving on, it's necessary to state that the Java compiler does not actually create different versions of **Gen**, or of any other generic class. Although it's helpful to think in these terms, it is not what actually happens. Instead, the compiler removes all generic type information, substituting the necessary casts, to make your code *behave as if* a specific version of **Gen** were created. Thus, there is really only one version of **Gen** that actually exists in your program. The process of removing generic type information is called *erasure*, and we will return to this topic later in this chapter.

The next line assigns to **iOb** a reference to an instance of an **Integer** version of the **Gen** class:

```
iOb = new Gen<Integer>(88);
```

Notice that when the **Gen** constructor is called, the type argument **Integer** is also specified. This is necessary because the type of the object (in this case **iOb**) to which the reference is being assigned is of type **Gen<Integer>**. Thus, the reference returned by **new** must also be of type **Gen<Integer>**. If it isn't, a compile-time error will result. For example, the following assignment will cause a compile-time error:

```
iOb = new Gen<Double>(88.0); // Error!
```

Because **iOb** is of type **Gen<Integer>**, it can't be used to refer to an object of **Gen<Double>**. This type checking is one of the main benefits of generics because it ensures type safety.

As the comments in the program state, the assignment

```
iOb = new Gen<Integer>(88);
```

makes use of autoboxing to encapsulate the value 88, which is an **int**, into an **Integer**. This works because **Gen<Integer>** creates a constructor that takes an **Integer** argument. Because an **Integer** is expected, Java will automatically box 88 inside one. Of course, the assignment could also have been written explicitly, like this:

```
iOb = new Gen<Integer>(new Integer(88));
```

However, there would be no benefit to using this version.

The program then displays the type of **ob** within **iOb**, which is **Integer**. Next, the program obtains the value of **ob** by use of the following line:

```
int v = iOb.getob();
```

Because the return type of **getob( )** is **T**, which was replaced by **Integer** when **iOb** was declared, the return type of **getob( )** is also **Integer**, which unboxes into **int** when assigned to **v** (which is an **int**). Thus, there is no need to cast the return type of **getob( )** to **Integer**. Of course, it's not necessary to use the auto-unboxing feature. The preceding line could have been written like this, too:

```
int v = iOb.getob().intValue();
```

However, the auto-unboxing feature makes the code more compact.

Next, **GenDemo** declares an object of type **Gen<String>**:

```
Gen<String> strOb = new Gen<String>("Generics Test");
```

Because the type argument is **String**, **String** is substituted for **T** inside **Gen**. This creates (conceptually) a **String** version of **Gen**, as the remaining lines in the program demonstrate.

Generics Work Only with Objects

When declaring an instance of a generic type, the type argument passed to the type parameter must be a class type. You cannot use a primitive type, such as **int** or **char**. For example, with **Gen**, it is possible to pass any class type to **T**, but you cannot pass a primitive type to a type parameter. Therefore, the following declaration is illegal:

```
Gen<int> strOb = new Gen<int>(53); // Error, can't use primitive type
```

Of course, not being able to specify a primitive type is not a serious restriction because you can use the type wrappers (as the preceding example did) to encapsulate a primitive type. Further, Java's autoboxing and auto-unboxing mechanism makes the use of the type wrapper transparent.

Generic Types Differ Based on Their Type Arguments

A key point to understand about generic types is that a reference of one specific version of a generic type is not type compatible with another version of the same generic type. For example, assuming the program just shown, the following line of code is in error and will not compile:

```
iOb = strOb; // Wrong!
```

Even though both **iOb** and **strOb** are of type **Gen<T>**, they are references to different types because their type parameters differ. This is part of the way that generics add type safety and prevent errors.

How Generics Improve Type Safety

At this point, you might be asking yourself the following question: Given that the same functionality found in the generic **Gen** class can be achieved without generics, by simply specifying **Object** as the data type and employing the proper casts, what is the benefit of making **Gen** generic? The answer is that generics automatically ensure the type safety of all operations involving **Gen**. In the process, they eliminate the need for you to enter casts and to type-check code by hand.

To understand the benefits of generics, first consider the following program that creates a non-generic equivalent of **Gen**:

```
// NonGen is functionally equivalent to Gen
// but does not use generics.
class NonGen {
  Object ob; // ob is now of type Object

  // Pass the constructor a reference to
  // an object of type Object
  NonGen(Object o) {
    ob = o;
  }

  // Return type Object.
  Object getob() {
    return ob;
```

```
  }

  // Show type of ob.
  void showType() {
    System.out.println("Type of ob is " +
                       ob.getClass().getName());
  }
}

// Demonstrate the non-generic class.
class NonGenDemo {
  public static void main(String args[]) {
    NonGen iOb;

    // Create NonGen Object and store
    // an Integer in it. Autoboxing still occurs.
    iOb = new NonGen(88);

    // Show the type of data used by iOb.
    iOb.showType();

    // Get the value of iOb.
    // This time, a cast is necessary.
    int v = (Integer) iOb.getob();
    System.out.println("value: " + v);

    System.out.println();

    // Create another NonGen object and
    // store a String in it.
    NonGen strOb = new NonGen("Non-Generics Test");

    // Show the type of data used by strOb.
    strOb.showType();

    // Get the value of strOb.
    // Again, notice that a cast is necessary.
    String str = (String) strOb.getob();
    System.out.println("value: " + str);

    // This compiles, but is conceptually wrong!
    iOb = strOb;
    v = (Integer) iOb.getob(); // run-time error!
  }
}
```

There are several things of interest in this version. First, notice that **NonGen** replaces all uses of **T** with **Object**. This makes **NonGen** able to store any type of object, as can the generic version. However, it also prevents the Java compiler from having any real knowledge about the type of data actually stored in **NonGen**, which is bad for two reasons. First, explicit casts must be employed to retrieve the stored data. Second, many kinds of type mismatch errors cannot be found until run time. Let's look closely at each problem.

Notice this line:

```
int v = (Integer) iOb.getob();
```

Because the return type of **getob( )** is **Object**, the cast to **Integer** is necessary to enable that value to be auto-unboxed and stored in **v**. If you remove the cast, the program will not compile. With the generic version, this cast was implicit. In the non-generic version, the cast must be explicit. This is not only an inconvenience, but also a potential source of error.

Now, consider the following sequence from near the end of the program:

```
// This compiles, but is conceptually wrong!
iOb = strOb;
v = (Integer) iOb.getob(); // run-time error!
```

Here, **strOb** is assigned to **iOb**. However, **strOb** refers to an object that contains a string, not an integer. This assignment is syntactically valid because all **NonGen** references are the same, and any **NonGen** reference can refer to any other **NonGen** object. However, the statement is semantically wrong, as the next line shows. Here, the return type of **getob( )** is cast to **Integer**, and then an attempt is made to assign this value to **v**. The trouble is that **iOb** now refers to an object that stores a **String**, not an **Integer**. Unfortunately, without the use of generics, the Java compiler has no way to know this. Instead, a run-time exception occurs when the cast to **Integer** is attempted. As you know, it is extremely bad to have run-time exceptions occur in your code!

The preceding sequence can't occur when generics are used. If this sequence were attempted in the generic version of the program, the compiler would catch it and report an error, thus preventing a serious bug that results in a run-time exception. The ability to create type-safe code in which type-mismatch errors are caught at compile time is a key advantage of generics. Although using **Object** references to create "generic" code has always been possible, that code was not type safe, and its misuse could result in run-time exceptions. Generics prevent this from occurring. In essence, through generics, what were once run-time errors have become compile-time errors. This is a major advantage.

A Generic Class with Two Type Parameters

You can declare more than one type parameter in a generic type. To specify two or more type parameters, simply use a comma-separated list. For example, the following **TwoGen** class is a variation of the **Gen** class that has two type parameters:

```
// A simple generic class with two type
// parameters: T and V.
class TwoGen<T, V> {
  T ob1;
  V ob2;

  // Pass the constructor a reference to
  // an object of type T and an object of type V.
  TwoGen(T o1, V o2) {
    ob1 = o1;
    ob2 = o2;
  }
```

```
  // Show types of T and V.
  void showTypes() {
    System.out.println("Type of T is " +
                          ob1.getClass().getName());

    System.out.println("Type of V is " +
                          ob2.getClass().getName());
  }

  T getob1() {
    return ob1;
  }

  V getob2() {
    return ob2;
  }
}

// Demonstrate TwoGen.
class SimpGen {
  public static void main(String args[]) {

    TwoGen<Integer, String> tgObj =
      new TwoGen<Integer, String>(88, "Generics");

    // Show the types.
    tgObj.showTypes();

    // Obtain and show values.
    int v = tgObj.getob1();
    System.out.println("value: " + v);

    String str = tgObj.getob2();
    System.out.println("value: " + str);
  }
}
```

The output from this program is shown here:

```
Type of T is java.lang.Integer
Type of V is java.lang.String
value: 88
value: Generics
```

Notice how **TwoGen** is declared:

```
class TwoGen<T, V> {
```

It specifies two type parameters: **T** and **V**, separated by a comma. Because it has two type parameters, two type arguments must be passed to **TwoGen** when an object is created, as shown next:

```
TwoGen<Integer, String> tgObj =
  new TwoGen<Integer, String>(88, "Generics");
```

In this case, **Integer** is substituted for **T**, and **String** is substituted for **V**.

Although the two type arguments differ in this example, it is possible for both types to be the same. For example, the following line of code is valid:

```
TwoGen<String, String> x = new TwoGen<String, String>("A", "B");
```

In this case, both **T** and **V** would be of type **String**. Of course, if the type arguments were always the same, then two type parameters would be unnecessary.

The General Form of a Generic Class

The generics syntax shown in the preceding examples can be generalized. Here is the syntax for declaring a generic class:

class *class-name<type-param-list>* { // ...

Here is the syntax for declaring a reference to a generic class:

class-name<type-arg-list> var-name =
    new *class-name<type-arg-list>(cons-arg-list);*

Bounded Types

In the preceding examples, the type parameters could be replaced by any class type. This is fine for many purposes, but sometimes it is useful to limit the types that can be passed to a type parameter. For example, assume that you want to create a generic class that contains a method that returns the average of an array of numbers. Furthermore, you want to use the class to obtain the average of an array of any type of number, including integers, floats, and doubles. Thus, you want to specify the type of the numbers generically, using a type parameter. To create such a class, you might try something like this:

```
// Stats attempts (unsuccessfully) to
// create a generic class that can compute
// the average of an array of numbers of
// any given type.
//
// The class contains an error!
class Stats<T> {
  T[] nums; // nums is an array of type T

  // Pass the constructor a reference to
  // an array of type T.
  Stats(T[] o) {
    nums = o;
  }

  // Return type double in all cases.
  double average() {
    double sum = 0.0;
```

```
    for(int i=0; i < nums.length; i++)
      sum += nums[i].doubleValue(); // Error!!!

    return sum / nums.length;
  }
}
```

In **Stats**, the **average( )** method attempts to obtain the **double** version of each number in the **nums** array by calling **doubleValue( )**. Because all numeric classes, such as **Integer** and **Double**, are subclasses of **Number**, and **Number** defines the **doubleValue( )** method, this method is available to all numeric wrapper classes. The trouble is that the compiler has no way to know that you are intending to create **Stats** objects using only numeric types. Thus, when you try to compile **Stats**, an error is reported that indicates that the **doubleValue( )** method is unknown. To solve this problem, you need some way to tell the compiler that you intend to pass only numeric types to **T**. Furthermore, you need some way to *ensure* that *only* numeric types are actually passed.

To handle such situations, Java provides *bounded types*. When specifying a type parameter, you can create an upper bound that declares the superclass from which all type arguments must be derived. This is accomplished through the use of an **extends** clause when specifying the type parameter, as shown here:

<T extends *superclass*>

This specifies that *T* can only be replaced by *superclass*, or subclasses of *superclass*. Thus, *superclass* defines an inclusive, upper limit.

You can use an upper bound to fix the **Stats** class shown earlier by specifying **Number** as an upper bound, as shown here:

```
// In this version of Stats, the type argument for
// T must be either Number, or a class derived
// from Number.
class Stats<T extends Number> {
  T[] nums; // array of Number or subclass

  // Pass the constructor a reference to
  // an array of type Number or subclass.
  Stats(T[] o) {
    nums = o;
  }

  // Return type double in all cases.
  double average() {
    double sum = 0.0;

    for(int i=0; i < nums.length; i++)
      sum += nums[i].doubleValue();

    return sum / nums.length;
  }
}
```

```
// Demonstrate Stats.
class BoundsDemo {
  public static void main(String args[]) {

    Integer inums[] = { 1, 2, 3, 4, 5 };
    Stats<Integer> iob = new Stats<Integer>(inums);
    double v = iob.average();
    System.out.println("iob average is " + v);

    Double dnums[] = { 1.1, 2.2, 3.3, 4.4, 5.5 };
    Stats<Double> dob = new Stats<Double>(dnums);
    double w = dob.average();
    System.out.println("dob average is " + w);

    // This won't compile because String is not a
    // subclass of Number.
//    String strs[] = { "1", "2", "3", "4", "5" };
//    Stats<String> strob = new Stats<String>(strs);

//    double x = strob.average();
//    System.out.println("strob average is " + v);

  }
}
```

The output is shown here:

```
Average is 3.0
Average is 3.3
```

Notice how **Stats** is now declared by this line:

```
class Stats<T extends Number> {
```

Because the type **T** is now bounded by **Number**, the Java compiler knows that all objects of type **T** can call **doubleValue( )** because it is a method declared by **Number**. This is, by itself, a major advantage. However, as an added bonus, the bounding of **T** also prevents nonnumeric **Stats** objects from being created. For example, if you try removing the comments from the lines at the end of the program, and then try recompiling, you will receive compile-time errors because **String** is not a subclass of **Number**.

In addition to using a class type as a bound, you can also use an interface type. In fact, you can specify multiple interfaces as bounds. Furthermore, a bound can include both a class type and one or more interfaces. In this case, the class type must be specified first. When a bound includes an interface type, only type arguments that implement that interface are legal. When specifying a bound that has a class and an interface, or multiple interfaces, use the **&** operator to connect them. For example,

```
class Gen<T extends MyClass & MyInterface> { // ...
```

Here, **T** is bounded by a class called **MyClass** and an interface called **MyInterface**. Thus, any type argument passed to **T** must be a subclass of **MyClass** and implement **MyInterface**.

Using Wildcard Arguments

As useful as type safety is, sometimes it can get in the way of perfectly acceptable constructs. For example, given the **Stats** class shown at the end of the preceding section, assume that you want to add a method called **sameAvg( )** that determines if two **Stats** objects contain arrays that yield the same average, no matter what type of numeric data each object holds. For example, if one object contains the **double** values 1.0, 2.0, and 3.0, and the other object contains the integer values 2, 1, and 3, then the averages will be the same. One way to implement **sameAvg( )** is to pass it a **Stats** argument, and then compare the average of that argument against the invoking object, returning true only if the averages are the same. For example, you want to be able to call **sameAvg( )**, as shown here:

```
Integer inums[] = { 1, 2, 3, 4, 5 };
Double dnums[] = { 1.1, 2.2, 3.3, 4.4, 5.5 };

Stats<Integer> iob = new Stats<Integer>(inums);
Stats<Double> dob = new Stats<Double>(dnums);

if(iob.sameAvg(dob))
  System.out.println("Averages are the same.");
else
  System.out.println("Averages differ.");
```

At first, creating **sameAvg( )** seems like an easy problem. Because **Stats** is generic and its **average( )** method can work on any type of **Stats** object, it seems that creating **sameAvg( )** would be straightforward. Unfortunately, trouble starts as soon as you try to declare a parameter of type **Stats**. Because **Stats** is a parameterized type, what do you specify for **Stats'** type parameter when you declare a parameter of that type?

At first, you might think of a solution like this, in which **T** is used as the type parameter:

```
// This won't work!
// Determine if two averages are the same.
boolean sameAvg(Stats<T> ob) {
  if(average() == ob.average())
    return true;

  return false;
}
```

The trouble with this attempt is that it will work only with other **Stats** objects whose type is the same as the invoking object. For example, if the invoking object is of type **Stats<Integer>**, then the parameter **ob** must also be of type **Stats<Integer>**. It can't be used to compare the average of an object of type **Stats<Double>** with the average of an object of type **Stats<Short>**, for example. Therefore, this approach won't work except in a very narrow context and does not yield a general (that is, generic) solution.

To create a generic **sameAvg( )** method, you must use another feature of Java generics: the *wildcard* argument. The wildcard argument is specified by the **?**, and it represents an unknown type. Using a wildcard, here is one way to write the **sameAvg( )** method:

```
// Determine if two averages are the same.
// Notice the use of the wildcard.
boolean sameAvg(Stats<?> ob) {
  if(average() == ob.average())
    return true;

  return false;
}
```

Here, **Stats<?>** matches any **Stats** object, allowing any two **Stats** objects to have their averages compared. The following program demonstrates this:

```
// Use a wildcard.
class Stats<T extends Number> {
  T[] nums; // array of Number or subclass

  // Pass the constructor a reference to
  // an array of type Number or subclass.
  Stats(T[] o) {
    nums = o;
  }

  // Return type double in all cases.
  double average() {
    double sum = 0.0;

    for(int i=0; i < nums.length; i++)
      sum += nums[i].doubleValue();

    return sum / nums.length;
  }

  // Determine if two averages are the same.
  // Notice the use of the wildcard.
  boolean sameAvg(Stats<?> ob) {
    if(average() == ob.average())
      return true;

    return false;
  }
}

// Demonstrate wildcard.
class WildcardDemo {
  public static void main(String args[]) {
    Integer inums[] = { 1, 2, 3, 4, 5 };
    Stats<Integer> iob = new Stats<Integer>(inums);
    double v = iob.average();
    System.out.println("iob average is " + v);
```

```
    Double dnums[] = { 1.1, 2.2, 3.3, 4.4, 5.5 };
    Stats<Double> dob = new Stats<Double>(dnums);
    double w = dob.average();
    System.out.println("dob average is " + w);

    Float fnums[] = { 1.0F, 2.0F, 3.0F, 4.0F, 5.0F };
    Stats<Float> fob = new Stats<Float>(fnums);
    double x = fob.average();
    System.out.println("fob average is " + x);

    // See which arrays have same average.
    System.out.print("Averages of iob and dob ");
    if(iob.sameAvg(dob))
      System.out.println("are the same.");
    else
      System.out.println("differ.");

    System.out.print("Averages of iob and fob ");
    if(iob.sameAvg(fob))
      System.out.println("are the same.");
    else
      System.out.println("differ.");
  }
}
```

The output is shown here:

```
iob average is 3.0
dob average is 3.3
fob average is 3.0
Averages of iob and dob differ.
Averages of iob and fob are the same.
```

One last point: It is important to understand that the wildcard does not affect what type of **Stats** objects can be created. This is governed by the **extends** clause in the **Stats** declaration. The wildcard simply matches any *valid* **Stats** object.

Bounded Wildcards

Wildcard arguments can be bounded in much the same way that a type parameter can be bounded. A bounded wildcard is especially important when you are creating a generic type that will operate on a class hierarchy. To understand why, let's work through an example. Consider the following hierarchy of classes that encapsulate coordinates:

```
// Two-dimensional coordinates.
class TwoD {
  int x, y;

  TwoD(int a, int b) {
    x = a;
    y = b;
  }
}
```

```
// Three-dimensional coordinates.
class ThreeD extends TwoD {
  int z;

  ThreeD(int a, int b, int c) {
    super(a, b);
    z = c;
  }
}

// Four-dimensional coordinates.
class FourD extends ThreeD {
  int t;

  FourD(int a, int b, int c, int d) {
    super(a, b, c);
    t = d;
  }
}
```

At the top of the hierarchy is **TwoD**, which encapsulates a two-dimensional, XY coordinate. **TwoD** is inherited by **ThreeD**, which adds a third dimension, creating an XYZ coordinate. **ThreeD** is inherited by **FourD**, which adds a fourth dimension (time), yielding a four-dimensional coordinate.

Shown next is a generic class called **Coords**, which stores an array of coordinates:

```
// This class holds an array of coordinate objects.
class Coords<T extends TwoD> {
  T[] coords;

  Coords(T[] o) { coords = o; }
}
```

Notice that **Coords** specifies a type parameter bounded by **TwoD**. This means that any array stored in a **Coords** object will contain objects of type **TwoD** or one of its subclasses.

Now, assume that you want to write a method that displays the X and Y coordinates for each element in the **coords** array of a **Coords** object. Because all types of **Coords** objects have at least two coordinates (X and Y), this is easy to do using a wildcard, as shown here:

```
static void showXY(Coords<?> c) {
  System.out.println("X Y Coordinates:");
  for(int i=0; i < c.coords.length; i++)
    System.out.println(c.coords[i].x + " " +
                       c.coords[i].y);
  System.out.println();
}
```

Because **Coords** is a bounded generic type that specifies **TwoD** as an upper bound, all objects that can be used to create a **Coords** object will be arrays of type **TwoD**, or of classes derived from **TwoD**. Thus, **showXY( )** can display the contents of any **Coords** object.

However, what if you want to create a method that displays the X, Y, and Z coordinates of a **ThreeD** or **FourD** object? The trouble is that not all **Coords** objects will have three coordinates, because a **Coords<TwoD>** object will only have X and Y. Therefore, how do you write a method that displays the X, Y, and Z coordinates for **Coords<ThreeD>** and **Coords<FourD>** objects, while preventing that method from being used with **Coords<TwoD>** objects? The answer is the *bounded wildcard argument*.

A bounded wildcard specifies either an upper bound or a lower bound for the type argument. This enables you to restrict the types of objects upon which a method will operate. The most common bounded wildcard is the upper bound, which is created using an **extends** clause in much the same way it is used to create a bounded type.

Using a bounded wildcard, it is easy to create a method that displays the X, Y, and Z coordinates of a **Coords** object, if that object actually has those three coordinates. For example, the following **showXYZ( )** method shows the X, Y, and Z coordinates of the elements stored in a **Coords** object, if those elements are actually of type **ThreeD** (or are derived from **ThreeD**):

```
static void showXYZ(Coords<? extends ThreeD> c) {
  System.out.println("X Y Z Coordinates:");
  for(int i=0; i < c.coords.length; i++)
    System.out.println(c.coords[i].x + " " +
                       c.coords[i].y + " " +
                       c.coords[i].z);
  System.out.println();
}
```

Notice that an **extends** clause has been added to the wildcard in the declaration of parameter **c**. It states that the **?** can match any type as long as it is **ThreeD**, or a class derived from **ThreeD**. Thus, the **extends** clause establishes an upper bound that the **?** can match. Because of this bound, **showXYZ( )** can be called with references to objects of type **Coords<ThreeD>** or **Coords<FourD>**, but not with a reference of type **Coords<TwoD>**. Attempting to call **showXZY( )** with a **Coords<TwoD>** reference results in a compile-time error, thus ensuring type safety.

Here is an entire program that demonstrates the actions of a bounded wildcard argument:

```
// Bounded Wildcard arguments.

// Two-dimensional coordinates.
class TwoD {
  int x, y;

  TwoD(int a, int b) {
    x = a;
    y = b;
  }
}

// Three-dimensional coordinates.
class ThreeD extends TwoD {
  int z;

  ThreeD(int a, int b, int c) {
```

```
    super(a, b);
    z = c;
  }
}

// Four-dimensional coordinates.
class FourD extends ThreeD {
  int t;

  FourD(int a, int b, int c, int d) {
    super(a, b, c);
    t = d;
  }
}

// This class holds an array of coordinate objects.
class Coords<T extends TwoD> {
  T[] coords;

  Coords(T[] o) { coords = o; }
}

// Demonstrate a bounded wildcard.
class BoundedWildcard {
  static void showXY(Coords<?> c) {
    System.out.println("X Y Coordinates:");
    for(int i=0; i < c.coords.length; i++)
      System.out.println(c.coords[i].x + " " +
                         c.coords[i].y);
    System.out.println();
  }

  static void showXYZ(Coords<? extends ThreeD> c) {
    System.out.println("X Y Z Coordinates:");
    for(int i=0; i < c.coords.length; i++)
      System.out.println(c.coords[i].x + " " +
                         c.coords[i].y + " " +
                         c.coords[i].z);
    System.out.println();
  }

  static void showAll(Coords<? extends FourD> c) {
    System.out.println("X Y Z T Coordinates:");
    for(int i=0; i < c.coords.length; i++)
      System.out.println(c.coords[i].x + " " +
                         c.coords[i].y + " " +
                         c.coords[i].z + " " +
                         c.coords[i].t);
    System.out.println();
  }

  public static void main(String args[]) {
    TwoD td[] = {
```

```
      new TwoD(0, 0),
      new TwoD(7, 9),
      new TwoD(18, 4),
      new TwoD(-1, -23)
    };

    Coords<TwoD> tdlocs = new Coords<TwoD>(td);

    System.out.println("Contents of tdlocs.");
    showXY(tdlocs); // OK, is a TwoD
//  showXYZ(tdlocs); // Error, not a ThreeD
//  showAll(tdlocs); // Error, not a FourD

    // Now, create some FourD objects.
    FourD fd[] = {
      new FourD(1, 2, 3, 4),
      new FourD(6, 8, 14, 8),
      new FourD(22, 9, 4, 9),
      new FourD(3, -2, -23, 17)
    };

    Coords<FourD> fdlocs = new Coords<FourD>(fd);

    System.out.println("Contents of fdlocs.");
    // These are all OK.
    showXY(fdlocs);
    showXYZ(fdlocs);
    showAll(fdlocs);
  }
}
```

The output from the program is shown here:

```
Contents of tdlocs.
X Y Coordinates:
0 0
7 9
18 4
-1 -23

Contents of fdlocs.
X Y Coordinates:
1 2
6 8
22 9
3 -2

X Y Z Coordinates:
1 2 3
6 8 14
22 9 4
3 -2 -23
```

```
X Y Z T Coordinates:
1 2 3 4
6 8 14 8
22 9 4 9
3 -2 -23 17
```

Notice these commented-out lines:

```
//  showXYZ(tdlocs); // Error, not a ThreeD
//  showAll(tdlocs); // Error, not a FourD
```

Because **tdlocs** is a **Coords(TwoD)** object, it cannot be used to call **showXYZ( )** or **showAll( )** because bounded wildcard arguments in their declarations prevent it. To prove this to yourself, try removing the comment symbols, and then attempt to compile the program. You will receive compilation errors because of the type mismatches.

In general, to establish an upper bound for a wildcard, use the following type of wildcard expression:

> <? extends *superclass*>

where *superclass* is the name of the class that serves as the upper bound. Remember, this is an inclusive clause because the class forming the upper bound (that is, specified by *superclass*) is also within bounds.

You can also specify a lower bound for a wildcard by adding a **super** clause to a wildcard declaration. Here is its general form:

> <? super *subclass*>

In this case, only classes that are superclasses of *subclass* are acceptable arguments. This is an exclusive clause, because it will not match the class specified by *subclass*.

Creating a Generic Method

As the preceding examples have shown, methods inside a generic class can make use of a class' type parameter and are, therefore, automatically generic relative to the type parameter. However, it is possible to declare a generic method that uses one or more type parameters of its own. Furthermore, it is possible to create a generic method that is enclosed within a non-generic class.

Let's begin with an example. The following program declares a non-generic class called **GenMethDemo** and a static generic method within that class called **isIn( )**. The **isIn( )** method determines if an object is a member of an array. It can be used with any type of object and array as long as the array contains objects that are compatible with the type of the object being sought.

```
// Demonstrate a simple generic method.
class GenMethDemo {

  // Determine if an object is in an array.
  static <T, V extends T> boolean isIn(T x, V[] y) {
```

```
     for(int i=0; i < y.length; i++)
       if(x.equals(y[i])) return true;

     return false;
   }

  public static void main(String args[]) {

     // Use isIn() on Integers.
     Integer nums[] = { 1, 2, 3, 4, 5 };

     if(isIn(2, nums))
       System.out.println("2 is in nums");

     if(!isIn(7, nums))
       System.out.println("7 is not in nums");

     System.out.println();

     // Use isIn() on Strings.
     String strs[] = { "one", "two", "three",
                       "four", "five" };

     if(isIn("two", strs))
       System.out.println("two is in strs");

     if(!isIn("seven", strs))
       System.out.println("seven is not in strs");

     // Oops! Won't compile! Types must be compatible.
//     if(isIn("two", nums))
//       System.out.println("two is in strs");
   }
}
```

The output from the program is shown here:

```
2 is in nums
7 is not in nums

two is in strs
seven is not in strs
```

Let's examine **isIn( )** closely. First, notice how it is declared by this line:

```
static <T, V extends T> boolean isIn(T x, V[] y) {
```

The type parameters are declared *before* the return type of the method. Second, notice that the type **V** is upper-bounded by **T**. Thus, **V** must either be the same as type **T**, or a subclass of **T**. This relationship enforces that **isIn( )** can be called only with arguments that are compatible with each other. Also notice that **isIn( )** is static, enabling it to be called independently of any object. Understand, though, that generic methods can be either static or non-static. There is no restriction in this regard.

Now, notice how **isIn( )** is called within **main( )** by use of the normal call syntax, without the need to specify type arguments. This is because the types of the arguments are automatically discerned, and the types of **T** and **V** are adjusted accordingly. For example, in the first call:

```
if(isIn(2, nums))
```

the type of the first argument is **Integer** (due to autoboxing), which causes **Integer** to be substituted for **T**. The base type of the second argument is also **Integer**, which makes **Integer** a substitute for **V**, too.

In the second call, **String** types are used, and the types of **T** and **V** are replaced by **String**. Now, notice the commented-out code, shown here:

```
//    if(isIn("two", nums))
//      System.out.println("two is in strs");
```

If you remove the comments and then try to compile the program, you will receive an error. The reason is that the type parameter **V** is bounded by **T** in the **extends** clause in **V**'s declaration. This means that **V** must be either type **T**, or a subclass of **T**. In this case, the first argument is of type **String**, making **T** into **String**, but the second argument is of type **Integer**, which is not a subclass of **String**. This causes a compile-time type-mismatch error. This ability to enforce type safety is one of the most important advantages of generic methods.

The syntax used to create **isIn( )** can be generalized. Here is the syntax for a generic method:

<type-param-list> ret-type meth-name(param-list) { // ...

In all cases, *type-param-list* is a comma-separated list of type parameters. Notice that for a generic method, the type parameter list precedes the return type.

Generic Constructors

It is also possible for constructors to be generic, even if their class is not. For example, consider the following short program:

```
// Use a generic constructor.
class GenCons {
  private double val;

  <T extends Number> GenCons(T arg) {
    val = arg.doubleValue();
  }

  void showval() {
    System.out.println("val: " + val);
  }
}

class GenConsDemo {
  public static void main(String args[]) {

    GenCons test = new GenCons(100);
    GenCons test2 = new GenCons(123.5F);
```

```
      test.showval();
      test2.showval();
   }
}
```

The output is shown here:

```
val: 100.0
val: 123.5
```

Because **GenCons( )** specifies a parameter of a generic type, which must be a subclass of **Number**, **GenCons( )** can be called with any numeric type, including **Integer**, **Float**, or **Double**. Therefore, even though **GenCons** is not a generic class, its constructor is generic.

Generic Interfaces

In addition to generic classes and methods, you can also have generic interfaces. Generic interfaces are specified just like generic classes. Here is an example. It creates an interface called **MinMax** that declares the methods **min( )** and **max( )**, which are expected to return the minimum and maximum value of some set of objects.

```
// A generic interface example.

// A Min/Max interface.
interface MinMax<T extends Comparable<T>> {
  T min();
  T max();
}

// Now, implement MinMax
class MyClass<T extends Comparable<T>> implements MinMax<T> {
  T[] vals;

  MyClass(T[] o) { vals = o; }

  // Return the minimum value in vals.
  public T min() {
    T v = vals[0];

    for(int i=1; i < vals.length; i++)
      if(vals[i].compareTo(v) < 0) v = vals[i];

    return v;
  }

  // Return the maximum value in vals.
  public T max() {
    T v = vals[0];

    for(int i=1; i < vals.length; i++)
      if(vals[i].compareTo(v) > 0) v = vals[i];
```

```
        return v;
    }
}

class GenIFDemo {
  public static void main(String args[]) {
    Integer inums[] = {3, 6, 2, 8, 6 };
    Character chs[] = {'b', 'r', 'p', 'w' };

    MyClass<Integer> iob = new MyClass<Integer>(inums);
    MyClass<Character> cob = new MyClass<Character>(chs);

    System.out.println("Max value in inums: " + iob.max());
    System.out.println("Min value in inums: " + iob.min());

    System.out.println("Max value in chs: " + cob.max());
    System.out.println("Min value in chs: " + cob.min());
  }
}
```

The output is shown here:

```
Max value in inums: 8
Min value in inums: 2
Max value in chs: w
Min value in chs: b
```

Although most aspects of this program should be easy to understand, a couple of key points need to be made. First, notice that **MinMax** is declared like this:

```
interface MinMax<T extends Comparable<T>> {
```

In general, a generic interface is declared in the same way as is a generic class. In this case, the type parameter is **T**, and its upper bound is **Comparable**, which is an interface defined by **java.lang**. A class that implements **Comparable** defines objects that can be ordered. Thus, requiring an upper bound of **Comparable** ensures that **MinMax** can be used only with objects that are capable of being compared. (See Chapter 16 for more information on **Comparable**.) Notice that **Comparable** is also generic. (It was retrofitted for generics by JDK 5.) It takes a type parameter that specifies the type of the objects being compared.

Next, **MinMax** is implemented by **MyClass**. Notice the declaration of **MyClass**, shown here:

```
class MyClass<T extends Comparable<T>> implements MinMax<T> {
```

Pay special attention to the way that the type parameter **T** is declared by **MyClass** and then passed to **MinMax**. Because **MinMax** requires a type that implements **Comparable**, the implementing class (**MyClass** in this case) must specify the same bound. Furthermore, once this bound has been established, there is no need to specify it again in the **implements** clause. In fact, it would be wrong to do so. For example, this line is incorrect and won't compile:

```
// This is wrong!
class MyClass<T extends Comparable<T>>
        implements MinMax<T extends Comparable<T>> {
```

Once the type parameter has been established, it is simply passed to the interface without further modification.

In general, if a class implements a generic interface, then that class must also be generic, at least to the extent that it takes a type parameter that is passed to the interface. For example, the following attempt to declare **MyClass** is in error:

```
class MyClass implements MinMax<T> { // Wrong!
```

Because **MyClass** does not declare a type parameter, there is no way to pass one to **MinMax**. In this case, the identifier **T** is simply unknown, and the compiler reports an error. Of course, if a class implements a *specific type* of generic interface, such as shown here:

```
class MyClass implements MinMax<Integer> { // OK
```

then the implementing class does not need to be generic.

The generic interface offers two benefits. First, it can be implemented for different types of data. Second, it allows you to put constraints (that is, bounds) on the types of data for which the interface can be implemented. In the **MinMax** example, only types that implement the **Comparable** interface can be passed to **T**.

Here is the generalized syntax for a generic interface:

interface *interface-name<type-param-list>* { // ...

Here, *type-param-list* is a comma-separated list of type parameters. When a generic interface is implemented, you must specify the type arguments, as shown here:

class *class-name<type-param-list>*
        implements *interface-name<type-arg-list>* {

Raw Types and Legacy Code

Because support for generics is a recent addition to Java, it was necessary to provide some transition path from old, pre-generics code. At the time of this writing, there are still millions and millions of lines of pre-generics legacy code that must remain both functional and compatible with generics. Pre-generics code must be able to work with generics, and generic code must be able to work with pre-generic code.

To handle the transition to generics, Java allows a generic class to be used without any type arguments. This creates a *raw type* for the class. This raw type is compatible with legacy code, which has no knowledge of generics. The main drawback to using the raw type is that the type safety of generics is lost.

Here is an example that shows a raw type in action:

```
// Demonstrate a raw type.
class Gen<T> {
```

```
    T ob; // declare an object of type T

    // Pass the constructor a reference to
    // an object of type T.
    Gen(T o) {
      ob = o;
    }

    // Return ob.
    T getob() {
      return ob;
    }
}

// Demonstrate raw type.
class RawDemo {
  public static void main(String args[]) {

    // Create a Gen object for Integers.
    Gen<Integer> iOb = new Gen<Integer>(88);

    // Create a Gen object for Strings.
    Gen<String> strOb = new Gen<String>("Generics Test");

    // Create a raw-type Gen object and give it
    // a Double value.
    Gen raw = new Gen(new Double(98.6));

    // Cast here is necessary because type is unknown.
    double d = (Double) raw.getob();
    System.out.println("value: " + d);

    // The use of a raw type can lead to run-time
    // exceptions.  Here are some examples.

    // The following cast causes a run-time error!
//    int i = (Integer) raw.getob(); // run-time error

    // This assignment overrides type safety.
    strOb = raw; // OK, but potentially wrong
//    String str = strOb.getob(); // run-time error

    // This assignment also overrides type safety.
    raw = iOb; // OK, but potentially wrong
//    d = (Double) raw.getob(); // run-time error
  }
}
```

This program contains several interesting things. First, a raw type of the generic **Gen** class is created by the following declaration:

```
Gen raw = new Gen(new Double(98.6));
```

Notice that no type arguments are specified. In essence, this creates a **Gen** object whose type **T** is replaced by **Object**.

A raw type is not type safe. Thus, a variable of a raw type can be assigned a reference to any type of **Gen** object. The reverse is also allowed; a variable of a specific **Gen** type can be assigned a reference to a raw **Gen** object. However, both operations are potentially unsafe because the type checking mechanism of generics is circumvented.

This lack of type safety is illustrated by the commented-out lines at the end of the program. Let's examine each case. First, consider the following situation:

```
//    int i = (Integer) raw.getob(); // run-time error
```

In this statement, the value of **ob** inside **raw** is obtained, and this value is cast to **Integer**. The trouble is that **raw** contains a **Double** value, not an integer value. However, this cannot be detected at compile time because the type of **raw** is unknown. Thus, this statement fails at run time.

The next sequence assigns to a **strOb** (a reference of type **Gen<String>**) a reference to a raw **Gen** object:

```
strOb = raw; // OK, but potentially wrong
//    String str = strOb.getob(); // run-time error
```

The assignment, itself, is syntactically correct, but questionable. Because **strOb** is of type **Gen<String>**, it is assumed to contain a **String**. However, after the assignment, the object referred to by **strOb** contains a **Double**. Thus, at run time, when an attempt is made to assign the contents of **strOb** to **str**, a run-time error results because **strOb** now contains a **Double**. Thus, the assignment of a raw reference to a generic reference bypasses the type-safety mechanism.

The following sequence inverts the preceding case:

```
    raw = iOb; // OK, but potentially wrong
//    d = (Double) raw.getob(); // run-time error
```

Here, a generic reference is assigned to a raw reference variable. Although this is syntactically correct, it can lead to problems, as illustrated by the second line. In this case, **raw** now refers to an object that contains an **Integer** object, but the cast assumes that it contains a **Double**. This error cannot be prevented at compile time. Rather, it causes a run-time error.

Because of the potential for danger inherent in raw types, **javac** displays *unchecked warnings* when a raw type is used in a way that might jeopardize type safety. In the preceding program, these lines generate unchecked warnings:

```
Gen raw = new Gen(new Double(98.6));

strOb = raw; // OK, but potentially wrong
```

In the first line, it is the call to the **Gen** constructor without a type argument that causes the warning. In the second line, it is the assignment of a raw reference to a generic variable that generates the warning.

At first, you might think that this line should also generate an unchecked warning, but it does not:

```
raw = iOb; // OK, but potentially wrong
```

No compiler warning is issued because the assignment does not cause any *further* loss of type safety than had already occurred when **raw** was created.

One final point: You should limit the use of raw types to those cases in which you must mix legacy code with newer, generic code. Raw types are simply a transitional feature and not something that should be used for new code.

Generic Class Hierarchies

Generic classes can be part of a class hierarchy in just the same way as a non-generic class. Thus, a generic class can act as a superclass or be a subclass. The key difference between generic and non-generic hierarchies is that in a generic hierarchy, any type arguments needed by a generic superclass must be passed up the hierarchy by all subclasses. This is similar to the way that constructor arguments must be passed up a hierarchy.

Using a Generic Superclass

Here is a simple example of a hierarchy that uses a generic superclass:

```
// A simple generic class hierarchy.
class Gen<T> {
  T ob;

  Gen(T o) {
    ob = o;
  }

  // Return ob.
  T getob() {
    return ob;
  }
}

// A subclass of Gen.
class Gen2<T> extends Gen<T> {
  Gen2(T o) {
    super(o);
  }
}
```

In this hierarchy, **Gen2** extends the generic class **Gen**. Notice how **Gen2** is declared by the following line:

```
class Gen2<T> extends Gen<T> {
```

The type parameter **T** is specified by **Gen2** and is also passed to **Gen** in the **extends** clause. This means that whatever type is passed to **Gen2** will also be passed to **Gen**. For example, this declaration,

```
Gen2<Integer> num = new Gen2<Integer>(100);
```

passes **Integer** as the type parameter to **Gen**. Thus, the **ob** inside the **Gen** portion of **Gen2** will be of type **Integer**.

Notice also that **Gen2** does not use the type parameter **T** except to pass it to the **Gen** superclass. Thus, even if a subclass of a generic superclass would otherwise not need to be generic, it still must specify the type parameter(s) required by its generic superclass.

Of course, a subclass is free to add its own type parameters, if needed. For example, here is a variation on the preceding hierarchy in which **Gen2** adds a type parameter of its own:

```
// A subclass can add its own type parameters.
class Gen<T> {
  T ob; // declare an object of type T

  // Pass the constructor a reference to
  // an object of type T.
  Gen(T o) {
    ob = o;
  }

  // Return ob.
  T getob() {
    return ob;
  }
}

// A subclass of Gen that defines a second
// type parameter, called V.
class Gen2<T, V> extends Gen<T> {
  V ob2;

  Gen2(T o, V o2) {
    super(o);
    ob2 = o2;
  }

  V getob2() {
    return ob2;
  }
}

// Create an object of type Gen2.
class HierDemo {
  public static void main(String args[]) {
```

```
    // Create a Gen2 object for String and Integer.
    Gen2<String, Integer> x =
      new Gen2<String, Integer>("Value is: ", 99);

    System.out.print(x.getob());
    System.out.println(x.getob2());
  }
}
```

Notice the declaration of this version of **Gen2**, which is shown here:

```
class Gen2<T, V> extends Gen<T> {
```

Here, **T** is the type passed to **Gen**, and **V** is the type that is specific to **Gen2**. **V** is used to declare an object called **ob2**, and as a return type for the method **getob2( )**. In **main( )**, a **Gen2** object is created in which type parameter **T** is **String**, and type parameter **V** is **Integer**. The program displays the following, expected, result:

```
    Value is: 99
```

A Generic Subclass

It is perfectly acceptable for a non-generic class to be the superclass of a generic subclass. For example, consider this program:

```
// A non-generic class can be the superclass
// of a generic subclass.

// A non-generic class.
class NonGen {
  int num;

  NonGen(int i) {
    num = i;
  }

  int getnum() {
    return num;
  }
}

// A generic subclass.
class Gen<T> extends NonGen {
  T ob; // declare an object of type T

  // Pass the constructor a reference to
  // an object of type T.
  Gen(T o, int i) {
    super(i);
    ob = o;
  }
```

```
    // Return ob.
    T getob() {
      return ob;
    }
}

// Create a Gen object.
class HierDemo2 {
  public static void main(String args[]) {

    // Create a Gen object for String.
    Gen<String> w = new Gen<String>("Hello", 47);

    System.out.print(w.getob() + " ");
    System.out.println(w.getnum());
  }
}
```

The output from the program is shown here:

```
    Hello 47
```

In the program, notice how **Gen** inherits **NonGen** in the following declaration:

```
class Gen<T> extends NonGen {
```

Because **NonGen** is not generic, no type argument is specified. Thus, even though **Gen** declares the type parameter **T**, it is not needed by (nor can it be used by) **NonGen**. Thus, **NonGen** is inherited by **Gen** in the normal way. No special conditions apply.

Run-Time Type Comparisons Within a Generic Hierarchy

Recall the run-time type information operator **instanceof** that was described in Chapter 13. As explained, **instanceof** determines if an object is an instance of a class. It returns true if an object is of the specified type or can be cast to the specified type. The **instanceof** operator can be applied to objects of generic classes. The following class demonstrates some of the type compatibility implications of a generic hierarchy:

```
// Use the instanceof operator with a generic class hierarchy.
class Gen<T> {
  T ob;

  Gen(T o) {
    ob = o;
  }

  // Return ob.
  T getob() {
    return ob;
  }
}
```

```java
// A subclass of Gen.
class Gen2<T> extends Gen<T> {
  Gen2(T o) {
    super(o);
  }
}

// Demonstrate run-time type ID implications of generic
// class hierarchy.
class HierDemo3 {
  public static void main(String args[]) {

    // Create a Gen object for Integers.
    Gen<Integer> iOb = new Gen<Integer>(88);

    // Create a Gen2 object for Integers.
    Gen2<Integer> iOb2 = new Gen2<Integer>(99);

    // Create a Gen2 object for Strings.
    Gen2<String> strOb2 = new Gen2<String>("Generics Test");

    // See if iOb2 is some form of Gen2.
    if(iOb2 instanceof Gen2<?>)
      System.out.println("iOb2 is instance of Gen2");

    // See if iOb2 is some form of Gen.
    if(iOb2 instanceof Gen<?>)
      System.out.println("iOb2 is instance of Gen");

    System.out.println();

    // See if strOb2 is a Gen2.
    if(strOb2 instanceof Gen2<?>)
      System.out.println("strOb2 is instance of Gen2");

    // See if strOb2 is a Gen.
    if(strOb2 instanceof Gen<?>)
      System.out.println("strOb2 is instance of Gen");

    System.out.println();

    // See if iOb is an instance of Gen2, which it is not.
    if(iOb instanceof Gen2<?>)
      System.out.println("iOb is instance of Gen2");

    // See if iOb is an instance of Gen, which it is.
    if(iOb instanceof Gen<?>)
      System.out.println("iOb is instance of Gen");

    // The following can't be compiled because
    // generic type info does not exist at run time.
//    if(iOb2 instanceof Gen2<Integer>)
//      System.out.println("iOb2 is instance of Gen2<Integer>");
  }
}
```

The output from the program is shown here:

```
iOb2 is instance of Gen2
iOb2 is instance of Gen

strOb2 is instance of Gen2
strOb2 is instance of Gen

iOb is instance of Gen
```

In this program, **Gen2** is a subclass of **Gen**, which is generic on type parameter **T**. In **main( )**, three objects are created. The first is **iOb**, which is an object of type **Gen<Integer>**. The second is **iOb2**, which is an instance of **Gen2<Integer>**. Finally, **strOb2** is an object of type **Gen2<String>**.

Then, the program performs these **instanceof** tests on the type of **iOb2**:

```
// See if iOb2 is some form of Gen2.
if(iOb2 instanceof Gen2<?>)
  System.out.println("iOb2 is instance of Gen2");

// See if iOb2 is some form of Gen.
if(iOb2 instanceof Gen<?>)
  System.out.println("iOb2 is instance of Gen");
```

As the output shows, both succeed. In the first test, **iOb2** is checked against **Gen2<?>**. This test succeeds because it simply confirms that **iOb2** is an object of some type of **Gen2** object. The use of the wildcard enables **instanceof** to determine if **iOb2** is an object of any type of **Gen2**. Next, **iOb2** is tested against **Gen<?>**, the superclass type. This is also true because **iOb2** is some form of **Gen**, the superclass. The next few lines in **main( )** show the same sequence (and same results) for **strOb2**.

Next, **iOb**, which is an instance of **Gen<Integer>** (the superclass), is tested by these lines:

```
// See if iOb is an instance of Gen2, which it is not.
if(iOb instanceof Gen2<?>)
  System.out.println("iOb is instance of Gen2");

// See if iOb is an instance of Gen, which it is.
if(iOb instanceof Gen<?>)
  System.out.println("iOb is instance of Gen");
```

The first **if** fails because **iOb** is not some type of **Gen2** object. The second test succeeds because **iOb** is some type of **Gen** object.

Now, look closely at these commented-out lines:

```
    // The following can't be compiled because
    // generic type info does not exist at run time.
//    if(iOb2 instanceof Gen2<Integer>)
//      System.out.println("iOb2 is instance of Gen2<Integer>");
```

As the comments indicate, these lines can't be compiled because they attempt to compare **iOb2** with a specific type of **Gen2**, in this case, **Gen2<Integer>**. Remember, there is no generic type information available at run time. Therefore, there is no way for **instanceof** to know if iOb2 is an instance of **Gen2<Integer>** or not.

Casting

You can cast one instance of a generic class into another only if the two are otherwise compatible and their type arguments are the same. For example, assuming the foregoing program, this cast is legal:

```
(Gen<Integer>) iOb2 // legal
```

because **iOb2** is an instance of **Gen<Integer>**. But, this cast:

```
(Gen<Long>) iOb2 // illegal
```

is not legal because **iOb2** is not an instance of **Gen<Long>**.

Overriding Methods in a Generic Class

A method in a generic class can be overridden just like any other method. For example, consider this program in which the method **getob( )** is overridden:

```
// Overriding a generic method in a generic class.
class Gen<T> {
  T ob; // declare an object of type T

  // Pass the constructor a reference to
  // an object of type T.
  Gen(T o) {
    ob = o;
  }

  // Return ob.
  T getob() {
    System.out.print("Gen's getob(): " );
    return ob;
  }
}

// A subclass of Gen that overrides getob().
class Gen2<T> extends Gen<T> {

  Gen2(T o) {
    super(o);
  }

  // Override getob().
  T getob() {
    System.out.print("Gen2's getob(): ");
    return ob;
  }
}
```

```
// Demonstrate generic method override.
class OverrideDemo {
  public static void main(String args[]) {

    // Create a Gen object for Integers.
    Gen<Integer> iOb = new Gen<Integer>(88);

    // Create a Gen2 object for Integers.
    Gen2<Integer> iOb2 = new Gen2<Integer>(99);

    // Create a Gen2 object for Strings.
    Gen2<String> strOb2 = new Gen2<String>("Generics Test");

    System.out.println(iOb.getob());
    System.out.println(iOb2.getob());
    System.out.println(strOb2.getob());
  }
}
```

The output is shown here:

```
Gen's getob(): 88
Gen2's getob(): 99
Gen2's getob(): Generics Test
```

As the output confirms, the overridden version of **getob( )** is called for objects of type **Gen2**, but the superclass version is called for objects of type **Gen**.

Erasure

Usually, it is not necessary to know the details about how the Java compiler transforms your source code into object code. However, in the case of generics, some general understanding of the process is important because it explains why the generic features work as they do—and why their behavior is sometimes a bit surprising. For this reason, a brief discussion of how generics are implemented in Java is in order.

An important constraint that governed the way that generics were added to Java was the need for compatibility with previous versions of Java. Simply put, generic code had to be compatible with preexisting, non-generic code. Thus, any changes to the syntax of the Java language, or to the JVM, had to avoid breaking older code. The way Java implements generics while satisfying this constraint is through the use of *erasure.*

In general, here is how erasure works. When your Java code is compiled, all generic type information is removed (erased). This means replacing type parameters with their bound type, which is **Object** if no explicit bound is specified, and then applying the appropriate casts (as determined by the type arguments) to maintain type compatibility with the types specified by the type arguments. The compiler also enforces this type compatibility. This approach to generics means that no type parameters exist at run time. They are simply a source-code mechanism.

To better understand how erasure works, consider the following two classes:

```
// Here, T is bound by Object by default.
class Gen<T> {
  T ob; // here, T will be replaced by Object

  Gen(T o) {
    ob = o;
  }

  // Return ob.
  T getob() {
    return ob;
  }
}

// Here, T is bound by String.
class GenStr<T extends String> {
  T str; // here, T will be replaced by String

  GenStr(T o) {
    str = o;
  }

  T getstr() { return str; }
}
```

After these two classes are compiled, the **T** in **Gen** will be replaced by **Object**. The **T** in **GenStr** will be replaced by **String**. You can confirm this by running **javap** on their compiled classes. The results are shown here:

```
class Gen extends java.lang.Object{
    java.lang.Object ob;
    Gen(java.lang.Object);
    java.lang.Object getob();
}

class GenStr extends java.lang.Object{
    java.lang.String str;
    GenStr(java.lang.String);
    java.lang.String getstr();
}
```

Within the code for **Gen** and **GenStr**, casts are employed to ensure proper typing. For example, this sequence:

```
Gen<Integer> iOb = new Gen<Integer>(99);

int x = iOb.getob();
```

would be compiled as if it were written like this:

```
Gen iOb = new Gen(99);

int x = (Integer) iOb.getob();
```

Because of erasure, some things work a bit differently than you might think. For example, consider this short program that creates two objects of the generic **Gen** class just shown:

```
class GenTypeDemo {
  public static void main(String args[]) {
    Gen<Integer> iOb = new Gen<Integer>(99);
    Gen<Float> fOb = new Gen<Float>(102.2F);

    System.out.println(iOb.getClass().getName());
    System.out.println(fOb.getClass().getName());
  }
}
```

The output from this program is shown here:

```
Gen
Gen
```

As you can see, the types of both **iOb** and **fOb** are **Gen**, not the **Gen<Integer>** and **Gen<Float>** that you might have expected. Remember, all type parameters are erased during compilation. At run time, only raw types actually exist.

Bridge Methods

Occasionally, the compiler will need to add a *bridge method* to a class to handle situations in which the type erasure of an overriding method in a subclass does not produce the same erasure as the method in the superclass. In this case, a method is generated that uses the type erasure of the superclass, and this method calls the method that has the type erasure specified by the subclass. Of course, bridge methods only occur at the bytecode level, are not seen by you, and are not available for your use.

Although bridge methods are not something that you will normally need to be concerned with, it is still instructive to see a situation in which one is generated. Consider the following program:

```
// A situation that creates a bridge method.
class Gen<T> {
  T ob; // declare an object of type T

  // Pass the constructor a reference to
  // an object of type T.
  Gen(T o) {
    ob = o;
  }

  // Return ob.
  T getob() {
    return ob;
  }
```

```
    }

// A subclass of Gen.
class Gen2 extends Gen<String> {

  Gen2(String o) {
    super(o);
  }

  // A String-specific override of getob().
  String getob() {
    System.out.print("You called String getob(): ");
    return ob;
  }
}

// Demonstrate a situation that requires a bridge method.
class BridgeDemo {
  public static void main(String args[]) {

    // Create a Gen2 object for Strings.
    Gen2 strOb2 = new Gen2("Generics Test");

    System.out.println(strOb2.getob());
  }
}
```

In the program, the subclass **Gen2** extends **Gen**, but does so using a **String**-specific version of **Gen**, as its declaration shows:

```
class Gen2 extends Gen<String> {
```

Furthermore, inside **Gen2**, **getob( )** is overridden with **String** specified as the return type:

```
// A String-specific override of getob().
String getob() {
  System.out.print("You called String getob(): ");
  return ob;
}
```

All of this is perfectly acceptable. The only trouble is that because of type erasure, the expected form of **getob( )** will be

```
Object getob() { // ...
```

To handle this problem, the compiler generates a bridge method with the preceding signature that calls the **String** version. Thus, if you examine the class file for **Gen2** by using **javap**, you will see the following methods:

```
    class Gen2 extends Gen{
        Gen2(java.lang.String);
        java.lang.String getob();
        java.lang.Object getob(); // bridge method
    }
```

As you can see, the bridge method has been included. (The comment was added by the author, and not by **javap**.)

There is one last point to make about bridge methods. Notice that the only difference between the two **getob( )** methods is their return type. Normally, this would cause an error, but because this does not occur in your source code, it does not cause a problem and is handled correctly by the JVM.

Ambiguity Errors

The inclusion of generics gives rise to a new type of error that you must guard against: *ambiguity.* Ambiguity errors occur when erasure causes two seemingly distinct generic declarations to resolve to the same erased type, causing a conflict. Here is an example that involves method overloading:

```
// Ambiguity caused by erasure on
// overloaded methods.
class MyGenClass<T, V> {
  T ob1;
  V ob2;

  // ...

  // These two overloaded methods are ambiguous
  // and will not compile.
  void set(T o) {
    ob1 = o;
  }

  void set(V o) {
    ob2 = o;
  }
}
```

Notice that **MyGenClass** declares two generic types: **T** and **V**. Inside **MyGenClass**, an attempt is made to overload **set( )** based on parameters of type **T** and **V**. This looks reasonable because **T** and **V** appear to be different types. However, there are two ambiguity problems here.

First, as **MyGenClass** is written, there is no requirement that **T** and **V** actually be different types. For example, it is perfectly correct (in principle) to construct a **MyGenClass** object as shown here:

```
MyGenClass<String, String> obj = new MyGenClass<String, String>()
```

In this case, both **T** and **V** will be replaced by **String**. This makes both versions of **set( )** identical, which is, of course, an error.

The second and more fundamental problem is that the type erasure of **set( )** reduces both versions to the following:

```
void set(Object o) { // ...
```

Thus, the overloading of **set( )** as attempted in **MyGenClass** is inherently ambiguous.

Ambiguity errors can be tricky to fix. For example, if you know that **V** will always be some type of **String**, you might try to fix **MyGenClass** by rewriting its declaration as shown here:

```
class MyGenClass<T, V extends String> {  // almost OK!
```

This change causes **MyGenClass** to compile, and you can even instantiate objects like the one shown here:

```
MyGenClass<Integer, String> x = new MyGenClass<Integer, String>();
```

This works because Java can accurately determine which method to call. However, ambiguity returns when you try this line:

```
MyGenClass<String, String> x = new MyGenClass<String, String>();
```

In this case, since both **T** and **V** are **String**, which version of **set( )** is to be called?

Frankly, in the preceding example, it would be much better to use two separate method names, rather than trying to overload **set( )**. Often, the solution to ambiguity involves the restructuring of the code, because ambiguity often means that you have a conceptual error in your design.

Some Generic Restrictions

There are a few restrictions that you need to keep in mind when using generics. They involve creating objects of a type parameter, static members, exceptions, and arrays. Each is examined here.

Type Parameters Can't Be Instantiated

It is not possible to create an instance of a type parameter. For example, consider this class:

```
// Can't create an instance of T.
class Gen<T> {
  T ob;
  Gen() {
    ob = new T(); // Illegal!!!
  }
}
```

Here, it is illegal to attempt to create an instance of **T**. The reason should be easy to understand: because **T** does not exist at run time, how would the compiler know what type of object to create? Remember, erasure removes all type parameters during the compilation process.

Restrictions on Static Members

No **static** member can use a type parameter declared by the enclosing class. For example, all of the **static** members of this class are illegal:

```
class Wrong<T> {
  // Wrong, no static variables of type T.
  static T ob;
```

```
  // Wrong, no static method can use T.
  static T getob() {
    return ob;
  }

  // Wrong, no static method can access object
  // of type T.
  static void showob() {
    System.out.println(ob);
  }
}
```

Although you can't declare **static** members that use a type parameter declared by the enclosing class, you *can* declare **static** generic methods, which define their own type parameters, as was done earlier in this chapter.

Generic Array Restrictions

There are two important generics restrictions that apply to arrays. First, you cannot instantiate an array whose base type is a type parameter. Second, you cannot create an array of type-specific generic references. The following short program shows both situations:

```
// Generics and arrays.
class Gen<T extends Number> {
  T ob;

  T vals[]; // OK

  Gen(T o, T[] nums) {
    ob = o;

    // This statement is illegal.
    // vals = new T[10]; // can't create an array of T

    // But, this statement is OK.
    vals = nums; // OK to assign reference to existent array
  }
}

class GenArrays {
  public static void main(String args[]) {
    Integer n[] = { 1, 2, 3, 4, 5 };

    Gen<Integer> iOb = new Gen<Integer>(50, n);

    // Can't create an array of type-specific generic references.
    // Gen<Integer> gens[] = new Gen<Integer>[10]; // Wrong!

    // This is OK.
    Gen<?> gens[] = new Gen<?>[10]; // OK
  }
}
```

As the program shows, it's valid to declare a reference to an array of type **T**, as this line does:

```
T vals[]; // OK
```

But, you cannot instantiate an array of **T**, as this commented-out line attempts:

```
// vals = new T[10]; // can't create an array of T
```

The reason you can't create an array of **T** is that **T** does not exist at run time, so there is no way for the compiler to know what type of array to actually create.

However, you can pass a reference to a type-compatible array to **Gen( )** when an object is created and assign that reference to **vals**, as the program does in this line:

```
vals = nums; // OK to assign reference to existent array
```

This works because the array passed to **Gen** has a known type, which will be the same type as **T** at the time of object creation.

Inside **main( )**, notice that you can't declare an array of references to a specific generic type. That is, this line

```
// Gen<Integer> gens[] = new Gen<Integer>[10]; // Wrong!
```

won't compile. Arrays of specific generic types simply aren't allowed, because they can lead to a loss of type safety.

You *can* create an array of references to a generic type if you use a wildcard, however, as shown here:

```
Gen<?> gens[] = new Gen<?>[10]; // OK
```

This approach is better than using an array of raw types, because at least some type checking will still be enforced.

Generic Exception Restriction

A generic class cannot extend **Throwable**. This means that you cannot create generic exception classes.

Final Thoughts on Generics

Generics are a powerful extension to Java because they streamline the creation of type-safe, reusable code. Although the generic syntax can seem a bit overwhelming at first, it will become second nature after you use it a while. Generic code will be a part of the future for all Java programmers.

PART

The Java Library

String Handling

A brief overview of Java's string handling was presented in Chapter 7. In this chapter, it is described in detail. As is the case in most other programming languages, in Java a *string* is a sequence of characters. But, unlike many other languages that implement strings as character arrays, Java implements strings as objects of type **String**.

Implementing strings as built-in objects allows Java to provide a full complement of features that make string handling convenient. For example, Java has methods to compare two strings, search for a substring, concatenate two strings, and change the case of letters within a string. Also, **String** objects can be constructed a number of ways, making it easy to obtain a string when needed.

Somewhat unexpectedly, when you create a **String** object, you are creating a string that cannot be changed. That is, once a **String** object has been created, you cannot change the characters that comprise that string. At first, this may seem to be a serious restriction. However, such is not the case. You can still perform all types of string operations. The difference is that each time you need an altered version of an existing string, a new **String** object is created that contains the modifications. The original string is left unchanged. This approach is used because fixed, immutable strings can be implemented more efficiently than changeable ones. For those cases in which a modifiable string is desired, Java provides two options: **StringBuffer** and **StringBuilder**. Both hold strings that can be modified after they are created.

The **String**, **StringBuffer**, and **StringBuilder** classes are defined in **java.lang**. Thus, they are available to all programs automatically. All are declared **final**, which means that none of these classes may be subclassed. This allows certain optimizations that increase performance to take place on common string operations. All three implement the **CharSequence** interface.

One last point: To say that the strings within objects of type **String** are unchangeable means that the contents of the **String** instance cannot be changed after it has been created. However, a variable declared as a **String** reference can be changed to point at some other **String** object at any time.

The String Constructors

The **String** class supports several constructors. To create an empty **String**, call the default constructor. For example,

```
String s = new String();
```

will create an instance of **String** with no characters in it.

Frequently, you will want to create strings that have initial values. The **String** class provides a variety of constructors to handle this. To create a **String** initialized by an array of characters, use the constructor shown here:

String(char *chars*[ ])

Here is an example:

```
char chars[] = { 'a', 'b', 'c' };
String s = new String(chars);
```

This constructor initializes **s** with the string "abc".

You can specify a subrange of a character array as an initializer using the following constructor:

String(char *chars*[ ], int *startIndex*, int *numChars*)

Here, *startIndex* specifies the index at which the subrange begins, and *numChars* specifies the number of characters to use. Here is an example:

```
char chars[] = { 'a', 'b', 'c', 'd', 'e', 'f' };
String s = new String(chars, 2, 3);
```

This initializes **s** with the characters **cde**.

You can construct a **String** object that contains the same character sequence as another **String** object using this constructor:

String(String *strObj*)

Here, *strObj* is a **String** object. Consider this example:

```
// Construct one String from another.
class MakeString {
  public static void main(String args[]) {
    char c[] = {'J', 'a', 'v', 'a'};
    String s1 = new String(c);
    String s2 = new String(s1);

    System.out.println(s1);
    System.out.println(s2);
  }
}
```

The output from this program is as follows:

```
Java
Java
```

As you can see, **s1** and **s2** contain the same string.

Even though Java's **char** type uses 16 bits to represent the basic Unicode character set, the typical format for strings on the Internet uses arrays of 8-bit bytes constructed from the

ASCII character set. Because 8-bit ASCII strings are common, the **String** class provides constructors that initialize a string when given a **byte** array. Their forms are shown here:

String(byte *asciiChars*[ ])
String(byte *asciiChars*[ ], int *startIndex*, int *numChars*)

Here, *asciiChars* specifies the array of bytes. The second form allows you to specify a subrange. In each of these constructors, the byte-to-character conversion is done by using the default character encoding of the platform. The following program illustrates these constructors:

```
// Construct string from subset of char array.
class SubStringCons {
  public static void main(String args[]) {
    byte ascii[] = {65, 66, 67, 68, 69, 70 };

    String s1 = new String(ascii);
    System.out.println(s1);

    String s2 = new String(ascii, 2, 3);
    System.out.println(s2);
  }
}
```

This program generates the following output:

```
ABCDEF
CDE
```

Extended versions of the byte-to-string constructors are also defined in which you can specify the character encoding that determines how bytes are converted to characters. However, most of the time, you will want to use the default encoding provided by the platform.

NOTE *The contents of the array are copied whenever you create a **String** object from an array. If you modify the contents of the array after you have created the string, the **String** will be unchanged.*

You can construct a **String** from a **StringBuffer** by using the constructor shown here:

String(StringBuffer *strBufObj*)

You can construct a **String** from a **StringBuilder** by using this constructor:

String(StringBuilder *strBuildobj*)

The following constructor supports the extended Unicode character set:

String(int *codePoints*[ ], int *startIndex*, int *numChars*)

Here, *codePoints* is an array that contains Unicode code points. The resulting string is constructed from the range that begins at *startIndex* and runs for *numChars*.

Java SE 6 also adds the ability to construct a **String** from a **Charset**.

PART II

> **NOTE** *A discussion of Unicode code points and how they are handled by Java is found in Chapter 16.*

String Length

The length of a string is the number of characters that it contains. To obtain this value, call the **length( )** method, shown here:

> int length( )

The following fragment prints "3", since there are three characters in the string **s**:

```
char chars[] = { 'a', 'b', 'c' };
String s = new String(chars);
System.out.println(s.length());
```

Special String Operations

Because strings are a common and important part of programming, Java has added special support for several string operations within the syntax of the language. These operations include the automatic creation of new **String** instances from string literals, concatenation of multiple **String** objects by use of the + operator, and the conversion of other data types to a string representation. There are explicit methods available to perform all of these functions, but Java does them automatically as a convenience for the programmer and to add clarity.

String Literals

The earlier examples showed how to explicitly create a **String** instance from an array of characters by using the **new** operator. However, there is an easier way to do this using a string literal. For each string literal in your program, Java automatically constructs a **String** object. Thus, you can use a string literal to initialize a **String** object. For example, the following code fragment creates two equivalent strings:

```
char chars[] = { 'a', 'b', 'c' };
String s1 = new String(chars);

String s2 = "abc"; // use string literal
```

Because a **String** object is created for every string literal, you can use a string literal any place you can use a **String** object. For example, you can call methods directly on a quoted string as if it were an object reference, as the following statement shows. It calls the **length( )** method on the string "abc". As expected, it prints "3".

```
System.out.println("abc".length());
```

String Concatenation

In general, Java does not allow operators to be applied to **String** objects. The one exception to this rule is the + operator, which concatenates two strings, producing a **String** object as the result. This allows you to chain together a series of + operations. For example, the following fragment concatenates three strings:

```
String age = "9";
String s = "He is " + age + " years old.";
System.out.println(s);
```

This displays the string "He is 9 years old."

One practical use of string concatenation is found when you are creating very long strings. Instead of letting long strings wrap around within your source code, you can break them into smaller pieces, using the + to concatenate them. Here is an example:

```
// Using concatenation to prevent long lines.
class ConCat {
  public static void main(String args[]) {
    String longStr = "This could have been " +
      "a very long line that would have " +
      "wrapped around.  But string concatenation " +
      "prevents this.";

    System.out.println(longStr);
  }
}
```

String Concatenation with Other Data Types

You can concatenate strings with other types of data. For example, consider this slightly different version of the earlier example:

```
int age = 9;
String s = "He is " + age + " years old.";
System.out.println(s);
```

In this case, **age** is an **int** rather than another **String**, but the output produced is the same as before. This is because the **int** value in **age** is automatically converted into its string representation within a **String** object. This string is then concatenated as before. The compiler will convert an operand to its string equivalent whenever the other operand of the + is an instance of **String**.

Be careful when you mix other types of operations with string concatenation expressions, however. You might get surprising results. Consider the following:

```
String s = "four: " + 2 + 2;
System.out.println(s);
```

This fragment displays

```
four: 22
```

rather than the

```
four: 4
```

that you probably expected. Here's why. Operator precedence causes the concatenation of "four" with the string equivalent of 2 to take place first. This result is then concatenated with the string equivalent of 2 a second time. To complete the integer addition first, you must use parentheses, like this:

```
String s = "four: " + (2 + 2);
```

Now **s** contains the string "four: 4".

String Conversion and toString( )

When Java converts data into its string representation during concatenation, it does so by calling one of the overloaded versions of the string conversion method **valueOf( )** defined by **String**. **valueOf( )** is overloaded for all the primitive types and for type **Object**. For the primitive types, **valueOf( )** returns a string that contains the human-readable equivalent of the value with which it is called. For objects, **valueOf( )** calls the **toString( )** method on the object. We will look more closely at **valueOf( )** later in this chapter. Here, let's examine the **toString( )** method, because it is the means by which you can determine the string representation for objects of classes that you create.

Every class implements **toString( )** because it is defined by **Object**. However, the default implementation of **toString( )** is seldom sufficient. For most important classes that you create, you will want to override **toString( )** and provide your own string representations. Fortunately, this is easy to do. The **toString( )** method has this general form:

String toString( )

To implement **toString( )**, simply return a **String** object that contains the human-readable string that appropriately describes an object of your class.

By overriding **toString( )** for classes that you create, you allow them to be fully integrated into Java's programming environment. For example, they can be used in **print( )** and **println( )** statements and in concatenation expressions. The following program demonstrates this by overriding **toString( )** for the **Box** class:

```
// Override toString() for Box class.
class Box {
  double width;
  double height;
  double depth;

  Box(double w, double h, double d) {
    width = w;
    height = h;
    depth = d;
  }

  public String toString() {
    return "Dimensions are " + width + " by " +
           depth + " by " + height + ".";
  }
}

class toStringDemo {
  public static void main(String args[]) {
    Box b = new Box(10, 12, 14);
    String s = "Box b: " + b; // concatenate Box object
```

```
      System.out.println(b); // convert Box to string
      System.out.println(s);
   }
}
```

The output of this program is shown here:

```
Dimensions are 10.0 by 14.0 by 12.0
Box b: Dimensions are 10.0 by 14.0 by 12.0
```

As you can see, **Box**'s **toString( )** method is automatically invoked when a **Box** object is used in a concatenation expression or in a call to **println( )**.

Character Extraction

The **String** class provides a number of ways in which characters can be extracted from a **String** object. Each is examined here. Although the characters that comprise a string within a **String** object cannot be indexed as if they were a character array, many of the **String** methods employ an index (or offset) into the string for their operation. Like arrays, the string indexes begin at zero.

charAt( )

To extract a single character from a **String**, you can refer directly to an individual character via the **charAt( )** method. It has this general form:

   char charAt(int *where*)

Here, *where* is the index of the character that you want to obtain. The value of *where* must be nonnegative and specify a location within the string. **charAt( )** returns the character at the specified location. For example,

```
char ch;
ch = "abc".charAt(1);
```

assigns the value "b" to **ch**.

getChars( )

If you need to extract more than one character at a time, you can use the **getChars( )** method. It has this general form:

   void getChars(int *sourceStart*, int *sourceEnd*, char *target*[ ], int *targetStart*)

Here, *sourceStart* specifies the index of the beginning of the substring, and *sourceEnd* specifies an index that is one past the end of the desired substring. Thus, the substring contains the characters from *sourceStart* through *sourceEnd*–1. The array that will receive the characters is specified by *target*. The index within *target* at which the substring will be copied is passed in *targetStart*. Care must be taken to assure that the *target* array is large enough to hold the number of characters in the specified substring.

The following program demonstrates **getChars( )**:

```
class getCharsDemo {
  public static void main(String args[]) {
    String s = "This is a demo of the getChars method.";
    int start = 10;
    int end = 14;
    char buf[] = new char[end - start];

    s.getChars(start, end, buf, 0);
    System.out.println(buf);
  }
}
```

Here is the output of this program:

```
demo
```

getBytes( )

There is an alternative to **getChars( )** that stores the characters in an array of bytes. This method is called **getBytes( )**, and it uses the default character-to-byte conversions provided by the platform. Here is its simplest form:

byte[ ] getBytes( )

Other forms of **getBytes( )** are also available. **getBytes( )** is most useful when you are exporting a **String** value into an environment that does not support 16-bit Unicode characters. For example, most Internet protocols and text file formats use 8-bit ASCII for all text interchange.

toCharArray( )

If you want to convert all the characters in a **String** object into a character array, the easiest way is to call **toCharArray( )**. It returns an array of characters for the entire string. It has this general form:

char[ ] toCharArray( )

This function is provided as a convenience, since it is possible to use **getChars( )** to achieve the same result.

String Comparison

The **String** class includes several methods that compare strings or substrings within strings. Each is examined here.

equals( ) and equalsIgnoreCase( )

To compare two strings for equality, use **equals( )**. It has this general form:

boolean equals(Object *str*)

Here, *str* is the **String** object being compared with the invoking **String** object. It returns **true** if the strings contain the same characters in the same order, and **false** otherwise. The comparison is case-sensitive.

To perform a comparison that ignores case differences, call **equalsIgnoreCase( )**. When it compares two strings, it considers **A-Z** to be the same as **a-z**. It has this general form:

boolean equalsIgnoreCase(String *str*)

Here, *str* is the **String** object being compared with the invoking **String** object. It, too, returns **true** if the strings contain the same characters in the same order, and **false** otherwise.

Here is an example that demonstrates **equals( )** and **equalsIgnoreCase( )**:

```
// Demonstrate equals() and equalsIgnoreCase().
class equalsDemo {
  public static void main(String args[]) {
    String s1 = "Hello";
    String s2 = "Hello";
    String s3 = "Good-bye";
    String s4 = "HELLO";
    System.out.println(s1 + " equals " + s2 + " -> " +
                       s1.equals(s2));
    System.out.println(s1 + " equals " + s3 + " -> " +
                       s1.equals(s3));
    System.out.println(s1 + " equals " + s4 + " -> " +
                       s1.equals(s4));
    System.out.println(s1 + " equalsIgnoreCase " + s4 + " -> " +
                       s1.equalsIgnoreCase(s4));
  }
}
```

The output from the program is shown here:

```
Hello equals Hello -> true
Hello equals Good-bye -> false
Hello equals HELLO -> false
Hello equalsIgnoreCase HELLO -> true
```

regionMatches( )

The **regionMatches( )** method compares a specific region inside a string with another specific region in another string. There is an overloaded form that allows you to ignore case in such comparisons. Here are the general forms for these two methods:

boolean regionMatches(int *startIndex*, String *str2*,
  int *str2StartIndex*, int *numChars*)

boolean regionMatches(boolean *ignoreCase*,
  int *startIndex*, String *str2*,
  int *str2StartIndex*, int *numChars*)

For both versions, *startIndex* specifies the index at which the region begins within the invoking **String** object. The **String** being compared is specified by *str2*. The index at which the comparison will start within *str2* is specified by *str2StartIndex*. The length of the substring being compared is passed in *numChars*. In the second version, if *ignoreCase* is **true**, the case of the characters is ignored. Otherwise, case is significant.

startsWith( ) and endsWith( )

String defines two routines that are, more or less, specialized forms of **regionMatches( )**. The **startsWith( )** method determines whether a given **String** begins with a specified string. Conversely, **endsWith( )** determines whether the **String** in question ends with a specified string. They have the following general forms:

boolean startsWith(String *str*)
boolean endsWith(String *str*)

Here, *str* is the **String** being tested. If the string matches, **true** is returned. Otherwise, **false** is returned. For example,

```
"Foobar".endsWith("bar")
```

and

```
"Foobar".startsWith("Foo")
```

are both **true**.

A second form of **startsWith( )**, shown here, lets you specify a starting point:

boolean startsWith(String *str*, int *startIndex*)

Here, *startIndex* specifies the index into the invoking string at which point the search will begin. For example,

```
"Foobar".startsWith("bar", 3)
```

returns **true**.

equals( ) Versus ==

It is important to understand that the **equals( )** method and the **==** operator perform two different operations. As just explained, the **equals( )** method compares the characters inside a **String** object. The **==** operator compares two object references to see whether they refer to the same instance. The following program shows how two different **String** objects can contain the same characters, but references to these objects will not compare as equal:

```
// equals() vs ==
class EqualsNotEqualTo {
  public static void main(String args[]) {
    String s1 = "Hello";
    String s2 = new String(s1);

    System.out.println(s1 + " equals " + s2 + " -> " +
                       s1.equals(s2));
    System.out.println(s1 + " == " + s2 + " -> " + (s1 == s2));
  }
}
```

The variable **s1** refers to the **String** instance created by "Hello". The object referred to by **s2** is created with **s1** as an initializer. Thus, the contents of the two **String** objects are identical, but they are distinct objects. This means that **s1** and **s2** do not refer to the same objects and are, therefore, not **==**, as is shown here by the output of the preceding example:

```
Hello equals Hello -> true
Hello == Hello -> false
```

compareTo( )

Often, it is not enough to simply know whether two strings are identical. For sorting applications, you need to know which is *less than, equal to,* or *greater than* the next. A string is less than another if it comes before the other in dictionary order. A string is greater than another if it comes after the other in dictionary order. The **String** method **compareTo( )** serves this purpose. It has this general form:

int compareTo(String *str*)

Here, *str* is the **String** being compared with the invoking **String**. The result of the comparison is returned and is interpreted, as shown here:

Value	Meaning
Less than zero	The invoking string is less than *str*.
Greater than zero	The invoking string is greater than *str*.
Zero	The two strings are equal.

Here is a sample program that sorts an array of strings. The program uses **compareTo( )** to determine sort ordering for a bubble sort:

```
// A bubble sort for Strings.
class SortString {
  static String arr[] = {
    "Now", "is", "the", "time", "for", "all", "good", "men",
    "to", "come", "to", "the", "aid", "of", "their", "country"
  };
  public static void main(String args[]) {
    for(int j = 0; j < arr.length; j++) {
      for(int i = j + 1; i < arr.length; i++) {
        if(arr[i].compareTo(arr[j]) < 0) {
          String t = arr[j];
          arr[j] = arr[i];
          arr[i] = t;
        }
      }
      System.out.println(arr[j]);
    }
  }
}
```

The output of this program is the list of words:

```
Now
aid
all
come
country
for
good
is
men
of
the
the
their
time
to
to
```

As you can see from the output of this example, **compareTo( )** takes into account uppercase and lowercase letters. The word "Now" came out before all the others because it begins with an uppercase letter, which means it has a lower value in the ASCII character set.

If you want to ignore case differences when comparing two strings, use **compareToIgnoreCase( )**, as shown here:

int compareToIgnoreCase(String *str*)

This method returns the same results as **compareTo( )**, except that case differences are ignored. You might want to try substituting it into the previous program. After doing so, "Now" will no longer be first.

Searching Strings

The **String** class provides two methods that allow you to search a string for a specified character or substring:

- **indexOf( )** Searches for the first occurrence of a character or substring.
- **lastIndexOf( )** Searches for the last occurrence of a character or substring.

These two methods are overloaded in several different ways. In all cases, the methods return the index at which the character or substring was found, or –1 on failure.

To search for the first occurrence of a character, use

int indexOf(int *ch*)

To search for the last occurrence of a character, use

int lastIndexOf(int *ch*)

Here, *ch* is the character being sought.

To search for the first or last occurrence of a substring, use

int indexOf(String *str*)
int lastIndexOf(String *str*)

Here, *str* specifies the substring.

You can specify a starting point for the search using these forms:

int indexOf(int *ch*, int *startIndex*)
int lastIndexOf(int *ch*, int *startIndex*)

int indexOf(String *str*, int *startIndex*)
int lastIndexOf(String *str*, int *startIndex*)

Here, *startIndex* specifies the index at which point the search begins. For **indexOf( )**, the search runs from *startIndex* to the end of the string. For **lastIndexOf( )**, the search runs from *startIndex* to zero.

The following example shows how to use the various index methods to search inside of **String**s:

```
// Demonstrate indexOf() and lastIndexOf().
class indexOfDemo {
  public static void main(String args[]) {
    String s = "Now is the time for all good men " +
               "to come to the aid of their country.";

    System.out.println(s);
    System.out.println("indexOf(t) = " +
                       s.indexOf('t'));
    System.out.println("lastIndexOf(t) = " +
                       s.lastIndexOf('t'));
    System.out.println("indexOf(the) = " +
                       s.indexOf("the"));
    System.out.println("lastIndexOf(the) = " +
                       s.lastIndexOf("the"));
    System.out.println("indexOf(t, 10) = " +
                       s.indexOf('t', 10));
    System.out.println("lastIndexOf(t, 60) = " +
                       s.lastIndexOf('t', 60));
    System.out.println("indexOf(the, 10) = " +
                       s.indexOf("the", 10));
    System.out.println("lastIndexOf(the, 60) = " +
                       s.lastIndexOf("the", 60));
  }
}
```

Here is the output of this program:

```
Now is the time for all good men to come to the aid of their country.
indexOf(t) = 7
lastIndexOf(t) = 65
indexOf(the) = 7
```

```
lastIndexOf(the) = 55
indexOf(t, 10) = 11
lastIndexOf(t, 60) = 55
indexOf(the, 10) = 44
lastIndexOf(the, 60) = 55
```

Modifying a String

Because **String** objects are immutable, whenever you want to modify a **String**, you must either copy it into a **StringBuffer** or **StringBuilder**, or use one of the following **String** methods, which will construct a new copy of the string with your modifications complete.

substring( )

You can extract a substring using **substring( )**. It has two forms. The first is

String substring(int *startIndex*)

Here, *startIndex* specifies the index at which the substring will begin. This form returns a copy of the substring that begins at *startIndex* and runs to the end of the invoking string.

The second form of **substring( )** allows you to specify both the beginning and ending index of the substring:

String substring(int *startIndex*, int *endIndex*)

Here, *startIndex* specifies the beginning index, and *endIndex* specifies the stopping point. The string returned contains all the characters from the beginning index, up to, but not including, the ending index.

The following program uses **substring( )** to replace all instances of one substring with another within a string:

```java
// Substring replacement.
class StringReplace {
  public static void main(String args[]) {
    String org = "This is a test. This is, too.";
    String search = "is";
    String sub = "was";
    String result = "";
    int i;

    do { // replace all matching substrings
      System.out.println(org);
      i = org.indexOf(search);
      if(i != -1) {
        result = org.substring(0, i);
        result = result + sub;
        result = result + org.substring(i + search.length());
        org = result;
      }
    } while(i != -1);

  }
}
```

The output from this program is shown here:

```
This is a test. This is, too.
Thwas is a test. This is, too.
Thwas was a test. This is, too.
Thwas was a test. Thwas is, too.
Thwas was a test. Thwas was, too.
```

concat( )

You can concatenate two strings using **concat( )**, shown here:

String concat(String *str*)

This method creates a new object that contains the invoking string with the contents of *str* appended to the end. **concat( )** performs the same function as **+**. For example,

```
String s1 = "one";
String s2 = s1.concat("two");
```

puts the string "onetwo" into **s2**. It generates the same result as the following sequence:

```
String s1 = "one";
String s2 = s1 + "two";
```

replace( )

The **replace( )** method has two forms. The first replaces all occurrences of one character in the invoking string with another character. It has the following general form:

String replace(char *original*, char *replacement*)

Here, *original* specifies the character to be replaced by the character specified by *replacement*. The resulting string is returned. For example,

```
String s = "Hello".replace('l', 'w');
```

puts the string "Hewwo" into **s**.

The second form of **replace( )** replaces one character sequence with another. It has this general form:

String replace(CharSequence *original*, CharSequence *replacement*)

trim( )

The **trim( )** method returns a copy of the invoking string from which any leading and trailing whitespace has been removed. It has this general form:

String trim( )

Here is an example:

```
String s = "   Hello World    ".trim();
```

This puts the string "Hello World" into **s**.

The **trim( )** method is quite useful when you process user commands. For example, the following program prompts the user for the name of a state and then displays that state's capital. It uses **trim( )** to remove any leading or trailing whitespace that may have inadvertently been entered by the user.

```java
// Using trim() to process commands.
import java.io.*;

class UseTrim {
  public static void main(String args[])
    throws IOException
  {
    // create a BufferedReader using System.in
    BufferedReader br = new
      BufferedReader(new InputStreamReader(System.in));
    String str;

    System.out.println("Enter 'stop' to quit.");
    System.out.println("Enter State: ");
    do {
      str = br.readLine();
      str = str.trim(); // remove whitespace

      if(str.equals("Illinois"))
        System.out.println("Capital is Springfield.");
      else if(str.equals("Missouri"))
        System.out.println("Capital is Jefferson City.");
      else if(str.equals("California"))
        System.out.println("Capital is Sacramento.");
      else if(str.equals("Washington"))
        System.out.println("Capital is Olympia.");
      // ...
    } while(!str.equals("stop"));
  }
}
```

Data Conversion Using valueOf( )

The **valueOf( )** method converts data from its internal format into a human-readable form. It is a static method that is overloaded within **String** for all of Java's built-in types so that each type can be converted properly into a string. **valueOf( )** is also overloaded for type **Object**, so an object of any class type you create can also be used as an argument. (Recall that **Object** is a superclass for all classes.) Here are a few of its forms:

static String valueOf(double *num*)
static String valueOf(long *num*)
static String valueOf(Object *ob*)
static String valueOf(char *chars*[ ])

As we discussed earlier, **valueOf( )** is called when a string representation of some other type of data is needed—for example, during concatenation operations. You can call this method directly with any data type and get a reasonable **String** representation. All of the simple types are converted to their common **String** representation. Any object that you pass to **valueOf( )** will return the result of a call to the object's **toString( )** method. In fact, you could just call **toString( )** directly and get the same result.

For most arrays, **valueOf( )** returns a rather cryptic string, which indicates that it is an array of some type. For arrays of **char**, however, a **String** object is created that contains the characters in the **char** array. There is a special version of **valueOf( )** that allows you to specify a subset of a **char** array. It has this general form:

static String valueOf(char *chars*[ ], int *startIndex*, int *numChars*)

Here, *chars* is the array that holds the characters, *startIndex* is the index into the array of characters at which the desired substring begins, and *numChars* specifies the length of the substring.

Changing the Case of Characters Within a String

The method **toLowerCase( )** converts all the characters in a string from uppercase to lowercase. The **toUpperCase( )** method converts all the characters in a string from lowercase to uppercase. Nonalphabetical characters, such as digits, are unaffected. Here are the general forms of these methods:

String toLowerCase( )
String toUpperCase( )

Both methods return a **String** object that contains the uppercase or lowercase equivalent of the invoking **String**. The default locale governs the conversion in both cases.

Here is an example that uses **toLowerCase( )** and **toUpperCase( )**:

```
// Demonstrate toUpperCase() and toLowerCase().

class ChangeCase {
  public static void main(String args[])
  {
    String s = "This is a test.";

    System.out.println("Original: " + s);

    String upper = s.toUpperCase();
    String lower = s.toLowerCase();

    System.out.println("Uppercase: " + upper);
    System.out.println("Lowercase: " + lower);
  }
}
```

The output produced by the program is shown here:

```
Original: This is a test.
Uppercase: THIS IS A TEST.
Lowercase: this is a test.
```

PART II

One other point: Overloaded versions of **toLowerCase( )** and **toUpperCase( )** that let you specify a **Locale** object to govern the conversion are also supplied.

Additional String Methods

In addition to those methods discussed earlier, **String** includes several other methods. These are summarized in the following table.

Method	Description
int codePointAt(int *i*)	Returns the Unicode code point at the location specified by *i*.
int codePointBefore(int *i*)	Returns the Unicode code point at the location that precedes that specified by *i*.
int codePointCount(int *start*, int *end*)	Returns the number of code points in the portion of the invoking **String** that are between *start* and *end*–1.
boolean contains(CharSequence *str*)	Returns **true** if the invoking object contains the string specified by *str*. Returns **false**, otherwise.
boolean contentEquals(CharSequence *str*)	Returns **true** if the invoking string contains the same string as *str*. Otherwise, returns **false**.
boolean contentEquals(StringBuffer *str*)	Returns **true** if the invoking string contains the same string as *str*. Otherwise, returns **false**.
static String format(String *fmtstr*, Object ... *args*)	Returns a string formatted as specified by *fmtstr*. (See Chapter 18 for details on formatting.)
static String format(Locale *loc*, String *fmtstr*, Object ... *args*)	Returns a string formatted as specified by *fmtstr*. Formatting is governed by the locale specified by *loc*. (See Chapter 18 for details on formatting.)
boolean isEmpty( )	Returns **true** if the invoking string contains no characters and has a length of zero. Added by Java SE 6.
boolean matches(string *regExp*)	Returns **true** if the invoking string matches the regular expression passed in *regExp*. Otherwise, returns **false**.
int offsetByCodePoints(int *start*, int *num*)	Returns the index within the invoking string that is *num* code points beyond the starting index specified by *start*.
String replaceFirst(String *regExp*, String *newStr*)	Returns a string in which the first substring that matches the regular expression specified by *regExp* is replaced by *newStr*.
String replaceAll(String *regExp*, String *newStr*)	Returns a string in which all substrings that match the regular expression specified by *regExp* are replaced by *newStr*.
String[ ] split(String *regExp*)	Decomposes the invoking string into parts and returns an array that contains the result. Each part is delimited by the regular expression passed in *regExp*.

Method	Description
String[ ] split(String *regExp*, int *max*)	Decomposes the invoking string into parts and returns an array that contains the result. Each part is delimited by the regular expression passed in *regExp*. The number of pieces is specified by *max*. If *max* is negative, then the invoking string is fully decomposed. Otherwise, if *max* contains a nonzero value, the last entry in the returned array contains the remainder of the invoking string. If *max* is zero, the invoking string is fully decomposed.

CharSequence
    subSequence(int *startIndex*,
                  int *stopIndex*)
	Returns a substring of the invoking string, beginning at *startIndex* and stopping at *stopIndex*. This method is required by the **CharSequence** interface, which is implemented by **String**.

Notice that several of these methods work with regular expressions. Regular expressions are described in Chapter 27.

StringBuffer

StringBuffer is a peer class of **String** that provides much of the functionality of strings. As you know, **String** represents fixed-length, immutable character sequences. In contrast, **StringBuffer** represents growable and writeable character sequences. **StringBuffer** may have characters and substrings inserted in the middle or appended to the end. **StringBuffer** will automatically grow to make room for such additions and often has more characters preallocated than are actually needed, to allow room for growth. Java uses both classes heavily, but many programmers deal only with **String** and let Java manipulate **StringBuffer**s behind the scenes by using the overloaded + operator.

StringBuffer Constructors

StringBuffer defines these four constructors:

```
StringBuffer( )
StringBuffer(int size)
StringBuffer(String str)
StringBuffer(CharSequence chars)
```

The default constructor (the one with no parameters) reserves room for 16 characters without reallocation. The second version accepts an integer argument that explicitly sets the size of the buffer. The third version accepts a **String** argument that sets the initial contents of the **StringBuffer** object and reserves room for 16 more characters without reallocation. **StringBuffer** allocates room for 16 additional characters when no specific buffer length is requested, because reallocation is a costly process in terms of time. Also, frequent reallocations can fragment memory. By allocating room for a few extra characters, **StringBuffer** reduces the number of reallocations that take place. The fourth constructor creates an object that contains the character sequence contained in *chars*.

length( ) and capacity( )

The current length of a **StringBuffer** can be found via the **length( )** method, while the total allocated capacity can be found through the **capacity( )** method. They have the following general forms:

```
int length( )
int capacity( )
```

Here is an example:

```
// StringBuffer length vs. capacity.
class StringBufferDemo {
  public static void main(String args[]) {
    StringBuffer sb = new StringBuffer("Hello");

    System.out.println("buffer = " + sb);
    System.out.println("length = " + sb.length());
    System.out.println("capacity = " + sb.capacity());
  }
}
```

Here is the output of this program, which shows how **StringBuffer** reserves extra space for additional manipulations:

```
buffer = Hello
length = 5
capacity = 21
```

Since **sb** is initialized with the string "Hello" when it is created, its length is 5. Its capacity is 21 because room for 16 additional characters is automatically added.

ensureCapacity( )

If you want to preallocate room for a certain number of characters after a **StringBuffer** has been constructed, you can use **ensureCapacity( )** to set the size of the buffer. This is useful if you know in advance that you will be appending a large number of small strings to a **StringBuffer**. **ensureCapacity( )** has this general form:

```
void ensureCapacity(int capacity)
```

Here, *capacity* specifies the size of the buffer.

setLength( )

To set the length of the string within a **StringBuffer** object, use **setLength( )**. Its general form is shown here:

```
void setLength(int len)
```

Here, *len* specifies the length of the string. This value must be nonnegative.

When you increase the size of the string, null characters are added to the end. If you call **setLength( )** with a value less than the current value returned by **length( )**, then the characters stored beyond the new length will be lost. The **setCharAtDemo** sample program in the following section uses **setLength( )** to shorten a **StringBuffer**.

charAt( ) and setCharAt( )

The value of a single character can be obtained from a **StringBuffer** via the **charAt( )** method. You can set the value of a character within a **StringBuffer** using **setCharAt( )**. Their general forms are shown here:

char charAt(int *where*)
void setCharAt(int *where*, char *ch*)

For **charAt( )**, *where* specifies the index of the character being obtained. For **setCharAt( )**, *where* specifies the index of the character being set, and *ch* specifies the new value of that character. For both methods, *where* must be nonnegative and must not specify a location beyond the end of the buffer.

The following example demonstrates **charAt( )** and **setCharAt( )**:

```
// Demonstrate charAt() and setCharAt().
class setCharAtDemo {
  public static void main(String args[]) {
    StringBuffer sb = new StringBuffer("Hello");
    System.out.println("buffer before = " + sb);
    System.out.println("charAt(1) before = " + sb.charAt(1));
    sb.setCharAt(1, 'i');
    sb.setLength(2);
    System.out.println("buffer after = " + sb);
    System.out.println("charAt(1) after = " + sb.charAt(1));
  }
}
```

Here is the output generated by this program:

```
buffer before = Hello
charAt(1) before = e
buffer after = Hi
charAt(1) after = i
```

getChars( )

To copy a substring of a **StringBuffer** into an array, use the **getChars( )** method. It has this general form:

void getChars(int *sourceStart*, int *sourceEnd*, char *target*[ ], int *targetStart*)

Here, *sourceStart* specifies the index of the beginning of the substring, and *sourceEnd* specifies an index that is one past the end of the desired substring. This means that the substring contains the characters from *sourceStart* through *sourceEnd*–1. The array that will receive the characters is specified by *target*. The index within *target* at which the substring will be copied is passed in *targetStart*. Care must be taken to assure that the *target* array is large enough to hold the number of characters in the specified substring.

append( )

The **append( )** method concatenates the string representation of any other type of data to the end of the invoking **StringBuffer** object. It has several overloaded versions. Here are a few of its forms:

StringBuffer append(String *str*)
StringBuffer append(int *num*)
StringBuffer append(Object *obj*)

String.valueOf( ) is called for each parameter to obtain its string representation. The result is appended to the current **StringBuffer** object. The buffer itself is returned by each version of **append( )**. This allows subsequent calls to be chained together, as shown in the following example:

```
// Demonstrate append().
class appendDemo {
  public static void main(String args[]) {
    String s;
    int a = 42;
    StringBuffer sb = new StringBuffer(40);

    s = sb.append("a = ").append(a).append("!").toString();
    System.out.println(s);
  }
}
```

The output of this example is shown here:

```
a = 42!
```

The **append( )** method is most often called when the + operator is used on **String** objects. Java automatically changes modifications to a **String** instance into similar operations on a **StringBuffer** instance. Thus, a concatenation invokes **append( )** on a **StringBuffer** object. After the concatenation has been performed, the compiler inserts a call to **toString( )** to turn the modifiable **StringBuffer** back into a constant **String**. All of this may seem unreasonably complicated. Why not just have one string class and have it behave more or less like **StringBuffer**? The answer is performance. There are many optimizations that the Java run time can make knowing that **String** objects are immutable. Thankfully, Java hides most of the complexity of conversion between **String**s and **StringBuffer**s. Actually, many programmers will never feel the need to use **StringBuffer** directly and will be able to express most operations in terms of the + operator on **String** variables.

insert( )

The **insert( )** method inserts one string into another. It is overloaded to accept values of all the primitive types, plus **String**s, **Object**s, and **CharSequence**s. Like **append( )**, it calls **String.valueOf( )** to obtain the string representation of the value it is called with. This string is then inserted into the invoking **StringBuffer** object. These are a few of its forms:

StringBuffer insert(int *index*, String *str*)
StringBuffer insert(int *index*, char *ch*)
StringBuffer insert(int *index*, Object *obj*)

Here, *index* specifies the index at which point the string will be inserted into the invoking **StringBuffer** object.

The following sample program inserts "like" between "I" and "Java":

```
// Demonstrate insert().
class insertDemo {
  public static void main(String args[]) {
    StringBuffer sb = new StringBuffer("I Java!");

    sb.insert(2, "like ");
    System.out.println(sb);
  }
}
```

The output of this example is shown here:

```
I like Java!
```

reverse( )

You can reverse the characters within a **StringBuffer** object using **reverse( )**, shown here:

StringBuffer reverse( )

This method returns the reversed object on which it was called. The following program demonstrates **reverse( )**:

```
// Using reverse() to reverse a StringBuffer.
class ReverseDemo {
  public static void main(String args[]) {
    StringBuffer s = new StringBuffer("abcdef");

    System.out.println(s);
    s.reverse();
    System.out.println(s);
  }
}
```

Here is the output produced by the program:

```
abcdef
fedcba
```

delete( ) and deleteCharAt( )

You can delete characters within a **StringBuffer** by using the methods **delete( )** and **deleteCharAt( )**. These methods are shown here:

StringBuffer delete(int *startIndex*, int *endIndex*)
StringBuffer deleteCharAt(int *loc*)

The **delete( )** method deletes a sequence of characters from the invoking object. Here, *startIndex* specifies the index of the first character to remove, and *endIndex* specifies an index one past the last character to remove. Thus, the substring deleted runs from *startIndex* to *endIndex*–1. The resulting **StringBuffer** object is returned.

The **deleteCharAt( )** method deletes the character at the index specified by *loc*. It returns the resulting **StringBuffer** object.

Here is a program that demonstrates the **delete( )** and **deleteCharAt( )** methods:

```
// Demonstrate delete() and deleteCharAt()
class deleteDemo {
  public static void main(String args[]) {
    StringBuffer sb = new StringBuffer("This is a test.");

    sb.delete(4, 7);
    System.out.println("After delete: " + sb);

    sb.deleteCharAt(0);
    System.out.println("After deleteCharAt: " + sb);
  }
}
```

The following output is produced:

```
After delete: This a test.
After deleteCharAt: his a test.
```

replace( )

You can replace one set of characters with another set inside a **StringBuffer** object by calling **replace( )**. Its signature is shown here:

StringBuffer replace(int *startIndex*, int *endIndex*, String *str*)

The substring being replaced is specified by the indexes *startIndex* and *endIndex*. Thus, the substring at *startIndex* through *endIndex*–1 is replaced. The replacement string is passed in *str*. The resulting **StringBuffer** object is returned.

The following program demonstrates **replace( )**:

```
// Demonstrate replace()
class replaceDemo {
  public static void main(String args[]) {
    StringBuffer sb = new StringBuffer("This is a test.");
```

```
    sb.replace(5, 7, "was");
    System.out.println("After replace: " + sb);
  }
}
```

Here is the output:

```
After replace: This was a test.
```

substring( )

You can obtain a portion of a **StringBuffer** by calling **substring( )**. It has the following two forms:

String substring(int *startIndex*)
String substring(int *startIndex*, int *endIndex*)

The first form returns the substring that starts at *startIndex* and runs to the end of the invoking **StringBuffer** object. The second form returns the substring that starts at *startIndex* and runs through *endIndex*–1. These methods work just like those defined for **String** that were described earlier.

Additional StringBuffer Methods

In addition to those methods just described, **StringBuffer** includes several others. They are summarized in the following table.

Method	Description
StringBuffer appendCodePoint(int *ch*)	Appends a Unicode code point to the end of the invoking object. A reference to the object is returned.
int codePointAt(int *i*)	Returns the Unicode code point at the location specified by *i*.
int codePointBefore(int *i*)	Returns the Unicode code point at the location that precedes that specified by *i*.
int codePointCount(int *start*, int *end*)	Returns the number of code points in the portion of the invoking **String** that are between *start* and *end*–1.
int indexOf(String *str*)	Searches the invoking **StringBuffer** for the first occurrence of *str*. Returns the index of the match, or –1 if no match is found.
int indexOf(String *str*, int *startIndex*)	Searches the invoking **StringBuffer** for the first occurrence of *str*, beginning at *startIndex*. Returns the index of the match, or –1 if no match is found.
int lastIndexOf(String *str*)	Searches the invoking **StringBuffer** for the last occurrence of *str*. Returns the index of the match, or –1 if no match is found.
int lastIndexOf(String *str*, int *startIndex*)	Searches the invoking **StringBuffer** for the last occurrence of *str*, beginning at *startIndex*. Returns the index of the match, or –1 if no match is found.
int offsetByCodePoints(int *start*, int *num*)	Returns the index with the invoking string that is *num* code points beyond the starting index specified by *start*.

Method	Description
CharSequence subSequence(int *startIndex*, int *stopIndex*)	Returns a substring of the invoking string, beginning at *startIndex* and stopping at *stopIndex*. This method is required by the **CharSequence** interface, which is implemented by **StringBuffer**.
void trimToSize( )	Reduces the size of the character buffer for the invoking object to exactly fit the current contents.

The following program demonstrates **indexOf( )** and **lastIndexOf( )**:

```
class IndexOfDemo {
  public static void main(String args[]) {
    StringBuffer sb = new StringBuffer("one two one");
    int i;

    i = sb.indexOf("one");
    System.out.println("First index: " + i);

    i = sb.lastIndexOf("one");
    System.out.println("Last index: " + i);
  }
}
```

The output is shown here:

```
First index: 0
Last index: 8
```

StringBuilder

Introduced by JDK 5, **StringBuilder** is a recent addition to Java's string handling capabilities. **StringBuilder** is identical to **StringBuffer** except for one important difference: it is not synchronized, which means that it is not thread-safe. The advantage of **StringBuilder** is faster performance. However, in cases in which you are using multithreading, you must use **StringBuffer** rather than **StringBuilder**.

Exploring java.lang

This chapter discusses thos e classes and interfaces defined by **java.lang**. As you know, **java.lang** is automatically imported into all programs. It contains classes and interfaces that are fundamental to virtually all of Java programming. It is Java's most widely used package.

java.lang includes the following classes:

Boolean	InheritableThreadLocal	Runtime	System
Byte	Integer	RuntimePermission	Thread
Character	Long	SecurityManager	ThreadGroup
Class	Math	Short	ThreadLocal
ClassLoader	Number	StackTraceElement	Throwable
Compiler	Object	StrictMath	Void
Double	Package	String	
Enum	Process	StringBuffer	
Float	ProcessBuilder	StringBuilder	

There are also two classes defined by the **Character** class: **Character.Subset** and **Character.UnicodeBlock**.

java.lang defines the following interfaces:

Appendable	Comparable	Runnable
CharSequence	Iterable	
Cloneable	Readable	

Several of the classes contained in **java.lang** contain deprecated methods, most dating back to Java 1.0. These deprecated methods are still provided by Java to support an ever-shrinking pool of legacy code and are not recommended for new code. Most of the deprecations took place prior to Java SE 6, and these deprecated methods are not discussed here.

Primitive Type Wrappers

As mentioned in Part I of this book, Java uses primitive types, such as **int** and **char**, for performance reasons. These data types are not part of the object hierarchy. They are passed by value to methods and cannot be directly passed by reference. Also, there is no way for two methods to refer to the *same instance* of an **int**. At times, you will need to create an object representation for one of these primitive types. For example, there are collection classes discussed in Chapter 17 that deal only with objects; to store a primitive type in one of these classes, you need to wrap the primitive type in a class. To address this need, Java provides classes that correspond to each of the primitive types. In essence, these classes encapsulate, or *wrap,* the primitive types within a class. Thus, they are commonly referred to as *type wrappers.* The type wrappers were introduced in Chapter 12. They are examined in detail here.

Number

The abstract class **Number** defines a superclass that is implemented by the classes that wrap the numeric types **byte**, **short**, **int**, **long**, **float**, and **double**. **Number** has abstract methods that return the value of the object in each of the different number formats. For example, **doubleValue( )** returns the value as a **double**, **floatValue( )** returns the value as a **float**, and so on. These methods are shown here:

```
byte byteValue( )
double doubleValue( )
float floatValue( )
int intValue( )
long longValue( )
short shortValue( )
```

The values returned by these methods can be rounded.

Number has six concrete subclasses that hold explicit values of each numeric type: **Double**, **Float**, **Byte**, **Short**, **Integer**, and **Long**.

Double and Float

Double and **Float** are wrappers for floating-point values of type **double** and **float**, respectively. The constructors for **Float** are shown here:

```
Float(double num)
Float(float num)
Float(String str) throws NumberFormatException
```

As you can see, **Float** objects can be constructed with values of type **float** or **double**. They can also be constructed from the string representation of a floating-point number.

The constructors for **Double** are shown here:

```
Double(double num)
Double(String str) throws NumberFormatException
```

Double objects can be constructed with a **double** value or a string containing a floating-point value.

The methods defined by **Float** are shown in Table 16-1. The methods defined by **Double** are shown in Table 16-2. Both **Float** and **Double** define the following constants:

MAX_EXPONENT	Maximum exponent (Added by Java SE 6.)
MAX_VALUE	Maximum positive value
MIN_EXPONENT	Minimum exponent (Added by Java SE 6.)
MIN_NORMAL	Minimum positive normal value (Added by Java SE 6.)
MIN_VALUE	Minimum positive value
NaN	Not a number
POSITIVE_INFINITY	Positive infinity
NEGATIVE_INFINITY	Negative infinity
SIZE	The bit width of the wrapped value
TYPE	The **Class** object for **float** or **double**

Method	Description
byte byteValue( )	Returns the value of the invoking object as a **byte**.
static int compare(float *num1*, float *num2*)	Compares the values of *num1* and *num2*. Returns 0 if the values are equal. Returns a negative value if *num1* is less than *num2*. Returns a positive value if *num1* is greater than *num2*.
int compareTo(Float *f*)	Compares the numerical value of the invoking object with that of *f*. Returns 0 if the values are equal. Returns a negative value if the invoking object has a lower value. Returns a positive value if the invoking object has a greater value.
double doubleValue( )	Returns the value of the invoking object as a **double**.
boolean equals(Object *FloatObj*)	Returns **true** if the invoking **Float** object is equivalent to *FloatObj*. Otherwise, it returns **false**.
static int floatToIntBits(float *num*)	Returns the IEEE-compatible, single-precision bit pattern that corresponds to *num*.
static int floatToRawIntBits(float *num*)	Returns the IEEE-compatible single-precision bit pattern that corresponds to *num*. A NaN value is preserved.
float floatValue( )	Returns the value of the invoking object as a **float**.
int hashCode( )	Returns the hash code for the invoking object.
static float intBitsToFloat(int *num*)	Returns **float** equivalent of the IEEE-compatible, single-precision bit pattern specified by *num*.
int intValue( )	Returns the value of the invoking object as an **int**.
boolean isInfinite( )	Returns **true** if the invoking object contains an infinite value. Otherwise, it returns **false**.
static boolean isInfinite(float *num*)	Returns **true** if *num* specifies an infinite value. Otherwise, it returns **false**.

TABLE 16-1   The Methods Defined by **Float**

Method	Description
boolean isNaN( )	Returns **true** if the invoking object contains a value that is not a number. Otherwise, it returns **false**.
static boolean isNaN(float *num*)	Returns **true** if *num* specifies a value that is not a number. Otherwise, it returns **false**.
long longValue( )	Returns the value of the invoking object as a **long**.
static float parseFloat(String *str*) throws NumberFormatException	Returns the **float** equivalent of the number contained in the string specified by *str* using radix 10.
short shortValue( )	Returns the value of the invoking object as a **short**.
static String toHexString(float *num*)	Returns a string containing the value of *num* in hexadecimal format.
String toString( )	Returns the string equivalent of the invoking object.
static String toString(float *num*)	Returns the string equivalent of the value specified by *num*.
static Float valueOf(float *num*)	Returns a **Float** object containing the value passed in *num*.
static Float valueOf(String *str*) throws NumberFormatException	Returns the **Float** object that contains the value specified by the string in *str*.

TABLE 16-1   The Methods Defined by **Float** *(continued)*

Method	Description
byte byteValue( )	Returns the value of the invoking object as a **byte**.
static int compare(double *num1*, double *num2*)	Compares the values of *num1* and *num2*. Returns 0 if the values are equal. Returns a negative value if *num1* is less than *num2*. Returns a positive value if *num1* is greater than *num2*.
int compareTo(Double *d*)	Compares the numerical value of the invoking object with that of *d*. Returns 0 if the values are equal. Returns a negative value if the invoking object has a lower value. Returns a positive value if the invoking object has a greater value.
static long doubleToLongBits(double *num*)	Returns the IEEE-compatible, double-precision bit pattern that corresponds to *num*.
static long doubleToRawLongBits(double *num*)	Retuns the IEEE-compatible double-precision bit pattern that corresponds to *num*. A NaN value is preserved.
double doubleValue( )	Returns the value of the invoking object as a **double**.
boolean equals(Object *DoubleObj*)	Returns **true** if the invoking **Double** object is equivalent to *DoubleObj*. Otherwise, it returns **false**.
float floatValue( )	Returns the value of the invoking object as a **float**.
int hashcode( )	Returns the hash code for the invoking object.
int intValue( )	Returns the value of the invoking object as an **int**.

TABLE 16-2   The Methods Defined by **Double**

Method	Description
boolean isInfinite( )	Returns **true** if the invoking object contains an infinite value. Otherwise, it returns **false**.
static boolean isInfinite(double *num*)	Returns **true** if *num* specifies an infinite value. Otherwise, it returns **false**.
boolean isNaN( )	Returns **true** if the invoking object contains a value that is not a number. Otherwise, it returns **false**.
static boolean isNaN(double *num*)	Returns **true** if *num* specifies a value that is not a number. Otherwise, it returns **false**.
static double longBitsToDouble(long *num*)	Returns **double** equivalent of the IEEE-compatible, double-precision bit pattern specified by *num*.
long longValue( )	Returns the value of the invoking object as a **long**.
static double parseDouble(String *str*) throws NumberFormatException	Returns the **double** equivalent of the number contained in the string specified by *str* using radix 10.
short shortValue( )	Returns the value of the invoking object as a **short**.
static String toHexString(double *num*)	Returns a string containing the value of *num* in hexadecimal format.
String toString( )	Returns the string equivalent of the invoking object.
static String toString(double *num*)	Returns the string equivalent of the value specified by *num*.
static Double valueOf(double *num*)	Returns a **Double** object containing the value passed in *num*.
static Double valueOf(String *str*) throws NumberFormatException	Returns a **Double** object that contains the value specified by the string in *str*.

TABLE 16-2 The Methods Defined by **Double** *(continued)*

The following example creates two **Double** objects—one by using a **double** value and the other by passing a string that can be parsed as a **double**:

```
class DoubleDemo {
  public static void main(String args[]) {
    Double d1 = new Double(3.14159);
    Double d2 = new Double("314159E-5");

    System.out.println(d1 + " = " + d2 + " -> " + d1.equals(d2));
  }
}
```

As you can see from the following output, both constructors created identical **Double** instances, as shown by the **equals( )** method returning **true**:

```
3.14159 = 3.14159 -> true
```

Understanding isInfinite( ) and isNaN( )

Float and **Double** provide the methods **isInfinite( )** and **isNaN( )**, which help when manipulating two special **double** and **float** values. These methods test for two unique values defined by the IEEE floating-point specification: infinity and NaN (not a number). **isInfinite( )** returns **true** if the value being tested is infinitely large or small in magnitude. **isNaN( )** returns **true** if the value being tested is not a number.

The following example creates two **Double** objects; one is infinite, and the other is not a number:

```
// Demonstrate isInfinite() and isNaN()
class InfNaN {
  public static void main(String args[]) {
    Double d1 = new Double(1/0.);
    Double d2 = new Double(0/0.);

    System.out.println(d1 + ": " + d1.isInfinite() + ", " + d1.isNaN());
    System.out.println(d2 + ": " + d2.isInfinite() + ", " + d2.isNaN());
  }
}
```

This program generates the following output:

```
Infinity: true, false
NaN: false, true
```

Byte, Short, Integer, and Long

The **Byte**, **Short**, **Integer**, and **Long** classes are wrappers for **byte**, **short**, **int**, and **long** integer types, respectively. Their constructors are shown here:

Byte(byte *num*)
Byte(String *str*) throws NumberFormatException

Short(short *num*)
Short(String *str*) throws NumberFormatException

Integer(int *num*)
Integer(String *str*) throws NumberFormatException

Long(long *num*)
Long(String *str*) throws NumberFormatException

As you can see, these objects can be constructed from numeric values or from strings that contain valid whole number values.

The methods defined by these classes are shown in Tables 16-3 through 16-6. As you can see, they define methods for parsing integers from strings and converting strings back into integers. Variants of these methods allow you to specify the *radix*, or numeric base, for conversion. Common radixes are 2 for binary, 8 for octal, 10 for decimal, and 16 for hexadecimal.

The following constants are defined:

MIN_VALUE	Minimum value
MAX_VALUE	Maximum value
SIZE	The bit width of the wrapped value
TYPE	The **Class** object for **byte**, **short**, **int**, or **long**

Method	Description
byte byteValue( )	Returns the value of the invoking object as a **byte**.
int compareTo(Byte *b*)	Compares the numerical value of the invoking object with that of *b*. Returns 0 if the values are equal. Returns a negative value if the invoking object has a lower value. Returns a positive value if the invoking object has a greater value.
static Byte decode(String *str*) throws NumberFormatException	Returns a **Byte** object that contains the value specified by the string in *str*.
double doubleValue( )	Returns the value of the invoking object as a **double**.
boolean equals(Object *ByteObj*)	Returns **true** if the invoking **Byte** object is equivalent to *ByteObj*. Otherwise, it returns **false**.
float floatValue( )	Returns the value of the invoking object as a **float**.
int hashCode( )	Returns the hash code for the invoking object.
int intValue( )	Returns the value of the invoking object as an **int**.
long longValue( )	Returns the value of the invoking object as a **long**.
static byte parseByte(String *str*) throws NumberFormatException	Returns the **byte** equivalent of the number contained in the string specified by *str* using radix 10.
static byte parseByte(String *str*, int *radix*) throws NumberFormatException	Returns the **byte** equivalent of the number contained in the string specified by *str* using the specified radix.
short shortValue( )	Returns the value of the invoking object as a **short**.
String toString( )	Returns a string that contains the decimal equivalent of the invoking object.
static String toString(byte *num*)	Returns a string that contains the decimal equivalent of *num*.
static Byte valueOf(byte *num*)	Returns a **Byte** object containing the value passed in *num*.
static Byte valueOf(String *str*) throws NumberFormatException	Returns a **Byte** object that contains the value specified by the string in *str*.
static Byte valueOf(String *str*, int *radix*) throws NumberFormatException	Returns a **Byte** object that contains the value specified by the string in *str* using the specified *radix*.

TABLE 16-3   The Methods Defined by **Byte**

Method	Description
byte byteValue( )	Returns the value of the invoking object as a **byte**.
int compareTo(Short *s*)	Compares the numerical value of the invoking object with that of *s*. Returns 0 if the values are equal. Returns a negative value if the invoking object has a lower value. Returns a positive value if the invoking object has a greater value.
static Short decode(String *str*) throws NumberFormatException	Returns a **Short** object that contains the value specified by the string in *str*.
double doubleValue( )	Returns the value of the invoking object as a **double**.
boolean equals(Object *ShortObj*)	Returns **true** if the invoking **Short** object is equivalent to *ShortObj*. Otherwise, it returns **false**.
float floatValue( )	Returns the value of the invoking object as a **float**.
int hashCode( )	Returns the hash code for the invoking object.
int intValue( )	Returns the value of the invoking object as an **int**.
long longValue( )	Returns the value of the invoking object as a **long**.
static short parseShort(String *str*) throws NumberFormatException	Returns the **short** equivalent of the number contained in the string specified by *str* using radix 10.
static short parseShort(String *str*, int *radix*) throws NumberFormatException	Returns the **short** equivalent of the number contained in the string specified by *str* using the specified *radix*.
static short reverseBytes(short *num*)	Exchanges the high- and low-order bytes of *num* and returns the result.
short shortValue( )	Returns the value of the invoking object as a **short**.
String toString( )	Returns a string that contains the decimal equivalent of the invoking object.
static String toString(short *num*)	Returns a string that contains the decimal equivalent of *num*.
static Short valueOf(short *num*)	Returns a **Short** object containing the value passed in *num*.
static Short valueOf(String *str*) throws NumberFormatException	Returns a **Short** object that contains the value specified by the string in *str* using radix 10.
static Short valueOf(String *str*, int *radix*) throws NumberFormatException	Returns a **Short** object that contains the value specified by the string in *str* using the specified *radix*.

TABLE 16-4   The Methods Defined by **Short**

Method	Description
static int bitCount(int *num*)	Returns the number of set bits in *num*.
byte byteValue( )	Returns the value of the invoking object as a **byte**.
int compareTo(Integer *i*)	Compares the numerical value of the invoking object with that of *i*. Returns 0 if the values are equal. Returns a negative value if the invoking object has a lower value. Returns a positive value if the invoking object has a greater value.
static Integer decode(String *str*) throws NumberFormatException	Returns an **Integer** object that contains the value specified by the string in *str*.
double doubleValue( )	Returns the value of the invoking object as a **double**.
boolean equals(Object *IntegerObj*)	Returns **true** if the invoking **Integer** object is equivalent to *IntegerObj*. Otherwise, it returns **false**.
float floatValue( )	Returns the value of the invoking object as a **float**.
static Integer getInteger(String *propertyName*)	Returns the value associated with the environmental property specified by *propertyName*. A **null** is returned on failure.
static Integer getInteger(String *propertyName*, int *default*)	Returns the value associated with the environmental property specified by *propertyName*. The value of *default* is returned on failure.
static Integer getInteger(String *propertyName*, Integer *default*)	Returns the value associated with the environmental property specified by *propertyName*. The value of *default* is returned on failure.
int hashCode( )	Returns the hash code for the invoking object.
static int highestOneBit(int *num*)	Determines the position of the highest order set bit in *num*. It returns a value in which only this bit is set. If no bit is set to one, then zero is returned.
int intValue( )	Returns the value of the invoking object as an **int**.
long longValue( )	Returns the value of the invoking object as a **long**.
static int lowestOneBit(int *num*)	Determines the position of the lowest order set bit in *num*. It returns a value in which only this bit is set. If no bit is set to one, then zero is returned.
static int numberOfLeadingZeros(int *num*)	Returns the number of high-order zero bits that precede the first high-order set bit in *num*. If *num* is zero, 32 is returned.

TABLE 16-5   The Methods Defined by **Integer**

Method	Description
static int numberOfTrailingZeros(int *num*)	Returns the number of low-order zero bits that precede the first low-order set bit in *num*. If *num* is zero, 32 is returned.
static int parseInt(String *str*) throws NumberFormatException	Returns the integer equivalent of the number contained in the string specified by *str* using radix 10.
static int parseInt(String *str*, int *radix*) throws NumberFormatException	Returns the integer equivalent of the number contained in the string specified by *str* using the specified *radix*.
static int reverse(int *num*)	Reverses the order of the bits in *num* and returns the result.
static int reverseBytes(int *num*)	Reverses the order of the bytes in *num* and returns the result.
static int rotateLeft(int *num*, int *n*)	Returns the result of rotating *num* left *n* positions.
static int rotateRight(int *num*, int *n*)	Returns the result of rotating *num* right *n* positions.
static int signum(int *num*)	Returns –1 if *num* is negative, 0 if it is zero, and 1 if it is positive.
short shortValue( )	Returns the value of the invoking object as a **short**.
static String toBinaryString(int *num*)	Returns a string that contains the binary equivalent of *num*.
static String toHexString(int *num*)	Returns a string that contains the hexadecimal equivalent of *num*.
static String toOctalString(int *num*)	Returns a string that contains the octal equivalent of *num*.
String toString( )	Returns a string that contains the decimal equivalent of the invoking object.
static String toString(int *num*)	Returns a string that contains the decimal equivalent of *num*.
static String toString(int *num*, int *radix*)	Returns a string that contains the decimal equivalent of *num* using the specified *radix*.
static Integer valueOf(int *num*)	Returns an **Integer** object containing the value passed in *num*.
static Integer valueOf(String *str*) throws NumberFormatException	Returns an **Integer** object that contains the value specified by the string in *str*.
static Integer valueOf(String *str*, int *radix*) throws NumberFormatException	Returns an **Integer** object that contains the value specified by the string in *str* using the specified *radix*.

TABLE 16-5   The Methods Defined by **Integer** *(continued)*

Method	Description
static int bitCount(long *num*)	Returns the number of set bits in *num*.
byte byteValue( )	Returns the value of the invoking object as a **byte**.
int compareTo(Long *l*)	Compares the numerical value of the invoking object with that of *l*. Returns 0 if the values are equal. Returns a negative value if the invoking object has a lower value. Returns a positive value if the invoking object has a greater value.
static Long decode(String *str*) throws NumberFormatException	Returns a **Long** object that contains the value specified by the string in *str*.
double doubleValue( )	Returns the value of the invoking object as a **double**.
boolean equals(Object *LongObj*)	Returns **true** if the invoking **Long** object is equivalent to *LongObj*. Otherwise, it returns **false**.
float floatValue( )	Returns the value of the invoking object as a **float**.
static Long getLong(String *propertyName*)	Returns the value associated with the environmental property specified by *propertyName*. A **null** is returned on failure.
static Long getLong(String *propertyName*, long *default*)	Returns the value associated with the environmental property specified by *propertyName*. The value of *default* is returned on failure.
static Long getLong(String *propertyName*, Long *default*)	Returns the value associated with the environmental property specified by *propertyName*. The value of *default* is returned on failure.
int hashCode( )	Returns the hash code for the invoking object.
static long highestOneBit(long *num*)	Determines the position of the highest-order set bit in *num*. It returns a value in which only this bit is set. If no bit is set to one, then zero is returned.
int intValue( )	Returns the value of the invoking object as an **int**.
long longValue( )	Returns the value of the invoking object as a **long**.
static long lowestOneBit(long *num*)	Determines the position of the lowest-order set bit in *num*. It returns a value in which only this bit is set. If no bit is set to one, then zero is returned.
static int numberOfLeadingZeros(long *num*)	Returns the number of high-order zero bits that precede the first high-order set bit in *num*. If *num* is zero, 64 is returned.
static int numberOfTrailingZeros(long *num*)	Returns the number of low-order zero bits that precede the first low-order set bit in *num*. If *num* is zero, 64 is returned.

TABLE 16-6 The Methods Defined by **Long**

Method	Description
static long parseLong(String *str*) throws NumberFormatException	Returns the **long** equivalent of the number contained in the string specified by *str* in radix 10.
static long parseLong(String *str*, int *radix*) throws NumberFormatException	Returns the **long** equivalent of the number contained in the string specified by *str* using the specified *radix*.
static long reverse(long *num*)	Reverses the order of the bits in *num* and returns the result.
static long reverseBytes(long *num*)	Reverses the order of the bytes in *num* and returns the result.
static long rotateLeft(long *num*, int *n*)	Returns the result of rotating *num* left *n* positions.
static long rotateRight(long *num*, int *n*)	Returns the result of rotating *num* right *n* positions.
static int signum(long *num*)	Returns –1 if *num* is negative, 0 if it is zero, and 1 if it is positive.
short shortValue( )	Returns the value of the invoking object as a **short**.
static String toBinaryString(long *num*)	Returns a string that contains the binary equivalent of *num*.
static String toHexString(long *num*)	Returns a string that contains the hexadecimal equivalent of *num*.
static String toOctalString(long *num*)	Returns a string that contains the octal equivalent of *num*.
String toString( )	Returns a string that contains the decimal equivalent of the invoking object.
static String toString(long *num*)	Returns a string that contains the decimal equivalent of *num*.
static String toString(long *num*, int *radix*)	Returns a string that contains the decimal equivalent of *num* using the specified *radix*.
static Long valueOf(long *num*)	Returns a **Long** object containing the value passed in *num*.
static Long valueOf(String *str*) throws NumberFormatException	Returns a **Long** object that contains the value specified by the string in *str*.
static Long valueOf(String *str*, int *radix*) throws NumberFormatException	Returns a **Long** object that contains the value specified by the string in *str* using the specified *radix*.

TABLE 16-6 The Methods Defined by **Long** *(continued)*

Converting Numbers to and from Strings

One of the most common programming chores is converting the string representation of a number into its internal, binary format. Fortunately, Java provides an easy way to accomplish this. The **Byte**, **Short**, **Integer**, and **Long** classes provide the **parseByte( )**, **parseShort( )**, **parseInt( )**, and **parseLong( )** methods, respectively. These methods return the **byte**, **short**,

int, or **long** equivalent of the numeric string with which they are called. (Similar methods also exist for the **Float** and **Double** classes.)

The following program demonstrates **parseInt( )**. It sums a list of integers entered by the user. It reads the integers using **readLine( )** and uses **parseInt( )** to convert these strings into their **int** equivalents.

```
/* This program sums a list of numbers entered
   by the user.  It converts the string representation
   of each number into an int using parseInt().
*/

import java.io.*;

class ParseDemo {
  public static void main(String args[])
    throws IOException
  {
    // create a BufferedReader using System.in
    BufferedReader br = new
      BufferedReader(new InputStreamReader(System.in));
    String str;
    int i;
    int sum=0;

    System.out.println("Enter numbers, 0 to quit.");
    do {
      str = br.readLine();
      try {
        i = Integer.parseInt(str);
      } catch(NumberFormatException e) {
        System.out.println("Invalid format");
        i = 0;
      }
      sum += i;
      System.out.println("Current sum is: " + sum);
    } while(i != 0);
  }
}
```

To convert a whole number into a decimal string, use the versions of **toString( )** defined in the **Byte**, **Short**, **Integer**, or **Long** classes. The **Integer** and **Long** classes also provide the methods **toBinaryString( )**, **toHexString( )**, and **toOctalString( )**, which convert a value into a binary, hexadecimal, or octal string, respectively.

The following program demonstrates binary, hexadecimal, and octal conversion:

```
/* Convert an integer into binary, hexadecimal,
   and octal.
*/

class StringConversions {
  public static void main(String args[]) {
    int num = 19648;
```

```
System.out.println(num + " in binary: " +
                   Integer.toBinaryString(num));

System.out.println(num + " in octal: " +
                   Integer.toOctalString(num));

System.out.println(num + " in hexadecimal: " +
                   Integer.toHexString(num));
  }
}
```

The output of this program is shown here:

```
19648 in binary: 100110011000000
19648 in octal: 46300
19648 in hexadecimal: 4cc0
```

Character

Character is a simple wrapper around a **char**. The constructor for **Character** is

Character(char *ch*)

Here, *ch* specifies the character that will be wrapped by the **Character** object being created. To obtain the **char** value contained in a **Character** object, call **charValue( )**, shown here:

char charValue( )

It returns the character.

The **Character** class defines several constants, including the following:

MAX_RADIX	The largest radix
MIN_RADIX	The smallest radix
MAX_VALUE	The largest character value
MIN_VALUE	The smallest character value
TYPE	The **Class** object for **char**

Character includes several static methods that categorize characters and alter their case. They are shown in Table 16-7. The following example demonstrates several of these methods:

```
// Demonstrate several Is... methods.

class IsDemo {
  public static void main(String args[]) {
    char a[] = {'a', 'b', '5', '?', 'A', ' '};

    for(int i=0; i<a.length; i++) {
      if(Character.isDigit(a[i]))
        System.out.println(a[i] + " is a digit.");
      if(Character.isLetter(a[i]))
```

```
      System.out.println(a[i] + " is a letter.");
    if(Character.isWhitespace(a[i]))
      System.out.println(a[i] + " is whitespace.");
    if(Character.isUpperCase(a[i]))
      System.out.println(a[i] + " is uppercase.");
    if(Character.isLowerCase(a[i]))
      System.out.println(a[i] + " is lowercase.");
    }
  }
}
```

The output from this program is shown here:

```
a is a letter.
a is lowercase.
b is a letter.
b is lowercase.
5 is a digit.
A is a letter.
A is uppercase.
  is whitespace.
```

Method	Description
static boolean isDefined(char *ch*)	Returns **true** if *ch* is defined by Unicode. Otherwise, it returns **false**.
static boolean isDigit(char *ch*)	Returns **true** if *ch* is a digit. Otherwise, it returns **false**.
static boolean isIdentifierIgnorable(char *ch*)	Returns **true** if *ch* should be ignored in an identifier. Otherwise, it returns **false**.
static boolean isISOControl(char *ch*)	Returns **true** if *ch* is an ISO control character. Otherwise, it returns **false**.
static boolean isJavaIdentifierPart(char *ch*)	Returns **true** if *ch* is allowed as part of a Java identifier (other than the first character). Otherwise, it returns **false**.
static boolean isJavaIdentifierStart(char *ch*)	Returns **true** if *ch* is allowed as the first character of a Java identifier. Otherwise, it returns **false**.
static boolean isLetter(char *ch*)	Returns **true** if *ch* is a letter. Otherwise, it returns **false**.
static boolean isLetterOrDigit(char *ch*)	Returns **true** if *ch* is a letter or a digit. Otherwise, it returns **false**.
static boolean isLowerCase(char *ch*)	Returns **true** if *ch* is a lowercase letter. Otherwise, it returns **false**.

TABLE 16-7   Various **Character** Methods

Method	Description
static boolean isMirrored(char *ch*)	Returns **true** if *ch* is a mirrored Unicode character. A mirrored character is one that is reversed for text that is displayed right-to-left.
static boolean isSpaceChar(char *ch*)	Returns **true** if *ch* is a Unicode space character. Otherwise, it returns **false**.
static boolean isTitleCase(char *ch*)	Returns **true** if *ch* is a Unicode titlecase character. Otherwise, it returns **false**.
static boolean isUnicodeIdentifierPart(char *ch*)	Returns **true** if *ch* is allowed as part of a Unicode identifier (other than the first character). Otherwise, it returns **false**.
static boolean isUnicodeIdentifierStart(char *ch*)	Returns **true** if *ch* is allowed as the first character of a Unicode identifier. Otherwise, it returns **false**.
static boolean isUpperCase(char *ch*)	Returns **true** if *ch* is an uppercase letter. Otherwise, it returns **false**.
static boolean isWhitespace(char *ch*)	Returns **true** if *ch* is whitespace. Otherwise, it returns **false**.
static char toLowerCase(char *ch*)	Returns lowercase equivalent of *ch*.
static char toTitleCase(char *ch*)	Returns titlecase equivalent of *ch*.
static char toUpperCase(char *ch*)	Returns uppercase equivalent of *ch*.

TABLE 16-7 Various **Character** Methods *(continued)*

Character defines two methods, **forDigit( )** and **digit( )**, that enable you to convert between integer values and the digits they represent. They are shown here:

static char forDigit(int *num*, int *radix*)
static int digit(char *digit*, int *radix*)

forDigit( ) returns the digit character associated with the value of *num*. The radix of the conversion is specified by *radix*. **digit( )** returns the integer value associated with the specified character (which is presumably a digit) according to the specified radix.

Another method defined by **Character** is **compareTo( )**, which has the following form:

int compareTo(Character *c*)

It returns zero if the invoking object and *c* have the same value. It returns a negative value if the invoking object has a lower value. Otherwise, it returns a positive value.

Character includes a method called **getDirectionality( )** which can be used to determine the direction of a character. Several constants are defined that describe directionality. Most programs will not need to use character directionality.

Character also overrides the **equals( )** and **hashCode( )** methods.

Two other character-related classes are **Character.Subset**, used to describe a subset of Unicode, and **Character.UnicodeBlock**, which contains Unicode character blocks.

Recent Additions to Character for Unicode Code Point Support

Recently, major additions have been made to **Character**. Beginning with JDK 5, the **Character** class has included support for 32-bit Unicode characters. In the past, all Unicode characters could be held by 16 bits, which is the size of a **char** (and the size of the value encapsulated within a **Character**), because those values ranged from 0 to FFFF. However, the Unicode character set has been expanded, and more than 16 bits are required. Characters can now range from 0 to 10FFFF.

Here are two important terms: code point and supplemental character. A *code point* is a character in the range 0 to 10FFFF. Characters that have values greater than FFFF are called *supplemental characters.*

The expansion of the Unicode character set caused a fundamental problem for Java. Because a supplemental character has a value greater than a **char** can hold, some means of handling the supplemental characters was needed. Java addressed this problem two ways. First, Java uses two **char**s to represent a supplemental character. The first **char** is called the *high surrogate,* and the second is called the *low surrogate.* New methods, such as **codePointAt( )**, were provided to translate between code points and supplemental characters.

Secondly, Java overloaded several preexisting methods in the **Character** class. The overloaded forms use **int** rather than **char** data. Because an **int** is large enough to hold any character as a single value, it can be used to store any character. For example, all of the methods in Table 16-7 have overloaded forms that operate on **int**. Here is a sampling:

```
static boolean isDigit(int cp)
static boolean isLetter(int cp)
static int toLowerCase(int cp)
```

In addition to the methods overloaded to accept code points, **Character** adds methods that provide additional support for code points. A sampling is shown in Table 16-8.

Method	Description
static int charCount(int *cp*)	Returns 1 if *cp* can be represented by a single **char**. It returns 2 if two **chars** are needed.
static int codePointAt(CharSequence *chars*, int *loc*)	Returns the code point at the location specified by *loc*.
static int codePointAt(char *chars*[ ], int *loc*)	Returns the code point at the location specified by *loc*.
static int codePointBefore(CharSequence *chars*, int *loc*)	Returns the code point at the location that precedes that specified by *loc*.
static int codePointBefore(char *chars*[ ], int *loc*)	Returns the code point at the location that precedes that specified by *loc*.
static boolean isHighSurrogate(char *ch*)	Returns **true** if *ch* contains a valid high surrogate character.

TABLE 16-8 A Sampling of Methods That Provide Support for 32-Bit Unicode Code Points

Method	Description
static boolean isLowSurrogate(char *ch*)	Returns **true** if *ch* contains a valid low surrogate character.
static boolean isSupplementaryCodePoint(int *cp*)	Returns **true** if *cp* contains a supplemental character.
static boolean isSurrogatePair(char *highCh*, char *lowCh*)	Returns **true** if *highCh* and *lowCh* form a valid surrogate pair.
static boolean isValidCodePoint(int *cp*)	Returns **true** if *cp* contains a valid code point.
static char[ ] toChars(int *cp*)	Converts the code point in *cp* into its **char** equivalent, which might require two **chars**. An array holding the result is returned.
static int toChars(int *cp*, char *target*[ ], int *loc*)	Converts the code point in *cp* into its **char** equivalent, storing the result in *target*, beginning at *loc*. Returns 1 if *cp* can be represented by a single **char**. It returns 2 otherwise.
static int toCodePoint(char *highCh*, char *lowCh*)	Converts *highCh* and *lowCh* into their equivalent code point.

TABLE 16-8   A Sampling of Methods That Provide Support for 32-Bit Unicode Code Points *(continued)*

Boolean

Boolean is a very thin wrapper around **boolean** values, which is useful mostly when you want to pass a **boolean** variable by reference. It contains the constants **TRUE** and **FALSE**, which define true and false **Boolean** objects. **Boolean** also defines the **TYPE** field, which is the **Class** object for **boolean**. **Boolean** defines these constructors:

    Boolean(boolean *boolValue*)
    Boolean(String *boolString*)

In the first version, *boolValue* must be either **true** or **false**. In the second version, if *boolString* contains the string "true" (in uppercase or lowercase), then the new **Boolean** object will be true. Otherwise, it will be false.

    Boolean defines the methods shown in Table 16-9.

Method	Description
boolean booleanValue( )	Returns **boolean** equivalent.
int compareTo(Boolean *b*)	Returns zero if the invoking object and *b* contain the same value. Returns a positive value if the invoking object is **true** and *b* is **false**. Otherwise, returns a negative value.
boolean equals(Object *boolObj*)	Returns **true** if the invoking object is equivalent to *boolObj*. Otherwise, it returns **false**.

TABLE 16-9   The Methods Defined by **Boolean**

Method	Description
static boolean getBoolean(String *propertyName*)	Returns **true** if the system property specified by *propertyName* is **true**. Otherwise, it returns **false**.
int hashCode( )	Returns the hash code for the invoking object.
static boolean parseBoolean(String *str*)	Returns **true** if *str* contains the string "true". Case is not significant. Otherwise, returns **false**.
String toString( )	Returns the string equivalent of the invoking object.
static String toString(boolean *boolVal*)	Returns the string equivalent of *boolVal*.
static Boolean valueOf(boolean *boolVal*)	Returns the **Boolean** equivalent of *boolVal*.
static Boolean valueOf(String *boolString*)	Returns **true** if *boolString* contains the string "true" (in uppercase or lowercase). Otherwise, it returns **false**.

TABLE 16-9   The Methods Defined by **Boolean** *(continued)*

Void

The **Void** class has one field, **TYPE**, which holds a reference to the **Class** object for type **void**. You do not create instances of this class.

Process

The abstract **Process** class encapsulates a *process*—that is, an executing program. It is used primarily as a superclass for the type of objects created by **exec( )** in the **Runtime** class, or by **start( )** in the **ProcessBuilder** class. **Process** contains the abstract methods shown in Table 16-10.

Method	Description
void destroy( )	Terminates the process.
int exitValue( )	Returns an exit code obtained from a subprocess.
InputStream getErrorStream( )	Returns an input stream that reads input from the process' **err** output stream.
InputStream getInputStream( )	Returns an input stream that reads input from the process' **out** output stream.
OutputStream getOutputStream( )	Returns an output stream that writes output to the process' **in** input stream.
int waitFor( ) throws InterruptedException	Returns the exit code returned by the process. This method does not return until the process on which it is called terminates.

TABLE 16-10   The Methods Defined by **Process**

Runtime

The **Runtime** class encapsulates the run-time environment. You cannot instantiate a **Runtime** object. However, you can get a reference to the current **Runtime** object by calling the static method **Runtime.getRuntime( )**. Once you obtain a reference to the current **Runtime** object, you can call several methods that control the state and behavior of the Java Virtual Machine. Applets and other untrusted code typically cannot call any of the **Runtime** methods without raising a **SecurityException**. Commonly used methods defined by **Runtime** are shown in Table 16-11.

Method	Description
void addShutdownHook(Thread *thrd*)	Registers *thrd* as a thread to be run when the Java Virtual Machine terminates.
Process exec(String *progName*) throws IOException	Executes the program specified by *progName* as a separate process. An object of type **Process** is returned that describes the new process.
Process exec(String *progName*, String *environment*[ ]) throws IOException	Executes the program specified by *progName* as a separate process with the environment specified by *environment*. An object of type **Process** is returned that describes the new process.
Process exec(String *comLineArray*[ ]) throws IOException	Executes the command line specified by the strings in *comLineArray* as a separate process. An object of type **Process** is returned that describes the new process.
Process exec(String *comLineArray*[ ], String *environment*[ ]) throws IOException	Executes the command line specified by the strings in *comLineArray* as a separate process with the environment specified by *environment*. An object of type **Process** is returned that describes the new process.
void exit(int *exitCode*)	Halts execution and returns the value of *exitCode* to the parent process. By convention, 0 indicates normal termination. All other values indicate some form of error.
long freeMemory( )	Returns the approximate number of bytes of free memory available to the Java run-time system.
void gc( )	Initiates garbage collection.
static Runtime getRuntime( )	Returns the current **Runtime** object.
void halt(int *code*)	Immediately terminates the Java Virtual Machine. No termination threads or finalizers are run. The value of *code* is returned to the invoking process.
void load(String *libraryFileName*)	Loads the dynamic library whose file is specified by *libraryFileName*, which must specify its complete path.
void loadLibrary(String *libraryName*)	Loads the dynamic library whose name is associated with *libraryName*.

TABLE 16-11   A Sampling of Methods Defined by **Runtime**

Method	Description
boolean removeShutdownHook(Thread *thrd*)	Removes *thrd* from the list of threads to run when the Java Virtual Machine terminates. It returns **true** if successful—that is, if the thread was removed.
void runFinalization( )	Initiates calls to the **finalize( )** methods of unused but not yet recycled objects.
long totalMemory( )	Returns the total number of bytes of memory available to the program.
void traceInstructions(boolean *traceOn*)	Turns on or off instruction tracing, depending upon the value of *traceOn*. If *traceOn* is **true**, the trace is displayed. If it is **false**, tracing is turned off.
void traceMethodCalls(boolean *traceOn*)	Turns on or off method call tracing, depending upon the value of *traceOn*. If *traceOn* is **true**, the trace is displayed. If it is **false**, tracing is turned off.

TABLE 16-11   A Sampling of Methods Defined by **Runtime** *(continued)*

Let's look at two of the most common uses of the **Runtime** class: memory management and executing additional processes.

Memory Management

Although Java provides automatic garbage collection, sometimes you will want to know how large the object heap is and how much of it is left. You can use this information, for example, to check your code for efficiency or to approximate how many more objects of a certain type can be instantiated. To obtain these values, use the **totalMemory( )** and **freeMemory( )** methods.

As mentioned in Part I, Java's garbage collector runs periodically to recycle unused objects. However, sometimes you will want to collect discarded objects prior to the collector's next appointed rounds. You can run the garbage collector on demand by calling the **gc( )** method. A good thing to try is to call **gc( )** and then call **freeMemory( )** to get a baseline memory usage. Next, execute your code and call **freeMemory( )** again to see how much memory it is allocating. The following program illustrates this idea:

```
// Demonstrate totalMemory(), freeMemory() and gc().

class MemoryDemo {
  public static void main(String args[]) {
    Runtime r = Runtime.getRuntime();
    long mem1, mem2;
    Integer someints[] = new Integer[1000];

    System.out.println("Total memory is: " +
                  r.totalMemory());
```

```
    mem1 = r.freeMemory();
    System.out.println("Initial free memory: " + mem1);
    r.gc();
    mem1 = r.freeMemory();
    System.out.println("Free memory after garbage collection: "
                        + mem1);

    for(int i=0; i<1000; i++)
      someints[i] = new Integer(i); // allocate integers

    mem2 = r.freeMemory();
    System.out.println("Free memory after allocation: "
                        + mem2);
    System.out.println("Memory used by allocation: "
                        + (mem1-mem2));

    // discard Integers
    for(int i=0; i<1000; i++) someints[i] = null;

    r.gc(); // request garbage collection

    mem2 = r.freeMemory();
    System.out.println("Free memory after collecting" +
                        " discarded Integers: " + mem2);

  }
}
```

Sample output from this program is shown here (of course, your actual results may vary):

```
    Total memory is: 1048568
    Initial free memory: 751392
    Free memory after garbage collection: 841424
    Free memory after allocation: 824000
    Memory used by allocation: 17424
    Free memory after collecting discarded Integers: 842640
```

Executing Other Programs

In safe environments, you can use Java to execute other heavyweight processes (that is, programs) on your multitasking operating system. Several forms of the **exec( )** method allow you to name the program you want to run as well as its input parameters. The **exec( )** method returns a **Process** object, which can then be used to control how your Java program interacts with this new running process. Because Java can run on a variety of platforms and under a variety of operating systems, **exec( )** is inherently environment-dependent.

The following example uses **exec( )** to launch **notepad**, Windows' simple text editor. Obviously, this example must be run under the Windows operating system.

```
// Demonstrate exec().
class ExecDemo {
  public static void main(String args[]) {
    Runtime r = Runtime.getRuntime();
    Process p = null;
```

```
  try {
    p = r.exec("notepad");
  } catch (Exception e) {
    System.out.println("Error executing notepad.");
  }
  }
}
```

There are several alternative forms of **exec( )**, but the one shown in the example is the most common. The **Process** object returned by **exec( )** can be manipulated by **Process'** methods after the new program starts running. You can kill the subprocess with the **destroy( )** method. The **waitFor( )** method causes your program to wait until the subprocess finishes. The **exitValue( )** method returns the value returned by the subprocess when it is finished. This is typically 0 if no problems occur. Here is the preceding **exec( )** example modified to wait for the running process to exit:

```
// Wait until notepad is terminated.
class ExecDemoFini {
  public static void main(String args[]) {
    Runtime r = Runtime.getRuntime();
    Process p = null;

    try {
      p = r.exec("notepad");
      p.waitFor();
    } catch (Exception e) {
      System.out.println("Error executing notepad.");
    }
    System.out.println("Notepad returned " + p.exitValue());
  }
}
```

While a subprocess is running, you can write to and read from its standard input and output. The **getOutputStream( )** and **getInputStream( )** methods return the handles to standard **in** and **out** of the subprocess. (I/O is examined in detail in Chapter 19.)

ProcessBuilder

ProcessBuilder provides another way to start and manage processes (that is, programs). As explained earlier, all processes are represented by the **Process** class, and a process can be started by **Runtime.exec( )**. **ProcessBuilder** offers more control over the processes. For example, you can set the current working directory and change environmental parameters.

ProcessBuilder defines these constructors:

ProcessBuilder(List<String> *args*)
ProccessBuilder(String ... *args*)

Here, *args* is a list of arguments that specify the name of the program to be executed along with any required command-line arguments. In the first constructor, the arguments are passed in a **List**. In the second, they are specified through a varargs parameter. Table 16-12 describes the methods defined by **ProcessBuilder**.

To create a process using **ProcessBuilder**, simply create an instance of **ProcessBuilder**, specifying the name of the program and any needed arguments. To begin execution of the program, call **start( )** on that instance. Here is an example that executes the Windows text editor **notepad**. Notice that it specifies the name of the file to edit as an argument.

```
class PBDemo {
public static void main(String args[]) {

    try {
      ProcessBuilder proc =
        new ProcessBuilder("notepad.exe", "testfile");
      proc.start();
    } catch (Exception e) {
      System.out.println("Error executing notepad.");
    }
  }
}
```

Method	Description
List<String> command( )	Returns a reference to a **List** that contains the name of the program and its arguments. Changes to this list affect the invoking process.
ProcessBuilder command(List<String> *args*)	Sets the name of the program and its arguments to those specified by *args*. Changes to this list affect the invoking process. Returns a reference to the invoking object.
ProcessBuilder command(String ... *args*)	Sets the name of the program and its arguments to those specified by *args*. Returns a reference to the invoking object.
File directory( )	Returns the current working directory of the invoking object. This value will be **null** if the directory is the same as that of the Java program that started the process.
ProcessBuilder directory(File *dir*)	Sets the current working directory of the invoking object. Returns a reference to the invoking object.
Map<String, String> environment( )	Returns the environmental variables associated with the invoking object as key/value pairs.
boolean redirectErrorStream( )	Returns **true** if the standard error stream has been redirected to the standard output stream. Returns **false** if the streams are separate.
ProcessBuilder redirectErrorStream(boolean *merge*)	If *merge* is **true**, then the standard error stream is redirected to standard output. If *merge* is **false**, the streams are separated, which is the default state. Returns a reference to the invoking object.
Process start( ) throws IOException	Begins the process specified by the invoking object. In other words, it runs the specified program.

TABLE 16-12   The Methods Defined by **ProcessBuilder**

System

The **System** class holds a collection of static methods and variables. The standard input, output, and error output of the Java run time are stored in the **in**, **out**, and **err** variables. The methods defined by **System** are shown in Table 16-13. Many of the methods throw a **SecurityException** if the operation is not permitted by the security manager.

Let's look at some common uses of **System**.

Method	Description
static void arraycopy(Object *source*, int *sourceStart*, Object *target*, int *targetStart*, int *size*)	Copies an array. The array to be copied is passed in *source*, and the index at which point the copy will begin within *source* is passed in *sourceStart*. The array that will receive the copy is passed in *target*, and the index at which point the copy will begin within *target* is passed in *targetStart*. *size* is the number of elements that are copied.
static String clearProperty(String *which*)	Deletes the environmental variable specified by *which*. The previous value associated with *which* is returned.
static Console console ( )	Returns the console associated with the JVM. **null** is returned if the JVM currently has no console. (Added by Java SE 6.)
static long currentTimeMillis( )	Returns the current time in terms of milliseconds since midnight, January 1, 1970.
static void exit(int *exitCode*)	Halts execution and returns the value of *exitCode* to the parent process (usually the operating system). By convention, 0 indicates normal termination. All other values indicate some form of error.
static void gc( )	Initiates garbage collection.
static Map<String, String> getenv( )	Returns a **Map** that contains the current environmental variables and their values.
static String getenv(String *which*)	Returns the value associated with the environmental variable passed in *which*.
static Properties getProperties( )	Returns the properties associated with the Java run-time system. (The **Properties** class is described in Chapter 17.)
static String getProperty(String *which*)	Returns the property associated with *which*. A **null** object is returned if the desired property is not found.
static String getProperty(String *which*, String *default*)	Returns the property associated with *which*. If the desired property is not found, *default* is returned.
static SecurityManager getSecurityManager( )	Returns the current security manager or a **null** object if no security manager is installed.
static int identityHashCode(Object *obj*)	Returns the identity hash code for *obj*.

TABLE 16-13   The Methods Defined by **System**

Method	Description
static Channel inheritedChannel( ) throws IOException	Returns the channel inherited by the Java Virtual Machine. Returns **null** if no channel is inherited.
static void load(String *libraryFileName*)	Loads the dynamic library whose file is specified by *libraryFileName*, which must specify its complete path.
static void loadLibrary(String *libraryName*)	Loads the dynamic library whose name is associated with *libraryName*.
static String mapLibraryName(String *lib*)	Returns a platform-specific name for the library named *lib*.
static long nanoTime( )	Obtains the most precise timer in the system and returns its value in terms of nanoseconds since some arbitrary starting point. The accuracy of the timer is unknowable.
static void runFinalization( )	Initiates calls to the **finalize( )** methods of unused but not yet recycled objects.
static void setErr(PrintStream *eStream*)	Sets the standard **err** stream to *eStream*.
static void setIn(InputStream *iStream*)	Sets the standard **in** stream to *iStream*.
static void setOut(PrintStream *oStream*)	Sets the standard **out** stream to *oStream*.
static void setProperties(Properties *sysProperties*)	Sets the current system properties as specified by *sysProperties*.
static String setProperty(String *which*, String *v*)	Assigns the value *v* to the property named *which*.
static void setSecurityManager(SecurityManager *secMan*)	Sets the security manager to that specified by *secMan*.

TABLE 16-13   The Methods Defined by **System** *(continued)*

Using currentTimeMillis( ) to Time Program Execution

One use of the **System** class that you might find particularly interesting is to use the **currentTimeMillis( )** method to time how long various parts of your program take to execute. The **currentTimeMillis( )** method returns the current time in terms of milliseconds since midnight, January 1, 1970. To time a section of your program, store this value just before beginning the section in question. Immediately upon completion, call **currentTimeMillis( )** again. The elapsed time will be the ending time minus the starting time. The following program demonstrates this:

```
// Timing program execution.

class Elapsed {
  public static void main(String args[]) {
    long start, end;

    System.out.println("Timing a for loop from 0 to 1,000,000");

    // time a for loop from 0 to 1,000,000
```

```
    start = System.currentTimeMillis(); // get starting time
    for(int i=0; i < 1000000; i++) ;
    end = System.currentTimeMillis(); // get ending time

    System.out.println("Elapsed time: " + (end-start));
  }
}
```

Here is a sample run (remember that your results probably will differ):

```
Timing a for loop from 0 to 1,000,000
Elapsed time: 10
```

If your system has a timer that offers nanosecond precision, then you could rewrite the preceding program to use **nanoTime( )** rather than **currentTimeMillis( )**. For example, here is the key portion of the program rewritten to use **nanoTime( )**:

```
start = System.nanoTime(); // get starting time
for(int i=0; i < 1000000; i++) ;
end = System.nanoTime(); // get ending time
```

Using arraycopy( )

The **arraycopy( )** method can be used to copy quickly an array of any type from one place to another. This is much faster than the equivalent loop written out longhand in Java. Here is an example of two arrays being copied by the **arraycopy( )** method. First, **a** is copied to **b**. Next, all of **a**'s elements are shifted *down* by one. Then, **b** is shifted *up* by one.

```
// Using arraycopy().

class ACDemo {
  static byte a[] = { 65, 66, 67, 68, 69, 70, 71, 72, 73, 74 };
  static byte b[] = { 77, 77, 77, 77, 77, 77, 77, 77, 77, 77 };

  public static void main(String args[]) {
    System.out.println("a = " + new String(a));
    System.out.println("b = " + new String(b));
    System.arraycopy(a, 0, b, 0, a.length);
    System.out.println("a = " + new String(a));
    System.out.println("b = " + new String(b));
    System.arraycopy(a, 0, a, 1, a.length - 1);
    System.arraycopy(b, 1, b, 0, b.length - 1);
    System.out.println("a = " + new String(a));
    System.out.println("b = " + new String(b));
  }
}
```

As you can see from the following output, you can copy using the same source and destination in either direction:

```
a = ABCDEFGHIJ
b = MMMMMMMMMM
```

```
a = ABCDEFGHIJ
b = ABCDEFGHIJ
a = AABCDEFGHI
b = BCDEFGHIJJ
```

Environment Properties

The following properties are available:

file.separator	java.specification.version	java.vm.version
java.class.path	java.vendor	line.separator
java.class.version	java.vendor.url	os.arch
java.compiler	java.version	os.name
java.ext.dirs	java.vm.name	os.version
java.home	java.vm.specification.name	path.separator
java.io.tmpdir	java.vm.specification.vendor	user.dir
java.library.path	java.vm.specification.version	user.home
java.specification.name	java.vm.vendor	user.name
java.specification.vendor		

You can obtain the values of various environment variables by calling the **System.getProperty( )** method. For example, the following program displays the path to the current user directory:

```java
class ShowUserDir {
  public static void main(String args[]) {
    System.out.println(System.getProperty("user.dir"));
  }
}
```

Object

As mentioned in Part I, **Object** is a superclass of all other classes. **Object** defines the methods shown in Table 16-14, which are available to every object.

Method	Description

Object clone( )
    throws
       CloneNotSupportedException
	Creates a new object that is the same as the invoking object.

boolean equals(Object *object*)	Returns **true** if the invoking object is equivalent to *object*.
void finalize( ) throws Throwable	Default **finalize( )** method. This is usually overridden by subclasses.

TABLE 16-14 The Methods Defined by **Object**

Method	Description
final Class<?> getClass( )	Obtains a **Class** object that describes the invoking object.
int hashCode( )	Returns the hash code associated with the invoking object.
final void notify( )	Resumes execution of a thread waiting on the invoking object.
final void notifyAll( )	Resumes execution of all threads waiting on the invoking object.
String toString( )	Returns a string that describes the object.
final void wait( ) throws InterruptedException	Waits on another thread of execution.
final void wait(long *milliseconds*) throws InterruptedException	Waits up to the specified number of *milliseconds* on another thread of execution.

final void wait(long *milliseconds*,
            int *nanoseconds*)
    throws InterruptedException
	Waits up to the specified number of *milliseconds* plus *nanoseconds* on another thread of execution.

TABLE 16-14   The Methods Defined by **Object** *(continued)*

Using clone( ) and the Cloneable Interface

Most of the methods defined by **Object** are discussed elsewhere in this book. However, one deserves special attention: **clone( )**. The **clone( )** method generates a duplicate copy of the object on which it is called. Only classes that implement the **Cloneable** interface can be cloned.

The **Cloneable** interface defines no members. It is used to indicate that a class allows a bitwise copy of an object (that is, a *clone*) to be made. If you try to call **clone( )** on a class that does not implement **Cloneable**, a **CloneNotSupportedException** is thrown. When a clone is made, the constructor for the object being cloned is *not* called. A clone is simply an exact copy of the original.

Cloning is a potentially dangerous action, because it can cause unintended side effects. For example, if the object being cloned contains a reference variable called *obRef*, then when the clone is made, *obRef* in the clone will refer to the same object as does *obRef* in the original. If the clone makes a change to the contents of the object referred to by *obRef*, then it will be changed for the original object, too. Here is another example: If an object opens an I/O stream and is then cloned, two objects will be capable of operating on the same stream. Further, if one of these objects closes the stream, the other object might still attempt to write to it, causing an error. In some cases, you will need to override the **clone( )** method defined by **Object** to handle these types of problems.

Because cloning can cause problems, **clone( )** is declared as **protected** inside **Object**. This means that it must either be called from within a method defined by the class that implements **Cloneable**, or it must be explicitly overridden by that class so that it is public. Let's look at an example of each approach.

The following program implements **Cloneable** and defines the method **cloneTest( )**, which calls **clone( )** in **Object**:

```
// Demonstrate the clone() method.

class TestClone implements Cloneable {
  int a;
  double b;

  // This method calls Object's clone().
  TestClone cloneTest() {
    try {
      // call clone in Object.
      return (TestClone) super.clone();
    } catch(CloneNotSupportedException e) {
      System.out.println("Cloning not allowed.");
      return this;
    }
  }
}

class CloneDemo {
  public static void main(String args[]) {
    TestClone x1 = new TestClone();
    TestClone x2;

    x1.a = 10;
    x1.b = 20.98;

    x2 = x1.cloneTest(); // clone x1

    System.out.println("x1: " + x1.a + " " + x1.b);
    System.out.println("x2: " + x2.a + " " + x2.b);
  }
}
```

Here, the method **cloneTest( )** calls **clone( )** in **Object** and returns the result. Notice that the object returned by **clone( )** must be cast into its appropriate type (**TestClone**).

The following example overrides **clone( )** so that it can be called from code outside of its class. To do this, its access specifier must be **public**, as shown here:

```
// Override the clone() method.

class TestClone implements Cloneable {
  int a;
  double b;

  // clone() is now overridden and is public.
  public Object clone() {
    try {
      // call clone in Object.
      return super.clone();
    } catch(CloneNotSupportedException e) {
```

```
      System.out.println("Cloning not allowed.");
      return this;
    }
  }
}

class CloneDemo2 {
  public static void main(String args[]) {
    TestClone x1 = new TestClone();
    TestClone x2;

    x1.a = 10;
    x1.b = 20.98;

    // here, clone() is called directly.
    x2 = (TestClone) x1.clone();

    System.out.println("x1: " + x1.a + " " + x1.b);
    System.out.println("x2: " + x2.a + " " + x2.b);
  }
}
```

The side effects caused by cloning are sometimes difficult to see at first. It is easy to think that a class is safe for cloning when it actually is not. In general, you should not implement **Cloneable** for any class without good reason.

Class

Class encapsulates the run-time state of an object or interface. Objects of type **Class** are created automatically, when classes are loaded. You cannot explicitly declare a **Class** object. Generally, you obtain a **Class** object by calling the **getClass( )** method defined by **Object**. **Class** is a generic type that is declared as shown here:

class Class<T>

Here, **T** is the type of the class or interface represented. A sampling of commonly used methods defined by **Class** is shown in Table 16-15.

Method	Description
static Class<?> forName(String *name*) throws ClassNotFoundException	Returns a **Class** object given its complete name.
static Class<?> forName(String *name*, boolean *how*, ClassLoader *ldr*) throws ClassNotFoundException	Returns a **Class** object given its complete name. The object is loaded using the loader specified by *ldr*. If *how* is **true**, the object is initialized; otherwise, it is not.
<A extends Annotation> A getAnnotation(Class<A> *annoType*)	Returns an **Annotation** object that contains the annotation associated with *annoType* for the invoking object.

TABLE 16-15 A Sampling of Methods Defined by **Class**

Method	Description
Annotation[ ] getAnnotations( )	Obtains all annotations associated with the invoking object and stores them in an array of **Annotation** objects. Returns a reference to this array.
Class<?>[ ] getClasses( )	Returns a **Class** object for each of the public classes and interfaces that are members of the invoking object.
ClassLoader getClassLoader( )	Returns the **ClassLoader** object that loaded the class or interface used to instantiate the invoking object.
Constructor<T> getConstructor(Class<?> ... *paramTypes*) throws NoSuchMethodException, SecurityException	Returns a **Constructor** object that represents the constructor for the invoking object that has the parameter types specified by *paramTypes*.
Constructor<?>[ ] getConstructors( ) throws SecurityException	Obtains a **Constructor** object for each public constructor of the invoking object and stores them in an array. Returns a reference to this array.
Annotation[ ] getDeclaredAnnotations( )	Obtains an **Annotation** object for all the annotations that are declared by the invoking object and stores them in an array. Returns a reference to this array. (Inherited annotations are ignored.)
Constructor<?>[ ] getDeclaredConstructors( ) throws SecurityException	Obtains a **Constructor** object for each constructor declared by the invoking object and stores them in an array. Returns a reference to this array. (Superclass constructors are ignored.)
Field[ ] getDeclaredFields( ) throws SecurityException	Obtains a **Field** object for each field declared by this class and stores them in an array. Returns a reference to this array. (Inherited fields are ignored.)
Method[ ] getDeclaredMethods( ) throws SecurityException	Obtains a **Method** object for each method declared by this class or interface and stores them in an array. Returns a reference to this array. (Inherited methods are ignored.)
Field getField(String *fieldName*) throws NoSuchMethodException, SecurityException	Returns a **Field** object that represents the field specified by *fieldName* for the invoking object.
Field[ ] getFields( ) throws SecurityException	Obtains a **Field** object for each public field of the invoking object and stores them in an array. Returns a reference to this array.
Class<?>[ ] getInterfaces( )	When invoked on an object, this method returns an array of the interfaces implemented by the class type of the object. When invoked on an interface, this method returns an array of interfaces extended by the interface.

TABLE 16-15 A Sampling of Methods Defined by **Class** *(continued)*

Method	Description
Method getMethod(String *methName*, Class<?> ... *paramTypes*) throws NoSuchMethodException, SecurityException	Returns a **Method** object that represents the method specified by *methName* and having the parameter types specified by *paramTypes*.
Method[ ] getMethods( ) throws SecurityException	Obtains a **Method** object for each public method of the invoking object and stores them in an array. Returns a reference to this array.
String getName( )	Returns the complete name of the class or interface of the invoking object.
ProtectionDomain getProtectionDomain( )	Returns the protection domain associated with the invoking object.
Class<? super T> getSuperclass( )	Returns the superclass of the invoking object. The return value is **null** if the invoking object is of type **Object**.
boolean isInterface( )	Returns **true** if the invoking object is an interface. Otherwise, it returns **false**.
T newInstance( ) throws IllegalAccessException, InstantiationException	Creates a new instance (i.e., a new object) that is of the same type as the invoking object. This is equivalent to using **new** with the class' default constructor. The new object is returned.
String toString( )	Returns the string representation of the invoking object or interface.

TABLE 16-15   A Sampling of Methods Defined by **Class** *(continued)*

The methods defined by **Class** are often useful in situations where run-time type information about an object is required. As Table 16-15 shows, methods are provided that allow you to determine additional information about a particular class, such as its public constructors, fields, and methods. Among other things, this is important for the Java Beans functionality, which is discussed later in this book.

The following program demonstrates **getClass( )** (inherited from **Object**) and **getSuperclass( )** (from **Class**):

```
// Demonstrate Run-Time Type Information.

class X {
  int a;
  float b;
}

class Y extends X {
  double c;
}

class RTTI {
```

```
public static void main(String args[]) {
  X x = new X();
  Y y = new Y();
  Class<?> clObj;

  clObj = x.getClass(); // get Class reference
  System.out.println("x is object of type: " +
                        clObj.getName());

  clObj = y.getClass(); // get Class reference
  System.out.println("y is object of type: " +
                        clObj.getName());
  clObj = clObj.getSuperclass();
  System.out.println("y's superclass is " +
                        clObj.getName());
  }
}
```

The output from this program is shown here:

```
x is object of type: X
y is object of type: Y
y's superclass is X
```

ClassLoader

The abstract class **ClassLoader** defines how classes are loaded. Your application can create subclasses that extend **ClassLoader**, implementing its methods. Doing so allows you to load classes in some way other than the way they are normally loaded by the Java run-time system. However, this is not something that you will normally need to do.

Math

The **Math** class contains all the floating-point functions that are used for geometry and trigonometry, as well as several general-purpose methods. **Math** defines two **double** constants: **E** (approximately 2.72) and **PI** (approximately 3.14).

Transcendental Functions

The following methods accept a **double** parameter for an angle in radians and return the result of their respective transcendental function:

Method	Description
static double sin(double *arg*)	Returns the sine of the angle specified by *arg* in radians.
static double cos(double *arg*)	Returns the cosine of the angle specified by *arg* in radians.
static double tan(double *arg*)	Returns the tangent of the angle specified by *arg* in radians.

The next methods take as a parameter the result of a transcendental function and return, in radians, the angle that would produce that result. They are the inverse of their non-arc companions.

Method	Description
static double asin(double *arg*)	Returns the angle whose sine is specified by *arg*.
static double acos(double *arg*)	Returns the angle whose cosine is specified by *arg*.
static double atan(double *arg*)	Returns the angle whose tangent is specified by *arg*.
static double atan2(double *x*, double *y*)	Returns the angle whose tangent is *x/y*.

The next methods compute the hyperbolic sine, cosine, and tangent of an angle.

Method	Description
static double sinh(double *arg*)	Returns the hyperbolic sine of the angle specified by *arg*.
static double cosh(double *arg*)	Returns the hyperbolic cosine of the angle specified by *arg*.
static double tanh(double *arg*)	Returns the hyperbolic tangent of the angle specified by *arg*.

Exponential Functions

Math defines the following exponential methods:

Method	Description
static double cbrt(double *arg*)	Returns the cube root of *arg*.
static double exp(double *arg*)	Returns e to the *arg*.
static double expm1(double *arg*)	Returns e to the *arg*–1
static double log(double *arg*)	Returns the natural logarithm of *arg*.
static double log10(double *arg*)	Returns the base 10 logarithm for *arg*.
static double log1p(double *arg*)	Returns the natural logarithm for *arg* + 1.
static double pow(double *y*, double *x*)	Returns *y* raised to the *x*; for example, pow(2.0, 3.0) returns 8.0.
static double scalb(double *arg*, int *factor*)	Returns *val* $\times$ 2^{factor}. (Added by Java SE 6.)
static float scalb(float *arg*, int *factor*)	Returns *val* $\times$ 2^{factor}. (Added by Java SE 6.)
static double sqrt(double *arg*)	Returns the square root of *arg*.

Rounding Functions

The **Math** class defines several methods that provide various types of rounding operations. They are shown in Table 16-16. Notice the two **ulp( )** methods at the end of the table. In this context, *ulp* stands for *units in the last place*. It indicates the number of units between a value and the next higher value. It can be used to help assess the accuracy of a result.

Method	Description
static int abs(int *arg*)	Returns the absolute value of *arg*.
static long abs(long *arg*)	Returns the absolute value of *arg*.
static float abs(float *arg*)	Returns the absolute value of *arg*.
static double abs(double *arg*)	Returns the absolute value of *arg*.
static double ceil(double *arg*)	Returns the smallest whole number greater than or equal to *arg*.
static double floor(double *arg*)	Returns the largest whole number less than or equal to *arg*.
static int max(int *x*, int *y*)	Returns the maximum of *x* and *y*.
static long max(long *x*, long *y*)	Returns the maximum of *x* and *y*.
static float max(float *x*, float *y*)	Returns the maximum of *x* and *y*.
static double max(double *x*, double *y*)	Returns the maximum of *x* and *y*.
static int min(int *x*, int *y*)	Returns the minimum of *x* and *y*.
static long min(long *x*, long *y*)	Returns the minimum of *x* and *y*.
static float min(float *x*, float *y*)	Returns the minimum of *x* and *y*.
static double min(double *x*, double *y*)	Returns the minimum of *x* and *y*.
static double nextAfter(double *arg*, double *toward*)	Beginning with the value of *arg*, returns the next value in the direction of *toward*. If *arg* == *toward*, then *toward* is returned. (Added by Java SE 6.)
static float nextAfter(float *arg*, double *toward*)	Beginning with the value of *arg*, returns the next value in the direction of *toward*. If *arg* == *toward*, then *toward* is returned. (Added by Java SE 6.)
static double nextUp(double *arg*)	Returns the next value in the positive direction from *arg*. (Added by Java SE 6.)
static float nextUp(float *arg*)	Returns the next value in the positive direction from *arg*. (Added by Java SE 6.)
static double rint(double *arg*)	Returns the integer nearest in value to *arg*.
static int round(float *arg*)	Returns *arg* rounded up to the nearest **int**.
static long round(double *arg*)	Returns *arg* rounded up to the nearest **long**.
static float ulp(float *arg*)	Returns the ulp for *arg*.
static double ulp(double *arg*)	Returns the ulp for *arg*.

TABLE 16-16 The Rounding Methods Defined by **Math**

Miscellaneous Math Methods

In addition to the methods just shown, **Math** defines several other methods, which are shown here:

Method	Description
static double copySign(double *arg*, double *signarg*)	Returns *arg* with same sign as that of *signarg*. (Added by Java SE 6.)
static float copySign(float *arg*, float *signarg*)	Returns *arg* with same sign as that of *signarg*. (Added by Java SE 6.)
static int getExponent(double *arg*)	Returns the base-2 exponent used by the binary representation of *arg*. (Added by Java SE 6.)
static int getExponent(float *arg*)	Returns the base-2 exponent used by the binary representation of *arg*. (Added by Java SE 6.)

static double
    IEEEremainder(double *dividend*,
                      double *divisor*)
	Returns the remainder of *dividend / divisor*.

static hypot(double *side1*, double *side2*)	Returns the length of the hypotenuse of a right triangle given the length of the two opposing sides.
static double random( )	Returns a pseudorandom number between 0 and 1.
static float signum(double *arg*)	Determines the sign of a value. It returns 0 if *arg* is 0, 1 if *arg* is greater than 0, and –1 if *arg* is less than 0.
static float signum(float *arg*)	Determines the sign of a value. It returns 0 if *arg* is 0, 1 if *arg* is greater than 0, and –1 if *arg* is less than 0.
static double toDegrees(double *angle*)	Converts radians to degrees. The angle passed to *angle* must be specified in radians. The result in degrees is returned.
static double toRadians(double *angle*)	Converts degrees to radians. The angle passed to *angle* must be specified in degrees. The result in radians is returned.

The following program demonstrates **toRadians( )** and **toDegrees( )**:

```
// Demonstrate toDegrees() and toRadians().
class Angles {
  public static void main(String args[]) {
    double theta = 120.0;

    System.out.println(theta + " degrees is " +
                   Math.toRadians(theta) + " radians.");

    theta = 1.312;
    System.out.println(theta + " radians is " +
                   Math.toDegrees(theta) + " degrees.");
  }
}
```

The output is shown here:

```
120.0 degrees is 2.0943951023931953 radians.
1.312 radians is 75.17206272116401 degrees.
```

StrictMath

The **StrictMath** class defines a complete set of mathematical methods that parallel those in **Math**. The difference is that the **StrictMath** version is guaranteed to generate precisely identical results across all Java implementations, whereas the methods in **Math** are given more latitude in order to improve performance.

Compiler

The **Compiler** class supports the creation of Java environments in which Java bytecode is compiled into executable code rather than interpreted. It is not for normal programming use.

Thread, ThreadGroup, and Runnable

The **Runnable** interface and the **Thread** and **ThreadGroup** classes support multithreaded programming. Each is examined next.

NOTE *An overview of the techniques used to manage threads, implement the **Runnable** interface, and create multithreaded programs is presented in Chapter 11.*

The Runnable Interface

The **Runnable** interface must be implemented by any class that will initiate a separate thread of execution. **Runnable** only defines one abstract method, called **run( )**, which is the entry point to the thread. It is defined like this:

    void run( )

Threads that you create must implement this method.

Thread

Thread creates a new thread of execution. It defines the following commonly used constructors:

    Thread( )
    Thread(Runnable threadOb)
    Thread(Runnable threadOb, String threadName)
    Thread(String threadName)
    Thread(ThreadGroup groupOb, Runnable threadOb)
    Thread(ThreadGroup groupOb, Runnable threadOb, String threadName)
    Thread(ThreadGroup groupOb, String threadName)

threadOb is an instance of a class that implements the **Runnable** interface and defines where execution of the thread will begin. The name of the thread is specified by *threadName*. When a name is not specified, one is created by the Java Virtual Machine. *groupOb* specifies the thread group to which the new thread will belong. When no thread group is specified, the new thread belongs to the same group as the parent thread.

The following constants are defined by **Thread**:

    MAX_PRIORITY
    MIN_PRIORITY
    NORM_PRIORITY

As expected, these constants specify the maximum, minimum, and default thread priorities.

The methods defined by **Thread** are shown in Table 16-17. In early versions of Java, **Thread** also included the methods **stop( )**, **suspend( )**, and **resume( )**. However, as explained in Chapter 11, these were deprecated because they were inherently unstable. Also deprecated are **countStackFrames( )**, because it calls **suspend( )**, and **destroy( )**, because it can cause deadlock.

Method	Description
static int activeCount( )	Returns the number of threads in the group to which the thread belongs.
final void checkAccess( )	Causes the security manager to verify that the current thread can access and/or change the thread on which **checkAccess( )** is called.
static Thread currentThread( )	Returns a **Thread** object that encapsulates the thread that calls this method.
static void dumpStack( )	Displays the call stack for the thread.
static int enumerate(Thread *threads*[ ])	Puts copies of all **Thread** objects in the current thread's group into *threads*. The number of threads is returned.
static Map<Thread, StackTraceElement[ ]> getAllStackTraces( )	Returns a **Map** that contains the stack traces for all active threads. In the map, each entry consists of a key, which is the **Thread** object, and its value, which is an array of **StackTraceElement**.
ClassLoader getContextClassLoader( )	Returns the class loader that is used to load classes and resources for this thread.
static Thread.UncaughtExceptionHandler getDefaultUncaughtExceptionHandler( )	Returns the default uncaught exception handler.
long getID( )	Returns the ID of the invoking thread.
final String getName( )	Returns the thread's name.
final int getPriority( )	Returns the thread's priority setting.
StackTraceElement[ ] getStackTrace( )	Returns an array containing the stack trace for the invoking thread.
Thread.State getState( )	Returns the invoking thread's state.
final ThreadGroup getThreadGroup( )	Returns the **ThreadGroup** object of which the invoking thread is a member.
Thread.UncaughtExceptionHandler getUncaughtExceptionHandler( )	Returns the invoking thread's uncaught exception handler.
static boolean holdsLock(Object *ob*)	Returns **true** if the invoking thread owns the lock on *ob*. Returns **false** otherwise.
void interrupt( )	Interrupts the thread.
static boolean interrupted( )	Returns **true** if the currently executing thread has been scheduled for interruption. Otherwise, it returns **false**.

TABLE 16-17   The Methods Defined by **Thread**

Method	Description
final boolean isAlive( )	Returns **true** if the thread is still active. Otherwise, it returns **false**.
final boolean isDaemon( )	Returns **true** if the thread is a daemon thread. Otherwise, it returns **false**.
boolean isInterrupted( )	Returns **true** if the thread is interrupted. Otherwise, it returns **false**.
final void join( ) throws InterruptedException	Waits until the thread terminates.
final void join(long *milliseconds*) throws InterruptedException	Waits up to the specified number of milliseconds for the thread on which it is called to terminate.

final void join(long *milliseconds*,
            int *nanoseconds*)
    throws InterruptedException
	Waits up to the specified number of milliseconds plus nanoseconds for the thread on which it is called to terminate.

void run( )	Begins execution of a thread.
void setContextClassLoader(ClassLoader *cl*)	Sets the class loader that will be used by the invoking thread to *cl*.
final void setDaemon(boolean *state*)	Flags the thread as a daemon thread.

static void
    setDefaultUncaughtExceptionHandler(
        Thread.UncaughtExceptionHandler *e*)
	Sets the default uncaught exception handler to *e*.

final void setName(String *threadName*)	Sets the name of the thread to that specified by *threadName*.
final void setPriority(int *priority*)	Sets the priority of the thread to that specified by *priority*.

void
    setUncaughtExceptionHandler(
        Thread.UncaughtExceptionHandler *e*)
	Sets the invoking thread's default uncaught exception handler to *e*.

static void sleep(long *milliseconds*) throws InterruptedException	Suspends execution of the thread for the specified number of milliseconds.

static void sleep(long *milliseconds*,
            int *nanoseconds*)
    throws InterruptedException
	Suspends execution of the thread for the specified number of milliseconds plus nanoseconds.

void start( )	Starts execution of the thread.
String toString( )	Returns the string equivalent of a thread.
static void yield( )	The calling thread yields the CPU to another thread.

TABLE 16-17   The Methods Defined by **Thread** *(continued)*

ThreadGroup

ThreadGroup creates a group of threads. It defines these two constructors:

    ThreadGroup(String *groupName*)
    ThreadGroup(ThreadGroup *parentOb*, String *groupName*)

For both forms, *groupName* specifies the name of the thread group. The first version creates a new group that has the current thread as its parent. In the second form, the parent is specified by *parentOb*. The non-deprecated methods defined by **ThreadGroup** are shown in Table 16-18.

Thread groups offer a convenient way to manage groups of threads as a unit. This is particularly valuable in situations in which you want to suspend and resume a number of related threads. For example, imagine a program in which one set of threads is used for printing a document, another set is used to display the document on the screen, and another set saves the document to a disk file. If printing is aborted, you will want an easy way to

Method	Description
int activeCount( )	Returns the number of threads in the group plus any groups for which this thread is a parent.
int activeGroupCount( )	Returns the number of groups for which the invoking thread is a parent.
final void checkAccess( )	Causes the security manager to verify that the invoking thread may access and/or change the group on which **checkAccess( )** is called.
final void destroy( )	Destroys the thread group (and any child groups) on which it is called.
int enumerate(Thread *group*[ ])	The threads that comprise the invoking thread group are put into the *group* array.
int enumerate(Thread *group*[ ], boolean *all*)	The threads that comprise the invoking thread group are put into the *group* array. If *all* is **true**, then threads in all subgroups of the thread are also put into *group*.
int enumerate(ThreadGroup *group*[ ])	The subgroups of the invoking thread group are put into the *group* array.
int enumerate(ThreadGroup *group*[ ], boolean *all*)	The subgroups of the invoking thread group are put into the *group* array. If *all* is **true**, then all subgroups of the subgroups (and so on) are also put into *group*.
final int getMaxPriority( )	Returns the maximum priority setting for the group.
final String getName( )	Returns the name of the group.
final ThreadGroup getParent( )	Returns **null** if the invoking **ThreadGroup** object has no parent. Otherwise, it returns the parent of the invoking object.
final void interrupt( )	Invokes the **interrupt( )** method of all threads in the group.

TABLE 16-18   The Methods Defined by **ThreadGroup**

Method	Description
final boolean isDaemon( )	Returns **true** if the group is a daemon group. Otherwise, it returns **false**.
boolean isDestroyed( )	Returns **true** if the group has been destroyed. Otherwise, it returns **false**.
void list( )	Displays information about the group.
final boolean parentOf(ThreadGroup *group*)	Returns **true** if the invoking thread is the parent of *group* (or *group,* itself). Otherwise, it returns **false**.
final void setDaemon(boolean *isDaemon*)	If *isDaemon* is **true**, then the invoking group is flagged as a daemon group.
final void setMaxPriority(int *priority*)	Sets the maximum priority of the invoking group to *priority*.
String toString( )	Returns the string equivalent of the group.
void uncaughtException(Thread *thread,* Throwable *e*)	This method is called when an exception goes uncaught.

TABLE 16-18   The Methods Defined by **ThreadGroup** *(continued)*

stop all threads related to printing. Thread groups offer this convenience. The following program, which creates two thread groups of two threads each, illustrates this usage:

```
// Demonstrate thread groups.
class NewThread extends Thread {
  boolean suspendFlag;

  NewThread(String threadname, ThreadGroup tgOb) {
    super(tgOb, threadname);
    System.out.println("New thread: " + this);
    suspendFlag = false;
    start(); // Start the thread
  }

  // This is the entry point for thread.
  public void run() {
    try {
      for(int i = 5; i > 0; i--) {
        System.out.println(getName() + ": " + i);
        Thread.sleep(1000);
        synchronized(this) {
          while(suspendFlag) {
            wait();
          }
        }
      }
    } catch (Exception e) {
      System.out.println("Exception in " + getName());
    }
```

```
      System.out.println(getName() + " exiting.");
    }

    void mysuspend() {
      suspendFlag = true;
    }

    synchronized void myresume() {
      suspendFlag = false;
      notify();
    }
}

class ThreadGroupDemo {
  public static void main(String args[]) {
    ThreadGroup groupA = new ThreadGroup("Group A");
    ThreadGroup groupB = new ThreadGroup("Group B");

    NewThread ob1 = new NewThread("One", groupA);
    NewThread ob2 = new NewThread("Two", groupA);
    NewThread ob3 = new NewThread("Three", groupB);
    NewThread ob4 = new NewThread("Four", groupB);

    System.out.println("\nHere is output from list():");
    groupA.list();
    groupB.list();
    System.out.println();

    System.out.println("Suspending Group A");
    Thread tga[] = new Thread[groupA.activeCount()];
    groupA.enumerate(tga); // get threads in group
    for(int i = 0; i < tga.length; i++) {
      ((NewThread)tga[i]).mysuspend(); // suspend each thread
    }

    try {
      Thread.sleep(4000);
    } catch (InterruptedException e) {
      System.out.println("Main thread interrupted.");
    }

    System.out.println("Resuming Group A");
    for(int i = 0; i < tga.length; i++) {
      ((NewThread)tga[i]).myresume(); // resume threads in group
    }

    // wait for threads to finish
    try {
      System.out.println("Waiting for threads to finish.");
      ob1.join();
      ob2.join();
      ob3.join();
      ob4.join();
```

```
    } catch (Exception e) {
      System.out.println("Exception in Main thread");
    }

    System.out.println("Main thread exiting.");
  }
}
```

Sample output from this program is shown here (the precise ouput you see may differ):

```
New thread: Thread[One,5,Group A]
New thread: Thread[Two,5,Group A]
New thread: Thread[Three,5,Group B]
New thread: Thread[Four,5,Group B]
Here is output from list():
java.lang.ThreadGroup[name=Group A,maxpri=10]
   Thread[One,5,Group A]
   Thread[Two,5,Group A]
java.lang.ThreadGroup[name=Group B,maxpri=10]
   Thread[Three,5,Group B]
   Thread[Four,5,Group B]
Suspending Group A
Three: 5
Four: 5
Three: 4
Four: 4
Three: 3
Four: 3
Three: 2
Four: 2
Resuming Group A
Waiting for threads to finish.
One: 5
Two: 5
Three: 1
Four: 1
One: 4
Two: 4
Three exiting.
Four exiting.
One: 3
Two: 3
One: 2
Two: 2
One: 1
Two: 1
One exiting.
```

```
Two exiting.
Main thread exiting.
```

Inside the program, notice that thread group A is suspended for four seconds. As the output confirms, this causes threads One and Two to pause, but threads Three and Four continue running. After the four seconds, threads One and Two are resumed. Notice how thread group A is suspended and resumed. First, the threads in group A are obtained by calling **enumerate( )** on group A. Then, each thread is suspended by iterating through the resulting array. To resume the threads in A, the list is again traversed and each thread is resumed. One last point: this example uses the recommended approach to suspending and resuming threads. It does not rely upon the deprecated methods **suspend( )** and **resume( )**.

ThreadLocal and InheritableThreadLocal

Java defines two additional thread-related classes in **java.lang**:

- **ThreadLocal**   Used to create thread local variables. Each thread will have its own copy of a thread local variable.

- **InheritableThreadLocal**   Creates thread local variables that may be inherited.

Package

Package encapsulates version data associated with a package. Package version information is becoming more important because of the proliferation of packages and because a Java program may need to know what version of a package is available. The methods defined by **Package** are shown in Table 16-19. The following program demonstrates **Package**, displaying the packages about which the program currently is aware:

```
// Demonstrate Package
class PkgTest {
  public static void main(String args[]) {
    Package pkgs[];

    pkgs = Package.getPackages();

    for(int i=0; i < pkgs.length; i++)
      System.out.println(
            pkgs[i].getName() + " " +
            pkgs[i].getImplementationTitle() + " " +
            pkgs[i].getImplementationVendor() + " " +
            pkgs[i].getImplementationVersion()
      );

  }
}
```

Method	Description
<A extends Annotation> A getAnnotation(Class<A> *annoType*)	Returns an **Annotation** object that contains the annotation associated with *annoType* for the invoking object.
Annotation[ ] getAnnotations( )	Returns all annotations associated with the invoking object in an array of **Annotation** objects. Returns a reference to this array.
Annotation[ ] getDeclaredAnnotations( )	Returns an **Annotation** object for all the annotations that are declared by the invoking object. (Inherited annotations are ignored.)
String getImplementationTitle( )	Returns the title of the invoking package.
String getImplementationVendor( )	Returns the name of the implementor of the invoking package.
String getImplementationVersion( )	Returns the version number of the invoking package.
String getName( )	Returns the name of the invoking package.
static Package getPackage(String *pkgName*)	Returns a **Package** object with the name specified by *pkgName*.
static Package[ ] getPackages( )	Returns all packages about which the invoking program is currently aware.
String getSpecificationTitle( )	Returns the title of the invoking package's specification.
String getSpecificationVendor( )	Returns the name of the owner of the specification for the invoking package.
String getSpecificationVersion( )	Returns the invoking package's specification version number.
int hashCode( )	Returns the hash code for the invoking package.
boolean isAnnotationPresent(Class<? extends Annotation> *anno*)	Returns **true** if the annotation described by *anno* is associated with the invoking object. Returns **false**, otherwise.
boolean isCompatibleWith(String *verNum*) throws NumberFormatException	Returns **true** if *verNum* is less than or equal to the invoking package's version number.
boolean isSealed( )	Returns **true** if the invoking package is sealed. Returns **false** otherwise.
boolean isSealed(URL *url*)	Returns **true** if the invoking package is sealed relative to *url*. Returns **false** otherwise.
String toString( )	Returns the string equivalent of the invoking package.

TABLE 16-19 The Methods Defined by **Package**

RuntimePermission

RuntimePermission relates to Java's security mechanism and is not examined further here.

Throwable

The **Throwable** class supports Java's exception-handling system and is the class from which all exception classes are derived. It is discussed in Chapter 10.

SecurityManager

SecurityManager is a class that your classes can subclass to create a security manager. Generally, you don't need to implement your own security manager. If you do, you need to consult the documentation that comes with your Java development system.

StackTraceElement

The **StackTraceElement** class describes a single *stack frame,* which is an individual element of a stack trace when an exception occurs. Each stack frame represents an *execution point,* which includes such things as the name of the class, the name of the method, the name of the file, and the source-code line number. An array of **StackTraceElement**s is returned by the **getStackTrace( )** method of the **Throwable** class.

StackTraceElement has one constructor:

StackTraceElement(String *className,* String *methName,* string *fileName,* int *line*)

Here, the name of the class is specified by *className,* the name of the method is specified in *methName,* the name of the file is specified by *fileName,* and the line number is passed in *line.* If there is no valid line number, use a negative value for *line.* Furthermore, a value of –2 for *line* indicates that this frame refers to a native method.

The methods supported by **StackTraceElement** are shown in Table 16-20. These methods give you programmatic access to a stack trace.

Method	Description
boolean equals(Object *ob*)	Returns **true** if the invoking **StackTraceElement** is the same as the one passed in *ob*. Otherwise, it returns **false**.
String getClassName( )	Returns the class name of the execution point described by the invoking **StackTraceElement**.
String getFileName( )	Returns the filename of the execution point described by the invoking **StackTraceElement**.

TABLE 16-20   The Methods Defined by **StackTraceElement**

Method	Description
int getLineNumber( )	Returns the source-code line number of the execution point described by the invoking **StackTraceElement**. In some situations, the line number will not be available, in which case a negative value is returned.
String getMethodName( )	Returns the method name of the execution point described by the invoking **StackTraceElement**.
int hashCode( )	Returns the hash code for the invoking **StackTraceElement**.
boolean isNativeMethod( )	Returns **true** if the invoking **StackTraceElement** describes a native method. Otherwise, returns **false**.
String toString( )	Returns the **String** equivalent of the invoking sequence.

TABLE 16-20   The Methods Defined by **StackTraceElement** *(continued)*

Enum

As described in Chapter 12, enumerations were recently added to the Java language. (Recall that an enumeration is created by using the keyword **enum**.) All enumerations automatically inherit **Enum**. **Enum** is a generic class that is declared as shown here:

    class Enum<E extends Enum<E>>

Here, **E** stands for the enumeration type. **Enum** has no public constructors.

   Enum defines several methods that are available for use by all enumerations, which are shown in Table 16-21.

Method	Description
protected final Object clone( ) throws CloneNotSupportedException	Invoking this method causes a **CloneNotSupportedException** to be thrown. This prevents enumerations from being cloned.
final int compareTo(E *e*)	Compares the ordinal value of two constants of the same enumeration. Returns a negative value if the invoking constant has an ordinal value less than *e*'s, zero if the two ordinal values are the same, and a positive value if the invoking constant has an ordinal value greater than *e*'s.
final boolean equals(Object *obj*)	Returns true if *obj* and the invoking object refer to the same constant.
final Class<E> getDeclaringClass( )	Returns the type of enumeration of which the invoking constant is a member.
final int hashCode( )	Returns the hash code for the invoking object.

TABLE 16-21   The Methods Defined by **Enum**

Method	Description
final String name( )	Returns the unaltered name of the invoking constant.
final int ordinal( )	Returns a value that indicates an enumeration constant's position in the list of constants.
String toString( )	Returns the name of the invoking constant. This name may differ from the one used in the enumeration's declaration.
static \<T extends Enum\<T>> T valueOf(Class\<T> *e-type*, String *name*)	Returns the constant associated with *name* in the enumeration type specified by *e-type*.

TABLE 16-21   The Methods Defined by **Enum** *(continued)*

The CharSequence Interface

The **CharSequence** interface defines methods that grant read-only access to a sequence of characters. These methods are shown in Table 16-22. This interface is implemented by **String**, **StringBuffer**, and **StringBuilder**. It is also implemented by **CharBuffer**, which is in the **java.nio** package (described later in this book).

The Comparable Interface

Objects of classes that implement **Comparable** can be ordered. In other words, classes that implement **Comparable** contain objects that can be compared in some meaningful manner. Comparable is generic and is declared like this:

interface Comparable\<T>

Here, **T** represents the type of objects being compared.

The **Comparable** interface declares one method that is used to determine what Java calls the *natural ordering* of instances of a class. The signature of the method is shown here:

int compareTo(T *obj*)

Method	Description
char charAt(int *idx*)	Returns the character at the index specified by *idx*.
int length( )	Returns the number of characters in the invoking sequence.
CharSequence subSequence(int *startIdx*, int *stopIdx*)	Returns a subset of the invoking sequence beginning at *startIdx* and ending at *stopIdx*–1.
String toString( )	Returns the **String** equivalent of the invoking sequence.

TABLE 16-22   The Methods Defined by **CharSequence**

This method compares the invoking object with *obj*. It returns 0 if the values are equal. A negative value is returned if the invoking object has a lower value. Otherwise, a positive value is returned.

This interface is implemented by several of the classes already reviewed in this book. Specifically, the **Byte**, **Character**, **Double**, **Float**, **Long**, **Short**, **String**, and **Integer** classes define a **compareTo( )** method. In addition, as the next chapter explains, objects that implement this interface can be used in various collections.

The Appendable Interface

Objects of a class that implements **Appendable** can have a character or character sequences appended to it. **Appendable** defines these three methods:

Appendable append(char *ch*) throws IOException
Appendable append(CharSequence *chars*) throws IOException
Appendable append(CharSequence *chars*, int *begin*, int *end*) throws IOException

In the first form, the character *ch* is appended to the invoking object. In the second form, the character sequence *chars* is appended to the invoking object. The third form allows you to indicate a portion (specified by *begin* and *end*) of the sequence specified by *chars*. In all cases, a reference to the invoking object is returned.

The Iterable Interface

Iterable must be implemented by any class whose objects will be used by the for-each version of the **for** loop. In other words, in order for an object to be used within a for-each style **for** loop, its class must implement **Iterable**. **Iterable** is a generic interface that has this declaration:

interface Iterable<T>

Here, **T** is the type of the object being iterated. It defines one method, **iterator( )**, which is shown here:

Iterator<T> iterator( )

It returns an iterator to the elements contained in the invoking object.

NOTE   *Iterators are described in detail in Chapter 17.*

The Readable Interface

The **Readable** interface indicates that an object can be used as a source for characters. It defines one method called **read( )**, which is shown here:

int read(CharBuffer *buf*) throws IOException

This method reads characters into *buf.* It returns the number of characters read, or –1 if an EOF is encountered.

The java.lang Subpackages

Java defines several subpackages:

- java.lang.annotation
- java.lang.instrument
- java.lang.management
- java.lang.ref
- java.lang.reflect

Each is briefly described here.

java.lang.annotation

Java's annotation facility is supported by **java.lang.annotation**. It defines the **Annotation** interface, and the **ElementType** and **RetentionPolicy** enumerations. Annotations are described in Chapter 12.

java.lang.instrument

java.lang.instrument defines features that can be used to add instrumentation to various aspects of program execution. It defines the **Instrumentation** and **ClassFileTransformer** interfaces, and the **ClassDefinition** class.

java.lang.management

The **java.lang.management** package provides management support for the JVM and the execution environment. Using the features in **java.lang.management**, you can observe and manage various aspects of program execution.

java.lang.ref

You learned earlier that the garbage collection facilities in Java automatically determine when no references exist to an object. The object is then assumed to be no longer needed and its memory is reclaimed. The classes in the **java.lang.ref** package provide more flexible control over the garbage collection process. For example, assume that your program has created numerous objects that you want to reuse at some later time. You can continue to hold references to these objects, but that may require too much memory.

Instead, you can define "soft" references to these objects. An object that is "softly reachable" can be reclaimed by the garbage collector, if available memory runs low. In that case, the garbage collector sets the "soft" references to that object to **null**. Otherwise, the garbage collector saves the object for possible future use.

A programmer has the ability to determine whether a "softly reachable" object has been reclaimed. If it has been reclaimed, it can be re-created. Otherwise, the object is still available for reuse. You may also create "weak" and "phantom" references to objects. Discussion of these and other features of the **java.lang.ref** package is beyond the scope of this book.

java.lang.reflect

Reflection is the ability of a program to analyze itself. The **java.lang.reflect** package provides the ability to obtain information about the fields, constructors, methods, and modifiers of a class. Among other reasons, you need this information to build software tools that enable you to work with Java Beans components. The tools use reflection to determine dynamically the characteristics of a component. Reflection was introduced in Chapter 12 and is also examined in Chapter 27.

java.lang.reflect defines several classes, including **Method**, **Field**, and **Constructor**. It also defines several interfaces, including **AnnotatedElement**, **Member**, and **Type**. In addition, the **java.lang.reflect** package includes the **Array** class that enables you to create and access arrays dynamically.

java.util Part 1:
The Collections Framework

This chapter begins our examination of **java.util**. This important package contains a large assortment of classes and interfaces that support a broad range of functionality. For example, **java.util** has classes that generate pseudorandom numbers, manage date and time, observe events, manipulate sets of bits, tokenize strings, and handle formatted data. The **java.util** package also contains one of Java's most powerful subsystems: The *Collections Framework.* The Collections Framework is a sophisticated hierarchy of interfaces and classes that provide state-of-the-art technology for managing groups of objects. It merits close attention by all programmers.

Because **java.util** contains a wide array of functionality, it is quite large. Here is a list of its classes:

AbstractCollection	EventObject	Random
AbstractList	FormattableFlags	ResourceBundle
AbstractMap	Formatter	Scanner
AbstractQueue	GregorianCalendar	ServiceLoader (Added by Java SE 6.)
AbstractSequentialList	HashMap	SimpleTimeZone
AbstractSet	HashSet	Stack
ArrayDeque (Added by Java SE 6.)	Hashtable	StringTokenizer
ArrayList	IdentityHashMap	Timer
Arrays	LinkedHashMap	TimerTask
BitSet	LinkedHashSet	TimeZone
Calendar	LinkedList	TreeMap
Collections	ListResourceBundle	TreeSet
Currency	Locale	UUID
Date	Observable	Vector
Dictionary	PriorityQueue	WeakHashMap
EnumMap	Properties	
EnumSet	PropertyPermission	
EventListenerProxy	PropertyResourceBundle	

The interfaces defined by **java.util** are shown next:

Collection	List	Queue
Comparator	ListIterator	RandomAccess
Deque (Added by Java SE 6.)	Map	Set
Enumeration	Map.Entry	SortedMap
EventListener	NavigableMap (Added by Java SE 6.)	SortedSet
Formattable	NavigableSet (Added by Java SE 6.)	
Iterator	Observer	

Because of its size, the description of **java.util** is broken into two chapters. This chapter examines those members of **java.util** that are part of the Collections Framework. Chapter 18 discusses its other classes and interfaces.

Collections Overview

The Java Collections Framework standardizes the way in which groups of objects are handled by your programs. Collections were not part of the original Java release, but were added by J2SE 1.2. Prior to the Collections Framework, Java provided ad hoc classes such as **Dictionary**, **Vector**, **Stack**, and **Properties** to store and manipulate groups of objects. Although these classes were quite useful, they lacked a central, unifying theme. The way that you used **Vector** was different from the way that you used **Properties**, for example. Also, this early, ad hoc approach was not designed to be easily extended or adapted. Collections are an answer to these (and other) problems.

The Collections Framework was designed to meet several goals. First, the framework had to be high-performance. The implementations for the fundamental collections (dynamic arrays, linked lists, trees, and hash tables) are highly efficient. You seldom, if ever, need to code one of these "data engines" manually. Second, the framework had to allow different types of collections to work in a similar manner and with a high degree of interoperability. Third, extending and/or adapting a collection had to be easy. Toward this end, the entire Collections Framework is built upon a set of standard interfaces. Several standard implementations (such as **LinkedList**, **HashSet**, and **TreeSet**) of these interfaces are provided that you may use as-is. You may also implement your own collection, if you choose. Various special-purpose implementations are created for your convenience, and some partial implementations are provided that make creating your own collection class easier. Finally, mechanisms were added that allow the integration of standard arrays into the Collections Framework.

Algorithms are another important part of the collection mechanism. Algorithms operate on collections and are defined as static methods within the **Collections** class. Thus, they are available for all collections. Each collection class need not implement its own versions. The algorithms provide a standard means of manipulating collections.

Another item closely associated with the Collections Framework is the **Iterator** interface. An *iterator* offers a general-purpose, standardized way of accessing the elements within a collection, one at a time. Thus, an iterator provides a means of *enumerating the contents of a collection*. Because each collection implements **Iterator**, the elements of any collection class can be accessed through the methods defined by **Iterator**. Thus, with only small changes, the code that cycles through a set can also be used to cycle through a list, for example.

In addition to collections, the framework defines several map interfaces and classes. *Maps* store key/value pairs. Although maps are part of the Collections Framework, they are not "collections" in the strict use of the term. You can, however, obtain a *collection-view* of a map. Such a view contains the elements from the map stored in a collection. Thus, you can process the contents of a map as a collection, if you choose.

The collection mechanism was retrofitted to some of the original classes defined by **java.util** so that they too could be integrated into the new system. It is important to understand that although the addition of collections altered the architecture of many of the original utility classes, it did not cause the deprecation of any. Collections simply provide a better way of doing several things.

NOTE   *If you are familiar with C++, then you will find it helpful to know that the Java collections technology is similar in spirit to the Standard Template Library (STL) defined by C++. What C++ calls a container, Java calls a collection. However, there are significant differences between the Collections Framework and the STL. It is important to not jump to conclusions.*

Recent Changes to Collections

Recently, the Collections Framework underwent a fundamental change that significantly increased its power and streamlined its use. The changes were caused by the addition of generics, autoboxing/unboxing, and the for-each style **for** loop, by JDK 5. Although we will be revisiting these topics throughout the course of this chapter, a brief overview is warranted now.

Generics Fundamentally Change the Collections Framework

The addition of generics caused a significant change to the Collections Framework because the entire Collections Framework has been reengineered for it. All collections are now generic, and many of the methods that operate on collections take generic type parameters. Simply put, the addition of generics has affected every part of the Collections Framework.

Generics add the one feature that collections had been missing: type safety. Prior to generics, all collections stored **Object** references, which meant that any collection could store any type of object. Thus, it was possible to accidentally store incompatible types in a collection. Doing so could result in run-time type mismatch errors. With generics, it is possible to explicitly state the type of data being stored, and run-time type mismatch errors can be avoided.

Although the addition of generics changed the declarations of most of its classes and interfaces, and several of their methods, overall, the Collections Framework still works the same as it did prior to generics. However, if you are familiar with the pre-generics version of the Collections Framework, you might find the new syntax a bit intimidating. Don't worry; over time, the generic syntax will become second nature.

One other point: to gain the advantages that generics bring collections, older code will need to be rewritten. This is also important because pre-generics code will generate warning messages when compiled by a modern Java compiler. To eliminate these warnings, you will need to add type information to all your collections code.

Autoboxing Facilitates the Use of Primitive Types

Autoboxing/unboxing facilitates the storing of primitive types in collections. As you will see, a collection can store only references, not primitive values. In the past, if you wanted to store a primitive value, such as an **int**, in a collection, you had to manually box it into its type wrapper. When the value was retrieved, it needed to be manually unboxed (by using an explicit cast) into its proper primitive type. Because of autoboxing/unboxing, Java can automatically perform the proper boxing and unboxing needed when storing or retrieving primitive types. There is no need to manually perform these operations.

The For-Each Style for Loop

All collection classes in the Collections Framework have been retrofitted to implement the **Iterable** interface, which means that a collection can be cycled through by use of the for-each style **for** loop. In the past, cycling through a collection required the use of an iterator (described later in this chapter), with the programmer manually constructing the loop. Although iterators are still needed for some uses, in many cases, iterator-based loops can be replaced by **for** loops.

The Collection Interfaces

The Collections Framework defines several interfaces. This section provides an overview of each interface. Beginning with the collection interfaces is necessary because they determine the fundamental nature of the collection classes. Put differently, the concrete classes simply provide different implementations of the standard interfaces. The interfaces that underpin collections are summarized in the following table:

Interface	Description
Collection	Enables you to work with groups of objects; it is at the top of the collections hierarchy.
Deque	Extends **Queue** to handle a double-ended queue. (Added by Java SE 6.)
List	Extends **Collection** to handle sequences (lists of objects).
NavigableSet	Extends **SortedSet** to handle retrieval of elements based on closest-match searches. (Added by Java SE 6.)
Queue	Extends **Collection** to handle special types of lists in which elements are removed only from the head.
Set	Extends **Collection** to handle sets, which must contain unique elements.
SortedSet	Extends **Set** to handle sorted sets.

In addition to the collection interfaces, collections also use the **Comparator**, **RandomAccess**, **Iterator**, and **ListIterator** interfaces, which are described in depth later in this chapter. Briefly, **Comparator** defines how two objects are compared; **Iterator** and **ListIterator** enumerate the objects within a collection. By implementing **RandomAccess**, a list indicates that it supports efficient, random access to its elements.

To provide the greatest flexibility in their use, the collection interfaces allow some methods to be optional. The optional methods enable you to modify the contents of a collection. Collections that support these methods are called *modifiable*. Collections that do not allow their contents to be changed are called *unmodifiable*. If an attempt is made to use one of these methods on an unmodifiable collection, an **UnsupportedOperationException** is thrown. All the built-in collections are modifiable.

The following sections examine the collection interfaces.

The Collection Interface

The **Collection** interface is the foundation upon which the Collections Framework is built because it must be implemented by any class that defines a collection. **Collection** is a generic interface that has this declaration:

interface Collection<E>

Here, **E** specifies the type of objects that the collection will hold. **Collection** extends the **Iterable** interface. This means that all collections can be cycled through by use of the for-each style **for** loop. (Recall that only classes that implement **Iterable** can be cycled through by the **for**.)

Collection declares the core methods that all collections will have. These methods are summarized in Table 17-1. Because all collections implement **Collection**, familiarity with its methods is necessary for a clear understanding of the framework. Several of these methods can throw an **UnsupportedOperationException**. As explained, this occurs if a collection cannot be modified. A **ClassCastException** is generated when one object is incompatible with another, such as when an attempt is made to add an incompatible object to a collection. A **NullPointerException** is thrown if an attempt is made to store a **null** object and **null** elements are not allowed in the collection. An **IllegalArgumentException** is thrown if an invalid argument is used. An **IllegalStateException** is thrown if an attempt is made to add an element to a fixed-length collection that is full.

Objects are added to a collection by calling **add( )**. Notice that **add( )** takes an argument of type **E**, which means that objects added to a collection must be compatible with the type of data expected by the collection. You can add the entire contents of one collection to another by calling **addAll( )**.

You can remove an object by using **remove( )**. To remove a group of objects, call **removeAll( )**. You can remove all elements except those of a specified group by calling **retainAll( )**. To empty a collection, call **clear( )**.

You can determine whether a collection contains a specific object by calling **contains( )**. To determine whether one collection contains all the members of another, call **containsAll( )**. You can determine when a collection is empty by calling **isEmpty( )**. The number of elements currently held in a collection can be determined by calling **size( )**.

The **toArray( )** methods return an array that contains the elements stored in the invoking collection. The first returns an array of **Object**. The second returns an array of elements that have the same type as the array specified as a parameter. Normally, the second form is more convenient because it returns the desired array type. These methods are more important than it might at first seem. Often, processing the contents of a collection by using array-like syntax is advantageous. By providing a pathway between collections and arrays, you can have the best of both worlds.

Two collections can be compared for equality by calling **equals( )**. The precise meaning of "equality" may differ from collection to collection. For example, you can implement **equals( )** so that it compares the values of elements stored in the collection. Alternatively, **equals( )** can compare references to those elements.

One more very important method is **iterator( )**, which returns an iterator to a collection. Iterators are frequently used when working with collections.

The List Interface

The **List** interface extends **Collection** and declares the behavior of a collection that stores a sequence of elements. Elements can be inserted or accessed by their position in the list, using

Method	Description
boolean add(E *obj*)	Adds *obj* to the invoking collection. Returns **true** if *obj* was added to the collection. Returns **false** if *obj* is already a member of the collection and the collection does not allow duplicates.
boolean addAll(Collection<? extends E> *c*)	Adds all the elements of *c* to the invoking collection. Returns **true** if the operation succeeded (i.e., the elements were added). Otherwise, returns **false**.
void clear( )	Removes all elements from the invoking collection.
boolean contains(Object *obj*)	Returns **true** if *obj* is an element of the invoking collection. Otherwise, returns **false**.
boolean containsAll(Collection<?> *c*)	Returns **true** if the invoking collection contains all elements of *c*. Otherwise, returns **false**.
boolean equals(Object *obj*)	Returns **true** if the invoking collection and *obj* are equal. Otherwise, returns **false**.
int hashCode( )	Returns the hash code for the invoking collection.
boolean isEmpty( )	Returns **true** if the invoking collection is empty. Otherwise, returns **false**.
Iterator<E> iterator( )	Returns an iterator for the invoking collection.
boolean remove(Object *obj*)	Removes one instance of *obj* from the invoking collection. Returns **true** if the element was removed. Otherwise, returns **false**.
boolean removeAll(Collection<?> *c*)	Removes all elements of *c* from the invoking collection. Returns **true** if the collection changed (i.e., elements were removed). Otherwise, returns **false**.
boolean retainAll(Collection<?> *c*)	Removes all elements from the invoking collection except those in *c*. Returns **true** if the collection changed (i.e., elements were removed). Otherwise, returns **false**.
int size( )	Returns the number of elements held in the invoking collection.
Object[ ] toArray( )	Returns an array that contains all the elements stored in the invoking collection. The array elements are copies of the collection elements.
<T> T[ ] toArray(T *array*[ ])	Returns an array that contains the elements of the invoking collection. The array elements are copies of the collection elements. If the size of *array* equals the number of elements, these are returned in *array*. If the size of *array* is less than the number of elements, a new array of the necessary size is allocated and returned. If the size of *array* is greater than the number of elements, the array element following the last collection element is set to **null**. An **ArrayStoreException** is thrown if any collection element has a type that is not a subtype of *array*.

TABLE 17-1   The Methods Defined by **Collection**

a zero-based index. A list may contain duplicate elements. **List** is a generic interface that has this declaration:

    interface List<E>

Here, **E** specifies the type of objects that the list will hold.

In addition to the methods defined by **Collection**, **List** defines some of its own, which are summarized in Table 17-2. Note again that several of these methods will throw an **UnsupportedOperationException** if the list cannot be modified, and a **ClassCastException** is

Method	Description
void add(int *index*, E *obj*)	Inserts *obj* into the invoking list at the index passed in *index*. Any preexisting elements at or beyond the point of insertion are shifted up. Thus, no elements are overwritten.
boolean addAll(int *index*, Collection<? extends E> *c*)	Inserts all elements of *c* into the invoking list at the index passed in *index*. Any preexisting elements at or beyond the point of insertion are shifted up. Thus, no elements are overwritten. Returns **true** if the invoking list changes and returns **false** otherwise.
E get(int *index*)	Returns the object stored at the specified index within the invoking collection.
int indexOf(Object *obj*)	Returns the index of the first instance of *obj* in the invoking list. If *obj* is not an element of the list, −1 is returned.
int lastIndexOf(Object *obj*)	Returns the index of the last instance of *obj* in the invoking list. If *obj* is not an element of the list, −1 is returned.
ListIterator<E> listIterator( )	Returns an iterator to the start of the invoking list.
ListIterator<E> listIterator(int *index*)	Returns an iterator to the invoking list that begins at the specified index.
E remove(int *index*)	Removes the element at position *index* from the invoking list and returns the deleted element. The resulting list is compacted. That is, the indexes of subsequent elements are decremented by one.
E set(int *index*, E *obj*)	Assigns *obj* to the location specified by *index* within the invoking list.
List<E> subList(int *start*, int *end*)	Returns a list that includes elements from *start* to *end*−1 in the invoking list. Elements in the returned list are also referenced by the invoking object.

TABLE 17-2   The Methods Defined by **List**

generated when one object is incompatible with another, such as when an attempt is made to add an incompatible object to a list. Also, several methods will throw an **IndexOutOfBoundsException** if an invalid index is used. A **NullPointerException** is thrown if an attempt is made to store a **null** object and **null** elements are not allowed in the list. An **IllegalArgumentException** is thrown if an invalid argument is used.

To the versions of **add( )** and **addAll( )** defined by **Collection**, **List** adds the methods **add(int, E)** and **addAll(int, Collection)**. These methods insert elements at the specified index. Also, the semantics of **add(E)** and **addAll(Collection)** defined by **Collection** are changed by **List** so that they add elements to the end of the list.

To obtain the object stored at a specific location, call **get( )** with the index of the object. To assign a value to an element in the list, call **set( )**, specifying the index of the object to be changed. To find the index of an object, use **indexOf( )** or **lastIndexOf( )**.

You can obtain a sublist of a list by calling **subList( )**, specifying the beginning and ending indexes of the sublist. As you can imagine, **subList( )** makes list processing quite convenient.

The Set Interface

The **Set** interface defines a set. It extends **Collection** and declares the behavior of a collection that does not allow duplicate elements. Therefore, the **add( )** method returns **false** if an attempt is made to add duplicate elements to a set. It does not define any additional methods of its own. **Set** is a generic interface that has this declaration:

    interface Set<E>

Here, **E** specifies the type of objects that the set will hold.

The SortedSet Interface

The **SortedSet** interface extends **Set** and declares the behavior of a set sorted in ascending order. **SortedSet** is a generic interface that has this declaration:

    interface SortedSet<E>

Here, **E** specifies the type of objects that the set will hold.

In addition to those methods defined by **Set**, the **SortedSet** interface declares the methods summarized in Table 17-3. Several methods throw a **NoSuchElementException** when no items are contained in the invoking set. A **ClassCastException** is thrown when an object is incompatible with the elements in a set. A **NullPointerException** is thrown if an attempt is made to use a **null** object and **null** is not allowed in the set. An **IllegalArgumentException** is thrown if an invalid argument is used.

SortedSet defines several methods that make set processing more convenient. To obtain the first object in the set, call **first( )**. To get the last element, use **last( )**. You can obtain a subset of a sorted set by calling **subSet( )**, specifying the first and last object in the set. If you need the subset that starts with the first element in the set, use **headSet( )**. If you want the subset that ends the set, use **tailSet( )**.

The NavigableSet Interface

The **NavigableSet** interface was added by Java SE 6. It extends **SortedSet** and declares the behavior of a collection that supports the retrieval of elements based on the closest match to a given value or values. **NavigableSet** is a generic interface that has this declaration:

    interface NavigableSet<E>

Here, **E** specifies the type of objects that the set will hold. In addition to the methods that it inherits from **SortedSet**, **NavigableSet** adds those summarized in Table 17-4. A

Method	Description
Comparator<? super E> comparator( )	Returns the invoking sorted set's comparator. If the natural ordering is used for this set, **null** is returned.
E first( )	Returns the first element in the invoking sorted set.
SortedSet<E> headSet(E *end*)	Returns a **SortedSet** containing those elements less than *end* that are contained in the invoking sorted set. Elements in the returned sorted set are also referenced by the invoking sorted set.
E last( )	Returns the last element in the invoking sorted set.
SortedSet<E> subSet(E *start*, E *end*)	Returns a **SortedSet** that includes those elements between *start* and *end*–1. Elements in the returned collection are also referenced by the invoking object.
SortedSet<E> tailSet(E *start*)	Returns a **SortedSet** that contains those elements greater than or equal to *start* that are contained in the sorted set. Elements in the returned set are also referenced by the invoking object.

TABLE 17-3   The Methods Defined by **SortedSet**

Method	Description
E ceiling(E *obj*)	Searches the set for the smallest element *e* such that *e* >= *obj*. If such an element is found, it is returned. Otherwise, **null** is returned.
Iterator<E> descendingIterator( )	Returns an iterator that moves from the greatest to least. In other words, it returns a reverse iterator.
NavigableSet<E> descendingSet( )	Returns a **NavigableSet** that is the reverse of the invoking set. The resulting set is backed by the invoking set.
E floor(E *obj*)	Searches the set for the largest element *e* such that *e* <= *obj*. If such an element is found, it is returned. Otherwise, **null** is returned.
NavigableSet<E> headSet(E *upperBound*, boolean *incl*)	Returns a **NavigableSet** that includes all elements from the invoking set that are less than *upperBound*. If *incl* is **true**, then an element equal to *upperBound* is included. The resulting set is backed by the invoking set.
E higher(E *obj*)	Searches the set for the largest element *e* such that *e* > *obj*. If such an element is found, it is returned. Otherwise, **null** is returned.
E lower(E *obj*)	Searches the set for the largest element *e* such that *e* < *obj*. If such an element is found, it is returned. Otherwise, **null** is returned.
E pollFirst( )	Returns the first element, removing the element in the process. Because the set is sorted, this is the element with the least value. **null** is returned if the set is empty.
E pollLast( )	Returns the last element, removing the element in the process. Because the set is sorted, this is the element with the greatest value. **null** is returned if the set is empty.

NavigableSet<E>
  subSet(E *lowerBound*,
    boolean *lowIncl*,
    E *upperBound*,
    boolean *highIncl*)
	Returns a **NavigableSet** that includes all elements from the invoking set that are greater than *lowerBound* and less than *upperBound*. If *lowIncl* is **true**, then an element equal to *lowerBound* is included. If *highIncl* is **true**, then an element equal to *upperBound* is included. The resulting set is backed by the invoking set.

NavigableSet<E> tailSet(E *lowerBound*, boolean *incl*)	Returns a **NavigableSet** that includes all elements from the invoking set that are greater than *lowerBound*. If *incl* is **true**, then an element equal to **lowerBound** is included. The resulting set is backed by the invoking set.

TABLE 17-4   The Methods Defined by **NavigableSet**

ClassCastException is thrown when an object is incompatible with the elements in the set. A **NullPointerException** is thrown if an attempt is made to use a null object and null is not allowed in the set. An **IllegalArgumentException** is thrown if an invalid argument is used.

The Queue Interface

The **Queue** interface extends **Collection** and declares the behavior of a queue, which is often a first-in, first-out list. However, there are types of queues in which the ordering is based upon other criteria. **Queue** is a generic interface that has this declaration:

    interface Queue<E>

Method	Description
E element( )	Returns the element at the head of the queue. The element is not removed. It throws **NoSuchElementException** if the queue is empty.
boolean offer(E *obj*)	Attempts to add *obj* to the queue. Returns **true** if *obj* was added and **false** otherwise.
E peek( )	Returns the element at the head of the queue. It returns **null** if the queue is empty. The element is not removed.
E poll( )	Returns the element at the head of the queue, removing the element in the process. It returns **null** if the queue is empty.
E remove( )	Removes the element at the head of the queue, returning the element in the process. It throws **NoSuchElementException** if the queue is empty.

TABLE 17-5 The Methods Defined by **Queue**

Here, **E** specifies the type of objects that the queue will hold. The methods defined by Queue are shown in Table 17-5.

Several methods throw a **ClassCastException** when an object is incompatible with the elements in the queue. A **NullPointerException** is thrown if an attempt is made to store a **null** object and **null** elements are not allowed in the queue. An **IllegalArgumentException** is thrown if an invalid argument is used. An **IllegalStateException** is thrown if an attempt is made to add an element to a fixed-length queue that is full. A **NoSuchElementException** is thrown if an attempt is made to remove an element from an empty queue.

Despite its simplicity, **Queue** offers several points of interest. First, elements can only be removed from the head of the queue. Second, there are two methods that obtain and remove elements: **poll( )** and **remove( )**. The difference between them is that **poll( )** returns **null** if the queue is empty, but **remove( )** throws an exception. Third, there are two methods, **element( )** and **peek( )**, that obtain but don't remove the element at the head of the queue. They differ only in that **element( )** throws an exception if the queue is empty, but **peek( )** returns **null**. Finally, notice that **offer( )** only attempts to add an element to a queue. Because some queues have a fixed length and might be full, **offer( )** can fail.

The Deque Interface

The **Deque** interface was added by Java SE 6. It extends **Queue** and declares the behavior of a double-ended queue. Double-ended queues can function as standard, first-in, first-out queues or as last-in, first-out stacks. **Deque** is a generic interface that has this declaration:

interface Deque<E>

Here, **E** specifies the type of objects that the deque will hold. In addition to the methods that it inherits from **Queue**, **Deque** adds those methods summarized in Table 17-6. Several methods throw a **ClassCastException** when an object is incompatible with the elements in the deque. A **NullPointerException** is thrown if an attempt is made to store a **null** object and **null** elements are not allowed in the deque. An **IllegalArgumentException** is thrown if an invalid argument is used. An **IllegalStateException** is thrown if an attempt is made to add an element to a fixed-length deque that is full. A **NoSuchElementException** is thrown if an attempt is made to remove an element from an empty deque.

Notice that **Deque** includes the methods **push( )** and **pop( )**. These methods enable a **Deque** to function as a stack. Also, notice the **descendingIterator( )** method. It returns an iterator that returns elements in reverse order. In other words, it returns an iterator that moves from the end of the collection to the start. A **Deque** implementation can be *capacity-restricted*, which means that only a limited number of elements can be added to the deque. When this is the case, an attempt to add an element to the deque can fail. **Deque** allows you to handle such a failure in two ways. First, methods such as **addFirst( )** and **addLast( )** throw an **IllegalStateException** if a

Method	Description
void addFirst(E *obj*)	Adds *obj* to the head of the deque. Throws an **IllegaiStateException** if a capacity-restricted deque is out of space.
void addLast(E *obj*)	Adds *obj* to the tail of the deque. Throws an **IllegalStateException** if a capacity-restricted deque is out of space.
Iterator<E> descendingIterator( )	Returns an iterator that moves from the tail to the head of the deque. In other words, it returns a reverse iterator.
E getFirst( )	Returns the first element in the deque. The object is not removed from the deque. It throws **NoSuchElementException** if the deque is empty.
E getLast( )	Returns the last element in the deque. The object is not removed from the deque. It throws **NoSuchElementException** if the deque is empty.
boolean offerFirst(E *obj*)	Attempts to add *obj* to the head of the deque. Returns **true** if *obj* was added and **false** otherwise. Therefore, this method returns **false** when an attempt is made to add *obj* to a full, capacity-restricted deque.
boolean offerLast(E *obj*)	Attempts to add *obj* to the tail of the deque. Returns **true** if *obj* was added and **false** otherwise.
E peekFirst( )	Returns the element at the head of the deque. It returns **null** if the deque is empty. The object is not removed.
E peekLast( )	Returns the element at the tail of the deque. It returns **null** if the deque is empty. The object is not removed.
E pollFirst( )	Returns the element at the head of the deque, removing the element in the process. It returns **null** if the deque is empty.
E pollLast( )	Returns the element at the tail of the deque, removing the element in the process. It returns **null** if the deque is empty.
E pop( )	Returns the element at the head of the deque, removing it in the process. It throws **NoSuchElementException** if the deque is empty.
void push(E *obj*)	Adds *obj* to the head of the deque. Throws an **IllegalStateException** if a capacity-restricted deque is out of space.
E removeFirst( )	Returns the element at the head of the deque, removing the element in the process. It throws **NoSuchElementException** if the deque is empty.
boolean removeFirstOccurrence(Object *obj*)	Removes the first occurrence of *obj* from the deque. Returns **true** if successful and **false** if the deque did not contain *obj*.
E removeLast( )	Returns the element at the tail of the deque, removing the element in the process. It throws **NoSuchElementException** if the deque is empty.
boolean removeLastOccurrence(Object *obj*)	Removes the last occurrence of *obj* from the deque. Returns **true** if successful and **false** if the deque did not contain *obj*.

TABLE 17-6   The Methods Defined by **Deque**

capacity-restricted deque is full. Second, methods such as **offerFirst( )** and **offerLast( )** return false if the element can not be added.

The Collection Classes

Now that you are familiar with the collection interfaces, you are ready to examine the standard classes that implement them. Some of the classes provide full implementations that can be used as-is. Others are abstract, providing skeletal implementations that are used as starting points for creating concrete collections. None of the collection classes are synchronized, but as you will see later in this chapter, it is possible to obtain synchronized versions.

The standard collection classes are summarized in the following table:

Class	Description
AbstractCollection	Implements most of the **Collection** interface.
AbstractList	Extends **AbstractCollection** and implements most of the **List** interface.
AbstractQueue	Extends **AbstractCollection** and implements parts of the **Queue** interface.
AbstractSequentialList	Extends **AbstractList** for use by a collection that uses sequential rather than random access of its elements.
LinkedList	Implements a linked list by extending **AbstractSequentialList**.
ArrayList	Implements a dynamic array by extending **AbstractList**.
ArrayDeque	Implements a dynamic double-ended queue by extending **AbstractCollection** and implementing the **Deque** interface. (Added by Java SE 6.)
AbstractSet	Extends **AbstractCollection** and implements most of the **Set** interface.
EnumSet	Extends **AbstractSet** for use with **enum** elements.
HashSet	Extends **AbstractSet** for use with a hash table.
LinkedHashSet	Extends **HashSet** to allow insertion-order iterations.
PriorityQueue	Extends **AbstractQueue** to support a priority-based queue.
TreeSet	Implements a set stored in a tree. Extends **AbstractSet**.

The following sections examine the concrete collection classes and illustrate their use.

NOTE *In addition to the collection classes, several legacy classes, such as **Vector**, **Stack**, and **Hashtable**, have been reengineered to support collections. These are examined later in this chapter.*

The ArrayList Class

The **ArrayList** class extends **AbstractList** and implements the **List** interface. **ArrayList** is a generic class that has this declaration:

    class ArrayList<E>

Here, **E** specifies the type of objects that the list will hold.

ArrayList supports dynamic arrays that can grow as needed. In Java, standard arrays are of a fixed length. After arrays are created, they cannot grow or shrink, which means that you must know in advance how many elements an array will hold. But, sometimes, you may not know until run time precisely how large an array you need. To handle this situation, the Collections Framework defines **ArrayList**. In essence, an **ArrayList** is a variable-length array of object references. That is, an **ArrayList** can dynamically increase or decrease in size. Array lists are created with an initial size. When this size is exceeded, the collection is automatically enlarged. When objects are removed, the array can be shrunk.

NOTE *Dynamic arrays are also supported by the legacy class **Vector**, which is described later in this chapter.*

ArrayList has the constructors shown here:

ArrayList( )
ArrayList(Collection<? extends E> c)
ArrayList(int *capacity*)

The first constructor builds an empty array list. The second constructor builds an array list that is initialized with the elements of the collection c. The third constructor builds an array list that has the specified initial *capacity*. The capacity is the size of the underlying array that is used to store the elements. The capacity grows automatically as elements are added to an array list.

The following program shows a simple use of **ArrayList**. An array list is created for objects of type **String**, and then several strings are added to it. (Recall that a quoted string is translated into a **String** object.) The list is then displayed. Some of the elements are removed and the list is displayed again.

```
// Demonstrate ArrayList.
import java.util.*;

class ArrayListDemo {
  public static void main(String args[]) {
    // Create an array list.
    ArrayList<String> al = new ArrayList<String>();

    System.out.println("Initial size of al: " +
                       al.size());

    // Add elements to the array list.
    al.add("C");
    al.add("A");
    al.add("E");
    al.add("B");
    al.add("D");
    al.add("F");
    al.add(1, "A2");

    System.out.println("Size of al after additions: " +
                       al.size());

    // Display the array list.
    System.out.println("Contents of al: " + al);

    // Remove elements from the array list.
    al.remove("F");
    al.remove(2);

    System.out.println("Size of al after deletions: " +
                       al.size());
```

```
    System.out.println("Contents of al: " + al);
    }
}
```

The output from this program is shown here:

```
Initial size of al: 0
Size of al after additions: 7
Contents of al: [C, A2, A, E, B, D, F]
Size of al after deletions: 5
Contents of al: [C, A2, E, B, D]
```

Notice that **a1** starts out empty and grows as elements are added to it. When elements are removed, its size is reduced.

In the preceding example, the contents of a collection are displayed using the default conversion provided by **toString( )**, which was inherited from **AbstractCollection**. Although it is sufficient for short, sample programs, you seldom use this method to display the contents of a real-world collection. Usually, you provide your own output routines. But, for the next few examples, the default output created by **toString( )** is sufficient.

Although the capacity of an **ArrayList** object increases automatically as objects are stored in it, you can increase the capacity of an **ArrayList** object manually by calling **ensureCapacity( )**. You might want to do this if you know in advance that you will be storing many more items in the collection than it can currently hold. By increasing its capacity once, at the start, you can prevent several reallocations later. Because reallocations are costly in terms of time, preventing unnecessary ones improves performance. The signature for **ensureCapacity( )** is shown here:

void ensureCapacity(int *cap*)

Here, *cap* is the new capacity.

Conversely, if you want to reduce the size of the array that underlies an **ArrayList** object so that it is precisely as large as the number of items that it is currently holding, call **trimToSize( )**, shown here:

void trimToSize( )

Obtaining an Array from an ArrayList

When working with **ArrayList**, you will sometimes want to obtain an actual array that contains the contents of the list. You can do this by calling **toArray( )**, which is defined by **Collection**. Several reasons exist why you might want to convert a collection into an array, such as:

- To obtain faster processing times for certain operations
- To pass an array to a method that is not overloaded to accept a collection
- To integrate collection-based code with legacy code that does not understand collections

Whatever the reason, converting an **ArrayList** to an array is a trivial matter.

As explained earlier, there are two versions of **toArray( )**, which are shown again here for your convenience:

Object[ ] toArray( )
<T> T[ ] toArray(T *array*[ ])

The first returns an array of **Object**. The second returns an array of elements that have the same type as **T**. Normally, the second form is more convenient because it returns the proper type of array. The following program demonstrates its use:

```
// Convert an ArrayList into an array.
import java.util.*;

class ArrayListToArray {
  public static void main(String args[]) {
    // Create an array list.
    ArrayList<Integer> al = new ArrayList<Integer>();

    // Add elements to the array list.
    al.add(1);
    al.add(2);
    al.add(3);
    al.add(4);

    System.out.println("Contents of al: " + al);

    // Get the array.
    Integer ia[] = new Integer[al.size()];
    ia = al.toArray(ia);

    int sum = 0;

    // Sum the array.
    for(int i : ia) sum += i;

    System.out.println("Sum is: " + sum);
  }
}
```

The output from the program is shown here:

```
Contents of al: [1, 2, 3, 4]
Sum is: 10
```

The program begins by creating a collection of integers. Next, **toArray( )** is called and it obtains an array of **Integer**s. Then, the contents of that array are summed by use of a for-each style **for** loop.

There is something else of interest in this program. As you know, collections can store only references to, not values of, primitive types. However, autoboxing makes it possible to pass values of type **int** to **add( )** without having to manually wrap them within an **Integer**, as the program shows. Autoboxing causes them to be automatically wrapped. In this way, autoboxing significantly improves the ease with which collections can be used to store primitive values.

The LinkedList Class

The **LinkedList** class extends **AbstractSequentialList** and implements the **List**, **Deque**, and **Queue** interfaces. It provides a linked-list data structure. **LinkedList** is a generic class that has this declaration:

    class LinkedList<E>

Here, **E** specifies the type of objects that the list will hold. **LinkedList** has the two constructors shown here:

LinkedList( )
LinkedList(Collection<? extends E> c)

The first constructor builds an empty linked list. The second constructor builds a linked list that is initialized with the elements of the collection c.

Because **LinkedList** implements the **Deque** interface, you have access to the methods defined by **Deque**. For example, to add elements to the start of a list you can use **addFirst( )** or **offerFirst( )**. To add elements to the end of the list, use **addLast( )** or **offerLast( )**. To obtain the first element, you can use **getFirst( )** or **peekFirst( )**. To obtain the last element, use **getLast( )** or **peekLast( )**. To remove the first element, use **removeFirst( )** or **pollFirst( )**. To remove the last element, use **removeLast( )** or **pollLast( )**.

The following program illustrates **LinkedList**:

```
// Demonstrate LinkedList.
import java.util.*;

class LinkedListDemo {
  public static void main(String args[]) {
    // Create a linked list.
    LinkedList<String> ll = new LinkedList<String>();

    // Add elements to the linked list.
    ll.add("F");
    ll.add("B");
    ll.add("D");
    ll.add("E");
    ll.add("C");
    ll.addLast("Z");
    ll.addFirst("A");

    ll.add(1, "A2");

    System.out.println("Original contents of ll: " + ll);

    // Remove elements from the linked list.
    ll.remove("F");
    ll.remove(2);

    System.out.println("Contents of ll after deletion: "
                       + ll);

    // Remove first and last elements.
    ll.removeFirst();
    ll.removeLast();

    System.out.println("ll after deleting first and last: "
                       + ll);

    // Get and set a value.
```

```
    String val = ll.get(2);
    ll.set(2, val + " Changed");

    System.out.println("ll after change: " + ll);
  }
}
```

The output from this program is shown here:

```
Original contents of ll: [A, A2, F, B, D, E, C, Z]
Contents of ll after deletion: [A, A2, D, E, C, Z]
ll after deleting first and last: [A2, D, E, C]
ll after change: [A2, D, E Changed, C]
```

Because **LinkedList** implements the **List** interface, calls to **add(E)** append items to the end of the list, as do calls to **addLast( )**. To insert items at a specific location, use the **add(int, E)** form of **add( )**, as illustrated by the call to **add(1, "A2")** in the example.

Notice how the third element in **ll** is changed by employing calls to **get( )** and **set( )**. To obtain the current value of an element, pass **get( )** the index at which the element is stored. To assign a new value to that index, pass **set( )** the index and its new value.

The HashSet Class

HashSet extends **AbstractSet** and implements the **Set** interface. It creates a collection that uses a hash table for storage. **HashSet** is a generic class that has this declaration:

class HashSet<E>

Here, **E** specifies the type of objects that the set will hold.

As most readers likely know, a hash table stores information by using a mechanism called hashing. In *hashing,* the informational content of a key is used to determine a unique value, called its *hash code.* The hash code is then used as the index at which the data associated with the key is stored. The transformation of the key into its hash code is performed automatically— you never see the hash code itself. Also, your code can't directly index the hash table. The advantage of hashing is that it allows the execution time of **add( )**, **contains( )**, **remove( )**, and **size( )** to remain constant even for large sets.

The following constructors are defined:

HashSet( )
HashSet(Collection<? extends E> c)
HashSet(int *capacity*)
HashSet(int *capacity*, float *fillRatio*)

The first form constructs a default hash set. The second form initializes the hash set by using the elements of *c.* The third form initializes the capacity of the hash set to *capacity.* (The default capacity is 16.) The fourth form initializes both the capacity and the fill ratio (also called *load capacity*) of the hash set from its arguments. The fill ratio must be between 0.0 and 1.0, and it determines how full the hash set can be before it is resized upward. Specifically, when the number of elements is greater than the capacity of the hash set multiplied by its fill ratio, the hash set is expanded. For constructors that do not take a fill ratio, 0.75 is used.

HashSet does not define any additional methods beyond those provided by its superclasses and interfaces.

It is important to note that **HashSet** does not guarantee the order of its elements, because the process of hashing doesn't usually lend itself to the creation of sorted sets. If you need sorted storage, then another collection, such as **TreeSet**, is a better choice.

Here is an example that demonstrates **HashSet**:

```
// Demonstrate HashSet.
import java.util.*;

class HashSetDemo {
  public static void main(String args[]) {
    // Create a hash set.
    HashSet<String> hs = new HashSet<String>();

    // Add elements to the hash set.
    hs.add("B");
    hs.add("A");
    hs.add("D");
    hs.add("E");
    hs.add("C");
    hs.add("F");

    System.out.println(hs);
  }
}
```

The following is the output from this program:

```
[D, A, F, C, B, E]
```

As explained, the elements are not stored in sorted order, and the precise output may vary.

The LinkedHashSet Class

The **LinkedHashSet** class extends **HashSet** and adds no members of its own. It is a generic class that has this declaration:

    class LinkedHashSet<E>

Here, **E** specifies the type of objects that the set will hold. Its constructors parallel those in **HashSet**.

LinkedHashSet maintains a linked list of the entries in the set, in the order in which they were inserted. This allows insertion-order iteration over the set. That is, when cycling through a **LinkedHashSet** using an iterator, the elements will be returned in the order in which they were inserted. This is also the order in which they are contained in the string returned by **toString( )** when called on a **LinkedHashSet** object. To see the effect of **LinkedHashSet**, try substituting **LinkedHashSet** for **HashSet** in the preceding program. The output will be

```
[B, A, D, E, C, F]
```

which is the order in which the elements were inserted.

The TreeSet Class

TreeSet extends **AbstractSet** and implements the **NavigableSet** interface. It creates a collection that uses a tree for storage. Objects are stored in sorted, ascending order. Access and retrieval times are quite fast, which makes **TreeSet** an excellent choice when storing large amounts of sorted information that must be found quickly.

TreeSet is a generic class that has this declaration:

class TreeSet<E>

Here, **E** specifies the type of objects that the set will hold.

TreeSet has the following constructors:

TreeSet( )
TreeSet(Collection<? extends E> c)
TreeSet(Comparator<? super E> comp)
TreeSet(SortedSet<E> ss)

The first form constructs an empty tree set that will be sorted in ascending order according to the natural order of its elements. The second form builds a tree set that contains the elements of c. The third form constructs an empty tree set that will be sorted according to the comparator specified by comp. (Comparators are described later in this chapter.) The fourth form builds a tree set that contains the elements of ss.

Here is an example that demonstrates a **TreeSet**:

```
// Demonstrate TreeSet.
import java.util.*;

class TreeSetDemo {
  public static void main(String args[]) {
    // Create a tree set.
    TreeSet<String> ts = new TreeSet<String>();

    // Add elements to the tree set.
    ts.add("C");
    ts.add("A");
    ts.add("B");
    ts.add("E");
    ts.add("F");
    ts.add("D");

    System.out.println(ts);
  }
}
```

The output from this program is shown here:

    [A, B, C, D, E, F]

As explained, because **TreeSet** stores its elements in a tree, they are automatically arranged in sorted order, as the output confirms.

Because **TreeSet** implements the **NavigableSet** interface (which was added by Java SE 6), you can use the methods defined by **NavigableSet** to retrieve elements of a **TreeSet**. For example, assuming the preceding program, the following statement uses **subSet( )** to obtain a subset of **ts** that contains the elements between **C** (inclusive) and **F** (exclusive). It then displays the resulting set.

```
System.out.println(ts.subSet()("C", "F"));
```

The output from this statement is shown here:

```
[C, D, E]
```

You might want to experiment with the other methods defined by **NavigableSet**.

The PriorityQueue Class

PriorityQueue extends **AbstractQueue** and implements the **Queue** interface. It creates a queue that is prioritized based on the queue's comparator. **PriorityQueue** is a generic class that has this declaration:

class PriorityQueue<E>

Here, **E** specifies the type of objects stored in the queue. **PriorityQueue**s are dynamic, growing as necessary.

PriorityQueue defines the six constructors shown here:

PriorityQueue( )
PriorityQueue(int *capacity*)
PriorityQueue(int *capacity*, Comparator<? super E> *comp*)
PriorityQueue(Collection<? extends E> *c*)
PriorityQueue(PriorityQueue<? extends E> *c*)
PriorityQueue(SortedSet<? extends E> *c*)

The first constructor builds an empty queue. Its starting capacity is 11. The second constructor builds a queue that has the specified initial capacity. The third constructor builds a queue with the specified capacity and comparator. The last three constructors create queues that are initialized with the elements of the collection passed in *c*. In all cases, the capacity grows automatically as elements are added.

If no comparator is specified when a **PriorityQueue** is constructed, then the default comparator for the type of data stored in the queue is used. The default comparator will order the queue in ascending order. Thus, the head of the queue will be the smallest value. However, by providing a custom comparator, you can specify a different ordering scheme. For example, when storing items that include a time stamp, you could prioritize the queue such that the oldest items are first in the queue.

You can obtain a reference to the comparator used by a **PriorityQueue** by calling its **comparator( )** method, shown here:

Comparator<? super E> comparator( )

It returns the comparator. If natural ordering is used for the invoking queue, **null** is returned.

One word of caution: although you can iterate through a **PriorityQueue** using an iterator, the order of that iteration is undefined. To properly use a **PriorityQueue**, you must call methods such as **offer( )** and **poll( )**, which are defined by the **Queue** interface.

The ArrayDeque Class

Java SE 6 added the **ArrayDeque** class, which extends **AbstractCollection** and implements the **Deque** interface. It adds no methods of its own. **ArrayDeque** creates a dynamic array and has no capacity restrictions. (The **Deque** interface supports implementations that restrict capacity, but does not require such restrictions.) **ArrayDeque** is a generic class that has this declaration:

    class ArrayDeque<E>

Here, **E** specifies the type of objects stored in the collection.

ArrayDeque defines the following constructors:

ArrayDeque( )

ArrayDeque(int *size*)

ArrayDeque(Collection<? extends E> *c*)

The first constructor builds an empty deque. Its starting capacity is 16. The second constructor builds a deque that has the specified initial capacity. The third constructor creates a deque that is initialized with the elements of the collection passed in *c*. In all cases, the capacity grows as needed to handle the elements added to the deque.

The following program demonstrates **ArrayDeque** by using it to create a stack:

```
// Demonstrate ArrayDeque.
import java.util.*;

class ArrayDequeDemo {
  public static void main(String args[]) {
    // Create a tree set.
    ArrayDeque<String> adq = new ArrayDeque<String>();

    // Use an ArrayDeque like a stack.
    adq.push("A");
    adq.push("B");
    adq.push("D");
    adq.push("E");
    adq.push("F");

    System.out.print("Popping the stack: ");

    while(adq.peek() != null)
      System.out.print(adq.pop() + " ");

    System.out.println();
  }
}
```

The output is shown here:

```
Popping the stack: F E D B A
```

The EnumSet Class

EnumSet extends **AbstractSet** and implements **Set**. It is specifically for use with keys of an **enum** type. It is a generic class that has this declaration:

    class EnumSet<E extends Enum<E>>

Here, **E** specifies the elements. Notice that **E** must extend **Enum<E>**, which enforces the requirement that the elements must be of the specified **enum** type.

    EnumSet defines no constructors. Instead, it uses the factory methods shown in Table 17-7 to create objects. All methods can throw **NullPointerException**. The **copyOf( )** and **range( )** methods can also throw **IllegalArgumentException**. Notice that the **of( )** method is overloaded a number of times. This is in the interest of efficiency. Passing a known number of arguments can be faster than using a vararg parameter when the number of arguments is small.

Accessing a Collection via an Iterator

Often, you will want to cycle through the elements in a collection. For example, you might want to display each element. One way to do this is to employ an *iterator,* which is an object that implements either the **Iterator** or the **ListIterator** interface. **Iterator** enables you to cycle through a collection, obtaining or removing elements. **ListIterator** extends **Iterator** to allow

Method	Description
static <E extends Enum<E>> EnumSet<E> allOf(Class<E> *t*)	Creates an **EnumSet** that contains the elements in the enumeration specified by *t*.
static <E extends Enum<E>> EnumSet<E> complementOf(EnumSet<E> *e*)	Creates an **EnumSet** that is comprised of those elements not stored in *e*.
static <E extends Enum<E>> EnumSet<E> copyOf(EnumSet<E> *c*)	Creates an **EnumSet** from the elements stored in *c*.
static <E extends Enum<E>> EnumSet<E> copyOf(Collection<E> *c*)	Creates an **EnumSet** from the elements stored in *c*.
static <E extends Enum<E>> EnumSet<E> noneOf(Class<E> *t*)	Creates an **EnumSet** that contains the elements that are not in the enumeration specified by *t*, which is an empty set by definition.
static <E extends Enum<E>> EnumSet<E> of(E *v*, E ... *varargs*)	Creates an **EnumSet** that contains *v* and zero or more additional enumeration values.
static <E extends Enum<E>> EnumSet<E> of(E *v*)	Creates an **EnumSet** that contains *v*.
static <E extends Enum<E>> EnumSet<E> of(E *v1*, E *v2*)	Creates an **EnumSet** that contains *v1* and *v2*.
static <E extends Enum<E>> EnumSet<E> of(E *v1*, E *v2*, E *v3*)	Creates an **EnumSet** that contains *v1* through *v3*.
static <E extends Enum<E>> EnumSet<E> of(E *v1*, E *v2*, E *v3*, E *v4*)	Creates an **EnumSet** that contains *v1* through *v4*.
static <E extends Enum<E>> EnumSet<E> of(E *v1*, E *v2*, E *v3*, E *v4*, E *v5*)	Creates an **EnumSet** that contains *v1* through *v5*.
static <E extends Enum<E>> EnumSet<E> range(E *start*, E *end*)	Creates an **EnumSet** that contains the elements in the range specified by *start* and *end*.

TABLE 17-7   The Methods Defined by **EnumSet**

Method	Description
boolean hasNext( )	Returns **true** if there are more elements. Otherwise, returns **false**.
E next( )	Returns the next element. Throws **NoSuchElementException** if there is not a next element.
void remove( )	Removes the current element. Throws **IllegalStateException** if an attempt is made to call **remove( )** that is not preceded by a call to **next( )**.

TABLE 17-8   The Methods Defined by **Iterator**

bidirectional traversal of a list, and the modification of elements. **Iterator** and **ListIterator** are generic interfaces which are declared as shown here:

    interface Iterator<E>
    interface ListIterator<E>

Here, **E** specifies the type of objects being iterated. The **Iterator** interface declares the methods shown in Table 17-8. The methods declared by **ListIterator** are shown in Table 17-9. In both cases, operations that modify the underlying collection are optional. For example, **remove( )** will throw **UnsupportedOperationException** when used with a read-only collection. Various other exceptions are possible.

Using an Iterator

Before you can access a collection through an iterator, you must obtain one. Each of the collection classes provides an **iterator( )** method that returns an iterator to the start of the collection. By using this iterator object, you can access each element in the collection, one

Method	Description
void add(E *obj*)	Inserts *obj* into the list in front of the element that will be returned by the next call to **next( )**.
boolean hasNext( )	Returns **true** if there is a next element. Otherwise, returns **false**.
boolean hasPrevious( )	Returns **true** if there is a previous element. Otherwise, returns **false**.
E next( )	Returns the next element. A **NoSuchElementException** is thrown if there is not a next element.
int nextIndex( )	Returns the index of the next element. If there is not a next element, returns the size of the list.
E previous( )	Returns the previous element. A **NoSuchElementException** is thrown if there is not a previous element.
int previousIndex( )	Returns the index of the previous element. If there is not a previous element, returns −1.
void remove( )	Removes the current element from the list. An **IllegalStateException** is thrown if **remove( )** is called before **next( )** or **previous( )** is invoked.
void set(E *obj*)	Assigns *obj* to the current element. This is the element last returned by a call to either **next( )** or **previous( )**.

TABLE 17-9   The Methods Defined by **ListIterator**

element at a time. In general, to use an iterator to cycle through the contents of a collection, follow these steps:

1. Obtain an iterator to the start of the collection by calling the collection's **iterator( )** method.

2. Set up a loop that makes a call to **hasNext( )**. Have the loop iterate as long as **hasNext( )** returns **true**.

3. Within the loop, obtain each element by calling **next( )**.

For collections that implement **List**, you can also obtain an iterator by calling **listIterator( )**. As explained, a list iterator gives you the ability to access the collection in either the forward or backward direction and lets you modify an element. Otherwise, **ListIterator** is used just like **Iterator**.

The following example implements these steps, demonstrating both the **Iterator** and **ListIterator** interfaces. It uses an **ArrayList** object, but the general principles apply to any type of collection. Of course, **ListIterator** is available only to those collections that implement the **List** interface.

```java
// Demonstrate iterators.
import java.util.*;

class IteratorDemo {
  public static void main(String args[]) {
    // Create an array list.
    ArrayList<String> al = new ArrayList<String>();

    // Add elements to the array list.
    al.add("C");
    al.add("A");
    al.add("E");
    al.add("B");
    al.add("D");
    al.add("F");

    // Use iterator to display contents of al.
    System.out.print("Original contents of al: ");
    Iterator<String> itr = al.iterator();
    while(itr.hasNext()) {
      String element = itr.next();
      System.out.print(element + " ");
    }
    System.out.println();

    // Modify objects being iterated.
    ListIterator<String> litr = al.listIterator();
    while(litr.hasNext()) {
      String element = litr.next();
      litr.set(element + "+");
    }

    System.out.print("Modified contents of al: ");
    itr = al.iterator();
    while(itr.hasNext()) {
```

```
      String element = itr.next();
      System.out.print(element + " ");
    }
    System.out.println();

    // Now, display the list backwards.
    System.out.print("Modified list backwards: ");
    while(litr.hasPrevious()) {
      String element = litr.previous();
      System.out.print(element + " ");
    }
    System.out.println();
  }
}
```

The output is shown here:

```
Original contents of al: C A E B D F
Modified contents of al: C+ A+ E+ B+ D+ F+
Modified list backwards: F+ D+ B+ E+ A+ C+
```

Pay special attention to how the list is displayed in reverse. After the list is modified, **litr** points to the end of the list. (Remember, **litr.hasNext( )** returns **false** when the end of the list has been reached.) To traverse the list in reverse, the program continues to use **litr**, but this time it checks to see whether it has a previous element. As long as it does, that element is obtained and displayed.

The For-Each Alternative to Iterators

If you won't be modifying the contents of a collection or obtaining elements in reverse order, then the for-each version of the **for** loop is often a more convenient alternative to cycling through a collection than is using an iterator. Recall that the **for** can cycle through any collection of objects that implement the **Iterable** interface. Because all of the collection classes implement this interface, they can all be operated upon by the **for**.

The following example uses a **for** loop to sum the contents of a collection:

```
// Use the for-each for loop to cycle through a collection.
import java.util.*;

class ForEachDemo {
  public static void main(String args[]) {
    // Create an array list for integers.
    ArrayList<Integer> vals = new ArrayList<Integer>();

    // Add values to the array list.
    vals.add(1);
    vals.add(2);
    vals.add(3);
    vals.add(4);
    vals.add(5);

    // Use for loop to display the values.
    System.out.print("Original contents of vals: ");
    for(int v : vals)
      System.out.print(v + " ");
```

```
    System.out.println();

    // Now, sum the values by using a for loop.
    int sum = 0;
    for(int v : vals)
      sum += v;

    System.out.println("Sum of values: " + sum);
  }
}
```

The output from the program is shown here:

```
Original contents of vals: 1 2 3 4 5
Sum of values: 15
```

As you can see, the **for** loop is substantially shorter and simpler to use than the iterator-based approach. However, it can only be used to cycle through a collection in the forward direction, and you can't modify the contents of the collection.

Storing User-Defined Classes in Collections

For the sake of simplicity, the foregoing examples have stored built-in objects, such as **String** or **Integer**, in a collection. Of course, collections are not limited to the storage of built-in objects. Quite the contrary. The power of collections is that they can store any type of object, including objects of classes that you create. For example, consider the following example that uses a **LinkedList** to store mailing addresses:

```java
// A simple mailing list example.
import java.util.*;

class Address {
  private String name;
  private String street;
  private String city;
  private String state;
  private String code;

  Address(String n, String s, String c,
          String st, String cd) {
    name = n;
    street = s;
    city = c;
    state = st;
    code = cd;
  }

  public String toString() {
    return name + "\n" + street + "\n" +
           city + " " + state + " " + code;
  }
}
```

```
class MailList {
  public static void main(String args[]) {
    LinkedList<Address> ml = new LinkedList<Address>();

    // Add elements to the linked list.
    ml.add(new Address("J.W. West", "11 Oak Ave",
                       "Urbana", "IL", "61801"));
    ml.add(new Address("Ralph Baker", "1142 Maple Lane",
                       "Mahomet", "IL", "61853"));
    ml.add(new Address("Tom Carlton", "867 Elm St",
                       "Champaign", "IL", "61820"));

    // Display the mailing list.
    for(Address element : ml)
      System.out.println(element + "\n");

    System.out.println();
  }
}
```

The output from the program is shown here:

```
J.W. West
11 Oak Ave
Urbana IL 61801

Ralph Baker
1142 Maple Lane
Mahomet IL 61853

Tom Carlton
867 Elm St
Champaign IL 61820
```

Aside from storing a user-defined class in a collection, another important thing to notice about the preceding program is that it is quite short. When you consider that it sets up a linked list that can store, retrieve, and process mailing addresses in about 50 lines of code, the power of the Collections Framework begins to become apparent. As most readers know, if all of this functionality had to be coded manually, the program would be several times longer. Collections offer off-the-shelf solutions to a wide variety of programming problems. You should use them whenever the situation presents itself.

The RandomAccess Interface

The **RandomAccess** interface contains no members. However, by implementing this interface, a collection signals that it supports efficient random access to its elements. Although a collection might support random access, it might not do so efficiently. By checking for the **RandomAccess** interface, client code can determine at run time whether a collection is suitable for certain types of random access operations—especially as they apply to large collections. (You can use **instanceof** to determine if a class implements an interface.) **RandomAccess** is implemented by **ArrayList** and by the legacy **Vector** class, among others.

Working with Maps

A *map* is an object that stores associations between keys and values, or *key/value pairs*. Given a key, you can find its value. Both keys and values are objects. The keys must be unique, but the values may be duplicated. Some maps can accept a **null** key and **null** values, others cannot.

There is one key point about maps that is important to mention at the outset: they don't implement the **Iterable** interface. This means that you *cannot* cycle through a map using a for-each style **for** loop. Furthermore, you can't obtain an iterator to a map. However, as you will soon see, you can obtain a collection-view of a map, which does allow the use of either the **for** loop or an iterator.

The Map Interfaces

Because the map interfaces define the character and nature of maps, this discussion of maps begins with them. The following interfaces support maps:

Interface	Description
Map	Maps unique keys to values.
Map.Entry	Describes an element (a key/value pair) in a map. This is an inner class of **Map**.
NavigableMap	Extends **SortedMap** to handle the retrieval of entries based on closest-match searches. (Added by Java SE 6.)
SortedMap	Extends **Map** so that the keys are maintained in ascending order.

Each interface is examined next, in turn.

The Map Interface

The **Map** interface maps unique keys to values. A *key* is an object that you use to retrieve a value at a later date. Given a key and a value, you can store the value in a **Map** object. After the value is stored, you can retrieve it by using its key. **Map** is generic and is declared as shown here:

interface Map<K, V>

Here, **K** specifies the type of keys, and **V** specifies the type of values.

The methods declared by **Map** are summarized in Table 17-10. Several methods throw a **ClassCastException** when an object is incompatible with the elements in a map. A **NullPointerException** is thrown if an attempt is made to use a **null** object and **null** is not allowed in the map. An **UnsupportedOperationException** is thrown when an attempt is made to change an unmodifiable map. An **IllegalArgumentException** is thrown if an invalid argument is used.

Maps revolve around two basic operations: **get( )** and **put( )**. To put a value into a map, use **put( )**, specifying the key and the value. To obtain a value, call **get( )**, passing the key as an argument. The value is returned.

As mentioned earlier, although part of the Collections Framework, maps are not, themselves, collections because they do not implement the **Collection** interface. However, you can obtain a collection-view of a map. To do this, you can use the **entrySet( )** method. It returns a **Set** that contains the elements in the map. To obtain a collection-view of the keys,

Method	Description
void clear( )	Removes all key/value pairs from the invoking map.
boolean containsKey(Object *k*)	Returns **true** if the invoking map contains *k* as a key. Otherwise, returns **false**.
boolean containsValue(Object *v*)	Returns **true** if the map contains *v* as a value. Otherwise, returns **false**.
Set<Map.Entry<K, V>> entrySet( )	Returns a **Set** that contains the entries in the map. The set contains objects of type **Map.Entry**. Thus, this method provides a set-view of the invoking map.
boolean equals(Object *obj*)	Returns **true** if *obj* is a **Map** and contains the same entries. Otherwise, returns **false**.
V get(Object *k*)	Returns the value associated with the key *k*. Returns **null** if the key is not found.
int hashCode( )	Returns the hash code for the invoking map.
boolean isEmpty( )	Returns **true** if the invoking map is empty. Otherwise, returns **false**.
Set<K> keySet( )	Returns a **Set** that contains the keys in the invoking map. This method provides a set-view of the keys in the invoking map.
V put(K *k*, V *v*)	Puts an entry in the invoking map, overwriting any previous value associated with the key. The key and value are *k* and *v*, respectively. Returns **null** if the key did not already exist. Otherwise, the previous value linked to the key is returned.
void putAll(Map<? extends K, ? extends V> *m*)	Puts all the entries from *m* into this map.
V remove(Object *k*)	Removes the entry whose key equals *k*.
int size( )	Returns the number of key/value pairs in the map.
Collection<V> values( )	Returns a collection containing the values in the map. This method provides a collection-view of the values in the map.

TABLE 17-10   The Methods Defined by **Map**

use **keySet( )**. To get a collection-view of the values, use **values( )**. Collection-views are the means by which maps are integrated into the larger Collections Framework.

The SortedMap Interface

The **SortedMap** interface extends **Map**. It ensures that the entries are maintained in ascending order based on the keys. **SortedMap** is generic and is declared as shown here:

interface SortedMap<K, V>

Here, **K** specifies the type of keys, and **V** specifies the type of values.

The methods declared by **SortedMap** are summarized in Table 17-11. Several methods throw a **NoSuchElementException** when no items are in the invoking map. A **ClassCastException** is thrown when an object is incompatible with the elements in a map. A **NullPointerException** is thrown if an attempt is made to use a **null** object when **null** is not allowed in the map. An **IllegalArgumentException** is thrown if an invalid argument is used.

Sorted maps allow very efficient manipulations of *submaps* (in other words, subsets of a map). To obtain a submap, use **headMap( )**, **tailMap( )**, or **subMap( )**. To get the first key in the set, call **firstKey( )**. To get the last key, use **lastKey( )**.

Method	Description
Comparator<? super K> comparator( )	Returns the invoking sorted map's comparator. If natural ordering is used for the invoking map, **null** is returned.
K firstKey( )	Returns the first key in the invoking map.
SortedMap<K, V> headMap(K *end*)	Returns a sorted map for those map entries with keys that are less than *end*.
K lastKey( )	Returns the last key in the invoking map.
SortedMap<K, V> subMap(K *start*, K *end*)	Returns a map containing those entries with keys that are greater than or equal to *start* and less than *end*.
SortedMap<K, V> tailMap(K *start*)	Returns a map containing those entries with keys that are greater than or equal to *start*.

TABLE 17-11   The Methods Defined by **SortedMap**

The NavigableMap Interface

The **NavigableMap** interface was added by Java SE 6. It extends **SortedMap** and declares the behavior of a map that supports the retrieval of entries based on the closest match to a given key or keys. **NavigableMap** is a generic interface that has this declaration:

    interface NavigableMap<K,V>

Here, **K** specifies the type of the keys, and **V** specifies the type of the values associated with the keys. In addition to the methods that it inherits from **SortedMap**, **NavigableMap** adds those summarized in Table 17-12. Several methods throw a **ClassCastException** when an object is incompatible with the keys in the map. A **NullPointerException** is thrown if an attempt is made to use a **null** object and **null** keys are not allowed in the set. An **IllegalArgumentException** is thrown if an invalid argument is used.

Method	Description
Map.Entry<K,V> ceilingEntry(K *obj*)	Searches the map for the smallest key *k* such that *k* >= *obj*. If such a key is found, its entry is returned. Otherwise, **null** is returned.
K ceilingKey(K *obj*)	Searches the map for the smallest key *k* such that *k* >= *obj*. If such a key is found, it is returned. Otherwise, **null** is returned.
NavigableSet<K> descendingKeySet( )	Returns a **NavigableSet** that contains the keys in the invoking map in reverse order. Thus, it returns a reverse set-view of the keys. The resulting set is backed by the map.
NavigableMap<K,V> descendingMap( )	Returns a **NavigableMap** that is the reverse of the invoking map. The resulting map is backed by the invoking map.
Map.Entry<K,V> firstEntry( )	Returns the first entry in the map. This is the entry with the least key.
Map.Entry<K,V> floorEntry(K *obj*)	Searches the map for the largest key *k* such that *k* <= *obj*. If such a key is found, its entry is returned. Otherwise, **null** is returned.
K floorKey(K *obj*)	Searches the map for the largest key *k* such that *k* <= *obj*. If such a key is found, it is returned. Otherwise, **null** is returned.
NavigableMap<K,V> headMap(K *upperBound*, boolean *incl*)	Returns a **NavigableMap** that includes all entries from the invoking map that have keys that are less than *upperBound*. If *incl* is **true**, then an element equal to *upperBound* is included. The resulting map is backed by the invoking map.
Map.Entry<K,V> higherEntry(K *obj*)	Searches the set for the largest key *k* such that *k* > *obj*. If such a key is found, its entry is returned. Otherwise, **null** is returned.

TABLE 17-12   The Methods defined by **NavigableMap**

Method	Description
K higherKey(K *obj*)	Searches the set for the largest key *k* such that *k* > *obj*. If such a key is found, it is returned. Otherwise, **null** is returned.
Map.Entry<K,V> lastEntry( )	Returns the last entry in the map. This is the entry with the largest key.
Map.Entry<K,V> lowerEntry(K *obj*)	Searches the set for the largest key *k* such that *k* < *obj*. If such a key is found, its entry is returned. Otherwise, **null** is returned.
K lowerKey(K *obj*)	Searches the set for the largest key *k* such that *k* < *obj*. If such a key is found, it is returned. Otherwise, **null** is returned.
NavigableSet<K> navigableKeySet( )	Returns a **NavigableSet** that contains the keys in the invoking map. The resulting set is backed by the invoking map.
Map.Entry<K,V> pollFirstEntry( )	Returns the first entry, removing the entry in the process. Because the map is sorted, this is the entry with the least key value. **null** is returned if the map is empty.
Map.Entry<K,V> pollLastEntry( )	Returns the last entry, removing the entry in the process. Because the map is sorted, this is the entry with the greatest key value. **null** is returned if the map is empty.

NavigableMap<K,V>
    subMap(K *lowerBound*,
        boolean *lowIncl*,
        K *upperBound*
        boolean *highIncl*)
	Returns a **NavigableMap** that includes all entries from the invoking map that have keys that are greater than *lowerBound* and less than *upperBound*. If *lowIncl* is **true**, then an element equal to *lowerBound* is included. If *highIncl* is **true**, then an element equal to *highIncl* is included. The resulting map is backed by the invoking map.

NavigableMap<K,V> tailMap(K *lowerBound*, boolean *incl*)	Returns a **NavigableMap** that includes all entries from the invoking map that have keys that are greater than *lowerBound*. If *incl* is **true**, then an element equal to *lowerBound* is included. The resulting map is backed by the invoking map.

TABLE 17-12   The Methods defined by **NavigableMap** *(continued)*

The Map.Entry Interface

The **Map.Entry** interface enables you to work with a map entry. Recall that the **entrySet( )** method declared by the **Map** interface returns a **Set** containing the map entries. Each of these set elements is a **Map.Entry** object. **Map.Entry** is generic and is declared like this:

interface Map.Entry<K, V>

Here, **K** specifies the type of keys, and **V** specifies the type of values. Table 17-13 summarizes the methods declared by **Map.Entry**. Various exceptions are possible.

Method	Description
boolean equals(Object *obj*)	Returns **true** if *obj* is a **Map.Entry** whose key and value are equal to that of the invoking object.
K getKey( )	Returns the key for this map entry.
V getValue( )	Returns the value for this map entry.
int hashCode( )	Returns the hash code for this map entry.
V setValue(V *v*)	Sets the value for this map entry to *v*. A **ClassCastException** is thrown if *v* is not the correct type for the map. An **IllegalArgumentException** is thrown if there is a problem with *v*. A **NullPointerException** is thrown if *v* is **null** and the map does not permit **null** keys. An **UnsupportedOperationException** is thrown if the map cannot be changed.

TABLE 17-13   The Methods Defined by **Map.Entry**

The Map Classes

Several classes provide implementations of the map interfaces. The classes that can be used for maps are summarized here:

Class	Description
AbstractMap	Implements most of the **Map** interface.
EnumMap	Extends **AbstractMap** for use with **enum** keys.
HashMap	Extends **AbstractMap** to use a hash table.
TreeMap	Extends **AbstractMap** to use a tree.
WeakHashMap	Extends **AbstractMap** to use a hash table with weak keys.
LinkedHashMap	Extends **HashMap** to allow insertion-order iterations.
IdentityHashMap	Extends **AbstractMap** and uses reference equality when comparing documents.

Notice that **AbstractMap** is a superclass for all concrete map implementations.

WeakHashMap implements a map that uses "weak keys," which allows an element in a map to be garbage-collected when its key is otherwise unused. This class is not discussed further here. The other map classes are described next.

The HashMap Class

The **HashMap** class extends **AbstractMap** and implements the **Map** interface. It uses a hash table to store the map. This allows the execution time of **get( )** and **put( )** to remain constant even for large sets. **HashMap** is a generic class that has this declaration:

    class HashMap<K, V>

Here, **K** specifies the type of keys, and **V** specifies the type of values.

The following constructors are defined:

    HashMap( )
    HashMap(Map<? extends K, ? extends V> m)
    HashMap(int capacity)
    HashMap(int capacity, float fillRatio)

The first form constructs a default hash map. The second form initializes the hash map by using the elements of *m*. The third form initializes the capacity of the hash map to *capacity*. The fourth form initializes both the capacity and fill ratio of the hash map by using its arguments. The meaning of capacity and fill ratio is the same as for **HashSet**, described earlier. The default capacity is 16. The default fill ratio is 0.75.

HashMap implements **Map** and extends **AbstractMap**. It does not add any methods of its own.

You should note that a hash map does *not* guarantee the order of its elements. Therefore, the order in which elements are added to a hash map is not necessarily the order in which they are read by an iterator.

The following program illustrates **HashMap**. It maps names to account balances. Notice how a set-view is obtained and used.

```
import java.util.*;

class HashMapDemo {
  public static void main(String args[]) {

    // Create a hash map.
    HashMap<String, Double> hm = new HashMap<String, Double>();

    // Put elements to the map
    hm.put("John Doe", new Double(3434.34));
    hm.put("Tom Smith", new Double(123.22));
    hm.put("Jane Baker", new Double(1378.00));
    hm.put("Tod Hall", new Double(99.22));
    hm.put("Ralph Smith", new Double(-19.08));

    // Get a set of the entries.
    Set<Map.Entry<String, Double>> set = hm.entrySet();

    // Display the set.
    for(Map.Entry<String, Double> me : set) {
      System.out.print(me.getKey() + ": ");
      System.out.println(me.getValue());
    }

    System.out.println();

    // Deposit 1000 into John Doe's account.
    double balance = hm.get("John Doe");
    hm.put("John Doe", balance + 1000);

    System.out.println("John Doe's new balance: " +
      hm.get("John Doe"));
  }
}
```

Output from this program is shown here (the precise order may vary):

```
Ralph Smith: -19.08
Tom Smith: 123.22
John Doe: 3434.34
Tod Hall: 99.22
Jane Baker: 1378.0

John Doe's new balance: 4434.34
```

The program begins by creating a hash map and then adds the mapping of names to balances. Next, the contents of the map are displayed by using a set-view, obtained by calling **entrySet( )**. The keys and values are displayed by calling the **getKey( )** and **getValue( )** methods that are defined by **Map.Entry**. Pay close attention to how the deposit is made into John Doe's account. The **put( )** method automatically replaces any preexisting value that is associated with the specified key with the new value. Thus, after John Doe's account is updated, the hash map will still contain just one "John Doe" account.

The TreeMap Class

The **TreeMap** class extends **AbstractMap** and implements the **NavigableMap** interface. It creates maps stored in a tree structure. A **TreeMap** provides an efficient means of storing key/value pairs in sorted order and allows rapid retrieval. You should note that, unlike a hash map, a tree map guarantees that its elements will be sorted in ascending key order. **TreeMap** is a generic class that has this declaration:

    class TreeMap<K, V>

Here, **K** specifies the type of keys, and **V** specifies the type of values.

The following **TreeMap** constructors are defined:

    TreeMap( )
    TreeMap(Comparator<? super K> *comp*)
    TreeMap(Map<? extends K, ? extends V> *m*)
    TreeMap(SortedMap<K, ? extends V> *sm*)

The first form constructs an empty tree map that will be sorted by using the natural order of its keys. The second form constructs an empty tree-based map that will be sorted by using the **Comparator** *comp*. (Comparators are discussed later in this chapter.) The third form initializes a tree map with the entries from *m*, which will be sorted by using the natural order of the keys. The fourth form initializes a tree map with the entries from *sm*, which will be sorted in the same order as *sm*.

TreeMap has no methods beyond those specified by the **NavigableMap** interface and the **AbstractMap** class.

The following program reworks the preceding example so that it uses **TreeMap**:

```
import java.util.*;

class TreeMapDemo {
  public static void main(String args[]) {

    // Create a tree map.
    TreeMap<String, Double> tm = new TreeMap<String, Double>();

    // Put elements to the map.
    tm.put("John Doe", new Double(3434.34));
    tm.put("Tom Smith", new Double(123.22));
    tm.put("Jane Baker", new Double(1378.00));
    tm.put("Tod Hall", new Double(99.22));
    tm.put("Ralph Smith", new Double(-19.08));

    // Get a set of the entries.
    Set<Map.Entry<String, Double>> set = tm.entrySet();

    // Display the elements.
    for(Map.Entry<String, Double> me : set) {
      System.out.print(me.getKey() + ": ");
      System.out.println(me.getValue());
    }
    System.out.println();
```

```
    // Deposit 1000 into John Doe's account.
    double balance = tm.get("John Doe");
    tm.put("John Doe", balance + 1000);

    System.out.println("John Doe's new balance: " +
      tm.get("John Doe"));
  }
}
```

The following is the output from this program:

```
Jane Baker: 1378.0
John Doe: 3434.34
Ralph Smith: -19.08
Todd Hall: 99.22
Tom Smith: 123.22

John Doe's current balance: 4434.34
```

Notice that **TreeMap** sorts the keys. However, in this case, they are sorted by first name instead of last name. You can alter this behavior by specifying a comparator when the map is created, as described shortly.

The LinkedHashMap Class

LinkedHashMap extends **HashMap**. It maintains a linked list of the entries in the map, in the order in which they were inserted. This allows insertion-order iteration over the map. That is, when iterating through a collection-view of a **LinkedHashMap**, the elements will be returned in the order in which they were inserted. You can also create a **LinkedHashMap** that returns its elements in the order in which they were last accessed. **LinkedHashMap** is a generic class that has this declaration:

  class LinkedHashMap<K, V>

Here, **K** specifies the type of keys, and **V** specifies the type of values.
  LinkedHashMap defines the following constructors:

  LinkedHashMap( )
  LinkedHashMap(Map<? extends K, ? extends V> *m*)
  LinkedHashMap(int *capacity*)
  LinkedHashMap(int *capacity*, float *fillRatio*)
  LinkedHashMap(int *capacity*, float *fillRatio*, boolean *Order*)

The first form constructs a default **LinkedHashMap**. The second form initializes the **LinkedHashMap** with the elements from *m*. The third form initializes the capacity. The fourth form initializes both capacity and fill ratio. The meaning of capacity and fill ratio are the same as for **HashMap**. The default capactiy is 16. The default ratio is 0.75. The last form allows you to specify whether the elements will be stored in the linked list by insertion order, or by order of last access. If *Order* is **true**, then access order is used. If *Order* is **false**, then insertion order is used.

LinkedHashMap adds only one method to those defined by **HashMap**. This method is **removeEldestEntry( )** and it is shown here:

protected boolean removeEldestEntry(Map.Entry<K, V> e)

This method is called by **put( )** and **putAll( )**. The oldest entry is passed in e. By default, this method returns **false** and does nothing. However, if you override this method, then you can have the **LinkedHashMap** remove the oldest entry in the map. To do this, have your override return **true**. To keep the oldest entry, return **false**.

The IdentityHashMap Class

IdentityHashMap extends **AbstractMap** and implements the **Map** interface. It is similar to **HashMap** except that it uses reference equality when comparing elements. **IdentityHashMap** is a generic class that has this declaration:

class IdentityHashMap<K, V>

Here, **K** specifies the type of key, and **V** specifies the type of value. The API documentation explicitly states that **IdentityHashMap** is not for general use.

The EnumMap Class

EnumMap extends **AbstractMap** and implements **Map**. It is specifically for use with keys of an **enum** type. It is a generic class that has this declaration:

class EnumMap<K extends Enum<K>, V>

Here, **K** specifies the type of key, and **V** specifies the type of value. Notice that **K** must extend **Enum<K>**, which enforces the requirement that the keys must be of an **enum** type.
  EnumMap defines the following constructors:

EnumMap(Class<K> kType)
EnumMap(Map<K, ? extends V> m)
EnumMap(EnumMap<K, ? extends V> em)

The first constructor creates an empty **EnumMap** of type kType. The second creates an **EnumMap** map that contains the same entries as m. The third creates an **EnumMap** initialized with the values in em.
  EnumMap defines no methods of its own.

Comparators

Both **TreeSet** and **TreeMap** store elements in sorted order. However, it is the comparator that defines precisely what "sorted order" means. By default, these classes store their elements by using what Java refers to as "natural ordering," which is usually the ordering that you would expect (A before B, 1 before 2, and so forth). If you want to order elements a different way, then specify a **Comparator** when you construct the set or map. Doing so gives you the ability to govern precisely how elements are stored within sorted collections and maps.
  Comparator is a generic interface that has this declaration:

interface Comparator<T>

Here, **T** specifies the type of objects being compared.

The **Comparator** interface defines two methods: **compare( )** and **equals( )**. The **compare( )** method, shown here, compares two elements for order:

    int compare(T *obj1*, T *obj2*)

obj1 and *obj2* are the objects to be compared. This method returns zero if the objects are equal. It returns a positive value if *obj1* is greater than *obj2*. Otherwise, a negative value is returned. The method can throw a **ClassCastException** if the types of the objects are not compatible for comparison. By overriding **compare( )**, you can alter the way that objects are ordered. For example, to sort in reverse order, you can create a comparator that reverses the outcome of a comparison.

The **equals( )** method, shown here, tests whether an object equals the invoking comparator:

    boolean equals(Object *obj*)

Here, *obj* is the object to be tested for equality. The method returns **true** if *obj* and the invoking object are both **Comparator** objects and use the same ordering. Otherwise, it returns **false**. Overriding **equals( )** is unnecessary, and most simple comparators will not do so.

Using a Comparator

The following is an example that demonstrates the power of a custom comparator. It implements the **compare( )** method for strings that operates in reverse of normal. Thus, it causes a tree set to be stored in reverse order.

```
// Use a custom comparator.
import java.util.*;

// A reverse comparator for strings.
class MyComp implements Comparator<String> {
  public int compare(String a, String b) {
    String aStr, bStr;

    aStr = a;
    bStr = b;

    // Reverse the comparison.
    return bStr.compareTo(aStr);
  }

  // No need to override equals.
}

class CompDemo {
  public static void main(String args[]) {
    // Create a tree set.
    TreeSet<String> ts = new TreeSet<String>(new MyComp());

    // Add elements to the tree set.
    ts.add("C");
    ts.add("A");
    ts.add("B");
    ts.add("E");
    ts.add("F");
    ts.add("D");
```

PART II

```
    // Display the elements.
    for(String element : ts)
      System.out.print(element + " ");

    System.out.println();
  }
}
```

As the following output shows, the tree is now stored in reverse order:

```
F E D C B A
```

Look closely at the **MyComp** class, which implements **Comparator** and overrides **compare( )**. (As explained earlier, overriding **equals( )** is neither necessary nor common.) Inside **compare( )**, the **String** method **compareTo( )** compares the two strings. However, **bStr**— not **aStr**—invokes **compareTo( )**. This causes the outcome of the comparison to be reversed.

For a more practical example, the following program is an updated version of the **TreeMap** program shown earlier that stores account balances. In the previous version, the accounts were sorted by name, but the sorting began with the first name. The following program sorts the accounts by last name. To do so, it uses a comparator that compares the last name of each account. This results in the map being sorted by last name.

```
// Use a comparator to sort accounts by last name.
import java.util.*;

// Compare last whole words in two strings.
class TComp implements Comparator<String> {
  public int compare(String a, String b) {
    int i, j, k;
    String aStr, bStr;

    aStr = a;
    bStr = b;

    // Find index of beginning of last name.
    i = aStr.lastIndexOf(' ');
    j = bStr.lastIndexOf(' ');

    k = aStr.substring(i).compareTo(bStr.substring(j));
    if(k==0) // last names match, check entire name
      return aStr.compareTo(bStr);
    else
      return k;
  }

  // No need to override equals.
}

class TreeMapDemo2 {
  public static void main(String args[]) {
    // Create a tree map.
    TreeMap<String, Double> tm = new TreeMap<String, Double>(new TComp());
```

```
// Put elements to the map.
tm.put("John Doe", new Double(3434.34));
tm.put("Tom Smith", new Double(123.22));
tm.put("Jane Baker", new Double(1378.00));
tm.put("Tod Hall", new Double(99.22));
tm.put("Ralph Smith", new Double(-19.08));

// Get a set of the entries.
Set<Map.Entry<String, Double>> set = tm.entrySet();

// Display the elements.
for(Map.Entry<String, Double> me : set) {
  System.out.print(me.getKey() + ": ");
  System.out.println(me.getValue());
}
System.out.println();

// Deposit 1000 into John Doe's account.
double balance =  tm.get("John Doe");
tm.put("John Doe", balance + 1000);

System.out.println("John Doe's new balance: " +
  tm.get("John Doe"));
  }
}
```

Here is the output; notice that the accounts are now sorted by last name:

```
Jane Baker: 1378.0
John Doe: 3434.34
Todd Hall: 99.22
Ralph Smith: -19.08
Tom Smith: 123.22

John Doe's new balance: 4434.34
```

The comparator class **TComp** compares two strings that hold first and last names. It does so by first comparing last names. To do this, it finds the index of the last space in each string and then compares the substrings of each element that begin at that point. In cases where last names are equivalent, the first names are then compared. This yields a tree map that is sorted by last name, and within last name by first name. You can see this because Ralph Smith comes before Tom Smith in the output.

The Collection Algorithms

The Collections Framework defines several algorithms that can be applied to collections and maps. These algorithms are defined as static methods within the **Collections** class. They are summarized in Table 17-14. As explained earlier, beginning with JDK 5 all of the algorithms have been retrofitted for generics. Although the generic syntax might seem a bit intimidating at first, the algorithms are as simple to use as they were before generics. It's just that now, they are type safe.

Method	Description

static <T> boolean
    addAll(Collection <? super T> c,
        T ... elements)
	Inserts the elements specified by elements into the collection specified by c. Returns **true** if the elements were added and **false** otherwise.

static <T> Queue<T> asLifoQueue(Deque<T> c)	Returns a last-in, first-out view of c. (Added by Java SE 6.)

static <T>
    int binarySearch(List<? extends T> list,
        T value,
        Comparator<? super T> c)
	Searches for value in list ordered according to c. Returns the position of value in list, or a negative value if value is not found.

static <T>
    int binarySearch(List<? extends
        Comparable<? super T>> list,
        T value)
	Searches for value in list. The list must be sorted. Returns the position of value in list, or a negative value if value is not found.

static <E> Collection<E>
    checkedCollection(Collection<E> c,
        Class<E> t)
	Returns a run-time type-safe view of a collection. An attempt to insert an incompatible element will cause a **ClassCastException**.

static <E> List<E> checkedList(List<E> c, Class<E> t)	Returns a run-time type-safe view of a **List**. An attempt to insert an incompatible element will cause a **ClassCastException**.

static <K, V> Map<K, V>
    checkedMap(Map<K, V> c,
        Class<K> keyT,
        Class<V> valueT)
	Returns a run-time type-safe view of a **Map**. An attempt to insert an incompatible element will cause a **ClassCastException**.

static <E> List<E> checkedSet(Set<E> c, Class<E> t)	Returns a run-time type-safe view of a **Set**. An attempt to insert an incompatible element will cause a **ClassCastException**.

static <K, V> SortedMap<K, V>
    checkedSortedMap(SortedMap<K, V> c,
        Class<K> keyT,
        Class<V> valueT)
	Returns a run-time type-safe view of a **SortedMap**. An attempt to insert an incompatible element will cause a **ClassCastException**.

static <E> SortedSet<E> checkedSortedSet(SortedSet<E> c, Class<E> t)	Returns a run-time type-safe view of a **SortedSet**. An attempt to insert an incompatible element will cause a **ClassCastException**.
static <T> void copy(List<? super T> list1, List<? extends T> list2)	Copies the elements of list2 to list1.
static boolean disjoint(Collection<?> a, Collection<?> b)	Compares the elements in a to elements in b. Returns **true** if the two collections contain no common elements (i.e., the collections contain disjoint sets of elements). Otherwise, returns **true**.
static <T> List<T> emptyList( )	Returns an immutable, empty **List** object of the inferred type.
static <K, V> Map<K, V> emptyMap( )	Returns an immutable, empty **Map** object of the inferred type.
static <T> Set<T> emptySet( )	Returns an immutable, empty **Set** object of the inferred type.
static <T> Enumeration<T> enumeration(Collection<T> c)	Returns an enumeration over c. (See "The Enumeration Interface," later in this chapter.)
static <T> void fill(List<? super T> list, T obj)	Assigns obj to each element of list.

TABLE 17-14   The Algorithms Defined by **Collections**

Method	Description
static int frequency(Collection<?> *c*, Object *obj*)	Counts the number of occurrences of *obj* in *c* and returns the result.
static int indexOfSubList(List<?> *list*, List<?> *subList*)	Searches *list* for the first occurrence of *subList*. Returns the index of the first match, or −1 if no match is found.
static int lastIndexOfSubList(List<?> *list*, List<?> *subList*)	Searches list for the last occurrence of *subList*. Returns the index of the last match, or −1 if no match is found.
static <T> ArrayList<T> list(Enumeration<T> *enum*)	Returns an **ArrayList** that contains the elements of *enum*.
static <T> T max(Collection<? extends T> *c*, Comparator<? super T> *comp*)	Returns the maximum element in *c* as determined by *comp*.
static <T extends Object & Comparable<? super T>> T max(Collection<? extends T> *c*)	Returns the maximum element in *c* as determined by natural ordering. The collection need not be sorted.
static <T> T min(Collection<? extends T> *c*, Comparator<? super T> *comp*)	Returns the minimum element in *c* as determined by *comp*. The collection need not be sorted.
static <T extends Object & Comparable<? superT>> T min(Collection<? extends T> *c*)	Returns the minimum element in *c* as determined by natural ordering.
static <T> List<T> nCopies(int *num*, T *obj*)	Returns *num* copies of *obj* contained in an immutable list. *num* must be greater than or equal to zero.
static <E> Set<E> newSetFromMap(Map<E, Boolean> *m*)	Creates and returns a set backed by the map specified by *m*, which must be empty at the time this method is called. (Added by Java SE 6.)
static <T> boolean replaceAll(List<T> *list*, T *old*, T *new*)	Replaces all occurrences of *old* with *new* in *list*. Returns **true** if at least one replacement occurred. Returns **false**, otherwise.
static void reverse(List<T> *list*)	Reverses the sequence in *list*.
static <T> Comparator<T> reverseOrder(Comparator<T> *comp*)	Returns a reverse comparator based on the one passed in *comp*. That is, the returned comparator reverses the outcome of a comparison that uses *comp*.
static <T> Comparator<T> reverseOrder( )	Returns a reverse comparator, which is a comparator that reverses the outcome of a comparison between two elements.
static void rotate(List<T> *list*, int *n*)	Rotates *list* by *n* places to the right. To rotate left, use a negative value for *n*.
static void shuffle(List<T> *list*, Random *r*)	Shuffles (i.e., randomizes) the elements in *list* by using *r* as a source of random numbers.
static void shuffle(List<T> *list*)	Shuffles (i.e., randomizes) the elements in *list*.
static <T> Set<T> singleton(T *obj*)	Returns *obj* as an immutable set. This is an easy way to convert a single object into a set.
static <T> List<T> singletonList(T *obj*)	Returns *obj* as an immutable list. This is an easy way to convert a single object into a list.
static <K, V> Map<K, V> singletonMap(K *k*, V *v*)	Returns the key/value pair *k/v* as an immutable map. This is an easy way to convert a single key/value pair into a map.

TABLE 17-14 The Algorithms Defined by **Collections** (continued)

Method	Description
static \<T\> void sort(List\<T\> *list*, Comparator\<? super T\> *comp*)	Sorts the elements of *list* as determined by *comp*.
static \<T extends Comparable\<? super T\>\> void sort(List\<T\> *list*)	Sorts the elements of *list* as determined by their natural ordering.
static void swap(List\<?\> *list*, int *idx1*, int *idx2*)	Exchanges the elements in *list* at the indices specified by *idx1* and *idx2*.
static \<T\> Collection\<T\> synchronizedCollection(Collection\<T\> *c*)	Returns a thread-safe collection backed by *c*.
static \<T\> List\<T\> synchronizedList(List\<T\> *list*)	Returns a thread-safe list backed by *list*.
static \<K, V\> Map\<K, V\> synchronizedMap(Map\<K, V\> *m*)	Returns a thread-safe map backed by *m*.
static \<T\> Set\<T\> synchronizedSet(Set\<T\> *s*)	Returns a thread-safe set backed by *s*.
static \<K, V\> SortedMap\<K, V\> synchronizedSortedMap(SortedMap\<K, V\> *sm*)	Returns a thread-safe sorted map backed by *sm*.
static \<T\> SortedSet\<T\> synchronizedSortedSet(SortedSet\<T\> *ss*)	Returns a thread-safe set backed by *ss*.
static \<T\> Collection\<T\> unmodifiableCollection(Collection\<? extends T\> *c*)	Returns an unmodifiable collection backed by *c*.
static \<T\> List\<T\> unmodifiableList(List\<? extends T\> *list*)	Returns an unmodifiable list backed by *list*.
static \<K, V\> Map\<K, V\> unmodifiableMap(Map\<? extends K, ? extends V\> *m*)	Returns an unmodifiable map backed by *m*.
static \<T\> Set\<T\> unmodifiableSet(Set\<? extends T\> *s*)	Returns an unmodifiable set backed by *s*.
static \<K, V\> SortedMap\<K, V\> unmodifiableSortedMap(SortedMap\<K, ? extends V\> *sm*)	Returns an unmodifiable sorted map backed by *sm*.
static \<T\> SortedSet\<T\> unmodifiableSortedSet(SortedSet\<T\> *ss*)	Returns an unmodifiable sorted set backed by *ss*.

TABLE 17-14   The Algorithms Defined by **Collections** *(continued)*

Several of the methods can throw a **ClassCastException**, which occurs when an attempt is made to compare incompatible types, or an **UnsupportedOperationException**, which occurs when an attempt is made to modify an unmodifiable collection. Other exceptions are possible, depending on the method.

One thing to pay special attention to is the set of **checked** methods, such as **checkedCollection( )**, which returns what the API documentation refers to as a "dynamically typesafe view" of a collection. This view is a reference to the collection that monitors insertions into the collection for type compatibility at run time. An attempt to insert an incompatible element will cause a **ClassCastException**. Using such a view is especially helpful during debugging because it ensures that the collection always contains valid elements. Related methods include **checkedSet( )**, **checkedList( )**, **checkedMap( )**, and so on. They obtain a type-safe view for the indicated collection.

Notice that several methods, such as **synchronizedList( )** and **synchronizedSet( )**, are used to obtain synchronized (*thread-safe*) copies of the various collections. As explained, none of the standard collections implementations are synchronized. You must use the synchronization algorithms to provide synchronization. One other point: iterators to synchronized collections must be used within **synchronized** blocks.

The set of methods that begins with **unmodifiable** returns views of the various collections that cannot be modified. These will be useful when you want to grant some process read— but not write—capabilities on a collection.

Collections defines three static variables: **EMPTY_SET**, **EMPTY_LIST**, and **EMPTY_MAP**. All are immutable.

The following program demonstrates some of the algorithms. It creates and initializes a linked list. The **reverseOrder( )** method returns a **Comparator** that reverses the comparison of **Integer** objects. The list elements are sorted according to this comparator and then are displayed. Next, the list is randomized by calling **shuffle( )**, and then its minimum and maximum values are displayed.

```
// Demonstrate various algorithms.
import java.util.*;

class AlgorithmsDemo {
  public static void main(String args[]) {

    // Create and initialize linked list.
    LinkedList<Integer> ll = new LinkedList<Integer>();
    ll.add(-8);
    ll.add(20);
    ll.add(-20);
    ll.add(8);

    // Create a reverse order comparator.
    Comparator<Integer> r = Collections.reverseOrder();

    // Sort list by using the comparator.
    Collections.sort(ll, r);

    System.out.print("List sorted in reverse: ");
    for(int i : ll)
      System.out.print(i+ " ");

    System.out.println();

    // Shuffle list.
    Collections.shuffle(ll);

    // Display randomized list.
    System.out.print("List shuffled: ");
    for(int i : ll)
      System.out.print(i + " ");

    System.out.println();
```

```
      System.out.println("Minimum: " + Collections.min(ll));
      System.out.println("Maximum: " + Collections.max(ll));
   }
}
```

Output from this program is shown here:

```
List sorted in reverse: 20 8 -8 -20
List shuffled: 20 -20 8 -8
Minimum: -20
Maximum: 20
```

Notice that **min( )** and **max( )** operate on the list after it has been shuffled. Neither requires a sorted list for its operation.

Arrays

The **Arrays** class provides various methods that are useful when working with arrays. These methods help bridge the gap between collections and arrays. Each method defined by **Arrays** is examined in this section.

The **asList( )** method returns a **List** that is backed by a specified array. In other words, both the list and the array refer to the same location. It has the following signature:

static <T> List asList(T ... *array*)

Here, *array* is the array that contains the data.

The **binarySearch( )** method uses a binary search to find a specified value. This method must be applied to sorted arrays. Here are some of its forms. (Java SE 6 adds several others.)

static int binarySearch(byte *array*[ ], byte *value*)
static int binarySearch(char *array*[ ], char *value*)
static int binarySearch(double *array*[ ], double *value*)
static int binarySearch(float *array*[ ], float *value*)
static int binarySearch(int *array*[ ], int *value*)
static int binarySearch(long *array*[ ], long *value*)
static int binarySearch(short *array*[ ], short *value*)
static int binarySearch(Object *array*[ ], Object *value*)
static <T> int binarySearch(T[ ] *array*, T *value*, Comparator<? super T> *c*)

Here, *array* is the array to be searched, and *value* is the value to be located. The last two forms throw a **ClassCastException** if *array* contains elements that cannot be compared (for example, **Double** and **StringBuffer**) or if *value* is not compatible with the types in *array*. In the last form, the **Comparator** *c* is used to determine the order of the elements in *array*. In all cases, if *value* exists in *array*, the index of the element is returned. Otherwise, a negative value is returned.

The **copyOf( )** method was added by Java SE 6. It returns a copy of an array and has the following forms:

static boolean[ ] copyOf(boolean[ ] *source*, int *len*)
static byte[ ] copyOf(byte[ ] *source*, int *len*)
static char[ ] copyOf(char[ ] *source*, int *len*)
static double[ ] copyOf(double[ ] *source*, int *len*)
static float[ ] copyOf(float[ ] *source*, int *len*)

```
static int[ ] copyOf(int[ ] source, int len)
static long[ ] copyOf(long[ ] source, int len)
static short[ ] copyOf(short[ ] source, int len)
static <T> T[ ] copyOf(T[ ] source, int len)
static <T,U> T[ ] copyOf(U[ ] source, int len, Class<? extends T[ ]> resultT)
```

The original array is specified by *source,* and the length of the copy is specified by *len*. If the copy is longer than *source,* then the copy is padded with zeros (for numeric arrays), **nulls** (for object arrays), or **false** (for boolean arrays). If the copy is shorter than *source,* then the copy is truncated. In the last form, the type of *resultT* becomes the type of the array returned. If *len* is negative, a **NegativeArraySizeException** is thrown. If *source* is **null**, a **NullPointerException** is thrown. If *resultT* is incompatible with the type of *source,* an **ArrayStoreException** is thrown.

The **copyOfRange( )** method was also added by Java SE 6. It returns a copy of a range within an array and has the following forms:

```
static boolean[ ] copyOfRange(boolean[ ] source, int start, int end)
static byte[ ] copyOfRange(byte[ ] source, int start, int end)
static char[ ] copyOfRange(char[ ] source, int start, int end)
static double[ ] copyOfRange(double[ ] source, int start, int end)
static float[ ] copyOfRange(float[ ] source, int start, int end)
static int[ ] copyOfRange(int[ ] source, int start, int end)
static long[ ] copyOfRange(long[ ] source, int start, int end)
static short[ ] copyOfRange(short[ ] source, int start, int end)
static <T> T[ ] copyOfRange(T[ ] source, int start, int end)
static <T,U> T[ ] copyOfRange(U[ ] source, int start, int end,
                              Class<? extends T[ ]> resultT)
```

The original array is specified by *source*. The range to copy is specified by the indices passed via *start* and *end*. The range runs from *start* to *end* – 1. If the range is longer than *source,* then the copy is padded with zeros (for numeric arrays), **nulls** (for object arrays), or **false** (for boolean arrays). In the last form, the type of *resultT* becomes the type of the array returned. If *start* is negative or greater than the length of *source,* an **ArrayIndexOutOfBoundsException** is thrown. If *start* is greater than *end,* an **IllegalArgumentException** is thrown. If *source* is **null**, a **NullPointerException** is thrown. If *resultT* is incompatible with the type of *source,* an **ArrayStoreException** is thrown.

The **equals( )** method returns **true** if two arrays are equivalent. Otherwise, it returns **false**. The **equals( )** method has the following forms:

```
static boolean equals(boolean array1[ ], boolean array2[ ])
static boolean equals(byte array1[ ], byte array2[ ])
static boolean equals(char array1[ ], char array2[ ])
static boolean equals(double array1[ ], double array2[ ])
static boolean equals(float array1[ ], float array2[ ])
static boolean equals(int array1[ ], int array2[ ])
static boolean equals(long array1[ ], long array2[ ])
static boolean equals(short array1[ ], short array2[ ])
static boolean equals(Object array1[ ], Object array2[ ])
```

Here, *array1* and *array2* are the two arrays that are compared for equality.

The **deepEquals( )** method can be used to determine if two arrays, which might contain nested arrays, are equal. It has this declaration:

static boolean deepEquals(Object[ ] *a*, Object[ ] *b*)

It returns **true** if the arrays passed in *a* and *b* contain the same elements. If *a* and *b* contain nested arrays, then the contents of those nested arrays are also checked. It returns **false** if the arrays, or any nested arrays, differ.

The **fill( )** method assigns a value to all elements in an array. In other words, it fills an array with a specified value. The **fill( )** method has two versions. The first version, which has the following forms, fills an entire array:

static void fill(boolean *array*[ ], boolean *value*)
static void fill(byte *array*[ ], byte *value*)
static void fill(char *array*[ ], char *value*)
static void fill(double *array*[ ], double *value*)
static void fill(float *array*[ ], float *value*)
static void fill(int *array*[ ], int *value*)
static void fill(long *array*[ ], long *value*)
static void fill(short *array*[ ], short *value*)
static void fill(Object *array*[ ], Object *value*)

Here, *value* is assigned to all elements in *array*.

The second version of the **fill( )** method assigns a value to a subset of an array. Its forms are shown here:

static void fill(boolean *array*[ ], int *start*, int *end*, boolean *value*)
static void fill(byte *array*[ ], int *start*, int *end*, byte *value*)
static void fill(char *array*[ ], int *start*, int *end*, char *value*)
static void fill(double *array*[ ], int *start*, int *end*, double *value*)
static void fill(float *array*[ ], int *start*, int *end*, float *value*)
static void fill(int *array*[ ], int *start*, int *end*, int *value*)
static void fill(long *array*[ ], int *start*, int *end*, long *value*)
static void fill(short *array*[ ], int *start*, int *end*, short *value*)
static void fill(Object *array*[ ], int *start*, int *end*, Object *value*)

Here, *value* is assigned to the elements in *array* from position *start* to position *end*–1. These methods may all throw an **IllegalArgumentException** if *start* is greater than *end*, or an **ArrayIndexOutOfBoundsException** if *start* or *end* is out of bounds.

The **sort( )** method sorts an array so that it is arranged in ascending order. The **sort( )** method has two versions. The first version, shown here, sorts the entire array:

static void sort(byte *array*[ ])
static void sort(char *array*[ ])
static void sort(double *array*[ ])
static void sort(float *array*[ ])
static void sort(int *array*[ ])
static void sort(long *array*[ ])
static void sort(short *array*[ ])
static void sort(Object *array*[ ])
static <T> void sort(T *array*[ ], Comparator<? super T> *c*)

Here, *array* is the array to be sorted. In the last form, *c* is a **Comparator** that is used to order the elements of *array.* The last two forms can throw a **ClassCastException** if elements of the array being sorted are not comparable.

The second version of **sort( )** enables you to specify a range within an array that you want to sort. Its forms are shown here:

static void sort(byte *array*[ ], int *start,* int *end)*
static void sort(char *array*[ ], int *start,* int *end)*
static void sort(double *array*[ ], int *start,* int *end)*
static void sort(float *array*[ ], int *start,* int *end)*
static void sort(int *array*[ ], int *start,* int *end)*
static void sort(long *array*[ ], int *start,* int *end)*
static void sort(short *array*[ ], int *start,* int *end)*
static void sort(Object *array*[ ], int *start,* int *end)*
static <T> void sort(T *array*[ ], int *start,* int *end,* Comparator<? super T> *c)*

Here, the range beginning at *start* and running through *end*–1 within *array* will be sorted. In the last form, *c* is a **Comparator** that is used to order the elements of *array.* All of these methods can throw an **IllegalArgumentException** if *start* is greater than *end,* or an **ArrayIndexOutOfBoundsException** if *start* or *end* is out of bounds. The last two forms can also throw a **ClassCastException** if elements of the array being sorted are not comparable.

Arrays also overrides **toString( )** and **hashCode( )** for the various types of arrays. In addition, **deepToString( )** and **deepHashCode( )** are provided, which operate effectively on arrays that contain nested arrays.

The following program illustrates how to use some of the methods of the **Arrays** class:

```
// Demonstrate Arrays
import java.util.*;

class ArraysDemo {
  public static void main(String args[]) {

    // Allocate and initialize array.
    int array[] = new int[10];
    for(int i = 0; i < 10; i++)
      array[i] = -3 * i;

    // Display, sort, and display the array.
    System.out.print("Original contents: ");
    display(array);
    Arrays.sort(array);
    System.out.print("Sorted: ");
    display(array);

    // Fill and display the array.
    Arrays.fill(array, 2, 6, -1);
    System.out.print("After fill(): ");
    display(array);

    // Sort and display the array.
    Arrays.sort(array);
    System.out.print("After sorting again: ");
    display(array);
```

```
      // Binary search for -9.
      System.out.print("The value -9 is at location ");
      int index =
        Arrays.binarySearch(array, -9);

      System.out.println(index);
    }

  static void display(int array[]) {
    for(int i: array)
      System.out.print(i + " ");

    System.out.println();
  }
}
```

The following is the output from this program:

```
Original contents: 0 -3 -6 -9 -12 -15 -18 -21 -24 -27
Sorted: -27 -24 -21 -18 -15 -12 -9 -6 -3 0
After fill(): -27 -24 -1 -1 -1 -1 -9 -6 -3 0
After sorting again: -27 -24 -9 -6 -3 -1 -1 -1 -1 0
The value -9 is at location 2
```

Why Generic Collections?

As mentioned at the start of this chapter, the entire Collections Framework was refitted for
generics when JDK 5 was released. Furthermore, the Collections Framework is arguably
the single most important use of generics in the Java API. The reason for this is that generics
add type safety to the Collections Framework. Before moving on, it is worth taking some
time to examine in detail the significance of this improvement.

Let's begin with an example that uses pre-generics code. The following program stores
a list of strings in an **ArrayList** and then displays the contents of the list:

```
// Pre-generics example that uses a collection.
import java.util.*;

class OldStyle {
  public static void main(String args[]) {
    ArrayList list = new ArrayList();

    // These lines store strings, but any type of object
    // can be stored.  In old-style code, there is no
    // convenient way to restrict the type of objects stored
    // in a collection
    list.add("one");
    list.add("two");
    list.add("three");
    list.add("four");

    Iterator itr = list.iterator();
    while(itr.hasNext()) {
```

```
      // To retrieve an element, an explicit type cast is needed
      // because the collection stores only Object.
      String str = (String) itr.next(); // explicit cast needed here.

      System.out.println(str + " is " + str.length() + " chars long.");
    }
  }
}
```

Prior to generics, all collections stored references of type **Object**. This allowed any type of reference to be stored in the collection. The preceding program uses this feature to store references to objects of type **String** in **list**, but any type of reference could have been stored.

Unfortunately, the fact that a pre-generics collection stored **Object** references could easily lead to errors. First, it required that you, rather than the compiler, ensure that only objects of the proper type be stored in a specific collection. For example, in the preceding example, **list** is clearly intended to store **String**s, but there is nothing that actually prevents another type of reference from being added to the collection. For example, the compiler will find nothing wrong with this line of code:

```
list.add(new Integer(100));
```

Because **list** stores **Object** references, it can store a reference to **Integer** as well as it can store a reference to **String**. However, if you intended **list** to hold only strings, then the preceding statement would corrupt the collection. Again, the compiler had no way to know that the preceding statement is invalid.

The second problem with pre-generics collections is that when you retrieve a reference from the collection, you must manually cast that reference into the proper type. This is why the preceding program casts the reference returned by **next( )** into **String**. Prior to generics, collections simply stored **Object** references. Thus, the cast was necessary when retrieving objects from a collection.

Aside from the inconvenience of always having to cast a retrieved reference into its proper type, this lack of type safety often led to a rather serious, but surprisingly easy-to-create, error. Because **Object** can be cast into any type of object, it was possible to cast a reference obtained from a collection into the *wrong type*. For example, if the following statement were added to the preceding example, it would still compile without error, but generate a run-time exception when executed:

```
Integer i = (Integer) itr.next();
```

Recall that the preceding example stored only references to instances of type **String** in **list**. Thus, when this statement attempts to cast a **String** into an **Integer**, an invalid cast exception results! Because this happens at run time, this is a very serious error.

The addition of generics fundamentally improves the usability and safety of collections because it

- Ensures that only references to objects of the proper type can actually be stored in a collection. Thus, a collection will always contain references of a known type.

- Eliminates the need to cast a reference retrieved from a collection. Instead, a reference retrieved from a collection is automatically cast into the proper type. This prevents run-time errors due to invalid casts and avoids an entire category of errors.

These two improvements are made possible because each collection class has been given a type parameter that specifies the type of the collection. For example, **ArrayList** is now declared like this:

    class ArrayList<E>

Here, **E** is the type of element stored in the collection. Therefore, the following declares an **ArrayList** for objects of type **String**:

```
ArrayList<String> list = new ArrayList<String>();
```

Now, only references of type **String** can be added to **list**.

The **Iterator** and **ListIterator** interfaces are now also generic. This means that the type parameter must agree with the type of the collection for which the iterator is obtained. Furthermore, this type compatibility is enforced at compile time.

The following program shows the modern, generic form of the preceding program:

```
// Modern, generics version.
import java.util.*;

class NewStyle {
  public static void main(String args[]) {

    // Now, list holds references of type String.
    ArrayList<String> list = new ArrayList<String>();

    list.add("one");
    list.add("two");
    list.add("three");
    list.add("four");

    // Notice that Iterator is also generic.
    Iterator<String> itr = list.iterator();

    // The following statement will now cause a compile-time error.
//    Iterator<Integer> itr = list.iterator(); // Error!

    while(itr.hasNext()) {
      String str = itr.next(); // no cast needed

      // Now, the following line is a compile-time,
      // rather than run-time, error.
//      Integer i = itr.next(); // this won't compile

      System.out.println(str + " is " + str.length() + " chars long.");
    }
  }
}
```

Now, **list** can hold only references to objects of type **String**. Furthermore, as the following line shows, there is no need to cast the return value of **next( )** into **String**:

```
String str = itr.next(); // no cast needed
```

The cast is performed automatically.

Because of support for raw types, it is not necessary to immediately update older collection code. However, all new code should use generics, and you should update older code as soon as time permits. The addition of generics to the Collections Framework is a fundamental improvement that should be utilized wherever possible.

The Legacy Classes and Interfaces

As explained at the start of this chapter, early versions of **java.util** did not include the Collections Framework. Instead, it defined several classes and an interface that provided an ad hoc method of storing objects. When collections were added (by J2SE 1.2), several of the original classes were reengineered to support the collection interfaces. Thus, they are fully compatible with the framework. While no classes have actually been deprecated, one has been rendered obsolete. Of course, where a collection duplicates the functionality of a legacy class, you will usually want to use the collection for new code. In general, the legacy classes are supported because there is still code that uses them.

One other point: none of the collection classes are synchronized, but all the legacy classes are synchronized. This distinction may be important in some situations. Of course, you can easily synchronize collections, too, by using one of the algorithms provided by **Collections**.

The legacy classes defined by **java.util** are shown here:

Dictionary	Hashtable	Properties	Stack	Vector

There is one legacy interface called **Enumeration**. The following sections examine **Enumeration** and each of the legacy classes, in turn.

The Enumeration Interface

The **Enumeration** interface defines the methods by which you can *enumerate* (obtain one at a time) the elements in a collection of objects. This legacy interface has been superseded by **Iterator**. Although not deprecated, **Enumeration** is considered obsolete for new code. However, it is used by several methods defined by the legacy classes (such as **Vector** and **Properties**), is used by several other API classes, and is currently in widespread use in application code. Because it is still in use, it was retrofitted for generics by JDK 5. It has this declaration:

    interface Enumeration<E>

where **E** specifies the type of element being enumerated.

Enumeration specifies the following two methods:

    boolean hasMoreElements( )
    E nextElement( )

When implemented, **hasMoreElements( )** must return **true** while there are still more elements to extract, and **false** when all the elements have been enumerated. **nextElement( )** returns the next object in the enumeration. That is, each call to **nextElement( )** obtains the next object in the enumeration. It throws **NoSuchElementException** when the enumeration is complete.

Vector

Vector implements a dynamic array. It is similar to **ArrayList**, but with two differences: **Vector** is synchronized, and it contains many legacy methods that are not part of the Collections

Framework. With the advent of collections, **Vector** was reengineered to extend **AbstractList** and to implement the **List** interface. With the release of JDK 5, it was retrofitted for generics and reengineered to implement **Iterable**. This means that **Vector** is fully compatible with collections, and a **Vector** can have its contents iterated by the enhanced **for** loop.

Vector is declared like this:

```
class Vector<E>
```

Here, **E** specifies the type of element that will be stored.

Here are the **Vector** constructors:

```
Vector( )
Vector(int size)
Vector(int size, int incr)
Vector(Collection<? extends E> c)
```

The first form creates a default vector, which has an initial size of 10. The second form creates a vector whose initial capacity is specified by *size*. The third form creates a vector whose initial capacity is specified by *size* and whose increment is specified by *incr*. The increment specifies the number of elements to allocate each time that a vector is resized upward. The fourth form creates a vector that contains the elements of collection *c*.

All vectors start with an initial capacity. After this initial capacity is reached, the next time that you attempt to store an object in the vector, the vector automatically allocates space for that object plus extra room for additional objects. By allocating more than just the required memory, the vector reduces the number of allocations that must take place. This reduction is important, because allocations are costly in terms of time. The amount of extra space allocated during each reallocation is determined by the increment that you specify when you create the vector. If you don't specify an increment, the vector's size is doubled by each allocation cycle.

Vector defines these protected data members:

```
int capacityIncrement;
int elementCount;
Object[ ] elementData;
```

The increment value is stored in **capacityIncrement**. The number of elements currently in the vector is stored in **elementCount**. The array that holds the vector is stored in **elementData**.

In addition to the collections methods defined by **List**, **Vector** defines several legacy methods, which are summarized in Table 17-15.

Because **Vector** implements **List**, you can use a vector just like you use an **ArrayList** instance. You can also manipulate one using its legacy methods. For example, after you instantiate a **Vector**, you can add an element to it by calling **addElement( )**. To obtain the element at a specific location, call **elementAt( )**. To obtain the first element in the vector, call **firstElement( )**. To retrieve the last element, call **lastElement( )**. You can obtain the index of an element by using **indexOf( )** and **lastIndexOf( )**. To remove an element, call **removeElement( )** or **removeElementAt( )**.

Method	Description
void addElement(E *element*)	The object specified by *element* is added to the vector.
int capacity( )	Returns the capacity of the vector.
Object clone( )	Returns a duplicate of the invoking vector.
boolean contains(Object *element*)	Returns **true** if *element* is contained by the vector, and returns **false** if it is not.
void copyInto(Object *array*[ ])	The elements contained in the invoking vector are copied into the array specified by *array*.
E elementAt(int *index*)	Returns the element at the location specified by *index*.
Enumeration<E> elements( )	Returns an enumeration of the elements in the vector.
void ensureCapacity(int *size*)	Sets the minimum capacity of the vector to *size*.
E firstElement( )	Returns the first element in the vector.
int indexOf(Object *element*)	Returns the index of the first occurrence of *element*. If the object is not in the vector, –1 is returned.
int indexOf(Object *element*, int *start*)	Returns the index of the first occurrence of *element* at or after *start*. If the object is not in that portion of the vector, –1 is returned.
void insertElementAt(E *element*, int *index*)	Adds *element* to the vector at the location specified by *index*.
boolean isEmpty( )	Returns **true** if the vector is empty, and returns **false** if it contains one or more elements.
E lastElement( )	Returns the last element in the vector.
int lastIndexOf(Object *element*)	Returns the index of the last occurrence of *element*. If the object is not in the vector, –1 is returned.
int lastIndexOf(Object *element*, int *start*)	Returns the index of the last occurrence of *element* before *start*. If the object is not in that portion of the vector, –1 is returned.
void removeAllElements( )	Empties the vector. After this method executes, the size of the vector is zero.
boolean removeElement(Object *element*)	Removes *element* from the vector. If more than one instance of the specified object exists in the vector, then it is the first one that is removed. Returns **true** if successful and **false** if the object is not found.
void removeElementAt(int *index*)	Removes the element at the location specified by *index*.
void setElementAt(E *element*, int *index*)	The location specified by *index* is assigned *element*.
void setSize(int *size*)	Sets the number of elements in the vector to *size*. If the new size is less than the old size, elements are lost. If the new size is larger than the old size, **null** elements are added.
int size( )	Returns the number of elements currently in the vector.
String toString( )	Returns the string equivalent of the vector.
void trimToSize( )	Sets the vector's capacity equal to the number of elements that it currently holds.

TABLE 17-15 The Legacy Methods Defined by **Vector**

The following program uses a vector to store various types of numeric objects. It demonstrates several of the legacy methods defined by **Vector**. It also demonstrates the **Enumeration** interface.

```
// Demonstrate various Vector operations.
import java.util.*;

class VectorDemo {
  public static void main(String args[]) {

    // initial size is 3, increment is 2
```

```
    Vector<Integer> v = new Vector<Integer>(3, 2);

    System.out.println("Initial size: " + v.size());
    System.out.println("Initial capacity: " +
                       v.capacity());

    v.addElement(1);
    v.addElement(2);
    v.addElement(3);
    v.addElement(4);

    System.out.println("Capacity after four additions: " +
                       v.capacity());
    v.addElement(5);
    System.out.println("Current capacity: " +
                       v.capacity());
    v.addElement(6);
    v.addElement(7);

    System.out.println("Current capacity: " +
                       v.capacity());
    v.addElement(9);
    v.addElement(10);

    System.out.println("Current capacity: " +
                       v.capacity());
    v.addElement(11);
    v.addElement(12);


    System.out.println("First element: " + v.firstElement());
    System.out.println("Last element: " + v.lastElement());

    if(v.contains(3))
      System.out.println("Vector contains 3.");

    // Enumerate the elements in the vector.
    Enumeration vEnum = v.elements();

    System.out.println("\nElements in vector:");
    while(vEnum.hasMoreElements())
      System.out.print(vEnum.nextElement() + " ");
    System.out.println();
  }
}
```

The output from this program is shown here:

```
    Initial size: 0
    Initial capacity: 3
    Capacity after four additions: 5
    Current capacity: 5
    Current capacity: 7
    Current capacity: 9
```

```
First element: 1
Last element: 12
Vector contains 3.

Elements in vector:
1 2 3 4 5 6 7 9 10 11 12
```

Instead of relying on an enumeration to cycle through the objects (as the preceding program does), you can use an iterator. For example, the following iterator-based code can be substituted into the program:

```
// Use an iterator to display contents.
Iterator<Integer> vItr = v.iterator();

System.out.println("\nElements in vector:");
while(vItr.hasNext())
  System.out.print(vItr.next() + " ");
System.out.println();
```

You can also use a for-each **for** loop to cycle through a **Vector**, as the following version of the preceding code shows:

```
// Use an enhanced for loop to display contents.
System.out.println("\nElements in vector:");
for(int i : v)
  System.out.print(i + " ");

System.out.println();
```

Because the **Enumeration** interface is not recommended for new code, you will usually use an iterator or a for-each **for** loop to enumerate the contents of a vector. Of course, much legacy code exists that employs **Enumeration**. Fortunately, enumerations and iterators work in nearly the same manner.

Stack

Stack is a subclass of **Vector** that implements a standard last-in, first-out stack. **Stack** only defines the default constructor, which creates an empty stack. With the release of JDK 5, **Stack** was retrofitted for generics and is declared as shown here:

    class Stack<E>

Here, **E** specifies the type of element stored in the stack.

    Stack includes all the methods defined by **Vector** and adds several of its own, shown in Table 17-16.

    To put an object on the top of the stack, call **push( )**. To remove and return the top element, call **pop( )**. An **EmptyStackException** is thrown if you call **pop( )** when the invoking stack is empty. You can use **peek( )** to return, but not remove, the top object. The **empty( )** method returns **true** if nothing is on the stack. The **search( )** method determines whether an object exists on the stack and returns the number of pops that are required to bring it to the top of

Method	Description
boolean empty( )	Returns **true** if the stack is empty, and returns **false** if the stack contains elements.
E peek( )	Returns the element on the top of the stack, but does not remove it.
E pop( )	Returns the element on the top of the stack, removing it in the process.
E push(E *element*)	Pushes *element* onto the stack. *element* is also returned.
int search(Object *element*)	Searches for *element* in the stack. If found, its offset from the top of the stack is returned. Otherwise, –1 is returned.

TABLE 17-16   The Methods Defined by **Stack**

the stack. Here is an example that creates a stack, pushes several **Integer** objects onto it, and then pops them off again:

```
// Demonstrate the Stack class.
import java.util.*;

class StackDemo {
  static void showpush(Stack<Integer> st, int a) {
    st.push(a);
    System.out.println("push(" + a + ")");
    System.out.println("stack: " + st);
  }

  static void showpop(Stack<Integer> st) {
    System.out.print("pop -> ");
    Integer a = st.pop();
    System.out.println(a);
    System.out.println("stack: " + st);
  }

  public static void main(String args[]) {
    Stack<Integer> st = new Stack<Integer>();

    System.out.println("stack: " + st);
    showpush(st, 42);
    showpush(st, 66);
    showpush(st, 99);
    showpop(st);
    showpop(st);
    showpop(st);

    try {
      showpop(st);
    } catch (EmptyStackException e) {
      System.out.println("empty stack");
    }
  }
}
```

The following is the output produced by the program; notice how the exception handler for **EmptyStackException** is caught so that you can gracefully handle a stack underflow:

```
stack: [ ]
push(42)
stack: [42]
push(66)
stack: [42, 66]
push(99)
stack: [42, 66, 99]
pop -> 99
stack: [42, 66]
pop -> 66
stack: [42]
pop -> 42
stack: [ ]
pop -> empty stack
```

One other point: Although **Stack** is not deprecated, with the release of Java SE 6, **ArrayDeque** is a better choice.

Dictionary

Dictionary is an abstract class that represents a key/value storage repository and operates much like **Map**. Given a key and value, you can store the value in a **Dictionary** object. Once the value is stored, you can retrieve it by using its key. Thus, like a map, a dictionary can be thought of as a list of key/value pairs. Although not currently deprecated, **Dictionary** is classified as obsolete, because it is fully superseded by **Map**. However, **Dictionary** is still in use and thus is fully discussed here.

With the advent of JDK 5, **Dictionary** was made generic. It is declared as shown here:

class Dictionary<K, V>

Here, **K** specifies the type of keys, and **V** specifies the type of values. The abstract methods defined by **Dictionary** are listed in Table 17-17.

Method	Purpose
Enumeration<V> elements( )	Returns an enumeration of the values contained in the dictionary.
V get(Object *key*)	Returns the object that contains the value associated with *key*. If *key* is not in the dictionary, a **null** object is returned.
boolean isEmpty( )	Returns **true** if the dictionary is empty, and returns **false** if it contains at least one key.
Enumeration<K> keys( )	Returns an enumeration of the keys contained in the dictionary.
V put(K *key*, V *value*)	Inserts a key and its value into the dictionary. Returns **null** if *key* is not already in the dictionary; returns the previous value associated with *key* if *key* is already in the dictionary.
V remove(Object *key*)	Removes *key* and its value. Returns the value associated with *key*. If *key* is not in the dictionary, a **null** is returned.
int size( )	Returns the number of entries in the dictionary.

TABLE 17-17   The Abstract Methods Defined by **Dictionary**

To add a key and a value, use the **put( )** method. Use **get( )** to retrieve the value of a given key. The keys and values can each be returned as an **Enumeration** by the **keys( )** and **elements( )** methods, respectively. The **size( )** method returns the number of key/value pairs stored in a dictionary, and **isEmpty( )** returns **true** when the dictionary is empty. You can use the **remove( )** method to delete a key/value pair.

REMEMBER   *The **Dictionary** class is obsolete. You should implement the **Map** interface to obtain key/value storage functionality.*

Hashtable

Hashtable was part of the original **java.util** and is a concrete implementation of a **Dictionary**. However, with the advent of collections, **Hashtable** was reengineered to also implement the **Map** interface. Thus, **Hashtable** is now integrated into the Collections Framework. It is similar to **HashMap**, but is synchronized.

Like **HashMap**, **Hashtable** stores key/value pairs in a hash table. However, neither keys nor values can be **null**. When using a **Hashtable**, you specify an object that is used as a key, and the value that you want linked to that key. The key is then hashed, and the resulting hash code is used as the index at which the value is stored within the table.

Hashtable was made generic by JDK 5. It is declared like this:

class Hashtable<K, V>

Here, **K** specifies the type of keys, and **V** specifies the type of values.

A hash table can only store objects that override the **hashCode( )** and **equals( )** methods that are defined by **Object**. The **hashCode( )** method must compute and return the hash code for the object. Of course, **equals( )** compares two objects. Fortunately, many of Java's built-in classes already implement the **hashCode( )** method. For example, the most common type of **Hashtable** uses a **String** object as the key. **String** implements both **hashCode( )** and **equals( )**.

The **Hashtable** constructors are shown here:

Hashtable( )
Hashtable(int *size*)
Hashtable(int *size*, float *fillRatio*)
Hashtable(Map<? extends K, ? extends V> *m*)

The first version is the default constructor. The second version creates a hash table that has an initial size specified by *size*. (The default size is 11.) The third version creates a hash table that has an initial size specified by *size* and a fill ratio specified by *fillRatio*. This ratio must be between 0.0 and 1.0, and it determines how full the hash table can be before it is resized upward. Specifically, when the number of elements is greater than the capacity of the hash table multiplied by its fill ratio, the hash table is expanded. If you do not specify a fill ratio, then 0.75 is used. Finally, the fourth version creates a hash table that is initialized with the elements in *m*. The capacity of the hash table is set to twice the number of elements in *m*. The default load factor of 0.75 is used.

In addition to the methods defined by the **Map** interface, which **Hashtable** now implements, **Hashtable** defines the legacy methods listed in Table 17-18. Several methods throw **NullPointerException** if an attempt is made to use a **null** key or value.

Method	Description
void clear( )	Resets and empties the hash table.
Object clone( )	Returns a duplicate of the invoking object.
boolean contains(Object *value*)	Returns **true** if some value equal to *value* exists within the hash table. Returns **false** if the value isn't found.
boolean containsKey(Object *key*)	Returns **true** if some key equal to *key* exists within the hash table. Returns **false** if the key isn't found.
boolean containsValue(Object *value*)	Returns **true** if some value equal to *value* exists within the hash table. Returns **false** if the value isn't found.
Enumeration<V> elements( )	Returns an enumeration of the values contained in the hash table.
V get(Object *key*)	Returns the object that contains the value associated with *key*. If *key* is not in the hash table, a **null** object is returned.
boolean isEmpty( )	Returns **true** if the hash table is empty; returns **false** if it contains at least one key.
Enumeration<K> keys( )	Returns an enumeration of the keys contained in the hash table.
V put(K *key*, V *value*)	Inserts a key and a value into the hash table. Returns **null** if *key* isn't already in the hash table; returns the previous value associated with *key* if *key* is already in the hash table.
void rehash( )	Increases the size of the hash table and rehashes all of its keys.
V remove(Object *key*)	Removes *key* and its value. Returns the value associated with *key*. If *key* is not in the hash table, a **null** object is returned.
int size( )	Returns the number of entries in the hash table.
String toString( )	Returns the string equivalent of a hash table.

TABLE 17-18   The Legacy Methods Defined by **Hashtable**

The following example reworks the bank account program, shown earlier, so that it uses a **Hashtable** to store the names of bank depositors and their current balances:

```
// Demonstrate a Hashtable.
import java.util.*;

class HTDemo {
  public static void main(String args[]) {
    Hashtable<String, Double> balance =
      new Hashtable<String, Double>();

    Enumeration<String> names;
    String str;
    double bal;

    balance.put("John Doe", 3434.34);
    balance.put("Tom Smith", 123.22);
    balance.put("Jane Baker", 1378.00);
    balance.put("Tod Hall", 99.22);
    balance.put("Ralph Smith", -19.08);

    // Show all balances in hashtable.
    names = balance.keys();
```

```
    while(names.hasMoreElements()) {
      str = names.nextElement();
      System.out.println(str + ": " +
                          balance.get(str));
    }

    System.out.println();

    // Deposit 1,000 into John Doe's account.
    bal = balance.get("John Doe");
    balance.put("John Doe", bal+1000);
    System.out.println("John Doe's new balance: " +
                        balance.get("John Doe"));
  }
}
```

The output from this program is shown here:

```
    Todd Hall: 99.22
    Ralph Smith: -19.08
    John Doe: 3434.34
    Jane Baker: 1378.0
    Tom Smith: 123.22

    John Doe's new balance: 4434.34
```

One important point: like the map classes, **Hashtable** does not directly support iterators. Thus, the preceding program uses an enumeration to display the contents of **balance**. However, you can obtain set-views of the hash table, which permits the use of iterators. To do so, you simply use one of the collection-view methods defined by **Map**, such as **entrySet( )** or **keySet( )**. For example, you can obtain a set-view of the keys and cycle through them using either an iterator or an enhanced **for** loop. Here is a reworked version of the program that shows this technique:

```
// Use iterators with a Hashtable.
import java.util.*;

class HTDemo2 {
  public static void main(String args[]) {
    Hashtable<String, Double> balance =
      new Hashtable<String, Double>();

    String str;
    double bal;

    balance.put("John Doe", 3434.34);
    balance.put("Tom Smith", 123.22);
    balance.put("Jane Baker", 1378.00);
    balance.put("Tod Hall", 99.22);
    balance.put("Ralph Smith", -19.08);

    // Show all balances in hashtable.
    // First, get a set view of the keys.
```

```
    Set<String> set = balance.keySet();

    // Get an iterator.
    Iterator<String> itr = set.iterator();
    while(itr.hasNext()) {
      str = itr.next();
      System.out.println(str + ": " +
                         balance.get(str));
    }

    System.out.println();

    // Deposit 1,000 into John Doe's account.
    bal = balance.get("John Doe");
    balance.put("John Doe", bal+1000);
    System.out.println("John Doe's new balance: " +
                       balance.get("John Doe"));
  }
}
```

Properties

Properties is a subclass of **Hashtable**. It is used to maintain lists of values in which the key is a **String** and the value is also a **String**. The **Properties** class is used by many other Java classes. For example, it is the type of object returned by **System.getProperties( )** when obtaining environmental values. Although the **Properties** class, itself, is not generic, several of its methods are.

Properties defines the following instance variable:

Properties defaults;

This variable holds a default property list associated with a **Properties** object. **Properties** defines these constructors:

Properties( )
Properties(Properties *propDefault*)

The first version creates a **Properties** object that has no default values. The second creates an object that uses *propDefault* for its default values. In both cases, the property list is empty.

In addition to the methods that **Properties** inherits from **Hashtable**, **Properties** defines the methods listed in Table 17-19. **Properties** also contains one deprecated method: **save( )**. This was replaced by **store( )** because **save( )** did not handle errors correctly.

One useful capability of the **Properties** class is that you can specify a default property that will be returned if no value is associated with a certain key. For example, a default value can be specified along with the key in the **getProperty( )** method—such as **getProperty("name"**, **"default value")**. If the "name" value is not found, then "default value" is returned. When you construct a **Properties** object, you can pass another instance of **Properties** to be used as the default properties for the new instance. In this case, if you call **getProperty("foo")** on a given **Properties** object, and "foo" does not exist, Java looks for "foo" in the default **Properties** object. This allows for arbitrary nesting of levels of default properties.

Method	Description
String getProperty(String *key*)	Returns the value associated with *key*. A **null** object is returned if *key* is neither in the list nor in the default property list.
String getProperty(String *key*, String *defaultProperty*)	Returns the value associated with *key*. *defaultProperty* is returned if *key* is neither in the list nor in the default property list.
void list(PrintStream *streamOut*)	Sends the property list to the output stream linked to *streamOut*.
void list(PrintWriter *streamOut*)	Sends the property list to the output stream linked to *streamOut*.
void load(InputStream *streamIn*) throws IOException	Inputs a property list from the input stream linked to *streamIn*.
void load(Reader *streamIn*) throws IOException	Inputs a property list from the input stream linked to *streamIn*. (Added by Java SE 6.)
void loadFromXML(InputStream *streamIn*) throws IOException, InvalidPropertiesFormatException	Inputs a property list from an XML document linked to *streamIn*.
Enumeration<?> propertyNames( )	Returns an enumeration of the keys. This includes those keys found in the default property list, too.
Object setProperty(String *key*, String *value*)	Associates *value* with *key*. Returns the previous value associated with *key*, or returns null if no such association exists.
void store(OutputStream *streamOut*, String *description*) throws IOException	After writing the string specified by *description*, the property list is written to the output stream linked to *streamOut*.
void store(Writer *streamOut*, String *description*) throws IOException	After writing the string specified by *description*, the property list is written to the output stream linked to *streamOut*. (Added by Java SE 6.)
void storeToXML(OutputStream *streamOut*, String *description*) throws IOException	After writing the string specified by *description*, the property list is written to the XML document linked to *streamOut*.
void storeToXML(OutputStream *streamOut*, String *description*, String *enc*)	The property list and the string specified by *description* is written to the XML document linked to *streamOut* using the specified character encoding.
Set<String> stringPropertyNames( )	Returns a set of keys. (Added by Java SE 6.)

TABLE 17-19 The Methods Defined by **Properties**

The following example demonstrates **Properties**. It creates a property list in which the keys are the names of states and the values are the names of their capitals. Notice that the attempt to find the capital for Florida includes a default value.

```
// Demonstrate a Property list.
import java.util.*;

class PropDemo {
  public static void main(String args[]) {
    Properties capitals = new Properties();

    capitals.put("Illinois", "Springfield");
    capitals.put("Missouri", "Jefferson City");
    capitals.put("Washington", "Olympia");
    capitals.put("California", "Sacramento");
    capitals.put("Indiana", "Indianapolis");

    // Get a set-view of the keys.
    Set states = capitals.keySet();
```

```
    // Show all of the states and capitals.
    for(Object name : states)
      System.out.println("The capital of " +
                         name + " is " +
                         capitals.getProperty((String)name)
                         + ".");

    System.out.println();

    // Look for state not in list -- specify default.
    String str = capitals.getProperty("Florida", "Not Found");
    System.out.println("The capital of Florida is "
                       + str + ".");
  }
}
```

The output from this program is shown here:

```
    The capital of Missouri is Jefferson City.
    The capital of Illinois is Springfield.
    The capital of Indiana is Indianapolis.
    The capital of California is Sacramento.
    The capital of Washington is Olympia.

    The capital of Florida is Not Found.
```

Since Florida is not in the list, the default value is used.

Although it is perfectly valid to use a default value when you call **getProperty( )**, as the preceding example shows, there is a better way of handling default values for most applications of property lists. For greater flexibility, specify a default property list when constructing a **Properties** object. The default list will be searched if the desired key is not found in the main list. For example, the following is a slightly reworked version of the preceding program, with a default list of states specified. Now, when Florida is sought, it will be found in the default list:

```
// Use a default property list.
import java.util.*;

class PropDemoDef {
  public static void main(String args[]) {
    Properties defList = new Properties();
    defList.put("Florida", "Tallahassee");
    defList.put("Wisconsin", "Madison");

    Properties capitals = new Properties(defList);

    capitals.put("Illinois", "Springfield");
    capitals.put("Missouri", "Jefferson City");
    capitals.put("Washington", "Olympia");
    capitals.put("California", "Sacramento");
    capitals.put("Indiana", "Indianapolis");
```

```
   // Get a set-view of the keys.
   Set states = capitals.keySet();

   // Show all of the states and capitals.
   for(Object name : states)
     System.out.println("The capital of " +
                          name + " is " +
                          capitals.getProperty((String)name)
                          + ".");

   System.out.println();

   // Florida will now be found in the default list.
   String str = capitals.getProperty("Florida");
   System.out.println("The capital of Florida is "
                          + str + ".");
   }
}
```

Using store( ) and load( )

One of the most useful aspects of **Properties** is that the information contained in a **Properties** object can be easily stored to or loaded from disk with the **store( )** and **load( )** methods. At any time, you can write a **Properties** object to a stream or read it back. This makes property lists especially convenient for implementing simple databases. For example, the following program uses a property list to create a simple computerized telephone book that stores names and phone numbers. To find a person's number, you enter his or her name. The program uses the **store( )** and **load( )** methods to store and retrieve the list. When the program executes, it first tries to load the list from a file called **phonebook.dat**. If this file exists, the list is loaded. You can then add to the list. If you do, the new list is saved when you terminate the program. Notice how little code is required to implement a small, but functional, computerized phone book.

```
/* A simple telephone number database that uses
   a property list. */
import java.io.*;
import java.util.*;

class Phonebook {
  public static void main(String args[])
    throws IOException
  {
    Properties ht = new Properties();
    BufferedReader br =
      new BufferedReader(new InputStreamReader(System.in));
    String name, number;
    FileInputStream fin = null;
    boolean changed = false;

    // Try to open phonebook.dat file.
    try {
      fin = new FileInputStream("phonebook.dat");
    } catch(FileNotFoundException e) {
```

```
      // ignore missing file
    }

    /* If phonebook file already exists,
       load existing telephone numbers. */
    try {
      if(fin != null) {
        ht.load(fin);
        fin.close();
      }
    } catch(IOException e) {
      System.out.println("Error reading file.");
    }

    // Let user enter new names and numbers.
    do {
      System.out.println("Enter new name" +
                         " ('quit' to stop): ");
      name = br.readLine();
      if(name.equals("quit")) continue;

      System.out.println("Enter number: ");
      number = br.readLine();

      ht.put(name, number);
      changed = true;
    } while(!name.equals("quit"));

    // If phone book data has changed, save it.
    if(changed) {
      FileOutputStream fout = new FileOutputStream("phonebook.dat");

      ht.store(fout, "Telephone Book");
      fout.close();
    }

    // Look up numbers given a name.
    do {
      System.out.println("Enter name to find" +
                         " ('quit' to quit): ");
      name = br.readLine();
      if(name.equals("quit")) continue;

      number = (String) ht.get(name);
      System.out.println(number);
    } while(!name.equals("quit"));
  }
}
```

Parting Thoughts on Collections

The Collections Framework gives you, the programmer, a powerful set of well-engineered solutions to some of programming's most common tasks. Now that the Collections Framework is generic, it can be used with complete type safety, which further contributes to its value.

Consider using a collection the next time that you need to store and retrieve information. Remember, collections need not be reserved for only the "large jobs," such as corporate databases, mailing lists, or inventory systems. They are also effective when applied to smaller jobs. For example, a **TreeMap** would make an excellent collection to hold the directory structure of a set of files. A **TreeSet** could be quite useful for storing project-management information. Frankly, the types of problems that will benefit from a collections-based solution are limited only by your imagination.

java.util Part 2: More Utility Classes

This chapter continues our discussion of **java.util** by examining those classes and interfaces that are not part of the Collections Framework. These include classes that tokenize strings, work with dates, compute random numbers, bundle resources, and observe events. Also covered are the **Formatter** and **Scanner** classes which make it easy to write and read formatted data. Finally, the subpackages of **java.util** are briefly mentioned at the end of this chapter.

StringTokenizer

The processing of text often consists of parsing a formatted input string. *Parsing* is the division of text into a set of discrete parts, or *tokens,* which in a certain sequence can convey a semantic meaning. The **StringTokenizer** class provides the first step in this parsing process, often called the *lexer* (lexical analyzer) or *scanner.* **StringTokenizer** implements the **Enumeration** interface. Therefore, given an input string, you can enumerate the individual tokens contained in it using **StringTokenizer**.

To use **StringTokenizer**, you specify an input string and a string that contains delimiters. *Delimiters* are characters that separate tokens. Each character in the delimiters string is considered a valid delimiter—for example, "*,;:*" sets the delimiters to a comma, semicolon, and colon. The default set of delimiters consists of the whitespace characters: space, tab, newline, and carriage return.

The **StringTokenizer** constructors are shown here:

StringTokenizer(String *str*)
StringTokenizer(String *str*, String *delimiters*)
StringTokenizer(String *str*, String *delimiters*, boolean *delimAsToken*)

In all versions, *str* is the string that will be tokenized. In the first version, the default delimiters are used. In the second and third versions, *delimiters* is a string that specifies the delimiters. In the third version, if *delimAsToken* is **true**, then the delimiters are also returned as tokens when the string is parsed. Otherwise, the delimiters are not returned. Delimiters are not returned as tokens by the first two forms.

Once you have created a **StringTokenizer** object, the **nextToken( )** method is used to extract consecutive tokens. The **hasMoreTokens( )** method returns **true** while there are more tokens to be extracted. Since **StringTokenizer** implements **Enumeration**, the **hasMoreElements( )** and **nextElement( )** methods are also implemented, and they act the same as **hasMoreTokens( )** and **nextToken( )**, respectively. The **StringTokenizer** methods are shown in Table 18-1.

Here is an example that creates a **StringTokenizer** to parse "key=value" pairs. Consecutive sets of "key=value" pairs are separated by a semicolon.

```
// Demonstrate StringTokenizer.
import java.util.StringTokenizer;

class STDemo {
  static String in = "title=Java: The Complete Reference;" +
    "author=Schildt;" +
    "publisher=Osborne/McGraw-Hill;" +
    "copyright=2007";

  public static void main(String args[]) {
    StringTokenizer st = new StringTokenizer(in, "=;");

    while(st.hasMoreTokens()) {
      String key = st.nextToken();
      String val = st.nextToken();
      System.out.println(key + "\t" + val);
    }
  }
}
```

The output from this program is shown here:

```
title   Java: The Complete Reference
author  Schildt
publisher  Osborne/McGraw-Hill
copyright  2007
```

Method	Description
int countTokens( )	Using the current set of delimiters, the method determines the number of tokens left to be parsed and returns the result.
boolean hasMoreElements( )	Returns **true** if one or more tokens remain in the string and returns **false** if there are none.
boolean hasMoreTokens( )	Returns **true** if one or more tokens remain in the string and returns **false** if there are none.
Object nextElement( )	Returns the next token as an **Object**.
String nextToken( )	Returns the next token as a **String**.
String nextToken(String *delimiters*)	Returns the next token as a **String** and sets the delimiters string to that specified by *delimiters*.

TABLE 18-1 The Methods Defined by **StringTokenizer**

BitSet

A **BitSet** class creates a special type of array that holds bit values. This array can increase in size as needed. This makes it similar to a vector of bits. The **BitSet** constructors are shown here:

BitSet( )
BitSet(int *size*)

The first version creates a default object. The second version allows you to specify its initial size (that is, the number of bits that it can hold). All bits are initialized to zero.

BitSet defines the methods listed in Table 18-2.

Method	Description
void and(BitSet *bitSet*)	ANDs the contents of the invoking **BitSet** object with those specified by *bitSet*. The result is placed into the invoking object.
void andNot(BitSet *bitSet*)	For each 1 bit in *bitSet,* the corresponding bit in the invoking **BitSet** is cleared.
int cardinality( )	Returns the number of set bits in the invoking object.
void clear( )	Zeros all bits.
void clear(int *index*)	Zeros the bit specified by *index.*
void clear(int *startIndex,* int *endIndex*)	Zeros the bits from *startIndex* to *endIndex*–1.
Object clone( )	Duplicates the invoking **BitSet** object.
boolean equals(Object *bitSet*)	Returns **true** if the invoking bit set is equivalent to the one passed in *bitSet*. Otherwise, the method returns **false**.
void flip(int *index*)	Reverses the bit specified by *index.*
void flip(int *startIndex,* int *endIndex*)	Reverses the bits from *startIndex* to *endIndex*–1.
boolean get(int *index*)	Returns the current state of the bit at the specified index.
BitSet get(int *startIndex,* int *endIndex*)	Returns a **BitSet** that consists of the bits from *startIndex* to *endIndex*–1. The invoking object is not changed.
int hashCode( )	Returns the hash code for the invoking object.
boolean intersects(BitSet *bitSet*)	Returns **true** if at least one pair of corresponding bits within the invoking object and *bitSet* are 1.
boolean isEmpty( )	Returns **true** if all bits in the invoking object are zero.
int length( )	Returns the number of bits required to hold the contents of the invoking **BitSet**. This value is determined by the location of the last 1 bit.
int nextClearBit(int *startIndex*)	Returns the index of the next cleared bit (that is, the next zero bit), starting from the index specified by *startIndex*.

TABLE 18-2   The Methods Defined by **BitSet**

Method	Description
int nextSetBit(int *startIndex*)	Returns the index of the next set bit (that is, the next 1 bit), starting from the index specified by *startIndex*. If no bit is set, –1 is returned.
void or(BitSet *bitSet*)	ORs the contents of the invoking **BitSet** object with that specified by *bitSet*. The result is placed into the invoking object.
void set(int *index*)	Sets the bit specified by *index*.
void set(int *index*, boolean *v*)	Sets the bit specified by *index* to the value passed in *v*. **true** sets the bit, **false** clears the bit.
void set(int *startIndex*, int *endIndex*)	Sets the bits from *startIndex* to *endIndex*–1.
void set(int *startIndex*, int *endIndex*, boolean *v*)	Sets the bits from *startIndex* to *endIndex*–1, to the value passed in *v*. **true** sets the bits, **false** clears the bits.
int size( )	Returns the number of bits in the invoking **BitSet** object.
String toString( )	Returns the string equivalent of the invoking **BitSet** object.
void xor(BitSet *bitSet*)	XORs the contents of the invoking **BitSet** object with that specified by *bitSet*. The result is placed into the invoking object.

TABLE 18-2   The Methods Defined by **BitSet** *(continued)*

Here is an example that demonstrates **BitSet**:

```
// BitSet Demonstration.
import java.util.BitSet;

class BitSetDemo {
  public static void main(String args[]) {
    BitSet bits1 = new BitSet(16);
    BitSet bits2 = new BitSet(16);

    // set some bits
    for(int i=0; i<16; i++) {
      if((i%2) == 0) bits1.set(i);
      if((i%5) != 0) bits2.set(i);
    }

    System.out.println("Initial pattern in bits1: ");
    System.out.println(bits1);
    System.out.println("\nInitial pattern in bits2: ");
    System.out.println(bits2);

    // AND bits
    bits2.and(bits1);
    System.out.println("\nbits2 AND bits1: ");
    System.out.println(bits2);
```

```
    // OR bits
    bits2.or(bits1);
    System.out.println("\nbits2 OR bits1: ");
    System.out.println(bits2);

    // XOR bits
    bits2.xor(bits1);
    System.out.println("\nbits2 XOR bits1: ");
    System.out.println(bits2);
  }
}
```

The output from this program is shown here. When **toString( )** converts a **BitSet** object to its string equivalent, each set bit is represented by its bit position. Cleared bits are not shown.

```
Initial pattern in bits1:
{0, 2, 4, 6, 8, 10, 12, 14}

Initial pattern in bits2:
{1, 2, 3, 4, 6, 7, 8, 9, 11, 12, 13, 14}

bits2 AND bits1:
{2, 4, 6, 8, 12, 14}

bits2 OR bits1:
{0, 2, 4, 6, 8, 10, 12, 14}

bits2 XOR bits1:
{}
```

Date

The **Date** class encapsulates the current date and time. Before beginning our examination of **Date**, it is important to point out that it has changed substantially from its original version defined by Java 1.0. When Java 1.1 was released, many of the functions carried out by the original **Date** class were moved into the **Calendar** and **DateFormat** classes, and as a result, many of the original 1.0 **Date** methods were deprecated. Since the deprecated 1.0 methods should not be used for new code, they are not described here.

Date supports the following constructors:

Date( )
Date(long *millisec*)

The first constructor initializes the object with the current date and time. The second constructor accepts one argument that equals the number of milliseconds that have elapsed since midnight, January 1, 1970. The nondeprecated methods defined by **Date** are shown in Table 18-3. **Date** also implements the **Comparable** interface.

Method	Description
boolean after(Date *date*)	Returns **true** if the invoking **Date** object contains a date that is later than the one specified by *date*. Otherwise, it returns **false**.
boolean before(Date *date*)	Returns **true** if the invoking **Date** object contains a date that is earlier than the one specified by *date*. Otherwise, it returns **false**.
Object clone( )	Duplicates the invoking **Date** object.
int compareTo(Date *date*)	Compares the value of the invoking object with that of *date*. Returns 0 if the values are equal. Returns a negative value if the invoking object is earlier than *date*. Returns a positive value if the invoking object is later than *date*.
boolean equals(Object *date*)	Returns **true** if the invoking **Date** object contains the same time and date as the one specified by *date*. Otherwise, it returns **false**.
long getTime( )	Returns the number of milliseconds that have elapsed since January 1, 1970.
int hashCode( )	Returns a hash code for the invoking object.
void setTime(long *time*)	Sets the time and date as specified by *time*, which represents an elapsed time in milliseconds from midnight, January 1, 1970.
String toString( )	Converts the invoking **Date** object into a string and returns the result.

TABLE 18-3   The Nondeprecated Methods Defined by **Date**

As you can see by examining Table 18-3, the **Date** features do not allow you to obtain the individual components of the date or time. As the following program demonstrates, you can only obtain the date and time in terms of milliseconds or in its default string representation as returned by **toString( )**. To obtain more-detailed information about the date and time, you will use the **Calendar** class.

```
// Show date and time using only Date methods.
import java.util.Date;

class DateDemo {
  public static void main(String args[]) {
    // Instantiate a Date object
    Date date = new Date();

    // display time and date using toString()
    System.out.println(date);

    // Display number of milliseconds since midnight, January 1, 1970 GMT
    long msec = date.getTime();
    System.out.println("Milliseconds since Jan. 1, 1970 GMT = " + msec);
  }
}
```

Sample output is shown here:

```
Mon Jan 01 16:28:16 CST 2007
Milliseconds since Jan. 1, 1970 GMT = 1167690496023
```

Calendar

The abstract **Calendar** class provides a set of methods that allows you to convert a time in milliseconds to a number of useful components. Some examples of the type of information that can be provided are year, month, day, hour, minute, and second. It is intended that subclasses of **Calendar** will provide the specific functionality to interpret time information according to their own rules. This is one aspect of the Java class library that enables you to write programs that can operate in international environments. An example of such a subclass is **GregorianCalendar**.

Calendar provides no public constructors.

Calendar defines several protected instance variables. **areFieldsSet** is a **boolean** that indicates if the time components have been set. **fields** is an array of **int**s that holds the components of the time. **isSet** is a **boolean** array that indicates if a specific time component has been set. **time** is a **long** that holds the current time for this object. **isTimeSet** is a **boolean** that indicates if the current time has been set.

Some commonly used methods defined by **Calendar** are shown in Table 18-4.

Method	Description
abstract void add(int *which*, int *val*)	Adds *val* to the time or date component specified by *which*. To subtract, add a negative value. *which* must be one of the fields defined by **Calendar**, such as **Calendar.HOUR**.
boolean after(Object *calendarObj*)	Returns **true** if the invoking **Calendar** object contains a date that is later than the one specified by *calendarObj*. Otherwise, it returns **false**.
boolean before(Object *calendarObj*)	Returns **true** if the invoking **Calendar** object contains a date that is earlier than the one specified by *calendarObj*. Otherwise, it returns **false**.
final void clear( )	Zeros all time components in the invoking object.
final void clear(int *which*)	Zeros the time component specified by *which* in the invoking object.
Object clone( )	Returns a duplicate of the invoking object.
boolean equals(Object *calendarObj*)	Returns **true** if the invoking **Calendar** object contains a date that is equal to the one specified by *calendarObj*. Otherwise, it returns **false**.

TABLE 18-4   Commonly Used Methods Defined by **Calendar**

Method	Description
int get(int *calendarField*)	Returns the value of one component of the invoking object. The component is indicated by *calendarField*. Examples of the components that can be requested are **Calendar.YEAR**, **Calendar.MONTH**, **Calendar.MINUTE**, and so forth.
static Locale[ ] getAvailableLocales( )	Returns an array of **Locale** objects that contains the locales for which calendars are available.
static Calendar getInstance( )	Returns a **Calendar** object for the default locale and time zone.
static Calendar getInstance(TimeZone *tz*)	Returns a **Calendar** object for the time zone specified by *tz*. The default locale is used.
static Calendar getInstance(Locale *locale*)	Returns a **Calendar** object for the locale specified by *locale*. The default time zone is used.
static Calendar getInstance(TimeZone *tz*, Locale *locale*)	Returns a **Calendar** object for the time zone specified by *tz* and the locale specified by *locale*.
final Date getTime( )	Returns a **Date** object equivalent to the time of the invoking object.
TimeZone getTimeZone( )	Returns the time zone for the invoking object.
final boolean isSet(int *which*)	Returns **true** if the specified time component is set. Otherwise, it returns **false**.
void set(int *which*, int *val*)	Sets the date or time component specified by *which* to the value specified by *val* in the invoking object. *which* must be one of the fields defined by **Calendar**, such as **Calendar.HOUR**.
final void set(int *year*, int *month*, int *dayOfMonth*)	Sets various date and time components of the invoking object.
final void set(int *year*, int *month*, int *dayOfMonth*, int *hours*, int *minutes*)	Sets various date and time components of the invoking object.
final void set(int *year*, int *month*, int *dayOfMonth*, int *hours*, int *minutes*, int *seconds*)	Sets various date and time components of the invoking object.
final void setTime(Date *d*)	Sets various date and time components of the invoking object. This information is obtained from the **Date** object *d*.
void setTimeZone(TimeZone *tz*)	Sets the time zone for the invoking object to that specified by *tz*.

TABLE 18-4   Commonly Used Methods Defined by **Calendar** *(continued)*

Calendar defines the following **int** constants, which are used when you get or set components of the calendar:

ALL_STYLES	FRIDAY	PM
AM	HOUR	SATURDAY
AM_PM	HOUR_OF_DAY	SECOND
APRIL	JANUARY	SEPTEMBER
AUGUST	JULY	SHORT
DATE	JUNE	SUNDAY
DAY_OF_MONTH	LONG	THURSDAY
DAY_OF_WEEK	MARCH	TUESDAY
DAY_OF_WEEK_IN_MONTH	MAY	UNDECIMBER
DAY_OF_YEAR	MILLISECOND	WEDNESDAY
DECEMBER	MINUTE	WEEK_OF_MONTH
DST_OFFSET	MONDAY	WEEK_OF_YEAR
ERA	MONTH	YEAR
FEBRUARY	NOVEMBER	ZONE_OFFSET
FIELD_COUNT	OCTOBER	

The following program demonstrates several **Calendar** methods:

```
// Demonstrate Calendar
import java.util.Calendar;

class CalendarDemo {
  public static void main(String args[]) {
    String months[] = {
            "Jan", "Feb", "Mar", "Apr",
            "May", "Jun", "Jul", "Aug",
            "Sep", "Oct", "Nov", "Dec"};

    // Create a calendar initialized with the
    // current date and time in the default
    // locale and timezone.
    Calendar calendar = Calendar.getInstance();

    // Display current time and date information.
    System.out.print("Date: ");
    System.out.print(months[calendar.get(Calendar.MONTH)]);
    System.out.print(" " + calendar.get(Calendar.DATE) + " ");
    System.out.println(calendar.get(Calendar.YEAR));

    System.out.print("Time: ");
    System.out.print(calendar.get(Calendar.HOUR) + ":");
    System.out.print(calendar.get(Calendar.MINUTE) + ":");
    System.out.println(calendar.get(Calendar.SECOND));

    // Set the time and date information and display it.
    calendar.set(Calendar.HOUR, 10);
    calendar.set(Calendar.MINUTE, 29);
    calendar.set(Calendar.SECOND, 22);
```

```
    System.out.print("Updated time: ");
    System.out.print(calendar.get(Calendar.HOUR) + ":");
    System.out.print(calendar.get(Calendar.MINUTE) + ":");
    System.out.println(calendar.get(Calendar.SECOND));
  }
}
```

Sample output is shown here:

```
Date: Jan 1 2007
Time: 11:24:25
Updated time: 10:29:22
```

GregorianCalendar

GregorianCalendar is a concrete implementation of a **Calendar** that implements the normal Gregorian calendar with which you are familiar. The **getInstance( )** method of **Calendar** will typically return a **GregorianCalendar** initialized with the current date and time in the default locale and time zone.

GregorianCalendar defines two fields: **AD** and **BC**. These represent the two eras defined by the Gregorian calendar.

There are also several constructors for **GregorianCalendar** objects. The default, **GregorianCalendar( )**, initializes the object with the current date and time in the default locale and time zone. Three more constructors offer increasing levels of specificity:

GregorianCalendar(int *year*, int *month*, int *dayOfMonth*)
GregorianCalendar(int *year*, int *month*, int *dayOfMonth*, int *hours*,
                  int *minutes*)
GregorianCalendar(int *year*, int *month*, int *dayOfMonth*, int *hours*,
                  int *minutes*, int *seconds*)

All three versions set the day, month, and year. Here, *year* specifies the year. The month is specified by *month*, with zero indicating January. The day of the month is specified by *dayOfMonth*. The first version sets the time to midnight. The second version also sets the hours and the minutes. The third version adds seconds.

You can also construct a **GregorianCalendar** object by specifying the locale and/or time zone. The following constructors create objects initialized with the current date and time using the specified time zone and/or locale:

GregorianCalendar(Locale *locale*)
GregorianCalendar(TimeZone *timeZone*)
GregorianCalendar(TimeZone *timeZone*, Locale *locale*)

GregorianCalendar provides an implementation of all the abstract methods in **Calendar**. It also provides some additional methods. Perhaps the most interesting is **isLeapYear( )**, which tests if the year is a leap year. Its form is

boolean isLeapYear(int *year*)

This method returns **true** if *year* is a leap year and **false** otherwise.

The following program demonstrates **GregorianCalendar**:

```
// Demonstrate GregorianCalendar
import java.util.*;

class GregorianCalendarDemo {
  public static void main(String args[]) {
    String months[] = {
            "Jan", "Feb", "Mar", "Apr",
            "May", "Jun", "Jul", "Aug",
            "Sep", "Oct", "Nov", "Dec"};
    int year;

    // Create a Gregorian calendar initialized
    // with the current date and time in the
    // default locale and timezone.
    GregorianCalendar gcalendar = new GregorianCalendar();

    // Display current time and date information.
    System.out.print("Date: ");
    System.out.print(months[gcalendar.get(Calendar.MONTH)]);
    System.out.print(" " + gcalendar.get(Calendar.DATE) + " ");
    System.out.println(year = gcalendar.get(Calendar.YEAR));

    System.out.print("Time: ");
    System.out.print(gcalendar.get(Calendar.HOUR) + ":");
    System.out.print(gcalendar.get(Calendar.MINUTE) + ":");
    System.out.println(gcalendar.get(Calendar.SECOND));

    // Test if the current year is a leap year
    if(gcalendar.isLeapYear(year)) {
      System.out.println("The current year is a leap year");
    }
    else {
      System.out.println("The current year is not a leap year");
    }
  }
}
```

Sample output is shown here:

```
Date: Jan 1 2007
Time: 11:25:27
The current year is not a leap year
```

TimeZone

Another time-related class is **TimeZone**. The **TimeZone** class allows you to work with time zone offsets from Greenwich mean time (GMT), also referred to as Coordinated Universal Time (UTC). It also computes daylight saving time. **TimeZone** only supplies the default constructor.

A sampling of methods defined by **TimeZone** is given in Table 18-5.

Method	Description
Object clone( )	Returns a **TimeZone**-specific version of **clone( )**.
static String[ ] getAvailableIDs( )	Returns an array of **String** objects representing the names of all time zones.
static String[ ] getAvailableIDs(int *timeDelta*)	Returns an array of **String** objects representing the names of all time zones that are *timeDelta* offset from GMT.
static TimeZone getDefault( )	Returns a **TimeZone** object that represents the default time zone used on the host computer.
String getID( )	Returns the name of the invoking **TimeZone** object.
abstract int getOffset(int *era*, int *year*, int *month*, int *dayOfMonth*, int *dayOfWeek*, int *millisec*)	Returns the offset that should be added to GMT to compute local time. This value is adjusted for daylight saving time. The parameters to the method represent date and time components.
abstract int getRawOffset( )	Returns the raw offset that should be added to GMT to compute local time. This value is not adjusted for daylight saving time.
static TimeZone getTimeZone(String *tzName*)	Returns the **TimeZone** object for the time zone named *tzName*.
abstract boolean inDaylightTime(Date *d*)	Returns **true** if the date represented by *d* is in daylight saving time in the invoking object. Otherwise, it returns **false**.
static void setDefault(TimeZone *tz*)	Sets the default time zone to be used on this host. *tz* is a reference to the **TimeZone** object to be used.
void setID(String *tzName*)	Sets the name of the time zone (that is, its ID) to that specified by *tzName*.
abstract void setRawOffset(int *millis*)	Sets the offset in milliseconds from GMT.
abstract boolean useDaylightTime( )	Returns **true** if the invoking object uses daylight saving time. Otherwise, it returns **false**.

TABLE 18-5 Some of the Methods Defined by **TimeZone**

SimpleTimeZone

The **SimpleTimeZone** class is a convenient subclass of **TimeZone**. It implements **TimeZone**'s abstract methods and allows you to work with time zones for a Gregorian calendar. It also computes daylight saving time.

SimpleTimeZone defines four constructors. One is

SimpleTimeZone(int *timeDelta*, String *tzName*)

This constructor creates a **SimpleTimeZone** object. The offset relative to Greenwich mean time (GMT) is *timeDelta*. The time zone is named *tzName*.

The second **SimpleTimeZone** constructor is

SimpleTimeZone(int *timeDelta*, String *tzId*, int *dstMonth0*,
        int *dstDayInMonth0*, int *dstDay0*, int *time0*,
        int *dstMonth1*, int *dstDayInMonth1*, int *dstDay1*,
        int *time1*)

Here, the offset relative to GMT is specified in *timeDelta*. The time zone name is passed in *tzId*. The start of daylight saving time is indicated by the parameters *dstMonth0*, *dstDayInMonth0*, *dstDay0*, and *time0*. The end of daylight saving time is indicated by the parameters *dstMonth1*, *dstDayInMonth1*, *dstDay1*, and *time1*.

The third **SimpleTimeZone** constructor is

SimpleTimeZone(int *timeDelta*, String *tzId*, int *dstMonth0*,
        int *dstDayInMonth0*, int *dstDay0*, int *time0*,
        int *dstMonth1*, int *dstDayInMonth1*, int *dstDay1*,
        int *time1*, int *dstDelta*)

Here, *dstDelta* is the number of milliseconds saved during daylight saving time.

The fourth **SimpleTimeZone** constructor is

SimpleTimeZone(int *timeDelta*, String *tzId*, int *dstMonth0*,
        int *dstDayInMonth0*, int *dstDay0*, int *time0*,
        int *time0mode*, int *dstMonth1*, int *dstDayInMonth1*,
        int *dstDay1*, int *time1*, int *time1mode*, int *dstDelta*)

Here, *time0mode* specifies the mode of the starting time, and *time1mode* specifies the mode of the ending time. Valid mode values include

STANDARD_TIME	WALL_TIME	UTC_TIME

The time mode indicates how the time values are interpreted. The default mode used by the other constructors is **WALL_TIME**.

Locale

The **Locale** class is instantiated to produce objects that describe a geographical or cultural region. It is one of several classes that provide you with the ability to write programs that can execute in different international environments. For example, the formats used to display dates, times, and numbers are different in various regions.

Internationalization is a large topic that is beyond the scope of this book. However, many programs will only need to deal with its basics, which include setting the current locale.

The **Locale** class defines the following constants that are useful for dealing with the most common locales:

CANADA	GERMAN	KOREAN
CANADA_FRENCH	GERMANY	PRC

CHINA	ITALIAN	SIMPLIFIED_CHINESE
CHINESE	ITALY	TAIWAN
ENGLISH	JAPAN	TRADITIONAL_CHINESE
FRANCE	JAPANESE	UK
FRENCH	KOREA	US

For example, the expression **Locale.CANADA** represents the **Locale** object for Canada.
The constructors for **Locale** are

Locale(String *language*)
Locale(String *language*, String *country*)
Locale(String *language*, String *country*, String *data*)

These constructors build a **Locale** object to represent a specific *language* and in the case
of the last two, *country*. These values must contain ISO-standard language and country codes.
Auxiliary browser and vendor-specific information can be provided in *data*.
   Locale defines several methods. One of the most important is **setDefault( )**, shown here:

static void setDefault(Locale *localeObj*)

This sets the default locale to that specified by *localeObj*.
   Some other interesting methods are the following:

final String getDisplayCountry( )
final String getDisplayLanguage( )
final String getDisplayName( )

These return human-readable strings that can be used to display the name of the country,
the name of the language, and the complete description of the locale.
   The default locale can be obtained using **getDefault( )**, shown here:

static Locale getDefault( )

Calendar and **GregorianCalendar** are examples of classes that operate in a locale-
sensitive manner. **DateFormat** and **SimpleDateFormat** also depend on the locale.

Random

The **Random** class is a generator of pseudorandom numbers. These are called *pseudorandom*
numbers because they are simply uniformly distributed sequences. **Random** defines the
following constructors:

Random( )
Random(long *seed*)

The first version creates a number generator that uses the current time as the starting, or *seed*,
value. The second form allows you to specify a seed value manually.

Method	Description
boolean nextBoolean( )	Returns the next **boolean** random number.
void nextBytes(byte *vals*[ ])	Fills *vals* with randomly generated values.
double nextDouble( )	Returns the next **double** random number.
float nextFloat( )	Returns the next **float** random number.
double nextGaussian( )	Returns the next Gaussian random number.
int nextInt( )	Returns the next **int** random number.
int nextInt(int *n*)	Returns the next **int** random number within the range zero to *n*.
long nextLong( )	Returns the next **long** random number.
void setSeed(long *newSeed*)	Sets the seed value (that is, the starting point for the random number generator) to that specified by *newSeed*.

TABLE 18-6   The Methods Defined by **Random**

If you initialize a **Random** object with a seed, you define the starting point for the random sequence. If you use the same seed to initialize another **Random** object, you will extract the same random sequence. If you want to generate different sequences, specify different seed values. The easiest way to do this is to use the current time to seed a **Random** object. This approach reduces the possibility of getting repeated sequences.

The public methods defined by **Random** are shown in Table 18-6.

As you can see, there are seven types of random numbers that you can extract from a **Random** object. Random Boolean values are available from **nextBoolean( )**. Random bytes can be obtained by calling **nextBytes( )**. Integers can be extracted via the **nextInt( )** method. Long integers, uniformly distributed over their range, can be obtained with **nextLong( )**. The **nextFloat( )** and **nextDouble( )** methods return a uniformly distributed **float** and **double**, respectively, between 0.0 and 1.0. Finally, **nextGaussian( )** returns a **double** value centered at 0.0 with a standard deviation of 1.0. This is what is known as a *bell curve*.

Here is an example that demonstrates the sequence produced by **nextGaussian( )**. It obtains 100 random Gaussian values and averages these values. The program also counts the number of values that fall within two standard deviations, plus or minus, using increments of 0.5 for each category. The result is graphically displayed sideways on the screen.

```java
// Demonstrate random Gaussian values.
import java.util.Random;
class RandDemo {
  public static void main(String args[]) {
    Random r = new Random();
    double val;
    double sum = 0;
    int bell[] = new int[10];

    for(int i=0; i<100; i++) {
      val = r.nextGaussian();
      sum += val;
      double t = -2;
```

```
        for(int x=0; x<10; x++, t += 0.5)
          if(val < t) {
            bell[x]++;
            break;
          }
      }
      System.out.println("Average of values: " +
                              (sum/100));

      // display bell curve, sideways
      for(int i=0; i<10; i++) {
        for(int x=bell[i]; x>0; x--)
          System.out.print("*");
        System.out.println();
      }
    }
  }
}
```

Here is a sample program run. As you can see, a bell-like distribution of numbers is obtained.

```
Average of values: 0.0702235271133344
**
*******
******
**************
*****************
****************
*************
**********
********
***
```

Observable

The **Observable** class is used to create subclasses that other parts of your program can observe. When an object of such a subclass undergoes a change, observing classes are notified. Observing classes must implement the **Observer** interface, which defines the **update( )** method. The **update( )** method is called when an observer is notified of a change in an observed object.

Observable defines the methods shown in Table 18-7. An object that is being observed must follow two simple rules. First, if it has changed, it must call **setChanged( )**. Second, when it is ready to notify observers of this change, it must call **notifyObservers( )**. This causes the **update( )** method in the observing object(s) to be called. Be careful—if the object calls **notifyObservers( )** without having previously called **setChanged( )**, no action will take place. The observed object must call both **setChanged( )** and **notifyObservers( )** before **update( )** will be called.

Notice that **notifyObservers( )** has two forms: one that takes an argument and one that does not. If you call **notifyObservers( )** with an argument, this object is passed to the observer's **update( )** method as its second parameter. Otherwise, **null** is passed to **update( )**. You can use the second parameter for passing any type of object that is appropriate for your application.

Method	Description
void addObserver(Observer *obj*)	Adds *obj* to the list of objects observing the invoking object.
protected void clearChanged( )	Calling this method returns the status of the invoking object to "unchanged."
int countObservers( )	Returns the number of objects observing the invoking object.
void deleteObserver(Observer *obj*)	Removes *obj* from the list of objects observing the invoking object.
void deleteObservers( )	Removes all observers for the invoking object.
boolean hasChanged( )	Returns **true** if the invoking object has been modified and **false** if it has not.
void notifyObservers( )	Notifies all observers of the invoking object that it has changed by calling **update( )**. A **null** is passed as the second argument to **update( )**.
void notifyObservers(Object *obj*)	Notifies all observers of the invoking object that it has changed by calling **update( )**. *obj* is passed as an argument to **update( )**.
protected void setChanged( )	Called when the invoking object has changed.

TABLE 18-7   The Methods Defined by **Observable**

The Observer Interface

To observe an observable object, you must implement the **Observer** interface. This interface defines only the one method shown here:

> void update(Observable *observOb*, Object *arg*)

Here, *observOb* is the object being observed, and *arg* is the value passed by **notifyObservers( )**. The **update( )** method is called when a change in the observed object takes place.

An Observer Example

Here is an example that demonstrates an observable object. It creates an observer class, called **Watcher**, that implements the **Observer** interface. The class being monitored is called **BeingWatched**. It extends **Observable**. Inside **BeingWatched** is the method **counter( )**, which simply counts down from a specified value. It uses **sleep( )** to wait a tenth of a second between counts. Each time the count changes, **notifyObservers( )** is called with the current count passed as its argument. This causes the **update( )** method inside **Watcher** to be called, which displays the current count. Inside **main( )**, a **Watcher** and a **BeingWatched** object, called **observing** and **observed**, respectively, are created. Then, **observing** is added to the list of observers for **observed**. This means that **observing.update( )** will be called each time **counter( )** calls **notifyObservers( )**.

```
/* Demonstrate the Observable class and the
   Observer interface.
*/
```

```java
import java.util.*;

// This is the observing class.
class Watcher implements Observer {
  public void update(Observable obj, Object arg) {
    System.out.println("update() called, count is " +
                       ((Integer)arg).intValue());
  }
}

/ This is the class being observed.
class BeingWatched extends Observable {
  void counter(int period) {
    for( ; period >=0; period--) {
      setChanged();
      notifyObservers(new Integer(period));
      try {
        Thread.sleep(100);
      } catch(InterruptedException e) {
        System.out.println("Sleep interrupted");
      }
    }
  }
}

class ObserverDemo {
  public static void main(String args[]) {
    BeingWatched observed = new BeingWatched();
    Watcher observing = new Watcher();

    /* Add the observing to the list of observers for
       observed object.  */
    observed.addObserver(observing);

    observed.counter(10);
  }
}
```

The output from this program is shown here:

```
update() called, count is 10
update() called, count is 9
update() called, count is 8
update() called, count is 7
update() called, count is 6
update() called, count is 5
update() called, count is 4
update() called, count is 3
update() called, count is 2
update() called, count is 1
update() called, count is 0
```

More than one object can be an observer. For example, the following program implements two observing classes and adds an object of each class to the **BeingWatched** observer list. The second observer waits until the count reaches zero and then rings the bell.

```
/* An object may be observed by two or more
   observers.
*/

import java.util.*;

// This is the first observing class.
class Watcher1 implements Observer {
  public void update(Observable obj, Object arg) {
    System.out.println("update() called, count is " +
                        ((Integer)arg).intValue());
  }
}

// This is the second observing class.
class Watcher2 implements Observer {
  public void update(Observable obj, Object arg) {
    // Ring bell when done
    if(((Integer)arg).intValue() == 0)
      System.out.println("Done" + '\7');
  }
}

// This is the class being observed.
class BeingWatched extends Observable {
  void counter(int period) {
    for( ; period >=0; period--) {
      setChanged();
      notifyObservers(new Integer(period));
      try {
        Thread.sleep(100);
      } catch(InterruptedException e) {
        System.out.println("Sleep interrupted");
      }
    }
  }
}

class TwoObservers {
  public static void main(String args[]) {
    BeingWatched observed = new BeingWatched();
    Watcher1 observing1 = new Watcher1();
    Watcher2 observing2 = new Watcher2();

    // add both observers
    observed.addObserver(observing1);
    observed.addObserver(observing2);

    observed.counter(10);
  }
}
```

The **Observable** class and the **Observer** interface allow you to implement sophisticated program architectures based on the document/view methodology. They are also useful in multithreaded situations.

Timer and TimerTask

An interesting and useful feature offered by **java.util** is the ability to schedule a task for execution at some future time. The classes that support this are **Timer** and **TimerTask**. Using these classes, you can create a thread that runs in the background, waiting for a specific time. When the time arrives, the task linked to that thread is executed. Various options allow you to schedule a task for repeated execution, and to schedule a task to run on a specific date. Although it was always possible to manually create a task that would be executed at a specific time using the **Thread** class, **Timer** and **TimerTask** greatly simplify this process.

Timer and **TimerTask** work together. **Timer** is the class that you will use to schedule a task for execution. The task being scheduled must be an instance of **TimerTask**. Thus, to schedule a task, you will first create a **TimerTask** object and then schedule it for execution using an instance of **Timer**.

TimerTask implements the **Runnable** interface; thus, it can be used to create a thread of execution. Its constructor is shown here:

TimerTask( )

TimerTask defines the methods shown in Table 18-8. Notice that **run( )** is abstract, which means that it must be overridden. The **run( )** method, defined by the **Runnable** interface, contains the code that will be executed. Thus, the easiest way to create a timer task is to extend **TimerTask** and override **run( )**.

Once a task has been created, it is scheduled for execution by an object of type **Timer**. The constructors for **Timer** are shown here:

Timer( )
Timer(boolean *DThread*)
Timer(String *tName*)
Timer(String *tName*, boolean *DThread*)

The first version creates a **Timer** object that runs as a normal thread. The second uses a daemon thread if *DThread* is **true**. A daemon thread will execute only as long as the rest of the program continues to execute. The third and fourth constructors allow you to specify a name for the **Timer** thread. The methods defined by **Timer** are shown in Table 18-9.

Method	Description
boolean cancel( )	Terminates the task. Returns **true** if an execution of the task is prevented. Otherwise, returns **false**.
abstract void run( )	Contains the code for the timer task.
long scheduledExecutionTime( )	Returns the time at which the last execution of the task was scheduled to have occurred.

TABLE 18-8   The Methods Defined by **TimerTask**

Method	Description
void cancel( )	Cancels the timer thread.
int purge( )	Deletes cancelled tasks from the timer's queue.
void schedule(TimerTask *TTask*, long *wait*)	*TTask* is scheduled for execution after the period passed in *wait* has elapsed. The *wait* parameter is specified in milliseconds.
void schedule(TimerTask *TTask*, long *wait*, long *repeat*)	*TTask* is scheduled for execution after the period passed in *wait* has elapsed. The task is then executed repeatedly at the interval specified by *repeat*. Both *wait* and *repeat* are specified in milliseconds.
void schedule(TimerTask *TTask*, Date *targetTime*)	*TTask* is scheduled for execution at the time specified by *targetTime*.
void schedule(TimerTask *TTask*, Date *targetTime*, long *repeat*)	*TTask* is scheduled for execution at the time specified by *targetTime*. The task is then executed repeatedly at the interval passed in *repeat*. The *repeat* parameter is specified in milliseconds.
void scheduleAtFixedRate(TimerTask *TTask*, long *wait*, long *repeat*)	*TTask* is scheduled for execution after the period passed in *wait* has elapsed. The task is then executed repeatedly at the interval specified by *repeat*. Both *wait* and *repeat* are specified in milliseconds. The time of each repetition is relative to the first execution, not the preceding execution. Thus, the overall rate of execution is fixed.
void scheduleAtFixedRate(TimerTask *TTask*, Date *targetTime*, long *repeat*)	*TTask* is scheduled for execution at the time specified by *targetTime*. The task is then executed repeatedly at the interval passed in *repeat*. The *repeat* parameter is specified in milliseconds. The time of each repetition is relative to the first execution, not the preceding execution. Thus, the overall rate of execution is fixed.

TABLE 18-9   The Methods Defined by **Timer**

Once a **Timer** has been created, you will schedule a task by calling **schedule( )** on the **Timer** that you created. As Table 18-9 shows, there are several forms of **schedule( )** which allow you to schedule tasks in a variety of ways.

If you create a non-daemon task, then you will want to call **cancel( )** to end the task when your program ends. If you don't do this, then your program may "hang" for a period of time.

The following program demonstrates **Timer** and **TimerTask**. It defines a timer task whose **run( )** method displays the message "Timer task executed." This task is scheduled to run once every half second after an initial delay of one second.

```
// Demonstrate Timer and TimerTask.

import java.util.*;

class MyTimerTask extends TimerTask {
```

```
    public void run() {
      System.out.println("Timer task executed.");
    }
}

class TTest {
  public static void main(String args[]) {
    MyTimerTask myTask = new MyTimerTask();
    Timer myTimer = new Timer();

    /* Set an initial delay of 1 second,
       then repeat every half second.
    */
    myTimer.schedule(myTask, 1000, 500);

    try {
      Thread.sleep(5000);
    } catch (InterruptedException exc) {}

    myTimer.cancel();
  }
}
```

Currency

The **Currency** class encapsulates information about a currency. It defines no constructors. The methods supported by **Currency** are shown in Table 18-10. The following program demonstrates **Currency**:

```
// Demonstrate Currency.
import java.util.*;

class CurDemo {
  public static void main(String args[]) {
    Currency c;

    c = Currency.getInstance(Locale.US);

    System.out.println("Symbol: " + c.getSymbol());
    System.out.println("Default fractional digits: " +
                        c.getDefaultFractionDigits());
  }
}
```

The output is shown here:

```
Symbol: $
Default fractional digits: 2
```

Method	Description
String getCurrencyCode( )	Returns the code (as defined by ISO 4217) that describes the invoking currency.
int getDefaultFractionDigits( )	Returns the number of digits after the decimal point that are normally used by the invoking currency. For example, there are 2 fractional digits normally used for dollars.
static Currency getInstance(Locale *localeObj*)	Returns a **Currency** object for the locale specified by *localeObj*.
static Currency getInstance(String *code*)	Returns a **Currency** object associated with the currency code passed in *code*.
String getSymbol( )	Returns the currency symbol (such as $) for the invoking object.
String getSymbol(Locale *localeObj*)	Returns the currency symbol (such as $) for the locale passed in *localeObj*.
String toString( )	Returns the currency code for the invoking object.

TABLE 18-10   The Methods Defined by **Currency**

Formatter

With the release of JDK 5, Java added a capability long desired by programmers: the ability to easily create formatted output. Since the beginning, Java has offered a rich and varied API, but it had not always offered an easy way to create formatted text output, especially for numeric values. Classes such as **NumberFormat**, **DateFormat**, and **MessageFormat** provided by earlier versions of Java do have useful formatting capabilities, but they were not especially convenient to use. Furthermore, unlike C and C++ that support the widely understood and used **printf( )** family of functions which offers a simple way to format output, Java had previously not offered such methods. One reason for this is that **printf**-style formatting requires the use of variable-length arguments (varargs), which Java did not support until the release of JDK 5. Once varargs were available, it was a simple matter to add a general-purpose formatter.

At the core of Java's support for creating formatted output is the **Formatter** class. It provides *format conversions* that let you display numbers, strings, and time and date in virtually any format you like. It operates in a manner similar to the C/C++ **printf( )** function, which means that if you are familiar with C/C++, then learning to use **Formatter** will be very easy. It also further streamlines the conversion of C/C++ code to Java. If you are not familiar with C/C++, it is still quite easy to format data.

NOTE   *Although Java's **Formatter** class operates in a manner very similar to the C/C++ **printf( )** function, there are some differences, and some new features. Therefore, if you have a C/C++ background, a careful reading is advised.*

The Formatter Constructors

Before you can use **Formatter** to format output, you must create a **Formatter** object. In general, **Formatter** works by converting the binary form of data used by a program into formatted text. It stores the formatted text in a buffer, the contents of which can be obtained by your program whenever they are needed. It is possible to let **Formatter** supply this buffer automatically, or you can specify the buffer explicitly when a **Formatter** object is created. It is also possible to have **Formatter** output its buffer to a file.

The **Formatter** class defines many constructors, which enable you to construct a **Formatter** in a variety of ways. Here is a sampling:

Formatter( )

Formatter(Appendable *buf*)

Formatter(Appendable *buf*, Locale *loc*)

Formatter(String *filename*)
   throws FileNotFoundException

Formatter(String *filename*, String *charset*)
   throws FileNotFoundException, UnsupportedEncodingException

Formatter(File *outF*)
   throws FileNotFoundException

Formatter(OutputStream *outStrm*)

Here, *buf* specifies a buffer for the formatted output. If *buf* is null, then **Formatter** automatically allocates a **StringBuilder** to hold the formatted output. The *loc* parameter specifies a locale. If no locale is specified, the default locale is used. The *filename* parameter specifies the name of a file that will receive the formatted output. The *charset* parameter specifies the character set. If no character set is specified, then the default character set is used. The *outF* parameter specifies a reference to an open file that will receive output. The *outStrm* parameter specifies a reference to an output stream that will receive output. When using a file, output is also written to the file.

Perhaps the most widely used constructor is the first, which has no parameters. It automatically uses the default locale and allocates a **StringBuilder** to hold the formatted output.

The Formatter Methods

Formatter defines the methods shown in Table 18-11.

Formatting Basics

After you have created a **Formatter**, you can use it to create a formatted string. To do so, use the **format( )** method. The most commonly used version is shown here:

Formatter format(String *fmtString*, Object ... *args*)

Method	Description
void close( )	Closes the invoking **Formatter**. This causes any resources used by the object to be released. After a **Formatter** has been closed, it cannot be reused. An attempt to use a closed **Formatter** results in a **FormatterClosedException**.
void flush( )	Flushes the format buffer. This causes any output currently in the buffer to be written to the destination. This applies mostly to a **Formatter** tied to a file.
Formatter format(String *fmtString*, Object ... *args*)	Formats the arguments passed via *args* according to the format specifiers contained in *fmtString*. Returns the invoking object.
Formatter format(Locale *loc*, String *fmtString*, Object ... *args*)	Formats the arguments passed via *args* according to the format specifiers contained in *fmtString*. The locale specified by *loc* is used for this format. Returns the invoking object.
IOException ioException( )	If the underlying object that is the destination for output throws an **IOException**, then this exception is returned. Otherwise, null is returned.
Locale locale( )	Returns the invoking object's locale.
Appendable out( )	Returns a reference to the underlying object that is the destination for output.
String toString( )	Returns a **String** containing the formatted output.

TABLE 18-11 The Methods Defined by **Formatter**

The *fmtSring* consists of two types of items. The first type is composed of characters that are simply copied to the output buffer. The second type contains *format specifiers* that define the way the subsequent arguments are displayed.

In its simplest form, a format specifier begins with a percent sign followed by the format *conversion specifier*. All format conversion specifiers consist of a single character. For example, the format specifier for floating-point data is **%f**. In general, there must be the same number of arguments as there are format specifiers, and the format specifiers and the arguments are matched in order from left to right. For example, consider this fragment:

```
Formatter fmt = new Formatter();
fmt.format("Formatting %s is easy %d %f", "with Java", 10, 98.6);
```

This sequence creates a **Formatter** that contains the following string:

```
Formatting with Java is easy 10 98.600000
```

In this example, the format specifiers, **%s**, **%d**, and **%f**, are replaced with the arguments that follow the format string. Thus, **%s** is replaced by "with Java", **%d** is replaced by 10, and **%f** is replaced by 98.6. All other characters are simply used as-is. As you might guess, the format specifier **%s** specifies a string, and **%d** specifies an integer value. As mentioned earlier, the **%f** specifies a floating-point value.

TABLE 18-12
The Format
Specifiers

Format Specifier	Conversion Applied
%a %A	Floating-point hexadecimal
%b %B	Boolean
%c	Character
%d	Decimal integer
%h %H	Hash code of the argument
%e %E	Scientific notation
%f	Decimal floating-point
%g %G	Uses **%e** or **%f**, whichever is shorter
%o	Octal integer
%n	Inserts a newline character
%s %S	String
%t %T	Time and date
%x %X	Integer hexadecimal
%%	Inserts a % sign

The **format( )** method accepts a wide variety of format specifiers, which are shown in Table 18-12. Notice that many specifiers have both upper- and lowercase forms. When an uppercase specifier is used, then letters are shown in uppercase. Otherwise, the upper- and lowercase specifiers perform the same conversion. It is important to understand that Java type-checks each format specifier against its corresponding argument. If the argument doesn't match, an **IllegalFormatException** is thrown.

Once you have formatted a string, you can obtain it by calling **toString( )**. For example, continuing with the preceding example, the following statement obtains the formatted string contained in **fmt**:

```
String str = fmt.toString();
```

Of course, if you simply want to display the formatted string, there is no reason to first assign it to a **String** object. When a **Formatter** object is passed to **println( )**, for example, its **toString( )** method is automatically called.

Here is a short program that puts together all of the pieces, showing how to create and display a formatted string:

```
// A very simple example that uses Formatter.
import java.util.*;

class FormatDemo {
  public static void main(String args[]) {
    Formatter fmt = new Formatter();

    fmt.format("Formatting %s is easy %d %f", "with Java", 10, 98.6);

    System.out.println(fmt);
  }
}
```

One other point: You can obtain a reference to the underlying output buffer by calling **out( )**. It returns a reference to an **Appendable** object.

Now that you know the general mechanism used to create a formatted string, the remainder of this section discusses in detail each conversion. It also describes various options, such as justification, minimum field width, and precision.

Formatting Strings and Characters

To format an individual character, use **%c**. This causes the matching character argument to be output, unmodified. To format a string, use **%s**.

Formatting Numbers

To format an integer in decimal format, use **%d**. To format a floating-point value in decimal format, use **%f**. To format a floating-point value in scientific notation, use **%e**. Numbers represented in scientific notation take this general form:

$$x.ddddd\text{d}e+/-yy$$

The **%g** format specifier causes **Formatter** to use either **%f** or **%e**, whichever is shorter. The following program demonstrates the effect of the **%g** format specifier:

```
// Demonstrate the %g format specifier.
import java.util.*;

class FormatDemo2 {
  public static void main(String args[]) {
    Formatter fmt = new Formatter();

    for(double i=1000; i < 1.0e+10; i *= 100) {
      fmt.format("%g ", i);
      System.out.println(fmt);
    }

  }
}
```

It produces the following output:

```
1000.000000
1000.000000 100000.000000
1000.000000 100000.000000 1.000000e+07
1000.000000 100000.000000 1.000000e+07 1.000000e+09
```

You can display integers in octal or hexadecimal format by using **%o** and **%x**, respectively. For example, this fragment:

```
fmt.format("Hex: %x, Octal: %o", 196, 196);
```

produces this output:

```
Hex: c4, Octal: 304
```

You can display floating-point values in hexadecimal format by using **%a**. The format produced by **%a** appears a bit strange at first glance. This is because its representation uses a form similar to scientific notation that consists of a significand and an exponent, both in hexadecimal. Here is the general format:

0x1.*sigpexp*

Here, *sig* contains the fractional portion of the significand and *exp* contains the exponent. The **p** indicates the start of the exponent. For example, this call:

```
fmt.format("%a", 123.123);
```

produces this output:

```
0x1.ec7df3b645a1dp6
```

Formatting Time and Date

One of the more powerful conversion specifiers is **%t**. It lets you format time and date information. The **%t** specifier works a bit differently than the others because it requires the use of a suffix to describe the portion and precise format of the time or date desired. The suffixes are shown in Table 18-13. For example, to display minutes, you would use **%tM**, where **M** indicates minutes in a two-character field. The argument corresponding to the **%t** specifier must be of type **Calendar**, **Date**, **Long**, or **long**.

Here is a program that demonstrates several of the formats:

```
// Formatting time and date.
import java.util.*;

class TimeDateFormat {
  public static void main(String args[]) {
    Formatter fmt = new Formatter();
    Calendar cal = Calendar.getInstance();
```

```
    // Display standard 12-hour time format.
    fmt.format("%tr", cal);
    System.out.println(fmt);

    // Display complete time and date information.
    fmt = new Formatter();
    fmt.format("%tc", cal);
    System.out.println(fmt);

    // Display just hour and minute.
    fmt = new Formatter();
    fmt.format("%tl:%tM", cal, cal);
    System.out.println(fmt);

    // Display month by name and number.
    fmt = new Formatter();
    fmt.format("%tB %tb %tm", cal, cal, cal);
    System.out.println(fmt);
  }
}
```

Sample output is shown here:

```
09:17:15 AM
Mon Jan 01 09:17:15 CST 2007
9:17
January Jan 01
```

	Suffix	Replaced By
TABLE 18-13 The Time and Date Format Suffixes	a	Abbreviated weekday name
	A	Full weekday name
	b	Abbreviated month name
	B	Full month name
	c	Standard date and time string formatted as *day month date hh::mm:ss tzone year*
	C	First two digits of year
	d	Day of month as a decimal (01–31)
	D	month/day/year
	e	Day of month as a decimal (1–31)
	F	year-month-day
	h	Abbreviated month name
	H	Hour (00 to 23)
	I	Hour (01 to 12)
	j	Day of year as a decimal (001 to 366)
	k	Hour (0 to 23)
	l	Hour (1 to 12)

PART II

Suffix	Replaced By
L	Millisecond (000 to 999)
m	Month as decimal (01 to 13)
M	Minute as decimal (00 to 59)
N	Nanosecond (000000000 to 999999999)
p	Locale's equivalent of AM or PM in lowercase
Q	Milliseconds from 1/1/1970
r	*hh:mm:ss* (12-hour format)
R	*hh:mm* (24-hour format)
S	Seconds (00 to 60)
s	Seconds from 1/1/1970 UTC
T	*hh:mm:ss* (24-hour format)
y	Year in decimal without century (00 to 99)
Y	Year in decimal including century (0001 to 9999)
z	Offset from UTC
Z	Time zone name

The %n and %% Specifiers

The **%n** and **%%** format specifiers differ from the others in that they do not match an argument. Instead, they are simply escape sequences that insert a character into the output sequence. The **%n** inserts a newline. The **%%** inserts a percent sign. Neither of these characters can be entered directly into the format string. Of course, you can also use the standard escape sequence \n to embed a newline character.

Here is an example that demonstrates the **%n** and **%%** format specifiers:

```
// Demonstrate the %n and %% format specifiers.
import java.util.*;

class FormatDemo3 {
  public static void main(String args[]) {
    Formatter fmt = new Formatter();

    fmt.format("Copying file%nTransfer is %d%% complete", 88);
    System.out.println(fmt);
  }
}
```

It displays the following output:

```
Copying file
Transfer is 88% complete
```

Specifying a Minimum Field Width

An integer placed between the % sign and the format conversion code acts as a *minimum field-width specifier.* This pads the output with spaces to ensure that it reaches a certain minimum length. If the string or number is longer than that minimum, it will still be printed in full. The default padding is done with spaces. If you want to pad with 0's, place a 0 before the field-width specifier. For example, **%05d** will pad a number of less than five digits with 0's so that its total length is five. The field-width specifier can be used with all format specifiers except **%n**.

The following program demonstrates the minimum field-width specifier by applying it to the **%f** conversion:

```
// Demonstrate a field-width specifier.
import java.util.*;

class FormatDemo4 {
  public static void main(String args[]) {
    Formatter fmt = new Formatter();

    fmt.format("|%f|%n|%12f|%n|%012f|",
               10.12345, 10.12345, 10.12345);

    System.out.println(fmt);

  }
}
```

This program produces the following output:

```
|10.123450|
|   10.123450|
|00010.123450|
```

The first line displays the number 10.12345 in its default width. The second line displays that value in a 12-character field. The third line displays the value in a 12-character field, padded with leading zeros.

The minimum field-width modifier is often used to produce tables in which the columns line up. For example, the next program produces a table of squares and cubes for the numbers between 1 and 10:

```
// Create a table of squares and cubes.
import java.util.*;

class FieldWidthDemo {
  public static void main(String args[]) {
    Formatter fmt;

    for(int i=1; i <= 10; i++) {
      fmt = new Formatter();
```

PART II

```
    fmt.format("%4d %4d %4d", i, i*i, i*i*i);
    System.out.println(fmt);
  }


 }
}
```

Its output is shown here:

```
 1    1    1
 2    4    8
 3    9   27
 4   16   64
 5   25  125
 6   36  216
 7   49  343
 8   64  512
 9   81  729
10  100 1000
```

Specifying Precision

A *precision specifier* can be applied to the **%f**, **%e**, **%g**, and **%s** format specifiers. It follows the minimum field-width specifier (if there is one) and consists of a period followed by an integer. Its exact meaning depends upon the type of data to which it is applied.

When you apply the precision specifier to floating-point data using the **%f** or **%e** specifiers, it determines the number of decimal places displayed. For example, **%10.4f** displays a number at least ten characters wide with four decimal places. When using **%g**, the precision determines the number of significant digits. The default precision is 6.

Applied to strings, the precision specifier specifies the maximum field length. For example, **%5.7s** displays a string at least five and not exceeding seven characters long. If the string is longer than the maximum field width, the end characters will be truncated.

The following program illustrates the precision specifier:

```
// Demonstrate the precision modifier.
import java.util.*;

class PrecisionDemo {
  public static void main(String args[]) {
    Formatter fmt = new Formatter();

    // Format 4 decimal places.
    fmt.format("%.4f", 123.1234567);
    System.out.println(fmt);

    // Format to 2 decimal places in a 16 character field.
    fmt = new Formatter();
    fmt.format("%16.2e", 123.1234567);
    System.out.println(fmt);

    // Display at most 15 characters in a string.
    fmt = new Formatter();
```

```
      fmt.format("%.15s", "Formatting with Java is now easy.");
      System.out.println(fmt);
  }
}
```

It produces the following output:

```
123.1235
         1.23e+02
Formatting with
```

Using the Format Flags

Formatter recognizes a set of format *flags* that lets you control various aspects of a conversion. All format flags are single characters, and a format flag follows the % in a format specification. The flags are shown here:

Flag	Effect
–	Left justification
#	Alternate conversion format
0	Output is padded with zeros rather than spaces
space	Positive numeric output is preceded by a space
+	Positive numeric output is preceded by a + sign
,	Numeric values include grouping separators
(	Negative numeric values are enclosed within parentheses

Not all flags apply to all format specifiers. The following sections explain each in detail.

Justifying Output

By default, all output is right-justified. That is, if the field width is larger than the data printed, the data will be placed on the right edge of the field. You can force output to be left-justified by placing a minus sign directly after the %. For instance, **%–10.2f** left-justifies a floating-point number with two decimal places in a 10-character field. For example, consider this program:

```
// Demonstrate left justification.
import java.util.*;

class LeftJustify {
  public static void main(String args[]) {
    Formatter fmt = new Formatter();

    // Right justify by default
    fmt.format("|%10.2f|", 123.123);
    System.out.println(fmt);

    // Now, left justify.
    fmt = new Formatter();
```

```
    fmt.format("|%-10.2f|", 123.123);
    System.out.println(fmt);
  }
}
```

It produces the following output:

```
|    123.12|
|123.12    |
```

As you can see, the second line is left-justified within a 10-character field.

The Space, +, 0, and (Flags

To cause a + sign to be shown before positive numeric values, add the + flag. For example,

```
fmt.format("%+d", 100);
```

creates this string:

```
+100
```

When creating columns of numbers, it is sometimes useful to output a space before positive values so that positive and negative values line up. To do this, add the space flag. For example,

```
// Demonstrate the space format specifiers.
import java.util.*;

class FormatDemo5 {
  public static void main(String args[]) {
    Formatter fmt = new Formatter();

    fmt.format("% d", -100);
    System.out.println(fmt);

    fmt = new Formatter();
    fmt.format("% d", 100);
    System.out.println(fmt);

    fmt = new Formatter();
    fmt.format("% d", -200);
    System.out.println(fmt);

    fmt = new Formatter();
    fmt.format("% d", 200);
    System.out.println(fmt);
  }
}
```

The output is shown here:

```
-100
 100
-200
 200
```

Notice that the positive values have a leading space, which causes the digits in the column to line up properly.

To show negative numeric output inside parentheses, rather than with a leading –, use the **(** flag. For example,

```
fmt.format("%(d", -100);
```

creates this string:

```
(100)
```

The 0 flag causes output to be padded with zeros rather than spaces.

The Comma Flag

When displaying large numbers, it is often useful to add grouping separators, which in English are commas. For example, the value 1234567 is more easily read when formatted as 1,234,567. To add grouping specifiers, use the comma (,) flag. For example,

```
fmt.format("%,.2f", 4356783497.34);
```

creates this string:

```
4,356,783,497.34
```

The # Flag

The **#** can be applied to **%o**, **%x**, **%e**, and **%f**. For **%e** and **%f**, the **#** ensures that there will be a decimal point even if there are no decimal digits. If you precede the **%x** format specifier with a **#**, the hexadecimal number will be printed with a **0x** prefix. Preceding the **%o** specifier with **#** causes the number to be printed with a leading zero.

The Uppercase Option

As mentioned earlier, several of the format specifiers have uppercase versions that cause the conversion to use uppercase where appropriate. The following table describes the effect.

Specifier	Effect
%A	Causes the hexadecimal digits *a* through *f* to be displayed in uppercase as *A* through *F*. Also, the prefix **0x** is displayed as **0X**, and the **p** will be displayed as **P**.
%B	Uppercases the values **true** and **false**.

Specifier	Effect
%E	Causes the *e* symbol that indicates the exponent to be displayed in uppercase.
%G	Causes the *e* symbol that indicates the exponent to be displayed in uppercase.
%H	Causes the hexadecimal digits *a* through *f* to be displayed in uppercase as *A* through *F*.
%S	Uppercases the corresponding string.
%T	Causes all alphabetical output to be displayed in uppercase.
%X	Causes the hexadecimal digits *a* through *f* to be displayed in uppercase as *A* through *F*. Also, the optional prefix **0x** is displayed as **0X**, if present.

For example, this call:

```
fmt.format("%X", 250);
```

creates this string:

```
FA
```

This call:

```
fmt.format("%E", 123.1234);
```

creates this string:

```
1.231234E+02
```

Using an Argument Index

Formatter includes a very useful feature that lets you specify the argument to which a format specifier applies. Normally, format specifiers and arguments are matched in order, from left to right. That is, the first format specifier matches the first argument, the second format specifier matches the second argument, and so on. However, by using an *argument index,* you can explicitly control which argument a format specifier matches.

An argument index immediately follows the % in a format specifier. It has the following format:

n$

where *n* is the index of the desired argument, beginning with 1. For example, consider this example:

```
fmt.format("%3$d %1$d %2$d", 10, 20, 30);
```

It produces this string:

```
30 10 20
```

In this example, the first format specifier matches 30, the second matches 10, and the third matches 20. Thus, the arguments are used in an order other than strictly left to right.

One advantage of argument indexes is that they enable you to reuse an argument without having to specify it twice. For example, consider this line:

```
fmt.format("%d in hex is %1$x", 255);
```

It produces the following string:

```
255 in hex is ff
```

As you can see, the argument 255 is used by both format specifiers.

There is a convenient shorthand called a *relative index* that enables you to reuse the argument matched by the preceding format specifier. Simply specify < for the argument index. For example, the following call to **format( )** produces the same results as the previous example:

```
fmt.format("%d in hex is %<x", 255);
```

Relative indexes are especially useful when creating custom time and date formats. Consider the following example:

```
// Use relative indexes to simplify the
// creation of a custom time and date format.
import java.util.*;

class FormatDemo6 {
  public static void main(String args[]) {
    Formatter fmt = new Formatter();
    Calendar cal = Calendar.getInstance();

    fmt.format("Today is day %te of %<tB, %<tY", cal);
    System.out.println(fmt);
  }
}
```

Here is sample output:

```
Today is day 1 of Jan, 2007
```

Because of relative indexing, the argument **cal** need only be passed once, rather than three times.

The Java printf( ) Connection

Although there is nothing technically wrong with using **Formatter** directly (as the preceding examples have done) when creating output that will be displayed on the console, there is a more convenient alternative: the **printf( )** method. The **printf( )** method automatically uses **Formatter** to create a formatted string. It then displays that string on **System.out**, which is the console by default. The **printf( )** method is defined by both **PrintStream** and **PrintWriter**. The **printf( )** method is described in Chapter 19.

Scanner

Scanner is the complement of **Formatter**. Added by JDK 5, **Scanner** reads formatted input and converts it into its binary form. Although it has always been possible to read formatted input, it required more effort than most programmers would prefer. Because of the addition of **Scanner**, it is now easy to read all types of numeric values, strings, and other types of data, whether it comes from a disk file, the keyboard, or another source.

Scanner can be used to read input from the console, a file, a string, or any source that implements the **Readable** interface or **ReadableByteChannel**. For example, you can use **Scanner** to read a number from the keyboard and assign its value to a variable. As you will see, given its power, **Scanner** is surprisingly easy to use.

The Scanner Constructors

Scanner defines the constructors shown in Table 18-14. In general, a **Scanner** can be created for a **String**, an **InputStream**, a **File**, or any object that implements the **Readable** or **ReadableByteChannel** interfaces. Here are some examples.

The following sequence creates a **Scanner** that reads the file **Test.txt**:

```
FileReader fin = new FileReader("Test.txt");
Scanner src = new Scanner(fin);
```

This works because **FileReader** implements the **Readable** interface. Thus, the call to the constructor resolves to **Scanner(Readable)**.

Method	Description
Scanner(File *from*) throws FileNotFoundException	Creates a **Scanner** that uses the file specified by *from* as a source for input.
Scanner(File *from*, String *charset*) throws FileNotFoundException	Creates a **Scanner** that uses the file specified by *from* with the encoding specified by *charset* as a source for input.
Scanner(InputStream *from*)	Creates a **Scanner** that uses the stream specified by *from* as a source for input.
Scanner(InputStream *from*, String *charset*)	Creates a **Scanner** that uses the stream specified by *from* with the encoding specified by *charset* as a source for input.
Scanner(Readable *from*)	Creates a **Scanner** that uses the **Readable** object specified by *from* as a source for input.
Scanner (ReadableByteChannel *from*)	Creates a **Scanner** that uses the **ReadableByteChannel** specified by *from* as a source for input.
Scanner(ReadableByteChannel *from*, String *charset*)	Creates a **Scanner** that uses the **ReadableByteChannel** specified by *from* with the encoding specified by *charset* as a source for input.
Scanner(String *from*)	Creates a **Scanner** that uses the string specified by *from* as a source for input.

TABLE 18-14   The **Scanner** Constructors

This next line creates a **Scanner** that reads from standard input, which is the keyboard by default:

```
Scanner conin = new Scanner(System.in);
```

This works because **System.in** is an object of type **InputStream**. Thus, the call to the constructor maps to **Scanner(InputStream)**.

The next sequence creates a **Scanner** that reads from a string.

```
String instr = "10 99.88 scanning is easy.";
Scanner conin = new Scanner(instr);
```

Scanning Basics

Once you have created a **Scanner**, it is a simple matter to use it to read formatted input. In general, a **Scanner** reads *tokens* from the underlying source that you specified when the **Scanner** was created. As it relates to **Scanner**, a token is a portion of input that is delineated by a set of delimiters, which is whitespace by default. A token is read by matching it with a particular *regular expression*, which defines the format of the data. Although **Scanner** allows you to define the specific type of expression that its next input operation will match, it includes many predefined patterns, which match the primitive types, such as **int** and **double**, and strings. Thus, often you won't need to specify a pattern to match.

In general, to use **Scanner**, follow this procedure:

1. Determine if a specific type of input is available by calling one of **Scanner**'s **hasNext**X methods, where X is the type of data desired.

2. If input is available, read it by calling one of **Scanner**'s **next**X methods.

3. Repeat the process until input is exhausted.

As the preceding indicates, **Scanner** defines two sets of methods that enable you to read input. The first are the **hasNext**X methods, which are shown in Table 18-15. These methods determine if the specified type of input is available. For example, calling **hasNextInt( )** returns **true** only if the next token to be read is an integer. If the desired data is available, then you read it by calling one of **Scanner**'s **next**X methods, which are shown in Table 18-16. For example, to read the next integer, call **nextInt( )**. The following sequence shows how to read a list of integers from the keyboard.

```
Scanner conin = new Scanner(System.in);
int i;

// Read a list of integers.
while(conin.hasNextInt()) {
  i = conin.nextInt();
  // ...
}
```

Method	Description
boolean hasNext( )	Returns **true** if another token of any type is available to be read. Returns **false** otherwise.
boolean hasNext(Pattern *pattern*)	Returns **true** if a token that matches the pattern passed in *pattern* is available to be read. Returns **false** otherwise.
boolean hasNext(String *pattern*)	Returns **true** if a token that matches the pattern passed in *pattern* is available to be read. Returns **false** otherwise.
boolean hasNextBigDecimal( )	Returns **true** if a value that can be stored in a **BigDecimal** object is available to be read. Returns **false** otherwise.
boolean hasNextBigInteger( )	Returns **true** if a value that can be stored in a **BigInteger** object is available to be read. Returns **false** otherwise. The default radix is used. (Unless changed, the default radix is 10.)
boolean hasNextBigInteger(int *radix*)	Returns **true** if a value in the specified radix that can be stored in a **BigInteger** object is available to be read. Returns **false** otherwise.
boolean hasNextBoolean( )	Returns **true** if a **boolean** value is available to be read. Returns **false** otherwise.
boolean hasNextByte( )	Returns **true** if a **byte** value is available to be read. Returns **false** otherwise. The default radix is used. (Unless changed, the default radix is 10.)
boolean hasNextByte(int *radix*)	Returns **true** if a **byte** value in the specified radix is available to be read. Returns **false** otherwise.
boolean hasNextDouble( )	Returns **true** if a **double** value is available to be read. Returns **false** otherwise.
boolean hasNextFloat( )	Returns **true** if a **float** value is available to be read. Returns **false** otherwise.
boolean hasNextInt( )	Returns **true** if an **int** value is available to be read. Returns **false** otherwise. The default radix is used. (Unless changed, the default radix is 10.)
boolean hasNextInt(int *radix*)	Returns **true** if an **int** value in the specified radix is available to be read. Returns **false** otherwise.
boolean hasNextLine( )	Returns **true** if a line of input is available.
boolean hasNextLong( )	Returns **true** if a **long** value is available to be read. Returns **false** otherwise. The default radix is used. (Unless changed, the default radix is 10.)
boolean hasNextLong(int *radix*)	Returns **true** if a **long** value in the specified radix is available to be read. Returns **false** otherwise.
boolean hasNextShort( )	Returns **true** if a **short** value is available to be read. Returns **false** otherwise. The default radix is used. (Unless changed, the default radix is 10.)
boolean hasNextShort(int *radix*)	Returns **true** if a **short** value in the specified radix is available to be read. Returns **false** otherwise.

TABLE 18-15   The **Scanner hasNext** Methods

Method	Description
String next( )	Returns the next token of any type from the input source.
String next(Pattern *pattern*)	Returns the next token that matches the pattern passed in *pattern* from the input source.
String next(String *pattern*)	Returns the next token that matches the pattern passed in *pattern* from the input source.
BigDecimal nextBigDecimal( )	Returns the next token as a **BigDecimal** object.
BigInteger nextBigInteger( )	Returns the next token as a **BigInteger** object. The default radix is used. (Unless changed, the default radix is 10.)
BigInteger nextBigInteger(int *radix*)	Returns the next token (using the specified radix) as a **BigInteger** object.
boolean nextBoolean( )	Returns the next token as a **boolean** value.
byte nextByte( )	Returns the next token as a **byte** value. The default radix is used. (Unless changed, the default radix is 10.)
byte nextByte(int *radix*)	Returns the next token (using the specified radix) as a **byte** value.
double nextDouble( )	Returns the next token as a **double** value.
float nextFloat( )	Returns the next token as a **float** value.
int nextInt( )	Returns the next token as an **int** value. The default radix is used. (Unless changed, the default radix is 10.)
int nextInt(int *radix*)	Returns the next token (using the specified radix) as an **int** value.
String nextLine( )	Returns the next line of input as a string.
long nextLong( )	Returns the next token as a **long** value. The default radix is used. (Unless changed, the default radix is 10.)
long nextLong(int *radix*)	Returns the next token (using the specified radix) as a **long** value.
short nextShort( )	Returns the next token as a **short** value. The default radix is used. (Unless changed, the default radix is 10.)
short nextShort(int *radix*)	Returns the next token (using the specified radix) as a **short** value.

TABLE 18-16   The **Scanner next** Methods

The **while** loop stops as soon as the next token is not an integer. Thus, the loop stops reading integers as soon as a non-integer is encountered in the input stream.

If a **next** method cannot find the type of data it is looking for, it throws a **NoSuchElementException**. For this reason, it is best to first confirm that the desired type of data is available by calling a **hasNext** method before calling its corresponding **next** method.

Some Scanner Examples

The addition of **Scanner** to Java makes what was formerly a tedious task into an easy one. To understand why, let's look at some examples. The following program averages a list of numbers entered at the keyboard:

```java
// Use Scanner to compute an average of the values.
import java.util.*;

class AvgNums {
  public static void main(String args[]) {
    Scanner conin = new Scanner(System.in);

    int count = 0;
    double sum = 0.0;

    System.out.println("Enter numbers to average.");

    // Read and sum numbers.
    while(conin.hasNext()) {
      if(conin.hasNextDouble()) {
        sum += conin.nextDouble();
        count++;
      }
      else {
        String str = conin.next();
        if(str.equals("done")) break;
        else {
          System.out.println("Data format error.");
          return;
        }
      }
    }

    System.out.println("Average is " + sum / count);
  }
}
```

The program reads numbers from the keyboard, summing them in the process, until the user enters the string "done". It then stops input and displays the average of the numbers. Here is a sample run:

```
Enter numbers to average.
1.2
2
3.4
4
done
Average is 2.65
```

The program reads numbers until it encounters a token that does not represent a valid **double** value. When this occurs, it confirms that the token is the string "done". If it is, the program terminates normally. Otherwise, it displays an error.

Notice that the numbers are read by calling **nextDouble( )**. This method reads any number that can be converted into a **double** value, including an integer value, such as 2, and a floating-point value like 3.4. Thus, a number read by **nextDouble( )** need not specify a decimal point. This same general principle applies to all **next** methods. They will match and read any data format that can represent the type of value being requested.

One thing that is especially nice about **Scanner** is that the same technique used to read from one source can be used to read from another. For example, here is the preceding program reworked to average a list of numbers contained in a text file:

```
// Use Scanner to compute an average of the values in a file.
import java.util.*;
import java.io.*;

class AvgFile {
  public static void main(String args[])
    throws IOException {

    int count = 0;
    double sum = 0.0;

    // Write output to a file.
    FileWriter fout = new FileWriter("test.txt");
    fout.write("2 3.4 5 6 7.4 9.1 10.5 done");
    fout.close();

    FileReader fin = new FileReader("Test.txt");

    Scanner src = new Scanner(fin);

    // Read and sum numbers.
    while(src.hasNext()) {
      if(src.hasNextDouble()) {
        sum += src.nextDouble();
        count++;
      }
      else {
        String str = src.next();
        if(str.equals("done")) break;
        else {
          System.out.println("File format error.");
          return;
        }
      }
    }

    fin.close();
    System.out.println("Average is " + sum / count);
  }
}
```

Here is the output:

```
Average is 6.2
```

You can use **Scanner** to read input that contains several different types of data—even if the order of that data is unknown in advance. You must simply check what type of data is available before reading it. For example, consider this program:

```
// Use Scanner to read various types of data from a file.
import java.util.*;
import java.io.*;

class ScanMixed {
  public static void main(String args[])
    throws IOException {

    int i;
    double d;
    boolean b;
    String str;

    // Write output to a file.
    FileWriter fout = new FileWriter("test.txt");
    fout.write("Testing Scanner 10 12.2 one true two false");
    fout.close();

    FileReader fin = new FileReader("Test.txt");

    Scanner src = new Scanner(fin);


    // Read to end.
    while(src.hasNext()) {
      if(src.hasNextInt()) {
        i = src.nextInt();
        System.out.println("int: " + i);
      }
      else if(src.hasNextDouble()) {
        d = src.nextDouble();
        System.out.println("double: " + d);
      }
      else if(src.hasNextBoolean()) {
        b = src.nextBoolean();
        System.out.println("boolean: " + b);
      }
      else {
        str = src.next();
        System.out.println("String: " + str);
      }
    }

    fin.close();
  }
}
```

Here is the output:

```
String: Testing
String: Scanner
```

```
int: 10
double: 12.2
String: one
boolean: true
String: two
boolean: false
```

When reading mixed data types, as the preceding program does, you need to be a bit careful about the order in which you call the **next** methods. For example, if the loop reversed the order of the calls to **nextInt( )** and **nextDouble( )**, both numeric values would have been read as **double**s, because **nextDouble( )** matches any numeric string that can be represented as a **double**.

Setting Delimiters

Scanner defines where a token starts and ends based on a set of *delimiters*. The default delimiters are the whitespace characters, and this is the delimiter set that the preceding examples have used. However, it is possible to change the delimiters by calling the **useDelimiter( )** method, shown here:

Scanner useDelimiter(String *pattern*)

Scanner useDelimiter(Pattern *pattern*)

Here, *pattern* is a regular expression that specifies the delimiter set.

Here is the program that reworks the average program shown earlier so that it reads a list of numbers that are separated by commas, and any number of spaces:

```
// Use Scanner to compute an average a list of
// comma-separated values.
import java.util.*;
import java.io.*;

class SetDelimiters {
  public static void main(String args[])
    throws IOException {

    int count = 0;
    double sum = 0.0;

    // Write output to a file.
    FileWriter fout = new FileWriter("test.txt");

    // Now, store values in comma-separated list.
    fout.write("2, 3.4,    5,6, 7.4, 9.1, 10.5, done");
    fout.close();

    FileReader fin = new FileReader("Test.txt");

    Scanner src = new Scanner(fin);

    // Set delimiters to space and comma.
    src.useDelimiter(", *");
```

```
  // Read and sum numbers.
  while(src.hasNext()) {
    if(src.hasNextDouble()) {
      sum += src.nextDouble();
      count++;
    }
    else {
      String str = src.next();
      if(str.equals("done")) break;
      else {
        System.out.println("File format error.");
        return;
      }
    }
  }

  fin.close();
  System.out.println("Average is " + sum / count);
  }
}
```

In this version, the numbers written to **test.txt** are separated by commas and spaces. The use of the delimiter pattern ", *" tells **Scanner** to match a comma and zero or more spaces as delimiters. The output is the same as before.

You can obtain the current delimiter pattern by calling **delimiter( )**, shown here:

Pattern delimiter( )

Other Scanner Features

Scanner defines several other methods in addition to those already discussed. One that is particularly useful in some circumstances is **findInLine( )**. Its general forms are shown here:

String findInLine(Pattern *pattern*)
String findInLine(String *pattern*)

This method searches for the specified pattern within the next line of text. If the pattern is found, the matching token is consumed and returned. Otherwise, null is returned. It operates independently of any delimiter set. This method is useful if you want to locate a specific pattern. For example, the following program locates the Age field in the input string and then displays the age:

```
// Demonstrate findInLine().
import java.util.*;

class FindInLineDemo {
  public static void main(String args[]) {
    String instr = "Name: Tom Age: 28 ID: 77";

    Scanner conin = new Scanner(instr);

    // Find and display age.
    conin.findInLine("Age:"); // find Age

    if(conin.hasNext())
```

```
      System.out.println(conin.next());
    else
      System.out.println("Error!");

  }
}
```

The output is **28**. In the program, **findInLine( )** is used to find an occurrence of the pattern "Age". Once found, the next token is read, which is the age.

Related to **findInLine( )** is **findWithinHorizon( )** It is shown here:

String findWithinHorizon(Pattern *pattern*, int *count*)

String findWithinHorizon(String *pattern*, int *count*)

This method attempts to find an occurrence of the specified pattern within the next *count* characters. If successful, it returns the matching pattern. Otherwise, it returns null. If *count* is zero, then all input is searched until either a match is found or the end of input is encountered.

You can bypass a pattern using **skip( )**, shown here:

Scanner skip(Pattern *pattern*)

Scanner skip(String *pattern*)

If *pattern* is matched, **skip( )** simply advances beyond it and returns a reference to the invoking object. If pattern is not found, **skip( )** throws **NoSuchElementException**.

Other **Scanner** methods include **radix( )**, which returns the default radix used by the **Scanner**; **useRadix( )**, which sets the radix; **reset( )**, which resets the scanner; and **close( )**, which closes the scanner.

The ResourceBundle, ListResourceBundle, and PropertyResourceBundle Classes

The **java.util** package includes three classes that aid in the internationalization of your program. The first is the abstract class **ResourceBundle**. It defines methods that enable you to manage a collection of locale-sensitive resources, such as the strings that are used to label the user interface elements in your program. You can define two or more sets of translated strings that support various languages, such as English, German, or Chinese, with each translation set residing in its own bundle. You can then load the bundle appropriate to the current locale and use the strings to construct the program's user interface.

Resource bundles are identified by their *family name* (also called their *base name*). To the family name can be added a two-character lowercase *language code* which specifies the language. In this case, if a requested locale matches the language code, then that version of the resource bundle is used. For example, a resource bundle with a family name of **SampleRB** could have a German version called **SampleRB_de** and a Russian version called **SampleRB_ru**. (Notice that an underscore links the family name to the language code.) Therefore, if the locale is **Locale.GERMAN**, **SampleRB_de** will be used.

It is also possible to indicate specific variants of a language that relate to a specific country by specifying a *country code* after the language code. A country code is a two-character uppercase identifier, such as **AU** for Australia or **IN** for India. A country code is also preceded by an underscore when linked to the resource bundle name. A resource bundle that has only the family name is the default bundle. It is used when no language-specific bundles are applicable.

> **NOTE** *The language codes are defined by ISO standard 639 and the country codes by ISO standard 3166.*

The methods defined by **ResourceBundle** are summarized in Table 18-17. One important point: **null** keys are not allowed and several of the methods will throw a **NullPointerException** if **null** is passed as the key. Notice the nested class **ResourceBundle.Control**. It was added by Java SE 6 and is used to control the resource-bundle loading process.

There are two subclasses of **ResourceBundle**. The first is **PropertyResourceBundle**, which manages resources by using property files. **PropertyResourceBundle** adds no methods of

Method	Description
static final void clearCache( )	Deletes all resource bundles from the cache that were loaded by the default class loader. (Added by Java SE 6.)
static final void clearCache(ClassLoader *ldr*)	Deletes all resource bundles from the cache that were loaded by *ldr*. (Added by Java SE 6.)
boolean containsKey(String *k*)	Returns **true** if *k* is a key within the invoking resource bundle (or its parent). (Added by Java SE 6.)
static final ResourceBundle getBundle(String *familyName*)	Loads the resource bundle with a family name of *familyName* using the default locale and the default class loader. Throws **MissingResourceException** if no resource bundle matching the family name specified by *familyName* is available.
static final ResourceBundle getBundle(String *familyName*, Locale *loc*)	Loads the resource bundle with a family name of *familyName* using the specified locale and the default class loader. Throws **MissingResourceException** if no resource bundle matching the family name specified by *familyName* is available.
static ResourceBundle getBundle(String *familyName*, Locale *loc*, ClassLoader *ldr*)	Loads the resource bundle with a family name of *familyName* using the specified locale and the specified class loader. Throws **MissingResourceException** if no resource bundle matching the family name specified by *familyName* is available.
static final ResourceBundle getBundle(String *familyName*, ResourceBundle.Control *cntl*)	Loads the resource bundle with a family name of *familyName* using the default locale and the default class loader. The loading process is under the control of *cntl*. Throws **MissingResourceException** if no resource bundle matching the family name specified by *familyName* is available. (Added by Java SE 6.)
static final ResourceBundle getBundle(String *familyName*, Locale *loc*, ResourceBundle.Control *cntl*)	Loads the resource bundle with a family name of *familyName* using the specified locale and the default class loader. The loading process is under the control of *cntl*. Throws **MissingResourceException** if no resource bundle matching the family name specified by *familyName* is available. (Added by Java SE 6.)

TABLE 18-17 The Methods Defined by **ResourceBundle**

Method	Description

static ResourceBundle
    getBundle(String *familyName*,
                  Locale *loc*,
                  ClassLoader *ldr*,
                  ResourceBundle.Control *cntl*)
	Loads the resource bundle with a family name of *familyName* using the specified locale and the specified class loader. The loading process is under the control of *cntl*. Throws **MissingResourceException** if no resource bundle matching the family name specified by *familyName* is available. (Added by Java SE 6.)

abstract Enumeration<String> getKeys( )	Returns the resource bundle keys as an enumeration of strings. Any parent's keys are also obtained.
Locale getLocale( )	Returns the locale supported by the resource bundle.
final Object getObject(String *k*)	Returns the object associated with the key passed via *k*. Throws **MissingResourceException** if *k* is not in the resource bundle.
final String getString(String *k*)	Returns the string associated with the key passed via *k*. Throws **MissingResourceException** if *k* is not in the resource bundle. Throws **ClassCastException** if the object associated with *k* is not a string.
final String[ ] getStringArray(String *k*)	Returns the string array associated with the key passed via *k*. Throws **MissingResourceException** if *k* is not in the resource bundle. Throws **ClassCastException** if the object associated with *k* is not a string array.
protected abstract Object handleGetObject(String *k*)	Returns the object associated with the key passed via *k*. Returns **null** if *k* is not in the resource bundle.
protected Set<String> handleKeySet( )	Returns the resource bundle keys as a set of strings. No parent's keys are obtained. Also, keys with **null** values are not obtained. (Added by Java SE 6.)
Set<String> keySet( )	Returns the resource bundle keys as a set of strings. Any parent keys are also obtained. (Added by Java SE 6.)
protected void setParent(ResourceBundle *parent*)	Sets *parent* as the parent bundle for the resource bundle. When a key is looked up, the parent will be searched if the key is not found in the invoking resource object.

TABLE 18-17   The Methods Defined by **ResourceBundle** *(continued)*

its own. The second is the abstract class **ListResourceBundle**, which manages resources in an array of key/value pairs. **ListResourceBundle** adds the method **getContents( )**, which all subclasses must implement. It is shown here:

protected abstract Object[ ][ ] getContents( )

It returns a two-dimensional array that contains key/value pairs that represent resources. The keys must be strings. The values are typically strings, but can be other types of objects.

Here is an example that demonstrates using a resource bundle. The resource bundle has the family name **SampleRB**. Two resource bundle classes of this family are created by extending **ListResourceBundle**. The first is called **SampleRB**, and it is the default bundle (which uses English). It is shown here:

```
import java.util.*;
```

```java
public class SampleRB extends ListResourceBundle {
  protected Object[][] getContents() {
    Object[][] resources = new Object[3][2];

    resources[0][0] = "title";
    resources[0][1] = "My Program";

    resources[1][0] = "StopText";
    resources[1][1] = "Stop";

    resources[2][0] = "StartText";
    resources[2][1] = "Start";

    return resources;
  }
}
```

The second resource bundle, shown next, is called **SampleRB_de**. It contains the German translation.

```java
import java.util.*;

// German version.
public class SampleRB_de extends ListResourceBundle {
  protected Object[][] getContents() {
    Object[][] resources = new Object[3][2];

    resources[0][0] = "title";
    resources[0][1] = "Mein Programm";

    resources[1][0] = "StopText";
    resources[1][1] = "Anschlag";

    resources[2][0] = "StartText";
    resources[2][1] = "Anfang";

    return resources;
  }
}
```

The following program demonstrates these two resource bundles by displaying the string associated with each key for both the default (English) version and the German version:

```java
// Demonstrate a resource bundle.
import java.util.*;

class LRBDemo {
  public static void main(String args[]) {
    // Load the default bundle.
    ResourceBundle rd = ResourceBundle.getBundle("SampleRB");

    System.out.println("English version: ");
    System.out.println("String for Title key : " +
                       rd.getString("title"));
```

```
    System.out.println("String for StopText key: " +
                     rd.getString("StopText"));

    System.out.println("String for StartText key: " +
                     rd.getString("StartText"));

    // Load the German bundle.
    rd = ResourceBundle.getBundle("SampleRB", Locale.GERMAN);

    System.out.println("\nGerman version: ");
    System.out.println("String for Title key : " +
                     rd.getString("title"));

    System.out.println("String for StopText key: " +
                     rd.getString("StopText"));

    System.out.println("String for StartText key: " +
                     rd.getString("StartText"));
  }
}
```

The output from the program is shown here:

```
English version:
String for Title key : My Program
String for StopText key: Stop
String for StartText key: Start

German version:
String for Title key : Mein Programm
String for StopText key: Anschlag
String for StartText key: Anfang
```

Miscellaneous Utility Classes and Interfaces

In addition to the classes already discussed, **java.util** includes the following classes:

EventListenerProxy	Extends the **EventListener** class to allow additional parameters. See Chapter 22 for a discussion of event listeners.
EventObject	The superclass for all event classes. Events are discussed in Chapter 22.
FormattableFlags	Defines formatting flags that are used with the **Formattable** interface.
PropertyPermission	Manages property permissions.
ServiceLoader	Provides a means of finding service providers. (Added by Java SE 6.)
UUID	Encapsulates and manages Universally Unique Identifiers (UUIDs).

The following interfaces are also packaged in **java.util**:

EventListener	Indicates that a class is an event listener. Events are discussed in Chapter 22.
Formattable	Enables a class to provide custom formatting.

The java.util Subpackages

Java defines the following subpackages to **java.util**:

- java.util.concurrent
- java.util.concurrent.atomic
- java.util.concurrent.locks
- java.util.jar
- java.util.logging
- java.util.prefs
- java.util.regex
- java.util.spi
- java.util.zip

Each is briefly examined here.

java.util.concurrent, java.util.concurrent.atomic, and java.util.concurrent.locks

The **java.util.concurrent** package along with its two subpackages, **java.util.concurrent.atomic** and **java.util.concurrent.locks**, support concurrent programming. These packages provide a high-performance alternative to using Java's built-in synchronization features when thread-safe operation is required. These packages are examined in detail in Chapter 26.

java.util.jar

The **java.util.jar** package provides the ability to read and write Java Archive (JAR) files.

java.util.logging

The **java.util.logging** package provides support for program activity logs, which can be used to record program actions, and to help find and debug problems.

java.util.prefs

The **java.util.prefs** package provides support for user preferences. It is typically used to support program configuration.

java.util.regex

The **java.util.regex** package provides support for regular expression handling. It is described in detail in Chapter 27.

java.util.spi

The **java.util.spi** package provides support for service providers. (Added by Java SE 6.)

java.util.zip

The **java.util.zip** package provides the ability to read and write files in the popular ZIP and GZIP formats. Both ZIP and GZIP input and output streams are available.

Input/Output: Exploring java.io

This chapter explores **java.io**, which provides support for I/O operations. In Chapter 13, we presented an overview of Java's I/O system. Here, we will examine the Java I/O system in greater detail.

As all programmers learn early on, most programs cannot accomplish their goals without accessing external data. Data is retrieved from an *input* source. The results of a program are sent to an *output* destination. In Java, these sources or destinations are defined very broadly. For example, a network connection, memory buffer, or disk file can be manipulated by the Java I/O classes. Although physically different, these devices are all handled by the same abstraction: the *stream*. A stream, as explained in Chapter 13, is a logical entity that either produces or consumes information. A stream is linked to a physical device by the Java I/O system. All streams behave in the same manner, even if the actual physical devices they are linked to differ.

NOTE *In addition to the I/O capabilities discussed here, Java provides further I/O support in the* **java.nio** *package, which is described in Chapter 27.*

The Java I/O Classes and Interfaces

The I/O classes defined by **java.io** are listed here:

BufferedInputStream	FileWriter	PipedOutputStream
BufferedOutputStream	FilterInputStream	PipedReader
BufferedReader	FilterOutputStream	PipedWriter
BufferedWriter	FilterReader	PrintStream
ByteArrayInputStream	FilterWriter	PrintWriter
ByteArrayOutputStream	InputStream	PushbackInputStream
CharArrayReader	InputStreamReader	PushbackReader
CharArrayWriter	LineNumberReader	RandomAccessFile

Console	ObjectInputStream	Reader
DataInputStream	ObjectInputStream.GetField	SequenceInputStream
DataOutputStream	ObjectOutputStream	SerializablePermission
File	ObjectOutputStream.PutField	StreamTokenizer
FileDescriptor	ObjectStreamClass	StringReader
FileInputStream	ObjectStreamField	StringWriter
FileOutputStream	OutputStream	Writer
FilePermission	OutputStreamWriter	
FileReader	PipedInputStream	

Console was added by Java SE 6.

The **java.io** package also contains two deprecated classes that are not shown in the preceding table: **LineNumberInputStream** and **StringBufferInputStream**. These classes should not be used for new code.

The following interfaces are defined by **java.io**:

Closeable	FileFilter	ObjectInputValidation
DataInput	FilenameFilter	ObjectOutput
DataOutput	Flushable	ObjectStreamConstants
Externalizable	ObjectInput	Serializable

As you can see, there are many classes and interfaces in the **java.io** package. These include byte and character streams, and object serialization (the storage and retrieval of objects). This chapter examines several of the most commonly used I/O components. The new **Console** class is also examined. We begin our discussion with one of the most distinctive I/O classes: **File**.

File

Although most of the classes defined by **java.io** operate on streams, the **File** class does not. It deals directly with files and the file system. That is, the **File** class does not specify how information is retrieved from or stored in files; it describes the properties of a file itself. A **File** object is used to obtain or manipulate the information associated with a disk file, such as the permissions, time, date, and directory path, and to navigate subdirectory hierarchies.

Files are a primary source and destination for data within many programs. Although there are severe restrictions on their use within applets for security reasons, files are still a central resource for storing persistent and shared information. A directory in Java is treated simply as a **File** with one additional property—a list of filenames that can be examined by the **list( )** method.

The following constructors can be used to create **File** objects:

File(String *directoryPath*)
File(String *directoryPath*, String *filename*)
File(File *dirObj*, String *filename*)
File(URI *uriObj*)

Here, *directoryPath* is the path name of the file, *filename* is the name of the file or subdirectory, *dirObj* is a **File** object that specifies a directory, and *uriObj* is a **URI** object that describes a file.

The following example creates three files: **f1**, **f2**, and **f3**. The first **File** object is constructed with a directory path as the only argument. The second includes two arguments—the path and the filename. The third includes the file path assigned to **f1** and a filename; **f3** refers to the same file as **f2**.

```
File f1 = new File("/");
File f2 = new File("/","autoexec.bat");
File f3 = new File(f1,"autoexec.bat");
```

Note *Java does the right thing with path separators between UNIX and Windows conventions. If you use a forward slash (/) on a Windows version of Java, the path will still resolve correctly. Remember, if you are using the Windows convention of a backslash character (\\), you will need to use its escape sequence (\\\\) within a string.*

File defines many methods that obtain the standard properties of a **File** object. For example, **getName( )** returns the name of the file, **getParent( )** returns the name of the parent directory, and **exists( )** returns **true** if the file exists, **false** if it does not. The **File** class, however, is not symmetrical. By this, we mean that there are a few methods that allow you to *examine* the properties of a simple file object, but no corresponding function exists to change those attributes. The following example demonstrates several of the **File** methods:

```
// Demonstrate File.
import java.io.File;

class FileDemo {
  static void p(String s) {
    System.out.println(s);
  }

  public static void main(String args[]) {
    File f1 = new File("/java/COPYRIGHT");
    p("File Name: " + f1.getName());
    p("Path: " + f1.getPath());
    p("Abs Path: " + f1.getAbsolutePath());
    p("Parent: " + f1.getParent());
    p(f1.exists() ? "exists" : "does not exist");
    p(f1.canWrite() ? "is writeable" : "is not writeable");
    p(f1.canRead() ? "is readable" : "is not readable");
    p("is " + (f1.isDirectory() ? "" : "not" + " a directory"));
    p(f1.isFile() ? "is normal file" : "might be a named pipe");
    p(f1.isAbsolute() ? "is absolute" : "is not absolute");
    p("File last modified: " + f1.lastModified());
    p("File size: " + f1.length() + " Bytes");
  }
}
```

When you run this program, you will see something similar to the following:

```
File Name: COPYRIGHT
Path: /java/COPYRIGHT
Abs Path: /java/COPYRIGHT
Parent: /java
exists
is writeable
is readable
is not a directory
is normal file
is absolute
File last modified: 812465204000
File size: 695 Bytes
```

Most of the **File** methods are self-explanatory. **isFile( )** and **isAbsolute( )** are not. **isFile( )** returns **true** if called on a file and **false** if called on a directory. Also, **isFile( )** returns **false** for some special files, such as device drivers and named pipes, so this method can be used to make sure the file will behave as a file. The **isAbsolute( )** method returns **true** if the file has an absolute path and **false** if its path is relative.

File also includes two useful utility methods. The first is **renameTo( )**, shown here:

boolean renameTo(File *newName*)

Here, the filename specified by *newName* becomes the new name of the invoking **File** object. It will return **true** upon success and **false** if the file cannot be renamed (if you either attempt to rename a file so that it moves from one directory to another or use an existing filename, for example).

The second utility method is **delete( )**, which deletes the disk file represented by the path of the invoking **File** object. It is shown here:

boolean delete( )

You can also use **delete( )** to delete a directory if the directory is empty. **delete( )** returns **true** if it deletes the file and **false** if the file cannot be removed.

Here are some other **File** methods that you will find helpful.

Method	Description
void deleteOnExit( )	Removes the file associated with the invoking object when the Java Virtual Machine terminates.
long getFreeSpace( )	Returns the number of free bytes of storage available on the partition associated with the invoking object. (Added by Java SE 6.)
long getTotalSpace( )	Returns the storage capacity of the partition associated with the invoking object. (Added by Java SE 6.)
long getUsableSpace( )	Returns the number of usable free bytes of storage available on the partition associated with the invoking object. (Added by Java SE 6.)

Method	Description
boolean isHidden( )	Returns **true** if the invoking file is hidden. Returns **false** otherwise.
boolean setLastModified(long *millisec*)	Sets the time stamp on the invoking file to that specified by *millisec*, which is the number of milliseconds from January 1, 1970, Coordinated Universal Time (UTC).
boolean setReadOnly( )	Sets the invoking file to read-only.

Methods also exist to mark files as readable, writable, and executable. Because **File** implements the **Comparable** interface, the method **compareTo( )** is also supported.

Directories

A directory is a **File** that contains a list of other files and directories. When you create a **File** object and it is a directory, the **isDirectory( )** method will return **true**. In this case, you can call **list( )** on that object to extract the list of other files and directories inside. It has two forms. The first is shown here:

    String[ ] list( )

The list of files is returned in an array of **String** objects.

The program shown here illustrates how to use **list( )** to examine the contents of a directory:

```
// Using directories.
import java.io.File;

class DirList {
  public static void main(String args[]) {
    String dirname = "/java";
    File f1 = new File(dirname);

    if (f1.isDirectory()) {
      System.out.println("Directory of " + dirname);
      String s[] = f1.list();

      for (int i=0; i < s.length; i++) {
        File f = new File(dirname + "/" + s[i]);
        if (f.isDirectory()) {
          System.out.println(s[i] + " is a directory");
        } else {
          System.out.println(s[i] + " is a file");
        }
      }
    } else {
      System.out.println(dirname + " is not a directory");
    }
  }
}
```

Here is sample output from the program. (Of course, the output you see will be different, based on what is in the directory.)

```
Directory of /java
bin is a directory
lib is a directory
demo is a directory
COPYRIGHT is a file
README is a file
index.html is a file
include is a directory
src.zip is a file
src is a directory
```

Using FilenameFilter

You will often want to limit the number of files returned by the **list( )** method to include only those files that match a certain filename pattern, or *filter*. To do this, you must use a second form of **list( )**, shown here:

String[ ] list(FilenameFilter *FFObj*)

In this form, *FFObj* is an object of a class that implements the **FilenameFilter** interface.

FilenameFilter defines only a single method, **accept( )**, which is called once for each file in a list. Its general form is given here:

boolean accept(File *directory*, String *filename*)

The **accept( )** method returns **true** for files in the directory specified by *directory* that should be included in the list (that is, those that match the *filename* argument), and returns **false** for those files that should be excluded.

The **OnlyExt** class, shown next, implements **FilenameFilter**. It will be used to modify the preceding program so that it restricts the visibility of the filenames returned by **list( )** to files with names that end in the file extension specified when the object is constructed.

```java
import java.io.*;

public class OnlyExt implements FilenameFilter {
  String ext;

  public OnlyExt(String ext) {
    this.ext = "." + ext;
  }

  public boolean accept(File dir, String name) {
    return name.endsWith(ext);
  }
}
```

The modified directory listing program is shown here. Now it will only display files that use the **.html** extension.

```
// Directory of .HTML files.
import java.io.*;

class DirListOnly {
  public static void main(String args[]) {
    String dirname = "/java";
    File f1 = new File(dirname);
    FilenameFilter only = new OnlyExt("html");
    String s[] = f1.list(only);

    for (int i=0; i < s.length; i++) {
      System.out.println(s[i]);
    }
  }
}
```

The listFiles( ) Alternative

There is a variation to the **list( )** method, called **listFiles( )**, which you might find useful. The signatures for **listFiles( )** are shown here:

File[ ] listFiles( )
File[ ] listFiles(FilenameFilter *FFObj*)
File[ ] listFiles(FileFilter *FObj*)

These methods return the file list as an array of **File** objects instead of strings. The first method returns all files, and the second returns those files that satisfy the specified **FilenameFilter**. Aside from returning an array of **File** objects, these two versions of **listFiles( )** work like their equivalent **list( )** methods.

The third version of **listFiles( )** returns those files with path names that satisfy the specified **FileFilter**. **FileFilter** defines only a single method, **accept( )**, which is called once for each file in a list. Its general form is given here:

boolean accept(File *path*)

The **accept( )** method returns **true** for files that should be included in the list (that is, those that match the *path* argument), and **false** for those that should be excluded.

Creating Directories

Another two useful **File** utility methods are **mkdir( )** and **mkdirs( )**. The **mkdir( )** method creates a directory, returning **true** on success and **false** on failure. Failure indicates that the path specified in the **File** object already exists, or that the directory cannot be created because the entire path does not exist yet. To create a directory for which no path exists, use the **mkdirs( )** method. It creates both a directory and all the parents of the directory.

The Closeable and Flushable Interfaces

Recently (with the release of JDK 5), two interfaces were added to **java.io**: **Closeable** and **Flushable**. The interfaces are implemented by several of the I/O classes. Their inclusion does not add new functionality to the stream classes. They simply offer a uniform way of specifying that a stream can be closed or flushed.

Objects of a class that implements **Closeable** can be closed. It defines the **close( )** method, shown here:

void close( ) throws IOException

This method closes the invoking stream, releasing any resources that it may hold. This interface is implemented by all of the I/O classes that open a stream that can be closed.

Objects of a class that implements **Flushable** can force buffered output to be written to the stream to which the object is attached. It defines the **flush( )** method, shown here:

void flush( ) throws IOException

Flushing a stream typically causes buffered output to be physically written to the underlying device. This interface is implemented by all of the I/O classes that write to a stream.

The Stream Classes

Java's stream-based I/O is built upon four abstract classes: **InputStream**, **OutputStream**, **Reader**, and **Writer**. These classes were briefly discussed in Chapter 13. They are used to create several concrete stream subclasses. Although your programs perform their I/O operations through concrete subclasses, the top-level classes define the basic functionality common to all stream classes.

InputStream and **OutputStream** are designed for byte streams. **Reader** and **Writer** are designed for character streams. The byte stream classes and the character stream classes form separate hierarchies. In general, you should use the character stream classes when working with characters or strings, and use the byte stream classes when working with bytes or other binary objects.

In the remainder of this chapter, both the byte- and character-oriented streams are examined.

The Byte Streams

The byte stream classes provide a rich environment for handling byte-oriented I/O. A byte stream can be used with any type of object, including binary data. This versatility makes byte streams important to many types of programs. Since the byte stream classes are topped by **InputStream** and **OutputStream**, our discussion will begin with them.

InputStream

InputStream is an abstract class that defines Java's model of streaming byte input. It implements the **Closeable** interface. Most of the methods in this class will throw an **IOException** on error conditions. (The exceptions are **mark( )** and **markSupported( )**.) Table 19-1 shows the methods in **InputStream**.

OutputStream

OutputStream is an abstract class that defines streaming byte output. It implements the **Closeable** and **Flushable** interfaces. Most of the methods in this class return **void** and throw an **IOException** in the case of errors. (The exceptions are **mark( )** and **markSupported( )**.) Table 19-2 shows the methods in **OutputStream**.

Method	Description
int available( )	Returns the number of bytes of input currently available for reading.
void close( )	Closes the input source. Further read attempts will generate an **IOException**.
void mark(int *numBytes*)	Places a mark at the current point in the input stream that will remain valid until *numBytes* bytes are read.
boolean markSupported( )	Returns **true** if **mark( )**/**reset( )** are supported by the invoking stream.
int read( )	Returns an integer representation of the next available byte of input. –1 is returned when the end of the file is encountered.
int read(byte *buffer*[ ])	Attempts to read up to *buffer.length* bytes into *buffer* and returns the actual number of bytes that were successfully read. –1 is returned when the end of the file is encountered.
int read(byte *buffer*[ ], int *offset*, int *numBytes*)	Attempts to read up to *numBytes* bytes into *buffer* starting at *buffer*[*offset*], returning the number of bytes successfully read. –1 is returned when the end of the file is encountered.
void reset( )	Resets the input pointer to the previously set mark.
long skip(long *numBytes*)	Ignores (that is, skips) *numBytes* bytes of input, returning the number of bytes actually ignored.

TABLE 19-1   The Methods Defined by **InputStream**

NOTE   *Most of the methods described in Tables 19-1 and 19-2 are implemented by the subclasses of **InputStream** and **OutputStream**. The **mark( )** and **reset( )** methods are exceptions; notice their use or lack thereof by each subclass in the discussions that follow.*

Method	Description
void close( )	Closes the output stream. Further write attempts will generate an **IOException**.
void flush( )	Finalizes the output state so that any buffers are cleared. That is, it flushes the output buffers.
void write(int *b*)	Writes a single byte to an output stream. Note that the parameter is an **int**, which allows you to call **write( )** with expressions without having to cast them back to **byte**.
void write(byte *buffer*[ ])	Writes a complete array of bytes to an output stream.
void write(byte *buffer*[ ], int *offset*, int *numBytes*)	Writes a subrange of *numBytes* bytes from the array *buffer*, beginning at *buffer*[*offset*].

TABLE 19-2   The Methods Defined by **OutputStream**

FileInputStream

The **FileInputStream** class creates an **InputStream** that you can use to read bytes from a file. Its two most common constructors are shown here:

FileInputStream(String *filepath*)
FileInputStream(File *fileObj*)

Either can throw a **FileNotFoundException**. Here, *filepath* is the full path name of a file, and *fileObj* is a **File** object that describes the file.

The following example creates two **FileInputStream**s that use the same disk file and each of the two constructors:

```
FileInputStream f0 = new FileInputStream("/autoexec.bat")
File f = new File("/autoexec.bat");
FileInputStream f1 = new FileInputStream(f);
```

Although the first constructor is probably more commonly used, the second allows us to closely examine the file using the **File** methods, before we attach it to an input stream. When a **FileInputStream** is created, it is also opened for reading. **FileInputStream** overrides six of the methods in the abstract class **InputStream**. The **mark( )** and **reset( )** methods are not overridden, and any attempt to use **reset( )** on a **FileInputStream** will generate an **IOException**.

The next example shows how to read a single byte, an array of bytes, and a subrange array of bytes. It also illustrates how to use **available( )** to determine the number of bytes remaining, and how to use the **skip( )** method to skip over unwanted bytes. The program reads its own source file, which must be in the current directory.

```
// Demonstrate FileInputStream.
import java.io.*;

class FileInputStreamDemo {
  public static void main(String args[]) throws IOException {
    int size;
    InputStream f =
      new FileInputStream("FileInputStreamDemo.java");

    System.out.println("Total Available Bytes: " +
                       (size = f.available()));
    int n = size/40;
    System.out.println("First " + n +
                       " bytes of the file one read() at a time");
    for (int i=0; i < n; i++) {
      System.out.print((char) f.read());
    }
    System.out.println("\nStill Available: " + f.available());
    System.out.println("Reading the next " + n +
                       " with one read(b[])");
    byte b[] = new byte[n];
    if (f.read(b) != n) {
      System.err.println("couldn't read " + n + " bytes.");
    }
    System.out.println(new String(b, 0, n));
    System.out.println("\nStill Available: " + (size = f.available()));
    System.out.println("Skipping half of remaining bytes with skip()");
```

```
   f.skip(size/2);
   System.out.println("Still Available: " + f.available());
   System.out.println("Reading " + n/2 + " into the end of array");
   if (f.read(b, n/2, n/2) != n/2) {
     System.err.println("couldn't read " + n/2 + " bytes.");
   }
   System.out.println(new String(b, 0, b.length));
   System.out.println("\nStill Available: " + f.available());
   f.close();
  }
}
```

Here is the output produced by this program:

```
Total Available Bytes: 1433
First 35 bytes of the file one read() at a time
// Demonstrate FileInputStream.
im
Still Available: 1398
Reading the next 35 with one read(b[])
port java.io.*;

class FileInputS

Still Available: 1363
Skipping half of remaining bytes with skip()
Still Available: 682
Reading 17 into the end of array
port java.io.*;
read(b) != n) {
S

Still Available: 665
```

This somewhat contrived example demonstrates how to read three ways, to skip input, and to inspect the amount of data available on a stream.

NOTE   *The preceding example (and the other examples in this chapter) handle any I/O exceptions that might occur by throwing **IOException** out of **main( )**, which means that they are handled by the JVM. This is fine for simple demonstration programs (and for small utility programs that you write for your own use), but commercial applications will normally need to handle I/O exceptions within the program.*

FileOutputStream

FileOutputStream creates an **OutputStream** that you can use to write bytes to a file. Its most commonly used constructors are shown here:

FileOutputStream(String *filePath*)
FileOutputStream(File *fileObj*)
FileOutputStream(String *filePath*, boolean *append*)
FileOutputStream(File *fileObj*, boolean *append*)

They can throw a **FileNotFoundException**. Here, *filePath* is the full path name of a file, and *fileObj* is a **File** object that describes the file. If *append* is **true**, the file is opened in append mode.

Creation of a **FileOutputStream** is not dependent on the file already existing. **FileOutputStream** will create the file before opening it for output when you create the object. In the case where you attempt to open a read-only file, an **IOException** will be thrown.

The following example creates a sample buffer of bytes by first making a **String** and then using the **getBytes( )** method to extract the byte array equivalent. It then creates three files. The first, **file1.txt**, will contain every other byte from the sample. The second, **file2.txt**, will contain the entire set of bytes. The third and last, **file3.txt**, will contain only the last quarter.

```
// Demonstrate FileOutputStream.
import java.io.*;

class FileOutputStreamDemo {
  public static void main(String args[]) throws IOException {
    String source = "Now is the time for all good men\n"
      + " to come to the aid of their country\n"
      + " and pay their due taxes.";
    byte buf[] = source.getBytes();
    OutputStream f0 = new FileOutputStream("file1.txt");
    for (int i=0; i < buf.length; i += 2) {
      f0.write(buf[i]);
    }
    f0.close();

    OutputStream f1 = new FileOutputStream("file2.txt");
    f1.write(buf);
    f1.close();

    OutputStream f2 = new FileOutputStream("file3.txt");
    f2.write(buf,buf.length-buf.length/4,buf.length/4);
    f2.close();
  }
}
```

Here are the contents of each file after running this program. First, **file1.txt**:

```
Nwi h iefralgo e
t oet h i ftercuty n a hi u ae.
```

Next, **file2.txt**:

```
Now is the time for all good men
 to come to the aid of their country
 and pay their due taxes.
```

Finally, **file3.txt**:

```
nd pay their due taxes.
```

ByteArrayInputStream

ByteArrayInputStream is an implementation of an input stream that uses a byte array as the source. This class has two constructors, each of which requires a byte array to provide the data source:

> ByteArrayInputStream(byte *array*[ ])
> ByteArrayInputStream(byte *array*[ ], int *start*, int *numBytes*)

Here, *array* is the input source. The second constructor creates an **InputStream** from a subset of your byte array that begins with the character at the index specified by *start* and is *numBytes* long.

The following example creates a pair of **ByteArrayInputStream**s, initializing them with the byte representation of the alphabet:

```
// Demonstrate ByteArrayInputStream.
import java.io.*;

class ByteArrayInputStreamDemo {
  public static void main(String args[]) throws IOException {
    String tmp = "abcdefghijklmnopqrstuvwxyz";
    byte b[] = tmp.getBytes();
    ByteArrayInputStream input1 = new ByteArrayInputStream(b);
    ByteArrayInputStream input2 = new ByteArrayInputStream(b,0,3);
  }
}
```

The **input1** object contains the entire lowercase alphabet, while **input2** contains only the first three letters.

A **ByteArrayInputStream** implements both **mark( )** and **reset( )**. However, if **mark( )** has not been called, then **reset( )** sets the stream pointer to the start of the stream—which in this case is the start of the byte array passed to the constructor. The next example shows how to use the **reset( )** method to read the same input twice. In this case, we read and print the letters "abc" once in lowercase and then again in uppercase.

```
import java.io.*;

class ByteArrayInputStreamReset {
  public static void main(String args[]) throws IOException {
    String tmp = "abc";
    byte b[] = tmp.getBytes();
    ByteArrayInputStream in = new ByteArrayInputStream(b);

    for (int i=0; i<2; i++) {
      int c;
      while ((c = in.read()) != -1) {
        if (i == 0) {
          System.out.print((char) c);
        } else {
          System.out.print(Character.toUpperCase((char) c));
        }
      }
      System.out.println();
      in.reset();
```

```
      }
    }
}
```

This example first reads each character from the stream and prints it as-is, in lowercase.
It then resets the stream and begins reading again, this time converting each character to
uppercase before printing. Here's the output:

```
abc
ABC
```

ByteArrayOutputStream

ByteArrayOutputStream is an implementation of an output stream that uses a byte array
as the destination. **ByteArrayOutputStream** has two constructors, shown here:

ByteArrayOutputStream( )
ByteArrayOutputStream(int *numBytes*)

In the first form, a buffer of 32 bytes is created. In the second, a buffer is created with
a size equal to that specified by *numBytes*. The buffer is held in the protected **buf** field
of **ByteArrayOutputStream**. The buffer size will be increased automatically, if needed.
The number of bytes held by the buffer is contained in the protected **count** field of
ByteArrayOutputStream.
The following example demonstrates **ByteArrayOutputStream**:

```
// Demonstrate ByteArrayOutputStream.
import java.io.*;

class ByteArrayOutputStreamDemo {
  public static void main(String args[]) throws IOException {
    ByteArrayOutputStream f = new ByteArrayOutputStream();
    String s = "This should end up in the array";
    byte buf[] = s.getBytes();

    f.write(buf);
    System.out.println("Buffer as a string");
    System.out.println(f.toString());
    System.out.println("Into array");
    byte b[] = f.toByteArray();
    for (int i=0; i<b.length; i++) {
      System.out.print((char) b[i]);
    }
    System.out.println("\nTo an OutputStream()");
    OutputStream f2 = new FileOutputStream("test.txt");

    f.writeTo(f2);
    f2.close();
    System.out.println("Doing a reset");
    f.reset();
    for (int i=0; i<3; i++)
      f.write('X');
    System.out.println(f.toString());
  }
}
```

When you run the program, you will create the following output. Notice how after the call
to **reset( )**, the three *X*'s end up at the beginning.

```
Buffer as a string
This should end up in the array
Into array
This should end up in the array
To an OutputStream()
Doing a reset
XXX
```

This example uses the **writeTo( )** convenience method to write the contents of **f** to **test.txt**.
Examining the contents of the **test.txt** file created in the preceding example shows the result
we expected:

```
This should end up in the array
```

Filtered Byte Streams

Filtered streams are simply wrappers around underlying input or output streams that
transparently provide some extended level of functionality. These streams are typically
accessed by methods that are expecting a generic stream, which is a superclass of the
filtered streams. Typical extensions are buffering, character translation, and raw data
translation. The filtered byte streams are **FilterInputStream** and **FilterOutputStream**. Their
constructors are shown here:

FilterOutputStream(OutputStream *os*)
FilterInputStream(InputStream *is*)

The methods provided in these classes are identical to those in **InputStream** and **OutputStream**.

Buffered Byte Streams

For the byte-oriented streams, a *buffered stream* extends a filtered stream class by attaching
a memory buffer to the I/O streams. This buffer allows Java to do I/O operations on more
than a byte at a time, hence increasing performance. Because the buffer is available, skipping,
marking, and resetting of the stream become possible. The buffered byte stream classes are
BufferedInputStream and **BufferedOutputStream**. **PushbackInputStream** also implements
a buffered stream.

BufferedInputStream

Buffering I/O is a very common performance optimization. Java's **BufferedInputStream** class
allows you to "wrap" any **InputStream** into a buffered stream and achieve this performance
improvement.

    BufferedInputStream has two constructors:

BufferedInputStream(InputStream *inputStream*)
BufferedInputStream(InputStream *inputStream*, int *bufSize*)

The first form creates a buffered stream using a default buffer size. In the second, the size
of the buffer is passed in *bufSize*. Use of sizes that are multiples of a memory page, a disk

block, and so on, can have a significant positive impact on performance. This is, however, implementation-dependent. An optimal buffer size is generally dependent on the host operating system, the amount of memory available, and how the machine is configured. To make good use of buffering doesn't necessarily require quite this degree of sophistication. A good guess for a size is around 8,192 bytes, and attaching even a rather small buffer to an I/O stream is always a good idea. That way, the low-level system can read blocks of data from the disk or network and store the results in your buffer. Thus, even if you are reading the data a byte at a time out of the **InputStream**, you will be manipulating fast memory most of the time.

Buffering an input stream also provides the foundation required to support moving backward in the stream of the available buffer. Beyond the **read( )** and **skip( )** methods implemented in any **InputStream, BufferedInputStream** also supports the **mark( )** and **reset( )** methods. This support is reflected by **BufferedInputStream.markSupported( )** returning **true**.

The following example contrives a situation where we can use **mark( )** to remember where we are in an input stream and later use **reset( )** to get back there. This example is parsing a stream for the HTML entity reference for the copyright symbol. Such a reference begins with an ampersand (&) and ends with a semicolon (;) without any intervening whitespace. The sample input has two ampersands to show the case where the **reset( )** happens and where it does not.

```
// Use buffered input.
import java.io.*;

class BufferedInputStreamDemo {
  public static void main(String args[]) throws IOException {
    String s = "This is a &copy; copyright symbol " +
      "but this is &copy not.\n";
    byte buf[] = s.getBytes();
    ByteArrayInputStream in = new ByteArrayInputStream(buf);
    BufferedInputStream f = new BufferedInputStream(in);
    int c;
    boolean marked = false;

    while ((c = f.read()) != -1) {
      switch(c) {
      case '&':
        if (!marked) {
          f.mark(32);
          marked = true;
        } else {
          marked = false;
        }
        break;
      case ';':
        if (marked) {
          marked = false;
          System.out.print("(c)");
        } else
          System.out.print((char) c);
        break;
```

```
      case ' ':
        if (marked) {
          marked = false;
          f.reset();
          System.out.print("&");
        } else
          System.out.print((char) c);
        break;
      default:
        if (!marked)
            System.out.print((char) c);
        break;
      }
    }
  }
}
```

Notice that this example uses **mark(32)**, which preserves the mark for the next 32 bytes read (which is enough for all entity references). Here is the output produced by this program:

```
This is a (c) copyright symbol but this is &copy not.
```

BufferedOutputStream

A **BufferedOutputStream** is similar to any **OutputStream** with the exception of an added **flush( )** method that is used to ensure that data buffers are physically written to the actual output device. Since the point of a **BufferedOutputStream** is to improve performance by reducing the number of times the system actually writes data, you may need to call **flush( )** to cause any data that is in the buffer to be immediately written.

Unlike buffered input, buffering output does not provide additional functionality. Buffers for output in Java are there to increase performance. Here are the two available constructors:

BufferedOutputStream(OutputStream *outputStream*)
BufferedOutputStream(OutputStream *outputStream*, int *bufSize*)

The first form creates a buffered stream using the default buffer size. In the second form, the size of the buffer is passed in *bufSize*.

PushbackInputStream

One of the novel uses of buffering is the implementation of pushback. *Pushback* is used on an input stream to allow a byte to be read and then returned (that is, "pushed back") to the stream. The **PushbackInputStream** class implements this idea. It provides a mechanism to "peek" at what is coming from an input stream without disrupting it.

PushbackInputStream has the following constructors:

PushbackInputStream(InputStream *inputStream*)
PushbackInputStream(InputStream *inputStream*, int *numBytes*)

The first form creates a stream object that allows one byte to be returned to the input stream. The second form creates a stream that has a pushback buffer that is *numBytes* long. This allows multiple bytes to be returned to the input stream.

Beyond the familiar methods of **InputStream**, **PushbackInputStream** provides **unread( )**, shown here:

void unread(int *ch*)
void unread(byte *buffer*[ ])
void unread(byte *buffer*, int *offset*, int *numChars*)

The first form pushes back the low-order byte of *ch*. This will be the next byte returned by a subsequent call to **read( )**. The second form returns the bytes in *buffer*. The third form pushes back *numChars* bytes beginning at *offset* from *buffer*. An **IOException** will be thrown if there is an attempt to return a byte when the pushback buffer is full.

Here is an example that shows how a programming language parser might use a **PushbackInputStream** and **unread( )** to deal with the difference between the = = operator for comparison and the = operator for assignment:

```
// Demonstrate unread().
import java.io.*;

class PushbackInputStreamDemo {
  public static void main(String args[]) throws IOException {
    String s = "if (a == 4) a = 0;\n";
    byte buf[] = s.getBytes();
    ByteArrayInputStream in = new ByteArrayInputStream(buf);
    PushbackInputStream f = new PushbackInputStream(in);
    int c;

    while ((c = f.read()) != -1) {
      switch(c) {
      case '=':
        if ((c = f.read()) == '=')
          System.out.print(".eq.");
        else {
          System.out.print("<-");
          f.unread(c);
        }
        break;
      default:
        System.out.print((char) c);
        break;
      }
    }
  }
}
```

Here is the output for this example. Notice that = = was replaced by ".eq." and = was replaced by "<-".

```
if (a .eq. 4) a <- 0;
```

CAUTION *PushbackInputStream has the side effect of invalidating the* **mark( )** *or* **reset( )** *methods of the* **InputStream** *used to create it. Use* **markSupported( )** *to check any stream on which you are going to use* **mark( )**/**reset( )**.

SequenceInputStream

The **SequenceInputStream** class allows you to concatenate multiple **InputStream**s. The construction of a **SequenceInputStream** is different from any other **InputStream**. A **SequenceInputStream** constructor uses either a pair of **InputStream**s or an **Enumeration** of **InputStream**s as its argument:

SequenceInputStream(InputStream *first*, InputStream *second*)
SequenceInputStream(Enumeration <? extends InputStream> *streamEnum*)

Operationally, the class fulfills read requests from the first **InputStream** until it runs out and then switches over to the second one. In the case of an **Enumeration**, it will continue through all of the **InputStream**s until the end of the last one is reached.

Here is a simple example that uses a **SequenceInputStream** to output the contents of two files:

```
// Demonstrate sequenced input.
import java.io.*;
import java.util.*;

class InputStreamEnumerator implements Enumeration<FileInputStream> {
  private Enumeration<String> files;

  public InputStreamEnumerator(Vector<String> files) {
    this.files = files.elements();
  }

  public boolean hasMoreElements() {
    return files.hasMoreElements();
  }

  public FileInputStream nextElement() {
    try {
      return new FileInputStream(files.nextElement().toString());
    } catch (IOException e) {
      return null;
    }
  }
}

class SequenceInputStreamDemo {
  public static void main(String args[])
    throws IOException {

    int c;
    Vector<String> files = new Vector<String>();

    files.addElement("/autoexec.bat");
    files.addElement("/config.sys");
    InputStreamEnumerator e = new InputStreamEnumerator(files);
    InputStream input = new SequenceInputStream(e);

    while ((c = input.read()) != -1) {
      System.out.print((char) c);
```

```
    }

    input.close();
  }
}
```

This example creates a **Vector** and then adds two filenames to it. It passes that vector of names to the **InputStreamEnumerator** class, which is designed to provide a wrapper on the vector where the elements returned are not the filenames but rather, open **FileInputStream**s on those names. The **SequenceInputStream** opens each file in turn, and this example prints the contents of the two files.

PrintStream

The **PrintStream** class provides all of the output capabilities we have been using from the **System** file handle, **System.out**, since the beginning of the book. This makes **PrintStream** one of Java's most often used classes. It implements the **Appendable**, **Closeable**, and **Flushable** interfaces.

PrintStream defines several constructors. The ones shown next have been specified from the start:

PrintStream(OutputStream *outputStream*)
PrintStream(OutputStream *outputStream*, boolean *flushOnNewline*)
PrintStream(OutputStream *outputStream*, boolean *flushOnNewline*,
      String *charSet*)

Here, *outputStream* specifies an open **OutputStream** that will receive output. The *flushOnNewline* parameter controls whether the output buffer is automatically flushed every time a newline (**\n**) character or a byte array is written, or when **println( )** is called. If *flushOnNewline* is **true**, flushing automatically takes place. If it is **false**, flushing is not automatic. The first constructor does not automatically flush. You can specify a character encoding by passing its name in *charSet*.

The next set of constructors give you an easy way to construct a **PrintStream** that writes its output to a file.

PrintStream(File *outputFile*) throws FileNotFoundException
PrintStream(File *outputFile*, String *charSet*)
  throws FileNotFoundException, UnsupportedEncodingException

PrintStream(String *outputFileName*) throws FileNotFoundException
PrintStream(String *outputFileName*, String *charSet*)
  throws FileNotFoundException, UnsupportedEncodingException

These allow a **PrintStream** to be created from a **File** object or by specifying the name of a file. In either case, the file is automatically created. Any preexisting file by the same name is destroyed. Once created, the **PrintStream** object directs all output to the specified file. You can specify a character encoding by passing its name in *charSet*.

PrintStream supports the **print( )** and **println( )** methods for all types, including **Object**. If an argument is not a primitive type, the **PrintStream** methods will call the object's **toString( )** method and then display the result.

Recently (with the release of JDK 5), the **printf( )** method was added to **PrintStream**. It allows you to specify the precise format of the data to be written. The **printf( )** method uses the **Formatter** class (described in Chapter 18) to format data. It then writes this data to the invoking stream. Although formatting can be done manually, by using **Formatter** directly, **printf( )** streamlines the process. It also parallels the C/C++ **printf( )** function, which makes it easy to convert existing C/C++ code into Java. Frankly, **printf( )** is a much welcome addition to the Java API because it greatly simplifies the output of formatted data to the console.

The **printf( )** method has the following general forms:

PrintStream printf(String *fmtString*, Object ... *args*)

PrintStream printf(Locale *loc*, String *fmtString*, Object ... *args*)

The first version writes *args* to standard output in the format specified by *fmtString*, using the default locale. The second lets you specify a locale. Both return the invoking **PrintStream**.

In general, **printf( )** works in a manner similar to the **format( )** method specified by **Formatter**. The *fmtString* consists of two types of items. The first type is composed of characters that are simply copied to the output buffer. The second type contains format specifiers that define the way the subsequent arguments, specified by *args*, are displayed. For complete information on formatting output, including a description of the format specifiers, see the **Formatter** class in Chapter 18.

Because **System.out** is a **PrintStream**, you can call **printf( )** on **System.out**. Thus, **printf( )** can be used in place of **println( )** when writing to the console whenever formatted output is desired. For example, the following program uses **printf( )** to output numeric values in various formats. In the past, such formatting required a bit of work. With the addition of **printf( )**, this now becomes an easy task.

```
// Demonstrate printf().

class PrintfDemo {
  public static void main(String args[]) {
    System.out.println("Here are some numeric values " +
                       "in different formats.\n");

    System.out.printf("Various integer formats: ");
    System.out.printf("%d %(d %+d %05d\n", 3, -3, 3, 3);

    System.out.println();

    System.out.printf("Default floating-point format: %f\n",
                   1234567.123);
    System.out.printf("Floating-point with commas: %,f\n",
                   1234567.123);
    System.out.printf("Negative floating-point default: %,f\n",
                   -1234567.123);
    System.out.printf("Negative floating-point option: %,(f\n",
                   -1234567.123);

    System.out.println();

    System.out.printf("Line up positive and negative values:\n");
    System.out.printf("% ,.2f\n% ,.2f\n",
```

```
                           1234567.123, -1234567.123);

    }
}
```

The output is shown here:

```
Here are some numeric values in different formats.

Various integer formats: 3 (3) +3 00003

Default floating-point format: 1234567.123000
Floating-point with commas: 1,234,567.123000
Negative floating-point default: -1,234,567.123000
Negative floating-point option: (1,234,567.123000)

Line up positive and negative values:
 1,234,567.12
-1,234,567.12
```

PrintStream also defines the **format( )** method. It has these general forms:

PrintStream format(String *fmtString*, Object ... *args*)

PrintStream format(Locale *loc*, String *fmtString*, Object ... *args*)

It works exactly like **printf( )**.

DataOutputStream and DataInputStream

DataOutputStream and **DataInputStream** enable you to write or read primitive data to or from a stream. They implement the **DataOutput** and **DataInput** interfaces, respectively. These interfaces define methods that convert primitive values to or from a sequence of bytes. These streams make it easy to store binary data, such as integers or floating-point values, in a file. Each is examined here.

DataOutputStream extends **FilterOutputStream**, which extends **OutputStream**. **DataOutputStream** defines the following constructor:

DataOutputStream(OutputStream *outputStream*)

Here, *outputStream* specifies the output stream to which data will be written.

DataOutputStream supports all of the methods defined by it superclasses. However, it is the methods defined by the **DataOutput** interface, which it implements, that make it interesting. **DataOutput** defines methods that convert values of a primitive type into a byte sequence and then writes it to the underlying stream. Here is a sampling of these methods:

final void writeDouble(double *value*) throws IOException
final void writeBoolean(boolean *value*) throws IOException
final void writeInt(int *value*) throws IOException

Here, *value* is the value written to the stream.

DataInputStream is the complement of **DataOuputStream**. It extends **FilterInputStream**, which extends **InputStream**, and it implements the **DataInput** interface. Here is its only constructor:

DataInputStream(InputStream *inputStream*)

Here, *inputStream* specifies the input stream from which data will be read.

Like **DataOutputStream**, **DataInputStream** supports all of the methods of its superclasses, but it is the methods defined by the **DataInput** interface that make it unique. These methods read a sequence of bytes and convert them into values of a primitive type. Here is a sampling of these methods:

double readDouble( ) throws IOException
boolean readBoolean( ) throws IOException
int readInt( ) throws IOException

The following program demonstrates the use of **DataOutputStream** and **DataInputStream**:

```java
import java.io.*;

class DataIODemo {
  public static void main(String args[])
    throws IOException {

    FileOutputStream fout = new FileOutputStream("Test.dat");
    DataOutputStream out = new DataOutputStream(fout);

    out.writeDouble(98.6);
    out.writeInt(1000);
    out.writeBoolean(true);

    out.close();

    FileInputStream fin = new FileInputStream("Test.dat");
    DataInputStream in = new DataInputStream(fin);

    double d = in.readDouble();
    int i = in.readInt();
    boolean b = in.readBoolean();

    System.out.println("Here are the values:  " +
                  d + " " + i + " " + b);

    in.close();
  }
}
```

The output is shown here:

```
Here are the values:  98.6 1000 true
```

RandomAccessFile

RandomAccessFile encapsulates a random-access file. It is not derived from **InputStream** or **OutputStream**. Instead, it implements the interfaces **DataInput** and **DataOutput**, which define the basic I/O methods. It also implements the **Closeable** interface. **RandomAccessFile** is special because it supports positioning requests—that is, you can position the *file pointer* within the file. It has these two constructors:

RandomAccessFile(File *fileObj*, String *access*)
    throws FileNotFoundException

RandomAccessFile(String *filename*, String *access*)
    throws FileNotFoundException

In the first form, *fileObj* specifies the name of the file to open as a **File** object. In the second form, the name of the file is passed in *filename*. In both cases, *access* determines what type of file access is permitted. If it is "r", then the file can be read, but not written. If it is "rw", then the file is opened in read-write mode. If it is "rws", the file is opened for read-write operations and every change to the file's data or metadata will be immediately written to the physical device. If it is "rwd", the file is opened for read-write operations and every change to the file's data will be immediately written to the physical device.

The method **seek( )**, shown here, is used to set the current position of the file pointer within the file:

void seek(long *newPos*) throws IOException

Here, *newPos* specifies the new position, in bytes, of the file pointer from the beginning of the file. After a call to **seek( )**, the next read or write operation will occur at the new file position.

RandomAccessFile implements the standard input and output methods, which you can use to read and write to random access files. It also includes some additional methods. One is **setLength( )**. It has this signature:

void setLength(long *len*) throws IOException

This method sets the length of the invoking file to that specified by *len*. This method can be used to lengthen or shorten a file. If the file is lengthened, the added portion is undefined.

The Character Streams

While the byte stream classes provide sufficient functionality to handle any type of I/O operation, they cannot work directly with Unicode characters. Since one of the main purposes of Java is to support the "write once, run anywhere" philosophy, it was necessary to include direct I/O support for characters. In this section, several of the character I/O classes are discussed. As explained earlier, at the top of the character stream hierarchies are the **Reader** and **Writer** abstract classes. We will begin with them.

NOTE   *As discussed in Chapter 13, the character I/O classes were added by the 1.1 release of Java. Because of this, you may still find legacy code that uses byte streams where character streams would be more appropriate. When working on such code, it is a good idea to update it.*

Reader

Reader is an abstract class that defines Java's model of streaming character input. It implements the **Closeable** and **Readable** interfaces. All of the methods in this class (except for **markSupported( )**) will throw an **IOException** on error conditions. Table 19-3 provides a synopsis of the methods in **Reader**.

Writer

Writer is an abstract class that defines streaming character output. It implements the **Closeable**, **Flushable**, and **Appendable** interfaces. All of the methods in this class throw an **IOException** in the case of errors. Table 19-4 shows a synopsis of the methods in **Writer**.

FileReader

The **FileReader** class creates a **Reader** that you can use to read the contents of a file. Its two most commonly used constructors are shown here:

FileReader(String *filePath*)
FileReader(File *fileObj*)

Either can throw a **FileNotFoundException**. Here, *filePath* is the full path name of a file, and *fileObj* is a **File** object that describes the file.

The following example shows how to read lines from a file and print these to the standard output stream. It reads its own source file, which must be in the current directory.

```
// Demonstrate FileReader.
import java.io.*;

class FileReaderDemo {
  public static void main(String args[]) throws IOException {
    FileReader fr = new FileReader("FileReaderDemo.java");
    BufferedReader br = new BufferedReader(fr);
    String s;

    while((s = br.readLine()) != null) {
      System.out.println(s);
    }

    fr.close();
  }
}
```

FileWriter

FileWriter creates a **Writer** that you can use to write to a file. Its most commonly used constructors are shown here:

FileWriter(String *filePath*)
FileWriter(String *filePath*, boolean *append*)
FileWriter(File *fileObj*)
FileWriter(File *fileObj*, boolean *append*)

They can throw an **IOException**. Here, *filePath* is the full path name of a file, and *fileObj* is a **File** object that describes the file. If *append* is **true**, then output is appended to the end of the file.

Method	Description
abstract void close( )	Closes the input source. Further read attempts will generate an **IOException**.
void mark(int *numChars*)	Places a mark at the current point in the input stream that will remain valid until *numChars* characters are read.
boolean markSupported( )	Returns **true** if **mark( )/reset( )** are supported on this stream.
int read( )	Returns an integer representation of the next available character from the invoking input stream. –1 is returned when the end of the file is encountered.
int read(char *buffer*[ ])	Attempts to read up to *buffer.length* characters into *buffer* and returns the actual number of characters that were successfully read. –1 is returned when the end of the file is encountered.
abstract int read(char *buffer*[ ], int *offset*, int *numChars*)	Attempts to read up to *numChars* characters into *buffer* starting at *buffer*[*offset*], returning the number of characters successfully read. –1 is returned when the end of the file is encountered.
boolean ready( )	Returns **true** if the next input request will not wait. Otherwise, it returns **false**.
void reset( )	Resets the input pointer to the previously set mark.
long skip(long *numChars*)	Skips over *numChars* characters of input, returning the number of characters actually skipped.

TABLE 19-3   The Methods Defined by **Reader**

Method	Description
Writer append(char *ch*)	Appends *ch* to the end of the invoking output stream. Returns a reference to the invoking stream.
Writer append(CharSequence *chars*)	Appends *chars* to the end of the invoking output stream. Returns a reference to the invoking stream.
Writer append(CharSequence *chars*, int *begin*, int *end*)	Appends the subrange of *chars* specified by *begin* and *end*–1 to the end of the invoking ouput stream. Returns a reference to the invoking stream.
abstract void close( )	Closes the output stream. Further write attempts will generate an **IOException**.
abstract void flush( )	Finalizes the output state so that any buffers are cleared. That is, it flushes the output buffers.
void write(int *ch*)	Writes a single character to the invoking output stream. Note that the parameter is an **int**, which allows you to call **write** with expressions without having to cast them back to **char**.

TABLE 19-4   The Methods Defined by **Writer**

Method	Description
void write(char *buffer*[ ])	Writes a complete array of characters to the invoking output stream.
abstract void write(char *buffer*[ ], int *offset*, int *numChars*)	Writes a subrange of *numChars* characters from the array *buffer*, beginning at *buffer*[*offset*] to the invoking output stream.
void write(String *str*)	Writes *str* to the invoking output stream.
void write(String *str*, int *offset*, int *numChars*)	Writes a subrange of *numChars* characters from the string *str*, beginning at the specified *offset*.

TABLE 19-4   The Methods Defined by **Writer** *(continued)*

Creation of a **FileWriter** is not dependent on the file already existing. **FileWriter** will create the file before opening it for output when you create the object. In the case where you attempt to open a read-only file, an **IOException** will be thrown.

The following example is a character stream version of an example shown earlier when **FileOutputStream** was discussed. This version creates a sample buffer of characters by first making a **String** and then using the **getChars( )** method to extract the character array equivalent. It then creates three files. The first, **file1.txt**, will contain every other character from the sample. The second, **file2.txt**, will contain the entire set of characters. Finally, the third, **file3.txt**, will contain only the last quarter.

```
// Demonstrate FileWriter.
import java.io.*;

class FileWriterDemo {
  public static void main(String args[]) throws IOException {
    String source = "Now is the time for all good men\n"
      + " to come to the aid of their country\n"
      + " and pay their due taxes.";
    char buffer[] = new char[source.length()];
    source.getChars(0, source.length(), buffer, 0);

    FileWriter f0 = new FileWriter("file1.txt");
    for (int i=0; i < buffer.length; i += 2) {
      f0.write(buffer[i]);
    }
    f0.close();

    FileWriter f1 = new FileWriter("file2.txt");
    f1.write(buffer);
    f1.close();

    FileWriter f2 = new FileWriter("file3.txt");

    f2.write(buffer,buffer.length-buffer.length/4,buffer.length/4);
    f2.close();
  }
}
```

CharArrayReader

CharArrayReader is an implementation of an input stream that uses a character array as the source. This class has two constructors, each of which requires a character array to provide the data source:

CharArrayReader(char *array*[ ])
CharArrayReader(char *array*[ ], int *start*, int *numChars*)

Here, *array* is the input source. The second constructor creates a **Reader** from a subset of your character array that begins with the character at the index specified by *start* and is *numChars* long.

The following example uses a pair of **CharArrayReader**s:

```
// Demonstrate CharArrayReader.
import java.io.*;

public class CharArrayReaderDemo {
  public static void main(String args[]) throws IOException {
    String tmp = "abcdefghijklmnopqrstuvwxyz";
    int length = tmp.length();
    char c[] = new char[length];

    tmp.getChars(0, length, c, 0);
    CharArrayReader input1 = new CharArrayReader(c);
    CharArrayReader input2 = new CharArrayReader(c, 0, 5);

    int i;
    System.out.println("input1 is:");
    while((i = input1.read()) != -1) {
      System.out.print((char)i);
    }
    System.out.println();

    System.out.println("input2 is:");
    while((i = input2.read()) != -1) {
      System.out.print((char)i);
    }
    System.out.println();
  }
}
```

The **input1** object is constructed using the entire lowercase alphabet, while **input2** contains only the first five letters. Here is the output:

```
input1 is:
abcdefghijklmnopqrstuvwxyz
input2 is:
abcde
```

CharArrayWriter

CharArrayWriter is an implementation of an output stream that uses an array as the destination. **CharArrayWriter** has two constructors, shown here:

CharArrayWriter( )
CharArrayWriter(int *numChars*)

In the first form, a buffer with a default size is created. In the second, a buffer is created with a size equal to that specified by *numChars*. The buffer is held in the **buf** field of **CharArrayWriter**. The buffer size will be increased automatically, if needed. The number of characters held by the buffer is contained in the **count** field of **CharArrayWriter**. Both **buf** and **count** are protected fields.

The following example demonstrates **CharArrayWriter** by reworking the sample program shown earlier for **ByteArrayOutputStream**. It produces the same output as the previous version.

```
// Demonstrate CharArrayWriter.
import java.io.*;

class CharArrayWriterDemo {
  public static void main(String args[]) throws IOException {
    CharArrayWriter f = new CharArrayWriter();
    String s = "This should end up in the array";
    char buf[] = new char[s.length()];

    s.getChars(0, s.length(), buf, 0);
    f.write(buf);
    System.out.println("Buffer as a string");
    System.out.println(f.toString());
    System.out.println("Into array");

    char c[] = f.toCharArray();
    for (int i=0; i<c.length; i++) {
      System.out.print(c[i]);
    }

    System.out.println("\nTo a FileWriter()");
    FileWriter f2 = new FileWriter("test.txt");
    f.writeTo(f2);
    f2.close();
    System.out.println("Doing a reset");
    f.reset();
    for (int i=0; i<3; i++)
      f.write('X');
    System.out.println(f.toString());
  }
}
```

BufferedReader

BufferedReader improves performance by buffering input. It has two constructors:

BufferedReader(Reader *inputStream*)
BufferedReader(Reader *inputStream*, int *bufSize*)

The first form creates a buffered character stream using a default buffer size. In the second, the size of the buffer is passed in *bufSize*.

As is the case with the byte-oriented stream, buffering an input character stream also provides the foundation required to support moving backward in the stream within the available buffer. To support this, **BufferedReader** implements the **mark( )** and **reset( )** methods, and **BufferedReader.markSupported( )** returns **true**.

The following example reworks the **BufferedInputStream** example, shown earlier, so that it uses a **BufferedReader** character stream rather than a buffered byte stream. As before, it uses **mark( )** and **reset( )** methods to parse a stream for the HTML entity reference for the copyright symbol. Such a reference begins with an ampersand (&) and ends with a semicolon (;) without any intervening whitespace. The sample input has two ampersands, to show the case where the **reset( )** happens and where it does not. Output is the same as that shown earlier.

```
// Use buffered input.
import java.io.*;

class BufferedReaderDemo {
  public static void main(String args[]) throws IOException {
    String s = "This is a &copy; copyright symbol " +
      "but this is &copy not.\n";
    char buf[] = new char[s.length()];
    s.getChars(0, s.length(), buf, 0);
    CharArrayReader in = new CharArrayReader(buf);
    BufferedReader f = new BufferedReader(in);
    int c;
    boolean marked = false;

    while ((c = f.read()) != -1) {
      switch(c) {
      case '&':
        if (!marked) {

          f.mark(32);
          marked = true;
        } else {
          marked = false;
        }
        break;
      case ';':
        if (marked) {
          marked = false;
          System.out.print("(c)");
        } else
          System.out.print((char) c);
        break;
      case ' ':
        if (marked) {
          marked = false;
          f.reset();
          System.out.print("&");
        } else
          System.out.print((char) c);
        break;
```

```
      default:
        if (!marked)
            System.out.print((char) c);
        break;
      }
    }
  }
}
```

BufferedWriter

A **BufferedWriter** is a **Writer** that buffers ouput. Using a **BufferedWriter** can increase performance by reducing the number of times data is actually physically written to the output stream.

A **BufferedWriter** has these two constructors:

BufferedWriter(Writer *outputStream*)
BufferedWriter(Writer *outputStream*, int *bufSize*)

The first form creates a buffered stream using a buffer with a default size. In the second, the size of the buffer is passed in *bufSize*.

PushbackReader

The **PushbackReader** class allows one or more characters to be returned to the input stream. This allows you to look ahead in the input stream. Here are its two constructors:

PushbackReader(Reader *inputStream*)
PushbackReader(Reader *inputStream*, int *bufSize*)

The first form creates a buffered stream that allows one character to be pushed back. In the second, the size of the pushback buffer is passed in *bufSize*.

PushbackReader provides **unread( )**, which returns one or more characters to the invoking input stream. It has the three forms shown here:

void unread(int *ch*)
void unread(char *buffer*[ ])
void unread(char *buffer*[ ], int *offset*, int *numChars*)

The first form pushes back the character passed in *ch*. This will be the next character returned by a subsequent call to **read( )**. The second form returns the characters in *buffer*. The third form pushes back *numChars* characters beginning at *offset* from *buffer*. An **IOException** will be thrown if there is an attempt to return a character when the pushback buffer is full.

The following program reworks the earlier **PushBackInputStream** example by replacing **PushBackInputStream** with a **PushbackReader**. As before, it shows how a programming language parser can use a pushback stream to deal with the difference between the == operator for comparison and the = operator for assignment.

```
// Demonstrate unread().
import java.io.*;

class PushbackReaderDemo {
  public static void main(String args[]) throws IOException {
    String s = "if (a == 4) a = 0;\n";
```

```
       char buf[] = new char[s.length()];
       s.getChars(0, s.length(), buf, 0);
       CharArrayReader in = new CharArrayReader(buf);
       PushbackReader f = new PushbackReader(in);
       int c;

       while ((c = f.read()) != -1) {
         switch(c) {
         case '=':
           if ((c = f.read()) == '=')
             System.out.print(".eq.");
           else {
             System.out.print("<-");
             f.unread(c);
           }
           break;
        default:
          System.out.print((char) c);
          break;
         }
       }
     }
   }
}
```

PrintWriter

PrintWriter is essentially a character-oriented version of **PrintStream**. It implements the **Appendable**, **Closeable**, and **Flushable** interfaces. **PrintWriter** has several constructors. The following have been supplied by **PrintWriter** from the start:

PrintWriter(OutputStream *outputStream*)
PrintWriter(OutputStream *outputStream*, boolean *flushOnNewline*)

PrintWriter(Writer *outputStream*)
PrintWriter(Writer *outputStream*, boolean *flushOnNewline*)

Here, *outputStream* specifies an open **OutputStream** that will receive output. The *flushOnNewline* parameter controls whether the output buffer is automatically flushed every time **println( )**, **printf( )**, or **format( )** is called. If *flushOnNewline* is **true**, flushing automatically takes place. If **false**, flushing is not automatic. Constructors that do not specify the *flushOnNewline* parameter do not automatically flush.

The next set of constructors give you an easy way to construct a **PrintWriter** that writes its output to a file.

PrintWriter(File *outputFile*) throws FileNotFoundException
PrintWriter(File *outputFile*, String *charSet*)
    throws FileNotFoundException, UnsupportedEncodingException

PrintWriter(String *outputFileName*) throws FileNotFoundException
PrintWriter(String *outputFileName*, String *charSet*)
    throws FileNotFoundException, UnsupportedEncodingException

These allow a **PrintWriter** to be created from a **File** object or by specifying the name of a file. In either case, the file is automatically created. Any preexisting file by the same name is destroyed. Once created, the **PrintWriter** object directs all output to the specified file. You can specify a character encoding by passing its name in *charSet*.

PrintWriter supports the **print( )** and **println( )** methods for all types, including **Object**. If an argument is not a primitive type, the **PrintWriter** methods will call the object's **toString( )** method and then output the result.

PrintWriter also supports the **printf( )** method. It works the same way it does in the **PrintStream** class described earlier: it allows you to specify the precise format of the data. Here is how **printf( )** is declared in **PrintWriter**:

PrintWriter printf(String *fmtString*, Object ... *args*)

PrintWriter printf(Locale *loc*, String *fmtString*, Object ... *args*)

The first version writes *args* to standard output in the format specified by *fmtString*, using the default locale. The second lets you specify a locale. Both return the invoking **PrintWriter**.

The **format( )** method is also supported. It has these general forms:

PrintWriter format(String *fmtString*, Object ... *args*)

PrintWriter format(Locale *loc*, String *fmtString*, Object ... *args*)

It works exactly like **printf( )**.

The Console Class

Java SE 6 adds the **Console** class. It is used to read from and write to the console, if one exists. It implements the **Flushable** interface. **Console** is primarily a convenience class because most of its functionality is available through **System.in** and **System.out**. However, its use can simplify some types of console interactions, especially when reading strings from the console.

Console supplies no constructors. Instead, a **Console** object is obtained by calling **System.console( )**, which is shown here:

static Console console( )

If a console is available, then a reference to it is returned. Otherwise, **null** is returned. A console will not be available in all cases. Thus, if **null** is returned, no console I/O is possible.

Console defines the methods shown in Table 19-5. Notice that the input methods, such as **readLine( )**, throw **IOError** if an input error occurs. **IOError** is a new exception added by Java SE 6, and it is a subclass of **Error**. It indicates an I/O failure that is beyond the control of your program. Thus, you will not normally catch an **IOError**. Frankly, if an **IOError** is thrown while accessing the console, it usually means that there has been a catastrophic system failure.

Also notice the **readPassword( )** methods. These methods let your application read a password without echoing what is typed. When reading passwords, you should "zero-out" both the array that holds the string entered by the user and the array that holds the password that the string is tested against. This reduces the chance that a malicious program will be able to obtain a password by scanning memory.

Method	Description
void flush( )	Causes buffered output to be written physically to the console.
Console format(String *fmtString,* Object...*args*)	Writes *args* to the console using the format specified by *fmtString.*
Console printf(String *fmtString,* Object...*args*)	Writes *args* to the console using the format specified by *fmtString.*
Reader reader( )	Returns a reference to a **Reader** connected to the console.
String readLine( )	Reads and returns a string entered at the keyboard. Input stops when the user presses ENTER. If the end of the console input stream has been reached, **null** is returned. An **IOError** is thrown on failure.
String readLine(String *fmtString,* Object...*args*)	Displays a prompting string formatted as specified by *fmtString* and *args,* and then reads and returns a string entered at the keyboard. Input stops when the user presses ENTER. If the end of the console input stream has been reached, **null** is returned. An **IOError** is thrown on failure.
char[ ] readPassword( )	Reads a string entered at the keyboard. Input stops when the user presses ENTER. The string is not displayed. If the end of the console input stream has been reached, **null** is returned. An **IOError** is thrown on failure.
char[ ] readPassword(String *fmtString,* Object... *args*)	Displays a prompting string formatted as specified by *fmtString* and *args,* and then reads a string entered at the keyboard. Input stops when the user presses ENTER. The string is not displayed. If the end of the console input stream has been reached, **null** is returned. An **IOError** is thrown on failure.
PrintWriter writer( )	Returns a reference to a **Writer** connected to the console.

TABLE 19-5   The Methods Defined by **Console**

Here is an example that demonstrates the **Console** class:

```
// Demonstrate Console.
import java.io.*;

class ConsoleDemo {
  public static void main(String args[]) {
    String str;
    Console con;

    // Obtain a reference to the console.
    con = System.console();
```

```
    // If no console available, exit.
    if(con == null) return;

    // Read a string and then display it.
    str = con.readLine("Enter a string: ");
    con.printf("Here is your string: %s\n", str);
  }
}
```

Here is sample output:

```
Enter a string: This is a test.
Here is your string: This is a test.
```

Using Stream I/O

The following example demonstrates several of Java's I/O character stream classes and methods. This program implements the standard **wc** (word count) command. The program has two modes: If no filenames are provided as arguments, the program operates on the standard input stream. If one or more filenames are specified, the program operates on each of them.

```
// A word counting utility.
import java.io.*;

class WordCount {
  public static int words = 0;
  public static int lines = 0;
  public static int chars = 0;

  public static void wc(InputStreamReader isr)
    throws IOException {
    int c = 0;
    boolean lastWhite = true;
    String whiteSpace = " \t\n\r";

    while ((c = isr.read()) != -1) {
      // Count characters
      chars++;
      // Count lines
      if (c == '\n') {
        lines++;
      }
      // Count words by detecting the start of a word
      int index = whiteSpace.indexOf(c);
      if(index == -1) {
        if(lastWhite == true) {
          ++words;
        }
        lastWhite = false;
      }
      else {
        lastWhite = true;
```

PART II

```
      }
    }
    if(chars != 0) {
      ++lines;
    }
  }

  public static void main(String args[]) {
    FileReader fr;
    try {
      if (args.length == 0) { // We're working with stdin
        wc(new InputStreamReader(System.in));
      }
      else { // We're working with a list of files
        for (int i = 0; i < args.length; i++) {
          fr = new FileReader(args[i]);
          wc(fr);
        }
      }
    }
    catch (IOException e) {
      return;
    }
    System.out.println(lines + " " + words + " " + chars);
  }
}
```

The **wc( )** method operates on any input stream and counts the number of characters, lines, and words. It tracks the parity of words and whitespace in the **lastNotWhite** variable.

When executed with no arguments, **WordCount** creates an **InputStreamReader** object using **System.in** as the source for the stream. This stream is then passed to **wc( )**, which does the actual counting. When executed with one or more arguments, **WordCount** assumes that these are filenames and creates **FileReader**s for each of them, passing the resultant **FileReader** objects to the **wc( )** method. In either case, it prints the results before exiting.

Improving wc( ) Using a StreamTokenizer

An even better way to look for patterns in an input stream is to use another of Java's I/O classes: **StreamTokenizer**. Similar to **StringTokenizer** from Chapter 18, **StreamTokenizer** breaks up the input stream into *tokens* that are delimited by sets of characters. It has this constructor:

StreamTokenizer(Reader *inStream*)

Here, *inStream* must be some form of **Reader**.

StreamTokenizer defines several methods. In this example, we will use only a few. To reset the default set of delimiters, we will employ the **resetSyntax( )** method. The default set of delimiters is finely tuned for tokenizing Java programs and is thus too specialized for this example. We declare that our tokens, or "words," are any consecutive string of visible characters delimited on both sides by whitespace.

We use the **eolIsSignificant( )** method to ensure that newline characters will be delivered as tokens, so we can count the number of lines as well as words. It has this general form:

void eolIsSignificant(boolean *eolFlag*)

If *eolFlag* is **true**, the end-of-line characters are returned as tokens. If *eolFlag* is **false**, the end-of-line characters are ignored.

The **wordChars( )** method is used to specify the range of characters that can be used in words. Its general form is shown here:

void wordChars(int *start*, int *end*)

Here, *start* and *end* specify the range of valid characters. In this program, characters in the range 33 to 255 are valid word characters.

The whitespace characters are specified using **whitespaceChars( )**. It has this general form:

void whitespaceChars(int *start*, int *end*)

Here, *start* and *end* specify the range of valid whitespace characters.

The next token is obtained from the input stream by calling **nextToken( )**. It returns the type of token.

StreamTokenizer defines four **int** constants: **TT_EOF, TT_EOL, TT_NUMBER,** and **TT_WORD.** There are three instance variables. **nval** is a public **double** used to hold the values of numbers as they are recognized. **sval** is a public **String** used to hold the value of any words as they are recognized. **ttype** is a public **int** indicating the type of token that has just been read by the **nextToken( )** method. If the token is a word, **ttype** equals **TT_WORD.** If the token is a number, **ttype** equals **TT_NUMBER.** If the token is a single character, **ttype** contains its value. If an end-of-line condition has been encountered, **ttype** equals **TT_EOL.** (This assumes that **eolIsSignificant( )** was invoked with a **true** argument.) If the end of the stream has been encountered, **ttype** equals **TT_EOF.**

The word count program revised to use a **StreamTokenizer** is shown here:

```
// Enhanced word count program that uses a StreamTokenizer
import java.io.*;

class WordCount {
  public static int words=0;
  public static int lines=0;
  public static int chars=0;

  public static void wc(Reader r) throws IOException {
    StreamTokenizer tok = new StreamTokenizer(r);

    tok.resetSyntax();
    tok.wordChars(33, 255);
    tok.whitespaceChars(0, ' ');
    tok.eolIsSignificant(true);

    while (tok.nextToken() != tok.TT_EOF) {
      switch (tok.ttype) {
        case StreamTokenizer.TT_EOL:
          lines++;
          chars++;
          break;
        case StreamTokenizer.TT_WORD:
          words++;
```

PART II

```
            default: // FALLSTHROUGH
              chars += tok.sval.length();
              break;
        }
      }
    }

    public static void main(String args[]) {
      if (args.length == 0) { // We're working with stdin
        try {
          wc(new InputStreamReader(System.in));
          System.out.println(lines + " " + words + " " + chars);
        } catch (IOException e) {};
      } else { // We're working with a list of files
        int twords = 0, tchars = 0, tlines = 0;
        for (int i=0; i<args.length; i++) {
          try {
            words = chars = lines = 0;
            wc(new FileReader(args[i]));
            twords += words;
            tchars += chars;
            tlines += lines;
            System.out.println(args[i] + ": " +
              lines + " " + words + " " + chars);
          } catch (IOException e) {
            System.out.println(args[i] + ": error.");
          }
        }
        System.out.println("total: " +
        tlines + " " + twords + " " + tchars);
      }
    }
  }
```

Serialization

Serialization is the process of writing the state of an object to a byte stream. This is useful when you want to save the state of your program to a persistent storage area, such as a file. At a later time, you may restore these objects by using the process of deserialization.

Serialization is also needed to implement Remote Method Invocation (RMI). RMI allows a Java object on one machine to invoke a method of a Java object on a different machine. An object may be supplied as an argument to that remote method. The sending machine serializes the object and transmits it. The receiving machine deserializes it. (More information about RMI appears in Chapter 27.)

Assume that an object to be serialized has references to other objects, which, in turn, have references to still more objects. This set of objects and the relationships among them form a directed graph. There may also be circular references within this object graph. That is, object X may contain a reference to object Y, and object Y may contain a reference back to object X. Objects may also contain references to themselves. The object serialization and deserialization facilities have been designed to work correctly in these scenarios. If you attempt to serialize an object at the top of an object graph, all of the other referenced objects are recursively located and serialized. Similarly, during the process of deserialization, all of these objects and their references are correctly restored.

An overview of the interfaces and classes that support serialization follows.

Serializable

Only an object that implements the **Serializable** interface can be saved and restored by the serialization facilities. The **Serializable** interface defines no members. It is simply used to indicate that a class may be serialized. If a class is serializable, all of its subclasses are also serializable.

Variables that are declared as **transient** are not saved by the serialization facilities. Also, **static** variables are not saved.

Externalizable

The Java facilities for serialization and deserialization have been designed so that much of the work to save and restore the state of an object occurs automatically. However, there are cases in which the programmer may need to have control over these processes. For example, it may be desirable to use compression or encryption techniques. The **Externalizable** interface is designed for these situations.

The **Externalizable** interface defines these two methods:

```
void readExternal(ObjectInput inStream)
    throws IOException, ClassNotFoundException

void writeExternal(ObjectOutput outStream)
    throws IOException
```

In these methods, *inStream* is the byte stream from which the object is to be read, and *outStream* is the byte stream to which the object is to be written.

ObjectOutput

The **ObjectOutput** interface extends the **DataOutput** interface and supports object serialization. It defines the methods shown in Table 19-6. Note especially the **writeObject( )** method. This is called to serialize an object. All of these methods will throw an **IOException** on error conditions.

ObjectOutputStream

The **ObjectOutputStream** class extends the **OutputStream** class and implements the **ObjectOutput** interface. It is responsible for writing objects to a stream. A constructor of this class is

```
ObjectOutputStream(OutputStream outStream) throws IOException
```

The argument *outStream* is the output stream to which serialized objects will be written.

Several commonly used methods in this class are shown in Table 19-7. They will throw an **IOException** on error conditions. There is also an inner class to **ObjectOuputStream** called **PutField**. It facilitates the writing of persistent fields, and its use is beyond the scope of this book.

Method	Description
void close( )	Closes the invoking stream. Further write attempts will generate an **IOException**.
void flush( )	Finalizes the output state so that any buffers are cleared. That is, it flushes the output buffers.
void write(byte *buffer*[ ])	Writes an array of bytes to the invoking stream.
void write(byte *buffer*[ ], int *offset*, int *numBytes*)	Writes a subrange of *numBytes* bytes from the array *buffer*, beginning at *buffer*[*offset*].
void write(int *b*)	Writes a single byte to the invoking stream. The byte written is the low-order byte of *b*.
void writeObject(Object *obj*)	Writes object *obj* to the invoking stream.

TABLE 19-6   The Methods Defined by **ObjectOutput**

Method	Description
void close( )	Closes the invoking stream. Further write attempts will generate an **IOException**.
void flush( )	Finalizes the output state so that any buffers are cleared. That is, it flushes the output buffers.
void write(byte *buffer*[ ])	Writes an array of bytes to the invoking stream.
void write(byte *buffer*[ ], int *offset*, int *numBytes*)	Writes a subrange of *numBytes* bytes from the array *buffer*, beginning at *buffer*[*offset*].
void write(int *b*)	Writes a single **byte** to the invoking stream. The byte written is the low-order byte of *b*.
void writeBoolean(boolean *b*)	Writes a **boolean** to the invoking stream.
void writeByte(int *b*)	Writes a **byte** to the invoking stream. The byte written is the low-order byte of *b*.
void writeBytes(String *str*)	Writes the bytes representing *str* to the invoking stream.
void writeChar(int *c*)	Writes a **char** to the invoking stream.
void writeChars(String *str*)	Writes the characters in *str* to the invoking stream.
void writeDouble(double *d*)	Writes a **double** to the invoking stream.
void writeFloat(float *f*)	Writes a **float** to the invoking stream.
void writeInt(int *i*)	Writes an **int** to the invoking stream.
void writeLong(long *l*)	Writes a **long** to the invoking stream.
final void writeObject(Object *obj*)	Writes *obj* to the invoking stream.
void writeShort(int *i*)	Writes a **short** to the invoking stream.

TABLE 19-7   Commonly Used Methods Defined by **ObjectOutputStream**

ObjectInput

The **ObjectInput** interface extends the **DataInput** interface and defines the methods shown in Table 19-8. It supports object serialization. Note especially the **readObject( )** method. This is called to deserialize an object. All of these methods will throw an **IOException** on error conditions. The **readObject( )** method can also throw **ClassNotFoundException**.

ObjectInputStream

The **ObjectInputStream** class extends the **InputStream** class and implements the **ObjectInput** interface. **ObjectInputStream** is responsible for reading objects from a stream. A constructor of this class is

ObjectInputStream(InputStream *inStream*)
    throws IOException

The argument *inStream* is the input stream from which serialized objects should be read.

Several commonly used methods in this class are shown in Table 19-9. They will throw an **IOException** on error conditions. The **readObject( )** method can also throw **ClassNotFoundException**. There is also an inner class to **ObjectInputStream** called **GetField**. It facilitates the reading of persistent fields, and its use is beyond the scope of this book.

A Serialization Example

The following program illustrates how to use object serialization and deserialization. It begins by instantiating an object of class **MyClass**. This object has three instance variables that are of types **String**, **int**, and **double**. This is the information we want to save and restore.

Method	Description
int available( )	Returns the number of bytes that are now available in the input buffer.
void close( )	Closes the invoking stream. Further read attempts will generate an **IOException**.
int read( )	Returns an integer representation of the next available byte of input. −1 is returned when the end of the file is encountered.
int read(byte *buffer*[ ])	Attempts to read up to *buffer.length* bytes into *buffer*, returning the number of bytes that were successfully read. −1 is returned when the end of the file is encountered.
int read(byte *buffer*[ ], int *offset*, int *numBytes*)	Attempts to read up to *numBytes* bytes into *buffer* starting at *buffer*[*offset*], returning the number of bytes that were successfully read. −1 is returned when the end of the file is encountered.
Object readObject( )	Reads an object from the invoking stream.
long skip(long *numBytes*)	Ignores (that is, skips) *numBytes* bytes in the invoking stream, returning the number of bytes actually ignored.

TABLE 19-8   The Methods Defined by **ObjectInput**

Method	Description
int available( )	Returns the number of bytes that are now available in the input buffer.
void close( )	Closes the invoking stream. Further read attempts will generate an **IOException**.
int read( )	Returns an integer representation of the next available byte of input. −1 is returned when the end of the file is encountered.
int read(byte *buffer*[ ], int *offset*, int *numBytes*)	Attempts to read up to *numBytes* bytes into *buffer* starting at *buffer*[*offset*], returning the number of bytes successfully read. −1 is returned when the end of the file is encountered.
boolean readBoolean( )	Reads and returns a **boolean** from the invoking stream.
byte readByte( )	Reads and returns a **byte** from the invoking stream.
char readChar( )	Reads and returns a **char** from the invoking stream.
double readDouble( )	Reads and returns a **double** from the invoking stream.
float readFloat( )	Reads and returns a **float** from the invoking stream.
void readFully(byte *buffer*[ ])	Reads *buffer.length* bytes into *buffer*. Returns only when all bytes have been read.
void readFully(byte *buffer*[ ], int *offset*, int *numBytes*)	Reads *numBytes* bytes into *buffer* starting at *buffer*[*offset*]. Returns only when *numBytes* have been read.
int readInt( )	Reads and returns an **int** from the invoking stream.
long readLong( )	Reads and returns a **long** from the invoking stream.
final Object readObject( )	Reads and returns an object from the invoking stream.
short readShort( )	Reads and returns a **short** from the invoking stream.
int readUnsignedByte( )	Reads and returns an unsigned **byte** from the invoking stream.
int readUnsignedShort( )	Reads and returns an unsigned **short** from the invoking stream.

TABLE 19-9   Commonly Used Methods Defined by **ObjectInputStream**

A **FileOutputStream** is created that refers to a file named "serial," and an **ObjectOutputStream** is created for that file stream. The **writeObject( )** method of **ObjectOutputStream** is then used to serialize our object. The object output stream is flushed and closed.

A **FileInputStream** is then created that refers to the file named "serial," and an **ObjectInputStream** is created for that file stream. The **readObject( )** method of **ObjectInputStream** is then used to deserialize our object. The object input stream is then closed.

Note that **MyClass** is defined to implement the **Serializable** interface. If this is not done, a **NotSerializableException** is thrown. Try experimenting with this program by declaring some of the **MyClass** instance variables to be **transient**. That data is then not saved during serialization.

```java
import java.io.*;

public class SerializationDemo {
  public static void main(String args[]) {

    // Object serialization
    try {
      MyClass object1 = new MyClass("Hello", -7, 2.7e10);
      System.out.println("object1: " + object1);
      FileOutputStream fos = new FileOutputStream("serial");
      ObjectOutputStream oos = new ObjectOutputStream(fos);
      oos.writeObject(object1);
      oos.flush();
      oos.close();
    }
    catch(IOException e) {
      System.out.println("Exception during serialization: " + e);
      System.exit(0);
    }

    // Object deserialization
    try {
      MyClass object2;
      FileInputStream fis = new FileInputStream("serial");
      ObjectInputStream ois = new ObjectInputStream(fis);
      object2 = (MyClass)ois.readObject();
      ois.close();
      System.out.println("object2: " + object2);
    }
    catch(Exception e) {
      System.out.println("Exception during deserialization: " + e);
      System.exit(0);
    }
  }
}

class MyClass implements Serializable {
  String s;
  int i;
  double d;
  public MyClass(String s, int i, double d) {
    this.s = s;
    this.i = i;
    this.d = d;
  }
  public String toString() {
    return "s=" + s + "; i=" + i + "; d=" + d;
  }
}
```

This program demonstrates that the instance variables of **object1** and **object2** are identical. The output is shown here:

```
object1: s=Hello; i=-7; d=2.7E10
object2: s=Hello; i=-7; d=2.7E10
```

Stream Benefits

The streaming interface to I/O in Java provides a clean abstraction for a complex and often cumbersome task. The composition of the filtered stream classes allows you to dynamically build the custom streaming interface to suit your data transfer requirements. Java programs written to adhere to the abstract, high-level **InputStream**, **OutputStream**, **Reader**, and **Writer** classes will function properly in the future even when new and improved concrete stream classes are invented. As you will see in the next chapter, this model works very well when we switch from a file system–based set of streams to the network and socket streams. Finally, serialization of objects plays an important role in many types of Java programs. Java's serialization I/O classes provide a portable solution to this sometimes tricky task.

Networking

As all readers know, Java is practically a synonym for Internet programming. There are a number of reasons for this, not the least of which is its ability to generate secure, cross-platform, portable code. However, one of the most important reasons that Java is the premier language for network programming are the classes defined in the **java.net** package. They provide an easy-to-use means by which programmers of all skill levels can access network resources.

This chapter explores the **java.net** package. It is important to emphasize that networking is a very large and at times complicated topic. It is not possible for this book to discuss all of the capabilities contained in **java.net**. Instead, this chapter focuses on several of its core classes and interfaces.

Networking Basics

Before we begin, it will be useful to review some key networking concepts and terms. At the core of Java's networking support is the concept of a *socket*. A socket identifies an endpoint in a network. The socket paradigm was part of the 4.2BSD Berkeley UNIX release in the early 1980s. Because of this, the term *Berkeley socket* is also used. Sockets are at the foundation of modern networking because a socket allows a single computer to serve many different clients at once, as well as to serve many different types of information. This is accomplished through the use of a *port*, which is a numbered socket on a particular machine. A server process is said to "listen" to a port until a client connects to it. A server is allowed to accept multiple clients connected to the same port number, although each session is unique. To manage multiple client connections, a server process must be multithreaded or have some other means of multiplexing the simultaneous I/O.

Socket communication takes place via a protocol. *Internet Protocol (IP)* is a low-level routing protocol that breaks data into small packets and sends them to an address across a network, which does not guarantee to deliver said packets to the destination. *Transmission Control Protocol* (TCP) is a higher-level protocol that manages to robustly string together these packets, sorting and retransmitting them as necessary to reliably transmit data. A third protocol, *User Datagram Protocol (UDP)*, sits next to TCP and can be used directly to support fast, connectionless, unreliable transport of packets.

Once a connection has been established, a higher-level protocol ensues, which is dependent on which port you are using. TCP/IP reserves the lower 1,024 ports for specific protocols. Many of these will seem familiar to you if you have spent any time surfing the Internet. Port number 21 is for FTP; 23 is for Telnet; 25 is for e-mail; 43 is for whois; 79 is for finger; 80 is for HTTP; 119 is for netnews—and the list goes on. It is up to each protocol to determine how a client should interact with the port.

For example, HTTP is the protocol that web browsers and servers use to transfer hypertext pages and images. It is a quite simple protocol for a basic page-browsing web server. Here's how it works. When a client requests a file from an HTTP server, an action known as a *hit*, it simply sends the name of the file in a special format to a predefined port and reads back the contents of the file. The server also responds with a status code to tell the client whether or not the request can be fulfilled and why.

A key component of the Internet is the *address*. Every computer on the Internet has one. An Internet address is a number that uniquely identifies each computer on the Net. Originally, all Internet addresses consisted of 32-bit values, organized as four 8-bit values. This address type was specified by IPv4 (Internet Protocol, version 4). However, a new addressing scheme, called IPv6 (Internet Protocol, version 6) has come into play. IPv6 uses a 128-bit value to represent an address, organized into eight 16-bit chunks. Although there are several reasons for and advantages to IPv6, the main one is that it supports a much larger address space than does IPv4.

To provide backward compatibility with IPv4, the low-order 32 bits of an IPv6 address can contain a valid IPv4 address. Thus, IPv4 is upwardly compatible with IPv6. Fortunately, when using Java, you won't normally need to worry about whether IPv4 or IPv6 addresses are used because Java handles the details for you.

Just as the numbers of an IP address describe a network hierarchy, the name of an Internet address, called its *domain name,* describes a machine's location in a name space. For example, **www.osborne.com** is in the *COM* domain (reserved for U.S. commercial sites); it is called *osborne* (after the company name), and *www* identifies the server for web requests. An Internet domain name is mapped to an IP address by the *Domain Naming Service (DNS)*. This enables users to work with domain names, but the Internet operates on IP addresses.

The Networking Classes and Interfaces

Java supports TCP/IP both by extending the already established stream I/O interface introduced in Chapter 19 and by adding the features required to build I/O objects across the network. Java supports both the TCP and UDP protocol families. TCP is used for reliable stream-based I/O across the network. UDP supports a simpler, hence faster, point-to-point datagram-oriented model. The classes contained in the **java.net** package are shown here:

Authenticator	Inet6Address	ServerSocket
CacheRequest	InetAddress	Socket
CacheResponse	InetSocketAddress	SocketAddress
ContentHandler	InterfaceAddress (Added by Java SE 6.)	SocketImpl
CookieHandler	JarURLConnection	SocketPermission
CookieManager (Added by Java SE 6.)	MulticastSocket	URI
DatagramPacket	NetPermission	URL

DatagramSocket	NetworkInterface	URLClassLoader
DatagramSocketImpl	PasswordAuthentication	URLConnection
HttpCookie (Added by Java SE 6.)	Proxy	URLDecoder
HttpURLConnection	ProxySelector	URLEncoder
IDN (Added by Java SE 6.)	ResponseCache	URLStreamHandler
Inet4Address	SecureCacheResponse	

The **java.net** package's interfaces are listed here:

ContentHandlerFactory	DatagramSocketImplFactory	SocketOptions
CookiePolicy (Added by Java SE 6.)	FileNameMap	URLStreamHandlerFactory
CookieStore (Added by Java SE 6.)	SocketImplFactory	

In the sections that follow, we will examine the main networking classes and show several examples that apply to them. Once you understand these core networking classes, you will be able to easily explore the others on your own.

InetAddress

The **InetAddress** class is used to encapsulate both the numerical IP address and the domain name for that address. You interact with this class by using the name of an IP host, which is more convenient and understandable than its IP address. The **InetAddress** class hides the number inside. **InetAddress** can handle both IPv4 and IPv6 addresses.

Factory Methods

The **InetAddress** class has no visible constructors. To create an **InetAddress** object, you have to use one of the available factory methods. *Factory methods* are merely a convention whereby static methods in a class return an instance of that class. This is done in lieu of overloading a constructor with various parameter lists when having unique method names makes the results much clearer. Three commonly used **InetAddress** factory methods are shown here:

static InetAddress getLocalHost( )
    throws UnknownHostException

static InetAddress getByName(String *hostName*)
    throws UnknownHostException

static InetAddress[ ] getAllByName(String *hostName*)
    throws UnknownHostException

The **getLocalHost( )** method simply returns the **InetAddress** object that represents the local host. The **getByName( )** method returns an **InetAddress** for a host name passed to it. If these methods are unable to resolve the host name, they throw an **UnknownHostException**.

On the Internet, it is common for a single name to be used to represent several machines. In the world of web servers, this is one way to provide some degree of scaling. The **getAllByName( )** factory method returns an array of **InetAddress**es that represent all of the addresses that a particular name resolves to. It will also throw an **UnknownHostException** if it can't resolve the name to at least one address.

InetAddress also includes the factory method **getByAddress( )**, which takes an IP address and returns an **InetAddress** object. Either an IPv4 or an IPv6 address can be used.

The following example prints the addresses and names of the local machine and two well-known Internet web sites:

```
// Demonstrate InetAddress.
import java.net.*;

class InetAddressTest
{
  public static void main(String args[]) throws UnknownHostException {
    InetAddress Address = InetAddress.getLocalHost();
    System.out.println(Address);
    Address = InetAddress.getByName("osborne.com");
    System.out.println(Address);
    InetAddress SW[] = InetAddress.getAllByName("www.nba.com");
    for (int i=0; i<SW.length; i++)
      System.out.println(SW[i]);
  }
}
```

Here is the output produced by this program. (Of course, the output you see may be slightly different.)

```
default/206.148.209.138
osborne.com/198.45.24.162
www.nba.com/64.5.96.214
www.nba.com/64.5.96.216
```

Instance Methods

The **InetAddress** class has several other methods, which can be used on the objects returned by the methods just discussed. Here are some of the more commonly used methods:

Method	Description
boolean equals(Object *other*)	Returns **true** if this object has the same Internet address as *other*.
byte[ ] getAddress( )	Returns a byte array that represents the object's IP address in network byte order.
String getHostAddress( )	Returns a string that represents the host address associated with the **InetAddress** object.
String getHostName( )	Returns a string that represents the host name associated with the **InetAddress** object.
boolean isMulticastAddress( )	Returns **true** if this address is a multicast address. Otherwise, it returns **false**.
String toString( )	Returns a string that lists the host name and the IP address for convenience.

Internet addresses are looked up in a series of hierarchically cached servers. That means that your local computer might know a particular name-to-IP-address mapping automatically, such as for itself and nearby servers. For other names, it may ask a local DNS server for IP address information. If that server doesn't have a particular address, it can go to a remote site and ask for it. This can continue all the way up to the root server. This process might take a long time, so it is wise to structure your code so that you cache IP address information locally rather than look it up repeatedly.

Inet4Address and Inet6Address

Beginning with version 1.4, Java has included support for IPv6 addresses. Because of this, two subclasses of **InetAddress** were created: **Inet4Address** and **Inet6Address**. **Inet4Address** represents a traditional-style IPv4 address. **Inet6Address** encapsulates a new-style IPv6 address. Because they are subclasses of **InetAddress**, an **InetAddress** reference can refer to either. This is one way that Java was able to add IPv6 functionality without breaking existing code or adding many more classes. For the most part, you can simply use **InetAddress** when working with IP addresses because it can accommodate both styles.

TCP/IP Client Sockets

TCP/IP sockets are used to implement reliable, bidirectional, persistent, point-to-point, stream-based connections between hosts on the Internet. A socket can be used to connect Java's I/O system to other programs that may reside either on the local machine or on any other machine on the Internet.

NOTE   *Applets may only establish socket connections back to the host from which the applet was downloaded. This restriction exists because it would be dangerous for applets loaded through a firewall to have access to any arbitrary machine.*

There are two kinds of TCP sockets in Java. One is for servers, and the other is for clients. The **ServerSocket** class is designed to be a "listener," which waits for clients to connect before doing anything. Thus, **ServerSocket** is for servers. The **Socket** class is for clients. It is designed to connect to server sockets and initiate protocol exchanges. Because client sockets are the most commonly used by Java applications, they are examined here.

The creation of a **Socket** object implicitly establishes a connection between the client and server. There are no methods or constructors that explicitly expose the details of establishing that connection. Here are two constructors used to create client sockets:

Socket(String *hostName*, int *port*)
    throws UnknownHostException,
        IOException
	Creates a socket connected to the named host and port.

Socket(InetAddress *ipAddress*, int *port*) throws IOException	Creates a socket using a preexisting **InetAddress** object and a port.

Socket defines several instance methods. For example, a **Socket** can be examined at any time for the address and port information associated with it, by use of the following methods:

InetAddress getInetAddress( )	Returns the **InetAddress** associated with the **Socket** object. It returns null if the socket is not connected.
int getPort( )	Returns the remote port to which the invoking **Socket** object is connected. It returns 0 if the socket is not connected.
int getLocalPort( )	Returns the local port to which the invoking **Socket** object is bound. It returns –1 if the socket is not bound.

You can gain access to the input and output streams associated with a **Socket** by use of the **getInputStream( )** and **getOuputStream( )** methods, as shown here. Each can throw an **IOException** if the socket has been invalidated by a loss of connection. These streams are used exactly like the I/O streams described in Chapter 19 to send and receive data.

InputStream getInputStream( ) throws IOException	Returns the **InputStream** associated with the invoking socket.
OutputStream getOutputStream( ) throws IOException	Returns the **OutputStream** associated with the invoking socket.

Several other methods are available, including **connect( )**, which allows you to specify a new connection; **isConnected( )**, which returns true if the socket is connected to a server; **isBound( )**, which returns true if the socket is bound to an address; and **isClosed( )**, which returns true if the socket is closed.

The following program provides a simple **Socket** example. It opens a connection to a "whois" port (port 43) on the InterNIC server, sends the command-line argument down the socket, and then prints the data that is returned. InterNIC will try to look up the argument as a registered Internet domain name, and then send back the IP address and contact information for that site.

```
// Demonstrate Sockets.
import java.net.*;
import java.io.*;

class Whois {
  public static void main(String args[]) throws Exception {
    int c;

    // Create a socket connected to internic.net, port 43.
    Socket s = new Socket("internic.net", 43);

    // Obtain input and output streams.
    InputStream in = s.getInputStream();
    OutputStream out = s.getOutputStream();

    // Construct a request string.
```

```
      String str = (args.length == 0 ? "osborne.com" : args[0]) + "\n";
      // Convert to bytes.
      byte buf[] = str.getBytes();

      // Send request.
      out.write(buf);

      // Read and display response.
      while ((c = in.read()) != -1) {
        System.out.print((char) c);
      }
      s.close();
    }
}
```

If, for example, you obtained information about **osborne.com**, you'd get something similar to the following:

```
Whois Server Version 1.3

Domain names in the .com, .net, and .org domains can now be registered
with many different competing registrars. Go to http://www.internic.net
for detailed information.

    Domain Name: OSBORNE.COM
    Registrar: NETWORK SOLUTIONS, INC.
    Whois Server: whois.networksolutions.com
    Referral URL: http://www.networksolutions.com
    Name Server: NS1.EPPG.COM
    Name Server: NS2.EPPG.COM
    .
    .
    .
```

Here is how the program works. First, a **Socket** is constructed that specifies the host name "internic.net" and the port number 43. **Internic.net** is the InterNIC web site that handles whois requests. Port 43 is the whois port. Next, both input and output streams are opened on the socket. Then, a string is constructed that contains the name of the web site you want to obtain information about. In this case, if no web site is specified on the command line, then "osborne.com" is used. The string is converted into a **byte** array and then sent out of the socket. The response is read by inputting from the socket, and the results are displayed.

URL

The preceding example was rather obscure because the modern Internet is not about the older protocols such as whois, finger, and FTP. It is about WWW, the World Wide Web. The Web is a loose collection of higher-level protocols and file formats, all unified in a web browser. One of the most important aspects of the Web is that Tim Berners-Lee devised a scaleable way to locate all of the resources of the Net. Once you can reliably name anything and everything, it becomes a very powerful paradigm. The Uniform Resource Locator (URL) does exactly that.

The URL provides a reasonably intelligible form to uniquely identify or address information on the Internet. URLs are ubiquitous; every browser uses them to identify information on the Web. Within Java's network class library, the **URL** class provides a simple, concise API to access information across the Internet using URLs.

All URLs share the same basic format, although some variation is allowed. Here are two examples: **http://www.osborne.com/** and **http://www.osborne.com:80/index.htm**. A URL specification is based on four components. The first is the protocol to use, separated from the rest of the locator by a colon (:). Common protocols are HTTP, FTP, gopher, and file, although these days almost everything is being done via HTTP (in fact, most browsers will proceed correctly if you leave off the "http://" from your URL specification). The second component is the host name or IP address of the host to use; this is delimited on the left by double slashes (//) and on the right by a slash (/) or optionally a colon (:). The third component, the port number, is an optional parameter, delimited on the left from the host name by a colon (:) and on the right by a slash (/). (It defaults to port 80, the predefined HTTP port; thus, ":80" is redundant.) The fourth part is the actual file path. Most HTTP servers will append a file named **index.html** or **index.htm** to URLs that refer directly to a directory resource. Thus, **http://www.osborne.com/** is the same as **http://www.osborne.com/index.htm**.

Java's **URL** class has several constructors; each can throw a **MalformedURLException**. One commonly used form specifies the URL with a string that is identical to what you see displayed in a browser:

URL(String *urlSpecifier*) throws MalformedURLException

The next two forms of the constructor allow you to break up the URL into its component parts:

URL(String *protocolName*, String *hostName*, int *port*, String *path*)
   throws MalformedURLException

URL(String *protocolName*, String *hostName*, String *path*)
   throws MalformedURLException

Another frequently used constructor allows you to use an existing URL as a reference context and then create a new URL from that context. Although this sounds a little contorted, it's really quite easy and useful.

URL(URL *urlObj*, String *urlSpecifier*) throws MalformedURLException

The following example creates a URL to Osborne's download page and then examines its properties:

```
// Demonstrate URL.
import java.net.*;
class URLDemo {
  public static void main(String args[]) throws MalformedURLException {
    URL hp = new URL("http://www.osborne.com/downloads");

    System.out.println("Protocol: " + hp.getProtocol());
    System.out.println("Port: " + hp.getPort());
```

```
    System.out.println("Host: " + hp.getHost());
    System.out.println("File: " + hp.getFile());
    System.out.println("Ext:" + hp.toExternalForm());
  }
}
```

When you run this, you will get the following output:

```
Protocol: http
Port: -1
Host: www.osborne
File: /downloads
Ext:http://www.osborne/downloads
```

Notice that the port is –1; this means that a port was not explicitly set. Given a **URL** object, you can retrieve the data associated with it. To access the actual bits or content information of a **URL**, create a **URLConnection** object from it, using its **openConnection( )** method, like this:

```
urlc = url.openConnection()
```

openConnection( ) has the following general form:

URLConnection openConnection( ) throws IOException

It returns a **URLConnection** object associated with the invoking **URL** object. Notice that it may throw an **IOException**.

URLConnection

URLConnection is a general-purpose class for accessing the attributes of a remote resource. Once you make a connection to a remote server, you can use **URLConnection** to inspect the properties of the remote object before actually transporting it locally. These attributes are exposed by the HTTP protocol specification and, as such, only make sense for **URL** objects that are using the HTTP protocol.

URLConnection defines several methods. Here is a sampling:

int getContentLength( )	Returns the size in bytes of the content associated with the resource. If the length is unavailable, –1 is returned.
String getContentType( )	Returns the type of content found in the resource. This is the value of the **content-type** header field. Returns null if the content type is not available.
long getDate( )	Returns the time and date of the response represented in terms of milliseconds since January 1, 1970 GMT.
long getExpiration( )	Returns the expiration time and date of the resource represented in terms of milliseconds since January 1, 1970 GMT. Zero is returned if the expiration date is unavailable.

String getHeaderField(int *idx*)	Returns the value of the header field at index *idx*. (Header field indexes begin at 0.) Returns null if the value of *idx* exceeds the number of fields.
String getHeaderField(String *fieldName*)	Returns the value of header field whose name is specified by *fieldName*. Returns null if the specified name is not found.
String getHeaderFieldKey(int *idx*)	Returns the header field key at index *idx*. (Header field indexes begin at 0.) Returns null if the value of *idx* exceeds the number of fields.
Map<String, List<String>> getHeaderFields( )	Returns a map that contains all of the header fields and values.
long getLastModified( )	Returns the time and date, represented in terms of milliseconds since January 1, 1970 GMT, of the last modification of the resource. Zero is returned if the last-modified date is unavailable.
InputStream getInputStream( ) throws IOException	Returns an **InputStream** that is linked to the resource. This stream can be used to obtain the content of the resource.

Notice that **URLConnection** defines several methods that handle header information. A header consists of pairs of keys and values represented as strings. By using **getHeaderField( )**, you can obtain the value associated with a header key. By calling **getHeaderFields( )**, you can obtain a map that contains all of the headers. Several standard header fields are available directly through methods such as **getDate( )** and **getContentType( )**.

The following example creates a **URLConnection** using the **openConnection( )** method of a **URL** object and then uses it to examine the document's properties and content:

```
// Demonstrate URLConnection.
import java.net.*;
import java.io.*;
import java.util.Date;

class UCDemo
{
  public static void main(String args[]) throws Exception {
    int c;
    URL hp = new URL("http://www.internic.net");
    URLConnection hpCon = hp.openConnection();

    // get date
    long d = hpCon.getDate();
    if(d==0)
      System.out.println("No date information.");
    else
      System.out.println("Date: " + new Date(d));

    // get content type
    System.out.println("Content-Type: " + hpCon.getContentType());
```

```
  // get expiration date
  d = hpCon.getExpiration();
  if(d==0)
    System.out.println("No expiration information.");
  else
    System.out.println("Expires: " + new Date(d));

  // get last-modified date
  d = hpCon.getLastModified();
  if(d==0)
    System.out.println("No last-modified information.");
  else
    System.out.println("Last-Modified: " + new Date(d));

  // get content length
  int len = hpCon.getContentLength();
  if(len == -1)
    System.out.println("Content length unavailable.");
  else
    System.out.println("Content-Length: " + len);

  if(len != 0) {
    System.out.println("=== Content ===");
    InputStream input = hpCon.getInputStream();
    int i = len;
    while (((c = input.read()) != -1)) { // && (--i > 0)) {
      System.out.print((char) c);
    }
    input.close();

  } else {
    System.out.println("No content available.");
  }

  }
}
```

The program establishes an HTTP connection to **www.internic.net** over port 80. It then displays several header values and retrieves the content. Here are the first lines of the output (the precise output will vary over time).

```
Date: Thu Jun 08 14:41:35 CDT 2006
Content-Type: text/html
No expiration information.
Last-Modified: Wed Oct 05 19:49:29 CDT 2005
Content-Length: 4917
=== Content ===
<html>
<head>
<title>InterNIC | The Internet's Network Information Center</title>
<meta name="keywords"
      content="internic,network information, domain registration">
```

```
<style type="text/css">
<!--
p, li, td, ul { font-family: Arial, Helvetica, sans-serif}
-->
</style>
</head>
```

HttpURLConnection

Java provides a subclass of **URLConnection** that provides support for HTTP connections. This class is called **HttpURLConnection**. You obtain an **HttpURLConnection** in the same way just shown, by calling **openConnection( )** on a **URL** object, but you must cast the result to **HttpURLConnection**. (Of course, you must make sure that you are actually opening an HTTP connection.) Once you have obtained a reference to an **HttpURLConnection** object, you can use any of the methods inherited from **URLConnection**. You can also use any of the several methods defined by **HttpURLConnection**. Here is a sampling:

static boolean getFollowRedirects( )	Returns **true** if redirects are automatically followed and **false** otherwise. This feature is on by default.
String getRequestMethod( )	Returns a string representing how URL requests are made. The default is GET. Other options, such as POST, are available.
int getResponseCode( ) throws IOException	Returns the HTTP response code. –1 is returned if no response code can be obtained. An **IOException** is thrown if the connection fails.
String getResponseMessage( ) throws IOException	Returns the response message associated with the response code. Returns null if no message is available. An **IOException** is thrown if the connection fails.
static void setFollowRedirects(boolean *how*)	If *how* is **true**, then redirects are automatically followed. If how is **false**, redirects are not automatically followed. By default, redirects are automatically followed.
void setRequestMethod(String *how*) throws ProtocolException	Sets the method by which HTTP requests are made to that specified by *how*. The default method is GET, but other options, such as POST, are available. If *how* is invalid, a **ProtocolException** is thrown.

The following program demonstrates **HttpURLConnection**. It first establishes a connection to **www.google.com**. Then it displays the request method, the response code, and the response message. Finally, it displays the keys and values in the response header.

```
// Demonstrate HttpURLConnection.
import java.net.*;
import java.io.*;
import java.util.*;

class HttpURLDemo
{
```

```
public static void main(String args[]) throws Exception {
  URL hp = new URL("http://www.google.com");

  HttpURLConnection hpCon = (HttpURLConnection) hp.openConnection();

  // Display request method.
  System.out.println("Request method is " +
                     hpCon.getRequestMethod());

  // Display response code.
  System.out.println("Response code is " +
                     hpCon.getResponseCode());

  // Display response message.
  System.out.println("Response Message is " +
                     hpCon.getResponseMessage());

  // Get a list of the header fields and a set
  // of the header keys.
  Map<String, List<String>> hdrMap = hpCon.getHeaderFields();
  Set<String> hdrField = hdrMap.keySet();

  System.out.println("\nHere is the header:");

  // Display all header keys and values.
  for(String k : hdrField) {
    System.out.println("Key: " + k +
                       " Value: " + hdrMap.get(k));
  }
 }
}
```

The output produced by the program is shown here. (Of course, the exact response returned by **www.google.com** will vary over time.)

```
Request method is GET
Response code is 200
Response Message is OK

Here is the header:
Key: Set-Cookie  Value:
[PREF=ID=4fbe939441ed966b:TM=1150213711:LM=1150213711:S=Qk81
WCVtvYkJOdh3; expires=Sun, 17-Jan-2038 19:14:07 GMT; path=/;
 domain=.google.com]
Key: null  Value: [HTTP/1.1 200 OK]
Key: Date  Value: [Tue, 13 Jun 2006 15:48:31 GMT]
Key: Content-Type  Value: [text/html]
Key: Server  Value: [GWS/2.1]
Key: Transfer-Encoding  Value: [chunked]
Key: Cache-Control  Value: [private]
```

Notice how the header keys and values are displayed. First, a map of the header keys and values is obtained by calling **getHeaderFields( )** (which is inherited from **URLConnection**). Next, a set of the header keys is retrieved by calling **keySet( )** on the map. Then the key set is cycled through by using a for-each style **for** loop. The value associated with each key is obtained by calling **get( )** on the map.

The URI Class

A relatively recent addition to Java is the **URI** class, which encapsulates a *Uniform Resource Identifier (URI)*. URIs are similar to URLs. In fact, URLs constitute a subset of URIs. A URI represents a standard way to identify a resource. A URL also describes how to access the resource.

Cookies

The **java.net** package includes classes and interfaces that help manage cookies and can be used to create a stateful (as opposed to stateless) HTTP session. The classes are **CookieHandler**, **CookieManager**, and **HttpCookie**. The interfaces are **CookiePolicy** and **CookieStore**. All but **CookieHandler** was added by Java SE 6. (**CookieHandler** was added by JDK 5.) The creation of a stateful HTTP session is beyond the scope of this book.

NOTE *For information about using cookies with servlets, see Chapter 31.*

TCP/IP Server Sockets

As mentioned earlier, Java has a different socket class that must be used for creating server applications. The **ServerSocket** class is used to create servers that listen for either local or remote client programs to connect to them on published ports. **ServerSocket**s are quite different from normal **Socket**s. When you create a **ServerSocket**, it will register itself with the system as having an interest in client connections. The constructors for **ServerSocket** reflect the port number that you want to accept connections on and, optionally, how long you want the queue for said port to be. The queue length tells the system how many client connections it can leave pending before it should simply refuse connections. The default is 50. The constructors might throw an **IOException** under adverse conditions. Here are three of its constructors:

ServerSocket(int *port*) throws IOException	Creates server socket on the specified port with a queue length of 50.
ServerSocket(int *port*, int *maxQueue*) throws IOException	Creates a server socket on the specified port with a maximum queue length of *maxQueue*.
ServerSocket(int *port*, int *maxQueue*, InetAddress *localAddress*) throws IOException	Creates a server socket on the specified port with a maximum queue length of *maxQueue*. On a multihomed host, *localAddress* specifies the IP address to which this socket binds.

ServerSocket has a method called **accept( )**, which is a blocking call that will wait for a client to initiate communications and then return with a normal **Socket** that is then used for communication with the client.

Datagrams

TCP/IP-style networking is appropriate for most networking needs. It provides a serialized, predictable, reliable stream of packet data. This is not without its cost, however. TCP includes many complicated algorithms for dealing with congestion control on crowded networks, as well as pessimistic expectations about packet loss. This leads to a somewhat inefficient way to transport data. Datagrams provide an alternative.

Datagrams are bundles of information passed between machines. They are somewhat like a hard throw from a well-trained but blindfolded catcher to the third baseman. Once the datagram has been released to its intended target, there is no assurance that it will arrive or even that someone will be there to catch it. Likewise, when the datagram is received, there is no assurance that it hasn't been damaged in transit or that whoever sent it is still there to receive a response.

Java implements datagrams on top of the UDP protocol by using two classes: the **DatagramPacket** object is the data container, while the **DatagramSocket** is the mechanism used to send or receive the **DatagramPacket**s. Each is examined here.

DatagramSocket

DatagramSocket defines four public constructors. They are shown here:

DatagramSocket( ) throws SocketException

DatagramSocket(int *port*) throws SocketException

DatagramSocket(int *port*, InetAddress *ipAddress*) throws SocketException

DatagramSocket(SocketAddress *address*) throws SocketException

The first creates a **DatagramSocket** bound to any unused port on the local computer. The second creates a **DatagramSocket** bound to the port specified by *port*. The third constructs a **DatagramSocket** bound to the specified port and **InetAddress**. The fourth constructs a **DatagramSocket** bound to the specified **SocketAddress**. **SocketAddress** is an abstract class that is implemented by the concrete class **InetSocketAddress**. **InetSocketAddress** encapsulates an IP address with a port number. All can throw a **SocketException** if an error occurs while creating the socket.

DatagramSocket defines many methods. Two of the most important are **send( )** and **receive( )**, which are shown here:

void send(DatagramPacket *packet*) throws IOException

void receive(DatagramPacket *packet*) throws IOException

The **send( )** method sends packet to the port specified by *packet*. The receive method waits for a packet to be received from the port specified by *packet* and returns the result.

Other methods give you access to various attributes associated with a **DatagramSocket**. Here is a sampling:

InetAddress getInetAddress( )	If the socket is connected, then the address is returned. Otherwise, null is returned.
int getLocalPort( )	Returns the number of the local port.
int getPort( )	Returns the number of the port to which the socket is connected. It returns −1 if the socket is not connected to a port.
boolean isBound( )	Returns **true** if the socket is bound to an address. Returns **false** otherwise.
boolean isConnected( )	Returns **true** if the socket is connected to a server. Returns **false** otherwise.
void setSoTimeout(int *millis*) throws SocketException	Sets the time-out period to the number of milliseconds passed in *millis*.

DatagramPacket

DatagramPacket defines several constructors. Four are shown here:

DatagramPacket(byte *data*[ ], int *size*)
DatagramPacket(byte *data*[ ], int *offset*, int *size*)
DatagramPacket(byte *data*[ ], int *size*, InetAddress *ipAddress*, int *port*)
DatagramPacket(byte *data*[ ], int *offset*, int *size*, InetAddress *ipAddress*, int *port*)

The first constructor specifies a buffer that will receive data and the size of a packet. It is used for receiving data over a **DatagramSocket**. The second form allows you to specify an offset into the buffer at which data will be stored. The third form specifies a target address and port, which are used by a **DatagramSocket** to determine where the data in the packet will be sent. The fourth form transmits packets beginning at the specified offset into the data. Think of the first two forms as building an "in box," and the second two forms as stuffing and addressing an envelope.

DatagramPacket defines several methods, including those shown here, that give access to the address and port number of a packet, as well as the raw data and its length. In general, the **get** methods are used on packets that are received and the **set** methods are used on packets that will be sent.

InetAddress getAddress( )	Returns the address of the source (for datagrams being received) or destination (for datagrams being sent).
byte[ ] getData( )	Returns the byte array of data contained in the datagram. Mostly used to retrieve data from the datagram after it has been received.
int getLength( )	Returns the length of the valid data contained in the byte array that would be returned from the **getData( )** method. This may not equal the length of the whole byte array.

int getOffset( )	Returns the starting index of the data.
int getPort( )	Returns the port number.
void setAddress(InetAddress *ipAddress*)	Sets the address to which a packet will be sent. The address is specified by *ipAddress*.
void setData(byte[ ] *data*)	Sets the data to *data*, the offset to zero, and the length to number of bytes in *data*.
void setData(byte[ ] *data*, int *idx*, int *size*)	Sets the data to *data*, the offset to *idx*, and the length to *size*.
void setLength(int *size*)	Sets the length of the packet to *size*.
void setPort(int *port*)	Sets the port to *port*.

A Datagram Example

The following example implements a very simple networked communications client and server. Messages are typed into the window at the server and written across the network to the client side, where they are displayed.

```
// Demonstrate datagrams.
import java.net.*;

class WriteServer {
  public static int serverPort = 998;
  public static int clientPort = 999;
  public static int buffer_size = 1024;
  public static DatagramSocket ds;
  public static byte buffer[] = new byte[buffer_size];

  public static void TheServer() throws Exception {
    int pos=0;
    while (true) {
      int c = System.in.read();
      switch (c) {
        case -1:
          System.out.println("Server Quits.");
          return;
        case '\r':
          break;
        case '\n':
          ds.send(new DatagramPacket(buffer,pos,
              InetAddress.getLocalHost(),clientPort));
          pos=0;
          break;
        default:
          buffer[pos++] = (byte) c;
      }
    }
  }
}
```

```
public static void TheClient() throws Exception {
  while(true) {
    DatagramPacket p = new DatagramPacket(buffer, buffer.length);
    ds.receive(p);
    System.out.println(new String(p.getData(), 0, p.getLength()));
  }
}

public static void main(String args[]) throws Exception {
  if(args.length == 1) {
    ds = new DatagramSocket(serverPort);
    TheServer();
  } else {
    ds = new DatagramSocket(clientPort);
    TheClient();
  }
}
}
```

This sample program is restricted by the **DatagramSocket** constructor to running between two ports on the local machine. To use the program, run

```
java WriteServer
```

in one window; this will be the client. Then run

```
java WriteServer 1
```

This will be the server. Anything that is typed in the server window will be sent to the client window after a newline is received.

The Applet Class

This chapter examines the **Applet** class, which provides the foundation for applets. The **Applet** class is contained in the **java.applet** package. **Applet** contains several methods that give you detailed control over the execution of your applet. In addition, **java.applet** also defines three interfaces: **AppletContext**, **AudioClip**, and **AppletStub**.

Two Types of Applets

It is important to state at the outset that there are two varieties of applets. The first are those based directly on the **Applet** class described in this chapter. These applets use the Abstract Window Toolkit (AWT) to provide the graphic user interface (or use no GUI at all). This style of applet has been available since Java was first created.

The second type of applets are those based on the Swing class **JApplet**. Swing applets use the Swing classes to provide the GUI. Swing offers a richer and often easier-to-use user interface than does the AWT. Thus, Swing-based applets are now the most popular. However, traditional AWT-based applets are still used, especially when only a very simple user interface is required. Thus, both AWT- and Swing-based applets are valid.

Because **JApplet** inherits **Applet**, all the features of **Applet** are also available in **JApplet**, and most of the information in this chapter applies to both types of applets. Therefore, even if you are interested in only Swing applets, the information in this chapter is still relevant and necessary. Understand, however, that when creating Swing-based applets, some additional constraints apply and these are described later in this book, when Swing is covered.

NOTE *For information on building applets when using Swing, see Chapter 29.*

Applet Basics

Chapter 13 introduced the general form of an applet and the steps necessary to compile and run one. Let's begin by reviewing this information.

All applets are subclasses (either directly or indirectly) of **Applet**. Applets are not stand-alone programs. Instead, they run within either a web browser or an applet viewer. The illustrations shown in this chapter were created with the standard applet viewer, called **appletviewer**, provided by the JDK. But you can use any applet viewer or browser you like.

Execution of an applet does not begin at **main( )**. Actually, few applets even have **main( )** methods. Instead, execution of an applet is started and controlled with an entirely different mechanism, which will be explained shortly. Output to your applet's window is not performed by **System.out.println( )**. Rather, in non-Swing applets, output is handled with various AWT methods, such as **drawString( )**, which outputs a string to a specified X,Y location. Input is also handled differently than in a console application. (Remember, Swing-based applets use the Swing classes to handle user interactions, and they are described later in this book.)

To use an applet, it is specified in an HTML file. One way to do this is by using the APPLET tag. (The OBJECT tag can also be used, but Sun currently recommends the APPLET tag and this is the tag used by examples in this book.) The applet will be executed by a Java-enabled web browser when it encounters the APPLET tag within the HTML file. To view and test an applet more conveniently, simply include a comment at the head of your Java source code file that contains the APPLET tag. This way, your code is documented with the necessary HTML statements needed by your applet, and you can test the compiled applet by starting the applet viewer with your Java source code file specified as the target. Here is an example of such a comment:

```
/*
<applet code="MyApplet" width=200 height=60>
</applet>
*/
```

This comment contains an APPLET tag that will run an applet called **MyApplet** in a window that is 200 pixels wide and 60 pixels high. Because the inclusion of an APPLET command makes testing applets easier, all of the applets shown in this book will contain the appropriate APPLET tag embedded in a comment.

The Applet Class

The **Applet** class defines the methods shown in Table 21-1. **Applet** provides all necessary support for applet execution, such as starting and stopping. It also provides methods that load and display images, and methods that load and play audio clips. **Applet** extends the AWT class **Panel**. In turn, **Panel** extends **Container**, which extends **Component**. These classes provide support for Java's window-based, graphical interface. Thus, **Applet** provides all of the necessary support for window-based activities. (The AWT is described in detail in following chapters.)

Method	Description
void destroy( )	Called by the browser just before an applet is terminated. Your applet will override this method if it needs to perform any cleanup prior to its destruction.
AccessibleContext getAccessibleContext( )	Returns the accessibility context for the invoking object.
AppletContext getAppletContext( )	Returns the context associated with the applet.
String getAppletInfo( )	Returns a string that describes the applet.
AudioClip getAudioClip(URL *url*)	Returns an **AudioClip** object that encapsulates the audio clip found at the location specified by *url*.

TABLE 21-1   The Methods Defined by **Applet**

Method	Description
AudioClip getAudioClip(URL *url*, String *clipName*)	Returns an **AudioClip** object that encapsulates the audio clip found at the location specified by *url* and having the name specified by *clipName*.
URL getCodeBase( )	Returns the URL associated with the invoking applet.
URL getDocumentBase( )	Returns the URL of the HTML document that invokes the applet.
Image getImage(URL *url*)	Returns an **Image** object that encapsulates the image found at the location specified by *url*.
Image getImage(URL *url*, String *imageName*)	Returns an **Image** object that encapsulates the image found at the location specified by *url* and having the name specified by *imageName*.
Locale getLocale( )	Returns a **Locale** object that is used by various locale-sensitive classes and methods.
String getParameter(String *paramName*)	Returns the parameter associated with *paramName*. **null** is returned if the specified parameter is not found.
String[ ] [ ] getParameterInfo( )	Returns a **String** table that describes the parameters recognized by the applet. Each entry in the table must consist of three strings that contain the name of the parameter, a description of its type and/or range, and an explanation of its purpose.
void init( )	Called when an applet begins execution. It is the first method called for any applet.
boolean isActive( )	Returns **true** if the applet has been started. It returns **false** if the applet has been stopped.
static final AudioClip newAudioClip(URL *url*)	Returns an **AudioClip** object that encapsulates the audio clip found at the location specified by *url*. This method is similar to **getAudioClip( )** except that it is static and can be executed without the need for an **Applet** object.
void play(URL *url*)	If an audio clip is found at the location specified by *url*, the clip is played.
void play(URL *url*, String *clipName*)	If an audio clip is found at the location specified by *url* with the name specified by *clipName*, the clip is played.
void resize(Dimension *dim*)	Resizes the applet according to the dimensions specified by *dim*. **Dimension** is a class stored inside **java.awt**. It contains two integer fields: **width** and **height**.
void resize(int *width*, int *height*)	Resizes the applet according to the dimensions specified by *width* and *height*.
final void setStub(AppletStub *stubObj*)	Makes *stubObj* the stub for the applet. This method is used by the run-time system and is not usually called by your applet. A *stub* is a small piece of code that provides the linkage between your applet and the browser.

TABLE 21-1   The Methods Defined by **Applet** *(continued)*

Method	Description
void showStatus(String *str*)	Displays *str* in the status window of the browser or applet viewer. If the browser does not support a status window, then no action takes place.
void start( )	Called by the browser when an applet should start (or resume) execution. It is automatically called after **init( )** when an applet first begins.
void stop( )	Called by the browser to suspend execution of the applet. Once stopped, an applet is restarted when the browser calls **start( )**.

TABLE 21-1   The Methods Defined by **Applet** *(continued)*

Applet Architecture

An applet is a window-based program. As such, its architecture is different from the console-based programs shown in the first part of this book. If you are familiar with Windows programming, you will be right at home writing applets. If not, then there are a few key concepts you must understand.

First, applets are event driven. Although we won't examine event handling until the following chapter, it is important to understand in a general way how the event-driven architecture impacts the design of an applet. An applet resembles a set of interrupt service routines. Here is how the process works. An applet waits until an event occurs. The run-time system notifies the applet about an event by calling an event handler that has been provided by the applet. Once this happens, the applet must take appropriate action and then quickly return. This is a crucial point. For the most part, your applet should not enter a "mode" of operation in which it maintains control for an extended period. Instead, it must perform specific actions in response to events and then return control to the run-time system. In those situations in which your applet needs to perform a repetitive task on its own (for example, displaying a scrolling message across its window), you must start an additional thread of execution. (You will see an example later in this chapter.)

Second, the user initiates interaction with an applet—not the other way around. As you know, in a nonwindowed program, when the program needs input, it will prompt the user and then call some input method, such as **readLine( )**. This is not the way it works in an applet. Instead, the user interacts with the applet as he or she wants, when he or she wants. These interactions are sent to the applet as events to which the applet must respond. For example, when the user clicks the mouse inside the applet's window, a mouse-clicked event is generated. If the user presses a key while the applet's window has input focus, a keypress event is generated. As you will see in later chapters, applets can contain various controls, such as push buttons and check boxes. When the user interacts with one of these controls, an event is generated.

While the architecture of an applet is not as easy to understand as that of a console-based program, Java makes it as simple as possible. If you have written programs for Windows, you know how intimidating that environment can be. Fortunately, Java provides a much cleaner approach that is more quickly mastered.

An Applet Skeleton

All but the most trivial applets override a set of methods that provides the basic mechanism by which the browser or applet viewer interfaces to the applet and controls its execution. Four of these methods, **init( )**, **start( )**, **stop( )**, and **destroy( )**, apply to all applets and are defined by **Applet**. Default implementations for all of these methods are provided. Applets do not need to override those methods they do not use. However, only very simple applets will not need to define all of them.

AWT-based applets (such as those discussed in this chapter) will also override the **paint( )** method, which is defined by the AWT **Component** class. This method is called when the applet's output must be redisplayed. (Swing-based applets use a different mechanism to accomplish this task.) These five methods can be assembled into the skeleton shown here:

```
// An Applet skeleton.
import java.awt.*;
import java.applet.*;
/*
<applet code="AppletSkel" width=300 height=100>
</applet>
*/

public class AppletSkel extends Applet {
  // Called first.
  public void init() {
    // initialization
  }

  /* Called second, after init().  Also called whenever
     the applet is restarted. */
  public void start() {
    // start or resume execution
  }

  // Called when the applet is stopped.
  public void stop() {
    // suspends execution
  }

  /* Called when applet is terminated.  This is the last
     method executed. */
  public void destroy() {
    // perform shutdown activities
  }

  // Called when an applet's window must be restored.
  public void paint(Graphics g) {
    // redisplay contents of window
  }
}
```

Although this skeleton does not do anything, it can be compiled and run. When run, it generates the following window when viewed with an applet viewer:

Applet Initialization and Termination

It is important to understand the order in which the various methods shown in the skeleton are called. When an applet begins, the following methods are called, in this sequence:

1. **init( )**
2. **start( )**
3. **paint( )**

When an applet is terminated, the following sequence of method calls takes place:

1. **stop( )**
2. **destroy( )**

Let's look more closely at these methods.

init( )

The **init( )** method is the first method to be called. This is where you should initialize variables. This method is called only once during the run time of your applet.

start( )

The **start( )** method is called after **init( )**. It is also called to restart an applet after it has been stopped. Whereas **init( )** is called once—the first time an applet is loaded—**start( )** is called each time an applet's HTML document is displayed onscreen. So, if a user leaves a web page and comes back, the applet resumes execution at **start( )**.

paint( )

The **paint( )** method is called each time your applet's output must be redrawn. This situation can occur for several reasons. For example, the window in which the applet is running may be overwritten by another window and then uncovered. Or the applet window may be minimized and then restored. **paint( )** is also called when the applet begins execution. Whatever the cause, whenever the applet must redraw its output, **paint( )** is called. The **paint( )** method has one parameter of type **Graphics**. This parameter will contain the graphics context, which describes the graphics environment in which the applet is running. This context is used whenever output to the applet is required.

stop( )

The **stop( )** method is called when a web browser leaves the HTML document containing the applet—when it goes to another page, for example. When **stop( )** is called, the applet is probably running. You should use **stop( )** to suspend threads that don't need to run when the applet is not visible. You can restart them when **start( )** is called if the user returns to the page.

destroy( )

The **destroy( )** method is called when the environment determines that your applet needs to be removed completely from memory. At this point, you should free up any resources the applet may be using. The **stop( )** method is always called before **destroy( )**.

Overriding update( )

In some situations, your applet may need to override another method defined by the AWT, called **update( )**. This method is called when your applet has requested that a portion of its window be redrawn. The default version of **update( )** simply calls **paint( )**. However, you can override the **update( )** method so that it performs more subtle repainting. In general, overriding **update( )** is a specialized technique that is not applicable to all applets, and the examples in this book do not override **update( )**.

Simple Applet Display Methods

As we've mentioned, applets are displayed in a window, and AWT-based applets use the AWT to perform input and output. Although we will examine the methods, procedures, and techniques necessary to fully handle the AWT windowed environment in subsequent chapters, a few are described here, because we will use them to write sample applets. (Remember, Swing-based applets are described later in this book.)

As described in Chapter 13, to output a string to an applet, use **drawString( )**, which is a member of the **Graphics** class. Typically, it is called from within either **update( )** or **paint( )**. It has the following general form:

   void drawString(String *message*, int *x*, int *y*)

Here, *message* is the string to be output beginning at *x,y*. In a Java window, the upper-left corner is location 0,0. The **drawString( )** method will not recognize newline characters. If you want to start a line of text on another line, you must do so manually, specifying the precise X,Y location where you want the line to begin. (As you will see in later chapters, there are techniques that make this process easy.)

To set the background color of an applet's window, use **setBackground( )**. To set the foreground color (the color in which text is shown, for example), use **setForeground( )**. These methods are defined by **Component**, and they have the following general forms:

   void setBackground(Color *newColor*)
   void setForeground(Color *newColor*)

Here, *newColor* specifies the new color. The class **Color** defines the constants shown here that can be used to specify colors:

Color.black	Color.magenta
Color.blue	Color.orange
Color.cyan	Color.pink
Color.darkGray	Color.red

Color.gray	Color.white
Color.green	Color.yellow
Color.lightGray	

Uppercase versions of the constants are also defined.

The following example sets the background color to green and the text color to red:

```
setBackground(Color.green);
setForeground(Color.red);
```

A good place to set the foreground and background colors is in the **init( )** method. Of course, you can change these colors as often as necessary during the execution of your applet.

You can obtain the current settings for the background and foreground colors by calling **getBackground( )** and **getForeground( )**, respectively. They are also defined by **Component** and are shown here:

Color getBackground( )
Color getForeground( )

Here is a very simple applet that sets the background color to cyan, the foreground color to red, and displays a message that illustrates the order in which the **init( )**, **start( )**, and **paint( )** methods are called when an applet starts up:

```
/* A simple applet that sets the foreground and
   background colors and outputs a string. */
import java.awt.*;
import java.applet.*;
/*
<applet code="Sample" width=300 height=50>
</applet>
*/

public class Sample extends Applet{
  String msg;

  // set the foreground and background colors.
  public void init() {
    setBackground(Color.cyan);
    setForeground(Color.red);
    msg = "Inside init( ) --";
  }

  // Initialize the string to be displayed.
  public void start() {
    msg += " Inside start( ) --";
  }

  // Display msg in applet window.
  public void paint(Graphics g) {
    msg += " Inside paint( ).";
    g.drawString(msg, 10, 30);
  }
}
```

This applet generates the window shown here:

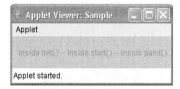

The methods **stop( )** and **destroy( )** are not overridden, because they are not needed by this simple applet.

Requesting Repainting

As a general rule, an applet writes to its window only when its **update( )** or **paint( )** method is called by the AWT. This raises an interesting question: How can the applet itself cause its window to be updated when its information changes? For example, if an applet is displaying a moving banner, what mechanism does the applet use to update the window each time this banner scrolls? Remember, one of the fundamental architectural constraints imposed on an applet is that it must quickly return control to the run-time system. It cannot create a loop inside **paint( )** that repeatedly scrolls the banner, for example. This would prevent control from passing back to the AWT. Given this constraint, it may seem that output to your applet's window will be difficult at best. Fortunately, this is not the case. Whenever your applet needs to update the information displayed in its window, it simply calls **repaint( )**.

The **repaint( )** method is defined by the AWT. It causes the AWT run-time system to execute a call to your applet's **update( )** method, which, in its default implementation, calls **paint( )**. Thus, for another part of your applet to output to its window, simply store the output and then call **repaint( )**. The AWT will then execute a call to **paint( )**, which can display the stored information. For example, if part of your applet needs to output a string, it can store this string in a **String** variable and then call **repaint( )**. Inside **paint( )**, you will output the string using **drawString( )**.

The **repaint( )** method has four forms. Let's look at each one, in turn. The simplest version of **repaint( )** is shown here:

    void repaint( )

This version causes the entire window to be repainted. The following version specifies a region that will be repainted:

    void repaint(int *left*, int *top*, int *width*, int *height*)

Here, the coordinates of the upper-left corner of the region are specified by *left* and *top*, and the width and height of the region are passed in *width* and *height*. These dimensions are specified in pixels. You save time by specifying a region to repaint. Window updates are costly in terms of time. If you need to update only a small portion of the window, it is more efficient to repaint only that region.

Calling **repaint( )** is essentially a request that your applet be repainted sometime soon. However, if your system is slow or busy, **update( )** might not be called immediately. Multiple requests for repainting that occur within a short time can be collapsed by the AWT in a manner such that **update( )** is only called sporadically. This can be a problem in many situations, including animation, in which a consistent update time is necessary. One solution to this problem is to use the following forms of **repaint( )**:

> void repaint(long *maxDelay*)
> void repaint(long *maxDelay*, int *x*, int *y*, int *width*, int *height*)

Here, *maxDelay* specifies the maximum number of milliseconds that can elapse before **update( )** is called. Beware, though. If the time elapses before **update( )** can be called, it isn't called. There's no return value or exception thrown, so you must be careful.

NOTE   *It is possible for a method other than **paint( )** or **update( )** to output to an applet's window. To do so, it must obtain a graphics context by calling **getGraphics( )** (defined by **Component**) and then use this context to output to the window. However, for most applications, it is better and easier to route window output through **paint( )** and to call **repaint( )** when the contents of the window change.*

A Simple Banner Applet

To demonstrate **repaint( )**, a simple banner applet is developed. This applet scrolls a message, from right to left, across the applet's window. Since the scrolling of the message is a repetitive task, it is performed by a separate thread, created by the applet when it is initialized. The banner applet is shown here:

```
/* A simple banner applet.

   This applet creates a thread that scrolls
   the message contained in msg right to left
   across the applet's window.
*/
import java.awt.*;
import java.applet.*;
/*
<applet code="SimpleBanner" width=300 height=50>
</applet>
*/

public class SimpleBanner extends Applet implements Runnable {
  String msg = " A Simple Moving Banner.";
  Thread t = null;
  int state;
  boolean stopFlag;

  // Set colors and initialize thread.
  public void init() {
    setBackground(Color.cyan);
    setForeground(Color.red);
  }

  // Start thread
  public void start() {
    t = new Thread(this);
    stopFlag = false;
    t.start();
```

```
  }

  // Entry point for the thread that runs the banner.
  public void run() {
    char ch;

    // Display banner
    for( ; ; ) {
      try {
        repaint();
        Thread.sleep(250);
        ch = msg.charAt(0);
        msg = msg.substring(1, msg.length());
        msg += ch;
        if(stopFlag)
          break;
      } catch(InterruptedException e) {}
    }
  }

  // Pause the banner.
  public void stop() {
    stopFlag = true;
    t = null;
  }

  // Display the banner.
  public void paint(Graphics g) {
    g.drawString(msg, 50, 30);
  }
}
```

Following is sample output:

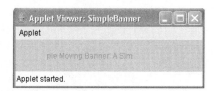

Let's take a close look at how this applet operates. First, notice that **SimpleBanner**
extends **Applet**, as expected, but it also implements **Runnable**. This is necessary, since the
applet will be creating a second thread of execution that will be used to scroll the banner.
Inside **init( )**, the foreground and background colors of the applet are set.

After initialization, the run-time system calls **start( )** to start the applet running. Inside
start( ), a new thread of execution is created and assigned to the **Thread** variable **t**. Then, the
boolean variable **stopFlag**, which controls the execution of the applet, is set to **false**. Next,
the thread is started by a call to **t.start( )**. Remember that **t.start( )** calls a method defined by
Thread, which causes **run( )** to begin executing. It does not cause a call to the version of
start( ) defined by **Applet**. These are two separate methods.

Inside **run( )**, the characters in the string contained in **msg** are repeatedly rotated left. Between each rotation, a call to **repaint( )** is made. This eventually causes the **paint( )** method to be called, and the current contents of **msg** are displayed. Between each iteration, **run( )** sleeps for a quarter of a second. The net effect of **run( )** is that the contents of **msg** are scrolled right to left in a constantly moving display. The **stopFlag** variable is checked on each iteration. When it is **true**, the **run( )** method terminates.

If a browser is displaying the applet when a new page is viewed, the **stop( )** method is called, which sets **stopFlag** to **true**, causing **run( )** to terminate. This is the mechanism used to stop the thread when its page is no longer in view. When the applet is brought back into view, **start( )** is once again called, which starts a new thread to execute the banner.

Using the Status Window

In addition to displaying information in its window, an applet can also output a message to the status window of the browser or applet viewer on which it is running. To do so, call **showStatus( )** with the string that you want displayed. The status window is a good place to give the user feedback about what is occurring in the applet, suggest options, or possibly report some types of errors. The status window also makes an excellent debugging aid, because it gives you an easy way to output information about your applet.

The following applet demonstrates **showStatus( )**:

```
// Using the Status Window.
import java.awt.*;
import java.applet.*;
/*
<applet code="StatusWindow" width=300 height=50>
</applet>
*/

public class StatusWindow extends Applet{
  public void init() {
    setBackground(Color.cyan);
  }

  // Display msg in applet window.
  public void paint(Graphics g) {
    g.drawString("This is in the applet window.", 10, 20);
    showStatus("This is shown in the status window.");
  }
}
```

Sample output from this program is shown here:

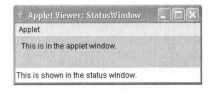

The HTML APPLET Tag

As mentioned earlier, Sun currently recommends that the APPLET tag be used to start an applet from both an HTML document and from an applet viewer. An applet viewer will execute each APPLET tag that it finds in a separate window, while web browsers will allow many applets on a single page. So far, we have been using only a simplified form of the APPLET tag. Now it is time to take a closer look at it.

The syntax for a fuller form of the APPLET tag is shown here. Bracketed items are optional.

```
< APPLET
 [CODEBASE = codebaseURL]
 CODE = appletFile
 [ALT = alternateText]
 [NAME = appletInstanceName]
 WIDTH = pixels HEIGHT = pixels
 [ALIGN = alignment]
 [VSPACE = pixels] [HSPACE = pixels]
 >
 [< PARAM NAME = AttributeName VALUE = AttributeValue>]
 [< PARAM NAME = AttributeName2 VALUE = AttributeValue>]
 . . .
 [HTML Displayed in the absence of Java]
 </APPLET>
```

Let's take a look at each part now.

CODEBASE   CODEBASE is an optional attribute that specifies the base URL of the applet code, which is the directory that will be searched for the applet's executable class file (specified by the CODE tag). The HTML document's URL directory is used as the CODEBASE if this attribute is not specified. The CODEBASE does not have to be on the host from which the HTML document was read.

CODE   CODE is a required attribute that gives the name of the file containing your applet's compiled **.class** file. This file is relative to the code base URL of the applet, which is the directory that the HTML file was in or the directory indicated by CODEBASE if set.

ALT   The ALT tag is an optional attribute used to specify a short text message that should be displayed if the browser recognizes the APPLET tag but can't currently run Java applets. This is distinct from the alternate HTML you provide for browsers that don't support applets.

NAME   NAME is an optional attribute used to specify a name for the applet instance. Applets must be named in order for other applets on the same page to find them by name and communicate with them. To obtain an applet by name, use **getApplet( )**, which is defined by the **AppletContext** interface.

WIDTH and HEIGHT   WIDTH and HEIGHT are required attributes that give the size (in pixels) of the applet display area.

ALIGN ALIGN is an optional attribute that specifies the alignment of the applet. This attribute is treated the same as the HTML IMG tag with these possible values: LEFT, RIGHT, TOP, BOTTOM, MIDDLE, BASELINE, TEXTTOP, ABSMIDDLE, and ABSBOTTOM.

VSPACE and HSPACE These attributes are optional. VSPACE specifies the space, in pixels, above and below the applet. HSPACE specifies the space, in pixels, on each side of the applet. They're treated the same as the IMG tag's VSPACE and HSPACE attributes.

PARAM NAME and VALUE The PARAM tag allows you to specify applet-specific arguments in an HTML page. Applets access their attributes with the **getParameter( )** method.

Other valid APPLET attributes include ARCHIVE, which lets you specify one or more archive files, and OBJECT, which specifies a saved version of the applet. In general, an APPLET tag should include only a CODE or an OBJECT attribute, but not both.

Passing Parameters to Applets

As just discussed, the APPLET tag in HTML allows you to pass parameters to your applet. To retrieve a parameter, use the **getParameter( )** method. It returns the value of the specified parameter in the form of a **String** object. Thus, for numeric and **boolean** values, you will need to convert their string representations into their internal formats. Here is an example that demonstrates passing parameters:

```
// Use Parameters
import java.awt.*;
import java.applet.*;
/*
<applet code="ParamDemo" width=300 height=80>
<param name=fontName value=Courier>
<param name=fontSize value=14>
<param name=leading value=2>
<param name=accountEnabled value=true>
</applet>
*/

public class ParamDemo extends Applet{
  String fontName;
  int fontSize;
  float leading;
  boolean active;

  // Initialize the string to be displayed.
  public void start() {
    String param;

    fontName = getParameter("fontName");
    if(fontName == null)
      fontName = "Not Found";

    param = getParameter("fontSize");
    try {
      if(param != null) // if not found
        fontSize = Integer.parseInt(param);
      else
```

```
      fontSize = 0;
  } catch(NumberFormatException e) {
    fontSize = -1;
  }

  param = getParameter("leading");
  try {
    if(param != null) // if not found
      leading = Float.valueOf(param).floatValue();
    else
      leading = 0;
  } catch(NumberFormatException e) {
    leading = -1;
  }

  param = getParameter("accountEnabled");
  if(param != null)
    active = Boolean.valueOf(param).booleanValue();
}

// Display parameters.
public void paint(Graphics g) {
  g.drawString("Font name: " + fontName, 0, 10);
  g.drawString("Font size: " + fontSize, 0, 26);
  g.drawString("Leading: " + leading, 0, 42);
  g.drawString("Account Active: " + active, 0, 58);
}
}
```

Sample output from this program is shown here:

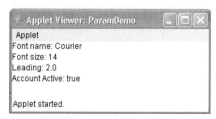

As the program shows, you should test the return values from **getParameter( )**. If a
parameter isn't available, **getParameter( )** will return **null**. Also, conversions to numeric
types must be attempted in a **try** statement that catches **NumberFormatException**. Uncaught
exceptions should never occur within an applet.

Improving the Banner Applet

It is possible to use a parameter to enhance the banner applet shown earlier. In the previous
version, the message being scrolled was hard-coded into the applet. However, passing the
message as a parameter allows the banner applet to display a different message each time it
is executed. This improved version is shown here. Notice that the APPLET tag at the top of
the file now specifies a parameter called **message** that is linked to a quoted string.

```
// A parameterized banner
import java.awt.*;
```

```
import java.applet.*;
/*
<applet code="ParamBanner" width=300 height=50>
<param name=message value="Java makes the Web move!">
</applet>
*/

public class ParamBanner extends Applet implements Runnable {
  String msg;
  Thread t = null;
  int state;
  boolean stopFlag;

  // Set colors and initialize thread.
  public void init() {
    setBackground(Color.cyan);
    setForeground(Color.red);
  }

  // Start thread
  public void start() {
    msg = getParameter("message");
    if(msg == null) msg = "Message not found.";
    msg = " " + msg;
    t = new Thread(this);
    stopFlag = false;
    t.start();
  }

  // Entry point for the thread that runs the banner.
  public void run() {
    char ch;

    // Display banner
    for( ; ; ) {
      try {
        repaint();
        Thread.sleep(250);
        ch = msg.charAt(0);
        msg = msg.substring(1, msg.length());
        msg += ch;
        if(stopFlag)
          break;
      } catch(InterruptedException e) {}
    }
  }

  // Pause the banner.
  public void stop() {
    stopFlag = true;
    t = null;
  }
```

```
  // Display the banner.
  public void paint(Graphics g) {
    g.drawString(msg, 50, 30);
  }
}
```

getDocumentBase( ) and getCodeBase( )

Often, you will create applets that will need to explicitly load media and text. Java will allow the applet to load data from the directory holding the HTML file that started the applet (the *document base*) and the directory from which the applet's class file was loaded (the *code base*). These directories are returned as **URL** objects (described in Chapter 20) by **getDocumentBase( )** and **getCodeBase( )**. They can be concatenated with a string that names the file you want to load. To actually load another file, you will use the **showDocument( )** method defined by the **AppletContext** interface, discussed in the next section.

The following applet illustrates these methods:

```
// Display code and document bases.
import java.awt.*;
import java.applet.*;
import java.net.*;
/*
<applet code="Bases" width=300 height=50>
</applet>
*/

public class Bases extends Applet{
  // Display code and document bases.
  public void paint(Graphics g) {
    String msg;

    URL url = getCodeBase(); // get code base
    msg = "Code base: " + url.toString();
    g.drawString(msg, 10, 20);

    url = getDocumentBase(); // get document base
    msg = "Document base: " + url.toString();
    g.drawString(msg, 10, 40);
  }
}
```

Sample output from this program is shown here:

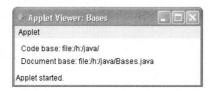

AppletContext and showDocument( )

One application of Java is to use active images and animation to provide a graphical means of navigating the Web that is more interesting than simple text-based links. To allow your applet to transfer control to another URL, you must use the **showDocument( )** method defined by the **AppletContext** interface. **AppletContext** is an interface that lets you get information from the applet's execution environment. The methods defined by **AppletContext** are shown in Table 21-2. The context of the currently executing applet is obtained by a call to the **getAppletContext( )** method defined by **Applet**.

Within an applet, once you have obtained the applet's context, you can bring another document into view by calling **showDocument( )**. This method has no return value and throws no exception if it fails, so use it carefully. There are two **showDocument( )** methods. The method **showDocument(URL)** displays the document at the specified **URL**. The method **showDocument(URL, String)** displays the specified document at the specified location within the browser window. Valid arguments for *where* are "_self" (show in current frame), "_parent" (show in parent frame), "_top" (show in topmost frame), and "_blank" (show in new browser window). You can also specify a name, which causes the document to be shown in a new browser window by that name.

The following applet demonstrates **AppletContext** and **showDocument( )**. Upon execution, it obtains the current applet context and uses that context to transfer control to a file called **Test.html**. This file must be in the same directory as the applet. **Test.html** can contain any valid hypertext that you like.

```
/* Using an applet context, getCodeBase(),
   and showDocument() to display an HTML file.
*/

import java.awt.*;
import java.applet.*;
import java.net.*;
/*
<applet code="ACDemo" width=300 height=50>
</applet>
*/

public class ACDemo extends Applet{
  public void start() {
    AppletContext ac = getAppletContext();
    URL url = getCodeBase(); // get url of this applet

    try {
      ac.showDocument(new URL(url+"Test.html"));
    } catch(MalformedURLException e) {
      showStatus("URL not found");
    }
  }
}
```

Method	Description
Applet getApplet(String *appletName*)	Returns the applet specified by *appletName* if it is within the current applet context. Otherwise, **null** is returned.
Enumeration<Applet> getApplets( )	Returns an enumeration that contains all of the applets within the current applet context.
AudioClip getAudioClip(URL *url*)	Returns an **AudioClip** object that encapsulates the audio clip found at the location specified by *url*.
Image getImage(URL *url*)	Returns an **Image** object that encapsulates the image found at the location specified by *url*.
InputStream getStream(String *key*)	Returns the stream linked to *key*. Keys are linked to streams by using the **setStream( )** method. A **null** reference is returned if no stream is linked to *key*.
Iterator<String> getStreamKeys( )	Returns an iterator for the keys associated with the invoking object. The keys are linked to streams. See **getStream( )** and **setStream( )**.
void setStream(String *key*, InputStream *strm*)	Links the stream specified by *strm* to the key passed in *key*. The *key* is deleted from the invoking object if *strm* is **null**.
void showDocument(URL *url*)	Brings the document at the **URL** specified by *url* into view. This method may not be supported by applet viewers.
void showDocument(URL *url*, String *where*)	Brings the document at the **URL** specified by *url* into view. This method may not be supported by applet viewers. The placement of the document is specified by *where* as described in the text.
void showStatus(String *str*)	Displays *str* in the status window.

TABLE 21-2   The Methods Defined by the **AppletContext** Interface

The AudioClip Interface

The **AudioClip** interface defines these methods: **play( )** (play a clip from the beginning), **stop( )** (stop playing the clip), and **loop( )** (play the loop continuously). After you have loaded an audio clip using **getAudioClip( )**, you can use these methods to play it.

The AppletStub Interface

The **AppletStub** interface provides the means by which an applet and the browser (or applet viewer) communicate. Your code will not typically implement this interface.

Outputting to the Console

Although output to an applet's window must be accomplished through GUI-based methods, such as **drawString( )**, it is still possible to use console output in your applet—especially for debugging purposes. In an applet, when you call a method such as **System.out.println( )**, the output is not sent to your applet's window. Instead, it appears either in the console session in which you launched the applet viewer or in the Java console that is available in some browsers. Use of console output for purposes other than debugging is discouraged, since it violates the design principles of the graphical interface most users will expect.

22

Event Handling

This chapter examines an important aspect of Java: the event. Event handling is fundamental to Java programming because it is integral to the creation of applets and other types of GUI-based programs. As explained in Chapter 21, applets are event-driven programs that use a graphical user interface to interact with the user. Furthermore, any program that uses a graphical user interface, such as a Java application written for Windows, is event driven. Thus, you cannot write these types of programs without a solid command of event handling. Events are supported by a number of packages, including **java.util**, **java.awt**, and **java.awt.event**.

Most events to which your program will respond are generated when the user interacts with a GUI-based program. These are the types of events examined in this chapter. They are passed to your program in a variety of ways, with the specific method dependent upon the actual event. There are several types of events, including those generated by the mouse, the keyboard, and various GUI controls, such as a push button, scroll bar, or check box.

This chapter begins with an overview of Java's event handling mechanism. It then examines the main event classes and interfaces used by the AWT and develops several examples that demonstrate the fundamentals of event processing. This chapter also explains how to use adapter classes, inner classes, and anonymous inner classes to streamline event handling code. The examples provided in the remainder of this book make frequent use of these techniques.

NOTE *This chapter focuses on events related to GUI-based programs. However, events are also occasionally used for purposes not directly related to GUI-based programs. In all cases, the same basic event handling techniques apply.*

Two Event Handling Mechanisms

Before beginning our discussion of event handling, an important point must be made: The way in which events are handled changed significantly between the original version of Java (1.0) and modern versions of Java, beginning with version 1.1. The 1.0 method of event handling is still supported, but it is not recommended for new programs. Also, many of the methods that support the old 1.0 event model have been deprecated. The modern approach is the way that events should be handled by all new programs and thus is the method employed by programs in this book.

The Delegation Event Model

The modern approach to handling events is based on the *delegation event model,* which defines standard and consistent mechanisms to generate and process events. Its concept is quite simple: a *source* generates an event and sends it to one or more *listeners.* In this scheme, the listener simply waits until it receives an event. Once an event is received, the listener processes the event and then returns. The advantage of this design is that the application logic that processes events is cleanly separated from the user interface logic that generates those events. A user interface element is able to "delegate" the processing of an event to a separate piece of code.

In the delegation event model, listeners must register with a source in order to receive an event notification. This provides an important benefit: notifications are sent only to listeners that want to receive them. This is a more efficient way to handle events than the design used by the old Java 1.0 approach. Previously, an event was propagated up the containment hierarchy until it was handled by a component. This required components to receive events that they did not process, and it wasted valuable time. The delegation event model eliminates this overhead.

NOTE *Java also allows you to process events without using the delegation event model. This can be done by extending an AWT component. This technique is discussed at the end of Chapter 24. However, the delegation event model is the preferred design for the reasons just cited.*

The following sections define events and describe the roles of sources and listeners.

Events

In the delegation model, an *event* is an object that describes a state change in a source. It can be generated as a consequence of a person interacting with the elements in a graphical user interface. Some of the activities that cause events to be generated are pressing a button, entering a character via the keyboard, selecting an item in a list, and clicking the mouse. Many other user operations could also be cited as examples.

Events may also occur that are not directly caused by interactions with a user interface. For example, an event may be generated when a timer expires, a counter exceeds a value, a software or hardware failure occurs, or an operation is completed. You are free to define events that are appropriate for your application.

Event Sources

A *source* is an object that generates an event. This occurs when the internal state of that object changes in some way. Sources may generate more than one type of event.

A source must register listeners in order for the listeners to receive notifications about a specific type of event. Each type of event has its own registration method. Here is the general form:

public void add*Type*Listener(*Type*Listener *el*)

Here, *Type* is the name of the event, and *el* is a reference to the event listener. For example, the method that registers a keyboard event listener is called **addKeyListener( )**. The method that registers a mouse motion listener is called **addMouseMotionListener( )**. When an event occurs, all registered listeners are notified and receive a copy of the event object. This is known as *multicasting* the event. In all cases, notifications are sent only to listeners that register to receive them.

Some sources may allow only one listener to register. The general form of such a method is this:

public void add*Type*Listener(*Type*Listener *el*)
   throws java.util.TooManyListenersException

Here, *Type* is the name of the event, and *el* is a reference to the event listener. When such an event occurs, the registered listener is notified. This is known as *unicasting* the event.

A source must also provide a method that allows a listener to unregister an interest in a specific type of event. The general form of such a method is this:

public void remove*Type*Listener(*Type*Listener *el*)

Here, *Type* is the name of the event, and *el* is a reference to the event listener. For example, to remove a keyboard listener, you would call **removeKeyListener( )**.

The methods that add or remove listeners are provided by the source that generates events. For example, the **Component** class provides methods to add and remove keyboard and mouse event listeners.

Event Listeners

A *listener* is an object that is notified when an event occurs. It has two major requirements. First, it must have been registered with one or more sources to receive notifications about specific types of events. Second, it must implement methods to receive and process these notifications.

The methods that receive and process events are defined in a set of interfaces found in **java.awt.event**. For example, the **MouseMotionListener** interface defines two methods to receive notifications when the mouse is dragged or moved. Any object may receive and process one or both of these events if it provides an implementation of this interface. Many other listener interfaces are discussed later in this and other chapters.

Event Classes

The classes that represent events are at the core of Java's event handling mechanism. Thus, a discussion of event handling must begin with the event classes. It is important to understand, however, that Java defines several types of events and that not all event classes can be discussed in this chapter. The most widely used events are those defined by the AWT and those defined by Swing. This chapter focuses on the AWT events. (Most of these events also apply to Swing.) Several Swing-specific events are described in Chapter 29, when Swing is covered.

At the root of the Java event class hierarchy is **EventObject**, which is in **java.util**. It is the superclass for all events. Its one constructor is shown here:

EventObject(Object *src*)

Here, *src* is the object that generates this event.

EventObject contains two methods: **getSource( )** and **toString( )**. The **getSource( )** method returns the source of the event. Its general form is shown here:

Object getSource( )

As expected, **toString( )** returns the string equivalent of the event.

The class **AWTEvent**, defined within the **java.awt** package, is a subclass of **EventObject**. It is the superclass (either directly or indirectly) of all AWT-based events used by the delegation event model. Its **getID( )** method can be used to determine the type of the event. The signature of this method is shown here:

   int getID( )

Additional details about **AWTEvent** are provided at the end of Chapter 24. At this point, it is important to know only that all of the other classes discussed in this section are subclasses of **AWTEvent**.

To summarize:

- **EventObject** is a superclass of all events.
- **AWTEvent** is a superclass of all AWT events that are handled by the delegation event model.

The package **java.awt.event** defines many types of events that are generated by various user interface elements. Table 22-1 shows several commonly used event classes and provides a brief description of when they are generated. Commonly used constructors and methods in each class are described in the following sections.

The ActionEvent Class

An **ActionEvent** is generated when a button is pressed, a list item is double-clicked, or a menu item is selected. The **ActionEvent** class defines four integer constants that can be used to identify any modifiers associated with an action event: **ALT_MASK**, **CTRL_MASK**, **META_MASK**, and **SHIFT_MASK**. In addition, there is an integer constant, **ACTION_ PERFORMED**, which can be used to identify action events.

Event Class	Description
ActionEvent	Generated when a button is pressed, a list item is double-clicked, or a menu item is selected.
AdjustmentEvent	Generated when a scroll bar is manipulated.
ComponentEvent	Generated when a component is hidden, moved, resized, or becomes visible.
ContainerEvent	Generated when a component is added to or removed from a container.
FocusEvent	Generated when a component gains or loses keyboard focus.
InputEvent	Abstract superclass for all component input event classes.
ItemEvent	Generated when a check box or list item is clicked; also occurs when a choice selection is made or a checkable menu item is selected or deselected.
KeyEvent	Generated when input is received from the keyboard.
MouseEvent	Generated when the mouse is dragged, moved, clicked, pressed, or released; also generated when the mouse enters or exits a component.
MouseWheelEvent	Generated when the mouse wheel is moved.
TextEvent	Generated when the value of a text area or text field is changed.
WindowEvent	Generated when a window is activated, closed, deactivated, deiconified, iconified, opened, or quit.

TABLE 22-1   Main Event Classes in **java.awt.event**

ActionEvent has these three constructors:

ActionEvent(Object *src*, int *type*, String *cmd*)
ActionEvent(Object *src*, int *type*, String *cmd*, int *modifiers*)
ActionEvent(Object *src*, int *type*, String *cmd*, long *when*, int *modifiers*)

Here, *src* is a reference to the object that generated this event. The type of the event is specified by *type*, and its command string is *cmd*. The argument *modifiers* indicates which modifier keys (ALT, CTRL, META, and/or SHIFT) were pressed when the event was generated. The *when* parameter specifies when the event occurred.

You can obtain the command name for the invoking **ActionEvent** object by using the **getActionCommand( )** method, shown here:

String getActionCommand( )

For example, when a button is pressed, an action event is generated that has a command name equal to the label on that button.

The **getModifiers( )** method returns a value that indicates which modifier keys (ALT, CTRL, META, and/or SHIFT) were pressed when the event was generated. Its form is shown here:

int getModifiers( )

The method **getWhen( )** returns the time at which the event took place. This is called the event's *timestamp*. The **getWhen( )** method is shown here:

long getWhen( )

The AdjustmentEvent Class

An **AdjustmentEvent** is generated by a scroll bar. There are five types of adjustment events. The **AdjustmentEvent** class defines integer constants that can be used to identify them. The constants and their meanings are shown here:

BLOCK_DECREMENT	The user clicked inside the scroll bar to decrease its value.
BLOCK_INCREMENT	The user clicked inside the scroll bar to increase its value.
TRACK	The slider was dragged.
UNIT_DECREMENT	The button at the end of the scroll bar was clicked to decrease its value.
UNIT_INCREMENT	The button at the end of the scroll bar was clicked to increase its value.

In addition, there is an integer constant, **ADJUSTMENT_VALUE_CHANGED**, that indicates that a change has occurred.

Here is one **AdjustmentEvent** constructor:

AdjustmentEvent(Adjustable *src*, int *id*, int *type*, int *data*)

Here, *src* is a reference to the object that generated this event. The *id* specifies the event. The type of the adjustment is specified by *type*, and its associated data is *data*.

The **getAdjustable( )** method returns the object that generated the event. Its form is shown here:

Adjustable getAdjustable( )

The type of the adjustment event may be obtained by the **getAdjustmentType( )** method. It returns one of the constants defined by **AdjustmentEvent**. The general form is shown here:

    int getAdjustmentType( )

The amount of the adjustment can be obtained from the **getValue( )** method, shown here:

    int getValue( )

For example, when a scroll bar is manipulated, this method returns the value represented by that change.

The ComponentEvent Class

A **ComponentEvent** is generated when the size, position, or visibility of a component is changed. There are four types of component events. The **ComponentEvent** class defines integer constants that can be used to identify them. The constants and their meanings are shown here:

COMPONENT_HIDDEN	The component was hidden.
COMPONENT_MOVED	The component was moved.
COMPONENT_RESIZED	The component was resized.
COMPONENT_SHOWN	The component became visible.

ComponentEvent has this constructor:

    ComponentEvent(Component *src*, int *type*)

Here, *src* is a reference to the object that generated this event. The type of the event is specified by *type*.

ComponentEvent is the superclass either directly or indirectly of **ContainerEvent**, **FocusEvent**, **KeyEvent**, **MouseEvent**, and **WindowEvent**.

The **getComponent( )** method returns the component that generated the event. It is shown here:

    Component getComponent( )

The ContainerEvent Class

A **ContainerEvent** is generated when a component is added to or removed from a container. There are two types of container events. The **ContainerEvent** class defines **int** constants that can be used to identify them: **COMPONENT_ADDED** and **COMPONENT_REMOVED**. They indicate that a component has been added to or removed from the container.

ContainerEvent is a subclass of **ComponentEvent** and has this constructor:

    ContainerEvent(Component *src*, int *type*, Component *comp*)

Here, *src* is a reference to the container that generated this event. The type of the event is specified by *type*, and the component that has been added to or removed from the container is *comp*.

You can obtain a reference to the container that generated this event by using the **getContainer( )** method, shown here:

Container getContainer( )

The **getChild( )** method returns a reference to the component that was added to or removed from the container. Its general form is shown here:

Component getChild( )

The FocusEvent Class

A **FocusEvent** is generated when a component gains or loses input focus. These events are identified by the integer constants **FOCUS_GAINED** and **FOCUS_LOST**.

FocusEvent is a subclass of **ComponentEvent** and has these constructors:

FocusEvent(Component *src*, int *type*)
FocusEvent(Component *src*, int *type*, boolean *temporaryFlag*)
FocusEvent(Component *src*, int *type*, boolean *temporaryFlag*, Component *other*)

Here, *src* is a reference to the component that generated this event. The type of the event is specified by *type*. The argument *temporaryFlag* is set to **true** if the focus event is temporary. Otherwise, it is set to **false**. (A temporary focus event occurs as a result of another user interface operation. For example, assume that the focus is in a text field. If the user moves the mouse to adjust a scroll bar, the focus is temporarily lost.)

The other component involved in the focus change, called the *opposite component,* is passed in *other*. Therefore, if a **FOCUS_GAINED** event occurred, *other* will refer to the component that lost focus. Conversely, if a **FOCUS_LOST** event occurred, *other* will refer to the component that gains focus.

You can determine the other component by calling **getOppositeComponent( )**, shown here:

Component getOppositeComponent( )

The opposite component is returned.

The **isTemporary( )** method indicates if this focus change is temporary. Its form is shown here:

boolean isTemporary( )

The method returns **true** if the change is temporary. Otherwise, it returns **false**.

The InputEvent Class

The abstract class **InputEvent** is a subclass of **ComponentEvent** and is the superclass for component input events. Its subclasses are **KeyEvent** and **MouseEvent**.

InputEvent defines several integer constants that represent any modifiers, such as the control key being pressed, that might be associated with the event. Originally, the **InputEvent** class defined the following eight values to represent the modifiers:

ALT_MASK	BUTTON2_MASK	META_MASK
ALT_GRAPH_MASK	BUTTON3_MASK	SHIFT_MASK
BUTTON1_MASK	CTRL_MASK	

However, because of possible conflicts between the modifiers used by keyboard events and mouse events, and other issues, the following extended modifier values were added:

ALT_DOWN_MASK	BUTTON2_DOWN_MASK	META_DOWN_MASK
ALT_GRAPH_DOWN_MASK	BUTTON3_DOWN_MASK	SHIFT_DOWN_MASK
BUTTON1_DOWN_MASK	CTRL_DOWN_MASK	

When writing new code, it is recommended that you use the new, extended modifiers rather than the original modifiers.

To test if a modifier was pressed at the time an event is generated, use the **isAltDown( )**, **isAltGraphDown( )**, **isControlDown( )**, **isMetaDown( )**, and **isShiftDown( )** methods. The forms of these methods are shown here:

```
boolean isAltDown( )
boolean isAltGraphDown( )
boolean isControlDown( )
boolean isMetaDown( )
boolean isShiftDown( )
```

You can obtain a value that contains all of the original modifier flags by calling the **getModifiers( )** method. It is shown here:

```
int getModifiers( )
```

You can obtain the extended modifiers by calling **getModifiersEx( )**, which is shown here:

```
int getModifiersEx( )
```

The ItemEvent Class

An **ItemEvent** is generated when a check box or a list item is clicked or when a checkable menu item is selected or deselected. (Check boxes and list boxes are described later in this book.) There are two types of item events, which are identified by the following integer constants:

DESELECTED	The user deselected an item.
SELECTED	The user selected an item.

In addition, **ItemEvent** defines one integer constant, **ITEM_STATE_CHANGED**, that signifies a change of state.

ItemEvent has this constructor:

ItemEvent(ItemSelectable *src*, int *type*, Object *entry*, int *state*)

Here, *src* is a reference to the component that generated this event. For example, this might be a list or choice element. The type of the event is specified by *type*. The specific item that generated the item event is passed in *entry*. The current state of that item is in *state*.

The **getItem( )** method can be used to obtain a reference to the item that generated an event. Its signature is shown here:

Object getItem( )

The **getItemSelectable( )** method can be used to obtain a reference to the **ItemSelectable** object that generated an event. Its general form is shown here:

ItemSelectable getItemSelectable( )

Lists and choices are examples of user interface elements that implement the **ItemSelectable** interface.

The **getStateChange( )** method returns the state change (that is, **SELECTED** or **DESELECTED**) for the event. It is shown here:

int getStateChange( )

The KeyEvent Class

A **KeyEvent** is generated when keyboard input occurs. There are three types of key events, which are identified by these integer constants: **KEY_PRESSED**, **KEY_RELEASED**, and **KEY_TYPED**. The first two events are generated when any key is pressed or released. The last event occurs only when a character is generated. Remember, not all keypresses result in characters. For example, pressing SHIFT does not generate a character.

There are many other integer constants that are defined by **KeyEvent**. For example, **VK_0** through **VK_9** and **VK_A** through **VK_Z** define the ASCII equivalents of the numbers and letters. Here are some others:

VK_ALT	VK_DOWN	VK_LEFT	VK_RIGHT
VK_CANCEL	VK_ENTER	VK_PAGE_DOWN	VK_SHIFT
VK_CONTROL	VK_ESCAPE	VK_PAGE_UP	VK_UP

The **VK** constants specify *virtual key codes* and are independent of any modifiers, such as control, shift, or alt.

KeyEvent is a subclass of **InputEvent**. Here is one of its constructors:

KeyEvent(Component *src*, int *type*, long *when*, int *modifiers*, int *code*, char *ch*)

Here, *src* is a reference to the component that generated the event. The type of the event is specified by *type*. The system time at which the key was pressed is passed in *when*. The *modifiers* argument indicates which modifiers were pressed when this key event occurred. The virtual key code, such as **VK_UP**, **VK_A**, and so forth, is passed in *code*. The character equivalent (if one exists) is passed in *ch*. If no valid character exists, then *ch* contains **CHAR_UNDEFINED**. For **KEY_TYPED** events, *code* will contain **VK_UNDEFINED**.

The **KeyEvent** class defines several methods, but the most commonly used ones are **getKeyChar( )**, which returns the character that was entered, and **getKeyCode( )**, which returns the key code. Their general forms are shown here:

char getKeyChar( )
int getKeyCode( )

If no valid character is available, then **getKeyChar( )** returns **CHAR_UNDEFINED**. When a **KEY_TYPED** event occurs, **getKeyCode( )** returns **VK_UNDEFINED**.

The MouseEvent Class

There are eight types of mouse events. The **MouseEvent** class defines the following integer constants that can be used to identify them:

MOUSE_CLICKED	The user clicked the mouse.
MOUSE_DRAGGED	The user dragged the mouse.
MOUSE_ENTERED	The mouse entered a component.
MOUSE_EXITED	The mouse exited from a component.
MOUSE_MOVED	The mouse moved.
MOUSE_PRESSED	The mouse was pressed.
MOUSE_RELEASED	The mouse was released.
MOUSE_WHEEL	The mouse wheel was moved.

MouseEvent is a subclass of **InputEvent**. Here is one of its constructors:

MouseEvent(Component *src*, int *type*, long *when*, int *modifiers*,
                     int *x*, int *y*, int *clicks*, boolean *triggersPopup*)

Here, *src* is a reference to the component that generated the event. The type of the event is specified by *type*. The system time at which the mouse event occurred is passed in *when*. The *modifiers* argument indicates which modifiers were pressed when a mouse event occurred. The coordinates of the mouse are passed in *x* and *y*. The click count is passed in *clicks*. The *triggersPopup* flag indicates if this event causes a pop-up menu to appear on this platform.

Two commonly used methods in this class are **getX( )** and **getY( )**. These return the X and Y coordinates of the mouse within the component when the event occurred. Their forms are shown here:

int getX( )
int getY( )

Alternatively, you can use the **getPoint( )** method to obtain the coordinates of the mouse. It is shown here:

Point getPoint( )

It returns a **Point** object that contains the X,Y coordinates in its integer members: **x** and **y**. The **translatePoint( )** method changes the location of the event. Its form is shown here:

void translatePoint(int *x*, int *y*)

Here, the arguments *x* and *y* are added to the coordinates of the event. The **getClickCount( )** method obtains the number of mouse clicks for this event. Its signature is shown here:

int getClickCount( )

The **isPopupTrigger( )** method tests if this event causes a pop-up menu to appear on this platform. Its form is shown here:

boolean isPopupTrigger( )

Also available is the **getButton( )** method, shown here:

int getButton( )

It returns a value that represents the button that caused the event. The return value will be one of these constants defined by **MouseEvent**:

NOBUTTON	BUTTON1	BUTTON2	BUTTON3

The **NOBUTTON** value indicates that no button was pressed or released.

Java SE 6 added three methods to **MouseEvent** that obtain the coordinates of the mouse relative to the screen rather than the component. They are shown here:

Point getLocationOnScreen( )

int getXOnScreen( )

int getYOnScreen( )

The **getLocationOnScreen( )** method returns a **Point** object that contains both the X and Y coordinate. The other two methods return the indicated coordinate.

The MouseWheelEvent Class

The **MouseWheelEvent** class encapsulates a mouse wheel event. It is a subclass of **MouseEvent**. Not all mice have wheels. If a mouse has a wheel, it is located between the left and right buttons. Mouse wheels are used for scrolling. **MouseWheelEvent** defines these two integer constants:

WHEEL_BLOCK_SCROLL	A page-up or page-down scroll event occurred.
WHEEL_UNIT_SCROLL	A line-up or line-down scroll event occurred.

Here is one of the constructors defined by **MouseWheelEvent**:

MouseWheelEvent(Component *src*, int *type*, long *when*, int *modifiers*,
        int *x*, int *y*, int *clicks*, boolean *triggersPopup*,
        int *scrollHow*, int *amount*, int *count*)

Here, *src* is a reference to the object that generated the event. The type of the event is specified by *type*. The system time at which the mouse event occurred is passed in *when*. The *modifiers* argument indicates which modifiers were pressed when the event occurred. The coordinates of the mouse are passed in *x* and *y*. The number of clicks the wheel has rotated is passed in *clicks*. The *triggersPopup* flag indicates if this event causes a pop-up menu to appear on this platform. The *scrollHow* value must be either **WHEEL_UNIT_SCROLL** or **WHEEL_BLOCK_SCROLL**. The number of units to scroll is passed in *amount*. The *count* parameter indicates the number of rotational units that the wheel moved.

MouseWheelEvent defines methods that give you access to the wheel event. To obtain the number of rotational units, call **getWheelRotation( )**, shown here:

int getWheelRotation( )

It returns the number of rotational units. If the value is positive, the wheel moved counterclockwise. If the value is negative, the wheel moved clockwise.

To obtain the type of scroll, call **getScrollType( )**, shown next:

int getScrollType( )

It returns either **WHEEL_UNIT_SCROLL** or **WHEEL_BLOCK_SCROLL**.

If the scroll type is **WHEEL_UNIT_SCROLL**, you can obtain the number of units to scroll by calling **getScrollAmount( )**. It is shown here:

int getScrollAmount( )

The TextEvent Class

Instances of this class describe text events. These are generated by text fields and text areas when characters are entered by a user or program. **TextEvent** defines the integer constant **TEXT_VALUE_CHANGED**.

The one constructor for this class is shown here:

TextEvent(Object *src*, int *type*)

Here, *src* is a reference to the object that generated this event. The type of the event is specified by *type*.

The **TextEvent** object does not include the characters currently in the text component that generated the event. Instead, your program must use other methods associated with the text component to retrieve that information. This operation differs from other event objects discussed in this section. For this reason, no methods are discussed here for the **TextEvent** class. Think of a text event notification as a signal to a listener that it should retrieve information from a specific text component.

The WindowEvent Class

There are ten types of window events. The **WindowEvent** class defines integer constants that can be used to identify them. The constants and their meanings are shown here:

WINDOW_ACTIVATED	The window was activated.
WINDOW_CLOSED	The window has been closed.
WINDOW_CLOSING	The user requested that the window be closed.
WINDOW_DEACTIVATED	The window was deactivated.
WINDOW_DEICONIFIED	The window was deiconified.
WINDOW_GAINED_FOCUS	The window gained input focus.
WINDOW_ICONIFIED	The window was iconified.
WINDOW_LOST_FOCUS	The window lost input focus.
WINDOW_OPENED	The window was opened.
WINDOW_STATE_CHANGED	The state of the window changed.

WindowEvent is a subclass of **ComponentEvent**. It defines several constructors. The first is

WindowEvent(Window *src*, int *type*)

Here, *src* is a reference to the object that generated this event. The type of the event is *type*.
The next three constructors offer more detailed control:

WindowEvent(Window *src*, int *type*, Window *other*)
WindowEvent(Window *src*, int *type*, int *fromState*, int *toState*)
WindowEvent(Window *src*, int *type*, Window *other*, int *fromState*, int *toState*)

Here, *other* specifies the opposite window when a focus or activation event occurs. The *fromState* specifies the prior state of the window, and *toState* specifies the new state that the window will have when a window state change occurs.

A commonly used method in this class is **getWindow( )**. It returns the **Window** object that generated the event. Its general form is shown here:

Window getWindow( )

WindowEvent also defines methods that return the opposite window (when a focus or activation event has occurred), the previous window state, and the current window state. These methods are shown here:

Window getOppositeWindow( )
int getOldState( )
int getNewState( )

Sources of Events

Table 22-2 lists some of the user interface components that can generate the events described in the previous section. In addition to these graphical user interface elements, any class derived

Event Source	Description
Button	Generates action events when the button is pressed.
Check box	Generates item events when the check box is selected or deselected.
Choice	Generates item events when the choice is changed.
List	Generates action events when an item is double-clicked; generates item events when an item is selected or deselected.
Menu Item	Generates action events when a menu item is selected; generates item events when a checkable menu item is selected or deselected.
Scroll bar	Generates adjustment events when the scroll bar is manipulated.
Text components	Generates text events when the user enters a character.
Window	Generates window events when a window is activated, closed, deactivated, deiconified, iconified, opened, or quit.

TABLE 22-2   Event Source Examples

from **Component**, such as **Applet**, can generate events. For example, you can receive key and mouse events from an applet. (You may also build your own components that generate events.) In this chapter, we will be handling only mouse and keyboard events, but the following two chapters will be handling events from the sources shown in Table 22-2.

Event Listener Interfaces

As explained, the delegation event model has two parts: sources and listeners. Listeners are created by implementing one or more of the interfaces defined by the **java.awt.event** package. When an event occurs, the event source invokes the appropriate method defined by the listener and provides an event object as its argument. Table 22-3 lists commonly used listener interfaces and provides a brief description of the methods that they define. The following sections examine the specific methods that are contained in each interface.

The ActionListener Interface

This interface defines the **actionPerformed( )** method that is invoked when an action event occurs. Its general form is shown here:

        void actionPerformed(ActionEvent *ae*)

Interface	Description
ActionListener	Defines one method to receive action events.
AdjustmentListener	Defines one method to receive adjustment events.
ComponentListener	Defines four methods to recognize when a component is hidden, moved, resized, or shown.
ContainerListener	Defines two methods to recognize when a component is added to or removed from a container.
FocusListener	Defines two methods to recognize when a component gains or loses keyboard focus.
ItemListener	Defines one method to recognize when the state of an item changes.
KeyListener	Defines three methods to recognize when a key is pressed, released, or typed.
MouseListener	Defines five methods to recognize when the mouse is clicked, enters a component, exits a component, is pressed, or is released.
MouseMotionListener	Defines two methods to recognize when the mouse is dragged or moved.
MouseWheelListener	Defines one method to recognize when the mouse wheel is moved.
TextListener	Defines one method to recognize when a text value changes.
WindowFocusListener	Defines two methods to recognize when a window gains or loses input focus.
WindowListener	Defines seven methods to recognize when a window is activated, closed, deactivated, deiconified, iconified, opened, or quit.

TABLE 22-3   Commonly Used Event Listener Interfaces

The AdjustmentListener Interface

This interface defines the **adjustmentValueChanged( )** method that is invoked when an adjustment event occurs. Its general form is shown here:

void adjustmentValueChanged(AdjustmentEvent *ae*)

The ComponentListener Interface

This interface defines four methods that are invoked when a component is resized, moved, shown, or hidden. Their general forms are shown here:

void componentResized(ComponentEvent *ce*)
void componentMoved(ComponentEvent *ce*)
void componentShown(ComponentEvent *ce*)
void componentHidden(ComponentEvent *ce*)

The ContainerListener Interface

This interface contains two methods. When a component is added to a container, **componentAdded( )** is invoked. When a component is removed from a container, **componentRemoved( )** is invoked. Their general forms are shown here:

void componentAdded(ContainerEvent *ce*)
void componentRemoved(ContainerEvent *ce*)

The FocusListener Interface

This interface defines two methods. When a component obtains keyboard focus, **focusGained( )** is invoked. When a component loses keyboard focus, **focusLost( )** is called. Their general forms are shown here:

void focusGained(FocusEvent *fe*)
void focusLost(FocusEvent *fe*)

The ItemListener Interface

This interface defines the **itemStateChanged( )** method that is invoked when the state of an item changes. Its general form is shown here:

void itemStateChanged(ItemEvent *ie*)

The KeyListener Interface

This interface defines three methods. The **keyPressed( )** and **keyReleased( )** methods are invoked when a key is pressed and released, respectively. The **keyTyped( )** method is invoked when a character has been entered.

For example, if a user presses and releases the A key, three events are generated in sequence: key pressed, typed, and released. If a user presses and releases the HOME key, two key events are generated in sequence: key pressed and released.

The general forms of these methods are shown here:

void keyPressed(KeyEvent *ke*)
void keyReleased(KeyEvent *ke*)
void keyTyped(KeyEvent *ke*)

The MouseListener Interface

This interface defines five methods. If the mouse is pressed and released at the same point, **mouseClicked( )** is invoked. When the mouse enters a component, the **mouseEntered( )** method is called. When it leaves, **mouseExited( )** is called. The **mousePressed( )** and **mouseReleased( )** methods are invoked when the mouse is pressed and released, respectively.

The general forms of these methods are shown here:

void mouseClicked(MouseEvent *me*)
void mouseEntered(MouseEvent *me*)
void mouseExited(MouseEvent *me*)
void mousePressed(MouseEvent *me*)
void mouseReleased(MouseEvent *me*)

The MouseMotionListener Interface

This interface defines two methods. The **mouseDragged( )** method is called multiple times as the mouse is dragged. The **mouseMoved( )** method is called multiple times as the mouse is moved. Their general forms are shown here:

void mouseDragged(MouseEvent *me*)
void mouseMoved(MouseEvent *me*)

The MouseWheelListener Interface

This interface defines the **mouseWheelMoved( )** method that is invoked when the mouse wheel is moved. Its general form is shown here:

void mouseWheelMoved(MouseWheelEvent *mwe*)

The TextListener Interface

This interface defines the **textChanged( )** method that is invoked when a change occurs in a text area or text field. Its general form is shown here:

void textChanged(TextEvent *te*)

The WindowFocusListener Interface

This interface defines two methods: **windowGainedFocus( )** and **windowLostFocus( )**. These are called when a window gains or loses input focus. Their general forms are shown here:

void windowGainedFocus(WindowEvent *we*)
void windowLostFocus(WindowEvent *we*)

The WindowListener Interface

This interface defines seven methods. The **windowActivated( )** and **windowDeactivated( )** methods are invoked when a window is activated or deactivated, respectively. If a window is iconified, the **windowIconified( )** method is called. When a window is deiconified, the **windowDeiconified( )** method is called. When a window is opened or closed, the **windowOpened( )** or **windowClosed( )** methods are called, respectively. The **windowClosing( )** method is called when a window is being closed. The general forms of these methods are

```
void windowActivated(WindowEvent we)
void windowClosed(WindowEvent we)
void windowClosing(WindowEvent we)
void windowDeactivated(WindowEvent we)
void windowDeiconified(WindowEvent we)
void windowIconified(WindowEvent we)
void windowOpened(WindowEvent we)
```

Using the Delegation Event Model

Now that you have learned the theory behind the delegation event model and have had an overview of its various components, it is time to see it in practice. Using the delegation event model is actually quite easy. Just follow these two steps:

1. Implement the appropriate interface in the listener so that it will receive the type of event desired.

2. Implement code to register and unregister (if necessary) the listener as a recipient for the event notifications.

Remember that a source may generate several types of events. Each event must be registered separately. Also, an object may register to receive several types of events, but it must implement all of the interfaces that are required to receive these events.

To see how the delegation model works in practice, we will look at examples that handle two commonly used event generators: the mouse and keyboard.

Handling Mouse Events

To handle mouse events, you must implement the **MouseListener** and the **MouseMotionListener** interfaces. (You may also want to implement **MouseWheelListener**, but we won't be doing so, here.) The following applet demonstrates the process. It displays the current coordinates of the mouse in the applet's status window. Each time a button is pressed, the word "Down" is displayed at the location of the mouse pointer. Each time the button is released, the word "Up" is shown. If a button is clicked, the message "Mouse clicked" is displayed in the upper-left corner of the applet display area.

As the mouse enters or exits the applet window, a message is displayed in the upper-left corner of the applet display area. When dragging the mouse, a * is shown, which tracks with the mouse pointer as it is dragged. Notice that the two variables, **mouseX** and **mouseY**, store the location of the mouse when a mouse pressed, released, or dragged event occurs. These coordinates are then used by **paint( )** to display output at the point of these occurrences.

```
// Demonstrate the mouse event handlers.
import java.awt.*;
```

```
import java.awt.event.*;
import java.applet.*;
/*
  <applet code="MouseEvents" width=300 height=100>
  </applet>
*/

public class MouseEvents extends Applet
  implements MouseListener, MouseMotionListener {

  String msg = "";
  int mouseX = 0, mouseY = 0; // coordinates of mouse

  public void init() {
     addMouseListener(this);
     addMouseMotionListener(this);
  }

  // Handle mouse clicked.
  public void mouseClicked(MouseEvent me) {
    // save coordinates
    mouseX = 0;
    mouseY = 10;
    msg = "Mouse clicked.";
    repaint();
  }

  // Handle mouse entered.
  public void mouseEntered(MouseEvent me) {
    // save coordinates
    mouseX = 0;
    mouseY = 10;
    msg = "Mouse entered.";
    repaint();
  }

  // Handle mouse exited.
  public void mouseExited(MouseEvent me) {
    // save coordinates
    mouseX = 0;
    mouseY = 10;
    msg = "Mouse exited.";
    repaint();
  }

  // Handle button pressed.
  public void mousePressed(MouseEvent me) {
    // save coordinates
    mouseX = me.getX();
    mouseY = me.getY();
    msg = "Down";
    repaint();
  }
```

```
  // Handle button released.
  public void mouseReleased(MouseEvent me) {
    // save coordinates
    mouseX = me.getX();
    mouseY = me.getY();
    msg = "Up";
    repaint();
  }

  // Handle mouse dragged.
  public void mouseDragged(MouseEvent me) {
    // save coordinates
    mouseX = me.getX();
    mouseY = me.getY();
    msg = "*";
    showStatus("Dragging mouse at " + mouseX + ", " + mouseY);
    repaint();
  }

  // Handle mouse moved.
  public void mouseMoved(MouseEvent me) {
    // show status
    showStatus("Moving mouse at " + me.getX() + ", " + me.getY());
  }

  // Display msg in applet window at current X,Y location.
  public void paint(Graphics g) {
    g.drawString(msg, mouseX, mouseY);
  }
}
```

Sample output from this program is shown here:

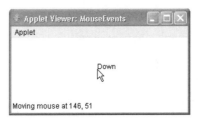

Let's look closely at this example. The **MouseEvents** class extends **Applet** and implements both the **MouseListener** and **MouseMotionListener** interfaces. These two interfaces contain methods that receive and process the various types of mouse events. Notice that the applet is both the source and the listener for these events. This works because **Component**, which supplies the **addMouseListener( )** and **addMouseMotionListener( )** methods, is a superclass of **Applet**. Being both the source and the listener for events is a common situation for applets.

Inside **init( )**, the applet registers itself as a listener for mouse events. This is done by using **addMouseListener( )** and **addMouseMotionListener( )**, which, as mentioned, are members of **Component**. They are shown here:

    void addMouseListener(MouseListener *ml*)
    void addMouseMotionListener(MouseMotionListener *mml*)

Here, *ml* is a reference to the object receiving mouse events, and *mml* is a reference to the object receiving mouse motion events. In this program, the same object is used for both.

The applet then implements all of the methods defined by the **MouseListener** and **MouseMotionListener** interfaces. These are the event handlers for the various mouse events. Each method handles its event and then returns.

Handling Keyboard Events

To handle keyboard events, you use the same general architecture as that shown in the mouse event example in the preceding section. The difference, of course, is that you will be implementing the **KeyListener** interface.

Before looking at an example, it is useful to review how key events are generated. When a key is pressed, a **KEY_PRESSED** event is generated. This results in a call to the **keyPressed( )** event handler. When the key is released, a **KEY_RELEASED** event is generated and the **keyReleased( )** handler is executed. If a character is generated by the keystroke, then a **KEY_TYPED** event is sent and the **keyTyped( )** handler is invoked. Thus, each time the user presses a key, at least two and often three events are generated. If all you care about are actual characters, then you can ignore the information passed by the keypress and release events. However, if your program needs to handle special keys, such as the arrow or function keys, then it must watch for them through the **keyPressed( )** handler.

The following program demonstrates keyboard input. It echoes keystrokes to the applet window and shows the pressed/released status of each key in the status window.

```
// Demonstrate the key event handlers.
import java.awt.*;
import java.awt.event.*;
import java.applet.*;
/*
  <applet code="SimpleKey" width=300 height=100>
  </applet>
*/

public class SimpleKey extends Applet
  implements KeyListener {

  String msg = "";
  int X = 10, Y = 20; // output coordinates

  public void init() {
    addKeyListener(this);
  }

  public void keyPressed(KeyEvent ke) {
    showStatus("Key Down");
  }

  public void keyReleased(KeyEvent ke) {
    showStatus("Key Up");
  }

  public void keyTyped(KeyEvent ke) {
    msg += ke.getKeyChar();
```

```
    repaint();
  }

  // Display keystrokes.
  public void paint(Graphics g) {
    g.drawString(msg, X, Y);
  }
}
```

Sample output is shown here:

If you want to handle the special keys, such as the arrow or function keys, you need to respond to them within the **keyPressed( )** handler. They are not available through **keyTyped( )**. To identify the keys, you use their virtual key codes. For example, the next applet outputs the name of a few of the special keys:

```
// Demonstrate some virtual key codes.
import java.awt.*;
import java.awt.event.*;
import java.applet.*;
/*
  <applet code="KeyEvents" width=300 height=100>
  </applet>
*/

public class KeyEvents extends Applet
  implements KeyListener {

  String msg = "";
  int X = 10, Y = 20; // output coordinates

  public void init() {
    addKeyListener(this);
  }

  public void keyPressed(KeyEvent ke) {
    showStatus("Key Down");

    int key = ke.getKeyCode();
    switch(key) {
      case KeyEvent.VK_F1:
        msg += "<F1>";
        break;
      case KeyEvent.VK_F2:
```

```
      msg += "<F2>";
      break;
    case KeyEvent.VK_F3:
      msg += "<F3>";
      break;
    case KeyEvent.VK_PAGE_DOWN:
      msg += "<PgDn>";
      break;
    case KeyEvent.VK_PAGE_UP:
      msg += "<PgUp>";
      break;
    case KeyEvent.VK_LEFT:
      msg += "<Left Arrow>";
      break;
    case KeyEvent.VK_RIGHT:
      msg += "<Right Arrow>";
      break;
    }

    repaint();
  }

  public void keyReleased(KeyEvent ke) {
    showStatus("Key Up");
  }

  public void keyTyped(KeyEvent ke) {
    msg += ke.getKeyChar();
    repaint();
  }

  // Display keystrokes.
  public void paint(Graphics g) {
    g.drawString(msg, X, Y);
  }
}
```

Sample output is shown here:

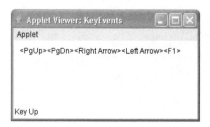

The procedures shown in the preceding keyboard and mouse event examples can be generalized to any type of event handling, including those events generated by controls. In later chapters, you will see many examples that handle other types of events, but they will all follow the same basic structure as the programs just described.

Adapter Class	Listener Interface
ComponentAdapter	ComponentListener
ContainerAdapter	ContainerListener
FocusAdapter	FocusListener
KeyAdapter	KeyListener
MouseAdapter	MouseListener
MouseMotionAdapter	MouseMotionListener
WindowAdapter	WindowListener

TABLE 22-4
Commonly Used
Listener Interfaces
Implemented by
Adapter Classes

Adapter Classes

Java provides a special feature, called an *adapter class,* that can simplify the creation of event handlers in certain situations. An adapter class provides an empty implementation of all methods in an event listener interface. Adapter classes are useful when you want to receive and process only some of the events that are handled by a particular event listener interface. You can define a new class to act as an event listener by extending one of the adapter classes and implementing only those events in which you are interested.

For example, the **MouseMotionAdapter** class has two methods, **mouseDragged( )** and **mouseMoved( )**, which are the methods defined by the **MouseMotionListener** interface. If you were interested in only mouse drag events, then you could simply extend **MouseMotionAdapter** and override **mouseDragged( )**. The empty implementation of **mouseMoved( )** would handle the mouse motion events for you.

Table 22-4 lists the commonly used adapter classes in **java.awt.event** and notes the interface that each implements.

The following example demonstrates an adapter. It displays a message in the status bar of an applet viewer or browser when the mouse is clicked or dragged. However, all other mouse events are silently ignored. The program has three classes. **AdapterDemo** extends **Applet**. Its **init( )** method creates an instance of **MyMouseAdapter** and registers that object to receive notifications of mouse events. It also creates an instance of **MyMouseMotionAdapter** and registers that object to receive notifications of mouse motion events. Both of the constructors take a reference to the applet as an argument.

MyMouseAdapter extends **MouseAdapter** and overrides the **mouseClicked( )** method. The other mouse events are silently ignored by code inherited from the **MouseAdapter** class. **MyMouseMotionAdapter** extends **MouseMotionAdapter** and overrides the **mouseDragged( )** method. The other mouse motion event is silently ignored by code inherited from the **MouseMotionAdapter** class.

Note that both of the event listener classes save a reference to the applet. This information is provided as an argument to their constructors and is used later to invoke the **showStatus( )** method.

```
// Demonstrate an adapter.
import java.awt.*;
import java.awt.event.*;
import java.applet.*;
/*
```

```
   <applet code="AdapterDemo" width=300 height=100>
   </applet>
*/

public class AdapterDemo extends Applet {
  public void init() {
     addMouseListener(new MyMouseAdapter(this));
     addMouseMotionListener(new MyMouseMotionAdapter(this));
  }
}

class MyMouseAdapter extends MouseAdapter {

  AdapterDemo adapterDemo;
  public MyMouseAdapter(AdapterDemo adapterDemo) {
    this.adapterDemo = adapterDemo;
  }

  // Handle mouse clicked.
  public void mouseClicked(MouseEvent me) {
    adapterDemo.showStatus("Mouse clicked");
  }
}

class MyMouseMotionAdapter extends MouseMotionAdapter {
  AdapterDemo adapterDemo;
  public MyMouseMotionAdapter(AdapterDemo adapterDemo) {
    this.adapterDemo = adapterDemo;
  }

  // Handle mouse dragged.
  public void mouseDragged(MouseEvent me) {
    adapterDemo.showStatus("Mouse dragged");
  }
}
```

As you can see by looking at the program, not having to implement all of the methods defined by the **MouseMotionListener** and **MouseListener** interfaces saves you a considerable amount of effort and prevents your code from becoming cluttered with empty methods. As an exercise, you might want to try rewriting one of the keyboard input examples shown earlier so that it uses a **KeyAdapter**.

Inner Classes

In Chapter 7, the basics of inner classes were explained. Here you will see why they are important. Recall that an *inner class* is a class defined within another class, or even within an expression. This section illustrates how inner classes can be used to simplify the code when using event adapter classes.

To understand the benefit provided by inner classes, consider the applet shown in the following listing. It *does not* use an inner class. Its goal is to display the string "Mouse Pressed" in the status bar of the applet viewer or browser when the mouse is pressed. There are two top-level classes in this program. **MousePressedDemo** extends **Applet**, and **MyMouseAdapter** extends **MouseAdapter**. The **init( )** method of **MousePressedDemo** instantiates **MyMouseAdapter** and provides this object as an argument to the **addMouseListener( )** method.

Notice that a reference to the applet is supplied as an argument to the **MyMouseAdapter** constructor. This reference is stored in an instance variable for later use by the **mousePressed( )** method. When the mouse is pressed, it invokes the **showStatus( )** method of the applet through the stored applet reference. In other words, **showStatus( )** is invoked relative to the applet reference stored by **MyMouseAdapter**.

```java
// This applet does NOT use an inner class.
import java.applet.*;
import java.awt.event.*;
/*
  <applet code="MousePressedDemo" width=200 height=100>
  </applet>
*/

public class MousePressedDemo extends Applet {
  public void init() {
    addMouseListener(new MyMouseAdapter(this));
  }
}

class MyMouseAdapter extends MouseAdapter {
  MousePressedDemo mousePressedDemo;
  public MyMouseAdapter(MousePressedDemo mousePressedDemo) {
    this.mousePressedDemo = mousePressedDemo;
  }
  public void mousePressed(MouseEvent me) {
    mousePressedDemo.showStatus("Mouse Pressed.");
  }
}
```

The following listing shows how the preceding program can be improved by using an inner class. Here, **InnerClassDemo** is a top-level class that extends **Applet**. **MyMouseAdapter** is an inner class that extends **MouseAdapter**. Because **MyMouseAdapter** is defined within the scope of **InnerClassDemo**, it has access to all of the variables and methods within the scope of that class. Therefore, the **mousePressed( )** method can call the **showStatus( )** method directly. It no longer needs to do this via a stored reference to the applet. Thus, it is no longer necessary to pass **MyMouseAdapter( )** a reference to the invoking object.

```java
// Inner class demo.
import java.applet.*;
import java.awt.event.*;
/*
  <applet code="InnerClassDemo" width=200 height=100>
  </applet>
*/

public class InnerClassDemo extends Applet {
```

```
  public void init() {
    addMouseListener(new MyMouseAdapter());
  }
  class MyMouseAdapter extends MouseAdapter {
    public void mousePressed(MouseEvent me) {
      showStatus("Mouse Pressed");
    }
  }
}
```

Anonymous Inner Classes

An *anonymous* inner class is one that is not assigned a name. This section illustrates how an anonymous inner class can facilitate the writing of event handlers. Consider the applet shown in the following listing. As before, its goal is to display the string "Mouse Pressed" in the status bar of the applet viewer or browser when the mouse is pressed.

```
// Anonymous inner class demo.
import java.applet.*;
import java.awt.event.*;
/*
  <applet code="AnonymousInnerClassDemo" width=200 height=100>
  </applet>
*/

public class AnonymousInnerClassDemo extends Applet {
  public void init() {
    addMouseListener(new MouseAdapter() {
      public void mousePressed(MouseEvent me) {
        showStatus("Mouse Pressed");
      }
    });
  }
}
```

There is one top-level class in this program: **AnonymousInnerClassDemo**. The **init( )** method calls the **addMouseListener( )** method. Its argument is an expression that defines and instantiates an anonymous inner class. Let's analyze this expression carefully.

The syntax **new MouseAdapter( ) { ... }** indicates to the compiler that the code between the braces defines an anonymous inner class. Furthermore, that class extends **MouseAdapter**. This new class is not named, but it is automatically instantiated when this expression is executed.

Because this anonymous inner class is defined within the scope of **AnonymousInnerClassDemo**, it has access to all of the variables and methods within the scope of that class. Therefore, it can call the **showStatus( )** method directly.

As just illustrated, both named and anonymous inner classes solve some annoying problems in a simple yet effective way. They also allow you to create more efficient code.

Introducing the AWT: Working with Windows, Graphics, and Text

T he Abstract Window Toolkit (AWT) was introduced in Chapter 21, where it was used in several example applets. This chapter begins its in-depth examination. The AWT contains numerous classes and methods that allow you to create and manage windows. It is also the foundation upon which Swing is built. The AWT is quite large and a full description would easily fill an entire book. Therefore, it is not possible to describe in detail every AWT class, method, or instance variable. However, this and the following two chapters explain the basic techniques needed to use the AWT effectively when creating your own applets or stand-alone GUI-based applications. From there, you will be able to explore other parts of the AWT on your own. You will also be ready to move on to Swing.

In this chapter, you will learn how to create and manage windows, manage fonts, output text, and utilize graphics. Chapter 24 describes the various controls, such as scroll bars and push buttons, supported by the AWT. It also explains further aspects of Java's event handling mechanism. Chapter 25 examines the AWT's imaging subsystem and animation.

Although a common use of the AWT is in applets, it is also used to create stand-alone windows that run in a GUI environment, such as Windows. For the sake of convenience, most of the examples in this chapter are contained in applets. To run them, you need to use an applet viewer or a Java-compatible web browser. A few examples will demonstrate the creation of stand-alone, windowed programs.

One other point before beginning. Today, most Java programs employ user interfaces based on Swing. Because Swing provides richer implementations than does the AWT of some common GUI controls, such as buttons, lists, and check boxes, it is easy to jump to the conclusion that the AWT is no longer important, that it has been superseded by Swing. This assumption is, however, quite wrong. As mentioned, Swing is built on top of the AWT. Thus, many aspects of the AWT are also aspects of Swing. Furthermore, many AWT classes are used either directly or indirectly by Swing. Finally, for some types of small programs (especially small applets) that make only minimal use of a GUI, using the AWT rather than Swing still makes sense. Therefore, even though most interfaces today will be based on Swing, a solid knowledge of the AWT is still required. Simply put, you can't be a great Java programmer without knowing the AWT.

NOTE   *If you have not yet read Chapter 22, please do so now. It provides an overview of event handling, which is used by many of the examples in this chapter.*

AWT Classes

The AWT classes are contained in the **java.awt** package. It is one of Java's largest packages. Fortunately, because it is logically organized in a top-down, hierarchical fashion, it is easier to understand and use than you might at first believe. Table 23-1 lists some of the many AWT classes.

Class	Description
AWTEvent	Encapsulates AWT events.
AWTEventMulticaster	Dispatches events to multiple listeners.
BorderLayout	The border layout manager. Border layouts use five components: North, South, East, West, and Center.
Button	Creates a push button control.
Canvas	A blank, semantics-free window.
CardLayout	The card layout manager. Card layouts emulate index cards. Only the one on top is showing.
Checkbox	Creates a check box control.
CheckboxGroup	Creates a group of check box controls.
CheckboxMenuItem	Creates an on/off menu item.
Choice	Creates a pop-up list.
Color	Manages colors in a portable, platform-independent fashion.
Component	An abstract superclass for various AWT components.
Container	A subclass of **Component** that can hold other components.
Cursor	Encapsulates a bitmapped cursor.
Dialog	Creates a dialog window.
Dimension	Specifies the dimensions of an object. The width is stored in **width**, and the height is stored in **height**.
Event	Encapsulates events.
EventQueue	Queues events.
FileDialog	Creates a window from which a file can be selected.
FlowLayout	The flow layout manager. Flow layout positions components left to right, top to bottom.
Font	Encapsulates a type font.
FontMetrics	Encapsulates various information related to a font. This information helps you display text in a window.
Frame	Creates a standard window that has a title bar, resize corners, and a menu bar.

TABLE 23-1   A Sampling of AWT Classes

Class	Description
Graphics	Encapsulates the graphics context. This context is used by the various output methods to display output in a window.
GraphicsDevice	Describes a graphics device such as a screen or printer.
GraphicsEnvironment	Describes the collection of available **Font** and **GraphicsDevice** objects.
GridBagConstraints	Defines various constraints relating to the **GridBagLayout** class.
GridBagLayout	The grid bag layout manager. Grid bag layout displays components subject to the constraints specified by **GridBagConstraints**.
GridLayout	The grid layout manager. Grid layout displays components in a two-dimensional grid.
Image	Encapsulates graphical images.
Insets	Encapsulates the borders of a container.
Label	Creates a label that displays a string.
List	Creates a list from which the user can choose. Similar to the standard Windows list box.
MediaTracker	Manages media objects.
Menu	Creates a pull-down menu.
MenuBar	Creates a menu bar.
MenuComponent	An abstract class implemented by various menu classes.
MenuItem	Creates a menu item.
MenuShortcut	Encapsulates a keyboard shortcut for a menu item.
Panel	The simplest concrete subclass of **Container**.
Point	Encapsulates a Cartesian coordinate pair, stored in **x** and **y**.
Polygon	Encapsulates a polygon.
PopupMenu	Encapsulates a pop-up menu.
PrintJob	An abstract class that represents a print job.
Rectangle	Encapsulates a rectangle.
Robot	Supports automated testing of AWT-based applications.
Scrollbar	Creates a scroll bar control.
ScrollPane	A container that provides horizontal and/or vertical scroll bars for another component.
SystemColor	Contains the colors of GUI widgets such as windows, scroll bars, text, and others.
TextArea	Creates a multiline edit control.
TextComponent	A superclass for **TextArea** and **TextField**.
TextField	Creates a single-line edit control.
Toolkit	Abstract class implemented by the AWT.
Window	Creates a window with no frame, no menu bar, and no title.

TABLE 23-1 A Sampling of AWT Classes *(continued)*

Although the basic structure of the AWT has been the same since Java 1.0, some of the original methods were deprecated and replaced by new ones. For backward-compatibility, Java still supports all the original 1.0 methods. However, because these methods are not for use with new code, this book does not describe them.

Window Fundamentals

The AWT defines windows according to a class hierarchy that adds functionality and specificity with each level. The two most common windows are those derived from **Panel**, which is used by applets, and those derived from **Frame**, which creates a standard application window. Much of the functionality of these windows is derived from their parent classes. Thus, a description of the class hierarchies relating to these two classes is fundamental to their understanding. Figure 23-1 shows the class hierarchy for **Panel** and **Frame**. Let's look at each of these classes now.

Component

At the top of the AWT hierarchy is the **Component** class. **Component** is an abstract class that encapsulates all of the attributes of a visual component. All user interface elements that are displayed on the screen and that interact with the user are subclasses of **Component**. It defines over a hundred public methods that are responsible for managing events, such as mouse and keyboard input, positioning and sizing the window, and repainting. (You already used many of these methods when you created applets in Chapters 21 and 22.) A **Component** object is responsible for remembering the current foreground and background colors and the currently selected text font.

Container

The **Container** class is a subclass of **Component**. It has additional methods that allow other **Component** objects to be nested within it. Other **Container** objects can be stored inside of a **Container** (since they are themselves instances of **Component**). This makes for a multileveled containment system. A container is responsible for laying out (that is, positioning) any

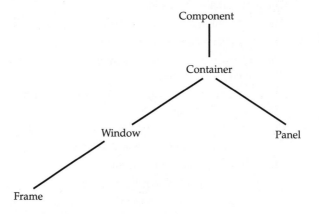

FIGURE 23-1   The class hierarchy for **Panel** and **Frame**

components that it contains. It does this through the use of various layout managers, which you will learn about in Chapter 24.

Panel

The **Panel** class is a concrete subclass of **Container**. It doesn't add any new methods; it simply implements **Container**. A **Panel** may be thought of as a recursively nestable, concrete screen component. **Panel** is the superclass for **Applet**. When screen output is directed to an applet, it is drawn on the surface of a **Panel** object. In essence, a **Panel** is a window that does not contain a title bar, menu bar, or border. This is why you don't see these items when an applet is run inside a browser. When you run an applet using an applet viewer, the applet viewer provides the title and border.

Other components can be added to a **Panel** object by its **add( )** method (inherited from **Container**). Once these components have been added, you can position and resize them manually using the **setLocation( )**, **setSize( )**, **setPreferredSize( )**, or **setBounds( )** methods defined by **Component**.

Window

The **Window** class creates a top-level window. A *top-level window* is not contained within any other object; it sits directly on the desktop. Generally, you won't create **Window** objects directly. Instead, you will use a subclass of **Window** called **Frame**, described next.

Frame

Frame encapsulates what is commonly thought of as a "window." It is a subclass of **Window** and has a title bar, menu bar, borders, and resizing corners. If you create a **Frame** object from within an applet, it will contain a warning message, such as "Java Applet Window," to the user that an applet window has been created. This message warns users that the window they see was started by an applet and not by software running on their computer. (An applet that could masquerade as a host-based application could be used to obtain passwords and other sensitive information without the user's knowledge.) When a **Frame** window is created by a stand-alone application rather than an applet, a normal window is created.

Canvas

Although it is not part of the hierarchy for applet or frame windows, there is one other type of window that you will find valuable: **Canvas**. **Canvas** encapsulates a blank window upon which you can draw. You will see an example of **Canvas** later in this book.

Working with Frame Windows

After the applet, the type of window you will most often create is derived from **Frame**. You will use it to create child windows within applets, and top-level or child windows for stand-alone applications. As mentioned, it creates a standard-style window.

Here are two of **Frame**'s constructors:

Frame( )
Frame(String *title*)

The first form creates a standard window that does not contain a title. The second form creates a window with the title specified by *title*. Notice that you cannot specify the dimensions of the window. Instead, you must set the size of the window after it has been created.

There are several key methods you will use when working with **Frame** windows. They are examined here.

Setting the Window's Dimensions

The **setSize( )** method is used to set the dimensions of the window. Its signature is shown here:

> void setSize(int *newWidth*, int *newHeight*)
> void setSize(Dimension *newSize*)

The new size of the window is specified by *newWidth* and *newHeight*, or by the **width** and **height** fields of the **Dimension** object passed in *newSize*. The dimensions are specified in terms of pixels.

The **getSize( )** method is used to obtain the current size of a window. Its signature is shown here:

> Dimension getSize( )

This method returns the current size of the window contained within the **width** and **height** fields of a **Dimension** object.

Hiding and Showing a Window

After a frame window has been created, it will not be visible until you call **setVisible( )**. Its signature is shown here:

> void setVisible(boolean *visibleFlag*)

The component is visible if the argument to this method is **true**. Otherwise, it is hidden.

Setting a Window's Title

You can change the title in a frame window using **setTitle( )**, which has this general form:

> void setTitle(String *newTitle*)

Here, *newTitle* is the new title for the window.

Closing a Frame Window

When using a frame window, your program must remove that window from the screen when it is closed, by calling **setVisible(false)**. To intercept a window-close event, you must implement the **windowClosing( )** method of the **WindowListener** interface. Inside **windowClosing( )**, you must remove the window from the screen. The example in the next section illustrates this technique.

Creating a Frame Window in an Applet

While it is possible to simply create a window by creating an instance of **Frame**, you will seldom do so, because you will not be able to do much with it. For example, you will not be able to receive or process events that occur within it or easily output information to it. Most of the time, you will create a subclass of **Frame**. Doing so lets you override **Frame**'s methods and provide event handling.

Creating a new frame window from within an applet is actually quite easy. First, create a subclass of **Frame**. Next, override any of the standard applet methods, such as **init( )**, **start( )**, and **stop( )**, to show or hide the frame as needed. Finally, implement the **windowClosing( )** method of the **WindowListener** interface, calling **setVisible(false)** when the window is closed.

Once you have defined a **Frame** subclass, you can create an object of that class. This causes a frame window to come into existence, but it will not be initially visible. You make it visible by calling **setVisible( )**. When created, the window is given a default height and width. You can set the size of the window explicitly by calling the **setSize( )** method.

The following applet creates a subclass of **Frame** called **SampleFrame**. A window of this subclass is instantiated within the **init( )** method of **AppletFrame**. Notice that **SampleFrame** calls **Frame**'s constructor. This causes a standard frame window to be created with the title passed in **title**. This example overrides the applet's **start( )** and **stop( )** methods so that they show and hide the child window, respectively. This causes the window to be removed automatically when you terminate the applet, when you close the window, or, if using a browser, when you move to another page. It also causes the child window to be shown when the browser returns to the applet.

```java
//  Create a child frame window from within an applet.
import java.awt.*;
import java.awt.event.*;
import java.applet.*;
/*
  <applet code="AppletFrame" width=300 height=50>
  </applet>
*/

// Create a subclass of Frame.
class SampleFrame extends Frame {
  SampleFrame(String title) {
    super(title);
    // create an object to handle window events
    MyWindowAdapter adapter = new MyWindowAdapter(this);
     // register it to receive those events
    addWindowListener(adapter);
  }
  public void paint(Graphics g) {
    g.drawString("This is in frame window", 10, 40);
  }
}

class MyWindowAdapter extends WindowAdapter {
  SampleFrame sampleFrame;
  public MyWindowAdapter(SampleFrame sampleFrame) {
    this.sampleFrame = sampleFrame;
  }
  public void windowClosing(WindowEvent we) {
    sampleFrame.setVisible(false);
  }
}

// Create frame window.
```

```
public class AppletFrame extends Applet {
  Frame f;
  public void init() {
    f = new SampleFrame("A Frame Window");

    f.setSize(250, 250);
    f.setVisible(true);
  }
  public void start() {
    f.setVisible(true);
  }
  public void stop() {
    f.setVisible(false);
  }
  public void paint(Graphics g) {
    g.drawString("This is in applet window", 10, 20);
  }
}
```

Sample output from this program is shown here:

Handling Events in a Frame Window

Since **Frame** is a subclass of **Component**, it inherits all the capabilities defined by **Component**. This means that you can use and manage a frame window just like you manage an applet's main window. For example, you can override **paint( )** to display output, call **repaint( )** when you need to restore the window, and add event handlers. Whenever an event occurs in a window, the event handlers defined by that window will be called. Each window handles its own events. For example, the following program creates a window that responds to mouse events. The main applet window also responds to mouse events. When you experiment with this program, you will see that mouse events are sent to the window in which the event occurs.

```
// Handle mouse events in both child and applet windows.
import java.awt.*;
import java.awt.event.*;
import java.applet.*;
/*
  <applet code="WindowEvents" width=300 height=50>
  </applet>
*/

// Create a subclass of Frame.
class SampleFrame extends Frame
```

```
implements MouseListener, MouseMotionListener {

String msg = "";
int mouseX=10, mouseY=40;
int movX=0, movY=0;

SampleFrame(String title) {
  super(title);
  // register this object to receive its own mouse events
  addMouseListener(this);
  addMouseMotionListener(this);
  // create an object to handle window events
  MyWindowAdapter adapter = new MyWindowAdapter(this);
  // register it to receive those events
  addWindowListener(adapter);
}

// Handle mouse clicked.
public void mouseClicked(MouseEvent me) {
}

// Handle mouse entered.
public void mouseEntered(MouseEvent evtObj) {
  // save coordinates
  mouseX = 10;
  mouseY = 54;
  msg = "Mouse just entered child.";
  repaint();
}

// Handle mouse exited.
public void mouseExited(MouseEvent evtObj) {
  // save coordinates
  mouseX = 10;
  mouseY = 54;
  msg = "Mouse just left child window.";
  repaint();
}

// Handle mouse pressed.
public void mousePressed(MouseEvent me) {
  // save coordinates
  mouseX = me.getX();
  mouseY = me.getY();
  msg = "Down";
  repaint();
}
// Handle mouse released.
public void mouseReleased(MouseEvent me) {
  // save coordinates
  mouseX = me.getX();
  mouseY = me.getY();
  msg = "Up";
  repaint();
}
```

```java
    // Handle mouse dragged.
    public void mouseDragged(MouseEvent me) {
      // save coordinates
      mouseX = me.getX();
      mouseY = me.getY();
      movX = me.getX();
      movY = me.getY();
      msg = "*";
      repaint();
    }

    // Handle mouse moved.
    public void mouseMoved(MouseEvent me) {
      // save coordinates
      movX = me.getX();
      movY = me.getY();
      repaint(0, 0, 100, 60);
    }

    public void paint(Graphics g) {
      g.drawString(msg, mouseX, mouseY);
      g.drawString("Mouse at " + movX + ", " + movY, 10, 40);
    }
}

class MyWindowAdapter extends WindowAdapter {
  SampleFrame sampleFrame;
  public MyWindowAdapter(SampleFrame sampleFrame) {
    this.sampleFrame = sampleFrame;
  }
  public void windowClosing(WindowEvent we) {
    sampleFrame.setVisible(false);
  }
}

// Applet window.
public class WindowEvents extends Applet
  implements MouseListener, MouseMotionListener {

  SampleFrame f;
  String msg = "";
  int mouseX=0, mouseY=10;
  int movX=0, movY=0;

  // Create a frame window.
  public void init() {
    f = new SampleFrame("Handle Mouse Events");
    f.setSize(300, 200);
    f.setVisible(true);

    // register this object to receive its own mouse events
    addMouseListener(this);
    addMouseMotionListener(this);
  }
```

```
// Remove frame window when stopping applet.
public void stop() {
  f.setVisible(false);
}

// Show frame window when starting applet.
public void start() {
  f.setVisible(true);
}

// Handle mouse clicked.
public void mouseClicked(MouseEvent me) {
}

// Handle mouse entered.
public void mouseEntered(MouseEvent me) {
  // save coordinates
  mouseX = 0;
  mouseY = 24;
  msg = "Mouse just entered applet window.";
  repaint();
}

// Handle mouse exited.
public void mouseExited(MouseEvent me) {
  // save coordinates
  mouseX = 0;
  mouseY = 24;
  msg = "Mouse just left applet window.";
  repaint();
}

// Handle button pressed.
public void mousePressed(MouseEvent me) {
  // save coordinates
  mouseX = me.getX();
  mouseY = me.getY();
  msg = "Down";
  repaint();
}

// Handle button released.
public void mouseReleased(MouseEvent me) {
  // save coordinates
  mouseX = me.getX();
  mouseY = me.getY();
  msg = "Up";
  repaint();
}

// Handle mouse dragged.
public void mouseDragged(MouseEvent me) {
  // save coordinates
  mouseX = me.getX();
  mouseY = me.getY();
```

```
      movX = me.getX();
      movY = me.getY();
      msg = "*";
      repaint();
  }

  // Handle mouse moved.
  public void mouseMoved(MouseEvent me) {
    // save coordinates
    movX = me.getX();
    movY = me.getY();
    repaint(0, 0, 100, 20);
  }

  // Display msg in applet window.
  public void paint(Graphics g) {
    g.drawString(msg, mouseX, mouseY);
    g.drawString("Mouse at " + movX + ", " + movY, 0, 10);
  }
}
```

Sample output from this program is shown here:

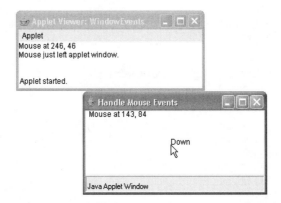

Creating a Windowed Program

Although creating applets is a common use for Java's AWT, it is also possible to create
stand-alone AWT-based applications. To do this, simply create an instance of the window
or windows you need inside **main( )**. For example, the following program creates a frame
window that responds to mouse clicks and keystrokes:

```
// Create an AWT-based application.
import java.awt.*;
import java.awt.event.*;
import java.applet.*;

// Create a frame window.
public class AppWindow extends Frame {
  String keymsg = "This is a test.";
```

```
    String mousemsg = "";
    int mouseX=30, mouseY=30;

    public AppWindow() {
      addKeyListener(new MyKeyAdapter(this));
      addMouseListener(new MyMouseAdapter(this));
      addWindowListener(new MyWindowAdapter());
    }

    public void paint(Graphics g) {
      g.drawString(keymsg, 10, 40);
      g.drawString(mousemsg, mouseX, mouseY);
    }

    // Create the window.
    public static void main(String args[]) {
      AppWindow appwin = new AppWindow();

      appwin.setSize(new Dimension(300, 200));
      appwin.setTitle("An AWT-Based Application");
      appwin.setVisible(true);
    }
  }

  class MyKeyAdapter extends KeyAdapter {
    AppWindow appWindow;
    public MyKeyAdapter(AppWindow appWindow) {
      this.appWindow = appWindow;
    }
    public void keyTyped(KeyEvent ke) {
      appWindow.keymsg += ke.getKeyChar();
      appWindow.repaint();
    };
  }

  class MyMouseAdapter extends MouseAdapter {
    AppWindow appWindow;
    public MyMouseAdapter(AppWindow appWindow) {
      this.appWindow = appWindow;
    }
    public void mousePressed(MouseEvent me) {
      appWindow.mouseX = me.getX();
      appWindow.mouseY = me.getY();
      appWindow.mousemsg = "Mouse Down at " + appWindow.mouseX +
                           ", " + appWindow.mouseY;
      appWindow.repaint();
    }
  }

  class MyWindowAdapter extends WindowAdapter {
    public void windowClosing(WindowEvent we) {
      System.exit(0);
    }
  }
```

Sample output from this program is shown here:

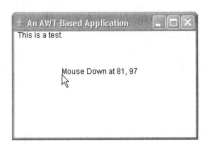

Once created, a frame window takes on a life of its own. Notice that **main( )** ends with the call to **appwin.setVisible(true)**. However, the program keeps running until you close the window. In essence, when creating a windowed application, you will use **main( )** to launch its top-level window. After that, your program will function as a GUI-based application, not like the console-based programs used earlier.

Displaying Information Within a Window

In the most general sense, a window is a container for information. Although we have already output small amounts of text to a window in the preceding examples, we have not begun to take advantage of a window's ability to present high-quality text and graphics. Indeed, much of the power of the AWT comes from its support for these items. For this reason, the remainder of this chapter discusses Java's text-, graphics-, and font-handling capabilities. As you will see, they are both powerful and flexible.

Working with Graphics

The AWT supports a rich assortment of graphics methods. All graphics are drawn relative to a window. This can be the main window of an applet, a child window of an applet, or a stand-alone application window. The origin of each window is at the top-left corner and is 0,0. Coordinates are specified in pixels. All output to a window takes place through a graphics context. A *graphics context* is encapsulated by the **Graphics** class and is obtained in two ways:

- It is passed to an applet when one of its various methods, such as **paint( )** or **update( )**, is called.
- It is returned by the **getGraphics( )** method of **Component**.

For the sake of convenience the remainder of the examples in this chapter will demonstrate graphics in the main applet window. However, the same techniques will apply to any other window.

The **Graphics** class defines a number of drawing functions. Each shape can be drawn edge-only or filled. Objects are drawn and filled in the currently selected graphics color, which is black by default. When a graphics object is drawn that exceeds the dimensions of the window, output is automatically clipped. Let's take a look at several of the drawing methods.

Drawing Lines

Lines are drawn by means of the **drawLine( )** method, shown here:

void drawLine(int *startX*, int *startY*, int *endX*, int *endY*)

drawLine( ) displays a line in the current drawing color that begins at *startX,startY* and ends at *endX,endY*.

The following applet draws several lines:

```
// Draw lines
import java.awt.*;
import java.applet.*;
/*
<applet code="Lines" width=300 height=200>
</applet>
*/
public class Lines extends Applet {
  public void paint(Graphics g) {
    g.drawLine(0, 0, 100, 100);
    g.drawLine(0, 100, 100, 0);
    g.drawLine(40, 25, 250, 180);
    g.drawLine(75, 90, 400, 400);
    g.drawLine(20, 150, 400, 40);
    g.drawLine(5, 290, 80, 19);
  }
}
```

Sample output from this program is shown here:

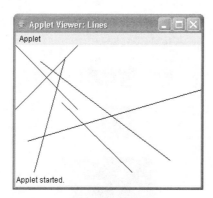

Drawing Rectangles

The **drawRect( )** and **fillRect( )** methods display an outlined and filled rectangle, respectively. They are shown here:

void drawRect(int *top*, int *left*, int *width*, int *height*)
void fillRect(int *top*, int *left*, int *width*, int *height*)

The upper-left corner of the rectangle is at *top,left*. The dimensions of the rectangle are specified by *width* and *height*.

To draw a rounded rectangle, use **drawRoundRect( )** or **fillRoundRect( )**, both shown here:

void drawRoundRect(int *top*, int *left*, int *width*, int *height*,
int *xDiam*, int *yDiam*)

void fillRoundRect(int *top*, int *left*, int *width*, int *height*,
int *xDiam*, int *yDiam*)

A rounded rectangle has rounded corners. The upper-left corner of the rectangle is at *top,left*. The dimensions of the rectangle are specified by *width* and *height*. The diameter of the rounding arc along the X axis is specified by *xDiam*. The diameter of the rounding arc along the Y axis is specified by *yDiam*.

The following applet draws several rectangles:

```
// Draw rectangles
import java.awt.*;
import java.applet.*;
/*
<applet code="Rectangles" width=300 height=200>
</applet>
*/

public class Rectangles extends Applet {
  public void paint(Graphics g) {
    g.drawRect(10, 10, 60, 50);
    g.fillRect(100, 10, 60, 50);
    g.drawRoundRect(190, 10, 60, 50, 15, 15);
    g.fillRoundRect(70, 90, 140, 100, 30, 40);
  }
}
```

Sample output from this program is shown here:

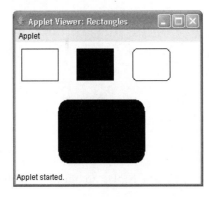

Drawing Ellipses and Circles

To draw an ellipse, use **drawOval( )**. To fill an ellipse, use **fillOval( )**. These methods are shown here:

```
void drawOval(int top, int left, int width, int height)
void fillOval(int top, int left, int width, int height)
```

The ellipse is drawn within a bounding rectangle whose upper-left corner is specified by
top,left and whose width and height are specified by *width* and *height*. To draw a circle, specify
a square as the bounding rectangle.

The following program draws several ellipses:

```
// Draw Ellipses
import java.awt.*;
import java.applet.*;
/*
<applet code="Ellipses" width=300 height=200>
</applet>
*/

public class Ellipses extends Applet {
  public void paint(Graphics g) {
    g.drawOval(10, 10, 50, 50);
    g.fillOval(100, 10, 75, 50);
    g.drawOval(190, 10, 90, 30);
    g.fillOval(70, 90, 140, 100);
  }
}
```

Sample output from this program is shown here:

Drawing Arcs

Arcs can be drawn with **drawArc( )** and **fillArc( )**, shown here:

void drawArc(int *top*, int *left*, int *width*, int *height*, int *startAngle*,
      int *sweepAngle*)

void fillArc(int *top*, int *left*, int *width*, int *height*, int *startAngle*,
      int *sweepAngle*)

The arc is bounded by the rectangle whose upper-left corner is specified by *top,left* and whose width and height are specified by *width* and *height*. The arc is drawn from *startAngle* through the angular distance specified by *sweepAngle*. Angles are specified in degrees. Zero degrees is on the horizontal, at the three o'clock position. The arc is drawn counterclockwise if *sweepAngle* is positive, and clockwise if *sweepAngle* is negative. Therefore, to draw an arc from twelve o'clock to six o'clock, the start angle would be 90 and the sweep angle 180.

The following applet draws several arcs:

```
// Draw Arcs
import java.awt.*;
import java.applet.*;
/*
<applet code="Arcs" width=300 height=200>
</applet>
*/

public class Arcs extends Applet {
  public void paint(Graphics g) {
    g.drawArc(10, 40, 70, 70, 0, 75);
    g.fillArc(100, 40, 70, 70, 0, 75);
    g.drawArc(10, 100, 70, 80, 0, 175);
    g.fillArc(100, 100, 70, 90, 0, 270);
    g.drawArc(200, 80, 80, 80, 0, 180);
  }
}
```

Sample output from this program is shown here:

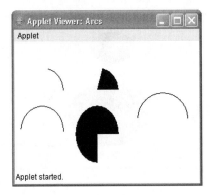

Drawing Polygons

It is possible to draw arbitrarily shaped figures using **drawPolygon( )** and **fillPolygon( )**, shown here:

    void drawPolygon(int *x*[ ], int *y*[ ], int *numPoints*)
    void fillPolygon(int *x*[ ], int *y*[ ], int *numPoints*)

The polygon's endpoints are specified by the coordinate pairs contained within the *x* and *y* arrays. The number of points defined by *x* and *y* is specified by *numPoints*. There are alternative forms of these methods in which the polygon is specified by a **Polygon** object.

The following applet draws an hourglass shape:

```
// Draw Polygon
import java.awt.*;
import java.applet.*;
/*
<applet code="HourGlass" width=230 height=210>
</applet>
*/

public class HourGlass extends Applet {
  public void paint(Graphics g) {
    int xpoints[] = {30, 200, 30, 200, 30};
    int ypoints[] = {30, 30, 200, 200, 30};
    int num = 5;

    g.drawPolygon(xpoints, ypoints, num);
  }
}
```

Sample output from this program is shown here:

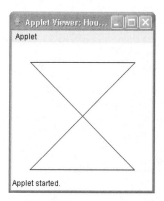

Sizing Graphics

Often, you will want to size a graphics object to fit the current size of the window in which it is drawn. To do so, first obtain the current dimensions of the window by calling **getSize( )** on the window object. It returns the dimensions of the window encapsulated within a **Dimension** object. Once you have the current size of the window, you can scale your graphical output accordingly.

To demonstrate this technique, here is an applet that will start as a 200×200-pixel square and grow by 25 pixels in width and height with each mouse click until the applet gets larger than 500×500. At that point, the next click will return it to 200×200, and the process starts over.

Within the window, a rectangle is drawn around the inner border of the window; within that rectangle, an *X* is drawn so that it fills the window. This applet works in **appletviewer**, but it may not work in a browser window.

```
// Resizing output to fit the current size of a window.
import java.applet.*;
import java.awt.*;
import java.awt.event.*;
/*
  <applet code="ResizeMe" width=200 height=200>
  </applet>
 */

public class ResizeMe extends Applet {
  final int inc = 25;
  int max = 500;
  int min = 200;
  Dimension d;

  public ResizeMe() {
    addMouseListener(new MouseAdapter() {
      public void mouseReleased(MouseEvent me) {
        int w = (d.width + inc) > max?min :(d.width + inc);
        int h = (d.height + inc) > max?min :(d.height + inc);
        setSize(new Dimension(w, h));
      }
    });
  }
  public void paint(Graphics g) {
    d = getSize();

    g.drawLine(0, 0, d.width-1, d.height-1);
    g.drawLine(0, d.height-1, d.width-1, 0);
    g.drawRect(0, 0, d.width-1, d.height-1);
  }
}
```

Working with Color

Java supports color in a portable, device-independent fashion. The AWT color system allows you to specify any color you want. It then finds the best match for that color, given the limits of the display hardware currently executing your program or applet. Thus, your code does not need to be concerned with the differences in the way color is supported by various hardware devices. Color is encapsulated by the **Color** class.

As you saw in Chapter 21, **Color** defines several constants (for example, **Color.black**) to specify a number of common colors. You can also create your own colors, using one of the color constructors. Three commonly used forms are shown here:

Color(int *red*, int *green*, int *blue*)
Color(int *rgbValue*)
Color(float *red*, float *green*, float *blue*)

The first constructor takes three integers that specify the color as a mix of red, green, and blue. These values must be between 0 and 255, as in this example:

```
new Color(255, 100, 100); // light red
```

The second color constructor takes a single integer that contains the mix of red, green, and blue packed into an integer. The integer is organized with red in bits 16 to 23, green in bits 8 to 15, and blue in bits 0 to 7. Here is an example of this constructor:

```
int newRed = (0xff000000 | (0xc0 << 16) | (0x00 << 8) | 0x00);
Color darkRed = new Color(newRed);
```

The final constructor, **Color(float, float, float)**, takes three float values (between 0.0 and 1.0) that specify the relative mix of red, green, and blue.

Once you have created a color, you can use it to set the foreground and/or background color by using the **setForeground( )** and **setBackground( )** methods described in Chapter 21. You can also select it as the current drawing color.

Color Methods

The **Color** class defines several methods that help manipulate colors. They are examined here.

Using Hue, Saturation, and Brightness

The *hue-saturation-brightness (HSB)* color model is an alternative to red-green-blue (RGB) for specifying particular colors. Figuratively, *hue* is a wheel of color. The hue is specified with a number between 0.0 and 1.0 (the colors are approximately red, orange, yellow, green, blue, indigo, and violet). *Saturation* is another scale ranging from 0.0 to 1.0, representing light pastels to intense hues. *Brightness* values also range from 0.0 to 1.0, where 1 is bright white and 0 is black. **Color** supplies two methods that let you convert between RGB and HSB. They are shown here:

> static int HSBtoRGB(float *hue*, float *saturation*, float *brightness*)
> static float[ ] RGBtoHSB(int *red*, int *green*, int *blue*, float *values*[ ])

HSBtoRGB( ) returns a packed RGB value compatible with the **Color(int)** constructor. **RGBtoHSB( )** returns a float array of HSB values corresponding to RGB integers. If *values* is not **null**, then this array is given the HSB values and returned. Otherwise, a new array is created and the HSB values are returned in it. In either case, the array contains the hue at index 0, saturation at index 1, and brightness at index 2.

getRed( ), getGreen( ), getBlue( )

You can obtain the red, green, and blue components of a color independently using **getRed( )**, **getGreen( )**, and **getBlue( )**, shown here:

> int getRed( )
> int getGreen( )
> int getBlue( )

Each of these methods returns the RGB color component found in the invoking **Color** object in the lower 8 bits of an integer.

getRGB( )

To obtain a packed, RGB representation of a color, use **getRGB( )**, shown here:

    int getRGB( )

The return value is organized as described earlier.

Setting the Current Graphics Color

By default, graphics objects are drawn in the current foreground color. You can change this color by calling the **Graphics** method **setColor( )**:

    void setColor(Color *newColor*)

Here, *newColor* specifies the new drawing color.

You can obtain the current color by calling **getColor( )**, shown here:

    Color getColor( )

A Color Demonstration Applet

The following applet constructs several colors and draws various objects using these colors:

```
// Demonstrate color.
import java.awt.*;
import java.applet.*;
/*
<applet code="ColorDemo" width=300 height=200>
</applet>
*/

public class ColorDemo extends Applet {
  // draw lines
  public void paint(Graphics g) {
    Color c1 = new Color(255, 100, 100);
    Color c2 = new Color(100, 255, 100);
    Color c3 = new Color(100, 100, 255);

    g.setColor(c1);
    g.drawLine(0, 0, 100, 100);
    g.drawLine(0, 100, 100, 0);

    g.setColor(c2);
    g.drawLine(40, 25, 250, 180);
    g.drawLine(75, 90, 400, 400);

    g.setColor(c3);
    g.drawLine(20, 150, 400, 40);
    g.drawLine(5, 290, 80, 19);

    g.setColor(Color.red);
    g.drawOval(10, 10, 50, 50);
    g.fillOval(70, 90, 140, 100);
```

```
      g.setColor(Color.blue);
      g.drawOval(190, 10, 90, 30);
      g.drawRect(10, 10, 60, 50);

      g.setColor(Color.cyan);
      g.fillRect(100, 10, 60, 50);
      g.drawRoundRect(190, 10, 60, 50, 15, 15);
  }
}
```

Setting the Paint Mode

The *paint mode* determines how objects are drawn in a window. By default, new output to
a window overwrites any preexisting contents. However, it is possible to have new objects
XORed onto the window by using **setXORMode( )**, as follows:

> void setXORMode(Color *xorColor*)

Here, *xorColor* specifies the color that will be XORed to the window when an object is drawn.
The advantage of XOR mode is that the new object is always guaranteed to be visible no matter
what color the object is drawn over.

To return to overwrite mode, call **setPaintMode( )**, shown here:

> void setPaintMode( )

In general, you will want to use overwrite mode for normal output, and XOR mode for special
purposes. For example, the following program displays cross hairs that track the mouse
pointer. The cross hairs are XORed onto the window and are always visible, no matter what
the underlying color is.

```
// Demonstrate XOR mode.
import java.awt.*;
import java.awt.event.*;
import java.applet.*;
/*
  <applet code="XOR" width=400 height=200>
  </applet>
*/

public class XOR extends Applet {
  int chsX=100, chsY=100;

  public XOR() {
    addMouseMotionListener(new MouseMotionAdapter() {
      public void mouseMoved(MouseEvent me) {
        int x = me.getX();
        int y = me.getY();
        chsX = x-10;
        chsY = y-10;
        repaint();
      }
    });
  }
```

```
public void paint(Graphics g) {
  g.drawLine(0, 0, 100, 100);
  g.drawLine(0, 100, 100, 0);
  g.setColor(Color.blue);
  g.drawLine(40, 25, 250, 180);
  g.drawLine(75, 90, 400, 400);
  g.setColor(Color.green);
  g.drawRect(10, 10, 60, 50);
  g.fillRect(100, 10, 60, 50);
  g.setColor(Color.red);
  g.drawRoundRect(190, 10, 60, 50, 15, 15);
  g.fillRoundRect(70, 90, 140, 100, 30, 40);
  g.setColor(Color.cyan);
  g.drawLine(20, 150, 400, 40);
  g.drawLine(5, 290, 80, 19);

  // xor cross hairs
  g.setXORMode(Color.black);
  g.drawLine(chsX-10, chsY, chsX+10, chsY);
  g.drawLine(chsX, chsY-10, chsX, chsY+10);
  g.setPaintMode();
  }
}
```

Sample output from this program is shown here:

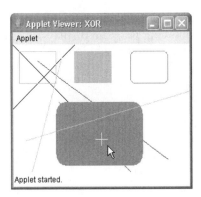

Working with Fonts

The AWT supports multiple type fonts. Years ago, fonts emerged from the domain of traditional typesetting to become an important part of computer-generated documents and displays. The AWT provides flexibility by abstracting font-manipulation operations and allowing for dynamic selection of fonts.

Fonts have a family name, a logical font name, and a face name. The *family name* is the general name of the font, such as Courier. The *logical name* specifies a category of font, such as Monospaced. The *face name* specifies a specific font, such as Courier Italic.

Fonts are encapsulated by the **Font** class. Several of the methods defined by **Font** are listed in Table 23-2.

Method	Description
static Font decode(String *str*)	Returns a font given its name.
boolean equals(Object *FontObj*)	Returns **true** if the invoking object contains the same font as that specified by *FontObj*. Otherwise, it returns **false**.
String getFamily( )	Returns the name of the font family to which the invoking font belongs.
static Font getFont(String *property*)	Returns the font associated with the system property specified by *property*. **null** is returned if *property* does not exist.
static Font getFont(String *property*, Font *defaultFont*)	Returns the font associated with the system property specified by *property*. The font specified by *defaultFont* is returned if *property* does not exist.
String getFontName()	Returns the face name of the invoking font.
String getName( )	Returns the logical name of the invoking font.
int getSize( )	Returns the size, in points, of the invoking font.
int getStyle( )	Returns the style values of the invoking font.
int hashCode( )	Returns the hash code associated with the invoking object.
boolean isBold( )	Returns **true** if the font includes the **BOLD** style value. Otherwise, **false** is returned.
boolean isItalic( )	Returns **true** if the font includes the **ITALIC** style value. Otherwise, **false** is returned.
boolean isPlain( )	Returns **true** if the font includes the **PLAIN** style value. Otherwise, **false** is returned.
String toString( )	Returns the string equivalent of the invoking font.

TABLE 23-2   A Sampling of Methods Defined by **Font**

The **Font** class defines these variables:

Variable	Meaning
String name	Name of the font
float pointSize	Size of the font in points
int size	Size of the font in points
int style	Font style

Determining the Available Fonts

When working with fonts, often you need to know which fonts are available on your machine. To obtain this information, you can use the **getAvailableFontFamilyNames( )** method defined by the **GraphicsEnvironment** class. It is shown here:

String[ ] getAvailableFontFamilyNames( )

This method returns an array of strings that contains the names of the available font families.

In addition, the **getAllFonts( )** method is defined by the **GraphicsEnvironment** class. It is shown here:

Font[ ] getAllFonts( )

This method returns an array of **Font** objects for all of the available fonts.

Since these methods are members of **GraphicsEnvironment**, you need a **GraphicsEnvironment** reference to call them. You can obtain this reference by using the **getLocalGraphicsEnvironment( )** static method, which is defined by **GraphicsEnvironment**. It is shown here:

static GraphicsEnvironment getLocalGraphicsEnvironment( )

Here is an applet that shows how to obtain the names of the available font families:

```
// Display Fonts
/*
<applet code="ShowFonts" width=550 height=60>
</applet>
*/
import java.applet.*;
import java.awt.*;

public class ShowFonts extends Applet {
  public void paint(Graphics g) {
    String msg = "";
    String FontList[];

    GraphicsEnvironment ge =
      GraphicsEnvironment.getLocalGraphicsEnvironment();
    FontList = ge.getAvailableFontFamilyNames();
    for(int i = 0; i < FontList.length; i++)
      msg += FontList[i] + " ";

    g.drawString(msg, 4, 16);
  }
}
```

Sample output from this program is shown next. However, when you run this program, you may see a different list of fonts than the one shown in this illustration.

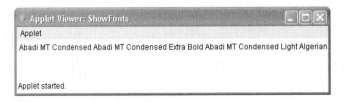

Creating and Selecting a Font

To select a new font, you must first construct a **Font** object that describes that font. One **Font** constructor has this general form:

Font(String *fontName*, int *fontStyle*, int *pointSize*)

Here, *fontName* specifies the name of the desired font. The name can be specified using either the logical or face name. All Java environments will support the following fonts: Dialog, DialogInput, Sans Serif, Serif, and Monospaced. Dialog is the font used by your system's dialog boxes. Dialog is also the default if you don't explicitly set a font. You can also use any other fonts supported by your particular environment, but be careful—these other fonts may not be universally available.

The style of the font is specified by *fontStyle*. It may consist of one or more of these three constants: **Font.PLAIN**, **Font.BOLD**, and **Font.ITALIC**. To combine styles, OR them together. For example, **Font.BOLD | Font.ITALIC** specifies a bold, italics style.

The size, in points, of the font is specified by *pointSize.*

To use a font that you have created, you must select it using **setFont( )**, which is defined by **Component**. It has this general form:

void setFont(Font *fontObj*)

Here, *fontObj* is the object that contains the desired font.

The following program outputs a sample of each standard font. Each time you click the mouse within its window, a new font is selected and its name is displayed.

```
// Show fonts.
import java.applet.*;
import java.awt.*;
import java.awt.event.*;
/*
  <applet code="SampleFonts" width=200 height=100>
  </applet>
*/

public class SampleFonts extends Applet {
  int next = 0;
  Font f;
  String msg;
  public void init() {
    f = new Font("Dialog", Font.PLAIN, 12);
    msg = "Dialog";
    setFont(f);
    addMouseListener(new MyMouseAdapter(this));
  }

  public void paint(Graphics g) {
    g.drawString(msg, 4, 20);
  }
}
```

PART II

```
class MyMouseAdapter extends MouseAdapter {
  SampleFonts sampleFonts;
  public MyMouseAdapter(SampleFonts sampleFonts) {
    this.sampleFonts = sampleFonts;
  }
  public void mousePressed(MouseEvent me) {
    // Switch fonts with each mouse click.
    sampleFonts.next++;
    switch(sampleFonts.next) {
    case 0:
      sampleFonts.f = new Font("Dialog", Font.PLAIN, 12);
      sampleFonts.msg = "Dialog";
      break;
    case 1:
      sampleFonts.f = new Font("DialogInput", Font.PLAIN, 12);
      sampleFonts.msg = "DialogInput";
      break;
    case 2:
      sampleFonts.f = new Font("SansSerif", Font.PLAIN, 12);
      sampleFonts.msg = "SansSerif";
      break;
    case 3:
      sampleFonts.f = new Font("Serif", Font.PLAIN, 12);
      sampleFonts.msg = "Serif";
      break;
    case 4:
      sampleFonts.f = new Font("Monospaced", Font.PLAIN, 12);
      sampleFonts.msg = "Monospaced";
      break;
    }
    if(sampleFonts.next == 4) sampleFonts.next = -1;
    sampleFonts.setFont(sampleFonts.f);
    sampleFonts.repaint();
  }
}
```

Sample output from this program is shown here:

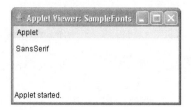

Obtaining Font Information

Suppose you want to obtain information about the currently selected font. To do this, you must first get the current font by calling **getFont( )**. This method is defined by the **Graphics** class, as shown here:

PART II

Font getFont( )

Once you have obtained the currently selected font, you can retrieve information about it using various methods defined by **Font**. For example, this applet displays the name, family, size, and style of the currently selected font:

```
// Display font info.
import java.applet.*;
import java.awt.*;
/*
<applet code="FontInfo" width=350 height=60>
</applet>
*/

public class FontInfo extends Applet {
  public void paint(Graphics g) {
    Font f = g.getFont();
    String fontName = f.getName();
    String fontFamily = f.getFamily();
    int fontSize = f.getSize();
    int fontStyle = f.getStyle();

    String msg = "Family: " + fontName;
    msg += ", Font: " + fontFamily;
    msg += ", Size: " + fontSize + ", Style: ";
    if((fontStyle & Font.BOLD) == Font.BOLD)
      msg += "Bold ";
    if((fontStyle & Font.ITALIC) == Font.ITALIC)
      msg += "Italic ";
    if((fontStyle & Font.PLAIN) == Font.PLAIN)
      msg += "Plain ";

    g.drawString(msg, 4, 16);
  }
}
```

Managing Text Output Using FontMetrics

As just explained, Java supports a number of fonts. For most fonts, characters are not all the same dimension—most fonts are proportional. Also, the height of each character, the length of *descenders* (the hanging parts of letters, such as *y*), and the amount of space between horizontal lines vary from font to font. Further, the point size of a font can be changed. That these (and other) attributes are variable would not be of too much consequence except that Java demands that you, the programmer, manually manage virtually all text output.

Given that the size of each font may differ and that fonts may be changed while your program is executing, there must be some way to determine the dimensions and various other attributes of the currently selected font. For example, to write one line of text after another implies that you have some way of knowing how tall the font is and how many pixels are needed between lines. To fill this need, the AWT includes the **FontMetrics** class, which encapsulates various information about a font. Let's begin by defining the common terminology used when describing fonts:

Height	The top-to-bottom size of a line of text
Baseline	The line that the bottoms of characters are aligned to (not counting descent)
Ascent	The distance from the baseline to the top of a character
Descent	The distance from the baseline to the bottom of a character
Leading	The distance between the bottom of one line of text and the top of the next

As you know, we have used the **drawString( )** method in many of the previous examples. It paints a string in the current font and color, beginning at a specified location. However, this location is at the left edge of the baseline of the characters, not at the upper-left corner as is usual with other drawing methods. It is a common error to draw a string at the same coordinate that you would draw a box. For example, if you were to draw a rectangle at coordinate 0,0, you would see a full rectangle. If you were to draw the string "Typesetting" at 0,0, you would only see the tails (or descenders) of the *y, p,* and *g.* As you will see, by using font metrics, you can determine the proper placement of each string that you display.

FontMetrics defines several methods that help you manage text output. Several commonly used ones are listed in Table 23-3. These methods help you properly display text in a window. Let's look at some examples.

Method	Description
int bytesWidth(byte *b*[ ], int *start*, int *numBytes*)	Returns the width of *numBytes* characters held in array *b*, beginning at *start*.
int charWidth(char *c*[ ], int *start*, int *numChars*)	Returns the width of *numChars* characters held in array *c*, beginning at *start*.
int charWidth(char *c*)	Returns the width of *c*.
int charWidth(int *c*)	Returns the width of *c*.
int getAscent( )	Returns the ascent of the font.
int getDescent( )	Returns the descent of the font.
Font getFont( )	Returns the font.
int getHeight( )	Returns the height of a line of text. This value can be used to output multiple lines of text in a window.
int getLeading( )	Returns the space between lines of text.
int getMaxAdvance( )	Returns the width of the widest character. −1 is returned if this value is not available.
int getMaxAscent( )	Returns the maximum ascent.
int getMaxDescent( )	Returns the maximum descent.
int[ ] getWidths( )	Returns the widths of the first 256 characters.
int stringWidth(String *str*)	Returns the width of the string specified by *str*.
String toString( )	Returns the string equivalent of the invoking object.

TABLE 23-3   A Sampling of Methods Defined by **FontMetrics**

Displaying Multiple Lines of Text

Perhaps the most common use of **FontMetrics** is to determine the spacing between lines of text. The second most common use is to determine the length of a string that is being displayed. Here, you will see how to accomplish these tasks.

In general, to display multiple lines of text, your program must manually keep track of the current output position. Each time a newline is desired, the Y coordinate must be advanced to the beginning of the next line. Each time a string is displayed, the X coordinate must be set to the point at which the string ends. This allows the next string to be written so that it begins at the end of the preceding one.

To determine the spacing between lines, you can use the value returned by **getLeading( )**. To determine the total height of the font, add the value returned by **getAscent( )** to the value returned by **getDescent( )**. You can then use these values to position each line of text you output. However, in many cases, you will not need to use these individual values. Often, all that you will need to know is the total height of a line, which is the sum of the leading space and the font's ascent and descent values. The easiest way to obtain this value is to call **getHeight( )**. Simply increment the Y coordinate by this value each time you want to advance to the next line when outputting text.

To start output at the end of previous output on the same line, you must know the length, in pixels, of each string that you display. To obtain this value, call **stringWidth( )**. You can use this value to advance the X coordinate each time you display a line.

The following applet shows how to output multiple lines of text in a window. It also displays multiple sentences on the same line. Notice the variables **curX** and **curY**. They keep track of the current text output position.

```
// Demonstrate multiline output.
import java.applet.*;
import java.awt.*;
/*
<applet code="MultiLine" width=300 height=100>
</applet>
*/

public class MultiLine extends Applet {
  int curX=0, curY=0; // current position

  public void init() {
    Font f = new Font("SansSerif", Font.PLAIN, 12);
    setFont(f);
  }
  public void paint(Graphics g) {
    FontMetrics fm = g.getFontMetrics();

    nextLine("This is on line one.", g);
    nextLine("This is on line two.", g);
    sameLine(" This is on same line.", g);
    sameLine(" This, too.", g);
    nextLine("This is on line three.", g);
  }
```

```
    // Advance to next line.
    void nextLine(String s, Graphics g) {
      FontMetrics fm = g.getFontMetrics();

      curY += fm.getHeight(); // advance to next line
      curX = 0;
      g.drawString(s, curX, curY);
      curX = fm.stringWidth(s); // advance to end of line
    }

    // Display on same line.
    void sameLine(String s, Graphics g) {
      FontMetrics fm = g.getFontMetrics();

      g.drawString(s, curX, curY);
      curX += fm.stringWidth(s); // advance to end of line
    }
}
```

Sample output from this program is shown here:

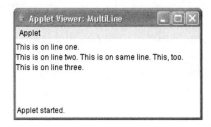

Centering Text

Here is an example that centers text, left to right, top to bottom, in a window. It obtains the ascent, descent, and width of the string and computes the position at which it must be displayed to be centered.

```
// Center text.
import java.applet.*;
import java.awt.*;
/*
  <applet code="CenterText" width=200 height=100>
  </applet>
*/

public class CenterText extends Applet {
  final Font f = new Font("SansSerif", Font.BOLD, 18);

  public void paint(Graphics g) {
    Dimension d = this.getSize();

    g.setColor(Color.white);
    g.fillRect(0, 0, d.width,d.height);
    g.setColor(Color.black);
```

```
      g.setFont(f);
      drawCenteredString("This is centered.", d.width, d.height, g);
      g.drawRect(0, 0, d.width-1, d.height-1);
  }

  public void drawCenteredString(String s, int w, int h,
                                   Graphics g) {
    FontMetrics fm = g.getFontMetrics();
    int x = (w - fm.stringWidth(s)) / 2;
    int y = (fm.getAscent() + (h - (fm.getAscent()
            + fm.getDescent()))/2);
    g.drawString(s, x, y);
  }
}
```

Following is a sample output from this program:

Multiline Text Alignment

If you've used a word processor, you've seen text aligned so that one or more of the edges of the text make a straight line. For example, most word processors can left-justify and/or right-justify text. Most can also center text. In the following program, you will see how to accomplish these actions.

In the program, the string to be justified is broken into individual words. For each word, the program keeps track of its length in the current font and automatically advances to the next line if the word will not fit on the current line. Each completed line is displayed in the window in the currently selected alignment style. Each time you click the mouse in the applet's window, the alignment style is changed. Sample output from this program is shown here:

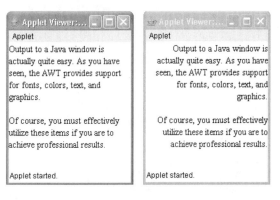

```
// Demonstrate text alignment.
import java.applet.*;
import java.awt.*;
import java.awt.event.*;
import java.util.*;
/* <title>Text Layout</title>
   <applet code="TextLayout" width=200 height=200>
   <param name="text" value="Output to a Java window is actually
      quite easy.
      As you have seen, the AWT provides support for
      fonts, colors, text, and graphics. <P>  Of course,
      you must effectively utilize these items
      if you are to achieve professional results.">
    <param name="fontname" value="Serif">
    <param name="fontSize" value="14">
   </applet>
*/

public class TextLayout extends Applet {
  final int LEFT = 0;
  final int RIGHT = 1;
  final int CENTER = 2;
  final int LEFTRIGHT =3;
  int align;
  Dimension d;
  Font f;
  FontMetrics fm;
  int fontSize;
  int fh, bl;
  int space;
  String text;

  public void init() {
    setBackground(Color.white);
    text = getParameter("text");
    try {
      fontSize = Integer.parseInt(getParameter("fontSize"));}
    catch (NumberFormatException e) {
      fontSize=14;
    }
    align = LEFT;
    addMouseListener(new MyMouseAdapter(this));
  }

  public void paint(Graphics g) {
    update(g);
  }

  public void update(Graphics g) {
    d = getSize();
    g.setColor(getBackground());
    g.fillRect(0,0,d.width, d.height);
    if(f==null) f = new Font(getParameter("fontname"),
                          Font.PLAIN, fontSize);
```

```
    g.setFont(f);
    if(fm == null) {
        fm = g.getFontMetrics();
        bl = fm.getAscent();
        fh = bl + fm.getDescent();
        space = fm.stringWidth(" ");
    }

    g.setColor(Color.black);
    StringTokenizer st = new StringTokenizer(text);
    int x = 0;
    int nextx;
    int y = 0;
    String word, sp;
    int wordCount = 0;
    String line = "";
    while (st.hasMoreTokens()) {
      word = st.nextToken();
      if(word.equals("<P>")) {
        drawString(g, line, wordCount,
                   fm.stringWidth(line), y+bl);
        line = "";
        wordCount = 0;
        x = 0;
        y = y + (fh * 2);
      }
      else {
        int w = fm.stringWidth(word);
        if(( nextx = (x+space+w)) > d.width ) {
          drawString(g, line, wordCount,
                     fm.stringWidth(line), y+bl);
          line = "";
          wordCount = 0;
          x = 0;
          y = y + fh;
        }
        if(x!=0) {sp = " ";} else {sp = "";}
        line = line + sp + word;
        x = x + space + w;
        wordCount++;
      }
    }
    drawString(g, line, wordCount, fm.stringWidth(line), y+bl);
}

public void drawString(Graphics g, String line,
                       int wc, int lineW, int y) {
  switch(align) {
    case LEFT: g.drawString(line, 0, y);
      break;
    case RIGHT: g.drawString(line, d.width-lineW ,y);
      break;
    case CENTER: g.drawString(line, (d.width-lineW)/2, y);
      break;
```

```
      case LEFTRIGHT:
        if(lineW < (int)(d.width*.75)) {
          g.drawString(line, 0, y);
        }
        else {
          int toFill = (d.width - lineW)/wc;
          int nudge = d.width - lineW - (toFill*wc);
          int s = fm.stringWidth(" ");
          StringTokenizer st = new StringTokenizer(line);
          int x = 0;
          while(st.hasMoreTokens()) {
            String word = st.nextToken();
            g.drawString(word, x, y);
            if(nudge>0) {
              x = x + fm.stringWidth(word) + space + toFill + 1;
              nudge--;
            } else {
              x = x + fm.stringWidth(word) + space + toFill;
            }
          }
        }
        break;
      }

  }

}

class MyMouseAdapter extends MouseAdapter {
  TextLayout tl;
  public MyMouseAdapter(TextLayout tl) {
    this.tl = tl;
  }
  public void mouseClicked(MouseEvent me) {
    tl.align = (tl.align + 1) % 4;
    tl.repaint();
  }
}
```

Let's take a closer look at how this applet works. The applet first creates several constants that will be used to determine the alignment style, and then declares several variables. The **init( )** method obtains the text that will be displayed. It then initializes the font size in a **try-catch** block, which will set the font size to 14 if the **fontSize** parameter is missing from the HTML. The **text** parameter is a long string of text, with the HTML tag **<P>** as a paragraph separator.

The **update( )** method is the engine for this example. It sets the font and gets the baseline and font height from a font metrics object. Next, it creates a **StringTokenizer** and uses it to retrieve the next token (a string separated by whitespace) from the string specified by **text**. If the next token is **<P>**, it advances the vertical spacing. Otherwise, **update( )** checks to see if the length of this token in the current font will go beyond the width of the column. If the line is full of text or if there are no more tokens, the line is output by a custom version of **drawString( )**.

The first three cases in **drawString( )** are simple. Each aligns the string that is passed in **line** to the left or right edge or to the center of the column, depending upon the alignment style. The **LEFTRIGHT** case aligns both the left and right sides of the string. This means that we need to calculate the remaining whitespace (the difference between the width of the string and the width of the column) and distribute that space between each of the words. The last method in this class advances the alignment style each time you click the mouse on the applet's window.

PART II

Using AWT Controls, Layout Managers, and Menus

T his chapter continues our exploration of the Abstract Window Toolkit (AWT). It begins with an examination of the standard controls and layout managers. It then discusses menus and the menu bar. The chapter also includes a discussion of two high-level components: the dialog box and the file dialog box. It concludes with another look at event handling.

Controls are components that allow a user to interact with your application in various ways—for example, a commonly used control is the push button. A *layout manager* automatically positions components within a container. Thus, the appearance of a window is determined by a combination of the controls that it contains and the layout manager used to position them.

In addition to the controls, a frame window can also include a standard-style *menu bar*. Each entry in a menu bar activates a drop-down menu of options from which the user can choose. A menu bar is always positioned at the top of a window. Although different in appearance, menu bars are handled in much the same way as are the other controls.

While it is possible to manually position components within a window, doing so is quite tedious. The layout manager automates this task. For the first part of this chapter, which introduces the various controls, the default layout manager will be used. This displays components in a container using left-to-right, top-to-bottom organization. Once the controls have been covered, the layout managers will be examined. There you will see how to better manage the positioning of your controls.

Control Fundamentals

The AWT supports the following types of controls:

- Labels
- Push buttons
- Check boxes
- Choice lists
- Lists

- Scroll bars
- Text editing

These controls are subclasses of **Component**.

Adding and Removing Controls

To include a control in a window, you must add it to the window. To do this, you must first create an instance of the desired control and then add it to a window by calling **add( )**, which is defined by **Container**. The **add( )** method has several forms. The following form is the one that is used for the first part of this chapter:

Component add(Component *compObj*)

Here, *compObj* is an instance of the control that you want to add. A reference to *compObj* is returned. Once a control has been added, it will automatically be visible whenever its parent window is displayed.

Sometimes you will want to remove a control from a window when the control is no longer needed. To do this, call **remove( )**. This method is also defined by **Container**. It has this general form:

void remove(Component *obj*)

Here, *obj* is a reference to the control you want to remove. You can remove all controls by calling **removeAll( )**.

Responding to Controls

Except for labels, which are passive, all controls generate events when they are accessed by the user. For example, when the user clicks on a push button, an event is sent that identifies the push button. In general, your program simply implements the appropriate interface and then registers an event listener for each control that you need to monitor. As explained in Chapter 22, once a listener has been installed, events are automatically sent to it. In the sections that follow, the appropriate interface for each control is specified.

The HeadlessException

Most of the AWT controls described in this chapter now have constructors that can throw a **HeadlessException** when an attempt is made to instantiate a GUI component in a non-interactive environment (such as one in which no display, mouse, or keyboard is present). The **HeadlessException** was added by Java 1.4. You can use this exception to write code that can adapt to non-interactive environments. (Of course, this is not always possible.) This exception is not handled by the programs in this chapter because an interactive environment is required to demonstrate the AWT controls.

Labels

The easiest control to use is a label. A *label* is an object of type **Label**, and it contains a string, which it displays. Labels are passive controls that do not support any interaction with the user. **Label** defines the following constructors:

Label( ) throws HeadlessException
Label(String *str*) throws HeadlessException
Label(String *str*, int *how*) throws HeadlessException

The first version creates a blank label. The second version creates a label that contains the string specified by *str*. This string is left-justified. The third version creates a label that contains the string specified by *str* using the alignment specified by *how*. The value of *how* must be one of these three constants: **Label.LEFT**, **Label.RIGHT**, or **Label.CENTER**.

You can set or change the text in a label by using the **setText( )** method. You can obtain the current label by calling **getText( )**. These methods are shown here:

void setText(String *str*)
String getText( )

For **setText( )**, *str* specifies the new label. For **getText( )**, the current label is returned.

You can set the alignment of the string within the label by calling **setAlignment( )**. To obtain the current alignment, call **getAlignment( )**. The methods are as follows:

void setAlignment(int *how*)
int getAlignment( )

Here, *how* must be one of the alignment constants shown earlier.

The following example creates three labels and adds them to an applet window:

```
// Demonstrate Labels
import java.awt.*;
import java.applet.*;
/*
<applet code="LabelDemo" width=300 height=200>
</applet>
*/

public class LabelDemo extends Applet {
  public void init() {
    Label one = new Label("One");
    Label two = new Label("Two");
    Label three = new Label("Three");

    // add labels to applet window
    add(one);
    add(two);
    add(three);
  }
}
```

Here is the window created by the **LabelDemo** applet. Notice that the labels are organized in the window by the default layout manager. Later, you will see how to control more precisely the placement of the labels.

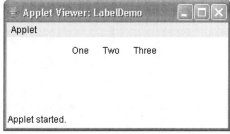

Using Buttons

Perhaps the most widely used control is the push button. A *push button* is a component that contains a label and that generates an event when it is pressed. Push buttons are objects of type **Button**. **Button** defines these two constructors:

Button( ) throws HeadlessException
Button(String *str*) throws HeadlessException

The first version creates an empty button. The second creates a button that contains *str* as a label.

After a button has been created, you can set its label by calling **setLabel( )**. You can retrieve its label by calling **getLabel( )**. These methods are as follows:

void setLabel(String *str*)
String getLabel( )

Here, *str* becomes the new label for the button.

Handling Buttons

Each time a button is pressed, an action event is generated. This is sent to any listeners that previously registered an interest in receiving action event notifications from that component. Each listener implements the **ActionListener** interface. That interface defines the **actionPerformed( )** method, which is called when an event occurs. An **ActionEvent** object is supplied as the argument to this method. It contains both a reference to the button that generated the event and a reference to the *action command string* associated with the button. By default, the action command string is the label of the button. Usually, either the button reference or the action command string can be used to identify the button. (You will soon see examples of each approach.)

Here is an example that creates three buttons labeled "Yes", "No", and "Undecided". Each time one is pressed, a message is displayed that reports which button has been pressed. In this version, the action command of the button (which, by default, is its label) is used to determine which button has been pressed. The label is obtained by calling the **getActionCommand( )** method on the **ActionEvent** object passed to **actionPerformed( )**.

```
// Demonstrate Buttons
import java.awt.*;
import java.awt.event.*;
import java.applet.*;
/*
  <applet code="ButtonDemo" width=250 height=150>
  </applet>
*/

public class ButtonDemo extends Applet implements ActionListener {
  String msg = "";
  Button yes, no, maybe;

  public void init() {
    yes = new Button("Yes");
```

```
    no = new Button("No");
    maybe = new Button("Undecided");

    add(yes);
    add(no);
    add(maybe);

    yes.addActionListener(this);
    no.addActionListener(this);
    maybe.addActionListener(this);
  }

  public void actionPerformed(ActionEvent ae) {
    String str = ae.getActionCommand();
    if(str.equals("Yes")) {
      msg = "You pressed Yes.";
    }
    else if(str.equals("No")) {
      msg = "You pressed No.";
    }
    else {
      msg = "You pressed Undecided.";
    }

    repaint();
  }

  public void paint(Graphics g) {
    g.drawString(msg, 6, 100);
  }
}
```

Sample output from the **ButtonDemo** program is shown in Figure 24-1.

As mentioned, in addition to comparing button action command strings, you can also determine which button has been pressed, by comparing the object obtained from the

FIGURE 24-1   Sample output from the **ButtonDemo** applet

getSource( ) method to the button objects that you added to the window. To do this, you must keep a list of the objects when they are added. The following applet shows this approach:

```
// Recognize Button objects.
import java.awt.*;
import java.awt.event.*;
import java.applet.*;
/*
  <applet code="ButtonList" width=250 height=150>
  </applet>
*/

public class ButtonList extends Applet implements ActionListener {
  String msg = "";
  Button bList[] = new Button[3];

  public void init() {
    Button yes = new Button("Yes");
    Button no = new Button("No");
    Button maybe = new Button("Undecided");

    // store references to buttons as added
    bList[0] = (Button) add(yes);
    bList[1] = (Button) add(no);
    bList[2] = (Button) add(maybe);

    // register to receive action events
    for(int i = 0; i < 3; i++) {
      bList[i].addActionListener(this);
    }
  }

  public void actionPerformed(ActionEvent ae) {
    for(int i = 0; i < 3; i++) {
      if(ae.getSource() == bList[i]) {
        msg = "You pressed " + bList[i].getLabel();
      }
    }
    repaint();
  }

  public void paint(Graphics g) {
      g.drawString(msg, 6, 100);
  }
}
```

In this version, the program stores each button reference in an array when the buttons are added to the applet window. (Recall that the **add( )** method returns a reference to the button when it is added.) Inside **actionPerformed( )**, this array is then used to determine which button has been pressed.

For simple programs, it is usually easier to recognize buttons by their labels. However, in situations in which you will be changing the label inside a button during the execution of your program, or using buttons that have the same label, it may be easier to determine which button has been pushed by using its object reference. It is also possible to set the action command string associated with a button to something other than its label by calling **setActionCommand( )**. This method changes the action command string, but does not affect the string used to label the button. Thus, setting the action command enables the action command and the label of a button to differ.

Applying Check Boxes

A *check box* is a control that is used to turn an option on or off. It consists of a small box that can either contain a check mark or not. There is a label associated with each check box that describes what option the box represents. You change the state of a check box by clicking on it. Check boxes can be used individually or as part of a group. Check boxes are objects of the **Checkbox** class.

Checkbox supports these constructors:

Checkbox( ) throws HeadlessException
Checkbox(String *str*) throws HeadlessException
Checkbox(String *str*, boolean *on*) throws HeadlessException
Checkbox(String *str*, boolean *on*, CheckboxGroup *cbGroup*) throws HeadlessException
Checkbox(String *str*, CheckboxGroup *cbGroup*, boolean *on*) throws HeadlessException

The first form creates a check box whose label is initially blank. The state of the check box is unchecked. The second form creates a check box whose label is specified by *str*. The state of the check box is unchecked. The third form allows you to set the initial state of the check box. If *on* is **true**, the check box is initially checked; otherwise, it is cleared. The fourth and fifth forms create a check box whose label is specified by *str* and whose group is specified by *cbGroup*. If this check box is not part of a group, then *cbGroup* must be **null**. (Check box groups are described in the next section.) The value of *on* determines the initial state of the check box.

To retrieve the current state of a check box, call **getState( )**. To set its state, call **setState( )**. You can obtain the current label associated with a check box by calling **getLabel( )**. To set the label, call **setLabel( )**. These methods are as follows:

boolean getState( )
void setState(boolean *on*)
String getLabel( )
void setLabel(String *str*)

Here, if *on* is **true**, the box is checked. If it is **false**, the box is cleared. The string passed in *str* becomes the new label associated with the invoking check box.

Handling Check Boxes

Each time a check box is selected or deselected, an item event is generated. This is sent to any listeners that previously registered an interest in receiving item event notifications from that component. Each listener implements the **ItemListener** interface. That interface defines the **itemStateChanged( )** method. An **ItemEvent** object is supplied as the argument to this method. It contains information about the event (for example, whether it was a selection or deselection).

The following program creates four check boxes. The initial state of the first box is checked. The status of each check box is displayed. Each time you change the state of a check box, the status display is updated.

```java
// Demonstrate check boxes.
import java.awt.*;
import java.awt.event.*;
import java.applet.*;
/*
  <applet code="CheckboxDemo" width=250 height=200>
  </applet>
*/

public class CheckboxDemo extends Applet implements ItemListener {
  String msg = "";
  Checkbox winXP, winVista, solaris, mac;

  public void init() {
    winXP = new Checkbox("Windows XP", null, true);
    winVista = new Checkbox("Windows Vista");
    solaris = new Checkbox("Solaris");
    mac = new Checkbox("Mac OS");

    add(winXP);
    add(winVista);
    add(solaris);
    add(mac);

    winXP.addItemListener(this);
    winVista.addItemListener(this);
    solaris.addItemListener(this);
    mac.addItemListener(this);
  }

  public void itemStateChanged(ItemEvent ie) {
    repaint();
  }

  // Display current state of the check boxes.
  public void paint(Graphics g) {
    msg = "Current state: ";
    g.drawString(msg, 6, 80);
    msg = "  Windows XP: " + winXP.getState();
    g.drawString(msg, 6, 100);
    msg = "  Windows Vista: " + winVista.getState();
    g.drawString(msg, 6, 120);
    msg = "  Solaris: " + solaris.getState();
    g.drawString(msg, 6, 140);
    msg = "  Mac OS: " + mac.getState();
    g.drawString(msg, 6, 160);
  }
}
```

Sample output is shown in Figure 24-2.

PART II

FIGURE 24-2   Sample output from the **CheckboxDemo** applet

CheckboxGroup

It is possible to create a set of mutually exclusive check boxes in which one and only one
check box in the group can be checked at any one time. These check boxes are often called
radio buttons, because they act like the station selector on a car radio—only one station can
be selected at any one time. To create a set of mutually exclusive check boxes, you must first
define the group to which they will belong and then specify that group when you construct
the check boxes. Check box groups are objects of type **CheckboxGroup**. Only the default
constructor is defined, which creates an empty group.

You can determine which check box in a group is currently selected by calling
getSelectedCheckbox( ). You can set a check box by calling **setSelectedCheckbox( )**.
These methods are as follows:

    Checkbox getSelectedCheckbox( )
    void setSelectedCheckbox(Checkbox *which*)

Here, *which* is the check box that you want to be selected. The previously selected check box
will be turned off.

Here is a program that uses check boxes that are part of a group:

```
// Demonstrate check box group.
import java.awt.*;
import java.awt.event.*;
import java.applet.*;
/*
  <applet code="CBGroup" width=250 height=200>
  </applet>
*/

public class CBGroup extends Applet implements ItemListener {
  String msg = "";
  Checkbox winXP, winVista, solaris, mac;
```

```
CheckboxGroup cbg;

public void init() {
  cbg = new CheckboxGroup();
  winXP = new Checkbox("Windows XP", cbg, true);
  winVista = new Checkbox("Windows Vista", cbg, false);
  solaris = new Checkbox("Solaris", cbg, false);
  mac = new Checkbox("Mac OS", cbg, false);

  add(winXP);
  add(winVista);
  add(solaris);
  add(mac);

  winXP.addItemListener(this);
  winVista.addItemListener(this);
  solaris.addItemListener(this);
  mac.addItemListener(this);
}

public void itemStateChanged(ItemEvent ie) {
  repaint();
}

// Display current state of the check boxes.
public void paint(Graphics g) {
  msg = "Current selection: ";
  msg += cbg.getSelectedCheckbox().getLabel();
  g.drawString(msg, 6, 100);
}
}
```

Output generated by the **CBGroup** applet is shown in Figure 24-3. Notice that the check boxes are now circular in shape.

FIGURE 24-3 Sample output from the **CBGroup** applet

Choice Controls

The **Choice** class is used to create a *pop-up list* of items from which the user may choose. Thus, a **Choice** control is a form of menu. When inactive, a **Choice** component takes up only enough space to show the currently selected item. When the user clicks on it, the whole list of choices pops up, and a new selection can be made. Each item in the list is a string that appears as a left-justified label in the order it is added to the **Choice** object. **Choice** only defines the default constructor, which creates an empty list.

To add a selection to the list, call **add( )**. It has this general form:

void add(String *name*)

Here, *name* is the name of the item being added. Items are added to the list in the order in which calls to **add( )** occur.

To determine which item is currently selected, you may call either **getSelectedItem( )** or **getSelectedIndex( )**. These methods are shown here:

String getSelectedItem( )
int getSelectedIndex( )

The **getSelectedItem( )** method returns a string containing the name of the item. **getSelectedIndex( )** returns the index of the item. The first item is at index 0. By default, the first item added to the list is selected.

To obtain the number of items in the list, call **getItemCount( )**. You can set the currently selected item using the **select( )** method with either a zero-based integer index or a string that will match a name in the list. These methods are shown here:

int getItemCount( )
void select(int *index*)
void select(String *name*)

Given an index, you can obtain the name associated with the item at that index by calling **getItem( )**, which has this general form:

String getItem(int *index*)

Here, *index* specifies the index of the desired item.

Handling Choice Lists

Each time a choice is selected, an item event is generated. This is sent to any listeners that previously registered an interest in receiving item event notifications from that component. Each listener implements the **ItemListener** interface. That interface defines the **itemStateChanged( )** method. An **ItemEvent** object is supplied as the argument to this method.

Here is an example that creates two **Choice** menus. One selects the operating system. The other selects the browser.

```
// Demonstrate Choice lists.
import java.awt.*;
import java.awt.event.*;
```

```java
import java.applet.*;
/*
  <applet code="ChoiceDemo" width=300 height=180>
  </applet>
*/

public class ChoiceDemo extends Applet implements ItemListener {
  Choice os, browser;
  String msg = "";

  public void init() {
    os = new Choice();
    browser = new Choice();

    // add items to os list
    os.add("Windows XP");
    os.add("Windows Vista");
    os.add("Solaris");
    os.add("Mac OS");

    // add items to browser list
    browser.add("Internet Explorer");
    browser.add("Firefox");
    browser.add("Opera");

    // add choice lists to window
    add(os);
    add(browser);

    // register to receive item events
    os.addItemListener(this);
    browser.addItemListener(this);
  }

  public void itemStateChanged(ItemEvent ie) {
    repaint();
  }

  // Display current selections.
  public void paint(Graphics g) {
    msg = "Current OS: ";
    msg += os.getSelectedItem();
    g.drawString(msg, 6, 120);
    msg = "Current Browser: ";
    msg += browser.getSelectedItem();
    g.drawString(msg, 6, 140);
  }
}
```

Sample output is shown in Figure 24-4.

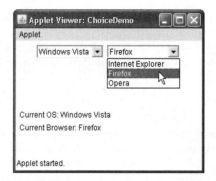

FIGURE 24-4 Sample output from the **ChoiceDemo** applet

Using Lists

The **List** class provides a compact, multiple-choice, scrolling selection list. Unlike the **Choice** object, which shows only the single selected item in the menu, a **List** object can be constructed to show any number of choices in the visible window. It can also be created to allow multiple selections. **List** provides these constructors:

List( ) throws HeadlessException
List(int *numRows*) throws HeadlessException
List(int *numRows*, boolean *multipleSelect*) throws HeadlessException

The first version creates a **List** control that allows only one item to be selected at any one time. In the second form, the value of *numRows* specifies the number of entries in the list that will always be visible (others can be scrolled into view as needed). In the third form, if *multipleSelect* is **true**, then the user may select two or more items at a time. If it is **false**, then only one item may be selected.

To add a selection to the list, call **add( )**. It has the following two forms:

void add(String *name*)
void add(String *name*, int *index*)

Here, *name* is the name of the item added to the list. The first form adds items to the end of the list. The second form adds the item at the index specified by *index*. Indexing begins at zero. You can specify –1 to add the item to the end of the list.

For lists that allow only single selection, you can determine which item is currently selected by calling either **getSelectedItem( )** or **getSelectedIndex( )**. These methods are shown here:

String getSelectedItem( )
int getSelectedIndex( )

The **getSelectedItem( )** method returns a string containing the name of the item. If more than one item is selected, or if no selection has yet been made, **null** is returned. **getSelectedIndex( )**

returns the index of the item. The first item is at index 0. If more than one item is selected, or if no selection has yet been made, –1 is returned.

For lists that allow multiple selection, you must use either **getSelectedItems( )** or **getSelectedIndexes( )**, shown here, to determine the current selections:

```
String[ ] getSelectedItems( )
int[ ] getSelectedIndexes( )
```

getSelectedItems( ) returns an array containing the names of the currently selected items. **getSelectedIndexes( )** returns an array containing the indexes of the currently selected items.

To obtain the number of items in the list, call **getItemCount( )**. You can set the currently selected item by using the **select( )** method with a zero-based integer index. These methods are shown here:

```
int getItemCount( )
void select(int index)
```

Given an index, you can obtain the name associated with the item at that index by calling **getItem( )**, which has this general form:

```
String getItem(int index)
```

Here, *index* specifies the index of the desired item.

Handling Lists

To process list events, you will need to implement the **ActionListener** interface. Each time a **List** item is double-clicked, an **ActionEvent** object is generated. Its **getActionCommand( )** method can be used to retrieve the name of the newly selected item. Also, each time an item is selected or deselected with a single click, an **ItemEvent** object is generated. Its **getStateChange( )** method can be used to determine whether a selection or deselection triggered this event. **getItemSelectable( )** returns a reference to the object that triggered this event.

Here is an example that converts the **Choice** controls in the preceding section into **List** components, one multiple choice and the other single choice:

```
// Demonstrate Lists.
import java.awt.*;
import java.awt.event.*;
import java.applet.*;
/*
  <applet code="ListDemo" width=300 height=180>
  </applet>
*/

public class ListDemo extends Applet implements ActionListener {
  List os, browser;
```

```
String msg = "";

public void init() {
  os = new List(4, true);
  browser = new List(4, false);

  // add items to os list
  os.add("Windows XP");
  os.add("Windows Vista");
  os.add("Solaris");
  os.add("Mac OS");

  // add items to browser list
  browser.add("Internet Explorer");
  browser.add("Firefox");
  browser.add("Opera");

  browser.select(1);

  // add lists to window
  add(os);
  add(browser);

  // register to receive action events
  os.addActionListener(this);
  browser.addActionListener(this);
}

public void actionPerformed(ActionEvent ae) {
  repaint();
}

// Display current selections.
public void paint(Graphics g) {
  int idx[];

  msg = "Current OS: ";
  idx = os.getSelectedIndexes();
  for(int i=0; i<idx.length; i++)
    msg += os.getItem(idx[i]) + "   ";
  g.drawString(msg, 6, 120);
  msg = "Current Browser: ";
  msg += browser.getSelectedItem();
  g.drawString(msg, 6, 140);
}
}
```

Sample output generated by the **ListDemo** applet is shown in Figure 24-5.

FIGURE 24-5   Sample output from the **ListDemo** applet

Managing Scroll Bars

Scroll bars are used to select continuous values between a specified minimum and maximum. Scroll bars may be oriented horizontally or vertically. A scroll bar is actually a composite of several individual parts. Each end has an arrow that you can click to move the current value of the scroll bar one unit in the direction of the arrow. The current value of the scroll bar relative to its minimum and maximum values is indicated by the *slider box* (or *thumb*) for the scroll bar. The slider box can be dragged by the user to a new position. The scroll bar will then reflect this value. In the background space on either side of the thumb, the user can click to cause the thumb to jump in that direction by some increment larger than 1. Typically, this action translates into some form of page up and page down. Scroll bars are encapsulated by the **Scrollbar** class.

Scrollbar defines the following constructors:

Scrollbar( ) throws HeadlessException
Scrollbar(int *style*) throws HeadlessException
Scrollbar(int *style*, int *initialValue*, int *thumbSize*, int *min*, int *max*)
      throws HeadlessException

The first form creates a vertical scroll bar. The second and third forms allow you to specify the orientation of the scroll bar. If *style* is **Scrollbar.VERTICAL**, a vertical scroll bar is created. If *style* is **Scrollbar.HORIZONTAL**, the scroll bar is horizontal. In the third form of the constructor, the initial value of the scroll bar is passed in *initialValue*. The number of units represented by the height of the thumb is passed in *thumbSize*. The minimum and maximum values for the scroll bar are specified by *min* and *max*.

If you construct a scroll bar by using one of the first two constructors, then you need to set its parameters by using **setValues( )**, shown here, before it can be used:

void setValues(int *initialValue*, int *thumbSize*, int *min*, int *max*)

The parameters have the same meaning as they have in the third constructor just described. To obtain the current value of the scroll bar, call **getValue( )**. It returns the current setting. To set the current value, call **setValue( )**. These methods are as follows:

int getValue( )
void setValue(int *newValue*)

Here, *newValue* specifies the new value for the scroll bar. When you set a value, the slider box inside the scroll bar will be positioned to reflect the new value.

You can also retrieve the minimum and maximum values via **getMinimum( )** and **getMaximum( )**, shown here:

```
int getMinimum( )
int getMaximum( )
```

They return the requested quantity.

By default, 1 is the increment added to or subtracted from the scroll bar each time it is scrolled up or down one line. You can change this increment by calling **setUnitIncrement( )**. By default, page-up and page-down increments are 10. You can change this value by calling **setBlockIncrement( )**. These methods are shown here:

```
void setUnitIncrement(int newIncr)
void setBlockIncrement(int newIncr)
```

Handling Scroll Bars

To process scroll bar events, you need to implement the **AdjustmentListener** interface. Each time a user interacts with a scroll bar, an **AdjustmentEvent** object is generated. Its **getAdjustmentType( )** method can be used to determine the type of the adjustment. The types of adjustment events are as follows:

BLOCK_DECREMENT	A page-down event has been generated.
BLOCK_INCREMENT	A page-up event has been generated.
TRACK	An absolute tracking event has been generated.
UNIT_DECREMENT	The line-down button in a scroll bar has been pressed.
UNIT_INCREMENT	The line-up button in a scroll bar has been pressed.

The following example creates both a vertical and a horizontal scroll bar. The current settings of the scroll bars are displayed. If you drag the mouse while inside the window, the coordinates of each drag event are used to update the scroll bars. An asterisk is displayed at the current drag position.

```
// Demonstrate scroll bars.
import java.awt.*;
import java.awt.event.*;
import java.applet.*;
/*
  <applet code="SBDemo" width=300 height=200>
  </applet>
*/

public class SBDemo extends Applet
  implements AdjustmentListener, MouseMotionListener {
  String msg = "";
```

```
Scrollbar vertSB, horzSB;

public void init() {
  int width = Integer.parseInt(getParameter("width"));
  int height = Integer.parseInt(getParameter("height"));

  vertSB = new Scrollbar(Scrollbar.VERTICAL,
                         0, 1, 0, height);
  horzSB = new Scrollbar(Scrollbar.HORIZONTAL,
                         0, 1, 0, width);
  add(vertSB);
  add(horzSB);

  // register to receive adjustment events
  vertSB.addAdjustmentListener(this);
  horzSB.addAdjustmentListener(this);

  addMouseMotionListener(this);
}

public void adjustmentValueChanged(AdjustmentEvent ae) {
  repaint();
}

// Update scroll bars to reflect mouse dragging.
public void mouseDragged(MouseEvent me) {
  int x = me.getX();
  int y = me.getY();
  vertSB.setValue(y);
  horzSB.setValue(x);
  repaint();
}

// Necessary for MouseMotionListener
public void mouseMoved(MouseEvent me) {
}

// Display current value of scroll bars.
public void paint(Graphics g) {
  msg = "Vertical: " + vertSB.getValue();
  msg += ",  Horizontal: " + horzSB.getValue();
  g.drawString(msg, 6, 160);

  // show current mouse drag position
  g.drawString("*", horzSB.getValue(),
                    vertSB.getValue());
}
}
```

Sample output from the **SBDemo** applet is shown in Figure 24-6.

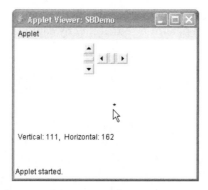

FIGURE 24-6   Sample output from the **SBDemo** applet

Using a TextField

The **TextField** class implements a single-line text-entry area, usually called an *edit control*. Text fields allow the user to enter strings and to edit the text using the arrow keys, cut and paste keys, and mouse selections. **TextField** is a subclass of **TextComponent**. **TextField** defines the following constructors:

TextField( ) throws HeadlessException
TextField(int *numChars*) throws HeadlessException
TextField(String *str*) throws HeadlessException
TextField(String *str*, int *numChars*) throws HeadlessException

The first version creates a default text field. The second form creates a text field that is *numChars* characters wide. The third form initializes the text field with the string contained in *str*. The fourth form initializes a text field and sets its width.

   TextField (and its superclass **TextComponent**) provides several methods that allow you to utilize a text field. To obtain the string currently contained in the text field, call **getText( )**. To set the text, call **setText( )**. These methods are as follows:

String getText( )
void setText(String *str*)

Here, *str* is the new string.

   The user can select a portion of the text in a text field. Also, you can select a portion of text under program control by using **select( )**. Your program can obtain the currently selected text by calling **getSelectedText( )**. These methods are shown here:

String getSelectedText( )
void select(int *startIndex*, int *endIndex*)

getSelectedText( ) returns the selected text. The **select( )** method selects the characters beginning at *startIndex* and ending at *endIndex*–1.

You can control whether the contents of a text field may be modified by the user by calling **setEditable( )**. You can determine editability by calling **isEditable( )**. These methods are shown here:

boolean isEditable( )
void setEditable(boolean *canEdit*)

isEditable( ) returns **true** if the text may be changed and **false** if not. In **setEditable( )**, if *canEdit* is **true**, the text may be changed. If it is **false**, the text cannot be altered.

There may be times when you will want the user to enter text that is not displayed, such as a password. You can disable the echoing of the characters as they are typed by calling **setEchoChar( )**. This method specifies a single character that the **TextField** will display when characters are entered (thus, the actual characters typed will not be shown). You can check a text field to see if it is in this mode with the **echoCharIsSet( )** method. You can retrieve the echo character by calling the **getEchoChar( )** method. These methods are as follows:

void setEchoChar(char *ch*)
boolean echoCharIsSet( )
char getEchoChar( )

Here, *ch* specifies the character to be echoed.

Handling a TextField

Since text fields perform their own editing functions, your program generally will not respond to individual key events that occur within a text field. However, you may want to respond when the user presses ENTER. When this occurs, an action event is generated.

Here is an example that creates the classic user name and password screen:

```
// Demonstrate text field.
import java.awt.*;
import java.awt.event.*;
import java.applet.*;
/*

  <applet code="TextFieldDemo" width=380 height=150>
  </applet>
*/

public class TextFieldDemo extends Applet
  implements ActionListener {

  TextField name, pass;

  public void init() {
    Label namep = new Label("Name: ", Label.RIGHT);
    Label passp = new Label("Password: ", Label.RIGHT);
    name = new TextField(12);
    pass = new TextField(8);
    pass.setEchoChar('?');

    add(namep);
```

```
      add(name);
      add(passp);
      add(pass);

      // register to receive action events
      name.addActionListener(this);
      pass.addActionListener(this);
    }

    // User pressed Enter.
    public void actionPerformed(ActionEvent ae) {
      repaint();
    }

    public void paint(Graphics g) {
        g.drawString("Name: " + name.getText(), 6, 60);
        g.drawString("Selected text in name: "
                      + name.getSelectedText(), 6, 80);
        g.drawString("Password: " + pass.getText(), 6, 100);
    }
}
```

Sample output from the **TextFieldDemo** applet is shown in Figure 24-7.

Using a TextArea

Sometimes a single line of text input is not enough for a given task. To handle these situations, the AWT includes a simple multiline editor called **TextArea**. Following are the constructors for **TextArea**:

TextArea( ) throws HeadlessException
TextArea(int *numLines*, int *numChars*) throws HeadlessException
TextArea(String *str*) throws HeadlessException
TextArea(String *str*, int *numLines*, int *numChars*) throws HeadlessException
TextArea(String *str*, int *numLines*, int *numChars*, int *sBars*) throws HeadlessException

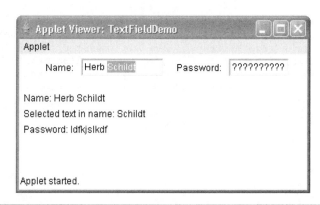

FIGURE 24-7   Sample output from the **TextFieldDemo** applet

Here, *numLines* specifies the height, in lines, of the text area, and *numChars* specifies its width, in characters. Initial text can be specified by *str*. In the fifth form, you can specify the scroll bars that you want the control to have. *sBars* must be one of these values:

SCROLLBARS_BOTH	SCROLLBARS_NONE
SCROLLBARS_HORIZONTAL_ONLY	SCROLLBARS_VERTICAL_ONLY

TextArea is a subclass of **TextComponent**. Therefore, it supports the **getText( )**, **setText( )**, **getSelectedText( )**, **select( )**, **isEditable( )**, and **setEditable( )** methods described in the preceding section.

TextArea adds the following methods:

> void append(String *str*)
> void insert(String *str*, int *index*)
> void replaceRange(String *str*, int *startIndex*, int *endIndex*)

The **append( )** method appends the string specified by *str* to the end of the current text. **insert( )** inserts the string passed in *str* at the specified index. To replace text, call **replaceRange( )**. It replaces the characters from *startIndex* to *endIndex*–1, with the replacement text passed in *str*.

Text areas are almost self-contained controls. Your program incurs virtually no management overhead. Text areas only generate got-focus and lost-focus events. Normally, your program simply obtains the current text when it is needed.

The following program creates a **TextArea** control:

```
// Demonstrate TextArea.
import java.awt.*;
import java.applet.*;
/*
<applet code="TextAreaDemo" width=300 height=250>
</applet>
*/

public class TextAreaDemo extends Applet {
  public void init() {
    String val =
      "Java SE 6 is the latest version of the most\n" +
      "widely-used computer language for Internet programming.\n" +
      "Building on a rich heritage, Java has advanced both\n" +
      "the art and science of computer language design.\n\n" +
      "One of the reasons for Java's ongoing success is its\n" +
      "constant, steady rate of evolution. Java has never stood\n" +
      "still. Instead, Java has consistently adapted to the\n" +
      "rapidly changing landscape of the networked world.\n" +
      "Moreover, Java has often led the way, charting the\n" +
      "course for others to follow.";

    TextArea text = new TextArea(val, 10, 30);
    add(text);
  }
}
```

Here is sample output from the **TextAreaDemo** applet:

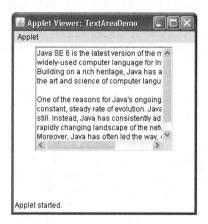

Understanding Layout Managers

All of the components that we have shown so far have been positioned by the default layout manager. As we mentioned at the beginning of this chapter, a layout manager automatically arranges your controls within a window by using some type of algorithm. If you have programmed for other GUI environments, such as Windows, then you are accustomed to laying out your controls by hand. While it is possible to lay out Java controls by hand, too, you generally won't want to, for two main reasons. First, it is very tedious to manually lay out a large number of components. Second, sometimes the width and height information is not yet available when you need to arrange some control, because the native toolkit components haven't been realized. This is a chicken-and-egg situation; it is pretty confusing to figure out when it is okay to use the size of a given component to position it relative to another.

Each **Container** object has a layout manager associated with it. A layout manager is an instance of any class that implements the **LayoutManager** interface. The layout manager is set by the **setLayout( )** method. If no call to **setLayout( )** is made, then the default layout manager is used. Whenever a container is resized (or sized for the first time), the layout manager is used to position each of the components within it.

The **setLayout( )** method has the following general form:

void setLayout(LayoutManager *layoutObj*)

Here, *layoutObj* is a reference to the desired layout manager. If you wish to disable the layout manager and position components manually, pass **null** for *layoutObj*. If you do this, you will need to determine the shape and position of each component manually, using the **setBounds( )** method defined by **Component**. Normally, you will want to use a layout manager.

Each layout manager keeps track of a list of components that are stored by their names. The layout manager is notified each time you add a component to a container. Whenever the container needs to be resized, the layout manager is consulted via its **minimumLayoutSize( )** and **preferredLayoutSize( )** methods. Each component that is being managed by a layout manager contains the **getPreferredSize( )** and **getMinimumSize( )** methods. These return the preferred and minimum size required to display each component. The layout manager will honor these requests if at all possible, while maintaining the integrity of the layout policy. You may override these methods for controls that you subclass. Default values are provided otherwise.

Java has several predefined **LayoutManager** classes, several of which are described next. You can use the layout manager that best fits your application.

FlowLayout

FlowLayout is the default layout manager. This is the layout manager that the preceding examples have used. **FlowLayout** implements a simple layout style, which is similar to how words flow in a text editor. The direction of the layout is governed by the container's component orientation property, which, by default, is left to right, top to bottom. Therefore, by default, components are laid out line-by-line beginning at the upper-left corner. In all cases, when a line is filled, layout advances to the next line. A small space is left between each component, above and below, as well as left and right. Here are the constructors for **FlowLayout**:

FlowLayout( )
FlowLayout(int *how*)
FlowLayout(int *how*, int *horz*, int *vert*)

The first form creates the default layout, which centers components and leaves five pixels of space between each component. The second form lets you specify how each line is aligned. Valid values for *how* are as follows:

FlowLayout.LEFT
FlowLayout.CENTER
FlowLayout.RIGHT
FlowLayout.LEADING
FlowLayout.TRAILING

These values specify left, center, right, leading edge, and trailing edge alignment, respectively. The third constructor allows you to specify the horizontal and vertical space left between components in *horz* and *vert*, respectively.

Here is a version of the **CheckboxDemo** applet shown earlier in this chapter, modified so that it uses left-aligned flow layout:

```
// Use left-aligned flow layout.
import java.awt.*;
import java.awt.event.*;
import java.applet.*;
/*
  <applet code="FlowLayoutDemo" width=250 height=200>
  </applet>
*/

public class FlowLayoutDemo extends Applet
  implements ItemListener {

  String msg = "";
  Checkbox winXP, winVista, solaris, mac;
```

```
public void init() {
  // set left-aligned flow layout
  setLayout(new FlowLayout(FlowLayout.LEFT));

  winXP = new Checkbox("Windows XP", null, true);
  winVista = new Checkbox("Windows Vista");
  solaris = new Checkbox("Solaris");
  mac = new Checkbox("Mac OS");

  add(winXP);
  add(winVista);
  add(solaris);
  add(mac);

  // register to receive item events
  winXP.addItemListener(this);
  winVista.addItemListener(this);
  solaris.addItemListener(this);
  mac.addItemListener(this);
}

// Repaint when status of a check box changes.
public void itemStateChanged(ItemEvent ie) {
  repaint();
}

// Display current state of the check boxes.
public void paint(Graphics g) {

  msg = "Current state: ";
  g.drawString(msg, 6, 80);
  msg = "  Windows XP: " + winXP.getState();
  g.drawString(msg, 6, 100);
  msg = "  Windows Vista: " + winVista.getState();
  g.drawString(msg, 6, 120);
  msg = "  Solaris: " + solaris.getState();
  g.drawString(msg, 6, 140);
  msg = "  Mac: " + mac.getState();
  g.drawString(msg, 6, 160);
  }
}
```

Here is sample output generated by the **FlowLayoutDemo** applet. Compare this with the output from the **CheckboxDemo** applet, shown earlier in Figure 24-2.

BorderLayout

The **BorderLayout** class implements a common layout style for top-level windows. It has four narrow, fixed-width components at the edges and one large area in the center. The four sides are referred to as north,

south, east, and west. The middle area is called the center. Here are the constructors defined by **BorderLayout**:

BorderLayout( )
BorderLayout(int *horz*, int *vert*)

The first form creates a default border layout. The second allows you to specify the horizontal and vertical space left between components in *horz* and *vert,* respectively.

BorderLayout defines the following constants that specify the regions:

BorderLayout.CENTER	BorderLayout.SOUTH
BorderLayout.EAST	BorderLayout.WEST
BorderLayout.NORTH	

When adding components, you will use these constants with the following form of **add( )**, which is defined by **Container**:

void add(Component *compObj*, Object *region*)

Here, *compObj* is the component to be added, and *region* specifies where the component will be added.

Here is an example of a **BorderLayout** with a component in each layout area:

```
// Demonstrate BorderLayout.
import java.awt.*;
import java.applet.*;
import java.util.*;
/*
<applet code="BorderLayoutDemo" width=400 height=200>
</applet>
*/

public class BorderLayoutDemo extends Applet {
  public void init() {
    setLayout(new BorderLayout());

    add(new Button("This is across the top."),
        BorderLayout.NORTH);
    add(new Label("The footer message might go here."),
        BorderLayout.SOUTH);
    add(new Button("Right"), BorderLayout.EAST);
    add(new Button("Left"), BorderLayout.WEST);

    String msg = "The reasonable man adapts " +
      "himself to the world;\n" +
      "the unreasonable one persists in " +
      "trying to adapt the world to himself.\n" +
      "Therefore all progress depends " +
      "on the unreasonable man.\n\n" +
      "         - George Bernard Shaw\n\n";

    add(new TextArea(msg), BorderLayout.CENTER);
  }
}
```

Sample output from the **BorderLayoutDemo** applet is shown here:

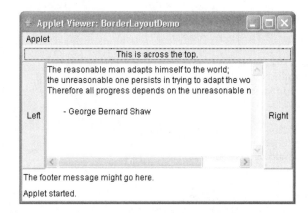

Using Insets

Sometimes you will want to leave a small amount of space between the container that holds your components and the window that contains it. To do this, override the **getInsets( )** method that is defined by **Container**. This method returns an **Insets** object that contains the top, bottom, left, and right inset to be used when the container is displayed. These values are used by the layout manager to inset the components when it lays out the window. The constructor for **Insets** is shown here:

   Insets(int *top*, int *left*, int *bottom*, int *right*)

The values passed in *top, left, bottom,* and *right* specify the amount of space between the container and its enclosing window.

   The **getInsets( )** method has this general form:

   Insets getInsets( )

When overriding this method, you must return a new **Insets** object that contains the inset spacing you desire.

   Here is the preceding **BorderLayout** example modified so that it insets its components ten pixels from each border. The background color has been set to cyan to help make the insets more visible.

```
// Demonstrate BorderLayout with insets.
import java.awt.*;
import java.applet.*;
import java.util.*;
/*
<applet code="InsetsDemo" width=400 height=200>
</applet>
*/

public class InsetsDemo extends Applet {
  public void init() {
    // set background color so insets can be easily seen
```

```
   setBackground(Color.cyan);

   setLayout(new BorderLayout());

   add(new Button("This is across the top."),
      BorderLayout.NORTH);
   add(new Label("The footer message might go here."),
      BorderLayout.SOUTH);
   add(new Button("Right"), BorderLayout.EAST);
   add(new Button("Left"), BorderLayout.WEST);

   String msg = "The reasonable man adapts " +
     "himself to the world;\n" +
     "the unreasonable one persists in " +
     "trying to adapt the world to himself.\n" +
     "Therefore all progress depends " +
     "on the unreasonable man.\n\n" +
     "          - George Bernard Shaw\n\n";

   add(new TextArea(msg), BorderLayout.CENTER);
 }
 // add insets
 public Insets getInsets() {
   return new Insets(10, 10, 10, 10);
 }
}
```

Output from the **InsetsDemo** applet is shown here:

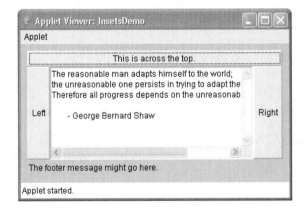

GridLayout

GridLayout lays out components in a two-dimensional grid. When you instantiate a
GridLayout, you define the number of rows and columns. The constructors supported
by **GridLayout** are shown here:

GridLayout( )
GridLayout(int *numRows*, int *numColumns*)
GridLayout(int *numRows*, int *numColumns*, int *horz*, int *vert*)

The first form creates a single-column grid layout. The second form creates a grid layout with the specified number of rows and columns. The third form allows you to specify the horizontal and vertical space left between components in *horz* and *vert*, respectively. Either *numRows* or *numColumns* can be zero. Specifying *numRows* as zero allows for unlimited-length columns. Specifying *numColumns* as zero allows for unlimited-length rows.

Here is a sample program that creates a 4×4 grid and fills it in with 15 buttons, each labeled with its index:

```java
// Demonstrate GridLayout
import java.awt.*;
import java.applet.*;
/*
<applet code="GridLayoutDemo" width=300 height=200>
</applet>
*/

public class GridLayoutDemo extends Applet {
  static final int n = 4;
  public void init() {
    setLayout(new GridLayout(n, n));

    setFont(new Font("SansSerif", Font.BOLD, 24));

    for(int i = 0; i < n; i++) {
      for(int j = 0; j < n; j++) {
        int k = i * n + j;
        if(k > 0)
          add(new Button("" + k));
      }
    }
  }
}
```

Following is the output generated by the **GridLayoutDemo** applet:

TIP   *You might try using this example as the starting point for a 15-square puzzle.*

CardLayout

The **CardLayout** class is unique among the other layout managers in that it stores several different layouts. Each layout can be thought of as being on a separate index card in a deck that can be shuffled so that any card is on top at a given time. This can be useful for user interfaces with optional components that can be dynamically enabled and disabled upon user input. You can prepare the other layouts and have them hidden, ready to be activated when needed.

CardLayout provides these two constructors:

CardLayout( )
CardLayout(int *horz*, int *vert*)

The first form creates a default card layout. The second form allows you to specify the horizontal and vertical space left between components in *horz* and *vert*, respectively.

Use of a card layout requires a bit more work than the other layouts. The cards are typically held in an object of type **Panel**. This panel must have **CardLayout** selected as its layout manager. The cards that form the deck are also typically objects of type **Panel**. Thus, you must create a panel that contains the deck and a panel for each card in the deck. Next, you add to the appropriate panel the components that form each card. You then add these panels to the panel for which **CardLayout** is the layout manager. Finally, you add this panel to the window. Once these steps are complete, you must provide some way for the user to select between cards. One common approach is to include one push button for each card in the deck.

When card panels are added to a panel, they are usually given a name. Thus, most of the time, you will use this form of **add( )** when adding cards to a panel:

void add(Component *panelObj*, Object *name*)

Here, *name* is a string that specifies the name of the card whose panel is specified by *panelObj*.

After you have created a deck, your program activates a card by calling one of the following methods defined by **CardLayout**:

void first(Container *deck*)
void last(Container *deck*)
void next(Container *deck*)
void previous(Container *deck*)
void show(Container *deck*, String *cardName*)

Here, *deck* is a reference to the container (usually a panel) that holds the cards, and *cardName* is the name of a card. Calling **first( )** causes the first card in the deck to be shown. To show the last card, call **last( )**. To show the next card, call **next( )**. To show the previous card, call **previous( )**. Both **next( )** and **previous( )** automatically cycle back to the top or bottom of the deck, respectively. The **show( )** method displays the card whose name is passed in *cardName*.

The following example creates a two-level card deck that allows the user to select an operating system. Windows-based operating systems are displayed in one card. Macintosh and Solaris are displayed in the other card.

```
// Demonstrate CardLayout.
import java.awt.*;
import java.awt.event.*;
```

```java
import java.applet.*;
/*
  <applet code="CardLayoutDemo" width=300 height=100>
  </applet>
*/

public class CardLayoutDemo extends Applet
  implements ActionListener, MouseListener {

  Checkbox winXP, winVista, solaris, mac;
  Panel osCards;
  CardLayout cardLO;
  Button Win, Other;

  public void init() {
    Win = new Button("Windows");
    Other = new Button("Other");
    add(Win);
    add(Other);

    cardLO = new CardLayout();
    osCards = new Panel();
    osCards.setLayout(cardLO); // set panel layout to card layout

    winXP = new Checkbox("Windows XP", null, true);
    winVista = new Checkbox("Windows Vista");
    solaris = new Checkbox("Solaris");
    mac = new Checkbox("Mac OS");

    // add Windows check boxes to a panel
    Panel winPan = new Panel();
    winPan.add(winXP);
    winPan.add(winVista);

    // add other OS check boxes to a panel
    Panel otherPan = new Panel();
    otherPan.add(solaris);
    otherPan.add(mac);

    // add panels to card deck panel
    osCards.add(winPan, "Windows");
    osCards.add(otherPan, "Other");

    // add cards to main applet panel
    add(osCards);

    // register to receive action events
    Win.addActionListener(this);
    Other.addActionListener(this);

    // register mouse events
    addMouseListener(this);
  }

  // Cycle through panels.
```

```
public void mousePressed(MouseEvent me) {
  cardLO.next(osCards);
}

// Provide empty implementations for the other MouseListener methods.
public void mouseClicked(MouseEvent me) {
}
public void mouseEntered(MouseEvent me) {
}
public void mouseExited(MouseEvent me) {
}
public void mouseReleased(MouseEvent me) {
}

public void actionPerformed(ActionEvent ae) {
  if(ae.getSource() == Win) {

    cardLO.show(osCards, "Windows");
  }
  else {
    cardLO.show(osCards, "Other");
  }
}
}
```

Here is the output generated by the **CardLayoutDemo** applet. Each card is activated by pushing its button. You can also cycle through the cards by clicking the mouse.

GridBagLayout

Although the preceding layouts are perfectly acceptable for many uses, some situations will require that you take a bit more control over how the components are arranged. A good way to do this is to use a grid bag layout, which is specified by the **GridBagLayout** class. What makes the grid bag useful is that you can specify the relative placement of components by specifying their positions within cells inside a grid. The key to the grid bag is that each component can be a different size, and each row in the grid can have a different number of columns. This is why the layout is called a *grid bag*. It's a collection of small grids joined together.

The location and size of each component in a grid bag are determined by a set of constraints linked to it. The constraints are contained in an object of type **GridBagConstraints**. Constraints include the height and width of a cell, and the placement of a component, its alignment, and its anchor point within the cell.

The general procedure for using a grid bag is to first create a new **GridBagLayout** object and to make it the current layout manager. Then, set the constraints that apply to each component that will be added to the grid bag. Finally, add the components to the layout manager. Although **GridBagLayout** is a bit more complicated than the other layout managers, it is still quite easy to use once you understand how it works.

GridBagLayout defines only one constructor, which is shown here:

GridBagLayout( )

GridBagLayout defines several methods, of which many are protected and not for general use. There is one method, however, that you must use: **setConstraints( )**. It is shown here:

void setConstraints(Component *comp*, GridBagConstraints *cons*)

Here, *comp* is the component for which the constraints specified by *cons* apply. This method sets the constraints that apply to each component in the grid bag.

The key to successfully using **GridBagLayout** is the proper setting of the constraints, which are stored in a **GridBagConstraints** object. **GridBagConstraints** defines several fields that you can set to govern the size, placement, and spacing of a component. These are shown in Table 24-1. Several are described in greater detail in the following discussion.

Field	Purpose
int anchor	Specifies the location of a component within a cell. The default is **GridBagConstraints.CENTER**.
int fill	Specifies how a component is resized if the component is smaller than its cell. Valid values are **GridBagConstraints.NONE** (the default), **GridBagConstraints.HORIZONTAL**, **GridBagConstraints.VERTICAL**, **GridBagConstraints.BOTH**.
int gridheight	Specifies the height of component in terms of cells. The default is 1.
int gridwidth	Specifies the width of component in terms of cells. The default is 1.
int gridx	Specifies the X coordinate of the cell to which the component will be added. The default value is **GridBagConstraints.RELATIVE**.
int gridy	Specifies the Y coordinate of the cell to which the component will be added. The default value is **GridBagConstraints.RELATIVE**.
Insets insets	Specifies the insets. Default insets are all zero.
int ipadx	Specifies extra horizontal space that surrounds a component within a cell. The default is 0.
int ipady	Specifies extra vertical space that surrounds a component within a cell. The default is 0.
double weightx	Specifies a weight value that determines the horizontal spacing between cells and the edges of the container that holds them. The default value is 0.0. The greater the weight, the more space that is allocated. If all values are 0.0, extra space is distributed evenly between the edges of the window.
double weighty	Specifies a weight value that determines the vertical spacing between cells and the edges of the container that holds them. The default value is 0.0. The greater the weight, the more space that is allocated. If all values are 0.0, extra space is distributed evenly between the edges of the window.

TABLE 24-1   Constraint Fields Defined by **GridBagConstraints**

GridBagConstraints also defines several static fields that contain standard constraint values, such as **GridBagConstraints.CENTER** and **GridBagConstraints.VERTICAL**.

When a component is smaller than its cell, you can use the **anchor** field to specify where within the cell the component's top-left corner will be located. There are three types of values that you can give to **anchor**. The first are absolute:

GridBagConstraints.CENTER	GridBagConstraints.SOUTH
GridBagConstraints.EAST	GridBagConstraints.SOUTHEAST
GridBagConstraints.NORTH	GridBagConstraints.SOUTHWEST
GridBagConstraints.NORTHEAST	GridBagConstraints.WEST
GridBagConstraints.NORTHWEST	

As their names imply, these values cause the component to be placed at the specific locations.

The second type of values that can be given to **anchor** is relative, which means the values are relative to the container's orientation, which might differ for non-Western languages. The relative values are shown here:

GridBagConstraints.FIRST_LINE_END	GridBagConstraints.LINE_END
GridBagConstraints.FIRST_LINE_START	GridBagConstraints.LINE_START
GridBagConstraints.LAST_LINE_END	GridBagConstraints.PAGE_END
GridBagConstraints.LAST_LINE_START	GridBagConstraints.PAGE_START

Their names describe the placement.

The third type of values that can be given to **anchor** were added by Java SE 6. They allow you to position components vertically relative to the baseline of the row. They are shown here:

GridBagConstraints.BASELINE	GridBagConstraints.BASELINE_LEADING
GridBagConstraints.BASELINE_TRAILING	GridBagConstraints.ABOVE_BASELINE
GridBagConstraints.ABOVE_BASELINE_LEADING	GridBagConstraints.ABOVE_BASELINE_TRAILING
GridBagConstraints.BELOW_BASELINE	GridBagConstraints.BELOW_BASELINE_LEADING
GridBagConstraints. BELOW_BASELINE_TRAILING	

The horizontal position can be either centered, against the leading edge (LEADING), or against the trailing edge (TRAILING).

The **weightx** and **weighty** fields are both quite important and quite confusing at first glance. In general, their values determine how much of the extra space within a container is allocated to each row and column. By default, both these values are zero. When all values within a row or a column are zero, extra space is distributed evenly between the edges of the window. By increasing the weight, you increase that row or column's allocation of space proportional to the other rows or columns. The best way to understand how these values work is to experiment with them a bit.

The **gridwidth** variable lets you specify the width of a cell in terms of cell units. The default is 1. To specify that a component use the remaining space in a row, use **GridBagConstraints.REMAINDER**. To specify that a component use the next-to-last cell in a row, use **GridBagConstraints.RELATIVE**. The **gridheight** constraint works the same way, but in the vertical direction.

You can specify a padding value that will be used to increase the minimum size of a cell. To pad horizontally, assign a value to **ipadx**. To pad vertically, assign a value to **ipady**.

Here is an example that uses **GridBagLayout** to demonstrate several of the points just discussed:

```java
// Use GridBagLayout.
import java.awt.*;
import java.awt.event.*;
import java.applet.*;
/*
  <applet code="GridBagDemo" width=250 height=200>
  </applet>
*/

public class GridBagDemo extends Applet
  implements ItemListener {

  String msg = "";
  Checkbox winXP, winVista, solaris, mac;

  public void init() {
    GridBagLayout gbag = new GridBagLayout();
    GridBagConstraints gbc = new GridBagConstraints();
    setLayout(gbag);

    // Define check boxes.
    winXP = new Checkbox("Windows XP ", null, true);
    winVista = new Checkbox("Windows Vista");
    solaris = new Checkbox("Solaris");
    mac = new Checkbox("Mac OS");

    // Define the grid bag.

    // Use default row weight of 0 for first row.
    gbc.weightx = 1.0; // use a column weight of 1
    gbc.ipadx = 200; // pad by 200 units
    gbc.insets = new Insets(4, 4, 0, 0); // inset slightly from top left

    gbc.anchor = GridBagConstraints.NORTHEAST;

    gbc.gridwidth = GridBagConstraints.RELATIVE;
    gbag.setConstraints(winXP, gbc);

    gbc.gridwidth = GridBagConstraints.REMAINDER;
    gbag.setConstraints(winVista, gbc);

    // Give second row a weight of 1.
    gbc.weighty = 1.0;
```

```
    gbc.gridwidth = GridBagConstraints.RELATIVE;
    gbag.setConstraints(solaris, gbc);

    gbc.gridwidth = GridBagConstraints.REMAINDER;
    gbag.setConstraints(mac, gbc);

    // Add the components.
    add(winXP);
    add(winVista);
    add(solaris);
    add(mac);

    // Register to receive item events.
    winXP.addItemListener(this);
    winVista.addItemListener(this);
    solaris.addItemListener(this);
    mac.addItemListener(this);
  }

  // Repaint when status of a check box changes.
  public void itemStateChanged(ItemEvent ie) {
    repaint();
  }

  // Display current state of the check boxes.
  public void paint(Graphics g) {
    msg = "Current state: ";
    g.drawString(msg, 6, 80);
    msg = "  Windows XP: " + winXP.getState();
    g.drawString(msg, 6, 100);
    msg = "  Windows Vista: " + winVista.getState();
    g.drawString(msg, 6, 120);
    msg = "  Solaris: " + solaris.getState();
    g.drawString(msg, 6, 140);
    msg = "  Mac: " + mac.getState();
    g.drawString(msg, 6, 160);
  }
}
```

The output produced by the program is shown here.

In this layout, the operating system check boxes are positioned in a 2×2 grid. Each cell has a horizontal padding of 200. Each component is inset slightly (by 4 units) from the top left. The column weight is set to 1, which causes any extra horizontal space to be distributed evenly between the columns. The first row uses a default weight of 0; the second has a weight of 1. This means that any extra vertical space is added to the second row.

GridBagLayout is a powerful layout manager. It

is worth taking some time to experiment with and explore. Once you understand what the various settings do, you can use **GridBagLayout** to position components with a high degree of precision.

Menu Bars and Menus

A top-level window can have a menu bar associated with it. A menu bar displays a list of top-level menu choices. Each choice is associated with a drop-down menu. This concept is implemented in the AWT by the following classes: **MenuBar**, **Menu**, and **MenuItem**. In general, a menu bar contains one or more **Menu** objects. Each **Menu** object contains a list of **MenuItem** objects. Each **MenuItem** object represents something that can be selected by the user. Since **Menu** is a subclass of **MenuItem**, a hierarchy of nested submenus can be created. It is also possible to include checkable menu items. These are menu options of type **CheckboxMenuItem** and will have a check mark next to them when they are selected.

To create a menu bar, first create an instance of **MenuBar**. This class only defines the default constructor. Next, create instances of **Menu** that will define the selections displayed on the bar. Following are the constructors for **Menu**:

Menu( ) throws HeadlessException
Menu(String *optionName*) throws HeadlessException
Menu(String *optionName*, boolean *removable*) throws HeadlessException

Here, *optionName* specifies the name of the menu selection. If *removable* is **true**, the menu can be removed and allowed to float free. Otherwise, it will remain attached to the menu bar. (Removable menus are implementation-dependent.) The first form creates an empty menu.

Individual menu items are of type **MenuItem**. It defines these constructors:

MenuItem( ) throws HeadlessException
MenuItem(String *itemName*) throws HeadlessException
MenuItem(String *itemName*, MenuShortcut *keyAccel*) throws HeadlessException

Here, *itemName* is the name shown in the menu, and *keyAccel* is the menu shortcut for this item.

You can disable or enable a menu item by using the **setEnabled( )** method. Its form is shown here:

void setEnabled(boolean *enabledFlag*)

If the argument *enabledFlag* is **true**, the menu item is enabled. If **false**, the menu item is disabled.

You can determine an item's status by calling **isEnabled( )**. This method is shown here:

boolean isEnabled( )

isEnabled( ) returns **true** if the menu item on which it is called is enabled. Otherwise, it returns **false**.

You can change the name of a menu item by calling **setLabel( )**. You can retrieve the current name by using **getLabel( )**. These methods are as follows:

void setLabel(String *newName*)
String getLabel( )

Here, *newName* becomes the new name of the invoking menu item. **getLabel( )** returns the current name.

You can create a checkable menu item by using a subclass of **MenuItem** called **CheckboxMenuItem**. It has these constructors:

CheckboxMenuItem( ) throws HeadlessException
CheckboxMenuItem(String *itemName*) throws HeadlessException
CheckboxMenuItem(String *itemName*, boolean *on*) throws HeadlessException

Here, *itemName* is the name shown in the menu. Checkable items operate as toggles. Each time one is selected, its state changes. In the first two forms, the checkable entry is unchecked. In the third form, if *on* is **true**, the checkable entry is initially checked. Otherwise, it is cleared.

You can obtain the status of a checkable item by calling **getState( )**. You can set it to a known state by using **setState( )**. These methods are shown here:

boolean getState( )
void setState(boolean *checked*)

If the item is checked, **getState( )** returns **true**. Otherwise, it returns **false**. To check an item, pass **true** to **setState( )**. To clear an item, pass **false**.

Once you have created a menu item, you must add the item to a **Menu** object by using **add( )**, which has the following general form:

MenuItem add(MenuItem *item*)

Here, *item* is the item being added. Items are added to a menu in the order in which the calls to **add( )** take place. The *item* is returned.

Once you have added all items to a **Menu** object, you can add that object to the menu bar by using this version of **add( )** defined by **MenuBar**:

Menu add(Menu *menu*)

Here, *menu* is the menu being added. The *menu* is returned.

Menus only generate events when an item of type **MenuItem** or **CheckboxMenuItem** is selected. They do not generate events when a menu bar is accessed to display a drop-down menu, for example. Each time a menu item is selected, an **ActionEvent** object is generated. By default, the action command string is the name of the menu item. However, you can specify a different action command string by calling **setActionCommand( )** on the menu item. Each time a check box menu item is checked or unchecked, an **ItemEvent** object is generated. Thus, you must implement the **ActionListener** and/or **ItemListener** interfaces in order to handle these menu events.

The **getItem( )** method of **ItemEvent** returns a reference to the item that generated this event. The general form of this method is shown here:

Object getItem( )

Following is an example that adds a series of nested menus to a pop-up window. The item selected is displayed in the window. The state of the two check box menu items is also displayed.

```
// Illustrate menus.
import java.awt.*;
import java.awt.event.*;
import java.applet.*;
/*
```

```
    <applet code="MenuDemo" width=250 height=250>
    </applet>
*/

// Create a subclass of Frame.
class MenuFrame extends Frame {
  String msg = "";
  CheckboxMenuItem debug, test;

  MenuFrame(String title) {
    super(title);

    // create menu bar and add it to frame
    MenuBar mbar = new MenuBar();
    setMenuBar(mbar);

    // create the menu items
    Menu file = new Menu("File");
    MenuItem item1, item2, item3, item4, item5;
    file.add(item1 = new MenuItem("New..."));
    file.add(item2 = new MenuItem("Open..."));
    file.add(item3 = new MenuItem("Close"));
    file.add(item4 = new MenuItem("-"));
    file.add(item5 = new MenuItem("Quit..."));
    mbar.add(file);

    Menu edit = new Menu("Edit");
    MenuItem item6, item7, item8, item9;
    edit.add(item6 = new MenuItem("Cut"));
    edit.add(item7 = new MenuItem("Copy"));
    edit.add(item8 = new MenuItem("Paste"));
    edit.add(item9 = new MenuItem("-"));

    Menu sub = new Menu("Special");
    MenuItem item10, item11, item12;
    sub.add(item10 = new MenuItem("First"));
    sub.add(item11 = new MenuItem("Second"));
    sub.add(item12 = new MenuItem("Third"));
    edit.add(sub);

    // these are checkable menu items
    debug = new CheckboxMenuItem("Debug");
    edit.add(debug);
    test = new CheckboxMenuItem("Testing");
    edit.add(test);

    mbar.add(edit);

    // create an object to handle action and item events
    MyMenuHandler handler = new MyMenuHandler(this);
    // register it to receive those events
    item1.addActionListener(handler);
    item2.addActionListener(handler);
    item3.addActionListener(handler);
    item4.addActionListener(handler);
```

```java
    item5.addActionListener(handler);
    item6.addActionListener(handler);
    item7.addActionListener(handler);
    item8.addActionListener(handler);
    item9.addActionListener(handler);
    item10.addActionListener(handler);
    item11.addActionListener(handler);
    item12.addActionListener(handler);
    debug.addItemListener(handler);
    test.addItemListener(handler);

    // create an object to handle window events
    MyWindowAdapter adapter = new MyWindowAdapter(this);
     // register it to receive those events
    addWindowListener(adapter);
  }

  public void paint(Graphics g) {
    g.drawString(msg, 10, 200);

   if(debug.getState())
      g.drawString("Debug is on.", 10, 220);
    else
      g.drawString("Debug is off.", 10, 220);

    if(test.getState())
      g.drawString("Testing is on.", 10, 240);
    else
      g.drawString("Testing is off.", 10, 240);
  }
}

class MyWindowAdapter extends WindowAdapter {
  MenuFrame menuFrame;
  public MyWindowAdapter(MenuFrame menuFrame) {
    this.menuFrame = menuFrame;
  }
  public void windowClosing(WindowEvent we) {
    menuFrame.setVisible(false);
  }
}

class MyMenuHandler implements ActionListener, ItemListener {
  MenuFrame menuFrame;
  public MyMenuHandler(MenuFrame menuFrame) {
    this.menuFrame = menuFrame;
  }
  // Handle action events.
  public void actionPerformed(ActionEvent ae) {
      String msg = "You selected ";
      String arg = ae.getActionCommand();
      if(arg.equals("New..."))
        msg += "New.";
      else if(arg.equals("Open..."))
        msg += "Open.";
```

```
          else if(arg.equals("Close"))
            msg += "Close.";
          else if(arg.equals("Quit..."))
            msg += "Quit.";
          else if(arg.equals("Edit"))
            msg += "Edit.";
          else if(arg.equals("Cut"))
            msg += "Cut.";
          else if(arg.equals("Copy"))
            msg += "Copy.";
          else if(arg.equals("Paste"))
            msg += "Paste.";
          else if(arg.equals("First"))
            msg += "First.";
          else if(arg.equals("Second"))
            msg += "Second.";
          else if(arg.equals("Third"))
            msg += "Third.";
          else if(arg.equals("Debug"))
            msg += "Debug.";
          else if(arg.equals("Testing"))
            msg += "Testing.";
        menuFrame.msg = msg;
        menuFrame.repaint();
      }
      // Handle item events.
      public void itemStateChanged(ItemEvent ie) {
        menuFrame.repaint();
      }
    }

    // Create frame window.
    public class MenuDemo extends Applet {
      Frame f;

      public void init() {
        f = new MenuFrame("Menu Demo");
        int width = Integer.parseInt(getParameter("width"));
        int height = Integer.parseInt(getParameter("height"));

        setSize(new Dimension(width, height));

        f.setSize(width, height);
        f.setVisible(true);
      }

      public void start() {
        f.setVisible(true);
      }

      public void stop() {
        f.setVisible(false);
      }
    }
```

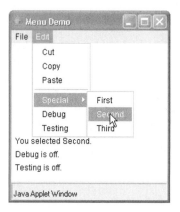

FIGURE 24-8   Sample output from the **MenuDemo** applet

Sample output from the **MenuDemo** applet is shown in Figure 24-8.

There is one other menu-related class that you might find interesting: **PopupMenu**. It works just like **Menu**, but produces a menu that can be displayed at a specific location. **PopupMenu** provides a flexible, useful alternative for some types of menuing situations.

Dialog Boxes

Often, you will want to use a *dialog box* to hold a set of related controls. Dialog boxes are primarily used to obtain user input and are often child windows of a top-level window. Dialog boxes don't have menu bars, but in other respects, they function like frame windows. (You can add controls to them, for example, in the same way that you add controls to a frame window.) Dialog boxes may be modal or modeless. When a *modal* dialog box is active, all input is directed to it until it is closed. This means that you cannot access other parts of your program until you have closed the dialog box. When a *modeless* dialog box is active, input focus can be directed to another window in your program. Thus, other parts of your program remain active and accessible. Dialog boxes are of type **Dialog**. Two commonly used constructors are shown here:

Dialog(Frame *parentWindow*, boolean *mode*)
Dialog(Frame *parentWindow*, String *title*, boolean *mode*)

Here, *parentWindow* is the owner of the dialog box. If *mode* is **true**, the dialog box is modal. Otherwise, it is modeless. The title of the dialog box can be passed in *title*. Generally, you will subclass **Dialog**, adding the functionality required by your application.

Following is a modified version of the preceding menu program that displays a modeless dialog box when the New option is chosen. Notice that when the dialog box is closed, **dispose( )** is called. This method is defined by **Window**, and it frees all system resources associated with the dialog box window.

```
// Demonstrate Dialog box.
import java.awt.*;
import java.awt.event.*;
```

```
import java.applet.*;
/*
  <applet code="DialogDemo" width=250 height=250>
  </applet>
*/

// Create a subclass of Dialog.
class SampleDialog extends Dialog implements ActionListener {
  SampleDialog(Frame parent, String title) {
    super(parent, title, false);
    setLayout(new FlowLayout());
    setSize(300, 200);

    add(new Label("Press this button:"));
    Button b;
    add(b = new Button("Cancel"));
    b.addActionListener(this);
  }

  public void actionPerformed(ActionEvent ae) {
     dispose();
  }

  public void paint(Graphics g) {
    g.drawString("This is in the dialog box", 10, 70);
  }
}

// Create a subclass of Frame.
class MenuFrame extends Frame {
  String msg = "";
  CheckboxMenuItem debug, test;

  MenuFrame(String title) {
    super(title);

    // create menu bar and add it to frame
    MenuBar mbar = new MenuBar();
    setMenuBar(mbar);

    // create the menu items
    Menu file = new Menu("File");
    MenuItem item1, item2, item3, item4;
    file.add(item1 = new MenuItem("New..."));
    file.add(item2 = new MenuItem("Open..."));
    file.add(item3 = new MenuItem("Close"));
    file.add(new MenuItem("-"));
    file.add(item4 = new MenuItem("Quit..."));
    mbar.add(file);

    Menu edit = new Menu("Edit");
    MenuItem item5, item6, item7;
    edit.add(item5 = new MenuItem("Cut"));
    edit.add(item6 = new MenuItem("Copy"));
```

```
      edit.add(item7 = new MenuItem("Paste"));
      edit.add(new MenuItem("-"));

      Menu sub = new Menu("Special", true);
      MenuItem item8, item9, item10;
      sub.add(item8 = new MenuItem("First"));
      sub.add(item9 = new MenuItem("Second"));
      sub.add(item10 = new MenuItem("Third"));
      edit.add(sub);

      // these are checkable menu items
      debug = new CheckboxMenuItem("Debug");
      edit.add(debug);
      test = new CheckboxMenuItem("Testing");
      edit.add(test);

      mbar.add(edit);

      // create an object to handle action and item events
      MyMenuHandler handler = new MyMenuHandler(this);
      // register it to receive those events
      item1.addActionListener(handler);
      item2.addActionListener(handler);
      item3.addActionListener(handler);
      item4.addActionListener(handler);
      item5.addActionListener(handler);
      item6.addActionListener(handler);
      item7.addActionListener(handler);
      item8.addActionListener(handler);
      item9.addActionListener(handler);
      item10.addActionListener(handler);
      debug.addItemListener(handler);
      test.addItemListener(handler);

      // create an object to handle window events
      MyWindowAdapter adapter = new MyWindowAdapter(this);
       // register it to receive those events
      addWindowListener(adapter);
    }
  public void paint(Graphics g) {
    g.drawString(msg, 10, 200);

    if(debug.getState())
      g.drawString("Debug is on.", 10, 220);
    else
      g.drawString("Debug is off.", 10, 220);

    if(test.getState())
      g.drawString("Testing is on.", 10, 240);
    else
      g.drawString("Testing is off.", 10, 240);
  }
}
```

```
class MyWindowAdapter extends WindowAdapter {
  MenuFrame menuFrame;
  public MyWindowAdapter(MenuFrame menuFrame) {
    this.menuFrame = menuFrame;
  }
  public void windowClosing(WindowEvent we) {
    menuFrame.dispose();
  }
}

class MyMenuHandler implements ActionListener, ItemListener {
  MenuFrame menuFrame;
  public MyMenuHandler(MenuFrame menuFrame) {
    this.menuFrame = menuFrame;
  }
  // Handle action events.
  public void actionPerformed(ActionEvent ae) {
      String msg = "You selected ";
      String arg = ae.getActionCommand();
     // Activate a dialog box when New is selected.
     if(arg.equals("New...")) {
        msg += "New.";
        SampleDialog d = new
          SampleDialog(menuFrame, "New Dialog Box");
        d.setVisible(true);
     }
     // Try defining other dialog boxes for these options.
     else if(arg.equals("Open..."))
       msg += "Open.";
     else if(arg.equals("Close"))
       msg += "Close.";
     else if(arg.equals("Quit..."))
       msg += "Quit.";
     else if(arg.equals("Edit"))
       msg += "Edit.";
     else if(arg.equals("Cut"))
       msg += "Cut.";
     else if(arg.equals("Copy"))
       msg += "Copy.";
     else if(arg.equals("Paste"))
       msg += "Paste.";
     else if(arg.equals("First"))
       msg += "First.";
     else if(arg.equals("Second"))
       msg += "Second.";
     else if(arg.equals("Third"))
       msg += "Third.";
     else if(arg.equals("Debug"))
       msg += "Debug.";
     else if(arg.equals("Testing"))
       msg += "Testing.";
     menuFrame.msg = msg;
     menuFrame.repaint();
  }
```

PART II

```
    public void itemStateChanged(ItemEvent ie) {
        menuFrame.repaint();
    }
}

// Create frame window.
public class DialogDemo extends Applet {
  Frame f;

  public void init() {
    f = new MenuFrame("Menu Demo");
    int width = Integer.parseInt(getParameter("width"));
    int height = Integer.parseInt(getParameter("height"));

    setSize(width, height);

    f.setSize(width, height);
    f.setVisible(true);
  }

  public void start() {
    f.setVisible(true);
  }

  public void stop() {
    f.setVisible(false);
  }
}
```

Here is sample output from the **DialogDemo** applet:

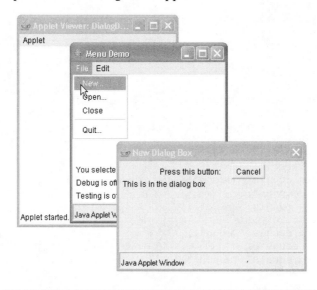

TIP *On your own, try defining dialog boxes for the other options presented by the menus.*

FileDialog

Java provides a built-in dialog box that lets the user specify a file. To create a file dialog box, instantiate an object of type **FileDialog**. This causes a file dialog box to be displayed. Usually, this is the standard file dialog box provided by the operating system. Here are three **FileDialog** constructors:

FileDialog(Frame *parent*)
FileDialog(Frame *parent*, String *boxName*)
FileDialog(Frame *parent*, String *boxName*, int *how*)

Here, *parent* is the owner of the dialog box. The *boxName* parameter specifies the name displayed in the box's title bar. If *boxName* is omitted, the title of the dialog box is empty. If *how* is **FileDialog.LOAD**, then the box is selecting a file for reading. If *how* is **FileDialog.SAVE**, the box is selecting a file for writing. If *how* is omitted, the box is selecting a file for reading.

FileDialog provides methods that allow you to determine the name of the file and its path as selected by the user. Here are two examples:

String getDirectory( )
String getFile( )

These methods return the directory and the filename, respectively.

The following program activates the standard file dialog box:

```
/* Demonstrate File Dialog box.

   This is an application, not an applet.
*/
import java.awt.*;
import java.awt.event.*;

// Create a subclass of Frame.
class SampleFrame extends Frame {
  SampleFrame(String title) {
    super(title);

    // remove the window when closed
    addWindowListener(new WindowAdapter() {
      public void windowClosing(WindowEvent we) {
        System.exit(0);
      }
    });

  }
}

// Demonstrate FileDialog.
class FileDialogDemo {
  public static void main(String args[]) {
    // create a frame that owns the dialog
    Frame f = new SampleFrame("File Dialog Demo");
    f.setVisible(true);
```

```
    f.setSize(100, 100);

    FileDialog fd = new FileDialog(f, "File Dialog");

    fd.setVisible(true);
  }
}
```

The output generated by this program is shown here. (The precise configuration of the
dialog box may vary.)

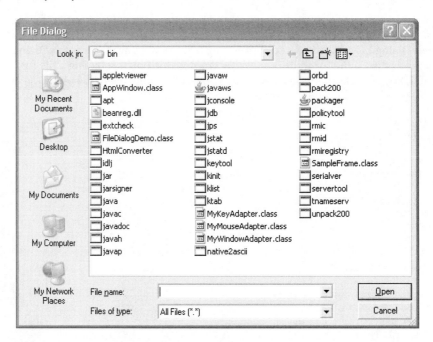

Handling Events by Extending AWT Components

Before concluding our look at the AWT, one more topic needs to be discussed: handling
events by extending AWT components. The delegation event model was introduced in
Chapter 22, and all of the programs in this book so far have used that design. But Java also
allows you to handle events by subclassing AWT components. Doing so allows you to
handle events in much the same way as they were handled under the original 1.0 version of
Java. Of course, this technique is discouraged, because it has the same disadvantages of the
Java 1.0 event model, the main one being inefficiency. Handling events by extending AWT
components is described in this section for completeness. However, this technique is not
used in any other sections of this book.

When extending an AWT component, you must call the **enableEvents( )** method of
Component. Its general form is shown here:

protected final void enableEvents(long *eventMask*)

The *eventMask* argument is a bit mask that defines the events to be delivered to this component. The **AWTEvent** class defines **int** constants for making this mask. Several are shown here:

ACTION_EVENT_MASK	KEY_EVENT_MASK
ADJUSTMENT_EVENT_MASK	MOUSE_EVENT_MASK
COMPONENT_EVENT_MASK	MOUSE_MOTION_EVENT_MASK
CONTAINER_EVENT_MASK	MOUSE_WHEEL_EVENT_MASK
FOCUS_EVENT_MASK	TEXT_EVENT_MASK
INPUT_METHOD_EVENT_MASK	WINDOW_EVENT_MASK
ITEM_EVENT_MASK	

You must also override the appropriate method from one of your superclasses in order to process the event. Table 24-2 lists the methods most commonly used and the classes that provide them.

The following sections provide simple programs that show how to extend several AWT components.

Extending Button

The following program creates an applet that displays a button labeled "Test Button". When the button is pressed, the string "action event: " is displayed on the status line of the applet viewer or browser, followed by a count of the number of button presses.

The program has one top-level class named **ButtonDemo2** that extends **Applet**. A static integer variable named **i** is defined and initialized to zero. This records the number of button pushes. The **init( )** method instantiates **MyButton** and adds it to the applet.

Class	Processing Methods
Button	processActionEvent( )
Checkbox	processItemEvent( )
CheckboxMenuItem	processItemEvent( )
Choice	processItemEvent( )
Component	processComponentEvent( ), processFocusEvent( ), processKeyEvent( ), processMouseEvent( ), processMouseMotionEvent( ), processMouseWheelEvent( )
List	processActionEvent( ), processItemEvent( )
MenuItem	processActionEvent( )
Scrollbar	processAdjustmentEvent( )
TextComponent	processTextEvent( )

TABLE 24-2   Commonly Used Event Processing Methods

MyButton is an inner class that extends **Button**. Its constructor uses **super** to pass the label of the button to the superclass constructor. It calls **enableEvents( )** so that action events may be received by this object. When an action event is generated, **processActionEvent( )** is called. That method displays a string on the status line and calls **processActionEvent( )** for the superclass. Because **MyButton** is an inner class, it has direct access to the **showStatus( )** method of **ButtonDemo2**.

```
/*
* <applet code=ButtonDemo2 width=200 height=100>
* </applet>
*/
import java.awt.*;
import java.awt.event.*;
import java.applet.*;

public class ButtonDemo2 extends Applet {
  MyButton myButton;
  static int i = 0;
  public void init() {
    myButton = new MyButton("Test Button");
    add(myButton);
  }
  class MyButton extends Button {
    public MyButton(String label) {
      super(label);
      enableEvents(AWTEvent.ACTION_EVENT_MASK);
    }
    protected void processActionEvent(ActionEvent ae) {
      showStatus("action event: " + i++);
      super.processActionEvent(ae);
    }
  }
}
```

Extending Checkbox

The following program creates an applet that displays three check boxes labeled "Item 1", "Item 2", and "Item 3". When a check box is selected or deselected, a string containing the name and state of that check box is displayed on the status line of the applet viewer or browser.

The program has one top-level class named **CheckboxDemo2** that extends **Applet**. Its **init( )** method creates three instances of **MyCheckbox** and adds these to the applet. **MyCheckbox** is an inner class that extends **Checkbox**. Its constructor uses **super** to pass the label of the check box to the superclass constructor. It calls **enableEvents( )** so that item events may be received by this object. When an item event is generated, **processItemEvent( )** is called. That method displays a string on the status line and calls **processItemEvent( )** for the superclass.

```
/*
* <applet code=CheckboxDemo2 width=300 height=100>
* </applet>
*/
import java.awt.*;
```

```
import java.awt.event.*;
import java.applet.*;

public class CheckboxDemo2 extends Applet {
  MyCheckbox myCheckbox1, myCheckbox2, myCheckbox3;
  public void init() {
    myCheckbox1 = new MyCheckbox("Item 1");
    add(myCheckbox1);
    myCheckbox2 = new MyCheckbox("Item 2");
    add(myCheckbox2);
    myCheckbox3 = new MyCheckbox("Item 3");
    add(myCheckbox3);
  }
  class MyCheckbox extends Checkbox {
    public MyCheckbox(String label) {
      super(label);
      enableEvents(AWTEvent.ITEM_EVENT_MASK);
    }
    protected void processItemEvent(ItemEvent ie) {
      showStatus("Checkbox name/state: " + getLabel() +
                 "/" + getState());
      super.processItemEvent(ie);
    }
  }
}
```

Extending a Check Box Group

The following program reworks the preceding check box example so that the check boxes
form a check box group. Thus, only one of the check boxes may be selected at any time.

```
/*
* <applet code=CheckboxGroupDemo2 width=300 height=100>
* </applet>
*/
import java.awt.*;
import java.awt.event.*;
import java.applet.*;

public class CheckboxGroupDemo2 extends Applet {
  CheckboxGroup cbg;
  MyCheckbox myCheckbox1, myCheckbox2, myCheckbox3;
  public void init() {
    cbg = new CheckboxGroup();
    myCheckbox1 = new MyCheckbox("Item 1", cbg, true);
    add(myCheckbox1);
    myCheckbox2 = new MyCheckbox("Item 2", cbg, false);
    add(myCheckbox2);
    myCheckbox3 = new MyCheckbox("Item 3", cbg, false);
    add(myCheckbox3);
  }
  class MyCheckbox extends Checkbox {
    public MyCheckbox(String label, CheckboxGroup cbg,
                      boolean flag) {
      super(label, cbg, flag);
```

```
            enableEvents(AWTEvent.ITEM_EVENT_MASK);
        }
        protected void processItemEvent(ItemEvent ie) {
            showStatus("Checkbox name/state: " + getLabel() +
                    "/" + getState());
            super.processItemEvent(ie);
        }
    }
}
```

Extending Choice

The following program creates an applet that displays a choice list with items labeled "Red", "Green", and "Blue". When an entry is selected, a string that contains the name of the color is displayed on the status line of the applet viewer or browser.

There is one top-level class named **ChoiceDemo2** that extends **Applet**. Its **init( )** method creates a choice element and adds it to the applet. **MyChoice** is an inner class that extends **Choice**. It calls **enableEvents( )** so that item events may be received by this object. When an item event is generated, **processItemEvent( )** is called. That method displays a string on the status line and calls **processItemEvent( )** for the superclass.

```
/*
 * <applet code=ChoiceDemo2 width=300 height=100>
 * </applet>
 */
import java.awt.*;
import java.awt.event.*;
import java.applet.*;

public class ChoiceDemo2 extends Applet {
    MyChoice choice;
    public void init() {
        choice = new MyChoice();
        choice.add("Red");
        choice.add("Green");
        choice.add("Blue");
        add(choice);
    }
    class MyChoice extends Choice {
        public MyChoice() {
            enableEvents(AWTEvent.ITEM_EVENT_MASK);
        }
        protected void processItemEvent(ItemEvent ie) {
            showStatus("Choice selection: " + getSelectedItem());
            super.processItemEvent(ie);
        }
    }
}
```

Extending List

The following program modifies the preceding example so that it uses a list instead of a choice menu. There is one top-level class named **ListDemo2** that extends **Applet**. Its **init( )** method creates a list element and adds it to the applet. **MyList** is an inner class that extends

List. It calls **enableEvents( )** so that both action and item events may be received by this object. When an entry is selected or deselected, **processItemEvent( )** is called. When an entry is double-clicked, **processActionEvent( )** is also called. Both methods display a string and then hand control to the superclass.

```
/*
 * <applet code=ListDemo2 width=300 height=100>
 * </applet>
*/
import java.awt.*;
import java.awt.event.*;
import java.applet.*;

public class ListDemo2 extends Applet {
  MyList list;
  public void init() {
    list = new MyList();
    list.add("Red");
    list.add("Green");
    list.add("Blue");
    add(list);
  }
  class MyList extends List {
    public MyList() {
      enableEvents(AWTEvent.ITEM_EVENT_MASK |
                   AWTEvent.ACTION_EVENT_MASK);
    }
    protected void processActionEvent(ActionEvent ae) {
      showStatus("Action event: " + ae.getActionCommand());
      super.processActionEvent(ae);
    }
    protected void processItemEvent(ItemEvent ie) {
      showStatus("Item event: " + getSelectedItem());
      super.processItemEvent(ie);
    }
  }
}
```

Extending Scrollbar

The following program creates an applet that displays a scroll bar. When this control is manipulated, a string is displayed on the status line of the applet viewer or browser. That string includes the value represented by the scroll bar.

There is one top-level class named **ScrollbarDemo2** that extends **Applet**. Its **init( )** method creates a scroll bar element and adds it to the applet. **MyScrollbar** is an inner class that extends **Scrollbar**. It calls **enableEvents( )** so that adjustment events may be received by this object. When the scroll bar is manipulated, **processAdjustmentEvent( )** is called. When an entry is selected, **processAdjustmentEvent( )** is called. It displays a string and then hands control to the superclass.

```
/*
 * <applet code=ScrollbarDemo2 width=300 height=100>
 * </applet>
```

```
*/
import java.awt.*;
import java.awt.event.*;
import java.applet.*;

public class ScrollbarDemo2 extends Applet {
  MyScrollbar myScrollbar;
  public void init() {
    myScrollbar = new MyScrollbar(Scrollbar.HORIZONTAL,
                                  0, 1, 0, 100);
    add(myScrollbar);
  }
  class MyScrollbar extends Scrollbar {
    public MyScrollbar(int style, int initial, int thumb,
                       int min, int max) {
      super(style, initial, thumb, min, max);
      enableEvents(AWTEvent.ADJUSTMENT_EVENT_MASK);
    }
    protected void processAdjustmentEvent(AdjustmentEvent ae) {
      showStatus("Adjustment event: " + ae.getValue());
      setValue(getValue());
      super.processAdjustmentEvent(ae);
    }
  }
}
```

Images

This chapter examines the AWT's **Image** class and the **java.awt.image** package. Together, they provide support for *imaging* (the display and manipulation of graphical images). An *image* is simply a rectangular graphical object. Images are a key component of web design. In fact, the inclusion of the **<img>** tag in the Mosaic browser at NCSA (National Center for Supercomputer Applications) is what caused the Web to begin to grow explosively in 1993. This tag was used to include an image *inline* with the flow of hypertext. Java expands upon this basic concept, allowing images to be managed under program control. Because of its importance, Java provides extensive support for imaging.

Images are objects of the **Image** class, which is part of the **java.awt** package. Images are manipulated using the classes found in the **java.awt.image** package. There are a large number of imaging classes and interfaces defined by **java.awt.image**, and it is not possible to examine them all. Instead, we will focus on those that form the foundation of imaging. Here are the **java.awt.image** classes discussed in this chapter:

CropImageFilter	MemoryImageSource
FilteredImageSource	PixelGrabber
ImageFilter	RGBImageFilter

These are the interfaces that we will use:

ImageConsumer	ImageObserver	ImageProducer

Also examined is the **MediaTracker** class, which is part of **java.awt**.

File Formats

Originally, web images could only be in GIF format. The GIF image format was created by CompuServe in 1987 to make it possible for images to be viewed while online, so it was well suited to the Internet. GIF images can have only up to 256 colors each. This limitation caused the major browser vendors to add support for JPEG images in 1995. The JPEG format was created by a group of photographic experts to store full-color-spectrum, continuous-tone images. These images, when properly created, can be of much higher fidelity as well as more highly compressed than a GIF encoding of the same source image. Another file format is PNG. It too is an alternative to GIF. In almost all cases, you will never care or notice which format is being used in your programs. The Java image classes abstract the differences behind a clean interface.

Image Fundamentals: Creating, Loading, and Displaying

There are three common operations that occur when you work with images: creating an image, loading an image, and displaying an image. In Java, the **Image** class is used to refer to images in memory and to images that must be loaded from external sources. Thus, Java provides ways for you to create a new image object and ways to load one. It also provides a means by which an image can be displayed. Let's look at each.

Creating an Image Object

You might expect that you create a memory image using something like the following:

```
Image test = new Image(200, 100); // Error -- won't work
```

Not so. Because images must eventually be painted on a window to be seen, the **Image** class doesn't have enough information about its environment to create the proper data format for the screen. Therefore, the **Component** class in **java.awt** has a factory method called **createImage( )** that is used to create **Image** objects. (Remember that all of the AWT components are subclasses of **Component**, so all support this method.)

The **createImage( )** method has the following two forms:

Image createImage(ImageProducer *imgProd*)
Image createImage(int *width*, int *height*)

The first form returns an image produced by *imgProd*, which is an object of a class that implements the **ImageProducer** interface. (We will look at image producers later.) The second form returns a blank (that is, empty) image that has the specified width and height. Here is an example:

```
Canvas c = new Canvas();
Image test = c.createImage(200, 100);
```

This creates an instance of **Canvas** and then calls the **createImage( )** method to actually make an **Image** object. At this point, the image is blank. Later you will see how to write data to it.

Loading an Image

The other way to obtain an image is to load one. One way to do this is to use the **getImage( )** method defined by the **Applet** class. It has the following forms:

Image getImage(URL *url*)
Image getImage(URL *url*, String *imageName*)

The first version returns an **Image** object that encapsulates the image found at the location specified by *url*. The second version returns an **Image** object that encapsulates the image found at the location specified by *url* and having the name specified by *imageName*.

Displaying an Image

Once you have an image, you can display it by using **drawImage( )**, which is a member of the **Graphics** class. It has several forms. The one we will be using is shown here:

   boolean drawImage(Image *imgObj*, int *left*, int *top*, ImageObserver *imgOb*)

This displays the image passed in *imgObj* with its upper-left corner specified by *left* and *top*. *imgOb* is a reference to a class that implements the **ImageObserver** interface. This interface is implemented by all AWT components. An *image observer* is an object that can monitor an image while it loads. **ImageObserver** is described in the next section.

   With **getImage( )** and **drawImage( )**, it is actually quite easy to load and display an image. Here is a sample applet that loads and displays a single image. The file **seattle.jpg** is loaded, but you can substitute any GIF, JPG, or PNG file you like (just make sure it is available in the same directory with the HTML file that contains the applet).

```
/*
 * <applet code="SimpleImageLoad" width=248 height=146>
 *   <param name="img" value="seattle.jpg">
 * </applet>
 */
import java.awt.*;
import java.applet.*;

public class SimpleImageLoad extends Applet
{
  Image img;

  public void init() {
    img = getImage(getDocumentBase(), getParameter("img"));
  }

  public void paint(Graphics g) {
    g.drawImage(img, 0, 0, this);
  }
}
```

   In the **init( )** method, the **img** variable is assigned to the image returned by **getImage( )**. The **getImage( )** method uses the string returned by **getParameter("img")** as the filename for the image. This image is loaded from a **URL** that is relative to the result of **getDocumentBase( )**, which is the **URL** of the HTML page this applet tag was in. The filename returned by **getParameter("img")** comes from the applet tag **<param name= "img" value="seattle.jpg">**. This is the equivalent, if a little slower, of using the HTML tag **<img src="seattle.jpg" width=248 height=146>**. Figure 25-1 shows what it looks like when you run the program.

FIGURE 25-1
Sample
output from
SimpleImageLoad

When this applet runs, it starts loading **img** in the **init( )** method. Onscreen you can see the image as it loads from the network, because **Applet**'s implementation of the **ImageObserver** interface calls **paint( )** every time more image data arrives.

Seeing the image load is somewhat informative, but it might be better if you use the time it takes to load the image to do other things in parallel. That way, the fully formed image can simply appear on the screen in an instant, once it is fully loaded. You can use **ImageObserver**, described next, to monitor loading an image while you paint the screen with other information.

ImageObserver

ImageObserver is an interface used to receive notification as an image is being generated, and it defines only one method: **imageUpdate( )**. Using an image observer allows you to perform other actions, such as show a progress indicator or an attract screen, as you are informed of the progress of the download. This kind of notification is very useful when an image is being loaded over the network, where the content designer rarely appreciates that people are often trying to load applets over a slow modem.

The **imageUpdate( )** method has this general form:

boolean imageUpdate(Image *imgObj*, int *flags*, int *left*, int *top*, int *width*, int *height*)

Here, *imgObj* is the image being loaded, and *flags* is an integer that communicates the status of the update report. The four integers *left, top, width,* and *height* represent a rectangle that contains different values depending on the values passed in *flags*. **imageUpdate( )** should return **false** if it has completed loading, and **true** if there is more image to process.

The *flags* parameter contains one or more bit flags defined as static variables inside the **ImageObserver** interface. These flags and the information they provide are listed in Table 25-1.

The **Applet** class has an implementation of the **imageUpdate( )** method for the **ImageObserver** interface that is used to repaint images as they are loaded. You can override this method in your class to change that behavior.

Flag	Meaning
WIDTH	The *width* parameter is valid and contains the width of the image.
HEIGHT	The *height* parameter is valid and contains the height of the image.
PROPERTIES	The properties associated with the image can now be obtained using **imgObj.getProperty( )**.
SOMEBITS	More pixels needed to draw the image have been received. The parameters *left, top, width,* and *height* define the rectangle containing the new pixels.
FRAMEBITS	A complete frame that is part of a multiframe image, which was previously drawn, has been received. This frame can be displayed. The *left, top, width,* and *height* parameters are not used.
ALLBITS	The image is now complete. The *left, top, width,* and *height* parameters are not used.
ERROR	An error has occurred to an image that was being tracked asynchronously. The image is incomplete and cannot be displayed. No further image information will be received. The **ABORT** flag will also be set to indicate that the image production was aborted.
ABORT	An image that was being tracked asynchronously was aborted before it was complete. However, if an error has not occurred, accessing any part of the image's data will restart the production of the image.

TABLE 25-1   Bit Flags of the **imageUpdate( )** *flags* Parameter

Here is a simple example of an **imageUpdate( )** method:

```
public boolean imageUpdate(Image img, int flags,
                           int x, int y, int w, int h) {
  if ((flags & ALLBITS) == 0) {
    System.out.println("Still processing the image.");
    return true;
  } else {
    System.out.println("Done processing the image.");
    return false;
  }
}
```

Double Buffering

Not only are images useful for storing pictures, as we've just shown, but you can also use them as offscreen drawing surfaces. This allows you to render any image, including text and graphics, to an offscreen buffer that you can display at a later time. The advantage to doing this is that the image is seen only when it is complete. Drawing a complicated image could take several milliseconds or more, which can be seen by the user as flashing or flickering.

This flashing is distracting and causes the user to perceive your rendering as slower than it actually is. Use of an offscreen image to reduce flicker is called *double buffering,* because the screen is considered a buffer for pixels, and the offscreen image is the second buffer, where you can prepare pixels for display.

Earlier in this chapter, you saw how to create a blank **Image** object. Now you will see how to draw on that image rather than the screen. As you recall from earlier chapters, you need a **Graphics** object in order to use any of Java's rendering methods. Conveniently, the **Graphics** object that you can use to draw on an **Image** is available via the **getGraphics( )** method. Here is a code fragment that creates a new image, obtains its graphics context, and fills the entire image with red pixels:

```
Canvas c = new Canvas();
Image test = c.createImage(200, 100);
Graphics gc = test.getGraphics();
gc.setColor(Color.red);
gc.fillRect(0, 0, 200, 100);
```

Once you have constructed and filled an offscreen image, it will still not be visible. To actually display the image, call **drawImage( )**. Here is an example that draws a time-consuming image, to demonstrate the difference that double buffering can make in perceived drawing time:

```
/*
 * <applet code=DoubleBuffer width=250 height=250>
 * </applet>
 */
import java.awt.*;
import java.awt.event.*;
import java.applet.*;

public class DoubleBuffer extends Applet {
  int gap = 3;
  int mx, my;
  boolean flicker = true;
  Image buffer = null;
  int w, h;

  public void init() {
    Dimension d = getSize();
    w = d.width;
    h = d.height;
    buffer = createImage(w, h);
    addMouseMotionListener(new MouseMotionAdapter() {
      public void mouseDragged(MouseEvent me) {
        mx = me.getX();
        my = me.getY();
        flicker = false;
        repaint();
      }
      public void mouseMoved(MouseEvent me) {
        mx = me.getX();
        my = me.getY();
```

```
          flicker = true;
          repaint();
        }
    });
  }

  public void paint(Graphics g) {
    Graphics screengc = null;

    if (!flicker) {
      screengc = g;
      g = buffer.getGraphics();
    }

    g.setColor(Color.blue);
    g.fillRect(0, 0, w, h);

    g.setColor(Color.red);
    for (int i=0; i<w; i+=gap)
      g.drawLine(i, 0, w-i, h);
    for (int i=0; i<h; i+=gap)
      g.drawLine(0, i, w, h-i);

    g.setColor(Color.black);
    g.drawString("Press mouse button to double buffer", 10, h/2);

    g.setColor(Color.yellow);
    g.fillOval(mx - gap, my - gap, gap*2+1, gap*2+1);

    if (!flicker) {
      screengc.drawImage(buffer, 0, 0, null);
    }
  }
  public void update(Graphics g) {
    paint(g);
  }
}
```

This simple applet has a complicated **paint( )** method. It fills the background with blue
and then draws a red moiré pattern on top of that. It paints some black text on top of that and
then paints a yellow circle centered at the coordinates **mx,my**. The **mouseMoved( )** and
mouseDragged( ) methods are overridden to track the mouse position. These methods are
identical, except for the setting of the **flicker** Boolean variable. **mouseMoved( )** sets **flicker**
to **true**, and **mouseDragged( )** sets it to **false**. This has the effect of calling **repaint( )** with
flicker set to **true** when the mouse is moved (but no button is pressed) and set to **false** when
the mouse is dragged with any button pressed.

When **paint( )** gets called with **flicker** set to **true**, we see each drawing operation as it
is executed on the screen. In the case where a mouse button is pressed and **paint( )** is called
with **flicker** set to **false**, we see quite a different picture. The **paint( )** method swaps the
Graphics reference **g** with the graphics context that refers to the offscreen canvas, **buffer**,
which we created in **init( )**. Then all of the drawing operations are invisible. At the end of
paint( ), we simply call **drawImage( )** to show the results of these drawing methods all at once.

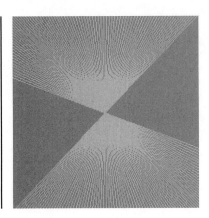

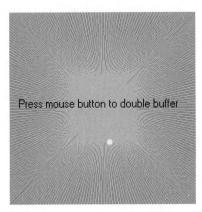

FIGURE 25-2
Output from
DoubleBuffer
without (left) and
with (right) double
buffering

Notice that it is okay to pass in a **null** as the fourth parameter to **drawImage( )**. This is the parameter used to pass an **ImageObserver** object that receives notification of image events. Since this is an image that is not being produced from a network stream, we have no need for notification. The left snapshot in Figure 25-2 is what the applet looks like with the mouse button not pressed. As you can see, the image was in the middle of repainting when this snapshot was taken. The right snapshot shows how, when a mouse button is pressed, the image is always complete and clean due to double buffering.

MediaTracker

Many early Java developers found the **ImageObserver** interface far too difficult to understand and manage when there were multiple images to be loaded. The developer community asked for a simpler solution that would allow programmers to load all of their images synchronously, without having to worry about **imageUpdate( )**. In response to this, Sun Microsystems added a class to **java.awt** called **MediaTracker** in a subsequent release of the JDK. A **MediaTracker** is an object that will check the status of an arbitrary number of images in parallel.

To use **MediaTracker**, you create a new instance and use its **addImage( )** method to track the loading status of an image. **addImage( )** has the following general forms:

    void addImage(Image *imgObj*, int *imgID*)
    void addImage(Image *imgObj*, int *imgID*, int *width*, int *height*)

Here, *imgObj* is the image being tracked. Its identification number is passed in *imgID*. ID numbers do not need to be unique. You can use the same number with several images as a means of identifying them as part of a group. In the second form, *width* and *height* specify the dimensions of the object when it is displayed.

Once you've registered an image, you can check whether it's loaded, or you can wait for it to completely load. To check the status of an image, call **checkID( )**. The version used in this chapter is shown here:

    boolean checkID(int *imgID*)

Here, *imgID* specifies the ID of the image you want to check. The method returns **true** if all images that have the specified ID have been loaded (or if an error or user-abort has terminated loading). Otherwise, it returns **false**. You can use the **checkAll( )** method to see if all images being tracked have been loaded.

You should use **MediaTracker** when loading a group of images. If all of the images that you're interested in aren't downloaded, you can display something else to entertain the user until they all arrive.

CAUTION   *If you use **MediaTracker** once you've called **addImage( )** on an image, a reference in **MediaTracker** will prevent the system from garbage collecting it. If you want the system to be able to garbage collect images that were being tracked, make sure it can collect the **MediaTracker** instance as well.*

Here's an example that loads a seven-image slide show and displays a nice bar chart of the loading progress:

```
/*
 * <applet code="TrackedImageLoad" width=300 height=400>
 * <param name="img"
 * value="vincent+leonardo+matisse+picasso+renoir+seurat+vermeer">
 * </applet>
 */
import java.util.*;
import java.applet.*;
import java.awt.*;

public class TrackedImageLoad extends Applet implements Runnable {
  MediaTracker tracker;
  int tracked;
  int frame_rate = 5;
  int current_img = 0;
  Thread motor;
  static final int MAXIMAGES = 10;
  Image img[] = new Image[MAXIMAGES];
  String name[] = new String[MAXIMAGES];
  boolean stopFlag;

  public void init() {
    tracker = new MediaTracker(this);
    StringTokenizer st = new StringTokenizer(getParameter("img"),
                                             "+");

    while(st.hasMoreTokens() && tracked <= MAXIMAGES) {
      name[tracked] = st.nextToken();
      img[tracked] = getImage(getDocumentBase(),
                              name[tracked] + ".jpg");
      tracker.addImage(img[tracked], tracked);
      tracked++;
    }
  }

  public void paint(Graphics g) {
    String loaded = "";
    int donecount = 0;

    for(int i=0; i<tracked; i++) {
```

```java
        if (tracker.checkID(i, true)) {
          donecount++;
          loaded += name[i] + " ";
        }
      }

    Dimension d = getSize();
    int w = d.width;
    int h = d.height;

    if (donecount == tracked) {
      frame_rate = 1;
      Image i = img[current_img++];
      int iw = i.getWidth(null);
      int ih = i.getHeight(null);
      g.drawImage(i, (w - iw)/2, (h - ih)/2, null);
      if (current_img >= tracked)
        current_img = 0;
    } else {
      int x = w * donecount / tracked;
      g.setColor(Color.black);
      g.fillRect(0, h/3, x, 16);
      g.setColor(Color.white);
      g.fillRect(x, h/3, w-x, 16);
      g.setColor(Color.black);
      g.drawString(loaded, 10, h/2);
    }
  }

  public void start() {
    motor = new Thread(this);
    stopFlag = false;
    motor.start();
  }

  public void stop() {
    stopFlag = true;
  }

  public void run() {
    motor.setPriority(Thread.MIN_PRIORITY);
    while (true) {
      repaint();
      try {
        Thread.sleep(1000/frame_rate);
      } catch (InterruptedException e) {
        System.out.println("Interrupted");
        return;
      }
      if(stopFlag)
        return;
    }
  }
}
```

FIGURE 25-3
Sample
output from
TrackedImageLoad

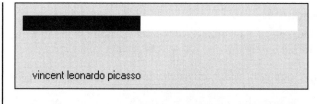

This example creates a new **MediaTracker** in the **init( )** method and then adds each of the named images as a tracked image with **addImage( )**. In the **paint( )** method, it calls **checkID( )** on each of the images that we're tracking. If all of the images are loaded, they are displayed. If not, a simple bar chart of the number of images loaded is shown, with the names of the fully loaded images displayed underneath the bar. Figure 25-3 shows two scenes from this applet running. One is the bar chart, displaying that three of the images have been loaded. The other is the Van Gogh self-portrait during the slide show.

ImageProducer

ImageProducer is an interface for objects that want to produce data for images. An object that implements the **ImageProducer** interface will supply integer or byte arrays that represent image data and produce **Image** objects. As you saw earlier, one form of the **createImage( )** method takes an **ImageProducer** object as its argument. There are two image producers contained in **java.awt.image**: **MemoryImageSource** and **FilteredImageSource**. Here, we will examine **MemoryImageSource** and create a new **Image** object from data generated in an applet.

MemoryImageSource

MemoryImageSource is a class that creates a new **Image** from an array of data. It defines several constructors. Here is the one we will be using:

   MemoryImageSource(int *width*, int *height*, int *pixel*[ ], int *offset*, int *scanLineWidth*)

The **MemoryImageSource** object is constructed out of the array of integers specified by *pixel*, in the default RGB color model to produce data for an **Image** object. In the default color model, a pixel is an integer with Alpha, Red, Green, and Blue (0xAARRGGBB). The Alpha value represents a degree of transparency for the pixel. Fully transparent is 0 and fully opaque is 255. The width and height of the resulting image are passed in *width* and *height.* The starting point in the pixel array to begin reading data is passed in *offset.* The width of a scan line (which is often the same as the width of the image) is passed in *scanLineWidth.*

   The following short example generates a **MemoryImageSource** object using a variation on a simple algorithm (a bitwise-exclusive-OR of the x and y address of each pixel) from the book *Beyond Photography, The Digital Darkroom* by Gerard J. Holzmann (Prentice Hall, 1988).

```
/*
 * <applet code="MemoryImageGenerator" width=256 height=256>
 * </applet>
 */
import java.applet.*;
import java.awt.*;
import java.awt.image.*;

public class MemoryImageGenerator extends Applet {
  Image img;
  public void init() {
    Dimension d = getSize();
    int w = d.width;
    int h = d.height;
    int pixels[] = new int[w * h];
    int i = 0;

    for(int y=0; y<h; y++) {
      for(int x=0; x<w; x++) {
        int r = (x^y)&0xff;
        int g = (x*2^y*2)&0xff;
        int b = (x*4^y*4)&0xff;
        pixels[i++] = (255 << 24) | (r << 16) | (g << 8) | b;
      }
    }
    img = createImage(new MemoryImageSource(w, h, pixels, 0, w));
  }
  public void paint(Graphics g) {
    g.drawImage(img, 0, 0, this);
  }
}
```

FIGURE 25-4
Sample output from
MemoryImageGenerator

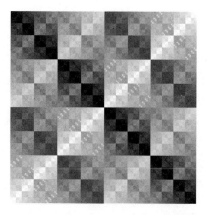

The data for the new **MemoryImageSource** is created in the **init( )** method. An array of integers is created to hold the pixel values; the data is generated in the nested **for** loops where the **r, g,** and **b** values get shifted into a pixel in the **pixels** array. Finally, **createImage( )** is called with a new instance of a **MemoryImageSource** created from the raw pixel data as its parameter. Figure 25-4 shows the image when we run the applet. (It looks much nicer in color.)

ImageConsumer

ImageConsumer is an abstract interface for objects that want to take pixel data from images and supply it as another kind of data. This, obviously, is the opposite of **ImageProducer**, described earlier. An object that implements the **ImageConsumer** interface is going to create **int** or **byte** arrays that represent pixels from an **Image** object. We will examine the **PixelGrabber** class, which is a simple implementation of the **ImageConsumer** interface.

PixelGrabber

The **PixelGrabber** class is defined within **java.lang.image**. It is the inverse of the **MemoryImageSource** class. Rather than constructing an image from an array of pixel values, it takes an existing image and *grabs* the pixel array from it. To use **PixelGrabber**, you first create an array of **int**s big enough to hold the pixel data, and then you create a **PixelGrabber** instance passing in the rectangle that you want to grab. Finally, you call **grabPixels( )** on that instance.

The **PixelGrabber** constructor that is used in this chapter is shown here:

PixelGrabber(Image *imgObj*, int *left*, int *top*, int *width*, int *height*, int *pixel*[ ],
        int *offset*, int *scanLineWidth*)

Here, *imgObj* is the object whose pixels are being grabbed. The values of *left* and *top* specify the upper-left corner of the rectangle, and *width* and *height* specify the dimensions of the rectangle from which the pixels will be obtained. The pixels will be stored in *pixel* beginning at *offset*. The width of a scan line (which is often the same as the width of the image) is passed in *scanLineWidth*.

grabPixels( ) is defined like this:

boolean grabPixels( )
  throws InterruptedException

boolean grabPixels(long *milliseconds*)
  throws InterruptedException

Both methods return **true** if successful and **false** otherwise. In the second form, *milliseconds* specifies how long the method will wait for the pixels. Both throw **InterruptedException** if execution is interrupted by another thread.

Here is an example that grabs the pixels from an image and then creates a histogram of pixel brightness. The *histogram* is simply a count of pixels that are a certain brightness for all brightness settings between 0 and 255. After the applet paints the image, it draws the histogram over the top.

```
/*
 * <applet code=HistoGrab.class width=341 height=400>
 * <param name=img value=vermeer.jpg>
 * </applet> */
import java.applet.*;
import java.awt.* ;
import java.awt.image.* ;

public class HistoGrab extends Applet {
  Dimension d;
  Image img;
  int iw, ih;
  int pixels[];
  int w, h;
  int hist[] = new int[256];
  int max_hist = 0;

  public void init() {
    d = getSize();
    w = d.width;
    h = d.height;

    try {
      img = getImage(getDocumentBase(), getParameter("img"));
      MediaTracker t = new MediaTracker(this);
      t.addImage(img, 0);
      t.waitForID(0);
      iw = img.getWidth(null);
      ih = img.getHeight(null);
      pixels = new int[iw * ih];
      PixelGrabber pg = new PixelGrabber(img, 0, 0, iw, ih,
                                         pixels, 0, iw);
      pg.grabPixels();
    } catch (InterruptedException e) {
      System.out.println("Interrupted");
      return;
    }
```

```
    for (int i=0; i<iw*ih; i++) {
      int p = pixels[i];
      int r = 0xff & (p >> 16);
      int g = 0xff & (p >> 8);
      int b = 0xff & (p);
      int y = (int) (.33 * r + .56 * g + .11 * b);
      hist[y]++;
    }
    for (int i=0; i<256; i++) {
      if (hist[i] > max_hist)
        max_hist = hist[i];
    }
  }

  public void update() {}

  public void paint(Graphics g) {
    g.drawImage(img, 0, 0, null);
    int x = (w - 256) / 2;
    int lasty = h - h * hist[0] / max_hist;
    for (int i=0; i<256; i++, x++) {
      int y = h - h * hist[i] / max_hist;
      g.setColor(new Color(i, i, i));
      g.fillRect(x, y, 1, h);
      g.setColor(Color.red);
      g.drawLine(x-1,lasty,x,y);
      lasty = y;
    }
  }
}
```

Figure 25-5 shows the image and histogram for a famous Vermeer painting.

FIGURE 25-5
Sample output
from **HistoGrab**

ImageFilter

Given the **ImageProducer** and **ImageConsumer** interface pair—and their concrete classes **MemoryImageSource** and **PixelGrabber**—you can create an arbitrary set of translation filters that takes a source of pixels, modifies them, and passes them on to an arbitrary consumer. This mechanism is analogous to the way concrete classes are created from the abstract I/O classes **InputStream**, **OutputStream**, **Reader**, and **Writer** (described in Chapter 19). This stream model for images is completed by the introduction of the **ImageFilter** class. Some subclasses of **ImageFilter** in the **java.awt.image** package are **AreaAveragingScaleFilter**, **CropImageFilter**, **ReplicateScaleFilter**, and **RGBImageFilter**. There is also an implementation of **ImageProducer** called **FilteredImageSource**, which takes an arbitrary **ImageFilter** and wraps it around an **ImageProducer** to filter the pixels it produces. An instance of **FilteredImageSource** can be used as an **ImageProducer** in calls to **createImage( )**, in much the same way that **BufferedInputStream**s can be passed off as **InputStream**s.

In this chapter, we examine two filters: **CropImageFilter** and **RGBImageFilter**.

CropImageFilter

CropImageFilter filters an image source to extract a rectangular region. One situation in which this filter is valuable is where you want to use several small images from a single, larger source image. Loading twenty 2K images takes much longer than loading a single 40K image that has many frames of an animation tiled into it. If every subimage is the same size, then you can easily extract these images by using **CropImageFilter** to disassemble the block once your applet starts. Here is an example that creates 16 images taken from a single image. The tiles are then scrambled by swapping a random pair from the 16 images 32 times.

```
/*
 * <applet code=TileImage.class width=288 height=399>
 * <param name=img value=picasso.jpg>
 * </applet>
 */
import java.applet.*;
import java.awt.*;
import java.awt.image.*;

public class TileImage extends Applet {
  Image img;
  Image cell[] = new Image[4*4];
  int iw, ih;
  int tw, th;

  public void init() {
    try {
      img = getImage(getDocumentBase(), getParameter("img"));
      MediaTracker t = new MediaTracker(this);
      t.addImage(img, 0);
      t.waitForID(0);
      iw = img.getWidth(null);
      ih = img.getHeight(null);
      tw = iw / 4;
      th = ih / 4;
      CropImageFilter f;
      FilteredImageSource fis;
```

```
      t = new MediaTracker(this);
      for (int y=0; y<4; y++) {
        for (int x=0; x<4; x++) {
          f = new CropImageFilter(tw*x, th*y, tw, th);
          fis = new FilteredImageSource(img.getSource(), f);
          int i = y*4+x;
          cell[i] = createImage(fis);
          t.addImage(cell[i], i);
        }
      }
      t.waitForAll();
      for (int i=0; i<32; i++) {
        int si = (int)(Math.random() * 16);
        int di = (int)(Math.random() * 16);
        Image tmp = cell[si];
        cell[si] = cell[di];
        cell[di] = tmp;
      }
    } catch (InterruptedException e) {
      System.out.println("Interrupted");
    }
  }

  public void update(Graphics g) {
    paint(g);
  }

  public void paint(Graphics g) {
    for (int y=0; y<4; y++) {
      for (int x=0; x<4; x++) {
        g.drawImage(cell[y*4+x], x * tw, y * th, null);
      }
    }
  }
}
```

Figure 25-6 shows a famous Picasso painting scrambled by the **TileImage** applet.

FIGURE 25-6
Sample output
from **TileImage**

RGBImageFilter

The **RGBImageFilter** is used to convert one image to another, pixel by pixel, transforming the colors along the way. This filter could be used to brighten an image, to increase its contrast, or even to convert it to grayscale.

To demonstrate **RGBImageFilter**, we have developed a somewhat complicated example that employs a dynamic plug-in strategy for image-processing filters. We've created an interface for generalized image filtering so that an applet can simply load these filters based on <param> tags without having to know about all of the **ImageFilter**s in advance. This example consists of the main applet class called **ImageFilterDemo**, the interface called **PlugInFilter**, and a utility class called **LoadedImage**, which encapsulates some of the **MediaTracker** methods we've been using in this chapter. Also included are three filters—**Grayscale**, **Invert**, and **Contrast**— which simply manipulate the color space of the source image using **RGBImageFilter**s, and two more classes—**Blur** and **Sharpen**—which do more complicated "convolution" filters that change pixel data based on the pixels surrounding each pixel of source data. **Blur** and **Sharpen** are subclasses of an abstract helper class called **Convolver**. Let's look at each part of our example.

ImageFilterDemo.java

The **ImageFilterDemo** class is the applet framework for our sample image filters. It employs a simple **BorderLayout**, with a **Panel** at the *South* position to hold the buttons that will represent each filter. A **Label** object occupies the *North* slot for informational messages about filter progress. The *Center* is where the image (which is encapsulated in the **LoadedImage Canvas** subclass, described later) is put. We parse the buttons/filters out of the **filters <param>** tag, separating them with +'s using a **StringTokenizer**.

The **actionPerformed( )** method is interesting because it uses the label from a button as the name of a filter class that it tries to load with **(PlugInFilter) Class.forName(a).newInstance( )**. This method is robust and takes appropriate action if the button does not correspond to a proper class that implements **PlugInFilter**.

```
/*
 * <applet code=ImageFilterDemo width=350 height=450>
 * <param name=img value=vincent.jpg>
 * <param name=filters value="Grayscale+Invert+Contrast+Blur+ Sharpen">
 * </applet>
 */
import java.applet.*;
import java.awt.*;
import java.awt.event.*;
import java.util.*;

public class ImageFilterDemo extends Applet implements ActionListener {
  Image img;
  PlugInFilter pif;
  Image fimg;
  Image curImg;
  LoadedImage lim;
  Label lab;
  Button reset;
```

```
public void init() {
  setLayout(new BorderLayout());
  Panel p = new Panel();
  add(p, BorderLayout.SOUTH);
  reset = new Button("Reset");
  reset.addActionListener(this);
  p.add(reset);
  StringTokenizer st = new StringTokenizer(getParameter("filters"), "+");
  while(st.hasMoreTokens()) {
    Button b = new Button(st.nextToken());
    b.addActionListener(this);
    p.add(b);
  }

  lab = new Label("");
  add(lab, BorderLayout.NORTH);

  img = getImage(getDocumentBase(), getParameter("img"));
  lim = new LoadedImage(img);
  add(lim, BorderLayout.CENTER);

}

public void actionPerformed(ActionEvent ae) {
  String a = "";

  try {
    a = ae.getActionCommand();
    if (a.equals("Reset")) {
      lim.set(img);
      lab.setText("Normal");
    }
    else {
      pif = (PlugInFilter) Class.forName(a).newInstance();
      fimg = pif.filter(this, img);
      lim.set(fimg);
      lab.setText("Filtered: " + a);
    }
    repaint();
  } catch (ClassNotFoundException e) {
    lab.setText(a + " not found");
    lim.set(img);
    repaint();
  } catch (InstantiationException e) {
    lab.setText("couldn't new " + a);
  } catch (IllegalAccessException e) {
    lab.setText("no access: " + a);
  }
}
}
```

Figure 25-7 shows what the applet looks like when it is first loaded using the applet tag shown at the top of this source file.

FIGURE 25-7
Sample normal
output from
ImageFilterDemo

FIGURE 25-7
Sample normal
output from
ImageFilterDemo

PlugInFilter.java

PlugInFilter is a simple interface used to abstract image filtering. It has only one method, **filter( )**, which takes the applet and the source image and returns a new image that has been filtered in some way.

```
interface PlugInFilter {
  java.awt.Image filter(java.applet.Applet a, java.awt.Image in);
}
```

LoadedImage.java

LoadedImage is a convenient subclass of **Canvas**, which takes an image at construction time and synchronously loads it using **MediaTracker**. **LoadedImage** then behaves properly inside of **LayoutManager** control, because it overrides the **getPreferredSize( )** and **getMinimumSize( )** methods. Also, it has a method called **set( )** that can be used to set a new **Image** to be displayed in this **Canvas**. That is how the filtered image is displayed after the plug-in is finished.

```
import java.awt.*;

public class LoadedImage extends Canvas {
  Image img;

  public LoadedImage(Image i) {
    set(i);
  }

  void set(Image i) {
    MediaTracker mt = new MediaTracker(this);
```

```
    mt.addImage(i, 0);
    try {
      mt.waitForAll();
    } catch (InterruptedException e) {
      System.out.println("Interrupted");
      return;
    }
    img = i;
    repaint();
  }

  public void paint(Graphics g) {
    if (img == null) {
      g.drawString("no image", 10, 30);
    } else {
      g.drawImage(img, 0, 0, this);
    }
  }

  public Dimension getPreferredSize()  {
    return new Dimension(img.getWidth(this), img.getHeight(this));
  }

  public Dimension getMinimumSize()  {
    return getPreferredSize();
  }
}
```

Grayscale.java

The **Grayscale** filter is a subclass of **RGBImageFilter**, which means that **Grayscale** can use itself as the **ImageFilter** parameter to **FilteredImageSource**'s constructor. Then all it needs to do is override **filterRGB( )** to change the incoming color values. It takes the red, green, and blue values and computes the brightness of the pixel, using the NTSC (National Television Standards Committee) color-to-brightness conversion factor. It then simply returns a gray pixel that is the same brightness as the color source.

```
import java.applet.*;
import java.awt.*;
import java.awt.image.*;

class Grayscale extends RGBImageFilter implements PlugInFilter {
  public Image filter(Applet a, Image in) {
    return a.createImage(new FilteredImageSource(in.getSource(), this));
  }

  public int filterRGB(int x, int y, int rgb) {
    int r = (rgb >> 16) & 0xff;
    int g = (rgb >> 8) & 0xff;
    int b = rgb & 0xff;
    int k = (int) (.56 * g + .33 * r + .11 * b);
    return (0xff000000 | k << 16 | k << 8 | k);
  }
}
```

Invert.java

The **Invert** filter is also quite simple. It takes apart the red, green, and blue channels and then inverts them by subtracting them from 255. These inverted values are packed back into a pixel value and returned.

```
import java.applet.*;
import java.awt.*;
import java.awt.image.*;

class Invert extends RGBImageFilter implements PlugInFilter {
  public Image filter(Applet a, Image in) {
    return a.createImage(new FilteredImageSource(in.getSource(), this));
  }
  public int filterRGB(int x, int y, int rgb) {
    int r = 0xff - (rgb >> 16) & 0xff;
    int g = 0xff - (rgb >> 8) & 0xff;
    int b = 0xff - rgb & 0xff;
    return (0xff000000 | r << 16 | g << 8 | b);
  }
}
```

Figure 25-8 shows the image after it has been run through the **Invert** filter.

FIGURE 25-8
Using the **Invert** filter with **ImageFilterDemo**

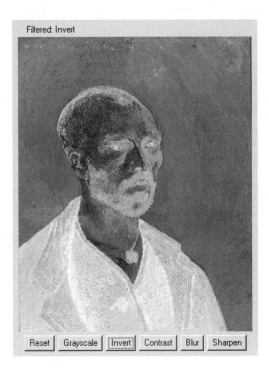

Filtered: Invert

Reset | Grayscale | Invert | Contrast | Blur | Sharpen

Contrast.java

The **Contrast** filter is very similar to **Grayscale**, except its override of **filterRGB( )** is slightly more complicated. The algorithm it uses for contrast enhancement takes the red, green, and blue values separately and boosts them by 1.2 times if they are already brighter than 128. If they are below 128, then they are divided by 1.2. The boosted values are properly clamped at 255 by the **multclamp( )** method.

```java
import java.applet.*;
import java.awt.*;
import java.awt.image.*;

public class Contrast extends RGBImageFilter implements PlugInFilter {

  public Image filter(Applet a, Image in) {
    return a.createImage(new FilteredImageSource(in.getSource(), this));
  }

  private int multclamp(int in, double factor) {
    in = (int) (in * factor);
    return in > 255 ? 255 : in;
  }

  double gain = 1.2;
  private int cont(int in) {
    return (in < 128) ? (int)(in/gain) : multclamp(in, gain);
  }

  public int filterRGB(int x, int y, int rgb) {
    int r = cont((rgb >> 16) & 0xff);
    int g = cont((rgb >> 8) & 0xff);
    int b = cont(rgb & 0xff);
    return (0xff000000 | r << 16 | g << 8 | b);
  }
}
```

Figure 25-9 shows the image after **Contrast** is pressed.

Convolver.java

The abstract class **Convolver** handles the basics of a convolution filter by implementing the **ImageConsumer** interface to move the source pixels into an array called **imgpixels**. It also creates a second array called **newimgpixels** for the filtered data. Convolution filters sample a small rectangle of pixels around each pixel in an image, called the *convolution kernel*. This area, 3×3 pixels in this demo, is used to decide how to change the center pixel in the area.

NOTE *The reason that the filter can't modify the **imgpixels** array in place is that the next pixel on a scan line would try to use the original value for the previous pixel, which would have just been filtered away.*

FIGURE 25-9
Using the **Contrast**
filter with
ImageFilterDemo

Filtered: Contrast

The two concrete subclasses, shown in the next section, simply implement the **convolve( )**
method, using **imgpixels** for source data and **newimgpixels** to store the result.

```
import java.applet.*;
import java.awt.*;
import java.awt.image.*;

abstract class Convolver implements ImageConsumer, PlugInFilter {
  int width, height;
  int imgpixels[], newimgpixels[];
  boolean imageReady = false;

  abstract void convolve();  // filter goes here...

  public Image filter(Applet a, Image in) {
    in.getSource().startProduction(this);
    imageReady = false;
    waitForImage();
    newimgpixels = new int[width*height];

    try {
      convolve();
    } catch (Exception e) {
      System.out.println("Convolver failed: " + e);
      e.printStackTrace();
    }
```

```
    return a.createImage(
      new MemoryImageSource(width, height, newimgpixels, 0, width));
}

synchronized void waitForImage() {
  try {
    while(!imageReady) wait();
  } catch (Exception e) {
    System.out.println("Interrupted");
  }
}

public void setProperties(java.util.Hashtable dummy) { }
public void setColorModel(ColorModel dummy) { }
public void setHints(int dummy) { }

public synchronized void imageComplete(int dummy) {
imageReady = true;
  notifyAll();
}

public void setDimensions(int x, int y) {
  width = x;
  height = y;
  imgpixels = new int[x*y];
}

public void setPixels(int x1, int y1, int w, int h,
  ColorModel model, byte pixels[], int off, int scansize) {
  int pix, x, y, x2, y2, sx, sy;

  x2 = x1+w;
  y2 = y1+h;
  sy = off;
  for(y=y1; y<y2; y++) {
    sx = sy;
    for(x=x1; x<x2; x++) {
      pix = model.getRGB(pixels[sx++]);
      if((pix & 0xff000000) == 0)
          pix = 0x00ffffff;
      imgpixels[y*width+x] = pix;
    }
    sy += scansize;
  }
}

public void setPixels(int x1, int y1, int w, int h,
  ColorModel model, int pixels[], int off, int scansize) {
  int pix, x, y, x2, y2, sx, sy;

  x2 = x1+w;
  y2 = y1+h;
  sy = off;
  for(y=y1; y<y2; y++) {
```

```
      sx = sy;
      for(x=x1; x<x2; x++) {
        pix = model.getRGB(pixels[sx++]);
        if((pix & 0xff000000) == 0)
            pix = 0x00ffffff;
        imgpixels[y*width+x] = pix;
      }
      sy += scansize;
    }
  }
}
```

Blur.java

The **Blur** filter is a subclass of **Convolver** and simply runs through every pixel in the source image array, **imgpixels**, and computes the average of the 3×3 box surrounding it. The corresponding output pixel in **newimgpixels** is that average value.

```
public class Blur extends Convolver {
  public void convolve() {
    for(int y=1; y<height-1; y++) {
      for(int x=1; x<width-1; x++) {
        int rs = 0;
        int gs = 0;
        int bs = 0;

        for(int k=-1; k<=1; k++) {
          for(int j=-1; j<=1; j++) {
            int rgb = imgpixels[(y+k)*width+x+j];
            int r = (rgb >> 16) & 0xff;
            int g = (rgb >> 8) & 0xff;
            int b = rgb & 0xff;
            rs += r;
            gs += g;
            bs += b;
          }
        }

        rs /= 9;
        gs /= 9;
        bs /= 9;

        newimgpixels[y*width+x] = (0xff000000 |
                              rs << 16 | gs << 8 | bs);
      }
    }
  }
}
```

Figure 25-10 shows the applet after **Blur**.

Sharpen.java

The **Sharpen** filter is also a subclass of **Convolver** and is (more or less) the inverse of **Blur**. It runs through every pixel in the source image array, **imgpixels**, and computes the average of the 3×3 box surrounding it, not counting the center. The corresponding output pixel in

PART II

FIGURE 25-10
Using the **Blur**
filter with
ImageFilterDemo

Filtered: Blur

| Reset | Grayscale | Invert | Contrast | Blur | Sharpen |

newimgpixels has the difference between the center pixel and the surrounding average added to it. This basically says that if a pixel is 30 brighter than its surroundings, make it another 30 brighter. If, however, it is 10 darker, then make it another 10 darker. This tends to accentuate edges while leaving smooth areas unchanged.

```java
public class Sharpen extends Convolver {

  private final int clamp(int c) {
    return (c > 255 ? 255 : (c < 0 ? 0 : c));
  }

  public void convolve() {
    int r0=0, g0=0, b0=0;
    for(int y=1; y<height-1; y++) {
      for(int x=1; x<width-1; x++) {
        int rs = 0;
        int gs = 0;
        int bs = 0;

        for(int k=-1; k<=1; k++) {
          for(int j=-1; j<=1; j++) {
            int rgb = imgpixels[(y+k)*width+x+j];
            int r = (rgb >> 16) & 0xff;
            int g = (rgb >> 8) & 0xff;
            int b = rgb & 0xff;
            if (j == 0 && k == 0) {
              r0 = r;
```

```
            g0 = g;
            b0 = b;
        } else {
          rs += r;
          gs += g;
          bs += b;
        }
      }
    }

    rs >>= 3;
    gs >>= 3;
    bs >>= 3;
    newimgpixels[y*width+x] = (0xff000000 |
                              clamp(r0+r0-rs) << 16 |
                              clamp(g0+g0-gs) << 8 |
                              clamp(b0+b0-bs));
        }
      }
    }
}
```

Figure 25-11 shows the applet after **Sharpen**.

FIGURE 25-11
Using the **Sharpen**
filter with
ImageFilterDemo

Cell Animation

Now that we have presented an overview of the image APIs, we can put together an interesting applet that will display a sequence of animation cells. The animation cells are taken from a single image that can arrange the cells in a grid specified via the **rows** and **cols** <param> tags. Each cell in the image is snipped out in a way similar to that used in the **TileImage** example earlier. We obtain the sequence in which to display the cells from the **sequence** <param> tag. This is a comma-separated list of cell numbers that is zero-based and proceeds across the grid from left to right, top to bottom.

Once the applet has parsed the <param> tags and loaded the source image, it cuts the image into a number of small subimages. Then, a thread is started that causes the images to be displayed according to the order described in **sequence**. The thread sleeps for enough time to maintain the **framerate**. Here is the source code:

```java
/ Animation example.
import java.applet.*;
import java.awt.*;
import java.awt.image.*;
import java.util.*;

public class Animation extends Applet implements Runnable {
  Image cell[];
  final int MAXSEQ = 64;
  int sequence[];
  int nseq;
  int idx;
  int framerate;
  boolean stopFlag;

  private int intDef(String s, int def) {
    int n = def;
    if (s != null)
      try {
        n = Integer.parseInt(s);
      } catch (NumberFormatException e) {
        System.out.println("Number Format Exception");
      }
    return n;
  }

  public void init() {
    framerate = intDef(getParameter("framerate"), 5);
    int tilex = intDef(getParameter("cols"), 1);
    int tiley = intDef(getParameter("rows"), 1);
    cell = new Image[tilex*tiley];

    StringTokenizer st = new
              StringTokenizer(getParameter("sequence"), ",");
    sequence = new int[MAXSEQ];
```

```
    nseq = 0;
    while(st.hasMoreTokens() && nseq < MAXSEQ) {
      sequence[nseq] = intDef(st.nextToken(), 0);
      nseq++;
    }

    try {
      Image img = getImage(getDocumentBase(), getParameter("img"));
      MediaTracker t = new MediaTracker(this);
      t.addImage(img, 0);
      t.waitForID(0);
      int iw = img.getWidth(null);
      int ih = img.getHeight(null);
      int tw = iw / tilex;
      int th = ih / tiley;
      CropImageFilter f;
      FilteredImageSource fis;
      for (int y=0; y<tiley; y++) {
        for (int x=0; x<tilex; x++) {
          f = new CropImageFilter(tw*x, th*y, tw, th);
          fis = new FilteredImageSource(img.getSource(), f);
          int i = y*tilex+x;
          cell[i] = createImage(fis);
          t.addImage(cell[i], i);
        }
      }
      t.waitForAll();
    } catch (InterruptedException e) {
      System.out.println("Image Load Interrupted");
    }
  }

  public void update(Graphics g) { }

  public void paint(Graphics g) {
      g.drawImage(cell[sequence[idx]], 0, 0, null);
  }

  Thread t;
  public void start() {
    t = new Thread(this);
    stopFlag = false;
    t.start();
  }

  public void stop() {
    stopFlag = true;
  }

  public void run() {
```

```
      idx = 0;
      while (true) {
        paint(getGraphics());
        idx = (idx + 1) % nseq;
        try {
          Thread.sleep(1000/framerate);
        } catch (InterruptedException e) {
          System.out.println("Animation Interrupted");
          return;
        }
        if(stopFlag)
          return;
      }
    }
  }
```

The following applet tag shows the famous locomotion study by Eadweard Muybridge, which proved that horses do, indeed, get all four hooves off the ground at once. (Of course, you can substitute another image file in your own applet.)

```
<applet code=Animation width=67 height=48>
<param name=img value=horse.gif>
<param name=rows value=3>
<param name=cols value=4>
<param name=sequence value=0,1,2,3,4,5,6,7,8,9,10,11>
<param name=framerate value=15>
</applet>
```

Figure 25-12 shows the applet running. Notice the source image that has been loaded below the applet using a normal **<img>** tag.

FIGURE 25-12
Sample output
of **Animation**

Additional Imaging Classes

In addition to the imaging classes described in this chapter, **java.awt.image** supplies several others that offer enhanced control over the imaging process and that support advanced imaging techniques. Also available is the imaging package called **javax.imageio**. This package supports plug-ins that handle various image formats. If sophisticated graphical output is of special interest to you, then you will want to explore the additional classes found in **java.awt.image** and **javax.imageio**.

The Concurrency Utilities

From the start, Java has provided built-in support for multithreading and synchronization. For example, new threads can be created by implementing **Runnable** or by extending **Thread**, synchronization is available by use of the **synchronized** keyword, and interthread communication is supported by the **wait( )** and **notify( )** methods that are defined by **Object**. In general, this built-in support for multithreading was one of Java's most important innovations and is still one of its major strengths.

However, as conceptually pure as Java's original support for multithreading is, it is not ideal for all applications—especially those that make extensive use of multiple threads. For example, the original multithreading support does not provide several high-level features, such as semaphores, thread pools, and execution managers, that facilitate the creation of intensive concurrent programs.

It is important to explain at the outset that many Java programs make use of multithreading and are therefore "concurrent." For example, most applets use multithreading. However, as it is used in this chapter, the term *concurrent program* refers to a program that makes *extensive, integral* use of concurrently executing threads of execution. An example of such a program is one that uses separate threads to simultaneously compute the partial results of a larger computation. Another example is a program that coordinates the activities of several threads, each of which seeks access to information in a database. In this case, read-only accesses might be handled differently from those that require read/write capabilities.

To handle the needs of a concurrent program, JDK 5 added the *concurrency utilities*, also commonly referred to as the *concurrent API*. The concurrency utilities supply many features that had long been wanted by programmers who develop concurrent applications. For example, they offer the semaphore, cyclic barriers, countdown latches, thread pools, execution managers, locks, several concurrent collections, and a streamlined way to use threads to obtain computational results.

The concurrent API is quite large, and many of the issues surrounding its use are quite complex. It is beyond the scope of this book to discuss all of its facets. Moreover, the alternatives offered by the concurrency utilities are not designed for use by most programs. Simply put: Unless you are writing programs with a significant amount of concurrency, in most cases, Java's traditional support for multithreading and synchronization is not only sufficient, but in many cases also is preferable to the capabilities offered by the concurrent API.

The preceding paragraph notwithstanding, it is important for all programmers to have a general, working knowledge of the concurrent API. Furthermore, there are some parts of it, such as its synchronizers, callable threads, and executors, that are applicable to a wide variety of situations. For these reasons, this chapter presents an overview of the concurrency utilities and shows several examples of their use.

The Concurrent API Packages

The concurrency utilities are contained in the **java.util.concurrent** package and in its two subpackages, **java.util.concurrent.atomic** and **java.util.concurrent.locks**. A brief overview of their contents is given here.

java.util.concurrent

java.util.concurrent defines the core features that support alternatives to the built-in approaches to synchronization and interthread communication. It defines the following key features:

Synchronizers
Executors
Concurrent collections

Synchronizers offer high-level ways of synchronizing the interactions between multiple threads. The synchronizer classes defined by **java.util.concurrent** are

Semaphore	Implements the classic semaphore
CountDownLatch	Waits until a specified number of events have occurred
CyclicBarrier	Enables a group of threads to wait at a predefined execution point
Exchanger	Exchanges data between two threads

Notice that each synchronizer provides a solution to a specific type of synchronization problem. This enables each synchronizer to be optimized for its intended use. In the past, these types of synchronization objects had to be crafted by hand. The concurrent API standardizes them and makes them available to all Java programmers.

Executors manage thread execution. At the top of the executor hierarchy is the **Executor** interface, which is used to initiate a thread. **ExecutorService** extends **Executor** and provides methods that manage execution. There are two implementations of **ExecutorService**: **ThreadPoolExecutor** and **ScheduledThreadPoolExecutor**. **java.util.concurrent** also defines the **Executors** utility class, which includes a number of static methods that simplify the creation of various executors.

Related to executors are the **Future** and **Callable** interfaces. A **Future** contains a value that is returned by a thread after it executes. Thus, its value becomes defined "in the future," when the thread terminates. **Callable** defines a thread that returns a value.

java.util.concurrent defines several concurrent collection classes, including **ConcurrentHashMap**, **ConcurrentLinkedQueue**, and **CopyOnWriteArraylist**. These offer concurrent alternatives to their related classes defined by the Collections Framework.

Finally, to better handle thread timing, **java.util.concurrent** defines the **TimeUnit** enumeration.

java.util.concurrent.atomic

java.util.concurrent.atomic facilitates the use of variables in a concurrent environment. It provides a means of efficiently updating the value of a variable without the use of locks. This is accomplished through the use of classes, such as **AtomicInteger** and **AtomicLong**, and methods, such as **compareAndSet( )**, **decrementAndGet( )**, and **getAndSet( )**. These methods execute as a single, non-interruptible operation.

java.util.concurrent.locks

java.util.concurrent.locks provides an alternative to the use of **synchronized** methods. At the core of this alternative is the **Lock** interface, which defines the basic mechanism used to acquire and relinquish access to an object. The key methods are **lock( )**, **tryLock( )**, and **unlock( )**. The advantage to using these methods is greater control over synchronization.

The remainder of this chapter takes a closer look at the constituents of the concurrent API.

Using Synchronization Objects

It is likely that the most widely used part of the concurrent API will be its synchronization objects. These are supported by the **Semaphore**, **CountDownLatch**, **CyclicBarrier**, and **Exchanger** classes. Collectively, they enable you to handle several formerly difficult synchronization situations with ease. They are also applicable to a wide range of programs—even those that contain only limited concurrency. Because the synchronization objects will be of interest to nearly all Java programs, each is examined here in some detail.

Semaphore

The synchronization object that many readers will immediately recognize is **Semaphore**, which implements a classic semaphore. A semaphore controls access to a shared resource through the use of a counter. If the counter is greater than zero, then access is allowed. If it is zero, then access is denied. What the counter is counting are *permits* that allow access to the shared resource. Thus, to access the resource, a thread must be granted a permit from the semaphore.

In general, to use a semaphore, the thread that wants access to the shared resource tries to acquire a permit. If the semaphore's count is greater than zero, then the thread acquires a permit, which causes the semaphore's count to be decremented. Otherwise, the thread will be blocked until a permit can be acquired. When the thread no longer needs access to the shared resource, it releases the permit, which causes the semaphore's count to be incremented. If there is another thread waiting for a permit, then that thread will acquire a permit at that time. Java's **Semaphore** class implements this mechanism.

Semaphore has the two constructors shown here:

Semaphore(int *num*)
Semaphore(int *num*, boolean *how*)

Here, *num* specifies the initial permit count. Thus, *num* specifies the number of threads that can access a shared resource at any one time. If *num* is one, then only one thread can access the resource at any one time. By default, waiting threads are granted a permit in an undefined order. By setting *how* to **true**, you can ensure that waiting threads are granted a permit in the order in which they requested access.

To acquire a permit, call the **acquire( )** method, which has these two forms:

```
void acquire( ) throws InterruptedException
void acquire(int num) throws InterruptedException
```

The first form acquires one permit. The second form acquires *num* permits. Most often, the first form is used. If the permit cannot be granted at the time of the call, then the invoking thread suspends until the permit is available.

To release a permit, call **release( )**, which has these two forms:

```
void release( )
void release(int num)
```

The first form releases one permit. The second form releases the number of permits specified by *num*.

To use a semaphore to control access to a resource, each thread that wants to use that resource must first call **acquire( )** before accessing the resource. When the thread is done with the resource, it must call **release( )**. Here is an example that illustrates the use of a semaphore:

```
// A simple semaphore example.

import java.util.concurrent.*;

class SemDemo {

  public static void main(String args[]) {
    Semaphore sem = new Semaphore(1);

    new IncThread(sem, "A");
    new DecThread(sem, "B");

  }
}

// A shared resource.
class Shared {
  static int count = 0;
}

// A thread of execution that increments count.
class IncThread implements Runnable {
  String name;
  Semaphore sem;

  IncThread(Semaphore s, String n) {
    sem = s;
    name = n;
    new Thread(this).start();
  }
```

```
  public void run() {

    System.out.println("Starting " + name);

    try {
      // First, get a permit.
      System.out.println(name + " is waiting for a permit.");
      sem.acquire();
      System.out.println(name + " gets a permit.");

      // Now, access shared resource.
      for(int i=0; i < 5; i++) {
        Shared.count++;
        System.out.println(name + ": " + Shared.count);

        // Now, allow a context switch -- if possible.
        Thread.sleep(10);
      }
    } catch (InterruptedException exc) {
      System.out.println(exc);
    }

    // Release the permit.
    System.out.println(name + " releases the permit.");
    sem.release();
  }
}

// A thread of execution that decrements count.
class DecThread implements Runnable {
  String name;
  Semaphore sem;

  DecThread(Semaphore s, String n) {
    sem = s;
    name = n;
    new Thread(this).start();
  }

  public void run() {

    System.out.println("Starting " + name);

    try {
      // First, get a permit.
      System.out.println(name + " is waiting for a permit.");
      sem.acquire();
      System.out.println(name + " gets a permit.");

      // Now, access shared resource.
      for(int i=0; i < 5; i++) {
        Shared.count--;
        System.out.println(name + ": " + Shared.count);
```

```
        // Now, allow a context switch -- if possible.
        Thread.sleep(10);
      }
    } catch (InterruptedException exc) {
      System.out.println(exc);
    }

    // Release the permit.
    System.out.println(name + " releases the permit.");
    sem.release();
  }
}
```

The output from the program is shown here. (The precise order in which the threads execute may vary.)

```
Starting A
A is waiting for a permit.
A gets a permit.
A: 1
Starting B
B is waiting for a permit.
A: 2
A: 3
A: 4
A: 5
A releases the permit.
B gets a permit.
B: 4
B: 3
B: 2
B: 1
B: 0
B releases the permit.
```

The program uses a semaphore to control access to the **count** variable, which is a static variable within the **Shared** class. **Shared.count** is incremented five times by the **run( )** method of **IncThread** and decremented five times by **DecThread**. To prevent these two threads from accessing **Shared.count** at the same time, access is allowed only after a permit is acquired from the controlling semaphore. After access is complete, the permit is released. In this way, only one thread at a time will access **Shared.count**, as the output shows.

In both **IncThread** and **DecThread**, notice the call to **sleep( )** within **run( )**. It is used to "prove" that accesses to **Shared.count** are synchronized by the semaphore. In **run( )**, the call to **sleep( )** causes the invoking thread to pause between each access to **Shared.count**. This would normally enable the second thread to run. However, because of the semaphore, the second thread must wait until the first has released the permit, which happens only after all accesses by the first thread are complete. Thus, **Shared.count** is first incremented five times by **IncThread** and then decremented five times by **DecThread**. The increments and decrements are *not* intermixed.

Without the use of the semaphore, accesses to **Shared.count** by both threads would have occurred simultaneously, and the increments and decrements would be intermixed. To confirm this, try commenting out the calls to **acquire( )** and **release( )**. When you run the program, you will see that access to **Shared.count** is no longer synchronized, and each thread accesses it as soon as it gets a timeslice.

Although many uses of a semaphore are as straightforward as that shown in the preceding program, more intriguing uses are also possible. Here is an example. The following program reworks the producer/consumer program shown in Chapter 11 so that it uses two semaphores to regulate the producer and consumer threads, ensuring that each call to **put( )** is followed by a corresponding call to **get( )**:

```
// An implementation of a producer and consumer
// that use semaphores to control synchronization.

import java.util.concurrent.Semaphore;

class Q {
  int n;

  // Start with consumer semaphore unavailable.
  static Semaphore semCon = new Semaphore(0);
  static Semaphore semProd = new Semaphore(1);

  void get() {
    try {
      semCon.acquire();
    } catch(InterruptedException e) {
      System.out.println("InterruptedException caught");
    }

    System.out.println("Got: " + n);
    semProd.release();
  }

  void put(int n) {
    try {
      semProd.acquire();
    } catch(InterruptedException e) {
      System.out.println("InterruptedException caught");
    }

    this.n = n;
    System.out.println("Put: " + n);
    semCon.release();
  }
}

class Producer implements Runnable {
  Q q;

  Producer(Q q) {
    this.q = q;
```

```
      new Thread(this, "Producer").start();
  }

  public void run() {
    for(int i=0; i < 20; i++) q.put(i);
  }
}

class Consumer implements Runnable {
  Q q;

  Consumer(Q q) {
    this.q = q;
    new Thread(this, "Consumer").start();
  }

  public void run() {
    for(int i=0; i < 20; i++)  q.get();
  }
}

class ProdCon {
  public static void main(String args[]) {
    Q q = new Q();
    new Consumer(q);
    new Producer(q);
  }
}
```

A portion of the output is shown here:

```
Put: 0
Got: 0
Put: 1
Got: 1
Put: 2
Got: 2
Put: 3
Got: 3
Put: 4
Got: 4
Put: 5
Got: 5
.
.
.
```

As you can see, the calls to **put( )** and **get( )** are synchronized. That is, each call to **put( )** is followed by a call to **get( )** and no values are missed. Without the semaphores, multiple calls to **put( )** would have occurred without matching calls to **get( )**, resulting in values being missed. (To prove this, remove the semaphore code and observe the results.)

The sequencing of **put( )** and **get( )** calls is handled by two semaphores: **semProd** and **semCon**. Before **put( )** can produce a value, it must acquire a permit from **semProd**. After it has set the value, it releases **semCon**. Before **get( )** can consume a value, it must acquire a permit from **semCon**. After it consumes the value, it releases **semProd**. This "give and take" mechanism ensures that each call to **put( )** must be followed by a call to **get( )**.

Notice that **semCon** is initialized with no available permits. This ensures that **put( )** executes first. The ability to set the initial synchronization state is one of the more powerful aspects of a semaphore.

CountDownLatch

Sometimes you will want a thread to wait until one or more events have occurred. To handle such a situation, the concurrent API supplies **CountDownLatch**. A **CountDownLatch** is initially created with a count of the number of events that must occur before the latch is released. Each time an event happens, the count is decremented. When the count reaches zero, the latch opens.

CountDownLatch has the following constructor:

CountDownLatch(int *num*)

Here, *num* specifies the number of events that must occur in order for the latch to open.

To wait on the latch, a thread calls **await( )**, which has the forms shown here:

void await( ) throws InterruptedException
void await(long *wait*, TimeUnit *tu*) throws InterruptedException

The first form waits until the count associated with the invoking **CountDownLatch** reaches zero. The second form waits only for the period of time specified by *wait*. The units represented by *wait* are specified by *tu*, which is an object the **TimeUnit** enumeration. (**TimeUnit** is described later in this chapter.)

To signal an event, call the **countDown( )** method, shown next:

void countDown( )

Each call to **countDown( )** decrements the count associated with the invoking object.

The following program demonstrates **CountDownLatch**. It creates a latch that requires five events to occur before it opens.

```
// An example of CountDownLatch.

import java.util.concurrent.CountDownLatch;

class CDLDemo {
  public static void main(String args[]) {
    CountDownLatch cdl = new CountDownLatch(5);

    System.out.println("Starting");

    new MyThread(cdl);
```

```
    try {
      cdl.await();
    } catch (InterruptedException exc) {
      System.out.println(exc);
    }

    System.out.println("Done");
  }
}

class MyThread implements Runnable {
  CountDownLatch latch;

  MyThread(CountDownLatch c) {
    latch = c;
    new Thread(this).start();
  }

  public void run() {
    for(int i = 0; i<5; i++) {
      System.out.println(i);
      latch.countDown(); // decrement count
    }
  }
}
```

The output produced by the program is shown here:

```
Starting
0
1
2
3
4
Done
```

Inside **main( )**, a **CountDownLatch** called **cdl** is created with an initial count of five. Next, an instance of **MyThread** is created, which begins execution of a new thread. Notice that **cdl** is passed as a parameter to **MyThread**'s constructor and stored in the **latch** instance variable. Then, the main thread calls **await( )** on **cdl**, which causes execution of the main thread to pause until **cdl**'s count has been decremented five times.

Inside the **run( )** method of **MyThread**, a loop is created that iterates five times. With each iteration, the **countDown( )** method is called on **latch**, which refers to **cdl** in **main( )**. After the fifth iteration, the latch opens, which allows the main thread to resume.

CountDownLatch is a powerful yet easy-to-use synchronization object that is appropriate whenever a thread must wait for one or more events to occur.

CyclicBarrier

A situation not uncommon in concurrent programming occurs when a set of two or more threads must wait at a predetermined execution point until all threads in the set have reached that point. To handle such a situation, the concurrent API supplies the **CyclicBarrier** class. It enables you to define a synchronization object that suspends until the specified number of threads has reached the barrier point.

CyclicBarrier has the following two constructors:

CyclicBarrier(int *numThreads*)
CyclicBarrier(int *numThreads*, Runnable *action*)

Here, *numThreads* specifies the number of threads that must reach the barrier before execution continues. In the second form, *action* specifies a thread that will be executed when the barrier is reached.

Here is the general procedure that you will follow to use **CyclicBarrier**. First, create a **CyclicBarrier** object, specifying the number of threads that you will be waiting for. Next, when each thread reaches the barrier, have it call **await( )** on that object. This will pause execution of the thread until all of the other threads also call **await( )**. Once the specified number of threads has reached the barrier, **await( )** will return, and execution will resume. Also, if you have specified an action, then that thread is executed.

The **await( )** method has the following two forms:

int await( ) throws InterruptedException, BrokenBarrierException

int await(long *wait*, TimeUnit *tu*)
    throws InterruptedException, BrokenBarrierException, TimeoutException

The first form waits until the all threads have reached the barrier point. The second form waits only for the period of time specified by *wait*. The units represented by *wait* are specified by *tu*. Both forms return a value that indicates the order that the threads arrive at the barrier point. The first thread returns a value equal to the number of threads waited upon minus one. The last thread returns zero.

Here is an example that illustrates **CyclicBarrier**. It waits until a set of three threads has reached the barrier. When that occurs, the thread specified by **BarAction** executes.

```
// An example of CyclicBarrier.

import java.util.concurrent.*;

class BarDemo {
  public static void main(String args[]) {
    CyclicBarrier cb = new CyclicBarrier(3, new BarAction() );

    System.out.println("Starting");

    new MyThread(cb, "A");
    new MyThread(cb, "B");
    new MyThread(cb, "C");

  }
}

// A thread of execution that uses a CyclicBarrier.
```

```
class MyThread implements Runnable {
  CyclicBarrier cbar;
  String name;

  MyThread(CyclicBarrier c, String n) {
    cbar = c;
    name = n;
    new Thread(this).start();
  }

  public void run() {

    System.out.println(name);

    try {
      cbar.await();
    } catch (BrokenBarrierException exc) {
      System.out.println(exc);
    } catch (InterruptedException exc) {
      System.out.println(exc);
    }
  }
}

// An object of this class is called when the
// CyclicBarrier ends.
class BarAction implements Runnable {
  public void run() {
    System.out.println("Barrier Reached!");
  }
}
```

The output is shown here. (The precise order in which the threads execute may vary.)

```
Starting
A
B
C
Barrier Reached!
```

A **CyclicBarrier** can be reused because it will release waiting threads each time the specified number of threads calls **await( )**. For example, if you change **main( )** in the preceding program so that it looks like this:

```
public static void main(String args[]) {
CyclicBarrier cb = new CyclicBarrier(3, new BarAction() );

  System.out.println("Starting");

  new MyThread(cb, "A");
  new MyThread(cb, "B");
  new MyThread(cb, "C");
```

```
new MyThread(cb, "X");
new MyThread(cb, "Y");
new MyThread(cb, "Z");

}
```

The following output will be produced. (The precise order in which the threads execute may vary.)

```
Starting
A
B
C
Barrier Reached!
X
Y
Z
Barrier Reached!
```

As the preceding example shows, the **CyclicBarrier** offers a streamlined solution to what was previously a complicated problem.

Exchanger

Perhaps the most interesting of the synchronization classes is **Exchanger**. It is designed to simplify the exchange of data between two threads. The operation of an **Exchanger** is astoundingly simple: it simply waits until two separate threads call its **exchange( )** method. When that occurs, it exchanges the data supplied by the threads. This mechanism is both elegant and easy to use. Uses for **Exchanger** are easy to imagine. For example, one thread might prepare a buffer for receiving information over a network connection. Another thread might fill that buffer with the information from the connection. The two threads work together so that each time a new buffer is needed, an exchange is made.

Exchanger is a generic class that is declared as shown here:

Exchanger<V>

Here, **V** specifies the type of the data being exchanged.

The only method defined by **Exchanger** is **exchange( )**, which has the two forms shown here:

V exchange(V *buffer*) throws InterruptedException

V exchange(V *buffer*, long *wait*, TimeUnit *tu*)
    throws InterruptedException, TimeoutException

Here, *buffer* is a reference to the data to exchange. The data received from the other thread is returned. The second form of **exchange( )** allows a time-out period to be specified. The key point about **exchange( )** is that it won't succeed until it has been called on the same **Exchanger** object by two separate threads. Thus, **exchange( )** synchronizes the exchange of the data.

Here is an example that demonstrates **Exchanger**. It creates two threads. One thread creates an empty buffer that will receive the data put into it by the second thread. Thus, the first thread exchanges an empty thread for a full one.

```java
// An example of Exchanger.

import java.util.concurrent.Exchanger;

class ExgrDemo {
  public static void main(String args[]) {
    Exchanger<String> exgr = new Exchanger<String>();

    new UseString(exgr);
    new MakeString(exgr);
  }
}

// A Thread that constructs a string.
class MakeString implements Runnable {
  Exchanger<String> ex;
  String str;

  MakeString(Exchanger<String> c) {
    ex = c;
    str = new String();

    new Thread(this).start();
  }

  public void run() {
    char ch = 'A';

    for(int i = 0; i < 3; i++) {

      // Fill Buffer
      for(int j = 0; j < 5; j++)
        str += ch++;

      try {
        // Exchange a full buffer for an empty one.
        str = ex.exchange(str);
      } catch(InterruptedException exc) {
        System.out.println(exc);
      }
    }
  }
}

// A Thread that uses a string.
class UseString implements Runnable {
  Exchanger<String> ex;
  String str;
```

```
UseString(Exchanger<String> c) {
  ex = c;
  new Thread(this).start();
}

public void run() {

  for(int i=0; i < 3; i++) {
    try {
      // Exchange an empty buffer for a full one.
      str = ex.exchange(new String());
      System.out.println("Got: " + str);
    } catch(InterruptedException exc) {
      System.out.println(exc);
    }
  }
}
}
```

Here is the output produced by the program:

```
Got: ABCDE
Got: FGHIJ
Got: KLMNO
```

In the program, the **main( )** method creates an **Exchanger** for strings. This object is then used to synchronize the exchange of strings between the **MakeString** and **UseString** classes. The **MakeString** class fills a string with data. The **UseString** exchanges an empty buffer for a full one. It then displays the contents of the newly constructed string. The exchange of empty and full buffers is synchronized by the **exchange( )** method, which is called by both class' **run( )** method.

Using an Executor

The concurrent API supplies a feature called an *executor* that initiates and controls the execution of threads. As such, an executor offers an alternative to managing threads through the **Thread** class.

At the core of an executor is the **Executor** interface. It defines the following method:

void execute(Runnable *thread*)

The thread specified by *thread* is executed. Thus, **execute( )** starts the specified thread.

The **ExecutorService** interface extends **Executor** by adding methods that help manage and control the execution of threads. For example, **ExecutorService** defines **shutdown( )**, shown here, which stops the invoking **ExecutorService**.

void shutdown( )

ExecutorService also defines methods that execute threads that return results, that execute a set of threads, and that determine the shutdown status. We will look at several of these methods a little later.

Also defined is the interface **ScheduledExecutorService**, which extends **ExecutorService** to support the scheduling of threads.

The concurrent API defines two predefined executor classes: **ThreadPoolExecutor** and **ScheduledThreadPoolExecutor**. **ThreadPoolExecutor** implements the **Executor** and **ExecutorService** interfaces and provides support for a managed pool of threads. **ScheduledThreadPoolExecutor** also implements the **ScheduledExecutorService** interface to allow a pool of threads to be scheduled.

A thread pool provides a set of threads that is used to execute various tasks. Instead of each task using its own thread, the threads in the pool are used. This reduces the overhead associated with creating many separate threads. Although you can use **ThreadPoolExecutor** and **ScheduledThreadPoolExecutor** directly, most often you will want to obtain an executor by calling one of the following static factory methods defined by the **Executors** utility class. Here are some examples:

static ExecutorService newCachedThreadPool( )
static ExecutorService newFixedThreadPool(int *numThreads*)
static ScheduledExecutorService newScheduledThreadPool(int *numThreads*)

newCachedThreadPool( ) creates a thread pool that adds threads as needed but reuses threads if possible. **newFixedThreadPool( )** creates a thread pool that consists of a specified number of threads. **newScheduledThreadPool( )** creates a thread pool that supports thread scheduling. Each returns a reference to an **ExecutorService** that can be used to manage the pool.

A Simple Executor Example

Before going any further, a simple example that uses an executor will be of value. The following program creates a fixed thread pool that contains two threads. It then uses that pool to execute four tasks. Thus, four tasks share the two threads that are in the pool. After the tasks finish, the pool is shut down and the program ends.

```
// A simple example that uses an Executor.

import java.util.concurrent.*;

class SimpExec {
  public static void main(String args[]) {
    CountDownLatch cdl = new CountDownLatch(5);
    CountDownLatch cdl2 = new CountDownLatch(5);
    CountDownLatch cdl3 = new CountDownLatch(5);
    CountDownLatch cdl4 = new CountDownLatch(5);
    ExecutorService es = Executors.newFixedThreadPool(2);

    System.out.println("Starting");

    // Start the threads.
    es.execute(new MyThread(cdl, "A"));
    es.execute(new MyThread(cdl2, "B"));
    es.execute(new MyThread(cdl3, "C"));
    es.execute(new MyThread(cdl4, "D"));

    try {
      cdl.await();
```

```
      cdl2.await();
      cdl3.await();
      cdl4.await();
    } catch (InterruptedException exc) {
      System.out.println(exc);
    }

    es.shutdown();
    System.out.println("Done");
  }
}

class MyThread implements Runnable {
  String name;
  CountDownLatch latch;

  MyThread(CountDownLatch c, String n) {
    latch = c;
    name = n;

    new Thread(this);
  }

  public void run() {

    for(int i = 0; i < 5; i++) {
      System.out.println(name + ": " + i);
      latch.countDown();
    }
  }
}
```

The output from the program is shown here. (The precise order in which the threads execute may vary.)

```
Starting
A: 0
A: 1
A: 2
A: 3
A: 4
C: 0
C: 1
C: 2
C: 3
C: 4
D: 0
D: 1
D: 2
D: 3
D: 4
B: 0
```

```
B: 1
B: 2
B: 3
B: 4
Done
```

As the output shows, even though the thread pool contains only two threads, all four tasks are still executed. However, only two can run at the same time. The others must wait until one of the pooled threads is available for use.

The call to **shutdown( )** is important. If it were not present in the program, then the program would not terminate because the executor would remain active. To try this for yourself, simply comment out the call to **shutdown( )** and observe the result.

Using Callable and Future

One of the most innovative—and exciting—features of the concurrent API is the new **Callable** interface. This interface represents a thread that returns a value. An application can use **Callable** objects to compute results that are then returned to the invoking thread. This is a powerful mechanism because it facilitates the coding of many types of numerical computations in which partial results are computed simultaneously. It can also be used to run a thread that returns a status code that indicates the successful completion of the thread.

Callable is a generic interface that is defined like this:

interface Callable<V>

Here, **V** indicates the type of data returned by the task. **Callable** defines only one method, **call( )**, which is shown here:

V call( ) throws Exception

Inside **call( )**, you define the task that you want performed. After that task completes, you return the result. If the result cannot be computed, **call( )** must throw an exception.

A **Callable** task is executed by an **ExecutorService**, by calling its **submit( )** method. There are three forms of **submit( )**, but only one is used to execute a **Callable**. It is shown here:

<T> Future<T> submit(Callable<T> *task*)

Here, *task* is the **Callable** object that will be executed in its own thread. The result is returned through an object of type **Future**.

Future is a generic interface that represents the value that will be returned by a **Callable** object. Because this value is obtained at some future time, the name **Future** is appropriate. **Future** is defined like this:

interface Future<V>

Here, **V** specifies the type of the result.

To obtain the returned value, you will call **Future**'s **get( )** method, which has these two forms:

V get( )
    throws InterruptedException, ExecutionException

V get(long *wait*, TimeUnit *tu*)
    throws InterruptedException, ExecutionException, TimeoutException

The first form waits for the result indefinitely. The second form allows you to specify a time-out period in *wait*. The units of *wait* are passed in *tu*, which is an object of the **TimeUnit** enumeration, described later in this chapter.

The following program illustrates **Callable** and **Future** by creating three tasks that perform three different computations. The first returns the summation of a value, the second computes the length of the hypotenuse of a right triangle given the length of its sides, and the third computes the factorial of a value. All three computations occur simultaneously.

```java
// An example that uses a Callable.

import java.util.concurrent.*;

class CallableDemo {
  public static void main(String args[]) {
    ExecutorService es = Executors.newFixedThreadPool(3);
    Future<Integer> f;
    Future<Double> f2;
    Future<Integer> f3;

    System.out.println("Starting");

    f = es.submit(new Sum(10));
    f2 = es.submit(new Hypot(3, 4));
    f3 = es.submit(new Factorial(5));

    try {
      System.out.println(f.get());
      System.out.println(f2.get());
      System.out.println(f3.get());
    } catch (InterruptedException exc) {
      System.out.println(exc);
    }
    catch (ExecutionException exc) {
      System.out.println(exc);
    }

    es.shutdown();
    System.out.println("Done");
  }
}

// Following are three computational threads.

class Sum implements Callable<Integer> {
  int stop;

  Sum(int v) { stop = v; }

  public Integer call() {
    int sum = 0;
    for(int i = 1; i <= stop; i++) {
      sum += i;
    }
```

PART II

```
    return sum;
  }
}

class Hypot implements Callable<Double> {
  double side1, side2;

  Hypot(double s1, double s2) {
    side1 = s1;
    side2 = s2;
  }

  public Double call() {
    return Math.sqrt((side1*side1) + (side2*side2));
  }
}


class Factorial implements Callable<Integer> {
  int stop;

  Factorial(int v) { stop = v; }

  public Integer call() {
    int fact = 1;
    for(int i = 2; i <= stop; i++) {
      fact *= i;
    }
    return fact;
  }
}
```

The output is shown here:

```
Starting
55
5.0
120
Done
```

The TimeUnit Enumeration

The concurrent API defines several methods that take an argument of type **TimeUnit**, which indicates a time-out period. **TimeUnit** is an enumeration that is used to specify the *granularity* (or resolution) of the timing. **TimeUnit** is defined within **java.util.concurrent**. It can be one of the following values:

DAYS
HOURS
MINUTES
SECONDS
MICROSECONDS
MILLISECONDS
NANOSECONDS

The first three were added by Java SE 6.

Although **TimeUnit** lets you specify any of these values in calls to methods that take a timing argument, there is no guarantee that the system is capable of the specified resolution.

Here is an example that uses **TimeUnit**. The **CallableDemo** class, shown in the previous section, is modified as shown next to use the second form of **get( )** that takes a **TimeUnit** argument.

```
try {
  System.out.println(f.get(10, TimeUnit.MILLISECONDS));
  System.out.println(f2.get(10, TimeUnit.MILLISECONDS));
  System.out.println(f3.get(10, TimeUnit.MILLISECONDS));
} catch (InterruptedException exc) {
  System.out.println(exc);
}
catch (ExecutionException exc) {
  System.out.println(exc);
} catch (TimeoutException exc) {
  System.out.println(exc);
}
```

In this version, no call to **get( )** will wait more than 10 milliseconds.

The **TimeUnit** enumeration defines various methods that convert between units. These are shown here:

long convert(long *tval*, TimeUnit *tu*)
long toMicros(long *tval*)
long toMillis(long *tval*)
long toNanos(long *tval*)
long toSeconds(long *tval*)
long toDays(long *tval*)
long toHours(long *tval*)
long toMinutes(long *tval*)

The **convert( )** method converts *tval* into the specified unit and returns the result. The **to** methods perform the indicated conversion and return the result. The last three methods were added by Java SE 6.

TimeUnit also defines the following timing methods:

void sleep(long *delay*) throws InterruptedExecution
void timedJoin(Thread *thrd*, long *delay*) throws InterruptedExecution
void timedWait(Object *obj*, long *delay*) throws InterruptedExecution

Here, **sleep( )** pauses execution for the specified delay period, which is specified in terms of the invoking enumeration constant. It translates into a call to **Thread.sleep( )**. The **timedJoin( )** method is a specialized version of **Thread.join( )** in which *thrd* pauses for the time period specified by *delay*, which is described in terms of the invoking time unit. The **timedWait( )** method is a specialized version of **Object.wait( )** in which *obj* is waited on for the period of time specified by *delay*, which is described in terms of the invoking time unit.

The Concurrent Collections

As explained, the concurrent API defines several collection classes that have been engineered for concurrent operation. They are

ArrayBlockingQueue
ConcurrentHashMap
ConcurrentLinkedQueue
ConcurrentSkipListMap (Added by Java SE 6.)
ConcurrentSkipListSet (Added by Java SE 6.)
CopyOnWriteArraylist
CopyOnWriteArraySet
DelayQueue
LinkedBlockingDeque (Added by Java SE 6.)
LinkedBlockingQueue
PriorityBlockingQueue
SynchronousQueue

These offer concurrent alternatives to their related classes defined by the Collections Framework. These collections work much like the other collections except that they provide concurrency support. Programmers familiar with the Collections Framework will have no trouble using these concurrent collections.

Locks

The **java.util.concurrent.locks** package provides support for *locks*, which are objects that offer an alternative to using **synchronized** to control access to a shared resource. In general, here is how a lock works. Before accessing a shared resource, the lock that protects that resource is acquired. When access to the resource is complete, the lock is released. If a second thread attempts to acquire the lock when it is in use by another thread, the second thread will suspend until the lock is released. In this way, conflicting access to a shared resource is prevented.

Locks are particularly useful when multiple threads need to access the value of shared data. For example, an inventory application might have a thread that first confirms that an item is in stock and then decreases the number of items on hand as each sale occurs. If two or more of these threads are running, then without some form of synchronization, it would be possible for one thread to be in middle of a transaction when the second thread begins its transaction. The result could be that both threads would assume that adequate inventory exists, even if there is only sufficient inventory on hand to satisfy one sale. In this type of situation, a lock offers a convenient means of handling the needed synchronization.

All locks implement the **Lock** interface. The methods defined by **Lock** are shown in Table 26-1. In general, to acquire a lock, call **lock( )**. If the lock is unavailable, **lock( )** will wait. To release a lock, call **unlock( )**. To see if a lock is available, and to acquire it if it is, call **tryLock( )**. This method will not wait for the lock if it is unavailable. Instead, it returns **true** if the lock is acquired and **false** otherwise. The **newCondition( )** method returns a **Condition** object associated with the lock. Using a **Condition**, you gain detailed control of the lock through methods such as **await( )** and **signal( )**, which provide functionality similar to **Object.wait( )** and **Object.notify( )**.

Method	Description
void lock( )	Waits until the invoking lock can be acquired.
void lockInterruptibly( ) throws InterruptedException	Waits until the invoking lock can be acquired, unless interrupted.
Condition newCondition( )	Returns a **Condition** object that is associated with the invoking lock.
boolean tryLock( )	Attempts to acquire the lock. This method will not wait if the lock is unavailable. Instead, it returns **true** if the lock has been acquired and **false** if the lock is currently in use by another thread.
boolean tryLock(long *wait*, TimeUnit *tu*) throws InterruptedException	Attempts to acquire the lock. If the lock is unavailable, this method will wait no longer than the period specified by *wait*, which is in *tu* units. It returns **true** if the lock has been acquired and **false** if the lock cannot be acquired within the specified period.
void unlock( )	Releases the lock.

TABLE 26-1   The **Lock** Methods

java.util.concurrent.locks supplies an implementation of **Lock** called **ReentrantLock**. **ReentrantLock** implements a *reentrant lock,* which is a lock that can be repeatedly entered by the thread that currently holds the lock. (Of course, in the case of a thread reentering a lock, all calls to **lock( )** must be offset by an equal number of calls to **unlock( )**.) Otherwise, a thread seeking to acquire the lock will suspend until the lock is not in use.

The following program demonstrates the use of a lock. It creates two threads that access a shared resource called **Shared.count**. Before a thread can access **Shared.count**, it must obtain a lock. After obtaining the lock, **Shared.count** is incremented and then, before releasing the lock, the thread sleeps. This causes the second thread to attempt to obtain the lock. However, because the lock is still held by the first thread, the second thread must wait until the first thread stops sleeping and releases the lock. The output shows that access to **Shared.count** is, indeed, synchronized by the lock.

```
// A simple lock example.

import java.util.concurrent.locks.*;

class LockDemo {

  public static void main(String args[]) {
    ReentrantLock lock = new ReentrantLock();

    new LockThread(lock, "A");
    new LockThread(lock, "B");

  }
}
```

```java
// A shared resource.
class Shared {
  static int count = 0;
}

// A thread of execution that increments count.
class LockThread implements Runnable {
  String name;
  ReentrantLock lock;

  LockThread(ReentrantLock lk, String n) {
    lock = lk;
    name = n;
    new Thread(this).start();
  }

  public void run() {

    System.out.println("Starting " + name);

    try {
      // First, lock count.
      System.out.println(name + " is waiting to lock count.");
      lock.lock();
      System.out.println(name + " is locking count.");

      Shared.count++;
      System.out.println(name + ": " + Shared.count);

      // Now, allow a context switch -- if possible.
      System.out.println(name + " is sleeping.");
      Thread.sleep(1000);
    } catch (InterruptedException exc) {
      System.out.println(exc);
    } finally {
      // Unlock
      System.out.println(name + " is unlocking count.");
      lock.unlock();
    }
  }
}
```

The output is shown here. (The precise order in which the threads execute may vary.)

```
Starting A
A is waiting to lock count.
A is locking count.
A: 1
A is sleeping.
Starting B
B is waiting to lock count.
A is unlocking count.
B is locking count.
```

```
    B: 2
    B is sleeping.
    B is unlocking count.
```

java.util.concurrent.locks also defines the **ReadWriteLock** interface. This interface specifies a reentrant lock that maintains separate locks for read and write access. This enables multiple locks to be granted for readers of a resource as long as the resource is not being written. **ReentrantReadWriteLock** provides an implementation of **ReadWriteLock**.

Atomic Operations

java.util.concurrent.atomic offers an alternative to the other synchronization features when reading or writing the value of some types of variables. This package offers methods that get, set, or compare the value of a variable in one uninterruptible (that is, atomic) operation. This means that no lock or other synchronization mechanism is required.

Atomic operations are accomplished through the use of classes, such as **AtomicInteger** and **AtomicLong**, and methods such as **get( )**, **set( )**, **compareAndSet( )**, **decrementAndGet( )**, and **getAndSet( )**, which perform the action indicated by their names.

Here is an example that demonstrates how access to a shared integer can be synchronized by the use of **AtomicInteger**:

```
// A simple example of Atomic.

import java.util.concurrent.atomic.*;

class AtomicDemo {

  public static void main(String args[]) {
    new AtomThread("A");
    new AtomThread("B");
    new AtomThread("C");
  }
}

class Shared {
  static AtomicInteger ai = new AtomicInteger(0);
}

// A thread of execution that increments count.
class AtomThread implements Runnable {
  String name;

  AtomThread(String n) {
    name = n;
    new Thread(this).start();
  }

  public void run() {

    System.out.println("Starting " + name);

    for(int i=1; i <= 3; i++)
```

```
        System.out.println(name + " got: " +
            Shared.ai.getAndSet(i));
    }
}
```

In the program, a static **AtomicInteger** named **ai** is created by **Shared**. Then, three threads of type **AtomThread** are created. Inside **run( )**, **Shared.ai** is modified by calling **getAndSet( )**. This method returns the previous value and then sets the value to the one passed as an argument. The use of **AtomicInteger** prevents two threads from writing to **ai** at the same time.

In general, the atomic operations offer a convenient (and possibly more efficient) alternative to the other synchronization mechanisms when only a single variable is involved.

The Concurrency Utilities Versus Java's Traditional Approach

Given the power and flexibility found in the new concurrency utilities, it is natural to ask the following question: Do they replace Java's traditional approach to multithreading and synchronization? The answer is a resounding no! The original support for multithreading and the built-in synchronization features are still the mechanism that should be employed for many, many Java programs, applets, and servlets. For example, **synchronized**, **wait( )**, and **notify( )** offer elegant solutions to a wide range of problems. However, when extra control is needed, the concurrency utilities are now available to handle the chore.

CHAPTER

NIO, Regular Expressions, and Other Packages

When Java was originally released, it included a set of eight packages, called the *core API*. Each subsequent release added to the API. Today, the Java API contains a large number of packages. Many of the new packages support areas of specialization that are beyond the scope of this book. However, five packages warrant an examination here: **java.nio**, **java.util.regex**, **java.lang.reflect**, **java.rmi**, and **java.text**. They support NIO-based I/O, regular expression processing, reflection, Remote Method Invocation (RMI), and text formatting, respectively.

The *NIO* API offers a different way to look at and handle certain types of I/O operations. The *regular expression* package lets you perform sophisticated pattern matching operations. This chapter provides an in-depth discussion of both of these packages along with extensive examples. *Reflection* is the ability of software to analyze itself. It is an essential part of the Java Beans technology that is covered in Chapter 28. *Remote Method Invocation (RMI)* allows you to build Java applications that are distributed among several machines. This chapter provides a simple client/server example that uses RMI. The *text formatting* capabilities of **java.text** have many uses. The one examined here formats date and time strings.

The Core Java API Packages

Table 27-1 lists all of the core API packages defined by Java and summarizes their functions.

Package	Primary Function
java.applet	Supports construction of applets.
java.awt	Provides capabilities for graphical user interfaces.
java.awt.color	Supports color spaces and profiles.
java.awt.datatransfer	Transfers data to and from the system clipboard.
java.awt.dnd	Supports drag-and-drop operations.
java.awt.event	Handles events.

TABLE 27-1   The Core Java API Packages

Package	Primary Function
java.awt.font	Represents various types of fonts.
java.awt.geom	Allows you to work with geometric shapes.
java.awt.im	Allows input of Japanese, Chinese, and Korean characters to text editing components.
java.awt.im.spi	Supports alternative input devices.
java.awt.image	Processes images.
java.awt.image.renderable	Supports rendering-independent images.
java.awt.print	Supports general print capabilities.
java.beans	Allows you to build software components.
java.beans.beancontext	Provides an execution environment for Beans.
java.io	Inputs and outputs data.
java.lang	Provides core functionality.
java.lang.annotation	Supports annotations (metadata).
java.lang.instrument	Supports program instrumentation.
java.lang.management	Supports management of the execution environment.
java.lang.ref	Enables some interaction with the garbage collector.
java.lang.reflect	Analyzes code at run time.
java.math	Handles large integers and decimal numbers.
java.net	Supports networking.
java.nio	Top-level package for the NIO classes. Encapsulates buffers.
java.nio.channels	Encapsulates channels, which are used by the NIO system.
java.nio.channels.spi	Supports service providers for channels.
java.nio.charset	Encapsulates character sets.
java.nio.charset.spi	Supports service providers for character sets.
java.rmi	Provides remote method invocation.
java.rmi.activation	Activates persistent objects.
java.rmi.dgc	Manages distributed garbage collection.
java.rmi.registry	Maps names to remote object references.
java.rmi.server	Supports remote method invocation.
java.security	Handles certificates, keys, digests, signatures, and other security functions.
java.security.acl	Manages access control lists.
java.security.cert	Parses and manages certificates.
java.security.interfaces	Defines interfaces for DSA (Digital Signature Algorithm) keys.
java.security.spec	Specifies keys and algorithm parameters.
java.sql	Communicates with a SQL (Structured Query Language) database.

TABLE 27-1   The Core Java API Packages *(continued)*

Package	Primary Function
java.text	Formats, searches, and manipulates text.
java.text.spi	Supports service providers for text formatting classes in **java.text**. (Added by Java SE 6.)
java.util	Contains common utilities.
java.util.concurrent	Supports the concurrent utilities.
java.util.concurrent.atomic	Supports atomic (that is, indivisible) operations on variables without the use of locks.
java.util.concurrent.locks	Supports synchronization locks.
java.util.jar	Creates and reads JAR files.
java.util.logging	Supports logging of information related to a program's execution.
java.util.prefs	Encapsulates information relating to user preference.
java.util.regex	Supports regular expression processing.
java.util.spi	Supports service providers for the utility classes in **java.util**. (Addded by Java SE 6.)
java.util.zip	Reads and writes compressed and uncompressed ZIP files.

TABLE 27-1   The Core Java API Packages *(continued)*

NIO

A relatively new addition to Java is called *NIO (New I/O)*, and it is one of the more interesting packages because it supports a channel-based approach to I/O operations. The NIO classes are contained in the five packages shown here:

Package	Purpose
java.nio	Top-level package for the NIO system. Encapsulates various types of buffers that contain data operated upon by the NIO system.
java.nio.channels	Supports channels, which are essentially open I/O connections.
java.nio.channels.spi	Supports service providers for channels.
java.nio.charset	Encapsulates character sets. Also supports encoders and decoders that convert characters to bytes and bytes to characters, respectively.
java.nio.charset.spi	Supports service providers for character sets.

Before we begin, it is important to emphasize that the NIO subsystem is not intended to replace the I/O classes found in **java.io**, which are discussed in Chapter 19. Instead, the NIO classes supplement the standard I/O system, giving you an alternative approach, which can be beneficial in some circumstances.

NIO Fundamentals

The NIO system is built on two foundational items: buffers and channels. A *buffer* holds data. A *channel* represents an open connection to an I/O device, such as a file or a socket. In general, to use the NIO system, you obtain a channel to an I/O device and a buffer to hold data. You then operate on the buffer, inputting or outputting data as needed. The following sections examine buffers and channels in more detail.

Buffers

Buffers are defined in the **java.nio** package. All buffers are subclasses of the **Buffer** class, which defines the core functionality common to all buffers: current position, limit, and capacity. The *current position* is the index within the buffer at which the next read or write operation will take place. The current position is advanced by most read or write operations. The *limit* is the index of the end of the buffer. The *capacity* is the number of elements that the buffer can hold. **Buffer** also supports mark and reset. **Buffer** defines several methods, which are shown in Table 27-2.

Method	Description
abstract Object array( )	If the invoking buffer is backed by an array, a reference to the array is returned. Otherwise, an **UnsupportedOperationException** is thrown. If the array is read-only, a **ReadOnlyBufferException** is thrown. (Added by Java SE 6.)
abstract int arrayOffset( )	If the invoking buffer is backed by an array, the index of the first element is returned. Otherwise, an **UnsupportedOperationException** is thrown. If the array is read-only, a **ReadOnlyBufferException** is thrown. (Added by Java SE 6.)
final int capacity( )	Returns the number of elements that the invoking buffer is capable of holding.
final Buffer clear( )	Clears the invoking buffer and returns a reference to the buffer.
final Buffer flip( )	Sets the invoking buffer's limit to the current position and resets the current position to 0. Returns a reference to the buffer.
abstract boolean hasArray( )	Returns **true** if the invoking buffer is backed by a read/write array and **false** otherwise. (Added by Java SE 6.)
final boolean hasRemaining( )	Returns **true** if there are elements remaining in the invoking buffer. Returns **false** otherwise.
abstract isDirect( )	Returns **true** if the invoking buffer is direct, which means that it can often be operated upon directly, rather than through a copy. Returns **false** otherwise. (Added by Java SE 6.)
abstract boolean isReadOnly( )	Returns **true** if the invoking buffer is read-only. Returns **false** otherwise.
final int limit( )	Returns the invoking buffer's limit.
final Buffer limit(int *n*)	Sets the invoking buffer's limit to *n*. Returns a reference to the buffer.
final Buffer mark( )	Sets the mark and returns a reference to the invoking buffer.
final int position( )	Returns the current position.
final Buffer position(int *n*)	Sets the invoking buffer's current position to *n*. Returns a reference to the buffer.
final Buffer reset( )	Resets the current position of the invoking buffer to the previously set mark. Returns a reference to the buffer.
final Buffer rewind( )	Sets the position of the invoking buffer to 0. Returns a reference to the buffer.

TABLE 27-2 The Methods Defined by **Buffer**

From **Buffer** are derived the following specific buffer classes, which hold the type of data that their names imply:

ByteBuffer	CharBuffer	DoubleBuffer	FloatBuffer
IntBuffer	LongBuffer	MappedByteBuffer	ShortBuffer

MappedByteBuffer is a subclass of **ByteBuffer** that is used to map a file to a buffer.

All buffers support various **get( )** and **put( )** methods, which allow you to get data from a buffer or put data into a buffer. For example, Table 27-3 shows the **get( )** and **put( )** methods defined by **ByteBuffer**. (The other buffer classes have similar methods.) All buffer classes also support methods that perform various buffer operations. For example, you can allocate a buffer manually using **allocate( )**. You can wrap an array inside a buffer using **wrap( )**. You can create a subsequence of a buffer using **slice( )**.

Method	Description
abstract byte get( )	Returns the byte at the current position.
ByteBuffer get(byte *vals*[ ])	Copies the invoking buffer into the array referred to by *vals*. Returns a reference to the buffer.
ByteBuffer get(byte *vals*[ ], int *start*, int *num*)	Copies *num* elements from the invoking buffer into the array referred to by *vals*, beginning at the index specified by *start*. Returns a reference to the buffer. If there are not *num* elements remaining in the buffer, a **BufferUnderflowException** is thrown.
abstract byte get(int *idx*)	Returns the byte at the index specified by *idx* within the invoking buffer.
abstract ByteBuffer put(byte *b*)	Copies *b* into the invoking buffer at the current position. Returns a reference to the buffer.
final ByteBuffer put(byte vals[ ])	Copies all elements of *vals* into the invoking buffer, beginning at the current position. Returns a reference to the buffer.
ByteBuffer put(byte *vals*[ ], int *start*, int *num*)	Copies *num* elements from *vals*, beginning at *start*, into the invoking buffer. Returns a reference to the buffer. If the buffer cannot hold all of the elements, a **BufferOverflowException** is thrown.
ByteBuffer put(ByteBuffer bb)	Copies the elements in *bb* to the invoking buffer, beginning at the current position. If the buffer cannot hold all of the elements, a **BufferOverflowException** is thrown. Returns a reference to the buffer.
abstract ByteBuffer put(int *idx*, byte *b*)	Copies *b* into the invoking buffer at the location specified by *idx*. Returns a reference to the buffer.

TABLE 27-3   The **get( )** and **put( )** Methods Defined for **ByteBuffer**

Channels

Channels are defined in **java.nio.channels**. A channel represents an open connection to an I/O source or destination. You obtain a channel by calling **getChannel( )** on an object that supports channels. For example, **getChannel( )** is supported by following I/O classes.

DatagramSocket	FileInputStream	FileOutputStream
RandomAccessFile	ServerSocket	Socket

Thus, to obtain a channel, you first obtain an object of one of these classes and then call **getChannel( )** on that object.

The specific type of channel returned depends upon the type of object **getChannel( )** is called on. For example, when called on a **FileInputStream**, **FileOutputStream**, or **RandomAccessFile**, **getChannel( )** returns a channel of type **FileChannel**. When called on a **Socket**, **getChannel( )** returns a **SocketChannel**.

Channels such as **FileChannel** and **SocketChannel** support various **read( )** and **write( )** methods that enable you to perform I/O operations through the channel. For example, here are a few of the **read( )** and **write( )** methods defined for **FileChannel**. All can throw an **IOException**.

Method	Description
abstract int read(ByteBuffer *bb*)	Reads bytes from the invoking channel into *bb* until the buffer is full or there is no more input. Returns the number of bytes actually read.
abstract int read(ByteBuffer *bb*, long *start*)	Beginning at the file location specified by *start*, reads bytes from the invoking channel into *bb* until the buffer is full or there is no more input. The current position is unchanged. Returns the number of bytes actually read or –1 if *start* is beyond the end of the file.
abstract int write(ByteBuffer *bb*)	Writes the contents of *bb* to the invoking channel, starting at the current position. Returns the number of bytes written.
abstract int write(ByteBuffer *bb*, long *start*)	Beginning at the file location specified by *start*, writes the contents of *bb* to the invoking channel. The current position is unchanged. Returns the number of bytes written.

All channels support additional methods that give you access to and control over the channel. For example, **FileChannel** supports methods to get or set the current position, transfer information between file channels, obtain the current size of the channel, and lock the channel, among others. **FileChannel** also provides the **map( )** method, which lets you map a file to a buffer.

Charsets and Selectors

Two other entities used by NIO are charsets and selectors. A *charset* defines the way that bytes are mapped to characters. You can encode a sequence of characters into bytes using an *encoder*. You can decode a sequence of bytes into characters using a *decoder*. Charsets, encoders, and decoders are supported by classes defined in the **java.nio.charset** package.

Because default encoders and decoders are provided, you will not often need to work explicitly with charsets.

A *selector* supports key-based, non-blocking, multiplexed I/O. In other words, selectors enable you to perform I/O through multiple channels. Selectors are supported by classes defined in the **java.nio.channels** package. Selectors are most applicable to socket-backed channels.

We will not use charsets or selectors in this chapter, but you might find them useful in your own applications.

Using the NIO System

Because the most common I/O device is the disk file, the rest of this section examines how to access a disk file using NIO. Because all file channel operations are byte-based, the type of buffers that we will be using are of type **ByteBuffer**.

Reading a File

There are several ways to read data from a file using NIO. We will look at two. The first reads a file by manually allocating a buffer and then performing an explicit read operation. The second uses a mapped file, which automates the process.

To read a file using a channel and a manually allocated buffer, follow this procedure. First, open the file for input using **FileInputStream**. Then, obtain a channel to this file by calling **getChannel( )**. It has this general form:

FileChannel getChannel( )

It returns a **FileChannel** object, which encapsulates the channel for file operations. Once a file channel has been opened, obtain the size of the file by calling **size( )**, shown here:

long size( ) throws IOException

It returns the current size, in bytes, of the channel, which reflects the underlying file. Next, call **allocate( )** to allocate a buffer large enough to hold the file's contents. Because file channels operate on byte buffers, you will use the **allocate( )** method defined by **ByteBuffer**. It has this general form:

static ByteBuffer allocate(int *cap*)

Here, *cap* specifies the capacity of the buffer. A reference to the buffer is returned. After you have created the buffer, call **read( )** on the channel, passing a reference to the buffer.

The following program shows how to read a text file called **test.txt** through a channel using explicit input operations:

```
// Use NIO to read a text file.
import java.io.*;
import java.nio.*;
import java.nio.channels.*;

public class ExplicitChannelRead {
  public static void main(String args[])
    FileInputStream fIn;
```

```
    FileChannel fChan;
    long fSize;
    ByteBuffer mBuf;

    try
      // First, open a file for input.
      fIn = new FileInputStream("test.txt");

      // Next, obtain a channel to that file.
      fChan = fIn.getChannel();

      // Now, get the file's size.
      fSize = fChan.size();

      // Allocate a buffer of the necessary size.
      mBuf = ByteBuffer.allocate((int)fSize);

      // Read the file into the buffer.
      fChan.read(mBuf);

      // Rewind the buffer so that it can be read.
      mBuf.rewind();

      // Read bytes from the buffer.
      for(int i=0; i < fSize; i++)
        System.out.print((char)mBuf.get());

      System.out.println();

      fChan.close(); // close channel
      fIn.close();    // close file
    } catch (IOException exc) {
      System.out.println(exc);
      System.exit(1);
    }
  }
}
```

Here is how the program works. First, a file is opened by using the **FileInputStream** constructor, and a reference to that object is assigned to **fIn**. Next, a channel connected to the file is obtained by calling **getChannel( )** on **fIn**, and the size of the file is obtained by calling **size( )**. The program then calls the **allocate( )** method of **ByteBuffer** to allocate a buffer that will hold the contents of the file when it is read. A byte buffer is used because **FileChannel** operates on bytes. A reference to this buffer is stored in **mBuf**. The contents of the file are then read into **mBuf** through a call to **read( )**. Next, the buffer is rewound through a call to **rewind( )**. This call is necessary because the current position is at the end of the buffer after the call to **read( )**. It must be reset to the start of the buffer in order for the bytes in **mBuf** to be read by calling **get( )**. Because **mBuf** is a byte buffer, the values returned by **get( )** are bytes. They are cast to **char** so that the file can be displayed as text. (Alternatively, it is possible to create a buffer that encodes the bytes into characters, and then reads that buffer.) The program ends by closing the channel and the file.

A second, and often easier, way to read a file is to map it to a buffer. The advantage to this approach is that the buffer automatically contains the contents of the file. No explicit read operation is necessary. To map and read the contents of a file, follow this general procedure. First, open the file using **FileInputStream**. Next, obtain a channel to that file by calling **getChannel( )** on the file object. Then, map the channel to a buffer by calling **map( )** on the **FileChannel** object. The **map( )** method is shown here:

MappedByteBuffer map(FileChannel.MapMode *how*,
                 long *pos*, long *size*) throws IOException

The **map( )** method causes the data in the file to be mapped into a buffer in memory. The value in *how* determines what type of operations are allowed. It must be one of these values:

MapMode.READ_ONLY	MapMode.READ_WRITE	MapMode.PRIVATE

For reading a file, use **MapMode.READ_ONLY**. To read and write, use **MapeMode.READ_ WRITE**. **MapMode.PRIVATE** causes a private copy of the file to be made, and changes to the buffer do not affect the underlying file. The location within the file to begin mapping is specified by *pos,* and the number of bytes to map are specified by *size.* A reference to this buffer is returned as a **MappedByteBuffer**, which is a subclass of **ByteBuffer**. Once the file has been mapped to a buffer, you can read the file from that buffer.

The following program reworks the first example so that it uses a mapped file:

```
// Use a mapped file to read a text file.
import java.io.*;
import java.nio.*;
import java.nio.channels.*;

public class MappedChannelRead {
  public static void main(String args[]) {
    FileInputStream fIn;
    FileChannel fChan;
    long fSize;
    MappedByteBuffer mBuf;

    try {
      // First, open a file for input.
      fIn = new FileInputStream("test.txt");

      // Next, obtain a channel to that file.
      fChan = fIn.getChannel();

      // Get the size of the file.
      fSize = fChan.size();

      // Now, map the file into a buffer.
      mBuf = fChan.map(FileChannel.MapMode.READ_ONLY,
                       0, fSize);
```

```
      // Read bytes from the buffer.
      for(int i=0; i < fSize; i++)
        System.out.print((char)mBuf.get());

      fChan.close(); // close channel
      fIn.close();   // close file
    } catch (IOException exc) {
      System.out.println(exc);
      System.exit(1);
    }
  }
}
```

As before, the file is opened by using the **FileInputStream** constructor, and a reference to that object is assigned to **fIn**. A channel connected to the file is obtained by calling **getChannel( )** on **fIn**, and the size of the file is obtained. Then the entire file is mapped into memory by calling **map( )**, and a reference to the buffer is stored in **mBuf**. The bytes in **mBuf** are read by calling **get( )**.

Writing to a File

There are several ways to write to a file through a channel. Again, we will look at two. First, you can write data to an output file through a channel, by using explicit write operations. Second, if the file is opened for read/write operations, you can map the file to a buffer and then write to that buffer. Changes to the buffer will automatically be reflected in the file. Both ways are described here.

To write to a file through a channel using explicit calls to **write( )**, follow these steps. First, open the file for output. Next, allocate a byte buffer, put the data you want to write into that buffer, and then call **write( )** on the channel. The following program demonstrates this procedure. It writes the alphabet to a file called **test.txt**.

```
// Write to a file using NIO.
import java.io.*;
import java.nio.*;
import java.nio.channels.*;

public class ExplicitChannelWrite {
  public static void main(String args[]) {
    FileOutputStream fOut;
    FileChannel fChan;
    ByteBuffer mBuf;

    try {
      fOut = new FileOutputStream("test.txt");

      // Get a channel to the output file.
      fChan = fOut.getChannel();

      // Create a buffer.
      mBuf = ByteBuffer.allocateDirect(26);
```

```
      // Write some bytes to the buffer.
      for(int i=0; i<26; i++)
        mBuf.put((byte)('A' + i));

      // Rewind the buffer so that it can be written.
      mBuf.rewind();

      // Write the buffer to the output file.
      fChan.write(mBuf);

      // close channel and file.
      fChan.close();
      fOut.close();
    } catch (IOException exc) {
      System.out.println(exc);
      System.exit(1);
    }
  }
}
```

The call to **rewind( )** on **mBuf** is necessary in order to reset the current position to zero after data has been written to **mBuf**. Remember, each call to **put( )** advances the current position. Therefore, it is necessary for the current position to be reset to the start of the buffer before calling **write( )**. If this is not done, **write( )** will think that there is no data in the buffer.

To write to a file using a mapped file, follow these steps. First, open the file for read/write operations. Next, map that file to a buffer by calling **map( )**. Then, write to the buffer. Because the buffer is mapped to the file, any changes to that buffer are automatically reflected in the file. Thus, no explicit write operations to the channel are necessary. Here is the preceding program reworked so that a mapped file is used. Notice that the file is opened as a **RandomAccessFile**. This is necessary to allow the file to be read and written.

```
// Write to a mapped file.
import java.io.*;
import java.nio.*;
import java.nio.channels.*;

public class MappedChannelWrite {
  public static void main(String args[]) {
    RandomAccessFile fOut;
    FileChannel fChan;
    ByteBuffer mBuf;

    try {
      fOut = new RandomAccessFile("test.txt", "rw");

      // Next, obtain a channel to that file.
      fChan = fOut.getChannel();

      // Then, map the file into a buffer.
      mBuf = fChan.map(FileChannel.MapMode.READ_WRITE,
                       0, 26);
```

```
    // Write some bytes to the buffer.
    for(int i=0; i<26; i++)
      mBuf.put((byte)('A' + i));

    // close channel and file.
    fChan.close();
    fOut.close();
  } catch (IOException exc) {
    System.out.println(exc);
    System.exit(1);
  }
 }
}
```

As you can see, there are no explicit write operations to the channel itself. Because **mBuf** is mapped to the file, changes to **mBuf** are automatically reflected in the underlying file.

Copying a File Using NIO

NIO simplifies some types of file operations. For example, the following program copies a file. It does so by opening an input channel to the source file and an output channel to the target file. It then writes the mapped input buffer to the output file in a single operation. You might want to compare this version of the file copy program to the one found in Chapter 13. As you will find, the part of the program that actually copies the file is substantially shorter.

```
// Copy a file using NIO.
import java.io.*;
import java.nio.*;
import java.nio.channels.*;

public class NIOCopy {

  public static void main(String args[]) {
    FileInputStream fIn;
    FileOutputStream fOut;
    FileChannel fIChan, fOChan;
    long fSize;
    MappedByteBuffer mBuf;

    try {
      fIn = new FileInputStream(args[0]);
      fOut = new FileOutputStream(args[1]);

      // Get channels to the input and output files.
      fIChan = fIn.getChannel();
      fOChan = fOut.getChannel();

      // Get the size of the file.
      fSize = fIChan.size();

      // Map the input file to a buffer.
      mBuf = fIChan.map(FileChannel.MapMode.READ_ONLY,
                        0, fSize);
```

```
    // Write the buffer to the output file.
    fOChan.write(mBuf); // this copies the file

    // Close the channels and files.
    fIChan.close();
    fIn.close();

    fOChan.close();
    fOut.close();
  } catch (IOException exc) {
    System.out.println(exc);
    System.exit(1);
  } catch (ArrayIndexOutOfBoundsException exc) {
    System.out.println("Usage: Copy from to");
    System.exit(1);
  }
  }
}
```

Because the input file is mapped to **mBuf**, it contains the entire source file. Thus, the call to **write( )** copies all of **mBuf** to the target file. This, of course, means that the target file is an identical copy of the source file.

Is NIO the Future of I/O Handling?

The NIO APIs offer an exciting new way to think about and handle some types of file operations. Because of this, it is natural to ask the question, "Is NIO the future of I/O handling?" Certainly, channels and buffers offer a clean way of thinking about I/O. However, they also add another layer of abstraction. Furthermore, the traditional stream-based approach is both well-understood and widely used. As explained at the outset, channel-based I/O is currently designed to supplement, not replace, the standard I/O mechanisms defined in **java.io**. In this role, the channel/buffer approach used by the NIO APIs succeeds admirably. Whether the new approach will someday supplant the traditional approach, only time and usage patterns will tell.

Regular Expression Processing

The **java.util.regex** package supports regular expression processing. As the term is used here, a *regular expression* is a string of characters that describes a character sequence. This general description, called a *pattern,* can then be used to find matches in other character sequences. Regular expressions can specify wildcard characters, sets of characters, and various quantifiers. Thus, you can specify a regular expression that represents a general form that can match several different specific character sequences.

There are two classes that support regular expression processing: **Pattern** and **Matcher**. These classes work together. Use **Pattern** to define a regular expression. Match the pattern against another sequence using **Matcher**.

Pattern

The **Pattern** class defines no constructors. Instead, a pattern is created by calling the **compile( )** factory method. One of its forms is shown here:

static Pattern compile(String *pattern*)

Here, *pattern* is the regular expression that you want to use. The **compile( )** method transforms the string in *pattern* into a pattern that can be used for pattern matching by the **Matcher** class. It returns a **Pattern** object that contains the pattern.

Once you have created a **Pattern** object, you will use it to create a **Matcher**. This is done by calling the **matcher( )** factory method defined by **Pattern**. It is shown here:

Matcher matcher(CharSequence *str*)

Here *str* is the character sequence that the pattern will be matched against. This is called the *input sequence*. **CharSequence** is an interface that defines a read-only set of characters. It is implemented by the **String** class, among others. Thus, you can pass a string to **matcher( )**.

Matcher

The **Matcher** class has no constructors. Instead, you create a **Matcher** by calling the **matcher( )** factory method defined by **Pattern**, as just explained. Once you have created a **Matcher**, you will use its methods to perform various pattern matching operations.

The simplest pattern matching method is **matches( )**, which simply determines whether the character sequence matches the pattern. It is shown here:

boolean matches( )

It returns **true** if the sequence and the pattern match, and **false** otherwise. Understand that the entire sequence must match the pattern, not just a subsequence of it.

To determine if a subsequence of the input sequence matches the pattern, use **find( )**. One version is shown here:

boolean find( )

It returns **true** if there is a matching subsequence and **false** otherwise. This method can be called repeatedly, allowing it to find all matching subsequences. Each call to **find( )** begins where the previous one left off.

You can obtain a string containing the last matching sequence by calling **group( )**. One of its forms is shown here:

String group( )

The matching string is returned. If no match exists, then an **IllegalStateException** is thrown.

You can obtain the index within the input sequence of the current match by calling **start( )**. The index one past the end of the current match is obtained by calling **end( )**. These methods are shown here:

int start( )
int end( )

Both throw **IllegalStateException** if no match exists.

You can replace all occurrences of a matching sequence with another sequence by calling **replaceAll( )**, shown here:

String replaceAll(String *newStr*)

Here, *newStr* specifies the new character sequence that will replace the ones that match the pattern. The updated input sequence is returned as a string.

Regular Expression Syntax

Before demonstrating **Pattern** and **Matcher**, it is necessary to explain how to construct a regular expression. Although no rule is complicated by itself, there are a large number of them, and a complete discussion is beyond the scope of this chapter. However, a few of the more commonly used constructs are described here.

In general, a regular expression is comprised of normal characters, character classes (sets of characters), wildcard characters, and quantifiers. A normal character is matched as-is. Thus, if a pattern consists of "xy", then the only input sequence that will match it is "xy". Characters such as newline and tab are specified using the standard escape sequences, which begin with a \. For example, a newline is specified by \n. In the language of regular expressions, a normal character is also called a *literal*.

A character class is a set of characters. A character class is specified by putting the characters in the class between brackets. For example, the class [wxyz] matches w, x, y, or z. To specify an inverted set, precede the characters with a ^. For example, [^wxyz] matches any character except w, x, y, or z. You can specify a range of characters using a hyphen. For example, to specify a character class that will match the digits 1 through 9, use [1-9].

The wildcard character is the **.** (dot) and it matches any character. Thus, a pattern that consists of "." will match these (and other) input sequences: "A", "a", "x", and so on.

A quantifier determines how many times an expression is matched. The quantifiers are shown here:

+	Match one or more.
*	Match zero or more.
?	Match zero or one.

For example, the pattern "x+" will match "x", "xx", and "xxx", among others.

One other point: In general, if you specify an invalid expression, a **PatternSyntaxException** will be thrown.

Demonstrating Pattern Matching

The best way to understand how regular expression pattern matching operates is to work through some examples. The first, shown here, looks for a match with a literal pattern:

```
// A simple pattern matching demo.
import java.util.regex.*;

class RegExpr {
  public static void main(String args[]) {
    Pattern pat;
    Matcher mat;
    boolean found;

    pat = Pattern.compile("Java");
    mat = pat.matcher("Java");
```

```
    found = mat.matches(); // check for a match

    System.out.println("Testing Java against Java.");
    if(found) System.out.println("Matches");
    else System.out.println("No Match");

    System.out.println();

    System.out.println("Testing Java against Java SE 6.");
    mat = pat.matcher("Java SE 6"); // create a new matcher

    found = mat.matches(); // check for a match

    if(found) System.out.println("Matches");
    else System.out.println("No Match");
  }
}
```

The output from the program is shown here:

```
Testing Java against Java.
Matches

Testing Java against Java SE 6.
No Match
```

Let's look closely at this program. The program begins by creating the pattern that contains the sequence "Java". Next, a **Matcher** is created for that pattern that has the input sequence "Java". Then, the **matches( )** method is called to determine if the input sequence matches the pattern. Because the sequence and the pattern are the same, **matches( )** returns **true**. Next, a new **Matcher** is created with the input sequence "Java SE 6" and **matches( )** is called again. In this case, the pattern and the input sequence differ, and no match is found. Remember, the **matches( )** function returns **true** only when the input sequence precisely matches the pattern. It will not return **true** just because a subsequence matches.

You can use **find( )** to determine if the input sequence contains a subsequence that matches the pattern. Consider the following program:

```
// Use find() to find a subsequence.
import java.util.regex.*;

class RegExpr2 {
  public static void main(String args[]) {
    Pattern pat = Pattern.compile("Java");
    Matcher mat = pat.matcher("Java SE 6");

    System.out.println("Looking for Java in Java SE 6.");

    if(mat.find()) System.out.println("subsequence found");
    else System.out.println("No Match");
  }
}
```

The output is shown here:

```
Looking for Java in Java SE 6.
subsequence found
```

In this case, **find( )** finds the subsequence "Java".

The **find( )** method can be used to search the input sequence for repeated occurrences of the pattern because each call to **find( )** picks up where the previous one left off. For example, the following program finds two occurrences of the pattern "test":

```
// Use find() to find multiple subsequences.
import java.util.regex.*;

class RegExpr3 {
  public static void main(String args[]) {
    Pattern pat = Pattern.compile("test");
    Matcher mat = pat.matcher("test 1 2 3 test");

    while(mat.find()) {
      System.out.println("test found at index " +
                         mat.start());
    }
  }
}
```

The output is shown here:

```
test found at index 0
test found at index 11
```

As the output shows, two matches were found. The program uses the **start( )** method to obtain the index of each match.

Using Wildcards and Quantifiers

Although the preceding programs show the general technique for using **Pattern** and **Matcher**, they don't show their power. The real benefit of regular expression processing is not seen until wildcards and quantifiers are used. To begin, consider the following example that uses the + quantifier to match any arbitrarily long sequence of Ws.

```
// Use a quantifier.
import java.util.regex.*;

class RegExpr4 {
  public static void main(String args[]) {
    Pattern pat = Pattern.compile("W+");
    Matcher mat = pat.matcher("W WW WWW");

    while(mat.find())
      System.out.println("Match: " + mat.group());
  }
}
```

The output from the program is shown here:

```
Match: W
Match: WW
Match: WWW
```

As the output shows, the regular expression pattern "W+" matches any arbitrarily long sequence of Ws.

The next program uses a wildcard to create a pattern that will match any sequence that begins with *e* and ends with *d*. To do this, it uses the dot wildcard character along with the + quantifier.

```java
// Use wildcard and quantifier.
import java.util.regex.*;

class RegExpr5 {
  public static void main(String args[]) {
    Pattern pat = Pattern.compile("e.+d");
    Matcher mat = pat.matcher("extend cup end table");

    while(mat.find())
      System.out.println("Match: " + mat.group());
  }
}
```

You might be surprised by the output produced by the program, which is shown here:

```
Match: extend cup end
```

Only one match is found, and it is the longest sequence that begins with *e* and ends with *d*. You might have expected two matches: "extend" and "end". The reason that the longer sequence is found is that by default, **find( )** matches the longest sequence that fits the pattern. This is called *greedy behavior*. You can specify *reluctant behavior* by adding the **?** quantifier to the pattern, as shown in this version of the program. It causes the shortest matching pattern to be obtained.

```java
// Use the ? quantifier.
import java.util.regex.*;

class RegExpr6 {
  public static void main(String args[]) {
    // Use reluctant matching behavior.
    Pattern pat = Pattern.compile("e.+?d");
    Matcher mat = pat.matcher("extend cup end table");

    while(mat.find())
      System.out.println("Match: " + mat.group());
  }
}
```

The output from the program is shown here:

```
Match: extend
Match: end
```

As the output shows, the pattern "e.+?d" will match the shortest sequence that begins with *e* and ends with *d*. Thus, two matches are found.

Working with Classes of Characters

Sometimes you will want to match any sequence that contains one or more characters, in any order, that are part of a set of characters. For example, to match whole words, you want to match any sequence of the letters of the alphabet. One of the easiest ways to do this is to use a character class, which defines a set of characters. Recall that a character class is created by putting the characters you want to match between brackets. For example, to match the lowercase characters a through z, use **[a-z]**. The following program demonstrates this technique:

```
// Use a character class.
import java.util.regex.*;

class RegExpr7 {
  public static void main(String args[]) {
    // Match lowercase words.
    Pattern pat = Pattern.compile("[a-z]+");
    Matcher mat = pat.matcher("this is a test.");

    while(mat.find())
      System.out.println("Match: " + mat.group());
  }
}
```

The output is shown here:

```
    Match: this
    Match: is
    Match: a
    Match: test
```

Using replaceAll( )

The **replaceAll( )** method supplied by **Matcher** lets you perform powerful search and replace operations that use regular expressions. For example, the following program replaces all occurrences of sequences that begin with "Jon" with "Eric":

```
// Use replaceAll().
import java.util.regex.*;

class RegExpr8 {
  public static void main(String args[]) {
    String str = "Jon Jonathan Frank Ken Todd";

    Pattern pat = Pattern.compile("Jon.*? ");
    Matcher mat = pat.matcher(str);

    System.out.println("Original sequence: " + str);

    str = mat.replaceAll("Eric ");
```

```
    System.out.println("Modified sequence: " + str);

  }
}
```

The output is shown here:

```
    Original sequence: Jon Jonathan Frank Ken Todd
    Modified sequence: Eric Eric Frank Ken Todd
```

Because the regular expression "Jon.*? " matches any string that begins with Jon followed by zero or more characters, ending in a space, it can be used to match and replace both Jon and Jonathan with the name Eric. Such a substitution is not possible without pattern matching capabilities.

Using split( )

You can reduce an input sequence into its individual tokens by using the **split( )** method defined by **Pattern**. One form of the **split( )** method is shown here:

String[ ] split(CharSequence *str*)

It processes the input sequence passed in *str*, reducing it into tokens based on the delimiters specified by the pattern.

For example, the following program finds tokens that are separated by spaces, commas, periods, and exclamation points:

```
// Use split().
import java.util.regex.*;

class RegExpr9 {
  public static void main(String args[]) {

    // Match lowercase words.
    Pattern pat = Pattern.compile("[ ,.!]");

    String strs[] = pat.split("one two,alpha9 12!done.");

    for(int i=0; i < strs.length; i++)
      System.out.println("Next token: " + strs[i]);

  }
}
```

The output is shown here:

```
    Next token: one
    Next token: two
    Next token: alpha9
    Next token: 12
    Next token: done
```

As the output shows, the input sequence is reduced to its individual tokens. Notice that the delimiters are not included.

Two Pattern-Matching Options

Although the pattern-matching techniques described in the foregoing offer the greatest flexibility and power, there are two alternatives which you might find useful in some circumstances. If you only need to perform a one-time pattern match, you can use the **matches( )** method defined by **Pattern**. It is shown here:

    static boolean matches(String *pattern*, CharSequence *str*)

It returns **true** if *pattern* matches *str* and **false** otherwise. This method automatically compiles *pattern* and then looks for a match. If you will be using the same pattern repeatedly, then using **matches( )** is less efficient than compiling the pattern and using the pattern-matching methods defined by **Matcher**, as described previously.

You can also perform a pattern match by using the **matches( )** method implemented by **String**. It is shown here:

    boolean matches(String *pattern*)

If the invoking string matches the regular expression in *pattern*, then **matches( )** returns **true**. Otherwise, it returns **false**.

Exploring Regular Expressions

The overview of regular expressions presented in this section only hints at their power. Since text parsing, manipulation, and tokenization are a large part of programming, you will likely find Java's regular expression subsystem a powerful tool that you can use to your advantage. It is, therefore, wise to explore the capabilities of regular expressions. Experiment with several different types of patterns and input sequences. Once you understand how regular expression pattern matching works, you will find it useful in many of your programming endeavors.

Reflection

Reflection is the ability of software to analyze itself. This is provided by the **java.lang.reflect** package and elements in **Class**. Reflection is an important capability, especially when using components called Java Beans. It allows you to analyze a software component and describe its capabilities dynamically, at run time rather than at compile time. For example, by using reflection, you can determine what methods, constructors, and fields a class supports. Reflection was introduced in Chapter 12. It is examined further here.

The package **java.lang.reflect** includes several interfaces. Of special interest is **Member**, which defines methods that allow you to get information about a field, constructor, or method of a class. There are also eight classes in this package. These are listed in Table 27-4.

The following application illustrates a simple use of the Java reflection capabilities. It prints the constructors, fields, and methods of the class **java.awt.Dimension**. The program begins by using the **forName( )** method of **Class** to get a class object for **java.awt.Dimension**. Once this is obtained, **getConstructors( )**, **getFields( )**, and **getMethods( )** are used to analyze this class object. They return arrays of **Constructor**, **Field**, and **Method** objects that provide the information about the object. The **Constructor**, **Field**, and **Method** classes define

Class	Primary Function
AccessibleObject	Allows you to bypass the default access control checks.
Array	Allows you to dynamically create and manipulate arrays.
Constructor	Provides information about a constructor.
Field	Provides information about a field.
Method	Provides information about a method.
Modifier	Provides information about class and member access modifiers.
Proxy	Supports dynamic proxy classes.
ReflectPermission	Allows reflection of private or protected members of a class.

TABLE 27-4   Classes Defined in **java.lang.reflect**

several methods that can be used to obtain information about an object. You will want to explore these on your own. However, each supports the **toString( )** method. Therefore, using **Constructor**, **Field**, and **Method** objects as arguments to the **println( )** method is straightforward, as shown in the program.

```java
// Demonstrate reflection.
import java.lang.reflect.*;
public class ReflectionDemo1 {
  public static void main(String args[]) {
    try {
      Class c = Class.forName("java.awt.Dimension");
      System.out.println("Constructors:");
      Constructor constructors[] = c.getConstructors();
      for(int i = 0; i < constructors.length; i++) {
        System.out.println(" " + constructors[i]);
      }

      System.out.println("Fields:");
      Field fields[] = c.getFields();
      for(int i = 0; i < fields.length; i++) {
        System.out.println(" " + fields[i]);
      }

      System.out.println("Methods:");
      Method methods[] = c.getMethods();
      for(int i = 0; i < methods.length; i++) {
        System.out.println(" " + methods[i]);
      }
    }
    catch(Exception e) {
      System.out.println("Exception: " + e);
    }
  }
}
```

Here is the output from this program. (The precise order may differ slightly from that shown.)

```
Constructors:
 public java.awt.Dimension(int,int)
 public java.awt.Dimension()
 public java.awt.Dimension(java.awt.Dimension)
Fields:
 public int java.awt.Dimension.width
 public int java.awt.Dimension.height
Methods:
 public int java.awt.Dimension.hashCode()
 public boolean java.awt.Dimension.equals(java.lang.Object)
 public java.lang.String java.awt.Dimension.toString()
 public java.awt.Dimension java.awt.Dimension.getSize()
 public void java.awt.Dimension.setSize(double,double)
 public void java.awt.Dimension.setSize(java.awt.Dimension)
 public void java.awt.Dimension.setSize(int,int)
 public double java.awt.Dimension.getHeight()
 public double java.awt.Dimension.getWidth()
 public java.lang.Object java.awt.geom.Dimension2D.clone()
 public void java.awt.geom.
             Dimension2D.setSize(java.awt.geom.Dimension2D)
 public final native java.lang.Class java.lang.Object.getClass()
 public final native void java.lang.Object.wait(long)
    throws java.lang.InterruptedException
 public final void java.lang.Object.wait()
    throws java.lang.InterruptedException
 public final void java.lang.Object.wait(long,int)
    throws java.lang.InterruptedException
 public final native void java.lang.Object.notify()
 public final native void java.lang.Object.notifyAll()
```

The next example uses Java's reflection capabilities to obtain the public methods of a class. The program begins by instantiating class **A**. The **getClass( )** method is applied to this object reference, and it returns the **Class** object for class **A**. The **getDeclaredMethods( )** method returns an array of **Method** objects that describe only the methods declared by this class. Methods inherited from superclasses such as **Object** are not included.

Each element of the **methods** array is then processed. The **getModifiers( )** method returns an **int** containing flags that describe which modifiers apply for this element. The **Modifier** class provides a set of methods, shown in Table 27-5, that can be used to examine this value. For example, the static method **isPublic( )** returns **true** if its argument includes the **public** modifier. Otherwise, it returns **false**. In the following program, if the method supports public access, its name is obtained by the **getName( )** method and is then printed.

```
// Show public methods.
import java.lang.reflect.*;
public class ReflectionDemo2 {
  public static void main(String args[]) {
```

```
try {
  A a = new A();
  Class c = a.getClass();
  System.out.println("Public Methods:");
  Method methods[] = c.getDeclaredMethods();
  for(int i = 0; i < methods.length; i++) {
    int modifiers = methods[i].getModifiers();
    if(Modifier.isPublic(modifiers)) {
      System.out.println(" " + methods[i].getName());
    }
  }
}
catch(Exception e) {
  System.out.println("Exception: " + e);
}
}
}

class A {
  public void a1() {
  }
  public void a2() {
  }
  protected void a3() {
  }
  private void a4() {
  }
}
```

Here is the output from this program:

```
Public Methods:
 a1
 a2
```

Method	Description
static boolean isAbstract(int *val*)	Returns **true** if *val* has the **abstract** flag set and **false** otherwise.
static boolean isFinal(int *val*)	Returns **true** if *val* has the **final** flag set and **false** otherwise.
static boolean isInterface(int *val*)	Returns **true** if *val* has the **interface** flag set and **false** otherwise.
static boolean isNative(int *val*)	Returns **true** if *val* has the **native** flag set and **false** otherwise.
static boolean isPrivate(int *val*)	Returns **true** if *val* has the **private** flag set and **false** otherwise.
static boolean isProtected(int *val*)	Returns **true** if *val* has the **protected** flag set and **false** otherwise.
static boolean isPublic(int *val*)	Returns **true** if *val* has the **public** flag set and **false** otherwise.
static boolean isStatic(int *val*)	Returns **true** if *val* has the **static** flag set and **false** otherwise.
static boolean isStrict(int *val*)	Returns **true** if *val* has the **strict** flag set and **false** otherwise.
static boolean isSynchronized(int *val*)	Returns **true** if *val* has the **synchronized** flag set and **false** otherwise.
static boolean isTransient(int *val*)	Returns **true** if *val* has the **transient** flag set and **false** otherwise.
static boolean isVolatile(int *val*)	Returns **true** if *val* has the **volatile** flag set and **false** otherwise.

TABLE 27-5 Methods Defined by **Modifier** That Determine Modifiers

Remote Method Invocation (RMI)

Remote Method Invocation (RMI) allows a Java object that executes on one machine to invoke a method of a Java object that executes on another machine. This is an important feature, because it allows you to build distributed applications. While a complete discussion of RMI is outside the scope of this book, the following example describes the basic principles involved.

A Simple Client/Server Application Using RMI

This section provides step-by-step directions for building a simple client/server application by using RMI. The server receives a request from a client, processes it, and returns a result. In this example, the request specifies two numbers. The server adds these together and returns the sum.

Step One: Enter and Compile the Source Code

This application uses four source files. The first file, **AddServerIntf.java**, defines the remote interface that is provided by the server. It contains one method that accepts two **double** arguments and returns their sum. All remote interfaces must extend the **Remote** interface, which is part of **java.rmi**. **Remote** defines no members. Its purpose is simply to indicate that an interface uses remote methods. All remote methods can throw a **RemoteException**.

```
import java.rmi.*;
public interface AddServerIntf extends Remote {
  double add(double d1, double d2) throws RemoteException;
}
```

The second source file, **AddServerImpl.java**, implements the remote interface. The implementation of the **add( )** method is straightforward. All remote objects must extend **UnicastRemoteObject**, which provides functionality that is needed to make objects available from remote machines.

```
import java.rmi.*;
import java.rmi.server.*;
public class AddServerImpl extends UnicastRemoteObject
  implements AddServerIntf {

  public AddServerImpl() throws RemoteException {
  }
  public double add(double d1, double d2) throws RemoteException {
    return d1 + d2;
  }
}
```

The third source file, **AddServer.java**, contains the main program for the server machine. Its primary function is to update the RMI registry on that machine. This is done by using the **rebind( )** method of the **Naming** class (found in **java.rmi**). That method associates a name with an object reference. The first argument to the **rebind( )** method is a string that names the server as "AddServer". Its second argument is a reference to an instance of **AddServerImpl**.

```
import java.net.*;
import java.rmi.*;
public class AddServer {
  public static void main(String args[]) {
```

```
    try {
      AddServerImpl addServerImpl = new AddServerImpl();
      Naming.rebind("AddServer", addServerImpl);
    }
    catch(Exception e) {
      System.out.println("Exception: " + e);
    }
  }
}
```

The fourth source file, **AddClient.java**, implements the client side of this distributed application. **AddClient.java** requires three command-line arguments. The first is the IP address or name of the server machine. The second and third arguments are the two numbers that are to be summed.

The application begins by forming a string that follows the URL syntax. This URL uses the **rmi** protocol. The string includes the IP address or name of the server and the string "AddServer". The program then invokes the **lookup( )** method of the **Naming** class. This method accepts one argument, the **rmi** URL, and returns a reference to an object of type **AddServerIntf**. All remote method invocations can then be directed to this object.

The program continues by displaying its arguments and then invokes the remote **add( )** method. The sum is returned from this method and is then printed.

```
import java.rmi.*;
public class AddClient {
  public static void main(String args[]) {
    try {
      String addServerURL = "rmi://" + args[0] + "/AddServer";
      AddServerIntf addServerIntf =
                      (AddServerIntf)Naming.lookup(addServerURL);
      System.out.println("The first number is: " + args[1]);
      double d1 = Double.valueOf(args[1]).doubleValue();
      System.out.println("The second number is: " + args[2]);

      double d2 = Double.valueOf(args[2]).doubleValue();
      System.out.println("The sum is: " + addServerIntf.add(d1, d2));
    }
    catch(Exception e) {
      System.out.println("Exception: " + e);
    }
  }
}
```

After you enter all the code, use **javac** to compile the four source files that you created.

Step Two: Generate a Stub

Before you can use the client and server, you must generate the necessary stub. In the context of RMI, a *stub* is a Java object that resides on the client machine. Its function is to present the same interfaces as the remote server. Remote method calls initiated by the client are actually directed to the stub. The stub works with the other parts of the RMI system to formulate a request that is sent to the remote machine.

A remote method may accept arguments that are simple types or objects. In the latter case, the object may have references to other objects. All of this information must be sent to the remote machine. That is, an object passed as an argument to a remote method call must be serialized and sent to the remote machine. Recall from Chapter 19 that the serialization facilities also recursively process all referenced objects.

If a response must be returned to the client, the process works in reverse. Note that the serialization and deserialization facilities are also used if objects are returned to a client.

To generate a stub, you use a tool called the *RMI compiler,* which is invoked from the command line, as shown here:

    rmic AddServerImpl

This command generates the file **AddServerImpl_Stub.class**. When using **rmic**, be sure that **CLASSPATH** is set to include the current directory.

Step Three: Install Files on the Client and Server Machines

Copy **AddClient.class**, **AddServerImpl_Stub.class**, and **AddServerIntf.class** to a directory on the client machine. Copy **AddServerIntf.class**, **AddServerImpl.class**, **AddServerImpl_Stub.class**, and **AddServer.class** to a directory on the server machine.

NOTE   *RMI has techniques for dynamic class loading, but they are not used by the example at hand. Instead, all of the files that are used by the client and server applications must be installed manually on those machines.*

Step Four: Start the RMI Registry on the Server Machine

Java SE 6 provides a program called **rmiregistry**, which executes on the server machine. It maps names to object references. First, check that the **CLASSPATH** environment variable includes the directory in which your files are located. Then, start the RMI Registry from the command line, as shown here:

    start rmiregistry

When this command returns, you should see that a new window has been created. You need to leave this window open until you are done experimenting with the RMI example.

Step Five: Start the Server

The server code is started from the command line, as shown here:

    java AddServer

Recall that the **AddServer** code instantiates **AddServerImpl** and registers that object with the name "AddServer".

Step Six: Start the Client

The **AddClient** software requires three arguments: the name or IP address of the server machine and the two numbers that are to be summed together. You may invoke it from the command line by using one of the two formats shown here:

    java AddClient server1 8 9
    java AddClient 11.12.13.14 8 9

In the first line, the name of the server is provided. The second line uses its IP address (11.12.13.14).

You can try this example without actually having a remote server. To do so, simply install all of the programs on the same machine, start **rmiregistry**, start **AddServer**, and then execute **AddClient** using this command line:

```
java AddClient 127.0.0.1 8 9
```

Here, the address 127.0.0.1 is the "loop back" address for the local machine. Using this address allows you to exercise the entire RMI mechanism without actually having to install the server on a remote computer.

In either case, sample output from this program is shown here:

```
The first number is: 8
The second number is: 9
The sum is: 17.0
```

Text Formatting

The package **java.text** allows you to format, search, and manipulate text. Chapter 32 illustrates its **NumberFormat** class, which is used to format numeric data. This section examines two more of its most commonly used classes: those that format date and time information.

DateFormat Class

DateFormat is an abstract class that provides the ability to format and parse dates and times. The **getDateInstance( )** method returns an instance of **DateFormat** that can format date information. It is available in these forms:

static final DateFormat getDateInstance( )
static final DateFormat getDateInstance(int *style*)
static final DateFormat getDateInstance(int *style*, Locale *locale*)

The argument *style* is one of the following values: **DEFAULT**, **SHORT**, **MEDIUM**, **LONG**, or **FULL**. These are **int** constants defined by **DateFormat**. They cause different details about the date to be presented. The argument *locale* is one of the static references defined by **Locale** (refer to Chapter 18 for details). If the *style* and/or *locale* is not specified, defaults are used.

One of the most commonly used methods in this class is **format( )**. It has several overloaded forms, one of which is shown here:

final String format(Date *d*)

The argument is a **Date** object that is to be displayed. The method returns a string containing the formatted information.

The following listing illustrates how to format date information. It begins by creating a **Date** object. This captures the current date and time information. Then it outputs the date information by using different styles and locales.

```
// Demonstrate date formats.
import java.text.*;
import java.util.*;

public class DateFormatDemo {
  public static void main(String args[]) {
    Date date = new Date();
```

```
    DateFormat df;

    df = DateFormat.getDateInstance(DateFormat.SHORT, Locale.JAPAN);
    System.out.println("Japan: " + df.format(date));

    df = DateFormat.getDateInstance(DateFormat.MEDIUM, Locale.KOREA);
    System.out.println("Korea: " + df.format(date));

    df = DateFormat.getDateInstance(DateFormat.LONG, Locale.UK);
    System.out.println("United Kingdom: " + df.format(date));

    df = DateFormat.getDateInstance(DateFormat.FULL, Locale.US);
    System.out.println("United States: " + df.format(date));
  }
}
```

Sample output from this program is shown here:

```
Japan: 06/07/12
Korea: 2006. 7. 12
United Kingdom: 12 July 2006
United States: Wednesday, July 12, 2006
```

The **getTimeInstance( )** method returns an instance of **DateFormat** that can format time information. It is available in these versions:

static final DateFormat getTimeInstance( )
static final DateFormat getTimeInstance(int *style*)
static final DateFormat getTimeInstance(int *style*, Locale *locale*)

The argument *style* is one of the following values: **DEFAULT**, **SHORT**, **MEDIUM**, **LONG**, or **FULL**. These are **int** constants defined by **DateFormat**. They cause different details about the time to be presented. The argument *locale* is one of the static references defined by **Locale**. If the *style* and/or *locale* is not specified, defaults are used.

The following listing illustrates how to format time information. It begins by creating a **Date** object. This captures the current date and time information and then outputs the time information by using different styles and locales.

```
// Demonstrate time formats.
import java.text.*;
import java.util.*;
public class TimeFormatDemo {
  public static void main(String args[]) {
    Date date = new Date();
    DateFormat df;

    df = DateFormat.getTimeInstance(DateFormat.SHORT, Locale.JAPAN);
    System.out.println("Japan: " + df.format(date));

    df = DateFormat.getTimeInstance(DateFormat.LONG, Locale.UK);
    System.out.println("United Kingdom: " + df.format(date));

    df = DateFormat.getTimeInstance(DateFormat.FULL, Locale.CANADA);
```

```
      System.out.println("Canada: " + df.format(date));
  }
}
```

Sample output from this program is shown here:

```
Japan: 20:25
United Kingdom: 20:25:14 CDT
Canada: 8:25:14 o'clock PM CDT
```

The **DateFormat** class also has a **getDateTimeInstance( )** method that can format both date and time information. You may wish to experiment with it on your own.

SimpleDateFormat Class

SimpleDateFormat is a concrete subclass of **DateFormat**. It allows you to define your own formatting patterns that are used to display date and time information.

One of its constructors is shown here:

SimpleDateFormat(String *formatString*)

The argument *formatString* describes how date and time information is displayed. An example of its use is given here:

```
SimpleDateFormat sdf = SimpleDateFormat("dd MMM yyyy hh:mm:ss zzz");
```

The symbols used in the formatting string determine the information that is displayed. Table 27-6 lists these symbols and gives a description of each.

In most cases, the number of times a symbol is repeated determines how that data is presented. Text information is displayed in an abbreviated form if the pattern letter is repeated less than four times. Otherwise, the unabbreviated form is used. For example, a zzzz pattern can display Pacific Daylight Time, and a zzz pattern can display PDT.

For numbers, the number of times a pattern letter is repeated determines how many digits are presented. For example, hh:mm:ss can present 01:51:15, but h:m:s displays the same time value as 1:51:15.

Finally, M or MM causes the month to be displayed as one or two digits. However, three or more repetitions of M cause the month to be displayed as a text string.

The following program shows how this class is used:

```
// Demonstrate SimpleDateFormat.
import java.text.*;
import java.util.*;

public class SimpleDateFormatDemo {
  public static void main(String args[]) {
    Date date = new Date();
    SimpleDateFormat sdf;
    sdf = new SimpleDateFormat("hh:mm:ss");
    System.out.println(sdf.format(date));
    sdf = new SimpleDateFormat("dd MMM yyyy hh:mm:ss zzz");
    System.out.println(sdf.format(date));
    sdf = new SimpleDateFormat("E MMM dd yyyy");
```

```
    System.out.println(sdf.format(date));
  }
}
```

Sample output from this program is shown here:

```
10:25:03
12 Jul 2006 10:25:03 CDT
Wed Jul 12 2006
```

TABLE 27-6
Formatting String
Symbols for
SimpleDateFormat

Symbol	Description
a	AM or PM
d	Day of month (1–31)
h	Hour in AM/PM (1–12)
k	Hour in day (1–24)
m	Minute in hour (0–59)
s	Second in minute (0–59)
w	Week of year (1–52)
y	Year
z	Time zone
D	Day of year (1–366)
E	Day of week (for example, Thursday)
F	Day of week in month
G	Era (that is, AD or BC)
H	Hour in day (0–23)
K	Hour in AM/PM (0–11)
M	Month
S	Millisecond in second
W	Week of month (1–5)
Z	Time zone in RFC822 format

PART

Software Development Using Java

Java Beans

This chapter provides an overview of Java Beans. Beans are important because they allow you to build complex systems from software components. These components may be provided by you or supplied by one or more different vendors. Java Beans defines an architecture that specifies how these building blocks can operate together.

To better understand the value of Beans, consider the following. Hardware designers have a wide variety of components that can be integrated together to construct a system. Resistors, capacitors, and inductors are examples of simple building blocks. Integrated circuits provide more advanced functionality. All of these different parts can be reused. It is not necessary or possible to rebuild these capabilities each time a new system is needed. Also, the same pieces can be used in different types of circuits. This is possible because the behavior of these components is understood and documented.

The software industry has also been seeking the benefits of reusability and interoperability of a component-based approach. To realize these benefits, a component architecture is needed that allows programs to be assembled from software building blocks, perhaps provided by different vendors. It must also be possible for a designer to select a component, understand its capabilities, and incorporate it into an application. When a new version of a component becomes available, it should be easy to incorporate this functionality into existing code. Fortunately, Java Beans provides just such an architecture.

What Is a Java Bean?

A *Java Bean* is a software component that has been designed to be reusable in a variety of different environments. There is no restriction on the capability of a Bean. It may perform a simple function, such as obtaining an inventory value, or a complex function, such as forecasting the performance of a stock portfolio. A Bean may be visible to an end user. One example of this is a button on a graphical user interface. A Bean may also be invisible to a user. Software to decode a stream of multimedia information in real time is an example of this type of building block. Finally, a Bean may be designed to work autonomously on a user's workstation or to work in cooperation with a set of other distributed components. Software to generate a pie chart from a set of data points is an example of a Bean that can execute locally. However, a Bean that provides real-time price information from a stock or commodities exchange would need to work in cooperation with other distributed software to obtain its data.

Advantages of Java Beans

The following list enumerates some of the benefits that Java Bean technology provides for a component developer:

- A Bean obtains all the benefits of Java's "write-once, run-anywhere" paradigm.
- The properties, events, and methods of a Bean that are exposed to another application can be controlled.
- Auxiliary software can be provided to help configure a Bean. This software is only needed when the design-time parameters for that component are being set. It does not need to be included in the run-time environment.
- The configuration settings of a Bean can be saved in persistent storage and restored at a later time.
- A Bean may register to receive events from other objects and can generate events that are sent to other objects.

Introspection

At the core of Java Beans is *introspection*. This is the process of analyzing a Bean to determine its capabilities. This is an essential feature of the Java Beans API because it allows another application, such as a design tool, to obtain information about a component. Without introspection, the Java Beans technology could not operate.

There are two ways in which the developer of a Bean can indicate which of its properties, events, and methods should be exposed. With the first method, simple naming conventions are used. These allow the introspection mechanisms to infer information about a Bean. In the second way, an additional class that extends the **BeanInfo** interface is provided that explicitly supplies this information. Both approaches are examined here.

Design Patterns for Properties

A *property* is a subset of a Bean's state. The values assigned to the properties determine the behavior and appearance of that component. A property is set through a *setter* method. A property is obtained by a *getter* method. There are two types of properties: simple and indexed.

Simple Properties

A simple property has a single value. It can be identified by the following design patterns, where **N** is the name of the property and **T** is its type:

```
public T getN( )
public void setN(T arg)
```

A read/write property has both of these methods to access its values. A read-only property has only a get method. A write-only property has only a set method.

Here are three read/write simple properties along with their getter and setter methods:

```
private double depth, height, width;

public double getDepth( ) {
  return depth;
}
```

```
public void setDepth(double d) {
  depth = d;
}

public double getHeight( ) {
  return height;
}
public void setHeight(double h) {
  height = h;
}

public double getWidth( ) {
  return width;
}
public void setWidth(double w) {
  width = w;
}
```

Indexed Properties

An indexed property consists of multiple values. It can be identified by the following design patterns, where **N** is the name of the property and **T** is its type:

> public T getN(int *index*);
> public void setN(int *index*, T *value*);
> public T[ ] getN( );
> public void setN(T *values*[ ]);

Here is an indexed property called **data** along with its getter and setter methods:

```
private double data[ ];

public double getData(int index) {
  return data[index];
}
public void setData(int index, double value) {
  data[index] = value;
}
public double[ ] getData( ) {
  return data;
}
public void setData(double[ ] values) {
  data = new double[values.length];
  System.arraycopy(values, 0, data, 0, values.length);
}
```

Design Patterns for Events

Beans use the delegation event model that was discussed earlier in this book. Beans can generate events and send them to other objects. These can be identified by the following design patterns, where **T** is the type of the event:

> public void addTListener(TListener *eventListener*)
> public void addTListener(TListener *eventListener*)
>   throws java.util.TooManyListenersException
> public void removeTListener(TListener *eventListener*)

These methods are used to add or remove a listener for the specified event. The version of **AddTListener( )** that does not throw an exception can be used to *multicast* an event, which means that more than one listener can register for the event notification. The version that throws **TooManyListenersException** *unicasts* the event, which means that the number of listeners is restricted to one. In either case, **removeTListener( )** is used to remove the listener. For example, assuming an event interface type called **TemperatureListener**, a Bean that monitors temperature might supply the following methods:

```
public void addTemperatureListener(TemperatureListener tl) {
  ...
}
public void removeTemperatureListener(TemperatureListener tl) {
  ...
}
```

Methods and Design Patterns

Design patterns are not used for naming nonproperty methods. The introspection mechanism finds all of the public methods of a Bean. Protected and private methods are not presented.

Using the BeanInfo Interface

As the preceding discussion shows, design patterns *implicitly* determine what information is available to the user of a Bean. The **BeanInfo** interface enables you to *explicitly* control what information is available. The **BeanInfo** interface defines several methods, including these:

>   PropertyDescriptor[ ] getPropertyDescriptors( )
>   EventSetDescriptor[ ] getEventSetDescriptors( )
>   MethodDescriptor[ ] getMethodDescriptors( )

They return arrays of objects that provide information about the properties, events, and methods of a Bean. The classes **PropertyDescriptor**, **EventSetDescriptor**, and **MethodDescriptor** are defined within the **java.beans** package, and they describe the indicated elements. By implementing these methods, a developer can designate exactly what is presented to a user, bypassing introspection based on design patterns.

When creating a class that implements **BeanInfo**, you must call that class *bname*BeanInfo, where *bname* is the name of the Bean. For example, if the Bean is called **MyBean**, then the information class must be called **MyBeanBeanInfo**.

To simplify the use of **BeanInfo**, JavaBeans supplies the **SimpleBeanInfo** class. It provides default implementations of the **BeanInfo** interface, including the three methods just shown. You can extend this class and override one or more of the methods to explicitly control what aspects of a Bean are exposed. If you don't override a method, then design-pattern introspection will be used. For example, if you don't override **getPropertyDescriptors( )**, then design patterns are used to discover a Bean's properties. You will see **SimpleBeanInfo** in action later in this chapter.

Bound and Constrained Properties

A Bean that has a *bound* property generates an event when the property is changed. The event is of type **PropertyChangeEvent** and is sent to objects that previously registered an interest in receiving such notifications. A class that handles this event must implement the **PropertyChangeListener** interface.

A Bean that has a *constrained* property generates an event when an attempt is made to change its value. It also generates an event of type **PropertyChangeEvent**. It too is sent to objects that previously registered an interest in receiving such notifications. However, those other objects have the ability to veto the proposed change by throwing a **PropertyVetoException**. This capability allows a Bean to operate differently according to its run-time environment. A class that handles this event must implement the **VetoableChangeListener** interface.

Persistence

Persistence is the ability to save the current state of a Bean, including the values of a Bean's properties and instance variables, to nonvolatile storage and to retrieve them at a later time. The object serialization capabilities provided by the Java class libraries are used to provide persistence for Beans.

The easiest way to serialize a Bean is to have it implement the **java.io.Serializable** interface, which is simply a marker interface. Implementing **java.io.Serializable** makes serialization automatic. Your Bean need take no other action. Automatic serialization can also be inherited. Therefore, if any superclass of a Bean implements **java.io.Serializable**, then automatic serialization is obtained. There is one important restriction: any class that implements **java.io.Serializable** must supply a parameterless constructor.

When using automatic serialization, you can selectively prevent a field from being saved through the use of the **transient** keyword. Thus, data members of a Bean specified as **transient** will not be serialized.

If a Bean does not implement **java.io.Serializable**, you must provide serialization yourself, such as by implementing **java.io.Externalizable**. Otherwise, containers cannot save the configuration of your component.

Customizers

A Bean developer can provide a *customizer* that helps another developer configure the Bean. A customizer can provide a step-by-step guide through the process that must be followed to use the component in a specific context. Online documentation can also be provided. A Bean developer has great flexibility to develop a customizer that can differentiate his or her product in the marketplace.

The Java Beans API

The Java Beans functionality is provided by a set of classes and interfaces in the **java.beans** package. This section provides a brief overview of its contents. Table 28-1 lists the interfaces in **java.beans** and provides a brief description of their functionality. Table 28-2 lists the classes in **java.beans**.

Although it is beyond the scope of this chapter to discuss all of the classes, four are of particular interest: **Introspector**, **PropertyDescriptor**, **EventSetDescriptor**, and **MethodDescriptor**. Each is briefly examined here.

Interface	Description
AppletInitializer	Methods in this interface are used to initialize Beans that are also applets.
BeanInfo	This interface allows a designer to specify information about the properties, events, and methods of a Bean.
Customizer	This interface allows a designer to provide a graphical user interface through which a Bean may be configured.
DesignMode	Methods in this interface determine if a Bean is executing in design mode.
ExceptionListener	A method in this interface is invoked when an exception has occurred.
PropertyChangeListener	A method in this interface is invoked when a bound property is changed.
PropertyEditor	Objects that implement this interface allow designers to change and display property values.
VetoableChangeListener	A method in this interface is invoked when a constrained property is changed.
Visibility	Methods in this interface allow a Bean to execute in environments where a graphical user interface is not available.

TABLE 28-1   The Interfaces in **java.beans**

Class	Description
BeanDescriptor	This class provides information about a Bean. It also allows you to associate a customizer with a Bean.
Beans	This class is used to obtain information about a Bean.
DefaultPersistenceDelegate	A concrete subclass of **PersistenceDelegate**.
Encoder	Encodes the state of a set of Beans. Can be used to write this information to a stream.
EventHandler	Supports dynamic event listener creation.
EventSetDescriptor	Instances of this class describe an event that can be generated by a Bean.
Expression	Encapsulates a call to a method that returns a result.
FeatureDescriptor	This is the superclass of the **PropertyDescriptor**, **EventSetDescriptor**, and **MethodDescriptor** classes.
IndexedPropertyChangeEvent	A subclass of **PropertyChangeEvent** that represents a change to an indexed property.
IndexedPropertyDescriptor	Instances of this class describe an indexed property of a Bean.
IntrospectionException	An exception of this type is generated if a problem occurs when analyzing a Bean.
Introspector	This class analyzes a Bean and constructs a **BeanInfo** object that describes the component.

TABLE 28-2   The Classes in **java.beans**

Class	Description
MethodDescriptor	Instances of this class describe a method of a Bean.
ParameterDescriptor	Instances of this class describe a method parameter.
PersistenceDelegate	Handles the state information of an object.
PropertyChangeEvent	This event is generated when bound or constrained properties are changed. It is sent to objects that registered an interest in these events and that implement either the **PropertyChangeListener** or **VetoableChangeListener** interfaces.
PropertyChangeListenerProxy	Extends **EventListenerProxy** and implements **PropertyChangeListener**.
PropertyChangeSupport	Beans that support bound properties can use this class to notify **PropertyChangeListener** objects.
PropertyDescriptor	Instances of this class describe a property of a Bean.
PropertyEditorManager	This class locates a **PropertyEditor** object for a given type.
PropertyEditorSupport	This class provides functionality that can be used when writing property editors.
PropertyVetoException	An exception of this type is generated if a change to a constrained property is vetoed.
SimpleBeanInfo	This class provides functionality that can be used when writing **BeanInfo** classes.
Statement	Encapsulates a call to a method.
VetoableChangeListenerProxy	Extends **EventListenerProxy** and implements **VetoableChangeListener**.
VetoableChangeSupport	Beans that support constrained properties can use this class to notify **VetoableChangeListener** objects.
XMLDecoder	Used to read a Bean from an XML document.
XMLEncoder	Used to write a Bean to an XML document.

TABLE 28-2   The Classes in **java.beans** *(continued)*

Introspector

The **Introspector** class provides several static methods that support introspection. Of most interest is **getBeanInfo( )**. This method returns a **BeanInfo** that can be used to obtain information about the Bean. The **getBeanInfo( )** method has several forms, including the one shown here:

    static BeanInfo getBeanInfo(Class<?> *bean*) throws IntrospectionException

The returned object contains information about the Bean specified by *bean*.

PropertyDescriptor

The **PropertyDescriptor** class describes a Bean property. It supports several methods that manage and describe properties. For example, you can determine if a property is bound by calling **isBound( )**. To determine if a property is constrained, call **isConstrained( )**. You can obtain the name of property by calling **getName( )**.

EventSetDescriptor

The **EventSetDescriptor** class represents a Bean event. It supports several methods that obtain the methods that a Bean uses to add or remove event listeners, and to otherwise manage events. For example, to obtain the method used to add listeners, call **getAddListenerMethod( )**. To obtain the method used to remove listeners, call **getRemoveListenerMethod( )**. To obtain the type of a listener, call **getListenerType( )**. You can obtain the name of an event by calling **getName( )**.

MethodDescriptor

The **MethodDescriptor** class represents a Bean method. To obtain the name of the method, call **getName( )**. You can obtain information about the method by calling **getMethod( )**, shown here:

    Method getMethod( )

An object of type **Method** that describes the method is returned.

A Bean Example

This chapter concludes with an example that illustrates various aspects of Bean programming, including introspection and using a **BeanInfo** class. It also makes use of the **Introspector**, **PropertyDescriptor**, and **EventSetDescriptor** classes. The example uses three classes. The first is a Bean called **Colors**, shown here:

```
// A simple Bean.
import java.awt.*;
import java.awt.event.*;
import java.io.Serializable;

public class Colors extends Canvas implements Serializable {
  transient private Color color; // not persistent
  private boolean rectangular; // is persistent

  public Colors() {
    addMouseListener(new MouseAdapter() {
      public void mousePressed(MouseEvent me) {
        change();
      }
    });
    rectangular = false;
    setSize(200, 100);
    change();
  }
```

```
public boolean getRectangular() {
  return rectangular;
}

public void setRectangular(boolean flag) {
  this.rectangular = flag;
  repaint();
}

public void change() {
  color = randomColor();
  repaint();
}

private Color randomColor() {
  int r = (int)(255*Math.random());
  int g = (int)(255*Math.random());
  int b = (int)(255*Math.random());
  return new Color(r, g, b);
}

public void paint(Graphics g) {
  Dimension d = getSize();
  int h = d.height;
  int w = d.width;
  g.setColor(color);
  if(rectangular) {
    g.fillRect(0, 0, w-1, h-1);
  }
  else {
    g.fillOval(0, 0, w-1, h-1);
  }
}
}
```

The **Colors** Bean displays a colored object within a frame. The color of the component is determined by the private **Color** variable **color**, and its shape is determined by the private **boolean** variable **rectangular**. The constructor defines an anonymous inner class that extends **MouseAdapter** and overrides its **mousePressed( )** method. The **change( )** method is invoked in response to mouse presses. It selects a random color and then repaints the component. The **getRectangular( )** and **setRectangular( )** methods provide access to the one property of this Bean. The **change( )** method calls **randomColor( )** to choose a color and then calls **repaint( )** to make the change visible. Notice that the **paint( )** method uses the **rectangular** and **color** variables to determine how to present the Bean.

The next class is **ColorsBeanInfo**. It is a subclass of **SimpleBeanInfo** that provides explicit information about **Colors**. It overrides **getPropertyDescriptors( )** in order to designate which properties are presented to a Bean user. In this case, the only property exposed is **rectangular**. The method creates and returns a **PropertyDescriptor** object for the **rectangular** property. The **PropertyDescriptor** constructor that is used is shown here:

PropertyDescriptor(String *property*, Class<?> *beanCls*)
    throws IntrospectionException

Here, the first argument is the name of the property, and the second argument is the class of the Bean.

```java
// A Bean information class.
import java.beans.*;
public class ColorsBeanInfo extends SimpleBeanInfo {
  public PropertyDescriptor[] getPropertyDescriptors() {
    try {
      PropertyDescriptor rectangular = new
          PropertyDescriptor("rectangular", Colors.class);
      PropertyDescriptor pd[] = {rectangular};
      return pd;
    }
    catch(Exception e) {
      System.out.println("Exception caught. " + e);
    }
    return null;
  }
}
```

The final class is called **IntrospectorDemo**. It uses introspection to display the properties and events that are available within the **Colors** Bean.

```java
// Show properties and events.
import java.awt.*;
import java.beans.*;

public class IntrospectorDemo {
  public static void main(String args[]) {
    try {
      Class c = Class.forName("Colors");
      BeanInfo beanInfo = Introspector.getBeanInfo(c);

      System.out.println("Properties:");
      PropertyDescriptor propertyDescriptor[] =
        beanInfo.getPropertyDescriptors();
      for(int i = 0; i < propertyDescriptor.length; i++) {
        System.out.println("\t" + propertyDescriptor[i].getName());
      }

      System.out.println("Events:");
      EventSetDescriptor eventSetDescriptor[] =
        beanInfo.getEventSetDescriptors();
      for(int i = 0; i < eventSetDescriptor.length; i++) {
        System.out.println("\t" + eventSetDescriptor[i].getName());
      }
    }
    catch(Exception e) {
      System.out.println("Exception caught. " + e);
    }
  }
}
```

The output from this program is the following:

```
Properties:
        rectangular
Events:
        mouseWheel
        mouse
        mouseMotion
        component
        hierarchyBounds
        focus
        hierarchy
        propertyChange
        inputMethod
        key
```

Notice two things in the output. First, because **ColorsBeanInfo** overrides **getPropertyDescriptors( )** such that the only property returned is **rectangular**, only the **rectangular** property is displayed. However, because **getEventSetDescriptors( )** is not overridden by **ColorsBeanInfo**, design-pattern introspection is used, and all events are found, including those in **Colors'** superclass, **Canvas**. Remember, if you don't override one of the "get" methods defined by **SimpleBeanInfo**, then the default, design-pattern introspection is used. To observe the difference that **ColorsBeanInfo** makes, erase its class file and then run **IntrospectorDemo** again. This time it will report more properties.

CHAPTER

Introducing Swing

In Part II, you saw how to build user interfaces with the AWT classes. Although the AWT is still a crucial part of Java, its component set is no longer widely used to create graphic user interfaces. Today, most programmers use Swing for this purpose. Swing is a set of classes that provides more powerful and flexible GUI components than does the AWT. Simply put, Swing provides the look and feel of the modern Java GUI.

Coverage of Swing is divided between two chapters. This chapter introduces Swing. It begins by describing Swing's core concepts. It then shows the general form of a Swing program, including both applications and applets. It concludes by explaining how painting is accomplished in Swing. The following chapter presents several commonly used Swing components. It is important to understand that the number of classes and interfaces in the Swing packages is quite large, and they can't all be covered in this book. (In fact, full coverage of Swing requires an entire book of its own.) However, these two chapters will give you a basic understanding of this important topic.

NOTE *For a comprehensive introduction to Swing, see my book* Swing: A Beginner's Guide *published by McGraw-Hill/Osborne (2007).*

The Origins of Swing

Swing did not exist in the early days of Java. Rather, it was a response to deficiencies present in Java's original GUI subsystem: the Abstract Window Toolkit. The AWT defines a basic set of controls, windows, and dialog boxes that support a usable, but limited graphical interface. One reason for the limited nature of the AWT is that it translates its various visual components into their corresponding, platform-specific equivalents, or *peers*. This means that the look and feel of a component is defined by the platform, not by Java. Because the AWT components use native code resources, they are referred to as *heavyweight*.

The use of native peers led to several problems. First, because of variations between operating systems, a component might look, or even act, differently on different platforms. This potential variability threatened the overarching philosophy of Java: write once, run anywhere. Second, the look and feel of each component was fixed (because it is defined by the platform) and could not be (easily) changed. Third, the use of heavyweight components caused some frustrating restrictions. For example, a heavyweight component is always rectangular and opaque.

Not long after Java's original release, it became apparent that the limitations and restrictions present in the AWT were sufficiently serious that a better approach was needed. The solution was Swing. Introduced in 1997, Swing was included as part of the Java Foundation Classes (JFC). Swing was initially available for use with Java 1.1 as a separate library. However, beginning with Java 1.2, Swing (and the rest of the JFC) was fully integrated into Java.

Swing Is Built on the AWT

Before moving on, it is necessary to make one important point: although Swing eliminates a number of the limitations inherent in the AWT, Swing *does not* replace it. Instead, Swing is built on the foundation of the AWT. This is why the AWT is still a crucial part of Java. Swing also uses the same event handling mechanism as the AWT. Therefore, a basic understanding of the AWT and of event handling is required to use Swing. (The AWT is covered in Chapters 23 and 24. Event handling is described in Chapter 22.)

Two Key Swing Features

As just explained, Swing was created to address the limitations present in the AWT. It does this through two key features: lightweight components and a pluggable look and feel. Together they provide an elegant, yet easy-to-use solution to the problems of the AWT. More than anything else, it is these two features that define the essence of Swing. Each is examined here.

Swing Components Are Lightweight

With very few exceptions, Swing components are *lightweight*. This means that they are written entirely in Java and do not map directly to platform-specific peers. Because lightweight components are rendered using graphics primitives, they can be transparent, which enables nonrectangular shapes. Thus, lightweight components are more efficient and more flexible. Furthermore, because lightweight components do not translate into native peers, the look and feel of each component is determined by Swing, not by the underlying operating system. This means that each component will work in a consistent manner across all platforms.

Swing Supports a Pluggable Look and Feel

Swing supports a *pluggable look and feel* (PLAF). Because each Swing component is rendered by Java code rather than by native peers, the look and feel of a component is under the control of Swing. This fact means that it is possible to separate the look and feel of a component from the logic of the component, and this is what Swing does. Separating out the look and feel provides a significant advantage: it becomes possible to change the way that a component is rendered without affecting any of its other aspects. In other words, it is possible to "plug in" a new look and feel for any given component without creating any side effects in the code that uses that component. Moreover, it becomes possible to define entire sets of look-and-feels that represent different GUI styles. To use a specific style, its look and feel is simply "plugged in." Once this is done, all components are automatically rendered using that style.

Pluggable look-and-feels offer several important advantages. It is possible to define a look and feel that is consistent across all platforms. Conversely, it is possible to create a look and feel that acts like a specific platform. For example, if you know that an application will be running only in a Windows environment, it is possible to specify the Windows look and feel. It is also possible to design a custom look and feel. Finally, the look and feel can be changed dynamically at run time.

Java SE 6 provides look-and-feels, such as metal and Motif, that are available to all Swing users. The metal look and feel is also called the *Java look and feel*. It is platform-independent and available in all Java execution environments. It is also the default look and feel. Windows environments also have access to the Windows and Windows Classic look and feel. This book uses the default Java look and feel (metal) because it is platform independent.

The MVC Connection

In general, a visual component is a composite of three distinct aspects:

- The way that the component looks when rendered on the screen
- The way that the component reacts to the user
- The state information associated with the component

No matter what architecture is used to implement a component, it must implicitly contain these three parts. Over the years, one component architecture has proven itself to be exceptionally effective: *Model-View-Controller*, or MVC for short.

The MVC architecture is successful because each piece of the design corresponds to an aspect of a component. In MVC terminology, the *model* corresponds to the state information associated with the component. For example, in the case of a check box, the model contains a field that indicates if the box is checked or unchecked. The *view* determines how the component is displayed on the screen, including any aspects of the view that are affected by the current state of the model. The *controller* determines how the component reacts to the user. For example, when the user clicks a check box, the controller reacts by changing the model to reflect the user's choice (checked or unchecked). This then results in the view being updated. By separating a component into a model, a view, and a controller, the specific implementation of each can be changed without affecting the other two. For instance, different view implementations can render the same component in different ways without affecting the model or the controller.

Although the MVC architecture and the principles behind it are conceptually sound, the high level of separation between the view and the controller is not beneficial for Swing components. Instead, Swing uses a modified version of MVC that combines the view and the controller into a single logical entity called the *UI delegate*. For this reason, Swing's approach is called either the *Model-Delegate* architecture or the *Separable Model* architecture. Therefore, although Swing's component architecture is based on MVC, it does not use a classical implementation of it.

Swing's pluggable look and feel is made possible by its Model-Delegate architecture. Because the view (look) and controller (feel) are separate from the model, the look and feel can be changed without affecting how the component is used within a program. Conversely, it is possible to customize the model without affecting the way that the component appears on the screen or responds to user input.

To support the Model-Delegate architecture, most Swing components contain two objects. The first represents the model. The second represents the UI delegate. Models are defined by interfaces. For example, the model for a button is defined by the **ButtonModel** interface. UI delegates are classes that inherit **ComponentUI**. For example, the UI delegate for a button is **ButtonUI**. Normally, your programs will not interact directly with the UI delegate.

Components and Containers

A Swing GUI consists of two key items: *components* and *containers*. However, this distinction is mostly conceptual because all containers are also components. The difference between the two is found in their intended purpose: As the term is commonly used, a *component* is an independent visual control, such as a push button or slider. A container holds a group of components. Thus, a container is a special type of component that is designed to hold other components. Furthermore, in order for a component to be displayed, it must be held within a container. Thus, all Swing GUIs will have at least one container. Because containers are components, a container can also hold other containers. This enables Swing to define what is called a *containment hierarchy*, at the top of which must be a *top-level container*.

Let's look a bit more closely at components and containers.

Components

In general, Swing components are derived from the **JComponent** class. (The only exceptions to this are the four top-level containers, described in the next section.) **JComponent** provides the functionality that is common to all components. For example, **JComponent** supports the pluggable look and feel. **JComponent** inherits the AWT classes **Container** and **Component**. Thus, a Swing component is built on and compatible with an AWT component.

All of Swing's components are represented by classes defined within the package **javax.swing**. The following table shows the class names for Swing components (including those used as containers).

JApplet	JButton	JCheckBox	JCheckBoxMenuItem
JColorChooser	JComboBox	JComponent	JDesktopPane
JDialog	JEditorPane	JFileChooser	JFormattedTextField
JFrame	JInternalFrame	JLabel	JLayeredPane
JList	JMenu	JMenuBar	JMenuItem
JOptionPane	JPanel	JPasswordField	JPopupMenu
JProgressBar	JRadioButton	JRadioButtonMenuItem	JRootPane
JScrollBar	JScrollPane	JSeparator	JSlider
JSpinner	JSplitPane	JTabbedPane	JTable
JTextArea	JTextField	JTextPane	JTogglebutton
JToolBar	JToolTip	JTree	JViewport
JWindow			

Notice that all component classes begin with the letter **J**. For example, the class for a label is **JLabel**; the class for a push button is **JButton**; and the class for a scroll bar is **JScrollBar**.

Containers

Swing defines two types of containers. The first are top-level containers: **JFrame**, **JApplet**, **JWindow**, and **JDialog**. These containers do not inherit **JComponent**. They do, however, inherit the AWT classes **Component** and **Container**. Unlike Swing's other components, which are lightweight, the top-level containers are heavyweight. This makes the top-level containers a special case in the Swing component library.

As the name implies, a top-level container must be at the top of a containment hierarchy. A top-level container is not contained within any other container. Furthermore, every containment hierarchy must begin with a top-level container. The one most commonly used for applications is **JFrame**. The one used for applets is **JApplet**.

The second type of containers supported by Swing are lightweight containers. Lightweight containers *do* inherit **JComponent**. An example of a lightweight container is **JPanel**, which is a general-purpose container. Lightweight containers are often used to organize and manage groups of related components because a lightweight container can be contained within another container. Thus, you can use lightweight containers such as **JPanel** to create subgroups of related controls that are contained within an outer container.

The Top-Level Container Panes

Each top-level container defines a set of *panes*. At the top of the hierarchy is an instance of **JRootPane**. **JRootPane** is a lightweight container whose purpose is to manage the other panes. It also helps manage the optional menu bar. The panes that comprise the root pane are called the *glass pane*, the *content pane*, and the *layered pane*.

The glass pane is the top-level pane. It sits above and completely covers all other panes. By default, it is a transparent instance of **JPanel**. The glass pane enables you to manage mouse events that affect the entire container (rather than an individual control) or to paint over any other component, for example. In most cases, you won't need to use the glass pane directly, but it is there if you need it.

The layered pane is an instance of **JLayeredPane**. The layered pane allows components to be given a depth value. This value determines which component overlays another. (Thus, the layered pane lets you specify a Z-order for a component, although this is not something that you will usually need to do.) The layered pane holds the content pane and the (optional) menu bar.

Although the glass pane and the layered panes are integral to the operation of a top-level container and serve important purposes, much of what they provide occurs behind the scene. The pane with which your application will interact the most is the content pane, because this is the pane to which you will add visual components. In other words, when you add a component, such as a button, to a top-level container, you will add it to the content pane. By default, the content pane is an opaque instance of **JPanel**.

The Swing Packages

Swing is a very large subsystem and makes use of many packages. These are the packages used by Swing that are defined by Java SE 6.

javax.swing	javax.swing.border	javax.swing.colorchooser
javax.swing.event	javax.swing.filechooser	javax.swing.plaf
javax.swing.plaf.basic	javax.swing.plaf.metal	javax.swing.plaf.multi
javax.swing.plaf.synth	javax.swing.table	javax.swing.text
javax.swing.text.html	javax.swing.text.html.parser	javax.swing.text.rtf
javax.swing.tree	javax.swing.undo	

The main package is **javax.swing**. This package must be imported into any program that uses Swing. It contains the classes that implement the basic Swing components, such as push buttons, labels, and check boxes.

A Simple Swing Application

Swing programs differ from both the console-based programs and the AWT-based programs shown earlier in this book. For example, they use a different set of components and a different container hierarchy than does the AWT. Swing programs also have special requirements that relate to threading. The best way to understand the structure of a Swing program is to work through an example. There are two types of Java programs in which Swing is typically used. The first is a desktop application. The second is the applet. This section shows how to create a Swing application. The creation of a Swing applet is described later in this chapter.

Although quite short, the following program shows one way to write a Swing application. In the process, it demonstrates several key features of Swing. It uses two Swing components: **JFrame** and **JLabel**. **JFrame** is the top-level container that is commonly used for Swing applications. **JLabel** is the Swing component that creates a label, which is a component that displays information. The label is Swing's simplest component because it is passive. That is, a label does not respond to user input. It just displays output. The program uses a **JFrame** container to hold an instance of a **JLabel**. The label displays a short text message.

```
// A simple Swing application.

import javax.swing.*;

class SwingDemo {

  SwingDemo() {

    // Create a new JFrame container.
    JFrame jfrm = new JFrame("A Simple Swing Application");

    // Give the frame an initial size.
    jfrm.setSize(275, 100);

    // Terminate the program when the user closes the application.
    jfrm.setDefaultCloseOperation(JFrame.EXIT_ON_CLOSE);

    // Create a text-based label.
```

```
    JLabel jlab = new JLabel(" Swing means powerful GUIs.");

    // Add the label to the content pane.
    jfrm.add(jlab);

    // Display the frame.
    jfrm.setVisible(true);
  }

  public static void main(String args[]) {
    // Create the frame on the event dispatching thread.
    SwingUtilities.invokeLater(new Runnable() {
      public void run() {
        new SwingDemo();
      }
    });
  }
}
```

Swing programs are compiled and run in the same way as other Java applications. Thus, to compile this program, you can use this command line:

```
javac SwingDemo.java
```

To run the program, use this command line:

```
java SwingDemo
```

When the program is run, it will produce the window shown in Figure 29-1.

Because the **SwingDemo** program illustrates several core Swing concepts, we will examine it carefully, line by line. The program begins by importing **javax.swing**. As mentioned, this package contains the components and models defined by Swing. For example, **javax.swing** defines classes that implement labels, buttons, text controls, and menus. It will be included in all programs that use Swing.

Next, the program declares the **SwingDemo** class and a constructor for that class. The constructor is where most of the action of the program occurs. It begins by creating a **JFrame**, using this line of code:

```
JFrame jfrm = new JFrame("A Simple Swing Application");
```

This creates a container called **jfrm** that defines a rectangular window complete with a title bar; close, minimize, maximize, and restore buttons; and a system menu. Thus, it creates a standard, top-level window. The title of the window is passed to the constructor.

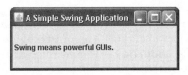

FIGURE 29-1   The window produced by the **SwingDemo** program

Next, the window is sized using this statement:

```
jfrm.setSize(275, 100);
```

The **setSize( )** method (which is inherited by **JFrame** from the AWT class **Component**) sets the dimensions of the window, which are specified in pixels. Its general form is shown here:

   void setSize(int *width*, int *height*)

In this example, the width of the window is set to 275 and the height is set to 100.

By default, when a top-level window is closed (such as when the user clicks the close box), the window is removed from the screen, but the application is not terminated. While this default behavior is useful in some situations, it is not what is needed for most applications. Instead, you will usually want the entire application to terminate when its top-level window is closed. There are a couple of ways to achieve this. The easiest way is to call **setDefaultCloseOperation( )**, as the program does:

```
jfrm.setDefaultCloseOperation(JFrame.EXIT_ON_CLOSE);
```

After this call executes, closing the window causes the entire application to terminate. The general form of **setDefaultCloseOperation( )** is shown here:

   void setDefaultCloseOperation(int *what*)

The value passed in *what* determines what happens when the window is closed. There are several other options in addition to **JFrame.EXIT_ON_CLOSE**. They are shown here:

   JFrame.DISPOSE_ON_CLOSE

   JFrame.HIDE_ON_CLOSE

   JFrame.DO_NOTHING_ON_CLOSE

Their names reflect their actions. These constants are declared in **WindowConstants**, which is an interface declared in **javax.swing** that is implemented by **JFrame**.

The next line of code creates a Swing **JLabel** component:

```
JLabel jlab = new JLabel(" Swing means powerful GUIs.");
```

JLabel is the simplest and easiest-to-use component because it does not accept user input. It simply displays information, which can consist of text, an icon, or a combination of the two. The label created by the program contains only text, which is passed to its constructor.

The next line of code adds the label to the content pane of the frame:

```
jfrm.add(jlab);
```

As explained earlier, all top-level containers have a content pane in which components are stored. Thus, to add a component to a frame, you must add it to the frame's content pane. This is accomplished by calling **add( )** on the **JFrame** reference (**jfrm** in this case). The general form of **add( )** is shown here:

   Component add(Component *comp*)

The **add( )** method is inherited by **JFrame** from the AWT class **Container**.

By default, the content pane associated with a **JFrame** uses border layout. The version of **add( )** just shown adds the label to the center location. Other versions of **add( )** enable you to specify one of the border regions. When a component is added to the center, its size is adjusted automatically to fit the size of the center.

Before continuing, an important historical point needs to be made. Prior to JDK 5, when adding a component to the content pane, you could not invoke the **add( )** method directly on a **JFrame** instance. Instead, you needed to call **add( )** on the content pane of the **JFrame** object. The content pane can be obtained by calling **getContentPane( )** on a **JFrame** instance. The **getContentPane( )** method is shown here:

    Container getContentPane( )

It returns a **Container** reference to the content pane. The **add( )** method was then called on that reference to add a component to a content pane. Thus, in the past, you had to use the following statement to add **jlab** to **jfrm**:

```
jfrm.getContentPane().add(jlab); // old-style
```

Here, **getContentPane( )** first obtains a reference to content pane, and then **add( )** adds the component to the container linked to this pane. This same procedure was also required to invoke **remove( )** to remove a component and **setLayout( )** to set the layout manager for the content pane. You will see explicit calls to **getContentPane( )** frequently throughout pre-5.0 code. Today, the use of **getContentPane( )** is no longer necessary. You can simply call **add( )**, **remove( )**, and **setLayout( )** directly on **JFrame** because these methods have been changed so that they operate on the content pane automatically.

The last statement in the **SwingDemo** constructor causes the window to become visible:

```
jfrm.setVisible(true);
```

The **setVisible( )** method is inherited from the AWT **Component** class. If its argument is **true**, the window will be displayed. Otherwise, it will be hidden. By default, a **JFrame** is invisible, so **setVisible(true)** must be called to show it.

Inside **main( )**, a **SwingDemo** object is created, which causes the window and the label to be displayed. Notice that the **SwingDemo** constructor is invoked using these lines of code:

```
SwingUtilities.invokeLater(new Runnable() {
  public void run() {
    new SwingDemo();
  }
});
```

This sequence causes a **SwingDemo** object to be created on the *event dispatching thread* rather than on the main thread of the application. Here's why. In general, Swing programs are event-driven. For example, when a user interacts with a component, an event is generated. An event is passed to the application by calling an event handler defined by the application. However, the handler is executed on the event dispatching thread provided by Swing and not on the main thread of the application. Thus, although event handlers are defined by your program, they are called on a thread that was not created by your program.

To avoid problems (including the potential for deadlock), all Swing GUI components must be created and updated from the event dispatching thread, not the main thread of the application. However, **main( )** is executed on the main thread. Thus, **main( )** cannot directly instantiate a **SwingDemo** object. Instead, it must create a **Runnable** object that executes on the event dispatching thread and have this object create the GUI.

To enable the GUI code to be created on the event dispatching thread, you must use one of two methods that are defined by the **SwingUtilities** class. These methods are **invokeLater( )** and **invokeAndWait( )**. They are shown here:

static void invokeLater(Runnable *obj*)

static void invokeAndWait(Runnable *obj*)
    throws InterruptedException, InvocationTargetException

Here, *obj* is a **Runnable** object that will have its **run( )** method called by the event dispatching thread. The difference between the two methods is that **invokeLater( )** returns immediately, but **invokeAndWait( )** waits until **obj.run( )** returns. You can use one of these methods to call a method that constructs the GUI for your Swing application, or whenever you need to modify the state of the GUI from code not executed by the event dispatching thread. You will normally want to use **invokeLater( )**, as the preceding program does. However, when constructing the initial GUI for an applet, you will need to use **invokeAndWait( )**.

Event Handling

The preceding example showed the basic form of a Swing program, but it left out one important part: event handling. Because **JLabel** does not take input from the user, it does not generate events, so no event handling was needed. However, the other Swing components *do* respond to user input and the events generated by those interactions need to be handled. Events can also be generated in ways not directly related to user input. For example, an event is generated when a timer goes off. Whatever the case, event handling is a large part of any Swing-based application.

The event handling mechanism used by Swing is the same as that used by the AWT. This approach is called the *delegation event model,* and it is described in Chapter 22. In many cases, Swing uses the same events as does the AWT, and these events are packaged in **java.awt.event**. Events specific to Swing are stored in **javax.swing.event**.

Although events are handled in Swing in the same way as they are with the AWT, it is still useful to work through a simple example. The following program handles the event generated by a Swing push button. Sample output is shown in Figure 29-2.

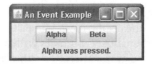

FIGURE 29-2 Output from the **EventDemo** program

```java
// Handle an event in a Swing program.

import java.awt.*;
import java.awt.event.*;
import javax.swing.*;

class EventDemo {

  JLabel jlab;

  EventDemo() {

    // Create a new JFrame container.
    JFrame jfrm = new JFrame("An Event Example");

    // Specify FlowLayout for the layout manager.
    jfrm.setLayout(new FlowLayout());

    // Give the frame an initial size.
    jfrm.setSize(220, 90);

    // Terminate the program when the user closes the application.
    jfrm.setDefaultCloseOperation(JFrame.EXIT_ON_CLOSE);

    // Make two buttons.
    JButton jbtnAlpha = new JButton("Alpha");
    JButton jbtnBeta = new JButton("Beta");

    // Add action listener for Alpha.
    jbtnAlpha.addActionListener(new ActionListener() {
      public void actionPerformed(ActionEvent ae) {
        jlab.setText("Alpha was pressed.");
      }
    });

    // Add action listener for Beta.
    jbtnBeta.addActionListener(new ActionListener() {
      public void actionPerformed(ActionEvent ae) {
        jlab.setText("Beta was pressed.");
      }
    });

    // Add the buttons to the content pane.
    jfrm.add(jbtnAlpha);
    jfrm.add(jbtnBeta);

    // Create a text-based label.
    jlab = new JLabel("Press a button.");

    // Add the label to the content pane.
    jfrm.add(jlab);

    // Display the frame.
```

```
    jfrm.setVisible(true);
  }

  public static void main(String args[]) {
    // Create the frame on the event dispatching thread.
    SwingUtilities.invokeLater(new Runnable() {
      public void run() {
        new EventDemo();
      }
    });
  }
}
```

First, notice that the program now imports both the **java.awt** and **java.awt.event** packages. The **java.awt** package is needed because it contains the **FlowLayout** class, which supports the standard flow layout manager used to lay out components in a frame. (See Chapter 24 for coverage of layout managers.) The **java.awt.event** package is needed because it defines the **ActionListener** interface and the **ActionEvent** class.

The **EventDemo** constructor begins by creating a **JFrame** called **jfrm**. It then sets the layout manager for the content pane of **jfrm** to **FlowLayout**. Recall that, by default, the content pane uses **BorderLayout** as its layout manager. However, for this example, **FlowLayout** is more convenient. Notice that **FlowLayout** is assigned using this statement:

```
jfrm.setLayout(new FlowLayout());
```

As explained, in the past you had to explicitly call **getContentPane( )** to set the layout manager for the content pane. This requirement was removed as of JDK 5.

After setting the size and default close operation, **EventDemo( )** creates two push buttons, as shown here:

```
JButton jbtnAlpha = new JButton("Alpha");
JButton jbtnBeta = new JButton("Beta");
```

The first button will contain the text "Alpha" and the second will contain the text "Beta." Swing push buttons are instances of **JButton**. **JButton** supplies several constructors. The one used here is

JButton(String *msg*)

The *msg* parameter specifies the string that will be displayed inside the button.

When a push button is pressed, it generates an **ActionEvent**. Thus, **JButton** provides the **addActionListener( )** method, which is used to add an action listener. (**JButton** also provides **removeActionListener( )** to remove a listener, but this method is not used by the program.) As explained in Chapter 22, the **ActionListener** interface defines only one method: **actionPerformed( )**. It is shown again here for your convenience:

void actionPerformed(ActionEvent *ae*)

This method is called when a button is pressed. In other words, it is the event handler that is called when a button press event has occurred.

Next, event listeners for the button's action events are added by the code shown here:

```
// Add action listener for Alpha.
jbtnAlpha.addActionListener(new ActionListener() {
  public void actionPerformed(ActionEvent ae) {
    jlab.setText("Alpha was pressed.");
  }
});

// Add action listener for Beta.
jbtnBeta.addActionListener(new ActionListener() {
  public void actionPerformed(ActionEvent ae) {
    jlab.setText("Beta was pressed.");
  }
});
```

Here, anonymous inner classes are used to provide the event handlers for the two buttons. Each time a button is pressed, the string displayed in **jlab** is changed to reflect which button was pressed.

Next, the buttons are added to the content pane of **jfrm**:

```
jfrm.add(jbtnAlpha);
jfrm.add(jbtnBeta);
```

Finally, **jlab** is added to the content pane and window is made visible. When you run the program, each time you press a button, a message is displayed in the label that indicates which button was pressed.

One last point: Remember that all event handlers, such as **actionPerformed( )**, are called on the event dispatching thread. Therefore, an event handler must return quickly in order to avoid slowing down the application. If your application needs to do something time consuming as the result of an event, it must use a separate thread.

Create a Swing Applet

The second type of program that commonly uses Swing is the applet. Swing-based applets are similar to AWT-based applets, but with an important difference: A Swing applet extends **JApplet** rather than **Applet**. **JApplet** is derived from **Applet**. Thus, **JApplet** includes all of the functionality found in **Applet** and adds support for Swing. **JApplet** is a top-level Swing container, which means that it is *not* derived from **JComponent**. Because **JApplet** is a top-level container, it includes the various panes described earlier. This means that all components are added to **JApplet**'s content pane in the same way that components are added to **JFrame**'s content pane.

Swing applets use the same four lifecycle methods as described in Chapter 21: **init( )**, **start( )**, **stop( )**, and **destroy( )**. Of course, you need override only those methods that are needed by your applet. Painting is accomplished differently in Swing than it is in the AWT, and a Swing applet will not normally override the **paint( )** method. (Painting in Swing is described later in this chapter.)

One other point: All interaction with components in a Swing applet must take place on the event dispatching thread, as described in the previous section. This threading issue applies to all Swing programs.

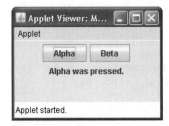

FIGURE 29-3   Output from the example Swing applet

Here is an example of a Swing applet. It provides the same functionality as the previous application, but does so in applet form. Figure 29-3 shows the program when executed by **appletviewer**.

```
// A simple Swing-based applet

import javax.swing.*;
import java.awt.*;
import java.awt.event.*;

/*
This HTML can be used to launch the applet:

<object code="MySwingApplet" width=220 height=90>
</object>
*/

public class MySwingApplet extends JApplet {
  JButton jbtnAlpha;
  JButton jbtnBeta;

  JLabel jlab;

  // Initialize the applet.
  public void init() {
    try {
      SwingUtilities.invokeAndWait(new Runnable () {
        public void run() {
          makeGUI(); // initialize the GUI
        }
      });
    } catch(Exception exc) {
      System.out.println("Can't create because of "+ exc);
    }
  }

  // This applet does not need to override start(), stop(),
  // or destroy().

  // Set up and initialize the GUI.
  private void makeGUI() {
```

```
    // Set the applet to use flow layout.
    setLayout(new FlowLayout());

    // Make two buttons.
    jbtnAlpha = new JButton("Alpha");
    jbtnBeta = new JButton("Beta");

    // Add action listener for Alpha.
    jbtnAlpha.addActionListener(new ActionListener() {
      public void actionPerformed(ActionEvent le) {
        jlab.setText("Alpha was pressed.");
      }
    });

    // Add action listener for Beta.
    jbtnBeta.addActionListener(new ActionListener() {
      public void actionPerformed(ActionEvent le) {
        jlab.setText("Beta was pressed.");
      }
    });

    // Add the buttons to the content pane.
    add(jbtnAlpha);
    add(jbtnBeta);

    // Create a text-based label.
    jlab = new JLabel("Press a button.");

    // Add the label to the content pane.
    add(jlab);
  }
}
```

There are two important things to notice about this applet. First, **MySwingApplet** extends **JApplet**. As explained, all Swing-based applets extend **JApplet** rather than **Applet**. Second, the **init( )** method initializes the Swing components on the event dispatching thread by setting up a call to **makeGUI( )**. Notice that this is accomplished through the use of **invokeAndWait( )** rather than **invokeLater( )**. Applets must use **invokeAndWait( )** because the **init( )** method must not return until the entire initialization process has been completed. In essence, the **start( )** method cannot be called until after initialization, which means that the GUI must be fully constructed.

Inside **makeGUI( )**, the two buttons and label are created, and the action listeners are added to the buttons. Finally, the components are added to the content pane. Although this example is quite simple, this same general approach must be used when building any Swing GUI that will be used by an applet.

Painting in Swing

Although the Swing component set is quite powerful, you are not limited to using it because Swing also lets you write directly into the display area of a frame, panel, or one of Swing's other components, such as **JLabel**. Although many (perhaps most) uses of Swing will *not* involve drawing directly to the surface of a component, it is available for those applications that need this capability. To write output directly to the surface of a component, you will use one or more drawing methods defined by the AWT, such as **drawLine( )** or **drawRect( )**. Thus, most of the techniques and methods described in Chapter 23 also apply to Swing. However, there are also some very important differences, and the process is discussed in detail in this section.

Painting Fundamentals

Swing's approach to painting is built on the original AWT-based mechanism, but Swing's implementation offers more finally grained control. Before examining the specifics of Swing-based painting, it is useful to review the AWT-based mechanism that underlies it.

The AWT class **Component** defines a method called **paint( )** that is used to draw output directly to the surface of a component. For the most part, **paint( )** is not called by your program. (In fact, only in the most unusual cases should it ever be called by your program.) Rather, **paint( )** is called by the run-time system whenever a component must be rendered. This situation can occur for several reasons. For example, the window in which the component is displayed can be overwritten by another window and then uncovered. Or, the window might be minimized and then restored. The **paint( )** method is also called when a program begins running. When writing AWT-based code, an application will override **paint( )** when it needs to write output directly to the surface of the component.

Because **JComponent** inherits **Component**, all Swing's lightweight components inherit the **paint( )** method. However, you *will not* override it to paint directly to the surface of a component. The reason is that Swing uses a bit more sophisticated approach to painting that involves three distinct methods: **paintComponent( )**, **paintBorder( )**, and **paintChildren( )**. These methods paint the indicated portion of a component and divide the painting process into its three distinct, logical actions. In a lightweight component, the original AWT method **paint( )** simply executes calls to these methods, in the order just shown.

To paint to the surface of a Swing component, you will create a subclass of the component and then override its **paintComponent( )** method. This is the method that paints the interior of the component. You will not normally override the other two painting methods. When overriding **paintComponent( )**, the first thing you must do is call **super.paintComponent( )**, so that the superclass portion of the painting process takes place. (The only time this is not required is when you are taking complete, manual control over how a component is displayed.) After that, write the output that you want to display. The **paintComponent( )** method is shown here:

protected void paintComponent(Graphics *g*)

The parameter *g* is the graphics context to which output is written.

To cause a component to be painted under program control, call **repaint( )**. It works in Swing just as it does for the AWT. The **repaint( )** method is defined by **Component**. Calling it causes the system to call **paint( )** as soon as it is possible to do so. Because painting is a time-consuming operation, this mechanism allows the run-time system to defer painting momentarily until some higher-priority task has completed, for example. Of course, in Swing the call to **paint( )** results in a call to **paintComponent( )**. Therefore, to output to the surface of a component, your program will store the output until **paintComponent( )** is called. Inside the overridden **paintComponent( )**, you will draw the stored output.

Compute the Paintable Area

When drawing to the surface of a component, you must be careful to restrict your output to the area that is inside the border. Although Swing automatically clips any output that will exceed the boundaries of a component, it is still possible to paint into the border, which will then get overwritten when the border is drawn. To avoid this, you must compute the *paintable area* of the component. This is the area defined by the current size of the component minus the space used by the border. Therefore, before you paint to a component, you must obtain the width of the border and then adjust your drawing accordingly.

To obtain the border width, call **getInsets( )**, shown here:

Insets getInsets( )

This method is defined by **Container** and overridden by **JComponent**. It returns an **Insets** object that contains the dimensions of the border. The inset values can be obtained by using these fields:

int top;

int bottom;

int left;

int right;

These values are then used to compute the drawing area given the width and the height of the component. You can obtain the width and height of the component by calling **getWidth( )** and **getHeight( )** on the component. They are shown here:

int getWidth( )

int getHeight( )

By subtracting the value of the insets, you can compute the usable width and height of the component.

A Paint Example

Here is a program that puts into action the preceding discussion. It creates a class called **PaintPanel** that extends **JPanel**. The program then uses an object of that class to display lines whose endpoints have been generated randomly. Sample output is shown in Figure 10-4.

FIGURE 29-4 Sample output from the **PaintPanel** program

```java
// Paint lines to a panel.

import java.awt.*;
import java.awt.event.*;
import javax.swing.*;
import java.util.*;

// This class extends JPanel. It overrides
// the paintComponent() method so that random
// lines are plotted in the panel.
class PaintPanel extends JPanel {
  Insets ins; // holds the panel's insets

  Random rand; // used to generate random numbers

  // Construct a panel.
  PaintPanel() {

    // Put a border around the panel.
    setBorder(
      BorderFactory.createLineBorder(Color.RED, 5));

    rand = new Random();
  }

  // Override the paintComponent() method.
  protected void paintComponent(Graphics g) {
    // Always call the superclass method first.
    super.paintComponent(g);

    int x, y, x2, y2;

    // Get the height and width of the component.
    int height = getHeight();
    int width = getWidth();

    // Get the insets.
    ins = getInsets();

    // Draw ten lines whose endpoints are randomly generated.
    for(int i=0; i < 10; i++) {
      // Obtain random coordinates that define
      // the endpoints of each line.
      x = rand.nextInt(width-ins.left);
      y = rand.nextInt(height-ins.bottom);
      x2 = rand.nextInt(width-ins.left);
      y2 = rand.nextInt(height-ins.bottom);

      // Draw the line.
      g.drawLine(x, y, x2, y2);
    }
  }
}
```

```
// Demonstrate painting directly onto a panel.
class PaintDemo {

  JLabel jlab;
  PaintPanel pp;

  PaintDemo() {

    // Create a new JFrame container.
    JFrame jfrm = new JFrame("Paint Demo");

    // Give the frame an initial size.
    jfrm.setSize(200, 150);

    // Terminate the program when the user closes the application.
    jfrm.setDefaultCloseOperation(JFrame.EXIT_ON_CLOSE);

    // Create the panel that will be painted.
    pp = new PaintPanel();

    // Add the panel to the content pane. Because the default
    // border layout is used, the panel will automatically be
    // sized to fit the center region.
    jfrm.add(pp);

    // Display the frame.
    jfrm.setVisible(true);
  }

  public static void main(String args[]) {
    // Create the frame on the event dispatching thread.
    SwingUtilities.invokeLater(new Runnable() {
      public void run() {
        new PaintDemo();
      }
    });
  }
}
```

Let's examine this program closely. The **PaintPanel** class extends **JPanel**. **JPanel** is one of Swing's lightweight containers, which means that it is a component that can be added to the content pane of a **JFrame**. To handle painting, **PaintPanel** overrides the **paintComponent( )** method. This enables **PaintPanel** to write directly to the surface of the component when painting takes place. The size of the panel is not specified because the program uses the default border layout and the panel is added to the center. This results in the panel being sized to fill the center. If you change the size of the window, the size of the panel will be adjusted accordingly.

Notice that the constructor also specifies a 5-pixel wide, red border. This is accomplished by setting the border by using the **setBorder( )** method, shown here:

void setBorder(Border *border*)

Border is the Swing interface that encapsulates a border. You can obtain a border by calling one of the factory methods defined by the **BorderFactory** class. The one used in the program is **createLineBorder( )**, which creates a simple line border. It is shown here:

static Border createLineBorder(Color *clr*, int *width*)

Here, *clr* specifies the color of the border and *width* specifies its width in pixels.

Inside the override of **paintComponent( )**, notice that it first calls **super.paintComponent( )**. As explained, this is necessary to ensure that the component is properly drawn. Next the width and height of the panel are obtained along with the insets. These values are used to ensure the lines lie within the drawing area of the panel. The drawing area is the overall width and height of a component less the border width. The computations are designed to work with differently sized **PaintPanel**s and borders. To prove this, try changing the size of the window. The lines will still all lie within the borders of the panel.

The **PaintDemo** class creates a **PaintPanel** and then adds the panel to the content pane. When the application is first displayed, the overridden **paintComponent( )** method is called, and the lines are drawn. Each time you resize or hide and restore the window, a new set of lines are drawn. In all cases, the lines fall within the paintable area.

CHAPTER 30

Exploring Swing

The previous chapter described several of the core concepts relating to Swing and showed the general form of both a Swing application and a Swing applet. This chapter continues the discussion of Swing by presenting an overview of several Swing components, such as buttons, check boxes, trees, and tables. The Swing components provide rich functionality and allow a high level of customization. Because of space limitations, it is not possible to describe all of their features and attributes. Rather, the purpose of this overview is to give you a feel for the capabilities of the Swing component set.

The Swing component classes described in this chapter are shown here:

JButton	JCheckBox	JComboBox	JLabel
JList	JRadioButton	JScrollPane	JTabbedPane
JTable	JTextField	JToggleButton	JTree

These components are all lightweight, which means that they are all derived from **JComponent**.

Also discussed is the **ButtonGroup** class, which encapsulates a mutually exclusive set of Swing buttons, and **ImageIcon**, which encapsulates a graphics image. Both are defined by Swing and packaged in **javax.swing**.

One other point: The Swing components are demonstrated in applets because the code for an applet is more compact than it is for a desktop application. However, the same techniques apply to both applets and applications.

JLabel and ImageIcon

JLabel is Swing's easiest-to-use component. It creates a label and was introduced in the preceding chapter. Here, we will look at **JLabel** a bit more closely. **JLabel** can be used to display text and/or an icon. It is a passive component in that it does not respond to user input. **JLabel** defines several constructors. Here are three of them:

JLabel(Icon *icon*)
JLabel(String *str*)
JLabel(String *str*, Icon *icon*, int *align*)

Here, *str* and *icon* are the text and icon used for the label. The *align* argument specifies the horizontal alignment of the text and/or icon within the dimensions of the label. It must be one of the following values: **LEFT**, **RIGHT**, **CENTER**, **LEADING**, or **TRAILING**. These constants are defined in the **SwingConstants** interface, along with several others used by the Swing classes.

Notice that icons are specified by objects of type **Icon**, which is an interface defined by Swing. The easiest way to obtain an icon is to use the **ImageIcon** class. **ImageIcon** implements **Icon** and encapsulates an image. Thus, an object of type **ImageIcon** can be passed as an argument to the **Icon** parameter of **JLabel**'s constructor. There are several ways to provide the image, including reading it from a file or downloading it from a URL. Here is the **ImageIcon** constructor used by the example in this section:

ImageIcon(String *filename*)

It obtains the image in the file named *filename.*

The icon and text associated with the label can be obtained by the following methods:

Icon getIcon( )
String getText( )

The icon and text associated with a label can be set by these methods:

void setIcon(Icon *icon*)
void setText(String *str*)

Here, *icon* and *str* are the icon and text, respectively. Therefore, using **setText( )** it is possible to change the text inside a label during program execution.

The following applet illustrates how to create and display a label containing both an icon and a string. It begins by creating an **ImageIcon** object for the file **france.gif**, which depicts the flag for France. This is used as the second argument to the **JLabel** constructor. The first and last arguments for the **JLabel** constructor are the label text and the alignment. Finally, the label is added to the content pane.

```
// Demonstrate JLabel and ImageIcon.
import java.awt.*;
import javax.swing.*;
/*
  <applet code="JLabelDemo" width=250 height=150>
  </applet>
*/

public class JLabelDemo extends JApplet {

  public void init() {
    try {
      SwingUtilities.invokeAndWait(
        new Runnable() {
          public void run() {
            makeGUI();
          }
        }
```

```
    );
  } catch (Exception exc) {
    System.out.println("Can't create because of " + exc);
  }
}

private void makeGUI() {

  // Create an icon.
  ImageIcon ii = new ImageIcon("france.gif");

  // Create a label.
  JLabel jl = new JLabel("France", ii, JLabel.CENTER);

  // Add the label to the content pane.
  add(jl);
  }
}
```

Output from the label example is shown here:

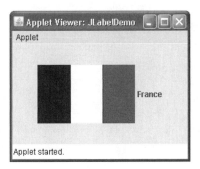

JTextField

JTextField is the simplest Swing text component. It is also probably its most widely used text component. **JTextField** allows you to edit one line of text. It is derived from **JTextComponent**, which provides the basic functionality common to Swing text components. **JTextField** uses the **Document** interface for its model.

Three of **JTextField**'s constructors are shown here:

JTextField(int *cols*)
JTextField(String *str*, int *cols*)
JTextField(String *str*)

Here, *str* is the string to be initially presented, and *cols* is the number of columns in the text field. If no string is specified, the text field is initially empty. If the number of columns is not specified, the text field is sized to fit the specified string.

JTextField generates events in response to user interaction. For example, an **ActionEvent** is fired when the user presses ENTER. A **CaretEvent** is fired each time the caret (i.e., the cursor) changes position. (**CaretEvent** is packaged in **javax.swing.event**.) Other events are also possible. In many cases, your program will not need to handle these events. Instead, you will simply obtain the string currently in the text field when it is needed. To obtain the text currently in the text field, call **getText( )**.

The following example illustrates **JTextField**. It creates a **JTextField** and adds it to the content pane. When the user presses ENTER, an action event is generated. This is handled by displaying the text in the status window.

```
// Demonstrate JTextField.
import java.awt.*;
import java.awt.event.*;
import javax.swing.*;
/*
  <applet code="JTextFieldDemo" width=300 height=50>
  </applet>
*/

public class JTextFieldDemo extends JApplet {
  JTextField jtf;

  public void init() {
    try {
      SwingUtilities.invokeAndWait(
        new Runnable() {
          public void run() {
            makeGUI();
          }
        }
      );
    } catch (Exception exc) {
      System.out.println("Can't create because of " + exc);
    }
  }

  private void makeGUI() {

    // Change to flow layout.
    setLayout(new FlowLayout());

    // Add text field to content pane.
    jtf = new JTextField(15);
    add(jtf);
    jtf.addActionListener(new ActionListener() {
      public void actionPerformed(ActionEvent ae) {
        // Show text when user presses ENTER.
        showStatus(jtf.getText());
      }
    });
  }
}
```

Output from the text field example is shown here:

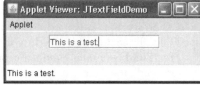

The Swing Buttons

Swing defines four types of buttons: **JButton**, **JToggleButton**, **JCheckBox**, and **JRadioButton**. All are subclasses of the **AbstractButton** class, which extends **JComponent**. Thus, all buttons share a set of common traits.

AbstractButton contains many methods that allow you to control the behavior of buttons. For example, you can define different icons that are displayed for the button when it is disabled, pressed, or selected. Another icon can be used as a *rollover* icon, which is displayed when the mouse is positioned over a button. The following methods set these icons:

> void setDisabledIcon(Icon *di*)
> void setPressedIcon(Icon *pi*)
> void setSelectedIcon(Icon *si*)
> void setRolloverIcon(Icon *ri*)

Here, *di*, *pi*, *si*, and *ri* are the icons to be used for the indicated purpose.

The text associated with a button can be read and written via the following methods:

> String getText( )
> void setText(String *str*)

Here, *str* is the text to be associated with the button.

The model used by all buttons is defined by the **ButtonModel** interface. A button generates an action event when it is pressed. Other events are possible. Each of the concrete button classes is examined next.

JButton

The **JButton** class provides the functionality of a push button. You have already seen a simple form of it in the preceding chapter. **JButton** allows an icon, a string, or both to be associated with the push button. Three of its constructors are shown here:

> JButton(Icon *icon*)
> JButton(String *str*)
> JButton(String *str*, Icon *icon*)

Here, *str* and *icon* are the string and icon used for the button.

When the button is pressed, an **ActionEvent** is generated. Using the **ActionEvent** object passed to the **actionPerformed( )** method of the registered **ActionListener**, you can obtain the *action command* string associated with the button. By default, this is the string displayed inside the button. However, you can set the action command by calling **setActionCommand( )** on the button. You can obtain the action command by calling **getActionCommand( )** on the event object. It is declared like this:

> String getActionCommand( )

The action command identifies the button. Thus, when using two or more buttons within the same application, the action command gives you an easy way to determine which button was pressed.

In the preceding chapter, you saw an example of a text-based button. The following demonstrates an icon-based button. It displays four push buttons and a label. Each button displays an icon that represents the flag of a country. When a button is pressed, the name of that country is displayed in the label.

```
// Demonstrate an icon-based JButton.
import java.awt.*;
import java.awt.event.*;
import javax.swing.*;
/*
  <applet code="JButtonDemo" width=250 height=450>
  </applet>
*/

public class JButtonDemo extends JApplet
implements ActionListener {
  JLabel jlab;

  public void init() {
    try {
      SwingUtilities.invokeAndWait(
        new Runnable() {
          public void run() {
            makeGUI();
          }
        }
      );
    } catch (Exception exc) {
      System.out.println("Can't create because of " + exc);
    }
  }

private void makeGUI() {

    // Change to flow layout.
    setLayout(new FlowLayout());

    // Add buttons to content pane.
    ImageIcon france = new ImageIcon("france.gif");
    JButton jb = new JButton(france);
    jb.setActionCommand("France");
    jb.addActionListener(this);
    add(jb);

    ImageIcon germany = new ImageIcon("germany.gif");
    jb = new JButton(germany);
    jb.setActionCommand("Germany");
    jb.addActionListener(this);
    add(jb);

    ImageIcon italy = new ImageIcon("italy.gif");
    jb = new JButton(italy);
    jb.setActionCommand("Italy");
```

```
    jb.addActionListener(this);
    add(jb);

    ImageIcon japan = new ImageIcon("japan.gif");
    jb = new JButton(japan);
    jb.setActionCommand("Japan");
    jb.addActionListener(this);
    add(jb);

    // Create and add the label to content pane.
    jlab = new JLabel("Choose a Flag");
    add(jlab);
  }

  // Handle button events.
  public void actionPerformed(ActionEvent ae) {
    jlab.setText("You selected " + ae.getActionCommand());
  }
}
```

Output from the button example is shown here:

JToggleButton

A useful variation on the push button is called a
toggle button. A toggle button looks just like a push
button, but it acts differently because it has two
states: pushed and released. That is, when you press
a toggle button, it stays pressed rather than popping
back up as a regular push button does. When you
press the toggle button a second time, it releases
(pops up). Therefore, each time a toggle button is
pushed, it toggles between its two states.

Toggle buttons are objects of the **JToggleButton**
class. **JToggleButton** implements **AbstractButton**.
In addition to creating standard toggle buttons,
JToggleButton is a superclass for two other Swing
components that also represent two-state controls.
These are **JCheckBox** and **JRadioButton**, which are
described later in this chapter. Thus, **JToggleButton**
defines the basic functionality of all two-state
components.

JToggleButton defines several constructors. The
one used by the example in this section is shown here:

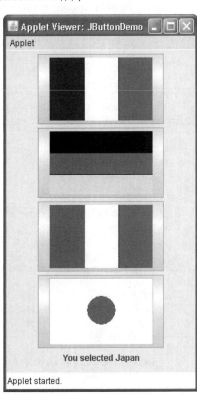

JToggleButton(String *str*)

This creates a toggle button that contains the text passed in *str*. By default, the button is in
the off position. Other constructors enable you to create toggle buttons that contain images,
or images and text.

JToggleButton uses a model defined by a nested class called **JToggleButton** **.ToggleButtonModel**. Normally, you won't need to interact directly with the model to use a standard toggle button.

Like **JButton**, **JToggleButton** generates an action event each time it is pressed. Unlike **JButton**, however, **JToggleButton** also generates an item event. This event is used by those components that support the concept of selection. When a **JToggleButton** is pressed in, it is selected. When it is popped out, it is deselected.

To handle item events, you must implement the **ItemListener** interface. Recall from Chapter 22, that each time an item event is generated, it is passed to the **itemStateChanged( )** method defined by **ItemListener**. Inside **itemStateChanged( )**, the **getItem( )** method can be called on the **ItemEvent** object to obtain a reference to the **JToggleButton** instance that generated the event. It is shown here:

Object getItem( )

A reference to the button is returned. You will need to cast this reference to **JToggleButton**.

The easiest way to determine a toggle button's state is by calling the **isSelected( )** method (inherited from **AbstractButton**) on the button that generated the event. It is shown here:

boolean isSelected( )

It returns **true** if the button is selected and **false** otherwise.

Here is an example that uses a toggle button. Notice how the item listener works. It simply calls **isSelected( )** to determine the button's state.

```java
// Demonstrate JToggleButton.
import java.awt.*;
import java.awt.event.*;
import javax.swing.*;
/*
  <applet code="JToggleButtonDemo" width=200 height=80>
  </applet>
*/

public class JToggleButtonDemo extends JApplet {

  JLabel jlab;
  JToggleButton jtbn;

  public void init() {
    try {
      SwingUtilities.invokeAndWait(
        new Runnable() {
          public void run() {
            makeGUI();
          }
        }
      );
    } catch (Exception exc) {
      System.out.println("Can't create because of " + exc);
    }
```

```
  }

  private void makeGUI() {

    // Change to flow layout.
    setLayout(new FlowLayout());

    // Create a label.
    jlab = new JLabel("Button is off.");

    // Make a toggle button.
    jtbn =  new JToggleButton("On/Off");

    // Add an item listener for the toggle button.
    jtbn.addItemListener(new ItemListener() {
      public void itemStateChanged(ItemEvent ie) {
        if(jtbn.isSelected())
          jlab.setText("Button is on.");
        else
          jlab.setText("Button is off.");
      }

    });

    // Add the toggle button and label to the content pane.
    add(jtbn);
    add(jlab);
  }
}
```

The output from the toggle button example is shown here:

Check Boxes

The **JCheckBox** class provides the functionality of a check box. Its immediate superclass is **JToggleButton**, which provides support for two-state buttons, as just described. **JCheckBox** defines several constructors. The one used here is

JCheckBox(String *str*)

It creates a check box that has the text specified by *str* as a label. Other constructors let you specify the initial selection state of the button and specify an icon.

When the user selects or deselects a check box, an **ItemEvent** is generated. You can obtain a reference to the **JCheckBox** that generated the event by calling **getItem( )** on the **ItemEvent** passed to the **itemStateChanged( )** method defined by **ItemListener**. The easiest way to determine the selected state of a check box is to call **isSelected( )** on the **JCheckBox** instance.

In addition to supporting the normal check box operation, **JCheckBox** lets you specify the icons that indicate when a check box is selected, cleared, and rolled-over. We won't be using this capability here, but it is available for use in your own programs.

The following example illustrates check boxes. It displays four check boxes and a label. When the user clicks a check box, an **ItemEvent** is generated. Inside the **itemStateChanged( )** method, **getItem( )** is called to obtain a reference to the **JCheckBox** object that generated the event. Next, a call to **isSelected( )** determines if the box was selected or cleared. The **getText( )** method gets the text for that check box and uses it to set the text inside the label.

```java
// Demonstrate JCheckbox.
import java.awt.*;
import java.awt.event.*;
import javax.swing.*;
/*
  <applet code="JCheckBoxDemo" width=270 height=50>
  </applet>
*/

public class JCheckBoxDemo extends JApplet
implements ItemListener {
  JLabel jlab;

  public void init() {
    try {
      SwingUtilities.invokeAndWait(
        new Runnable() {
          public void run() {
            makeGUI();
          }
        }
      );
    } catch (Exception exc) {
      System.out.println("Can't create because of " + exc);
    }
  }

  private void makeGUI() {

    // Change to flow layout.
    setLayout(new FlowLayout());

    // Add check boxes to the content pane.
    JCheckBox cb = new JCheckBox("C");
    cb.addItemListener(this);
    add(cb);

    cb = new JCheckBox("C++");
```

```
    cb.addItemListener(this);
    add(cb);

    cb = new JCheckBox("Java");
    cb.addItemListener(this);
    add(cb);

    cb = new JCheckBox("Perl");
    cb.addItemListener(this);
    add(cb);

    // Create the label and add it to the content pane.
    jlab = new JLabel("Select languages");
    add(jlab);
  }

  // Handle item events for the check boxes.
  public void itemStateChanged(ItemEvent ie) {
    JCheckBox cb = (JCheckBox)ie.getItem();

    if(cb.isSelected())
      jlab.setText(cb.getText() + " is selected");
    else
      jlab.setText(cb.getText() + " is cleared");
  }
}
```

Output from this example is shown here:

Radio Buttons

Radio buttons are a group of mutually exclusive buttons, in which only one button can be selected at any one time. They are supported by the **JRadioButton** class, which extends **JToggleButton**. **JRadioButton** provides several constructors. The one used in the example is shown here:

JRadioButton(String *str*)

Here, *str* is the label for the button. Other constructors let you specify the initial selection state of the button and specify an icon.

In order for their mutually exclusive nature to be activated, radio buttons must be configured into a group. Only one of the buttons in the group can be selected at any time. For example, if a user presses a radio button that is in a group, any previously selected button in that group is automatically deselected. A button group is created by the **ButtonGroup** class. Its default constructor is invoked for this purpose. Elements are then added to the button group via the following method:

void add(AbstractButton *ab*)

Here, *ab* is a reference to the button to be added to the group.

A **JRadioButton** generates action events, item events, and change events each time the button selection changes. Most often, it is the action event that is handled, which means that you will normally implement the **ActionListener** interface. Recall that the only method defined by **ActionListener** is **actionPerformed( )**. Inside this method, you can use a number of different ways to determine which button was selected. First, you can check its action command by calling **getActionCommand( )**. By default, the action command is the same as the button label, but you can set the action command to something else by calling **setActionCommand( )** on the radio button. Second, you can call **getSource( )** on the **ActionEvent** object and check that reference against the buttons. Finally, you can simply check each radio button to find out which one is currently selected by calling **isSelected( )** on each button. Remember, each time an action event occurs, it means that the button being selected has changed and that one and only one button will be selected.

The following example illustrates how to use radio buttons. Three radio buttons are created. The buttons are then added to a button group. As explained, this is necessary to cause their mutually exclusive behavior. Pressing a radio button generates an action event, which is handled by **actionPerformed( )**. Within that handler, the **getActionCommand( )** method gets the text that is associated with the radio button and uses it to set the text within a label.

```java
// Demonstrate JRadioButton
import java.awt.*;
import java.awt.event.*;
import javax.swing.*;
/*
  <applet code="JRadioButtonDemo" width=300 height=50>
  </applet>
*/

public class JRadioButtonDemo extends JApplet
implements ActionListener {
  JLabel jlab;

  public void init() {
    try {
      SwingUtilities.invokeAndWait(
        new Runnable() {
          public void run() {
            makeGUI();
          }
        }
      );
    } catch (Exception exc) {
      System.out.println("Can't create because of " + exc);
    }
  }

  private void makeGUI() {

    // Change to flow layout.
    setLayout(new FlowLayout());

    // Create radio buttons and add them to content pane.
    JRadioButton b1 = new JRadioButton("A");
    b1.addActionListener(this);
    add(b1);
```

```
      JRadioButton b2 = new JRadioButton("B");
      b2.addActionListener(this);
      add(b2);

      JRadioButton b3 = new JRadioButton("C");
      b3.addActionListener(this);
      add(b3);

      // Define a button group.
      ButtonGroup bg = new ButtonGroup();
      bg.add(b1);
      bg.add(b2);
      bg.add(b3);

      // Create a label and add it to the content pane.
      jlab = new JLabel("Select One");
      add(jlab);
   }

   // Handle button selection.
   public void actionPerformed(ActionEvent ae) {
      jlab.setText("You selected " + ae.getActionCommand());
   }
}
```

Output from the radio button example is shown here:

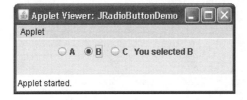

JTabbedPane

JTabbedPane encapsulates a *tabbed pane*. It manages a set of components by linking them with tabs. Selecting a tab causes the component associated with that tab to come to the forefront. Tabbed panes are very common in the modern GUI, and you have no doubt used them many times. Given the complex nature of a tabbed pane, they are surprisingly easy to create and use.

JTabbedPane defines three constructors. We will use its default constructor, which creates an empty control with the tabs positioned across the top of the pane. The other two constructors let you specify the location of the tabs, which can be along any of the four sides. **JTabbedPane** uses the **SingleSelectionModel** model.

Tabs are added by calling **addTab( )**. Here is one of its forms:

void addTab(String *name*, Component *comp*)

Here, *name* is the name for the tab, and *comp* is the component that should be added to the tab. Often, the component added to a tab is a **JPanel** that contains a group of related components. This technique allows a tab to hold a set of components.

The general procedure to use a tabbed pane is outlined here:

1. Create an instance of **JTabbedPane**.
2. Add each tab by calling **addTab( )**.
3. Add the tabbed pane to the content pane.

The following example illustrates a tabbed pane. The first tab is titled "Cities" and contains four buttons. Each button displays the name of a city. The second tab is titled "Colors" and contains three check boxes. Each check box displays the name of a color. The third tab is titled "Flavors" and contains one combo box. This enables the user to select one of three flavors.

```java
// Demonstrate JTabbedPane.
import javax.swing.*;
/*
  <applet code="JTabbedPaneDemo" width=400 height=100>
  </applet>
*/

public class JTabbedPaneDemo extends JApplet {

  public void init() {
    try {
      SwingUtilities.invokeAndWait(
        new Runnable() {
          public void run() {
            makeGUI();
          }
        }
      );
    } catch (Exception exc) {
      System.out.println("Can't create because of " + exc);
    }
  }

  private void makeGUI() {

    JTabbedPane jtp = new JTabbedPane();
    jtp.addTab("Cities", new CitiesPanel());
    jtp.addTab("Colors", new ColorsPanel());
    jtp.addTab("Flavors", new FlavorsPanel());
    add(jtp);
  }
}

// Make the panels that will be added to the tabbed pane.
class CitiesPanel extends JPanel {

  public CitiesPanel() {
    JButton b1 = new JButton("New York");
    add(b1);
    JButton b2 = new JButton("London");
    add(b2);
    JButton b3 = new JButton("Hong Kong");
```

```
        add(b3);
        JButton b4 = new JButton("Tokyo");
        add(b4);
    }
}

class ColorsPanel extends JPanel {

    public ColorsPanel() {
        JCheckBox cb1 = new JCheckBox("Red");
        add(cb1);
        JCheckBox cb2 = new JCheckBox("Green");
        add(cb2);
        JCheckBox cb3 = new JCheckBox("Blue");
        add(cb3);
    }
}

class FlavorsPanel extends JPanel {

    public FlavorsPanel() {
        JComboBox jcb = new JComboBox();
        jcb.addItem("Vanilla");
        jcb.addItem("Chocolate");
        jcb.addItem("Strawberry");
        add(jcb);
    }
}
```

Output from the tabbed pane example is shown in the following three illustrations:

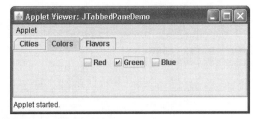

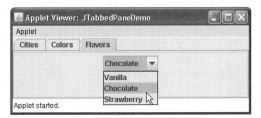

JScrollPane

JScrollPane is a lightweight container that automatically handles the scrolling of another component. The component being scrolled can either be an individual component, such as a table, or a group of components contained within another lightweight container, such as a **JPanel**. In either case, if the object being scrolled is larger than the viewable area, horizontal and/or vertical scroll bars are automatically provided, and the component can be scrolled through the pane. Because **JScrollPane** automates scrolling, it usually eliminates the need to manage individual scroll bars.

The viewable area of a scroll pane is called the *viewport*. It is a window in which the component being scrolled is displayed. Thus, the viewport displays the visible portion of the component being scrolled. The scroll bars scroll the component through the viewport. In its default behavior, a **JScrollPane** will dynamically add or remove a scroll bar as needed. For example, if the component is taller than the viewport, a vertical scroll bar is added. If the component will completely fit within the viewport, the scroll bars are removed.

JScrollPane defines several constructors. The one used in this chapter is shown here:

JScrollPane(Component *comp*)

The component to be scrolled is specified by *comp*. Scroll bars are automatically displayed when the content of the pane exceeds the dimensions of the viewport.

Here are the steps to follow to use a scroll pane:

1. Create the component to be scrolled.

2. Create an instance of **JScrollPane**, passing to it the object to scroll.

3. Add the scroll pane to the content pane.

The following example illustrates a scroll pane. First, a **JPanel** object is created, and 400 buttons are added to it, arranged into 20 columns. This panel is then added to a scroll pane, and the scroll pane is added to the content pane. Because the panel is larger than the viewport, vertical and horizontal scroll bars appear automatically. You can use the scroll bars to scroll the buttons into view.

```
// Demonstrate JScrollPane.
import java.awt.*;
import javax.swing.*;
/*
  <applet code="JScrollPaneDemo" width=300 height=250>
  </applet>
*/

public class JScrollPaneDemo extends JApplet {

  public void init() {
    try {
      SwingUtilities.invokeAndWait(
        new Runnable() {
          public void run() {
            makeGUI();
          }
        }
      );
    } catch (Exception exc) {
      System.out.println("Can't create because of " + exc);
    }
```

```
  }

  private void makeGUI() {

    // Add 400 buttons to a panel.
    JPanel jp = new JPanel();
    jp.setLayout(new GridLayout(20, 20));
    int b = 0;
    for(int i = 0; i < 20; i++) {
      for(int j = 0; j < 20; j++) {
        jp.add(new JButton("Button " + b));
        ++b;
      }
    }

    // Create the scroll pane.
    JScrollPane jsp = new JScrollPane(jp);

    // Add the scroll pane to the content pane.
    // Because the default border layout is used,
    // the scroll pane will be added to the center.
    add(jsp, BorderLayout.CENTER);
  }
}
```

Output from the scroll pane example is shown here:

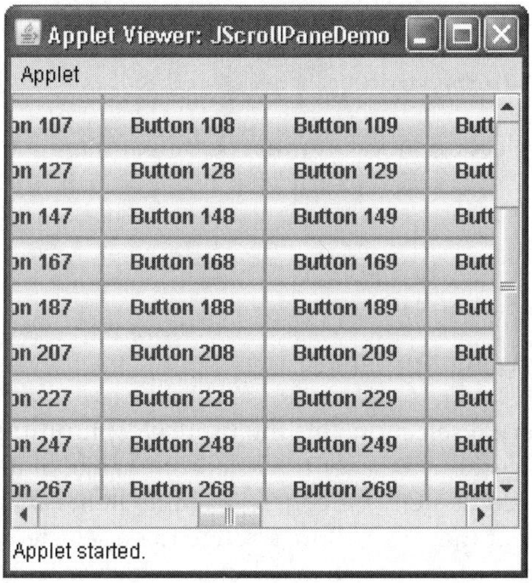

JList

In Swing, the basic list class is called **JList**. It supports the selection of one or more items from a list. Although the list often consists of strings, it is possible to create a list of just about any object that can be displayed. **JList** is so widely used in Java that it is highly unlikely that you have not seen one before.

JList provides several constructors. The one used here is

JList(Object[ ] *items*)

This creates a **JList** that contains the items in the array specified by *items*.

JList is based on two models. The first is **ListModel**. This interface defines how access to the list data is achieved. The second model is the **ListSelectionModel** interface, which defines methods that determine what list item or items are selected.

Although a **JList** will work properly by itself, most of the time you will wrap a **JList** inside a **JScrollPane**. This way, long lists will automatically be scrollable, which simplifies GUI design. It also makes it easy to change the number of entries in a list without having to change the size of the **JList** component.

A **JList** generates a **ListSelectionEvent** when the user makes or changes a selection. This event is also generated when the user deselects an item. It is handled by implementing **ListSelectionListener**. This listener specifies only one method, called **valueChanged( )**, which is shown here:

void valueChanged(ListSelectionEvent *le*)

Here, *le* is a reference to the object that generated the event. Although **ListSelectionEvent** does provide some methods of its own, normally you will interrogate the **JList** object itself to determine what has occurred. Both **ListSelectionEvent** and **ListSelectionListener** are packaged in **javax.swing.event**.

By default, a **JList** allows the user to select multiple ranges of items within the list, but you can change this behavior by calling **setSelectionMode( )**, which is defined by **JList**. It is shown here:

void setSelectionMode(int *mode*)

Here, *mode* specifies the selection mode. It must be one of these values defined by **ListSelectionModel**:

SINGLE_SELECTION

SINGLE_INTERVAL_SELECTION

MULTIPLE_INTERVAL_SELECTION

The default, multiple-interval selection, lets the user select multiple ranges of items within a list. With single-interval selection, the user can select one range of items. With single selection, the user can select only a single item. Of course, a single item can be selected in the other two modes, too. It's just that they also allow a range to be selected.

You can obtain the index of the first item selected, which will also be the index of the only selected item when using single-selection mode, by calling **getSelectedIndex( )**, shown here:

int getSelectedIndex( )

Indexing begins at zero. So, if the first item is selected, this method will return 0. If no item is selected, –1 is returned.

Instead of obtaining the index of a selection, you can obtain the value associated with the selection by calling **getSelectedValue( )**:

Object getSelectedValue( )

It returns a reference to the first selected value. If no value has been selected, it returns **null**.

The following applet demonstrates a simple **JList**, which holds a list of cities. Each time a city is selected in the list, a **ListSelectionEvent** is generated, which is handled by the **valueChanged( )** method defined by **ListSelectionListener**. It responds by obtaining the index of the selected item and displaying the name of the selected city in a label.

```
// Demonstrate JList.
import javax.swing.*;
import javax.swing.event.*;
import java.awt.*;
import java.awt.event.*;

/*
  <applet code="JListDemo" width=200 height=120>
  </applet>
*/

public class JListDemo extends JApplet {
  JList jlst;
  JLabel jlab;
  JScrollPane jscrlp;

  // Create an array of cities.
  String Cities[] = { "New York", "Chicago", "Houston",
                      "Denver", "Los Angeles", "Seattle",
                      "London", "Paris", "New Delhi",
                      "Hong Kong", "Tokyo", "Sydney" };

  public void init() {
    try {
      SwingUtilities.invokeAndWait(
        new Runnable() {
          public void run() {
            makeGUI();
          }
        }
      );
    } catch (Exception exc) {
      System.out.println("Can't create because of " + exc);
    }
  }

  private void makeGUI() {

    // Change to flow layout.
    setLayout(new FlowLayout());
```

```
    // Create a JList.
    jlst = new JList(Cities);

    // Set the list selection mode to single selection.
    jlst.setSelectionMode(ListSelectionModel.SINGLE_SELECTION);

    // Add the list to a scroll pane.
    jscrlp = new JScrollPane(jlst);

    // Set the preferred size of the scroll pane.
    jscrlp.setPreferredSize(new Dimension(120, 90));

    // Make a label that displays the selection.
    jlab = new JLabel("Choose a City");

    // Add selection listener for the list.
    jlst.addListSelectionListener(new ListSelectionListener() {
      public void valueChanged(ListSelectionEvent le) {
        // Get the index of the changed item.
        int idx = jlst.getSelectedIndex();

        // Display selection, if item was selected.
        if(idx != -1)
          jlab.setText("Current selection: " + Cities[idx]);
        else // Otherwise, reprompt.
          jlab.setText("Choose a City");

      }
    });

    // Add the list and label to the content pane.
    add(jscrlp);
    add(jlab);
  }
}
```

Output from the list example is shown here:

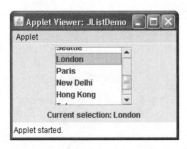

JComboBox

Swing provides a *combo box* (a combination of a text field and a drop-down list) through
the **JComboBox** class. A combo box normally displays one entry, but it will also display a
drop-down list that allows a user to select a different entry. You can also create a combo box

that lets the user enter a selection into the text field. The **JComboBox** constructor used by the example is shown here:

JComboBox(Object[ ] *items*)

Here, *items* is an array that initializes the combo box. Other constructors are available.

JComboBox uses the **ComboBoxModel**. Mutable combo boxes (those whose entries can be changed) use the **MutableComboBoxModel**.

In addition to passing an array of items to be displayed in the drop-down list, items can be dynamically added to the list of choices via the **addItem( )** method, shown here:

void addItem(Object *obj*)

Here, *obj* is the object to be added to the combo box. This method must be used only with mutable combo boxes.

JComboBox generates an action event when the user selects an item from the list. **JComboBox** also generates an item event when the state of selection changes, which occurs when an item is selected or deselected. Thus, changing a selection means that two item events will occur: one for the deselected item and another for the selected item. Often, it is sufficient to simply listen for action events, but both event types are available for your use.

One way to obtain the item selected in the list is to call **getSelectedItem( )** on the combo box. It is shown here:

Object getSelectedItem( )

You will need to cast the returned value into the type of object stored in the list.

The following example demonstrates the combo box. The combo box contains entries for "France," "Germany," "Italy," and "Japan." When a country is selected, an icon-based label is updated to display the flag for that country. You can see how little code is required to use this powerful component.

```
// Demonstrate JComboBox.
import java.awt.*;
import java.awt.event.*;
import javax.swing.*;
/*
  <applet code="JComboBoxDemo" width=300 height=100>
  </applet>
*/

public class JComboBoxDemo extends JApplet {
  JLabel jlab;
  ImageIcon france, germany, italy, japan;
  JComboBox jcb;

  String flags[] = { "France", "Germany", "Italy", "Japan" };

  public void init() {
    try {
      SwingUtilities.invokeAndWait(
        new Runnable() {
          public void run() {
```

```
        makeGUI();
      }
    }
  );
  } catch (Exception exc) {
    System.out.println("Can't create because of " + exc);
  }
}

private void makeGUI() {

  // Change to flow layout.
  setLayout(new FlowLayout());

  // Instantiate a combo box and add it to the content pane.
  jcb = new JComboBox(flags);
  add(jcb);

  // Handle selections.
  jcb.addActionListener(new ActionListener() {
    public void actionPerformed(ActionEvent ae) {
      String s = (String) jcb.getSelectedItem();
      jlab.setIcon(new ImageIcon(s + ".gif"));
    }
  });

  // Create a label and add it to the content pane.
  jlab = new JLabel(new ImageIcon("france.gif"));
  add(jlab);
  }
}
```

Output from the combo box example is shown here:

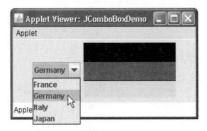

Trees

A *tree* is a component that presents a hierarchical view of data. The user has the ability to expand or collapse individual subtrees in this display. Trees are implemented in Swing by the **JTree** class. A sampling of its constructors is shown here:

JTree(Object *obj*[ ])
JTree(Vector<?> *v*)
JTree(TreeNode *tn*)

In the first form, the tree is constructed from the elements in the array *obj*. The second form constructs the tree from the elements of vector *v*. In the third form, the tree whose root node is specified by *tn* specifies the tree.

Although **JTree** is packaged in **javax.swing**, its support classes and interfaces are packaged in **javax.swing.tree**. This is because the number of classes and interfaces needed to support **JTree** is quite large.

JTree relies on two models: **TreeModel** and **TreeSelectionModel**. A **JTree** generates a variety of events, but three relate specifically to trees: **TreeExpansionEvent**, **TreeSelectionEvent**, and **TreeModelEvent**. **TreeExpansionEvent** events occur when a node is expanded or collapsed. A **TreeSelectionEvent** is generated when the user selects or deselects a node within the tree. A **TreeModelEvent** is fired when the data or structure of the tree changes. The listeners for these events are **TreeExpansionListener**, **TreeSelectionListener**, and **TreeModelListener**, respectively. The tree event classes and listener interfaces are packaged in **javax.swing.event**.

The event handled by the sample program shown in this section is **TreeSelectionEvent**. To listen for this event, implement **TreeSelectionListener**. It defines only one method, called **valueChanged( )**, which receives the **TreeSelectionEvent** object. You can obtain the path to the selected object by calling **getPath( )**, shown here, on the event object.

TreePath getPath( )

It returns a **TreePath** object that describes the path to the changed node. The **TreePath** class encapsulates information about a path to a particular node in a tree. It provides several constructors and methods. In this book, only the **toString( )** method is used. It returns a string that describes the path.

The **TreeNode** interface declares methods that obtain information about a tree node. For example, it is possible to obtain a reference to the parent node or an enumeration of the child nodes. The **MutableTreeNode** interface extends **TreeNode**. It declares methods that can insert and remove child nodes or change the parent node.

The **DefaultMutableTreeNode** class implements the **MutableTreeNode** interface. It represents a node in a tree. One of its constructors is shown here:

DefaultMutableTreeNode(Object *obj*)

Here, *obj* is the object to be enclosed in this tree node. The new tree node doesn't have a parent or children.

To create a hierarchy of tree nodes, the **add( )** method of **DefaultMutableTreeNode** can be used. Its signature is shown here:

void add(MutableTreeNode *child*)

Here, *child* is a mutable tree node that is to be added as a child to the current node.

JTree does not provide any scrolling capabilities of its own. Instead, a **JTree** is typically placed within a **JScrollPane**. This way, a large tree can be scrolled through a smaller viewport.

Here are the steps to follow to use a tree:

1. Create an instance of **JTree**.

2. Create a **JScrollPane** and specify the tree as the object to be scrolled.

3. Add the tree to the scroll pane.

4. Add the scroll pane to the content pane.

The following example illustrates how to create a tree and handle selections. The program creates a **DefaultMutableTreeNode** instance labeled "Options." This is the top node of the tree hierarchy. Additional tree nodes are then created, and the **add( )** method is called to connect these nodes to the tree. A reference to the top node in the tree is provided as the argument to the **JTree** constructor. The tree is then provided as the argument to the **JScrollPane** constructor. This scroll pane is then added to the content pane. Next, a label is created and added to the content pane. The tree selection is displayed in this label. To receive selection events from the tree, a **TreeSelectionListener** is registered for the tree. Inside the **valueChanged( )** method, the path to the current selection is obtained and displayed.

```java
// Demonstrate JTree.
import java.awt.*;
import javax.swing.event.*;
import javax.swing.*;
import javax.swing.tree.*;
/*
  <applet code="JTreeDemo" width=400 height=200>
  </applet>
*/


public class JTreeDemo extends JApplet {
  JTree tree;
  JLabel jlab;

  public void init() {
    try {
      SwingUtilities.invokeAndWait(
        new Runnable() {
          public void run() {
            makeGUI();
          }
        }
      );
    } catch (Exception exc) {
      System.out.println("Can't create because of " + exc);
    }
  }

  private void makeGUI() {

    // Create top node of tree.
    DefaultMutableTreeNode top = new DefaultMutableTreeNode("Options");

    // Create subtree of "A".
    DefaultMutableTreeNode a = new DefaultMutableTreeNode("A");
    top.add(a);
    DefaultMutableTreeNode a1 = new DefaultMutableTreeNode("A1");
    a.add(a1);
    DefaultMutableTreeNode a2 = new DefaultMutableTreeNode("A2");
    a.add(a2);
```

```
    // Create subtree of "B".
    DefaultMutableTreeNode b = new DefaultMutableTreeNode("B");
    top.add(b);
    DefaultMutableTreeNode b1 = new DefaultMutableTreeNode("B1");
    b.add(b1);
    DefaultMutableTreeNode b2 = new DefaultMutableTreeNode("B2");
    b.add(b2);
    DefaultMutableTreeNode b3 = new DefaultMutableTreeNode("B3");
    b.add(b3);

    // Create the tree.
    tree = new JTree(top);

    // Add the tree to a scroll pane.
    JScrollPane jsp = new JScrollPane(tree);

    // Add the scroll pane to the content pane.
    add(jsp);

    // Add the label to the content pane.
    jlab = new JLabel();
    add(jlab, BorderLayout.SOUTH);

    // Handle tree selection events.
    tree.addTreeSelectionListener(new TreeSelectionListener() {
      public void valueChanged(TreeSelectionEvent tse) {
        jlab.setText("Selection is " + tse.getPath());
      }
    });
  }
}
```

Output from the tree example is shown here:

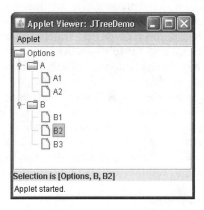

The string presented in the text field describes the path from the top tree node to the selected node.

JTable

JTable is a component that displays rows and columns of data. You can drag the cursor on column boundaries to resize columns. You can also drag a column to a new position. Depending on its configuration, it is also possible to select a row, column, or cell within the table, and to change the data within a cell. **JTable** is a sophisticated component that offers many more options and features than can be discussed here. (It is perhaps Swing's most complicated component.) However, in its default configuration, **JTable** still offers substantial functionality that is easy to use—especially if you simply want to use the table to present data in a tabular format. The brief overview presented here will give you a general understanding of this powerful component.

Like **JTree**, **JTable** has many classes and interfaces associated with it. These are packaged in **javax.swing.table**.

At its core, **JTable** is conceptually simple. It is a component that consists of one or more columns of information. At the top of each column is a heading. In addition to describing the data in a column, the heading also provides the mechanism by which the user can change the size of a column or change the location of a column within the table. **JTable** does not provide any scrolling capabilities of its own. Instead, you will normally wrap a **JTable** inside a **JScrollPane**.

JTable supplies several constructors. The one used here is

JTable(Object *data*[ ][ ], Object *colHeads*[ ])

Here, *data* is a two-dimensional array of the information to be presented, and *colHeads* is a one-dimensional array with the column headings.

JTable relies on three models. The first is the table model, which is defined by the **TableModel** interface. This model defines those things related to displaying data in a two-dimensional format. The second is the table column model, which is represented by **TableColumnModel**. **JTable** is defined in terms of columns, and it is **TableColumnModel** that specifies the characteristics of a column. These two models are packaged in **javax.swing.table**. The third model determines how items are selected, and it is specified by the **ListSelectionModel**, which was described when **JList** was discussed.

A **JTable** can generate several different events. The two most fundamental to a table's operation are **ListSelectionEvent** and **TableModelEvent**. A **ListSelectionEvent** is generated when the user selects something in the table. By default, **JTable** allows you to select one or more complete rows, but you can change this behavior to allow one or more columns, or one or more individual cells to be selected. A **TableModelEvent** is fired when that table's data changes in some way. Handling these events requires a bit more work than it does to handle the events generated by the previously described components and is beyond the scope of this book. However, if you simply want to use **JTable** to display data (as the following example does), then you don't need to handle any events.

Here are the steps required to set up a simple **JTable** that can be used to display data:

1. Create an instance of **JTable**.

2. Create a **JScrollPane** object, specifying the table as the object to scroll.

3. Add the table to the scroll pane.

4. Add the scroll pane to the content pane.

The following example illustrates how to create and use a simple table. A one-dimensional array of strings called **colHeads** is created for the column headings. A two-dimensional array of strings called **data** is created for the table cells. You can see that each element in the array is an array of three strings. These arrays are passed to the **JTable** constructor. The table is added to a scroll pane, and then the scroll pane is added to the content pane. The table displays the data in the **data** array. The default table configuration also allows the contents of a cell to be edited. Changes affect the underlying array, which is **data** in this case.

```java
// Demonstrate JTable.
import java.awt.*;
import javax.swing.*;
/*
  <applet code="JTableDemo" width=400 height=200>
  </applet>
*/

public class JTableDemo extends JApplet {

  public void init() {
    try {
      SwingUtilities.invokeAndWait(
        new Runnable() {
          public void run() {
            makeGUI();
          }
        }
      );
    } catch (Exception exc) {
      System.out.println("Can't create because of " + exc);
    }
  }

  private void makeGUI() {

    // Initialize column headings.
    String[] colHeads = { "Name", "Extension", "ID#" };

    // Initialize data.
    Object[][] data = {
      { "Gail", "4567", "865" },
      { "Ken", "7566", "555" },
      { "Viviane", "5634", "587" },
      { "Melanie", "7345", "922" },
      { "Anne", "1237", "333" },
      { "John", "5656", "314" },
      { "Matt", "5672", "217" },
      { "Claire", "6741", "444" },
      { "Erwin", "9023", "519" },
      { "Ellen", "1134", "532" },
      { "Jennifer", "5689", "112" },
      { "Ed", "9030", "133" },
      { "Helen", "6751", "145" }
    };
```

```
      // Create the table.
      JTable table = new JTable(data, colHeads);

      // Add the table to a scroll pane.
      JScrollPane jsp = new JScrollPane(table);

      // Add the scroll pane to the content pane.
      add(jsp);
   }
}
```

Output from this example is shown here:

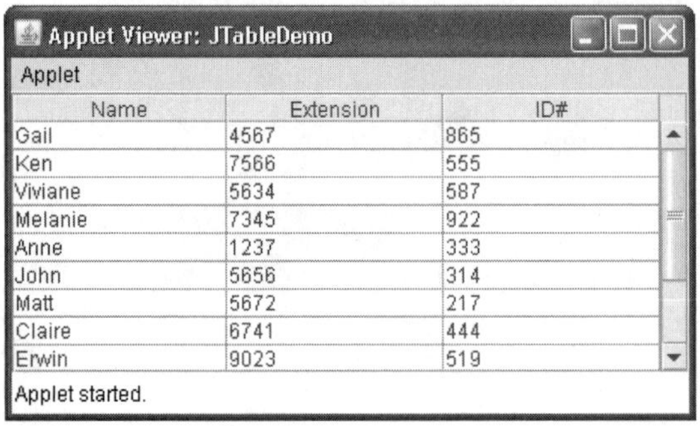

Continuing Your Exploration of Swing

Swing defines a very large GUI toolkit. It has many more features that you will want to explore on your own. For example, Swing provides toolbars, tooltips, and progress bars. It also provides a complete menu subsystem. Swing's pluggable look and feel lets you substitute another appearance and behavior for an element. You can define your own models for the various components, and you can change the way that cells are edited and rendered when working with tables and trees. The best way to become familiar with Swing's capabilities is to experiment with it.

CHAPTER

Servlets

This chapter presents an overview of *servlets*. Servlets are small programs that execute on the server side of a web connection. Just as applets dynamically extend the functionality of a web browser, servlets dynamically extend the functionality of a web server. The topic of servlets is quite large, and it is beyond the scope of this chapter to cover it all. Instead, we will focus on the core concepts, interfaces, and classes, and develop several examples.

Background

In order to understand the advantages of servlets, you must have a basic understanding of how web browsers and servers cooperate to provide content to a user. Consider a request for a static web page. A user enters a Uniform Resource Locator (URL) into a browser. The browser generates an HTTP request to the appropriate web server. The web server maps this request to a specific file. That file is returned in an HTTP response to the browser. The HTTP header in the response indicates the type of the content. The Multipurpose Internet Mail Extensions (MIME) are used for this purpose. For example, ordinary ASCII text has a MIME type of text/plain. The Hypertext Markup Language (HTML) source code of a web page has a MIME type of text/html.

Now consider dynamic content. Assume that an online store uses a database to store information about its business. This would include items for sale, prices, availability, orders, and so forth. It wishes to make this information accessible to customers via web pages. The contents of those web pages must be dynamically generated to reflect the latest information in the database.

In the early days of the Web, a server could dynamically construct a page by creating a separate process to handle each client request. The process would open connections to one or more databases in order to obtain the necessary information. It communicated with the web server via an interface known as the Common Gateway Interface (CGI). CGI allowed the separate process to read data from the HTTP request and write data to the HTTP response. A variety of different languages were used to build CGI programs. These included C, C++, and Perl.

However, CGI suffered serious performance problems. It was expensive in terms of processor and memory resources to create a separate process for each client request. It was also expensive to open and close database connections for each client request. In addition, the CGI programs were not platform-independent. Therefore, other techniques were introduced. Among these are servlets.

Servlets offer several advantages in comparison with CGI. First, performance is significantly better. Servlets execute within the address space of a web server. It is not necessary to create a separate process to handle each client request. Second, servlets are platform-independent because they are written in Java. Third, the Java security manager on the server enforces a set of restrictions to protect the resources on a server machine. Finally, the full functionality of the Java class libraries is available to a servlet. It can communicate with applets, databases, or other software via the sockets and RMI mechanisms that you have seen already.

The Life Cycle of a Servlet

Three methods are central to the life cycle of a servlet. These are **init( )**, **service( )**, and **destroy( )**. They are implemented by every servlet and are invoked at specific times by the server. Let us consider a typical user scenario to understand when these methods are called.

First, assume that a user enters a Uniform Resource Locator (URL) to a web browser. The browser then generates an HTTP request for this URL. This request is then sent to the appropriate server.

Second, this HTTP request is received by the web server. The server maps this request to a particular servlet. The servlet is dynamically retrieved and loaded into the address space of the server.

Third, the server invokes the **init( )** method of the servlet. This method is invoked only when the servlet is first loaded into memory. It is possible to pass initialization parameters to the servlet so it may configure itself.

Fourth, the server invokes the **service( )** method of the servlet. This method is called to process the HTTP request. You will see that it is possible for the servlet to read data that has been provided in the HTTP request. It may also formulate an HTTP response for the client.

The servlet remains in the server's address space and is available to process any other HTTP requests received from clients. The **service( )** method is called for each HTTP request.

Finally, the server may decide to unload the servlet from its memory. The algorithms by which this determination is made are specific to each server. The server calls the **destroy( )** method to relinquish any resources such as file handles that are allocated for the servlet. Important data may be saved to a persistent store. The memory allocated for the servlet and its objects can then be garbage collected.

Using Tomcat for Servlet Development

To create servlets, you will need access to a servlet development environment. The one used by this chapter is Tomcat. Tomcat is an open-source product maintained by the Jakarta Project of the Apache Software Foundation. It contains the class libraries, documentation, and run-time support that you will need to create and test servlets. At the time of this writing, the current version is 5.5.17, which supports servlet specification 2.4. You can download Tomcat from jakarta.apache.org.

The examples in this chapter assume a Windows environment. The default location for Tomcat 5.5.17 is

```
C:\Program Files\Apache Software Foundation\Tomcat 5.5\
```

This is the location assumed by the examples in this book. If you load Tomcat in a different location, you will need to make appropriate changes to the examples. You may need to set the environmental variable **JAVA_HOME** to the top-level directory in which the Java Development Kit is installed.

To start Tomcat, select Configure Tomcat in the Start | Programs menu, and then press Start in the Tomcat Properties dialog.

When you are done testing servlets, you can stop Tomcat by pressing Stop in the Tomcat Properties dialog.

The directory

```
C:\Program Files\Apache Software Foundation\Tomcat 5.5\common\lib\
```

contains **servlet-api.jar**. This JAR file contains the classes and interfaces that are needed to build servlets. To make this file accessible, update your **CLASSPATH** environment variable so that it includes

```
C:\Program Files\Apache Software Foundation\Tomcat 5.5\common\lib\servlet-api.jar
```

Alternatively, you can specify this file when you compile the servlets. For example, the following command compiles the first servlet example:

```
javac HelloServlet.java -classpath "C:\Program Files\Apache Software Foundation\
                         Tomcat 5.5\common\lib\servlet-api.jar"
```

Once you have compiled a servlet, you must enable Tomcat to find it. This means putting it into a directory under Tomcat's **webapps** directory and entering its name into a **web.xml** file. To keep things simple, the examples in this chapter use the directory and **web.xml** file that Tomcat supplies for its own example servlets. Here is the procedure that you will follow.

First, copy the servlet's class file into the following directory:

```
C:\Program Files\Apache Software Foundation\Tomcat 5.5\webapps\servlets-examples\WEB-INF\classes
```

Next, add the servlet's name and mapping to the **web.xml** file in the following directory:

```
C:\Program Files\Apache Software Foundation\Tomcat 5.5\webapps\servlets-examples\WEB-INF
```

For instance, assuming the first example, called **HelloServlet**, you will add the following lines in the section that defines the servlets:

```
<servlet>
  <servlet-name>HelloServlet</servlet-name>
  <servlet-class>HelloServlet</servlet-class>
</servlet>
```

Next, you will add the following lines to the section that defines the servlet mappings.

```
<servlet-mapping>
  <servlet-name>HelloServlet</servlet-name>
  <url-pattern>/servlet/HelloServlet</url-pattern>
</servlet-mapping>
```

Follow this same general procedure for all of the examples.

A Simple Servlet

To become familiar with the key servlet concepts, we will begin by building and testing a simple servlet. The basic steps are the following:

1. Create and compile the servlet source code. Then, copy the servlet's class file to the proper directory, and add the servlet's name and mappings to the proper **web.xml** file.

2. Start Tomcat.

3. Start a web browser and request the servlet.

Let us examine each of these steps in detail.

Create and Compile the Servlet Source Code

To begin, create a file named **HelloServlet.java** that contains the following program:

```
import java.io.*;
import javax.servlet.*;

public class HelloServlet extends GenericServlet {

  public void service(ServletRequest request,
    ServletResponse response)
  throws ServletException, IOException {
    response.setContentType("text/html");
    PrintWriter pw = response.getWriter();
    pw.println("<B>Hello!");
    pw.close();
  }
}
```

Let's look closely at this program. First, note that it imports the **javax.servlet** package. This package contains the classes and interfaces required to build servlets. You will learn more about these later in this chapter. Next, the program defines **HelloServlet** as a subclass of **GenericServlet**. The **GenericServlet** class provides functionality that simplifies the creation of a servlet. For example, it provides versions of **init( )** and **destroy( )**, which may be used as is. You need supply only the **service( )** method.

Inside **HelloServlet**, the **service( )** method (which is inherited from **GenericServlet**) is overridden. This method handles requests from a client. Notice that the first argument is a **ServletRequest** object. This enables the servlet to read data that is provided via the client request. The second argument is a **ServletResponse** object. This enables the servlet to formulate a response for the client.

The call to **setContentType( )** establishes the MIME type of the HTTP response. In this program, the MIME type is text/html. This indicates that the browser should interpret the content as HTML source code.

Next, the **getWriter( )** method obtains a **PrintWriter**. Anything written to this stream is sent to the client as part of the HTTP response. Then **println( )** is used to write some simple HTML source code as the HTTP response.

Compile this source code and place the **HelloServlet.class** file in the proper Tomcat directory as described in the previous section. Also, add **HelloServlet** to the **web.xml** file, as described earlier.

Start Tomcat

Start Tomcat as explained earlier. Tomcat must be running before you try to execute a servlet.

Start a Web Browser and Request the Servlet

Start a web browser and enter the URL shown here:

```
http://localhost:8080/servlets-examples/servlet/HelloServlet
```

Alternatively, you may enter the URL shown here:

```
http://127.0.0.1:8080/servlets-examples/servlet/HelloServlet
```

This can be done because 127.0.0.1 is defined as the IP address of the local machine.

You will observe the output of the servlet in the browser display area. It will contain the string **Hello!** in bold type.

The Servlet API

Two packages contain the classes and interfaces that are required to build servlets. These are **javax.servlet** and **javax.servlet.http**. They constitute the Servlet API. Keep in mind that these packages are not part of the Java core packages. Instead, they are standard extensions provided by Tomcat. Therefore, they are not included with Java SE 6.

The Servlet API has been in a process of ongoing development and enhancement. The current servlet specification is version 2.4, and that is the one used in this book. However, because changes happen fast in the world of Java, you will want to check for any additions or alterations. This chapter discusses the core of the Servlet API, which will be available to most readers.

The javax.servlet Package

The **javax.servlet** package contains a number of interfaces and classes that establish the framework in which servlets operate. The following table summarizes the core interfaces that are provided in this package. The most significant of these is **Servlet**. All servlets must implement this interface or extend a class that implements the interface. The **ServletRequest** and **ServletResponse** interfaces are also very important.

Interface	Description
Servlet	Declares life cycle methods for a servlet.
ServletConfig	Allows servlets to get initialization parameters.
ServletContext	Enables servlets to log events and access information about their environment.
ServletRequest	Used to read data from a client request.
ServletResponse	Used to write data to a client response.

The following table summarizes the core classes that are provided in the **javax.servlet** package:

Class	Description
GenericServlet	Implements the **Servlet** and **ServletConfig** interfaces.
ServletInputStream	Provides an input stream for reading requests from a client.
ServletOutputStream	Provides an output stream for writing responses to a client.
ServletException	Indicates a servlet error occurred.
UnavailableException	Indicates a servlet is unavailable.

Let us examine these interfaces and classes in more detail.

The Servlet Interface

All servlets must implement the **Servlet** interface. It declares the **init( )**, **service( )**, and **destroy( )** methods that are called by the server during the life cycle of a servlet. A method is also provided that allows a servlet to obtain any initialization parameters. The methods defined by **Servlet** are shown in Table 31-1.

The **init( )**, **service( )**, and **destroy( )** methods are the life cycle methods of the servlet. These are invoked by the server. The **getServletConfig( )** method is called by the servlet to obtain initialization parameters. A servlet developer overrides the **getServletInfo( )** method to provide a string with useful information (for example, author, version, date, copyright). This method is also invoked by the server.

The ServletConfig Interface

The **ServletConfig** interface allows a servlet to obtain configuration data when it is loaded. The methods declared by this interface are summarized here:

Method	Description
ServletContext getServletContext( )	Returns the context for this servlet.
String getInitParameter(String *param*)	Returns the value of the initialization parameter named *param*.
Enumeration getInitParameterNames( )	Returns an enumeration of all initialization parameter names.
String getServletName( )	Returns the name of the invoking servlet.

The ServletContext Interface

The **ServletContext** interface enables servlets to obtain information about their environment. Several of its methods are summarized in Table 31-2.

Method	Description
void destroy( )	Called when the servlet is unloaded.
ServletConfig getServletConfig( )	Returns a **ServletConfig** object that contains any initialization parameters.
String getServletInfo( )	Returns a string describing the servlet.
void init(ServletConfig *sc*) throws ServletException	Called when the servlet is initialized. Initialization parameters for the servlet can be obtained from *sc*. An **UnavailableException** should be thrown if the servlet cannot be initialized.
void service(ServletRequest *req*, ServletResponse *res*) throws ServletException, IOException	Called to process a request from a client. The request from the client can be read from *req*. The response to the client can be written to *res*. An exception is generated if a servlet or IO problem occurs.

TABLE 31-1   The Methods Defined by **Servlet**

The ServletRequest Interface

The **ServletRequest** interface enables a servlet to obtain information about a client request. Several of its methods are summarized in Table 31-3.

The ServletResponse Interface

The **ServletResponse** interface enables a servlet to formulate a response for a client. Several of its methods are summarized in Table 31-4.

Method	Description
Object getAttribute(String *attr*)	Returns the value of the server attribute named *attr*.
String getMimeType(String *file*)	Returns the MIME type of *file*.
String getRealPath(String *vpath*)	Returns the real path that corresponds to the virtual path *vpath*.
String getServerInfo( )	Returns information about the server.
void log(String *s*)	Writes *s* to the servlet log.
void log(String *s*, Throwable *e*)	Writes *s* and the stack trace for *e* to the servlet log.
void setAttribute(String *attr*, Object *val*)	Sets the attribute specified by *attr* to the value passed in *val*.

TABLE 31-2   Various Methods Defined by **ServletContext**

Method	Description
Object getAttribute(String *attr*)	Returns the value of the attribute named *attr*.
String getCharacterEncoding( )	Returns the character encoding of the request.
int getContentLength( )	Returns the size of the request. The value –1 is returned if the size is unavailable.
String getContentType( )	Returns the type of the request. A **null** value is returned if the type cannot be determined.
ServletInputStream getInputStream( ) throws IOException	Returns a **ServletInputStream** that can be used to read binary data from the request. An **IllegalStateException** is thrown if **getReader( )** has already been invoked for this request.
String getParameter(String *pname*)	Returns the value of the parameter named *pname*.
Enumeration getParameterNames( )	Returns an enumeration of the parameter names for this request.
String[ ] getParameterValues(String *name*)	Returns an array containing values associated with the parameter specified by *name*.
String getProtocol( )	Returns a description of the protocol.
BufferedReader getReader( ) throws IOException	Returns a buffered reader that can be used to read text from the request. An **IllegalStateException** is thrown if **getInputStream( )** has already been invoked for this request.
String getRemoteAddr( )	Returns the string equivalent of the client IP address.
String getRemoteHost( )	Returns the string equivalent of the client host name.
String getScheme( )	Returns the transmission scheme of the URL used for the request (for example, "http", "ftp").
String getServerName( )	Returns the name of the server.
int getServerPort( )	Returns the port number.

TABLE 31-3   Various Methods Defined by **ServletRequest**

The GenericServlet Class

The **GenericServlet** class provides implementations of the basic life cycle methods for a servlet. **GenericServlet** implements the **Servlet** and **ServletConfig** interfaces. In addition, a method to append a string to the server log file is available. The signatures of this method are shown here:

> void log(String *s*)
> void log(String *s*, Throwable *e*)

Here, *s* is the string to be appended to the log, and *e* is an exception that occurred.

Method	Description
String getCharacterEncoding( )	Returns the character encoding for the response.

ServletOutputStream
    getOutputStream( )
        throws IOException
	Returns a **ServletOutputStream** that can be used to write binary data to the response. An **IllegalStateException** is thrown if **getWriter( )** has already been invoked for this request.

PrintWriter getWriter( ) throws IOException	Returns a **PrintWriter** that can be used to write character data to the response. An **IllegalStateException** is thrown if **getOutputStream( )** has already been invoked for this request.
void setContentLength(int *size*)	Sets the content length for the response to *size*.
void setContentType(String *type*)	Sets the content type for the response to *type*.

TABLE 31-4   Various Methods Defined by **ServletResponse**

The ServletInputStream Class

The **ServletInputStream** class extends **InputStream**. It is implemented by the servlet container and provides an input stream that a servlet developer can use to read the data from a client request. It defines the default constructor. In addition, a method is provided to read bytes from the stream. It is shown here:

> int readLine(byte[ ] *buffer*, int *offset*, int *size*) throws IOException

Here, *buffer* is the array into which *size* bytes are placed starting at *offset*. The method returns the actual number of bytes read or –1 if an end-of-stream condition is encountered.

The ServletOutputStream Class

The **ServletOutputStream** class extends **OutputStream**. It is implemented by the servlet container and provides an output stream that a servlet developer can use to write data to a client response. A default constructor is defined. It also defines the **print( )** and **println( )** methods, which output data to the stream.

The Servlet Exception Classes

javax.servlet defines two exceptions. The first is **ServletException**, which indicates that a servlet problem has occurred. The second is **UnavailableException**, which extends **ServletException**. It indicates that a servlet is unavailable.

Reading Servlet Parameters

The **ServletRequest** interface includes methods that allow you to read the names and values of parameters that are included in a client request. We will develop a servlet that illustrates their use. The example contains two files. A web page is defined in **PostParameters.htm**, and a servlet is defined in **PostParametersServlet.java**.

The HTML source code for **PostParameters.htm** is shown in the following listing. It defines a table that contains two labels and two text fields. One of the labels is Employee and the other is Phone. There is also a submit button. Notice that the action parameter of the form tag specifies a URL. The URL identifies the servlet to process the HTTP POST request.

```
<html>
<body>
<center>
<form name="Form1"
  method="post"
  action="http://localhost:8080/servlets-examples/
          servlet/PostParametersServlet">
<table>
<tr>
  <td><B>Employee</td>
  <td><input type=textbox name="e" size="25" value=""></td>
</tr>
<tr>
  <td><B>Phone</td>
  <td><input type=textbox name="p" size="25" value=""></td>
</tr>
</table>
```

PART III

```
<input type=submit value="Submit">
</body>
</html>
```

The source code for **PostParametersServlet.java** is shown in the following listing. The **service( )** method is overridden to process client requests. The **getParameterNames( )** method returns an enumeration of the parameter names. These are processed in a loop. You can see that the parameter name and value are output to the client. The parameter value is obtained via the **getParameter( )** method.

```java
import java.io.*;
import java.util.*;
import javax.servlet.*;

public class PostParametersServlet
extends GenericServlet {

  public void service(ServletRequest request,
    ServletResponse response)
  throws ServletException, IOException {

    // Get print writer.
    PrintWriter pw = response.getWriter();

    // Get enumeration of parameter names.
    Enumeration e = request.getParameterNames();

    // Display parameter names and values.
    while(e.hasMoreElements()) {
      String pname = (String)e.nextElement();
      pw.print(pname + " = ");
      String pvalue = request.getParameter(pname);
      pw.println(pvalue);
    }
    pw.close();
  }
}
```

Compile the servlet. Next, copy it to the appropriate directory, and update the **web.xml** file, as previously described. Then, perform these steps to test this example:

1. Start Tomcat (if it is not already running).

2. Display the web page in a browser.

3. Enter an employee name and phone number in the text fields.

4. Submit the web page.

After following these steps, the browser will display a response that is dynamically generated by the servlet.

The javax.servlet.http Package

The **javax.servlet.http** package contains a number of interfaces and classes that are commonly used by servlet developers. You will see that its functionality makes it easy to build servlets that work with HTTP requests and responses.

The following table summarizes the core interfaces that are provided in this package:

Interface	Description
HttpServletRequest	Enables servlets to read data from an HTTP request.
HttpServletResponse	Enables servlets to write data to an HTTP response.
HttpSession	Allows session data to be read and written.
HttpSessionBindingListener	Informs an object that it is bound to or unbound from a session.

The following table summarizes the core classes that are provided in this package. The most important of these is **HttpServlet**. Servlet developers typically extend this class in order to process HTTP requests.

Class	Description
Cookie	Allows state information to be stored on a client machine.
HttpServlet	Provides methods to handle HTTP requests and responses.
HttpSessionEvent	Encapsulates a session-changed event.
HttpSessionBindingEvent	Indicates when a listener is bound to or unbound from a session value, or that a session attribute changed.

The HttpServletRequest Interface

The **HttpServletRequest** interface enables a servlet to obtain information about a client request. Several of its methods are shown in Table 31-5.

The HttpServletResponse Interface

The **HttpServletResponse** interface enables a servlet to formulate an HTTP response to a client. Several constants are defined. These correspond to the different status codes that can be assigned to an HTTP response. For example, **SC_OK** indicates that the HTTP request succeeded, and **SC_NOT_FOUND** indicates that the requested resource is not available. Several methods of this interface are summarized in Table 31-6.

The HttpSession Interface

The **HttpSession** interface enables a servlet to read and write the state information that is associated with an HTTP session. Several of its methods are summarized in Table 31-7. All of these methods throw an **IllegalStateException** if the session has already been invalidated.

Method	Description
String getAuthType( )	Returns authentication scheme.
Cookie[ ] getCookies( )	Returns an array of the cookies in this request.
long getDateHeader(String *field*)	Returns the value of the date header field named *field*.
String getHeader(String *field*)	Returns the value of the header field named *field*.
Enumeration getHeaderNames( )	Returns an enumeration of the header names.
int getIntHeader(String *field*)	Returns the **int** equivalent of the header field named *field*.
String getMethod( )	Returns the HTTP method for this request.
String getPathInfo( )	Returns any path information that is located after the servlet path and before a query string of the URL.
String getPathTranslated( )	Returns any path information that is located after the servlet path and before a query string of the URL after translating it to a real path.
String getQueryString( )	Returns any query string in the URL.
String getRemoteUser( )	Returns the name of the user who issued this request.
String getRequestedSessionId( )	Returns the ID of the session.
String getRequestURI( )	Returns the URI.
StringBuffer getRequestURL( )	Returns the URL.
String getServletPath( )	Returns that part of the URL that identifies the servlet.
HttpSession getSession( )	Returns the session for this request. If a session does not exist, one is created and then returned.
HttpSession getSession(boolean *new*)	If *new* is **true** and no session exists, creates and returns a session for this request. Otherwise, returns the existing session for this request.
boolean isRequestedSessionIdFromCookie( )	Returns **true** if a cookie contains the session ID. Otherwise, returns **false**.
boolean isRequestedSessionIdFromURL( )	Returns **true** if the URL contains the session ID. Otherwise, returns **false**.
boolean isRequestedSessionIdValid( )	Returns **true** if the requested session ID is valid in the current session context.

TABLE 31-5 Various Methods Defined by **HttpServletRequest**

Method	Description
void addCookie(Cookie *cookie*)	Adds *cookie* to the HTTP response.
boolean containsHeader(String *field*)	Returns **true** if the HTTP response header contains a field named *field*.
String encodeURL(String *url*)	Determines if the session ID must be encoded in the URL identified as *url*. If so, returns the modified version of *url*. Otherwise, returns *url*. All URLs generated by a servlet should be processed by this method.
String encodeRedirectURL(String *url*)	Determines if the session ID must be encoded in the URL identified as *url*. If so, returns the modified version of *url*. Otherwise, returns *url*. All URLs passed to **sendRedirect( )** should be processed by this method.

TABLE 31-6 Various Methods Defined by **HttpServletResponse**

Method	Description
void sendError(int *c*) throws IOException	Sends the error code *c* to the client.
void sendError(int *c*, String *s*) throws IOException	Sends the error code *c* and message *s* to the client.
void sendRedirect(String *url*) throws IOException	Redirects the client to *url*.
void setDateHeader(String *field*, long *msec*)	Adds *field* to the header with date value equal to *msec* (milliseconds since midnight, January 1, 1970, GMT).
void setHeader(String *field*, String *value*)	Adds *field* to the header with value equal to *value*.
void setIntHeader(String *field*, int *value*)	Adds *field* to the header with value equal to *value*.
void setStatus(int *code*)	Sets the status code for this response to *code*.

TABLE 31-6   Various Methods Defined by **HttpServletResponse** *(continued)*

The HttpSessionBindingListener Interface

The **HttpSessionBindingListener** interface is implemented by objects that need to be notified when they are bound to or unbound from an HTTP session. The methods that are invoked when an object is bound or unbound are

> void valueBound(HttpSessionBindingEvent *e*)
> void valueUnbound(HttpSessionBindingEvent *e*)

Here, *e* is the event object that describes the binding.

The Cookie Class

The **Cookie** class encapsulates a cookie. A *cookie* is stored on a client and contains state information. Cookies are valuable for tracking user activities. For example, assume that a

Method	Description
Object getAttribute(String *attr*)	Returns the value associated with the name passed in *attr*. Returns **null** if *attr* is not found.
Enumeration getAttributeNames( )	Returns an enumeration of the attribute names associated with the session.
long getCreationTime( )	Returns the time (in milliseconds since midnight, January 1, 1970, GMT) when this session was created.
String getId( )	Returns the session ID.
long getLastAccessedTime( )	Returns the time (in milliseconds since midnight, January 1, 1970, GMT) when the client last made a request for this session.
void invalidate( )	Invalidates this session and removes it from the context.
boolean isNew( )	Returns **true** if the server created the session and it has not yet been accessed by the client.
void removeAttribute(String *attr*)	Removes the attribute specified by *attr* from the session.
void setAttribute(String *attr*, Object *val*)	Associates the value passed in *val* with the attribute name passed in *attr*.

TABLE 31-7   The Methods Defined by **HttpSession**

user visits an online store. A cookie can save the user's name, address, and other information. The user does not need to enter this data each time he or she visits the store.

A servlet can write a cookie to a user's machine via the **addCookie( )** method of the **HttpServletResponse** interface. The data for that cookie is then included in the header of the HTTP response that is sent to the browser.

The names and values of cookies are stored on the user's machine. Some of the information that is saved for each cookie includes the following:

- The name of the cookie
- The value of the cookie
- The expiration date of the cookie
- The domain and path of the cookie

The expiration date determines when this cookie is deleted from the user's machine. If an expiration date is not explicitly assigned to a cookie, it is deleted when the current browser session ends. Otherwise, the cookie is saved in a file on the user's machine.

The domain and path of the cookie determine when it is included in the header of an HTTP request. If the user enters a URL whose domain and path match these values, the cookie is then supplied to the Web server. Otherwise, it is not.

There is one constructor for **Cookie**. It has the signature shown here:

Cookie(String *name*, String *value*)

Here, the name and value of the cookie are supplied as arguments to the constructor. The methods of the **Cookie** class are summarized in Table 31-8.

Method	Description
Object clone( )	Returns a copy of this object.
String getComment( )	Returns the comment.
String getDomain( )	Returns the domain.
int getMaxAge( )	Returns the maximum age (in seconds).
String getName( )	Returns the name.
String getPath( )	Returns the path.
boolean getSecure( )	Returns **true** if the cookie is secure. Otherwise, returns **false**.
String getValue( )	Returns the value.
int getVersion( )	Returns the version.
void setComment(String *c*)	Sets the comment to *c*.
void setDomain(String *d*)	Sets the domain to *d*.
void setMaxAge(int *secs*)	Sets the maximum age of the cookie to *secs*. This is the number of seconds after which the cookie is deleted.
void setPath(String *p*)	Sets the path to *p*.
void setSecure(boolean *secure*)	Sets the security flag to *secure*.
void setValue(String *v*)	Sets the value to *v*.
void setVersion(int *v*)	Sets the version to *v*.

TABLE 31-8 The Methods Defined by **Cookie**

The HttpServlet Class

The **HttpServlet** class extends **GenericServlet**. It is commonly used when developing servlets that receive and process HTTP requests. The methods of the **HttpServlet** class are summarized in Table 31-9.

The HttpSessionEvent Class

HttpSessionEvent encapsulates session events. It extends **EventObject** and is generated when a change occurs to the session. It defines this constructor:

HttpSessionEvent(HttpSession *session*)

Here, *session* is the source of the event.

HttpSessionEvent defines one method, **getSession( )**, which is shown here:

HttpSession getSession( )

It returns the session in which the event occurred.

Method	Description
void doDelete(HttpServletRequest *req*, HttpServletResponse *res*) throws IOException, ServletException	Handles an HTTP DELETE request.
void doGet(HttpServletRequest *req*, HttpServletResponse *res*) throws IOException, ServletException	Handles an HTTP GET request.
void doHead(HttpServletRequest *req*, HttpServletResponse *res*) throws IOException, ServletException	Handles an HTTP HEAD request.
void doOptions(HttpServletRequest *req*, HttpServletResponse *res*) throws IOException, ServletException	Handles an HTTP OPTIONS request.
void doPost(HttpServletRequest *req*, HttpServletResponse *res*) throws IOException, ServletException	Handles an HTTP POST request.
void doPut(HttpServletRequest *req*, HttpServletResponse *res*) throws IOException, ServletException	Handles an HTTP PUT request.
void doTrace(HttpServletRequest *req*, HttpServletResponse *res*) throws IOException, ServletException	Handles an HTTP TRACE request.
long getLastModified(HttpServletRequest *req*)	Returns the time (in milliseconds since midnight, January 1, 1970, GMT) when the requested resource was last modified.
void service(HttpServletRequest *req*, HttpServletResponse *res*) throws IOException, ServletException	Called by the server when an HTTP request arrives for this servlet. The arguments provide access to the HTTP request and response, respectively.

TABLE 31-9 The Methods Defined by **HttpServlet**

The HttpSessionBindingEvent Class

The **HttpSessionBindingEvent** class extends **HttpSessionEvent**. It is generated when a listener is bound to or unbound from a value in an **HttpSession** object. It is also generated when an attribute is bound or unbound. Here are its constructors:

```
HttpSessionBindingEvent(HttpSession session, String name)
HttpSessionBindingEvent(HttpSession session, String name, Object val)
```

Here, *session* is the source of the event, and *name* is the name associated with the object that is being bound or unbound. If an attribute is being bound or unbound, its value is passed in *val*.

The **getName( )** method obtains the name that is being bound or unbound. It is shown here:

```
String getName( )
```

The **getSession( )** method, shown next, obtains the session to which the listener is being bound or unbound:

```
HttpSession getSession( )
```

The **getValue( )** method obtains the value of the attribute that is being bound or unbound. It is shown here:

```
Object getValue( )
```

Handling HTTP Requests and Responses

The **HttpServlet** class provides specialized methods that handle the various types of HTTP requests. A servlet developer typically overrides one of these methods. These methods are **doDelete( )**, **doGet( )**, **doHead( )**, **doOptions( )**, **doPost( )**, **doPut( )**, and **doTrace( )**. A complete description of the different types of HTTP requests is beyond the scope of this book. However, the GET and POST requests are commonly used when handling form input. Therefore, this section presents examples of these cases.

Handling HTTP GET Requests

Here we will develop a servlet that handles an HTTP GET request. The servlet is invoked when a form on a web page is submitted. The example contains two files. A web page is defined in **ColorGet.htm**, and a servlet is defined in **ColorGetServlet.java**. The HTML source code for **ColorGet.htm** is shown in the following listing. It defines a form that contains a select element and a submit button. Notice that the action parameter of the form tag specifies a URL. The URL identifies a servlet to process the HTTP GET request.

```
<html>
<body>
<center>
<form name="Form1"
  action="http://localhost:8080/servlets-examples/servlet/ColorGetServlet">
<B>Color:</B>
<select name="color" size="1">
```

```
<option value="Red">Red</option>
<option value="Green">Green</option>
<option value="Blue">Blue</option>
</select>
<br><br>
<input type=submit value="Submit">
</form>
</body>
</html>
```

The source code for **ColorGetServlet.java** is shown in the following listing. The **doGet( )** method is overridden to process any HTTP GET requests that are sent to this servlet. It uses the **getParameter( )** method of **HttpServletRequest** to obtain the selection that was made by the user. A response is then formulated.

```
import java.io.*;
import javax.servlet.*;
import javax.servlet.http.*;

public class ColorGetServlet extends HttpServlet {

  public void doGet(HttpServletRequest request,
    HttpServletResponse response)
  throws ServletException, IOException {

    String color = request.getParameter("color");
    response.setContentType("text/html");
    PrintWriter pw = response.getWriter();
    pw.println("<B>The selected color is:  ");
    pw.println(color);
    pw.close();
  }
}
```

Compile the servlet. Next, copy it to the appropriate directory, and update the **web.xml** file, as previously described. Then, perform these steps to test this example:

1. Start Tomcat, if it is not already running.

2. Display the web page in a browser.

3. Select a color.

4. Submit the web page.

After completing these steps, the browser will display the response that is dynamically generated by the servlet.

One other point: Parameters for an HTTP GET request are included as part of the URL that is sent to the web server. Assume that the user selects the red option and submits the form. The URL sent from the browser to the server is

```
http://localhost:8080/servlets-examples/servlet/ColorGetServlet?color=Red
```

The characters to the right of the question mark are known as the *query string*.

Handling HTTP POST Requests

Here we will develop a servlet that handles an HTTP POST request. The servlet is invoked when a form on a web page is submitted. The example contains two files. A web page is defined in **ColorPost.htm**, and a servlet is defined in **ColorPostServlet.java**.

The HTML source code for **ColorPost.htm** is shown in the following listing. It is identical to **ColorGet.htm** except that the method parameter for the form tag explicitly specifies that the POST method should be used, and the action parameter for the form tag specifies a different servlet.

```
<html>
<body>
<center>
<form name="Form1"
  method="post"
  action="http://localhost:8080/servlets-examples/servlet/ColorPostServlet">
<B>Color:</B>
<select name="color" size="1">
<option value="Red">Red</option>
<option value="Green">Green</option>
<option value="Blue">Blue</option>
</select>
<br><br>
<input type=submit value="Submit">
</form>
</body>
</html>
```

The source code for **ColorPostServlet.java** is shown in the following listing. The **doPost( )** method is overridden to process any HTTP POST requests that are sent to this servlet. It uses the **getParameter( )** method of **HttpServletRequest** to obtain the selection that was made by the user. A response is then formulated.

```
import java.io.*;
import javax.servlet.*;
import javax.servlet.http.*;

public class ColorPostServlet extends HttpServlet {

  public void doPost(HttpServletRequest request,
    HttpServletResponse response)
  throws ServletException, IOException {

    String color = request.getParameter("color");
    response.setContentType("text/html");
    PrintWriter pw = response.getWriter();
    pw.println("<B>The selected color is:  ");
    pw.println(color);
    pw.close();
  }
}
```

Compile the servlet and perform the same steps as described in the previous section to test it.

NOTE *Parameters for an HTTP POST request are not included as part of the URL that is sent to the web server. In this example, the URL sent from the browser to the server is* `http://localhost:8080/servlets-examples/servlet/ColorPostServlet`. *The parameter names and values are sent in the body of the HTTP request.*

Using Cookies

Now, let's develop a servlet that illustrates how to use cookies. The servlet is invoked when a form on a web page is submitted. The example contains three files as summarized here:

File	Description
AddCookie.htm	Allows a user to specify a value for the cookie named **MyCookie**.
AddCookieServlet.java	Processes the submission of **AddCookie.htm**.
GetCookiesServlet.java	Displays cookie values.

The HTML source code for **AddCookie.htm** is shown in the following listing. This page contains a text field in which a value can be entered. There is also a submit button on the page. When this button is pressed, the value in the text field is sent to **AddCookieServlet** via an HTTP POST request.

```
<html>
<body>
<center>
<form name="Form1"
  method="post"
  action="http://localhost:8080/servlets-examples/servlet/AddCookieServlet">
<B>Enter a value for MyCookie:</B>
<input type=textbox name="data" size=25 value="">
<input type=submit value="Submit">
</form>
</body>
</html>
```

The source code for **AddCookieServlet.java** is shown in the following listing. It gets the value of the parameter named "data". It then creates a **Cookie** object that has the name "MyCookie" and contains the value of the "data" parameter. The cookie is then added to the header of the HTTP response via the **addCookie( )** method. A feedback message is then written to the browser.

```
import java.io.*;
import javax.servlet.*;
import javax.servlet.http.*;

public class AddCookieServlet extends HttpServlet {

  public void doPost(HttpServletRequest request,
```

```
      HttpServletResponse response)
  throws ServletException, IOException {

    // Get parameter from HTTP request.
    String data = request.getParameter("data");

    // Create cookie.
    Cookie cookie = new Cookie("MyCookie", data);

    // Add cookie to HTTP response.
    response.addCookie(cookie);

    // Write output to browser.
    response.setContentType("text/html");
    PrintWriter pw = response.getWriter();
    pw.println("<B>MyCookie has been set to");
    pw.println(data);
    pw.close();
  }
}
```

The source code for **GetCookiesServlet.java** is shown in the following listing. It invokes the **getCookies( )** method to read any cookies that are included in the HTTP GET request. The names and values of these cookies are then written to the HTTP response. Observe that the **getName( )** and **getValue( )** methods are called to obtain this information.

```
import java.io.*;
import javax.servlet.*;
import javax.servlet.http.*;

public class GetCookiesServlet extends HttpServlet {

  public void doGet(HttpServletRequest request,
    HttpServletResponse response)
  throws ServletException, IOException {

    // Get cookies from header of HTTP request.
    Cookie[] cookies = request.getCookies();

    // Display these cookies.
    response.setContentType("text/html");
    PrintWriter pw = response.getWriter();
    pw.println("<B>");
    for(int i = 0; i < cookies.length; i++) {
      String name = cookies[i].getName();
      String value = cookies[i].getValue();
      pw.println("name = " + name +
        "; value = " + value);
    }
    pw.close();
  }
}
```

Compile the servlets. Next, copy them to the appropriate directory, and update the **web.xml** file, as previously described. Then, perform these steps to test this example:

1. Start Tomcat, if it is not already running.

2. Display **AddCookie.htm** in a browser.

3. Enter a value for **MyCookie**.

4. Submit the web page.

After completing these steps, you will observe that a feedback message is displayed by the browser.

Next, request the following URL via the browser:

```
http://localhost:8080/servlets-examples/servlet/GetCookiesServlet
```

Observe that the name and value of the cookie are displayed in the browser.

In this example, an expiration date is not explicitly assigned to the cookie via the **setMaxAge( )** method of **Cookie**. Therefore, the cookie expires when the browser session ends. You can experiment by using **setMaxAge( )** and observe that the cookie is then saved to the disk on the client machine.

Session Tracking

HTTP is a stateless protocol. Each request is independent of the previous one. However, in some applications, it is necessary to save state information so that information can be collected from several interactions between a browser and a server. Sessions provide such a mechanism.

A session can be created via the **getSession( )** method of **HttpServletRequest**. An **HttpSession** object is returned. This object can store a set of bindings that associate names with objects. The **setAttribute( )**, **getAttribute( )**, **getAttributeNames( )**, and **removeAttribute( )** methods of **HttpSession** manage these bindings. It is important to note that session state is shared among all the servlets that are associated with a particular client.

The following servlet illustrates how to use session state. The **getSession( )** method gets the current session. A new session is created if one does not already exist. The **getAttribute( )** method is called to obtain the object that is bound to the name "date". That object is a **Date** object that encapsulates the date and time when this page was last accessed. (Of course, there is no such binding when the page is first accessed.) A **Date** object encapsulating the current date and time is then created. The **setAttribute( )** method is called to bind the name "date" to this object.

```
import java.io.*;
import java.util.*;
import javax.servlet.*;
import javax.servlet.http.*;

public class DateServlet extends HttpServlet {

  public void doGet(HttpServletRequest request,
    HttpServletResponse response)
  throws ServletException, IOException {
```

```
    // Get the HttpSession object.
    HttpSession hs = request.getSession(true);

    // Get writer.
    response.setContentType("text/html");
    PrintWriter pw = response.getWriter();
    pw.print("<B>");

    // Display date/time of last access.
    Date date = (Date)hs.getAttribute("date");
    if(date != null) {
      pw.print("Last access: " + date + "<br>");
    }

    // Display current date/time.
    date = new Date();
    hs.setAttribute("date", date);
    pw.println("Current date: " + date);
  }
}
```

When you first request this servlet, the browser displays one line with the current date and time information. On subsequent invocations, two lines are displayed. The first line shows the date and time when the servlet was last accessed. The second line shows the current date and time.

IV

PART

Applying Java

Financial Applets and Servlets

Despite all the large, sophisticated applications, such as word processors, databases, and accounting packages, that dominate much of the computing landscape, there has remained a class of programs that are both popular and small. These perform various financial calculations, such as the regular payments on a loan, the future value of an investment, or the remaining balance on a loan. None of these calculations are very complicated or require much code, yet they yield information that is quite useful.

As you know, Java was initially designed to support the creation of small, portable programs. Originally, these programs took the form of applets, but a few years later, servlets were added. (Recall that *applets* run on the local machine, inside the browser, and *servlets* execute on the server.) Because of their small size, many of the common financial calculations are right-sized for applets and servlets. Furthermore, including a financial applet/servlet in a web page is an amenity that many users will appreciate. A user will return again and again to a page that offers the calculation that he or she desires.

This chapter develops a number of applets that perform the financial calculations shown here:

- Regular payments on a loan
- Remaining balance on a loan
- Future value of an investment
- Initial investment needed to attain a desired future value
- Annuity from an investment
- Investment necessary for a desired annuity

The chapter ends by showing how to convert the financial applets into servlets.

Finding the Payments for a Loan

Perhaps the most popular financial calculation is the one that computes the regular payments on a loan, such as a car or house loan. The payments on a loan are found by using the following formula:

$$Payment = (intRate * (principal / payPerYear)) / (1 - ((intRate / payPerYear) + 1)^{-payPerYear * numYears})$$

where *intRate* specifies the interest rate, *principal* contains the starting balance, *payPerYear* specifies the number of payments per year, and *numYears* specifies the length of the loan in years.

The following applet called **RegPay** uses the preceding formula to compute the payments on a loan given the information entered by the user. Like all of the applets in this chapter, **RegPay** is a Swing-based applet. This means that it extends the **JApplet** class and uses the Swing classes to provide the user interface. Notice that it also implements the **ActionListener** interface.

```java
// A simple loan calculator applet.
import java.awt.*;
import java.awt.event.*;
import javax.swing.*;
import java.text.*;
/*
  <applet code="RegPay" width=320 height=200>
  </applet>
*/

public class RegPay extends JApplet
  implements ActionListener {

  JTextField amount Text, paymentText, periodText, rateText;
  JButton doIt;

  double principal; // original principal
  double intRate;   // interest rate
  double numYears;  // length of loan in years

  /* Number of payments per year. You could
     allow this value to be set by the user. */
  final int payPerYear = 12;

  NumberFormat nf;

  public void init() {
    try {
      SwingUtilities.invokeAndWait(new Runnable () {
        public void run() {
          makeGUI(); // initialize the GUI
        }
      });
    } catch(Exception exc) {
      System.out.println("Can't create because of "+ exc);
```

```java
    }
}

// Set up and initialize the GUI.
private void makeGUI() {

  // Use a grid bag layout.
  GridBagLayout gbag = new GridBagLayout();
  GridBagConstraints gbc = new GridBagConstraints();
  setLayout(gbag);

  JLabel heading = new
          JLabel("Compute Monthly Loan Payments");

  JLabel amountLab = new JLabel("Principal ");
  JLabel periodLab = new JLabel("Years ");
  JLabel rateLab = new JLabel("Interest Rate ");
  JLabel paymentLab = new JLabel("Monthly Payments ");

  amountText = new JTextField(10);
  periodText = new JTextField(10);
  paymentText = new JTextField(10);
  rateText = new JTextField(10);

  // Payment field for display only.
  paymentText.setEditable(false);

  doIt = new JButton("Compute");

  // Define the grid bag.
  gbc.weighty = 1.0; // use a row weight of 1
  gbc.gridwidth = GridBagConstraints.REMAINDER;
  gbc.anchor = GridBagConstraints.NORTH;
  gbag.setConstraints(heading, gbc);

  // Anchor most components to the right.
  gbc.anchor = GridBagConstraints.EAST;

  gbc.gridwidth = GridBagConstraints.RELATIVE;
  gbag.setConstraints(amountLab, gbc);
  gbc.gridwidth = GridBagConstraints.REMAINDER;
  gbag.setConstraints(amountText, gbc);

  gbc.gridwidth = GridBagConstraints.RELATIVE;
  gbag.setConstraints(periodLab, gbc);
  gbc.gridwidth = GridBagConstraints.REMAINDER;
  gbag.setConstraints(periodText, gbc);

  gbc.gridwidth = GridBagConstraints.RELATIVE;
  gbag.setConstraints(rateLab, gbc);
  gbc.gridwidth = GridBagConstraints.REMAINDER;
  gbag.setConstraints(rateText, gbc);

  gbc.gridwidth = GridBagConstraints.RELATIVE;
  gbag.setConstraints(paymentLab, gbc);
```

```
      gbc.gridwidth = GridBagConstraints.REMAINDER;
      gbag.setConstraints(paymentText, gbc);

      gbc.anchor = GridBagConstraints.CENTER;
      gbag.setConstraints(doIt, gbc);

      // Add all the components.
      add(heading);
      add(amountLab);
      add(amountText);
      add(periodLab);
      add(periodText);
      add(rateLab);
      add(rateText);
      add(paymentLab);
      add(paymentText);
      add(doIt);

      // Register to receive action events.
      amountText.addActionListener(this);
      periodText.addActionListener(this);
      rateText.addActionListener(this);
      doIt.addActionListener(this);

      // Create a number format.
      nf = NumberFormat.getInstance();
      nf.setMinimumFractionDigits(2);
      nf.setMaximumFractionDigits(2);
    }

    /* User pressed Enter on a text field or
       pressed Compute. Display the result if all
       fields are completed. */
    public void actionPerformed(ActionEvent ae) {
      double result = 0.0;

      String amountStr = amountText.getText();
      String periodStr = periodText.getText();
      String rateStr = rateText.getText();

      try {
        if(amountStr.length() != 0 &&
           periodStr.length() != 0 &&
           rateStr.length() != 0) {

          principal = Double.parseDouble(amountStr);
          numYears = Double.parseDouble(periodStr);
          intRate = Double.parseDouble(rateStr) / 100;

          result = compute();

          paymentText.setText(nf.format(result));
        }

        showStatus(""); // erase any previous error message
```

```
    } catch (NumberFormatException exc) {
      showStatus("Invalid Data");
      paymentText.setText("");
    }
  }

  // Compute the loan payment.
  double compute() {
    double numer;
    double denom;
    double b, e;

    numer = intRate * principal / payPerYear;

    e = -(payPerYear * numYears);
    b = (intRate / payPerYear) + 1.0;

    denom = 1.0 - Math.pow(b, e);

    return numer / denom;
  }
}
```

The applet produced by this program is shown in Figure 32-1. To use the applet, simply enter the loan principal, the length of the loan in years, and the interest rate. The payments are assumed to be monthly. Once the information is entered, press Compute to calculate the monthly payment.

The following sections examine the code to **RegPay** in detail. Because all the applets in this chapter use the same basic framework, much of the explanation presented here also applies to the other applets.

The RegPay Fields

RegPay begins by declaring a number of instance variables that hold references to the text fields into which the user will enter the loan information. Next, it declares the **doIt** variable that will hold a reference to the Compute button.

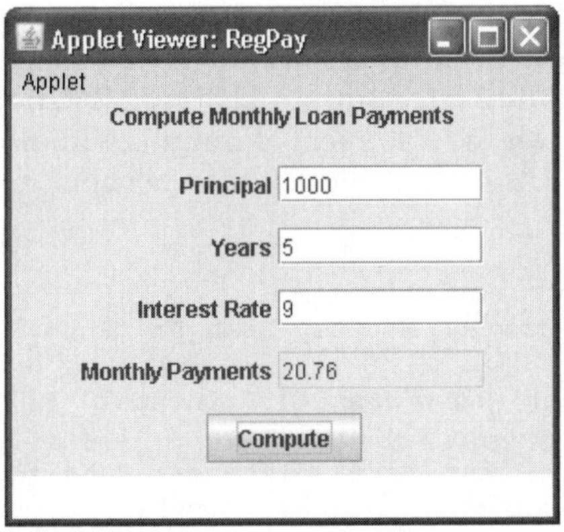

FIGURE 32-1
The **RegPay** applet

RegPay then declares three **double** variables that hold the loan values. The original principal is stored in **principal**, the interest rate is stored in **intRate**, and the length of the loan in years is stored in **numYears**. These values are entered by the user through the text fields. Next, the **final** integer variable **payPerYear** is declared and initialized to 12. Thus, the number of payments per year is hard-coded to monthly because this is the way that most loans are paid. As the comments suggest, you could allow the user to enter this value, but doing so will require another text field.

The last instance variable declared by **RegPay** is **nf**, a reference to an object of type **NumberFormat**, which will describe the number format used for output. **NumberFormat** is stored in the **java.text** package. Although there are other ways to format numeric output, such as by using the **Formatter** class, **NumberFormat** is a good choice in this case, because the same format is used repeatedly, and this format can be set once, at the start of the program. The financial applets also offer a good opportunity to demonstrate its use.

The init( ) Method

Like all applets, the **init( )** method is called when the applet first starts execution. This method simply invokes the **makeGUI( )** method on the event-dispatching thread. As explained in Chapter 29, Swing-based applets must construct and interact with GUI components only through the event-dispatching thread.

The makeGUI( ) Method

The **makeGUI( )** method sets up the user interface for the applet. It performs the following jobs:

1. It changes the layout manager to **GridBagLayout**.

2. It instantiates the various GUI components.

3. It adds the components to the grid bag.

4. It adds action listeners for the components.

Let's now look at **makeGUI( )** line by line. The method begins with these lines of code:

```
// Use a grid bag layout.
GridBagLayout gbag = new GridBagLayout();
GridBagConstraints gbc = new GridBagConstraints();
setLayout(gbag);
```

This sequence creates a **GridBagLayout** layout manager that will be used by the applet. (For details on using **GridBagLayout**, see Chapter 24.) **GrigBagLayout** is used because it allows detailed control over the placement of controls within an applet.

Next, **makeGUI( )** creates the label components, text fields, and Compute button, as shown here:

```
JLabel heading = new
     JLabel("Compute Monthly Loan Payments");

JLabel amountLab = new JLabel("Principal ");
JLabel periodLab = new JLabel("Years ");
JLabel rateLab = new JLabel("Interest Rate ");
JLabel paymentLab = new JLabel("Monthly Payments ");
```

```
amountText = new JTextField(10);
periodText = new JTextField(10);
paymentText = new JTextField(10);
rateText = new JTextField(10);

// Payment field for display only.
paymentText.setEditable(false);

doIt = new JButton("Compute");
```

Notice that the text field that displays the monthly payment is set to read-only by calling
setEditable(false). This causes the field to be grayed and no text can be entered into the
field by the user. However, the contents of the text field can still be set by calling **setText( )**.
Thus, when editing is disabled in a **JTextField**, the field can be used to display text, but the
text cannot be changed by the user.

Next, the grid bag constraints for each component are set by the following code sequence:

```
// Define the grid bag.
gbc.weighty = 1.0; // use a row weight of 1
gbc.gridwidth = GridBagConstraints.REMAINDER;
gbc.anchor = GridBagConstraints.NORTH;
gbag.setConstraints(heading, gbc);

// Anchor most components to the right.
gbc.anchor = GridBagConstraints.EAST;

gbc.gridwidth = GridBagConstraints.RELATIVE;
gbag.setConstraints(amountLab, gbc);
gbc.gridwidth = GridBagConstraints.REMAINDER;
gbag.setConstraints(amountText, gbc);

gbc.gridwidth = GridBagConstraints.RELATIVE;
gbag.setConstraints(periodLab, gbc);
gbc.gridwidth = GridBagConstraints.REMAINDER;
gbag.setConstraints(periodText, gbc);

gbc.gridwidth = GridBagConstraints.RELATIVE;
gbag.setConstraints(rateLab, gbc);
gbc.gridwidth = GridBagConstraints.REMAINDER;
gbag.setConstraints(rateText, gbc);

gbc.gridwidth = GridBagConstraints.RELATIVE;
gbag.setConstraints(paymentLab, gbc);
gbc.gridwidth = GridBagConstraints.REMAINDER;
gbag.setConstraints(paymentText, gbc);

gbc.anchor = GridBagConstraints.CENTER;
gbag.setConstraints(doIt, gbc);
```

Although this seems a bit complicated at first glance, it really isn't. Just remember that
each row in the grid is specified separately. Here is how the sequence works. First, the
weight of each row, contained in **gbc.weighty**, is set to 1. This tells the grid bag to distribute
extra space evenly when there is more vertical space than needed to hold the components.

Next, the **gbc.gridwidth** is set to **REMAINDER**, and **gbc.anchor** is set to **NORTH**. The label referred to by **heading** is added by calling **setConstraints( )** on **gbag**. This sequence sets the location of **heading** to the top of the grid (north) and gives it the remainder of the row. Thus, after this sequence executes, the heading will be at the top of the window and on a row by itself.

Next, the four text fields and their labels are added. First, **gbc.anchor** is set to **EAST**. This causes each component to be aligned to the right. Next, **gbc.gridWidth** is set to **RELATIVE**, and the label is added. Then, **gbc.gridWidth** is set to **REMAINDER**, and the text field is added. Thus, each text field and label pair occupies one row. This process repeats until all four text field and label pairs have been added. Finally, the Compute button is added in the center.

After the grid bag constraints have been set, the components are actually added to the window by the following code:

```
// Add all the components.
add(heading);
add(amountLab);
add(amountText);
add(periodLab);
add(periodText);
add(rateLab);
add(rateText);
add(paymentLab);
add(paymentText);
add(doIt);
```

Next, action listeners are registered for the three input text fields and the Compute button, as shown here:

```
// Register to receive action events.
amountText.addActionListener(this);
periodText.addActionListener(this);
rateText.addActionListener(this);
doIt.addActionListener(this);
```

Finally, a **NumberFormat** object is obtained and the format is set to two decimal digits:

```
// Create a number format.
nf = NumberFormat.getInstance();
nf.setMinimumFractionDigits(2);
nf.setMaximumFractionDigits(2);
```

The call to the factory method **getInstance( )** obtains a **NumberFormat** object suitable for the default locale. The calls to **setMinimumFractionDigits( )** and **setMaximumFractionDigits( )** set the minimum and maximum number of decimal digits to be displayed. Because both are set to two, this ensures that two decimal places will always be visible.

The actionPerformed( ) Method

The **actionPerformed( )** method is called whenever the user presses ENTER when in a text field or clicks the Compute button. This method performs three main functions: it obtains the loan information entered by the user, it calls **compute( )** to find the loan payments, and it displays the result. Let's now examine **actionPerformed( )** line by line.

After declaring the **result** variable, **actionperformed( )** begins by obtaining the strings from the three user-input text fields using the following sequence:

```
String amountStr = amountText.getText();
String periodStr = periodText.getText();
String rateStr = rateText.getText();
```

Next, it begins a **try** block and then verifies that all three fields actually contain information, as shown here:

```
try {
  if(amountStr.length() != 0 &&
     periodStr.length() != 0 &&
     rateStr.length() != 0) {
```

Recall that the user must enter the original loan amount, the number of years for the loan, and the interest rate. If all three text fields contain information, then the length of each string will be greater than zero.

If the user has entered all the loan data, then the numeric values corresponding to those strings are obtained and stored in the appropriate instance variable. Next, **compute( )** is called to compute the loan payment, and the result is displayed in the read-only text field referred to by **paymentText**, as shown here:

```
principal = Double.parseDouble(amountStr);
numYears = Double.parseDouble(periodStr);
intRate = Double.parseDouble(rateStr) / 100;

result = compute();

paymentText.setText(nf.format(result));
```

Notice the call to **nf.format(result)**. This causes the value in **result** to be formatted as previously specified (with two decimal digits) and the resulting string is returned. This string is then used to set the text in the **JTextField** specified by **paymentText**.

If the user has entered a nonnumeric value into one of the text fields, then **Double.parseDouble( )** will throw a **NumberFormatException**. If this happens, an error message will be displayed on the status line and the Payment text field will be emptied, as shown here:

```
    showStatus(""); // erase any previous error message
  } catch (NumberFormatException exc) {
    showStatus("Invalid Data");
    paymentText.setText("");
}
```

Otherwise, any previously reported error is removed.

The compute( ) Method

The calculation of the loan payment takes place in **compute( )**. It implements the formula shown earlier and operates on the values in **principal**, **intRate**, **numYears**, and **payPerYear**. It returns the result.

NOTE   *The basic skeleton used by* **RegPay** *is used by all the applets shown in this chapter.*

FIGURE 32-2
The **FutVal** applet

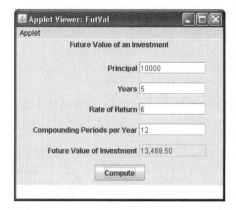

Finding the Future Value of an Investment

Another popular financial calculation finds the future value of an investment given the initial investment, the rate of return, the number of compounding periods per year, and the number of years the investment is held. For example, you might want to know what your retirement account will be worth in 12 years if it currently contains $98,000 and has an average annual rate of return of 6 percent. The **FutVal** applet developed here will supply the answer.

To compute the future value, use the following formula:

Future Value = $principal * ((rateOfRet / compPerYear) + 1)^{compPerYear * numYears}$

where *rateOfRet* specifies the rate of return, *principal* contains the initial value of the investment, *compPerYear* specifies the number of compounding periods per year, and *numYears* specifies the length of the investment in years. If you use an annualized rate of return for *rateOfRet,* then the number of compounding periods is 1.

The following applet called **FutVal** uses the preceding formula to compute the future value of an investment. The applet produced by this program is shown in Figure 32-2. Aside from the computational differences within the **compute( )** method, the applet is similar in operation to the **RegPay** applet described in the preceding section.

```java
// Compute the future value of an investment.
import java.awt.*;
import java.awt.event.*;
import javax.swing.*;
import java.text.*;
/*
   <applet code="FutVal" width=380 height=240>
   </applet>
*/

public class FutVal extends JApplet
   implements ActionListener {

   JTextField amountText, futvalText, periodText,
             rateText, compText;
   JButton doIt;
```

```java
double principal; // original principal
double rateOfRet; // rate of return
double numYears;  // length of investment in years
int compPerYear;  // number of compoundings per year

NumberFormat nf;

public void init() {
  try {
    SwingUtilities.invokeAndWait(new Runnable () {
      public void run() {
        makeGUI(); // initialize the GUI
      }
    });
  } catch(Exception exc) {
    System.out.println("Can't create because of "+ exc);
  }
}

// Set up and initialize the GUI.
private void makeGUI() {

  // Use a grid bag layout.
  GridBagLayout gbag = new GridBagLayout();
  GridBagConstraints gbc = new GridBagConstraints();
  setLayout(gbag);

  JLabel heading = new
        JLabel("Future Value of an Investment");

  JLabel amountLab = new JLabel("Principal ");
  JLabel periodLab = new JLabel("Years ");
  JLabel rateLab = new JLabel("Rate of Return ");
  JLabel futvalLab =
          new JLabel("Future Value of Investment ");
  JLabel compLab =
          new JLabel("Compounding Periods per Year ");

  amountText = new JTextField(10);
  periodText = new JTextField(10);
  futvalText = new JTextField(10);
  rateText = new JTextField(10);
  compText = new JTextField(10);

  // Future value field for display only.
  futvalText.setEditable(false);

  doIt = new JButton("Compute");

  // Define the grid bag.
  gbc.weighty = 1.0; // use a row weight of 1
  gbc.gridwidth = GridBagConstraints.REMAINDER;
  gbc.anchor = GridBagConstraints.NORTH;
  gbag.setConstraints(heading, gbc);
```

```
// Anchor most components to the right.
gbc.anchor = GridBagConstraints.EAST;

gbc.gridwidth = GridBagConstraints.RELATIVE;
gbag.setConstraints(amountLab, gbc);
gbc.gridwidth = GridBagConstraints.REMAINDER;
gbag.setConstraints(amountText, gbc);

gbc.gridwidth = GridBagConstraints.RELATIVE;
gbag.setConstraints(periodLab, gbc);
gbc.gridwidth = GridBagConstraints.REMAINDER;
gbag.setConstraints(periodText, gbc);

gbc.gridwidth = GridBagConstraints.RELATIVE;
gbag.setConstraints(rateLab, gbc);
gbc.gridwidth = GridBagConstraints.REMAINDER;
gbag.setConstraints(rateText, gbc);

gbc.gridwidth = GridBagConstraints.RELATIVE;
gbag.setConstraints(compLab, gbc);
gbc.gridwidth = GridBagConstraints.REMAINDER;
gbag.setConstraints(compText, gbc);

gbc.gridwidth = GridBagConstraints.RELATIVE;
gbag.setConstraints(futvalLab, gbc);
gbc.gridwidth = GridBagConstraints.REMAINDER;
gbag.setConstraints(futvalText, gbc);

gbc.anchor = GridBagConstraints.CENTER;
gbag.setConstraints(doIt, gbc);

add(heading);
add(amountLab);
add(amountText);
add(periodLab);
add(periodText);
add(rateLab);
add(rateText);
add(compLab);
add(compText);
add(futvalLab);
add(futvalText);
add(doIt);

// Register to receive action events.
amountText.addActionListener(this);
periodText.addActionListener(this);
rateText.addActionListener(this);
compText.addActionListener(this);
doIt.addActionListener(this);

// Create a number format.
nf = NumberFormat.getInstance();
nf.setMinimumFractionDigits(2);
```

```
      nf.setMaximumFractionDigits(2);
  }

  /* User pressed Enter on a text field or
     pressed Compute. Display the result if all
     fields are completed. */
  public void actionPerformed(ActionEvent ae) {
    double result = 0.0;

    String amountStr = amountText.getText();
    String periodStr = periodText.getText();
    String rateStr = rateText.getText();
    String compStr = compText.getText();

    try {
      if(amountStr.length() != 0 &&
         periodStr.length() != 0 &&
         rateStr.length() != 0 &&
         compStr.length() != 0) {

        principal = Double.parseDouble(amountStr);
        numYears = Double.parseDouble(periodStr);
        rateOfRet = Double.parseDouble(rateStr) / 100;
        compPerYear = Integer.parseInt(compStr);

        result = compute();

        futvalText.setText(nf.format(result));
      }

      showStatus(""); // erase any previous error message
    } catch (NumberFormatException exc) {
      showStatus("Invalid Data");
      futvalText.setText("");
    }
  }

  // Compute the future value.
  double compute() {
    double b, e;

    b = (1 + rateOfRet/compPerYear);
    e = compPerYear * numYears;

    return principal * Math.pow(b, e);
  }
}
```

Finding the Initial Investment Required to Achieve a Future Value

Sometimes you will want to know how large an initial investment is required to achieve some future value. For example, if you are saving for your child's college education and you know that you will need $75,000 in five years, how much money do you need to invest at 7 percent to reach that goal? The **InitInv** applet developed here can answer that question.

FIGURE 32-3
The **InitInv** applet

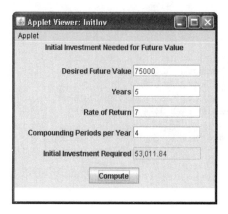

The formula to compute an initial investment is shown here:

$$\text{Initial Investment} = targetValue \; / \; (((rateOfRet \; / \; compPerYear) + 1)^{\,compPerYear \, * \, numYears})$$

where *rateOfRet* specifies the rate of return, *targetValue* contains the starting balance, *compPerYear* specifies the number of compounding periods per year, and *numYears* specifies the length of the investment in years. If you use an annualized rate of return for *rateOfRet,* then the number of compounding periods is 1.

The following applet called **InitInv** uses the preceding formula to compute the initial investment required to reach a desired future value. The applet produced by this program is shown in Figure 32-3.

```
/* Compute the initial investment necessary for
   a specified future value.  */
import java.awt.*;
import java.awt.event.*;
import javax.swing.*;
import java.text.*;
/*
  <applet code="InitInv" width=340 height=240>
  </applet>
*/

public class InitInv extends JApplet
  implements ActionListener {

  JTextField targetText, initialText, periodText,
             rateText, compText;
  JButton doIt;

  double targetValue; // original targetValue
  double rateOfRet;   // rate of return
  double numYears;    // length of loan in years
  int compPerYear;    // number of compoundings per year

  NumberFormat nf;
```

```java
public void init() {
  try {
    SwingUtilities.invokeAndWait(new Runnable () {
      public void run() {
        makeGUI(); // initialize the GUI
      }
    });
  } catch(Exception exc) {
    System.out.println("Can't create because of "+ exc);
  }
}

// Set up and initialize the GUI.
private void makeGUI() {

  // Use a grid bag layout.
  GridBagLayout gbag = new GridBagLayout();
  GridBagConstraints gbc = new GridBagConstraints();
  setLayout(gbag);

  JLabel heading = new
          JLabel("Initial Investment Needed for " +
                  "Future Value");

  JLabel targetLab = new JLabel("Desired Future Value ");
  JLabel periodLab = new JLabel("Years ");
  JLabel rateLab = new JLabel("Rate of Return ");
  JLabel compLab =
          new JLabel("Compounding Periods per Year ");
  JLabel initialLab =
          new  JLabel("Initial Investment Required ");

  targetText = new JTextField(10);
  periodText = new JTextField(10);
  initialText = new JTextField(10);
  rateText = new JTextField(10);
  compText = new JTextField(10);

  // Initial value field for display only.
  initialText.setEditable(false);

  doIt = new JButton("Compute");

  // Define the grid bag.
  gbc.weighty = 1.0; // use a row weight of 1

  gbc.gridwidth = GridBagConstraints.REMAINDER;
  gbc.anchor = GridBagConstraints.NORTH;
  gbag.setConstraints(heading, gbc);

  // Anchor most components to the right.
  gbc.anchor = GridBagConstraints.EAST;

  gbc.gridwidth = GridBagConstraints.RELATIVE;
```

```
        gbag.setConstraints(targetLab, gbc);
        gbc.gridwidth = GridBagConstraints.REMAINDER;
        gbag.setConstraints(targetText, gbc);

        gbc.gridwidth = GridBagConstraints.RELATIVE;
        gbag.setConstraints(periodLab, gbc);
        gbc.gridwidth = GridBagConstraints.REMAINDER;
        gbag.setConstraints(periodText, gbc);

        gbc.gridwidth = GridBagConstraints.RELATIVE;
        gbag.setConstraints(rateLab, gbc);
        gbc.gridwidth = GridBagConstraints.REMAINDER;
        gbag.setConstraints(rateText, gbc);

        gbc.gridwidth = GridBagConstraints.RELATIVE;
        gbag.setConstraints(compLab, gbc);
        gbc.gridwidth = GridBagConstraints.REMAINDER;
        gbag.setConstraints(compText, gbc);

        gbc.gridwidth = GridBagConstraints.RELATIVE;
        gbag.setConstraints(initialLab, gbc);
        gbc.gridwidth = GridBagConstraints.REMAINDER;
        gbag.setConstraints(initialText, gbc);

        gbc.anchor = GridBagConstraints.CENTER;
        gbag.setConstraints(doIt, gbc);

        // Add all the components.
        add(heading);
        add(targetLab);
        add(targetText);
        add(periodLab);
        add(periodText);
        add(rateLab);
        add(rateText);
        add(compLab);
        add(compText);
        add(initialLab);
        add(initialText);
        add(doIt);

        // Register to receive action events.
        targetText.addActionListener(this);
        periodText.addActionListener(this);
        rateText.addActionListener(this);
        compText.addActionListener(this);
        doIt.addActionListener(this);

        // Create a number format.
        nf = NumberFormat.getInstance();
        nf.setMinimumFractionDigits(2);
        nf.setMaximumFractionDigits(2);
    }

    /* User pressed Enter on a text field
```

```
     or pressed Compute. Display the result if all
     fields are completed. */
  public void actionPerformed(ActionEvent ae) {
    double result = 0.0;

    String targetStr = targetText.getText();
    String periodStr = periodText.getText();
    String rateStr = rateText.getText();
    String compStr = compText.getText();

    try {
      if(targetStr.length() != 0 &&
        periodStr.length() != 0 &&
        rateStr.length() != 0 &&
        compStr.length() != 0) {

        targetValue = Double.parseDouble(targetStr);
        numYears = Double.parseDouble(periodStr);
        rateOfRet = Double.parseDouble(rateStr) / 100;
        compPerYear = Integer.parseInt(compStr);

        result = compute();

        initialText.setText(nf.format(result));
      }

      showStatus(""); // erase any previous error message
    } catch (NumberFormatException exc) {
      showStatus("Invalid Data");
      initialText.setText("");
    }
  }

  // Compute the required initial investment.
  double compute() {
    double b, e;

    b = (1 + rateOfRet/compPerYear);
    e = compPerYear * numYears;

    return targetValue / Math.pow(b, e);
  }
}
```

Finding the Initial Investment Needed for a Desired Annuity

Another common financial calculation computes the amount of money that you must invest
so that a desired annuity, in terms of a regular withdrawal, can be paid. For example, you
might decide that you need $5,000 per month at retirement and that you will need that
amount for 20 years. The question is how much will you need to invest to secure that
annuity? The answer can be found using the following formula:

$$\text{Initial Investment} = ((regWD * wdPerYear) / rateOfRet) *$$
$$(1 - (1 / (rateOfRet / wdPerYear + 1)^{wdPerYear * numYears}))$$

FIGURE 32-4
The **Annuity** applet

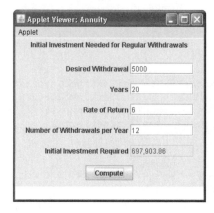

where *rateOfRet* specifies the rate of return, *regWD* contains the desired regular withdrawal, *wdPerYear* specifies the number of withdrawals per year, and *numYears* specifies the length of the annuity in years.

The **Annuity** applet shown here computes the initial investment required to produce the desired annuity. The applet produced by this program is shown in Figure 32-4.

```
/* Compute the initial investment necessary for
   a desired annuity. In other words, it finds
   the initial amount needed to allow the regular
   withdrawals of a desired amount over a period
   of time.   */
import java.awt.*;
import java.awt.event.*;
import javax.swing.*;
import java.text.*;
/*
   <applet code="Annuity" width=340 height=260>
   </applet>
*/

public class Annuity extends JApplet
  implements ActionListener {

  JTextField regWDText, initialText, periodText,
            rateText, numWDText;
  JButton doIt;

  double regWDAmount; // amount of each withdrawal
  double rateOfRet;   // rate of return
  double numYears;    // length of time in years
  int numPerYear;     // number of withdrawals per year

  NumberFormat nf;

   public void init() {
    try {
      SwingUtilities.invokeAndWait(new Runnable () {
```

```java
    public void run() {
      makeGUI(); // initialize the GUI
    }
  });
} catch(Exception exc) {
  System.out.println("Can't create because of "+ exc);
}
}

// Set up and initialize the GUI.
private void makeGUI() {

  // Use a grid bag layout.
  GridBagLayout gbag = new GridBagLayout();
  GridBagConstraints gbc = new GridBagConstraints();
  setLayout(gbag);

  JLabel heading = new
        JLabel("Initial Investment Needed for " +
               "Regular Withdrawals");

  JLabel regWDLab = new JLabel("Desired Withdrawal ");
  JLabel periodLab = new JLabel("Years ");
  JLabel rateLab = new JLabel("Rate of Return ");
  JLabel numWDLab =
          new JLabel("Number of Withdrawals per Year ");
  JLabel initialLab =
          new JLabel("Initial Investment Required ");

  regWDText = new JTextField(10);
  periodText = new JTextField(10);
  initialText = new JTextField(10);
  rateText = new JTextField(10);
  numWDText = new JTextField(10);

  // Initial investment field for display only.
  initialText.setEditable(false);

  doIt = new JButton("Compute");

  // Define the grid bag.

  gbc.weighty = 1.0; // use a row weight of 1

  gbc.gridwidth = GridBagConstraints.REMAINDER;
  gbc.anchor = GridBagConstraints.NORTH;
  gbag.setConstraints(heading, gbc);

  // Anchor most components to the right.
  gbc.anchor = GridBagConstraints.EAST;

  gbc.gridwidth = GridBagConstraints.RELATIVE;
  gbag.setConstraints(regWDLab, gbc);
  gbc.gridwidth = GridBagConstraints.REMAINDER;
```

```java
      gbag.setConstraints(regWDText, gbc);

      gbc.gridwidth = GridBagConstraints.RELATIVE;
      gbag.setConstraints(periodLab, gbc);
      gbc.gridwidth = GridBagConstraints.REMAINDER;
      gbag.setConstraints(periodText, gbc);

      gbc.gridwidth = GridBagConstraints.RELATIVE;
      gbag.setConstraints(rateLab, gbc);
      gbc.gridwidth = GridBagConstraints.REMAINDER;
      gbag.setConstraints(rateText, gbc);

      gbc.gridwidth = GridBagConstraints.RELATIVE;
      gbag.setConstraints(numWDLab, gbc);
      gbc.gridwidth = GridBagConstraints.REMAINDER;
      gbag.setConstraints(numWDText, gbc);

      gbc.gridwidth = GridBagConstraints.RELATIVE;
      gbag.setConstraints(initialLab, gbc);
      gbc.gridwidth = GridBagConstraints.REMAINDER;
      gbag.setConstraints(initialText, gbc);

      gbc.anchor = GridBagConstraints.CENTER;
      gbag.setConstraints(doIt, gbc);

      // Add all the components.
      add(heading);
      add(regWDLab);
      add(regWDText);
      add(periodLab);
      add(periodText);
      add(rateLab);
      add(rateText);
      add(numWDLab);
      add(numWDText);
      add(initialLab);
      add(initialText);
      add(doIt);

      // Register to receive text field action events.
      regWDText.addActionListener(this);
      periodText.addActionListener(this);
      rateText.addActionListener(this);
      numWDText.addActionListener(this);
      doIt.addActionListener(this);

      // Create a number format.
      nf = NumberFormat.getInstance();
      nf.setMinimumFractionDigits(2);
      nf.setMaximumFractionDigits(2);
    }

  /* User pressed Enter on a text field or
     pressed Compute. Display the result if all
```

```
      fields are completed. */
  public void actionPerformed(ActionEvent ae) {
    double result = 0.0;

    String regWDStr = regWDText.getText();
    String periodStr = periodText.getText();
    String rateStr = rateText.getText();
    String numWDStr = numWDText.getText();

    try {
      if(regWDStr.length() != 0 &&
         periodStr.length() != 0 &&
         rateStr.length() != 0 &&
         numWDStr.length() != 0) {

        regWDAmount = Double.parseDouble(regWDStr);
        numYears = Double.parseDouble(periodStr);
        rateOfRet = Double.parseDouble(rateStr) / 100;
        numPerYear = Integer.parseInt(numWDStr);

        result = compute();

        initialText.setText(nf.format(result));
      }

      showStatus(""); // erase any previous error message
    } catch (NumberFormatException exc) {
      showStatus("Invalid Data");
      initialText.setText("");
    }
  }

  // Compute the required initial investment.
  double compute() {
    double b, e;
    double t1, t2;

    t1 = (regWDAmount * numPerYear) / rateOfRet;

    b = (1 + rateOfRet/numPerYear);
    e = numPerYear * numYears;

    t2 = 1 - (1 / Math.pow(b, e));

    return t1 * t2;
  }
}
```

Finding the Maximum Annuity for a Given Investment

Another annuity calculation computes the maximum annuity (in terms of a regular withdrawal) available from a given investment over a specified period of time. For example, if you have

FIGURE 32-5
The **MaxWD**
applet

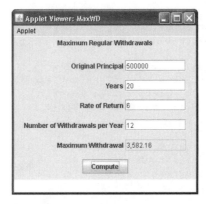

$500,000 in a retirement account, how much can you take out each month for 20 years, assuming a 6 percent rate of return? The formula that computes the maximum withdrawal is shown here:

$$\text{Maximum Withdrawal} = principal * (\,(\,(rateOfRet\,/\,wdPerYear)\,/ $$
$$(-1 + ((rateOfRet\,/\,wdPerYear) + 1)^{\,wdPerYear\,*\,numYears})\,) + $$
$$(rateOfRet\,/\,wdPerYear)\,)$$

where *rateOfRet* specifies the rate of return, *principal* contains the value of the initial investment, *wdPerYear* specifies the number of withdrawals per year, and *numYears* specifies the length of the annuity in years.

The **MaxWD** applet shown next computes the maximum periodic withdrawals that can be made over a specified length of time for an assumed rate of return. The applet produced by this program is shown in Figure 32-5.

```
/* Compute the maximum annuity that can
   be withdrawn from an investment over
   a period of time.   */
import java.awt.*;
import java.awt.event.*;
import javax.swing.*;
import java.text.*;
/*
  <applet code="MaxWD" width=340 height=260>
  </applet>
*/

public class MaxWD extends JApplet
  implements ActionListener {

  JTextField maxWDText, orgPText, periodText,
             rateText, numWDText;
  JButton doIt;

  double principal; // initial principal
  double rateOfRet; // annual rate of return
  double numYears;  // length of time in years
  int numPerYear;   // number of withdrawals per year

  NumberFormat nf;
```

```
public void init() {
  try {
    SwingUtilities.invokeAndWait(new Runnable () {
      public void run() {
        makeGUI(); // initialize the GUI
      }
    });
  } catch(Exception exc) {
    System.out.println("Can't create because of "+ exc);
  }
}

// Set up and initialize the GUI.
private void makeGUI() {

  // Use a grid bag layout.
  GridBagLayout gbag = new GridBagLayout();
  GridBagConstraints gbc = new GridBagConstraints();
  setLayout(gbag);

  JLabel heading = new
        JLabel("Maximum Regular Withdrawals");

  JLabel orgPLab = new JLabel("Original Principal ");
  JLabel periodLab = new JLabel("Years ");
  JLabel rateLab = new JLabel("Rate of Return ");
  JLabel numWDLab =
        new JLabel("Number of Withdrawals per Year ");
  JLabel maxWDLab = new JLabel("Maximum Withdrawal ");

  maxWDText = new JTextField(10);
  periodText = new JTextField(10);
  orgPText = new JTextField(10);
  rateText = new JTextField(10);
  numWDText = new JTextField(10);

  // Max withdrawal field for display only.
  maxWDText.setEditable(false);

  doIt = new JButton("Compute");

  // Define the grid bag.
  gbc.weighty = 1.0; // use a row weight of 1

  gbc.gridwidth = GridBagConstraints.REMAINDER;
  gbc.anchor = GridBagConstraints.NORTH;
  gbag.setConstraints(heading, gbc);

  // Anchor most components to the right.
  gbc.anchor = GridBagConstraints.EAST;

  gbc.gridwidth = GridBagConstraints.RELATIVE;
  gbag.setConstraints(orgPLab, gbc);
  gbc.gridwidth = GridBagConstraints.REMAINDER;
  gbag.setConstraints(orgPText, gbc);
```

```
      gbc.gridwidth = GridBagConstraints.RELATIVE;
      gbag.setConstraints(periodLab, gbc);
      gbc.gridwidth = GridBagConstraints.REMAINDER;
      gbag.setConstraints(periodText, gbc);

      gbc.gridwidth = GridBagConstraints.RELATIVE;
      gbag.setConstraints(rateLab, gbc);
      gbc.gridwidth = GridBagConstraints.REMAINDER;
      gbag.setConstraints(rateText, gbc);

      gbc.gridwidth = GridBagConstraints.RELATIVE;
      gbag.setConstraints(numWDLab, gbc);
      gbc.gridwidth = GridBagConstraints.REMAINDER;
      gbag.setConstraints(numWDText, gbc);

      gbc.gridwidth = GridBagConstraints.RELATIVE;
      gbag.setConstraints(maxWDLab, gbc);
      gbc.gridwidth = GridBagConstraints.REMAINDER;
      gbag.setConstraints(maxWDText, gbc);

      gbc.anchor = GridBagConstraints.CENTER;
      gbag.setConstraints(doIt, gbc);

      // Add all the components.
      add(heading);
      add(orgPLab);
      add(orgPText);
      add(periodLab);
      add(periodText);
      add(rateLab);
      add(rateText);
      add(numWDLab);
      add(numWDText);
      add(maxWDLab);
      add(maxWDText);
      add(doIt);

      // Register to receive action events.
      orgPText.addActionListener(this);
      periodText.addActionListener(this);
      rateText.addActionListener(this);
      numWDText.addActionListener(this);
      doIt.addActionListener(this);

      // Create a number format.
      nf = NumberFormat.getInstance();
      nf.setMinimumFractionDigits(2);
      nf.setMaximumFractionDigits(2);
    }

    /* User pressed Enter on a text field or
       pressed Compute. Display the result if all
       fields are completed. */
    public void actionPerformed(ActionEvent ae) {
      double result = 0.0;
```

```
      String orgPStr = orgPText.getText();
      String periodStr = periodText.getText();
      String rateStr = rateText.getText();
      String numWDStr = numWDText.getText();

      try {
        if(orgPStr.length() != 0 &&
           periodStr.length() != 0 &&
           rateStr.length() != 0 &&
           numWDStr.length() != 0) {

          principal = Double.parseDouble(orgPStr);
          numYears = Double.parseDouble(periodStr);
          rateOfRet = Double.parseDouble(rateStr) / 100;
          numPerYear = Integer.parseInt(numWDStr);

          result = compute();

          maxWDText.setText(nf.format(result));
        }

        showStatus(""); // erase any previous error message
      } catch (NumberFormatException exc) {
        showStatus("Invalid Data");
        maxWDText.setText("");
      }
    }

  // Compute the maximum regular withdrawals.
  double compute() {
    double b, e;
    double t1, t2;

    t1 = rateOfRet / numPerYear;

    b = (1 + t1);
    e = numPerYear * numYears;

    t2 = Math.pow(b, e) - 1;

    return principal * (t1/t2 + t1);
  }
}
```

Finding the Remaining Balance on a Loan

Often, you will want to know the remaining balance on a loan. This is easily calculated if you know the original principal, the interest rate, the loan length, and the number of payments made. To find the remaining balance, you must sum the payments, subtracting from each payment the amount allocated to interest, and then subtract that result from the principal.

The **RemBal** applet, shown next, finds the remaining balance of a loan. The applet produced by this program is shown in Figure 32-6.

FIGURE 32-6
The **RemBal**
applet

```java
// Find the remaining balance on a loan.
import java.awt.*;
import java.awt.event.*;
import javax.swing.*;
import java.text.*;
/*
  <applet code="RemBal" width=340 height=260>
  </applet>
*/

public class RemBal extends JApplet
  implements ActionListener {

  JTextField orgPText, paymentText, remBalText,
             rateText, numPayText;
  JButton doIt;

  double orgPrincipal; // original principal
  double intRate;      // interest rate
  double payment;      // amount of each payment
  double numPayments;  // number of payments made

  /* Number of payments per year. You could
     allow this value to be set by the user. */
  final int payPerYear = 12;

  NumberFormat nf;

  public void init() {
    try {
      SwingUtilities.invokeAndWait(new Runnable () {
        public void run() {
          makeGUI(); // initialize the GUI
        }
      });
    } catch(Exception exc) {
      System.out.println("Can't create because of "+ exc);
```

```
    }
}

// Set up and initialize the GUI.
private void makeGUI() {

  // Use a grid bag layout.
  GridBagLayout gbag = new GridBagLayout();
  GridBagConstraints gbc = new GridBagConstraints();
  setLayout(gbag);

  JLabel heading = new
        JLabel("Find Loan Balance ");

  JLabel orgPLab = new JLabel("Original Principal ");
  JLabel paymentLab = new JLabel("Amount of Payment ");
  JLabel numPayLab = new JLabel("Number of Payments Made ");
  JLabel rateLab = new JLabel("Interest Rate ");
  JLabel remBalLab = new JLabel("Remaining Balance ");

  orgPText = new JTextField(10);
  paymentText = new JTextField(10);
  remBalText = new JTextField(10);
  rateText = new JTextField(10);
  numPayText = new JTextField(10);

  // Payment field for display only.
  remBalText.setEditable(false);

  doIt = new JButton("Compute");

  // Define the grid bag.
   gbc.weighty = 1.0; // use a row weight of 1

  gbc.gridwidth = GridBagConstraints.REMAINDER;
  gbc.anchor = GridBagConstraints.NORTH;
  gbag.setConstraints(heading, gbc);

  // Anchor most components to the right.
  gbc.anchor = GridBagConstraints.EAST;

  gbc.gridwidth = GridBagConstraints.RELATIVE;
  gbag.setConstraints(orgPLab, gbc);
  gbc.gridwidth = GridBagConstraints.REMAINDER;
  gbag.setConstraints(orgPText, gbc);

  gbc.gridwidth = GridBagConstraints.RELATIVE;
  gbag.setConstraints(paymentLab, gbc);
  gbc.gridwidth = GridBagConstraints.REMAINDER;
  gbag.setConstraints(paymentText, gbc);

  gbc.gridwidth = GridBagConstraints.RELATIVE;
  gbag.setConstraints(rateLab, gbc);
```

```
      gbc.gridwidth = GridBagConstraints.REMAINDER;
      gbag.setConstraints(rateText, gbc);

      gbc.gridwidth = GridBagConstraints.RELATIVE;
      gbag.setConstraints(numPayLab, gbc);
      gbc.gridwidth = GridBagConstraints.REMAINDER;
      gbag.setConstraints(numPayText, gbc);

      gbc.gridwidth = GridBagConstraints.RELATIVE;
      gbag.setConstraints(remBalLab, gbc);
      gbc.gridwidth = GridBagConstraints.REMAINDER;
      gbag.setConstraints(remBalText, gbc);

      gbc.anchor = GridBagConstraints.CENTER;
      gbag.setConstraints(doIt, gbc);

      // Add all the components.
      add(heading);
      add(orgPLab);
      add(orgPText);
      add(paymentLab);
      add(paymentText);
      add(numPayLab);
      add(numPayText);
      add(rateLab);
      add(rateText);
      add(remBalLab);
      add(remBalText);
      add(doIt);

      // Register to receive action events.
      orgPText.addActionListener(this);
      numPayText.addActionListener(this);
      rateText.addActionListener(this);
      paymentText.addActionListener(this);
      doIt.addActionListener(this);

      // Create a number format.
      nf = NumberFormat.getInstance();
      nf.setMinimumFractionDigits(2);
      nf.setMaximumFractionDigits(2);
    }

    /* User pressed Enter on a text field
       or pressed Compute. Display the result if all
       fields are completed. */
    public void actionPerformed(ActionEvent ae) {
      double result = 0.0;

      String orgPStr = orgPText.getText();
      String numPayStr = numPayText.getText();
      String rateStr = rateText.getText();
```

```
    String payStr = paymentText.getText();

    try {
      if(orgPStr.length() != 0 &&
         numPayStr.length() != 0 &&
         rateStr.length() != 0 &&
         payStr.length() != 0) {

         orgPrincipal = Double.parseDouble(orgPStr);
         numPayments = Double.parseDouble(numPayStr);
         intRate = Double.parseDouble(rateStr) / 100;
         payment = Double.parseDouble(payStr);

         result = compute();

         remBalText.setText(nf.format(result));
      }

      showStatus(""); // erase any previous error message
    } catch (NumberFormatException exc) {
      showStatus("Invalid Data");
      remBalText.setText("");
    }
  }

  // Compute the loan balance.
  double compute() {
    double bal = orgPrincipal;
    double rate = intRate / payPerYear;

    for(int i = 0; i < numPayments; i++)
      bal -= payment - (bal * rate);

    return bal;
  }
}
```

Creating Financial Servlets

Although applets are easy to create and use, they are only one half of the Java Internet equation. The other half is servlets. Servlets execute on the server side of the connection, and they are more appropriate for some applications. Because many readers may want to use servlets rather than applets in their commercial applications, the remainder of this chapter shows how to convert the financial applets into servlets.

Because all the financial applets use the same basic skeleton, we will walk through the conversion of only one applet: **RegPay**. You can then apply the same basic process to convert any of the other applets into servlets on your own. As you will see, it's not hard to do.

NOTE *For information on creating, testing, and running servlets, see Chapter 31.*

Converting the RegPay Applet into a Servlet

It is fairly easy to convert the **RegPay** loan calculating applet into a servlet. First, the servlet must import the **javax.servlet** and **javax.servlet.http** packages. It must also extend **HttpServlet**, not **JApplet**. Next, you must remove all the GUI code. Then, you must add the code that obtains the parameters passed to the servlet by the HTML that calls the servlet. Finally, the servlet must send the HTML that displays the results. The basic financial calculations remain the same. It is only the way data is obtained and displayed that changes.

The RegPayS Servlet

The following **RegPayS** class is the servlet version of the **RegPay** applet. As the code is written, it assumes that **RegPayS.class** will be stored in Tomcat's example servlets directory, as described in Chapter 31. Remember to enter its name into the **web.xml** file, also as described in Chapter 31.

```
// A simple loan calculator servlet.
import javax.servlet.*;
import javax.servlet.http.*;
import java.io.*;
import java.text.*;

public class RegPayS extends HttpServlet {
  double principal; // original principal
  double intRate;   // interest rate
  double numYears;  // length of loan in years

  /* Number of payments per year. You could
     allow this value to be set by the user. */
  final int payPerYear = 12;

  NumberFormat nf;

  public void doGet(HttpServletRequest request,
                    HttpServletResponse response)
    throws ServletException, IOException {
    String payStr = "";

    // Create a number format.
    nf = NumberFormat.getInstance();
    nf.setMinimumFractionDigits(2);
    nf.setMaximumFractionDigits(2);

    // Get the parameters.
    String amountStr = request.getParameter("amount");
    String periodStr = request.getParameter("period");
    String rateStr = request.getParameter("rate");

    try {
      if(amountStr != null && periodStr != null &&
         rateStr != null) {
        principal = Double.parseDouble(amountStr);
```

```
      numYears = Double.parseDouble(periodStr);
      intRate = Double.parseDouble(rateStr) / 100;

      payStr = nf.format(compute());
    }
    else { // one or more parameters missing
      amountStr = "";
      periodStr = "";
      rateStr = "";
    }
  } catch (NumberFormatException exc) {
    // Take appropriate action here.
  }

  // Set the content type.
  response.setContentType("text/html");

  // Get the output stream.
  PrintWriter pw = response.getWriter();

  // Display the necessary HTML.
  pw.print("<html><body> <left>" +
          "<form name=\"Form1\"" +
          " action=\"http://localhost:8080/" +
          "servlets-examples/servlet/RegPayS\">" +
          "<B>Enter amount to finance:</B>" +
          " <input type=textbox name=\"amount\"" +
          " size=12 value=\"");
  pw.print(amountStr + "\">");
  pw.print("<BR><B>Enter term in years:</B>" +
          " <input type=textbox name=\"period\""+
          " size=12 value=\"");
  pw.println(periodStr + "\">");
  pw.print("<BR><B>Enter interest rate:</B>" +
          " <input type=textbox name=\"rate\"" +
          " size=12 value=\"");
  pw.print(rateStr + "\">");
  pw.print("<BR><B>Monthly Payment:</B>" +
          " <input READONLY type=textbox" +
          " name=\"payment\" size=12 value=\"");
  pw.print(payStr + "\">");
  pw.print("<BR><P><input type=submit value=\"Submit\">");
  pw.println("</form> </body> </html>");
}

// Compute the loan payment.
double compute() {
  double numer;
  double denom;
  double b, e;

  numer = intRate * principal / payPerYear;
```

```
    e = -(payPerYear * numYears);
    b = (intRate / payPerYear) + 1.0;

    denom = 1.0 - Math.pow(b, e);

    return numer / denom;
  }
}
```

The first thing to notice about **RegPayS** is that it has only two methods: **doGet( )** and **compute( )**. The **compute( )** method is the same as that used by the applet. The **doGet( )** method is defined by the **HttpServlet** class, which **RegPayS** extends. This method is called by the server when the servlet must respond to a GET request. Notice that it is passed a reference to the **HttpServletRequest** and **HttpServletResponse** objects associated with the request.

From the **request** parameter, the servlet obtains the arguments associated with the request. It does this by calling **getParameter( )**. The parameter is returned in its string form. Thus, a numeric value must be manually converted into its binary format. If no parameter is available, a **null** is returned.

From the **response** object, the servlet obtains a stream to which response information can be written. The response is then returned to the browser by outputting to that stream. Prior to obtaining a **PrintWriter** to the response stream, the output type should be set to text/html by calling **setContentType( )**.

RegPayS can be called with or without parameters. If called without parameters, the servlet responds with the necessary HTML to display an empty loan calculator form. Otherwise, if called with all needed parameters, **RegPayS** calculates the loan payment and redisplays the form, with the payment field filled in. Figure 32-7 shows the **RegPayS** servlet in action.

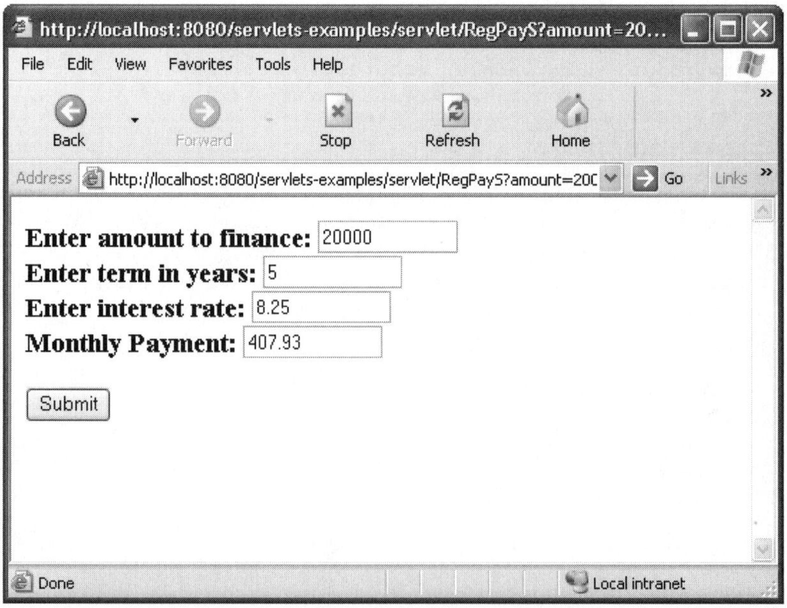

FIGURE 32-7
The **RegPayS**
servlet in action

The simplest way to invoke **RegPayS** is to link to its URL without passing any parameters. For example, assuming that you are using Tomcat, you can use this line to execute it:

```
<A HREF = "http://localhost:8080/servlets-examples/servlet/RegPayS">
Loan Calculator</A>
```

This displays a link called Loan Calculator that links to the **RegPayS** servlet in the Tomcat example servlets directory. Notice that no parameters are passed. This causes **RegPayS** to return the complete HTML that displays an empty loan calculator page.

You can also invoke **RegPayS** by first displaying an empty form manually, if you like. This approach is shown here, again using Tomcat's example servlets directory:

```
<html>
<body>
<form name="Form1"
  action="http://localhost:8080/servlets-examples/servlet/RegPayS">
<B>Enter amount to finance:</B>
<input type=textbox name="amount" size=12 value="">
<BR>
<B>Enter term in years:</B>
<input type=textbox name="period" size=12 value="">
<BR>
<B>Enter interest rate:</B>
<input type=textbox name="rate" size=12 value="">
<BR>
<B>Monthly Payment:</B>
<input READONLY type=textbox name="payment"
  size=12 value="">
<BR><P>
<input type=submit value="Submit">
</form>
</body>
</html>
```

Some Things to Try

The first thing you might want to try is converting the other financial applets into servlets. Because all the financial applets are built on the same skeleton, simply follow the same approach as used by **RegPayS**. There are many other financial calculations that you might find useful to implement as applets or servlets, such as the rate of return of an investment or the amount of a regular deposit needed over time to reach a future value. You could also print a loan amortization chart. You might want to try creating a larger application that offers all the calculations presented in this chapter, allowing the user to select the desired calculation from a menu.

Creating a Download Manager in Java

Have you ever had an Internet download interrupted, putting you back at square one? If you connect to the Internet with a dialup connection, it's very likely that you've run into this all too common nuisance. Everything from call-waiting disconnects to computer crashes can leave a download dead in its tracks. To say the least, restarting a download from scratch over and over can be a very time-consuming and frustrating experience.

A sometimes overlooked fact is that many interrupted downloads can be resumed. This allows you to recommence downloading from the point at which a download terminates instead of having to begin anew. In this chapter a tool called Download Manager is developed that manages Internet downloads for you and makes simple work of resuming interrupted downloads. It also lets you pause and then resume a download, and manage multiple downloads, simultaneously.

At the core of the Download Manager's usefulness is its ability to take advantage of downloading only specific portions of a file. In a classic download scenario, a whole file is downloaded from beginning to end. If the transmission of the file is interrupted for any reason, the progress made toward completing the downloading of the file is lost. The Download Manager, however, can pick up from where an interruption occurs and then download only the file's remaining fragment. Not all downloads are created equal, though, and there are some that simply cannot be restarted. Details on which files are and aren't resumable are explained in the following section.

Not only is the Download Manager a useful utility, it is an excellent illustration of the power and succinctness of Java's built-in APIs—especially as they apply to interfacing to the Internet. Because the Internet was a driving force behind the creation of Java, it should come as no surprise that Java's networking capabilities are unsurpassed. For example, attempting to create the Download Manager in another language, such as C++, would entail significantly more trouble and effort.

Understanding Internet Downloads

To understand and appreciate the Download Manager, it's necessary to shed some light on how Internet downloads really work.

Internet downloads in their simplest form are merely client/server transactions. The client, your browser, requests to download a file from a server on the Internet. The server then responds by sending the requested file to your browser. In order for clients to communicate with servers, they must have an established protocol for doing so. The most common protocols for downloading files are File Transfer Protocol (FTP) and Hypertext Transfer Protocol (HTTP). FTP is usually associated generically with exchanging files between computers, whereas HTTP is usually associated specifically with transferring web pages and their related files (that is, graphics, sounds, and so on). Over time, as the World Wide Web has grown in popularity, HTTP has become the dominant protocol for downloading files from the Internet. FTP is definitely not extinct, though.

For brevity's sake, the Download Manager developed in this chapter will only support HTTP downloads. Nonetheless, adding support for FTP would be an excellent exercise for extending the code. HTTP downloads come in two forms: resumable (HTTP 1.1) and nonresumable (HTTP 1.0). The difference between these two forms lies in the way files can be requested from servers. With the antiquated HTTP 1.0, a client can only request that a server send it a file, whereas with HTTP 1.1, a client can request that a server send it a complete file or *only a specific portion of a file.* This is the feature the Download Manager is built on.

An Overview of the Download Manager

The Download Manager uses a simple yet effective GUI interface built with Java's Swing libraries. The Download Manager window is shown in Figure 33-1. The use of Swing gives the interface a crisp, modern look and feel.

The GUI maintains a list of downloads that are currently being managed. Each download in the list reports its URL, size of the file in bytes, progress as a percentage toward completion, and current status. The downloads can each be in one of the following different states: Downloading, Paused, Complete, Error, or Cancelled. The GUI also has controls for adding downloads to the list and for changing the state of each download in the list. When a download in the list is selected, depending on its current state, it can be paused, resumed, cancelled, or removed from the list altogether.

The Download Manager is broken into a few classes for natural separation of functional components. These are the **Download**, **DownloadsTableModel**, **ProgressRenderer**, and **DownloadManager** classes, respectively. The **DownloadManager** class is responsible for the GUI interface and makes use of the **DownloadsTableModel** and **ProgressRenderer** classes for displaying the current list of downloads. The **Download** class represents a "managed" download and is responsible for performing the actual downloading of a file. In the following sections, we'll walk through each of these classes in detail, highlighting their inner workings and explaining how they relate to each other.

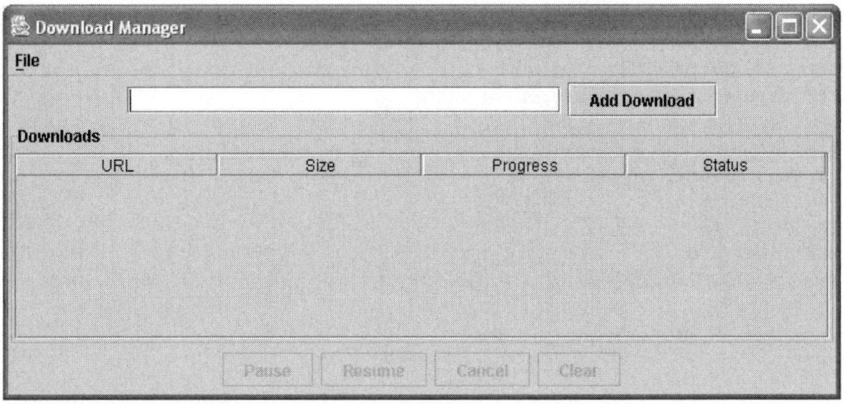

FIGURE 33-1   The Download Manager GUI interface

The Download Class

The **Download** class is the workhorse of the Download Manager. Its primary purpose is to download a file and save that file's contents to disk. Each time a new download is added to the Download Manager, a new **Download** object is instantiated to handle the download.

The Download Manager has the ability to download multiple files at once. To achieve this, it's necessary for each of the simultaneous downloads to run independently. It's also necessary for each individual download to manage its own state so that it can be reflected in the GUI. This is accomplished with the **Download** class.

The entire code for **Download** is shown here. Notice that it extends **Observable** and implements **Runnable**. Each part is examined in detail in the sections that follow.

```java
import java.io.*;
import java.net.*;
import java.util.*;

// This class downloads a file from a URL.
class Download extends Observable implements Runnable {
  // Max size of download buffer.
  private static final int MAX_BUFFER_SIZE = 1024;

  // These are the status names.
  public static final String STATUSES[] = {"Downloading",
    "Paused", "Complete", "Cancelled", "Error"};

  // These are the status codes.
  public static final int DOWNLOADING = 0;
  public static final int PAUSED = 1;
  public static final int COMPLETE = 2;
  public static final int CANCELLED = 3;
  public static final int ERROR = 4;
```

```java
private URL url; // download URL
private int size; // size of download in bytes
private int downloaded; // number of bytes downloaded
private int status; // current status of download

// Constructor for Download.
public Download(URL url) {
  this.url = url;
  size = -1;
  downloaded = 0;
  status = DOWNLOADING;

  // Begin the download.
  download();
}

// Get this download's URL.
public String getUrl() {
  return url.toString();
}

// Get this download's size.
public int getSize() {
  return size;
}

// Get this download's progress.
public float getProgress() {
  return ((float) downloaded / size) * 100;
}

// Get this download's status.
public int getStatus() {
  return status;
}

// Pause this download.
public void pause() {
  status = PAUSED;
  stateChanged();
}

// Resume this download.
public void resume() {
  status = DOWNLOADING;
  stateChanged();
  download();
}

// Cancel this download.
public void cancel() {
  status = CANCELLED;
  stateChanged();
}
```

```java
// Mark this download as having an error.
private void error() {
  status = ERROR;
  stateChanged();
}

// Start or resume downloading.
private void download() {
  Thread thread = new Thread(this);
  thread.start();
}

// Get file name portion of URL.
private String getFileName(URL url) {
  String fileName = url.getFile();
  return fileName.substring(fileName.lastIndexOf('/') + 1);
}

// Download file.
public void run() {
  RandomAccessFile file = null;
  InputStream stream = null;

  try {
    // Open connection to URL.
    HttpURLConnection connection =
      (HttpURLConnection) url.openConnection();

    // Specify what portion of file to download.
    connection.setRequestProperty("Range",
      "bytes=" + downloaded + "-");

    // Connect to server.
    connection.connect();

    // Make sure response code is in the 200 range.
    if (connection.getResponseCode() / 100 != 2) {
      error();
    }

    // Check for valid content length.
    int contentLength = connection.getContentLength();
    if (contentLength < 1) {
      error();
    }

    /* Set the size for this download if it
       hasn't been already set. */
    if (size == -1) {
      size = contentLength;
      stateChanged();
    }
```

```java
      // Open file and seek to the end of it.
      file = new RandomAccessFile(getFileName(url), "rw");
      file.seek(downloaded);

      stream = connection.getInputStream();
      while (status == DOWNLOADING) {
        /* Size buffer according to how much of the
           file is left to download. */
        byte buffer[];
        if (size - downloaded > MAX_BUFFER_SIZE) {
          buffer = new byte[MAX_BUFFER_SIZE];
        } else {
          buffer = new byte[size - downloaded];
        }

        // Read from server into buffer.
        int read = stream.read(buffer);
        if (read == -1)
          break;

        // Write buffer to file.
        file.write(buffer, 0, read);
        downloaded += read;
        stateChanged();
      }

      /* Change status to complete if this point was
         reached because downloading has finished. */
      if (status == DOWNLOADING) {
        status = COMPLETE;
        stateChanged();
      }
    } catch (Exception e) {
      error();
    } finally {
      // Close file.
      if (file != null) {
        try {
          file.close();
        } catch (Exception e) {}
      }

      // Close connection to server.
      if (stream != null) {
        try {
          stream.close();
        } catch (Exception e) {}
      }
    }
  }
```

```
// Notify observers that this download's status has changed.
private void stateChanged() {
  setChanged();
  notifyObservers();
}
}
```

The Download Variables

Download begins by declaring several **static final** variables that specify the various constants used by the class. Next, four instance variables are declared. The **url** variable holds the Internet URL for the file being downloaded; the **size** variable holds the size of the download file in bytes; the **downloaded** variable holds the number of bytes that have been downloaded thus far; and the **status** variable indicates the download's current status.

The Download Constructor

Download's constructor is passed a reference to the URL to download in the form of a **URL** object, which is assigned to the **url** instance variable. It then sets the remaining instance variables to their initial states and calls the **download()** method. Notice that **size** is set to –1 to indicate there is no size yet.

The download( ) Method

The **download()** method creates a new **Thread** object, passing it a reference to the invoking **Download** instance. As mentioned before, it's necessary for each download to run independently. In order for the **Download** class to act alone, it must execute in its own thread. Java has excellent built-in support for threads and makes using them a snap. To use threads, the **Download** class simply implements the **Runnable** interface by overriding the **run()** method. After the **download()** method has instantiated a new **Thread** instance, passing its constructor the **Runnable Download** class, it calls the thread's **start()** method. Invoking the **start()** method causes the **Runnable** instance's (the **Download** class') **run()** method to be executed.

The run( ) Method

When the **run()** method executes, the actual downloading gets under way. Because of its size and importance, we will examine it closely, line by line. The **run()** method begins with these lines:

```
RandomAccessFile file = null;
InputStream stream = null;

try {
  // Open connection to URL.
  HttpURLConnection connection =
    (HttpURLConnection) url.openConnection();
```

First, **run( )** sets up variables for the network stream that the download's contents will be read from and sets up the file that the download's contents will be written to. Next, a connection to the download's URL is opened by calling **url.openConnection( )**. Since we know that the Download Manager supports only HTTP downloads, the connection is cast to the **HttpURLConnection** type. Casting the connection as an **HttpURLConnection** allows us to take advantage of HTTP-specific connection features such as the **getResponseCode( )** method. Note that calling **url.openConnection( )** does not actually create a connection to the URL's server. It simply creates a new **URLConnection** instance associated with the URL that later will be used to connect to the server.

After the **HttpURLConnection** has been created, the connection request property is set by calling **connection.setRequestProperty( )**, as shown here:

```
// Specify what portion of file to download.
connection.setRequestProperty("Range",
  "bytes=" + downloaded + "-");
```

Setting request properties allows extra request information to be sent to the server the download will be coming from. In this case, the "Range" property is set. This is critically important, as the "Range" property specifies the range of bytes that is being requested for download from the server. Normally, all of a file's bytes are downloaded at once. However, if a download has been interrupted or paused, only the download's remaining bytes should be retrieved. Setting the "Range" property is the foundation for the Download Manager's operation.

The "Range" property is specified in this form:

start-byte – end-byte

For example, "0 – 12345". However, the end byte of the range is optional. If the end byte is absent, the range ends at the end of the file. The **run( )** method never specifies the end byte because downloads must run until the entire range is downloaded, unless paused or interrupted.

The next few lines are shown here:

```
// Connect to server.
connection.connect();

// Make sure response code is in the 200 range.
if (connection.getResponseCode() / 100 != 2) {
  error();
}

// Check for valid content length.
int contentLength = connection.getContentLength();
if (contentLength < 1) {
  error();
}
```

The **connection.connect( )** method is called to make the actual connection to the download's server. Next, the response code returned by the server is checked. The HTTP protocol has a list of response codes that indicate a server's response to a request. HTTP response codes are organized into numeric ranges of 100, and the 200 range indicates success. The server's response code is validated for being in the 200 range by calling **connection.getResponseCode( )** and dividing by 100. If the value of this division is 2, then the connection was successful.

Next, **run( )** gets the content length by calling **connection.getContentLength( )**. The content length represents the number of bytes in the requested file. If the content length is less than 1, the **error( )** method is called. The **error( )** method updates the download's status to **ERROR**, and then calls **stateChanged( )**. The **stateChanged( )** method will be described in detail later.

After getting the content length, the following code checks to see if it has already been assigned to the **size** variable:

```
/* Set the size for this download if it
   hasn't been already set. */
if (size == -1) {
  size = contentLength;
  stateChanged();
}
```

As you can see, instead of assigning the content length to the **size** variable unconditionally, it only gets assigned if it hasn't already been given a value. The reason for this is because the content length reflects how many bytes the server will be sending. If anything other than a 0-based start range is specified, the content length will only represent a portion of the file's size. The **size** variable has to be set to the complete size of the download's file.

The next few lines of code shown here create a new **RandomAccessFile** using the filename portion of the download's URL that is retrieved with a call to the **getFileName( )** method:

```
// Open file and seek to the end of it.
file = new RandomAccessFile(getFileName(url), "rw");
file.seek(downloaded);
```

The **RandomAccessFile** is opened in "rw" mode, which specifies that the file can be written to and read from. Once the file is open, **run( )** seeks to the end of the file by calling the **file.seek( )** method, passing in the **downloaded** variable. This tells the file to position itself at the number of bytes that have been downloaded—in other words, at the end. It's necessary to position the file at the end in case a download has been resumed. If a download is resumed, the newly downloaded bytes are appended to the file and they don't overwrite any previously downloaded bytes. After preparing the output file, a network stream handle to the open server connection is obtained by calling **connection.getInputStream( )**, as shown here:

```
stream = connection.getInputStream();
```

The heart of all the action begins next with a **while** loop:

```
while (status == DOWNLOADING) {
  /* Size buffer according to how much of the
     file is left to download. */
  byte buffer[];
  if (size - downloaded > MAX_BUFFER_SIZE) {
    buffer = new byte[MAX_BUFFER_SIZE];
```

PART IV

```
  } else {
    buffer = new byte[size - downloaded];
  }

  // Read from server into buffer.
  int read = stream.read(buffer);
  if (read == -1)
    break;

  // Write buffer to file.
  file.write(buffer, 0, read);
  downloaded += read;
  stateChanged();
}
```

This loop is set up to run until the download's **status** variable changes from **DOWNLOADING**. Inside the loop, a **byte** buffer array is created to hold the bytes that will be downloaded. The buffer is sized according to how much of the download is left to complete. If there is more left to download than the **MAX_BUFFER_SIZE**, the **MAX_ BUFFER_SIZE** is used to size the buffer. Otherwise, the buffer is sized exactly at the number of bytes left to download. Once the buffer is sized appropriately, the downloading takes place with a **stream.read( )** call. This call reads bytes from the server and places them into the buffer, returning the count of how many bytes were actually read. If the number of bytes read equals –1, then downloading has completed and the loop is exited. Otherwise, downloading is not finished and the bytes that have been read are written to disk with a call to **file.write( )**. Then the **downloaded** variable is updated, reflecting the number of bytes downloaded thus far. Finally, inside the loop, the **stateChanged( )** method is invoked. More on this later.

After the loop has exited, the following code checks to see why the loop was exited:

```
/* Change status to complete if this point was
   reached because downloading has finished. */
if (status == DOWNLOADING) {
  status = COMPLETE;
  stateChanged();
}
```

If the download's status is still **DOWNLOADING**, this means that the loop exited because downloading has been completed. Otherwise, the loop was exited because the download's status changed to something other than **DOWNLOADING**.

The **run( )** method wraps up with the **catch** and **finally** blocks shown here:

```
} catch (Exception e) {
  error();
} finally {
  // Close file.
  if (file != null) {
    try {
      file.close();
    } catch (Exception e) {}
  }
```

```
      // Close connection to server.
      if (stream != null) {
        try {
          stream.close();
        } catch (Exception e) {}
      }
    }
}
```

If an exception is thrown during the download process, the **catch** block captures the exception and calls the **error( )** method. The **finally** block ensures that if the **file** and **stream** connections have been opened, they get closed whether an exception has been thrown or not.

The stateChanged( ) Method

In order for the Download Manager to display up-to-date information on each of the downloads it's managing, it has to know each time a download's information changes. To handle this, the Observer software design pattern is used. The Observer pattern is analogous to an announcement's mailing list where several people register to receive announcements. Each time there's a new announcement, each person on the list receives a message with the announcement. In the Observer pattern's case, there's an observed class with which observer classes can register themselves to receive change notifications.

The **Download** class employs the Observer pattern by extending Java's built-in **Observable** utility class. Extending the **Observable** class allows classes that implement Java's **Observer** interface to register themselves with the **Download** class to receive change notifications. Each time the **Download** class needs to notify its registered **Observers** of a change, the **stateChanged( )** method is invoked. The **stateChanged( )** method first calls the **Observable** class' **setChanged( )** method to flag the class as having been changed. Next, the **stateChanged( )** method calls **Observable**'s **notifyObservers( )** method, which broadcasts the change notification to the registered **Observers**.

Action and Accessor Methods

The **Download** class has numerous action and accessor methods for controlling a download and getting data from it. Each of the **pause( )**, **resume( )**, and **cancel( )** action methods simply does as its name implies: pauses, resumes, or cancels the download, respectively. Similarly, the **error( )** method marks the download as having an error. The **getUrl( )**, **getSize( )**, **getProgress( )**, and **getStatus( )** accessor methods each return their current respective values.

The ProgressRenderer Class

The **ProgressRenderer** class is a small utility class that is used to render the current progress of a download listed in the GUI's "Downloads" **JTable** instance. Normally, a **JTable** instance renders each cell's data as text. However, often it's particularly useful to render a cell's data as something other than text. In the Download Manager's case, we want to render each of the table's Progress column cells as progress bars. The **ProgressRenderer** class shown here makes that possible. Notice that it extends **JProgressBar** and implements **TableCellRenderer**:

```
import java.awt.*;
import javax.swing.*;
import javax.swing.table.*;
```

```
// This class renders a JProgressBar in a table cell.
class ProgressRenderer extends JProgressBar
  implements TableCellRenderer
{
  // Constructor for ProgressRenderer.
  public ProgressRenderer(int min, int max) {
    super(min, max);
  }

  /* Returns this JProgressBar as the renderer
     for the given table cell. */
  public Component getTableCellRendererComponent(
    JTable table, Object value, boolean isSelected,
    boolean hasFocus, int row, int column)
  {
    // Set JProgressBar's percent complete value.
    setValue((int) ((Float) value).floatValue());
    return this;
  }
}
```

The **ProgressRenderer** class takes advantage of the fact that Swing's **JTable** class has a rendering system that can accept "plug-ins" for rendering table cells. To plug into this rendering system, first, the **ProgressRenderer** class has to implement Swing's **TableCellRenderer** interface. Second, a **ProgressRenderer** instance has to be registered with a **JTable** instance; doing so instructs the **JTable** instance as to which cells should be rendered with the "plug-in."

Implementing the **TableCellRenderer** interface requires the class to override the **getTableCellRendererComponent( )** method. The **getTableCellRendererComponent( )** method is invoked each time a **JTable** instance goes to render a cell for which this class has been registered. This method is passed several variables, but in this case, only the **value** variable is used. The **value** variable holds the data for the cell being rendered and is passed to **JProgressBar**'s **setValue( )** method. The **getTableCellRendererComponent( )** method wraps up by returning a reference to its class. This works because the **ProgressRenderer** class is a subclass of **JProgressBar**, which is a descendent of the AWT **Component** class.

The DownloadsTableModel Class

The **DownloadsTableModel** class houses the Download Manager's list of downloads and is the backing data source for the GUI's "Downloads" **JTable** instance.

The **DownloadsTableModel** class is shown here. Notice that it extends **AbstractTableModel** and implements the **Observer** interface:

```
import java.util.*;
import javax.swing.*;
import javax.swing.table.*;

// This class manages the download table's data.
class DownloadsTableModel extends AbstractTableModel
  implements Observer
{
```

```java
// These are the names for the table's columns.
private static final String[] columnNames = {"URL", "Size",
  "Progress", "Status"};

// These are the classes for each column's values.
private static final Class[] columnClasses = {String.class,
  String.class, JProgressBar.class, String.class};

// The table's list of downloads.
private ArrayList<Download> downloadList = new ArrayList<Download>();

// Add a new download to the table.
public void addDownload(Download download) {
  // Register to be notified when the download changes.
  download.addObserver(this);

  downloadList.add(download);

  // Fire table row insertion notification to table.
  fireTableRowsInserted(getRowCount() - 1, getRowCount() - 1);
}

// Get a download for the specified row.
public Download getDownload(int row) {
  return downloadList.get(row);
}

// Remove a download from the list.
public void clearDownload(int row) {
  downloadList.remove(row);

  // Fire table row deletion notification to table.
  fireTableRowsDeleted(row, row);
}

// Get table's column count.
public int getColumnCount() {
  return columnNames.length;
}

// Get a column's name.
public String getColumnName(int col) {
    return columnNames[col];
}

// Get a column's class.
public Class getColumnClass(int col) {
  return columnClasses[col];
}

// Get table's row count.
public int getRowCount() {
  return downloadList.size();
}
```

```
// Get value for a specific row and column combination.
public Object getValueAt(int row, int col) {
  Download download = downloadList.get(row);
  switch (col) {
    case 0: // URL
      return download.getUrl();
    case 1: // Size
      int size = download.getSize();
      return (size == -1) ? "" : Integer.toString(size);
    case 2: // Progress
      return new Float(download.getProgress());
    case 3: // Status
      return Download.STATUSES[download.getStatus()];
  }
  return "";
}

/* Update is called when a Download notifies its
   observers of any changes */
public void update(Observable o, Object arg) {
  int index = downloadList.indexOf(o);

  // Fire table row update notification to table.
  fireTableRowsUpdated(index, index);
}
}
```

The **DownloadsTableModel** class essentially is a utility class utilized by the "Downloads" **JTable** instance for managing data in the table. When the **JTable** instance is initialized, it is passed a **DownloadsTableModel** instance. The **JTable** then proceeds to call several methods on the **DownloadsTableModel** instance to populate itself. The **getColumnCount( )** method is called to retrieve the number of columns in the table. Similarly, **getRowCount( )** is used to retrieve the number of rows in the table. The **getColumnName( )** method returns a column's name given its ID. The **getDownload( )** method takes a row ID and returns the associated **Download** object from the list. The rest of the **DownloadsTableModel** class' methods, which are more involved, are detailed in the following sections.

The addDownload( ) Method

The **addDownload( )** method, shown here, adds a new **Download** object to the list of managed downloads and consequently a row to the table:

```
// Add a new download to the table.
public void addDownload(Download download) {
  // Register to be notified when the download changes.
  download.addObserver(this);

  downloadList.add(download);

  // Fire table row insertion notification to table.
  fireTableRowsInserted(getRowCount() - 1, getRowCount() - 1);
}
```

This method first registers itself with the new **Download** as an **Observer** interested in receiving change notifications. Next, the **Download** is added to the internal list of downloads being managed. Finally, a table row insertion event notification is fired to alert the table that a new row has been added.

The clearDownload( ) Method

The **clearDownload( )** method, shown next, removes a **Download** from the list of managed downloads:

```
// Remove a download from the list.
public void clearDownload(int row) {
  downloadList.remove(row);

  // Fire table row deletion notification to table.
  fireTableRowsDeleted(row, row);
}
```

After removing the **Download** from the internal list, a table row deleted event notification is fired to alert the table that a row has been deleted.

The getColumnClass( ) Method

The **getColumnClass( )** method, shown here, returns the class type for the data displayed in the specified column:

```
// Get a column's class.
public Class getColumnClass(int col) {
  return columnClasses[col];
}
```

All columns are displayed as text (that is, **String** objects) except for the Progress column, which is displayed as a progress bar (which is an object of type **JProgressBar**).

The getValueAt( ) Method

The **getValueAt( )** method, shown next, is called to get the current value that should be displayed for each of the table's cells:

```
// Get value for a specific row and column combination.
public Object getValueAt(int row, int col) {
  Download download = downloadList.get(row);
  switch (col) {
    case 0: // URL
      return download.getUrl();
    case 1: // Size
      int size = download.getSize();
      return (size == -1) ? "" : Integer.toString(size);
    case 2: // Progress
      return new Float(download.getProgress());
    case 3: // Status
```

PART IV

```
        return Download.STATUSES[download.getStatus()];
    }
    return "";
}
```

This method first looks up the **Download** corresponding to the row specified. Next, the column specified is used to determine which one of the **Download**'s property values to return.

The update( ) Method

The **update( )** method is shown here. It fulfills the **Observer** interface contract allowing the **DownloadsTableModel** class to receive notifications from **Download** objects when they change.

```
/* Update is called when a Download notifies its
   observers of any changes. */
public void update(Observable o, Object arg) {
  int index = downloadList.indexOf(o);

  // Fire table row update notification to table.
  fireTableRowsUpdated(index, index);
}
```

This method is passed a reference to the **Download** that has changed, in the form of an **Observable** object. Next, an index to that download is looked up in the list of downloads, and that index is then used to fire a table row update event notification, which alerts the table that the given row has been updated. The table will then rerender the row with the given index, reflecting its new values.

The DownloadManager Class

Now that the foundation has been laid by explaining each of the Download Manager's helper classes, we can look closely at the **DownloadManager** class. The **DownloadManager** class is responsible for creating and running the Download Manager's GUI. This class has a **main( )** method declared, so on execution it will be invoked first. The **main( )** method instantiates a new **DownloadManager** class instance and then calls its **show( )** method, which causes it to be displayed.

The **DownloadManager** class is shown here. Notice that it extends **JFrame** and implements **Observer**. The following sections examine it in detail.

```
import java.awt.*;
import java.awt.event.*;
import java.net.*;
import java.util.*;
import javax.swing.*;
import javax.swing.event.*;

// The Download Manager.
public class DownloadManager extends JFrame
  implements Observer
{
```

```java
// Add download text field.
private JTextField addTextField;

// Download table's data model.
private DownloadsTableModel tableModel;

// Table listing downloads.
private JTable table;

// These are the buttons for managing the selected download.
private JButton pauseButton, resumeButton;
private JButton cancelButton, clearButton;

// Currently selected download.
private Download selectedDownload;

// Flag for whether or not table selection is being cleared.
private boolean clearing;

// Constructor for Download Manager.
public DownloadManager()
{
  // Set application title.
  setTitle("Download Manager");

  // Set window size.
  setSize(640, 480);

  // Handle window closing events.
  addWindowListener(new WindowAdapter() {
    public void windowClosing(WindowEvent e) {
      actionExit();
    }
  });

  // Set up file menu.
  JMenuBar menuBar = new JMenuBar();
  JMenu fileMenu = new JMenu("File");
  fileMenu.setMnemonic(KeyEvent.VK_F);
  JMenuItem fileExitMenuItem = new JMenuItem("Exit",
    KeyEvent.VK_X);
  fileExitMenuItem.addActionListener(new ActionListener() {
    public void actionPerformed(ActionEvent e) {
      actionExit();
    }
  });
  fileMenu.add(fileExitMenuItem);
  menuBar.add(fileMenu);
  setJMenuBar(menuBar);

  // Set up add panel.
  JPanel addPanel = new JPanel();
  addTextField = new JTextField(30);
```

```
    addPanel.add(addTextField);
    JButton addButton = new JButton("Add Download");
    addButton.addActionListener(new ActionListener() {
      public void actionPerformed(ActionEvent e) {
        actionAdd();
      }
    });
    addPanel.add(addButton);

    // Set up Downloads table.
    tableModel = new DownloadsTableModel();
    table = new JTable(tableModel);
    table.getSelectionModel().addListSelectionListener(new
      ListSelectionListener() {
      public void valueChanged(ListSelectionEvent e) {
        tableSelectionChanged();
      }
    });
    // Allow only one row at a time to be selected.
    table.setSelectionMode(ListSelectionModel.SINGLE_SELECTION);

    // Set up ProgressBar as renderer for progress column.
    ProgressRenderer renderer = new ProgressRenderer(0, 100);
    renderer.setStringPainted(true); // show progress text
    table.setDefaultRenderer(JProgressBar.class, renderer);

    // Set table's row height large enough to fit JProgressBar.
    table.setRowHeight(
      (int) renderer.getPreferredSize().getHeight());

    // Set up downloads panel.
    JPanel downloadsPanel = new JPanel();
    downloadsPanel.setBorder(
      BorderFactory.createTitledBorder("Downloads"));
    downloadsPanel.setLayout(new BorderLayout());
    downloadsPanel.add(new JScrollPane(table),
      BorderLayout.CENTER);

    // Set up buttons panel.
    JPanel buttonsPanel = new JPanel();
    pauseButton = new JButton("Pause");
    pauseButton.addActionListener(new ActionListener() {
      public void actionPerformed(ActionEvent e) {
        actionPause();
      }
    });
    pauseButton.setEnabled(false);
    buttonsPanel.add(pauseButton);
    resumeButton = new JButton("Resume");
    resumeButton.addActionListener(new ActionListener() {
      public void actionPerformed(ActionEvent e) {
        actionResume();
      }
    });
```

```
    resumeButton.setEnabled(false);
    buttonsPanel.add(resumeButton);
    cancelButton = new JButton("Cancel");
    cancelButton.addActionListener(new ActionListener() {
      public void actionPerformed(ActionEvent e) {
        actionCancel();
      }
    });
    cancelButton.setEnabled(false);
    buttonsPanel.add(cancelButton);
    clearButton = new JButton("Clear");
    clearButton.addActionListener(new ActionListener() {
      public void actionPerformed(ActionEvent e) {
        actionClear();
      }
    });
    clearButton.setEnabled(false);
    buttonsPanel.add(clearButton);

    // Add panels to display.
    getContentPane().setLayout(new BorderLayout());
    getContentPane().add(addPanel, BorderLayout.NORTH);
    getContentPane().add(downloadsPanel, BorderLayout.CENTER);
    getContentPane().add(buttonsPanel, BorderLayout.SOUTH);
  }

  // Exit this program.
  private void actionExit() {
    System.exit(0);
  }

  // Add a new download.
  private void actionAdd() {
    URL verifiedUrl = verifyUrl(addTextField.getText());
    if (verifiedUrl != null) {
      tableModel.addDownload(new Download(verifiedUrl));
      addTextField.setText(""); // reset add text field
    } else {
      JOptionPane.showMessageDialog(this,
        "Invalid Download URL", "Error",
        JOptionPane.ERROR_MESSAGE);
    }
  }

  // Verify download URL.
  private URL verifyUrl(String url) {
    // Only allow HTTP URLs.
    if (!url.toLowerCase().startsWith("http://"))
      return null;

    // Verify format of URL.
    URL verifiedUrl = null;
    try {
```

```java
      verifiedUrl = new URL(url);
    } catch (Exception e) {
      return null;
    }

    // Make sure URL specifies a file.
    if (verifiedUrl.getFile().length() < 2)
      return null;

    return verifiedUrl;
  }

  // Called when table row selection changes.
  private void tableSelectionChanged() {
    /* Unregister from receiving notifications
       from the last selected download. */
    if (selectedDownload != null)
      selectedDownload.deleteObserver(DownloadManager.this);

    /* If not in the middle of clearing a download,
       set the selected download and register to
       receive notifications from it. */
    if (!clearing && table.getSelectedRow() > -1) {
      selectedDownload =
        tableModel.getDownload(table.getSelectedRow());
      selectedDownload.addObserver(DownloadManager.this);
      updateButtons();
    }
  }

  // Pause the selected download.
  private void actionPause() {
    selectedDownload.pause();
    updateButtons();
  }

  // Resume the selected download.
  private void actionResume() {
    selectedDownload.resume();
    updateButtons();
  }

  // Cancel the selected download.
  private void actionCancel() {
    selectedDownload.cancel();
    updateButtons();
  }

  // Clear the selected download.
  private void actionClear() {
    clearing = true;
    tableModel.clearDownload(table.getSelectedRow());
    clearing = false;
```

```java
      selectedDownload = null;
      updateButtons();
   }

   /* Update each button's state based off of the
      currently selected download's status. */
   private void updateButtons() {
      if (selectedDownload != null) {
         int status = selectedDownload.getStatus();
         switch (status) {
            case Download.DOWNLOADING:
              pauseButton.setEnabled(true);
              resumeButton.setEnabled(false);
              cancelButton.setEnabled(true);
              clearButton.setEnabled(false);
              break;
            case Download.PAUSED:
              pauseButton.setEnabled(false);
              resumeButton.setEnabled(true);
              cancelButton.setEnabled(true);
              clearButton.setEnabled(false);
              break;
            case Download.ERROR:
              pauseButton.setEnabled(false);
              resumeButton.setEnabled(true);
              cancelButton.setEnabled(false);
              clearButton.setEnabled(true);
              break;
            default: // COMPLETE or CANCELLED
              pauseButton.setEnabled(false);
              resumeButton.setEnabled(false);
              cancelButton.setEnabled(false);
              clearButton.setEnabled(true);
         }
      } else {
         // No download is selected in table.
         pauseButton.setEnabled(false);
         resumeButton.setEnabled(false);
         cancelButton.setEnabled(false);
         clearButton.setEnabled(false);
      }
   }

   /* Update is called when a Download notifies its
      observers of any changes. */
   public void update(Observable o, Object arg) {
      // Update buttons if the selected download has changed.
      if (selectedDownload != null && selectedDownload.equals(o))
         updateButtons();
   }

// Run the Download Manager.
   public static void main(String[] args) {
```

```
SwingUtilities.invokeLater(new Runnable() {
  public void run() {
    DownloadManager manager = new DownloadManager();
    manager.setVisible(true);
  }
});
}
}
```

The DownloadManager Variables

DownloadManager starts off by declaring several instance variables, most of which hold references to the GUI controls. The **selectedDownload** variable holds a reference to the **Download** object represented by the selected row in the table. Finally, the **clearing** instance variable is a **boolean** flag that tracks whether or not a download is currently being cleared from the Downloads table.

The DownloadManager Constructor

When the **DownloadManager** is instantiated, all of the GUI's controls are initialized inside its constructor. The constructor contains a lot of code, but most of it is straightforward. The following discussion gives an overview.

First, the window's title is set with a call to **setTitle( )**. Next, the **setSize( )** call establishes the window's width and height in pixels. After that, a window listener is added by calling **addWindowListener( )**, passing a **WindowAdapter** object that overrides the **windowClosing( )** event handler. This handler calls the **actionExit( )** method when the application's window is closed. Next, a menu bar with a "File" menu is added to the application's window. Then the "Add" panel, which has the Add Text field and button, is set up. An **ActionListener** is added to the "Add Download" button so that the **actionAdd( )** method is called each time the button is clicked.

The downloads table is constructed next. A **ListSelectionListener** is added to the table so that each time a row is selected in the table, the **tableSelectionChanged( )** method is invoked. The table's selection mode is also updated to **ListSelectionModel.SINGLE_SELECTION** so that only one row at a time can be selected in the table. Limiting row selection to only one row at a time simplifies the logic for determining which buttons should be enabled in the GUI when a row in the download table is selected. Next, a **ProgressRenderer** class is instantiated and registered with the table to handle the "Progress" column. The table's row height is updated to the **ProgressRenderer**'s height by calling **table.setRowHeight( )**. After the table has been assembled and tweaked, it is wrapped in a **JScrollPane** to make it scrollable and then added to a panel.

Finally, the buttons panel is created. The buttons panel has Pause, Resume, Cancel, and Clear buttons. Each of the buttons adds an **ActionListener** that invokes its respective action method when it is clicked. After creating the buttons panel, all of the panels that have been created are added to the window.

The verifyUrl( ) Method

The **verifyUrl( )** method is called by the **actionAdd( )** method each time a download is added to the Download Manager. The **verifyUrl( )** method is shown here:

```
// Verify download URL.
private URL verifyUrl(String url) {
  // Only allow HTTP URLs.
  if (!url.toLowerCase().startsWith("http://"))
    return null;

  // Verify format of URL.
  URL verifiedUrl = null;
  try {
    verifiedUrl = new URL(url);
  } catch (Exception e) {
    return null;
  }

  // Make sure URL specifies a file.
  if (verifiedUrl.getFile().length() < 2)
    return null;

  return verifiedUrl;
}
```

This method first verifies that the URL entered is an HTTP URL since only HTTP is supported. Next, the URL being verified is used to construct a new **URL** class instance. If the URL is malformed, the **URL** class constructor will throw an exception. Finally, this method verifies that a file is actually specified in the URL.

The tableSelectionChanged( ) Method

The **tableSelectionChanged( )** method, shown here, is called each time a row is selected in the downloads table:

```
// Called when table row selection changes.
private void tableSelectionChanged() {
  /* Unregister from receiving notifications
     from the last selected download. */
  if (selectedDownload != null)
    selectedDownload.deleteObserver(DownloadManager.this);

  /* If not in the middle of clearing a download,
     set the selected download and register to
     receive notifications from it. */
  if (!clearing && table.getSelectedRow() > -1) {
    selectedDownload =
      tableModel.getDownload(table.getSelectedRow());
    selectedDownload.addObserver(DownloadManager.this);
    updateButtons();
  }
}
```

This method starts by seeing if there is already a row currently selected by checking if the **selectedDownload** variable is **null**. If the **selectedDownload** variable is not **null**, **DownloadManager** removes itself as an observer of the download so that it no longer receives change notifications. Next the **clearing** flag is checked. If the table is not empty and the **clearing** flag is **false**, then first the **selectedDownload** variable is updated with the **Download** corresponding to the row selected. Second, the **DownloadManager** is registered as an **Observer** with the newly selected **Download**. Finally, **updateButtons( )** is called to update the button states based on the selected **Download**'s state.

The updateButtons( ) Method

The **updateButtons( )** method updates the state of all the buttons on the button panel based on the state of the selected download. The **updateButtons( )** method is shown here:

```
/* Update each button's state based on the
   currently selected download's status. */
private void updateButtons() {
  if (selectedDownload != null) {
    int status = selectedDownload.getStatus();
    switch (status) {
      case Download.DOWNLOADING:
        pauseButton.setEnabled(true);
        resumeButton.setEnabled(false);
        cancelButton.setEnabled(true);
        clearButton.setEnabled(false);
        break;
      case Download.PAUSED:
        pauseButton.setEnabled(false);
        resumeButton.setEnabled(true);
        cancelButton.setEnabled(true);
        clearButton.setEnabled(false);
        break;
      case Download.ERROR:
        pauseButton.setEnabled(false);
        resumeButton.setEnabled(true);
        cancelButton.setEnabled(false);
        clearButton.setEnabled(true);
        break;
      default: // COMPLETE or CANCELLED
        pauseButton.setEnabled(false);
        resumeButton.setEnabled(false);
        cancelButton.setEnabled(false);
        clearButton.setEnabled(true);
    }
  } else {
    // No download is selected in table.
    pauseButton.setEnabled(false);
    resumeButton.setEnabled(false);
    cancelButton.setEnabled(false);
    clearButton.setEnabled(false);
  }
}
```

If no download is selected in the downloads table, all of the buttons are disabled, giving them a grayed-out appearance. However, if there is a selected download, each button's state will be set based on whether the **Download** object has a status of **DOWNLOADING, PAUSED, ERROR, COMPLETE,** or **CANCELLED.**

Handling Action Events

Each of **DownloadManager**'s GUI controls registers an **ActionListener** that invokes its respective action method. **ActionListener**s are triggered each time an action event takes place on a GUI control. For example, when a button is clicked, an **ActionEvent** is generated and each of the button's registered **ActionListener**s is notified. You may have noticed a similarity between the way **ActionListener**s work and the Observer pattern discussed earlier. That is because they are the same pattern with two different naming schemes.

Compiling and Running the Download Manager

Compile **DownloadManager** like this:

```
javac DownloadManager.java DownloadsTableModel.java ProgressRenderer.java Download.java
```

Run **DownloadManager** like this:

```
javaw DownloadManager
```

The Download Manager is easy to use. First, enter the URL of a file that you want to download in the text field at the top of the screen. For example, to download a file called 0072229713_code.zip from the McGraw-Hill web site enter

http://books.mcgraw-hill.com/downloads/products/0072229713/0072229713_code.zip

This is the file that contains the code for my book *The Art of Java*, which I co-authored with James Holmes.

After adding a download to the Download Manager, you can manage it by selecting it in the table. Once selected, you can pause, cancel, resume, and clear a download. Figure 33-2 shows the Download Manager in action.

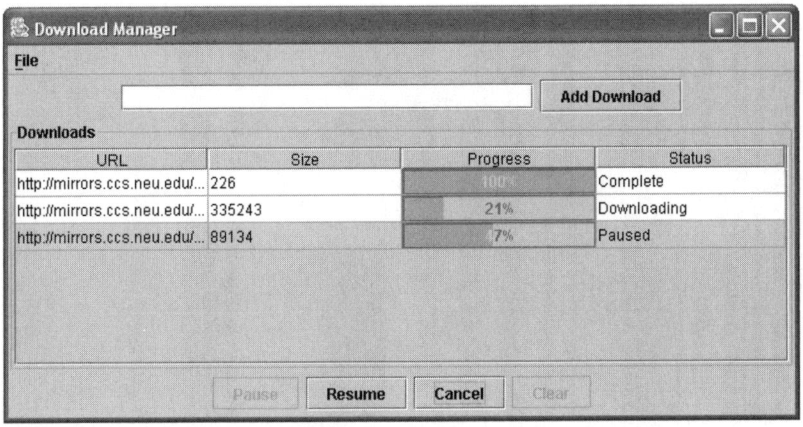

FIGURE 33-2   The Download Manager in action

Enhancing the Download Manager

The Download Manager as it stands is fully functional, with the ability to pause and resume downloads as well as download multiple files at once; however, there are several enhancements that you may want to try on your own. Here are some ideas: proxy server support, FTP and HTTPS support, and drag-and-drop support. A particularly appealing enhancement is a scheduling feature that lets you schedule a download at a specific time, perhaps in the middle of the night when system resources are plentiful.

Note that the techniques illustrated in this chapter are not limited to downloading files in the typical sense. There are many other practical uses for the code. For example, many software programs distributed over the Internet come in two pieces. The first piece is a small, compact application that can be downloaded quickly. This small application contains a mini download manager for downloading the second piece, which is generally much larger. This concept is quite useful, especially as the size of applications increases, which typically leads to an increase in the potential for download interruptions. You might want to try adapting the Download Manager for this purpose.

Using Java's Documentation Comments

A s explained in Part I, Java supports three types of comments. The first two are the //
and the /* */. The third type is called a *documentation comment*. It begins with the
character sequence /**. It ends with */. Documentation comments allow you to embed
information about your program into the program itself. You can then use the **javadoc** utility
program (supplied with the JDK) to extract the information and put it into an HTML file.
Documentation comments make it convenient to document your programs. You have almost
certainly seen documentation generated with **javadoc**, because that is the way the Java API
library was documented by Sun.

The javadoc Tags

The **javadoc** utility recognizes the following tags:

Tag	Meaning
@author	Identifies the author of a class.
{@code}	Displays information as-is, without processing HTML styles, in code font.
@deprecated	Specifies that a class or member is deprecated.
{@docRoot}	Specifies the path to the root directory of the current documentation.
@exception	Identifies an exception thrown by a method.
{@inheritDoc}	Inherits a comment from the immediate superclass.
{@link}	Inserts an in-line link to another topic.
{@linkplain}	Inserts an in-line link to another topic, but the link is displayed in a plain-text font.
{@literal}	Displays information as is, without processing HTML styles.
@param	Documents a method's parameter.
@return	Documents a method's return value.
@see	Specifies a link to another topic.

Tag	Meaning
@serial	Documents a default serializable field.
@serialData	Documents the data written by the **writeObject( )** or **writeExternal( )** methods.
@serialField	Documents an **ObjectStreamField** component.
@since	States the release when a specific change was introduced.
@throws	Same as **@exception**.
{@value}	Displays the value of a constant, which must be a **static** field.
@version	Specifies the version of a class.

Document tags that begin with an "at" sign (@) are called *stand-alone* tags, and they must be used on their own line. Tags that begin with a brace, such as {@code}, are called *in-line* tags, and they can be used within a larger description. You may also use other, standard HTML tags in a documentation comment. However, some tags, such as headings, should not be used because they disrupt the look of the HTML file produced by **javadoc**.

You can use documentation comments to document classes, interfaces, fields, constructors, and methods. In all cases, the documentation comment must immediately precede the item being documented. When you are documenting a variable, the documentation tags you can use are **@see**, **@serial**, **@serialField**, {**@value**}, and **@deprecated**. For classes and interfaces, you can use **@see**, **@author**, **@deprecated**, **@param**, and **@version**. Methods can be documented with **@see**, **@return**, **@param**, **@deprecated**, **@throws**, **@serialData**, {**@inheritDoc**}, and **@exception**. A {**@link**}, {**@docRoot**}, {**@code**}, {**@literal**}, **@since**, or {**@linkplain**} tag can be used anywhere. Each tag is examined next.

@author

The **@author** tag documents the author of a class or interface. It has the following syntax:

@author *description*

Here, *description* will usually be the name of the a uthor. You will need to specify the **-author** option when executing **javadoc** in order for the **@author** field to be included in the HTML documentation.

{@code}

The {**@code**} tag enables you to embed text, such as a snippet of code, into a comment. That text is then displayed as is in code font, without any further processing, such as HTML rendering. It has the following syntax:

{@code *code-snippet*}

@deprecated

The **@deprecated** tag specifies that a class, interface, or a member is deprecated. It is recommended that you include **@see** or {**@link**} tags to inform the programmer about available alternatives. The syntax is the following:

@deprecated *description*

Here, *description* is the message that describes the deprecation. The **@deprecated** tag can be used in documentation for variables, methods, classes, and interfaces.

{@docRoot}

{@docRoot} specifies the path to the root directory of the current documentation.

@exception

The **@exception** tag describes an exception to a method. It has the following syntax:

> @exception *exception-name explanation*

Here, the fully qualified name of the exception is specified by *exception-name,* and *explanation* is a string that describes how the exception can occur. The **@exception** tag can only be used in documentation for a method.

{@inheritDoc}

This tag inherits a comment from the immediate superclass.

{@link}

The {@link} tag provides an in-line link to additional information. It has the following syntax:

> {@link *pkg.class#member text*}

Here, *pkg.class#member* specifies the name of a class or method to which a link is added, and *text* is the string that is displayed.

{@linkplain}

Inserts an in-line link to another topic. The link is displayed in plain-text font. Otherwise, it is similar to {@link}.

{@literal}

The {@literal} tag enables you to embed text into a comment. That text is then displayed as is, without any further processing, such as HTML rendering. It has the following syntax:

> {@literal *description*}

Here, *description* is the text that is embedded.

@param

The **@param** tag documents a parameter to a method or a type parameter to a class or interface. It has the following syntax:

> @param *parameter-name explanation*

Here, *parameter-name* specifies the name of a parameter. The meaning of that parameter is described by *explanation*. The **@param** tag can be used only in documentation for a method or constructor, or a generic class or interface.

@return

The **@return** tag describes the return value of a method. It has the following syntax:

> @return *explanation*

Here, *explanation* describes the type and meaning of the value returned by a method. The **@return** tag can be used only in documentation for a method.

@see

The **@see** tag provides a reference to additional information. Its most commonly used forms are shown here:

@see *anchor*
@see *pkg.class#member text*

In the first form, *anchor* is a link to an absolute or relative URL. In the second form, *pkg.class#member* specifies the name of the item, and *text* is the text displayed for that item. The text parameter is optional, and if not used, then the item specified by *pkg.class#member* is displayed. The member name, too, is optional. Thus, you can specify a reference to a package, class, or interface in addition to a reference to a specific method or field. The name can be fully qualified or partially qualified. However, the dot that precedes the member name (if it exists) must be replaced by a hash character.

@serial

The **@serial** tag defines the comment for a default serializable field. It has the following syntax:

@serial *description*

Here, *description* is the comment for that field.

@serialData

The **@serialData** tag documents the data written by the **writeObject( )** and **writeExternal( )** methods. It has the following syntax:

@serialData *description*

Here, *description* is the comment for that data.

@serialField

For a class that implements **Serializable**, the **@serialField** tag provides comments for an **ObjectStreamField** component. It has the following syntax:

@serialField *name type description*

Here, *name* is the name of the field, *type* is its type, and *description* is the comment for that field.

@since

The **@since** tag states that a class or member was introduced in a specific release. It has the following syntax:

@since *release*

Here, *release* is a string that designates the release or version in which this feature became available.

@throws

The **@throws** tag has the same meaning as the **@exception** tag.

{@value}

{@value} has two forms. The first displays the value of the constant that it precedes, which must be a **static** field. It has this form:

{@value}

The second form displays the value of a specified **static** field. It has this form:

{@value *pkg.class#field*}

Here, *pkg.class#field* specifies the name of the **static** field.

@version

The **@version** tag specifies the version of a class. It has the following syntax:

@version *info*

Here, *info* is a string that contains version information, typically a version number, such as 2.2. You will need to specify the **-version** option when executing **javadoc** in order for the **@version** field to be included in the HTML documentation.

The General Form of a Documentation Comment

After the beginning /**, the first line or lines become the main description of your class, variable, or method. After that, you can include one or more of the various @ tags. Each @ tag must start at the beginning of a new line or follow one or more asterisks (*) that are at the start of a line. Multiple tags of the same type should be grouped together. For example, if you have three **@see** tags, put them one after the other. In-line tags (those that begin with a brace) can be used within any description.

Here is an example of a documentation comment for a class:

```
/**
 * This class draws a bar chart.
 * @author Herbert Schildt
 * @version 3.2
 */
```

What javadoc Outputs

The **javadoc** program takes as input your Java program's source file and outputs several HTML files that contain the program's documentation. Information about each class will be in its own HTML file. **javadoc** will also output an index and a hierarchy tree. Other HTML files can be generated.

An Example that Uses Documentation Comments

Following is a sample program that uses documentation comments. Notice the way each comment immediately precedes the item that it describes. After being processed by **javadoc**, the documentation about the **SquareNum** class will be found in **SquareNum.html**.

```java
import java.io.*;

/**
 * This class demonstrates documentation comments.
 * @author Herbert Schildt
 * @version 1.2
 */
public class SquareNum {
  /**
   * This method returns the square of num.
   * This is a multiline description.  You can use
   * as many lines as you like.
   * @param num The value to be squared.
   * @return num squared.
   */
  public double square(double num) {
    return num * num;
  }

  /**
   * This method inputs a number from the user.
   * @return The value input as a double.
   * @exception IOException On input error.
   * @see IOException
   */
  public double getNumber() throws IOException {
    // create a BufferedReader using System.in
    InputStreamReader isr = new InputStreamReader(System.in);
    BufferedReader inData = new BufferedReader(isr);
    String str;

    str = inData.readLine();
    return (new Double(str)).doubleValue();
  }
  /**
   * This method demonstrates square().
   * @param args Unused.
   * @exception IOException On input error.
   * @see IOException
   */

  public static void main(String args[])
    throws IOException
  {
    SquareNum ob = new SquareNum();
    double val;

    System.out.println("Enter value to be squared: ");
    val = ob.getNumber();
    val = ob.square(val);

    System.out.println("Squared value is " + val);
  }
}
```

Index